International Directory of
COMPANY
HISTORIES

International Directory of
COMPANY
HISTORIES

VOLUME 124

Editor

Drew D. Johnson

ST. JAMES PRESS
A part of Gale, Cengage Learning

GALE
CENGAGE Learning

Detroit • New York • San Francisco • New Haven, Conn • Waterville, Maine • London

International Directory of Company Histories, Volume 124

Drew D. Johnson, Editor

Project Editor: Miranda H. Ferrara

Editorial: Virgil Burton, Donna Craft, Peggy Geeseman, Julie Gough, Hillary Hentschel, Sonya Hill, Keith Jones, Matthew Miskelly, Lynn Pearce, Laura Peterson, Paul Schummer, Holly Selden

Production Technology Specialist: Mike Weaver

Imaging and Multimedia: John Watkins

Composition and Electronic Prepress: Gary Leach, Evi Seoud

Manufacturing: Rhonda Dover

Product Manager: Jenai Drouillard

For product information and technology assistance, contact us at
Gale Customer Support, 1-800-877-4253.
For permission to use material from this text or product,
submit all requests online at **www.cengage.com/permissions.**
Further permissions questions can be emailed to
permissionrequest@cengage.com

Gale
27500 Drake Rd.
Farmington Hills, MI, 48331-3535

LIBRARY OF CONGRESS CATALOG NUMBER 89-190943
ISBN-13: 978-1-55862-791-8
ISBN-10: 1-55862-791-X

This title is also available as an e-book
ISBN-13: 978-1-55862-806-9   ISBN-10: 1-55862-806-1
Contact your Gale, a part of Cengage Learning sales representative for ordering information.

BRITISH LIBRARY CATALOGUING IN PUBLICATION DATA
International directory of company histories, Vol. 124
Drew D. Johnson
33.87409

Printed in Mexico
1 2 3 4 5 6 7 15 14 13 12 11

Contents

Preface

The St. James Press series *The International Directory of Company Histories* (*IDCH*) is intended for reference use by students, business people, librarians, historians, economists, investors, job candidates, and others who seek to learn more about the historical development of the world's most important companies. To date, *IDCH* has profiled more than 11,610 companies in 124 volumes.

INCLUSION CRITERIA

Most companies chosen for inclusion in *IDCH* have achieved a minimum of US$25 million in annual sales and are leading influences in their industries or geographical locations. Companies may be publicly held, private, or nonprofit. State-owned companies that are important in their industries and that may operate much like public or private companies also are included. Wholly owned subsidiaries and divisions are profiled if they meet the requirements for inclusion. Entries on companies that have had major changes since they were last profiled may be selected for updating.

The *IDCH* series highlights 25% private and nonprofit companies, and features updated entries on approximately 35 companies per volume.

ENTRY FORMAT

Each entry begins with the company's legal name; the address of its headquarters; its telephone, toll-free, and fax numbers; and its web site. A statement of public, private, state, or parent ownership follows. A company with a legal name in both English and the language of its headquarters country is listed by the English name, with the native-language name in parentheses.

The company's founding or earliest incorporation date, the number of employees, and the most recent available sales figures follow. Sales figures are given in local currencies with equivalents in U.S. dollars. For some private companies, sales figures are estimates and indicated by the abbreviation *est*. The entry lists the exchanges on which the company's stock is traded and its ticker symbol, as well as the company's NAICS codes.

Entries generally contain a *Company Perspectives* box which provides a short summary of the company's mission, goals, and ideals; a *Key Dates* box highlighting milestones in the company's history; lists of *Principal Subsidiaries*, *Principal Divisions*, *Principal Operating Units*, *Principal Competitors*; and articles for *Further Reading*.

American spelling is used throughout *IDCH*, and the word "billion" is used in its U.S. sense of one thousand million.

SOURCES

Entries have been compiled from publicly accessible sources both in print and on the Internet such as general and academic periodicals, books, and annual reports, as well as material supplied by the companies themselves.

CUMULATIVE INDEXES

IDCH contains three indexes: the **Cumulative Index to Companies**, which provides an alphabetical index to companies profiled in the *IDCH* series, the **Index to Industries**, which allows researchers to locate companies by their principal industry, and the **Geographic Index**, which lists companies alphabetically by the country of their headquarters. The indexes are cumulative and specific instructions for using them are found immediately preceding each index.

SPECIAL TO THIS VOLUME

This volume of *IDCH* profiles two companies from Angola, a first for this series. Other companies throughout Africa are also given emphasis.

SUGGESTIONS WELCOME

Comments and suggestions from users of *IDCH* on any aspect of the product as well as suggestions for companies to be included or updated are cordially invited. Please write:

The Editor
International Directory of Company Histories
St. James Press
Gale, Cengage Learning
27500 Drake Rd.
Farmington Hills, Michigan 48331-3535

St. James Press does not endorse any of the companies or products mentioned in this series. Companies appearing in the *International Directory of Company Histories* were selected without reference to their wishes and have in no way endorsed their entries.

Notes on Contributors

Agata Antonow
A business writer and researcher based in Nova Scotia, Canada. Antonow works with clients all over North America.

Rhonda Campbell
Business writer and novelist. Campbell has written for and appeared in several periodicals including *Essence, Parade,* and the *Pittsburgh Quarterly.*

Aaron Hauser
Researcher, business writer, and novelist based in Austin, Texas.

Sara Huter
A professor of economics. Huter's background also includes risk management in the banking and energy industries with expertise in credit scores.

Paul Ingati
Business writer and researcher based in Nairobi. Ingati is a specialist in personal finance, business management, business planning, and project management.

David Larkins
Professional writer based in Santa Fe, New Mexico, where he contributes to a variety of books and publications. Larkins' most recent book is a collaboration with his father, *Startling Art: Revealing the Art of Dennis Larkins.*

Ian MacDonald
Contemporary writer with formal training in technical communications and an advance education in business administration. MacDonald is based in the island city of Richmond, British Columbia.

Diane Milne
Writer and researcher with a background in the field of education. Milne is currently living in Florida.

David Petechuk
Contributor to business, health care, and various educational publications. Petechuk is the author of a book on ethical issues in transplantation and a book about LSD, which is part of a drug education series targeting a young adult audience.

List of Abbreviations

€ European euro
¥ Japanese yen
£ United Kingdom pound
$ United States dollar

A

AB Aktiebolag (Finland, Sweden)
AB Oy Aktiebolag Osakeyhtiot (Finland)
A.E. Anonimos Eteria (Greece)
AED Emirati dirham
AG Aktiengesellschaft (Austria, Germany, Switzerland, Liechtenstein)
aG auf Gegenseitigkeit (Austria, Germany)
A.m.b.a. Andelsselskab med begraenset ansvar (Denmark)
A.O. Anonim Ortaklari/Ortakligi (Turkey)
ApS Amparteselskab (Denmark)
ARS Argentine peso
A.S. Anonim Sirketi (Turkey)
A/S Aksjeselskap (Norway)
A/S Aktieselskab (Denmark, Sweden)
Ay Avoinyhtio (Finland)
ATS Austrian shilling
AUD Australian dollar
Ay Avoinyhtio (Finland)

B

B.A. Buttengewone Aansprakeiijkheid (Netherlands)
BEF Belgian franc

BHD Bahraini dinar
Bhd. Berhad (Malaysia, Brunei)
BND Brunei dollar
BRL Brazilian real
B.V. Besloten Vennootschap (Belgium, Netherlands)
BWP Botswana pula

C

C. de R.L. Compania de Responsabilidad Limitada (Spain)
C. por A. Compania por Acciones (Dominican Republic)
C.A. Compania Anonima (Ecuador, Venezuela)
C.V. Commanditaire Vennootschap (Netherlands, Belgium)
CAD Canadian dollar
CEO Chief Executive Officer
CFO Chief Financial Officer
CHF Swiss franc
Cia. Compagnia (Italy)
Cia. Companhia (Brazil, Portugal)
Cia. Compania (Latin America [except Brazil], Spain)
Cie. Compagnie (Belgium, France, Luxembourg, Netherlands)
CIO Chief Information Officer
CLP Chilean peso
CNY Chinese yuan
Co. Company
COO Chief Operating Officer
Coop. Cooperative

COP Colombian peso
Corp. Corporation
CPT Cuideachta Phoibi Theoranta (Republic of Ireland)
CRL Companhia a Responsabilidao Limitida (Portugal, Spain)
CZK Czech koruna

D

D&B Dunn & Bradstreet
DEM German deutsche mark (W. Germany to 1990; unified Germany to 2002)
Div. Division (United States)
DKK Danish krone
DZD Algerian dinar

E

E.P.E. Etema Pemorismenis Evthynis (Greece)
EBIDTA Earnings before interest, taxes, depreciation, and amortization
EC Exempt Company (Arab countries)
Edms. Bpk. Eiendoms Beperk (South Africa)
EEK Estonian Kroon
eG eingetragene Genossenschaft (Germany)
EGMBH Eingetragene Genossenschaft mit beschraenkter Haftung (Austria, Germany)
EGP Egyptian pound

Ek For Ekonomisk Forening (Sweden)

EP Empresa Portuguesa (Portugal)

ESOP Employee Stock Options and Ownership

ESP Spanish peseta

Et(s). Etablissement(s) (Belgium, France, Luxembourg)

eV eingetragener Verein (Germany)

EUR European euro

F

FIM Finnish markka

FRF French franc

G

G.I.E. Groupement d'Interet Economique (France)

gGmbH gemeinnutzige Gesellschaft mit beschraenkter Haftung (Austria, Germany, Switzerland)

GmbH Gesellschaft mit beschraenkter Haftung (Austria, Germany, Switzerland)

GRD Greek drachma

GWA Gewerbte Amt (Austria, Germany)

H

HB Handelsbolag (Sweden)

HF Hlutafelag (Iceland)

HKD Hong Kong dollar

HUF Hungarian forint

I

IDR Indonesian rupiah

IEP Irish pound

ILS Israeli shekel (new)

Inc. Incorporated (United States, Canada)

INR Indian rupee

IPO Initial Public Offering

I/S Interesentselskap (Norway)

I/S Interessentselskab (Denmark)

ISK Icelandic krona

ITL Italian lira

J

JMD Jamaican dollar

JOD Jordanian dinar

K

KB Kommanditbolag (Sweden)

KES Kenyan schilling

Kft Korlatolt Felelossegu Tarsasag (Hungary)

KG Kommanditgesellschaft (Austria, Germany, Switzerland)

KGaA Kommanditgesellschaft auf Aktien (Austria, Germany, Switzerland)

KK Kabushiki Kaisha (Japan)

KPW North Korean won

KRW South Korean won

K/S Kommanditselskab (Denmark)

K/S Kommandittselskap (Norway)

KWD Kuwaiti dinar

Ky Kommandiitiyhtio (Finland)

L

L.L.C. Limited Liability Company (Arab countries, Egypt, Greece, United States)

L.L.P. Limited Liability Partnership (United States)

L.P. Limited Partnership (Canada, South Africa, United Kingdom, United States)

LBO Leveraged Buyout

Lda. Limitada (Spain)

Ltd. Limited

Ltda. Limitada (Brazil, Portugal)

Ltee. Limitee (Canada, France)

LUF Luxembourg franc

LYD Libyan dinar

M

MAD Moroccan dirham

mbH mit beschraenkter Haftung (Austria, Germany)

Mij. Maatschappij (Netherlands)

MUR Mauritian rupee

MXN Mexican peso

MYR Malaysian ringgit

N

N.A. National Association (United States)

N.V. Naamloze Vennootschap (Belgium, Netherlands)

NGN Nigerian naira

NLG Netherlands guilder

NOK Norwegian krone

NZD New Zealand dollar

O

OAO Otkrytoe Aktsionernoe Obshchestve (Russia)

OHG Offene Handelsgesellschaft (Austria, Germany, Switzerland)

OMR Omani rial

OOO Obschestvo s Ogranichennoi Otvetstvennostiu (Russia)

OOUR Osnova Organizacija Udruzenog Rada (Yugoslavia)

Oy Osakeyhtiö (Finland)

P

P.C. Private Corp. (United States)

P.L.L.C. Professional Limited Liability Corporation (United States)

P.T. Perusahaan/Perseroan Terbatas (Indonesia)

PEN Peruvian Nuevo Sol

PHP Philippine peso

PKR Pakistani rupee

P/L Part Lag (Norway)

PLC Public Limited Co. (United Kingdom, Ireland)

PLN Polish zloty

PTE Portuguese escudo

Pte. Private (Singapore)

Pty. Proprietary (Australia, South Africa, United Kingdom)

Pvt. Private (India, Zimbabwe)

PVBA Personen Vennootschap met Beperkte Aansprakelijkheid (Belgium)

PYG Paraguay guarani

Q

QAR Qatar riyal

R

REIT Real Estate Investment Trust

RMB Chinese renminbi

Rt Reszvenytarsasag (Hungary)

RUB Russian ruble

S

S.A. Sociedad Anónima (Latin America [except Brazil], Spain, Mexico)

S.A. Sociedades Anônimas (Brazil, Portugal)

S.A. Société Anonyme (Arab countries, Belgium, France, Jordan, Luxembourg, Switzerland)

S.A. de C.V. Sociedad Anonima de Capital Variable (Mexico)

S.A.B. de C.V. Sociedad Anónima Bursátil de Capital Variable (Mexico)

S.A.C. Sociedad Anonima Comercial (Latin America [except Brazil])

S.A.C.I. Sociedad Anonima Comercial e Industrial (Latin America [except Brazil])

S.A.C.I.y.F. Sociedad Anonima Comercial e Industrial y Financiera (Latin America [except Brazil])

S.A.R.L. Sociedade Anonima de Responsabilidade Limitada (Brazil, Portugal)

S.A.R.L. Société à Responsabilité Limitée (France, Belgium, Luxembourg)

S.A.S. Societe Anonyme Syrienne (Arab countries)

S.A.S. Societá in Accomandita Semplice (Italy)

S.C. Societe en Commandite (Belgium, France, Luxembourg)

S.C.A. Societe Cooperativa Agricole (France, Italy, Luxembourg)

S.C.I. Sociedad Cooperativa Ilimitada (Spain)

S.C.L. Sociedad Cooperativa Limitada (Spain)

S.C.R.L. Societe Cooperative a Responsabilite Limitee (Belgium)

S.E. Societas Europaea (European Union Member states)

S.L. Sociedad Limitada (Latin America [except Brazil], Portugal, Spain)

S.N.C. Société en Nom Collectif (France)

S.p.A. Società per Azioni (Italy)

S.R.L. Sociedad de Responsabilidad Limitada (Spain, Mexico, Latin America [except Brazil])

S.R.L. Società a Responsabilità Limitata (Italy)

S.R.O. Spolecnost s Rucenim Omezenym (Czechoslovakia)

S.S.K. Sherkate Sahami Khass (Iran)

S.V. Samemwerkende Vennootschap (Belgium)

S.Z.R.L. Societe Zairoise a Responsabilite Limitee (Zaire)

SAA Societe Anonyme Arabienne (Arab countries)

SAK Societe Anonyme Kuweitienne (Arab countries)

SAL Societe Anonyme Libanaise (Arab countries)

SAO Societe Anonyme Omanienne (Arab countries)

SAQ Societe Anonyme Qatarienne (Arab countries)

SAR Saudi riyal

Sdn. Bhd. Sendirian Berhad (Malaysia)

SEK Swedish krona

SGD Singapore dollar

S/L Salgslag (Norway)

Soc. Sociedad (Latin America [except Brazil], Spain)

Soc. Sociedade (Brazil, Portugal)

Soc. Societa (Italy)

Sp. z.o.o. Spólka z ograniczona odpowiedzialnoscia (Poland)

Ste. Societe (France, Belgium, Luxembourg, Switzerland)

Ste. Cve. Societe Cooperative (Belgium)

T

THB Thai baht

TND Tunisian dinar

TRL Turkish lira

TTD Trinidad and Tobago dollar

TWD Taiwan dollar (new)

TZS Tanzanian shilling

U

UGX Ugandan shilling

U.A. Uitgesloten Aansporakeiijkheid (Netherlands)

u.p.a. utan personligt ansvar (Sweden)

V

V.O.f. Vennootschap onder firma (Netherlands)

VAG Verein der Arbeitgeber (Austria, Germany)

VEB Venezuelan bolivar

VERTR Vertriebs (Austria, Germany)

VND Vietnamese dong

VVAG Versicherungsverein auf Gegenseitigkeit (Austria, Germany)

W – Z

WA Wettelika Aansprakalikhaed (Netherlands)

WLL With Limited Liability (Bahrain, Kuwait, Qatar, Saudi Arabia)

YK Yugen Kaisha (Japan)

ZAO Zakrytoe Aktsionernoe Obshchestve (Russia)

ZAR South African rand

ZMK Zambian kwacha

ZWD Zimbabwean dollar

155 East Tropicana, LLC

115 East Tropicana Avenue
Las Vegas, Nevada 89109
U.S.A.
Telephone: (702) 597-6076
Toll Free: (866) 584-6687
Web site: http://www.hooterscasinohotel.com

Private Company
Founded: 2004
Employees: 720 (2009)
Sales: $46.8 million (2009)
NAICS: 721120 Casino Hotels

■ ■ ■

155 East Tropicana, LLC, was formed for the single purpose of acquiring the property and asset's of the Hôtel San Rémo Casino and Resort in Las Vegas, Nevada, and redeveloping the property as the Hooters Casino Hotel. As the company name suggests, this Hooters Casino Hotel is located at 115 East Tropicana Avenue in Las Vegas, Nevada, about half a block off the famous Las Vegas "Strip."

In addition to a large Hooters restaurant, the property includes multiple bars (Dixie's Dam Country Bar, Pete & Shorty's Tavern) and other restaurants. The hotel has almost 700 rooms and the casino features the standard array of table games, slot and video poker machines, and a sports book.

155 East Tropicana is two-thirds owned by Florida Hooters LLC and one-third by EW Common LLC, a group which owned the previous Hôtel San Rémo.

OFTEN REBRANDED PROPERTY

While the Hooters Hotel and Casino opened its doors for business on February 3, 2006, the buildings and the property had been hotels of various names for over 30 years. The property was originally, in 1973, a Howard Johnson Hotel, and it became the Paradise Hotel and Casino three years later. The Paradise gave way to the 20th Century Hotel and Casino in 1977, the Treasury Hotel and Casino in 1979, and the Pacific Polynesian Hotel a bit later.

In 1989 the property was purchased by Sukeaki Izumi, a veteran hotel operator from Osaka, Japan, who had settled in Las Vegas. For $32 million, he purchased and reopened the property as the European-styled Hôtel San Rémo Casino and Resort. He also hired Michael J. Hessling, who became the Hôtel San Rémo 's first employee, as general manager.

Hessling had a great deal of experience in the Las Vegas gaming industry. He had done stints with Caesar's Palace, a large luxury casino resort, and with a management company that operated the Dunes Hotel and Casino. He had also operated several small casinos in the area.

Hessling, who would go on to become executive vice president and chief operating officer, was originally less than enthusiastic about the prospects for the San Rémo. He thought that the property itself was in a poor location and that the Hôtel San Rémo, which had no real brand identity, would have to compete on value alone. In many respects, he was correct, for while the Hôtel San Rémo was profitable, it lacked the resources for adequate reinvestment. In the highly competitive

COMPANY PERSPECTIVES

When you're ready to get your game on, Hooters Casino Hotel's got the goods. From one of the best players clubs in town and the coolest new slots and video poker, to our rockin' table games, you'll have no problem finding action no matter who you are. Add a hot sports book and a cool live poker room that's so alive you'll have fun no matter what you're playing. And did we mention that Hooters Girls bring the drinks around? Cocktails!

world of Las Vegas lodging and gaming, the ability to upgrade and improve property is vital. In theory, then, teaming up with the Hooters organization would solve two of the San Ramos' underlying flaws, as the partnership would provide both additional capital resources and a recognizable brand.

Hooters of America Inc. is a privately held corporation based in Atlanta, Georgia. The company is primarily in the restaurant business with more than 455 locations worldwide. It opened its first "casual, beach themed" restaurant in Clearwater, Florida, on October 4, 1983. Its key marketing ploy is its staff of "Hooters Girls" whose skimpy uniforms are targeted at a mostly male audience. The company is unabashed at its use of female sex appeal.

Investing the Hooters' name in Las Vegas hotel and casino seemed like a logical extension to its core business. Hooters' believed its clients were already Vegas-type customers, and they could attract business to their Las Vegas property from the 61 million people who annually visited their restaurants.

This was not the first time Hooters had invested outside of its core business. In 2003 Hooters Air began scheduled airline services in the southeastern United States. While other airlines were cutting costs, Hooters Air took to the sky with splashy painted aircraft, expensive interiors, and meal services in an attempt to buck the trend. The results were predictable, and in 2006 the airline ceased operations.

Some warned that the same fate could potentially befall the Hooters Hotel and Casino. While it might be able to attract some of its core customers to its Las Vegas property, critics said it seemed oblivious to the development of the "super casinos" which sprang up in Vegas, four of which were located a half a block away.

THE DEVELOPMENT OF LAS VEGAS

Despite the seemingly long history of the puritan work ethic, gambling has been part of life in the United States since colonial days. With little or no taxing power, colonial governments used lotteries as a means to finance development. Each of the 13 original colonies held lotteries. Until the end of the U.S. Civil War, state-sponsored gambling, most often in the form of lotteries, was used by governments to raise money. However, as gambling became associated with crime, violence, and poverty, governments began to legislate against gaming activities. The effect was to move gambling into the criminal realm.

In 1931 the State of Nevada, hoping to develop new sources of revenue, legalized casino gambling. The timing coincided with the plans of the federal government to undertake a massive new project to build a dam on the Colorado River. Thousands of people would be required to build the hydroelectric project at a place called Boulder, less than 50 miles from Las Vegas. While the rest of the nation was locked in the Great Depression, Vegas prospered.

The Hoover Dam, as it was called, was finished in 1936, and while Las Vegas suffered a slight downturn afterward, Lady Luck was not done with the city yet. With the outbreak of World War II, the government needed a location to train pilots. Las Vegas, with its seeming endless days of sunshine, was a perfect training ground. Nellis Air Force Base was built on the outskirts of Las Vegas, and the training schedule was rarely interrupted due to weather.

It was not until 1946 that Las Vegas drew the interest of organized crime groups in the United States. In many ways, the gaming industry was the perfect business for criminal gangs. It was largely a cash business, which offered the opportunity to skim money off the top, and it was an ideal vehicle in which to launder money from other illegal activities.

Benjamin "Bugsy" Siegel was a New York City gangster who opened the Flamingo Casino in Las Vegas in 1946. While the casino originally floundered and cost Siegel his life, the concept of legitimate business owned and controlled by criminal elements was too good to pass up. By 1950 Las Vegas was drawing 11 million visitors a year and gambling revenues were in excess of $50 million. Between 1950 and 1958, eight major new casinos opened, and according to the Federal Bureau of Investigation (FBI), nearly all were owned or controlled by organized crime.

Despite a 1950s' investigation into gambling and organized crime led by Senator Estes Kefauver (D-

KEY DATES

■

1973: Howard Johnson Hotel opens at 155 East Tropicana Avenue in Las Vegas.

1989: Hotel at 155 East Tropicana is redesigned as the European-styled Hôtel San Rémo Casino and Resort.

2004: 155 East Tropicana LLC is formed.

2006: Hooter Casino Hotel opens for business.

2010: 155 East Tropicana LCC considers bankruptcy as it struggles with excessive debt load.

Tenn.), not much would change in Las Vegas until the early 1960s. With the backing of Attorney General Robert Kennedy, the Federal Bureau of Investigation (FBI) under Director J. Edgar Hoover moved to rid the Nevada gaming industry of organized crime. It did so by concentrating on one resort at a time. The FBI would identify the criminals associated with the resort, and if prosecutors were unable to lay felony charges, they would pressure the State of Nevada to revoke the gaming licenses. Las Vegas became a very difficult place for organized crime to carry on business. The old Las Vegas was dying, but a new one was about to start under the control of a man who did not gamble.

THE NEW LAS VEGAS

Howard Hughes was a U.S. industrialist and investor who had inherited the Hughes Tool Company, a $100 million entity, and transformed it into a $2 billion conglomerate with interests in electronics, aeronautics, and airlines. In 1966 he relocated to Las Vegas, looking for new opportunities, having just sold his interests in Trans World Airlines for nearly half a billion dollars.

The arrival of Hughes seemed to come at a very fortunate time for both Nevada and the city of Las Vegas. The pressure being exerted by the federal authorities to rid the gaming industry of the organized crime element caused a vacuum in casino ownership. Under pressure to sell, the mobsters needed someone with Hughes' resources to buy. The problem was that Hughes, an eccentric recluse who did not gamble, was unwilling to appear at the public hearings required for a gaming license. It would take an act of the legislature to resolve the issue. In 1967 the State of Nevada enacted the Nevada Corporate Gaming Act, which allowed publicly traded corporations to obtain gaming licenses.

The world of corporate gaming had arrived. Howard Hughes would purchase the Desert Inn, the Sands, the Frontier, and several smaller casinos. By 1968 17 percent of Nevada's state revenues came from casinos owned or controlled by Hughes. By 1975 Nevada's gaming revenues topped $1 billion.

The new Las Vegas required a new type of casino. Whereas the criminal element had concentrated on high rollers, the new Las Vegas would cater to baby boomers and their families. A new facility, that some termed a super casino, came into existence.

One of the first examples of the new super casino was the Mirage Hotel and Casino, which opened in 1989. The three-million-square-foot property offered 3,049 guest rooms and in addition to its casino offered fine dining, retail stores, spectacular shows, pools, and a spa. There was no reason for a guest to ever have to leave the property, and in its first year, it recorded a $200 million profit.

Other super casinos would soon follow, and while games of chance were still the primary source of revenues, by the early 21st century visitors were spending in excess of $6 billion on rooms, meals, and non-gaming entertainment.

TURNING ORANGE RED

Given its brand name recognition and its reputation for being "delightfully tacky, yet unrefined," the management of 155 Tropicana were optimistic about the future of the Hooters Hotel and Casino. There were, however, some major hurdles to overcome.

The Hôtel San Rémo needed major renovations to be converted into a Hooters facility. In 2005 155 East Tropicana raised $130 million in a private placement to be used for renovations and to restructure debt from the original property.

The extensive renovations included a redesign of the main entrance and expansion of the casino from the original 24,000 square feet to 29,000 square feet. The original 532 slot machines and video terminals and 16 tables were increased to 658 machines and 31 gaming tables. The 711 guest rooms became 696 guest rooms and 17 suites. The original pool area was be expanded and renovated by the addition of a sand beach, palm trees, and a waterfall. To complete the renovations, several new restaurants, a retail store selling Hooters merchandise, and a day spa were added.

On February 3, 2006, the Hooters Hotel and Casino opened to the public, but 2005 had been a costly one for the company. Net losses for the year exceeded $13 million.

Another significant challenge facing the company was its location. It was half a block off the main Las Vegas strip and had four significant super casinos as neighbors. The New York New York, the MGM Grand, the Excalibur, and the Tropicana were all two to three times the size of Hooters. By its own admission, Hooters Hotel and Casino was within walking distance of an estimated 25,000 hotel rooms.

In mid-2006, 155 East Tropicana appointed Michael Hessling as president and chief operating officer of the company. Hessling, unlike the majority owners from Florida Hooters, was experienced in the Las Vegas gaming industry. It would not, however, be enough to stop the tide of red ink and 2006 ended with a net loss of $18.4 million.

In the face of mounting losses the company identified several remedial measures, which it implemented in 2007 to boost revenue. First, it increased its marketing efforts in the Southern California marketplace through television and radio ads, and interstate billboards. It was hoped this would stimulate walk-in traffic and raise the room occupancy levels, which stood at 81 percent. (In comparison, the Las Vegas norm was 95 percent occupancy.) Next, it converted the hotel's martini bar into the Night Owl Showroom and hired live entertainment. It also revamped its restaurant menus to feature more value-priced offerings.

In April 2007 Hedwigs Las Vegas Top Tier, part of the NTH Advisory Group, made an unsolicited offer to purchase 155 East Tropicana and the Hooters Hotel and Casino. The deal would see Hedwigs take over the property and all the debt, subject to completing due diligence. Although the deal was looked upon favorably by East Tropicana stakeholders, Hedwigs ultimately declined to purchase. East Tropicana's year-end net loss for 2007 was $14.1 million.

With the global recession that began in 2008, 155 East Tropicana found itself in an even worse position. Las Vegas as a whole suffered as tourism dropped, and many larger casinos hotels began decreasing their prices and offering bargains, thereby cutting into value-conscious clientele. Net losses occurred in both 2008 and 2009, and in 2009 the company missed payments due on its notes on both April 1 and October 1. By December 31, 2009, it had a combined debt of $146.1 million. In December 2010 the company publicly announced that if might have to seek protection under Chapter 11 of the U.S. Bankruptcy Code.

Although a buyer might be found who would be willing to inject more capital into the ailing hotel, in the early 2010s Hooters Casino Hotel was struggling in a weakened economy and with a burdensome level of debt.

Ian MacDonald

PRINCIPAL COMPETITORS

Caesars Entertainment Corporation; MGM Resorts International; Tropicana Las Vegas Hotel and Resort Inc.

FURTHER READING

Becker, Eric B. "Slots in the City: A Critical Look at the Balance of Decision-Making Power in Gaming Legislation." *Fordham Urban Law Journal,* October 2008. Accessed February 22, 2011. http://findarticles.com/p/articles/mi_hb6562/is_5_35/ai_n31061226/?tag=content;col1.

Covel, Simona. "Company Purchases Struggling Vegas Hooters." *USA Today,* January 23, 2007. Accessed February 22, 2011. http://www.usatoday.com/travel/hotels/2007-01-23-hooters-hotel_x.htm.

Early, Pete. Super Casino: *Inside the New Las Vegas.* New York: Bantam, 2000.

888 Holdings plc

601–701 Europort
Gibraltar
Telephone: (350) 2004-9800
Fax: (350) 2004-8280
Web site: http://www.888holdingsplc.com

Public Company
Founded: 1997
Employees: 947 (2009)
Sales: $246.7 million (2009)
Stock Exchanges: London
Ticker Symbol: 888 Hldgs
NAICS: 713290 Other Gambling Industries

■ ■ ■

888 Holdings plc is an online gaming company that principally provides globally accessible entertainment and solutions for online gaming. The company's varied product range is tailored to the needs of different customers and business to business (B2B) channels.

The company extends its B2B product range and solutions through Dragonfish, a division of the company tasked to provide total gaming services. As such, business partners seeking to establish an online gaming presence through 888's platform acquire access to Dragonfish's customizable solutions for monetizing their brands. 888 is credited for developing consumer Web sites equipped with world-class interactive platforms that provide optimized entertainment experience for online gaming enthusiasts. Dragonfish accounted for roughly one-fifth of all revenue in 2009.

The business operations of 888 are driven by the objective of gaining the leadership position in the online gaming industry's global market through the provision of gaming products that have wide appeal. 888casino, 888poker, 888bingo, and 888sport are the main online gaming segments of the company. The four distinctive gaming brands are accessible in the company's main gaming Web site (888.com) that serves as the central link for all its online gaming portals. Overall, online casino operations (excluding poker) accounted for about half of revenue in 2009.

888 evidently employs a niche market strategy through the 888ladies bingo gaming portal that targets the female population in the U.K. market. The company's Web site also provides access to mobile gaming portals and numerous online gaming proprietary products such as Pacific Poker and Casino-on-Net. 888 receives most of its business from the United Kingdom (37 percent in 2009) and continental Europe (46 percent in 2009), with North America accounting for only 8 percent of sales in 2009.

COMPANY FOUNDING AND EARLY YEARS: 1997–2002

The history of 888 Holdings plc dates back to 1997 when Virtual Holdings Limited was founded in the British Virgin Islands. The company was established by four brothers from the Shaked and Yitzchak families (Avi Shaked, Aaron Shaked, Shay Yitzchak, and Ron Yitzchak). The two sets of brothers reportedly mortgaged their homes to raise the start-up capital of the company. The company was based in Antigua and was granted a gaming license in 1997 at a cost of $100,000. The founders of the company opted to base the company's management operations, central deposit servers, and member support center in Antigua.

The launch of Casino-on-Net in May 1997 marked the company's debut in the provision of online proprietary casino gaming platforms. The newly founded company experienced a blessing in disguise when a serious error that occurred in the Lycos search engine delivered Casino-on-Net Internet advertisements to all parts of the world. The advertisement elicited instantaneous responses as unprecedented volumes of traffic visited the new Web site. The traffic was so heavy that it crashed the system, with statistics indicating that Web site had been visited by approximately 500,000 people before the system collapse. The founding brothers immediately embarked on intense Internet advertising for Casino-on-Net online, having experienced firsthand the power of advertising.

Virtual Holdings Limited began implementing an expansionist strategy within a year of its inception by acquiring Random Logic Limited in Tel Aviv in 1998. Random Logic had initially been founded in Israel as a small Internet technology business by a group of graduate students from the country's Institute of Technology. The Israel-based subsidiary became the company's nerve center for research and development (R&D).

Virtual Holdings Limited continued to exhibit signs of growth and success with the introduction of Reef Club Casino in June 2002. The Reef Club Casino became the second product launch for the company's proprietary casino gaming products. The company introduced the 888.com Web site as its main gaming brand in 2002.

Virtual Holdings Limited continued to pursue brand diversification strategies in 2002 by launching Pacific Poker, a gaming platform featuring online poker rooms for multiplayers. The company also enhanced its advertising market penetration capacity in the United Kingdom in 2002 by establishing the Virtual Marketing Services (UK) Limited in London. The London office

served as the U.K. sourcing center for the company's of-fline advertising segment.

RELOCATION AND LEGAL CHALLENGES: 2003–06

Cassava Enterprises, a company subsidiary in Gibraltar, finally secured a gaming license in July 2003. This development led to the transfer of the operational headquarters of the company to Gibraltar. The company consolidated and promoted its activities under the 888. com banner in Gibraltar while retaining Cassava Enterprises and Virtual Holdings Limited as its key subsidiaries. As such, the company managed its operations, central deposit servers, and member support center from Gibraltar. The company upgraded its Casino-on-Net proprietary brand in the fourth quarter of 2003 by introducing version seven of the gaming platform.

The introduction of the first phase of the skill games program in 888.com in August 2004 was a major achievement in the company's product diversification scheme. The skill games program was piloted by the 888.tv and 888.info gaming segments. In October 2004 the company added Betmate.com to its online range of gaming products and effectively provided a platform for betting exchange to its members outside the United States. 888.com also became a major participant in the sporting arena in the year by offering Middlesbrough Football Club in England a three-year sponsorship deal.

The initial public offering (IPO) for the sale of 25 percent of shares in 888 Holdings plc commenced in September 2005. The company, however, was forced to revise the offer price downwards following profit warnings by one of its competitors in the industry, PartyGaming plc. The profit warnings caused panic in the industry, forcing 888 Holdings to reduce its offer price by a total of £100 million. The IPO netted a total of £590 million, and in October 2005 the company's shares were finally listed on the London Stock Exchange.

The company also made clear its long-term objectives of developing its corporate social responsibility (CSR) programs by contributing toward the foundation of the eCommerce and Online Gaming Regulation and Assurance (eCOGRA) organization in 2005. eCOGRA is a nonprofit player protection and standards organization based in London. Founded by online gaming organizations, eCOGRA was mandated to establish and monitor the implementation of an internationally acceptable framework for ensuring fairness and responsibility in gambling. The founding of the eC-OGRA was necessitated by the need for greater levels of

KEY DATES

1997: Virtual Holdings Limited established.
2003: Operational headquarters relocates to Gibraltar.
2005: 888 Holdings listed on the London Stock Exchange.
2006: The United States enacts the Unlawful Internet Gambling Enforcement Act of 2006 (UIGEA).
2010: Acquisition of Mytopia strengthens company's mobile gaming platform options.

commitment by industry players to observing international consumer protection benchmarks.

888 began 2006 by signing a five-year sponsorship deal with the World Snooker Championship. The company kept pace with the fast-emerging information technology innovations by constantly adopting product upgrades for its online gaming platforms. The group further upgraded its casino gaming platform through the adoption of a highly interactive casino in January 2006. The company's gaming Web sites were also upgraded with extra entertainment features that allowed customers to launch both personalized and social networking activities. Customers were able to share their online gaming experiences through virtual community portals provided by the company's secure Web site environment. The online gaming channels of 888 were also highly secured to guarantee the privacy of customers' information.

Not all was rosy in 2006, however. The enactment of the Unlawful Internet Gambling Enforcement Act of 2006 (UIGEA) in the United States in September 2006 presented the company's international operations with new legal challenges. The UIGEA prohibited the acceptance by financial institutions of payments from any entity involved in the betting or wagering businesses, in effect outlawing gambling on the Internet. Consequently, the company canceled all its operations in the U.S. market. The group further adjusted its operational systems and barred all its sites from processing real money wagers from the United States.

The exit from the United States dealt a major blow to the 888's operating income because the country accounted for 48 percent of its overall revenues. The enactment of the UIGEA severely dented the company's share value as its stock prices fell to the lowest levels ever since its initial listing.

LIFE AFTER UIGEA: 2007

With a large geographical market denied to them, the company expanded through its product line. During the first quarter of 2007, the company fast-tracked the adoption of embedded video slots and blackjack. The company also made its first major acquisition in 2007 through the successful takeover of Globalcom Limited, a leading online bingo business, at a cost of $43.7 million.

The establishment of the Dragonfish brand in 2007 was a landmark strategic achievement by the company. Dragonfish was established to provide a technological product integration platform for the B2B segment of 888 Holdings plc. The Yitzchak brothers reduced their shareholding stake in the company from 17 percent to 13 percent in 2007 through the sale of 13.6 million shares. The share sale netted about $31 million for the two founder brothers as European fund managers expended their shareholding in the company.

The group continued to pursue measures that would guarantee full compliance with the UIGEA to avoid possibilities of future legal liabilities with the U.S. government. To this end, 888 entered discussions with the Office of the Attorney of the United States in June 2007 to ascertain the residual risks associated with the company's operations in the United States prior to the enactments of the UIGEA.

NICHE STRATEGY AND THE GLOBAL RECESSION: 2008–09

The product variety offering of 888 was enhanced when it implemented an industry-unique niche strategy at the beginning of 2008. The niche targeting strategy involved the introduction of the 888ladies product within its bingo brand segment in February 2008. The 888ladies was packaged with advanced social networking features tailored to suit the needs of female online gaming enthusiasts. The company also expanded its product segment in March 2008 through the launch of a sport betting online segment, the 888sport. Online betting for popular sports varieties such as soccer, rugby, basketball, and cricket were introduced with the 888sports.com gaming portal.

In May 2008 888 entered a licensing contract agreement of three years with Cryptologic's wholly owned subsidiary, WagerLogic. Cryptologic was an Internet gaming software development company based in Dublin, Ireland. The agreement licensed the selection and integration of Cryptologic's casino games by 888 to complement its product offerings. The partnership was announced by Cryptologic on May 12, 2008. 888 Holdings also entered into a commitment to use its expansive gaming sites to promote the principal business activities of Sportech plc through a marketing and distribution partnership agreement that was signed in June 2008. The company introduced its bingo segment in Spain for the first time in December 2008.

The adverse effects of the 2008 to 2009 global economic crisis in the financial sector prompted the management of 888 to employ numerous mitigation measures in 2009. Such measures involved the downward price adjustments on the Reef Casino Club with a view of providing customers with continued access to online gaming during the period of economic hardship. Although revenue from Dragonfish increased between 2008 and 2009, overall the company, like many gambling operations, suffered, with total revenue decreasing from $262.6 million in 2008 to $246.7 million a year later.

EXPANSION STRATEGY: 2009 AND BEYOND

888 Holdings plc acquired the Wink Online Bingo business in December 2009 as the company continued to pursue its expansion strategy. The acquisition significantly enhanced its service offerings under the bingo brand segment.

888 rolled out numerous strategic performance measures in 2010 as the company sought to stimulate growth in its core brand segments. In January 2010 the company relaunched all its core brand segments comprising 888casino, 888poker, 888bingo, and 888sport. The company also enhanced its poker gaming segment in France through a joint venture partnership with Microgaming in May 2010.

That same month 888 signed a joint venture with Endemol, Italy's largest private television company. The deal provided a platform for much-needed media exposure for the company's www.888.it online gaming subsidiary. The company further diversified its product portfolio towards social and mobile gaming when it acquired Mytopia in June 2010. Formerly owned by Real Dice Inc., Mytopia comprised a studio for games development of cross-platform, real-time social networking applications for mobile gadgets such as smartphones. 888 Holdings acquired Mytopia for a total cost of $18 million

Looking beyond 2010, the company planned to pursue a sustainable growth strategy through continuous expansions, partnerships and acquisitions. The company further planned to achieve the enhancement of the B2C and B2B business segments by continuously adopting new technological innovations. The introduction of 3-D virtual gaming was one of the priorities set by the management of the company.

Paul Ingati

PRINCIPLE SUBSIDIARIES

Active Media Limited (British Virgin Islands); Cassava Enterprises Limited (Antigua); Random Logic Limited (Israel); Virtual Marketing Services (UK) Limited.

PRINCIPAL DIVISIONS

888bingo; 888casino; 888poker; 888sport; Dragonfish.

PRINCIPAL COMPETITORS

Betonsports plc; Ladbrokes plc; Party Gaming plc; Playtech Ltd; The Rank Group plc.

FURTHER READING

"888 Holdings IPO Values Online Gaming Group at 590 mln stg." *AFX News Limited,* September 29, 2005. Accessed November 11, 2010. http://www.forbes.com/feeds/afx/2005/09/29/afx2250607.html.

"888 Holdings plc's Official Response to the Unlawful Internet Gambling Act." *Casino City Times,* October 3, 2006. Accessed November 12, 2010. http://www.casinocitytimes.com/news/article/888-holdings-plcs-official-response-to-the-unlawful-internet-gambling-act-161482?contentID=161482.

"888 Holdings Public Limited Company Announces Dividend Declaration." *Reuters,* March 23, 2010. Accessed February 7, 2011. http://www.reuters.com/finance/stocks/keyDevelopments?symbol=888.L.

"888sport." Bookie Rank. Accessed November 14, 2010. http://www.bookierank.com/888sport.html.

"Cryptologic Secures Agreement with 888 Holding plc." 24-7PressRelease.com, May 12, 2008. Accessed November 14, 2010. http://www.24-7pressrelease.com/press-release/cryptologic-secures-agreement-with-888-holdings-plc-49527.php.

eCommerce and Online Gaming Regulation and Assurance (eCOGRA). "Welcome to eCOGRA." London: eCOGRA. Accessed November 12, 2010. http://www.ecogra.org/Home.aspx.

Federal Deposit Insurance Corporation (FDIC). "Unlawful Internet Gambling Enforcement Act: Examination Guidance and Procedures." Washington, DC: FDIC, June 30, 2010. Accessed February 7, 2011. http://www.fdic.gov/news/news/financial/2010/fil10035.html.

Helyar, John. "New Anti-Gambling Law Won't Stop Online Bettors." ESPN.com, October 3, 2006. Accessed November 14, 2010. http://sports.espn.go.com/espn/news/story?id=2611872.

"History of 888 aka Casino on Net." gamblingsites.com. Accessed November 11, 2010. http://www.gamblingsites.com/history/888.

Kredell, Matthew. "UIGEA Goes into Full Effect." *Poker News,* June 1, 2010. Accessed February 7, 2011. http://www.poker news.com/news/2010/06/uigea-goes-into-full-effect-8378. htm.

Roger, S. "The Owners and Founders of 888 Holdings" gamblingsites.com, January 4, 2010. Accessed November 14, 2010. http://www.gamblingsites.com/bio/888.

"Strong Casino Revenue Lifts 888." *Market Watch,* October 31, 2010. Accessed November 14, 2010. http://www.market watch.com/story/strong-casino-revenue-lifts-888.

American Hospital Association

155 North Wacker Drive
Chicago, Illinois 60606
U.S.A.
Telephone: (312) 422-3000
Web site: http://www.aha.org

Private Association
Founded: 1898 (as the Association of Hospital Super-
intendents of the United States and Canada)
Employees: 450 (2010)
Revenues: $120.6 million (2010)
NAICS: 813920 Professional Organizations

■ ■ ■

The American Hospital Association (AHA) addresses and advocates health care policy issues on behalf of its members, some 5,000 hospitals, health care groups, and related health care providers. For example, in the early 2010s the AHA is continually addressing issues related to the Patient Protection and Affordable Care Act of 2010. Along with the hospitals and other organizational members, the AHA has about 37,000 individual members.

The organization works to influence legislative and regulatory policy through a variety of communication channels, from surveys and fact sheets to awards and opinion pieces. In addition, the AHA Resource Center contains books, journals, and other relevant reference material that members may use when researching a particular health care policy issue.

A PROFESSION DEVELOPS

Much like schools and churches, hospitals form an integral part of the communities they serve. For many small communities the closing of the local school or local hospital can mean the demise of the community itself.

In the latter half of the 19th century, as wave after wave of immigrants settled in North America, the demand for health care services began to escalate. While hospitals and health services did exist, there was not a formal profession for the administration of health care or hospital management. Hospitals were usually headed by superintendents who acted independently in attempting to solve the unique problems encountered by hospitals while serving their communities.

In 1899 a group of eight hospital superintendents met in Cleveland, Ohio, to form the Association of Hospital Superintendents of the United States and Canada. The group established its original mission as follows: "To facilitate the interchange of ideas comparing and contrasting methods of management, the discussion of hospital economics, the inspection of hospitals, suggestions of better plans of operating them and such matters as may affect the general interest of the membership."

The new profession of hospital management was born. Although early membership was limited to hospital superintendents, the organization grew. Within eight years, 234 hospital superintendents had joined, and in 1906 the organization renamed itself the American Hospital Association (AHA).

COMPANY PERSPECTIVES

The American Hospital Association (AHA) represents, leads, and serves hospitals, health systems, and other related organizations that are accountable to the community and are committed to health improvement. The AHA provides representation and advocacy for its members on issues of national health care policy development, legislation, regulatory affairs, and judicial matters. It is also a source of education and information on health care issues and trends for health care leaders. The AHA vision is of a society of healthy communities where all individuals reach their highest potential for health.

Interest in the field of hospital management began to expand to include health care management as membership continued to grow. In 1913 the AHA took the first tentative steps into the field of health care management when it opened membership to include not only hospital superintendents but also nursing superintendents, hospital trustees, and medical staff.

THE REALM OF PUBLIC POLICY

In 1917 the United States entered World War I as a combatant, and the American Hospital Association ventured into the realm of public policy for the first time. The organization passed a resolution to establish a war services committee for hospitals and called for greater cooperation between the government and hospitals in the care of soldiers and the health of the North American people.

While the focus remained on hospital management, a new motto called upon the organization to "promote the welfare of the people so far as may be done by the institution, care and management of hospitals," and " ...to do all things which may best promote hospital efficiency." This new wording suggested that the organization saw a broader role for itself.

In 1918 the organization would again expand its base and begin to admit institutional members. This would have a profound effect on expanding the AHA's scope and future resources. Within a decade, institutional memberships would become the organization's primary source of revenue.

Following World War I, the AHA began to work with other groups such as the American Medical As-

sociation and the American College of Surgeons to set standards for hospitals and medical education.

Internally, the organization began to develop. In the 1930s the AHA formed an internal council to examine such issues as administrative practices, professional practices, hospital planning, and operation. It began to investigate association development, public education, and the effects of government regulation. It developed manuals for hospitals, established guidelines for working with insurance organizations and local governments, and developed contracts to be used with medical doctors. It also created the Hospital Services Plan Commission, which would eventually lead to the Blue Cross and Blue Shield organizations.

As its main legislative body, the membership of the AHA created the House of Delegates to bring a more democratic approach to its discussions and process. The House of Delegates was based on the number of members, both individual and institutional, from each state.

By 1937 the American Hospital Association's annual convention attracted more than 4,000 people. Attendees came from not only Canada and the United States but from such diverse nations as Japan, Korea, Cuba, and Peru.

WAR AND ITS AFTERMATH

The years following the stock market crash of 1929 had been difficult for the AHA and its members. The economic depression, which had gripped the United States, placed a considerable strain on U.S. hospitals. As they were beginning to recover, the United States was again plunged into a world war.

Unlike World War I, World War II would put a much greater strain on U.S. resources. Facing the Axis powers in the Pacific and in Europe, the United States was at war on two fronts and geared its economy toward a total war effort.

In its own self-interest, the American Hospital Association became engaged in national issues concerning the war effort. Not only would medical supplies be in short supply on the home front, so would personnel as thousands of medically trained staff, doctors, nurses, and other medical professionals were called into the armed services.

In order to better represent its members and gain a voice at the center of the war effort, the AHA opened a Wartime Services Bureau in Washington, D.C. It hoped to reduce the stress to the domestic medical system caused by the war effort.

The experience gained by the AHA in dealing with the federal government during World War II would lead

KEY DATES

■

1899: The Association of Hospital Superintendents of the United States and Canada holds its first meeting in Cleveland, Ohio.

1906: Organization changes name to the American Hospital Association.

1938: The AHA begins to formally structure the organization with the creation of the House of Delegates as its main legislative body.

1943: Establishes a "Wartime Service Bureau" in Washington, D.C., which becomes the permanent Washington Service Bureau after the war.

1946: AHA plays a major role in development of the Hospital Survey and Construction Act (Hill-Burton Act).

1973: AHA drafts the Patient's Bill of Rights that endorses health care as an inherent right.

2005: AHA publishes "Health Care for Life: Better Health, Better Health Care," a five-point platform for reform.

it to make the Washington office a permanent fixture after the war. While maintaining its head office in Chicago, the AMA turned the Wartime Service Bureau into the Washington Service Bureau, creating a permanent presence at the center of U.S. executive and legislative power.

The AMA would begin to play a much greater role in public policy debates concerning health care and hospital services. George Bugbee, who had become chief executive, felt the most important functions of the organization were research, education, and advocacy.

In 1946 the American Hospital Association would play a key role in the development and passage of the "Hospital Survey and Construction Act," also known as the Hill-Burton Act. The act dealt with four basic points that would be very important to U.S. hospitals. These were the nature of federal funding for hospitals, the use of public funds by private hospitals, the oversight powers of a federal hospital council, and the provision of health services for the poor.

In 1949 the AHA would again exert its influence on national health policy when President Harry Truman proposed a national system of health insurance. While generally supportive of medical insurance, the AHA appeared to favor market forces over a government-mandated system. The Truman reforms met with strong

resistance from a nation in the midst of the cold war, where the idea of socialized medicine had a "red scare" quality about it.

Some progress on health care reform was achieved in the 1960s during the administration of President Lyndon Johnson. Under his "Great Society" program, Johnson was able to amend the Social Security Act to create Medicare and Medicaid.

Medicaid is a social insurance program that provides health and medical services for low-income persons based on each state's eligibility guidelines. Medicare is a federal health insurance program for the elderly and certain disabled U.S. citizens. When introduced in 1965, expenditures for Medicare were $2 billion, but by 2007 they would reach $432 billion. Both programs would begin to escalate federal spending in the health care field.

In the decades following, there was considerable concern about rising costs and the need for fiscal restraint. By 1974 the United States was spending $90 billion per year on health care, of which $41 billion or approximately 45 percent was spent on hospital care.

During the administration of President Richard M. Nixon (1969–74), the United States Economic Stabilization Act would introduce wage and price controls to the U.S. economy, a serious issue for U.S. hospitals. Successive administrations would also act on rising health care costs by attempting to cap or reduce payments for Medicare and Medicaid. This presented a serious challenge to the American Hospital Association. Wage and price controls and ceilings on Medicare and Medicaid payments would strain the resources of U.S. hospitals and affect the delivery of services. Economics and fiscal restraint were demanding issues for hospital administrators, and cost containment began to rival service delivery as an issue.

Patient care had always been the cornerstone of the American Hospital Association's philosophy. As early as 1903, then AHA president John Fehrenbaatch had declared, "The hospital is an institution in which the patient comes first. His interests and welfare are paramount."

In 1973 the AHA returned to its roots when it adopted "A Patient's Bill of Rights." In this document, the association recognized health care as an inherit right and identified effective health care as a collaborative effort between patients and health care professionals.

The Patient's Bill of Rights was revised and reaffirmed in 1992. It laid out a groundwork of health care ethics, which respected the role of the patient based on open and honest communication between parties, as well as respect for personal and professional values and sensitivity to differences. Age, gender, and the special needs of people with disabilities was also recognized.

Noble as the goals of the AHA's Patient's Bill of Rights were, in the real world of day-to-day politics, principles can become derailed. An act to enshrine patient's rights into law was defeated in the United States Congress in 2002, as was comprehensive health care reform in the United States.

HEALTH CARE REFORM AND THE AHA

In 1993 then President Bill Clinton undertook a major effort to reform the U.S. health care system. At the time, some 32 million U.S. citizens were uninsured. After the failure of the Clinton health care plan and the continuation of the free market model the number of uninsured rose to 46 million by 2007.

By 2005 more than a decade had passed since last major attempt at reform had been made. The American Hospital Association, discouraged by the lack of progress on national health care reform, decided to take matters into its own hands. The organization determined to take a greater leadership role in effecting change. In 2007 the AHA brought together a coalition of groups including consumers, physicians, nurses, and business, labor, and health advocates with the challenge of initiating reform. They produced a document titled "Health Care for Life: Better Health, Better Health Care" with the objective of creating better, safer, more efficient and affordable healthcare and a healthier United States.

The plan was composed of five basic elements. "Focus of Wellness" advocated health education, primary care, and the promotion of healthy lifestyles. The "Most Efficient, Affordable Care," focused on making health care costs affordable, and "Highest Quality Care" aimed to match the right care at the right time and in the right setting. "Best Information" was deemed a gateway to good care; and "Health Coverage for All: Paid for by All" laid out the conviction that health care was a shared responsibility. Individuals, businesses, insurers, and government all had a role and a responsibility for funding health care.

In 2008 Barack Obama, a Democrat and dedicated health reform advocate, was elected president of the United States. In addition, control of both the House of Representatives and the U.S. Senate passed to the Democratic Party. With the support of the American Hospital Association, in 2010 the U.S. Congress passed and President Obama signed into law the Patient Protection and Affordable Care Act, which would extend health care benefits to virtually every U.S. citizen.

Many provisions of this act were not scheduled to come into effect for several years, so it was unknown just how this piece of legislation would change the face of U.S. health care. Whatever the outcome, it was certain that the AHA would remain a powerful voice in this field, and its position on specific issues would continue to have an impact in the political arena.

Ian MacDonald

PRINCIPAL DIVISIONS

AHAPAC; Center for Healthcare Governance; Health Forum LLC; Health Research and Education Trust; Institute for Diversity in Health Care.

FURTHER READING

Eggen, Dan. "Hospital Lobbyists Try to Minimize Damage." *Washington Post*, July 25, 2009.

Fuch, Victor, and Emanuel Ezekiel. "Health Care Reform, Why, What, When." *Health Affairs*, 6, no. 1 (November 2005).

Lesparre, Michael. "A Century of the AHA." *Hospital & Health Networks*, January 20, 1998.

Perlstadt, Harry. "The Development of the Hill-Burton Legislation: Interest, Issues and Compromises." *Journal of Health and Social Policy* 6, no. 3 (1995): 77–96.

Picard, Andre. "Time to Get Our Health Act Together." *Globe & Mail*, November 8, 2010.

Ross, J. S. "Health Reform Redux: Learning from Experience and Politics." *American Journal of Public Health* 99, no. 5 (May 2009): 779–86.

Starr, Paul. "What Happened to Health Care Reform." *American Prospect*, December 1, 2004. Accessed February 14, 2011. http://www.prospect.org/cs/articles?article=what_happened_to_health_care_reform.

American Railcar
Industries, Inc.

■

100 Clark Street
St. Charles, Missouri 63301
U.S.A.
Telephone: (636) 940-6000
Fax: (636) 940-6030
Web site: http://www.americanrailcar.com

Public Company
Founded: 1864 as Milton Car Works
Employees: 1,335 (2009)
Sales: $365.3 million (2009)
Stock Exchanges: NASDAQ
Ticker Symbol: ARII
NAICS: 336510 Railroad Rolling Stock Manufacturing

■ ■ ■

A company with roots that date back to the mid-19th century, American Railcar Industries, Inc. (ARI), designs and manufactures railcars and their components, as well as repairing and refurbishing railcars. The business also offers fleet management and engineering services. ARI operates under two basic segments. The first is its manufacturing operations division, and the second is its railcar services. Manufacturing is the much larger operation, typically accounting for around 90 percent of all revenue. However, the economic recession that began in 2008 has led to a relative increase in railcar service revenue, as orders for new railcars dropped dramatically. (ARI received no new orders throughout 2009.)

The manufacturing operations division produces hopper railcars which transport, load, and unload products such as grains, cement, bulk powders, and plastic pallets. This division also produces tank railcars which handle liquid items ranging from ethanol to corn syrup to chlorine. This division is also responsible for manufacturing custom and standard railcar components for industrial and railroad customers, as well as aluminum and steel castings used in the trucking, construction, and mining markets.

The railcar services division of ARI is responsible for repairing and refurbishing railcars, and fleet management services including maintenance planning and engineering services for leasing, railroad, and industrial companies, as well as other companies outside of the railroad market.

Through Icahn Enterprises, L.P., billionaire investor Carl Icahn controls over half of ARI's stock (54.3%).

19TH CENTURY ROOTS

American Railcar Industries, Inc.'s founding dates back more than a century. In February 1864 Murray, Dougal & Company formed the Milton Car Works in the city of Milton, Pennsylvania. The following year, the company began selling some of the first railroad tank cars in the world. These cars were basically a flat car with two wood barrels mounted on them. These Densmore tank cars, named for their designer Amos Densmore, marked the beginning of a new era in railroads.

In 1899, 25 years after its founding, Milton Car Works, along with a dozen other builders of railcars, formed the American Car and Foundry Company (ACF). The previous year, these 13 companies had produced more than half of all freight cars that were built outside of railroad companies' own shops. ACF later built the first passenger car made completely of steel for the Interborough Rapid Transit system, the first subway of New York City, as well as more than 100 cars for London's Underground, the subway system for that city.

Within seven years, ACF had steel shops in a number of cities around the United States, including Detroit, Michigan; St. Louis; Berwick, Pennsylvania; Huntington, West Virginia; and Madison, Illinois. In 1907 the Berwick plant alone employed 5,700 people. By 1920 enough additional companies were added to ACF that it comprised 18 previously separate companies.

GROWTH AND CHANGE

In 1922 ACF acquired Carter Carburetor Corporation of St. Louis. This acquisition launched ACF into the automotive industry. Following this, the company continued to diversify and expand into bus and streetcar manufacturing. Also in this field, ACF acquired several other companies, including Fageol Motors and the Hall-Scott Motor Company. In 1927 Shippers Car Line, a tank car leasing company, was acquired. It was ACF's Shippers Carline Division that would later be spun off to become American Railcar Industries.

The diversity of ACF was especially notable during wartime. During World War I and World War II, ACF produced a variety of products for the Allied forces, including artillery gun mounts, ammunition, submarine chasers, wooden tent pegs, army tanks, tail assemblies for aircrafts, and hospital railcars. In fact, in 1941 ACF produced its 1,000th tank for the U.S. military. By the end of the war, the plant had produced as many as 15,000 tanks. The company's plant in Wilmington built Navy boats, then later switched to creating luxury wood yachts.

By the middle of the 20th century, the company had diversified so much that its name was changed to

reflect these new ventures. The company became ACF Industries, Inc., in 1954. Five years later, its last passenger railcar was produced.

AMERICAN RAILCAR INDUSTRIES: THE LATE 20TH CENTURY

Formed in 1988, American Railcar began as a provider of components for railcars and maintenance services. In 1994 American Railcar Industries, Inc. (ARI), "was formed from the acquisition of railcar component manufacturing and railcar maintenance assets from ACF Industries," according the company's Web site. ARI would manufacture railcars and railcar components, cast steel and aluminum, offer railcar maintenance for ACF's fleet as well as other costumers, operate mobile repair units, and paint and coat railcars. These activities would take place in several locations throughout the United States.

The following year, ARI spent in excess of $10 million on a hopper railcar manufacturing plant in Paragould, Arkansas. Three years after opening the plant in Paragould, ARI spent an additional $22 million to add a paint and lining facility at the same location, and another $20 million to build a tank car manufacturing plant just a few miles away in Marmaduke, Arkansas. That same year, the company announced construction of a railcar repair shop in Green River, Wyoming, and also acquired a paint, blast, and lining plant from another railcar company in Tennille, Georgia.

EXPANSION: 2005–06

In the early part of the new century, ARI found that the number of cars being produced was greater than the number it had room to paint. The company's facility in Paragould was only able to paint about two-thirds of the cars manufactured there. The railcars produced at this facility included covered hopper cars and 89-foot cars. To keep up with growing demand, ARI spent $13 million in 2005 on a 100,000- square-foot expansion to its Paragould plant, which added an additional paint shop. Following the expansion, the company expected to be able to paint all of the cars built at that location. During 2005 the company delivered 6,875 railcars, which was an increase of nearly 57 percent over the previous year's production. Nearly two-thirds of the cars were covered hoppers, and more than one-fourth were tank cars. The remainder of the deliveries were platform cars. Sales for the year reached more than $608 million.

Following this year of successful sales, ARI filed for an initial public offering (IPO) of stock worth as much as $150 million, in 2006. The proceeds from the IPO

KEY DATES

1864: Milton Car Works is founded.
1899: Milton Car Works, as well as 12 other railcar builders, form the American Car and Foundry Company.
1994: American Railcar Industries, Inc., is formed.
2006: American Railcar Industries, Inc., becomes a publicly traded company.
2009: Global economic recession leads to no new orders for entire year.

were to be used to reduce debt and redeem outstanding shares of preferred stock. At the time, the company's chairman, billionaire investor Carl Icahn, was the principal shareholder. Following the IPO, the company hoped to take advantage of the financial flexibility to pursue both internal and external growth opportunities, acquisitions, alliances, and other joint ventures.

Within three months of the IPO, ARI bought one of its suppliers, Steel Technologies Inc., a company that made fabricated parts for ARI. Custom Steel's plant was located beside the component manufacturing facility of ARI, and primarily supported ARI's factory. The purchase allowed ARI to manufacture more of its own railcar parts. The purchase was approximately $18 million.

Also in 2006 ARI announced it would build a new manufacturing plant for railcars adjacent to its existing tank car plant in Marmaduke. The new facility would build tank cars but also be flexible to build covered hoppers and intermodal cars as well. The new plant would be able to produce 2,500 cars each year, beginning in 2008.

At the same time, the company was expanding the tank car facility in Marmaduke to be able to produce an additional 1,000 cars each year. In the fall of 2006, large contracts for railcars were received by ARI. American Railcar Leasing placed orders for a total of 2,400 cars to be delivered during 2008 and 2009.

A YEAR OF PARTNERSHIP AND SUCCESS: 2007

The year 2007 proved to be successful, both in joint ventures and finances. ARI and freight car component supplier Amsted Industries formed a joint venture in 2007 to produce and sell railcar axles. The companies were equal partners in the venture, known as Axis LLC,

and ARI planned to use the products for its own railcar axle assembly business, as well as selling parts to other freight car builders. A $75 million factory was planned to be built early in the next year and to begin production by the end of the year. The plant was to be located in Paragould.

Despite slow production throughout the industry, ARI reported that its net earnings for the fourth quarter of 2007 had increased by 28 percent. The company attributed the increase to changes in the mix of the types of cars produced. The company had been making more tanker cars and fewer hopper cars. In fact, the company reported its best financial performance to date in 2007.

During this time, the company also began creating joint ventures with Amtek Auto Ltd. of New Delhi, India, which would take ARI's products into India and Southeast Asia. The partnership would produce and distribute freight cars and the components for these railcars. Both companies planned to use equal investments to build a manufacturing plant later in the year, with production scheduled to begin in India during the following year.

A DOWNTURN: 2008–09

ARI's impressive financial standing at the end of 2007 did not last long. By the second quarter of 2008, the company's revenue had dropped to approximately half of what it was during the same quarter of the previous year. A decrease in the number of hopper railcars being built at the Paragould plant was partly to blame for the drop in revenue. As a result, the company announced that it was preparing to lay off at least 200 employees at that location, which amounted to approximately one-third of the workers in that facility. Also, since demand and pricing for hopper cars had decreased, the company decreased production of these and produced more tank cars, which sold for higher prices.

Difficult financial times continued for the company. During the second quarter of 2009, ARI reported a decrease of nearly 53 percent in the number of railcars shipped, and a decrease in net income of nearly 82 percent, as compared to the same quarter of the previous year. In June the company reported that its backlog of railcars was reduced due to weak demand as a result of the struggling U.S. economy. Also, one of the company's largest customers announced that it was facing possible bankruptcy. This company had been responsible for 31 percent of ARI's revenue in the first half of the year, and 53 percent of the company's backlog of products.

Railcar shipments, as well as revenues and earnings, for 2009 were approximately half of what the company saw during the previous year, plunging from $808.8 million to $423.4 million. According to the company's annual report for 2009, this downturn followed that of the U.S. economy for that same period. Deliveries of new railcars decreased by about 65 percent from 2008, and no new orders were taken in 2009. However, the company remained profitable, and its railcar services division increased its earnings from $51.3 million in 2008 to $58.1 million in 2009.

PREPARING FOR THE FUTURE: 2010 AND BEYOND

As part of ARI's strategy for facing the future of the industry, the company found ways to diversify. In March 2010 ARI joined with US Railcar LLC to "compete for business in a growing U.S. passenger railcar market, marking the return to passenger railcar manufacturing for one of America's oldest railway supply companies," according to *Railway Age*. The companies planned to design, build, and sell diesel multiple units (DMU) for commuter and passenger rail services. DMUs, which are self-propelled passenger railcars, would be available in both single level and bi-level models. The joint venture was called US Railcar Company, LLC, and production was based in Arkansas. *Railway Age* explained that "The US Railcar DMU is designed to enable new, cost-effective, and environmentally friendly passenger rail service across a range of corridors and routes, all with a proven, existing equipment platform already in service." By becoming involved in this venture, ARI believed that the company would be able to expand its operations into developing markets.

In order to diversify its business further, ARI announced in December 2010 that it planned to invest in railcar leasing. This new venture would offer customers an additional way to use railcars produced by the company.

While ARI's primary business, railcar manufacturing, remained sluggish in the early 2010s, the company was still operating at a profit, and if any of its new ventures were to bear fruit, ARI would be able to diversify itself beneficially from the vagaries of its primary market.

Diane Milne

PRINCIPAL SUBSIDIARIES

Amrail Industries, Inc.; ARI Acquisition Sub, LLC; ARI Component Venture, LLC; ARI DMU, LLC; ARI Fleet Services of Canada, Inc.; ARI Longtrain, Inc.; ARI Mauritius I; Castings LLC; Southwest Steel I, LLC; Southwest Steel II, LLC; Southwest Steel III, LLC.

PRINCIPAL DIVISIONS

Manufacturing Operations; Railcar Services.

PRINCIPAL COMPETITORS

The Greenbrier Companies, Inc; National Steel Car Limited; Trinity Industries, Inc.; Union Tank Car Company.

FURTHER READING

"ARI, US Railcar Join Forces." *Railway Age* 211, no. 3 (2010): 8.

Boyd, John D. "Icahn Takes Greenbrier Stake." *Traffic World*, February 5, 2008.

"For ARI, a Strong Report Card." *Railway Age* 207 no. 4 (2006): 15.

Friedman, Mark. "American Railcar Completes Project." *Arkansas Business*, December 5, 2005, 13.

"Is an Initial Public Offering in ARI's Future?" *Railway Age* 207, no. 1 (2006): 16.

Wood, Jeffrey. "American Railcar Inc. Rolls On." *Arkansas Business*, September 28, 1998, 11.

Amscan Holdings, Inc.

———■———

80 Grasslands Road
Elmsford, New York 10523
U.S.A.
Telephone: (914) 345-2020
Toll Free: (800) 444-8887
Fax: (914) 345-3884
Web site: http://www.amscan.com

Subsidiary
Founded: 1948
Employees: 2,200 (est., 2009)
Sales: $1.48 billion (2009)
NAICS: 422130 Industrial and Personal Service Paper
Wholesalers; 322299 All Other Converted Paper
Product Manufacturing; 322291; Sanitary Paper
Product Manufacturing; 339999 All Other Miscel-
laneous Manufacturing

■ ■ ■

Amscan Holdings, Inc., designs, manufactures, and
distributes a wide variety of party items. Party goods
include tableware, centerpieces, candles, cutouts, crepe,
flags and banners, party hats, piñatas, and latex balloons.
Amscan's stationery items include invitations, decorative
tissues, gift wrapping, ribbons, photograph albums, baby
and wedding memory books, stickers, and confetti. The
company offers close to 400 product ensembles,
intended for seasonal events such as New Year's,
Valentine's Day, St. Patrick's Day, Easter, Passover,
Fourth of July, Halloween, Thanksgiving, Hanukkah,
and Christmas, as well as everyday occasions such as
birthdays, showers, christenings, graduations, an-

niversaries, retirements, first communions, bar mitzvahs,
confirmations, summer picnics and barbecues, and
theme parties such as Mardi Gras, Hawaiian luaus, and
1950s nostalgia. Each ensemble features from 30 to 150
coordinating items. The company also sells home, baby,
and wedding giftware, including plush toys, ceramic
items, mugs, decorative candles, and picture frames. It
manufactures more than 60 percent of its products, outsourcing labor-intensive items to other manufacturers,
located mostly in Asia.

Amscan sells to more than 40,000 retailers around
the world, including North America, Europe, Australia,
and Japan. In addition to its corporate headquarters, it
has locations in China, England, Canada, Germany,
Japan, Mexico, and Australia. The company has seven
distribution centers throughout the world and six
manufacturing facilities domestically. In addition, the
company operates retail party goods and social expressions supply stores in the United States under the names
Party City, Party America, the Paper Factory, Halloween
USA, and Factory Card & Party Outlet, and franchises
both individual stores and franchise areas throughout
the United States and Puerto Rico principally under the
names Party City and Party America. The company is a
wholly owned subsidiary of AAH Holdings
Corporation. Principal owners of Amscan Holdings,
Inc., are Berkshire Partners, Advent International, and
Weston Presidio.

COMPANY FOUNDING AND
DEVELOPMENT: 1947–95

Amscan was founded in 1947 by Elvera Svenningsen,
the mother of the company's longtime chief executive

COMPANY PERSPECTIVES

Our identity has a special meaning. Our founders were American and Scandinavian ... hence AMSCAN. Our in-house design staff continuously develops fresh, innovative, and contemporary product designs and concepts. Our continued investment in art and design results in a steady supply of fresh ideas and the creation of complex, unique ensembles that appeal to consumers. With Amscan you can offer your customers a full array of coordinating products for entertaining and home decoration, then let them mix and match to their heart's content, as they add on and on and on.

officer and chairman, John A. Svenningsen. With just $1,000 and operating out of her family garage in Bronxville, New York, she began to import and distribute such party items as honeycomb decorations like expandable turkeys and clowns. In 1948 she incorporated the business as Amscan Inc. and within a few years was showing modest success, generating some $60,000 in annual sales. After graduating from Swarthmore College in 1953, John Svenningsen joined the company. He was eager to grow the business, confident that the party goods industry, dominated at the time by Dennison Manufacturing Company, held great potential. He became president and chief executive officer in 1958.

Under John Svenningsen's leadership, Amscan moved to a new 600-square-foot facility in Tuckahoe, New York, in 1960 and began to increase the variety of party goods the company had to offer. In just four years, Amscan outgrew this space, relocated to a larger facility in New Rochelle, New York, and then in 1968 moved again, this time to Harrison, New York. Over the next 20 years the company enjoyed steady growth, due in large part to the leadership of Svenningsen. A self-acclaimed amateur psychologist, he gave a great deal of credit for the company's success to the people he hired and nurtured. In a 1993 profile of Amscan by *Party & Paper Retailers,* he explained, "I'm blessed with the ability to recognize people's strengths and place them in a job that will suit those strengths. Respect your employees—bring them in on decisions—and they will be stimulated to do a better job. Here, we run completely by committee—everybody can learn from everybody else." In addition, Svenningsen paid a great deal of attention to his customers, no matter how large or small. He said, "I've always tried to put the

customer's hat on and think like him. ... We have a great synergy with our customers. We offer them quality, price, and we know what will sell for them."

Over the years, many of those customers became large retailers dedicated solely to the sale of party goods. In 1986, for instance, Party City was founded as a single 4,000-square-foot store in New Jersey. Other Party City outlets would soon follow and other party goods retailing chains were also launched, looking to take advantage of a growing penchant of baby boomers attempting to outdo one another when it came to holding parties for their children and themselves. (Before its acquisition Party City emerged as Amscan's largest customer.) The resulting increase in retail sales fueled the steady growth of Amscan, which saw revenues reach $64 million in 1989, $68.5 million in 1990, and $75.5 million in 1991. Also during the late 1980s, the company looked overseas. In 1987 Amscan began to test the market in the United Kingdom, bringing out tableware and plastic cutlery in specially selected colors. British consumers, like their U.S. counterparts, were also becoming more affluent and increasingly engaged in hosting parties and barbecues.

In the early 1990s Amscan remained privately owned. Elvera Svenningsen died, leaving John Svenningsen as the last link to the founding of the company. He did not urge his children to become involved in the company, allowing them to pursue their own careers. Annual revenues topped the $100 million mark in 1993 ($108.9 million). The company enjoyed even stronger growth over the next two years, with revenues totaling $132 million in 1994 and $167.4 million in 1995. Moreover, net income jumped from nearly $10 million in 1994 to more than $17.4 million in 1995.

AN IPO AND DEATH OF CEO: 1996–97

John Svenningsen was diagnosed with lymphoma in the first quarter of 1996. In April of that year Gerald C. Rittenberg was promoted to the position of president of the company. Svenningsen remained CEO and chairman, and as he underwent treatment for his condition he continued to play a major role in running the company while others in the organization took on increasing levels of responsibility. Rittenberg, for instance, was a key player. Trained as a printer, he had headed product development since 1990. Another key executive was William S. Wilkey, senior vice president in charge of sales.

In October 1996 Amscan Holdings Inc. was formed as a holding company for Amscan and subsidiaries in preparation for taking the business public. The initial

KEY DATES

∎

1948: Amscan Inc. is formed by Elvera Svenningsen.
1958: John A. Svenningsen becomes CEO.
1968: Growing rapidly, company moves operations to Harrison, New York.
1986: Party City opens its first store in New Jersey.
1997: John Svenningsen dies of cancer.
1998: Anagram International is acquired.
2002: M&D Balloons is acquired.
2004: Boston buyout firms Berkshire Partners LLC and Weston Presidio purchase Amscan from Goldman Sachs.
2005: Amscan acquires Party City and its 500 stores.
2009: Amscan enters into a strategic alliance with American Greetings Corporation.

public offering (IPO) was completed in December. Amscan sold four million shares priced at $14 apiece, netting the company $48 million, which was then used to pay down debt and allow some shareholders, such as Svenningsen, to cash in some of their equity. The stock then began trading on the NASDAQ. The company finished 1996 producing record levels of sales ($192.7 million), although net income dropped to $2.1 million.

Amscan's tenure as a public company, however, would be short term. In May 1997, after a 15-month battle with cancer, John Svenningsen died at the age of 66. Rittenberg, the man who succeeded him as CEO (and filled in as chairman on an interim basis), commented at the time, "John was a true innovator and visionary for the party goods industry." By the end of 1997 Amscan was taken private again. GS Capital Partners II L.P., an investment fund managed by Goldman, Sachs & Co., formed Confetti Acquisition Inc. in order to acquire Amscan. Under terms of the $315 million transaction, shareholders were given their choice of tendering their stock for either $16.50 in cash or $9.33 plus a retained interest. At the end of the day, 83 percent of Amscan was owned by Goldman, Sachs. The estate of John A. Svenningsen owned 10 percent, and the company's management held a 7 percent stake. (A managing director of Goldman, Sachs, Terrence M. O'Toole, took over as chairman of the board, while Rittenberg continued to maintain operational control.)

Moreover, Amscan was infused with $75 million in capital in order to provide the financial clout the company needed to take advantage of the growing party goods industry, which was then responsible for around $3.5 billion in annual sales and was growing at a 10 percent rate each year. Superstores such as Party City not only continued to prosper, they promoted the celebration of an even larger number of occasions, which in turn greatly enhanced the prospects of Amscan with its well-entrenched position in the marketplace. Rittenberg also maintained that the party supplies market was actually "understored." As a result, Amscan was well positioned to enjoy even greater growth in the years to come.

ACQUISITION AND GROWTH: 1998–2001

In September 1998 Amscan expanded via external means, paying approximately $87 million for Minneapolis-based Anagram International, Inc., manufacturer and distributor of metallic balloons and other products made from synthetic materials. Anagram was founded in 1977 by Garry Kieves and family members. At the time of the acquisition the company was generating annual revenues in the $70 million range. While Rittenberg portrayed the acquisition as representing "a unique opportunity for Amscan to leverage its distribution in the party superstores," others outside the company were less enthusiastic. As reported by the *Westchester County Business Journal*, "'The outlook is negative,' according to a Standard & Poor's Rating Services report released six days after the deal was announced. S&P gave Amscan a single B plus corporate rating and single B minus subordinated debt rating. 'Ratings reflect Amscan's weak financial profile, stemming from its high debt leverage, and participation in the fragmented, highly competitive party goods industry,'" wrote S&P analyst Nicole Delz Lynch.

With Anagram contributing to the balance sheet for an entire year, Amscan saw its revenues improve from $235.3 million in 1998 to nearly $305 million in 1999. Net income also increased from $6.7 million to $10.2 million. These strong numbers were also the result of some internal changes. The company created a specialty sales force in 1999, targeting card and gift stores and other independent retailers. In addition, Amscan launched a gift line geared towards independents as a way to offer a one-stop shopping possibility. Amscan's balance sheet continue to show improvement in 2000 and 2001, when the company recorded sales of $323.5 million and $345.2 million. The company posted net income of $8.1 million in 2000 and $11 million in 2001.

M&D BALLOONS ACQUISITION: 2002

Early in 2002 Amscan completed another acquisition, paying $27.5 million in cash and stock for M&D Balloons Inc. to American Greetings Corporation. Based in Manteno, Illinois, M&D manufactured both metallic and plastic balloons. For American Greetings, the deal allowed it to continue a major cost-cutting effort while retaining the ability to distribute Mylar balloons through its Balloon Zone subsidiary by way of a supply contract with Amscan. The addition of M&D complemented Amscan's prior acquisition of Anagram, which ranked as the largest metallized balloon manufacturer in the world, with some $75 million in annual sales. M&D was second with $25 million, and together they formed a dominant force in the nonlatex party balloon segment. M&D also brought with it a patented film technology, Dynafloat, which enhanced the longevity of metallic balloons. Moreover, M&D possessed an impressive portfolio of licenses, including popular Disney and Nickelodeon characters. Within months, Amscan closed M&D's balloon-making factory, transferring operations to Anagram's more automated plant in Eden Prairie, Minnesota. For years, M&D had been at a competitive disadvantage, relying on its workers to lift, stack, and pack balloons manually.

In June 2002 Amscan took steps to once again become a publicly traded company, filing a registration for a projected $180 million stock offering. The $150 million net was earmarked to pay down debt. This time management planned on a New York Stock Exchange listing. Later in 2002, however, management dropped its plans for an offering, opting instead for a refinancing agreement with Goldman Sachs Credit Partners L.P., which extended the maturity of its senior debt facilities. However, this deal did not come to fruition, making the IPO operative once again. Finally, in March 2003 the offering was shelved permanently when Amscan and Goldman Sachs Credit Partners negotiated $200 million in loans.

NEW OWNERSHIP: 2004–07

Goldman Sachs announced in March 2004 that its private equity arm was selling Amscan to the Boston buyout firms Berkshire Partners LLC and Weston Presidio in a leveraged recapitalization. When the transaction was completed, it included equity and debt totaling approximately $560 million. "The recapitalization gives Amscan the continued financial strength and operating flexibility to allow the company to exploit new growth opportunities," Rittenberg said in a *Business Wire* article. In the same article, Robert J. Small, managing director at Berkshire Partners, noted that Amscan "is uniquely positioned for continued success and we are excited to support Amscan's growth plan as it focuses on new opportunities."

Although Amscan's various retail operations began as independent retailers and franchisors in the mid to late 1980s, Amscan started acquiring its own retail stores in 2005, beginning with the acquisition of Party City at that end of that year. Party City had 500 company-owned and franchise stores located throughout the United States. The following year, Amscan acquired PA Acquisition Corp., which did business as Party America, from the Gordong Brothers Group, LLC. Headquartered in Alameda, California, Party America was a leading chain of party supply stores that had a presence in 45 states with approximately 155 company-owned and franchise stories operating as Party America as well as 110 The Paper Factory stores.

Another major acquisition occurred in June 2007 when a leading retailer of Halloween and party goods, Gags & Games Inc., was purchased. The company operated approximately 20 party superstores in Michigan and Ohio under the name of Party USA and a chain of temporary Halloween stores throughout the Midwest. With this acquisition, Amscan had more than 770 company-owned and franchise party superstores. In November of the same year, Factory Card & Party Outlet, which had 185 stores in 19 states, became a wholly owned subsidiary of Amscan. In 2007 Amscan reported a profit of $19.3 million on 2007 sales of $1.22 billion.

A NEW STRATEGIC ALLIANCE: 2009

Amscan entered into a strategic alliance with American Greetings Corporation in December 2009. Through the alliance, Amscan acquired the inventory, equipment, and processes used by American Greetings in the manufacture and distribution of party goods, as well as exclusive rights to manufacture and distribute products into various channels. In turn, American Greetings began to source party goods from Amscan. Amscan also secured a $675 million secured term loan credit facility in 2010 to refinance indebtedness outstanding under an existing senior secured term loan facility, to pay special cash dividend to its shareholders and to improve the company's overall financial flexibility.

By the beginning of 2010, the company had a retail network of 386 party goods supply superstores, 161 party goods and social expressions supply stores, 54 party goods outlet stores, and 248 franchisee-owned party goods supply stores, as well as 247 temporary Halloween stores operating under the name Halloween USA. Nonseasonal merchandise accounted for approximately 70 percent of the company's retail net sales with the remaining 30 percent coming from seasonal merchandise for Halloween, Christmas, graduation, Easter, and other holidays. The company's future plans included building upon its position as a leading provider to party goods retailers, expanding its international presence, capitalizing on investments in infrastructures such as its distribution facility, and continuing to grow through targeted acquisitions.

Ed Dinger
Updated, David Petechuk

PRINCIPAL SUBSIDIARIES

Amscan Inc.; Anagram International, Inc.; Grasslands Road; Ya Otta Piñata.

PRINCIPAL COMPETITORS

American Greetings Corporation; Celebrate Express, Inc.; CSS Industries, Inc.; Hallmark Cards, Inc.

FURTHER READING

"Amscan Announces Strategic Alliance with American Greetings." *PR Newswire,* December 22, 2009. Accessed March 18, 2011. http://www.prnewswire.com/news-releases/amscan-announces-strategic-alliance-with-american-greetings-79909677.html.

"Amscan Is a Dominant Force in Party Supplies." *Chain Drug Review,* June 29, 1998, 16.

"Berkshire Partners and Weston Presidio Complete Recapitalization of Amscan Holdings, Inc." *Business Wire,* April 30, 2004, 5627.

Drain, Trisha McMahon. "Amscan-ning, the Horizon." *Party & Paper Retailer,* January, 1992, 68.

"Party America, a Leading Party Goods Retailer, Acquired by AAH Holdings Corporation." *PR Newswire,* September 29, 2006.

Phillippidis, Alex. "'Party People' Celebrate $48 Million Sale of Stock." *Westchester County Business Journal,* January 6, 1997, 3.

AuthenTec, Inc.

100 Rialto Place
Suite 100
Melbourne, Florida 32901
U.S.A.
Telephone: (321) 308-1300
Fax: (321) 308-1431
Web site: http://www.authentec.com

Public Company
Founded: 1998
Employees: 126 (2010)
Sales: $34.07 million (2010)
Stock Exchanges: NASDAQ
Ticker Symbol: AUTH
NAICS: 334413 Semiconductor and Related Device
Manufacturing

∎ ∎ ∎

AuthenTec, Inc., is the world's leading manufacturer of fingerprint sensors and identity management software. Products include security, identity management, and touch control applications for government, consumer, and corporate markets. AuthenTec's products are used for PCs and peripherals, wireless devices, and access control systems.

AuthenTec's fingerprint sensors are used in more than 50 million PCs and tablets, Wi-Fi access points, and other mobile devices. Sensors offer a secure method of identifying the intended user of a computer and user-friendly fingertip navigation.

AuthenTec's access control sensors are used to protect homes, corporate and government offices, and other secure facilities. AuthenTec's TrueSuite Identity management software is designed to simplify the experience of using computers and handheld devices by offering one-touch access to social networks and other password-protected applications without sacrificing the security a password provides.

AuthenTec maintains an Asian headquarters in Shanghai, China, and this geographic area (Asia and Oceania) accounted for 92 percent of revenue in 2010. Top customers that year included Edom Technology (27% of 2010 revenue), Fujitsu (19%), Lenovo (17%), and Richpower Electronic Devices (15%). After engaging in a battle of patent infringement lawsuits with competitor UPEK, the two companies merged in 2010.

A BETTER FINGERPRINT: 1995–99

In 1995 Dave Setlack was working as a software designer for Harris Semiconductor, an international communications and information technology company. His project, developing computer systems for electronic patient records, required that he find a more effective method for data security than passwords. He began testing a fingerprint sensor, soon finding that traditional methods of fingerprinting were prone to an error rate of up to 50 percent for his target market in hospital emergency rooms, where much of the population's fingertip surfaces were unreadable. (Fingerprinting in law enforcement was successful due to the relatively uniform population of prisoners and law enforcement officials, whose prints were usually unmarred.)

Setlack knew that a technology with such a high error rate would not be useful. Therefore, he began collaborating with antenna and semiconductor engineers to develop a technology that could read below the skin's outer service using electrical impulses.

Until 1996 the team worked on this fingerprinting project as a "skunkworks" project that lay outside their normal responsibilities. However, when Phillip W. Farmer took over as Harris' new chairman and CEO, he encouraged projects that collaborated across departments such as this one. Scott Moody, president of Harris Semiconductor Group's Core Products business unit, saw to it that Setlack's team received funding and authority to build the first FingerLoc sensor.

While the technology had a great deal of potential, it was a risky venture that did not quite fit Harris' product mix serving government markets. In 1998 Harris spun off the FingerLoc product to its own company, named AuthenTec, with Moody as its new president and Setlack as chief research officer. In 1999 the technology was perfected, and the FP-S1 went into production.

GROWTH, INNOVATION, AND AWARDS: 2000–06

In early 2000 AuthenTec started introducing kits for different industries so that clients could test the technology within their own companies. These Technology Evaluation Kits (TEKs) fitted into two categories. Software Design Kits (SDKs) were for software developers, and Reference Design Kits (RDKs) consisted of hardware and software designed to plug into existing software applications.

AuthenTec formed partnerships and generated venture capital to finance early growth. By the end of 2000, AuthenTec had partnerships with Biolink Technologies, Verification Media, and Arrow Electronics to integrate FingerLoc into personal computers and

eliminate the need for Internet passwords. Revenue had tripled each quarter in 2000, and the company doubled the size of its workforce from 25 to 55. While revenues poured in, so did venture funding. The company had acquired about $40 million in additional capital by March 2001, with the bulk coming from Texas Instruments (TI).

AuthenTec also focused on new product development. In 2001 the company introduced Entrepad AES3500, the smallest biometric device to that time that required minimal battery power. These two features made the new device a good fit for handheld devices. In 2002 AuthenTec introduced its first slide fingerprint sensor, introducing fingertip to screen navigation.

In 2003 AuthenTec made two critical strategic decisions. By focusing on the consumer market instead of corporate or government markets, AuthenTec captured 50 percent of the fingerprinting sensor sector by late 2003. In addition, a longtime relationship with Fujitsu allowed entrance to the Asian market, where consumer technology was more quickly accepted than in the United States. That year, Microsoft and AuthenTec joined up to develop authentication software for Microsoft's Windows operating system. Over 80 percent of AuthenTec's chips were for PCs and wireless devices, with the remaining 20 percent for security devices. In addition, over 93 percent of the company's customers were in Asia.

AuthenTec's technology potential applied to more than the computer and handheld industries. By 2006 it was not the mobile phone or computer industry driving demand for AuthenTec's products but the credit card industry. In Japan, transactions no longer used credit cards but instead mobile devices, using AuthenTec's products to provide data security device and customer identification. In addition, AuthenTec's Entrepad was used in 2006 by the U.S. government for its U.S. Census workers' PDAs, eliminating the need for paperwork while also providing necessary data protection.

In 2005 AuthenTec won the first of several prestigious awards for technology. *Fortune* named the company a breakout company for 2005 for its fingerprint swipe technology. In 2006 the *Wall Street Journal* awarded AuthenTec with its Technology Innovation Award.

GOING PUBLIC: 2007

Although the company had been awarded over $65 million in venture funding over the years, AuthenTec's growth potential needed more than venture capital In June 2007 the company completed its initial public of-

KEY DATES

1997: Engineers at Harris Semiconductor invent FingerLoc.

1998: Harris spins off FingerLoc product to form AuthenTec.

2002: AuthenTec introduces fingerprint sliding technology.

2007: AuthenTec begins trading on NASDAQ using ticker symbol AUTH.

2010: AuthenTec merges with competitor UPEK.

fering (IPO) and began trading on the NASDAQ under the ticker name AUTH. The IPO generated $57.5 million in proceeds. Sales exploded, increasing 250 percent in 18 months. In December 2007 AuthenTec sold its 25 millionth fingerprint sensor, up from 10 million in June 2006.

However, the IPO's success was marred by a class action lawsuit that alleged that company officers overstated its expectations for 2008, knowingly inflating its stock price by overproducing and flooding its clients with inventory. Furthermore, the company stated revenue expectations of $78 million for 2008 but later revised that projection downward. The company ended 2008 with a revenue of $63 million and net loss for the year due to softer demand in the PC market.

INTERNATIONAL EXPANSION AND ACQUISITIONS: 2008 AND BEYOND

In 2008 AuthenTec introduced Borah, a product that embedded two technologies, identification and navigation, on one chip. While seamless to the end-consumer, the invention reduced costs for both AuthenTec and its clients, allowing the final price for high-tech phones to go down even further. In 2009 AuthenTec introduced a new sensor called Mercy for netbooks, a part of its TruSuite software that automatically launched a user's favorite Web sites, such as Facebook or MySpace. However, the company began experiencing softening demand for its products. Consumers liked the applications, but netbook customers were price sensitive and did not want to pay a premium for Mercy. After all, entering passwords was a familiar process.

While AuthenTec continued product innovation, the company also focused on international expansion. In late 2008 AuthenTec teamed with Medion AG, based in Essen, Germany, to enhance Medion's fingerprint-

enabled personal navigation devices with a secure method of fingerprint identification. In addition, AuthenTec ventured into the African and Middle East markets by teaming up with Raydir Manufacturing to provide sensors for Raydir's Matrix M5 cell phone.

The most promising market for AuthenTec's international expansion was in Asia. In late 2009 the company pursued further expansion there, beginning with a distribution deal with Japanese component supplier Murata. Murata would offer AuthenTec's products to its customers that included Casio-Hitachi, Kyocera, NEC, Nintendo and others. In September the company hired Dr. Lunji Qiu as vice president and general manager of the Shanghai headquarters in order to develop further business in the area. Similarly, in October AuthenTec appointed Masatoshi Morishita as president of AuthenTec KK, the Japanese subsidiary. Japan, whose consumers are often early adapters of new technology, had long been a key market for AuthenTec's success. (In 2010 Japan accounted for 22 percent of all revenue.) Scott Deutsch was hired as vice president of worldwide sales to coordinate efforts to expand globally.

During this time, AuthenTec also began an acquisition spree. In April 2008 AuthenTec acquired the software assets of EzValidation, a company that had used fingerprinting technology for passport authentication. In July 2009 AuthenTec bought the assets of competing fingerprint technology company Atrua Technologies for a cash transaction of $4.9 million, an acquisition that provided access to the European market. In February 2010 AuthenTec announced that it had acquired the Embedded Security Solutions division of Safenet Inc. for $11.3 million in shares and cash.

However, AuthenTec was not agreeable to all mergers. In February 2010 AuthenTec's primary competitor, UPEK, proposed an unsolicited merger. AuthenTec rejected the offer. Days later, news reports revealed that AuthenTec had filed a lawsuit against UPEK for patent infringement a week earlier. In response, UPEK filed a similar claim against AuthenTec. Seven months later, the two companies finally merged, but not without casualties. Scott Moody stepped down as CEO but remained a board member. Larry Ciacca, AuthenTec's COO, stepped in to lead the company. Two new directors from UPEK joined the board of the new company. The patent infringement lawsuits were dropped, and the all-stock deal totaled $32.4 million. The merger combined AuthenTec's leading position in the PC and wireless market with UPEK's government market and software expertise. The combined company would retain the name of AuthenTec. With the merger, the new company held the largest patent portfolio in the biometrics industry.

In December 2010 the company announced that it would offer the world's first high-performance random number generator that complied with government standards for cryptographic security. This product was a departure from AuthenTec's traditional fingerprint biometric solutions. The merger with UPEK provided both the expertise and the government clientele for the product. The product could be used for statistical sampling, communication security, and random noise generation. Applications included secure military communication, banking and financial transactions, and digital content security.

Since its IPO, the company had posted a net loss for most quarters, and in the early 2010s it was operating in a U.S. market hesitant to pay for new technology. As a technology company, AuthenTec faced the challenge of predicting the future and developing technologies that would be most useful to a customer base that did not always know what it needed or wanted. The company's task was to continue to develop new products for the corporate and government markets that would pay for an application's potential before it was seen to be essential.

Sara K. Huter

PRINCIPAL SUBSIDIARIES

AuthenTec China; AuthenTec KK (Japan).

PRINCIPAL COMPETITORS

Atmel Corporation; EgisTec Inc.; Validity Sensors, Inc.

FURTHER READING

"AuthenTec Wins Fingerprint-Enabled Cell Phone Design Contract for Africa and the Middle East," *Health & Beauty Close-Up,* May 21, 2010.

"Census Taking Made Easier," *Sensors Magazine,* 23, no. 7 (2006).

LaPedus, Mark. "Chip Startups Sense Sales in Fingerprint ID." *Electronic Engineering Times,* March 3, 2008.

"Medion Debuts 3 New Fingerprint-Enabled Personal Navigation Devices." *Health & Beauty Close-Up,* December 8, 2008.

Ojo, Bolaji. "AuthenTec Leaves Mark in Sensors: Focus on Consumer Electronics Pushes Company into Fingerprint-IC Lead." *EBN,* 2003.

O'Melveny & Myers LLC. "O'Melveny Represents UPEK in Merger with AuthenTec." Washington, DC: O'Melveny & Myers LLC, September 7, 2010. Accessed February 14, 2011. http://www.pressreleasepoint.com/o039melveny-represents-upek-merger-authentec.

Quan, Margaret. "Identifying with Engineering," *Electronic Engineering Times,* 1998.

Sapp, Justin. "AuthenTec Posts Profits, Inks New Partnership." *Orlando Business Journal* 17, no. 6 (2000).

"Security issues … AuthenTec, a Provider of Bbiometric Security Solutions, Introduced FingerLoc Technology Evaluation Kits (TEKs), Software Design Kits (SDKs) and Reference Design Kits (RDKs) for Serial Bus and Universal Serial Bus (USB) Platforms." *Frontline Solutions,* June 1, 2000.

"Toshiba Lets Your Fingers Do the Working; Toshiba's Two Newest Notebook Computers Will Be Outfitted with Fingerprint Sensors, Assisting Users in Improving Productivity and Security, According to the PC Vendor." *InformationWeek,* April 28, 2005.

Yoshido, Junko. "Fingerprint Sensors Score in Handsets – AuthenTec Touts Tech's Benefits for Navigation, Game Play on Phones," *Electronic Engineering Times,* December 1, 2003.

Bank of Nova Scotia

———————— ∎ ————————

44 King Street West
Toronto, Ontario M5H 1H1
Canada
Telephone: (416) 866-6161
Fax: (416) 866-3750
Web site: http://www.scotiabank.com

Public Company
Founded: 1832
Employees: 70,772 (2010)
Sales: CAD 15.5 billion ($15.9 billion) (2010)
Stock Exchanges: New York Toronto
Ticker Symbol: BNS
NAICS: 522110 Commercial Banks

∎ ∎ ∎

Bank of Nova Scotia, also called Scotiabank, is a prominent Canadian commercial bank with a wide geographic reach. Scotiabank provides banking services for roughly 18.6 million customers through its 2,800 branches worldwide. While the company's Canadian banking segment captures the majority of revenues, Scotiabank's international banking segment cleared over CAD 1 billion in 2010, with operations in 45 countries in the Caribbean, Mexico, Latin America, and Asia. In addition, the Scotia Capital business segment offers wholesale banking services to corporate, government, and other institutional clients. In 2010 the bank introduced a Global Wealth Management segment which combined previously distinct insurance, transaction banking, and wealth management units.

PROVIDING SERVICES TO LOCAL MERCHANTS

The first public financial institution in the colonial port city of Halifax, the Bank of Nova Scotia was formed on March 30, 1832, to handle the economic activity associated with the area's lumber, fishing, farming, and foreign trade. None of the members of the first board of directors had any practical banking experience, but this did not deter them from setting up the necessary operations and appointing James Forman, a prominent citizen of Halifax, to serve as the first cashier (as the general manager was then called).

The bank officially opened in August 1832, a time of unfavorable economic conditions because of massive crop failures and a cholera outbreak. Early development, therefore, focused on establishing a foreign exchange business with agents in New York, London, and Boston, while local agencies and the main office in Halifax concentrated on making domestic loans.

Over the next 30 years, the bank grew slowly in the face of increased competition from existing institutions, such as the Halifax Banking Company and the Bank of British North America, as well as from new banks opening throughout Nova Scotia. It was not until the early 1870s that the staff also determined that growth had been stunted by Forman's embezzlement of CAD 315,000 since 1844.

The bank gradually recovered from these losses through the efforts of Forman's successor, William C. Menzies, who guided an expansion program that increased total assets to CAD 3.5 million by 1875. Although local industry was declining, growth

---

COMPANY PERSPECTIVES

Scotiabank is one of North America's leading financial institutions, and Canada's most international bank. We provide innovative financial products and services to individuals, small and medium-size businesses, corporations, and governments across Canada and around the world.

---

continued throughout the decade as the bank found opportunities in financing coal mining, iron, and steel businesses serving the railway and steamship lines. These improvements in transportation stimulated manufacturing throughout Canada, which also served to fuel the bank's development.

The Bank of Nova Scotia expanded outside the Maritime Provinces in 1882, when it opened a branch in Winnipeg to take advantage of opportunities created by a real estate boom in the area. The boom collapsed within six months, however, saddling the bank with enormous losses and forcing the branch to close three years later.

In 1883 the Bank of Nova Scotia acquired the Union Bank of Prince Edward Island. This bank had sought a larger, stronger institution to help it weather hard times that had forced the liquidation of one local bank and were seriously affecting others in the area. By the end of that year, the Bank of Nova Scotia was operating 23 branches in Prince Edward Island, New Brunswick, and Nova Scotia.

Although a depression in Canada in the early 1880s caused heavy losses stemming from the failure of several businesses, the bank had rebounded enough by 1885 to consider further expansion, this time in the United States. Minneapolis was chosen, because of its strong grain and manufacturing industries, to be the initial site for a direct lending and foreign exchange business. This office closed seven years later when the local environment became less favorable, and other cities, such as Chicago, showed more potential.

BRANCHING OUT TO MONTREAL

In 1888 the bank opened an office in Montreal in a second attempt to establish a domestic presence outside of the Maritime Provinces. This office was followed a year later by an office in Kingston, Jamaica, the first time a Canadian bank had expanded outside North America or the United Kingdom. The next new branch

opened in St. John's, Newfoundland, in 1894 to handle the business of two local institutions that had dissolved suddenly. This was the first move by a Canadian bank into Newfoundland, which would not become a province for another 55 years. Credit for this vigorous expansion goes to Thomas Fyshe, who became cashier in 1876 and resigned in 1897 after 21 years with the bank.

In March 1900 the bank moved its headquarters to Toronto, to be better able to take advantage of opportunities offered by the Klondike Gold Rush and the completion of the Canadian Pacific Railway, as well as to be closer to its other branches in Canada and the United States. Its move into Western Canada was only somewhat successful, however. Several unprofitable branches closed soon after they opened, while others in Edmonton, Calgary, and Vancouver were slow to make a profit. Nonetheless, the bank considered expansion a necessary part of its overall strategic plan to achieve national growth and avoid takeover by another institution. Development in the East was more successful, as 19 new branches opened in Nova Scotia and New Brunswick, 16 opened in Ontario, and four opened in Quebec between 1897 and 1909.

Beginning in 1901, Henry C. McLeod, who served as general manager from 1897 to 1910, waged a campaign to require all Canadian banks to undergo external inspection by the Canadian Department of Finance. This effort, prompted by the large number of bank failures that had occurred since 1895, was intended to win the public's confidence in its financial institutions. None of the other Canadian banks supported him, so, impatient with the government's inactivity on the issue, McLeod subjected the Bank of Nova Scotia to examination by two Scottish accountants, making his the first Canadian chartered bank to be verified by an independent, external audit. McLeod did not win his battle until 1913, when the Bank Act was revised and such inspection became compulsory.

Between 1910 and 1920 the bank embarked upon a series of major acquisitions that significantly altered its size and the scope of its operations. After two years of informal discussions, the bank officially merged with the oldest Canadian chartered bank, the Bank of New Brunswick, on December 11, 1912. Established in 1820, the Bank of New Brunswick was a relatively small institution, confined to 31 branches in a single region and lacking the resources to expand because of its traditional practice of returning capital to shareholders. In 1914, with the acquisition of the 12-year-old Toronto-based Metropolitan Bank, the Bank of Nova Scotia became the fourth-largest financial institution in Canada. Five years later, the Bank of Nova Scotia acquired the Bank

KEY DATES

1832: The Bank of Nova Scotia (or Scotiabank) is born; it is the first public financial institution in Halifax.

1883: The Union Bank of Prince Edward Island is acquired.

1900: Headquarters are moved to Toronto.

1912: Bank of Nova Scotia merges with the Bank of New Brunswick, the oldest Canadian chartered bank.

1914: Toronto-based Metropolitan Bank is acquired, making Scotiabank the fourth-largest financial institution in Canada.

1954: Passage of the National Housing Act leads Scotiabank to create a mortgage department.

1958: Changes to Bank Act of 1954 enable Scotiabank to introduce a consumer credit program.

1981: Bank of Nova Scotia expands into Asia with the opening of a branch in Japan.

1987: Scotia Securities is formed to provide discount brokerage and security underwriting services.

2000: Scotiabank increases to 55 percent its stake in Mexican bank Grupo Financiero Inverlat, which is subsequently renamed Grupo Financiero Scotiabank Inverlat.

2002: Economic turmoil in Argentina leads to the bank's sale of its subsidiary there and a CAD 540 million writedown on its investment.

2006: Bank of Nova Scotia purchases Maple Trust for CAD 233 million.

2007: Bank purchases 18 percent stake in Dundee Wealth Management for CAD 348 million.

2011: Bank announces plans to offer small loans and credit cards to customers in Mexico.

of Ottawa, allowing it to expand westward again without having to establish new branches.

Joining other Canadian financial institutions in the war effort during World War I, Scotiabank experienced only minor disruptions in operations and staffing and returned to normal upon the war's end.

During the early 1920s, the bank slowed the pace of external growth to focus its attention on consolidating the operations of its three prewar acquisitions and reorganizing its departments for greater efficiency. An Investment Department was formed to handle securities

transactions, which represented a significant amount of the bank's business in Toronto, Montreal, and New York.

The strong postwar recovery brought healthy earnings throughout most of the decade, until the 1929 stock market crash and subsequent depression. Between 1933 and 1935, the bank closed 19 domestic branches as profits dropped by half a million dollars, to CAD 1.8 million. Business conditions in Newfoundland deteriorated, the Social Credit Party rose to power in Alberta and enacted troublesome legislation there, and political difficulties in Cuba and Puerto Rico pressured international activities.

ECONOMIC RECOVERY

Economic recovery went up and down between 1936 and 1939 as the positive effects of the growing Canadian mining industry were offset by a drought in the West. The bank's asset base continued to grow, but not without some managerial concern since it consisted largely of loans to the government for relief funds, rather than higher-yielding commercial transactions.

World War II increased the demand for banking services, particularly by the government for financing the war. By the end of the war the bank's assets had surpassed CAD 600 million, with federal government securities representing 50 percent of the total.

In 1945 the new general manager, Horace L. Enman, renewed prewar efforts to explore new business opportunities and improve shareholders' returns. Buoyed by heavy immigration to Canada and the nation's need for capital, the bank's commercial loan activity increased after the war to restore a more favorable balance between lending to business concerns and to the government. In 1949 Enman became president, and C. Sydney Frost became general manager. By this time the bank's rapid growth and extensive reach demanded greater decentralization. Regional offices gradually assumed responsibility for staffing and maintaining branch activities and credit supervision. By 1950 the bank had opened 90 new branches, half in British Columbia and Alberta.

The 1950s were a period of economic prosperity throughout Canada. Resource development and improvements in transportation increased immigration levels in major Canadian cities and provided a stimulus to growth. The change from a fixed to a floating official exchange rate allowed the bank to take advantage of the open market for the Canadian dollar and enhance its exchange-trading skills. When the National Housing Act was passed in 1954, the bank established a mortgage department, and it later developed a secondary mortgage market among pension funds to offset decreased lending activity. The bank also introduced an insured savings plan that brought in a substantial amount of new business, and more importantly, gave the bank a competitive advantage in selling banking services.

A change in the Bank Act in 1954 permitted banks to make automobile and household loans, prompting the bank to introduce a consumer credit program in 1958. In order for the bank to observe the 6 percent interest rate ceiling mandated by the Bank Act yet successfully operate in the consumer lending area on a large scale, these loans required customers to deposit payments every month into a bank account that would pay off the loan by the due date and return a higher rate of interest to the bank over the life of the loan. By its second year, this plan had generated CAD 100 million in loans and become a major contributor to the bank's overall earnings. When, in 1959, a money squeeze threatened its lending activity volume, the bank introduced a one-to-six-year term note that allowed it to compete successfully with finance and trust companies.

The bank continued its international expansion during this period, particularly in Jamaica, Trinidad, and Barbados, although the nationalization of Cuban banks in 1961 forced it, regretfully, to close the eight branches it had established there at the beginning of the century.

In 1958 the bank joined with British financial interests to form the Bank of Nova Scotia Trust Company to engage in offshore and trust operations which were off-limits to foreign banks. A year later, the Bank of Nova Scotia Trust Company of New York was established.

ESTABLISHING NEW BRANCHES

Beginning in 1960, the bank aggressively pursued a strategy to increase its volume of deposits by resuming the establishment of new branches in Canada as well as abroad. This inflow of funds was required to support the bank's consumer credit operations while also meeting the demand for mortgages and short-term commercial loans. More than 60 percent of these new branches were in convenient suburban locations to attract new customers in and around Toronto, Montreal, Edmonton, and Calgary. Coupled with new products such as term notes, certificates of deposit, and six-year certificates, this campaign increased the volume of personal savings deposits by 50 percent between 1960 and 1965.

This increased activity also enabled the bank to maintain its presence in the financial services industry despite the ceiling on lending rates, which had virtually eliminated the bank from competing effectively against trust and finance companies in all areas except for

personal loans. During this time, the bank also increased its mortgage involvement by joining with two other partners to form three new ventures. These ventures were real estate company Markborough Properties, the Mortgage Insurance Company of Canada, and Central Covenants, a mortgage financing company.

RESTRUCTURING FROM WITHIN

In 1963 the bank underwent a major internal reorganization, and a new profit planning system was introduced that required each branch and region to submit annual loan and deposit forecasts to be incorporated into the bank's overall plan. This system allowed the bank to further decentralize operations, to encourage competition among branches, and to better identify the services its customers wanted.

Meanwhile, business in the Caribbean continued to grow, despite losses in Cuba. Much of this growth was hotel and resort financing in areas such as Jamaica and Puerto Rico, where tourism was becoming big business. The bank also opened branches in London, Glasgow, Amsterdam, Munich, Beirut, and Tokyo. Its international division became a major player in the Eurodollar market at this time.

During the early 1960s the bank also worked to establish a stronger presence in the United States, particularly in Los Angeles and Houston, by offering financing and deposit opportunities for U.S. corporations in addition to international tax services. These efforts fueled the bank's accelerated growth in the second half of the decade.

At home, the early 1970s saw strong personal and small-business lending activity, leading the bank to launch a number of new services, including automobile financing and a farm program to meet credit needs in the agricultural sector. Lending activity shifted significantly toward commercial concerns, particularly retail accounts, later that decade as inflation increased daily operational costs for Canadian businesses.

Actively involved in the precious metals market since 1958, the bank expanded this business throughout the 1970s by buying two-thirds of the country's annual production and then selling actual bullion and bullion certificates. It was also during this period that the rising expenses of branch development caused the bank to refocus its emphasis from opening new offices within Canada to improving existing operations and relocating branches to more lucrative areas.

A COURT CASE

In 1972 the bank was sued by VK Mason Construction Ltd. for negligent misrepresentation related to the building of an office and shopping complex. The contractor had required assurance from the bank that the developer, Courtot Investments, had sufficient financing to finish the construction before it would agree to take on the job, and Scotiabank had informed Mason that interim financing was available to Courtot if needed. When the project was completed, Mason was paid CAD 1 million less than had been agreed and found that, rather than helping the developer pay its creditors, the bank called in its own loan and sold the complex when Courtot defaulted.

The Supreme Court of Canada found against the bank, although it affirmed the bank's right of first claim on the developer's assets as the mortgagee. Mason was permitted to collect damages by placing a lien on the bank's assets without having to compete with other Courtot creditors.

INTERNATIONAL BUSINESS GROWS

The bank's total assets reached CAD 50 billion by the end of 1981, with international business growing twice as fast as domestic operations and at a higher rate than that of any other Canadian bank. This growth was attributed to many factors, including the bank's established European and North American presence, its expansion into the Asia-Pacific region with the 1981 opening of a branch in Japan, and the development of a worldwide foreign exchange and banking system that operated around the clock. The year also saw the historic opening of the first Canadian banking representative office in China.

Although a downturn in the economy during 1983 forced the bank to curtail expansion temporarily, its focus on smaller companies saved it from the large-scale losses other Canadian banks suffered from loans made to failing firms such as Dome Petroleum and Massey-Ferguson, and to Mexico, Brazil, and Poland.

This focus on smaller companies and individuals did create image problems in the corporate and commercial areas. To counter the perception that the bank was not fully committed to businesses, Scotiabank embarked upon an extensive, innovative advertising campaign in 1986 using customers' case histories and games of visual illusion to show the various ways that the bank had helped companies.

LEGAL CHALLENGES

During the first half of the 1980s, the bank was accused of wrongdoing in a series of cases stemming from its activities both at home and abroad. In March 1983 the bank was asked by a Miami court to release records from its Cayman Islands branch concerning certain customers under investigation for narcotics and tax violations. Although the bank was protected under Cayman Island law from such releases, a Florida judge ruled that the bank stood in contempt of court and fined it $25,000 a day, retroactive to November 1983, for each day it did not produce the records. In order to end a stalemate that could have forced the bank into bankruptcy, the Cayman Islands Governor-in-Council intervened to authorize the bank to supply the required information, but not before the fine had reached $1.8 million. The bank lost its appeal to the U.S. Supreme Court in January 1985.

In 1984 the bank, along with four other Canadian banks, was the subject of a one-year investigation by the Royal Commission of the Bahamas into drug dealing and money laundering by Bahamian prime minister Lynden Pindling and his wife. Scotiabank had lent more than CAD 1 million to Pindling between 1977 and 1983 and had also accepted deposits from the couple totaling CAD 114,000 from an unidentified source. Although the investigation was inconclusive, it cast a cloud on a 1985 case alleging that the bank had committed fraud against the Investment Dealers Association of Canada in its involvement in the failure of Atlantic Securities Ltd. in 1981. Although this case generated much controversy, the Nova Scotia County Court acquitted the bank.

In 1987 Scotiabank further penetrated the financial services market with the formation of Scotia Securities. That subsidiary, which provided discount brokerage and security underwriting services, allowed the bank to compete more effectively with investment banking firms. In addition to acquiring other banks during the late 1980s and early 1990s, the Bank of Nova Scotia pursued a strategy of global expansion to assure profitability regardless of any fluctuations in individual markets. It also worked to improve the quality of the loans in its portfolio and to increase the efficiency of its operations. Among the acquisitions during this period was the 1988 purchase for CAD 419 million of the brokerage firm McLeod Young Weir Ltd., which was later merged with Scotia Securities to form ScotiaMcLeod. Scotiabank also acquired a 40 percent stake in Solidbank Corp. in the Philippines in 1998 and a 24 percent stake in Banco Sud Americano, S.A., the sixth-largest bank in Chile, in 1991. Also, in 1992, in the wake of the enactment of the North American Free Trade Agreement, Scotiabank became the first Canadian bank to move into Mexico, spending $75 million for a 5 percent interest in Grupo Financiero Inverlat, S.A. de C.V. The Bank of Nova Scotia also opened its first bank branch in China, which it located in Guangzhou (formerly Canton).

Scotiabank's efforts during the late 1980s and early 1990s were clearly paying off by the mid-1990s. The bank's asset base ballooned from about CAD 94 billion in 1992 to nearly CAD 138 billion by early 1995, making it the third-largest Canadian bank. About CAD 12 billion in assets were gained in one fell swoop in 1994 when Scotiabank acquired Montreal Trustco Inc. for about CAD 290 million. The purchase bolstered two areas of weakness for Scotiabank, which were its retail banking presence in Central Canada and its wealth management operations. Also gained were Montreal Trustco's corporate trust services activities.

Following Mexico's peso crisis in 1994, that nation's banking industry collapsed under 100 percent interest rates and the inability of borrowers to repay their loans. Scotiabank's Mexican affiliate fell into bankruptcy and was put under the administration of the government, and Scotiabank took a CAD 145 million writedown on its investment in Grupo Financiero Inverlat in late 1995. The following year, however, the bank repurchased a 10 percent interest in Inverlat and also gained the right to increase its stake to 55 percent in 2000. Meantime, profits at the Bank of Nova Scotia surpassed the CAD 1 billion mark for the time in 1996.

AFTERSHOCKS OF REGIONAL ECONOMIC CRISIS

Scotiabank stepped up its acquisition activity in 1997. It spent $55 million for 35 percent of a small Indonesian bank, PT Bank Arya Panduarta, as well as CAD 260 million to acquire the 75 percent of Banco Quilmes, its Argentinean affiliate, it did not already own. The biggest deal that year, however, was Scotiabank's CAD 1.25 billion purchase of National Trustco Inc., the second-largest independent trust company in Canada with 175 branches and CAD 14.6 billion in assets. The operations of the two companies meshed well, given that 80 percent of National Trustco's branches were in Ontario, a historically weak market for the Bank of Nova Scotia. In the integration process over the next three years, about 50 overlapping branches were closed and about 1,000 jobs were eliminated. This acquisition helped propel Scotiabank's asset base beyond the CAD 200 billion mark by 1998.

The Canadian banking industry appeared to be headed for the largest shake-up in its history in 1998 when Royal Bank of Canada and Bank of Montreal agreed to a merger, as did the Toronto-Dominion Bank and Canadian Imperial Bank of Commerce. These two mergers involved the four other members of Canada's

"Big Five" banks, with Scotiabank the odd bank out. Scotiabank lobbied intensely in opposition to the mergers, arguing that they would lead to job cuts numbering 20,000, massive branch closures, and other negative outcomes not in the public interest. In December 1998 finance minister Paul Martin scotched both of the deals, having concluded that the mergers would create two banks wielding too much power in the Canadian market, with competition in the industry being severely reduced.

Scotiabank also felt some of the aftershocks of the Asian economic crisis that erupted in 1997. The bank was forced in 1998 to write off its equity stake in its Indonesia affiliate, PT Bank Arya, and to set aside provisions of $67 million for nonperforming loans in various emerging markets. On the positive side, however, the bank's stake in Banco Sud Americano was increased to 61 percent, and that Chilean bank was subsequently renamed Scotiabank Sud Americano, S.A. In 2000 the Bank of Nova Scotia sold its holding in Solidbank for CAD 140 million, a move that cleared the way for that bank to merge with a larger Philippine bank. It also exercised an option to increase its stake in Grupo Financiero Inverlat to 55 percent, with the purchase price being $184 million. The Mexican bank was subsequently renamed Grupo Financiero Scotiabank Inverlat. At the same time, Scotiabank also cut back on its Canadian operations, selling 43 branches in Quebec to Laurentian Bank.

During 2002 the Bank of Nova Scotia acquired Charles Schwab Canada Co. from the Charles Schwab Corporation, the huge U.S. discount broker. The newly acquired Canadian operations were merged with Scotiabank's existing discount brokerage, which was renamed ScotiaMcLeod Direct Investing. This meant that both the full-service and the discount brokerages of Scotiabank operated under the ScotiaMcLeod name. Also in 2002 Scotiabank bought a modest equity stake in Xi'an City Commercial Bank, which was based in the capital city of the Shaanxi province of northern China.

Another severe economic crisis, this time in Argentina, had a major impact on Scotiabank in 2002. In the political and economic chaos that followed Argentina's defaulting on its foreign debt in December 2001, the operations of Banco Scotiabank Quilmes were suspended by the local government because of liquidity problems, after Scotiabank refused to inject more capital into the troubled bank. In September 2002 Scotiabank sold the assets of its Argentinean bank to two small local banks, and it also took a CAD 540 million after-tax write-down on its investment there. One result was that net income fell to CAD 1.8 billion for the year, down

17 percent from the CAD 2.17 billion figure recorded the year previous.

FLURRY OF ACQUISITIONS

Acquisitions would take center stage again in 2006 after the Bank of Nova Scotia agreed to purchase one of Canada's lending businesses, Maple Trust Company. Most of Maple's customers lived in Ontario, British Columbia, and Alberta. At the time of the deal announcement in February 2006, Maple had nearly CAD 7.5 million in mortgages under administration. Purchase price for Maple was CAD 233 million.

Also in 2006 the Bank of Nova Scotia purchased Travelers Leasing Corporation (TLC), a Canadian automobile financing firm, and Dehring Bunting & Golding, the fourth-largest securities dealer in the Jamaican financial market. From 2005 through 2006, the Bank of Nova Scotia spent CAD 2.3 billion on acquisitions.

In 2007 ScotiaBank continued its efforts to grow by acquisition. This time the bank had its sights set on the Dundee Bank of Canada, particularly its wealth management division. The Bank of Nova Scotia was prepared to put up CAD 348 million for Dundee. However, days after The Bank of Nova Scotia announced plans to acquire Dundee, the CI Financial Income Fund, a Canadian diversified wealth management firm, made an unsolicited offer to acquire Dundee Wealth, Incorporated, the part of Dundee Bank that the Bank of Nova Scotia wanted as well. At the time, CI managed nearly CAD 68 billion in assets. Dundee Wealth, on the other hand, was valued at CAD 2.36 billion.

At the end of the bidding war, Bank of Nova Scotia walked away with an 18 percent stake in Dundee for CAD 348 million. CI would go on to purchase 2.67 million shares in Dundee in February 2008. As if to punish a competitor for going after the same wealth management division (Dundee) that it had, at the close of 2008 the Bank of Nova Scotia spent CAD 2.3 billion and bought 37 percent of Sun Life Financial Incorporated's stake in CI. The deal closed in December 2008.

PROFITABLE EVEN DURING RECESSION

Even with the global economic downturn, Bank of Nova Scotia managed to remain profitable. In 2009 the bank's assets totaled CAD 417.6 billion, making it Canada's third-largest bank. In its February 2009 article, "A Canadian Bank Plays It Safe ... and Smart," *Barron's*

wrote that Bank of Nova Scotia had less exposure to subprime mortgages than its neighboring banks in the United States did. "It (Bank of Nova Scotia) doesn't need billions in government aid to survive, and won't have to take huge write-downs on exotic instruments gone bad," the article claimed. However, Bank of Nova Scotia did not go completely unscathed by the recession. It charged off CAD 822 million in assets, after tax, to absorb losses related to the Lehmann Brothers' bankruptcy and collateralized debt obligations.

In January 2011 Bank of Nova Scotia announced plans to offer small loans and credit cards to customers in Mexico. The bank's executive vice president of sales and services, products and marketing, Wendy Hannam, told Sean P. Pasternak, in an article published by *Bloomberg,* "We are looking right now at Mexico, because it's the single-biggest population base for that business." Bank of Nova Scotia planned to offer the products to households with monthly incomes below $750.

Having weathered the financial crisis that began in 2008 better than many banks, Scotiabank sought to continue expanding its presence in Latin America and Asia while maintaining a prominent position in its home country as well.

Dave Mote
Updated, Rhonda Campbell; David E. S Salamie

PRINCIPAL SUBSIDIARIES

The Bank of Nova Scotia International Limited (Bahamas); BNS Capital Trust; Dundee Bank of Canada; Grupo Financiero Scotiabank Inverlat, S.A. de C.V. (93.7%, Mexico); Nova Scotia Inversiones Limitada (Chile); Scotia Capital Inc.; Scotiabank Europe plc (England).

PRINCIPAL DIVISIONS

Canadian Banking; Global Wealth Management; International Banking; Scotia Capital.

PRINCIPAL COMPETITORS

Bank of Montreal; Canadian Imperial Bank of Commerce; Royal Bank of Canada; The Toronto-Dominion Bank.

FURTHER READING

Anderson, Mark. "The Lost Picture Show." *Canadian Business,* May 1, 1997, 93.

Bandell, Brian. "Canada's Third-Largest Bank Wants Miami Office." *South Florida Business Journal,* February 9, 2009. Accessed March 7, 2011. http://www.bizjournals.com/southflorida/stories/2009/02/09/daily10.html.

"Bank of Nova Scotia Ends Cuba Banking in Jamaica Under US Pressure." *Havana Journal,* March 28, 2006. Accessed March 7, 2011. http://havanajournal.com/politics/entry/bank-of-nova-scotia-ends-cuba-banking-in-jamaica-under-us-pressure.

Blackwell, Richard. "Bank of Nova Scotia Looks to Branching Out." *Financial Post,* October 5, 1994, 8.

Darroch, James L. *Canadian Banks and Global Competitiveness.* Montreal: McGill-Queen's University Press, 1994.

Haliechuk, Rick. "Scotiabank Profit Hits Record in 4th Quarter." *Toronto Star,* December 1, 1994, E2.

Kalawsky, Keith. "Bank Mergers No Longer a Hot Political Issue." *Financial Post,* March 25, 2003, FP1.

Kraus, James R. "Scotiabank Weathers Growing Pains Overseas." *American Banker,* July 28, 1999, 4.

Laver, Ross. "Banking in Bad Times." *Maclean's,* November 26, 1990, 44+.

Luukko, Rudy. "CI's Hostile Takeover Bid Throws Wrench into DundeeWealth's Deal with Scotia." *MorningStar,* September 24, 2007. Accessed March 7, 2011. http://www.morningstar.ca/globalhome/industry/news.asp?ArticleId=ArticleID92120078411.

Partridge, John, Karen Howlett, and Sinclair Stewart. "Scotiabank Names President." *Globe and Mail,* January 16, 2003, B1.

Pasternak, Sean B. "Bank of Nova Scotia to Offer Credit Cards, Consumer Loans in Mexico Stores." *Bloomberg,* January 10, 2011. Accessed March 7, 2011. http://www.bloomberg.com/news/2011-01-10/bank-of-nova-scotia-to-offer-consumer-loans-cards-through-mexico-stores.html.

Posner, Michael. "Titans at the Altar: Two Financial Giants Link Up with New Partners." *Maclean's,* July 7, 1997, 50–51.

Racanelli, Vito. "A Canadian Bank Plays It Safe ... and Smart." *Barron's,* February 9, 2009. Accessed March 7, 2011. http://online.barrons.com/article/SB123397139248159425.html#articleTabs_panel_article%3D1.

Schull, Joseph, and J. Douglas Gibson. *The Scotiabank Story: A History of the Bank of Nova Scotia, 1832–1982.* Toronto: Macmillan of Canada, 1982.

Wood, Chris. "The Trials of a Banking Giant." *Maclean's,* November 18, 1985, 34+.

Best Western
International, Inc.

6201 North 24th Parkway
Phoenix, Arizona 85016-2023
U.S.A.
Telephone: (602) 957-4200
Fax: (602) 957-5641
Web site: http://www.bestwestern.com

Private Company
Founded: 1946
Employees: 1,000 (est., 2010)
Sales: $231 million (2009)
NAICS: 721110 Hotels (except Casino Hotels) and
    Motels

■ ■ ■

Best Western International, Inc., is a unique organization in the hotel industry. Boasting over 4,000 hotels spread throughout 80 countries around the world, the company operates as a nonprofit, cooperative association. Each of the hotels in its network is independently owned and operated and renews its association with the Best Western brand, headquartered in Phoenix, Arizona, on a yearly basis.

Member hotels pay a fee to join and agree to uphold Best Western's standards of operation. In return, they become a member of an internationally recognized hospitality brand while still remaining free to maintain their own individual identities. IThis is one of the selling points of Best Western's hotels, as no two are the same. Lodges in the Best Western chain range from

high-end luxury hotels (mostly located in Europe) to quaint roadside motor inns and motels.

GUERTIN'S VISION: 1946–62

This remarkable diversity of member lodges and the unique corporate model that oversees it all is owed to the singular vision of Best Western's founder, Merrill K. Guertin. Ever since the 1920s, the U.S. hotel industry had been expanding in time with the country's rapidly expanding love affair with the car and the road trip. Guertin had been there from the start, although he had gotten into the industry almost by accident. A single parent from Texas, he had traveled out to Long Beach, California, to join his sister in advertising in 1923. He ended up buying a "motor court," a precursor to the roadside motel, with $2,000 in cash that he kept pinned to the inside of his shirt.

Guertin and his daughter Ernestine effectively became business partners, and in 1938 they opened what would later become the first property in the Best Western chain, the 10-room Beach Motel in Long Beach. Later, when on a business trip to Tacoma, Washington (during which he found himself wondering if he would have enough gas to make it to the next motel), Guertin got the idea to publish the United Motor Court Guide. This was intended to provide local hoteliers with an authoritative list of other lodging establishments in their area.

In 1946, with the United States emerging from World War II as a global superpower, Guertin anticipated a boom in recreational and business travel that was very soon destined to become a reality. Taking

COMPANY PERSPECTIVES

Best Western International's uniqueness is found in each hotel's charm and local appeal while maintaining a commitment to quality, service, and value.

his ideas to the next logical level, he went from publishing a guide to founding an official network, which he dubbed Best Western. The name came from the fact that the hotels in the network were located in the western United States, most in the state of California.

Guertin set up Best Western with $2,332.62 of his own money. The initial network comprised 66 hotels selected from a pool of 507 (which Guertin personally visited over a period of 29 days), each of which contributed $10 to a general fund. By joining the network, the hotels agreed to serve as a mutual referral service, calling ahead on behalf of travelers to arrange for lodgings in the next hotel in the network down the road. They also agreed to help each other out by sharing expenses and promoting a unified vision of a high-quality hotel experience. The formula proved an immediate success. Within five years of its start, the Best Western network had spread far beyond its California base. The Best Western Motel Guide quickly became a standard reference for travelers and industry professionals, and hotels across the country were scrambling to be included.

Guertin continued to grow his vision throughout the 1950s. The company's first national "Round-Up" of member hotels was held in Las Vegas, Nevada, in 1951. Guertin helped to standardize a reservation system, promoted hotel advertising (a radical concept at the time) for members, established regional meetings, and first outlined what would become Best Western's well-known quality assurance guidelines. These included high-quality mattresses, clean linens, hot water, air conditioning, and, perhaps most famously, "Sanitized for Your Protection" toilet seat strips.

RISE TO PROMINENCE: 1963–73

By 1963 Best Western had built on its growing success and popularity to become the largest hotel chain in the United States. Nearly 700 hotels counted themselves as members, and Best Western could offer over 35,000 rooms to weary travelers from the West Coast to the East.

The operation had become so large that in 1964 it was decided to split off all member hotels that lay east of the Mississippi River into a separate venture titled, appropriately enough, Best Eastern. This proved to be a short-lived venture, however. In 1966 Best Western and Best Eastern were united under the Best Western brand once again. As part of the corporate reorganization, Guertin, now known in the industry as "Mr. Motel," stepped down from running the company, leaving an elected board of directors to take over. At the same time, company headquarters moved from Guertin's hometown of Long Beach, California, to Phoenix, Arizona, where it has remained to this day.

Despite the new leadership and headquarters location, Best Western managed to continue operating under the auspices that had brought it such success and attention through the first two decades of operation. In particular, Best Western continued to lead the way in innovations in the hotel industry. In 1965, for example, the company signed a deal with Standard Oil that mandated member hotels to accept gasoline credit cards. New customer appreciation policies were implemented as well, such as preferred customer cards, financial incentives for making early reservations, and reservation drawings that awarded cash prizes.

In 1966, the same year Best Western relocated to Phoenix, a set of ambitious goals was announced. A toll-free reservation call center was established, allowing travelers to arrange for reservations with any Best Western hotel in the country, a boon to travel agents and business travelers in particular. The new call center, facilitated through an arrangement with American Express, was part of an overall strategy to push hard in the business and tourism industries, including tie-ins and deals with airlines and travel industry reps.

Quality standards for member hotels were raised. New sales offices in Washington, D.C., Montreal, Phoenix, and Seattle were opened. Most notably, plans for international expansion into European markets as well as Caribbean and Pacific Rim nations were announced. In 1972 Best Western instituted a mandatory policy that required member hotels to accept six major credit cards, a method of payment that was still in a minority segment of American commerce transactions. As an incentive to travelers paying with credit cards, people who charged their rooms in advance would "guarantee" their room for the whole night. In return, the hotel could bill the cost of the room if the customer was a no-show.

FOREIGN EXPANSION: 1974–95

The 1970s saw Best Western using its strong base in the domestic hotel industry as a launching pad for international expansion. In 1974 the company

KEY DATES

1946: Best Western Motels is founded as an informal referral chain between associated hotels.

1963: With 699 member properties boasting over 35,000 rooms, Best Western is the largest hotel chain in the industry.

1966: Best Western moves its headquarters from Long Beach, California to Phoenix, Arizona, as a major expansion of services and standards is announced.

1976: Best Western begins its overseas expansion, signing affiliation agreements with 411 hotels in Australia and New Zealand.

2005: Hotel reservations made online through Best Western's Web site surpass $1 million per day for the first time.

simultaneously chose to abandon its corporate image as a mere referral chain and drop the word "motel," which had become associated with cheap motor lodges, from its logo and corporate branding. The company's Phoenix headquarters symbolized this growth and ambition with the opening of a massive new multimillion-dollar international headquarters complex, and the company's focus on facilitating reservations got a big boost from the opening of a 24-hour reservation call center.

By the time the new international headquarters opened in 1977, Best Western had taken the first steps toward expanding beyond the borders of the United States. In 1976 Best Western signed its first affiliation agreements with 411 lodging establishments in Australia and New Zealand. With the new overseas ventures, Best Western could justifiably adopt the phrase "world's largest lodging chain" for its advertisements and corporate branding. By the close of the 1970s, Best Western hotels were accommodating 15 million customers a year, bringing the company's total hotel room sales to the $1 billion mark for the first time.

The 1980s were the decade in which Best Western went international in a big way. The decade kicked off with 283 international properties joining Best Western in 1980 alone. There were 19 properties in Denmark, 120 properties in France, 19 properties in Finland, 23 properties in Spain, 19 properties in Sweden, and 93 properties in Switzerland. Worldwide, the Best Western network had risen to over 2,500 establishments, 34 percent of which were outside the United States.

In response to its international expansion, Best Western launched the Gold Crown Club International Program in 1988. In a sign of the strength of the company's brand overseas, the new program accumulated $40 million in sales during its first year of operation. During the 1980s, Best Western continued to strengthen its infrastructure domestically and abroad. New reservations branches were opened in Asia and Europe, corporate communications were strengthened, and deals were inked with airlines and member hotels in 29 countries. In 1993 the company's classic "gold crown" logo was retired in favor of a new, more modern design.

A GLOBAL HOTEL CHAIN: 1996–PRESENT

Fifty years after M. K. Guertin started Best Western, four of the original 66 hotels remained members of the network. These four constituted a drop in the bucket of Best Western's global presence of nearly 3,500 hotels. Yet the surviving hotels stood as a sign of how drastically the hotel industry had grown, thanks in large part to the pioneering efforts of Guertin and his company. The Hitching Post Inn in Cheyenne, Wyoming, for example, when it became one of the founding members of the chain, boasted a cafe, gas station, novelty shop, and 24 rooms that were available at a rate of $3 a night for two. Fifty years later, the Hitching Post could offer 166 rooms along with pools, a sauna, a fitness center, three restaurants, two lounges, and 13 banquet rooms. The rate, of course, had also increased. In 1996 two people looking for a room could expect to pay over 20 times the 1946 rate.

If the 1980s were about Best Western becoming an international organization, the 1990s were about the company focusing on sharpening the cutting edge of customer service. In the hotel industry, this often boiled down to making reserving rooms as easy and convenient as possible. Best Western had long maintained a large phone reservation network, but in 1995 the company took its first step into the new frontier of computer reservations with the debut of its Web site, BestWestern.com, which offered comprehensive hotel listings, information, and photographs to Internet users. The following year, the company implemented the LYNX system, a computerized reservation program that encompassed the company's worldwide hotel network under a single system.

By the first years of the 21st century, Best Western was seeing an average of $1 million a day in online hotel reservations coming through its Web site. The company launched a massive high-speed Internet initiative in 2004, with a stated goal of bringing free high-speed Web access to all of its hotels. Within eight months, every hotel in the company's North American network could boast free wireless, high-speed access in its public spaces, and 15 percent of the total rooms offered were wired for high-speed Internet.

A FORMULA FOR SUCCESS

In 1998, when Anupam Narayan came on board with Best Western as chief financial officer, the company had racked up $20 million in debt. This was considered unacceptable. As Narayan told *Hotel & Motel Management* magazine, "In most companies, you want a certain amount of debt, but in our case, we have no reason to carry debt. We're a net-cash investor, whereas most companies are net borrowers."

In just over two years, Narayan was able to eliminate Best Western's short-term debt and even establish a small cash reserve for making investments in infrastructure. Narayan's actions provided Best Western with a strong foundation heading into the 21st century.

In 2010, after years of debate, members voted to split Best Western's hotels into three tiers. Known as Best Western, Best Western Plus, and Best Western Premier, the goal was to distinguish the wide range of establishments under the brand's banner, from small roadside motels to luxurious European hotels. Best Western had come a long way from its humble origins as a telephone reference network of motor lodges, and

the company hoped to continue its success in the hotel industry.

David Larkins

PRINCIPAL DIVISIONS

Best Western Australia, New Zealand, Pacific Islands; Best Western Canada; Best Western Europe; Best Western North America.

PRINCIPAL COMPETITORS

Accor SA; LQ Management LLC; Super 8 Motels, Inc.; Wyndham Worldwide Corporation.

FURTHER READING

Bergsman, Steve. "Best Western Celebrates Golden Anniversary." *Hotel & Motel Management* 211, no. 9 (May 20, 1996): 3.

"Best Western International." *Hotel & Motel Management* 214, no. 14, (August 9, 1999): 98.

"Best Western International, Inc." hoovers.com. Accessed February 7, 2011. http://www.hoovers.com/company/Best_Western_International_Inc/ctxchi-1.html.

Higley, Jeff. " Debt-Free Best Western Builds on Basics." *Hotel & Motel Management* 215, no. 20 (November 20, 2000): 1.

Wolff, Carlo. "Going Golden with Best Western." *Lodging Hospitality* 52, no. 9 (September 1996): 34.

Boston Sox Baseball Club
Limited Partnership

—————————■—————————

4 Yawkey Way
Boston, Massachusetts 02215
U.S.A.
Telephone: (617) 267-9440
Fax: (617) 375-0944
Web site: http://boston.redsox.mlb.com

Private Company
Founded: 1901 as the Boston American League Baseball
    Club
Employees: 120 (est., 2010)
Sales: $266 million (2010)
NAICS: 711211 Sports Teams and Clubs

■ ■ ■

The Boston Sox Baseball Club Limited Partnership (Red Sox) is a professional baseball team located in Boston, Massachusetts, and is a member of Major League Baseball (MLB). The team competes within the East Division of the American League. The Red Sox was founded in 1901 as the Boston American League Baseball Club, and its home field has been the storied Fenway Park since 1912. The Red Sox is owned by partners John Henry, Tom Werner, and Larry Lucchino, who purchased the team in 2001. John Henry is the majority owner. The Red Sox is one of the few whose history is synonymous with the history of baseball in the United States, especially as one of the two teams that played in the very first World Series Championship against the Pittsburgh Athletic Company (Pittsburgh Pirates) in 1903.

A SECOND BOSTON TEAM

In 1901 former Cincinnati sports journalist Byron "Ban" Johnson reformed his regional minor league (the Western League) into the more ambitious American League (AL) by moving some of the teams from small towns to the larger cities. The AL was to compete with the already well-established National League (1876). When the NL saw the popularity of the AL growing it founded a sham league called the American Association, centered in Boston, supposedly to "compete" with the NL. As a countermove, Johnson decided the next team should be in Boston, but finding a place for them to play was a problem. The NL Boston Nationals were unwilling to share their stadium with another team, so Johnson asked Connie Mack, a native of East Brookfield, Massachusetts, and owner of the newly formed AL Philadelphia Athletics, to go to Boston and find a location. Mack found one on Huntington Avenue in Boston. This quickly assembled and modest ballpark became know as the Huntington Avenue Grounds.

Charles Somers was the team's first owner. Somers was a Cleveland business executive in the coal business and was the principle investor in Johnson's new league. Somers named the team the Boston American League Baseball Club, but journalists and fans used nicknames like the "Bostons," "Pilgrims," "Plymouth Rocks," "Puritans," "Somersets" (after the owner), and the "Collinsmen" (after the player-manager, Jimmy Collins). The most common nickname was the "Americans," and it stuck. The Boston Americans joined a league with teams in Baltimore, Chicago, Cleveland, Detroit, Milwaukee, Philadelphia, and Washington. The Americans played their first game at the Huntington Avenue Grounds on

COMPANY PERSPECTIVES

■

The Nation lives.

April 25, 1901. Somers sold the Americans to Milwaukee lawyer Henry J. Killilea in 1903.

After Johnson formed his league, the AL and NL engaged in a bitter fight for players, fan loyalty, and dollars. Johnson and the AL owners brazenly stole players from the NL, luring them away with much higher salaries. In 1903 the two leagues resolved to meet and work out their differences. They formed what became known as the "National Agreement." This agreement set forward employment, salary, and travel stipulations. It also created the World Championship Games between the best team from each league. In 1903 the NL Pittsburgh Athletic Company and the AL Boston Americans met for the very first World Championship Games, a best-of-nine series. The Boston Americans, led by pitcher Denton True "Cy" Young, won the series five games to three.

A NEW NAME AND THE GREEN MONSTER

Killilea gained a bad reputation for being a carpetbagger owner and skimping on salaries while raising ticket prices. After only a year as owner he sold the team to Boston native John I. Taylor for $145,000. Taylor was the son of the owner of the *Boston Globe* newspaper. Taylor proved to be an even worse owner than Killilea. He traded away the team's best talent and brought in aging veterans to replace them. He interfered with the management of the team until player-manager Jimmy Collins barred him from the clubhouse. Taylor resorted to sitting outside the door and berating players when they came out. Despite such antics, Taylor made two significant contributions to the team. He renamed the team the "Boston Red Sox" and built the team a new ballpark, Fenway Park.

The NL Boston Nationals wore red stockings at the time and had been a more successful team. Taylor thought he could make his team more successful by at least dressing them up like a successful team so he changed the uniforms and incorporated the Nationals' red stockings. The AL Chicago White Stockings had already had their name shortened by the press to the White Sox to make it fit headlines, so Taylor went ahead and made the team's name the Boston Red Sox.

In 1911 Taylor purchased property bordered by Brookline Avenue, Jersey Street, Van Ness Street, and Lansdowne Street. He named it Fenway Park because the area was known at the time as the Fens, because it had been created by filling in marshland. The construction of Fenway Park included erecting the "Green Monster," a thirty-seven-foot, three-inch-high left field wall, painted green. It was the highest outfield wall among professional fields.

Taylor sold the team to former Washington Senators manager James McAleer in 1912, but Fenway Park remained under the ownership of Taylor's Fenway Realty Trust. Regardless, it was McAleer who opened the new Fenway Park for play on April 20, 1912, the same day the *HMS Titanic* sunk. The newly named Red Sox played their first game at Fenway against the New York Highlanders (later renamed the New York Yankees) and won 7–6 in 11 innings before 27,000 fans. In the NL, the Boston Nationals changed their name to the Boston Braves.

Under manager Jacob Garland "Jake" Stahl, the Red Sox also won it's second World Series that season, defeating the New York Giants. Stahl had a falling out with the players and resigned in the middle of the 1913 season. He was replaced by player-manager Bill Carrigan.

McAleer did not get along with AL founder and president Ban Johnson, and at the end of the 1913 season, Johnson forced him out as owner. Johnson arranged for Joseph Lannin to purchase the team from McAleer for $200,000. Lannin became part-owner of Fenway Park by purchasing an interest in the Fenway Realty Trust. Lannin was the team's fifth owner in just 13 seasons, but his tenure only lasted three years, during which the team slumped to fourth place. Despite his poor management skills, Lannin made the most important acquisition in Red Sox history in the middle of the 1914 season. He acquired the 19-year-old lefty George Herman "Babe" Ruth for $2,900 from the Baltimore Orioles in the International League. Pitcher Ernie Shore came over in the same deal. Carrigan, Ruth, and Shores led the Red Sox to win two World Series in 1915 and 1916. Carrigan retired after the 1916 World Series and Jack Barry took over as player-manager. Barry had played shortstop on the 1915 and 1916 championship teams.

HARRY FRAZEE AND THE CURSE OF THE BAMBINO

In November 1916 Lannin sold the team due to health problems and Ban Johnson's constant interference with the management of the team. Lannin sold the team for $675,000 to Harry Frazee and his partners Hugh Ward

KEY DATES

1901: Ban Johnson and owner Charles Somers found the Boston American League Baseball Club.

1903: The Boston Americans win the first World Series over the National League Pittsburgh Athletic Company.

1907: Owner John Taylor renames team the Boston Red Sox.

1912: Fenway Park opens featuring the left field wall nicknamed "the Green Monster."

1914: Owner Joseph Lannin signs George Herman "Babe" Ruth to play for the team.

1916: Lannin sells the Red Sox to New York theatrical producer Harry Frazee.

1919: Frazee sells Babe Ruth to the New York Yankees. Brings upon the team the "curse of the bambino."

1933: Thomas A. Yawkey purchases the Red Sox for $1.2 million.

1959: Red Sox sign Elijah "Pumpsie" Green, becoming the last team in MLB to integrate.

1976: Tom Yawkey dies. Jean R. Yawkey inherits ownership of the team.

1992: Jean Yawkey dies. Ownership passes to the Jean R. Yawkey (JRY) Trust, John Harrington trustee.

2002: JRY Trust sells the Red Sox for $660 million to New England Sport Ventures.

2004: The Red Sox win the World Series, ending the 85-year curse of the bambino.

and G. M. Anderson. Lannin retained his ownership in Fenway Realty Trust. Frazee was a New York theatrical producer. The day Frazee bought the team he took the train back to New York, where he remained during most of his tenure as owner of the Red Sox.

The 1918 season got off to a dismal start, and Jack Barry retired rather than risk being traded. Ed Barrow took over and decided to play Ruth during every game. This started a downward spiral for relations between Frazee and the team's biggest star. Ruth was given a higher salary to meet the added workload, but Ruth's relationship with management became increasingly strained. After an argument with Barrow, Ruth walked out on the team and signed to play with the Chester Shipyards in the Delaware River Shipbuilding league.

He came back but the owners were not happy with Ruth's stunt. Regardless, Ruth led the team to its fifth World Series in 1918. They beat the Chicago Cubs in six games.

The year 1918 also brought an increasing estrangement between Frazee and league president Johnson. Johnson never wanted Frazee as an owner in the league and Frazee thought Johnson was mismanaging the league. At one point, Frazee and another team's owner asked former U.S. president Howard Taft to become a one-man commissioner of baseball, replacing the three-man National Commission headed by Johnson. This was in effect a coup and infuriated Johnson. Each tried to force the other out, but Johnson was fairly entrenched and powerful. While Frazee put together a coalition of supporters, they did not have enough voting power to overthrow Johnson. This bitter relationship eventually led to major battles in the press and in court over Johnson's interference in team management decisions and trades.

Before the 1919 season Babe Ruth demanded more money, this time $15,000 a year or $30,000 over three years. Frazee refused, and the team started playing without Ruth at the beginning of the season. Ruth took a trip to New York to demand the money face-to-face, and Frazee relented. Frazee agreed to pay Ruth $30,000 over three years. The team slumped during the 1919 season, but Ruth continued to put up record numbers. He finished the year with 29 home runs and 114 runs batted in (RBIs). By the end of the 1919 season Frazee's finances were in shambles and he was in dire need of cash. Also, Ruth's off-field behavior, which included high levels of alcohol intake and questionable female companions, had become increasingly reckless. New York Yankee's co-owner Col. T. L. Huston offered to solve both of Frazee's problems by purchasing Ruth from the Red Sox. They worked out a deal for the Yankees to pay Frazee $25,000 up front plus three promissory notes of $25,000 each. Ruth moved to New York, and the team received no players in return.

Selling Ruth was only the beginning of Frazee's gutting of the Red Sox. He sent many other star players to the Yankees for cash and little else in return. Red Sox fans look back on Frazee's fire sale, particularly Ruth, as the worst event in the history of the team and one that brought a curse upon all future Red Sox teams. Frazee could not show his face in Boston without drawing anger and derision. The Red Sox would not win a World Series for the next 85 years. This dry spell became known to fans as the "Curse of the Bambino," referring to the loss of the "Babe."

Another problem Frazee faced was that he did not own an interest in Fenway Park and rented the ballpark from Fenway Realty Trust for $30,000 a year. This put his ownership in a vulnerable position. If the team experienced further financial difficulties and defaulted on its obligations the league could easily push the Red Sox out and put another team in Fenway. In 1920 Frazee negotiated a deal with the Taylor family and Lannin to purchase Fenway Park. Later, as part of the sale of Ruth and the other players, Jake Rupert, another Yankees co-owner, agreed to loan Frazee $300,000. Since he now had ownership, Frazee put up Fenway Park as security for the loan. To the horror of Red Sox fans, their rival the Yankees now owned the mortgage on their home field.

During the 1920 season Ruth hit a league record 54 home runs and led the Yankees to a second-place finish. The Red Sox went 72–81 and finished 25 1/2 games out of first place. By the time Frazee sold the team in July 1923 not one player from the 1918 World Series team remained. Frazee sold the team for $1,250,000 to J. A. Robert Quin, who was the business manager for the St. Louis Browns (later, the Baltimore Orioles). Quin's fellow investors included former president of the Columbus Senators, Edward Schoenborn, Columbus physician Robert B. Drury, and St. Louis millionaire Palmer Winslow. Quin owned the team for a decade and tried to bring it back to its former glory, before Frazee's fire sale of star players, but the organization faced a constant shortage of funds that hindered his efforts. The team remained at the bottom of the AL through most of the 1920s and into the 1930s.

THE YAWKEY ERA BEGINS

In 1932 the team hit an all-time low, losing 111 games, and in 1933, Quin sold the team to Thomas "Tom" A. Yawkey, a South Carolina millionaire. Yawkey inherited his uncle's lumber and iron empire, a $40 million estate, when he turned 30, and four days after reaching that age he purchased the Red Sox for $1.2 million. Yawkey became president of the Red Sox organization. Yawkey used his deep pockets to improve the Red Sox. He hired his friend and former player Eddie Collins as general manager of the team. Collins was the person who gave Yawkey the idea to purchase the team. Then Yawkey paid $125,000 to acquire pitcher Lefty Grove, at the time one of the best pitchers in the league. A year later, he acquired shortstop Lyn Lary and player-manager Joe Cronin for $250,000 from the Washington Senators. In 1938 he paid more than $150,000 for first baseman and power hitter Jimmy Foxx and pitcher Johnny Marcum. Lastly, in 1939, the Red Sox signed left-hander Theodore Samuel "Ted" Williams from the minor league San Diego Padres. Williams would become one of the greatest hitters in Red Sox (and baseball) history. While

the Curse of the Bambino persisted, the Red Sox became synonymous with the hugely popular Ted Williams. Fans even referred to the team as the "Ted Sox."

Yawkey's player acquisitions turned the team around, but the team's fortunes seemed very much linked to Williams. When Williams was drafted to serve in World War II, the team slumped, but when he returned in 1946 the team won 104 games and the AL pennant, and played in the World Series. They lost to the St. Louis Cardinals in seven games. Cronin retired as a player in 1945 but continued managing the team until 1947. Williams and the team continued to play well over the next three years, coming very close to winning the AL pennant in 1947 and 1948. Then Williams was recalled to duty to serve in the Korean War in 1952. Cronin moved to the front office to become the Red Sox's general manager in 1947. Williams returned to the Red Sox in 1954. By then, most of the great players from the previous decade had retired or been traded, and Williams was the lone great player on a mediocre team. Also, in 1953, owner Lou Perini moved the Boston Braves to Milwaukee, Wisconsin, leaving the Red Sox as the sole Boston professional baseball team.

In 1959 the Red Sox became the last team in the league to integrate, hiring infielder Elijah "Pumpsie" Green. This was 12 years after Jackie Robinson had joined the league. The stain of racism was the one black eye upon the Yawkey era. Before Green joined the team Yawkey refused to hire black players. Players such as Jackie Robinson and Willie Mays tried out for the team, but Yawkey passed on them. Accusations of racism continued to plague the team even after hiring Green and into the 1970s.

Cronin retired from the Red Sox organization in 1959 after 12 years as general manager. Yawkey hired former Red Sox manager Stanley R. "Bucky" Harris to take over, but the team continued its slump during his two-year stint, and Yawkey fired Harris. Because Yawkey liked having current or future hall of fame players in the general manager position he offered the position to Ted Williams, who turned him down. The team was without a general manager for the 1961–62 seasons, but Dick O'Connell, the business manager for the team, served as a "de facto" general manager, mostly handling the business side. It was during this time that Yawkey acquired left fielder Carl Yastrzemski, who would become a pivotal figure in the rebuilding of the team in later years of the decade. The team continued to dwell at the bottom through the early part of the 1960s. In an attempt to improve the situation, Yawkey gave the general manager position to Michael F. "Pinky" Higgins, a former Red Sox manager. However, Higgins was a mediocre general manager whose few trades offered only slight improvements to the team. In 1965 the team lost 100 games, and Yawkey fired Higgins and replaced him with Dick O'Connell.

The 1966 season was not much better. The team lost 90 games, but O'Connell had already begun building what became known by the fans as the "impossible dream" Red Sox of 1967. O'Connell promoted Dick Williams to manager. He brought players up from the Red Sox's talent-rich farm system, and he traded for pitcher Gary Bell, infielder Jerry Adair, and catcher Elston Howard. The team also drafted catcher Carlton "Pudge" Fisk. At the beginning of the season, the press gave the team a 95-to-1 chance of winning the AL pennant. O'Connell had filled the team up with so many young players that they became known as the "Cardiac Kids" because of the excitement they added to the game. The team became one of four teams in a tight race for first place, and the Red Sox prevailed. They went on to win the AL pennant and played in the World Series, where they faced the much-favored St. Louis Cardinals. They lost in a hard-fought seven games.

The Red Sox continued to win after their magical 1967 season, but they never finished above second place. It was during this period that the team began integrating more than ever before, trying to make up for past years of racial bias. The team significantly increased the number of African American and Latin American players on the team. In 1975, under manager Darrell Johnson, the Red Sox won the AL pennant and made it to the World Series. This time they lost (4–3) to the heavily favored Cincinnati Reds.

JEAN YAWKEY AND THE COUP LEROUX

Tom Yawkey died of leukemia in July 1976. His wife Jean R. Yawkey inherited ownership of the team. O'Connell remained general manager, but in 1977 Jean Yawkey put the team up for sale. Edward "Buddy" LeRoux, a former Red Sox athletic trainer, put together an ownership group. The ownership group included Haywood Sullivan, the vice president of player personnel for the Red Sox. Jean Yawkey had a close relationship with Sullivan and accepted the offer from LeRoux even though their offer was lower than others. The AL rejected the deal but changed its mind when Jean Yawkey joined the investment group as a third general partner, thus continuing the Yawkey era of ownership. Yawkey fired O'Connell and replaced him with Sullivan. Despite the change in management, the mold formed by O'Connell carried the team forward, and they participated in a tough race for first place against the

Yankees in 1978. They ended the season tied and lost to the Yankees in a provisional one-game playoff.

After 1978 the team went into decline, mainly due to Sullivan's poor management of free agency. Free agency came to baseball in 1976, and Sullivan made poor decisions that cost the team valuable talent with little in return. Eventually, he refused to participate in the free agent market and chose to rely on the team's farm system to develop players. Unfortunately, the farm system was fairly dry of talent at the time. The early 1980s were a rebuilding period. Manager Ralph Houk fostered young players, including pitchers Wade Boggs and Roger Clemens.

On June 6, 1983, LeRoux held a press conference and announced that he and his partners were exercising a contract clause and taking control of the Red Sox. He also announced that Sullivan was fired and would be replaced by returning general manager O'Connell. The press called this "the Coup LeRoux," but Yawkey and Sullivan fought back in court, filing an injunction. Then, after a very public and nasty court battle, Yawkey and Sullivan won back the team and bought out LeRoux. Yawkey became once again the majority general partner and owner of the team. Soon after, Sullivan became chief executive officer and made James "Lou" Gorman the general manager. Houk retired in 1984 and handed off his rebuilt team to manager John McNamara. By 1986 the team had recovered with the help of a strong pitching staff. The Red Sox made it to the 1986 World Series and lost 4–3 to the New York Mets. McNamara was fired mid-season in 1988 and replaced by Joe Morgan who led the team to the AL Championship Series (ALCS). They went to the ALCS again in 1990. The team lost both times to the Oakland Athletics.

Jean Yawkey died in 1992, and ownership of the team passed to the Jean R. Yawkey (JRY) Trust with John Harrington as trustee. Harrington became CEO of the Red Sox. Harrington fired Gorman in 1994 and replaced him with Dan Duquette. Duquette was especially effective at developing players from the farm system and also made big deals on the free agent market. By the late 1990s his efforts came to fruition. In 1995 and 1998 the team made it to the League Divisional Series (LDS), and in 1999, they made it to the ALCS.

NEW OWNERS BRING AN END TO THE CURSE

In 2002 Johnson, as trustee of the JRY Trust, sold the Red Sox for $660 million to New England Sport Ventures, a consortium headed by John Henry. Henry was a futures and foreign exchange trading advisor. The deal was part of an ownership shift. At the time, Henry owned the MLB Florida Marlins. He sold the Marlins to Jeffrey Loria, who sold the Montreal Expos to MLB. The JRY Trust sold the Red Sox to Henry and his partners, ending 70 years of Yawkey ownership. The new owners appointed former Padres president Larry Lucchino as CEO of the Red Sox and fired Duquette, replacing him on an interim basis with Mike Port, former general manager for the Anaheim Angels (now the Los Angeles Angels of Anaheim).

By 2004 the owners settled on Theo Epstein to replace Port. Epstein, at 28, became the youngest general manager in MLB history. The team also fired manager Grady Little and replaced him with Terry Francona. Epstein and Francona had assembled a very talented team with star players like hitter David Ortiz, pitchers Curt Schilling and Pedro Martinez, and outfielders Manny Ramirez and Johnny Damon. The team made it to the ALCS against their archrival, the New York Yankees. The Red Sox lost the first three games in the series and at that time, no team had ever come back from a three-game deficit to win in the playoffs. However, the Red Sox not only came back to win the next four games, but they also won the 2004 World Series, defeating the St. Louis Cardinals 4–0. The 2004 Red Sox broke the Curse of the Bambino after 85 years.

At the end of the 2005 season Theo Epstein resigned on the last day of his contract, saying it was for "personal reasons," but almost three months later the Red Sox hired Epstein back with the added title of executive vice president. Two years later the team went on to win its seventh World Series, defeating the Colorado Rockies 4–0.

At the end of the 2010 season the Red Sox failed to make the playoffs, but the team was still performing well with 89 wins. Epstein remained general manager and executive vice president, having signed a new contract in 2008 (details undisclosed). Francona had served as manager for seven years, only two without a postseason. His return for the following season seemed assured. With the Curse of the Bambino growing smaller and smaller in the rearview mirror, the Boston Red Sox had a new life in a new millennium.

Aaron Hauser

PRINCIPAL COMPETITORS

Baltimore Orioles, LP; New York Yankees Partnership; Rogers Blue Jays Baseball Partnership; Tampa Bay Rays Baseball, Ltd.

FURTHER READING

Abrams, Roger I. "A Century Ago, It All Started Here." *Boston Globe,* October 1, 2003, p. A.13.

"Baseball: The Sale of the Red Sox – Red Sox Owners." *Providence Journal,* October 7, 2000, p. C–08.

"Boston Red Sox Team History & Encyclopedia," baseball-reference.com. Accessed January 14, 2011. http://www.baseball-reference.com/teams/BOS/.

Buckley, Steve. "Red Sox '99; A Century of Boston Baseball; The *Boston Herald* 100." *Boston Herald,* April 13, 1999, p. r38.

———. "Red Sox Turn 100; Boston Beats Out Buffalo." *Boston Herald,* January 29, 2001, p. O92.

———. "Red Sox Turn 100; 100 Years of Blood, Sweat and Cheers." *Boston Herald,* January 28, 2001, p. B02.

———. "Red Sox Turn 100; The 100 Most Significant Moments in Red Sox History." *Boston Herald,* January 30, 2001, p. O76.

"The Business of Baseball: #2 Boston Red Sox," Forbes.com. Accessed January 14, 2011. http://www.forbes.com/lists/2010/33/baseball-valuations-10_Boston-Red-Sox_330700.html.

Chass, Murray. "Red Sox Accept Bid from Group Headed by Marlins' Owner." *New York Times,* December 21, 2001, p. 1, col. 2.

Duffy, Bob. "Unwinding 100-Year-Old Yarn You Couldn't Even Call Them 'Sox' at the Start." *Boston Globe,* May 26, 2001, p. G.1.

"Fenway Fun Facts." *Boston Herald,* April 10, 2006, p. 4e6.

Johnson, Richard A., and Glenn Stout. *Red Sox Century.* Boston: Houghton Mifflin, 2000.

Leccese, Mark. "So Young and Bold, Behold the Curse." *Boston Globe,* February 16, 2003, p. 5.

Mulvoy, Tom. "Bring an End to the Mediocrity '67 Miracle." *Boston Globe,* April 3, 1992, p. 38.

Nowlin, Bill. "The Boston Pilgrims Never Existed." *Baseball Almanac.* Accessed January 14, 2011. http://www.baseball-almanac.com/articles/boston_pilgrims_story.shtml.

Shaughnessy, Dan. "The Curse of the Bambino; It Was the Dumbest Deal in the History of Baseball." *Boston Globe,* June 3, 1990, p. 23.

———. "The Impossible Dream." *Boston Globe,* April 3, 1992, p. 40.

Silverman, Michael. "Ownership Mired in World Series Slump." *Boston Herald,* October 8, 2000, p. O18.

———. "Red Sox '99; A Century of Boston Baseball; 1901–1920." *Boston Herald,* April 13, 1999, p. r28.

"World Series History." *Baseball Almanac.* Accessed January 14, 2011. http://www.baseball-almanac.com/ws/wsmenu.shtml.

Briggs Equipment, Inc.

—■—

10540 North Stemmons Freeway
Dallas, Texas 75220
U.S.A.
Telephone: (214) 630-0808
Toll Free: (888) 215-4530
Fax: (214) 631-3560
Web site: http://www.briggsequipment.com

Wholly Owned Subsidiary of Sammons Enterprises, Inc.
Founded: 1896 as Briggs-Weaver Machinery Company
Employees: 1,000 (est., 2009)
Sales: $290 million (est., 2009)
NAICS: 532412 Construction, Transportation, Mining, and Forestry Machinery and Equipment Rental and Leasing.

■ ■ ■

Briggs Equipment, Inc., is one of the largest industrial and construction dealers in North America. Briggs operates as a separate entity of Sammons Enterprises, its parent company. (Sammons, with assets of $40 billion, is one of the largest privately owned conglomerates in the world.) Both Briggs and Sammons offer employee stock ownership (ESOP) plans, allowing employees the opportunity to reap the rewards of their contributions to the company.

Briggs operates in the five primary sectors of industrial equipment, contractor rental, rail equipment, used equipment, and fleet management. The company offers well-known brands such as Yale forklifts, Trackmobile rail equipment, and Taylor industrial trucks. The

company operates about 20 locations throughout the United States and Mexico, with around half in Texas. Briggs maintains a parts inventory valued at more than $3 million.

Briggs Industrial Equipment supplies warehouse products and services. Products include forklift solutions, safety training, fleet management, and materials handling. Distribution centers are located throughout the southern United States and Mexico, providing terminal tractors, telescoping booms, scissor lifts, and railcar movers.

Briggs Contractor Rental offers short- and long-term equipment rental contracts to contractors in Texas, Mississippi, Louisiana, Alabama, and Georgia. With over 5,000 pieces of equipment, Briggs offers products for lifting, lighting, earth-moving, and cleanup.

Briggs Rail Equipment provides sales, leasing, and service for Trackmobile products. Trackmobile, owned by Marmon Transportation Services, is a line of railcars that can operate on both rail and road, using weight transfer and steel wheel technologies. Trackmobile is the worldwide leader in the railcar moving industry.

Briggs Used Equipment offers its equipment for sale through an online database. Equipment is inspected for quality and offers three levels of value, depending on customers' needs.

Briggs Fleet Management (BE Fleet) offers a Web-based management tool for customers to track equipment in real time. BE Fleet also offers cost analysis and online invoicing services.

EARLY YEARS: 1896–62

Briggs Equipment, originally named Briggs-Weaver Machinery Company, was established in 1896 by J. C. Weaver and C. H. Briggs. The company provided service for pump installations, cotton ginners, steam generators, lift trucks, and materials handling.

Prior to starting the company, J. C. Weaver designed and built cottonseed oil mills in Georgia. He moved to Dallas in 1892 where he met Briggs, who was starting a machinery business. After they became partners, Briggs was general manager until his death in 1909. Weaver was president until 1922.

During a tumultuous early history, the company had several different owners. In 1933 the firm was acquired by the Houston Oil Field Company (HOFC), which named Ashley Dewitt as president. In 1942 a group of investors headed by Dewitt purchased the company from HOFC.

Finally, Briggs-Weaver found its home with self-made billionaire Charles Sammons in 1952. Although the company was profitable, it faced a potentially devastating problem. Briggs built the bodies for Chrysler's Plymouths and Packards. Chrysler, a large customer, was dissatisfied with Brigg's workmanship and labor disputes. After Sammons purchased the company, he sold 19 Briggs plants to Chrysler a year later. Since the business would soon be lost, Sammons took the opportunity to sell rather than seek customers to replace Chrysler. Under Sammons's stewardship Briggs-Weaver thrived, with company resources growing a healthy rate for a decade after this sale.

NEW CEO AND NEW PRODUCTS

In 1968 Briggs-Weaver named 30-year-old Steve McKenney its president and CEO. McKenney had worked at Briggs-Weaver since the age of 17, went to Texas A&M on scholarship from Briggs, and returned to work at Briggs as a counter salesman. When he was promoted to a sales manager of the Dallas center in 1965, sales increased 40 percent each year, marking McKenney as a young talent with leadership potential. McKenney would serve in the CEO role until 1984.

In 1969 Briggs-Weaver acquired Mayse Industrial Equipment Co. With this acquisition, Briggs-Weaver obtained the rights to distribute the Automatic brand of lift trucks. Briggs was already the distributor for Yale forklift trucks. Both brands were owned by Eaton, Yale, & Town.

In 1972 Briggs-Weaver formed Systems Tooling Group in Austin, Texas. The purpose of the new division was to assist customers with design and technical applications for machine and cutting tools. The company also offered solutions to metal-working, aircraft companies, petrochemical, and electronics firms. "We're a productivity company," said President Steve McKenney in 1979. The company focused its efforts on providing new machines in Texas, where the average age of factory machinery was 20 years and forklifts 10 years, indicating a ripe market for Briggs-Weaver's products.

By 1977 the company was contributing over $100 million to Sammons's annual sales. The company's product line consisted of the distribution of machine tools, gloves, ladders, gears, and paint. The company also sold, serviced, and rented forklifts and rail-to-track locomotives.

GROWTH, AND SALE: 1980–96

In the 1980s and 1990s, Briggs-Weaver diversified into chemicals, electronics, and janitorial supplies in an effort to become a one-stop shop for its customers. However, foreign competition for inexpensive small tools and the loss of major customer W.W. Grainger began to erode the company's profitability. In 1984 CEO Rob Mellor indicated that the company had been operating at a loss for the past few years and hoped that diversification into electronics would return the company to profitability.

In 1994 Chrysler and Briggs found a reason to again do business together. Chrysler approached Briggs Equipment in Houston to purchase forklifts and other equipment to build a new plant in Saltillo, Mexico. Dave Bratton, the branch manager in Houston who would later become the president of Briggs Equipment, instead negotiated a long-term rental agreement with Chrysler. This marked Briggs Equipment's first expansion outside the United States.

In 1996 Briggs-Weaver became a separate business of Sammons Enterprises. Shortly thereafter, the company reorganized itself to focus its product mix and grow internationally. This relationship led to other relationships in Mexico. In 1996 the company purchased a Yale dealership in Mexico. Briggs Equipment Mexico was formed with a lucrative rental arrangement.

KEY DATES

1896: J. C. Weaver and C. H. Briggs establish Briggs-Weaver Machinery Company.

1952: Charles A. Sammons takes ownership of the company.

1994: Briggs Equipment signs a long-term rental contract with Chrysler for its new plant in Mexico, marking its expansion across the U.S. border.

1996: Briggs Equipment becomes a separate working operation of the Sammons Enterprises, Inc.

2001: Briggs-Weaver is sold to Hagemeyer NV, a Dutch trading company, leaving the assets of Briggs Equipment with Sammons.

2006: Briggs Equipment purchases the material handling division of Finning International, Inc., marking Brigg's overseas expansion to the United Kingdom.

NEW CENTURY, NEW OPPORTUNITIES

In 2001 Briggs-Weaver was sold to Hagemeyer NV, a Dutch trading company. Briggs Equipment, previously a division of Briggs-Weaver, stayed with Sammons but remained an independent operation.

Briggs Equipment also pursued growth opportunities in the United States, particularly in the southeast. In 1998 Briggs Equipment purchased a Yale dealership in Atlanta. In 2000 and 2001, Briggs Equipment purchased CASE Construction Equipment dealerships in North Carolina and Florida, respectively, adding 15 additional locations to the company's 21 material handling locations. In 2004 Briggs was chosen by Sennebogen to represent its "green line" material handlers in Florida. German company Sennebogen specialized in manufacturing cranes, hydraulic excavators, and other material handling machines. With this expansion, Briggs was able to add 15 sales and service locations to its product mix.

As Briggs expanded geographically, the company also enhanced its technology offerings to customers. In 2004 Briggs enhanced the capabilities of its rental equipment by equipping the fleet with GlobalTRACS equipment management software. GlobalTRACS collected and transmitted operating status data from the equipment and transferred the information to a Web-based application. This software allowed companies to track utilization hours, reducing manpower and downtime. In 2009 the company offered fleet management software to its customers that consolidated functions such as invoicing and reporting.

INTERNATIONAL EXPANSION: 2006 AND BEYOND

In September 2006 Sammons Enterprises purchased the materials handling assets of U.K.-based Finning International Inc. for $160 million, marking Briggs's first entry into the European market. In 2007 the company formed a separate arm of Briggs Equipment, named Briggs International, Inc. Dave Bratton became president of the newly formed company. The company's purpose was to pursue European expansion.

In 2009 Chris Meinecke took over as the chief operating officer of Briggs U.K. Meinecke was an 18-year veteran of Briggs Equipment U.S., serving in both operational and management positions. At the same time, Briggs hired Ben Wilson to head the national accounts business.

Soon after its arrival in the United Kingdom, Briggs received a warm reception. In September 2009 Finnforest, a Nordic timber company, awarded Briggs with a £4 million contract ($6.6 million) to replace 78 pieces of equipment. Later that year, Pinkerton Automotive named Briggs as its national Cat Lift distributor. The five-year contract, worth £1.2 million, was expected to reduce costs by £100,000 through damage prevention and battery management solutions. In 2010 the United Kingdom Warehousing Association awarded Briggs a technology innovation award for its "Speedshield" asset management tool. Introduced in 2008 in the United States, Speedshield provided real-time reporting so that customers could track their truck fleets. Data included speed, truck efficiency, misuse, and damage. By tracking this data, customers were able to pinpoint areas for cost reduction.

The construction industry, Briggs' primary revenue driver, struggled in the first decade of the 21st century. To combat this, Briggs tried to distinguish itself by offering a wide range of solutions to its customers through technology, leasing, and product offerings. Briggs' international expansion marked the company as a dominant player in the materials handling industry. By 2010 the company had three locations in Mexico (Mexico City, Monterrey, and Guadalajara), with rental volume totaling $29 million, accounting for 60 percent of Briggs Equipment's total revenue. Given these figures, it seemed likely that Briggs's international expansion would continue.

Sara K. Huter

PRINCIPAL SUBSIDIARIES

Briggs Equipment Mexico; Briggs Equipment U.K.; Briggs Equipment U.S.

PRINCIPAL DIVISIONS

Briggs Contractor Rental; Briggs Fleet Management; Briggs Industrial Equipment; Briggs Rail Equipment; Briggs Used Equipment.

PRINCIPAL COMPETITORS

Caterpillar Inc.; CNH Global N.V.; Sunbelt Rentals, Inc.

FURTHER READING

"Briggs Equipment Inc." In *American Wholesalers and Distributors Directory,* edited by Peggy Geeseman. 21st ed. Gale Cengage, 2010.

"Briggs Equipment Parent Acquires Finning U.K.'s Forklift Business." *Rental Equipment Register,* September 18, 2006.

"Briggs Equipment to Represent Sennebogen Green Line Material Handlers in Florida." *Dixie Contractor* 79, no. 8 (2004).

"Briggs Equipment Wins International Technology Award." *Rental Equipment Register,* August 27, 2010.

"Briggs International Acquires United Rentals' Mexico Operations." *Rental Equipment Register,* May 28, 2010.

"Briggs UK Inks $6.6 Million Fleet-Management Deal." *Rental Equipment Register,* September 21, 2009.

"Briggs UK Names Chief Operating Officer." *Rental Equipment Register,* February 13, 2010.

"Finning Sells Materials Arm to Sammons in [Pounds Sterling]85m Deal." *Plant Manager's Journal,* October 1, 2006.

British American Tobacco Uganda

———■———

Plot 69/71 Jinja Road
P.O. Box 7100
Kampala,
Uganda
Telephone: (256) 312 200100
Fax: (256) 414 256425
Web site: http://www.bateac.com

Wholly Owned Subsidiary of British American Tobacco
Founded: 1927
Sales: UGX 163.7 billion ($78.7 million) (2009)
Stock Exchanges: Uganda Securities Exchange
Ticker Symbol: BATU
NAICS: 111910 Tobacco Farming

■ ■ ■

British American Tobacco Uganda (BAT Uganda) is a subsidiary of British American Tobacco that principally operates in Uganda, exporting processed leaf tobacco globally. Headquartered in Kampala, Uganda' capital, BAT Uganda serves as a strategic unit for tobacco leaf purchasing and processing. The core activities of the company are split into leaf export and cigarette distribution. The company contracts more than 50,000 tobacco farmers spread in 18 districts across Uganda. Some of the Ugandan districts where BAT Uganda's tobacco is grown include Hoima, Lira, Rukungiri, Bunyoro, Masindi, Mubende, Kigezi, and West Nile.

The manufacture of cigarettes in BAT Uganda was stopped in 2006 following global operational and strategic overhauls that were implemented by BAT

Investments Limited. The structural and operational changes transformed BAT Uganda into a strategic leaf purchasing, processing, and exporting unit. The company's cigarette manufacturing operations were consequently transferred to its sister company in Nairobi, Kenya. As such, BAT Uganda supplies its domestic market with BAT-branded cigarettes imported from BAT Kenya Limited. Sportsman, Safari, Sweet Menthol (SM), Embassy Kings, and Embassy Lights are some of the leading cigarette brands distributed by the company in Uganda.

BAT Investments Limited UK, the investment branch of British American Tobacco plc, owns 70 percent of BAT Uganda and commands an additional 20 percent indirect shareholding in the company through its investments subsidiary Precis BV. The remaining 10 percent of the company's shares are owned by Ugandan and international investors and are traded in the country's bourse.

COMMERCIAL TOBACCO IN UGANDA: 1927–76

British American Tobacco Uganda (BAT Uganda) came into existence in 1927 following the introduction of commercial farming of tobacco in Uganda by BAT Investment Limited UK. Numerous varieties of commercial tobacco were first introduced to Hoima region in Uganda before gradually spreading to other fertile regions of the country. The bumper harvest that was realized from the pilot project of the commercial tobacco farms motivated the company to consider setting up a processing factory. The considerations were

COMPANY PERSPECTIVES

Our goal is to lead and excel in everything we do—through our people, through our products, and in support of the community—whilst ensuring profitable growth.

based on the need to achieve efficiency by exporting processed and value-added tobacco as opposed to exporting bulk unprocessed tobacco. In 1928 BAT Investment Limited UK established its first cigarette manufacturing company in East Africa by constructing a factory in Jinja, Uganda.

BAT Investment Limited UK concentrated on the Ugandan market through its subsidiary until 1949 when the company made its first major acquisition in Africa. The multinational acquired the East Africa Tobacco Limited, a Tanganyika-based (now Tanzania) company that also owned a cigarette production subsidiary in Kampala, Uganda. In 1965 BAT Investment Limited UK merged the Ugandan subsidiary and the East Africa Tobacco Limited to form BAT Uganda Limited.

The company's tobacco farming and cigarette manufacturing activities continued to flourish until 1972 when its operations were halted. BAT Uganda Limited was nationalized following the enactment of Properties and Business Decree Number 32 by President Idi Amin Dada. The decree that nationalized all privately owned companies in Uganda was unilaterally issued and all multinational corporations, including BAT Investment Limited UK, were ordered to surrender their rights in the companies.

The government of Uganda immediately initiated corporate restructuring programs that fully transformed BAT Uganda Limited into a parastatal. The restructuring process of the company resulted in the formation of three separate entities, which were the Smallholders Tobacco Program, Produce Marketing Board, and the Uganda National Tobacco Company. In 1976 the Ugandan government formed the National Tobacco Corporation (NTC) as part of institutional reforms that were implemented in its corporate sector and parastatal bodies. The NTC became the umbrella body that managed the farming, processing, and marketing activities of tobacco and tobacco products in the country.

PRIVATIZATION AND CIVIL WAR

Relative sanity was restored in Uganda's economic and political policies after the dictatorial government of

President Idi Amin was deposed by a revolution led by Milton Obote in 1979. Obote's government initiated numerous reform programs that were aimed at cleaning up the economic mess that had been created by Amin's government. The Ugandan parliament enacted the Expropriated Properties Rights Act in 1982, lifting the blanket ban that had been imposed on foreign-owned private enterprises in the country. BAT Investment Limited UK utilized the window of opportunity that was provided by the Properties Rights Act and applied for the restitution of its ownership rights in BAT Uganda Limited.

The efforts by BAT Investment Limited UK to reenter the Ugandan market finally materialized in July 1984 when the government agreed to disband the NTC through a privatization arrangement. BAT Uganda 1984 Limited was established in July 1984 under a joint venture agreement between the government of Uganda and BAT Investment Limited UK. The new company was established with a total authorized share capital of 64 million shares. The Ugandan government ceded ground and surrendered 70 percent of the ownership stake in BAT Uganda 1984 Limited to BAT Investment Limited UK under the joint venture arrangement. The government retained a 30 percent stake in the company that was designated for future divestment through a public rights issue.

In 1985 BAT Uganda 1984 Limited experienced more challenges as the country was ravaged by a lengthy civil war between government forces and the National Resistance Movement (NRM). The state of civil war affected tobacco production because many farmers in tobacco-growing regions were either displaced or fled to seek refuge in neighboring countries. The NRM finally overthrew Obote' government and installed NRM leader Yoweri Kaguta Museveni as the country's new president in 1986. Surprisingly, the Museveni-led government immediately adopted a friendlier stance toward private and foreign investments.

In 1987 the government initiated economic liberalization and reform programs in efforts to stimulate economic growth. Uganda gradually became a market-driven economy following the significant reduction of government control in the economy.

RISE OF DIRECT PARTNERSHIPS: 1995–99

In the mid-1990s, BAT Uganda 1984 Limited began reviewing the company's policies towards contract farming with the objective of developing direct contractual relationships with farmers. The company's management was concerned about the unnecessary bureaucracy that

KEY DATES

1927: Commercial tobacco farming is introduced in Uganda.

1984: BAT Uganda 1984 Limited Established.

1997: Company enters into direct partnerships with tobacco farmers.

2000: BAT Uganda shares list on the Uganda Securities Exchange.

2006: BAT Uganda ceases cigarette manufacturing operations.

2009: BAT Uganda posts profits despite the global economic crisis.

was caused by government-controlled cooperative organizations in the chain of growing and marketing of farmers' tobacco. Government interference and bureaucracy had inflated the costs of tobacco production and led to delays in remittance of farmers' payments.

The company was finally granted authorization to establish direct partnerships with farmers in 1997. As such, the cooperative movements were substituted by direct partnerships in all tobacco growing and marketing processes, including the provision of extension services. The strategy of direct contact with farmers was designed to reverse the declining tobacco production trend by motivating farmers through subsidized farm inputs, free extension services, and prompt payment for their tobacco produce.

The corporate identity of BAT Uganda 1984 Limited was transformed in April 1998 when its name was changed to British American Tobacco Limited Uganda. A subsequent change of name to British American Tobacco Uganda (BAT Uganda) was made in July 1998 following the adoption of BAT's universal tag and corporate identity. In 1999 BAT Uganda's cigarette products commanded 92.9 percent of market share in Uganda.

IPO AND INCREASED PRODUCTION: 2000–03

At the dawn of the 21st century the capitalist ideology had taken root in Uganda, and the private sector had become part of the country's vibrant economy. The government of Uganda continued to liberalize its economy through full privatization of major parastatals. The government's plans of completely divesting from BAT Uganda were in earnest right from the beginning of 2000. The successful filing of a resolution for the

conversion of BAT Uganda to a public limited company with the Registrar of Companies was made in May 2000. This paved the way for preparations of an initial public offering (IPO) for the 30 percent government's shareholding.

The IPO for the 30 percent of BAT Uganda shares was launched on June 28, 2000, and lasted until August 9, 2000. BAT Investments Limited expanded its controlling interests in BATU when it acquired 20 percent of the government shareholding through its subsidiary, Precis BV. The remaining 10 percent shareholding that represented 4,907,984 shares was floated to the public at an offer price of UGX 1,000 per share. The tremendous investor interest in BAT Uganda shares led to oversubscription of the IPO by 5 percent.

The success of the company's policy shifts in the 1990s became evident in 2001 when the tonnage of tobacco production increased threefold to 21,000 metric tons compared to 7,000 metric tons in 1995. The company also retained high volume of cigarette production by processing more than one billion sticks in 2001. BAT Uganda also launched a major tree planting program that would lead to the establishment of its own tree plantations in all tobacco growing districts in Uganda. The company was able to plant more than 700,000 indigenous trees and more than 2,000 hectares of eucalyptus trees in the year. (Farmers utilize a lot of firewood in the curing process of the Burley and Virginia tobacco varieties that are mainly grown in Uganda. As such, the company's decision to establish its own tree plantations was informed by the need to avoid the depletion of natural vegetation in tobacco growing areas of Uganda.)

The benefits of the direct partnerships with farmers increased tobacco production as the company purchased a total of 22,000 metric tons of tobacco in 2002. However, the company started experiencing the adverse effects of low-cost cigarette imports and counterfeits. These cheap cigarettes were gradually diminishing the company's market share. The trend prompted the Ugandan Revenue Authority (URA) to introduce the Minimum Specific Tax in 2002 to curb the dumping of cigarette products. The URA also adopted a host of other restrictive measures that included the introduction of tax stamps on cigarette packets and banned the sale of unstamped cigarettes in the country. These measures helped the company record sales of UGX 136 billion in 2002, up from UGX 66 billion in 1996.

BATU continued registering favorable production and sales performance in 2003 as the company revenues grew by 9.5 percent to reach UGX 149 billion. The company also made a significant concession in 2003 by accepting a change in the wording of the cigarette warning labels on its products and advertisements from "Smoking Can be Dangerous to Your Health"to "Smoking Is Dangerous to Your Health."

END OF MANUFACTURING AND AN AWARD: 2006–08

BAT Uganda faced litigation in April 2005 when a group of 2,838 farmers filed for a court injunction to prevent the company from buying tobacco from farmers until the company increased the buying price of the tobacco. In the case involving *Mwijakubi and Others vs. British American Tobacco Ltd,* the farmers accused the company of exploitation by offering very low prices for the tobacco grown by farmers. The judge, however, dismissed the case with cost, ruling that the farmers of lacked any basis for their application.

BAT Uganda stopped all cigarette manufacturing operations in 2006 and transferred the operations to BAT Kenya Ltd in the neighboring country. BAT Uganda would concentrate on the purchasing and exporting of tobacco leaf. The company's participation in the cigarette segment would be limited to the importation, marketing, and distribution of BAT cigarette brands in Uganda. The strategy shift was designed to optimize tobacco growing, leaf classification, and processing of bulk tobacco in Uganda, where the output of the produce was exceptionally high. The move also optimized the cigarette production potential of the Nairobi plant and reduced the overall operational expenses of the two subsidiaries.

The benefits of the operational and strategic adjustments that were implemented in BAT Uganda in 2006 became evident in 2007. In January of that year, the company sought to meet its strategic obligations by expanding its pool of contracted farmers by 40 percent to 40,000 farmers. As a result, the company recorded remarkable improvements in tobacco production by surpassing its annual production targets of 18,000 metric tons. The volume of green leaf tobacco BAT Uganda purchased from farmers in 2007 increased to 19,000 metric tons.

In 2008 the company won the Platinum Export Award for its achievement as the highest foreign exchange earner in Uganda. The company was honored with the prestigious award at a gala. The recognition came at a time when the company's total revenue contributions to the government had risen to $27 million.

MIXED RESULTS AND ENVIRONMENTAL ISSUES: 2009 AND BEYOND

BAT Uganda posted mixed results in the financial year 2009 as the company's net profits increased by 19 percent compared to 2008. The growth in profits was attributed to the success of the company's cost-cutting measures. BAT Uganda also recorded higher exports in the year as a result of enhanced competitiveness of the company in the global leaf export markets. The company's revenue, however, declined by 11.9 percent from UGX 185.9 billion in 2008 to 163.7 billion in 2009.

BAT Uganda encountered fresh accusations regarding its commitment to environmental preservation in an article published in the *East African* on August 16, 2010. Concerns emerged over the increased depletion of natural vegetation as farmers cut down trees for use in the curing process of tobacco. The company was quick to issue a press response through its corporate and regulatory affairs coordinator, Solomon Muyita. In a response published in the *East African* on September 6, 2010, the company outlined the various long-term measures it had instituted toward environmental preservation. For instance, BAT Uganda was emphatic that it had a sustainable initiative for generating sufficient wood fuel through a forestation plan implemented in 10-year phases. The company embraced measures that matched the firewood requirements to projections of quantities of tobacco to be produced in a given year. By its account, the company had achieved 92 percent self-sufficiency ratings in its wood requirements as of September 2010. The company distributed a total of 700,000 seedlings to farmers and planted a total of 165,000 indigenous tree seedlings in 2010.

BAT Uganda planned to enhance its environmental commitment standards by achieving 100 percent self-sufficiency in wood requirements by 2015. The company's process of outsourcing noncore services was well on course, and the company projected increased profit margins as a result of reduced operational costs and increased efficiencies.

Paul Ingati

PRINCIPAL DIVISIONS

Export Distribution: Leaf Export.

PRINCIPAL COMPETITORS

Alliance One International, Inc.; Mastermind Tobacco SA (Pty) Ltd.; Universal Corporation.

FURTHER READING

Barigaba, Julius. "BAT on a High Despite Freeze on '07 Dividends." allAfrica.com, January 7, 2008. Accessed November 5, 2010. http://allafrica.com/stories/2008010 71286.html.

"British American Tobacco Uganda Limited: Company Chart." FirstGlobalSelect.com. 2010. Accessed November 4, 2010. http://www.firstglobalselect.com/scripts/cgiip.wsc/globalone/htm/quote_and_news.r?pisharetype-id=15085.

"BAT Uganda–Profits Double." *Ugee! Uganda Online.* Accessed January 31, 2011. http://www.ugee.com/201003132734/Latest-News/BAT-UGANDA-PROFITS-DOUBLE.html.

"BAT Unveils Business Plans." *Tobacco International,* March 2007. Accessed November 7, 2010. http://www.tobaccointernational.com/0307/leaf.htm.

Google. "British American Tobacco Uganda Ltd." Accessed November 4, 2010. http://www.google.com/finance?q=UGA:BATU.

Muyita, Solomon. "BAT Uganda Not Destroying Forests." *East African,* September 6, 2010. Accessed November 7, 2010. http://www.theeastafrican.co.ke/OpEd/letters/-/434756/1004236/-/e3rftmz/-/index.html

"Mwijakubi and Others vs. British American Tobacco Ltd – HCT–00–CC–MA–0284–2005" Uganda Legal Information Institute.

Oketch, Martin Luther. "BAT Sets 21 Leaf Tobacco Standards." *Monitor,* January 24, 2007. Accessed January 31, 2011. http://allafrica.com/stories/200701240593.html.

Ojambo, Fred. "British American Tobacco Uganda Says Profit More Than Doubles." *Bloomberg BusinessWeek,* March 12, 2010. Accessed January 11, 2011. http://www.businessweek.com/news/2010-03-12/britist-american-tobacco-uganda-says-profit-more-than-doubles.html.

Sejjaaka, Samuel. "From Seed to Leaf: British American Tobacco and Supplier Relations in Uganda." Chap. 6 in *International Business and the Challenges of Poverty in Developing Areas,* edited by Frederick Bird and Stewart Herman. Basingstoke, Hampshire, UK: Palgrave Macmillan, 2004. Accessed November 5, 2010. http://www.cpa.ug/Herman_061.pdf.

Caché, Inc.

■

1440 Broadway
Fifth Floor
New York City, New York 10018
U.S.A.
Telephone: (212) 575-3248
Toll Free: (800) 788-2224
Web site: http://www.cache.com

Public Company
Founded: 1975 as Atours Incorporated
Employees: 1,072 (2010)
Sales: $219.8 million (2010)
Stock Exchanges: NASDAQ
Ticker Symbol: CACH
NAIC: 448120 Women's Clothing Stores

■ ■ ■

Caché, Inc., owns and operates a chain of upscale women's apparel stores. In 2010 the company had 286 stores (mostly in malls) in 43 U.S. states, Puerto Rico, and the U.S. Virgin Islands. Targeting women ages 25 to 45, Caché offers a variety of sportswear, dresses, and accessories. Its line of sportswear is its largest seller, accounting for 57 percent of revenue in 2010.

A ROUGH START FOR HIGH-END APPAREL

Caché was founded as Atours Incorporated in Miami, Florida, in 1975. Atours purchased high-end apparel from U.S. and European vendors, offering customers well-made, trendy daywear and eveningwear. Atours presented an alternative shopping experience to those weary of large, impersonal department stores. The company kept its stores small and emphasized customer service. The inventory exemplified a focus on style over quantity. The strategy worked and Atours went public in March 1981. Two years later the company changed its name to the more fashionable Caché Inc.

After a strong start, the 1980s proved to be a difficult decade for Caché. Department stores flourished and the upscale apparel industry faced increased competition from both individual designers and upstart small labels. By 1984 Caché was suffering a revenue slump. The company's revenues were down $1.7 million, and in 1985 they were down another $2 million. In 1985 Caché owned 30 stores located on the East Coast, but the company could not maintain operations while sustaining such losses. Caché had trouble finding credit to maintain inventory and paying off its creditors due to slow-moving inventory. In November 1986 the company sought protection from its creditors by filing for reorganization under Chapter 11 of the Federal Bankruptcy Code. Under Chapter 11, Caché was allowed to continue operations while working with its creditors and financial advisors to restore its financial viability.

In 1987 the company found two white knights. Joseph and Andrew Saul led an investment group to buy 78 percent of the company. The Sauls had a track record for buying companies and turning them around, including a company in the retail industry. They had recently sold their interest in Brooks Fashion Stores for $368 million and netted $125 million on the deal. The Sauls

COMPANY PERSPECTIVES

With sexy style and a bold attitude, Caché has the fashions of the moment. So, no matter the occasion, Caché provides the right look for the sexy modern woman who is dynamic in her interests and her activities.

initiated a restructuring plan and set a goal to expand the chain to 100 locations by 1991. They moved the company from its headquarters in Miami to New York City. They hired several executives from Bonwit Teller, a New York department store that specialized in women's high-end clothing. Among the transfers was Norman Polonofsky, Bonwit Teller's executive vice president. To execute their restructure the Sauls enlisted the help of Roy Chapman, a Caché chairman and a minority partner in the Sauls' investment group. Chapman had been chief financial officer for Brooks Fashion Stores.

The new owners shifted the company's merchandising strategy. Previously, the stores carried dresses priced between $4,000 and $6,000. The Sauls believed the merchandise narrowed the company's market too much. They scaled back the merchandise to an expensive but more realistic range, averaging around $500 a dress. Also, they made an effort to maintain most of the merchandise under their own private label. Within a year Caché pulled itself out of the red without having to close a single store. The company emerged from bankruptcy and was once again achieving solid growth.

LARGE SHOPPING MALLS BRING OPPORTUNITY

In the late 1980s and early 1990s the retail industry went through many changes. The most important change was the explosive growth of large shopping malls. The upscale malls were anchored by large national departments stores such as Saks Fifth Avenue and Neiman Marcus. Small, niche-market stores filled in the remaining retail space. Indoor malls offered customers more choices than ever before. They condensed a myriad of products and brands into a customer-friendly environment. No longer did a customer have to seek out a store or a particular product. Malls offered everything under one roof.

Malls may have made things easier for the consumer, but for retailers they meant more intense competition, and for the apparel industry the competi-

tion in malls was particularly intense. Stores like Caché faced competition from the large, increasing powerful department stores and the other boutiques that appealed to Caché's particular customers. To flourish, Caché strived to maintain a balance between offering merchandise similar to its competitors while marketing the merchandise as somehow unique and original so that it stood out in an increasingly crowded market. In 1990 Michael Warner became president and general merchandising manager of Caché. Warner had been a vice president of a women's apparel division at R.H. Macy & Co.

By the early 1990s Caché had proved its strength in the marketplace. Malls continued to grow and so did Caché by establishing a strong presence in upscale malls throughout the eastern part of the United States. The company focused on younger customers interested in trendy, dressy daywear and eveningwear. Caché opened 16 new stores nationwide in 1992 and another 16 stores in 1993. Also, Ray Chapman resigned as CEO and Andrew Saul took his place. At the time, Saul and his family owned 75 percent of the company's shares. Caché owned 93 stores and the company's net income rose to $1.9 million.

One advantage the company had over its competitors was that it did not maintain a warehouse of inventory. Instead, the company bought its inventory directly from vendors in the United States, Western Europe, and Asia. This enabled Caché to maintain a lower overhead than if it manufactured and stored its own merchandise. Another factor in its success was presentation. Caché kept its stores small with an average 2,000 square feet in floor space. The company designed the stores as intimate boutiques. The mix of effective operations management and store design proved mostly successful.

In 1995 Caché experienced slumping sales, and Warner resigned as president in September. No replacement was named but an executive vice president took over his responsibilities. The company continued to expand, opening 24 new stores.

CACHÉ ACQUIRES A NEW VENTURE

The company achieved $135 million in sales in 1997 and was looking for ways to expand without increasing overhead costs. The tough competition in malls had taken its toll on its competitors. In 1998 a small apparel chain, Lillie Rubin, declared bankruptcy and put itself up for sale. Lillie Rubin's stores sold expensive, high-quality apparel and accessories designed as "special occasion" ensembles. The stores appealed to high-income

```
┌─────────────────────────────────────────────┐
│                                               │
│              KEY DATES                        │
│                   ■                           │
│ ─────────────────────────────────────────    │
│  1975:  Founders start Atours Incorporated.   │
│  1981:  Atours goes public.                   │
│  1983:  Atours changes its name to Caché Inc. │
│  1986:  Caché files Chapter 11 bankruptcy.    │
│  1987:  Joseph and Andrew Saul buy a controlling │
│         interest.                             │
│  1998:  Caché acquires Lillie Rubin stores.   │
│  1999:  Caché launches e-commerce Web site.   │
│  2006:  Company closes Lillie Rubin stores and │
│         replaces them with Caché Luxe stores. │
│  2009:  Company begins to move away from its  │
│         Caché Luxe concept.                   │
│                                               │
└─────────────────────────────────────────────┘
```

women in their 40s and 50s. Lillie Rubin's inventory consisted of sequined, formal evening gowns, tailored pantsuits, and high quality faux jewelry. The company's stores were of similar design to Caché's. The difference lay with merchandise. Lillie Rubin offered higher priced merchandise, and this is what led to Lillie Rubin's financial difficulties. Its merchandise competed with department stores like Saks Fifth Avenue and Lord & Taylor rather than with other small boutiques like Caché. As the larger department stores became more powerful, Lillie Rubin lost out.

The 1998 bankruptcy filing was Rubin's second in two years. Buyers were wary of the beleaguered retail chain. A plus-sized apparel company, The Forgotten Woman, offered $2 million for the company but backed out at the last minute. Several months later Caché started negotiations and in August 1998 bought the company for only $775,000.

At the time of the purchase Lillie Rubin had closed all its stores, but after the purchase Caché reopened 12 of its stores. Caché marketed the new stores as a source of formal attire and clothing that appealed to a more mature clientele. The image of Lillie Rubin became more stylish and less flashy. Caché updated the stores' design and merchandise to fit the latest trends. With the Lillie Rubin's and Caché'slocations, Caché raised its number of locations to 172 stores, giving the company a significant presence in malls around the country.

In March 2002 the company acquired the leases of seven Mondi of America store locations and ran them under the Lilli Rubin name. The company continued to perform well during the first decade of the 21st century. In 2002, when many retailers were suffering because of the U.S. recession, Caché's sales increased to $216.2

million, an almost 11 percent increase over the previous year. Sales from existing locations rose 7 percent. The company's line of clothing for weddings and proms, which proved recession proof, helped the company make it through a difficult year. Also, net profit increased, mainly because the company's management lowered costs. They bought merchandise from fewer vendors and obtained volume discounts. Also, Caché increased its imports from overseas manufacturing plants that had lower labor costs.

SHEDDING ONE DIFFICULTY TO FACE ANOTHER

The company continued to enjoy strong growth over the next few years, but it became apparent to the company's leadership that the Lillie Rubin line of stores was dragging down earnings. In 2006 the company decided to convert the Lillie Rubin stores into a new line of stores under the name CachéLuxe. The CachéLuxe stores focused on daywear and eveningwear for its existing customer base but at higher price points. In 2007 the company launched the Caché Accents program, which was a loyalty program in which customers could earn a 5 percent lifetime discount on merchandise for as long as they were members. The company also launched a cobranded credit card with Visa U.S.A. Inc.

Caché experienced a slump in 2007. Sales dropped 1.6 percent and net income was reduced by 21.1 percent. In 2008 Brian Woolf resigned as CEO and Thomas Reinckens took over his position while remaining president of the company. Despite the change in leadership the company's slump worsened. The whole retail sector suffered a terrible slump as the United States began its descent into the worst economic downturn since the Great Depression. Even Caché's prom and wedding dress business failed to soften the blow as people severely cut back on expenses, including clothing for special events. Sales decreased 3 percent, and the company experienced a net loss of $7.1 million, with profits shifting from the black into the red.

The United States faced continuing economic uncertainty in 2009, and Caché's difficulties persisted. Company sales decreased significantly to $219.7 million, a loss of 17.2 percent, and the company experienced a net loss of $8.7 million. Sales at existing stores open more than a year decreased a dismal 18 percent. Caché began closing some of its Caché Luxe stores as the recession took its toll on luxury clothing lines nationwide.

In 2010 Caché showed further losses, but the bleeding had lessened somewhat. The U.S. economy started to show improvement, and the retail sector showed signs of recovery late in the year. At the end of the year the company faced uncertainty as to how deeply the recession had affected consumers' spending habits. As the United States emerged from the recession, retailers such as Caché faced a more budget-conscious woman who was less likely to pay for an expensive dress, no matter the occasion. (The price of the company's dresses have decreased over time, from averaging around $500 to a 2010 range of $75 to $420.) Another threat to Caché's long-term viability came from trends in retail. The primacy of the mall was waning, and this may affect the company's future store locations and possibly force the company to reassess its locations.

Rachel H. Martin
Updated, Aaron Hauser

PRINCIPAL DIVISIONS

Caché; Caché Luxe.

PRINCIPAL COMPETITORS

AnnTaylor Stores Corporation; bebe stores, inc.; Macy's, Inc.; Neiman Marcus, Inc.

FURTHER READING

"Caché Requests Chapter 11 Status." *Wall Street Journal,* November 13, 1986, 5.

"Dressy Retailer Is Life of the Party." *Crain's New York Business,* January 20, 2003, 19.

Lebow, Joan. "Pricey Niche Retailer Nabs Bonwit Execs." *Crain's New York Business,* June 22, 1987, 10.

Moin, David. "Caché Buys Lillie Rubin Chain." *Women's Wear Daily,* August 11, 1998, 16.

Saranow, Jennifer. "Retailers Downscale Their Luxury Lines. "*Wall Street Journal,* May 19, 2008, B1.

"US: Caché Inc to Exit Lillie Rubin, Launch CachéLuxe Concept." *Just-Style,* May 16, 2006.

Cascade Microtech, Inc.

———————■———————

2430 N.W. 206th Avenue
Beaverton, Oregon 97006
U.S.A.
Telephone: (503) 601-1000
Fax: (503) 601-1002
Web site: http://www.cmicro.com

■ ■ ■

Public Company
*Founded:*1983
Employees: 401 (2010)
Revenue: $95.8 million (2010)
Stock Exchanges: NASDAQ
Ticker Symbol: CSCD
NAICS: 334515 Instrument Manufacturing for Measuring and Testing Electricity and Electrical Signals

Cascade Microtech, Inc., designs, produces, and sells products which electrically measure and test semiconductor devices, such as high-performance chips, LED devices, and circuit boards. These products are designed and produced both in the United States and in Dresden, Germany. Centers which sell, service, and support these products are located in China, Germany, Japan, Singapore, and Taiwan, as well as in North America. Since 2005 more than 60 percent of the company's sales have been to overseas customers. In 2010 sales to the Asia/Pacific region accounted for 45 percent of total revenue, while sales to Europe and the United States were about 25 percent each.

Sales of Cascade Microtech's engineering probe stations depend greatly on the amount of money customers allocate to the research and development of semiconductors, which itself depends on the anticipated demand for chips. An increase in the demand for chips has occurred over the past decade as a result of growth in computer, telecommunications, and the electronics markets. Although Cascade Microtech's products are sold in most areas of the semiconductor industry, a significant percentage of the company's revenue is realized from sales to research and development departments of semiconductor companies as well as colleges and universities.

INVESTING IN A NEW COMPANY: 1983–90

Until 1983 it was not really possible to determine why a particular design for a high-speed integrated circuit worked, or to measure the electrical performance at the wafer level. Then Eric Strid and Reed Gleason, members of a research group at Tektronix, invented the first microwave wafer probe, which was able to test circuits prior to being cut into individual microchips. This advancement cut research and development times in half, while eliminating the high cost of creating new chips. However, Tektronix did not feel that the probe fit into its product line and was not interested in it. Strid and Gleason decided to produce the probes on their own, in their spare time. The following year, Cascade Microtech was incorporated. The company began realizing revenue and profits almost immediately.

For the first three years the company was in operation, Strid and Gleason put all revenues and profits back

COMPANY PERSPECTIVES

Cascade Microtech plays an essential role in the semiconductor industry by producing tough, reliable, innovative testing technologies for integrated circuit development and production.

into the business. They chose to fund the company without any outside capital. Instead, they used their own savings, home equity loans, and credit cards. They continued using their own money, and that raised by the company, until 1990, at which time Hewlett Packard (HP) made a minority equity investment in the company. HP bought a 20 percent equity stake in Cascade Microtech for $3 million. This purchase made HP the only outside investor in the company.

EXPANDING PRESENCE AND PRODUCTS: 1990–2000

During the next decade, Cascade Microtech continued to grow, both in the United States and abroad. The company's Japanese subsidiary, Cascade Microtech Japan, was formed in 1990 to sell the company's products in that country. One factor in establishing this subsidiary was the fact that a major competitor in that region, Tektronix Inc., was in negotiations to take over control of Sony/Tektronix Corp. of Japan. This move concerned Cascade's executives, due to the fact that the Japanese market was an important part of the company's business. Establishing a Japanese operation allowed Cascade to maintain its hold in that region. At the time, the company had a total of about 70 employees, including the five that worked in the new Japanese office.

Expansion of the company's product line also occurred during the 1990s. Alessi, a supplier of failure analysis systems in the market, was acquired by Cascade Microtech in 1995. Cascade believed that combining Alessi's failure analysis products with its own testing probes would help the company better integrate testing processes and therefore benefit customers. As new semiconductor products were being developed rapidly at that time, it was necessary to provide test equipment with greater automation capabilities.

Growing demand for digital cell phones and high-speed computer chips increased the demand for Cascade Microtech's testing equipment, causing considerable growth in the company. By 1997 the company had 185 employees, nearly triple the number employed three

years previously. With sales of high-speed chips accounting for nearly $1 billion in the industry each year, the company expected growth to continue. It was announced that Cascade Microtech was considering an initial public offering of its stock in 1998, although the IPO would not actually occur for several more years.

In 1999 the company raised $16 million in venture capital. Growth in the company made it necessary to expand its manufacturing capacity by nearly three times in 1999. Earnings were near $2.5 million, and sales approached $52 million. Hewlett Packard and Maristeth Ventures, a venture capital fund, invested in the company, and approximately $3 million of the investment was used to pay for the expansion.

In April of the following year, Cascade received $10 million in equity financing from the Teachers Insurance and Annuity Association of America. This money was earmarked for Cascade's marketing and manufacturing needs associated with the new Pyramid technology, which would offer advanced capabilities for testing semiconductors. A few months later, Electroglas, Inc., a supplier of process management tools, bought a minority equity share in Cascade by purchasing $3 million of the company's preferred stocks.

BECOMING A PUBLIC COMPANY: 2000–04

Approximately three years after originally announcing plans for the company to go public, Cascade filed with the SEC for its initial public offering in October 2000 but announced that the actual offering would wait until the stock market improved. The company hoped to raise about $69 million, to be used as working capital and for capital ventures. During the first half of the year, the company posted sales of $31.8 million, an increase from $20.7 million for the same period of the previous year.

Cascade Microtech, Inc., became a publicly traded company on December 15, 2004, under the symbol CSCD. During the IPO, 3.3 million shares of common stock were sold, with net proceeds for the company totaling $41.6 million.

RECOGNITION AND EXPANSION: 2005–08

Following more than two decades of work with the company, Cascade's founders were recognized in 2006 for their role in the industry. Strid and Gleason were awarded the Southwest Test Workshop (SWTW) Lifetime Achievement Award "for more than 25 years of outstanding technical contributions to the field of RF wafer-level measurements," according to *Microwaves and*

```
┌─────────────────────────────────────────────────┐
│                                                   │
│                KEY DATES                          │
│                    ▪                              │
│  ├────────────────────────────────────────────┤  │
│  1983:  Eric Strid and Reed Gleason found Cascade │
│         Microtech.                                │
│  1990:  Hewlett Packard becomes Cascade Micro-    │
│         tech's only outside investor when it buys a 20 │
│         percent equity stake in the company for $3 │
│         million.                                  │
│  2004:  Cascade Microtech becomes a publicly traded │
│         company.                                  │
│  2006:  Direct sales offices are opened in China and │
│         Taiwan to support Cascade Microtech's     │
│         customers in this region.                 │
│  2010:  Cascade Microtech acquires SUSS Test; the │
│         company begins restructuring plans in order │
│         to consolidate the businesses.            │
│                                                   │
└─────────────────────────────────────────────────┘
```

RF. The SWTW is a research forum that is sponsored by the Institute of Electrical and Electronics Engineers Computer Society.

The company's international expansion continued. As a result of Cascade's growing business overseas, direct sales and service offices were established in Shanghai, China, and Hsin Chu City, Taiwan, during 2006. Distributors had been selling the company's products in these areas for more than 10 years. The purpose of these offices was to provide support to existing customers in these areas, to strengthen customer relations, and to further expand Cascade's customer base.

Not only did Cascade continue to expand its footprint overseas, it also continued to expand its product offerings. Gryphics, Inc., a private company which specialized in developing high-performance test socket products for semiconductor integrated circuits, was acquired by Cascade Microtech for $13.7 million and became a wholly owned subsidiary of the company. At the time, there was a growing demand for new socket designs, and Gryphics was focused on supporting the industry's needs in this area. The acquisition allowed Cascade to increase its presence in the test consumables market, which was more stable than some other markets in which the company was involved.

Cascade's overseas expansion continued with the opening of the company's subsidiary, Cascade Microtech GmbH, in Munich, Germany, in 2007. This new company was created to provide sales and support to customers in Europe for both the engineering products and production products divisions. The company also continued to operate an office in the United Kingdom.

FACING ECONOMIC CHALLENGES: 2008–09

The global economic downturn impacted Cascade Microtech heavily, as lower demand for electronics led to a slump in demand for the company's products. Revenue went from $90 million in 2007 to $76.6 million in 2008. In response, Cascade Microtech restructured in 2008, changing from a divisional to a functional style of organization. The company's machine shop was also closed, as well as the sales and service office in England. Also, the manufacturing of some 150mm systems were outsourced. These changes eliminated redundancy in some of the positions within the divisions and lowered personnel expenses.

Economic conditions continued to negatively impact the sales of semiconductors in 2009. Revenue at Cascade Microtech plunged to $53.5 million in 2009. However, the Semiconductor Industry Association (SIA) reported that worldwide sales did surpass expectations for that year, reaching $226.3 billion, compared to $248.6 billion the previous year. Although this was a decline of 9 percent, it was considerably better than the 24 percent decline that had been predicted.

In 2010 sales rebounded to $95.8 million. This number was aided in part by Cascade's acquisition of the Test Systems Division of SUSS Microtec AG in January 2010. The division, known as SUSS Micro Tec Test Systems GmbH (SUSS Test), had long been a competitor in the area of engineering probe stations. The acquisition provided Cascade Microtech with an expanded product line in addition to engineering and technical resources.

LOOKING TOWARD THE FUTURE

As a result of plans to integrate Cascade's operations with those of SUSS Test, the company announced restructuring plans in the fall of 2010. Manufacturing operations for the company's Systems division would be consolidated at the facility in Germany over the course of the following year, and manufacturing for the Probes division would be consolidated at the Beaverton, Oregon, facility over the following six months. Two U.S. sales offices would be closed, resulting in the loss of 21 employees.

The company planned to step into the future by continuing to keep up with the technological advancements in the semiconductor industry through investments in research and development. Since engineering probing systems are mandatory in creating new chips, the demand for Cascade Microtech's products was expected to increase as more highly complex chip processes and designs were developed.

Diane Milne

PRINCIPAL SUBSIDIARIES

Cascade International Trading (Shanghai) Co., Ltd. (China); Cascade Microtech Dresden, GmbH (Germany); Cascade Microtech Japan, K.K.; Cascade Microtech Taiwan Co., Ltd.; Gryphics, Inc.

PRINCIPAL DIVISIONS

Systems; Probes and Sockets.

PRINCIPAL COMPETITORS

FormFactor Inc.; Lucas/Signatone Corp.; The Micromanipulator Co. Inc.; Vector Semiconductor Co. Ltd.; Wentworth Laboratories Inc.

FURTHER READING

"Cascade Microtech Inc." *Microwave Journal* 43 (2000): 64.

"Cascade Microtech Opens Two New Offices in Asia to Meet Rapid Regional Sales Growth." *PR Newswire,* July 5, 2006.

Curley, John. "Kudos." *Microwaves & RF,* July 2006, 22.

Goldfield, Robert. "Other Ways to Raise Funds for Start-Up." *Pacific Business News,* June 8, 2001, 15.

Strid, Eric. "An Interview with Eric Strid." *Microwaves & RF,* September 2009, 44+.

"Wafer Tester Cascade Tests the Financial Waters." *Electronics Times,* October 9, 2000, 14. PROMPT.

Cavaliers Operating Company, LLC

1 Center Court
Cleveland, Ohio 44115
U.S.A.
Telephone: (216) 420-2000
Toll Free: (800) 820-2287
Fax: (216) 420-2101
Web site: http://www.nba.com/cavaliers

Private Company
Founded: 1970
Employees: 225 (est., 2010)
Sales: $150 million (est., 2010)
NAICS: 711211 Sports Teams and Clubs

∎ ∎ ∎

The Cavaliers Operating Company, LLC, is a holding company that owns and operates the Cleveland Cavaliers (the Cavs), a professional basketball team with the United States National Basketball Association (NBA). The Cavs compete in the Central Division of the Eastern Conference of the NBA. The Cavaliers are owned by majority owner Dan Gilbert, founder of Quicken Loans. Minority owners include the musician Usher Raymond and the former majority owner Gordon Gund. The team's home court is in the Quicken Loans Arena (The Q) in downtown Cleveland, Ohio.

A ROUGH UP AND DOWN START: 1970–79

The NBA expanded the league from 14 to 17 teams in 1970, awarding the three new teams to Portland, Buf-

falo, and Cleveland. Nick Mileti paid the franchise fee of $3.7 million to become the owner of the Cleveland team. Mileti was a lawyer who could put together deals without putting much of his own money at risk, yet he retained majority ownership. At the time, he also owned the minor league hockey team the Cleveland Barons. Mileti held a contest sponsored by the *Cleveland Plain Dealer* newspaper to name the team and asked the people of Cleveland to contribute suggested names. Mileti narrowed the contributions down to five contenders, then chose "the Cavaliers." He also chose the colors wine and gold in honor of his high school team, which played wearing the same colors.

The team started playing in the league in 1970 under coach Bill Fitch. Their home court was Cleveland Arena, which was built during the Great Depression and offered a maximum of 9,900 seats. They played their first home game on October 28, 1970, after playing seven games on the road because the arena had been booked by other programs. The team got off to a dismal start with a 15–67 record in its first year and did not achieve a winning record until the 1975–76 season.

In 1973 Bill Fitch took over the general manager responsibilities from Mileti but remained as coach. Early on, the team experienced some bad luck. Its top draft pick, Austin Carr, experienced a rash of injuries that kept him off the court or hindered his play. The team acquired Lenny Wilkens from the Seattle SuperSonics, and Carr started to show potential, but early in the 1974–75 season he suffered a knee injury that ended his season.

In 1974 the team moved into the newly built Richfield Coliseum about 30 miles south of downtown Cleveland in Summit County. The new arena seated 20,000 and featured 96 private suites and a two-story apartment that could accommodate a 100-person party. The team improved to 40–42 thanks to the added talent of Bingo Smith, Jim Chones, Jim Cleamons, and Dick Snyder, but Carr's injury severely hurt their chances of making it to the playoffs. Cleamons and Chones also suffered injuries that kept the team from reaching its potential. For the 1975–76 season, the team acquired Nate Thurmond from the Chicago Bulls and achieved a 49–33 record and clinched the Central Division title. The Cavs made their first playoff appearance and won 4–3 over the Washington Bullets. This series became known to fans as the "Miracle of Richfield." However, the Cavs lost in the Eastern Conference Finals to the Boston Celtics. The team continued to play well over the next two years but failed to make it past the first round of the playoffs each year.

The Cavs 1978–79 season marked a return to losing ways, with a 30–52 season. Fitch resigned as coach. His replacement, Stan Albeck, did not do much better, with a 37–45 record. By 1979 the Cavaliers organization was in financial trouble, and Mileti sold his shares to Columbus, Ohio, businessman Louis Mitchell, who in turn sold the shares to Cleveland entrepreneur Joe Zingale. Zingale then sold the shares to Ted Stepien. In the end, Mileti reaped $1,395,000 for his shares in the team.

THE STEPIEN CHAOS: 1979–1983

Stepien was the millionaire founder of Nationwide Advertising Service. He was successful in advertising, but he did not show the same savvy in the professional basketball world. His one innovation that has now become commonplace in the NBA was a scantily clad troupe of dancers, similar to the famous National Football League Dallas Cowboys Cheerleaders. Stepien overpaid for players who played well but not well enough to make a significant impact. He also made some poor trades that caused the team to lose critical first-round draft opportunities. Stepien's hiring of Bill Musselman as coach, which was Musselman's first NBA post, was not a success. Musselman led the team to a

25–46 record before Stepien fired him and made him director of player personnel. Stepien made the general manager Don Delaney coach to finish out the season. Stepien then fired Delaney as coach and replaced him with Chuck Daly, an assistant coach for the Philadelphia 76ers. Daly began as coach for the 1981–82 season but was fired early on when the team went 9–32. Stepien brought back Musselman to replace Daly, and Musselman finished out the season with a 2–21 record.

Just days before the 1982–83 season started Musselman resigned, and Stepien replaced him with Tom Nissalke, a former American Basketball Association coach. Nissalke had one week to prepare the team for the season. The frequent changes in coaching had a negative effect on the fans and the team's morale. Attendance dropped to an average of 3,900, and the press and fans nicknamed the team the "Cleveland Cadavers." Don Delany left the organization and Harry Weltman took over as general manager.

Before the 1983–84 season, Stepien exhibited erratic behavior, saying he wanted to rename the team the Ohio Cavaliers and have them play in other cities throughout the state. Then he threatened to move the team to Toronto and rename them the Toronto Towers. In the end, he sold the team to Cleveland businessmen George and Gordon Gund, who wanted to keep the team in Cleveland, for $20 million. During Stepien's tenure as owner the team went 66–180, ran through five coaches, and lost $15 million.

THE GUNDS BRING A NEW ORDER: 1983–2003:

Gordon Gund, who went blind as a result of a genetic illness, served as majority owner and president of the Cavaliers. Gund changed the team colors to burnt orange and navy blue. However, coach Nissalke failed to turn the team around, and at the end of the 1983–84 season Weltman fired him and hired George Karl, who had been in the Continental Basketball Association (CBA) as coach of the Montana Golden Nuggets. Karl led the team through a transition period, and the Cavs made the playoffs in 1985, losing to the Boston Celtics in the first round. Then, 66 games into the 1986–87 season, Gund fired Karl. Interim coach Gene Littles finished out the season. In 1986 Weltman acquired Brad Daugherty, Mark Price, Ron Harper, and Larry Nance, a quartet who would become the heart of a strong Cavaliers team. Soon after what was considered a highly successful draft Gund fired Weltman for reasons that had to do with managerial issues rather than player acquisitions. Weltman's relationship with Gund has broken down as a result of various disagreements, including Weltman's firing of an assistant coach without

```
┌─────────────────────────────────────────────┐
│                                             │
│              KEY DATES                      │
│                  ─■─                        │
│                                             │
│  1970:  Nick Mileti purchases NBA franchise for │
│         Cleveland and names it the Cavaliers.  │
│  1976:  Team makes its first appearance in the NBA │
│         playoffs.                           │
│  1979:  Mileti sells the team to Ted Stepien. │
│  1983:  Stepien sells the team to George and Gordon │
│         Gund.                               │
│  2003:  The Cavaliers draft LeBron James.   │
│  2005:  George Gund sells his controlling interest to │
│         Dan Gilbert for $375 million.       │
│  2007:  The Cavaliers make their first trip to NBA │
│         Finals.                             │
│  2010:  LeBron James leaves the Cavaliers for the │
│         Miami Heat.                         │
│                                             │
└─────────────────────────────────────────────┘
```

consulting Gund. Also, Weltman's relationship with the players was rocky at best. Gund replaced Weltman with Wayne Embry, a former player and the first African American general manager in NBA history (when he became general manager of the Milwaukee Bucks in 1971). Embry and Gund began a search for a new coach and landed NBA legend Lenny Wilkens. Embry and Wilkens led what was arguably a team built by Weltman to the playoffs in five of the next seven seasons. In 1992 they made it to the Eastern Conference Finals and lost to the Chicago Bulls, who were led by star Michael Jordan. In 1993 they made it to the Conference semifinal but again lost to the Chicago Bulls.

At the end of the 1992–93 season Wilkens resigned as coach a week after losing to the Bulls in the playoffs. Gund hired Mike Fratello to take over. Fratello was an on-screen commentator for NBA games broadcast on the National Broadcasting Company (NBC). Previously, he was coach for the Atlanta Hawks. Fratello arrived in Cleveland with a very good team already established.

In 1992 the Gateway Economic Development Corporation broke ground on a new arena for the Cavaliers in downtown Cleveland. The Gateway Economic Development Corporation was formed to redevelop the downtown Cleveland area, channeling corporate investors' money to high-impact projects, including the Arena and a nearby ballpark for the Major League Baseball Cleveland Indians. Construction of the new arena, which featured 20,562 seats and 92 luxury suites, cost $100 million. The Gund Arena ("The Gund") opened for the 1994–95 season. The Cavaliers

leased the arena from the Gateway Economic Development Corporation.

Fratello coached a fairly successful team, leading them to the playoffs in four of his six seasons with the organization, but the team never made it past the first round. During the 1998–99 season, a labor dispute between the owners and players union led to a lockout that shortened the season by 50 games. After the team's listless start to this season Gund fired Fratello and replaced him with Randy Wittman, an assistant coach with the Minnesota Timberwolves. Embry, after 14 years in the position, left as general manager to be replaced by Jim Paxson, the team's vice president of basketball operations.

THE CAVS THRONE KING JAMES: 2003–10

The Cavaliers had a string of bad years at the beginning of the 21st century and in 2003 finished with a 17–65 record, one of the worst in the franchise's history. In what must have seemed a return to the Stepien days, Gund cycled through coaches during this period. He fired Wittman in 2001, after the team failed to make the playoffs three years in a row, and hired Denver Nuggets assistant coach John Lucas. Then in 2003, after a 8–34 start, the team became a laughing stock of the league, and Gund fired Lucas, promoting assistant coach Keith Smart to head coach on an interim basis.

The fortunes of the Cavaliers were soon to improve, if only temporarily. The team was awarded the first pick in the 2003 draft, which it used to select LeBron James, an Akron, Ohio, high school player who was considered to be the next Michael Jordan. After a lengthy search, Gund settled on Paul Silas as the new head coach to oversee the rebuilding of the Cavs with LeBron as the central player. That same year, Gund changed the colors of the team to wine, gold, and navy blue. He also had the logo redesigned. James proved to be as talented as expected and even surpassed many people's expectations. He won the 2003–04 Rookie of the Year Award, becoming the heart of the team, along with veteran Zydrunas Ilgauskas and Drew Gooden, However, after a promising start to the 2004–05 season the team slumped and finished with a 42–40 record and missed the playoffs. Gund fired coach Paul Silas and general manager Paxson.

In 2005 Gund stepped down as owner. He maintained a minority interest in the team but sold his controlling interest to Quicken Loans founder and owner Dan Gilbert and his group of investors for $375 million. Gilbert was from Detroit, and fans feared that he might move the team, but Gilbert committed to keeping the team in Cleveland, especially since the team had a lease agreement with the Gateway Economic Development Corporation that lasted until 2027. Gilbert hired Mike Brown as head coach and former Cavaliers forward Danny Ferry as general manager. He also renovated Gund Arena and renamed it Quicken Loans Arena or "The Q."

The mixture of a new owner, a new arena, and arguably the most exciting player in the league (James), gave the team new life. They made it to the playoffs and won the first round 4–2 against the Washington Wizards, but they lost 3–4 in the Conference Semifinal to the Detroit Pistons. Despite the loss, during the series James gave an impressive performance and increased his value to the team both as a player and as a marketing asset. The 2006–07 season marked the team's first trip to the NBA Finals. They lost 0–4 to the San Antonio Spurs, a more mature and stronger team with a deeper bench. The team continued to perform at a high level throughout the rest of the decade, making the playoffs for several years in a row.

LOSS OF JAMES BRINGS UNCERTAIN FUTURE: 2010 AND BEYOND

After losing the 2009 Conference Semifinal, in which they blew a 2–1 lead, Gilbert fired Brown, the most successful coach in the Cavaliers' history. Winning and losing had little to do with Brown's exit, however. Rather, the team wanted to keep their star player in Cleveland. James's contract made him a free agent on July 1, 2010, and the team wanted to give him the opportunity to participate in choosing the team's coach as an incentive to remain in Cleveland. In the lead up to James' decision, general manager Ferry resigned in the final month of his contract. He disagreed with Gilbert's decision to fire Brown and felt that his own authority as general manager had been undermined. Ferry's assistant, Chris Grant, took over as general manager. On July 2, the team hired Byron Scott, a highly successful coach who led the New Jersey Nets to two NBA finals and helped rebuild the New Orleans Hornets into a winning team. Gilbert believed hiring Scott would be a critical factor toward keeping James in Cleveland.

On July 8, 2010, ESPN aired an hour-long show, *The Decision,* focused entirely on what LeBron James would do with his career. The show culminated with James's announcement that he was leaving the Cavs to play for the Miami Heat. "I'm taking my talents to South Beach," declared James. The announcement attracted much attention and derision. The city of Cleveland went into a furor, and owner Gilbert wrote an open letter on the Cavs' Web site saying that James had committed a "cowardly betrayal" of the city. He also personally guaranteed that the team would win an NBA championship before James did with the Heat. The NBA fined Gilbert $100,000 for the letter and some scathing public statements he made regarding James. James also drew criticism across the nation for what many saw as flagrant self-promotion and the creation of a spectacle out of his decision.

The Cavs and the city of Cleveland prepared for the 2010–11 in a state of shell shock from the sudden loss of their beloved "King James." The team made several trades and acquisitions to make up for the loss, but in the early 2010s a big question mark stood over the team concerning whether it could return to winning ways without a player of the caliber of James on its roster.

Aaron Hauser

PRINCIPAL COMPETITORS

Chicago Professional Sports Limited Partnership; Detroit Pistons Basketball Company; Milwaukee Bucks, Inc.; Pacers Basketball, LLC.

FURTHER READING
"Cavaliers History." cavshistory.com.

"Dan Gilbert's Open Letter: LeBron James a 'Coward Betrayer'." *Meri News,* July 9, 2010.

Graeff, Burt. "Wilkens Resigns As Cavs Coach." *Plain Dealer,* May 25, 1993, p. 1A.

Kissling, Catherine. "Gateway Unveils Arena Design." *Plain Dealer,* January 4, 1992.

Patton, Paul. "Where Are They Now?" *Globe and Mail,* November 22, 1983, p. S4.

"Sports People; Cavaliers Coach Quits." *New York Times,* October 22, 1982.

Wise, Mike. "Having His Fun, but Losing His Legacy." *Washington Post,,* July 9, 2010, p. D01.

Creative Group, Inc.

619 North Lynndale Drive
Appleton, Wisconsin 54914
U.S.A.
Telephone: (920) 739-8850
Toll Free: (800) 236-2800
Fax: (920) 739-8817
Web site: http://www2.creativegroupinc.com

Private Company
Founded: 1970
Employees: 105 (est., 2011)
Sales: $80 million (est., 2010)
NAICS: 541611 Administrative Management and
General Management Consulting Services

■ ■ ■

Creative Group, Inc. (CGI), operates more than 400 programs to assist clients to motivate sales forces, enhance brand names, engage customers, and measure results. In theory, CGI improves its clients' businesses through meetings and communications. CGI offers services in performance improvement, strategic meetings management (SMM), meeting and event logistics, green initiatives, risk management, technology solutions, and performance evaluation and consulting.

Performance improvement services include consulting for employee retention, driving sales, improving safety, and grabbing customers' attention. Motivating sales force includes recommending rewards such as travel incentives and merchandise such as those offered in the company's product CreativeCollection. CreativeCollec-tion is a listing of over 5,000 motivational offerings that can be customized to the sales force of a company. Awards include merchandise, gift cards, travel, and others. The program tiers incentives to performance.

Strategic meetings management (SMM) services provide the logistics and management for meetings in which the objective is to obtain measurable results. This service includes benchmark data to allow clients to see the value of events directly. CGI can also provide services such as risk mitigation, compliance, and cost-savings that deal with the details of events. Related to that, the company organizes meetings by contracting with hotels and event location professionals, suppliers, and subcontractors to allow clients minimal organization duties and liability when unforeseen events happen.

CGI also offers services for clients that would like to pursue green initiatives for meetings, including reducing paper waste, serving food in recyclable products, and donating conference meal leftovers to the local food bank.

Risk Management Services provide protection against unforeseen circumstances when planning business meetings. Unforeseen events may include natural disasters, overbooked airlines, and food and beverage mishaps. As CGI is considered a national account for many hotel chains, they are able to negotiate contracts advantageous to the client.

CGI also operates as an agency to negotiate air travel, ticket prices, and arrange group programs. CGI's Creative Services designs communication strategies for clients. Communications include case studies, conference agenda packets, and travel packets. The primary objective of this group is to produce strategic communications for a target audience. All communications are provided in all available media, including video, print, podcast, digital, web flash animation, and RSS podcast.

CGI's proprietary CreativeEDGE provides an end-to-end solution for meeting administration. Features include registration systems, total event management solutions, database management, cost management, manage inventory, and conduct participant communications.

CGI offers performance measurement by partnering with MeetingMetrics, a performance measurement system that measures a hypothetical return on investment for events. MeetingMetrics is a tool that surveys performance measures prior to and after events. MeetingMetrics measures both quantifiable and abstract indications, including business results and impact, applied behaviors, abilities and skills, attitudes, intentions, commitments, options, perceptions, beliefs, and knowledge and understanding.

COMPANY FOUNDED: 1970

In 1961 Dick Baker was working at an advertising agency in Appleton, Wisconsin. One of his clients, a grocery wholesaler, asked Baker to find a way for grocery stores to buy a more diverse line of groceries in large quantities to cost-justify the recent purchase of a large warehouse.

Baker developed a program to create incentives for grocery retailers to buy from his client by offering an award. The leading purchaser would earn an all-expense paid trip to the Independent Grocers Association convention. The award included the payment for luxury transportation to the trip, including spouses, and tourist attractions.

At the time, such a reward program was rare. Wholesale grocers, noticing the success of the program at the convention, wanted Baker to do the same for their companies. In 1970 Baker opened his own company based on the concept, with a portfolio of wholesale grocer clients.

Soon, other industries followed. By 2011 63 percent of CGI's portfolio would consist of health care, insurance, and financial services companies. The technology, manufacturing, retail, and food service industries made up 31 percent of CGI's clients.

CGI thrived based on Baker's belief in sharing profits with employees and maintaining a debt-free capital structure. The company offered stock options to employees after two years of employment. The company has not had an unprofitable year since its founding, so profit sharing is a worthwhile incentive.

DEREGULATION AND PRODUCT EXPANSION: 1978–99

Naturally, CGI's product offering campaigns that centered around travel incentives led to its participation in the travel industry. CGI organized travel packages, providing many of the services offered by the traditional travel agency.

In 1978 the airline industry was deregulated. The next two decades presented challenges for the travel industry as the airline industry found its privatized footing. Carriers entered and exited the market. Bankruptcies and overbooked flights left travelers stranded. Increased security resulted in overall higher ticket prices, contrasting to the goals of deregulations. Both corporate and personal travel fell when the economy suffered.

CGI was one of the companies that offered products outside the travel industry, finding success by organizing meetings and designing incentive programs. Travel agencies that may have competed with CGI found benefits in using CGI's services. Since CGI specialized in organizing travel and incentive programs for business clients, travel agencies could outsource some of these services to CGI instead of handling nontravel services, such as organizing meetings. In 1995 Travel and Transport announced that it would outsource some of its meetings and incentives services to CGI.

Designing incentive packages focused on travel soon led to meeting planning, which had become another company mainstay. Clients such as Certco, Mutual of Omaha, and Baxter Healthcare were the first to use the progressive service.

The company's travel incentive programs offered cruises, which attracted clients because costs were all-inclusive. For example, in 1997 CGI organized a cruise for Tire Group International (TGI). The three objectives were a plant visit in Miami, a networking opportunity for salespeople and dealers, and an incentive trip. The success of this trip led to a similar one for the insurance company Aid Association for Lutherans in 1999.

```
┌─────────────────────────────────────────────┐
│                                             │
│              KEY DATES                      │
│                   ■                         │
│  ─────────────────────────────────────      │
│  1961:  Advertising executive Dick Baker    │
│         develops incentive campaign to      │
│         increase sales for wholesale        │
│         grocer client.                      │
│  1970:  Dick Baker founds Creative Group,   │
│         Inc.                                │
│  2001:  Terrorist attacks against the       │
│         United States on September 11,      │
│         2001, disrupt business travel.      │
│  2004:  Creative Group, Inc., adds          │
│         strategic meetings management       │
│         (SMM) to its service portfolio.     │
│  2010:  Company forms alliance with         │
│         incentive software developer        │
│         Tiger Solutions.                    │
│                                             │
└─────────────────────────────────────────────┘
```

DECLINE IN BUSINESS TRAVEL

In 2000 a study by the Incentive Federation found an unmet market need. Annually, companies spent $115 billion on incentives but without formal measures to determine the effectiveness of such programs. Since CGI designed incentive packages, a natural progression was to show tangible results of these packages.

In September 2000 CGI was the nation's eighth-largest incentive travel company. However, CGI struggled with airline customers' discontent. More people than ever were traveling, causing record number of cancellations and delays among airlines. CGI was often left with dealing with the fallout. Of course, this also created an opportunity to demonstrate the benefits of using a travel agency. Whereas airline employees could only resolve such problems by offering alternative flights within their own airline, travel agents could arrange alternatives with competing airlines. They could also proactively check flight schedules and prearrange another itinerary, minimizing the effects of travel delay on clients. These challenges also provided a foundation for CGI's risk management services.

Business seemed doomed for the company after the terrorist attacks against the United States on September 11, 2001. Companies, hesitant to send employees airborne, realized that technology might replace business conferences. E-mail, meeting software, and Web-conferencing seemed an adequate replacement. CGI did struggle for some years as business travel declined, but the company rebounded.

OPTIMAL INCENTIVES

The Incentive Federation published a study in 2003 that examined the effects of incentive programs. The study found that cash incentives, while effective, carried less weight than noncash incentives, which had the psychological effect of that of a gift. Cash incentives tended to be viewed as compensation instead of a reward, but employees attached a "trophy value" to non-cash incentives. The study also recommended "Best Practices in Incentive Management," providing statistical data for incentives that achieved the best results. With these results, CGI had statistical data that proved its tangible value.

Strategic meetings management (SMM) seemed a natural fit with CGI's product mix. SMM was first introduced in 2004 by the National Business Travel Association (NTBA), designed for the travel industry, and CGI developed a similar product that same year. By designing meetings that had specific and measurable results, clients could be assured that the cost would never outweigh the profits resulting from the meeting. In 2008 the company initiated the use of MeetingMetrics, an online pre- and postevent survey tool that measured the effectiveness of training programs, new product introductions, sales meetings, and other gatherings with measurable objectives.

ACCOLADES

In 2006 CGI won the Small Business Award from the Fox Cities Chamber of Commerce. CGI president and COO Brad Langley indicated that he believed his company had been a best kept secret until then.

In 2007 the company won the Innovative People Programs award from the Wisconsin 75. The Wisconsin 75 award is sponsored by the Milwaukee office of Deloitte & Touche and honors private companies with over $50 million in revenue. The award seeks Wisconsin companies that contribute to the home communities and the state's economy. Langley commented that CGI's employees were committed and creative due to the positive environment created by the company that included employee stock ownership, work/life balance, and an emphasis on learning and development, among other things.

STRATEGIC ALLIANCES: 2008 AND BEYOND

In April 2008 CGI and Adelman Travel formed a strategic alliance to mutually refer the other's services to clients. Adelman is a provider of travel management for corporations. The goal of the alliance was to increase each partner's client base and fill holes in services that each might otherwise outsource.

In 2009 two separate studies illustrated the case for face-to-face meetings and events. Boone Associates published a briefing paper that studied the difference in face-to-face communication and virtual conferencing. The study found that, while virtual conferencing did indeed have value, face-to-face meetings still exceeded virtual conferences when the goal was persuasion, inspiration, engagement, or decision making. (However, when the goal was information dissemination or data presentations, such as annual financial results, virtual meetings rated better.) In 2009 a study by the *Harvard Business Review* determined that fact-to-face meetings were necessary and measurably profitable in certain situations. Meetings where face-to-face engagement effectively met objectives were those where the engagement was necessary, such as new client meetings, client negotiations, and networking. The studies cemented CGI's business model but further indicated the need for measurable results.

The year 2010 saw a strategic alliance and another prestigious award. The company partnered with Tiger Solutions, a company that built software applications for the incentive and recognition industries. In March CGI was selected to receive the Sabre Travel Network Peak of Excellence Award for 2009. This award recognizes businesses in the travel agency industry for contribution to the industry.

The several awards CGI received were an indication that the company was on a firm footing and that its success was likely to continue in the early 2010s. Serving the needs of businesses that required meetings and conferences, the company had a large potential customer pool for future growth.

Sara K. Huter

PRINCIPAL COMPETITORS

Alcone Marketing Group; All Star Incentive Marketing; Loyaltyworks, Inc.; Pitney Bowes Marketing Solutions Group; Schoeneckers, Inc.

FURTHER READING

"The CMI 25." *Corporate Meetings & Incentives* 26, no. 9 (2007).

Eccles. "Adapt or Die." *Corporate Meetings & Incentives* 29, no. 1 (2010).

———. "Try This." *Corporate Meetings & Incentives* 29, no. 1 (2010).

Jackson, Nancy Mann. "15 Minutes with Brad Langley, President/COO, Creative Group, Inc." *Engagement Strategies Magazine.* Accessed March 16, 2011. http://www.engage mentstrategiesonline.com/15_Minutes_With_Brad_Langley. 709.0.html.

Stankewicz, Kristin. "Creative Group Rolls with Changes." *Post-Crescent,* September 3, 2006.

Stern, Avi. "Discontent among Airline Travelers Increases with Delays, Flight Loads." *Post-Crescent,* September 13, 2000.

"Testing the Waters: Tire Group International: Its First-Ever Incentive Destination? A Cruise." *Corporate Meetings & Incentives,* February 1, 1998.

Debswana Diamond Company Proprietary Limited

Debswana House, The Mall
P.O. Box 329
Gabarone, Botswana
Telephone: (267) 361 4200
Fax: (267) 318 0778
Web site: http://www.debswana.com

Joint Venture
Founded: 1969
Employees: 3,000 (est., 2010)
Sales: BWP 12.2 billion ($1.8 billion) (2009)
NAICS: 212399 All Other Nonmetallic Mineral Mining

■ ■ ■

Debswana Diamond Company Proprietary Limited is the world's largest diamond producer by value. The company accounts for 40 percent of the rough diamond market and 22 percent of the global diamond output and principally deals in the mining, recovery, and sorting of diamonds. Debswana is jointly owned by the government of Botswana and the multinational mining conglomerate De Beers S.A. Each of the two parties commands half of the company's shareholding through a 50-50 joint venture. Debswana's mining operations are based in four main diamond mines: Orapa, Jwaneng, Letlhakane, and Damtshaa.

Orapa is the oldest mine in Botswana and its pipe remains the second-largest kimberlite pipe in the world by production volume. (Kimberlite pipes are geological structures that may contain diamonds.) Jwaneng is located about 149 miles southwest of Gaborone, and its massive diamond deposits make it the most valuable diamond mine in the world. The Jwaneng Mine is also famed for its unique recovery plant, the Jwaneng Mine Aquarium, described as both a completely automated recovery plant (CARP) and a fully integrated sort house (FISH). Letlhakane and Damtshaa are considered to be offshoots of Orapa, and they are located in the same region, approximately 99 miles west of Francistown. Debswana also operates the Morupule Colliery as well as an insurance and diamond trading subsidiary.

Debswana operates as a monopoly in Botswana because no other companies participate in the mining and processing of diamond in the country. The company operates in an industry that is highly regulated by the government because diamond mining is the main economic activity in Botswana. Debswana is Botswana's largest source of revenue in addition to being the largest foreign exchange earner. Diamonds account for 33 percent of GDP in Botswana by contributing 50 percent and 70 percent of the country's revenue and foreign exchange earnings, respectively. The significance of the company to the country's economy is also underlined by its status as the biggest nongovernment employer in the country.

EARLIEST YEARS: 1969–73

The existence of diamonds in Botswana was first signaled by the finding of several diamondiferous alluvial stones in Tuli Block by the Selection Trust Company in 1955. This finding, made along the riverbanks of the Motloutse River, intensified the search for

COMPANY PERSPECTIVES

Our technology and innovation is at the forefront of its kind in the diamond industry.

the source of the valuable mineral. The efforts by the pioneer exploration activities finally paid off in 1967 when a team of De Beers Group geologists, led by Dr. Gavin Lamont, discovered some kimberlite pipes, near the villages of Letlhakane and Orapa, that were found to contain diamond deposits. De Beers launched preliminary formalities for the establishment of a diamond mine to exploit the voluminous diamondiferous deposits discovered in Orapa.

De Beers Consolidated Mines Limited entered negotiations with the government of Botswana, and the two parties formed a jointly owned diamond mining company. De Beers Botswana Mining Company was subsequently incorporated on June 23, 1969. De Beers Consolidated Mines Limited owned 85 percent while the Botswana government owned the remaining 15 percent shareholding interest in the company.

The country office of De Beers Botswana Mining Company was established in Botsalano. Geological explorations did not stop with the establishment of the Orapa Mine as the geologists from De Beers Group ventured farther into the southern district in 1969. The prospects of the De Beers geologists were guided by the unique rock formations in the southern district that were covered by a thin layer of sand.

The construction of the Orapa Mine was completed within two years, and the company was officially opened for production activities in July 1971. In a related development, De Beers Prospecting was formally registered as a foreign entity in Botswana in the same year. The company's head offices were established in Lobaste as the company sought to intensify its exploration activities in the area. The persistent exploration by the company's prospecting team eventually led to the discovery of another kimberlite pipe near the Kgalagadi Desert in 1972. The newly discovered kimberlite pipe was covered by layers of sand that averaged a thickness of 130 feet in Naledi River.

De Beers Botswana Mining Company moved to streamline its diamond sorting and marketing operations by establishing the Botswana Diamond Valuing Corporation (BDVC) in Lobaste in 1972. The relatively independent entity was formed as a joint venture between the Botswana Development Corporation and

De Beers Consolidated Mines Limited. The management team of De Beers Botswana Mining Company had their vision set into the future as the company diversified into coal mining by establishing the Morupule coal mine in 1973. The establishment of the coal mine was designed to contribute to the company's energy needs and revenue performance.

LETLKETHANE AND JWANENG MINES OPERATIONAL: 1970S–1980S

In 1974 the operations of BDVC were relocated to Consolidated Mines Limited's offices in Botsalano because of logistical constraints in Lobaste. By 1975 the government of Botswana had increased its ownership stake in De Beers Botswana Mining Company to 50 percent. De Beers Botswana Mining Company recorded a major expansion strategy achievement when the construction of its second mine, the Letlkethane Mine, was commissioned in 1975. The Letlkethane Mine was discovered at the same time as the Orapa Mine, but the company had decided to prioritize the Orapa Mine because of its voluminous diamondiferous deposits. Operations at the Letlkethane Mine were officially commenced in 1977 after the successful completion of construction activities in the mine.

De Beers Botswana Mining Company opened negotiations with the government for the conversion of BDVC into its fully owned subsidiary in 1977. The complete takeover bid of BDVC was made in recognition of the increasing significance of the subsidiary's operations, the company's expansion, and overall strategic pursuits. Preparations for the exploitation of the Jwaneng diamond fields were finally formalized in May 1978. The government of Botswana and De Beers Consolidated Mines Limited entered a partnership agreement for the establishment of Jwaneng Mine. The construction of the mine and an adjacent town were commenced immediately after the legal formalities involving the two joint venture partners. A major expansion project of the Orapa Mine was also commenced in 1978 and completed in 1979.

Jwaneng Mine began operations in 1982 after four years of intense construction activities. The mine was officially opened in August by the then president of Botswana, Sir Ketumile Masire. The opening of the Jwaneng Mine increased the company's overall annual production capacity to 18 million carats. The Jwaneng Mine was considered to be the richest mine in the world because of the high concentration of diamondiferous deposits in its pipes.

The Jwaneng Mine was able to achieve impressive progress in safety standards implementation as the

---

KEY DATES

1968: De Beers Botswana Mining Company is established.

1982: Diamond mining operations commence in Jwaneng Mines.

1992: Company changes name from De Beers Botswana Mining Company to Debswana.

2001: Debswana launches massive HIV/AIDS project.

2009: Debswana Diamond Company experiences steep decline in production.

---

company started recording the lowest incidents of disabling injuries in Botswana in 1984. De Beers Botswana Mining Company also commissioned a re-crush plant in the Jwaneng Mine in 1989 as part of its operations enhancement programs.

NEW NAME AND TECHNOLOGICAL ADVANCEMENTS: 1992–99

In 1992 De Beers Botswana Mining Company underwent minor legal and structural transformations that culminated in the changing of its name to Debswana Diamond Company (Pty) Limited. The company's head office was subsequently moved to Botswana's capital, Gaborone. Debswana experienced impressive production performance in the 1990s as the company's net profits kept on growing year over year. An increase in production operations prompted the management of the company to procure for mining equipments of higher capacity, such as 177-ton trucks in 1993. The company's overall production output increased from 14.7 million carats in 1993 to 16.5 million carats in 1994. This resulted in an increase in the annual profits of the company from BWP 1.5 billion in 1993 to BWP 1.8 billion in 1994.

Debswana continued to invest significant portions of its financial resources toward technological advancements that were aimed at enhancing diamond production processes. The company enhanced efficiency in its diamond mining processes by introducing the truck dispatch system in 1995. This was followed by the introduction of business unit divisions in the same year. The Orapa Mine was upgraded further with technologically advanced equipment that was designed to reduce the amount of water used in processes for recovering diamond. The completion of the Fourth Stream Project

in 1995 expanded the company's ore processing capacity by 33 percent. The Fourth Stream Project involved the installation of a crusher within the mining pit, an innovation that effectively reduced the distance of transporting ore to the first crushing phase.

Debswana Mining Company was granted a renewal of the mining lease for the Orapa Mine in August 1996. The new lease extended the company's mining rights in Orapa Mine to 2017. Debswana engaged a higher gear in its mining processes in 1997 by introducing round-the-clock operations to optimize production output. The move enhanced the company's diamond production output and also created more jobs.

The evolution of Botswana from an agricultural economy to a mining economy resulted in a record economic growth rate of 8.3 percent in 1998. The growth rate represented one of the highest economic transformation indices in the world at the time, thanks to the contribution of diamond mining to the country's economy. The simultaneous growth of Botswana's mining industry by more than 9 percent in 1998 was attributed to the nonstop mode of operations that was introduced in 1997.

Mining operations in the Jwaneng Mine were improved in 1998 through the commissioning of a second in-pit crusher. Debswana's overall production volume reached 24 million carats in 1999, the highest recorded in the 1990s. Debswana also enhanced its safety standards in the year by engaging the National Seismological Project in the process of monitoring the likelihood and frequency of earthquakes.

EXPANSION AND MASSIVE HIV/AIDS PROJECT: 2001–06

The dawn of the 21st century marked the beginning of the 2000–2005 Strategic Period for Debswana. The company had set priorities to improve diamond production from 24 million carats to 30 million carats in 2004.

The size of the Orapa Mine was expanded again in 2000 and as such retained its status as the largest diamond mine by size. The success of the mining sector in 2000 was evident, as an 11.9 percent growth in the mining sector in the year was spurred by Debswana's annual diamond production, which was in excess of 25 million carats. Jwaneng Mine made history in 2000 by becoming Botwana's first organization to achieve ISO 14001 accreditation standards. Debswana was credited for having contributed 80 percent of Botswana's foreign exchange earnings in 2000. The foreign earnings resulted from the transfer of entire production for the year to the London-based Diamond Trading Company.

In 2001 Debswana became one of the first companies in the world to provide free Highly Active

Anti–Retroviral Therapy (HAART) treatment services. The high rates of HIV/AIDS infection in Botswana prompted the company to undertake a massive launch of the HAART treatment program in May 2001. The HAART program was targeted at providing treatment to more than 100,000 HIV/AIDS-infected people who were not company employees. The project's main objective was to extend the company's employee HIV/AIDS programs to the community as part of its corporate social responsibility (CSR) initiatives.

However, the commitment of Debswana to the welfare of its employees was put in question in 2004 after the company's cruel response to a strike by its employees. The dispute that pitted the company against the Botswana Mining Workers' Union (BMWU) was centered on wage increment demands by the employees. Negotiations between the two parties did not reach an agreement, which led to the strike by workers. In a surprising turn of events, BMWU's industrial action was declared illegal by the court and as a result, more than 460 workers were dismissed. The incident attracted wide condemnation in Botswana and internationally. Many argued that Debswana demonstrated insensitivity toward economic realities by denying its employees pay increases and the right to industrial action.

In technical developments, the BK 9 pipe that was located between the Orapa Mine and Letlkathane Mine was upgraded to a full mine and renamed Damtshaa. Debswana also committed $40 million toward the construction of the Damtshaa Mine that was commissioned in October 2002. The Damtshaa Mine achieved full production capacity in March 2003. The mine, however, presented geographical challenges to the mining processes as the varying degrees of its rock formations affected the carat profile. Challenges notwithstanding, the Damtashaa Mine produced a total of 292,000 diamond carats in 2003.

Debswana adopted a new strategic orientation in 2006 as the company outlined its 2006 to 2010 strategy framework dubbed "Project North Star." The project was targeted toward eliminating all production-related inefficiencies in the company's operations with a view of enhancing production and maintaining the highest safety and environmental standards. The Botswana government and De Beers signed landmark agreements in May 2006 that included a 25-year extension of the mining licenses of Debswana and the establishment of an independent diamond sorting, valuation, and marketing unit, the Diamond Trading Company Botswana. The company's management hoped that the historic agreements would enable the company to maximize revenue from its value addition operations in addition to creating more job opportunities in the country.

PRODUCTION DECLINE AND FUTURE PLANS: 2008 AND BEYOND

The destination markets of Debswana's diamond product were badly hit by the global economic crisis that erupted in the third quarter of 2008. Consumer demand hit incredibly low levels, and the company could no longer afford to support unprofitable operations. Debswana consequently suspended its mining operations in Orapa, Jwaneng, and Letlhakane between December 2008 and April 2009. The suspension of mining activities in Orapa No. 2 was extended to August while Damtshaa's closure was extended until December 2009.

Debswana produced 17.7 million carats in 2009. The results represented a sharp decline in production compared to 2008 when the company produced more than 32 million carats. The company's revenue declined by a similar margin to BWP 12.2 b billion in 2009, compared to BWP 18.8 billion in 2008. These results led to a significant drop in the net profits of the company for the year. Even so, Debswana was able to keep its HIV/AIDS Impact Management program on course despite the financial constraints experienced throughout the year.

The company's performance recovery from the third quarter of 2009 resulted from the far reaching cost-containment and other mitigation measures that were adopted by the company in the first and second quarters of the year. Improved business opportunities in the third and fourth quarters of 2009 also contributed immensely to keeping the company stable.

In June 2010 Debswana disclosed its planned partnership with Firestone Diamonds plc for the construction of a Modular Tailings Treatment Project at the Jwaneng Mine. The project was estimated to cost $55 million by the time of its completion in 2012. After Eskom reduced its electricity power supply to Debswana by 29 percent from January 2010, the company pursued alternative sources of power, expanding its Morupule coal mine subsidiary to close the 100Mw electricity power supply gap created by Eskom's exit.

The company's plan to increase diamond production in the Jwaneng Mine through an expansion program dubbed "the Cut-8 Project" was approved by its principal shareholders on November 24, 2009. The Cut-8 Project involved the expansion of mining activities in the Jwaneng Mine between 2010 and 2025. According to information contained in the De Beers Web site, "the development will require the removal of over 700 million tons of waste between 2010 and 2024, exposing an additional 78 million tons of diamond bearing ore, and deepening the Jwaneng pit to a depth of 650 meters." The deepening of the mine was expected to facilitate access to an additional 95 million carats of diamond by 2025. The company committed an initial investment of $500 million in the project, which was expected to cost up to $3 billion by the time of its completion.

Paul Ingati

PRINCIPAL SUBSIDIARIES

Morupule Colliery Ltd.; Sesiro Insurance Company (Pty.) Ltd.

PRINCIPAL DIVISIONS

Damtshaa Mine; Jwaneng Mine; Letlhakane Mine; Orapa Mine.

PRINCIPAL COMPETITORS

Ashton Mining of Canada, Inc.; Rio Tinto Limited; Trans Hex Group Ltd.

FURTHER READING

Bruyn, Chanel de. "Debswana Delays $55m Jwaneng Tailings Project—Firestone." *Mining Weekly,* September 2, 2010. Accessed November 5, 2010. http://www.miningweekly.com/article/debswana-delays-55m-tailings-project-firestone-2010-09-02.

Bungu, Jerry. "Debswana Diamond Production Fell by Half in 2009 on Global Economics Crisis." *Bloomberg,* April 22, 2010. Accessed November 7, 2010. http://www.bloomberg.com/news/2010-04-22/debswana-diamond-production-fell-by-half-in-2009-on-global-economic-crisis.html.

Cropley, Ed. "World Diamond Prices Starting to Recover—Debswana." *Reuters,* September 10, 2009. Accessed November 7, 2010. http://in.reuters.com/article/idINIndia-42371220090910.

De Beers Group. "Debswana Observes 40 Years of Propelling the Nation to Greater Heights." De Beers Group, June 23, 2009. Accessed November 4, 2010. http://www.debeersgroup.com/en/Media-centre/Press-releases/2009/Debswana-observes-40-years-of-propelling-the-nation-to-greater-heights/.

———. "Diamond Trading Company Botswana." De Beers Group, 2008. Accessed November 3, 2010. http://www.debeersgroup.com/en/inside-de-beers/family-of-companies/Diamond-Trading-Company-Botswana/.

———. "Historic Investment in the World's Richest Diamond Mine." De Beers Group, November 24, 2009. http://www.debeersgroup.com/Media-centre/Press-releases/2009/Historic-Investment-in-Worlds-Richest-Diamond-Mine/.

"Debswana Approves Jwaneng Expansion Project." *Mining Weekly.com,* November 24, 2009. Accessed November 5, 2010. hhttp://www.miningweekly.com/article/debswana-approves-jwaneng-expansion-project-sees-3bn-investment-2009-11-24.

"Debswana Diamond Company (Pty) Ltd." Investments & Income.com. Accessed November 3, 2010. http://www.investmentsandincome.com/investments/debswana-diamonds-investment.html.

"Debswana Produces 17.7 Million Carats in 2009." *Botswana Gazette,* April 25, 2010. Accessed November 4, 2010. http://www.gazettebw.com.

"Expanded Community Initiatives Award Commended (2008): Debswana Diamond Company." Global Business Coalition. Accessed November 7, 2010. http://www.businessfightsaids.org/itcs_node/10/507,533/award/720.

"Firestone Diamonds Plc and Debswana Company (Pty) Ltd Plans to Construct Modular Tailings Treatment Project at the Jwaneng Mine." *Business Week,* June 30, 2010. Accessed November 7, 2010. http://investing.businessweek.com/research/stocks/private/snapshot.asp?privcapId=11500729.

Gannon, Suzanne. "De Beers Relieves Botswana of Diamond Wealth." *Diamond News Agency,* October 3, 2010. Accessed November 7, 2010. http://www.diamondnewsagency.com/Botswana–Cheated–on–Diamond–Deal.

"Labour Relations in Times of Industrial Crisis." *Mmegi Online* 24, no. 30, February 23, 2007. Accessed November 5, 2010. http://www.mmegi.bw/index.php?sid=6aid=2199dir=2010/May/Friday7&aid=120&dir=2007/February/Friday23.

Lute, Aubrey. "Debswana to Chop 1278 Jobs." *Botswana Gazette,* January 6, 2010. Accessed November 4, 2010. http://www.gazettebw.com/index.php?option=com_content&view=article&id=4964 percent3Adebswana–to–chop–1278–jobs–&catid=18 percent3Aheadlines&Itemid=2.

Newman, Harold R. "The Mineral Industry of Botswana." In *2008 Minerals Year Book.* US Geological Survey, January 2010. Accessed November 10, 2010. http://minerals.usgs.gov/minerals/pubs/country/2008/myb3-2008-bc.pdf.

United Nations Conference on Trade and Development. *World Investment Report 2007: Transition Corporations, Extractive Industries and Development.* New York: United Nations Publications, 2007.

Diversified Machine Inc.

28059 Center Oaks Court
Wixom, Michigan 48393
U.S.A.
Telephone: (248) 277-4400
Fax: (248) 277-4399
Web site: http://www.divmi.com

Private Company
Founded: 2005
Employees: 1,230 (2010)
Sales: $335 million (2009)
*NAICS:*331524 Aluminum Foundries (except Die-Casting); 333999 All Other Miscellaneous General Purpose Machinery Manufacturing

■ ■ ■

A global automotive supplier, Diversified Machine Inc. (DMI) develops, machines, and assembles engine transmission and driveline components for both the automotive and heavy truck industries. The company is a vertically integrated supplier of components and modules for both automotive original equipment manufacturers (OEMs) and Tier 1 suppliers. (Tier 1 suppliers are suppliers high up the supply chain.) DMI offers full service product design and testing.

In terms of products for the chassis, DMI is the largest manufacturer of steering knuckles in the world. Chassis products also include control arms, subframes and beams, corner modules, brake calipers and anchor brackets, and wheel hubs. Powertrain capabilities provide support for a wide range of markets, from high-volume aluminum front cover assemblies for the automotive business to special purpose International Traffic in Arms Regulations (ITAR) military cast iron housings. Powertrain products include bearing caps and bedplates, cylinder heads, engine blocks, flywheel housings, front covers, intake manifolds, differential cases, pinion flanges, power steering housings, transmission hubs, and tripots.

In addition to its corporate headquarters in Wixom, Michigan, the company has strategically located operations in Bristol, Indiana; Columbus, Georgia; Edon, Ohio; Howell and Montague, Michigan; and Milwaukee, Wisconsin. DMI's three largest customers are Ford Motor Co., General Motors Co., and TRW Automotive Inc. DMI also has facilities in Iztapalapa, Mexico, and Barcelona, Spain, and has formed a strategic alliance in China. The company's global operations include machining and assembly plants, aluminum foundries that cast and machine, a ductile iron foundry, and an engineering design and testing laboratory.

COMPANY FOUNDED: 2005

Diversified Machine Inc. was founded in 2005 by an investment group of experienced automotive executives who agreed to buy the auto supplier Uni Boring Co. out of bankruptcy. Automotive industry executive Bruce Swift helped spearhead the group. Swift previously held several positions at the Ford Motor Company, including vice president at Ford of Europe, director of Global Raw Material, and executive director of Powertrain Purchasing. He went on to become chairman and CEO of Covisint and, prior to establishing DMI, served as

COMPANY PERSPECTIVES

∎

Our strategic vision is to develop into a full service vertically integrated supplier of cast, machined, and assembled components to meet our customers' requirements globally. DMI provides a one-stop shopping experience for complex engineering driven solutions geared towards lighter weight, lower cost, and superior quality. The company believes quality is a fundamental requirement for customer satisfaction, global competitiveness, employee empowerment, and company success.

president of Metaldyne Driveline Division. The investing group also included the backing of the Carlyle Group and the Relativity Fund/JME.

Based in Howell, Michigan, Uni Boring was an automotive component and machining and manufacturing operation that employed approximately 500 people in three facilities in southeast Michigan. The company, which had been run by Facundo Bravo since 1983 and posted $195.6 million in sales in 2003, was forced to file for Chapter 11 bankruptcy protection in 2005. The primary causes were cash depletion after spending on capital equipment and then having customers delay and cancel some programs.

Uni Boring was purchased for $21 million and renamed Diversified Machine Inc. (DMI). Swift became the company's chief executive officer (CEO). Strategic and operational guidance fell under the direction of Stephen M. Bay, whose background included several senior roles at Metaldyne, including serving as vice president and general manager of Metaldyne's Drive Systems Group. Shakar Kiru, who held executive positions at Covisint and Allied Signa, was named chief financial officer (CFO). Prior to the creation of DMI, Kiru was vice president of engineering for Metalydyne. The new management team headed by Swift, Bay, and Kiru had an early vision to expand the company, making it a world-class operation with a global customer base in the process.

"We believe there's a major need in the auto industry to buy machining and manufacturing operations and grow this segment of the business," Swift told Gary Toushek in an article for the *Manufacturer Online* Web site. Swift went on to note that "there aren't a lot of players, and the OEMs [original equipment manufacturers] will hopefully continue to outsource more business to us as they develop new markets."

Swift felt that Uni Boring was a good buy because its workforce was experienced and talented and the company had "attract[ed] a substantial customer base," noted Swift, according to a *PR Newswire* story on the purchase. Swift added: "Second, the value-added component machining segment continues to grow, driven by the outsourcing trends of the major OEMS and their tiers."

WINNING NEW BUSINESS

Chief operating officer (COO) Bay implemented the Diversified Operating System, which enabled the company to record and analyze various operating metrics associated with the new company's three plants in Howell, Detroit, and Canton Township, all in Michigan. "We rolled it out to track the key metrics in every product line," Bay told the *Manufacturer Online* Web site contributor Toushek. Bay went on to note that they rolled the information "up into corporate scorecards, so we can look at … performance … on a daily and weekly basis."

The new management team saw Uni Boring as having the solid platform from which they could build a larger and more competitive company ready to take advantage of new trends in the auto industry. With a capital investment of $8 million and $140 in revenues, DMI set out to win new business while building on an agreement with the Big Three automakers in Detroit (General Motors, Ford, and Daimler Chrysler) to take on several overseas suppliers. As a result of the Big Three agreement, the company started on creating a global supply chain and also focused on regaining customer confidence to overcome the negative associations of being formed from a bankrupt operation.

IMPLEMENTING ADVANCED TECHNOLOGY

Technology was an integral part of the team's plan to modernize the new operations. Management at DMI focused primarily on employing lean techniques that included manufacturing cells and cutting costs via automation. Another goal was to improve cycle times.

Swift and his partners immediately set out to update Uni Boring's equipment, installing faster machines and integrated robotic loading and unloading to the operations. The upgrades had the desired effect. The Detroit plant previously had difficulty producing 40 cylinder heads daily to meet a 100-day demand, but the DMI team had the plant producing 140 cylinder heads daily after only one month. Meanwhile, the plant at Howell went from making 120 engine blocks daily at

KEY DATES

2005: Automobile industry executive Bruce Swift forms a partnership to purchase Uni Boring, renaming the company Diversified Machine Inc. (DMI).

2007: DMI purchases two automotive parts-making plants from Hayes Lemmerz Corp.

2008: DMI purchases the assets and equipment from Citation Corp.'s metal gravity casting facility.

2009: Company acquires Metaldyine's North America Chassis Division, enhancing DMI's machining capabilities.

2009: Purchase of Intermet's Columbus, Georgia, foundry adds ductile iron casting capabilities.

2010: Company expands into Europe to serve global platforms through the acquisition of Metaldyne's Barcelona plant.

2010: Company makes China alliance for expansion of aluminum casting and machining to serve global platforms.

the maximum to producing 210 daily on a consistent basis.

Overall, the planned improvements and changes to the former Uni Boring operations resulted in cutting cycle times dramatically, thus improving profit and operations. The company also succeeded in reducing inventory levels within the first few months of DMI's existence. As a result, inventory turns were boosted from 10 per year to 20. DMI also established an extensive continuous improvement program.

DIVERSIFYING THROUGH ACQUISITIONS

The team heading DMI wasted no time in living up to the company's name by diversifying product lineup and services. In addition to making new and strong partnerships with a growing list of suppliers, the company made a strategic acquisition on February 14, 2007, when it purchased two global automotive parts-making plants from Hayes Lemmerz Corp. DMI had primarily specialized in making components and modules, such as intake and exhaust manifolds, engine and cylinder blocks and heads, as well as various powertrain components. The newly acquired plants were the "Suspension Subsidiaries" of Hayes Lemmerz and

provided DMI with specialization in aluminum chassis parts and components.

"We're able to gain a lot of strong synergies from the way the products can work together," COO Bay was quoted as saying in an article for the *Manufacturer Online* Web site. The two former Hayes Lemmerz plants located in Montague, Michigan, and Bristol, Indiana, came with propriety technology and highly skilled manufacturing teams. Most importantly, the factory had an impressive reputation in the automotive industry for its aluminum casting capabilities.

In 2005 DMI had $140 million in sales. DMI's management team believed their new acquisition represented a significant potential for sales. The projected growth was based on DMI gaining recognition as a producer of aluminum permanent mold castings and suspension components. "I think there's a good fit, and the first couple of months are showing that's the case," Bay noted in the *Manufacturer Online* Web site article. "We're opening doors for our customers, and we're seeing a phenomenal amount of quotes coming in."

DMI continued to acquire companies that would help grow its customer base. In 2008 DMI purchased the assets and equipment from Citation Corp.'s metal-casting facility in Butler, Indiana. The facility manufactured semipermanent and permanent molded aluminum suspension and brake components. DMI incorporated the work and equipment at a facility in Bristol, Indiana, and another plant in Milwaukee, Wisconsin. The Milwaukee plant had been purchased by DMI from Aluminum Casting and Engineering Co. and was renamed Diversified Machine Milwaukee. In the final analysis, DMI had acquired a niche automotive casting and machining business focused on engine and transmission components. Overall, DMI paid $21.1 million and assumed approximately $5.1 million in debut under capital leases for equipment at the facilities.

CONVINCING THE BACKERS

The strategy behind DMI's acquisitions emphasized creating an expanded mix of automotive products and services. In a relatively short amount of time, DMI was operating plants in five Michigan locations and in Bristol, Indiana, and Milwaukee. In November 2009 DMI purchased Intermet Corp's Columbus, Georgia, ductile iron foundry. DMI's goal was to expand the business over the next year. Chairman and CEO Bruce Swift noted in a brief article for the *All About Auto Parts* Web site that he expected business to double within that time. Swift also remarked in an *Automotive News* article that DMI's growth was leading to a $300 million sales year for 2009.

Much of Swift's ability to rapidly expand the company was due to financial backing from the Carlyle Group, a large private-equity fund, and Relativity Fund/JME. This gave DMI the advantage of having capital available at a time when many casting and machining operations were struggling due to the overall collapse in automotive sales brought about by the economic recession of 2008 and 2009.

CONTINUING WITH THE PLAN

DMI continued to make acquisitions and new alliances in 2010. Interested in expanding its footprint into Europe to serve global platforms, the company purchased Metaldyne's plant in Barcelona, Spain, to create Diversified Machines Barcelona. The Spanish operation specializes in tight tolerance machining of aluminum, iron, and steel components. The facility machines high-integrity knuckles and chassis components. The company also has formed alliances in China as part of a global footprint expansion of aluminum casting and machining capabilities.

In 2010 DMI's CFO Shankar Kiru was named a CFO of the Year Awards winner by *Crain's Detroit Business*. Kiru, who started his career as a manufacturing engineer, worked at Covisint and then at Metaldyne with CEO Swift and COO Bay before the three quit to start DMI. Kiru told *Crain's Detroit Business* contributor Dustin Walsh that his experience as an engineer has helped him convince DMI customers that the company had "the industrial and financial means to win their business."

Kiru's aggressive benchmark strategy has resulted in numerous new contracts that generated $100 million in the first quarter of the new business year, compared to a total of $130 million in new contracts for all of 2009. Kiru noted in the *Crain's Detroit Business* article that the company constantly monitored emerging markets throughout the world with an eye on determining whether these new markets were competitors who could do what DMI did but at lower cost. "We do a lot of soul searching of how we can differentiate, and it really arms us with knowledge to provide a better service to our customers," Kiru told *Crain's Detroit Business* contributor Walsh.

In addition to acquiring new companies and facilities that met the company's goals, DMI was focusing on a company-wide succession plan while upholding DMI's financial liquidity to broaden its operations in Europe. The company projected continued growth worldwide during the 2010s.

David Petechuk

PRINCIPAL SUBSIDIARIES

Diversified Machine Inc. Barcelona (Spain); Diversified Machine Inc. Bristol; Diversified Machine Inc. Columbus; Diversified Machine Inc. Edon; Diversified Machine Inc. Howell; Diversified Machine Inc. Iztapalapa (Mexico); Diversified Machine Inc. Milwaukee; Diversified Machine Inc. Montague.

PRINCIPAL COMPETITORS

BorgWarner Inc.; Delphi Automotive, LLP; Linamar Corporation; Magna Powertrain; Robert Bosch GmbH.

FURTHER READING

"Michigan Auto Parts Supplier Purchases Columbus Foundry." *All About Auto Parts* (blog). Accessed February 8, 2011. http://allaboutautoparts.blog.com/2009/11/13/michigan-auto-parts-supplier-purchases-columbus-foundry/.

Regan, Keith. "Diversified Machine, Opportunity through Acquisition." *Manufacturer Online.* Accessed February 8, 2011. http://www.themanufacturer.com/us/profile/5491/Diversified_Machine.

Toushek, Gary. "Diversified Machine, Expand and Diversify." *Manufacturer Online.* Accessed February 8, 2011. http://www.themanufacturer.com/us/detail.html?contents_id=4326.

"UC Investors, Inc. Agrees to Purchase Uni Boring Company, Inc." *PR Newswire,* November 18, 2005.

Walsh, Dustin. "Private Companies Over $250 Million; Shankar Kiru." *Crain's Detroit Business,* May 24, 2010.

Dr Pepper Snapple Group, Inc.

5301 Legacy Drive
Plano, Texas 75024-3109
U.S.A.
Telephone: (972) 673-7000
Toll Free: (800) 527-7096
Fax: (972) 673-7980
Web site: http://www.drpeppersnapplegroup.com

Public Company
Founded: 1885 (Dr Pepper)
Employees: 19,000 (est., 2010)
Sales: $5.53 billion (2009)
Stock Exchanges: New York
Ticker Symbol: DPS
NAICS: 312111 Soft Drink Manufacturing; 311930 Flavoring Syrup and Concentrate Manufacturing

■ ■ ■

Dr Pepper Snapple Group, Inc., (DPS) is one of North America's leading refreshment beverage companies, manufacturing, bottling, and distributing more than 50 brands of carbonated soft drinks, juices, teas, mixers, waters, and other premium beverages. DPS was formed in 2008 as a spin-off of Cadbury Schweppes Americas Beverages (CSAB) from Cadbury Schweppes plc. CSAB was formed in 2003 with the combination of Cadbury Schweppes' four North American beverage businesses: Dr Pepper/Seven Up Inc., Snapple Beverage group, Mott's LLP, and Bebidas Mexico. In addition to the United States and Canada, DPS also distributes nonalcoholic beverages in Mexico and the Caribbean.

The company's three business segments are beverage concentrates, packaged beverages, and Latin American beverages. Key brands include 7 Up, Mott's, A&W, Sunkist Soda, Hawaiian Punch, Canada Dry, Schweppes, RC Cola, Diet Rite, Squirt Peñafiel, Yoohoo, Rose's, Clamato, and Mr & Mrs T. Headquartered in Plano, Texas, DPS has 23 manufacturing facilities in the United States and Mexico, and more than 200 distribution centers in North America.

EARLY DEVELOPMENT OF DR PEPPER

Dr Pepper was invented in Waco, Texas, at Morrison's Old Corner Drug Store. In 1885 a young pharmacist who worked for Morrison's, Charles C. Alderton, experimented on his own soft drink. He mixed phosphorescent water, fruit juice, sugar, and other ingredients to produce a new soft drink. With Morrison's approval, Alderton offered the drink to the store's customers. One of these jokingly called the concoction "Dr. Pepper's drink." This was a reference to Dr. Charles Pepper, the disapproving father of a woman Morrison had been courting. The hope was that Pepper might be flattered.

The name and the soft drink, with its tart yet sweet flavor became popular locally, and in 1887 Morrison offered beverage chemist Robert S. Lazenby the opportunity to participate in the marketing and development of this new product. After sampling "Dr. Pepper's drink," Lazenby agreed to go into partnership with Morrison to produce the beverage at his Circle A Ginger Ale Company, also in Waco. Alderton, the drink's inventor, dissociated himself from Dr Pepper, opting instead to turn his talents to the pharmaceutical trade.

The new product, "Dr. Pepper's Phos-Ferrates," was available only in soda fountains until 1891, when the manufacturers began bottling the beverage. With Lazenby handling the business end, Dr Pepper became a top seller in and around Texas. Expansion was inevitable, and Lazenby sought a marketing opportunity to introduce Dr Pepper to the world.

The ideal forum was the 1904 World's Fair, held in St. Louis. Lazenby and his son-in-law, J. B. O'Hara, demonstrated their product there, providing samples of Dr Pepper to some of the approximately 20 million World's Fair visitors. (Incidentally, the 1904 exhibition also showcased other innovations, including the ice-cream cone and buns for hot dogs and hamburgers.) Dr Pepper's success encouraged Lazenby and Morrison, who founded the Artesian Manufacturing and Bottling Company, which would eventually be renamed the Dr Pepper Company. By 1923, headquarters were moved from Waco to Dallas, Texas.

EARLY DEVELOPMENT OF 7 UP

Around 1920, while Dr Pepper was growing in favor, C. L. Grigg, an advertising veteran of 30 years, had formed the Howdy Company in St. Louis, Missouri. The company was named for the Howdy orange-flavored soft drink Grigg had developed, but Grigg wanted to sell more than one type of beverage. For two years, Grigg tested different combinations of lemon and other flavors. By the mid-1920s he had settled on a distinctive lemon-lime formula, and in 1929 the Howdy Company introduced the soda to the general public.

Grigg and company were confident of their invention's appeal. As an early sales bulletin noted, consumers "are tired of the insipid flavors, and the aftertaste of the heavy synthetic flavors is more objectionable. ... So in *our beverage* we have provided

seven natural flavors so blended and in such proportions that, when bottled, it produces a big natural flavor with a real taste that makes people remember it."

The only thing that might have stood in the way of the drink's early success was its name, "Bib-Label Lithiated Lemon-Lime Soda." Griggs derived the new and much simpler name, 7 Up, from the beverage's "seven natural flavors." The new name first appeared on the bottle later in 1929. The beverage sold well, and the new name made it easy for consumers to remember. In 1936 the Howdy Company became the Seven Up Company, and by the 1940s its product became the world's third-largest-selling soft drink.

MARKETING DEVELOPMENTS

Although what distinguished both drinks from the rest of the market was unique flavor, neither beverage was marketed simply as a refreshment. Both Dr Pepper and 7 Up were promoted as health drinks in their first decades. (The former beverage went by Dr. Pepper until the 1950s, when the period was dropped from its name.) In the 1930s, Dr Pepper's famous slogan "Drink a bite to eat at 10, 2 & 4" capitalized on the idea that one typically experienced an energy slump during those hours. A serving of Dr. Pepper would presumably provide the energy boost needed to make it through the day. At the same time, 7 Up boasted in ads that it "dispels brain cobwebs and muscular fatigue."

The fortunes of both companies grew during World War II, with Dr Pepper able to go public in 1946, The postwar period saw the baby boom, which produced an unprecedented number of soft drink consumers. In their marketing efforts, both beverage companies sought to appeal to this lucrative market. Dr Pepper, for instance, became a regular sponsor of the hit teen show "American Bandstand," while 7 Up became noted for its "uncola" campaign of the late 1960s, which capitalized on the individualistic tendencies of young people by distancing 7 Up from the cola market. In the 1970s Dr Pepper was marketed through the long-running "Be a Pepper" campaign.

Later advertising efforts avoided the so-called cola wars of the 1980s, focusing instead on what made Dr Pepper and 7 Up different. Dr Pepper ads declared the soft drink was "just what the doctor ordered," while Diet Dr Pepper was "the taste you've been looking for." 7 Up introduced an animated character, "Spot," derived from the its long-used logo, a large 7 with a red spot in the middle, that revitalized the "uncola" theme that worked so well in the 1970s. Both companies also spent years testing and introducing new products while refining existing ones. Both Dr Pepper and 7 Up brought

KEY DATES

∎

1885: Pharmacist Charles C. Alderton invents Dr Pepper soft drink in Waco, Texas.

1891: Bottling of Dr Pepper begins.

1929: Adman Charles L. Grigg introduces Bib-Label Lithiated Lemon-Lime Soda, soon renamed 7 Up, to the general public.

1936: Grigg's company, the Howdy Company, changes its name to the Seven Up Company.

1946: Dr Pepper Company goes public.

1978: Phillip Morris buys Seven Up.

1986: Hicks & Haas purchases Dr Pepper and Seven Up in separate transactions.

1988: Hicks & Haas merges Dr Pepper and Seven Up to form Dr Pepper/Seven Up Companies, Inc. (DPSU).

1995: Cadbury Schweppes acquires the company, with DPSU becoming a wholly owned subsidiary and being renamed Dr Pepper/Cadbury of North America, Inc.

1997: Company name is changed to Dr Pepper/Seven Up, Inc.

1998: 7 Up is reformulated for the first time ever.

2000: Cadbury Schweppes acquires Snapple Beverage Group.

2003: Four North American beverage companies under Cadbury Schweppes are unified to become Cadbury Schweppes Americas Beverages.

2008: Cadbury Schweppes plc spins off its Cadbury Schweppes Americas Beverages unit to create Dr Pepper Snapple Group

2010: Company celebrates 125-year history of Dr Pepper.

out "diet" versions by the early 1970s. In 1981 Dr Pepper purchased the rights to Welch's soft drinks.

OWNERSHIP CHANGES AND A MERGER: 1984–95

Dr Pepper was traded on the New York Stock Exchange until 1984, when it was taken private in a $615 million leveraged buyout by Forstmann Little & Co. Some of the company's assets were stripped to pay down debt, overhead was cut, and a new promotional campaign was launched. Meantime, Seven Up was a privately owned family business that did not avail itself of public trading

until 1967. In 1978 cigarette maker Philip Morris bought Seven Up, which soon went into a profit slide. By 1986 Philip Morris was set to sell the struggling Seven Up Company to PepsiCo, while Coca-Cola was seeking to buy Dr Pepper. The Federal Trade Commission, however, blocked both proposed acquisitions for antitrust reasons, although Philip Morris was allowed to sell Seven Up's international operations to PepsiCo. Dallas-based investment bank Hicks & Haas then entered the picture, purchasing Dr Pepper in another leveraged buyout for $406 million in August 1986. Participating in the buyout was Britain's Cadbury Schweppes, which gained a minority stake in Dr Pepper.

Later in 1986, Hicks & Haas struck again, purchasing the U.S. operations of Seven Up for $240 million. Two years later, Hicks & Haas merged Dr Pepper and Seven Up, forming the Dr Pepper/Seven Up Companies, Inc., on May 19, 1988. The combined market strength of the two companies created a stronger contender in the soft drink market, against Coke and Pepsi. The new company began with a brand portfolio that included Dr Pepper and 7 Up (both in regular and diet versions), caffeine-free Dr Pepper and diet Dr Pepper, Cherry 7 Up (introduced in 1987), Welch's, and IBC Root Beer and Cream Soda.

In 1990 Dr Pepper/Seven Up (DPSU) entered the sport drink field with Nautilus Thirst Quencher. Like rival Gatorade, Nautilus was promoted as a high-electrolyte, energy-producing beverage to revive athletes. However, Nautilus also stood out in its debut as the only major brand sport drink sweetened entirely by aspartame (the artificial sweetener marketed under the name NutraSweet).

In January 1993 Dr Pepper/Seven Up went public through an initial public offering. The $15 per share IPO raised $283.5 million, which was used to redeem the company's preferred stock and to retire debt. During the early 1990s DPSU enjoyed vigorous growth, with sales increasing from $658.7 million to $769 million from 1992 to 1994 alone. These gains came despite the continuing struggles of the 7 Up brand, which by this time had been surpassed by rival brand Sprite, owned by Coca-Cola. Dr Pepper's popularity, however, was on the increase, garnering a compound average growth of 8.5 percent a year from 1989 through 1993. Overall, DPSU's share of the domestic soft drink market increased from 9.8 percent in 1991 to 11.4 percent in 1994.

As of mid-1993 Cadbury Schweppes held a small stake in Dr Pepper/Seven Up, the holding stemming from its minority interest in Dr Pepper. Prudential Insurance Co. held a 22.2 percent stake in DPSU, which it sold to Cadbury in August 1993 for $231.8 million, raising Cadbury's stake in DPSU to 25.9

percent. Under the leadership of John Albers, DPSU quickly adopted a poison pill measure which discouraged Cadbury from making any immediate moves to further raise its stake or initiate a complete takeover. Albers also refused to grant its suitor a seat on the board as it had requested. Meantime, Cadbury in October 1993 further increased its presence in the U.S. market through the acquisition of A&W Brands Inc., thereby gaining U.S. ownership or rights to the flagship A&W root beer brand, the citrus-flavored Squirt, Vernors ginger ale, and Country Time lemonades. Cadbury already controlled the Schweppes, Canada Dry, Crush, Mott's, and Sunkist brands.

SUBSIDIARY OF CADBURY SCHWEPPES: 1995

The addition of A&W Brands increased Cadbury's share of the U.S. soft drink market to 5.6 percent. Nonetheless, the U.K. company aimed to become the leading producer of noncola soft drinks in the world. The emphasis on the noncola sector made particular sense in the U.S. market, where noncola sales were increasing at a rate of 10 percent per year while cola sales were merely edging ahead at 4 percent a year. The quickest path to achieving this goal was the acquisition of DPSU, particularly since Cadbury believed the Dr Pepper brand had untapped potential outside the United States, as it held a mere 1 percent of the world market.

In March 1995 Cadbury Schweppes acquired the 74 percent of Dr Pepper/Seven Up stock it did not already own for $33 per share, or $1.7 billion. Leading the newly named Dr Pepper/Cadbury of North America, Inc., was John F. Brock, a Cadbury veteran. Although it still lagged far behind industry behemoths Coca-Cola and Pepsi, Dr Pepper/Cadbury was a much stronger number three player in the United States, with a market share of 17 percent and a strong roster of brands. These included Dr Pepper, 7 Up, Welch's, IBC, Canada Dry, Schweppes, A&W, Crush, Sunkist, Squirt, Mott's, Hires, Vernors, and Country Time. During 1997 the name of the company was changed to Dr Pepper/Seven Up, Inc., and Todd Stitzer, another Cadbury veteran, was named president and CEO of the new DPSU.

During the late 1990s DPSU made several moves to solidify the bottling and distribution of its brands in the United States. In May 1996 Coca-Cola Enterprises Inc., the nation's largest soft drink distributor, agreed to manufacture and distribute Dr Pepper brand products until at least year-end 2000. The licensing agreement also covered several other DPSU brands, including Schweppes, Canada Dry, and Squirt, through the end of 1998. In January 1998 this licensing agreement was extended, with the above dates changed to year-end 2005 and year-end 2001, respectively.

Perhaps most importantly, Cadbury Schweppes and the Carlyle Group of Washington, D.C., in early 1998 formed a joint venture named the American Bottling Company, which initially consisted of the merger of two leading independent bottling groups in the Midwest, Beverage America and Select Beverages. A year later American Bottling was combined with another independent bottler, Dr Pepper Bottling Company of Texas. The creation of American Bottling, whereby the company gained ownership of at least part of its bottling system, was designed to give Dr Pepper/Seven Up greater control over the distribution of its brands.

As it headed into a new century, Dr Pepper/Seven Up faced a number of challenges, perhaps most importantly the continuing need to revitalize the 7 Up brand. By the end of the 1990s, the brand had fallen to the number nine position in the U.S. soft drink market. A series of ad campaigns in the 1990s, a 1998 formula change (the first for the brand), and such packaging changes as the dropping of the "Uncola" slogan all failed to stem the brand's decline.

UNIFICATION RESULTS IN CADBURY SCHWEPPES AMERICAS: 2003

In 2000 Cadbury Schweppes acquired Snapple Beverage Group. In addition to the namesake brand, the purchase included RC Cola, Diet Rite, and Stewart's, among others. The purchase, which was valued at $1.45 million, significantly expanded Cadbury Schweppes' portfolio in the United States. According to 1999 market share data for the carbonated soft drinks (CSD) category, as compiled by *Market Share Reporter 2001*, the move resulted in a slightly more than 1 percent market-share increase to almost 16 percent of the CSD business. Overall, the market segment remained dominated by the cola giants Coca-Cola and Pepsi-Cola, which held market shares of 44.1 percent and 31 percent, respectively.

Another major move was made in 2003 when the four North American beverage companies under Cadbury Schweppes (Dr. Pepper/Seven Up, Inc., Snapple Beverage Corp., Mott's, and Bebidas Mexico) were unified under a common management structure and business strategy to become Cadbury Schweppes Americas Beverages. The unification was part of an effort to establish one regional operating unit. The overall goal was to help the separate beverage businesses in the Americas work together better. Quoted in the *PR Newswire*, Gilbert M. Cassagne, Americas Beverages president and CEO, noted: "Our goal is to create a premier beverage marketing and sales organization that capitalizes on the terrific brand portfolios managed by the Dr Pepper/ Seven Up, Snapple, and Mott's organizations."

ANOTHER NEW BUSINESS STRUCTURE: 2006 AND BEYOND

In early 2006 parent company Cadbury Schweppes secured full ownership of the Dr Pepper/Seven Up Bottling Group (BG) when the Carlyle Group sold its 53 percent stake in the company for $353 million. Two years later, in 2008, Dr Pepper Snapple Group (DPS) was formed when Cadbury Schweppes plc spun off its Cadbury Schweppes Americas Beverages unit, with Wayne Sanders being named chairman of DPS. In April of that year, shareholders approved the spin-off Dr Pepper Snapple Group, thus creating a new company named Dr Pepper Snapple Group, Inc. The company was also listed on the New York Stock Exchange in 2008. In an article in *BusinessWorld*, Larry Young, president and CEO of DPS, noted that the separation marked a new era for the business. Young remarked: "We have confidence in the beverage industry and we are looking forward to seizing the opportunities as a stand-alone company."

Before the end of 2008, the company had relocated its research and development center from Trumbull, Connecticut, to the company's headquarters in Plano, Texas. The company also launched several new beverages, such as Canada Dry Green Tea Ginger ale and Venom Energy. In addition, DPS signed major distribution agreements for the Crush brand and secured equity positions in companies that owned and marketed Hydrive, Big Red, and All Sport brands. Although the company gained steadily on its cola sales over the previous two decades, by the end of 2009, the company's first full year of business as DPS, its flavors drinks overtook the colas and represented 50.4 percent of all its CSD sales.

Despite its many business maneuvers, revenue remained fairly flat for DPS. Revenue in 2007 was $5.70 billion, and 2008 revenue was $5.71 billion. In 2009 revenue dipped slightly to $5.53 billion, a decrease caused by lower sales in packaged beverages and the Latin American market.

Although revenue was sluggish, DPS remained the third-largest beverage company in the world. On January 25, 2010, the company celebrated the 125-year history of Dr Pepper by ringing the closing bell at the New York Stock Exchange. "We're going to be spending 10 to 15 percent more behind Dr Pepper this year versus last year," Jim Trebilcock, DPS's executive vice president of marketing, noted in a May 2010 *Beverage Industry* article, adding: "As we do well, we are going to reinvest in our brands to drive more growth." Overall, the company's plans for the future included expanding the distribution and availability of its products and capitalizing on the opportunity for growth in the U.S. West Coast. Susan Salter

Susan Salter
Updated, David E. Salamie; David Petechuk

PRINCIPAL SUBSIDIARIES

A&W Concentrate Company; Comercializadora de Bebidas, SA de CV (Mexico); DP Beverages, Inc.; Mott's LLP; Peñafiel Bebidas SA de CV (Mexico); Royal Crown Company, Inc.; Snapple Beverage Corp.

PRINCIPAL DIVISIONS

Beverage Concentrates; Latin American Beverages; Packaged Beverages.

PRINCIPAL COMPETITORS

The Coca–Cola Company; The Cott Corporation; PepsiCo, Inc.

FURTHER READING

"Cadbury Schweppes Americas Beverages Restructures for Growth, Changing Marketplace." *PR Newswire*, September 18, 2003.

"Cadbury-Schweppes Bottles Snapple Deal." *Drug Store News*, October 16, 2000, p. 45.

"DPS Puts the Flavor Back in CSDs; One Year after a Spin-Off from Cadbury, Dr Pepper Snapple Groups Is Focused on Flavor and Availability." *Beverage Industry*, July 2009, p. 16.

"DPS Reports Sales Increase in First Quarter." *Beverage World*, June 15, 2008, p. 16.

"Dr Pepper 125 Years of 23 Satisfying Flavors: Marketing, Flavors and Expanding Availability Push Brand Forward." *Beverage Industry*, May 2010, p. 26.

Duoyuan Global Water, Inc.

———■———

Number 3 Jinyuan Road
Fifth Floor
Daxing Industrial Development Zone
Beijing, China 102600
Telephone: (86) 10 6021 2222
Fax: (86) 10 6021 2164
Web site: http://www.duoyuan-hq.com

Public Company
Founded: 1992
Employees: 1,166 (2009)
Sales: $114.8 million (2009)
Stock Exchanges: New York
Ticker Symbol: DGW
NAICS: 334512 Automatic Environmental Control Manufacturing for Regulating Residential, Commercial, and Appliance Use

■ ■ ■

Duoyuan Global Water, Inc., is a Chinese company that manufactures equipment for water purification and treatment. The company has been enjoying steady growth in a crowded market ever since, meeting China's desperate need for clean, nonpolluted water. In 2009 Duoyuan became the first Chinese manufacturer of water treatment equipment to be listed on the New York Stock Exchange, and its initial public offering brought in much higher than expected returns. The enthusiasm expressed by investors was a reflection of the steadily increasing returns brought in by Duoyuan's

wide breadth of products made possible by its commitment to research and development, as well as its extensive distribution networks, both in China and abroad, that promised steadily increasing market share and attendant profits.

Through tough economic times, Duoyuan has continued to expand. As of 2011, it offered over 80 products broken up across three categories. Circulating Water Treatment Equipment includes devices such as electronic water conditioners, cyclone filters, water softeners, and other products designed to remove particulates and buildup from circulating systems. The company's Water Purification Equipment employ a variety of electrodeionization (EDI) techniques including ultraviolet, ozone, and membrane-based methods. The last category, Wastewater Treatment Equipment, includes grit separators and microporous aerators, among other things.

The company's broad customer base in China includes wastewater treatment plants, water utilities, factories and manufacturing plants, commercial and residential buildings, and individuals. Since 2007 Duoyuan has also been steadily expanding its international market share, first in North America and then in Europe.

COMPANY FOUNDING AND EARLY YEARS: 1989–97

Duoyuan was the brainchild of Wenhua Guo, a former physics teacher at Beijing Chemical Institute. Armed only with a bachelor's degree in physics, in 1989 Guo began researching the construction of water treatment engaged in an overhaul of its Beijing plant with an eye toward building a wider range of specialized machinery.

COMPANY PERSPECTIVES

Our philosophy is roughly translated to mean "Established in the market and innovators at heart." We at Duoyuan pursue continuous technological improvements to provide our customers excellent product quality and service. We have also adopted advanced international management systems and implemented Six Sigma methodology, achieving higher efficiency and further enhancing customer satisfaction. With the technology, quality, service and innovation, we have become a leading supplier in the industry in terms of manufacturing technology, product quality and production capacity.

PURIFICATION AND TREATMENT: 1998–2004

Duoyuan branched into water purification systems in 1998. That same year, Duoyuan became the first company in China to attain ISO 14001 certification. The certification, derived from a group of 16 international standards, was implemented to assist companies in reducing their environmental impact. A company, such as Duoyuan, that is ISO 14001 certified is one that has demonstrated compliance with environmental legislation and regulations. The certification and renewal process is also designed to encourage companies to continue to reduce their environmental impact through "continual improvement."

In 2000 Duoyuan expanded, building a 70,000-square-meter manufacturing facility at Langfang. The following year, the company branched out again, adding the manufacture of sewage waste treatment machinery to its matrix of goods. Its manufacturing facilities were state of the art, boasting individual workshops for circulating water treatment equipment, sludge-water separation machinery, water purifiers, disinfection machines, and aeration equipment, as well as the requisite in-house welding, machining, and rubber and plastic manufactories that all that equipment required.

Not only was Duoyuan expanding, but it was fast earning a reputation for quality products. Its Central Water Purifier was recognized by the Chinese government in 2001, and the following year its distinctively named Sludge Screw won an award for excellence. In 2004 the company itself was recognized by the Beijing government for its continued commitment to excellence. A sign of the company's ongoing drive toward improving and expanding its product line was the opening in 2003 of China's first postdoctoral research and development division for water treatment equipment.

apparatus. It was not long before he was building and producing circulating water treatment equipment, the first private supplier to do so in China. By 1992 Guo's cottage industry had grown successful enough to warrant founding Duoyuan.

When he started his business, Guo was among a small number of manufacturers in the water treatment industry. It was a niche that desperately needed to be filled. Within its borders, China's lakes and rivers comprise the fourth-largest collection of fresh water on the planet, yet nearly three-quarters of those waters are polluted. Half of the fresh water in China is so polluted, in fact, that it is not fit for human consumption. With its massive population, China's water needs are correspondingly acute. Due to the polluted condition of water sources, it is not uncommon for population centers to experience shortages. In other cases, water contaminated by pollutants or untreated sewage makes its way into the consumer market. Faced with a clearly unacceptable situation, the Chinese government has been steadily legislating and enforcing clean water laws in the country. As one U.S. reporter glibly summed it up in a headline, "China's Filthy Water Is Duoyuan's Niche."

In 1994 Duoyuan built its first manufacturing facility in Beijing. For its first five years, Duoyuan manufactured machinery to treat water used in industrial equipment as well as heating and cooling systems. However, with the ever-growing and drastic need for clean drinking water, it was perhaps inevitable that Duoyuan would make the move to manufacturing purification equipment for potable water. In 1996 the company began preparing to expand its scope as it

PRODUCTS AND STRATEGY

From the very beginning, Duoyuan stressed research and development as the core principle of its corporate strategy. As a result the company gradually expanded its range of equipment built and sold. In addition, the research and development team at Duoyuan focused on improving existing products. A key focus was on increasing automation of the machinery, as well as improving energy consumption. Duoyuan researchers also gave attention to developing equipment that can recycle and reuse sludge and waste materials generated by purification processes. Since standards for water

KEY DATES

1989: Founder Wenhua Guo begins research into water treatment equipment.

1992: Duoyuan Global Water is founded.

1998: Established in water treatment work, the company moves into water purification systems.

2002: Chinese government gives an award for excellence to Duoyuan for its Sludge Screw.

2007: In partnership with Global Environmental Fund, Duoyuan begins selling its products on the international market.

2009: Duoyuan becomes the first Chinese water treatment equipment manufacturing company to be listed on the New York Stock Exchange.

purification are constantly being raised and refined, there was also a demand for the company's research and development division to continually refine its existing product line, boosting performance.

By 2010 Duoyuan's research and development division was clearly paying dividends in the form of a vastly expanded range of products. Over 80 distinct equipment systems filled out Duoyuan's catalogue. These included grit separators, filters, conditioners, ultraviolet, ozone, and electrodeionization purification systems, disinfection systems, and other specialized equipment marketed to a wide range of municipal and industrial customers.

Research and development is all well and good, but it must be backed up by a solid sales strategy. Duoyuan's wide-ranging network of distributors gave the company access to vast swaths of China's residential, commercial, and industrial customers. In order to best stay in touch with its end-users, Duoyuan did not rely simply on its distributors to take care of sales. The company also assigned sales representatives to work on-site at distributors' offices, putting a personal face on the company's products and providing immediate, face-to-face support for customers.

EXPANSION AND GOING PUBLIC:
2007–10

As Duoyuan approached the end of the first decade of the 21st century, it found itself ready to expand once again. The market for water treatment and purification equipment, an untapped niche at the time the company

was founded, had become extremely competitive as the Chinese public and government alike clamored for cleaner water and more stringent environmental controls. Despite Duoyuan's success, it could still only claim a mere 1 percent of the market share.

This lack of market penetration was counterbalanced by the company's wide range of product and, most importantly, the distribution network it had built to get those products on the market. Duoyuan's distribution network was indeed formidable, as no fewer than 80 distributors across 28 provinces and districts in China carried its products. In response to such a crowded home market, Duoyuan looked to expand abroad. In 2007 the company signed a distribution partnership with the Global Environment Fund to help boost its international presence.

June 2009 brought Duoyuan's initial public offering (IPO). Set to list on the same day as another, more high-profile Chinese company, Chemspec International, Ltd., observers did not expect Duoyuan's IPO to perform especially well. Headlines were therefore made when Duoyuan not only bettered Chemspec's IPO, but rose 37 percent above its initial estimates by the close of trading. This outstanding performance was no doubt due in part to Duoyuan's commitment to excellent products and environmental compliance, but almost certainly had mostly to do with the company's rising financial fortunes. From 2007 to 2009, the company had seen its earnings per share rise first by 67 percent (2007), then 78 percent (2008), then 242 percent (2009).

Duoyuan's IPO brought in $88 million, and its stock continued to perform well for the remainder of 2009, jumping up 120 percent from its initial listing. Met with such success, Duoyuan put up a follow-on offering in January 2010 worth about $142 million.

LOOKING AHEAD

As Duoyuan looked to expand its market share in China, providing desperately needed (not to mention government-mandated) equipment, it continued to grow outside the borders of its home country. Despite the global recession, Duoyuan managed to continue to expand and perform well. Employee growth from 2009 to 2010 was over 25 percent, and Duoyuan looked to expand its international horizons. In November 2010 the company made further moves to open up foreign markets. Two companies, one American and one European (the latter a first for Duoyuan) entered into licensing agreements.

Duoyuan's stated strategies looking ahead were to more or less stay the course with an eye toward growth opportunities. In particular, after years of organic growth the company believed it was ready to start looking at opportunities for "selective strategic acquisition" of complementary product lines, new markets, and expanded research and development resources. The company was also looking to expand its in-house production capabilities by making more of its manufacturing processes in-house. Above all, Duoyuan hoped to grow its market share in China itself by increasing its product line and increasing sales of integrated systems.

David Larkins

PRINCIPAL SUBSIDIARIES

Duoyuan Clean Water Technology Industries (China) Co., Ltd.; Duoyuan Global Water Conservation Equipment (China) Co., Ltd.; Duoyuan Water Treatment Equipment Manufacturing (Langfang) Co., Ltd.; Langfang Duoyuan Aeration System and Equipment Manufacturing Co., Ltd.

PRINCIPAL DIVISIONS

Aeration System Machinery Division; Belt-type Press Division; Centrifuge Machinery Division; Circulating Water Division; Disinfection system Division; On-line Monitoring Division; Pure Water Division.

PRINCIPAL COMPETITORS

CANPURE Corporation; GE Water and Process Technologies; ITT Corporation; Siemens Water Technologies Corp; Wuxi Tongyong Machinery Co., Ltd.; Yixing Nopon Environment Co., Ltd; Zheijiang De'an New Technology Development Co., Ltd.

FURTHER READING

"Duoyuan Global Water Inc." hoovers.com, 2011.

"Duoyan Global Water Makes Fresh Offer on Back of Popularity." *Euroweek,* January 22, 2010.

"Duoyuan Global Water Signs Licensing Agreements with US and Dutch Companies." *Filtration Industry Analyst,* November 2010, 3–4.

"Duoyuan IPO Soars 37%; Chemspec Is Flat." *Wall Street Journal (Eastern Edition),* June 25, 2009, C3.

Gold, Donald H. "China's Filthy Water Is Duoyuan's Niche." *Investors Business Daily,* August 28, 2009.

Ecobank Transnational Incorporated

—————————■—————————

2 Rue du Commerce
P.O. Box 3261
Lomé, Togo
Telephone: (228) 221 03 03
Fax: (228) 222 24 34
Web site: http://www.ecobank.com

Public Company
Founded: 1985
Employees: 11,000 (2009)
Sales: $873 million (2009)
Stock Exchanges: Ghana Nigeria BRVM
Ticker Symbol: ETI (Ghana, Nigeria) ETIT (BVRM)
NAICS: 522110 Commercial Banking

■ ■ ■

Ecobank Transnational Incorporated (ETI) is an internationally renowned financial conglomerate headquartered in Lomé, Togo, with presence in Africa, Asia, and Europe. Famously tagged as the "Pan African Bank," ETI is a banking institution that provides a full range of banking services and products to individuals, multinational corporations, governments, nongovernmental institutions, and all sizes of business enterprises. The group's banking services are categorized into personal banking, business banking, corporate banking, and capital banking services. The operations of the ETI's subsidiaries and affiliates are supported by a common information technology platform headquartered in Accra, Ghana.

In 2010 ETI had 746 branches and offices supported by a workforce of more than 11,000 employees in approximately 30 countries. In addition to Togo, ETI had branches in Ghana, Nigeria, Ivory Coast, Kenya, Cape Verde, Tanzania, Chad, Burundi, Zambia, Malawi, Democratic Republic of Congo, Benin, Guinea, Cameroon, Uganda, Congo Brazzaville, Sierra Leone, Central African Republic, Senegal, Liberia, São Tomé and Principe, Malawi, Rwanda, Gabon, Niger, Guinea Bissau, Burkina Faso, Mali, and South Africa. The bank also has a subsidiary in Paris and representative offices in Johannesburg, in addition to possessing an approval to open a representative office in Dubai.

The operations and systems of ETI are supported by subsidiaries Ecobank Development Corporation (EDC) and eProcess International, specialized entities created to enhance the execution of the bank's core activities. The operations of EDC are managed through three key strategic units that include underwriting and trading sales and distribution, and investment and funds management. eProcess International, on the other hand, is entirely responsible for the management of all aspects of ETI information technology with reference to the achievement of centralized, efficient, and cost-effective standards.

FOUNDING AND EARLY YEARS: 1985–90

The founding of ETI can be traced back to 1984, when a consortium of investors, backed by the Federation of West African Chamber of Commerce, incorporated Eco-promotions S.A. The pioneer investors set the founda-

COMPANY PERSPECTIVES

Ecobank believes that its success depends for the most part on its ability to maintain a diverse, resourceful, and dynamic workforce to serve its customers. The bank has a strong policy in sourcing, attracting, developing and retaining the best talents.

tion of Ecopromotions by raising the initial capital, which was utilized to determine the feasibility of establishing a private financial institution in West Africa. The establishment of Ecopromotions was motivated by concerns over the domination of West Africa's banking industry by state-owned and foreign financial institutions. There was an urgent need to open up opportunities in West Africa's financial industry for African investors to participate in the development and management of the sector.

Ecopromotions successfully pursued and achieved the legal provisions for establishing a new financial institution, effectively setting the ground for the incorporation of ETI as a bank holding company in October 1985. The newly formed company declared an authorized share capital of $100 million and established its headquarters in Togo's capital, Lomé. The Economic Community of West African States (ECOWAS) Fund was visibly the largest contributor of the company's initial capital of $32 million following its acquisition of the majority shareholding in the company.

ETI secured a Headquarters Agreement with the Togolese government in 1985 for the recognition of its international status in line with its goal of expansion throughout the region. The granting of nonresident privileges and rights to ETI was one of the key aspects contained in the Headquarters 'Agreement. The process of laying the foundation for ETI's operations was enhanced in 1986 after Citibank offered to sign a two-year agreement for providing technical assistance to the bank. ETI finally launched operations in March 1988 when Ecobank Togo, the first branch that also doubled as the headquarters, was opened in Lomé, Togo. The bank opened subsidiaries in Nigeria and Ivory Coast in 1989 and spread its presence farther in West Africa in 1990 by opening subsidiaries in Ghana and Benin.

DIVIDENDS AND EXPANSION: 1991–99

The operations of ETI experienced tremendous growth in the early 1990s as a result of favorable rates of economic growth in West Africa. The rapid growth in the international operations of the company prompted the launch of a Rapid Transfer platform in 1994. The Rapid Transfer platform was a product that enhanced the bank's capacity to accelerate the transfer of funds in the West African subregion to within 24 hours. The product recorded instant success and largely contributed to the improved financial performance of the bank, which recorded net operating profit in excess of $5 million.

ETI diversified its options for international rapid funds transfer in 1995 through a partnership deal with Western Union. The group declared its first dividend in 1995 and clearly signaled stabilized operations in all its key markets. The bank embarked on its expansion strategy with the opening of a subsidiary in Burkina Faso in 1997. The value of ETI's total assets increased to $500 million as ETI proceeded to record operating profits in excess of $10 million. The group also initiated a motivation program for its employees in 1997 through the introduction of an employee share ownership program.

The International Finance Corporation (IFC) increased its stake in ETI in 1998 through a 6.25 percent and 10 percent share subscription in ETI and Ecobank Burkina, respectively. ETI also adopted a new strategic orientation in 1998 by splitting some of its core operations, creating the Economic Development Corporation (EDC) to take charge of its regional trading and investing activities. EDC was mandated to focus on the development of investment banking and advisory business interests in all the operational units of the bank.

As the twentieth century came to a close, the group consolidated its interests in the West African region by opening new subsidiaries in Guinea, Senegal, Mali, Niger and Liberia. The tremendous investor interest in ETI prompted its board to authorize the issue of shareholding stakes to numerous institutional investors. The West Africa Growth Fund and Kingdoms Holding Company were two of the institutional investors that were granted shareholding stakes in the group.

GROWTH IN A NEW CENTURY: 2001–07

ETI experienced successful growth in 2001 as the board of directors enhanced the company's operational strategies at the beginning of the decade. The group's shareholders' equity had grown to more than $70 million as the bank opened operations in Cameroon in 2001. The consolidated balance sheet of ETI exceeded $1 billion as the company's expansion strategy

KEY DATES

1985: Aided by the Federation of West African Chamber of Commerce, an investor group founds Ecobank Transnational Incorporated (ETI).

1998: ETI creates subsidiary Economic Development Corporation to take charge of its regional trading and investing activities.

2006: Company shares begin trading at multiple stock exchanges.

2009: Kolapo Lawson Appointed Group Chairman

2010: Ecobank Capital Launched

continued to bear fruit. The group registered a 29 percent increase in net profits in 2002 compared to financial year 2001. Unlike the previous years, however, the company declared a stock dividend of one share for every five shares held relative to the after-tax profits realized at the end of the financial year 2002.

The board and staff of ETI were accorded a morale-boosting visit by Prince Alwaleed Bin Talal Bin Abdulaziz Al-Saud in June 2003. The high-profile visit of the Saudi prince to the group's headquarters in Lomé was regarded as a significant vote of approval given his status of one of the ranking shareholders in the group. (Prince Alwaleed Bin Talal Bin Abdulaziz Al-Saud owned the Kingdom Hall Company, which accounted for 6.31 percent of ETI's capital at the time of his visit.) The prince expressed his optimism about the continued growth of the group and gave assurance of his willingness to facilitate the group's access to additional sources of capital.

The first decade of the 21st century continued to bring remarkable success for ETI. The successful cross-listing of ETI shares at the Ghana Stock Exchange (GSE) in Accra, Nigeria Stock Exchange (NSE) in Lagos, and Bourse Régionale des Valeurs Mobilières (BRVM) in Abidjan paved the way for the simultaneous commencement of trading of shares at all three bourses on September 11, 2006. The successful cross-listing was followed by the exit of Emerging Capital Partners (EMP), a firm that specialized in private equity.

Ecobank entered the Central African Republic's (CAR) banking industry in July 2007 through the acquisition of a 72 percent shareholding stake in the Banque Internationale Pour La Centrafrique (BICA). BICA operated three branches and was the largest private banking institution in CAR with a balance sheet

value of $54 million and approximately 85 employees at the time of the acquisition. The takeover raised ETI's presence in the Central Africa region to three countries and the total number of countries with the bank's subsidiaries to 17.

GROWTH IN A NEW CENTURY: 2001–07

The expansion strategy of ETI shifted to East Africa in 2008 when the bank launched a successful bid for the takeover of the East African Building Society (EABS). The EABS largely operated as a mortgage financing institution and had 10 branches in major towns in Kenya. ETI completed the acquisition of a 75 percent stake in EABS in 2008 and subsequently changed the subsidiary's name to Ecobank Kenya Limited.

The pursuit of product diversification in ETI was boosted with the signing of a partnership agreement between the bank and Nigeria's Bank of Industry (BOI) on July 1, 2008. The partnership expanded ETI's product portfolio by introducing project-oriented solutions for long-term financing into its range of products in Nigeria.

ETI launched the first phase of a planned three-tier public offering on August 25, 2008. The company hoped that the three phases of the offering would raise $2.5 billion additional capital in order to shore up the balance sheets of its subsidiaries and support new acquisitions. The offering was simultaneously carried out in Togo and 24 countries that hosted ETI subsidiaries. Contrary to expectations, however, the amount raised fell short of its goal, partly because of the global economic crisis that was taking shape at the time. ETI opted to extend the offer period until October 31, 2008, to allow the participation of more investors in the region. Dubbed "the biggest offering in Africa," the first phase of the public offering raised a total of $550 million.

ACROSS AFRICA AND TO OTHER CONTINENTS: 2009 AND BEYOND

ETI opened a representative office in Johannesburg in January 2009 as a strategic follow-up to an alliance it had made with South Africa's NedBank Group in December 2008. The bank further made a successful entry into the European market in June 2009 when it was granted a license to operate a subsidiary in Paris.

The Ugandan subsidiary was opened on January 19, 2009, with a total of six branches. The group was granted license to commence operations in Zambia in July 2009 and proceeded to establish a head office and two branches with 50 employees in the country's capital, Lusaka. Ecobank Zambia Limited planned to spread to other towns in the country by opening five new branches every year beginning in 2010, with the long-term objective of cross-listing at the Lusaka Stock Exchange.

ETI operations in Tanzania commenced in January 2010 after the company's successful bid to secure licensing from the largely government-protected economy. Ecobank immediately assumed a high-profile status in the Tanzanian banking industry upon its establishment of a subsidiary in the country, thanks to the group's huge capital base. The opening of the Tanzanian subsidiary involved the setting up of a new head office and countrywide branch network.

ETI's strategy to enter the Middle East market and expand its presence in Asia remained on course as the company secured an approval to open a representative office in Dubai in September 2010. In that month also, ETI launched Ecobank Capital, a new division that was created to facilitate EDC in the management of capital markets and investment banking. Launched during an African Investment Conference in New York, Ecobank Capital was designed to introduce sophistication and integration to its range of international financing products.

Ecobank Capital was mandated to consolidate trading in Middle Africa where there were as many as 16 different currencies, in addition to executing originated deals and market opportunities globally. Ecobank Capital began operations with 100 financial specialists stationed in major financial centers across the globe.

ETI's core expansion strategy for the future was defined by acquisitions, mergers, and entry into new markets. The bank planned to expand its international presence through acquisitions and the setting up of new subsidiaries in more countries in Sub-Saharan Africa. The Pan African Bank also planned to establish additional offices and facilities for international banking in globally recognized financial centers. Some of these financial centers provide transaction and trading platforms that are substantially linked to Africa such as London, Dubai, Beijing, and Paris. ETI also planned to cross-list in the Stock Exchanges of all the countries where it had subsidiaries.

Paul Ingati

PRINCIPAL SUBSIDIARIES

Ecobank Development Corporation; eProcess International S.A.

PRINCIPAL COMPETITORS

Bank of Africa Group; Barclays Bank PLC; Citibank, N.A.; Cooperative Bank of Kenya; Kenya Commercial Bank Group; Standard Bank Group Limited.

FURTHER READING

Bankelele. "Ecobank 2010 AGM." *GlobalPost (blog)*, June 11, 2010. Accessed October 27, 2010. http://www.globalpost.com/webblog/kenya/ecobank-2010-agm.

Constantine, Sebastian. "Tanzania: Pan-African Bank Set to Enter Local Market." allAfrica.com, December 4, 2009. Accessed October 27, 2010. http://allafrica.com/stories/200912040180.html.

"Ecobank Launches Pan-African Investment Banking Arm: Ecobank Capital." allAfrica.com, October 4, 2010. Accessed October 18, 2010. http://allafrica.com/stories/201010041517.html.

"Ecobank Nedbank Alliance Scoops Most Innovative Bank of the Year in Africa Award." allAfrica.com, October 15, 2010. Accessed October 18, 2010. http://allafrica.com/stories/201010151057.html.

Ecobank. "Ecobank Opens Dubai Office." Press Release, October 4, 2010. Accessed October 27, 2010. http://www.ecobank.com/upload/201010040207100604FtqhDA2sU3.pdf.

———. "Ecobank Opens Representative Office in South Africa–Group's Geographic Footprint Expands to 30 Countries." Press Release, January 22, 2009. Accessed October 26, 2010. http://www.ecobank.com/upload/20100205121306774279ghuEz9sNby.pdf.

———. "Ecobank Transnational Incorporated AGM Approves Dividend Increase." Press Release, August 3, 2010. Accessed October 17, 2010. www.ecobank.com/upload/20100615052012478467tvESKkCZnJ.pdf.

"Ecobank Signs Landmark U.S. $175M Capital Facilities with the IFC." allAfrica.com, August 3, 2010. Accessed October 27, 2010. http://allafrica.com/stories/201008031036.html.

"Ecobank Takes Over BICA." *Daily Express*, August 3, 2007. Accessed October 17, 2010. http://www.modernghana.com/GhanaHome/NewsArchive/news_details.asp?menu_id=1&id=VFZSUmQwMTZUVFE9.

"Ecobank to Open Subsidiary, Branches in Zambia." African Financial Markets, June 22, 2009. Accessed October 17, 2010. http://www.africanfinancialmarkets.com/front-news-detail.php?NewsID=49860.

"Ecobank Transnational Incorporated (ETI) Signs with Bank of Industry (BOI)." *Les Afriques*, July 22, 2008. Accessed October 17, 2010. http://www.lesafriques.com/en/africa/ecobank-transnational-incorporated-eti-signs-with-bank-of-industry-boi.html?Itemid=27?articleid=0149.

"Ecobank's USD 2.5bn Capital Raising Begins Today." *Frontier Markets* (blog), August 24, 2008. Accessed October 30, 2010. http://danfonds.blogspot.com/2008/08/ecobanks-usd-25bn-capital-raising.html.

Ekpe Arnold. "Motives for a Multiple Listing on African Stock Exchanges: The Ecobank Experience." *Proparco's Magazine*,

Issue 5, April 2010. Accessed February 7, 2011. http://www.cefeb.org/jahia/Jahia/site/proparco/lang/en/Numero-5-Revue-Secteur-prive-et-developpement-Les-marches-financiers-en-afrique-veritable-outil-de-developpement.

"Emerging Capital Partners Sells Stake in Ecobank Transnational Incorporated, Following IPO for 3x Initial Investment." *PRNewswire,* June 14, 2006. Accessed October 27, 2010. http://www.prnewswire.co.uk/cgi/news/release?id=200567.

"GEO Monitor Newsflash: Ecobank Transnational Incorporated (ETI)." Research Oracle, August 20, 2008. Accessed October 17, 2010. http://blogs.iirgroup.com/?p=3513.

"IPO Was Successful–Ecobank." GhanaWeb. Accessed October 27, 2010. http://mobile.ghanaweb.com/wap/article.php?ID=106341.

Kezio-Musoke, David. "Ecobank Extends $2.5 Billion IPO till Oct 31." allAfrica.com, October 12, 2008. Accessed October 26, 2010. http://allafrica.com/stories/200810130195.html.

Koranteng, Adu. " Ecobank IPO Receives Major Patronage." *Statesman Online,* September 1, 2008. Accessed October 27, 2010. http://www.thestatesmanonline.com/pages/news_detail.php?section=2&newsid=7149.

Latiff, Eric. "Pan African Bank Spreads East." *Capital Business,* October 2, 2008. Accessed February 4, 2011. http://www.capitalfm.co.ke/business_test/Features/Pan-African-Eco-Bank-spreads-east.html

Were, Emmanuel. "Kenya: Ecobank Makes Takeover Bid for EABS." *Business Daily (Nairobi),* January 27, 2008. Accessed October 17, 2010. http://allafrica.com/stories/200801280759.html.

Wessels, Vernon, and Eric Ombok. "Ecobank Says It Plans Africa's Biggest Stock Sale (Update3)." *Bloomberg,* August 20, 2008. Accessed October 30, 2010. http://www.bloomberg.com/apps/news?pid=newsarchive&sid=aj9tGNErIzR0&refer=africa.

"World Bank Lends $1.75 mln to Africa's Ecobank: IFC Loan to Help SME Lending in Impoverished Countries." *Reuters,* July 2, 2010. Accessed October 30, 2010. http://in.reuters.com/article/idINLDE6610MO20100702.

EG Systems LLC

30974 Santana Street
Hayward, California 94544
U.S.A.
Telephone: (408) 528-3000
Fax: (408) 528-3562
Web site: http://www.electroglas.com

Private Company
Founded: 1960 as Specialty Products
Sales: $45.4 million (2008)
NAICS: 333295 Semiconductor Machinery Manufacturing; 334413 Semiconductor and Related Device Manufacturing; 334419 Other Electronic Component Manufacturing

■ ■ ■

Semiconductor manufacturers worldwide depend on the wafer probing technologies of EG Systems, LLC. The company, formerly known as Electroglas, provides testing processes to examine the quality of semiconductor wafers and devices. This allows customers to improve their efficiency as well as the products they manufacture. Electroglas also offers software to help customers improve production yields of their chips.

More than half of this international company's sales are from outside the United States. Following several years of slow sales and financial challenges, Electroglas filed for Chapter 11 bankruptcy in 2009. Later that same year, it was purchased by private investors and renamed EG Systems LLC.

COMPANY FOUNDED: 1960

Specialty Products, a glass capillary producer, was founded in 1960 as a division of General Signal Corp. Before long, the company recognized the emergence of the computer age and shifted its focus to meet the rising need for wafer probing technology. As part of this change, the company also changed the name of this division to Electroglas. The first commercial prober used to test semiconductors was introduced by Electroglas in 1964. It was seven years before the first microprocessor was introduced.

General Signal Corp. later formed a new unit, known as the Semiconductor Assembly Factory Automation group, which included seven of the company's 13 semiconductor equipment operations, including Electroglas. The purpose of the organization was to integrate the equipment produced by General Signal's various operations and by other suppliers of equipment. The organization was to consist of representatives from each of the units, as well as several other employees. In theory, the group would establish standards for all of the company's semiconductor manufacturing equipment, as well as define its first set of integrated products to be offered.

SUCCESSES AND CHALLENGES: 1980–92

The first completely automated prober, used to analyze semiconductor wafers, was introduced in the early 1980s. It was called the 2001. The company continued to produce probers for nearly two decades and went on to sell almost 6,600 of the systems around the globe during those years. Another model, the 2010, was also introduced during this time. It used a robotic material handler to safely and efficiently process wafers.

Between 1986 and 1992, the company's 3001 model became the first prober in the world to handle 8-inch wafers. Also during this time, the Horizon 4060 and 4080 were the first of the company's EGCommander system software.

Despite the advanced products the company created, Electroglas was suffering. During this time the company was being "used 'as sort of a cash cow' to fund some of the less profitable West Coast companies in the semiconductor equipment group" of General Signal, according to *Electronic Business Buyer* in 1994. Neil Bonke, chairman and CEO of Electroglas at the time stated, "Electroglas suffered because its strategic issues were not the focus." He explained that Electroglas spent well below 10 percent of its budget on research and development, which was "sure death in the semiconductor equipment industry." As a result of this, the company's revenues and earnings decreased, despite the fact that industry revenues were increasing. General Signal's lack of emphasis on Electroglas' new products and the wrong marketing approach in Japan have also been blamed for the problems Electroglas faced during this period.

BECOMING A PUBLIC COMPANY

As a result of a broad plan to refocus General Signal, the company decided to sell off all of its integrated circuit production equipment operations. At the time, many in the field believed that the market for semiconductor equipment required a complete commitment from companies, and that trying to consolidate several product lines into a single company was not beneficial. One of the companies that was divested during this period was Electroglas, which had revenues of nearly $70 million at the time and was noted as General Signal's most financially successful division. According to *Electronic News*, Bonke said that Electroglas had "a profitable record, good market share, new products, and absolutely top-class customer relationships."

In 1993, following the decision to divest its semiconductor equipment operations, General Signal Corporation announced that its subsidiary Electroglas had filed with Securities and Exchange Commission for its initial public offering. Following the IPO, General Signal received gross proceeds in excess of $99 million, to be used to repay debts and for other corporate expenses.

INTERNATIONAL EXPANSION

The fourth quarter of 1994 showed record net sales for Electroglas, increasing 35 percent over the previous year to $30.7 million. Net income increased by 75 percent. The company showed increased sales within the United States, but a greater portion of the sales were in other countries. Forty seven percent of the total revenues for the year resulted from international sales, as compared to 33 percent in the previous year.

In order to meet the needs of its growing business in Singapore, Electroglas opened its Electroglas International Inc. facility there in 1995. At the time, the company had other satellite offices in Southeast Asia, including locations in Hong Kong, Korea, and Taiwan. The opening of these offices underscored the company's commitment to the Southeast Asia region.

EXPANDING PRODUCT OFFERINGS: 1997–2000

Electroglas acquired a yield management software manufacturing company, Knights Technology, in 1997. In an *Electronic News* article by Judy Erkanat, Electroglas CEO Curt Wozniak explained, "The semiconductor manufacturers are way behind in the use of software to manage yield information. Almost all of the companies have some kind of in-house software, but that in-house software is going the way of the dinosaur." He explained that his company would continue to pursue this type of acquisition. "We look at this as the beginning of our evolution." He also stated, "We believe Knights has pivotal yield management technology." At the time, it was predicted that the market served by Knights would be greater than $100 million within three years.

Over the next few years, Electroglas introduced a number of new products to the industry. In 1999 the company marketed a new prober on the market capable of exerting the exceptionally high probe loads needed to test multiple die and bumped wafers. Another product, the EG5 300, introduced the company in the 300mm market. The Horizon 4090f was introduced in 2000. It was an automatic film-frame prober used to test a single die after being cut (or ultra-thin wafers before the die

KEY DATES

1960: Specialty Products is founded as a division of General Signal Corp.

1964: Specialty Products is renamed Electroglas to reflect a change in company focus.

1993: General Signal divests Electroglas; Electroglas becomes a publicly traded company.

1991: Electroglas forms its EG Soft software division.

2009: Electroglas files for Chapter 11 bankruptcy.

were cut). It also tested for faulty semiconductor devices used for SmartCard and other telecommunication and computing products, before being assembled.

Electroglas also bought another software company, Statware, Inc., during 2000. The Oregon business provided Web-based software platforms that offered real-time access and data analysis from test equipment for its customers, which included Agilent Technologies.

NEW PRODUCTS AND A NEW DIVISION: 2001

The year 2001 proved to be significant for the company. Electroglas introduced several new products, including the EG4200e, which boasted lower levels of system noise and a Windows operating system that offered the option monitoring and control via the Internet. The QuickSilver inspection system was also introduced. This system identified and classified defects as small as 1 micron on wafers. The company's new 200mm Horizon 4090 micron Fast Probe system reduced die probe time by 40 percent, which allowed an increase in system throughput. The new, faster system improved rates to only 120 milliseconds between die.

Despite the introduction of these new systems, the third quarter revenues for 2001 decreased by 84 percent as compared to the same period for the previous year. According to the *Silicon Valley/San Jose Business Journal* in October 2001, Wozniak said, "The semiconductor equipment industry is currently experiencing the worst cyclical downturn in history." The company attributed this financial situation to the fact that customers drastically reduced the amount spent on new systems and service.

In November of that year, Electroglas formed its EG Soft division, which was dedicated to the company's software products. EG Soft incorporated "the develop-

ment and support organizations of Electroglas' existing software groups, including its soft floor automation group and subsidiaries Knight's Technology and Statware," according to *Electronic News*. Joe LaChapelle, the vice president of engineering for Electroglas, was tapped to serve as vice president and general manager of the new division. He explained, "Electroglas has spent time acquiring, building, and integrating a critical mass of data generations, collection and analysis software tools and applications. As a result, EG Soft is being launched with not just a vision and a road map, but is fully equipped to deliver collaborative process management capabilities today." He went on to say, "We're providing those capabilities with a cohesive software infrastructure that supports the semiconductor manufacturers' need for actionable information anywhere, anytime."

OVERSEAS EXPANSION AND REFOCUSED VISION: 2002–05

In anticipation of Southeast Asia and China becoming one of the fastest-growing areas in which the company's products were sold, Electroglas moved the manufacturing of its wafer probers from San Jose to Singapore in 2002. Some manufacturing continued in the California location, but the focus there was mainly on the development of new products.

In December of that year, the company continued its overseas expansion plans when it signed an exclusive agreement with Hakuto Co. Ltd. for the distribution of the full line of Electroglas' hardware products in Japan. Hakuto, an electronic equipment and industrial chemical distributor in that country, was already distributing Electroglas' inspection systems in Japan. The new agreement allowed Electroglas to increase its presence in that market.

During 2003 Electroglas altered its corporate strategy to refocus on wafer probers. Over the next two years, several new designs were introduced, representing significant advancements in the areas of design, automation, and performance. As part of this shift in focus, Electroglas sold two of its software product lines, Design for Manufacturing and Fab Solutions, in August 2003. These were purchased for $6 million in cash, as well as the assumption of some liabilities, by FEI. These, along with the company's Yield Manager and Merlin's Framework software, were the basis for a new division at FEI, which was staffed by some of Electroglas' employees who had worked on these product lines prior to their sale.

FINANCIAL CHALLENGES: 2006–09

Despite the company's positive feedback from customers, net sales for 2006 decreased by 30 percent from

2004, which the company blamed partially on customers' slow acceptance of some of the new products. Electroglas cited slow customer acceptance of its new products, as well as industry conditions, for weak sales worldwide from 2003 through 2008.

Net sales for 2007 were slightly higher than in 2006, and sales for 2008 did increase by about 2 percent over those for 2007. However, the company continued to report net losses annually. The company cited decreased volume of some its products and upgrades as the causes for this.

As a result of this financial downturn, in 2008 the company reduced its foreign workforce and closed its facility in Singapore. For the quarter ending in February 2009, net sales decreased by 81 percent as compared to the same period in the previous year. Electroglas stock was suspended in March 2009 then delisted from the NASDAQ in June of that year.

A NEW ERA: 2009 AND BEYOND

In July 2009 Electroglas filed for Chapter 11 Bankruptcy. The demand for semiconductor manufacturing equipment had decreased severely due to the global economic recession at the time. The filing followed months of efforts to decrease expenses, including reducing the workforce, salary cuts and mandatory time off for employees, as well as other measures to reduce other expenses unrelated to labor costs.

In October Electroglas was acquired by EG Systems, LLC, a private financial group which was formed for the purpose of acquiring Electroglas' prober business assets. The acquisition was approved by the Delaware Bankruptcy Court in the same month and included all business assets, the name, and trademarks of the company. Some of Electroglas' motion control automation technology (MCAT) assets, inventory, and intellectual property was sold to FormFactor, Inc., earlier in the same month, in a separate transaction. Raj Kaul became president and CEO of EG Systems. The *Internet*

Wire quoted Kaul's statement about the transaction: "Foremost, we will be bringing the company's focus back to concentrate on our worldwide customer base, which understandably was unclear during the turbulent financial times for the company and the industry in general."

Postbankruptcy, EG Systems still faced the challenges inherent in the semiconductor equipment manufacturer market. However, if consumer spending levels were to increase in the 2010s, heightened demand for new electronics may help EG Systems survive and thrive during the decade.

Diane Milne

PRINCIPAL COMPETITORS

KLA-Tencor Corporation; Tokyo Electron Limited; Tokyo Seimitsu Co., Ltd.

FURTHER READING

"Electroglas Combines Software Efforts, Forms EG Soft." *Electronic News 1991,* 47, no. 46 (2001): 28.

"Electroglas Inc. Files Registration Statement for Initial Public Offering of Common Stock of Electroglas Unit." *PR Newswire,* May 6, 1993: 506NY094.

"Electroglas Inc. Wafer Business Assets Have Been Sold to EG Systems, LLC." *Internet Wire,* October 23, 2009.

"Electroglas Opens New Customer Service Facility in Singapore." *Business Wire,* May 2, 1995: 5020234.

"Electroglas Reports Record Fourth Quarter Results." *Business Wire* February 2, 1995: 2020019.

Erkanat, Judy. "Electroglas to Buy Knights for $30m." *Electronic News 1991* 43, no. 2159 (1997): 8.

Feil, S. "General Signal Forms Automation Group." *Electronic News* 30, no. 1523 (1984): 92.

Holden, Daniel. "General Signal: 'Adios' to IC Production Units." *Electronic News 1991* 39, no. 1946 (1993): 1+.

Loffredo, Susan. "General Signal Learns High Tech the Hard Way." *Electronic Business Buyer,* September 1994, 61+.

"Revenues Plunge for Electroglas." *Silicon Valley/San Jose Business Journal* 19, no. 26 (2001): 24.

eLoyalty Corporation

150 Field Drive
Suite 250
Lake Forest, Illinois 60045
U.S.A.
Telephone: (877) 235-6925
Fax: (847) 582-7001
Web site: http://www.eloyalty.com

Public Company
Founded: 1999
Employees: 431 (2009)
Sales: $101.6 million (2009)
Stock Exchanges: NASDAQ
Ticker Symbol: ELOY
NAICS: 541611 Administrative Management and
General Management Consulting Services

■ ■ ■

A management consulting, systems integration, and managed services firm, eLoyalty Corporation uses analytics and advanced technologies to help clients achieve customer loyalty. eLoyalty offers services with names like Behavioral Analytics, Integrated Contact Solutions (ICS), and Consulting Services. Managed services revenue is recurring annuity revenue from longer-term contracts, generally one to five years. Consulting service revenue is typically on a shorter-term basis. The company also has product revenue, which it generates by reselling third-party hardware and software.

In addition to improving the reliability of call recording, the Behavioral Analytic business unit applies human behavioral modeling to analyze and improve customer interactions. The goal of this managed analytics service is to turn unstructured customer interaction content into structured actionable business insights. The service is used for all major business contact center applications such as customer services, sales, collections, and care management.

Behavioral Analytics begins by gathering large amounts of unstructured customer interactions inputs, from social media sites on the Web to phone conversations. This data is used to identify previously unknown patterns across a huge number and variety of customer interactions. This data can then be used to drive change and produce results. For example, the service can automatically measure customer satisfaction and agent performance on every call, identify and understand customer personality, improve rapport between customer and agent, and reduce call handling time while improving customer satisfaction. Clients for this service include health care financial services, utilities, and pharmaceutical companies.

Integrated Contact Solutions focuses on improving a company's customer experience involving contact centers, the Web, and speech self-service. Focusing on a company's applications and communications networks, eLoyalty employs advanced voice and data technologies, customer-focused business designs, engineered call and work flow processes, integration of disparate systems, and technical operations management. The company's Consulting Services division focuses on a holistic approach toward integrating people, technology, and processes. The mission is to help its clients achieve sustainable competitive advantage by creating customer

COMPANY PERSPECTIVES

The eLoyalty Corporationrsquo;s mission is to help customers achieve breakthrough results with revolutionary analytics and advanced technologies that drive ongoing business growth and improvement. The company has a long and deep history of customer experience and technology innovation. Shared values are the heart and soul of the culture and work environment at eLoyalty. Our values invest meaning in what we do and how we do it.

experiences on the Internet or other areas of customer contact to improve business results.

In addition to providing services to state and local government and federal agencies, eLoyalty clients include several private enterprises, including those in the insurance industry. eLoyalty generates approximately $100 million in revenues annually and operates primarily, but not solely, in the United States and Canada. In addition to its corporate headquarters in Lake Forest, Illinois, the company has branches in Austin, Texas, and Edina, Minnesota.

COMPANY FOUNDING AND EARLY YEARS: 1994–2000

Kelly Conway, president and CEO of eLoyalty, started the enterprise in 1994 as a division of the then publicly traded Technology Solutions Company (TSC) based in Chicago. Founded in 1988, TSC provided technology-enabled solutions to clients in the health care, financial services, manufacturing, and retail industries. Conway joined the company in November 1993 as senior vice president.

The new division created by Conway was called Enterprise Customer Management and started with only five employees. Over the next six years the division grew dramatically and became a wholly owned subsidiary of TSC. During that time, Conway assumed the position of executive vice president in July 1995 and then group president in October 1998.

In May 1999 Conway led the spin off of eLoyalty from TSC. eLoyalty became a publicly traded company in 2000, after earning $146 million in revenues in 1999. Although eLoyalty began as a consulting firm, Conway would head the successful repositioning of the company to also become known as a managed services company.

FOCUSING ON ATTAINING CUSTOMER LOYALTY

As the name of the company indicates, eLoyalty has been primarily concerned with helping its clients grow and maintain a loyal customer base. "Our company is all about loyalty," eLoyalty's senior vice president Craig Lashmet noted in a 2000 article in *Insurance & Technology*. "All about understanding who your customer is, and which ones you should be attracting, and how you can get the absolute highest relationship and profitability yield from that profit segment."

The company quickly became known for its pioneering efforts in contact center and customer relationship management (CRM) systems as a way to assist its clients in building customer loyalty. For example, in 1999, eLoyalty offered a Loyalty Suite that enabled users to integrate the Web with traditional CRM channels. The system allowed users to handle customer interactions consistently across key areas, including the Internet and e-mail. In addition, the suite included the Loyalty Outcome Manager and Loyalty Warehouse products to measure and report customer-related information.

In a January 2000 article in *Target Marketing*, eLoyalty's vice president of marketing, Julie Fitzpatrick, commented on the importance of developing loyal customers. "It's financially beneficial to build a loyal relationship with customers," Fitzpatrick said. "You sell more, upsell and cross-sell more, have more wallet share, and are able to sell them other things because you know them better." Fitzpatrick went on to point out: "You can do business more profitably with these customers by driving them to more personalized self-service more effectively."

SEEKING A MARKET ADVANTAGE

As a consulting service, eLoyalty found itself going head-to-head with a wide array of competitors, which included the Big Five consulting firms, IBM's consulting services, and a host of smaller consulting companies. eLoyalty saw its advantage over these over companies as residing in its comprehensive, one-stop services. In the *Insurance & Technology* article, Lashmet noted that the company's wide range of diverse services made it a competitor with a lot of companies but that eLoyalty offered a more complete approach than them.

The company was offering a total solution that included e-CRM strategy, process design, and technical aides. In addition, eLoyalty emphasized to its customers that it was not the ultimate solution but rather an enabler that helped companies use their services with strategic intent. As a result, the company established what it called the "active change and learning" program,

KEY DATES

1992: Kelly Conway starts the precursor to eLoyalty Corporation, Enterprise Customer Management, as a division of Technology Solutions Company.

1999: eLoyalty is spun off from Technology Solutions.

2000: eLoyalty becomes a publicly traded company on the NASDAQ.

2003: Company establishes the Behavioral Analytics concept.

2010: eLoyalty experiences a decrease in consulting services while managed services increase.

or training and consensus building, to interact with its clients.

Lashmet remarked in *Insurance & Technology* that more and more companies were realizing the need for their services. "All these organizations are beginning to realize that it's not the product that is really driving the buying decision," said Lashmet. "It's whether they are being more customer-centric and able to respond to the preferences—the values—the customer has to that company that they're doing business with."

BUILDING COLLABORATIONS AND PARTNERHSIPS

eLoyalty's first two years of operation as an independent company listed on NASDAQ featured collaborations and partnerships as the company sought to establish a firm foothold in business management consulting and systems integration. In May 2000 eLoyalty joined forces with Servigistics, which provided Web-based planning and forecasting logistics solutions. The agreement resulted in Servigistics' Web-based software becoming part of eLoyalty's Field Service & Logistics solution. The serviced focused on managing parts inventories and shipments with desired service levels while minimizing inventory costs and investment.

Another key alliance was made with Lucent Technologies to deliver a voice over Internet protocol (VOIP) integrated business solution, enabling eLoyalty to incorporate Lucent's VOIP technology features. Nortel Networks also agreed to include its complete e-CRM software in eLoyalty's electronic customer relationship management offering. The company entered into a worldwide partnership with Kana Communica-

tions, Inc., in which the two companies shared their respective technologies and expertise. By October 2000 eLoyalty had also formed a partnership with Epiphany, Inc., a provider of intelligent customer interaction software.

FACING AN EARLY CRISIS

Although in February 2001, eLoyalty announced stronger than expected fourth quarter earnings, by September of that year the company was facing a crisis. In June eLoyalty's largest client, Agilent Technologies Inc., severed ties with eLoyalty. Furthermore, the NASDAQ was threatening to delist the company, whose stock had fallen to around the 50-cent range. eLoyalty was also facing a credit crunch. Having nearly used up a $10 million line of credit, the company was in danger of violating the loan's covenants. "That's a sorry fall for a former star performer," wrote a contributor to *Crain's Chicago Business.*

eLoyalty was facing a potential fight for it young life. A major problem was that eLoyalty had only $700,000 of credit left of its $10 million unsecured bank loan. The company was required to maintain a tangible net worth as a company of $70 million. Although eLoyalty still exceeded that threshold by about $17 million, concerns were that losses could continue to occur and the bank could call in the loan before the end of the year.

To infuse cash and preserve its NASDAQ listing, in December 2001 eLoyalty made what a *Crain's Chicago Business* contributor called the "odd stock move of the month." The company proposed what appeared to be a contradictory move, namely to increase its common stock to 500 million shares from 100 million to cover a financing deal and then reduce the available common stock to 50 million shares through a 1-for-10 reverse stock split. The goal was to get $25 million cash infusion.

On December 20, 2001, eLoyalty announced that it had raised approximately $23.3 million. Part of the cash influx came from a private placement of convertible preferred stock purchased by funds affiliated with Technology Crossover Ventures and Sutter Hill Ventures. Also contributing was a concurrent rights offering to eLoyalty stockholders. The new funds helped eLoyalty avoid a credit crunch and bought the company time to rebuild its respected niche in managing customer relations.

KEEPING PACE AND MOVING AHEAD: 2002–05

In eLoyalty's CRM market, keeping pace with the rapid rate of technological innovation and change was essential. New products and services were continuously coming to the fore, and eLoyalty was dedicated to rapidly learning, using, and integrating software and other technology developed by third parties. The company continued to make alliances with other companies, such as Aspect Communications Corporation in 2002, with eLoyalty deploying Aspect's contact server solution for its business clients. Another major move was to form a partnership with Performix Technologies, a leader in enterprise performance management. Together, the companies set out to establish the first combined customer and employee management solution for contact centers.

In 2003, using an extensive set of proprietary models, software tools, and implementation methodologies, eLoyalty established a new set of offerings called Customer Connections. This service was designed to help eLoyalty's clients positively influence customer behavior by tailoring interactions to the specific personality traits of their customers.

In 2004 eLoyalty acquired nearly the complete net assets and business of Interlate, Inc., a provider of customer analytics solutions. eLoyalty agreed to pay approximately $4.9 million in cash plus the value of working capital at closing. Business continued to grow as the following year the company announced an agreement to provide services to Vodafone Ireland.

IMPROVING BEHAVIORAL ANALYTICS

By 2006 the company, which had never operated at a profit, remained focused on accelerating growth and improving its business model. It was focused primarily on the emerging market niches of behavioral analytics and converged IP for contact centers. The company also achieved a number of milestones in the first quarter of 2006, including signing a multiyear enterprise license and support contract to provide its behavioral analytic solution to Uniprise, a UnitedHealth Group company.

Since first developing behavioral analytics software in 2003, the company continuously sought to further develop and improve the program. Throughout 2008 the company announced various improvements to its behavioral analytics software. For example, one new version provided insights into customer attitude, customer service representative performance, and business process efficiency. The software also included the ability to automatically create alerts to identify customers who had significant customer service issues.

In May 2008 the company announced that its behavioral analytics service had surpassed 50 million analyzed calls, 150 million recorded calls, and 1,000

services in its Managed Services infrastructure. The milestones reflected the company's continued growth as well as market acceptance of Behavioral Analytics as a managed service. Overall, the company had invested more than $25 million in the behavioral analytics managed service.

LOOKING FORWARD IN A TOUGH ECONOMY

Like many companies, eLoyalty had a difficult 2008 due to the economic recession, with revenue decreasing from $102.1 million in 2007 to $91.2 million in 2008. However, one year later the company rebounded fairly well, posting a 2009 revenue ($101.6 million) quite close to where it had been in 2007. Much of the increased revenue resulted from substantially higher behavioral analytics service revenue. The company, however, did experience a decrease in consulting services revenue, down to $30.0 million in 2009 from $35.7 million in 2008. eLoyalty noted that the downturn in the economy had led to reduced spending by many of its consulting services clients. This pattern held true for most of 2010 as well, with revenue from managed services increasing while consulting revenues declined.

Despite not realizing a profit in its 11 years of existence as a separate publicly traded company, eLoyalty saw 2009 and 2010 as years of improved financial performance in a difficult economic environment. The company grew its cash balance and recognized record managed services revenues. As the company looked toward the future it expected to see further improvement in its profit and loss bottom line.

David Petechuk

PRINCIPAL DIVISIONS

Behavioral Analytics Service; Consulting Services; Integrated Contact Solutions (ICS).

PRINCIPAL COMPETITORS

Aspect Software, Inc.; Genesys Telecommunications Laboratories Inc.; NICE Systems Ltd.; SAS Institute Inc.

FURTHER READING

"eLoyalty Aims to Provide One-Stop E-CRM Solutions." *Insurance & Technology,* June 2000, 75.

"Steps to Create a Loyalty Solution." *Target Marketing,* January 2000, 24.

"Tech Watch: Online Publisher Eyes Nanotechnology World." *Crain's Chicago Business,* December 3, 2001, 6.

"Tech Watch: This Tech Consultancy Tests Limits of Loyalty." *Crain's Chicago Business,* September 3, 2001, 6.

Energy Future Holdings Corporation

1601 Bryan Street
Dallas, Texas 75201
U.S.A.
Telephone: (214) 812-4600
Toll Free: (800) 818-6132
Fax: (214) 812-7077
Web site: http://www.energyfutureholdings.com

Private Company
Founded: 1945 (as Texas Utilities Company)
Employees: 9,030 (2009)
Revenues: $9.55 billion (2009)
NAICS: 221112 Fossil Fuel Electric Power Generation; 221113 Nuclear Electric Power Generation; 221119 Other Electric Power Generation; 221122 Electric Power Distribution

■ ■ ■

Formerly Texas Utilities Corporation, Energy Future Holdings Corporation (EFH) is a privately held holding company with the three principal subsidiaries of Texas Utilities Energy, Luminant, and Oncor. The largest of these is Texas Utilities Energy (TXU Energy). TXU Energy produces and distributes electricity to more than two million customers in all major sections of Texas. Subsidiary Luminant operates power plants and mines that provide over 18,300 megawatts of energy generation. The company's facilities extend across the north-central region of the state. Managed by an independent board of directors, Oncor is a regulated electric distribution and transmission company. Energy Future Holdings (EFH) is a majority owner in Oncor, but the company does not manage Oncor.

EARLY HISTORY

Texas Utilities was formed in 1945 as a holding company for Dallas Power & Light Company (DP&L), Texas Electric Service Company (TESCO), and Texas Power & Light Company (TP&L). DP&L had been formed in 1917, TESCO in 1929, and TP&L in 1912, while predecessors of these companies dated back as far as the 1880s. Each company had its own electricity generation and distribution system.

Before the formation of Texas Utilities, DP&L had been a subsidiary of Electric Power & Light Company, while TESCO and TP&L had been subsidiaries of American Power & Light Company. Both parent companies, in turn, were subsidiaries of Electric Bond & Share Company, which had been set up by General Electric Company in 1905 to finance electrical power systems and form operating companies.

These holding companies were required to divest themselves of their utility operations under the Public Utility Holding Company Act of 1935. To that end, under an order of the Securities and Exchange Commission, Texas Utilities was formed in 1945 to acquire and run DP&L, TESCO, and TP&L. At the time, the utilities had combined revenues of $40.4 million, with about 427,000 electricity customers.

As the population and industry of Texas grew, so did the utilities. Sales surpassed $100 million in the mid-1950s, $200 million by 1960, and $400 million by

COMPANY PERSPECTIVES

Energy Future Holdings' vision is to be recognized, through its operating businesses, as a leader in the energy industry and an enabler of economic development and social progress by providing safe, reliable, affordable and environmentally sustainable power.

1969. During the 1960s, the number of customers grew to more than one million.

While D&L, TESCO, and TP&L retained their own identities, they often combined their efforts for acquisition of fuel and construction of power plants. Their parent company formed other subsidiaries to meet these needs, such as Texas Utilities Fuel Company, established in 1970 to provide natural gas to the utilities. Other subsidiaries formed during the 1970s included Chaco Energy Company, focusing on the production and delivery of coal and other fuels to the utilities, and Basic Resources Inc., with the purpose of developing additional energy sources and technology.

EXPANDING RESOURCES IN THE 1970S AND 1980S

At the beginning of the 1970s, Texas Utilities, like other utility operators in Texas, depended almost wholly on natural gas to run its electricity-generating plants. During the decade, as natural gas became increasingly scarce in Texas, the company turned to lignite, an inexpensive type of coal it already had in reserve. By 1975 Texas Utilities was meeting 25 percent of its fuel needs with lignite and was continuing to acquire lignite reserves. Texas Utilities won praise for its foresight in turning to this fuel, and its chairman and chief executive officer, T. L. Austin Jr., was named top utility executive for 1978 by *Financial World.* Even environmentalists approved of Austin and his company. Howard Saxton, chairman of the Lone Star Sierra Club, told *Financial World* in June 1979 that Austin represented "the good side of an industry that has been under continuous attack."

Texas Utilities also looked to nuclear power to reduce its use of natural gas. Its Comanche Peak nuclear plant, about 35 miles southwest of Fort Worth, was originally scheduled to begin operation in 1980. As was the case with many other utilities' nuclear plants, however, Comanche Peak had numerous delays and cost escalations, which Austin blamed on design changes ordered by the Nuclear Regulatory Commission (NRC).

By 1983 the plant was still not in operation, and its cost had risen from $787 million to $3.4 billion.

On the positive side, by 1983 Texas Utilities was using natural gas for only 45 percent of its fuel needs, with lignite supplying almost all of the remainder. Revenues had surpassed $3 billion, its earnings were rising steadily, and its credit rating was the highest possible. In 1984 the company reorganized, with each of the operating utilities becoming a division of a new subholding company, TU Electric. At that time Texas Utilities Mining Company, another subsidiary, took on the job of providing lignite to TU Electric's plants.

NUCLEAR START-UP PROBLEMS PERSIST

Comanche Peak continued to encounter rising costs and extended delays. In 1985 its estimated total cost was revised to $5.46 billion. Because of studies and inspections mandated by the NRC and the Atomic Safety Licensing Board, Comanche Peak's first unit was expected to go into operation in mid-1987 and the second about six months later. These dates passed without start-up of the units, however. By 1987 the NRC had identified a backlog of 20,000 problems the unit needed to correct.

In addition to regulatory hurdles, the plant was subject to continuing opposition by groups leery of the plant's safety and economic viability. One such group, Citizens Association for Sound Energy (CASE), had questioned the plant's safety numerous times during its construction. Juanita Ellis, a leader of the group, found that TU Electric employees who had made safety complaints had been fired. A total of 50 such employees sued the company.

TU Electric then took an unusual approach, deciding to negotiate with Ellis and the whistle-blowing employees. William G. Counsil, an executive vice-president of TU Electric, began meeting with Ellis in 1986 and providing her with information she requested. The NRC had certified CASE as an intervenor, with legal authority to raise questions and introduce evidence pertaining to the licensing of Comanche Peak. Until Counsil had begun meeting with Ellis, however, it had been difficult for CASE to obtain any TU Electric documents or to be taken seriously by the utility. In 1988 Ellis agreed to end her opposition to the licensing of Comanche Peak, and the utility made her a member of the plant's independent safety review committee. TU Electric also acknowledged the plant's past safety problems and paid $4.5 million to reimburse CASE for its expenses and $5.5 million to settle with the employees who had sued. The lavishness of the settle-

KEY DATES

1945: Texas Utilities (TXU) is founded as a holding company for three utilities.

1970: Subsidiary Texas Utilities Fuel Company created to supply natural gas to TXU operations.

1984: Subsidiary Texas Utilities Mining Company created to supply lignite coal to TXU operations.

1990: Years behind schedule, ComanchePeak nuclear plant begins electricity production.

2000: Company acquires all outstanding stock for Fort Bend Communications, Incorporated.

2007: Investors take TXU private in a leveraged buyout. Energy Future Holdings Corporation merges with Texas Holdings.

2008: John Young named company CEO and president.

2010: Energy Future Holdings Corporation completes its two-unit power plant in Robertson County, Texas.

ment was unprecedented in the history of U.S. nuclear energy.

Comanche Peak's first unit finally went into operation in August 1990, with a capability of producing 1,150 megawatts of electricity. The second unit was scheduled for startup in 1993. Overall, Texas Utilities had put more than $9 billion into the nuclear plant. TU Electric's use of lignite and nuclear energy had greatly reduced its dependence on natural gas. In 1990 TU Electric generated 44.4 percent of its power with lignite, 37.7 percent with natural gas, 3.9 percent with the nuclear unit (which was in use only part of the year), and 0.2 percent with oil. The remaining 13.8 percent was power purchased from other utilities.

In 1990 the utility had record electricity sales of 84 billion kilowatt hours, up 2.2 percent from 1989. It also had record hourly peak demand of 18 million kilowatts on August 30, 1990. This also was 2.2 percent more than the previous record, set in August 1988.

STRUGGLING FOR GROWTH: 1990–99

In January 1990 TU Electric requested a 10.2 percent rate increase, its first since 1984, from the Public Utility Commission (PUC) of Texas. The PUC allowed the utility to begin collecting this amount in August of that year. However, late in 1991 the PUC ordered the utility to write off $1.38 billion of its investment in Comanche Peak. PUC staff members had questioned some of the expenditures on the nuclear plant. The ordered write-off meant that, after accounting and tax adjustments, Texas Utilities would have to subtract $1 billion from a year's net income. This produced a net loss for 1991 of $410 million. The posting of such a loss rendered the company unable to raise capital through debt issues or preferred stock for at least a year.

Comanche Peak's second unit finally began commercial operation in the summer of 1993. When the unit went on line, TU imposed a 15 percent rate increase on its electric customers. This added as much as $11 a month to the average residential consumer's bill. Meanwhile TU began to look for expansion opportunities. In 1995 the company paid $65 million for Southwestern Electric Service Company. It also bought a 20 percent stake in PCS PrimeCo, a wireless telecommunications firm. This move cost the company $200 million. The next year TU bought the Lone Star Gas Co. and Lone Star Pipelines from ENSERCH Corp. for $1.7 billion. This increased TU's ability to produce and deliver natural gas. Texas Utilities also began its overseas expansion by buying an Australian electric utility, Eastern Energy Limited, for $1.5 billion.

The reason for the sudden burst of acquisition activity was that new laws deregulating the power industry threatened to bring TU more competition. Fearing that changes might mean a loss of its traditional business, the company aimed to break new ground. Not only did the company become bigger, it also got involved in telecommunications and overseas operations. After buying the share in PCS PrimeCo, TU went on to purchase another telecommunications entity, a privately held firm called Lufkin-Conroe Communications Company, in 1997. Lufkin-Conroe, based in Lufkin, Texas, was one of the state's largest phone companies, with annual revenue of close to $100 million. What apparently interested TU most was that Lufkin-Conroe served about 40,000 customers of TU Electric with local telephone service. TU hoped to take advantage of the customer overlap by offering a complete package of phone and energy use. Other utility companies around the country had been arranging similar deals in joint ventures or purchases of telecommunications businesses.

In 1998 TU offered to buy a large British utility company, the Energy Group PLC, for $6.9 billion. The Energy Group was one of 12 regional electric utilities in England, serving more than three million customers. It also owned Peabody Coal, one of the world's largest coal producers. The Energy Group was one of the last remaining utilities still in British hands after privatization of the industry began in 1990. Its assets were valued at $14 billion, with 1996 revenue at around $7.3 billion. It was considered quite a prize, and TU's offer started a bidding war with another interested U.S. utility, PacifiCorp of Portland, Oregon. After a series of offers and counteroffers, British utility regulators ordered a sealed bid, and TU won, paying $7.4 billion for the Energy Group. The enormous price was considered worthwhile, as international expansion was key to TU's business strategy. TU immediately announced that Peabody Coal was up for sale.

TEXAS LEGISLATURE CREATES RETAIL COMPETITION

The passing of Senate Bill 7 by the Texas legislature in 1999 restructured the state's electric industry, thereby increasing competition for retail customers amongst electric companies. Senator David Sibley championed the bill. Sibley said the bill was designed to help Texas avoid energy pricing and capacity issues that California faced. To position itself for the change and to expand its markets, Energy Future Holdings Corporation (EFH) acquired Fort Bend Communications in 2000. That same year the firm formed a joint venture with Pinnacle one, a telecommunications company. However, these relationships would prove to be short.

During 2002 EFH experienced some ups and downs. Texas' electric companies opened to competition on January 1, 2002. While competition opened in the United States, EFH shut down its European facilities due to mounting financial debt. Efforts to maintain a global presence were short-lived, and the company wrote off more than $3.9 billion in losses. The company then restructured and focused on increasing its liquidity and strengthening its credit. EFH's efforts to restructure included selling a branch of its Australian business, TKU Fuel, and TKU Gas. The company also exited the telecommunications business after less than five years in the market. In EFH's 2003 shareholder report, the company stated that left the telecommunications market in order to "focus on the company's core business in Texas and Australia." Money from the sales of the telecommunications businesses was used to pay off company debts.

When Hurricane Katrina struck the Gulf Coast (particularly Louisiana) in late August 2005, EFH was forced to significantly increase its energy output to meet the demands of Texas' growing population after thousands of Louisiana residents relocated to Texas. On September 14, 2005, EFH and the Texas Public Utility Commission agreed that the company would not request a change in its service prices until the first week of October 2005. The purpose of the delay was to ease the financial burden made on Texas residents post-Hurricane Katrina.

In 2007 EFH became a privately held company. Investors at various firms, including Goldman Sachs Capital Partners, Kohlberg Kravis Roberts & Company, and Texas Pacific Group led the charge on the private equity acquisition. At deal's end, TXU found itself rolled into EFH. The new company's three principal subsidiaries became Luminant (a business that focused on power generation), TXU Energy (a retail electric provider), and Oncor (a regulated electric delivery business). In 2008 John F. Young, former executive vice president of finance and markets at Exelon and a graduate of the U.S. Naval Academy in Annapolis, was named EFH's new president and CEO.

EFH positioned its market identity and electricity generation functions under Luminant, a business that generated 2,300 megawatts of nuclear energy, 7,217 megawatts of coal or lignite energy, and 8,002 megawatts of natural gas in Texas in 2009. By that same time, EFH's subsidiary Oncor had installed about 660,000 upgraded digital meters throughout Texas. Integrated energy readings and enhanced customer billing reports were key results realized after the digital meters were installed. Oncor expected to spend an additional $300 million through 2012 to improve customer electricity demands. Some of the money would be used to install more than two million additional digital meters.

In June 2010 William Reilly, a EFH board member, was named co-chairman on a commission created by the White House to investigate the BP oil spill. According to an article by Elizabeth Souder, published in the *Dallas Morning News* on June 2, 2010, President Barack Obama directed Reilly to "follow the facts wherever they lead, without fear, or favor."

In face of continued competition in 2010, EFH bolstered its green initiatives. Already the top purchaser of wind energy in the state of Texas, EFH also sought ways to conserve electricity through technology upgrades and conservation initiatives. With Texas one of the fastest-growing states in the country, it seemed likely that demand would remain high and that the influx of new customers would enable EFH to weather any losses in demand caused by competition.

Roger W. Rouland; Trudy Ring and Donald R. Stabile Updated, A. Woodward; Rhonda Campbell

PRINCIPAL SUBSIDIARIES

TXU Energy Retail Company LLC; Luminant Energy Company LLC; Oncor Electric Delivery Company LLC (80%).

PRINCIPAL COMPETITORS

American Electric Power Company, Inc.; CenterPoint Energy, Inc.; GenOnEnergy, Inc.

FURTHER READING

Aronson, Geoffrey. "The Co-Opting of CASE." *Nation,* December 4, 1989, pp. 678–82.

Kranhold, Kathryn. "Bidding War Erupts for Energy Group." *Wall Street Journal,* March 3, 1998, p. A3.

Levy, Robert. "Texas' Triple-A Utility." *Dun's Business Month,* June 1983.

Mason, Todd, and Corie Brown. "Juanita Ellis: Antinuke Saint or Sellout?" *Business Week,* October 24, 1988.

McKanic, Patricia Ann. "Texas Utilities Taking a Charge of $1 Billion." *Wall Street Journal,* August 9, 1991, p. A3.

O'Brian, Bridget. "Texas Utilities Posts Big Loss in 3rd Quarter." *Wall Street Journal,* October 28, 1991, p. A7.

Salpukas, Agis. "Texas Utilities Wins Fight for Energy Group." *New York Times,* May 1, 1998, p. D1.

Souder, Elizabeth. "Head of Commission to Investigate BP Oil Spill Also Sits on Energy Future Holdings Board." *Dallas Morning News,* June 2, 2010.

The Film Department
Holdings, Inc.

■

232 North Cañon Drive
Beverly Hills, California 90210
U.S.A.
Telephone: (424) 253-1100
Fax: (424) 253-1101
Web site: http://www.filmdept.com

Private Company
Founded: 2007
Employees: 23 (2009)
Revenues: $40.32 million (2009)
NAICS: 512110 Motion Picture and Video Production

■ ■ ■

The Film Department Holdings, Inc., is an independent motion picture company that finances and produces star-driven commercial films. The Film Department's goal has been to produce six motion pictures each year with budgets between $10 million and $45 million. From its inception, industry experts have compared The Film Department to the much-larger Miramax because of its concentration on wide-appeal, Oscar-worthy commercial films that have the potential to significantly exceed their production budgets.

THE RISE OF INDIE FILMS

Independent films are motion pictures produced without funding from a commercial film studio. The independent, or "indie," film industry first gained attention in the early 1920s, when the London Film Society was formed in order to recognize artistic achievement in filmmaking. Soon afterwards the concept reached Hollywood, where low-budget art house films, those movies that were aimed at niche rather than mass audiences, were screened in small theaters. Although this trend in entertainment lost momentum during World War II, postwar audiences were interested in films that explored society and the human experience, and independent films continued to enjoy a reputation of creative excellence.

In 1978 the independent film industry received widespread recognition when the Utah/U.S. Film Festival, which featured a film contest for unknown U.S. filmmakers, was founded in Salt Lake City, Utah. After the involvement of popular actor Robert Redford propelled the festival into the national spotlight, the event was renamed the Sundance Film Festival in 1985. It moved to Park City, Utah, and became a three-day event. Top studio executives took notice, as did Hollywood actors, and many increasingly sought roles in independent films.

By the middle of the first decade of the 21st century, indie films were being produced not only by small companies but also by the six major U.S. movie studios. By then 20th Century Fox, Walt Disney Studios, Paramount, Columbia, Universal Pictures, and Warner Bros. had all established their own independent film distribution subsidiaries. These divisions, such as Fox Searchlight or Sony's Screen Gems, concentrated primarily on star-driven art house motion pictures or genre films with midrange budgets of around $50 million or less. Whereas independent companies had historically played to smaller audiences, the "independent" studios backed by the big six production companies enjoyed major commercial box office success.

Even so, true independent production companies remained key players in the motion picture scene, especially as improvements in technology allowed films to be made on shoestring budgets. By 2008, however, the independent film industry was experiencing major setbacks in the midst of a worldwide economic downturn. Large commercial studios shut down or scaled back their independent divisions, advertising costs skyrocketed, and a glut of movies flooded the market. Additionally, the entire movie industry was competing against the video game, pay television, and home video markets. As a result, indie film companies in particular were struggling like never before, with a number of them, if they even remained in production, laying off employees and defaulting on loans. These were the kinds of challenges The Film Department faced from the time it was established.

THE FILM DEPARTMENT TEAM

Cofounders Mark Gill and Neil Sacker, both well-established and highly successful veterans of Hollywood's motion picture industry, saw such challenges as opportunities and in June 2007 announced the launch of The Film Department. Gill and Sacker had first worked together at Miramax in 1995. Between them, the two men brought over 40 years of experience to The Film Department partnership, with a combined 43 Academy Awards for films they had helped make during their careers. Gill assumed the position of chairman and CEO of The Film Department, while Sacker served as vice chairman and chief operating officer.

In the 1980s Gill worked in the marketing department at Columbia/Tri-Star Pictures. After being named a vice president in the publicity department in 1988, he handled the violent backlash sparked by the 1991 opening of *Boyz N the Hood* and was promoted to senior vice president for publicity and field operations that same year. In 1994 Gill took a job with Miramax, where he worked for eight years until moving on in 2003 to become founder and president of Warner Independent Pictures. While there, Gill acquired the documentary

March of the Penguins, which won an Oscar for Best Documentary and earned $129.4 million worldwide.

As chief operating officer of the Yari Film Group in the four years before his venture into The Film Department with Gill, Sacker oversaw the business, financial, and legal affairs of the company. It was during his tenure at the Yari Film Group that the critically acclaimed films *Crash* and *The Illusionist* debuted, both of which were commercially successful as well. Prior to that, Sacker worked at Miramax, where he was the head of business and legal affairs, and at Warner Bros. Pictures as theatrical counsel.

Other key players in The Film Department's operations were Robert Katz, Bernd Stephan, and Daniel Stutz, all of whom previously worked as part of the Yari Film Group. Before joining The Film Department, Katz served as executive vice president of production for the Yari Film Group, where he headed the production of 18 films. Known in the motion picture industry as a uniquely creative producer who could work within a prescribed budget, as well as attract high-profile talent, Katz's role at The Film Department was president of production. With a background in finance and tax consultation services, Stephan served as the Yari Film Group's senior vice president and controller, developing and managing the financial structures necessary for the creation of such movies as *The Matador.* Upon becoming a member of The Film Department, Stephan assumed the position of CFO. Legal representation for The Film Department was handled by attorney Stutz, who was the senior vice president of business and legal affairs at the Yari Film Group before accepting the position of executive vice president of business and legal affairs with The Film Department.

EARLY ACQUISITIONS: 2007–09

Gill and Sacker had procured $200 million in financing to launch The Film Department. Within the first five years, they projected, The Film Department's total production value would reach $725 million. Their proposed schedule, however, suffered a setback due to the 2007-08 Writers Guild of America strike, which left The Film Department short on scripts and projects going into 2008. Despite this situation, the studio was able to close several important deals during its first year of operations. In March 2008, for instance, the company paid a mid-six-figure amount in a bidding war for *Galahad,* a retelling of the Arthurian legend. Gill and Sacker were attracted to the universality of the well-known story of King Arthur and his knights, believing that the tale would appeal to a global audience and thus boost international sales.

```
╔══════════════════════════════════════╗
║                                      ║
║           KEY DATES                  ║
║              ━■━                     ║
║                                      ║
║  2007:  The Film Department is founded. ║
║  2008:  The studio wins a bidding war for Galahad, a ║
║         movie based on Arthurian legend. ║
║  2009:  Law Abiding Citizen is released. ║
║  2009:  The Rebound is released in foreign markets. ║
║  2009:  The company files an initial public offering ║
║         (IPO).                       ║
║  2010:  Production wraps on Earthbound. ║
║  2010:  The Film Department withdraws IPO. ║
║                                      ║
╚══════════════════════════════════════╝
```

In April 2008 The Film Department negotiated a guaranteed completion contract with the Screen Actors Guild. Available only to independent film companies that were not financially associated with major studios, guaranteed completion contracts allowed actors to continue working on indie films even if an actors' strike occurred. For The Film Department, this agreement meant that the company could begin to move forward with its production plans.

At the beginning of 2009 The Film Department acquired the screen rights to *Good People,* a crime novel by Marcus Sakey. Also in January, The Film Department prepared to shoot *The Beautiful and the Damned,* a biopic dramatizing the relationship of U.S. writer F. Scott Fitzgerald and his schizophrenic wife, Zelda, during the Roaring Twenties. The Film Department's executives were banking on the success of 2008's *The Curious Case of Benjamin Button,* a drama based on a Fitzgerald short story, to bolster interest in *The Beautiful and the Damned.* Featuring Keira Knightley, the film began production in March 2009. As of February 2011, however, the film had not been released.

FIRST MOTION PICTURES: 2009

The Film Department's first release was *Law Abiding Citizen,* a thriller that had a production budget of $53 million. Opening on October 16, 2009, the movie, which starred Gerard Butler and Jamie Foxx, was the second-highest-earning film of the weekend, beating out such films as *Where the Wild Things Are* and *The Stepfather,* both produced and distributed by major movie studios. Depicting the story of a man who takes revenge on the legal system that allowed his family's killers to go free in a plea bargain, the thriller brought in $21 million at the domestic box office the weekend it was released.

Law Abiding Citizen enjoyed international box-office success as well. Although the motion picture had a disappointing debut in the United Kingdom, bringing in only $2.46 million, it opened at number three in Brazil and number five in Russia. Overall, *Law Abiding Citizen* grossed over $45.32 million on the international market.

Domestically, the movie grossed more than $73.36 million at the box office. When the DVD was released on February 16, 2010, *Law Abiding Citizen* brought in an additional $21.36 million in sales. As a result of its mainstream success, the motion picture was considered a victory for independent film companies.

Although production wrapped on *The Rebound,* a romantic comedy starring Catherine Zeta-Jones and Justin Bartha, before *Law Abiding Citizen* was completed, *The Rebound* was not released until December 2009, and then only to foreign markets. International sales of the movie, which was about the relationship between a 40-year-old, recently divorced single mother and her 25-year-old neighbor, topped $11.7 million. When an expected December 2010 U.S. release date was missed, The Film Department announced that *The Rebound* would be released in April 2011.

BUSINESS OPERATIONS: 2009 AND BEYOND

In October 2009 The Film Department signed an agreement that would help it become a greater presence in foreign markets. The deal was made with independent film sales agent David Glasser, who served as international chief of The Weinstein Company, a highly successful independent film operation. According to terms of the contract, The Film Department would retain control of business affairs, which included delivery and collections, while Glasser's sales team would handle international licensing of The Film Department's movies. This strategic partnership would give The Film Department access to the Weinstein Company's network of international buyers.

The Film Department filed an initial public offering (IPO) in December 2009, seeking to raise approximately $85 million for paying off debts and expanding into distribution and marketing. According to the company's filing registration, it had suffered $34 million in losses and accrued over $40 million in debt in two years of operations due to the writers' strike, the threatened actors' strike, and an industry increase production costs. Additionally, the company had defaulted on debt payments during the summer of 2009. According to its IPO prospectus, The Film Department had plans to sign a contract with Gerry Rich, former president of marketing at Paramount

Pictures, to distribute between six and ten motion pictures per year. However, the agreement would take effect only if The Film Department could raise enough money to help ensure the company's viability.

Instead of going public in February 2010, The Film Department decided to wait until the IPO market stabilized. In March, the company cut the number of shares it was offering by 30 percent, a move that would have raised around $60 million. According to the *New York Times,* however, many investors were leery of The Film Department's capability to execute its business strategy due to its debt and the fact that it had not met its production schedule since its conception. Nevertheless, Gill and Sacker made a statement on August 5, 2010, one day after announcing The Film Department's withdrawal of its IPO, indicating that the company was in negotiations with private investors for $200 million.

With this capital, The Film Department planned to proceed with the production and release of more than 10 motion pictures. Several of these were romantic comedies, including *The Pre-Nup,* written and directed by Jordan Roberts of *March of the Penguins* fame. A sequel to *Law Abiding Citizen* was also planned, as well as a 3-D film set in the Himalayan Mountains. With these films The Film Department hoped it would be able to establish itself as a viable independent film company.

Alicia Elley

PRINCIPAL SUBSIDIARIES

Film Department Music LLC; TFD Literary Acquisitions, LLC; TFD Music, LLC; The Film Department International, LLC; 8439 Holdings, LLC; 8440 Holdings LLC.

PRINCIPAL COMPETITORS

CBS Films; Lionsgate Entertainment Corp.; Overture Films; Summit Entertainment; The Weinstein Company.

FURTHER READING

Cieply, Michael. "The Film Department Files for Possible Stock Offering." *New York Times,* December 7, 2009. Accessed February 28, 2011. http://mediadecoder.blogs.nytimes.com/2009/12/07/the-film-department-files-for-possible-stock-offering/.

Connelly, Michael P. *How to Make a Movie with a Very, Very Low Budget.* West Hills, CA: Uniconn Productions, 2005.

"The Film Cuts IPO." *New York Times,* March 9, 2010. Accessed February 28, 2011. http://dealbook.nytimes.com/2010/03/09/the-film-department-cuts-i-p-o/.

Fritz, Ben. "Independent Financier Film Department Plans IPO." *Los Angeles Times,* December 8, 2009.

Harding, Cortney. "Downtown Express: A Rising Indie Publisher Steps into the Spotlight." *Billboard,* August 15, 2009, 20.

Thompson, Anne. "LAFF: Mark Gill on Indie Film Crisis." *Variety,* June 21, 2008. Accessed February, 28, 2011. http://weblogs.variety.com/thompsononhollywood/2008/06/laff-mark-gill.html.

Fonterra Co-operative Group Limited

Private Bag 92032
9 Princes Street
Auckland, 1142
New Zealand
Telephone: (64) 9-374-9000
Fax: (64) 9-374-9001
Web site: http://www.fonterra.com

Co-operative
Founded: 2001
Employees: 15,800
Sales: NZD $16.73 billion ($12.1 billion) (2010)
*NAIC:*112120 Dairy Cattle and Milk Production;
311511 Fluid Milk Manufacturing; 311512
Creamery Butter Manufacturing; 311513 Cheese
Manufacturing; 311514 Dry, Condensed, and
Evaporated Dairy Product Manufacturing

■ ■ ■

Fonterra Co-operative Group Limited is one of the world's largest producers of dairy products. The group's co-operative consists of over 11,000 dairy farmers who sell their products under brands like Anchor, Anlene, and Anmum. In addition to milk, Fonterra also sells dairy products such as cheese, spreads, and yogurt, as well as more exotic items such as lactose excipients (inhalable lactose). The company's farms produce around 15 billion liters of milk annually, and Fonterra sells dairy products worldwide.

A BULL AND TWO HEIFERS

New Zealand's dairy industry got its start in the early 1800s. Samuel Marsden was a Christian missionary born in England, and he traveled to New Zealand to bring Christianity to the aboriginal Maori people living there. Little did he know that his gift of a bull and two heifers would mark the start of an industry that would eventually support much of New Zealand's economy.

The growth of the dairy industry coincided with a period of civil unrest in New Zealand. In 1840 Great Britain took control of the islands and formed settlements. The European settlers subjugated the aborigines and imposed their culture upon them. The aborigines fought back and war lasted until 1872 when the British declared victory.

Even as the conflict raged, a group of dairy farmers formed the first co-operative cheese company on the Ontago Peninsula in 1871. In 1882, the first refrigerated shipment of meat and butter sailed to London from Port Chalmers. The following year, the advent of the cream separator made it possible to separate skim milk from cream. In 1886 Henry Reynolds established a butter factory at Pukekura in the Waikato region. That same year dairy producers launched the Anchor brand, which soon became a leading brand across the globe. Anchor continued to be one of Fonterra's leading brands into the second decade of the twenty-first century.

By the early 1900s most of New Zealand's dairy factories were co-operatives. The government eyed the dairy industry as a key component to its economic development and took an active role in its performance.

COMPANY PERSPECTIVES

Dairy is our life's work. It's our passion and it's what we do best.

We are proud of our New Zealand roots. Year after year, our farmers in New Zealand work with the land and their cows to bring quality milk to millions of people around the world. They have passed their farming expertise down through the generations, keeping alive the time-honored traditions that have catapulted New Zealand to the forefront of the global dairy industry.

No matter where we are in the world, dairy is what makes us tick.

In 1923 the government established the Dairy Export Control Board to oversee all of New Zealand's dairy exports. In the 1930s there were more than 400 dairy co-operatives. The Labour government came to power in 1935 on the heels of strong support from farmers, who were enticed by the party's commitment to a guaranteed price for butterfat. The government took control of all export marketing that year.

Changes continued into the 1940s as dairy farmers demanded more control over their products. In 1947 the government launched the Dairy Products Marketing Commission, which empowered both industry leaders and government to make decisions related to export marketing. At the same time, new technological advances made their way to New Zealand. In 1948 the industry established an artificial breeding center with the promise of making the breeding of cows a more lucrative process. In 1951 farmers started collecting whole milk using tankers, which saved them time and money. In 1952 farmers started cooling milk on-farm.

MOVING MILK BEYOND NEW ZEALAND

During the 1960s the New Zealand dairy industry diversified its product line and sought international expansion. The country had started exporting butter and cheese to the United Kingdom in the 1920s, but dairy farmers wanted to extend their reach further. In 1961 the Dairy Board and Dairy Products Marketing Commission merged to form the Dairy Production and Marketing Board (Dairy Board). The Dairy Board launched an overseas milk recombining plant in Singapore, the industry's first move into Asia. The industry

grew at a rapid pace over the next few years. By 1964 New Zealand's dairy farmers had over two million cows producing. At the same time, the industry consolidated to 168 co-operatives.

In an effort to increase exports New Zealand took an active role in the General Agreement on Tariffs and Trade (GATT). In 1978 GATT started addressing agricultural trade and in 1994, after years of negotiations, agriculture was officially added to GATT's agenda at the Uruguay Round meetings.

Through the 1980s and 1990s the New Zealand dairy industry took measures to make itself competitive with dairy exporters in other nations. For decades the government had subsidized the dairy industry, which kept the farmers inefficient and uncompetitive. In 1984 a liberal government that supported free-market economics came to power and withdrew government subsidies for dairy farmers. In 1987 the government passed the Dairy Board Act, which gave the Dairy Board financial independence from the government. In 1992 the government further deregulated the milk and dairy products industry.

By 1995 the independent Dairy Board consisted of 80 subsidiaries and was the largest marketing network in the world. The network functioned as a co-operative. Local dairy farmers owned portions of their processing plants, and those plants owned part of the Dairy Board. The removal of government subsidies was good for New Zealand's dairy farmers. Output quintupled and their newfound financial agility allowed them to expand globally.

BUILDING A DAIRY POWERHOUSE

The dairy industry had become central to the overall health of the New Zealand economy. Dairy farmers remained heavily dependent on export trade, which left them vulnerable to economic fluctuations in the United States, Asia, and other parts of the world. During the late 1990s, industry leaders formulated a plan to secure New Zealand's place among the leading dairy exporters in the world. Their plan called for combining the nation's two largest dairy co-operatives, New Zealand Dairy Group (NZDG) and Kiwi Co-operative Dairies, and the marketing entity, New Zealand Dairy Board. The merger would create New Zealand's largest company and one of the largest dairy concerns in the world, with billions in assets. There were several conditions to the merger. The government needed to pass laws allowing competition in its domestic market to allay antitrust concerns. The Commerce Commission had to approve the merger. Seventy-five percent of the co-operative farmers had to vote in favor of the deal.

1814: Samuel Marsden brings a bull and two heifers to New Zealand.

1846: New Zealand ships its first export, a consignment of cheese, to Australia.

1886: New Zealand milk farmers launch Anchor brand.

1923: New Zealand establishes its first dairy board.

1935: New Zealand government takes over export marketing.

1961: Industry forms the Dairy Production and Marketing Board.

1987: Government passes the Dairy Board Act.

2001: The New Zealand Dairy Group, the Kiwi Co-operative Dairies, and the New Zealand Dairy Board merge to form the Fonterra Co-operative Group Ltd.

2007: Fonterra's first plan to bring in public investment fails under pressure from farmers.

2008: The Chinese government discovers melamine contamination in milk products, including those from Sanlu, Fonterra's Chinese subsidiary.

2010: Farmers approve new capital structure that allows for share trading among farmers.

Finally, NZDG and Kiwi needed to formulate an acceptable merger agreement.

The proposed deal was expected to increase industry earnings by NZD 300 million per year and was applauded by the farmers whose incomes were tumbling due to falling prices. Even though the merger seemed to be cut and dried, the deal nearly collapsed several times. NZDG and Kiwi had trouble settling on terms in the merger agreement. The negotiations became hostile at times, and several leading executives, including NZDG chairman Doug Leeder, resigned during the talks.

The co-operatives eventually reached an agreement. In a letter to shareholders, the heads of the merging companies (John Roadley, Henry van der Heyden, and Greg Gent) argued in favor of the merger. They asserted that the merger was crucial to the advancement of the industry and would point it in the right direction for future growth. They claimed the merger would increase global competitiveness, keep the assets of the NZDB in one piece, maintain a profitable co-operative structure, and integrate both manufacturing and marketing operations in a cost-effective fashion.

On June 18, 2001, the shareholders met and approved the deal. The new entity, named Fonterra Co-operative Group Ltd., started operations in October 2001. Fonterra rose to the upper echelon of dairy concerns and became the largest exporter of dairy products in the world. Fonterra's top exports were whole milk powder, cheese, skim milk powder, butter, casein, anhydrous milk fat, liquid milk and cream, buttermilk powder, prepared edible fat, and lactalbumin.

Fonterra spent its first year managing the integration of its joining entities. The company also forged partnerships to strengthen its presence in the international marketplace. In 2002 the company teamed up with Nestlé S.A. to create Dairy Partners America, an entity to manage exports to South America, the United States, and Canada. Fonterra took steps toward establishing sales in China, India, South America, and Eastern Europe. Sales in 2002 increased by almost 59 percent, but Fonterra reported a loss due to oversupply and falling prices. The rocky start for Fonterra made its shareholder farmers unhappy, and CEO Andrew Ferrier promised to improve the return on their investment.

The birth of the Fonterra group was a milestone for the country's dairy industry. Its future, however, was dependent on the health of global economies and its ability to transform itself from a commodities business into a multifaceted value-added concern with a broad range of branded consumer products.

ACQUISITIONS AND EXPANSION: 2002–09

The first few years of the 21st century were an expansionary period for Fonterra. In June 2002 Fonterra and Boniac, an Australian food company, merged their food operations to form Australasian Food Holdings, Australasia's largest dairy group. Fonterra already owned about 19 percent of National Foods, Australia's largest food company. In 2004 Fonterra offered $1.2 billion to acquire National Foods. National Foods rebuffed the offer, saying it was inadequate. Then San Miguel, a Philippine beverage and food company, offered $1.78 billion for National Foods, and a bidding war ensued. In April 2005 Fonterra backed out of the deal, and San Miguel acquired National Foods.

Fonterra redirected its energies toward Asia. In November 2005 the company bought 40 percent of Shijiazhuang Sanlu Group Co. (Sanlu) for $106.5 million. Located near Beijing, Sanlu was one of China's largest milk producers. Milk consumption was on the rise in China, and Fonterra saw a bright future there. Other companies saw the same trend and were quickly increasing investment in China's food and dairy companies. During the same year Groupe Danone (French) increased its stake in Shanghai-based Bright Dairy & Food Co. to 11.55 percent, and Aria Foods (Denmark) established a joint venture with China Mengniu Dairy Co. In China milk was considered a luxury item, and companies fought for consumer loyalty through huge advertising campaigns. In 2003 Mengniu spent over RMB 300 million ($37 million) for prime-time advertising on China Central Television.

Fonterra's growth eventually brought growing pains, and the company needed to raise capital to fund its global expansion and cope with increasing debt and fluctuating milk prices. In 2007 the company proposed a plan to raise capital by creating a second company that would be listed on the stock exchange. The co-operative would remain intact but the new company would take over the company's assets, liabilities, and operations. Sixty-five percent of the new company would be owned by the original co-operative, 15 percent by farmers, and 20 percent by the public. The plan was well received by everyone except the ones who counted: the dairy farmers. Their negative feedback forced the company to table the plan until it could figure out a better one.

In 2008 Fonterra's expansion continued. The company agreed to buy 42.6 percent of Soprole, a Chilean dairy company, for $201.9 million. Then, in September 2008 Fonterra became embroiled in a scandal. Its Chinese company, Sanlu, revealed that the toxic contamination of its milk products was responsible for the deaths of six infants and the illnesses of almost 300,000 people. The milk was contaminated with melamine, a toxic chemical added to create the false appearance of higher protein counts to meet nutrition standards. The scandal led to a recall of products around the world. By the end of the year the former chairwoman of Sanlu, Tian Wenhua, had been sentenced to life in prison for the contamination, the top Chinese food safety official had resigned, and Sanlu had declared bankruptcy. Fonterra wrote off its $201 million investment. Fonterra was not held directly responsible for the incident, but it was criticized for not alerting the public immediately when it discovered the contamination.

To make matters worse, milk commodity prices were falling. The average price of whole milk powder dropped 54 percent. In addition, the European Union restarted export refunds (subsidies) for dairy products, raising fears of a trade war. In early 2009 Fonterra announced a $500 million drop in profit from the previous year. The company dropped its payout to farmers from $7 per kilogram of milk solids to $6. By 2009 Fonterra was a large player in exports but small in

overall production. The company exported 4.5 million tons of dairy products, which represented a third of total world dairy exports, but its overall production was very small in comparison to world production since most dairy products were consumed within the market in which they were produced.

CAPITAL RESTRUCTURE: 2010 AND BEYOND

In 2010 Fonterra revisited its capital requirements. The company's equity had fallen by about $600 million between 2007 and 2008. By 2010 Fonterra had to work out a way to allow the public to invest in the company while maintaining the strength of its co-operative members. The leaders of the company presented a new plan. This plan allowed farmers to buy more shares than required by their production and changed the way shares were valued so they recognized that the market was restricted to the co-operative's owners. Farmers would trade shares among themselves rather than buying or redeeming them through the co-operative. In theory, such trading would give farmers more flexibility to buy and sell shares to match cash flow and give Fonterra stable share capital to grow returns. The company would set up the Fonterra Shareholders Fund. The fund would pay farmers for the right to receive dividends and the gain or loss from any change in value of shares. The fund would also sell investment units to sharemilkers, retired farmers, institutions, and the public. As in 2007 its member farmers were wary of the plan, but management presented its case to them and on July 1, 2010, the farmers approved the "trading among farmers" plan with almost 90 percent support.

Another area of change for the company was its move into online trading auctions for business-to-business trading. The company launched its first online auction in July 2008. In June 2010 the company increased the frequency from one auction a month to two auctions a month to create more price transparency. In the beginning, the auction was a Fonterra-only affair, but in March 2011, the company opened the action to international competition. At the time, the auction system had more than 300 registered bidders from 58 countries, but international sellers were slow to accept Fonterra's invitation to join its system.

Fonterra's business in China continued to experience quality problems. In August 2010, two years after the melamine scandal, several Chinese infants demonstrated early signs of puberty. The abnormality was attributed to unusual hormone levels and traced to milk products sold by Synutra International Inc., which bought its products from Fonterra. Fonterra denied responsibility.

Despite some setbacks, the company had strong prospects for growth in the early 2010s. Its new capital structure was likely to increase capital flow, which would help fund global expansion. At the same time, the company managed to maintain the happiness of its strongest asset, the large co-operative of dairy farmers. Fonterra continued to be New Zealand's major source of foreign trade, and the country's financial health depended on Fonterra's health. Fonterra seemed well placed to carry that burden.

Christina Stansell
Updated, Aaron Hauser

PRINCIPAL SUBSIDIARIES

Fonterra Brands (Australia) Pty Ltd. (Australia); Fonterra Brands Limited; Fonterra Commercial Trading (Shanghai) Company Limited (China); Fonterra (Europe) GmbH (Germany); Fonterra (USA) Inc.; New Zealand Dairy Board; Soprole S.A. (Chile); Vialactia Biosciences (NZ) Limited.

PRINCIPAL COMPETITORS

Groupe Danone; Goodman Fielder Limited; National Foods Limited.

FURTHER READING

"Aggressive Moves by the Dairy Sector." *Financial Times,* August 31, 1983.

Arnold, Wayne. "Surviving Without Subsidiaries." *New York Times,* August 2, 2007, 1.

"Changes Will Let Public Buy Into Fonterra." *New Zealand Herald,* April 8, 2010, 1.

"Defining Moment for Fonterra, Says Chairman." *New Zealand Herald,* July 1, 2010, 1.

"Farmers Wary of Share Trading." *New Zealand Herald,* April 6, 2010, 1.

"Fonterra Looking to China and India." *Grocer,* December 7, 2002, 47.

"Fonterra Plan Is Welcomed," *New Zealand Herald,* November 16, 2007, 2.

"Fonterra Small Fish in Big Ocean of Milk." *New Zealand Herald,* February 16, 2009, 2.

"Fonterra Throws Open Online Auction." *New Zealand Herald,* March 10, 2011, 1.

"Fonterra to Double Up on Internet Auctions." *New Zealand Herald,* June 10, 2010, 3.

"Fonterra to Make Up for Lost Time in Middle East." *New Zealand Herald,* August 3, 2007, 4.

"New Zealand Dairy Industry in Flux." *Ice Cream Reporter,* February 20, 2001, 2.

"New Zealand Dairy Mega Coop Named." *Agra Europe,* August 31, 2001.

"New Zealand to Deregulate the Dairy Industry." *Financial Times,* July 16, 1999, 36.

Santini, Laura. "China's Milk Industry Is Just Fonterra's Taste." *Wall Street Journal,* November 30, 2005, C5.

Wong, Edward. "Company at Core of China's Milk Scandal Is Declared Bankrupt." *New York Times,* December 25, 2008.

GameTech International, Inc.

8850 Double Diamond Parkway
Reno, Nevada 89521
U.S.A.
Telephone: (775) 850-6000
Toll Free: (800) 487-8510
Fax: (775) 850-6199
Web site: http://www.gametech-inc.com

Public Company
Founded: 1994
Employees: 190 (2010)
Net Revenues: $47.79 million (2009)
Stock Exchanges: NASDAQ
Ticker Symbol: GMTC
NAICS: 713290 Other Gambling Industries

■ ■ ■

GameTech International, Inc., designs, develops, and markets electronic bingo gaming equipment, slot machines, and video lottery terminals. The company's bingo games consist of stationary and portable (hand-held) systems designed with touch-screen monitors. Native American, military, and commercial bingo halls are the primary places where GameTech gaming system terminals are located. In the early 2010s the company had game systems in approximately 40 American states. Additionally, it had game systems in the United Kingdom, Mexico, Norway, the Philippines, Guam, Canada, and Japan.

LARGER THAN PROFESSIONAL SPORTS

Richard Fedor, Gary Held, Vern Blanchard, and Clare Thiesen founded GameTech in May 1994. The firm had a total of seven employees when it started. In a *Wall Street Journal* interview published on May 8, 2000, Fedor was asked why he and his three partners founded GameTech. Fedor replied, "There are approximately 60 million bingo players in the United States accounting for 1.2 billion visits annually to commercial, charitable, military and casino bingo operations. Bingo is more popular than the combined attendance of all NFL, NBA, Major League Baseball, hockey, NASCAR and thoroughbred racing events combined." To reach this market, GameTech developed wireless handheld bingo systems like PalmTop, The Electronic Dauber (TED), and TED2. It spent $1.9 million on research and development in 2000, a $700,000 increase over the previous year's $1.2 million. Software gaming systems GameTech designed to be used with its portable and stationary units included Diamond Bingo, AllTrack, and AllTrack 2.

Initially GameTech focused on the video lottery, slot machine, and electronic gaming industries in the United States. The company got out in front of the shift in consumer interest from table games to slot machines. GameTech's pentium-based computerized systems allowed people at bingo halls to play bingo with the touch of a button. Since the systems could be placed in several different locations throughout bingo halls, their appeal rose.

COMPANY PERSPECTIVES

GameTech International is dedicated to the development and manufacturing of cutting edge gaming entertainment products and systems.

Native American casinos were the primary locations where GameTech's initial gaming systems were placed. From a purely economic perspective, the choice was a wise one. In 1997, nine years after Congress passed the Indian Gaming Regulatory Act and three years after GameTech was founded, tribal casinos reported almost $7 billion in gross revenues.

The act was intended to promote economic growth for Native American tribes and protect Native American gaming systems from organized crime. Whether it was intended to or not, the act also opened the door for astute business leaders to get a slice of gains made from Native American gambling halls. With Native American bingo halls awarding prize winnings ranging from a few hundred dollars up to $1 million, GameTech took a chance on a growing opportunity. The early GameTech machines were the black and white fixed-based (stationary) units that operated off a local area network of microcomputers. The units were placed in nearly 275 Native American bingo halls.

Less than one year after it was founded, GameTech developed its first portable electronic bingo dauber (TED). Fifteen years later, TED was still the company's most popular portable bingo dauber. The colored, hand-held game came with stackable crates that stored, charged, and programmed the machine. The equipment could be used interchangeably with GameTech's Diamond, Diamond VIP, and AllTrak 2 gaming systems. The electronic games displayed card images players had purchased across their screens. This ease of use made it possible for players to play more bingo games simultaneously than they could using paper-based displays.

INROADS AND ACQUISITIONS

GameTech continued to compete with firms like Bingo Technologies Corporation, Konami, Bally Gaming, and Spielo for gaming equipment space in commercial casino halls, Native American bingo halls, and the nearly 60,000 licensed charitable organizations operating in North America. One year after GameTech debuted its first portable electronic bingo dauber, the company rolled out another bingo system (Diamond). At the

time, 34 states allowed gambling establishments to use electronic bingo gaming systems. Expanding the number of states that allowed for the use of electronic bingo gaming systems became one of GameTech's focuses. The company made handsome strides in this area, as Fedor told the *Wall Street Journal* during his May 8, 2000, interview: "We are working with the legislators in trying to get electronics rolled over into these venues. To date, GameTech has been very successful. We've been a leader in this area. GameTech played an active part in introducing electronic bingo in Texas. It took GameTech time to do that, but we were successful in helping to introduce electronics in Texas, and it's a very viable source of revenue now."

In February 1999 GameTech removed its largest competitor from the field when it purchased Bingo Technologies Corporation, a privately held company that developed and sold electronic bingo systems. The acquisition allowed GameTech to pick up Bingo Technologies' player tracking, accounting, and inventory control systems. The computerized systems streamlined the tracking and auditing process of monetary player transactions for gaming hall operators by allowing the usage and performance of individual game systems to be analyzed from a main console.

After acquiring Bingo Technologies, GameTech set its sights on gaming firms that operated in the slot machine arena. By this time GameTech had also begun to eye the international gaming market (approximately a $10 billion market). Diamond and Ted yielded significant returns for GameTech. The company's revenues in 2000 were $13.1 million, up from the previous year's $4.5 million. By October 31, 2000, GameTech had about 7,000 fixed-based units and more than 46,000 portable or handheld gaming units in Native American, commercial, and charitable bingo halls.

GameTech installed the equipment in the gaming halls at no cost. The company generated revenue by charging the hall operator a portion of the proceeds earned from the use of the game. A typical contract between GameTech and a hall operator extended from one to three years.

Despite gaining a presence in a growing number of casinos and bingo halls, GameTech did not escape its share of legal wrangling. In June 1995 a patent infringement was filed in the United States District Court (Nevada) against GameTech's wholly owned subsidiary, Bingo Card Minder Corporation, by FortuNet Incorporated. FortuNet sued for "punitive damages for willful infringement." FortuNet also brought the suit against Stuart Entertainment Incorporated (a company unrelated to GameTech). GameTech's Bingo Card Minder countered in February 1997 by stating that they

KEY DATES

1995: GameTech International develops its first portable electronic bingo dauber.

1999: GameTech International acquires competitor Bingo Technologies Corporation.

2007: Company acquires Summit Amusement & Distributing, Ltd, for $40.9 million in cash.

2008: Firm reports a $3.35 million decrease in revenue.

2010: Richard T. Fedor, company founder and chairman of the board, retires.

did not infringe upon two of Fortunet's patents when they created TED. All charges were dismissed out of court on January 22, 2001.

In 2002 GameTech realized profits in the slot machine industry when the company acquired International Gaming Systems, LLC. The deal closed in November of that year. GameTech paid $3.4 million in cash for International Gaming Systems. The deal added 1,400 fixed-based bingo units to GameTech.

ADDITIONAL LEGAL CHALLENGES

On October 30, 2002, Capital Gaming Supplies filed a lawsuit against GameTech in the United States District Court (Mississippi) claiming that GameTech "tortiously interfered with alleged existing and prospective customer accounts." GameTech filed a countersuit. Legal proceedings for GameTech did not improve over the ensuing months. In March 2003 the South Carolina Department of Revenue sent a notice to GameTech and other companies and persons that used electronic daubing devices to cease and desist using the equipment as of September 2003. The notice reversed the department's 1995 judgment stating that the use of such devices was permissible in the state of South Carolina. GameTech filed a Request for Contested Case Hearing regarding the notice.

GameTech would yield a win for their electronic daubers when the South Carolina General Assembly approved House Bill H3986 on February 24, 2004. The bill allowed for the use of electronic devices in charitable gaming halls. The law mandated that "All electronic dabbers must be tested and approved by an independent testing facility to be determined by the department within forty-five days of a written request. All costs for testing are the responsibility of the manufacturer wish-

ing to sell, lease, rent, or otherwise distribute the electronic dabber in South Carolina for the conduct of bingo."

GROWING MARKETS AND PRODUCTS

By October 2005 GameTech had systems in nearly 25 of the 30 states that allowed electronic bingo systems to operate in their jurisdictions. The company also broadened its use of its Bingo Enhanced Tab System. The pull tab system was used mainly by Native American gaming halls.

A newly developed GameTech product introduced in 2005 was the Crystal Ball Bingo system. The system allowed players to input their favorite numbers on the game's scantron card prior to the start of the game. The gaming hall cashier could scan the card into the system. Gamers had the option of playing the game on an electronic system or paper.

When it came to the international market, Game-Tech targeted the United Kingdom to roll out its two-way wireless Traveler color handheld terminals. The color games were designed with in-sales loading and an auto or manual daub option. Up to 21 cards could be displayed on the screen at one time, and 1,200 cards could be played in a single game.

In 2007 the company had products (electronic and nonelectronic) in 38 states and four foreign countries. Also that year the company picked up Summit Gaming for $41.7 million in cash.

One year later GameTech introduced GameTech Elite, a server-based game system that allowed Game-Tech to move further into the Class II and Class III gaming markets (e.g., slot machines). The system had a higher level of security and accountability than previous systems. With its new product line, GameTech expanded its capabilities. Customers now had the ability to play 2,000 bingo electronic game images during one game, in contrast to the initial 600-game image limit. GameTech also released Edge (another server-based system). The difference between GameTech Elite and Edge was that Edge was designed with Wi-Fi capabilities. Edge rolled out to domestic and international markets in 2008. It was GameTech's largest international introduction to date. Edge increased GameTech's international product line to nine products.

By 2009 GameTech had bingo terminals installed in international gaming locations in Asia, Canada, and Europe. Annual revenues generated from international product sales made up 7.2 percent of the company's total revenues in 2009, a slight decrease over the previous year's 9 percent of international revenues.

A ROUGH PATCH: 2008–10

The years 2008 and 2009 were not profitable for the company. Revenue decreased in both years, falling from $58.8 million in 2007 to $55.45 million in 2008 and $47.94 million in 2009. Net income suffered in both years as GameTech continued to suffer "goodwill impairment" losses as a result of its acquisition of Summit. Writedowns of $10.78 million and $15.72 million in 2008 and 2009 led to net losses of $11.16 million and $10.5 million, respectively.

In 2010 Fedor, one of GameTech's founders and its executive chairman of the board, announced his retirement from the firm. Fedor would continue to serve the company in a consulting role. He would also serve as a special advisor to the company's CEO, Bill Fasig. Fasig hoped to turn the company's fortunes around in the early 2010s by expanding into more markets and offering more new products.

Rhonda Campbell

PRINCIPAL SUBSIDIARIES

GameTech Arizona; GameTech Canada Corporation; GameTech Mexico S. de R.L. de C.V.

PRINCIPAL COMPETITORS

Applied Concepts, Inc.; eQube Technology and Software Inc.; FortuNet, Inc.; International Game Technology; Planet Bingo LLC.

FURTHER READING

Barlett, Donald. L., and James B. Steele. "Playing the Political Slots." *Time,* December 15, 2002. Accessed Fabruary 5, 2011. http://www.time.com/time/magazine/article/0,9171,1101021223-399923,00.html.

Dexhelmer, Eric. "State Determines Self-Described Gambler Isn't, Really." *Focal Point* (blog), May 5, 2009. Accessed February 5, 2011. http://www.statesman.com/blogs/content/shared-gen/blogs/austin/investigative/entries/2009/05/05/state_determines_selfdescribed.html.

"GameTech Completes Purchase of Bingo Technologies." *Casino City Times,* February 11, 1999. Accessed February 5, 2011. http://www.casinocitytimes.com/news/article/gametech-completes-purchase-of-bingo-technologies-116241.

"GameTech International, Inc. Announces Initial Delivery and Installation of New Operating System and Games in Montana." *PR Newswire,* September 10, 2010. Accessed February 5, 2011. http://www.prnewswire.com/news-releases/gametech-international-inc-announces-initial-delivery-and-installation-of-new-operating-system-and-games-in-montana-102667204.html.

"GameTech International Inc." *Market Watch.* Accessed February 5, 2011. http://www.marketwatch.com/investing/stock/GMTC/profile.

"Richard Fedor: GameTech international Inc (GMTC)." *Wall Street Transcript,* May 8, 2000. Accessed February 5, 2011. http://www.twst.com/ceos/GMTC.html.

Rimlinger, Craig, and Ian Salisbury. "Indian Gaming a Mixed Bag of Success, Controversy." *Medill News Service.* Accessed February 5, 2011. http://www.medillnewsdc.com/gambling/gambling_indian.shtml.

State of South Carolina. Department of Revenue. "SC Information Letter #04-4. Electronic Bingo – Implementation of House Bill 3986 (Bingo)," February 24, 2004. Accessed February 5, 2011. http://www.sctax.org/NR/rdonlyres/95E0777B-7A6E-4F2F-B819-261517166A91/0/IL044.pdf.

University of Nevada Las Vegas. Center for Gaming Research. "Research Companies; Gametech International." Last modified March 4, 2010. Accessed February 5, 2011. http://gaming.unlv.edu/abstract/fin_gmtc.html.

Herbst Gaming, Inc.

3440 West Russell Road
Las Vegas, Nevada 89118
U.S.A.
Telephone: (702) 889-7695
Fax: (702) 889-7691
Web site: http://www.herbstgaming.com

Private Company
Founded: 1987
Employees: 5,654 (2009)
Net Revenues: $668.56 million (2009)
NAICS: 713290 Other Gambling Industries; 721120
Casino Hotels

■ ■ ■

Herbst Gaming, Inc., owns casinos and operates slot routes. The company has 15 casinos, 12 of which are in Nevada. The slot route business consists of over 6,000 slot machines throughout Nevada in convenience stores, supermarkets, and gas stations. The slot operations are the largest in Nevada.

The company was owned and managed by brothers Ed, Troy, and Tim Herbst until 2009, when Herbst Gaming filed for Chapter 11 bankruptcy. The bankruptcy was brought about primarily by a decrease in gambling revenue as well as an acquisition strategy that backfired when the assets lost much of their value in the economic collapse in 2008, leaving the company mired in debt. In 2010 a court approved a reorganized Herbst Gaming, which is now owned by a group consisting of 140 different lenders. Under the approved plan the founding brothers have no ownership stake.

IT ALL STARTED IN CHICAGO

Brothers Ed, Troy, and Tim Herbst's entrepreneurial drive was ignited early on. Their grandfather, also named Ed, founded a gasoline station in Chicago in 1937. His penchant for lowering prices and making additional concessions to grow his customer base (he gave customers and their children free bubble gum, pony rides, and flowers) was not well received by competing business owners. Because of his customer appeasing antics Ed soon earned the nickname "Terrible" amongst competitors. Even when he moved the business to Los Angeles then finally Nevada, the name stuck. In 1959 Ed founded the Terrible Herbst Oil Company. He named his son, Jerry, as company president, even though Jerry was only 21 years old. The company featured a cartoonish, "bad guy" logo, an amusingly terrible desperado with a enormous handlebar mustache.

Ed and Jerry's focus on customer satisfaction would see the company grow from 1 to 120 gasoline stations over the next 20 years. The 1979 oil crisis that came in the wake of the Iranian Revolution and saw oil production in Iran and Iraq nearly grind to a halt resulted in a lack of growth in the number of Terrible Herbst Oil Company gasoline stations. Notwithstanding, car washes and convenience stores were added to the company's list of assets from 1980 through 1986.

In 1987, 50 years after the family started its first business, Jerry's sons, Troy, Ed, and Tim, founded Herbst Gaming. Jerry continued to own and operate

COMPANY PERSPECTIVES

Herbst Gaming offers the best value in the West.

the Terrible Herbst Oil Company. The first few years after Herbst Gaming was formed the brothers focused on getting slot machines into convenience stores, gasoline stations, and other installations. As might be expected, one of their early customers was Terrible Herbst Oil Company. Herbst Gaming paid Terrible Herbst Oil Company $9.2 million from 1999 through 2001 for exclusive placement of slot machines in their convenience stores. However, Herbst did not have the gaming market wrapped up. International Gaming Technology (IGT), a slot machine, blackjack and poker game designer and manufacturer, was one of Herbst Gaming's largest competitors.

Jackpot systems like IGT had nearly 60 percent of the slot machine market by 1988. This was the same year that the U.S. government passed the Indian Gaming Regulatory Act. The act was created to regulate the growing Native American gaming industry. Herbst Gaming and its competitors realized increased sales with the passing of the act. The gaming business also grew after states like Mississippi began to legalize riverboat gambling.

In 1997, nearly 40 years after Ed founded the family's first major company (Terrible Herbst Oil Company), Herbst Gaming was incorporated in Nevada. All gaming interests owned by the brothers was transferred and held under the newly incorporated firm. Revenues in 1999 for the company were $89.5 million. In November 2000 Herbst Gaming purchased Jackpot Enterprise's route operations for $45 million in cash. The acquisition gave Herbst an additional 3,200 slot machines, bringing the total of slot machines they owned to 5,400. By the end of 2000, annual revenues for Herbst Gaming reached $113.8 million. Revenues generated from route operations increased from $67.8 million in 1999 to $86.1 million in 2000.

GROWTH AND EXPANSION

In 2000 the company worked to complete a hotel-casino off the main Las Vegas Strip. The building that cost the Herbst brothers $65 million to construct went up at the corner of Flamingo and Paradise Roads in Las Vegas, the former location of the Continental. The hotel-casino opened in December 2000. About the opening Ed Herbst said, "We can't compete with a Sta-

tion or Coast (Resorts). But we're from Las Vegas, we know what local people like. We're price-conscious operators." Tim Herbst said, "We got our feet wet in Pahrump (with two smaller hotel-casinos). But you always have dreams of getting into the Las Vegas market."

Four years after it was incorporated, Herbst Gaming had 5,400 slot routes in 520 locations. Terrible's Hotel & Casino, less than two miles from the Las Vegas Strip, Terrible's Lakeside Casino & RV Park, Terrible's Town Casino in Pahrump, and Terrible's Casino & Bowl in Henderson were the four Nevada casinos that the company owned and operated as of December 31, 2001. In addition to its fledgling casino operations, Herbst Gaming had become one of the largest slot route operators in the state.

In efforts to expand its slot business, in 2002 Herbst Gaming agreed to purchase 1,100 slot machine routes from one of its major competitors, IGT, by acquiring IGT's Anchor Coin for $61 million. After this acquisition, the company would operate over 6,000 slot machines in Nevada.

To raise funds to pay for Anchor Coin, in January 2003 Herbst made a stock offering, raising approximately $47 million. One month later the Anchor Coin deal closed. In a press release Ed Herbst, president of Herbst Gaming, stated, "We are pleased to close the Anchor Coin transaction and look forward to the expansion of the number of our gaming locations, as we continue our efforts to provide an exciting and entertaining experience to our customers."

Grace Entertainment, a riverboat casino company, was Herbst's next acquisition. The deal was announced July 20, 2004 for a purchase price of nearly $287 million in cash. Through the deal Herbst picked up all of the Grace Entertainment assets, namely the St. Jo Frontier Casino, in St. Joseph, Missouri; the Mark Twain Casino in La Grange, Missouri; and the Lakeside Casino Resort in Osceola, Iowa. The deal closed on February 1, 2005. The amended aggregate cash purchase price was approximately $266.8 million.

Also in 2005 Herbst began work on a tri-level, 450-space parking lot and casino expansion at their Las Vegas property. This facility expansion and the various acquisitions gave Herbst an increased need to secure more loans. In January 2005 the company and its subsidiaries took on a $100 million loan to help pay for the Grace Entertainment acquisition.

Despite its burgeoning debt load, Herbst was not finished growing. In May 2006 MGM Mirage and Herbst entered into a purchase agreement. The deal gave Herbst ownership of MGM's Sands Regent for $148

KEY DATES

1959: Ed "Terrible" Herbst founds the Terrible Herbst Oil Company.

1987: Troy, Ed, and Tim Herbst, grandsons of Terrible Ed Herbst, start Herbst Gaming.

1999: Herbst Gaming reports $89.52 million in total revenues.

2005: Herbst Gaming acquires Grace Entertainment Riverboat Casinos.

2006: Herbst Gaming purchases MGM Mirage's Primm Valley Resorts.

2009: Herbst Gaming files for Chapter 11.

2010: Court approves bankruptcy plan that divests Herbst brothers of ownership.

million. Herbst would gain control of 12 casinos in Nevada, Iowa, and Missouri. In the May 18, 2006 *Las Vegas Review-Journal* article, "Herbst Gaming To Buy Sands Regent," President Ed Herbst noted, "This transaction will enable Herbst to further broaden and diversify its geographic presence within the state of Nevada and its cash flows as well as create cross-marketing and other growth opportunities."

NEW FINANCIAL CHALLENGES

Nearly six months after it entered into the purchase agreement with MGM Mirage, the two companies (Herbst and MGM Mirage) entered into another deal. MGM was selling its Buffalo Bill's, Primm Valley, and Whiskey Pete's hotel-casinos (also known as Primm Valley Resorts) to Herbst for $400 million. The deal was expected to close by the end of first quarter 2007. In addition to the hotels, Herbst would gain 2,900 slot machines, 98 gaming tables, three gas stations, and a convenience store from the deal. MGM Mirage's Primm Valley Golf Course was not part of the deal. Lehman Brothers and Wachovia Securities were Herbst Gaming's financial advisors in the deal. The deal was the largest that Herbst had undertaken. It gave the Herbst brothers a larger presence in Las Vegas, but it also threatened to cost Herbst Gaming more than the three Herbst brothers assumed.

Ed Herbst, president of Herbst Gaming, celebrated the deal by saying, "My brothers and I are extremely pleased about the acquisition of these three great assets. We look forward to continuing and building upon the legacy started at these properties by the Primm family."

The MGM Mirage Primm Valley deal closed in April 2007. The increased casino revenue in 2007 buffered the company from a dip in its slot route operations, but the interest expense was $85.63 million, a number that went a long way toward explaining the company's net loss of $127.2 million that year. This was only the start of a growing income challenge.

To help get a closer look at the financial challenges (and to find a solution to those challenges) Herbst retained the services of Goldman, Sachs & Company in February 2008. When the partnership was announced on February 28, Ed Herbst told the press, "The Company has a long history of providing gaming services in Nevada and we believe in the strength of the Terrible's brand; however, the recent impact from Question 5, the Nevada smoking ban, and general economic weakness has required us to explore our alternatives." It would be the last month that Ed Herbst would serve as president of the company.

In 2008, primarily in an effort to deal with its mounting debt, Herbst Gaming named Ferenc Szony as its president. Szony took over leadership effective March 5, 2008. Prior to joining Herbst Gaming in 2007 Szony had worked in a senior management position at Sands Regent. He had also worked as president of the Reno Hilton Resort from 1994 to 1997. Ed Herbst continued to serve as Herbst Gaming's chairman of the board and CEO. Due to the firm's financial challenges, the senior management ranks would not remain further unchanged for long.

BANKRUPTCY, REORGANIZATION, AND THE FUTURE

Financial figures for 2008 were even worse than 2007. Revenue decreased in both slots and casinos, and interest expense and asset devaluation increased. Herbst Gaming reported a net loss of $209.4 million that year. Ed Herbst took a leave of absence. However, he would continue to serve the firm as a director.

In March 2009 Herbst Gaming filed a prepackaged Chapter 11 reorganization plan. The company reached an agreement with lenders to whom it owed approximately 68 percent of its debt. Under the reorganization plan, the company would continue to operate under its current management team on a business as usual basis until it was completely restructured.

At the close of 2009 Herbst operated nearly 6,200 slot machines in Nevada. It continued to operate 15 casinos located in Nevada, Missouri, and Iowa. Total revenues at year end 2009 were $668.56 million. This represented a nearly $100 million loss over the previous year's $771.1 million in total revenues. However, the net loss slowed somewhat in 2009, with only $60.1 million reported.

In December 2010 the Nevada Gaming Commission agreed with a court-appointed plan to reduce the company's long-term debt. All three Herbst brothers lost their ownership stakes in the company. Instead, Herbst was owned by a group of 140 different lenders, the largest of which (a Connecticut investor group) owned 16 percent.

Although the company had less debt, Herbst Gaming faced an uncertain future in the 2010s. Its ability to create revenue had never been in doubt, but whether the company could keep costs down enough to become profitable again presented a challenge to its new management.

Rhonda Campbell

PRINCIPAL COMPETITORS

Harrah's Entertainment, Inc.; Las Vegas Sands Corporation; MGM Resorts International; Pinnacle Entertainment Incorporated.

FURTHER READING

Cooper, Sara. "The Wonderful World of Terrible's," *Modern Car Care,* November 1, 2001. Accessed February 5, 2011. http://www.moderncarcare.com/articles/2001/11/the-wonderful-world-of-terrible-s.aspx.

Finnegan, Amanda. "Herbst Gaming Swings to Profit on Cost-Cutting." *Las Vegas Sun,* May 13, 2010. Accessed February 5, 2011. http://www.lasvegassun.com/news/2010/may/13/herbst-gaming-swings-profit-cost-cutting.

Green, Steve. "Herbst Gaming Files For Bankruptcy Protection." *Las Vegas Sun,* March 22, 2009. Accessed February 5, 2011. http://www.lasvegassun.com/news/2009/mar/22/herbst-gaming-files-bankruptcy-protection.

"Herbst Gaming Inc." *Bloomberg BusinessWeek.* Accessed February 5, 2011. http://investing.businessweek.com/research/stocks/private/snapshot.asp?privcapId=3153346.

Stutz, Howard. "Herbst Gaming Files Chapter 11 Plan." *Las Vegas Review–Journal,* March 23, 2009. Accessed February 7, 2011. http://www.lvrj.com/news/41671192.html.

———. "Herbst Gaming Shuffling Managers." *Las Vegas Review–Journal,* May 3, 2008. Accessed February 5, 2011. http://www.lvrj.com/business/18544219.html.

———. "Herbst Gaming to Buy Primm Properties." *Las Vegas Review–Journal,* November 1, 2006. Accessed February 5, 2011. http://www.reviewjournal.com/lvrj_home/2006/Nov-01-Wed-2006/business/10558956.html.

——— "Herbst Gaming to Buy Sands Regent." *Las Vegas Review–Journal,* May 18, 2006. Accessed February 5, 2011. http://www.reviewjournal.com/lvrj_home/2006/May-18-Thu-2006/business/7466110.html.

Velotta, Richard. "Regulatory Board OKs Company to Run Herbst Gaming." *Las Vegas Sun,* December 2, 2010. Accessed February 5, 2011. http://www.lasvegassun.com/news/2010/dec/02/gaming-control-board-oks-company-run-herbst-gaming.

Hill International, Inc.

—————■—————

303 Lippincott Centre
Marlton, New Jersey 08053
U.S.A.
Telephone: (856) 810-6200
Toll Free: (800) 283-4088
Fax: (856) 810-1309
Web site: http://www.hillintl.com

Public Company
Founded: 1976
Employees: 2,356 (2010)
Sales: $421.8 million (2009)
Stock Exchanges: New York
Ticker Symbol: HIL
NAICS: 541330 Engineering Services

■ ■ ■

Hill International, Inc., offers comprehensive project management and construction claims consulting services worldwide. The company, which is one of the largest construction management firms in the United States, helps manage all aspects of the construction process, from initial feasibility studies to planning and design, procurement and construction, start-up and operation, and implementation and contract closeout, as well as troubled project turnaround. Hill International has served clients in a variety of different construction sectors, including buildings, transportation, power, industrial and process, oil and gas, manufacturing, telecom and technology, and environmental. The company also counts U.S. government agencies and international

governments among its clients, as these groups accounted for $189.3 million in revenue for 2009.

Hill International's construction claims services include expert witness testimony and litigation support. The company also advises clients on preventing and resolving claims based on delayed schedules, cost averages, and a variety of other issues and problems that occur during the construction process. Hill's construction claims segment earned $87.2 million in 2009.

Construction owners employ the company to help minimize risk and deliver projects on time, within budget with the highest quality deliverable. Hill International operates out of 80 offices in more than 30 countries. The company has offices in Africa, Asia, Australia, Europe, the Middle East and throughout North America.

COMPANY FOUNDED: 1976

Irvin E. Richter founded Hill International Inc. in 1976. In a brief portrait of Richter by Mia Geiger in the *Philadelphia Business Journal,* Richter recalled that a former boss did not like him attending law school at night. As a result, Richter was told to choose between school and his job. "I quit the job and started Hill," Richter told Geiger. "I didn't want anyone telling me what I could and couldn't do."

Richter obtained a $60,000 line of credit from a friend's consulting firm and, working out of his son's bedroom, decided to start a company based on his new idea. Richter had observed that many large construction companies were mired in lawsuits and other types of

COMPANY PERSPECTIVES

With more than 30 years of experience in construction claims and helping clients manage risk, Hill is uniquely suited to help insurers and their construction-industry clients navigate what could be complicated and costly terrain. Our formula is simple: we hire the best people, understand our clients' needs and objectives, then take ownership of each and every project where we are involved. No matter how large or small our role is in a project, our mission is to exceed our clients' expectations in every way possible. Our history is defined by thousands of successful projects. Our future is defined by the success of your next project.

litigation. Delayed projects and cost overruns had led to contractors, architects, owners, and subcontractors battling it out in court to determine who was at fault and financially responsible.

Hill came up with the idea of creating a team of outside experts who would visit sites to ascertain what caused problems and who was responsible. The team would assess all of the claims and estimate damages for a settlement. If a settlement could not be agreed upon, Richter and his team would testify to their findings in court. Richter, however, believed that many construction claims could be avoided through proper planning, well-drafted contracts, and constant monitoring.

Richter noted in an interview for *Inc.* magazine that the construction industry was in dire straits when he started Hill International. Construction had slowed down and increased competition among companies caused contractors to bid lower, leaving less of a margin for profits. If something went wrong, not only would profits disappear, but losses would often take their place. "Suddenly, it was a service everybody needed," Richter told *Inc.* contributor Curtis Hartman.

A FAST START: THE FIRST DECADE AND BEYOND

Following the completion of his company's first assignment involving a claim against Niagara Falls, New York, Richter, who was the only full-time employee of his company at the time, decided that he would help develop a seminar about construction claims. In addition to lawyers, contractors, insurance professionals, and

others, the 400 people who attended included important government officials, such as the chairman of the Armed Services Board of Contract Appeals and the director of the state construction office of New Jersey.

Richter continued to attend law school while he ran Hill International, participating in seminars and writing journal articles and two books on issues surrounding construction claims as well. He landed several high-profile clients for Hill International, including the Bechtel Group Inc. and the U.S. General Services Administration. Richter began to think that there was also a market for proactive services in which Hill International's services would be used earlier in the construction process. In essence, Richter's idea was to be a kind of babysitter for large construction projects, offering project management services from start to finish.

Hill International began offering project management services in 1980. By 1986 the service represented 25 percent of the company's business. Another major move was made in 1988 when the company purchased the engineering firm Gibbs & Hill, which specialized in power engineering, transportation, and environmental engineering. With this new acquisition came new capabilities, including nuclear power design and environmental engineering, particularly in the area of water quality. The purchase of Kaselaan & D'Angelo, an air-quality design firm specializing in consulting for asbestos cleanup, further enhanced Hill International's capabilities. Hill International's engineering acquisitions helped lead the company to $200 million in annual revenues with more than 2,000 employees.

FACING A CRISIS: 1991–97

By 1991 Hill was living up to its reputation as one of the fastest-growing companies in the country. The company had a total of 2,500 employees and offices throughout the United States and in various foreign countries. Hill International had established itself as an international force in construction claims management and project management oversight.

While it appeared to be smooth sailing for the company's future, an economic recession hit the construction industry hard as new office space sat vacant and financing for new projects disappeared. Hill International suffered, finally bottoming out with sales of $25 million and a workforce reduced to 250 employees. As a result, engineering firms acquired by Hill International were beginning to eat into the company's cash reserves. Richter and his management team sought and received a $7 million bank loan in 1994. The following year, holders of the debt, First Union Corp. of Charlotte, North Carolina, and Summit

KEY DATES

1976: Irvin E. Richter establishes Hill International, Inc.

1980: Company begins offering management services.

1997: Hill International agrees to pay $1.5 million to settle a lawsuit brought by two banks against the company.

2006: Company completes merger with Arpeggio Acquisition Corp. and goes public.

2010: Company acquires civil engineering and consulting management firm TRS Consultants.

Bancorp of Princeton, New Jersey, sued Hill International.

The banks claimed that Hill International had sold two of its subsidiaries that happened to be listed as collateral on a $7 million loan. Richter, who said he sold the subsidiaries because the company needed the money, realized Hill International was facing a serious threat. Richter was convinced the banks were intent on driving him out of business as the lenders' lawyers sought to have the courts declare Hill International in default of the loan.

Perhaps even more troubling to Richter was that he knew his company's reputation was on the line. "Our business depends on our integrity and credibility," Richter told Mary McInerney in an interview for the *Philadelphia Business Journal*. As a result, in March 1997, the company agreed to a settlement in which Hill would pay the banks $1.5 million.

FOREIGN PROJECTS BOLSTER BOTTOM LINE

With the lawsuit over, Hill International quickly turned its energies to an ambitious plan of growth, including establishing future offices in the midwestern and southwestern United States and around the world. The company had regained profitability largely due to its international business, including an estimated $350 million construction project in Seoul, South Korea.

Although Hill International had several large-scale projects in the United States, including the Tampa Bay Buccaneers' new football stadium and the Los Angeles Metro subway project, the U.S. construction industry was still languishing overall. Overseas construction, however, was booming due to infrastructure needs and the rapidly growing economies of Asia. As a result, Hill International had contracts to oversee major construction projects around the world, including the Latvian National Library, the Ukraine Power Redevelopment program, and the twin Petronas Towers in Kuala Lumpur, Malaysia.

In 1997 Hill International announced its plans to go public the following year. In addition to adding to the company's equity base, Richter was seeking to reward the employees who had remained dedicated to the company through the two years of legal problems. Richter thought stock options in the company was a good way to show his appreciation.

INTERNATIONAL EXPANSION AND GOING PUBLIC: 1997–2006

Despite Richter's plan to go public, it would be almost 10 years before Hill International would reach that goal. In the intervening years, Hill International continued on a steady pace of growth. By 2000 the company had worked on a number of high-profile projects, including international projects such as the Grand Mosque in Abu Dhabi. Projects in the United States included the Philadelphia International Airport and the Pennsylvania Convention Center.

Annual sales were approximately $60 million, and the company had 11 offices worldwide, including locations in Madrid, Athens, Abu Dhabi, Seoul, and Yerevan, Armenia. Commenting on the benefits of being both a nationwide and an international company, Irvin Richter told *Philadelphia Business Journal* contributor Paul Eisenberg: "If the economy is slow in the northeastern part of the U.S. and booming in the West, our risk is spread. Similarly, because we are in so many different countries worldwide, we also get the benefits of diversified risk; when the economy is down in one part of the world, it usually is on the rise somewhere else."

Although going public had been put on the backburner as the company's business and reputation burgeoned, it had not been forgotten. In December 2005, the company announced that it would merge with Arpeggio Acquisition Corp. as part of its plan to go public. Arpeggio was a "special purpose acquisition" firm trading on the NASDAQ. It was organized solely to go public as it raised funds and then searched for an acquisition or merger partner. Arpeggio had no operations. However, it did have $37 million in cash for a partner or purchaser to use for business growth.

Hill International planned to use the new funds to buy companies in the United States and overseas. In Richter's view, using a special purpose acquisition to go public was a faster and safer approach than the more traditional initial public offering (IPO). In 2006 the merger was completed and on July 26, 2006, Irvin Richter and his son, David Richter, who had become the company's president and COO, rang the opening bell for the NASDAQ in New York.

ACQUISITIONS DRIVE GROWTH

Hill International wasted little time after the merger to begin making acquisitions. Key among these were the 2006 acquisitions of James R. Knowles (Holdings) PLC and the Pickavance Group Ltd. Knowles gave the company a cost-effective way to bolster its presence in regional markets like Southeast Asia, Australia, and Canada. Pickavance added professional resources and client relationships in London, England, a key market in the claims industry.

Another major acquisition was KJM & Associates, Ltd., a firm based in Bellevue, Washington, that provided project management and project control services throughout the United States. The company had established a long list of big clients, including the U.S. Federal Transit Administration and the Washington State Department of Transportation. The stock market noticed and seemingly approved of these acquisitions, and Hill International stock rose 35 percent from the time the company went public in June 2006 to the end of the year.

As an economic downturn began in the U.S. construction industry in late 2007, Hill International's presence overseas once again paid off as the company's worldwide presence helped it weather the economic storm that followed in the banking industry and troubled economy. Hill continued to make numerous acquisitions, including the acquisition of Boyken International, a project management and claims consultancy with office in the Southern United States and the Caribbean. In January 2010 the company announced that it had acquired TRS Consultants, Inc., a firm specializing in civil engineering, program and construction management, and information technology services for the U.S. transportation and infrastructure markets.

By November 2010 Hill International was the third-fastest-growing company based in New Jersey. Its reputation was further enhanced in neighboring New York when the company received an Award of Merits in the "Best of 2010" issue of *New York Construction*

magazine. The company was recognized for managing two major projects in New York, the Queens Theater-in-the-Park in Corona, New York, and the Queens Community College Kupferberg Holocaust Resource Center in Bayside, New York.

By the early 2010s, Hill International had offices in 30 countries. The company planned to continue its expansion through organic growth and the acquisition of project management and claims consulting firms.

David Petechuk

PRINCIPAL SUBSIDIARIES

Boyken International, Inc.; Gerens Hill International S.A. (Spain); Hill International S.A. (Luxembourg); James R. Knowles Holdings Ltd. (England); KJM & Associates, Ltd.; Transportation Construction Services, Inc.

PRINCIPAL DIVISIONS

Construction Claims and Consulting Group; Corporate Group; Project Management Group.

PRINCIPAL COMPETITORS

AECOM Technology Corp.; Exponent, Inc.; FTI Consulting, Inc.; Jacobs Engineering Group; Navigant Consulting, Inc.; Parsons Brinckerhoff Inc.; Tishman Construction Corp.

FURTHER READING

Eisenberg, Paul. "For Hill Int'l., There's No Downside to Cycle." *Philadelphia Business Journal,* May 19, 2000, 18.

Fisher, Billy. "Hill International: The Houses Hill Built." *Daily Profit Blog,* Wyatt Investment Research, May 5, 2008. Accessed February 8, 2011. http://www.wyattresearch.com/article/hill_international_the_houses_that_hill_built/12294.

Geiger, Mia, "CEO Portrait," *Philadelphia Business Journal,* August 17, 2001, 12.

Hartman, Curtis, "The Inc. 500 Honor Roll: You Could Write the Book on Business Growth from the Strategies of the Companies That Have Made the Inc. 500 Five-Years Running." *Inc.,* December 1986, 90

McInerney, Mary. "Hill Readies to Go Public in 1998; The Company Is Eager to Put Bank Litigation behind It." *Philadelphia Business Journal,* March 28, 1997, C3.

HKS, Inc.

1919 McKinney Avenue
Dallas, Texas 75201-1610
U.S.A.
Telephone: (214) 969-5599
Fax: (214) 969-3397
Web site: http://hksinc.com

Private Company
Founded: 1939
Employees: 1,350
Sales: $418 million (2008)
NAICS: 541310 Architectural Services (Primary)

■ ■ ■

Consistently rated among the top 10 architectural firms in the world, HKS, Inc., has been building its reputation for architectural excellence for over 70 years from its headquarters in Dallas, Texas. HKS offers architectural design service at a full range of levels, from planning to structural engineering to interior and graphic design. Following a long-standing company precedent, the firm continues to offer a diverse range of project specialties, including commercial, health care, sports, hospitality, governmental, aviation, educational, retail, and mixed-use projects. Although the firm has a long-standing tradition in health care projects, it is probably best known to the average person for its work in sports architecture, having designed the high-profile Cowboys Stadium in Arlington, Texas.

For most of its existence, HKS focused on domestic products, but starting in 2002 the firm began an aggres-

sive expansion into worldwide markets. By 2010 the firm boasted 25 offices across the globe completing work in 59 foreign countries. At home, HKS has worked on projects in nearly every state in the United States. All together, the company has a completed project worth in excess of $45 billion.

A THREE-YEAR PLAN

HKS takes its name from its founder, Harwood K. Smith. Born in 1913 in Chicago, Smith moved with his family to Texas at the age of 15. While his family found success cultivating citrus orchards in the Rio Grande Valley, Smith aspired towards higher education and a career as an architect. He put himself through college at Texas A&M University by selling grapefruit and graduated in 1936 with a carefully thought out three-year plan which involved working for one year at each of Dallas's top three architectural firms. Having gained valuable experience in a range of specialties, he would then get licensed and go into business for himself.

Smith's plan worked like clockwork up to the point where he tried to get the nascent HKS, Inc., off the ground, as World War II interfered with his careful plans. The demands of total war meant that new architectural projects were quite thin on the ground. Contractors, on the other hand, were suddenly in great demand. Smith, always the pragmatist, saw where the winds were blowing and changed tack accordingly. Smith stated, "They all wanted contractors. So, hell, I became a contractor and built army camps all over the place."

COMPANY PERSPECTIVES

At HKS we listen, innovate, and deliver. Our philosophy is to design buildings of distinction that reflect the unique characteristics of both the location and the people who use them. HKS architects deliver imaginative, remarkable environments for work, play, and life.

With the end of the war in 1945, Smith had made a name for himself in the contracting industry. However, his first love, architecture, called him back despite lucrative offers from former clients. He was able to call on some of those contacts upon his return to Dallas. A local developer named Hugh Prather, for example, offered to finance any building project HKS wanted to undertake because, in Prather's words, "[Smith knew] how much it was going to cost, and how to achieve it." HKS was soon humming along with several apartment building projects as well as a 16-story office building for IBM.

DIVERSIFICATION: THE KEY TO SUCCESS

The architectural industry runs on a pattern of feast and famine. A particular sector might be generating an excess of projects one year and be completely flat the next. Smith recognized this pattern and tried to encourage a diverse range of specialties in his firm. The strategy saved HKS from going under in the 1950s when the commercial property design market in Dallas bottomed out. Nevertheless, Smith was forced to reduce his workforce by half. Vowing never to take such a big hit again, Smith began aggressively expanding into the health care market. Thanks to a rapidly expanding health care industry, the demand for new hospital, treatment, and diagnostic facilities was consistently on the rise. In addition to new projects, there was also great demand for updating and modernizing existing buildings. Smith pitched the firm's years of experience and design savvy to the medical professionals heading the design committees for these new projects.

He found entry into this promising new field tricky at best, despite having good connections. The big project in Dallas that every firm with an eye on health care facilities was angling for was the Texas Tech School of Medicine. Smith later recalled, "The head of the building committee was one of my buddies, I sought the job. He told me: 'Harwood, I can get you to first place from second, but I can't get you to first place from

fourth.'" Despite losing the initial bid, HKS caught a break several months later when the winning firm left the project, and Texas Tech tapped Smith and his firm to take its place.

The prestigious project proved to be the key that led to over six decades of continuing work in the health care facilities sector. By the end of the 20th century, HKS had built nearly $1 billion worth of health care facilities. In the 1990s alone, HKS built more than 20 million square feet of health care facilities for clients ranging from the George Washington University Medical Center to the MD Anderson Cancer Center. During that same decade, HKS also worked on prisons (an 8,000-bed facility), airports in Dallas and Orlando, and hotel rooms and entertainment venues at Disney's Boardwalk, Seuss Landing, and Milwaukee's Miller Ballpark.

The firm faced another period of drastic downsizing in the 1980s, seeing its number of employees drop from 500 to 225. Again, the culprit was a severe drop in the commercial property sector, although this time the loss in employees was not due to mass firings but simple attrition. In an effort to do more with less, HKS became a pioneer in the realm of architectural computer hardware and software, installing its first systems in 1983 at a time when most firms eschewed computer-assisted drafting. The firm would go on to make computer programs like AutoCAD, Microstation, and 3D-Studio an integral part of its team-based design approach. HKS continues to integrate computer software into all levels of its design process, utilizing programs designed exclusively for the firm such as ARCHengine and BIMMIT to communicate plans to clients in three dimensions and share building information, respectively.

By the time Smith handed over the reigns of the company he had started as a one-man, one-room operation, the firm had completed projects in 35 states totaling over $5 billion in construction costs. He left behind a strong vision of business philosophy, that his successors have continued to follow to this day.

MAKING IT WORK

In a 1999 interview published in *SMPS Marketer,* then chairman and CEO of HKS Ronald L. Skaggs summed up the firm's key to success: "We've always believed we should be in the business of architecture, as opposed to the practice of architecture." He went on to explain, "Our founder, Harwood K. Smith, didn't think marketing was a dirty word. He saw sales as a strong aspect of business and something that was necessary to grow the firm. He talked about marketing architectural services

KEY DATES

1939: HKS, Inc., founded by Harwood K. Smith, a Chicago native, in Dallas, Texas.
1947: HKS completes its first two projects, apartment buildings in Dallas.
2000: HKS grows to 26 principals, 500 employees, and seven offices across the United States.
2002: The company's first international branch, HKS Arquitectos, opens in Mexico City.
2009: Cowboys Stadium, one of HKS's most high-profile projects, becomes the new home of the Dallas Cowboys football team.

long before it was accepted. That set the basis for marketing for us. If you don't market, you don't really get the opportunity to realize your design goals. Those projects don't just walk in the door."

By pioneering concepts like marketing and computer-assisted design, HKS proved itself to be a trendsetter and trailblazer in the architectural industry. For decades, about 70 percent of its workload has been from repeat customers. The work model that has been developed and refined to bring such high levels of customer satisfaction is known in the firm as Continuous Process Improvement (CPI).

The basic idea behind CPI is to take no portion of a project for granted. Every step along the way must be continuously tested and reevaluated. Better ways of accomplishing a set goal are encouraged and rewarded. The CPI process operates on the foundation of a project team that is assigned to a given project from startup to completion. Every aspect of the project is overseen by the team. Scheduling, coordination, budget control, code compliance, details, materials selection, bidding, and construction are all part of the team's responsibilities, and it is all overseen by a project manager, principal-in-charge, and design architect.

DESIGN PHILOSOPHY

Teamwork is facilitated by project Web sites which allow not just the design team but in-house and subcontracted specialists as well as the client to keep up a steady flow of communication. Time and again, HKS pushes its commitment to the customer's vision, to flexibility and accessibility. This has resulted in a major architectural firm that has no single, easily recognizable visual style. A Frank Gehry building is instantly recognizable. An HKS building, on the other hand, is much more likely to

conform to the clients' vision. Compare, for example, two high-profile stadium projects taken on by HKS. Cowboys Stadium in Arlington, Texas, opened in 2009 after a five-year gestation. The facility immediately became one of the largest in the National Football League, boasting a seating capacity of 80,000 (110,000 with standing room) and costing $1.15 billion to build. The grandiose stadium was built entirely at the behest of HKS's client, Cowboys owner Jerry Jones, who told Rick Horrow and Karla Swatek of *Bloomberg Businessweek,* "It has a chance to be one of the most visible buildings in this country. I could have built this for $850 [million]. And it would have been a fabulous place to play football. But this was such an opportunity for the 'wow factor.'"

Meanwhile, in Liverpool, England, HKS, working for the Liverpool Football Club, submitted a design for the new Stanley Park Stadium in 2007 that met with wild acclaim. The firm, proving its adaptability, presented a design that honored traditional soccer pitch architecture while conveying a modern feel. Rick Parry, Liverpool FC's chief executive, praised the design. As quoted in Vicki Hodges' article in the *Telegraph,* Parry said the design "recognise[d] and [made] reference to the fact that English football grounds were historically asymmetric. … This new design will be unmistakably Liverpool and unmistakably recognisable as our stadium." Unfortunately, due to the global economic downturn, Liverpool and HKS were still waiting on beginning its stadium project four years later, despite an initial projected completion date of 2010.

These sort of unpredictable vicissitudes that can hang up or set back projects are one reason that HKS does not fault its project members for poor financial return. Project teams are given set benchmarks based on past projects, but recognition that performance can be affected by outside factors beyond the team's control is made, along with encouragment to innovate and take risks. This is perhaps the final ingredient in the long-standing success and client satisfaction rate at HKS.

LOOKING AHEAD

HKS opened its first foreign office (Mexico City) in 2002, ending a long-standing policy of focusing only on domestic projects. In 1999 CEO Skaggs had summed up his company's foreign policy in an interview as, "HKS does international work, but primarily when U.S. clients take us there. We've found it's easier on our staff and ourselves to work from this country where we can maintain our workload." The about-face that came three years later inaugurated a period of rapid global expansion. From the Mexico City office, HKS has gone on to open offices in London, Abu Dhabi, São Paulo, and Shanghai.

With the rising concern and focus on environmentally friendly, sustainable design, HKS has again shown itself a leader in an emerging industry movement. By 2010, over 30,000,000 feet of its completed or in-development space was sustainably designed. Heading into the second decade of the twenty-first century, HKS continued to set industry benchmarks.

David Larkins

PRINCIPAL COMPETITORS

Gsr Andrade Architects Inc.; HDR, Inc.; HOK Group, Inc.; Jacobs Engineering Group Inc.

FURTHER READING

Hodges, Vicki. "Liverpool Reveal New Stanley Park Stadium." *Telegraph,* July 25, 2007. Accessed February 14, 2011. http://www.telegraph.co.uk/sport/football/2317652/Liverpool-reveal-new-Stanley-Park-stadium.html.

Horrow, Rick, and Karla Swatek. "Welcome to the NFL's Biggest Stadium." *Bloomberg Businessweek,* August 21, 2009. Accessed February 14, 2011. http://www.businessweek.com/lifestyle/content/aug2009/bw20090820_764682.htm.

"Liverpool Over the Moon with Stadium Design." *Building Design,* July 27, 2007, 3.

"Liverpool Stadium Faces Delay." *BBC Sport,* August 29, 2008. Accessed February 14, 2011. http://news.bbc.co.uk/sport2/hi/football/teams/l/liverpool/7587609.stm.

Miller, L. Elaine, ed. *HKS: Selected and Current Works.* Mulgrave, Victoria, Australia: Images Publishing Group, 2001.

Usrey, Nancy J. "Flying with Eagles: An Interview with Ronald L. Skaggs, FAIA, Chairman & CEO, HKS Inc." *SMPS Marketer,* October 1999.

ICx Technologies, Inc.

———————————■———————————

2100 Crystal Drive
Suite 650
Arlington, Virginia 22202
U.S.A.
Telephone: (703) 678-2111
Fax: (703) 678-2112
Web site: http://www.icxt.com

Subsidiary of FLIR Systems, Inc.
Founded: 2003
Employees: 817 (2009)
Sales: $183.4 million (2009)
NAICS: 334516 Analytical Laboratory Instrument
   Manufacturing

■ ■ ■

ICx Technologies, Inc., began by acquiring other companies with an overarching goal of coordinating the products and services of various security technology companies. The company was divided into three operating segments to help it develop products used to detect and prevent critical threats to security around the world.

The Detection segment of ICx focuses on the detection of threats through biological, radiation, nuclear, and explosives sensors. The company's Surveillance segment focuses on products and services which offer not only perimeter security, but also wide area surveillance, including thermal imaging and radar products. The Solutions segment of ICx integrates the company's products and technologies to offer customers single source solutions to meet a wide range of needs in the areas of security and surveillance.

ICx develops sensor technologies used for homeland security, force protection, and also commercial applications. These sensors detect chemical, biological, radiation, nuclear, and explosive threats. The company also produces surveillance technology for both perimeter and area coverage. These products are marketed by a sales force that spans the globe, and through regional sales offices in Europe (Germany), the Middle East (Dubai), and Asia Pacific (Singapore). Although many of the company's products are used for homeland security and military purposes, other products address needs outside of these markets. ICx has developed chemical sensors which are used to detect the presence of pesticides. It has also developed thermal cameras which are able to inspect the brakes on commercial trucks. Some of the company's products are also integrated into products manufactured by other companies. ICx products and components are manufactured at 16 U.S. facilities as well as facilities located in Canada and Germany.

ICx customers include a number of government agencies, including the U.S. Department of Homeland Security, Border Patrol, the Transportation and Security Administration, and the Department of Defense. Private sector companies includes security and defense businesses as well as such well-known names as FedEx, The Walt Disney Corporation, Chevron, and Dow Chemical Supply Company. Two international airports are also ICx customers. Although the majority of the company's customers are in the United States, around 12 percent of sales are to international customers. A significant

COMPANY PERSPECTIVES

ICx Technologies is a leader in the development and integration of advanced sensor technologies for homeland security, force protection, and commercial applications. Our proprietary sensors detect and identify chemical, biological, radiological, nuclear, and explosive threats, and deliver superior awareness and actionable intelligence for wide-area surveillance, intrusion detection, and facility security. We then leverage our unparalleled technical expertise and government funding to address other emerging challenges of our time ranging from a cleaner environment and alternative energy, to life science.

percentage of the company's revenues result from sales to U.S. government agencies and departments.

ACQUISITIONS AND AN IPO:
2003–08

ICx was created by acquiring a number of companies. After its founding in 2003, ICx bought a stake in Amphitech, a sensor maker, that year. A stake in Ion Optics (gas sensors) was acquired one year later. However, it was not until 2005 that ICx would really expand its size, acquiring over 10 companies that year as well as completing its acquisitions of Amphitech and IonOptics. By 2006, when the dust had settled, seven acquired companies were integrated into ICx's Detection segment, five other companies became its Surveillance Unit, and four more were in its Solutions segment.

This method of company growth continued in 2007 and 2008. ICx acquired Pure Tech Systems, Inc (Pure Tech), a company focused on video analysis surveillance technologies, in October 2007 for $3.25 million. Pure Tech became ICx Vision Systems following the sale. Pure Tech's products were incorporated into ICx Vision's products and the company's existing product lines.

Several months later, at the end of May 2008, ICx acquired S3I, LLC (S3I), a company known for its Bio-aerosol Analyzer and Collector. This system detected anthrax and other potentially threatening agents. The majority of the company's customers were government agencies. The acquisition would enhance ICx's biological threat detection capabilities. The acquisition had a price tag of $5.3 million.

In addition to these acquisitions, ICx also had another significant development in the midst of these purchases. The company completed its initial public offering in November 2007 after registering to sell five million shares of common stock. Net proceeds from the IPO reached $72.2 million. The money was used to repay debts, for acquisitions, and as working capital. As of the end of 2009, nearly $26 million of the proceeds were invested in government securities.

GOVERNMENT CONTRACTS:
2007–08

During these same years, ICx was awarded a number of government contracts, and its products were used in a number of military devices. In January 2007 ICx's explosive-vapor detection technology was used by iRobot Corp. in robots used by the military to sniff out enemy explosive devices. More than 100 of the PackBot robots included ICx's Fido explosive detection systems. In the fall of that year, the Transportation Security Administration awarded ICx a contract to provide 200 handheld devices with the Fido technology, known as the Fido PaxPoint, to be used in airports to screen bottled liquids and to identify dangerous liquids and vapors.

In May 2008 ICx was awarded a $4.9 million contract from the Department of Homeland Security to provide sensors that would help to limit exposure to biological agents following an attack. The systems are able to identify 10 types of bioterrorism threats within 15 minutes.

The following month, ICx won a contract from the U.S. Army for $14 million to provide 22 of its Cerberus tower mobile surveillance units. These towers combine radar, thermal imaging, and cameras into a system that makes it easier to locate potential intruders. The systems were used to give advanced security to military bases located in Iraq and Afghanistan.

Within a short time, the company was awarded another military contract, this one worth $4.8 million to provide explosives detectors. The handheld systems were to be used to aid the military in the wars in Iraq and Afghanistan. The sensitivity qualities of these bomb-detection systems were comparable to those of specially trained bomb-detecting canines, which were considered to be the most effective means of identifying such devices. The system, known as Fido XT, was named the U.S. Army Top 10 Invention of the Year in both 2005 and 2006.

In December of that same year, ICx was awarded a $9.4 million contract by the U.S. Army to integrate its sensor technologies, as well as technologies from other

KEY DATES

2003: ICx Technologies is founded and incorporated.
2007: ICx acquires video surveillance company Pure Tech Systems, Inc.; the company completes its IPO.
2008: ICx acquires S3I, LLC, and the company continues to be granted a number of government and military contracts.
2009: ICx opens a regional Middle East office and an Asia Pacific office.
2010: ICx Technologies is acquired by FLIR Systems, Inc.; company becomes a wholly owned subsidiary.

companies, into the JFPASS Joint Capability Technology Demonstration. The company would also develop "sensor fusion and command-and-control logic-based algorithms to automate and speed up the link between the sensor information that comes in and the resulting emergency- and incident-response capabilities," according to *Energy Resource.*

POSITIVE FINANCIAL SITUATIONS: 2008–09

Although military contracts were an important part of ICx's business during 2008, contracts were awarded to the company for nonmilitary purposes as well. For example, the U.S. Department of Transportation awarded ICx a $12 million contract for a fog-detection and warning system to be used on the Highway 99 corridor located in central California. The "Fog Pilot" project was intended to improve safety for motorists along a 12-mile stretch of road known for having dangerous fog. The previous year, a deadly car accident involving 86 automobiles occurred along this same section of highway.

ICx posted a positive cash flow in the third quarter of 2008 for the first time in the history of the company. U.S. military contracts were noted as one reason for this success. The company's revenue for the first nine months of the year increased by 25 percent as compared to the same period of the previous year.

ICx invested about $79 million into research and development between 2004 and 2009. The company also received about $164 million in funding from contracts that offered this money for the purposes of

research and development during that period. The U.S. Department of Defense funded much of ICx's research.

In 2009 ICx continued its work on the Joint Nuclear, Biological, Chemical Reconnaissance System Increment II (JNBCRS 2 or J2) program, an award from the U.S. Army Research and Development Engineering Command Acquisition Center. The value of the award was estimated to be as much as $711 million over a period of seven years, beginning in 2009.

EXPANDING MARKETS: 2009

During 2009 ICx expanded its footprint into the Dubai Free Trade Zone. Opening a regional Middle East office in this area strengthened the company's presence in this part of the world and offered improved customer support. The company also opened its Asia Pacific office, located in Singapore.

In the fall of 2009, the company was awarded a contract by the Department of Homeland Security for a pilot program in the area of mass transit security. The program would test new sensors used to quickly identify the potential release of biological threats. The program was part of the DHS Detect-to-Protect (D2P) project, which focused on sensors to be used in indoor environments. These sensors were to be evaluated for use in a mass transit system.

Despite expanding into new markets, ICx product revenues decreased 9 percent in 2009 as compared to 2008, coming in at $81.6 million. The company did see an increase in sales in the Surveillance segment, yet sales in the Detection segment were lower, accounting for the overall decrease in revenue. ICx reported a net loss of $16.2 million for 2009, a decrease of 60 percent compared to the previous year. The improvement in this area was a result of decreased expenditure on internal research and development in favor of research that was externally funded, as well as decreases in personnel.

Since the company began, it has encountered notable operating losses. In 2009 consolidated operating losses totaled about $7.6 million, which was significantly lower than 2008's operating losses of $25.4 million, and $36.1 million in 2007. By the end of 2009, ICx faced a total deficit of $215.1 million.

NEW OWNERSHIP: 2010

ICx's strong government relationships and the company's footprint in this market were two of the factors that made the company desirable to others in similar fields. In the fall of 2010, FLIR Systems Inc., a company known for its thermal imaging products and infrared cameras, purchased ICx from Wexford Capital, the majority stakeholder in the company, for $268 million. ICx was merged with one of FLIR's subsidiaries and became part of FLIR's Government Systems Division.

Prior to the sale, Wexford owned approximately 62 percent of the outstanding common stock of ICx. FLIR had more than 1,900 employees around the globe and had revenues of $1.1 billion for 2008. The acquisition gave FLIR the opportunity to access the sensor technology market. It also allowed FLIR to advance its surveillance product line and to capitalize on the positive government relations that ICx had built.

Although ICx's board of directors unanimously supported the sale of the company to FLIR, the transaction did cause some negative repercussions. The board of directors was investigated "for possible breaches of fiduciary duty and other violations of state law in connection with their attempt to sell the company to FLIR," according to *Investment Weekly News*. The investigation considered the possibility that the board "breached their fiduciary duties to ICXT stockholders by failing to adequately shop the Company before entering into this transaction and whether FLIR is underpaying for ICXT shares, thus unlawfully harming ICXT stockholders." Estimates of the stock's value ranged between $9 and $10 per share at the time of the sale, yet FLIR paid only $7.55 per share. As of March 2011 no resolution to this investigation had been reached.

THE FUTURE OF ICX TECHNOLOGIES

Shortly after the acquisition, ICx Technologies, operating as a wholly owned subsidiary of FLIR, was awarded a $101.9 million contract from the U.S. Department of Homeland Security for mobile surveillance and detection systems to be used in some areas of the southern U.S. border. The five-year contract would help U.S. agents working in rugged areas to protect these borders.

Due to the importance of security, the company believed that many of its customers were not as strongly affected by the downturn of the global economy during the first decade of the 21st century as many other industries, and that the need for security products would continue to grow. Also, as many commercial products have had their origins in the government or military fields, ICx expected that their products would expand into other markets.

Diane Milne

PRINCIPAL DIVISIONS

Detection; Surveillance; Solutions.

PRINCIPAL COMPETITORS

American Science and Engineering, Inc.; BAE SYSTEMS plc; DRS Technologies, Inc.; Honeywell International Inc.; Smiths Detection

FURTHER READING

"Bomb-Sniffing Robots Are on the Way to the Troops in Iraq: More than 100 PackBot Robots Provided by iRobot Corp. Will Be Fitted with the Sniffing Technology." *Information Week,* January 29, 2007.

"ICx Technologies Awarded 49.4 Million Army Contract for Sensor Technologies." *Energy Resource,* December 3, 2008.

"ICx Technologies." *Security Distributing & Marketing,* 38, no. 7 (2008): 92.

"ICx Wins $14 Million Cerberus Mobile Surveillance Towers Contract for US Army." *Military & Aerospace Fiber Optics,* June 2008, 5+.

"Levi & Korsinsky, LLP Investigates Possible Breach of Fiduciary Duty by the Board of ICx Technologies, Inc. – ICXT." *Investment Weekly News,* September 4, 2010, 312.

Immersion Corporation

801 Fox Lane
San Jose, California 95131
U.S.A.
Telephone: (408) 467-1900
Fax: (408) 467-1901
Web site: http://www.immersion.com

Public Company
Founded: 1993
Employees: 124 (2010)
Total Assets: $27.72 million (2009)
Stock Exchanges: NASDAQ
Ticker Symbol: IMMR
NAICS: 334119 Other Computer Peripheral Equipment
Manufacturing

■ ■ ■

Touch sense technology and equipment are Immersion Corporation's primary products. Over 300 million devices (across the medical, gaming, automotive, and electronics industries) use the company's haptics, or touch feedback, technologies. Immersion's medical and surgical simulators are used within training programs created by health care organizations. Their mobile phone haptics are used with equipment like cellular phones. The haptics are designed so that users can dial telephone numbers by touching buttons on a screen. Approximately 20 percent of all Immersion revenue is derived from the PC and console gaming market, while around 30 percent comes from the mobile communications market.

Immersion licenses its technologies to manufacturers so that the manufacturers can sell equipment imbedded with Immersion technologies under their own company name. Product development is a core part of the company's business. As of 2010, Immersion had 800 issued or pending domestic and international patents.

Immersion Corporation has offices located throughout the United States. Its international offices are located in Canada, Korea, and Europe.

IMMERSION STARTS AT STANFORD

Dr. Louis Rosenberg was named Immersion's CEO and president in 1993, the same year he founded the company. Rosenberg had bachelor of science and master of science degrees from Stanford University. He later earned a doctorate in mechanical engineering from the university. Rosenberg's interests in research and virtual communications dated back to his days as a graduate student at Stanford. While there, Rosenberg invented computer-based and physical simulations of remote space environments. He focused more on how the simulations "felt" rather than on the visual steps users were required to follow to complete the space simulation activities.

Rosenberg worked with an advisor, Professor Larry Liefer, to learn more about human sensory gaps and the connections between human perception and touch. About those early experiments, Rosenberg told Stanford University's School of Engineering, "I was trying to understand conceptually how people decompose tactile feeling." Rosenberg asked himself questions like, "How do they (humans) sense a hard surface. Crispness? Sponginess?"

Rosenberg's curiosity led him to the U.S. National Aeronautics and Space Administration (NASA), where he once worked with a flight simulator joystick at a local NASA site. This would be a formative experience for Rosenberg. Before his work with the simulator ended, he had begun to wonder, "Why don't we make this (the joystick) a mass market product?"

The challenge to creating the joystick as a mass market product was the fact that the NASA simulation device cost $100,000. Rosenberg's goal was to create a similar device that cost as little as $99. His family supported his idea. In fact, his family and a group of friends gave him $60,000 to start his first company, Immersion. The engineering doctorate student who also had a keen interest in psychology used nearly half of the $60,000 to apply for patents.

By 1994 Rosenberg had raised an additional $700,000 from private investors. He spent nearly $220,000 of that to secure additional patents (for a total of 21 patents between 1993 and 1994). He also built a team of 20 employees, most of them Stanford graduates. The company started developing medical training and simulation technologies for the medical community.

A year after Immersion was founded, the company developed its first 3-D digitizer. The technology created three-dimensional computer images of small objects. Immersion also began developing its Softmouse product in 1994. This particular product was designed for mapmaking. Both products were used largely by video game and computer manufacturers. Revenues from the sale of the product were initially royalty based.

TURNING DOWN A GIANT'S DEAL

In 1995 Louis Rosenberg and his colleagues faced an unenviable challenge. Microsoft came knocking. The computer giant wanted to secure an exclusive license with Immersion, primarily for exclusive rights to the force-feedback joystick Immersion was creating. The deal could have brought Immersion millions of dollars. At the time Microsoft had 40 percent of the joystick

market. Immersion's focus on creating force-feedback joysticks was pioneering. The joystick allowed users to feel the action that took place across their computer or game system screens. For example. if a game user shot a gun while playing a video game, he or she would feel the recoil in the joystick.

This initial offer from Microsoft was rebuffed, although the two companies did continue to do business with each other. After Immersion walked away from the potentially lucrative licensing deal with Microsoft, it landed royalty-based deals for use of its joysticks with CH Products, SC&T International Incorporated, and Interactive I/O.

Immersion started to develop its TouchSense (formerly called FEELIt) force-feedback gaming system technology in 1996. The technology allowed game users to enjoy a personal, intuitive, and natural gaming experience. TouchSense technology could be synchronized with sound and images, features that made the tool even more attractive to gaming companies and consumers. However, nine years would pass before Immersion would roll the technology out for public usage. After that, the TouchSense technology was soon being used in automobiles (BMW, Rolls Royce, Volkswagon), video consoles, and medical simulation systems.

Nearly two years after it turned down Microsoft's initial exclusive licensing offer, Immersion renewed its discussions with Microsoft. This time the companies worked to integrate Immersion's TouchSense technology with Microsoft's DirectX application (a force feedback system that controlled joysticks, gamepads, and wheels). It was a natural fit. Microsoft had already incorporated Immersion's API application programming interface system into its DirectX system. Immersion also entered into contracts with the U.S. government to develop advanced simulated training technologies. Government contracts made up 24 percent of Immersion's 4.3 million total revenues in 1997. That same year, Immersion spent $1.5 million on research and development. It also reported losses in each quarter of 1997 citing research and development expenses.

In 1998 Immersion licensed its TouchSense technology to Logitech, a company that would go on to purchase 10 percent interest in Immersion later that same year. Logitech began selling computer mice using the Immersion technology in 1999. Before that year closed, Immersion was earning 32 percent of its royalty-based revenues from the sale of Logitech products that used Immersion technology.

Interest in Immersion grew. The firm went public on November 12, 1999. Per share price was $12 for a $53.68 million aggregate initial public offering.

KEY DATES

1993: Louis Rosenberg is named CEO and president at Immersion Corporation.

1994: Immersion Corporation develops its first 3D digitizer (Microscribe).

1999: Immersion Corporation completes its first public offering at $12 per share for an aggregate of $53.68 million.

2005: Sony Corporation is ordered to pay Immersion Corporation $90.7 million for patent infringement of the touch feedback technology Sony used in their PlayStation game consoles.

2009: Victor Viegas is named CEO at Immersion Corporation.

ACQUISITIONS

In 2000, the year that the Y2K bug was supposedly going to turn the technology world on its end because it was feared computer systems were not capable of recognizing dates later than December 31, 1999, Immersion strengthened its focus on generating revenue through royalty-based licensing deals with other equipment and technology firms. Immersion also focused on expanding market awareness of touch technology and products. Its icon- and menu-controlling software was already being used in the Microsoft Windows 98 and 2000 systems. The company had more than 95 patents and 230 pending patent applications in the United States and abroad. Its continuing growth included several acquisitions including HT Medical Systems, Haptic Technologies, and Virtual Technologies.

Haptic Technologies (renamed Immersion Canada) was a software application development firm based in Montreal, Canada. The company had 20 employees when Immersion purchased it. HT Medical Systems (renamed Immersion Medical) designed, manufactured, and sold computer-based medical simulators. The technology allowed medical professionals to conduct tests without using animals or cadavers. HT Medical Systems was based in Gaithersburg, Maryland, and had 60 employees at the time of the acquisition. Virtual Technologies had about 15 employees at the time of purchase and was based in Palo Alto, California. The company designed, manufactured, and sold high-end simulation software and hardware to equipment and technology firms.

GROWING PATENTS

Immersion secured a new patent for tactile sensation knobs to be used in cars in January 2001. Drivers would be able to send and receive information using the new technology. The device allowed drivers to control their automobile's entertainment systems, cell phone, temperature, windows, locks, seats, and GPS navigational systems using one unit, rather than reaching for seven separate devices. Louis Rosenberg told Sabra Chartrand, for the January 15, 2001 *New York Times* article, "Patents; A Multipurpose Device with One Objective: Letting Drivers Keep Their Eyes on the Road," "If you think of a desktop PC, you have one mouse to make it simpler. ... You wouldn't want to reach around for five different mice." The knob is installed in vehicles next to the driver for easy accessibility. Three car manufacturers, including BMW, were initially awarded licensing agreements from Immersion to use the technology.

Over the next two years Immersion increased the number of licensing and royalty-based agreements it had with firms operating in the video game industry. It was providing technology support for leaders in the gaming industry like Apple Macintosh's OS X Platform, Logitech's Wingman, and Microsoft's Cyborg 3D Force. Immersion also licensed its patents in more than 50 spinning tactile feedback game devices developed by companies like Intec, Mad, Saitek, and SpectraVideo.

TO THE COURTS

Company revenue was growing, but some of these earnings would go toward court fees when Immersion took on Sony Computer Entertainment and Microsoft in 2002, stating that both companies improperly used their patented technologies in video games. Immersion won the lawsuit against Microsoft in 2003. For infringing upon Immersion patents, Microsoft agreed to pay Immersion $26 million for the video game licensing rights. Sony would receive judgment on its lawsuit the following year.

In September 2004 an Oakland, California, jury found Sony guilty of patent infringement and ordered the electronic giant to pay Immersion $82 million. Upon receipt of the verdict, Immersion's shares rose 0.38 cents up to $6.20. However, the legal battle was not over. Sony appealed the lawsuit to a federal court. Its efforts were not met with success. In March 2005 federal district court judge Claudia Wilken ordered Sony to pay Immersion $90.7 million for patent infringement. The additional $8.7 million covered interest on the initial $82 million judgment Immersion was awarded by the Oakland, California, jury the previous year. Judge Wilken also ordered Sony to cease selling PlayStation consoles that used Immersion's patented technologies. The legal wrangling would continue into 2007.

Despite its legal battles, Immersion generated 18 percent of its total revenues from the sale of PC and gaming patent licenses and royalties in 2006, a 9 percent increase over the previous year's 27 percent total revenues generated from PC and gaming patent licenses and royalties. New product developments and releases would help the firm to generate even greater revenues in the coming years.

The introduction of its TouchSense vibration system in July 2006 led the way for the unveiling of several new products at Immersion. TouchSense's upgraded technology improved audio and graphic synchronizations used in gaming systems, meaning game players could feel with increased force the impact of movements they made. Other products that Immersion rolled out in 2006 included the MicroTouch system, which the firm introduced at the November 2006 Global Gaming Expo. Immersion's new VibeTonz System could be programmed using mobile handsets. VibeTonz was used primarily with portable game interfaces and ringtone playback devices. The embedded technology allowed users of mobile handsets (e.g., cell phones) to feel musical beats while they played on their mobile devices. Verizon Wireless started using the system in 2006. By the close of the year nearly 4 million mobile devices designed with the VibeTonz system had been distributed throughout the globe.

LEGAL VICTORY AND PRODUCT CHANGES

The first week in March 2007, Sony agreed to pay Immersion $150.3 million ($97.2 million from a court judgment and an additional $53.1 million in royalties) to settle its patent infringement lawsuit. Although it seemed the long court battle was over, there was one more lawsuit. Microsoft sued Immersion for breach of contract, claiming that it was owed a portion of the Sony money due to a sublicensing agreement. In 2008 Immersion paid Microsoft around $20 million to settle the claim.

Also that year Immersion announced that it would divest its 3-D product line. That same year nearly 33 million of the company's TouchSense portable devices were sold and distributed. Immersion was at that time generating 13 percent of its total revenues from the sale of mobile handheld devices. Immersion licensed its automobile rotary controls to various automotive manufacturers, including the makers of the Mercedes

Benz, Volkswagen, and Bentley. The company's rotary controls were now used in more than two million automobiles around the world. Automotive revenues comprised 9 percent of the company's total revenues in 2008.

Throughout 2009 and 2010 Immersion continued to focus on touch screen applications and technologies. It introduced its touch screen haptics computer processor (TouchSense 2500) in August 2010. Although company revenue was flat for 2008 and 2009, Immersion's haptics technology was well poised to take advantage of the continued popularity of handheld electronic devices in the early 2010s.

Rhonda Campbell

PRINCIPAL DIVISIONS

Medical; Touch.

PRINCIPAL COMPETITORS

LG Electronics Inc.; Logitech International S.A.; Microsoft Corporation; Nokia Corporation; Samsung Group.

FURTHER READING

Burrows, Peter. "Trying to Stick It to Microsoft." *Business Week,* June 14, 1997. Accessed February 6, 2011. http://www. businessweek.com/1996/43/b349846.htm.

"Immersion Corporation." *Bloomberg BusinessWeek.* Accessed February 6, 2011. http://investing.businessweek.com/res earch/stocks/snapshot/snapshot.asp?ticker=IMMR:US.

"Immersion Corporation." *New York Times.* Accessed February 6, 2011. http://topics.nytimes.com/topics/news/business/ companies/immersion-corporation/index.html.

"Immersion Corporation Mergers and Aquisitions." AlacraStore. com. Accessed February 6, 2011. http://www.alacrastore. com/mergers-acquisitions/Immersion_Corporation-2100221.

"Immersion Corporation: Turnaround on Track." *Seeking Alpha,* August 10, 2010. Accessed February 6, 2011. http://seeking alpha.com/article/219820-immersion-corporation-turna round-on-track.

"Logitech Gains Immersion Stake." *New York Times,* April 16, 1998. Accessed February 6, 2011. http://www.nytimes.com/ 1998/04/16/business/logitech-gains-immersion-stake.html? ref=immersion-corporation.

Noer, Michael. "Desktop Fingerprints." *Forbes,* September 21, 1998. Accessed February 6, 2011. http://www.forbes.com/ 1998/09/21/feat.html.

Stanford University School of Engineering. "Louis Rosenberg, Mechanical Engineering, Once More, With Feeling." Palo

Alto, CA: Stanford University School of Engineering, Annual Report, 1997–98. Accessed February 6, 2011. http://engineering.stanford.edu/about/AR97-98/rosenberg.html.

"Technology Briefing: Sony Ordered to Pay $90.7 Million."

New York Times, March 29, 2005. Accessed February 6, 2011. http://query.nytimes.com/gst/fullpage.html?res=9903E6DC123FF 93AA15750C0A9639C8B63&ref=immersion-corporation.

Industrial Acoustics
Company, Inc.

—■—

IAC House
Moorside Road
Winchester, Hampshire SO23 7US
United Kingdom
Telephone: (44) 0 1962 873000
Fax: (44) 0 1962 873111
Web site: http://www.industrialacoustics.com

Private Company
Founded: 1949
Employees: 700 (2010)
NAICS: 333999 All Other Miscellaneous General
    Purpose Machinery Manufacturing

■ ■ ■

Industrial Acoustics Company, Inc. (IAC), supplies noise control solutions throughout the world. With over 11 locations in Asia, Europe, the Americas, and Australia, IAC is the leading supplier of testing facilities, aero-testing solutions, and other acoustic products and structures.

For the manufacturing, power plant, and process industries, IAC supplies noise reduction barriers, silencers, and enclosures to silence noise pollution from machinery, railways, and roads.

For the architectural industry, IAC supplies noise reduction products for buildings with high populations, such as hotels, schools, and office buildings. These include acoustic doors and related products for conference rooms, study rooms, and music rooms. IAC provides solutions for the music and entertainment industry by building studios that provide total noise control from air conditioning, lighting, and other white noise. IAC also builds silenced windows, floors, and walls.

The medical and life sciences industry uses IAC's products for auditory testing, psychological examination, medical research, and speech therapy. The transportation and aviation industries utilize IAC products for testing facilities and turbine silencing. IAC provides standard products such as exhaust silencers, suppression systems, and aero-engine test facilities.

COMPANY FOUNDING AND
EARLY YEARS: 1949–68

IAC was founded by Martin Hirschorn, who was born and raised in Berlin. To escape the Nazi regime, his parents sent him to England in 1937 when he was 16 years old. Hirschorn earned his college degree in engineering from Woolwich Polytechnic College in England while working at Burt, Boulton, and Haywood (BB&H), a coal manufacturer. In 1944 he left BB&H to work for Nuswift Engineering Company before emigrating to the United States in 1947 to seek more lucrative opportunities.

Hirschorn moved to New York and resided with his aunt who had provided financial support for his escape from Berlin. He began work with M.W. Kellogg Company. There, Hirschorn developed an interest in noise pollution when he discovered that the business's processes caused problems for the local farmers. While his employer supported his efforts to develop a solution, he was laid off from the company in 1949 due to reduced contract work. That same year, he founded his own business, the Industrial Acoustics Company.

During the early years, Hirschorn published his ideas in trade journals such as *Chemical Engineering,* gaining credibility as an expert on the new concept of acoustics. When he lost his job at M.W. Kellogg, he was offered the opportunity to teach and research at New York University. However, Hirschorn instead decided to start his own company.

The time was right for Hirschorn's ideas, and he is considered the pioneer of industrial noise control. His products coincided with the postwar development of U.S. commercial industries such as air conditioning, aviation, and entertainment. The company began by providing customized acoustics for industrial companies that needed silencing solutions for factory machines and transportation noise. In 1952 the entertainment industry hired IAC to build acoustics for a new movie theatre format where three projectors would be run simultaneously. In 1958 and 1959, subsidiaries were established in London and California to serve IAC's expanding aviation business.

GOING PUBLIC, GOING PRIVATE: 1968–98

By 1968 Hirschorn had taken on two sets of partners and parted ways with both. He then decided to publicly offer company shares to obtain funding. However, Hirschorn retained a controlling interest.

After its IPO, the company pursued a strategy of expansion strategy into Europe and Asia. In 1973 the company opened a sales office in West Germany, and in 1980 a joint venture was established in Hong Kong. In 1995 the company purchased a 90,000-square-foot factory in Winchester for $3.1 million, financed with a short-term bank loan. In 1998 the company purchased a $4 million, 72,500-square-foot plant in the United States, also funded by a bank loan.

In IAC's own words, the company lost its way in the 1990s. The company's public SEC filings show overall losses between 1994 to 1997. Increasing long-term debt also contributed to the company's difficulties.

However, the company continued to introduce new products. During the late 1990s, it introduced fiber-free sound absorption walls, a fiber-free air flow attenuator, a new mini-booth for hearing testing, upgraded field testing anechoic products, and upgraded music recording studios.

IAC would remain a public company listed on the NASDAQ until 1998, when it was purchased by a European investment firm, effectively taking the company private. The move was an indication of the depth of IAC's financial plight, as the new owners provided subordinated debt and preferred equity, expensive financing obtained when bankrupcy is the likely alternative. Soon after, Hirschorn retired following a disagreement with the new owners over the CEO succession.

In 1999 the company built a new studio for the *Good Morning America* television show and developed new products specific to the task. The window behind the anchors, which would become famous, was conceived by IAC engineers using air pressure to open and close it, allowing the anchors access to fans outside while providing acoustic noise silencing inside.

In 2000 IAC acquired H M Akustik and Vikas, two companies in Copenhagen, Denmark, further expanding its European presence. In 2002 these companies were combined and named IAC Nordic.

A NEW PHASE OF EXPANSION: 2002–07

In January 2002 IAC announced the appointment of Brian Quarendon as its new CEO. While the company continued its aggressive international expansion, the company also obtained several prominent customers that would position IAC as the premier acoustics company in the world.

In December 2002 IAC made two significant moves to expand its international presence. A licensing agreement with Saudi-based Arabian Thermal Aire Industries Co. Lt. (ATAI) allowed ATAI the exclusive right to sell IAC products in the Middle East. At the same time, IAC acquired Boët Stopson (Boët), located in Lille, France. Boët, founded in 1872, specialized in large-scale projects such as intake and exhaust silencers, soundproof ceilings and walls, and custom solutions. Boët added 167 employees to the company and expanded IAC's European presence with plants in France, Spain, and Italy. The facilities included a modern research and development center and a 100,000-square-foot factory. Over the next few years, the Boët business segment brought in contracts from Japan, Austria, and Qatar.

```
┌─────────────────────────────────────────────┐
│                                               │
│              KEY DATES                        │
│                   ■                           │
│  ─────────────────────────────────────────    │
│                                               │
│  1949:  Martin Hirschorn founds Industrial Accous-  │
│         tics Company.                         │
│  1968:  Hirschorn takes company public, keeping a   │
│         majority interest.                    │
│  1998:  European investment company buys IAC,       │
│         taking the company private; Hirschorn retires. │
│  2000:  IAC relocates the Global Aviation division to │
│         the United Kingdom, and new headquarters    │
│         are established in Westchester, United       │
│         Kingdom.                              │
│  2002:  Brian Quarendon joins IAC as new CEO.  │
│  2010:  Founder Martin Hirschorn dies.        │
│                                               │
└─────────────────────────────────────────────┘
```

In July 2004 London's Heathrow Airport hired IAC for an air conditioning noise attenuation project for its terminal number five, with floor space equivalent to 50 soccer fields. That same month, the company announced the completion of projects for BMW for the supply of anechoic testing chambers for two manufacturing plants in Germany.

In February 2005 IAC expanded to Russia with a contract with international packaging giant Rexam Group. Rexam's Naro Fominsk plant manufactured cans specifically for the Russian market. The plant's large presses exceeded the Russian noise regulations, causing problems for workers in the factories and adjoining offices. IAC's customized solution won the bid for acoustics for the plant.

In October 2005 IAC initiated a relationship with GE that would lead to many lucrative opportunities, including reentry into China. In October, the Power Division of IAC Boët Stopson secured a contract with GE Jenbacher, a subsidiary of GE, to provide exhaust silencers. Later, IAC contracted with GE Electric Energy Europe to supply insulated enclosures for the company in September 2006. In June 2007 the company won the bid for GE's supply of three off-base noise-insulated enclosures for a GT25 gas turbine and compressor package.

In June 2007 IAC Aviation opened a new facility in Caerphilly, South Wales. The facility provided engineering services to clients west of England, and its location benefited from the closing of Curran Engineering in the area. The new facility employed three Curran engineers, including former director Glyn Price, who would head the team at IAC Aviation South Wales.

FURTHER EXPANSION: 2008 AND BEYOND

In August 2008 IAC announced a joint venture with Hong Kong-based company IAC China Holdings, previously owned by IAC but sold in 1997. The company's long-time relationship with GE resulted in the need to expand manufacturing capabilities for the power market worldwide. The joint venture would operate from Dongguan in Guangdong Province in South China, a fast-growing city with 5.4 million inhabitants and 15,000 international companies. Olivier Darrieus, general manager of IAC Boët Stopson, became the new chairman, while Fred Zhang was hired as general manager. By June 2009 the China joint venture operated at full capacity, necessitating a new plant.

IAC continued its expansion, targeting the Pacific Rim. In November 2008 IAC acquired the Australian company Colpro Engineering. Colpro designed performance silencers, exhaust systems, and thermal insulation blankets for the marine, mining, and transport industries in Australia. In August 2010 IAC acquired two more Australian companies, Acoustic Systems and Sound Attenuators Australia Pty Ltd (SAA). Both companies served the commercial building industry in New South Wales with noise control products. Acoustic Systems was established in 1994 and specialized in the commercial noise control equipment. SAA specialized in noise control products for the air conditioning and mechanical services.

On June 1, 2010, Martin Hirschorn died in New York at the age of 89. As a young man in Germany, he had dreamed of becoming a soldier to free his beloved country from the Nazis. He also wanted to become an artist and an explorer. At the end of his life, he believed he had achieved two of his dreams as an artist and explorer with the founding of IAC. He led the company through building standard industrial solutions for the commercial office, building high-rise sector, sound-absorbing linings for heavy machinery in factories, music practice rooms, and jet noise suppressors, including the supersonic aircraft Concorde. In 1999 the Martin Hirschorn IAC prize was established by the Institute of Noise Control Engineering Foundation (INCE) in recognition of his contribution to the industry. Hirschorn also published his research and memoirs. These publications include *Noise Control Reference Handbook* (1989), *The Standard of Silence: Recollections of the Early Years of Industrial Acoustics Company* (1991), and *Can You Hear Me? Making the World a Quieter Place; My Life as an Unwitting Entrepreneur* in 2007, just three years before his death.

As a dominant player in the field of noise reduction, it seemed likely that IAC would spend the 2010s acquiring smaller companies when economic conditions were suitable, using these smaller companies to increase its geographic reach.

Sara K. Huter

PRINCIPAL SUBSIDIARIES

IAC America, Inc.; IAC Boët Stopson SAS (France); IAC China; IAC Colpro Ltd. (Australia); IAC GmbH (Germany); IAC Nordic A/S (Denmark); IAC Sim Engineering & Soft SAS (France); IAC Stopson Espanola SA (Spain); IAC Stopson Italiana SpA (Italy); IAC Limited.

PRINCIPAL COMPETITORS

Acoustics Incorporated; Aero Systems Engineering, Inc.; Racal Acoustics Ltd.; Specialty Products & Insulation Co.

FURTHER READING

DeLasho, Ken. "Let the Sun Shine In … But." *Buildings* 94, no. 6 (2000).

Dinger, Ed. "IAC Group." In *International Directory of Company Histories*. Vol. 96. Detroit: St. James Press, 2009, 194–198.

Mowry, Jack K. "Martin Hirschorn— 1921–2010" *Sound & Vibration,* July 2010. Accessed March 12, 2011. www.sandv.com/downloads/1007edit.pdf.

Wetherill, Ewart A., and Warren E. Blazier Jr. "Book Review: Can You Hear Me? Making the World a Quieter Place — My Life as an Unwitting Entrepreneur." *Sound & Vibration* 2007. Accessed March 12, 2011. www.sandv.com/books/review01.pdf.

Inphi Corporation

3945 Freedom Circle
Suite 1100
Santa Clara, California 95054
U.S.A.
Telephone: (408) 217-7300
Web site: http://www.inphi.com

Public Company
Founded: 2000 as TCom Communications
Employees: 166 (2010)
Sales: $83.2 million (2010)
Stock Exchanges: New York
Ticker Symbol: IPHI
NAICS: 334413 Semiconductor and Related Device
  Manufacturing

∎ ∎ ∎

Inphi Corporation offers high-speed analog semiconductor solutions for the communications and computing industries, and provides an important interface between analog signals and information transmitted digitally. These semiconductor solutions boast high signal integrity and data speeds, as well as the ability to reduce the amount of power consumed by the system. The company also aims to provide products that handle bandwidth bottlenecks within networks.

Inphi offers more than 17 product lines and more than 170 products. Many of these products contain indium phosphide, or InP, from which the company derives its name. As a fabless semiconductor company, Inphi designs and markets its various devices (such as

demultiplexers, differential amplifiers, and logic gates) but does not actually fabricate the components itself. Inphi products are sold as components, which are then used for larger electronics sold by its customers. Two of Inphi's largest customers are Samsung and Micron Technology, the former accounting for about one-third of all total sales in multiple years. Sales in Asia account for the majority of Inphi's revenue.

THE EARLY YEARS: 2000–02

Three months after its incorporation, the privately held semiconductor company TCom Communications was renamed Inphi Corporation. After being in business for approximately a year and a half, the company raised $24 million during its second round of equity funding. This brought the total raised in an effort to develop Inphi's high-speed integrated circuits to be used with optical networks to $36 million. The lead investors were Walden International, Dali-Hook Partners, and Tallwood Venture Capital. Inphi chief financial officer Tim Semones stated in the *San Fernando Valley Business Journal* in June 2002 that "Given the current economic environment and reduced investment in telecommunications-related startups, our ability to close such a significant round with a lead investor ... validates our achievements over the past 18 months." Walden's chairman, Lip Bu Tan, cited the company's growth potential and technology as the main reasons for making the investment in Inphi: "We looked at a number of promising companies in the optical networking industry, but ultimately we were sold on Inphi's leading-edge technology and demonstrated customer traction." At the time, the company did not have much competition as not many other companies offered similar product lines.

In December 2002 Ashok Dhawan, former division president at Lucent Technologies, was named president and chief executive of Inphi. At the time, Inphi had a total of 40 employees, and Dhawan announced plans to help shift the focus of the company from technology to customers. Regarding Inphi, the *Los Angeles Business Journal* quoted Dhawan in December 2002 as saying, "They have been doing a lot of good work, but the company has been focused on technology and it has to be developed into more of a business." He went on to explain that "We have the technology, but nobody knows about us."

DEVELOPING NEW PRODUCTS: 2003–06

Over the next few years, Inphi expanded its product offerings. During its first few years, Inphi had focused on developing its core high-speed analog products as well as the proprietary system architectures which addressed bottlenecks in networks. In 2003 Inphi introduced products for communications, and test and measurement, as well as military markets.

Another funding round in December of 2004 secured an additional $18 million for Inphi. The money came from existing investors as well as Cadence Design Systems. The money was earmarked to expand products for some of its devices and to launch the company's Advanced Memory Buffer within the following months.

In 2005 the company introduced its first-generation high-speed phase lock loops (PLLs). It also "developed three differential amplifiers specifically to meet challenges in designing broadband test and measurement equipment, automatic test equipment, and a range of aerospace and military applications," according to *Electronic Engineering Times.*

In 2006 the company began developing its second-generation single chip high-speed PLLs. The company's visibility level was on the rise as well, as Inphi was recognized as one the greater San Fernando Valley's largest technology companies. The oldest company on the list had been in business for more than 100 years. Inphi was the newest company on the list. At that time, Inphi had annual revenues of $20 million, employed 60 people, and had five facilities.

GROWTH AND SUCCESS: 2007

The Fabless Semiconductor Association also awarded Inphi for its remarkable financial performance for doubled revenue or net income without any negative quarters for a period of eight quarters in a row. Readers of the *Electronic Engineering Times* also recognized Inphi, this time for its quality products. Two of the company's differential encoder integrated circuits (ICs) were recognized as two of the best analog products in the industry.

By the beginning of 2007, demand for Inphi's microchips had increased to the point that the company launched a hiring campaign, with plans to double its 60-employee workforce over the next two years. The focus was on hiring highly paid electrical engineers holding advanced degrees to develop microchips for optical communications and networks, as demand in these areas was increasing. These product developers would work in the company's California location where research and development were centered, while manufacturing would continue to be completed by overseas companies.

The company extended its expansion beyond simply increasing its employee base. Inphi also opened an office in Japan, in close proximity to corporations that depend on Inphi's products for their communications and computing systems. This new office would help the company to meet the ever-increasing need for Inphi's integrated circuits.

CONTINUED RECOGNITION AND EXPANSION: 2008–09

Positive recognition for the company continued in 2008. The Fabless Semiconductor Association recognized Inphi as the Most Respected Private Fabless Company. The award was given as a result of Inphi's "achievement in products, its vision and the company's considerable future opportunities in the semiconductor industry," according to the *San Fernando Valley Business Journal* on January 7, 2008. Soon after this, in April 2008, Inphi announced plans to acquire other electronic component manufacturing companies and to go public during 2009. However, the global economic recession created a slight delay to these plans, and the company's IPO did not happen that year.

As a result of increased sales of all of its product lines, Inphi expanded its worldwide sales and distribu-

KEY DATES

2000: TCom Communications is founded.
2001: The company name is changed to Inphi Corporation.
2007: Inphi launches a hiring campaign to double the size of its workforce over the next two years; opens an office in Japan.
2009: Distributors for Inphi products are added in Europe, Japan, China, and Canada, as well as in the United States.
2010: Inphi becomes a publicly traded company.

tion networks in 2009. New sales partners were added within the United States, as well as overseas, to offer a local presence for customers and to support further growth. Distributors for Inphi products were added in Europe, Japan, China, and Canada, as well as three distributors in the United States, located in Oregon, Washington, and Montana. Also, in response to the company's continued growth, a new vice president of operations, Atul Shingal, was hired in September 2009. Not only did Shingal have a proven track record in the field of global technology with more than two decades of experience in "international operations, engineering and quality management, and IT experience," but he had also successfully headed the initial public offerings of two other companies, according to *India Business Newsweekly.*

Inphi was once again recognized for its outstanding performance in the fall of 2009, by Deloitte and *Inc.* magazine. Over the previous five years, Inphi had enjoyed a healthy growth rate, despite a challenging economy. Deloitte listed Inphi at number 134 on its 2009 Technology Fast 500 list of the fastest-growing companies in the areas of technology, media, telecommunications, and life sciences companies. *Inc.* magazine ranked Inphi fourth on its 500/5000 list of the top computer hardware companies. (This list recognizes fast-growing companies.)

BUILDING NEW PARTNERSHIPS: 2009

At the end of 2009, Inphi sold its products to 160 customers, and its products were being designed into systems sold by a number of companies, including Dell Inc., Hewlett-Packard Company, and Agilent Technologies, Inc. At that time, Samsung Electronics Co. accounted for 36 percent of Inphi's annual revenues, and

Micron Technology, Inc., accounted for 17 percent. Between 2006 and 2009, Inphi shipped in excess of 90 million of its high-speed analog semiconductors. Revenue for 2009 was $58.9 million, an increase from revenues of $43.0 million for the previous year. For 2010 revenue increased to $83.2 million, a healthy increase over the previous years.

Between 2007 and 2009, sales to customers in Asia increased from 54 percent to 77 percent of Inphi's total revenue. In fact, the top five locations to which the company's products were shipped were China, Korea, the United States, Taiwan, and Japan. As a result, the company made plans to begin overseas operations in Asia. In April 2010 the government of Singapore approved the establishment of Inphi's international headquarters. Operations began the following month. Inphi expected to recruit new engineers from the universities and technology-based companies in Singapore. Another benefit of this location for conducting Inphi's international operations was its close proximity to Asian customers and suppliers.

A PUBLIC COMPANY: 2010 AND BEYOND

In May 2010 Inphi entered an agreement to acquire all outstanding shares of Winyatek Technology, Inc., for $3.5 million cash, as well as company stock. Winyatek was a manufacturer and wholesaler of flash memory products. The acquisition was finalized later that year.

In June 2010 Inphi filed with the U.S. Securities and Exchange Commission for an initial public offering (IPO) worth approximately $115 million. Money raised through the IPO was earmarked to be used as working capital. The company offered 6.8 million shares to the public at $12 per share. The stock was traded on the New York Stock Exchange under the symbol IPHI beginning in November of that year.

As the demand for mobile devices and wireless connectivity increased, Inphi expected to see an increase in demand for its products. The company expected that by 2014, mobile and wireless Internet traffic would increase by four times as compared to 2009. This, as well as growth in several other areas including cloud computing, would increase demand for Inphi's products and technologies. In fact, demand for cloud services was expected to grow at a compound annual rate of 37 percent between 2009 and 2013. All these factors boded well for Inphi's future in the 2010s.

Diane Milne

PRINCIPAL SUBSIDIARIES

Inphi International Pte. Ltd. (Singapore); Inphi Limited (UK).

PRINCIPAL COMPETITORS

Analog Devices, Inc.; Broadcom Corporation; Hittite Microwave Corporation; NXP Semiconductors N.V.; Texas Instruments Incorporated.

FURTHER READING

"Award: Inphi Corp. Was Named as the Most Respected Private Fabless Company by the Fabless Semiconductor Association. "*San Fernando Valley Business Journal* 13, no. 1 (2008): 5+.

"Chips — Differential Amps Span dc to 10 GHz."*Electronic Engineering Times,* November 21, 2005, 54.

Gianulias, Koula. "Start-up Lands Industry Vet as President." *Los Angeles Business Journal* 24, no. 49 (2002): 29.

Gold, Marty. "Readers Choose the Third Quarter's Best. "*Electronic Engineering Times,* December 18, 2006, 51.

"Inphi Expands Its Executive Staff with New VP of Operations. "*India Business Newsweekly,* September 15, 2009, 6.

Martinez, Carlos. "Inphi Raises $36 Million." *San Fernando Valley Business Journal* 11, no. 26 (2006): 4.

Insight Enterprises, Inc.

6820 South Harl Avenue
Tempe, Arizona 85283
U.S.A.
Telephone: (480) 902-1001
Toll Free: (800) 467-4448
Fax: (480) 902-1157
Web site: http://www.insight.com

Public Company
Incorporated: 1988
Employees: 4,900 (est., 2010)
Sales: $4.14 billion (2009)
Stock Exchanges: NASDAQ
Ticker Symbol: NSIT
NAICS: 454113 Mail-Order Houses; 541512 Computer Hardware and Software Consulting Services; 541511 Custom Computer Software Support Services; 518210 Computer Data Storage Services

∎ ∎ ∎

Insight Enterprises, Inc., (Insight) is one of the world's largest business-to-business distributors of information technology (IT) software and equipment. Its online catalog includes 200,000 products and 18,000 software titles from 3,700 publishers. The company provides IT hardware, software, and services. In 2009 these three groups accounted for 50 percent, 44 percent, and 6 percent of net sales, respectively. Insight's customer base covers a wide spectrum of small to midsize businesses and public sector organizations. It has clients in 190

countries, but North America accounts for over two-thirds of all revenue.

ENTREPRENEURIAL BEGINNINGS, THE 1980S

Eric Crown was working as a retail computer salesperson when, moved by the entrepreneurial spirit, he decided to earn more money for himself instead of someone else. Perhaps recalling a college paper he wrote, he started to act on his idea for a computer mail order company. Despite the paper's "C" grade, he went on to create a multimillion-dollar direct mail business, no small achievement given the challenges of direct marketing computers. As one industry executive told *Direct*: "Anybody can start a computer catalog—that's not difficult. What is difficult is to succeed against the inherent odds." To prosper as a direct marketer, Crown would need to overcome the notoriously small profit margins in computer catalogs and fierce competition from other catalogs, discount retailers, superstores, and resellers. Each of his direct marketing efforts would require a high response level and significant sales. Despite the odds, he succeeded brilliantly.

Crown and his brother Tim established Hard Drives International in 1986 and began selling mass storage computer products. They borrowed $2,000 on a credit card, rented 100 square feet of office space, and bought an ad in *Computer Shopper* magazine selling hard drives. Their advertised price was less than the brothers could buy the hard drives for, but the Crowns calculated that prices would drop between the time of buying the ad and its actual appearance. The result was $20,000 in

COMPANY PERSPECTIVES

Insight's unique model combines an array of advanced services and expert technical resources with a far-reaching supply chain to help its customers realize their information technology (IT) goals. The company's technology practices bring deep technical skills in vital solution areas to help customers implement strategic technologies, while Insight's Lifecycle and Management Services provide innovative ways to balance changing IT priorities and limited resources.

hard drive sales and a better profit than even they expected.

In 1988 Hard Drives International evolved into Insight Direct. Insight marketed mass storage products through ads in computer magazines and inbound toll-free telephone lines. In 1991 the company added product lines, including name-brand personal computers, software, and peripherals. By 1992 Insight spent $1.5 million each month on ads in print media.

GROWTH YEARS: 1990–96

In 1993 the company added catalogs to market more than 20,000 computer-related products, including hard drives, CD-ROM drives, and software. At this time, the company also began employing outbound telephone account executives who focused on larger, corporate customers.

Insight's account executives became one of the hallmarks of the company. They worked for volume sales and customer loyalty, hoping to establish long-term relationships with their customers. As Eric Crown explained: "We're not so much after market share as we are after customer share." Typically, two sales out of every three went to existing customers.

Experienced account executives cultivated strong relationships with their clients so that Insight would become the primary source for their computer-related purchases. Eric Crown termed the overriding principle of the sales force "solution selling." Insight routinely extended weekly training to its already knowledgeable account executives. Corporate goals for profitability were shared freely among sales staff. As Diane Cyr explained in *Direct,* "The sales model here is all Crown ... if you're good you get rich, and if you're not you get out. Miss your goal by one cent, no bonus. Exceed your goal, and you might go on a Caribbean cruise, take a

trip to New Orleans, or personally get handed 500 bucks by Eric Crown himself. The more you sell, the bigger the rewards, the bonuses, the commission percentage. Reps are even empowered to offer volume discounts, cut deals, do whatever it takes to get the customer." The result was an 8 percent call response rate to catalogs in 1995, with one-third converted to sales.

Insight's 800-number system contributed to establishing strong relationships between its 300 account representatives and customers. The company maintained more than 1,000 toll-free telephone numbers linked with specific catalogs and promotions. Each catalog or promotion was assigned an individual 800 number, which connected to specific account executives. This meant that account representatives were linked by their areas of expertise to a given catalog or promotion. This system made targeting and tracking customers easy. Account executives also had individual toll-free telephone numbers, so they could be contacted repeatedly, giving customers the opportunity to speak with an individual who was familiar with them instead of whichever representative just happened to answer the phone.

Another innovation, Insight's own brand of computer, debuted in 1993. Insight combined Intel Corporation's Pentium microprocessor and cutting-edge bus technology to create a state-of-the-art machine. The Pentium microprocessor provided the capabilities needed for three-dimensional graphics, calculating, and video applications, and the bus technology interfaced add-on cards (for example, graphics, networking, or modems) with the microprocessor. Priced lower than competitors' models, Insight's system offered high-speed graphics workstation applications, as well as use as a server for computer networks.

As time went on, Insight downplayed its own products. Sales of its computers eventually shrank from 30 percent of the company's total sales to less than 10 percent. The company discontinued the sale of Insight brand computers in 1996, opting to concentrate on its strengths in marketing and fulfillment instead of developing its own products.

In 1993 Insight first offered outsourcing services to leading manufacturers such as Toshiba, AST, Samsung, Conner Peripherals, and Motorola. Essentially, Insight assumed marketing, sales, accounting, and distribution functions for these manufacturers. Insight created catalogs or process orders from those catalogs for major industry players, with healthy results. Toshiba Accessories' sales, for example, increased tenfold after Insight took over some of its marketing operations. By 1995 12.2 percent of Insight's sales came from outsourcing.

Also by 1995, Insight had reduced its monthly spending on print ads to $150,000. The company

KEY DATES

1986: Eric Crown and his brother Tim establish Hard Drives International.

1988: Hard Drives International evolves into Insight Direct.

1991: The company adds product lines, including name-brand personal computers, software, and peripherals.

1993: The company adds catalogs to market more than 20,000 computer-related products, including hard drives, CD-ROM drives, and software. Insight creates its own brand of computer.

1995: Insight becomes a publicly traded company on NASDAQ.

1997: Insight signs deal to sponsor the Copper Bowl, which is renamed the Insight.com Bowl.

2002: Insight acquires Chicago-based rival, Comark.

2006: Insight acquires Plano-based Software Spectrum.

2008: Insight acquires Phoenix-based Calence LLC.

2010: Insight and Microsoft bolster partnership geared towards offering more cloud-based computing solutions internationally.

introduced its home page on the Web and issued the first Real Audio Talking Advertisement on the Internet. Insight's Internet marketing efforts drew thousands of hits and elicited about 500 catalog requests every day.

Insight also became a publicly traded company on NASDAQ in 1995. Insight accrued $245 million in sales that year, plus $6.1 million in operating earnings. Employees numbered more than 500, and the catalog house file held one million names.

Insight broke ground for a new headquarters for its corporate and sales staff in Tempe, Arizona, in January 1996. The 103,000-square foot facility featured "bull-pen" sales areas with training centers. At the ground-breaking, Eric Crown said, "This building will be a state-of-the-art facility. We expect to see higher sales productivity as a result of the move, as members of our sales force are motivated by the successes of other members of the team."

In 1996 Dataquest, a research firm, predicted that the demand for home personal computers would slow while the small and midsize business computer market

would grow. Since these were typically large repeat customers from corporations, government, and education, Insight initiated *The Business Computing Source Book,* a spin-off of its catalogue aimed directly at the business-to-business market. Featuring products exclusively for office applications and use, the catalog's average order was $1,000, more than $300 larger than orders from Insight's consumer-oriented catalog. Dan Sager, senior vice president of marketing for Insight, revealed: "Most computer catalogs are segmented by product category, such as Apple, PCs or UNIX. But this spin-off focuses on the target customer rather than the product."

The company also instituted a networking catalog and a network manager Web site targeted for local-area network managers. According to Insight's president Tim Crown, "As with the consumer catalog, we will use extensive targeting to reduce the number of 'cold' mailings necessary to meet our goals. This strategy ensures increased response rates at a lower cost. Our networking book will further pinpoint our business catalog offerings, reaching an elite group of network product buyers." As a result of this strategy, Insight's business-to-business sales grew from 33 percent of total sales to 67 percent by the end of 1995 to 80 percent by the fourth quarter of 1996. Insight also offered a leasing program in 1996 through PFO Capital Leasing of Newbury Park, California, to provide corporate customers with leasing options. Eric Crown noted: "Offering these aggressive leasing options through PFO will allow us to better meet the financing needs of business customers."

GAINING A WORLDWIDE PRESENCE

The late 1990s was a boom growth period for Insight. Sales grew 50 percent a year, faster than many competitors. The market continued to transition swiftly from computer dealers to online retailers. Also, the company made significant changes to its Web site as its business started a gradual shift from catalogs and salespeople to a self-serve Web site. Insight redesigned its Web site several times to cater to this changing dynamic. In a major site redesign, visitors to the site would navigate based on the size of their company and type of business and other preferences. Insight also ramped up its marketing efforts, becoming the first e-commerce site to become a sponsor of a college bowl game. The Tuscon-based Copper Bowl was renamed the Insight.com Bowl. Another marketing effort that made the news was offering a free computer to anyone who signed a three-year contract with Compuserve's Internet access service. The company also took steps to expand its international presence. In 1998 the company bought a German computer firm, Computerprofis of Frankfurt, Germany. Computerprofis was one of the largest direct marketers in Germany. Insight also expanded its operations in Canada and the United Kingdom. In 1999 Insight reached a record $1 billion in sales, and Web sales had increased 350 percent from the previous year. Its international sales were 7.5 percent of the total revenues. Ten percent of its revenue came from its Web site while the rest came from its various mail order catalogs.

SIGNS OF A CHANGING MISSION

The year 2000 brought several shifts in the company's focus. The Internet was becoming a larger portion of revenues and the company began reducing the number of catalogs it shipped. CEO Tim Crown said about catalogs, "It just wasn't profitable. You would mail 1,000 [catalogs] and you might get one customer." As Insight moved into the 21st century the company had already made small steps to venture beyond its retail focus and offer information technology services and solutions to its customers. In October 1999 the company formed an alliance with Concentric Network Corp. to offer its customers Concentric's e-commerce and Web hosting services, while Concentric agreed to offer Insight's equipment and services to their clients. In 2001 Insight bought Action PLC, a British computer reseller that it had tried and failed to purchase in the past. Upon completing this purchase Insight decided to close its German operation and concentrate its European efforts in the United Kingdom. These moves coincided with a downturn in computer sales. Revenues grew only 2 percent from 2000 to 2001. Insight's narrow focus on small and medium-sized businesses hampered its efforts to continue the substantial growth of the past. Its biggest competitor, CDW, had long ago diversified its client base to include governments and schools. While it also suffered under the downturn in computer sales, CDW managed to sustain good growth during this difficult time.

In April 2002 the company acquired a rival, Chicago-based Comark. Insight paid $100 million in cash and $50 million in Insight shares for the company. Comark added its expertise in the medium-to-large company market. Sales jumped almost 40 percent between 2001 and 2002, but a downturn in computer sales and the economic recession in the United States hit companies like Insight hard going into the next year. By 2003 annual sales growth had slowed considerably, growing only marginally. It became difficult to drive growth through just offering the lowest price. In 2004 Insight reported net sales of $3.082 billion, a growth of 6.8 percent, still considerably lower than only two years before.

In October 2004 Richard A. Fennessy became president and CEO of Insight. Before coming to Insight, Fennessy was head of International Business Machines Corp.'s direct telesales and Web channel. Fennessy brought a wave of change to increase growth during difficult times. He replaced 40 percent of management and invested $1.5 million to transform its sales force into one that sold services rather than products. In 2005 Insight announced that it was interested in teaming up with partners who offered services to small and midsize companies. Insight set up its structure to offer five service areas: security, storage, printing, mobility, and IT Management. The company's efforts faced competition, as rivals CDW and PC Connection made similar moves. All three firms were actively hunting for partners in the IT services industry.

SOFTWARE SPECTRUM ACQUISITION AND THE FUTURE

In September 2006 Insight purchased Plano, Texas-based Software Spectrum from Level 3 Communications Inc. for $287 million. This represented Insight's most significant move into the IT services business. Software Spectrum specialized in software and mobility solutions for midsize and large companies. The acquisition significantly increased the size of Insight, adding 1,300 employees in 24 countries. Software Spectrum reported $1.9 billion in revenue in 2005. The integration of Software Spectrum into Insight raised net sales from $3.6 billion in 2006 to $4.8 billion in 2007. In another sign that Insight was moving away from its catalog origins, the company sold its PC Wholesale unit, a product distribution network, to SYNNEX Corp., and in 2008, Insight acquired Phoenix-based Calence LLC. Calence was one of the largest Cisco Systems Inc. solution providers in the United States. Insight was moving fast toward becoming a major player in the IT services industry.

In December 2009 Kenneth Lamneck became president and CEO of Insight. Before coming to Insight, Lamneck was a leading manager at Tech Data, an international IT distributor. He took the helm of a company that with the purchase of Software Spectrum Insight had launched itself as a significant player in the IT solutions market. However, it was uncertain whether this major shift in focus would pay off and whether the company could match some of its larger competitors, like Hewlett Packard and Dell Computer. Net sales actually shrunk from $4.82 billion in 2008 to $4.14 billion in 2009, but this may have been due to the worldwide recession rather than Insight's decision to move into IT services.

Insight still was a significant player in the IT mail-order business, and in 2010 computer sales began a slow recovery. Also that year, with cloud computing becoming popular, Insight and Microsoft announced a reprioritized partnership to help garner new customers in Europe, the Middle East, and Africa. (Cloud computing refers to the storage of data and information not within a PC but in a "cloud" that can be accessed remotely from multiple locations.)

Over the years, Insight had built an excellent reputation for its sales associates, who offered an industry standard for customer service and IT expertise. With an army of energetic "teammates" (as the company refers to its employees), and a strong game plan for integrating services with its products business, there was reason to believe that in the 2010s Insight would return to strong growth once again.

Charity Anne Dorgan
Updated, Aaron Hauser

PRINCIPAL SUBSIDIARIES

Calence, LLC; Insight Consulting Services, LLC; Insight Direct Worldwide, Inc.; Insight Licensing, Inc.; Insight Technology Solutions, LLC; Kortex Computer Centre, Ltd. (Canada).

PRINCIPAL COMPETITORS

CDW Corp.; Dell Inc.; HP Enterprise Services, LLC; Lenovo Group Limited; Newegg.com Inc.; Softchoice Corp.; Symantec Corp.; Systemax, Inc.

FURTHER READING

Barrett, William P. "You Want Cables with That?" *Forbes,* August 24, 1998, p. 80a.

"A Bigger Prize For Insight." *Computer Reseller News,* January 28, 2008, p. 8.

Burke, Steven. "An Insightful Move?" *Computer Reseller News,* May 30, 2005, p. 72.

Campbell, Scott. "Insight Eyes VARs In SMB Bid — Company Is Investing $1.5 Million to Retrain Its Sales Staff to Work with Partners." *Computer Reseller News,* May 30, 2005, p. 5.

———. "Reliable Sources" *Computer Reseller News,* November 14, 2005, p. 52.

"CRN Interview: Tim Crown, Insight Enterprises." *Computer Reseller News,* April 21, 2003, p. 47.

Cruz, Mike, and Jerrry Rosa. "It's a Real Page-Turner —Insight, PC Connection Follow CDW's Lead in Cutting Back Number of Catalogs." *Computer Reseller News,* July 3, 2000, p. 12.

Estell, Libby. "Dialing up Devotion." *Incentive,* September 2000, p. 72.

"Insight Enterprises, Inc."*International Directory of Company Histories,* edited by Jay P. Pederson, Vol. 18, 259–261. Detroit: St. James Press, 1997. *Gale Virtual Reference Library.* Web. 12 Apr. 2010.

Insight Enterprises, Inc. "Microsoft Cloud Services Help Insight EMEA Drive Accelerated Growth into the Enterprise and SME Market Space." July 19, 2010. Accessed January 14, 2011. https://www.insight.com/pages/investor_relations.web?source=pressreleases.

"Insight to Buy Software Spectrum." *Computer Reseller News,* July 24, 2006, p. 84.

Kovar, Joseph F. "Insight Acquires Reseller Comark." *Computer Reseller News,* April 29, 2002, p. 4.

McWilliams, Gary. "Big Computer Dealers Feel Mail-Order Bite." *Wall Street Journal,* July 13, 2000, p. B6.

Stebbins, John. "CDW Bucks the Trend, Continues to Grow." *Chicago Sun-Times,* March 18, 2002, p. 55.

Interactive Data
Corporation

32 Crosby Drive
Bedford, Massachusetts 01730
U.S.A.
Telephone: (781) 687-8500
Fax: (781) 687-8005
Web site: http://www.interactivedata.com

Private Company
Founded: 2001
Employees: 2,500 (est., 2009)
Sales: $757.20 million (2009)
NAICS: 523920 Portfolio Management

■ ■ ■

Interactive Data Corporation (IDC) is a financial information company that provides financial market data, analytics, and related services to financial institutions, active traders, and individual investors. The corporation's services are provided by four companies that make up its two operating segments of institutional services and active trader services. IDC customers use their offerings to support their portfolio management and valuation, research and analysis, trading, wealth management, sales and marketing, and client service activities. Services are marketed either by direct subscriptions or through third-party business alliances.

Specific services subscribed to include fixed income evaluations, reference data, real-time market data, trading infrastructure services, fixed income analytics, desktop solutions, and Web-based solutions. The company's institutional clients include many of the larg-

est global mutual funds/investment funds, asset managers, securities firms, banks, and custodians. The company conducts business in the United States, the United Kingdom, Europe, and the Asia-Pacific region.

COMPANY ORIGINS

IDC's origins date back to 1992 when Allan Tessler, a company restructuring expert, was contacted by creditors of the bankrupt Financial News Network (FNN) to help salvage what they could from the failed company. Turnaround expert Tessler, who was initially contacted by FNN's creditors to handle the bankruptcy, brought in his friend, Alan Hirschfield, who had served as head of Columbia Pictures and Twentieth Century Fox Films, to help. The two began to sell off and reorganize the bankrupt Financial News Network (FNN), including the Learning Channel, which the pair sold to TCI's Discovery Channel.

Tessler and Hirschfield had no intention of starting a new company themselves but believed that some of FNN's holdings offered a good business opportunity. As a result, they decided to buy FNN's data broadcasting services division to establish the Data Broadcasting Corp. (DBC). Chief among these division's services were the Signal and QuoTrek brand services, which focused on providing investment information to private investors. These two services formed the foundation for the new Data Broadcasting Corp. The Signal service relayed information from the American, NASDAQ, and New York stock exchanges directly to desktop computers, and QuoTrek provided handheld wireless receivers

COMPANY PERSPECTIVES

Interactive Data Corp. is committed to data quality and reliable delivery, high-quality client service, flexible client relationships, and innovative technology and services. It is also dedicated to providing expertise and experience and developing strategic alliance worldwide. Interactive Data has distinguished itself by being open and flexible in the way it delivers its offerings to thousands of clients globally. Interactive Data works collaboratively with clients to integrate its market data services into time-sensitive operational workflows and help them address key business challenges. Through this approach, the company is focused on cultivating and maintaining mutually beneficial long-term relationships with clients as well as an ever-expanding range of partnerships and alliances with leading financial software and technology solutions providers. As a result, Interactive Data represents choice in an era when choices have been greatly diminished.

through which subscribers accessed stock data via FM transmission.

Tessler and Hirschfield each paid $1 million to acquire a 25 percent interest in the then public company. The remaining stock was distributed to FNN's creditors and former shareholders. The company was moved to Hirschfield's hometown of Jackson Hole, Wyoming, where the two men reportedly enjoyed outdoor activities such as skiing and fishing.

QUICK GROWTH: 1993–2000

Although the investment made by Tessler and Hirschfield was relatively modest, they were soon seeing significant financial rewards. In 1993 the company's revenues reached $14.8 million and a profit of $927,000. Much of the business came from the Signal real-time stock quote service, which provided private traders services similar to those that big brokerage firms and financial institutions enjoyed but without the high costs associated with the large company services. Over the next few years, the company focused on expanding, acquiring information companies such as Capital Management Sciences (CMS) and DataSport, which provided up-to-the minute information on sporting events and news. They also acquired Computer Sports World and Broadcast International Inc. in 1995.

DBC also established its own Web site in 1995, thus initiating its entry into Internet-based information delivery. The site offered a wide range of services that featured Brand Label Quotes, stock quotes on a 15-minute delay, and financial and sports news. The Web site also featured the ability to download free software to a desktop computer with the Windows 1.2 operating system, thus enabling reception of the Signal data feed. Chief among these division's services were the Signal and Quo Trek brand services that focused on private investors. The site was receiving more than two million "hits" a day by the middle of the year.

The company continued over the next few years to focus on delivery and content improvements. By 1999 DBC's sales reached $108 million. Sales had grown due to aggressive purchases of other information companies, such as the Federal News Service (FNS) in 1996 and ADP Global Treasury Information Services in 1998. The company also established a 1997 agreement with the Columbia Broadcasting System (CBS) to create CBS MarketWatch, which included contributions by CBS journalists, editors, and other staff. In addition, the company continued to aggressively expand its Internet-based information offerings through efforts such as StockEdge and StockEdge Online.

In 2000 DBS merged with Financial Times Asset Management, owned by Pearson plc. The move led to the company providing real-time financial data and information services targeting retail and institutional investors. Pearson retained a majority ownership of 60 percent. That same year, the company moved its headquarters to Bedford, Massachusetts, and acquired Itex Ltd. At around the same time, the company decided to focus on financial data service, thus ending its sports operations. The year also saw Stephen Hill named chairman of the company, and Stuart Clark was elected CEO and president. By the end of the year the company had offices in the United States, Europe, Asia, and Australia.

COMPANY RENAMED

In 2001 DBC changed its named to Interactive Data Corporation in order to reflect the company's new focus on supplying financial data primarily via the Internet. The following year, the company began trading on the New York Stock Exchange. By the end of 2002, company sales had grown 10 percent to $375 million. The company continued to expand its services when, in March 2003, IDC acquired ComStock Inc., a financial information service that had been owned by McGraw-Hill Companies. *Business Wire* reported that Clark noted: "The addition of ComStock's real-time market

REORGANIZATION AND ACQUISITIONS: 2007–08

By 2007 IDC, partly through company acquisitions that retained their own identities, had assembled a range of offerings in a variety of information-based areas, including pricing and reference data, valuation services, customized financial portals, and fixed-income analytics. In February 2007 the company announced a reorganization in its business lines. As a result, FT Interactive Data became Interactive Data Pricing and Reference Data, ComStock became Interactive Data Real-Time Services, and CMS BondEdge became Interactive Data Fixed Income Analytics.

As reported in *Security Industry News,* the move was meant to unify "the identities of the three institutionally oriented businesses," capitalize on the company's name recognition, and improve efficiency. "We believe that this new branding initiative will help us to build on the strengths of our company today, support our next phases of growth and expansion, and provide us with a framework to further align our organization from an operational, sales and marketing, and product development perspective," IDC's CEO Stuart Clark was quoted as saying in the *Security Industry News* article.

In a $25.3 million cash deal in 2007, IDC acquired the assets of Xcitek LLC's market data division and the market data assets of its affiliate Xcitax LLC. The purchase of Xcitek's market data division enhanced IDC's ability to provide a broad range of North American corporate actions data, from reorganization information to cost basis and class action data. This data service was provided via various platforms to more than 2,000 financial institutions throughout the world. The following year, 2008, found IDC acquiring the Rome-based reference data provider Kler's Financial Data Service S.R.l. for $29.6 million. The acquisition heightened IDC's capabilities to provide data on actions and taxation information, Italian and international securities, including coverage of equities and listed and unlisted Italian bonds, derivatives, warrants, and funds.

NEW OWNERSHIP: 2010

Looking toward the future, IDC announced in January 2010 that it was studying its strategic options. The announcement stirred interest from several private equity companies. On July 29, 2010, IDC was acquired by investment funds managed by Silver Lake and Warburg Pincus. IDC had been traded on the New York Stock Exchange (NYSE) since 2002 and on the NASDAQ prior to that. After the sale to the new investors, the company became privately owned by the Igloo Intermediate Corporation, which was wholly owned by

---

KEY DATES

1992: Allan Tessler and Alan Hirschfield create Data Broadcasting Corp. (DBS).

2000: DBS merges with Financial Times Asset Management owned by Pearson plc.

2001: DBS changes its name to Interactive Data Corp.

2003: Interactive Data acquires ComStock Inc. from McGraw-Hill Corp.

2010: Interactive Data is acquired by investment funds managed by Silver Lake and Warburg Pincus.

---

datafeeds rounds out our ability to serve the mission-critical operations of the global financial community."

The purchase of FutureSource LLC for $18 million in 2004 enabled the company to become a provider of real-time futures, commodities, and foreign exchange markets coverage. The company also purchased the datafeed customer base of HyperFeed Technologies. By the end of 2004 company profits exceeded $80 million on revenues of $485 million.

In July 2006 IDC announced that it had established the Interactive Data Managed Solutions AG group. The group's focus was to build and manage customized Web-based financial market data applications for a wide range of financial content. This content was to be presented within customized applications that could be used by various organizations around the world, such as retail and investment banks, online brokers, stock exchanges, and media portals. Interactive Data Managed Solutions AG was based on the technology and capabilities developed at IS.Teledata AG, which IDC had purchased in 2005.

In a *Business Wire* article, Mark Hepsworth, president of IDC's ComStock group, which was to oversee Interactive Data Managed Solutions, noted: "By offering these customized solutions tailored to customers' market data requirements we believe we are differentiating Interactive Data in the marketplace." Hepsworth also commented that the new group was "well positioned to build on its existing customer base in Europe and expand its business in North America." In addition to the main office in Germany that was formerly IS.Teledata, the group's subsidiaries included operations in France, Italy, United Kingdom, Spain, Finland, and Switzerland.

HG Investors LLC. The company was delisted from the NYSE, and stockholders received $33.86 per share for their stocks.

Commenting on Silver Lake and Warburg Pincus in an Interactive Data news release, IDC president and chief executive officer, Ray D'arcy, noted: "I believe that the collective experience and expertise of these firms in the financial services and technology sectors will enable us to take our company to a new level in terms of our size, capabilities and stature in the industry." Following the transaction, the company remained headquartered in Bedford, Massachusetts, and also maintained its various offices around the world.

In September 2010 the company announced that Mason Slaine had been named chairman, president, and chief executive officer of the company, replacing D'Arcy, who was named vice chairman of Interactive Data. Slaine was previously chairman of MLM Information Services, a vendor of corporate tax compliance software and services, which he founded in 2005 with Warburg Pincus. November 2010 saw IDC named the best third-party valuation provider as part of *Credit* magazine's Credit Awards Americas 2010.

GLOBAL EXPANSION

As a part of its global expansion program, Interactive Data added Equinix Inc. data centers in Tokyo and London in December 2010. These additions added to its existing presence with Equinix, a provider of data center services, in Hong Kong, Sydney, Chicago, New York, and Frankfurt. The new data centers enhanced the company's real-time market data and trading solutions, thus extending Interactive Data's capabilities to key financial markets across the world.

In addition to global expansion, the company continued to focus on enhancing its delivery platforms and technical infrastructure. In December 2010, the company announced that it had extended its mobile solutions suite for BlackBerry. The product, PrimeTerminal Mobile, featured a Blackberry application that enabled users to follow developments in the financial markets in real time and monitor their portfolios at any time and from anywhere. Specifically, PrimeTerminal Mobile offered access to a broad range of real-time quotes, historical and reference data, charts, business news and market overviews.

In January 2011 Interactive Data released a redesigned version of its eSignal software, the company's core information sharing software. The new version included an improved user-friendly interface that allowed user to focus entirely on market analysis and trading. The company's future plans were to accelerate its momentum in building the business globally and further enhance its overall capabilities, delivery platforms, and technical infrastructure.

David Petechuk

PRINCIPAL SUBSIDIARIES

Data Broadcasting Corp. (British Virgin Isles); eSignal, Inc.; GTIS Corporation; IDCO Canada Holdings Inc. (Canada); IDCO Worldwide Holdings Ltd. (UK); Infotec Holdings Corp.; Interactive Data Cayman Ltd. (Cayman Islands); Interactive Data Management & Services Verwaltung GmbH (Germany); Interactive Data Real Time Services, Inc.

PRINCIPAL DIVISIONS

Interactive Data Fixed Income Analytics; Interactive Data Pricing and Reference Data; Interactive Data Real-Time Services.

PRINCIPAL COMPETITORS

Barclays Bank PLC; Bloomberg, L.P.; CME Group Inc.; FactSet Research Systems Inc.; Standard & Poor's Financial Services LLC; Thomson Reuters Corporation.

FURTHER READING

"Interactive Data Completes Acquisition of S&P ComStock." *Business Week,* March 3, 2003, p. 5206.

Interactive Data Corp. "Interactive Data Announces Agreement to Be Acquired by Silver Lake and Warburg Pincus in a Transaction Valued at $3.4 Billion." May 4, 2010.

"Interactive Data Forms Managed Solutions Group; IS.Teledata Business Renamed; New Group Focused on Enabling Financial Institutions and Web Portals to Utilize a Wide Range of Financial Content within Customized Applications." *Business Wire,* July 11, 2006.

"One Interactive Brand," *Securities Industry News,* February 26, 2007.

Jackson Family Wines

421 Aviation Boulevard
Santa Rosa, California 95403
U.S.A.
Telephone: (707) 544-4000
Toll Free: (800) 544-4413
Fax: (707) 569-0105
Web site: http://wwwkj.com

Private Company
Incorporated: 1982 as Kendall-Jackson Vineyards and
    Winery.
Employees: 1,200
NAIC: 312130 Wineries

■ ■ ■

Jackson Family Wines is more widely known under the name Kendall-Jackson Winery and is one of the few remaining family-owned wineries in the United States. The company produces approximately five million cases of wine annually from the fruits of its more than 14,000 acres of vineyards, and it exports to at least 40 countries. The company remains in the control of billionaire Jess Jackson and his family.

THE LAWYER TURNED RELUCTANT VINTNER

Jesse "Jess" Stonestreet Jackson founded Kendall-Jackson Vineyards and Winery in 1982. Jackson was born in 1930 and grew up in San Francisco. He learned about winemaking from his family's Italian neighbors. Jackson earned a scholarship to attend the University of California at Berkeley where he studied law. He worked at the San Francisco docks to pay his living expenses. He also worked as a Berkeley policeman and as a legal researcher for then California attorney general, later governor, Pat Brown. Jackson passed the California bar exam in 1955 and became a respected attorney specializing in land use and property rights. One of his most famous cases was *Joe Gallo v. Ernest and Julio Gallo.* Jackson represented Joe Gallo in Gallo's failed attempt to take a one-third interest in his brothers' E. & J. Gallo winery, the world's largest.

In 1974 Jackson and his wife, Jane Kendall, purchased an 82-acre ranch near Lakeport in the Clear Lake region of northern California. They bought it as a weekend getaway and hobby farm for their family. Jackson's passion for grapes and winemaking fueled the family's decision to remove the trees and convert the crops to vineyards. The vineyards flourished, and for seven years Jackson's family sold grapes to local wineries such as Fetzer. In 1980 there was a wine glut that left most of their crop unsold, so Jackson decided to make wine. Jackson said, "I never intended to go into the winemaking business, but I was forced to. We couldn't sell our grapes for what it cost us to grow them. So we did the only thing we could to, we made wine." The family's first two chardonnays were bottled under the Chateau du Lac label. For almost a decade Jackson had experimented with different styles of wine, growing several varieties of grapes and supplementing them with grapes grown in vineyards throughout California's cool coastal regions. Most California wineries emphasized making wines from a single vineyard, but Jackson blended grapes grown in locations such as Santa

COMPANY PERSPECTIVES

Our family culture is built on the time-honored principles of hard work, integrity, an uncompromising desire for quality, and the long-term stewardship of the land. It takes a strong-willed family to live up to these principles. We take the no-compromise, high road approach to quality required to grow our world-class grapes and produce critically acclaimed wines.

What separates us further from our more corporate competitors is that we can put the long-term interests of future generations above short-term financial gains. Our success will be measured by generations of family rather than by numbers on quarterly reports.

Barbara, Monterey, Sonoma, and the Lake counties. He and his wife established the Kendall-Jackson Winery to satisfy a market niche for reasonably priced chardonnay wine.

In 1983 Jackson recruited winemaker Jedidiah "Jed" Steele to oversee processing. Kendall-Jackson chardonnay quickly became a success thanks to a fortunate mishap. Chardonnay is traditionally a dry white wine, but Jackson's fermentation became "stuck," meaning there was too much sugar left in the wine. The company brought in several winemakers to help save the wine, but they failed. The result was an off-dry chardonnay with some residual sugar that made it sweeter than traditional chardonnay wines. As it turned out, U.S. consumers liked the sweet taste, so much so that it became one of California's most popular wines. Soon, sweet and fruity chardonnays became the wine of choice for 60 percent of U.S. consumers. Later, a common phrase among vintners would be "Americans talk dry but drink sweet," which might as well have been the motto for Kendall-Jackson's chardonnay. The first Kendall-Jackson chardonnay vintage was introduced in 1983 under the name Vintner's Reserve Chardonnay. It won the American Wine Competition's first Platinum Medal. Jackson tells a story of how one day in 1983 he walked up and down the streets of Manhattan with an open bottle of chardonnay. He popped into fashionable bars and restaurants and poured free samples. He said, "it's $5 a bottle. How many cases do you want?" He sold 100 cases that day. Within six months he had sold 18,000 cases of chardonnay.

Jackson expanded the Vintner's Reserve line to include a sauvignon blanc, cabernet sauvignon, pinot noir, merlot, zinfandel, and riesling. The line was highly successful and after more experimentation Kendall-Jackson launched The Grand Reserve line, which was priced somewhat higher than the Vintner's Reserve. The Grand Reserve line of wines included a chardonnay, cabernet sauvignon, pinot noir, zinfandel, and merlot. The company marketed these wines as higher quality and as wines that the company would only produce in years when the wines could meet the higher standards that the company set for them.

When the Vintner Reserve wines proved their staying power in sales Jackson gave up his law practice and devoted all his time to winemaking. Jackson received praise even from his competitors. In an interview Michael Mondavi, president and CEO of Robert Mondavi Winery, said, "He's been creative when the industry's been lethargic." One advantage the company had was Jackson's ability to negotiate real estate deals. Kendall-Jackson acquired prime vineyards at bargain prices. Jackson and his wife divorced in the mid-1980s, but the company kept her maiden name on the wines.

GROWTH THROUGH ACQUISITIONS

In 1987 Jackson and Robert Mondavi Winery bought 1,000 acres in the Santa Maria Valley that included 700 acres of the bankrupt Tepusquet chardonnay vineyard. Nestle-owned Beringer Vineyards was on the verge of buying Tepusquet, but Jackson talked directly with the founder and manager of the property, who had the first right of refusal on the sale. The manager chose Jackson over Beringer, and Jackson compensated him generously for the favor. Jackson owned majority interest in the vineyard and renamed it the Cambria Winery and Vineyard. In 1988 Jackson acquired the Edmeades Winery in Mendocino County, and in 1989 he acquired the Stephen Zellerbach Winery for $3 million and renamed it the J. Stonestreet & Sons Winery in honor of his father. As he expanded the company's holdings Jackson also hired some of the best winemakers he could find, sometimes relying on the advice of Ric Forman, another Napa Valley winemaker. Foreman described Jackson as "a hard bargaining businessman ... he's outrageous. He thrives on the game. It's not the money for him, it's the game." Jackson's talents earned him a reputation as a cunning dealmaker with high energy and entrepreneurial skills. The enormous production facility he built and his speedy ascension to the top of the wine industry were no better evidence of those skills.

Some wine purists dismissed Kendall-Jackson wines as lower quality sweet wines, but Jackson insisted that

KEY DATES

1974: Jess Jackson purchases 82-acre ranch near Lakeport.
1980: Jackson founds the Kendall-Jackson Winery.
1982: Kendall-Jackson launches Vintner's Reserve Chardonnay.
1987: Company acquires Tepusquet chardonnay vineyard; *Wine & Spirits* magazine selects company as "Winery of the Year."
1988: Company acquires Edmeades Winery in Mendocino County.
1989: Company acquires Zellerbach Winery for $3 million and renames it J. Stonestreet & Sons Winery.
1992: Judge rules that Kendall-Jackson's recipe for chardonnay wine is a protected trade secret.
1993: Company moves headquarters to Santa Rosa, California.
1996: Kendall-Jackson forms its own distribution company for in-state sales; company acquires Chateau De Baun Winery.
2000: Company hires Lew Platt as CEO; Jess Jackson retires.
2007: *Wine Enthusiast* magazine gives Jackson its "LifetimeAchievement" award.
2008: Vintner Hall of Fame honors Jess Jackson as an inductee.

vinfera vines grew in the Caucasus Mountains of the former Soviet Georgia, grapes bear the best fruit in thinner, but well-drained soils." This statement gave insight as to why he tended to grow grapes on small slopes with drainages that mimicked mountain conditions.

THE TRADE SECRETS OF WINEMAKING

In 1990 Jed Steele left the company to start his own wine label, named simply Steele. The label would produce chardonnay, zinfandel, and cabernet sauvignon varieties. John Hawley, formerly of Cos du Bois, took over his position as chief winemaker for Kendall-Jackson. Steele remained a consultant with the company, but in May 1991 Jackson severed his relationship with Steele and refused to pay him an agreed severance package of $400,000 plus $10,000 for each month as he trained his successor. Jackson accused Steele of revealing trade secrets to new clients and of luring away grape suppliers. In 1992 Steele sued for the $275,000 he claimed Jackson still owed him, and Jackson countersued, claiming Steele disclosed trade secrets, interfered with the company's business relationships, and was negligent in his duties while preparing to quit.

The case drew wide attention from the California winemaking community. Many feared that a decision in favor of Jackson would change the way wine was made in California. The key issue was whether a winery could own a trade secret or whether some aspect of the winemaking process could be considered a trade secret. At the time, most of California's elite winemakers had graduated from the same schools of enology. They worked together during their formative years and rose up together as the industry grew and flourished. They called on each other when technical problems occurred. They lent each other equipment and even stored each other's wines when space was short. Many believed the industry's success had much to do with the free flow of ideas and technical expertise.

Jackson's lawyer argued that those days were long gone, that the industry had matured beyond the days when the free flow of ideas among a small group of winemakers was necessary to grow the industry. Jackson argued that his process was very specific and did not necessarily apply to other wineries. Jackson felt that the free flow of ideas and expertise among winemakers should and would continue even if the court found in his favor. The secret that Jackson felt Steele had divulged was the company's technique for making its off-dry chardonnay, specifically the method of stopping the fermentation before all the natural grape sugar was converted into alcohol and carbon dioxide. Steele's lawyer contended that every winemaker in California

his wines were made from the finest grapes and provided what the consumer desired. Virtually all the grapes that went into Kendall-Jackson wines came from two climatic zones in California, the coastal region and the temperate zone. The chardonnay, pinot noir, syrah, and zinfandel wines tasted best when made from grapes grown in the coastal region. These grapes benefited from the cooling breezes of the Pacific Ocean. The cabernet sauvignon, merlot, sangiovese, and sauvignon blanc wines tasted best when made from grapes grown in the temperate region. The company's vineyards stretched from Mendocino in the north to Santa Barbara in the south. The soils within zones varied, which was why a chardonnay from the Santa Maria Beach area tasted tropical, like guavas and mangos, while the more northern grown grapes tasted like pear and citrus. Kendall-Jackson took these factors into consideration as it blended its grapes to create its various wines. In an interview, Jackson said, "All good grapes are mountain grapes, because of natural selection. Because the first knew the process, and Kendall-Jackson's method was not a special formula that deserved protection. In August 1992 the judge ruled in favor of Kendall-Jackson, saying that the company did, in fact, possess a legally protected trade secret. The judge barred Steele from revealing Jackson's process, but he also ordered Jackson to pay Steele $312,000 in severance pay and bonuses.

MORE GROWTH THROUGH ACQUISITIONS

During the early 1990s Kendall-Jackson went on a buying spree. In 1991 Kendall-Jackson bought 1,300 acres and leased 1,200 acres of chardonnay vineyards in Monterey Country. In 1993 the company acquired Vinwood Cellars from the Chevron Corporation for $10 million. Vinwood produced 500,000 cases a year from its Geyserville winery. Jackson also acquired La Crema in Sebastopol. The year 1993 was also the year that Kendall-Jackson moved its corporate headquarters, retail shop, and tasting room from Lakeport to Santa Rosa. In 1994 the company acquired Domain Laurier in Forestville for $2.5 million, Mt. Veeder Vineyards in Napa Valley, Durell Vineyards in Sonoma County, and Robert Pepi Vinery in Napa Valley. Kendall-Jackson also won approval to build a 360,000-case winery in Windsor. The year 1994 also marked the company's first international ventures. The company bought Villa Arceno, a wine estate in the Tuscany region of Italy and VinaCalina, a winery in Chile.

The company continued to buy properties in 1995, but in that year Jackson took the company in a slightly different direction. For the California industry, the 1990s brought a move toward more traditional values in winemaking. Consumers and vintners recognized the advantage of specific vineyards devoted to producing particular wines. In 1995 Jackson structured eight of the company's smaller, start-up wineries into an international subsidiary named Artisans & Estates. The subsidiary included Jackson's own start-ups (Stonestreet, Cambria, Camelot, and Lakewood), recently acquired wineries, and its international assets. The company set up independent winemakers to run each winery, each specializing in making wines from single vineyards and viticultural regions. Among these winemakers was Charles Thomas, formerly from Robert Mondavi, and Tom Selfridge, formerly from Beaulieu. The new division launched Kristone, a sparkling wine from the Santa Maria region. They also introduced a new label, Hartford Court, specializing in Russian River Valley pinot noir. Jackson combined the blending of wines for the Kendall-Jackson label with the production of specialty wines from Artisan & Estates. The image of the Kendall-Jackson labels was reliable taste. The image of the Artisan & Estates label was that of more exclusive, handcrafted wines, and each wine offered what the company said was a "flavor domain."

Kendall Jackson acquired the 5,400-acre Gauer Ranch in 1995. Gauer was one of the largest agricultural holdings in Sonoma Country. Jackson bought the property from the Chevron Corporation as part of a deal worth $30 million. The company also bought the 580-acre Mission Trails Ranch in Santa Maria and the 208-acre Ahmann cattle ranch in Carneros. Much of the company's expansion was due to Jackson's opportunism. Increased competition in the California wine industry forced many smaller wineries into extinction. Jackson smartly scooped up some of the more valuable wineries at bargain prices. By 1995 analysts valued the Kendall-Jackson empire at $400 million. The company sold around 1.8 million cases and earned $120 million in revenues with 230 employees.

As chief vintner, John Hawley oversaw all of the Kendall-Jackson wine production. He believed there were advantages to handling the grapes as little as possible during the process, choosing not to filter or manipulate the wine needlessly. At the Vinwood facility, grapes were fed whole into the presses on a conveyer system, which allowed for more free-run juice and less sediment. The mixture's initial fermentation took place in 20,000-gallon stainless steel tanks. After fermentation, the wine was transferred to small oak barrels, for the majority of fermentation took place before the mixture was aged and bottled. The oak barrels imparted a spicy, toasty-oak flavor, sometimes compared to vanilla or butterscotch. The barrels also allowed a slow evaporation of water and alcohol. The flavor intensified with age. The shape of the barrels, grain density, oak source, thickness of stave, and level of toasting were some of the variables that contributed to a wine's taste. In the early 1990s Jackson saw the importance of the barrels to flavor, and he saw how much expense they added to the process. To reduce costs and improve quality the company formed a partnership with Independent Stave Company of Missouri. Together they bought Merrain International, a wine barrel making operation in Beaune, France. The move cut the cost of barrels in half.

A SHOT ACROSS THE BOW

Wine and Spirits magazine named Kendall-Jackson "Winery of the Year" at the end of 1995. In 1996 Kendall-Jackson made a change to its distribution network, in particular to in-state (California) distribution. The company believed that its brands were not receiving the attention they deserved from distributor Southern Wine and Spirits, so it ended its relationship with the company and replaced it with its own distribution network under a subsidiary called Regal Wine Company. Angry over Kendall-Jackson's decision, Southern campaigned to undermine the company's sales. Southern's salespeople urged some restaurant owners not to stock Kendall-Jackson wines, and some of them complied. Kendall-Jackson's move also caused some concern among distributors that the company was going to destroy the three-tier system (producer-distributor-retailer) that had been in place since the end of prohibition in the United States. With the growth of Internet and mail-order sales in a wide range of products wine aficionados were increasingly demanding the ability to order a particular vintage from wherever they could find it, even ordering it directly from the winery.

The alcohol industry had at one time been populated by a large number of small distributors scattered across the country, but over the years the industry became consolidated into a group of large entities. As these large entities commanded more control over the market they were able to demand a higher price for a product, which was passed on by the retailer to the consumer. A large distributor like Southern wanted to maintain its hegemony as the middleman and felt threatened by the growth of direct sales. A battle ensued between producers, distributors, and the state legislatures that wrote the laws governing the sale of alcohol within their borders. Southern mounted a lobbying effort that led several states to pass laws that made it a felony to sell alcohol across state lines, including direct sales from producer to consumer. Kendall-Jackson's decision to handle its own in-state distribution was seen as a shot across the bow. However, Southern's campaign to undermine sales failed, and Kendall-Jackson's sales returned to normal. Later, in 1997, Louisiana passed a law that was hailed as a harbinger of how states could resolve the dispute and end the war. The law allowed direct sales but assessed excise taxes on the transaction. Also, the buyer had to be of legal age and was limited to five cases per year.

In 1996 Kendall-Jackson continued to acquire more wineries and expand its operations. The company purchased the Fulton Winery Chateau De Baun, which would operate under the Artisans & Estates subsidiary. Other large wineries participated in the same land grab, and land prices skyrocketed. During that same month, the company sued E. & J. Gallo for trademark infringement, citing similar bottles and "colored leaf" logos on the bottles. Later in the year, the jury rejected the claim, and the judgment in favor of Gallo was affirmed on appeal. In May 1996 John Hawley left Kendall-Jackson to start his own winery. Steve Reeder replaced him as head winemaker. Reeder had been serving as winemaker at the Vinwood winery.

In February 1997, only 18 months after taking the position, Steve Reeder left Kendall-Jackson, and Randy Ullom took over as head winemaker. Ullom had been winemaker at Kendall-Jackson's Camelot Vineyards in Santa Barbara County.

STRENGTH IN A NEW CENTURY: 2000–08

In 2000 Foster's Brewing Group purchased Beringer Wine Estates Holdings for $1.14 billion, and analysts talked of further consolidation in the California wine industry. In November 2000 Jess Jackson, at the age of 70, retired from the company. He had already turned over his duties as chief executive officer to former Hewlett-Packard CEO Lew Platt. Platt was hired to help the company better manage its international holdings, explore growth opportunities, and potentially split up the company into public and private entities to better handle growth. An IPO plan was scrapped soon after an initial investigation into the idea. In February 2001 the company began seeking a buyer for its Kendall-Jackson Wine Estates unit, but after Jackson rejected three bids ranging from $1.5 to $2 billion, the company took itself off the sales block. A month later Platt resigned.

The middle of the first decade of the 21st century brought more consolidation to the California wine industry. Constellation Brands bought Robert Mondavi Corp, Diageo PLC bought Chalone Wine Group Ltd., and Wine Group LLC bought Golden State Vintners Inc. Despite the active market for mergers Kendall-Jackson remained immune to the barrage of deal making. Kendall-Jackson launched its Highland Estates label in 2005. Highland Estates joined the company's Grand Reserve and Stature lines in offering very expensive upper tier wines. By 2006 Kendall-Jackson's distribution arm had grown significantly and started distributing vodka in California and seven other states. This was the company's first foray into distributing a product other than wine. In December 2008 Jess Jackson was inducted into the Vintners Hall of Fame.

SURVIVING THE RECESSION: 2009 AND BEYOND

By 2009 Kendall-Jackson and its subsidiaries operated under the umbrella name of Jackson Family Wines. The company along with other California wineries suffered under the economic downturn. In previous recessions, high-end wines remained prosperous, but in 2009 even wealthy drinkers cut back spending on fine wines. While the overall volume of wine sales grew, sales of bottles priced at $25 and up fell about 12 percent. Retailers marked down their inventories significantly. Jackson was forced to lay off 12 percent of its staff, one of the largest layoffs among California wineries. The industry's woes continued into 2010 as the worldwide recession continued. Even the lower-priced bottles had trouble selling.

Falling wine prices affected every aspect of the wine industry. The value of vineyard lands dropped. Banks were less willing to lend to wineries. Grape prices dropped significantly. Although wine consumption grew 2.1 percent in the United States to 323 million cases, domestic wine shipments fell 4 percent due to competition from a flood of inexpensive foreign wine. It was the first such drop in 16 years. Jackson was close-mouthed about its sales but industry experts estimated that its shipments fell more than 20 percent. Analysts believed that the economic downturn would bring an industry shakeout, forcing smaller players out of the game and leaving. Also, the industry would see several of the founding members leave and hand over to a younger generation of wine executives.

Jackson had already gone through its internal transition. Jess Jackson was no longer at the helm, but he had handpicked his successors, and the Jackson family still retained control of the company. Much of his family, including Jackson's daughters, was still involved in the making of the company's wines.

Jackson Family Wines had endured some difficult financial hits, but in the early 2010s the company's wines still enjoyed a loyal following, and the company seemed hearty enough to weather the dismal economic conditions and thrive in a new and uncertain decade.

Terri Mozzone
Updated, Aaron Hauser

PRINCIPAL SUBSIDIARIES

Artisan & Estates Vineyards & Wineries; Jackson Family Farms; Kendall-Jackson Wine Estates; Majestic Marketing Group, Ltd.; Regal Sales Co.

PRINCIPAL COMPETITORS

Bronco Wine Company; Constellation Wines U.S., Inc.; Diageo Chateau & Estate Wines; E. & J. Gallo Winery; Foster's Wine Estates; Robert Mondavi Winery; Ste. Michelle Wine Estates; Trinchero Family Estates.

FURTHER READING

Appel, Ted. "K-J Creates Company for Small Wineries." *Press Democrat,* (Santa Rosa, CA), June 8, 1995, E1.

Berk, Christina Cheddar. "It Was a Good Year for Wine Mergers." *Wall Street Journal,* January 5, 2005.

Carlton, Jim, and David Kesmodel. "Luxury Wine Market Reels from Downturn." *Wall Street Journal,* July 8, 2009.

Deogun, Nikhil, and Jim Carlton. "Kendall-Jackson Seeks a Buyer." *Wall Street Journal,* February 9, 2001, B7.

"End of the Wine Wars." *San Francisco Chronicle,* June 25, 1997, A18.

Freedman, Alix M., and John R. Emshwiller. "Vintage System." *Wall Street Journal,* October 4, 1999, A1.

Frost, Bob. "Action Jackson." *San Jose Mercury News (West Magazine),* October 19, 1997.

Hinkle, Richard Paul. "Riding the Wine Trail With Jess Jackson." *Wines & Vines,* March 1, 1994, 20.

Marcus, Kim. "California's Mystery Vintner." *Wine Spectator,* July 31, 1995, 1+.

McCallum, Kevin. "Setbacks in Wine Country." *Press Democrat,* (Santa Rosa, CA), February 28, 2010.

Prial, Frank. "Wine Talk." *New York Times,* June 17, 1992, 10.

Tesconi, Tim. "Wine Industry Split on Standards." *Press Democrat,* (Santa Rosa, CA), May 16, 1996, E1.

———. "Wizard of Wine: Man Behind the Label Remains a Mystery." *Press Democrat,* (Santa Rosa, CA), June 25, 1995, A1.

Jones Day

—■—

901 Lakeside Avenue
Cleveland, Ohio 44114
U.S.A.
Telephone: (216) 586-3939
Fax: (216) 579-0212
Web site: http://www.jonesday.com

Private Company
Founded: 1893 as Reavis & Pogue
Employees: 2,500 attorneys (est., 2010)
Sales: $1.52 billion (2009)
NAICS: 541110 Offices of Lawyers

■ ■ ■

Ranked by revenue, Jones Day is the second-largest legal firm in the United States and the eighth-largest firm in the world. From its beginnings as a partnership in Cleveland, Ohio, the firm has gone on to establish 32 offices across the United States and around the world, earning a reputation as a legal powerhouse, particularly in the areas of litigation, corporate law, mergers and acquisitions, and antitrust law.

FOUNDING PARTNERS

Jones Day got its start in Cleveland, Ohio, in 1893 as a partnership between two respected and successful lawyers. Edwin J. Blandin, originally from New York, had been practicing law in Ohio for 23 years and had earned a reputation as a respected legal professional during that time, working as both a lawyer and a judge.

The firm's junior partner, Delaware native William Lowe Rice, had been admitted to the Ohio bar in 1883 and had focused his practice on the emerging realm of governmental regulations of businesses and corporations.

The firm of Blandin & Rice established a reputation early on for representing major utilities and railroads in the Cleveland area. Clients included the Lake Shore Electric Railway, the Baltimore & Ohio Railroad, the East Ohio Gas Company, Ohio Bell Telephone Company, and the Cleveland Electric Illuminating Company. Blandin & Rice was also active in Cleveland's growing status as one of the foremost cities in the United States, helping to write the Ohio Municipal Code and representing industrial and manufacturing interests such as Cleveland Trust Company, W.S. Tyler Company, and the Ohio & Pennsylvania Coal Company.

Unfortunately, the firm lost its founding partner William Rice to tragedy in 1910, when Rice was murdered during an evening stroll. The culprit was never caught. Three years later, a merger nearly quadrupled the firm's annual sales and brought its complement of attorneys up to 14. Among the new blood was Frank Ginn, who would go on to become one of the most influential managing partners in the history of Jones Day.

GINN AND THE ROARING TWENTIES

By the time World War I ended in 1918, the firm had begun representing the Van Sweringen brothers, Oris

COMPANY PERSPECTIVES

Jones Day is organized as a true partnership, and it operates as such, not as an LLP or LLC or some other quasi-corporate entity. We see ourselves as a global legal institution based on a set of principles to which a large number of men and women can commit— principles that have a social purpose and permanence, and that transcend individual interests.

and Mantis. These two men were tycoons of the Cleveland scene, railroad barons who exerted considerable influence on local business and development. The brothers controlled the "Nickel Plate" New York, Chicago, and St. Louis Railroad, along with Cleveland's Union Station and Terminal Tower transportation hub.

In the late 1920s, the firm's first nationally prominent case came from representing the Van Sweringen brothers and their railroad interests. In the case of *Snyder v. New York, Chicago, & St. Louis R.R.*, which went all the way to the Supreme Court, the firm successfully argued that the Nickel Plate's efforts to consolidate its many regional rail interests had not violated any antitrust laws.

Cleveland was the fifth-largest city in the United States by 1920, and the firm was increasingly finding itself representing nationally prominent clients and companies. Oil tycoon J. D. Rockefeller, whose Standard Oil had gotten its start in Ohio, was a client, as were local manufacturing corporations like the Weatherhead Company and Thompson Products, Inc., which would go on to become aereospace giant TRW. The 1920s also saw the firm, now known as Tolles, Hogsett, Ginn & Morley, beginning to represent steel interests, starting with the Otis Steel Company and the Midland Steel Products Company.

The firm also became actively involved in land trusts, the holding of a piece of real property on behalf of and for the benefit of another individual or company. Frank Ginn served as counsel to Cleveland's Union Trust Company when it opened on January 1, 1921. The company, which rose from the merger of 29 financial institutions, was fifth-largest among the nation's trust companies. During the twenties the firm also developed a special land trust certificate, which allowed trusts to finance real estate development without paying unnecessarily high state taxes.

MANAGING PARTNERS AND INDEPENDENCE

Perhaps the most lasting development during this period came from Frank Ginn's introduction of the managing partner system. Under this system, which continued to guide Jones Day policy in the 2010s, the firm was to be guided by a single managing partner who would be responsible for all management decisions. This allowed the other attorneys at the firm to focus solely on practicing law and serving clients' needs. This attitude was further encouraged by Ginn's rejection of compensation credit to individual attorneys for bringing in clients. Ginn established a culture of putting the needs of the firm as a whole as its clients ahead of individual interest.

Ginn also laid down a guiding principle that the firm had the right and obligation to turn away clients, no matter how powerful, wealthy, or influential. As Jones Day associate Marvin Bower summed up Ginn's philosophy, "If you are not willing to take pain to live by your principles, there is no point in having principles." This powerful example was carried on by later generations of Jones Day lawyers, most notably when the firm refused to represent President Richard Nixon during the Watergate crisis because of the White House's refusal to share the presidential tapes with its attorneys.

DEPRESSION AND WAR

The firm was not immune to the economic effects of the Great Depression of the 1930s, but the global crisis also ultimately proved to be an opportunity for growth. In 1933 the federal government ordered a mandatory "bank holiday" for all of the nation's financial institutions in order to give them a chance to reorganize and recapitalize and restore the public's faith in banks. Jones Day helped the Union Trust Company get through this difficult period and avoid federal foreclosure. The Wagner Act of 1935 reorganized labor laws and brought more work for the firm's labor lawyers. Throughout the 1930s, Jones Day lawyers represented companies like Republic Steel, whose 1930 formation it underwrote, and the Goodyear Tire & Rubber Company, which had run afoul of the Federal Trade Commission in a drawn-out antitrust case, a case Goodyear eventually won.

Frank Ginn died in 1938. In keeping with his managing partner system, he designated his successor to Thomas H. Jones. On January 1, 1939, the firm merged with another Cleveland firm, Day, Young, Veach & LeFever. With the merger, the firm's complement of attorneys grew to 22 partners and 20 associates. The merger brought together the original firm's focus on corporate law with the new firm's strong litigation

KEY DATES

1893: The law firm that would eventually become Jones Day is founded as a partnership by Cleveland lawyers Edwin J. Blandin and William Lowe Rice.

1939: Thomas H. Jones, having succeeded to leadership of the firm the previous year, merges with Luther Day's firm.

1973: Jones Day significantly expands its practice in the Washington, D.C. arena, marking the beginning of an era of high-profile clients and national growth.

1985: Tobacco company R.J. Reynolds chooses Jones Day as its national coordinating counsel in the wake of a wave of lawsuits.

2009: Jones Day opens foreign office in Dubai.

tradition. The following year, the firm enjoyed revenues of $1 million for the first time since the 1929 stock market crash.

World War II proved to a far more stressful time for Jones Day than the Great Depression had been. This was due to the fact that over a third of the firm's lawyers left to serve in the war in either military or governmental capacities. The firm instituted a hiring freeze for the duration of the war and got by with taking on associates from local law schools.

Even at reduced capacity, the firm proved able to handle major challenges, as in 1944 when one of its clients, the East Ohio Gas Company, found itself at the center of a tragic accident. An explosion at one of its plants killed 130 people and leveled two square blocks. Jones Day lawyers advised the company to admit culpability and settle victims' claims quickly, which the company did. Within three months, most claims had been settled without need for costly lawsuits. The strategy was widely credited with saving the company from bankruptcy.

POSTWAR GROWTH

After the end of World War II in 1945, Jones Day began looking toward establishing a national presence. Its first move in this direction came just a year later when, in 1946, a branch office was opened in Washington, D.C. This was a somewhat unusual move at the time, with the Washington, D.C., legal scene being viewed by most industry observers as largely shut off

to outsiders. However, the experience of Jones Day lawyers like H. Chapman "Chappie" Rose, who had served during the war as procurement agent for the government, told the firm there was room in the expanding role of the federal government, which Rose predicted correctly would not diminish just because the war had ended.

The firm's presence in Washington would prove to be a crucial piece of its successful fight against President Truman in 1952. With the Korean War raging, Truman wanted to nationalize the country's steel mills in order to fend off the threat of a strike that might shut down a vital wartime industry. Jones Day, with its long-standing tradition of representing steel interests, was hired to represent the steel industry in the subsequent case that sought to block the president's move. The case went before the Supreme Court, with Jones Day attorneys successfully arguing that the president had exceeded his authority. It was a landmark case in the definition of the powers of the executive branch, and the case made Jones Day a nationally recognized firm.

For the next 20 years, the firm continued to grow, taking on increasingly prominent clients. Financiers Abe List and Cyrus Eaton were represented by the firm, as were companies seeking securities financing such as American Greetings Corporation, TRW, National City Bank of Cleveland, Sherwin-Williams Company, and the J.M. Smucker Company. The firm helped companies like Midland-Ross Corporation in its mergers with Industrial Rayon Corporation and the National Casting Company. Other companies represented during this time included Diamond Alkali Company, Clevite Corporation, Scott & Fetzer Company, Diamond Shamrock Corporation, and Mogul Corporation.

The firm also began to flex its litigation muscles during the 1960s, most notably in its representation of General Motors during the lawsuits spawned by the early model Corvair and the subsequent firestorm when Ralph Nader's *Unsafe at Any Speed* dubbed the car the most dangerous vehicle on the road. It was the firm's first case of single-product, multidistrict litigation, and it won the first class action case brought against GM. Jones Day again represented a rubber and tire company, this time Firestone, in litigation with the federal government. In 1972, the firm successfully argued a case that allowed Ohio banks to open branches in counties other than their own.

THE D.C. SPLIT

Under the guidance of managing partner Jack Reavis, the firm had grown to nearly 200 lawyers, with many of the new blood drawn from the ranks of school law review editors and Supreme Court clerks, by the dawn of the 1970s. A small branch office had been opened in Los Angeles, and a merger bolstered the size of the Washington office.

In the late 1970s, the Supreme Court's rulings in the cases of *Goldfarb vs. Virginia State Bar* and *Bates vs. State of Arizona,* which eliminated minimum fee schedules and allowed lawyers to advertise, would soon prove instrumental in ushering in a new era in litigation practice. These long-term implications were not immediately appreciated by most of the legal world, however. Jones Day's new managing partner, Allen Holmes, was one of the few visionaries who understood the full implications of the court's decisions. Unfortunately, most of the staff of the Washington, D.C., office did not see eye to eye with Holmes' vision.

The resulting split in 1980 was the only such incident in the history of Jones Day. In the wake of the split, only 30 partners and associates remained at the Washington branch. The remainder left to start their own practice, Crowell & Moring.

NATIONAL AND INTERNATIONAL GROWTH

The D.C. split proved to be only a temporary setback for Jones Day, however. With Holmes leading the way into the new era of business law practice, the firm was soon experiencing an unprecedented period of geographical expansion. A branch in Columbus, Ohio, was opened in 1980, and in 1981 the firm expanded to Dallas, Texas, another region long considered hostile to outside attorneys. This move might have proved a dismal failure but for the assistance of local attorneys who had joined the firm and who helped ease the cultural gap between the locals and the new arrivals. Jones Day worked hard to integrate itself into the new community and its efforts paid off. In 1984 the firm opened a second Texas branch in Austin.

Throughout the 1980s, Jones Day continued to open new branches across the country, from New York to Chicago to Pittsburgh, Atlanta, and Irvine, California. It also opened offices abroad, starting with a Hong Kong branch and continuing on to Shanghai, Geneva, Brussels, Tokyo, Taipei, Frankfurt, and Madrid.

This rapid growth was part of an industry-wide trend fueled by escalating litigation and higher fees for top partners. By the late 1990s, Jones Day was involved in approximately 4,000 litigation cases worldwide, devoting 500 lawyers to litigation matters alone. During this period, Jones Day earned a reputation for defending large corporations that found themselves involved in highly charged, unpopular cases. For instance, the firm

continued to represent Firestone, this time over the course of 15 years of litigation over accidents involving the company's multipiece truck tires and rims. The firm also defended paint company Sherwin-Williams from lawsuits over lead content in its paint.

Perhaps most notoriously, starting in 1985 Jones Day served as national coordinating council for the tobacco company R.J. Reynolds (later RJR Nabisco Holdings Corporation) in a series of lawsuits involving claims of health damages caused by tobacco products. Jones Day lawyers successfully defended the company in the highly publicized Galbraith trial, and they won about 250 other cases for the company over the next 15 years. In the end, RJR Nabisco joined with other tobacco companies in reaching a $368.5 billion settlement.

ONE FIRM WORLDWIDE

In 2002 Stephen J. Brogan became the first Jones Day managing partner to reside outside of Cleveland, a sign of the firm's now global outlook. Since Brogan took the reins, the firm has continued to open new branches both at home and abroad. Offices opened in Houston, San Francisco, and San Diego between 2001 and 2004, and the 2009 opening of a branch office in Dubai completed a series of international openings throughout the decade that included Beijing, Munich, Moscow, and Mexico City.

Well over a century after its founding as a small-town partnership, the global powerhouse that is Jones Day continued to uphold its client-centered principles in the face of an ever more complex world of business law.

David Larkins

PRINCIPAL COMPETITORS

Akin Gump Strauss Hauer & Feld LLP; Baker & McKenzie, LLP; Clifford Chance LLP; Skadden, Arps, Slate, Meagher & Flom LLP.

FURTHER READING

Anderson, A. Donald, et al. "Jones, Day, Reavis & Pogue." In *Los Angeles: Realm of Possibility,* 320. Chatsworth, CA: Windsor Publications, 1991.

Borowitz, Albert. *Jones, Day, Reavis & Pogue: The First Century.* Cleveland: Jones, Day, Reavis & Pogue, 1993.

Dougan, Arthur L. *Jones, Day, Reavis & Pogue: A Slightly Irreverent History from the Beginning to 1975.* Cleveland: Jones, Day, Reavis & Pogue, 1985.

Haberman, Ian. *The Van Sweringens of Cleveland: The Biography of an Empire.* Cleveland: Western Reserve Historical Society, 1979.

Jackson, Harvey H. *Hansell & Post: From King & Anderson to Jones Day Reavis & Pogue 1890–1990.* Atlanta: 1989.

"Jones, Day, Reavis & Pogue." In *International Directory of Company Histories.* Vol. 33. St. James Press, 2000.

Mahar, Maggie. "Tobacco Showdown." *Barron's,* April 14, 1997, 15.

KEMET Corporation

2835 Kemet Way
Simponsonville, South Carolina 29681
U.S.A.
Telephone: (864) 963-6300
Web site: http://www.kemet.com

Public Company
Founded: 1987 as Kemet Electronics Corporation
Incorporated: 1919 as Kemet, a division of Union Carbide
Employees: 10,400 (2010)
Sales: $736.3 million (2010)
Stock Exchanges: New York
Ticker Symbol: KEM
NAICS: 334414 Electronic Capacitor Manufacturing

■ ■ ■

KEMET Corporation sells a wide variety of capacitors, a primary component of most electrical devices that can be used to smooth power output or filter interference, among other things. KEMET has three main business groups. Its Tantalum unit sells tantalum and aluminum capacitors, while its Ceramic group creates multilayer ceramic capacitors containing elements such as palladium. Its Film and Electrolytic Group builds film, paper, and wet aluminum capacitors which can be used in hybrid electric drive vehicles, for example. All told, the company produces around 30 billion units each year in the three divisions.

In addition to its headquarters in the United States, KEMET has locations in Mexico, China, Italy, Portugal,

Indonesia, Sweden, Finland, Bulgaria, Germany, and the United Kingdom. Roughly three-fourths of all sales are from outside North America.

THE BEGINNINGS OF A STAND-ALONE COMPANY

Kemet was created in 1987 when Union Carbide Corporation decided to jettison its "Kemet" capacitor manufacturing division. The capacitor industry was hurting at the time, and Union Carbide decided that the division no longer complemented its overall corporate goals. On April 1, 1987, the managers of the capacitor operation, with the cooperation of GE Capital Corp., bought out the subsidiary and renamed it Kemet Electronics Corporation. Kemet became a stand-alone company with Union Carbide as a 50 percent shareholder. Dave Maguire, the former leader of the unit, was named chief executive of the new company. Under his direction, Kemet accelerated its rate of investment in the burgeoning surface-mount capacitor business.

Maguire's decision to promote the surface-mount business was influenced by a number of trends that were emerging in the capacitor industry, an understanding of which provides insight into Kemet. Capacitors are among the most common components found in electronic circuits and are generally considered commodity items. They are named according to their dielectric, which is the material used to store and regulate the electricity. Different dielectrics include ceramic compounds, aluminum oxide, tantalum pentoxide, mica, plastic, paper, and even air. During the 1970s and

1980s, tantalum and ceramic capacitors became widely used in electronics industries for integrated circuits.

Most capacitors are mounted on a printed circuit board, which contains other electronic devices. A capacitor can be mounted by inserting lead wire "legs" extending from the dielectric through holes in the board, or by soldering the capacitor directly to the surface of the board. Capacitors used in the former technique are called "leaded" capacitors, whereas the devices utilized in the latter technique are known as "surface-mount" capacitors. Until the late 1980s leaded capacitors were considered conventional. In fact, not until the mid-1980s did surface-mount capacitors begin increasing in popularity with equipment manufacturers. A primary advantage of surface-mount devices is that they can be applied to both sides of a printed circuit board, whereas leaded capacitors can only be attached to one side. The dual-sided feature allows electronics manufacturers to build smaller devices.

EARLY HISTORY AS A SUBSIDIARY: 1919–45

The market switch from leaded to surface-mount capacitors complemented Kemet's operations, because Kemet had long been a leader in the production of tantalum and ceramic capacitors. Those two dielectrics are widely used with integrated circuits and possess characteristics that are particularly useful in surface-mount applications. In fact, Kemet, as a subsidiary of Union Carbide, had made the decision to target the tantalum capacitor industry shortly after Bell Laboratories invented the solid tantalum capacitor in the 1950s. The advantage of the tantalum dielectric was that it was useful in applications that required low-voltage semiconductors in electrical circuits. Kemet's decision was a sound one, as demand for high-tech tantalum capacitors mushroomed during the late 1950s and 1960s.

Kemet succeeded in the tantalum capacitor business for reasons dating back to the company's inception. Kemet was established as a division of Union Carbide in 1919. Union Carbide created the unit to purchase the assets of the Cooper Research Company of Cleveland, Ohio. Cooper had invented a promising high-

temperature alloy shortly before the buyout, and Union Carbide believed that it could integrate the technology into some of its operations. The name "Kemet" was derived from the words "chemical" and "metallurgy." Kemet used the advanced alloy to create high-performance grid wires utilized in triode vacuum tubes. The grids were used to regulate the flow of current in triodes, which were the precursor to the transistor. In 1930 Kemet's product line was broadened to include barium-aluminum alloy getters, which were an essential element in all vacuum tubes.

Kemet benefited during the 1930s and 1940s from the deep pockets of its parent, Union Carbide. That financial backing allowed Kemet to develop automatic machinery that made possible the production of high-quality getters in the massive quantities that were needed to match the rapid expansion of vacuum tube demand. Vacuum tubes were the basic building block of the electronics industry during the period. Importantly, demand for vacuum tubes during World War II exploded as production of communication, radar, and other types electronic equipment boomed. Evidencing the importance of Kemet's role in the vacuum tube industry, the company supplied an estimated 80 percent of all the vacuum tubes used by the Allies during the war.

DECADES OF GROWTH: 1945–79

Kemet continued to prosper selling vacuum tubes during the postwar economic boom. Interestingly, Kemet carved out a niche as a supplier for early vacuum-tube computer equipment. Then, in the early 1950s, Bell Telephone Laboratories invented the transistor. It soon became clear that the highly compact and efficient transistor was going to rapidly displace the vacuum tube. Kemet management foresaw the shift and decided to change its direction accordingly. Bell Laboratories had also invented the tantalum capacitor. Tantalum is a white, malleable, metallic element. When processed, the metallic substance offers specific characteristics needed for certain capacitor applications. Since Union Carbide had experience in the fields of high-temperature metals and alloys, the solid tantalum capacitor was chosen as Kemet's second-generation product to complement existing lines and eventually provide an alternative route to growth.

Kemet got into the solid-state capacitor industry on the ground floor. Demand for its capacitors ballooned during the late 1950s and early 1960s, and the devices quickly supplanted vacuum tubes as the company's core product. To keep pace with growth, Kemet built a 50,000-square-foot capacitor manufacturing facility in 1962 in Greenville, South Carolina. The plant opened

KEY DATES

1919: Kemet is created as a division of Union Carbide Corporation to manage assets of Cooper Research Company.

1930: Kemet produces getters, an essential element of a vacuum tube.

1963: Greenville Production plant opens.

1987: Kemet Electronics Corpration created when Union Carbide Corporation jettisons its "Kemet" capacitor manufacturing division.

1992: Kemet becomes a publicly traded company as KEMET Corporation.

2000: Sales for the year reach $1.4 billion, the company's most successful year to date.

2003: KEMET makes its first acquisition; the company buys some of the product lines from Greatbatch-Sierra Inc., a specialty capacitor and filter supplier.

2006: KEMET acquires companies that expand its product range into film, paper, and wet capacitors.

2009: The U.S. Department of Energy awards a $15.1 million grant to the company to support the production of film and electrolytic capacitors that will support electric drive vehicles.

in 1963 and remained Kemet's key production facility for several years. By the late 1960s Kemet had established itself as a leading U.S. capacitor manufacturer and the top producer of solid tantalum capacitors in the world.

In 1969 Kemet expanded its capacitor line to include multilayer ceramic capacitors. Kemet's sales continued to rise during the 1970s and into the early 1980s. Shortly after entering the ceramic capacitor industry, the company opened a new production facility in Matamoros, Mexico. The Cleveland plant was then phased out and all of its equipment and personnel were transferred to the South Carolina facility or to the Mexican plant. New plants were subsequently opened in Greenwood, South Carolina, and Columbus, Georgia, but the Georgia plant was later shuttered.

Increased capacity allowed Kemet to make heady advances in the market for high-tech ceramic capacitors. When Kemet entered the industry in 1969 there were 35 U.S. producers competing in that segment. By 1974

Kemet was the second-largest supplier of ceramic capacitors in the nation, a position that it would retain for the next 20 years.

COMPETITION IN THE INDUSTRY: THE 1980S

Kemet's success up until the 1980s was largely attributable to its savvy use of advanced capacitor technology, although its gains partially resulted from U.S. domination of many of the industries that incorporated capacitors. That situation began to change in the 1970s, when foreign manufacturers, particularly in Japan, began vying for U.S. market share. In fact, a number of Japanese and other Asian companies entered the electronic device industries during the late 1970s and 1980s and became tough competitors against companies like Kemet. Heightened competition placed downward pressure on prices and reduced profit margins. In the United States, the capacitor industry, like many other electronics sectors, became consolidated as companies joined forces to achieve economies of scale. By the mid-1980s only a handful of the several hundred companies that had competed earlier in the century remained.

Kemet managed to survive the industry shakeout for several reasons. Its sheer size was one important advantage. In addition, Kemet managed to keep costs down by having much of its more rudimentary assembly work done at its low-cost Mexican production facility. By the mid-1980s production of most types of capacitors had essentially become a commodity business. Large producers pumped out billions of capacitors for pennies apiece, and the companies that could create them at the lowest cost usually had the edge. To make matters worse, original equipment manufacturers that purchased most of the capacitors were increasingly moving to Asia and other low-cost manufacturing regions, which had the effect of depleting some of Kemet's U.S. customer base.

CHANGES FOR THE COMPANY

By the mid-1980s the capacitor industry had lost its luster in the eyes of Union Carbide executives. Profit margins were under pressure from foreign competitors, and the value of shipments by the U.S. capacitor industry was declining. In 1987 Union Carbide decided to sell the company by way of a management leveraged buyout. As described earlier, Union Carbide retained 50 percent of the newly formed Kemet Electronics Corporation until the company could get its feet on the ground, and former division head Dave Maguire took over as chief executive of the company. In 1990 Union Carbide completely divested itself of Kemet shares, and

Kemet management and other investors, including Citicorp Venture Capital, completed the leveraged buyout. Not until 1992 did Kemet go public, as KEMET Corporation, with a stock offering on the NASDAQ over-the-counter market.

Maguire believed that Kemet, under Union Carbide's ownership, had failed to take advantage of opportunities in the market. Although Kemet was operating in a depressed U.S. industry, the company maintained certain strategic advantages that could exempt it from the malaise. Chief among those advantages was Kemet's position as a leader in tantalum and multilayered ceramic technology. Those two technologies were of vital importance in the trend toward surface-mount circuits. Immediately after taking the helm, Maguire launched an aggressive drive to increase capacity for producing surface-mount ceramic and tantalum capacitors. During the next eight years KEMET would spend more than $175 million adding new production capacity, all of which was for surface-mount products.

In addition to redirecting KEMET's product mix, Maguire initiated a comprehensive quality program. During the early 1980s, U.S. and European producers had been left in the dust by Japanese competitors on the basis of quality. To recover lost ground, KEMET adopted a Total Quality Management plan designed to completely turn around its customer service and product quality. The effort worked. By the early 1990s KEMET was recognized as a global leader in quality. At least one analyst called KEMET's focus on quality and customer service obsessive and unsurpassed. Sales to what became one of KEMET's largest customers shot up more than eightfold during the late 1980s and early 1990s because of its quality and service, according to the buyer. In 1992 KEMET achieved registration to the stringent and respected ISO 9001 standards for quality. It also received Ford Motor Company's Total Quality Excellence Award, which was considered among the most prestigious awards of its kind in the country.

GLOBAL SUCCESS: 1994–95

KEMET's aggressive quality initiatives, combined with its emphasis on surface-mounted capacitors, supplied hefty sales and profit gains during the late 1980s and early 1990s, despite overall sluggishness in the U.S. capacitor industry. Demand for surface-mounted capacitors mushroomed during the period, and KEMET was among the best-positioned companies in the world to exploit the demand. KEMET's revenues from the sale of surface-mount capacitors shot up from about $30 million in 1988 to nearly $300 million in 1994. Meanwhile, sales of leaded capacitors declined only

slightly. The net result was that KEMET's sales mushroomed from less than $200 million in the late 1980s to about $475 million annually in 1994. Likewise, net income vaulted from a deficit in the mid-1980s to about $30 million annually by 1994.

KEMET entered 1995 as the largest manufacturer of tantalum capacitors in the world with 18 percent of that thriving market. It was also the fourth-largest global supplier of multilayered ceramic capacitors with about 7 percent of that segment. By 1995 KEMET was churning out 11.4 billion capacitors annually from 10 different manufacturing plants in the United States and Mexico, and was offering a total of 35,000 different types of capacitors.

COST-CUTTING AND RELOCATION: 1996–98

Over the next few years, the company's manufacturing operations were relocated to lower-cost facilities outside of the United States as a strategy to limit costs and maintain KEMET's competitive edge in the ever-changing electronics industry. Rising costs of palladium, as well as decreasing prices for capacitors were partly to blame for the company's need to find ways to cut costs. By moving manufacturing from the Carolinas to Mexico, the company expected savings of nearly $18 million per year. This move did, however, cause approximately 1,000 employees in the United States to be laid off, which equated to about one-fourth of the manufacturing staff in South Carolina. The move to Mexico was not the only one the company would make. By 2010 KEMET operated manufacturing facilities not only in Mexico, but also in China, Italy, England, Portugal, Sweden, Indonesia, Germany, and Bulgaria.

Decreasing demand for capacitor products caused KEMET to cut an additional 1,440 employees in 1998. While the company had expected a unit-volume increase of 40 percent, revenues actually dropped by 20 percent. Also, the cost of palladium had risen from $130 per ounce to $440 over the few previous years.

Believing that the company's stock was undervalued, KEMET repurchased two million of its shares. At the time, the stock had dropped to under $12, down from a high of over $25 within the previous year. Despite low earnings, the company continued to develop new products and replaced some of the palladium with other metals in all its ceramics. KEMET developed 50 new products during 1998.

FINANCIAL UPS AND DOWNS: 1999–2001

After several years of tightening its belt, KEMET began seeing financial improvements. The company enjoyed record sales during 1999 as cell phones and handheld electronics caused the demand for capacitors to skyrocket. As a result, the company built a 30,000-square-foot addition to its ceramic capacitor manufacturing facility in South Carolina in the spring of 2000. New equipment was also installed in two other plants, although expansion was not needed. Also in 2000 the board of directors announced a two-for-one stock split, the first in five years. At the time of the announcement, the company's stock was more than $78 per share.

In order to secure its supply of tantalum, KEMET entered an agreement with Australasian Gold Mines NL. Under the terms of the agreement, KEMET acquired 50 percent interest in Tantalum Australia, a joint venture which owned and operated a tantalum project in Australia, and KEMET gained access to the ore. However, the partnership was short-lived. Within two years, Australasian bought KEMET's interest in the venture as part of a restructuring plan.

The year 2000 proved to be KEMET's most financially successful to date, boasting sales of $1.4 billion, which was an increase of 71 percent over the previous year. At that time, the company had 16,000 employees. However, the celebration did not last long.

The cyclical nature of the industry resulted in lower sales and caused KEMET to lay off nearly 1,800 employees in June 2001 and to close its South Carolina manufacturing plant about a year later. The company also consolidated two of its operations in Mexico, cutting back to three plants from four in that location. This affected an additional 425 employees. Another round of cuts a few months later eliminated 280 more jobs, reducing the total number of employees to under 6,000, which was nearly 10,000 less than the company had two years before this time. Although a number of employees were shed due to layoffs, voluntary programs including special leave and programs focused on early retirement were also responsible for the reduction in workforce.

CHANGES IN LEADERSHIP AND PRODUCTS: 2003–07

Changes occur quickly in the electronics industry, and in order to remain at the forefront, KEMET made several major moves during 2003. Jeffrey Graves was named the new chief executive of KEMET in March 2003, replacing David Maguire. The company hoped that Graves's background in engineering, as well as his experience in the international market, would help turn the company around. Graves had previously served as the company's vice president of technology and

engineering as well as president and chief operating officer. Maguire remained as company chairman.

In July 2003 the company made its first acquisition when it bought some of the product lines from Greatbatch-Sierra Inc., a specialty capacitor and filter supplier, and set up the KEMET Innovation Center. The purpose of this venture was to develop higher margin products quickly. These steps not only helped the company produce proprietary products, it also increased KEMET's global manufacturing footprint. The next month, the company bought an equity stake in multilayer ceramic products manufacturer Lamina Ceramics. Also during this year, the company opened a manufacturing plant in China. This would allow the company to serve customers in Asia better, which at the time accounted for one-fourth of the company's revenue.

Following more losses for the company, Graves resigned from KEMET in January 2005, after less than two years in charge. The company began operating under new leadership later in the year when Per-Olof Loof became CEO.

KEMET quickly made several more acquisitions in order to strengthen its global position, especially in Europe, and to expand the company's existing product lines. The tantalum capacitor business of EPCOS AG was acquired in 2006, and the Evox Rifa Group Oyj companies and Arcotronics Italia S.p.A. were acquired in 2007. These acquisitions gave KEMET manufacturing operations in Europe. Two of these new companies also introduced KEMET into a new market segment. The purchase of Evox Rifa and Arcotronics put the company in the market of film, paper, and wet aluminum electrolytic capacitors, which were produced by the company's Film and Electrolytic business group. Net sales for 2007 reached nearly $660 million, up from approximately $490 million the previous year.

REDUCING COSTS: 2008–09

Several more cost-cutting measures were taken over the next few years. This included cutting 400 more jobs in December 2006, followed by closing two production facilities in Europe in early 2008, which affected about 420 more jobs. In addition, about 370 jobs in the United States and Mexico were also eliminated during early to mid-2008. Net sales for 2008 increased to more than $850 million. However, the company reported net losses of over $25 million for the year.

Plans were announced in 2009 to further reduce operating costs. One strategy for this was to consolidate manufacturing to lower-cost locations over the next several years. A reduction in the number of overall employees was also a part of the plan, and included 1,500 manufacturing employees, equaling about 14 percent of the total work force. Net sales for the year dropped to approximately $804.4 million, and the company reported a net loss of over $285.2 million.

LOOKING TO THE FUTURE: 2009 AND BEYOND

The U.S. Department of Energy awarded a $15.1 million grant to the company in 2009 to support the production of film and electrolytic capacitors that would support electric drive vehicles. These capacitors would be produced within the United States, reducing dependence on offshore suppliers and creating more jobs domestically. As a result, the company's South Carolina plant was expanded, and more than 100 jobs were expected to be added over the next three years.

In May 2010 the company completed a private placement of $230 million in aggregate principal of KEMET's 10.5 percent Senior Notes. This resulted in proceeds of $222.2 million for the company. Net sales for 2010 were $763.3 million, which was an 8.5 percent decrease from those of the previous year. Although the company reported a loss, it was not as significant as the loss from the year before.

In the early 2010s, KEMET remained a large producer in an industry that can be greatly affected by external forces. Analysts noted that an increase in demand for electronics should lead to an increase in company sales, but this was a factor largely beyond the company's control. Another factor outside of KEMET's control was the prices of the elements the company used to create its capacitors. A spike in price for one of these metals would often lead to reduced margins for KEMET.

Dave Mote
Updated, Diane Milne

PRINCIPAL SUBSIDIARIES

Arcotronics Italia S.p.A.; Dectron AB (Sweden); Evox Rifa Oy (Finland); KEMET de Mexico S.A.de C.V.; KEMET Electronics Asia Ltd. (Hong Kong); KEMET Electronics Corporation; KEMET Electronics Marketing (S) Pte Ltd. (Singapore); KEMET Electronics S.A. (Switzerland); KEMET Electronics (Suzhou) Co., Ltd. (China).

PRINCIPAL DIVISIONS

Ceramic; Film and Electrolytic; Tantalum.

PRINCIPAL COMPETITORS

AVX Corporation; EPCOS AG; Murata Manufacturing Co., Ltd; TDK Corporation; Vishay Intertechnology, Inc.

FURTHER READING

Brinton, James B. "Kemet Minds Its Business in a Tough Market — Strong Logistics and Other Customer-Service Programs Are Key to the Capacitor Maker's Stragegy." *Electronic Buyers' News,* November 30, 1998, 16E.

Chin, Spencer, and Bolaji Ojo. "Kemet Lands First Acquisition, Shifts Production Focus to China." *EBN,* July 7, 2003, 3.

Levine, Bernard. "Kemet Expands in Mexico and Shrinks in Carolinas." *Electronic News (1991),* November 17, 1997, 78+.

———. "Suppliers Restructure as Shakeout Accelerates." *Electronic News,* April 30, 1990, 30.

Spiegelman, Lisa L. "Adding Capacity to Meet Rising Demand." *Investor's Business Daily,* May 15, 1995.

Kenya Power and Lighting Company Limited

———— ■ ————

Stima Plaza, Kolobot Road, Parklands
P.O. Box 30099
Nairobi, 00100
Kenya
Telephone: (254) 20 320 1000
Fax: (254) 20 310336
Web site: http://www.kplc.co.ke

Public Company
Founded: 1908
Employees: 7,279 (2010)
Electricity sales: KES 39.1 billion ($488 million) (2010)
Stock Exchanges: Nairobi
Ticker Symbol: KPLC
NAICS: 221122 Electric Power Distribution

■ ■ ■

The Kenya Power and Lighting Company Limited (KPLC) transmits, distributes, and retails electricity to all parts of Kenya. The company purchases bulk electricity from Kenya Electricity Generating Company (KenGen) and independent power producers (IPPs). Uganda Electric Transmission Company and Tanzania Electric Supply Company Limited also supply electricity to KPLC. KPLC continuously provides and maintains the line network capacity required to support the effective and efficient supply of electricity throughout the country.

KPLC's national grid is serviced by an integrally linked transmission network of 220kV- and 132kV-rated power lines. The national grid is a very important component in the company's operations and strategic pursuits because it is the determining factor in capacity handling and expansion. Hydropower electricity accounts for more than 60 percent of the power transmitted by KPLC. Geothermal, thermal, diesel generators, and windmills are the other sources of power generation managed by KenGen and transmitted by KPLC.

COMPANY FOUNDING AND EARLY YEARS

The history of KPLC can be traced to as far back as 1875 when the sultan of Zanzibar, Seyyied Bargash, acquired a generator to light up his palace and its neighborhood. The generator supplied electric power to Seyyied Bargash's palace until 1908 when it was purchased by Harrali Esmailjee Jeevanjee, a wealthy Mombasa businessman. The generator set was transferred to the newly formed Mombasa Electric Power and Lighting Company. In a simultaneous development, Clement Hertzel, an engineering expert, acquired the rights to be the sole supplier of electricity to the Nairobi district. Hertzel proceeded to form the Nairobi Power and Lighting Syndicate in 1908 and used the company to set the foundation for electricity generation and supply in Nairobi District.

The Mombasa and Nairobi electricity companies were operated independently until January 6, 1922, when the two companies were merged and incorporated as the East African Power and Lighting Company (EAP&L). The company spread its presence to Tanzania in 1932 when it acquired the majority shareholding stake in the Tanganyika Electricity Supply Company

COMPANY PERSPECTIVES

Powering people for better lives.

Limited (TANESCO). EAP&L further expanded its interests in the East African region in 1936 when it was granted the license to generate and distribute electricity in Uganda.

In 1948 the regional growth and expansion prospects of EAP&L were curtailed by the establishment of the Uganda Electricity Board and the subsequent revocation of its license for generating, transmitting, and distributing power. EAP&L went back to Uganda in 1954 after a power sale agreement between Kenya and Uganda. In the agreement, Uganda offered to supply its surplus electricity power to Kenya via the Tororo-Juja line. The management of the transmission of the imported electricity energy was granted to EAP&L's newly formed Kenya Power Company. During the 1960s the Kenyan government expanded its ownership stake in EAP&L through gradual purchase of shares.

NATIONALIZATION AND FOCUS ON KENYA: 1964–99

The company's regional market was further diminished in 1964 following the acquisition of its majority stake in TANESCO by the Tanzanian government. The newly installed government in Tanzania enacted nationalization policies in line with its socialist ideology. As such, this government decreed that local and foreign private investors must forfeit their shareholding stakes in all the business enterprises in the country. The nationalization process of TANESCO commenced immediately with the exit of EAP&L from the Tanzanian market.

EAP&L entered an agreement with the government of Kenya in 1973 in which the company offered to implement rural electrification programs on behalf of the government. In the meantime, the Kenyan government continued increasing its shareholding in the company through the early 1970s. By 1975 the government's shareholding in EAP&L had grown to 32.9 million shares, representing 40.4 percent of the total shares. The shareholding stake of other government parastatals was also increased.

The exit of EAP&L from the Ugandan and Tanzanian market meant that the company's operations were restricted to Kenya. This prompted the change of the company's name from EAP&L to Kenya Power and Lighting Company (KPLC) on October 11, 1983. Samuel Gichuru was subsequently appointed to head the newly transformed entity as the managing director and CEO. Gichuru had served the company in different capacities as a senior manager before his eventual elevation to the position of CEO.

The Tana River Development Company (TRDC) was merged with the Kenya Power Company (KPC) in 1996 with the objective of harnessing the power generation potential of the two entities. In 1997 KPLC was subjected to additional structural and operational transformations that were aimed at optimizing efficiency in the generation and transmission of electricity. The KPC was unbundled from KPLC and converted into an independent entity to manage all the power generation installatons and projects funded by the public. The Kenya Power Company was transformed once again in 1998 when it was repackaged and its name changed to the Kenya Electricity Generating Company (KenGen).

EXPANSION IN A NEW CENTURY

At the dawn of the 21st century, KPLC was pursuing alternative and renewable sources of electricity energy to boost the capacity of the national grid. In 2000 KPLC entered a supply deal with Mumias Sugar Company Limited for the purchase of 10,000 MWh of electricity annually. The development followed the commissioning of a power cogeneration plant by Mumias Sugar Company. KPLC began initiating strategic approaches towards the management of costs associated with the purchase of power by constituting the IPP Committee in 2003. The committee was mandated with the responsibilities of forecasting future power needs and entering negotiations for reliable and affordable bulk power purchases.

The government's grip on KPLC was tightened in 2003 through the acquisition of noncumulative preference shares valued at KES 15.9 billion. Samuel Gichuru, the long-serving managing director, was forced to resign in February of that year after a government task force recommended his sacking for alleged abuse of office. Engineer Jasper Oduor was appointed in November 2003 to replace Gichuru as managing director. Simultaneous changes were also effected in the company's board of directors, and engineer Alfred Sambu was appointed to serve as chairman of the board.

KPLC partnered with the government of Kenya and other stakeholders to launch the Energy Sector Recovery Project (ESRP) in 2004. The $153 million ESRP program was mandated to undertake the rehabilitation of all the core components that affect the reliability, frequency, and quality of electricity supply. KPLC made

KEY DATES

1908: Clement Hertzel forms the Nairobi Power and Lighting Syndicate.
1922: East African Power and Lighting (EAP&L) Company incorporates.
1964: EAP&L exits the Tanzania market.
2006: KPLC Board enrolls Expatriate Management Services in a two-year management services agreement.
2010: Company completes its pilot project for prepaid metering technology.

commendable strides in the process of enhancing its energy transmission and distribution capacity of its network through the ESRP as system losses were drastically reduced.

In 2005 KPLC signed another contract for the importation of electricity from Mumias Sugar Company to the national grid at the rate of 2.2MWh. KPLC further harnessed its strategic management portfolio by establishing the Board Strategy and Customer Service Committee in February 2005. The committee was designed to provide facilitation to the board in the process of fast tracking all the annual and multiyear corporate projects and customer service enhancement programs.

The majority shareholding of the government and its parastatals was significantly reduced by 2.63 percent to 48.40 percent in October 2005 when the National Social Security Fund (NSSF) auctioned 2,139,367 shares to Transcentury Limited through the Nairobi Stock Exchange trading platform.

EXPATRIATES AND REFORM: 2006–08

In a strategy that was aimed at accelerating KPLC's turnaround and operational capacity, the Kenyan government contracted specialist management services from Canada. The specialist managers, consisting of expatriates from Manitoba Hydro International (MHI), were awarded a two-year contract on July 1, 2006. Under the provisions of the management services contract, the MHI team was expected to implement major transformations in KPLC, including connection of more than 300,000 new customers and reduction of losses from the transmission and distribution systems by 4 percent. Managing director Oduor was fired by the KPLC board in June 2006 following accusations of

indecisiveness, and Zachary Ayieko was immediately appointed to replace him.

The establishment of the Procurement Oversight Committee in January 2007 provided the company with a mechanism for streamlining procurement processes and activities in the company. The committee was charged with the responsibilities of reviewing and recommending to the board the appropriate strategic procurement framework. The committee was further tasked with the role of enforcing compliance in all routine and strategic procurement processes and providing approval for goods and services valued at KES 50 million or more. The move was particularly important because KPLC was gradually implementing an outsourcing program for its noncore services so as to meet the rapid growth in demand for electricity in urban and rural areas.

The Kenyan government implemented more reforms in KPLC in 2007 when it set up a parastatal, the Rural Electrification Authority, to provide oversight in the speedy and efficient implementation of electricity supply to rural areas in Kenya. Engineer Joseph K. Njoroge was appointed as the managing director and CEO in June 2007 following the exit of Ayieko. The company experienced a further change of management in June 2008 when the MHI team made an exit following the expiration of the management contract. The KPLC board declined to renew the MHI management services contract following operational misunderstandings between the two parties.

The Kenyan government further sanctioned the incorporation of Kenya Electricity Transmission Company (KETRACO) in 2008, as part of its energy sector reforms. KETRACO was designed to fast-track the government's objectives of accelerating the design and development of infrastructure for efficient transmission and distribution of electricity. The government also incorporated the Geothermal Development Company. This corporate entity was accorded the responsibilities of facilitating and actualizing the development of steam fields. The development would inhibit the risks associated with developing power upstream and eventually speed up the growth of geothermal electric power. KPLC also secured a partnership deal with the Postal Corporation of Kenya in 2008 to utilize the latter's countrywide network to facilitate customer bill payments.

NEW PROJECTS AND REVENUE GROWTH: 2009–10

The importation of electricity power from the Mumias Sugar Company's cogeneration plant to KPLC's national grid finally materialized on May 11, 2009, when the 40MWh cogeneration plant was officially opened. KPLC registered a major performance leap in 2009 when pretax profits increased from KES 2.7 billion in the 2008 financial year to KES 4.8 billion in the 2009 financial year. The launch of a pilot project for prepaid metering technology in April 2009 was a major achievement in the company's customer service strategy. Costing KES 388 million, the pilot project involved the installation of prepaid meters to 24,000 households and business premises within Nairobi. The project was successfully completed in February 2010, and the company prepared for a full-scale transition from the postpaid metering format. The main concept behind the pilot project for prepaid meters was to enable customers to determine and control the amount of money they spent monthly.

KPLC experienced a leadership transition in March 4, 2010, when Eliazar Ochola was elevated to chairman of the board of directors. Ochola had joined the company's board of directors in December 2006. The World Bank, through the Kenyan government, awarded a concessionary loan amounting to $102 million to KPLC in 2010 to support the company's Kenya Electricity Expansion Program (KEEP). The program was targeted at accelerating access to electricity in all parts of the country. The ESRP program also provided an additional $72.8 million to bolster the $153 million allocated to the program in 2004.

KPLC recorded improved performance in the financial year ending June 2010 following a 7.3 percent growth in revenue to KES 39.1 billion compared to KES 36.5 billion the previous financial year. The successful performance of the company resulted in after-tax profits of KES 3.7 billion, up from KES 3.2 billion in 2009. The company made a total of 214,288 new connections between July 2009 and June 2010, effectively raising the number of customers to 1.5 million.

EXPANSION PROJECTS: 2011 AND BEYOND

The future plans and strategies of KPLC were tagged to the expectations of infrastructure development in Kenya as espoused in the government's Vision 2030 economic development plan. KPLC had partnered with the Kenyan government in the development of sustainable and renewable sources of energy to replace fuel-generated electricity energy. In the financial year 2010–11, the government allocated KES 300 million toward the development of geothermal power and wind mills for the period from 2010 to 2016. The Kenyan government was also exploring the opportunities of investing in nuclear-generated electricity power by the year 2022.

KPLC planned to install a second Kenya-Uganda 220kV Lessos-Tororo transmission line by 2013 to facilitate importation of electricity from Uganda's Bujagaji Hydropower Project. Plans were also underway to commission the Kenya-Ethiopia 500kV transmission line by 2014. The project would involve the installation of a transmission line covering 1,200km to facilitate the importation of electricity from Ethiopia to northern and northeastern parts of Kenya. KPLC also planned to undertake extensive expansion of its electricity transmission capacity by 2014 in accordance with the projected of increase in power generation by KenGen and IPPs. KenGen was implementing various electricity generation projects that would increase power output by a total of 786MW by 2014. IPPs were projected to introduce an additional combined output of 800MW to the national grid.

Paul Ingati

PRINCIPAL DIVISIONS

Coast Region; Mount Kenya Region; Nairobi Region; West Kenya Region.

FURTHER READING

Departmental Committee on Energy, Communication and Information. "Report on Ownership and Status of the Kenya Power and Lighting Company Ltd (KPLC)." Kenya National Assembly, Tenth Parliament, Fourth Session, July 2010.

"FACTBOX-Upcoming Share Sales in East Africa." *Reuters*, July 13, 2010. Accessed October 25, 2010. http://uk.reuters.com/article/idUKLDE66B1BH20100713.

"Kenya Power & Lighting Co. Ltd (KPLC.NR)." *Reuters.*, Accessed October 27, 2010. http://www.reuters.com/finance/stocks/overview?symbol=KPLC.NR.

"KPLC, Ibesr Africa Deny Gichuru Link." *Kenya Times*, November 22, 2006.

"KPLC Share Capital Restructuring." Riba Capital, November 21, 2009. Accessed October 24, 2010. http://ribacapital.com/2009/11/21/kplc-share-capital-restructuring.

Macharia, James. "Kenya's KenGen Eyes Nuclear Power, Strategic Investor." *International Business Times*, October 15, 2010. Accessed October 26, 2010. http://uk.ibtimes.com/articles/72478/20101015/kenya-s-kengen-eyes-nuclear-power-strategic-investor.htm.

Musau, Michael. "Government Should Repurchase KenGen's Shares." *African Executive*, April 4, 2007. Accessed October 27, 2010. http://www.africanexecutive.com/modules/magazine/articles.php?article=2199.

"The Re-Incarnation of the Kenyan Capital Markets." Riba Capital, August 13, 2010. Accessed February 6, 2011. http://ribacapital.com/?s=Re-Incarnation+of+the+Kenyan+Capital+Markets.

Koninklijke Ahold N.V.

Piet Heinkade 167-173
Amsterdam, 1019 GM
The Netherlands
Telephone: (31) 20-509-5100
Toll Free: (800) 767-7772
Fax: (31) 20-509-5110
Web site: http://www.ahold.com

Public Company
Founded: 1887
Employees: 206,287 (2009)
Sales: EUR 27.92 billion ($36.1 billion) (2009)
Stock Exchanges: Euronext Amsterdam
Ticker Symbol: AH
NAICS: 445110 Supermarkets and Other Grocery
(except Convenience) Stores

∎∎∎

Koninklijke Ahold N.V. (known outside the Netherlands as Royal Ahold) operates more than 2,909 supermarket or specialty stores in the Netherlands and around the world. Its Albert Heijn, Alberto, and Etos units are familiar names throughout The Netherlands, where it is the country's largest grocer. (The company's Gall & Gall division is the largest wine and liquor chain in the country as well.) Royal Ahold also operates operates stores in the United States, Portugal, Czech Republic, the Baltic states, and Scandinavia.

In the United States, much of Royal Ahold's holdings are east of the Mississippi. Leading divisions include the Giant supermarket chain in the mid-Atlantic states and Stop & Shop in the New England region. Online grocery delivery division Peapod serves several cities in the Upper Midwest.

EARLY HISTORY

In 1887 Albert Heijn and his wife opened a small grocery store in Oostzan, the Netherlands. Holland was in the midst of an economic boom sustained by its colonial network. Heijn's grocery store prospered and soon became a chain, under the name Albert Heijn. By the end of World War I, Heijn was running a bakery and a confectionery to help supply his chain of 50 grocery stores.

Steady growth continued throughout the 1920s, as the company added new stores each year. In 1923 Heijn branched into the restaurant trade, providing his company with a new source of income. By the end of the decade, Albert Heijn was in a very solid position. As a result, the company was able not only to weather the worldwide Depression of the 1930s, but even to grow.

In 1941 the Nazi occupation of the Netherlands brought economic turmoil to the country. Dutch wealth was drained to fuel Germany's war machine. However, as during the Depression, the nature of the food business insulated Albert Heijn from the ruin faced by companies in other industries throughout Holland. By the end of World War II the chain had nearly 250 stores in operation.

In 1948 the company went public in preparation for the challenges of the postwar era. Self-service shop-

COMPANY PERSPECTIVES

We make it easy for our customers to choose the best, for themselves and the people they care about. We do this through our strong local brands and by putting the customer at the heart of every decision. We strive to stand out from the competition by providing the best products in a relevant range, the best quality, the best prices, and the best choices for a healthy lifestyle—all in the simplest way possible.

ping was clearly the trend. In 1952 the company opened its first self-service store, followed three years later by its first supermarket. Albert Heijn emerged from the 1950s as a leader in its industry, and expansion continued in the 1960s through diversification and the addition of new stores. In 1966 Albert Heijn acquired the Meester meatpacking plant, which produced a wide variety of processed meat products, delicatessen items, and sausages, among other things. In 1969 the company opened the first of its Alberto liquor stores.

EXPANSION IN THE 1970S

As the company began the 1970s it had a firm grip on about 20 percent of the Dutch market and was poised to expand. In 1971 Albeit Heijn opened the first Miro hypermarket. A year later the company acquired the Simon de Wit chain, bringing 137 new supermarkets under the Albert Heijn banner. In 1973 the company changed its name to Ahold N.V. It also entered the health and beauty care market that year with the purchase of the Etos chain.

A number of adverse conditions combined to slow growth just as Ahold digested its new acquisitions. The energy crisis of 1973 softened consumer demand somewhat, labor costs rose considerably, and the government removed artificial price supports. Ahold's management, accustomed to the often cyclical nature of the food retailing industry, rode out the storm. The company stepped up discount store activities and its roadside restaurant operations. By 1975 Ahold was enjoying rapid growth once again and was poised to make a major thrust overseas.

After carefully researching European markets, Ahold decided to establish a chain of supermarkets in Spain. Spain had a relatively undeveloped industry and Ahold believed its expertise would go the furthest there. In 1976 the company opened the first Cadadia store near

Madrid. Ahold planned to develop a major chain in the country, but the Spanish subsidiary got off to a sluggish start, hindered in part by a slow-moving Spanish bureaucracy and a depressed economy.

In 1977 Ahold made a major purchase in the United States when it acquired the Bi-Lo chain for $60 million. Bi-Lo operated 98 stores throughout North and South Carolina and Georgia. The Bi-Lo chain got off to a strong start within the Ahold group, returning a 3 percent profit margin, compared with 1.7 percent for Ahold's Dutch operations. Ahold retained Bi-Lo's management in the belief that local autonomy would best serve the company's interests. In 1981, however, the president of Bi-Lo resigned when the chain followed its competitors and began selling beer and wine.

Ahold continued its program of diversification when it purchased ten restaurants from the struggling Jacques Borel group of Belgium in 1978. The acquisition strengthened Ahold's network of restaurants located on roadsides throughout Europe. Ahold's Ostara holiday parks in West Germany and Holland provided strong earnings outside of the retail food sector for the company in the late 1970s.

In 1978 the company set up a foundation to hold DFL 100,000 in preferred stock as protection against hostile bids, after watching a number of hostile takeover attempts, including a particularly bitter battle between Heineken and Lucas Bols. To the company's relief, no hostile bids for Ahold actually materialized.

INTERNATIONAL GROWTH IN THE 1980S

In 1981 Ahold made its second major U.S. purchase, acquiring the Giant Food Stores chain, of Carlisle, Pennsylvania, for $35 million. Giant had 29 stores, mostly in Pennsylvania. As with the Bi-Lo purchase, the company's management remained autonomous.

That same year Ahold bought 50 percent of the Spanish sherry producer Luis Paez. By the end of the decade Ahold was producing one-third of all sherry sold in the Netherlands. In addition, the company's Alberto liquor store unit had grown to 89 stores in its first 20 years and continued to improve its share even in a shrinking market.

Ahold recorded vigorous profits in the early 1980s largely on the strength of its U.S. operations. Growth slowed a bit around 1984, as vicious competition in the Netherlands shaved already thin margins, and the Spanish chain Cadadia reported a loss. In 1985 the company sold the 38 Cadadia stores to the British Dee Corporation, having decided not to undertake a major expan-

```
┌─────────────────────────────────────────┐
│                                         │
│             KEY DATES                   │
│                 ■                       │
│                                         │
│  1887:  Albert Heijn and his wife open a small │
│         grocery store in Oostzan, the Netherlands. │
│  1923:  Heijn branches into the restaurant trade, │
│         providing his company with a new source of │
│         income.                         │
│  1948:  The company goes public in preparation for │
│         the challenges of the postwar era. │
│  1952:  The company opens its first self-service store, │
│         followed three years later by its first │
│         supermarket.                    │
│  1973:  The company changes its name to Ahold │
│         N.V. It also enters the health and beauty care │
│         market with the purchase of the Etos chain. │
│  1977:  Ahold makes a major purchase in the United │
│         States when it acquires the Bi-Lo chain for │
│         $60 million. Bi-Lo operates 98 stores │
│         throughout North and South Carolina and │
│         Georgia.                        │
│  1981:  Ahold makes its second major U.S. purchase: │
│         the Giant Food Stores chain, of Carlisle, │
│         Pennsylvania, for $35 million.  │
│  1989:  Pierre J. Everaert, formerly head of the │
│         company's overseas operations, replaces Albert │
│         Heijn, grandson of the company's founder, as │
│         president of Ahold.             │
│  2000:  Royal Ahold acquires a partnership stake in │
│         Scandinavian grocer ICA AB.     │
│  2003:  The company suffers multiple setbacks in its │
│         operations.                     │
│  2009:  Royal Ahold acquires 25 Ukrop supermarket │
│         stores in Virginia.             │
│                                         │
└─────────────────────────────────────────┘
```

sion in Spain. It kept its winery holdings, however. The company also acquired the Van Kok-Ede company, a major wholesale foods supplier in Holland, in 1985.

Ahold purchased 80 percent of the American First National Supermarkets chain in 1988, an acquisition which doubled the size of its U.S. operations. First National ran the Finast, Pick-n-Pay, and Edwards Food Warehouse chains. The deal gave Ahold a footing in New England, Ohio, and New York. Ahold slowed the expansion of its Giant and Bi-Lo chains in order to concentrate its resources on the First National stores.

Meanwhile Ahold increased its holding in the Dutch supplier Schuitema to 55 percent. Schuitema, Holland's largest supplier of independent supermarkets

in the country, gave Ahold an even stronger grip on the industry in Holland.

Ahold had always been committed to using the latest technology in its stores. In the late 1980s the company piloted a program which allowed customers to self-scan the items they wished to purchase. At the Albert Heijn store in Tilberg, the Netherlands, customers were offered the choice of self-scanning or traditional shopping. Self-scanning shoppers selected a cart equipped to scan each item before they put it in the cart. The scanner also kept a running total on an electronic readout. When customers finished shopping, they proceeded to a special line, where the cashier entered the data from the cart's scanner into the register. Customers liked the shorter lines at the checkout and the running total displayed at all times. However, self-scanning was still considered experimental through the early 1990s and was not tested at one of Ahold's U.S. supermarkets until 1995.

In 1989 Pierre J. Everaert, formerly head of the company's overseas operations, replaced Albert Heijn, grandson of the company's founder, as president of Ahold. Heijn had reached the company's mandatory retirement age of 62, and so the company passed out of the direct control of the Heijn family for the first time in three generations.

Ahold was well positioned for the integration of European markets in 1992. The company enjoyed substantial market share in the Netherlands, and in 1991 it founded a food retail and distribution company in the Czech Republic, called Euronova. Ahold bought 49 percent of a Portuguese food retailer in 1992. By 1995 Ahold ran four "supercenters" or "hypermarkets" in Portugal, 70,000-square-foot stores selling groceries and other household goods.

Royal Ahold's expansion into the U.S. market was its most dramatic. After acquiring Finast in 1988, Ahold purchased the Buffalo, New York-based Topps Markets in 1991. The chain had 168 stores and sales of $1.6 billion. Three years later, Ahold purchased the smaller Red Food Stores chain, based in Chattanooga, Tennessee, for about $125 million. Red Food had sales of $400 million and 55 stores. Ahold quickly merged Red Food into its larger Bi-Lo chain. The acquisition gave Ahold more than 600 food stores in the United States. Sales from its U.S. group were $6.6 billion before the purchase of Red Foods, making Ahold the ninth-largest grocery operator in the United States. After Ahold bought the Tennessee chain, the company announced its ambitious plan to become the largest supermarket group on the East Coast within 10 years.

Ahold worked to build up sales of private label items at all its stores. Private labels saved the company money. Thus, when approximately 15 percent of sales at its U.S. stores were of private label products by 1995, the company estimated it was able to lower prices overall by 7 percent. Sales at Ahold's Dutch supermarkets were close to 40 percent private label goods, and increasing the private label share at its U.S. markets was one way Ahold brought its European experience to bear on the U.S. market. For the most part, however, Ahold left management of its U.S. chains in local hands. In fact, Ahold USA, as the company's U.S. division was called, had 65,000 employees in 1995, but only two were Dutch.

In accord with its U.S. growth plan, Ahold bought a New Jersey chain, Mayfair supermarkets, in 1995. Mayfair operated 28 stores, with sales of $575 million. This purchase made Ahold the third-largest Eastern chain, close behind second-place Winn Dixie. Ahold was bringing in $8.3 billion in 1995 from its 650 stores. The next year, Ahold made its largest purchase in the United States when it bought Stop & Shop Companies Inc., the largest supermarket chain in New England. Stop & Shop had 1995 sales of $4.1 billion, brought in from its 116 Superstores, 43 Stop & Shop supermarkets, and 17 Mel's Foodtown supermarkets. The company also owned another chain of 28 Purity Supreme supermarkets and 64 convenience stores called Li'l Peach.

ROYAL AHOLD ACQUIRES STAKE IN ICA AB: 2000

Royal Ahold started the new millennium on a positive note when the group successfully sealed a partnership deal with Hakon Investment AB for 50 percent ownership of ICA AB in April 2000. ICA AB was the principal owner of the ICA Group, a food retail chain with headquarters in Stockholm, Sweden. The ICA Group boasted a retail network of more than 2,300 stores spread in Sweden, Norway, and Eastern Europe. As such, the joint venture agreement provided Royal Ahold with the much-needed impetus for expanding its presence in Sweden and Europe. Royal Ahold sold 93 million shares through a public offering in May 2000 to finance the purchase of the 50 percent stake in ICA.

Royal Ahold extended its market dominance in 2001 when it posted more than EUR 66 billion in sales. The positive growth trends of the company resulted in a record profit of more that EUR 1 billion that year. During the year, more than 5,000 supermarket stores operated under the Royal Ahold banner in 27 countries. Royal Ahold's capital base was largely boosted by the sale of 70 million shares through a public offering in September 2001 that generated slightly more than EUR 2 billion. The capital was used to finance the purchase

of Alliance Foodservices, Parkway Foodservices, and Bruno's food stores.

The rapid growth of Royal Ahold took a sudden downturn in 2003 when its capital might and financial strength were adversely affected by a rapid meltdown within its operational structure. The group was hit by a series of difficulties that included a massive accounting scandal, large-scale dismissal of the company's professional staff, and numerous court cases from investors. In the financial abstract *Royal Ahold: A Failure of Corporate Governance,* Abe de Jong and colleagues attributed the group's dismal performance to the failure of its corporate strategies. The authors particularly criticized the group's acquisition strategies, which they considered burdensome to the company's financial resources and long-term growth prospects. In December 2003, in order to reduce its debt of EUR 11 billion, Royal Ahold had to sell 621 million shares on a rights issue that generated more than EUR 2.9 billion.

The positive outcome of the Royal Ahold's partnership with Hakon Invest AB prompted the group to acquire an additional 10 percent stake of ICA in 2005. However, Royal Ahold's majority share ownership of the ICA did not give the group complete control over decision-making processes in ICA because the original agreement with Hakon Investment AB prevailed. The original partnership agreement stipulated that all operational, financial, and strategic decisions concerning ICA would be made through mutual approaches by Royal Ahold and Hakon Invest AB.

The introduction of a EUR 500 million program for reducing operational costs was one of the biggest announcements of Royal Ahold in 2007. The cost reduction program involved streamlining operations, cutting down on staff costs, and closing stores that were posting frequent losses. The strategy of cost reduction was influenced by the company's experience in 2003 when its excessive capital and operational expenditures led to its rapid meltdown.

IMPRESSIVE RESULTS IN A CHALLENGING YEAR: 2009

Royal Ahold registered impressive results in 2009 despite the economic difficulties that prevailed in its key markets in Europe and the United States. The retailing group posted total sales of EUR 27.9 billion, a figure that amounted to 8.9 percent growth compared to 2008. The group's favorable performance was largely occasioned by the success of its Project Fresh remodeling program that was used to expand the company's market share while enhancing its cost-cutting measures at the same time.

In Europe the company transformed its activities in the Czech Republic when all the Hypernova stores of the Albert & Hypernova segment were rebranded to Albert. This shift was aimed at consolidating activities in the country. The rebranding was closely followed by the completion of a process that downsized 12 hypermarket stores and the subsequent establishment of the Albert Foundation in the Czech Republic in 2009. The establishment of the Albert Foundation elevated the group's Corporate Social Responsibility exploits and also placed it in a better position to address the social welfare of communities in the country.

The administrative structure of Ahold USA was reviewed extensively in 2009 when the segment was divided into four main geographic areas that were placed under the charge of a single executive team. The new administrative structure was designed to enhance the quality of service delivery in the group's fast-expanding chain of stores. In 2009 Royal Ahold's operations in the United States expanded following its acquisition of 25 Ukrop supermarket stores in Virginia.

The end of 2009 also marked the end of the group's EUR 500 million cost reduction program and the subsequent launch of another cost-cutting program worth EUR 350 million, scheduled to run until 2012. Royal Ahold demonstrated its dominance in the retail industry by winning the 2009 Supermarket News' Retail Excellence Award. In the 2010s, Royal Ahold looked poised to begin expanding again in the United States and elsewhere but with the lessons of its earlier setback fresh in mind.

Tom Tucker
Updated, A. Woodward; Paul Ingati

PRINCIPAL SUBSIDIARIES

AHOLD Czech Republic, a.s. (Czech Republic); AHOLD Retail Slovakia (Slovakia); Albert Heijn B.V.; Albert Heijn Franchising B.V.; Etos, B.V.; Gall & Gall B.V.; Giant Food Stores LLC (USA); ICA AB (60%, Sweden); Peapod, LLC (USA); Stop & Shop Supermarket Company LLC (USA).

PRINCIPAL COMPETITORS

Carrefour SA; Kooperativa Förbundet; Safeway Inc.; Tesco PLC; Wal-Mart Stores, Inc.

FURTHER READING

Hoover's Inc. "Royal Ahold N.V.: Company Description." Accessed January 12, 2011. http://www.hoovers.com/company/Royal_Ahold_NV/ctysti-1.html.

Jong, Abe de, Douglas V. DeJong, Gerard Mertens, and Peter Roosenboom. "Royal Ahold: A Failure of Corporate Governance," Finance Working Paper No. 67/2005. Accessed January 11, 2011. http://homepage.univie.ac.at/klaus.gugler/public/SSRN-id663504.pdf.

"Koninklijke Ahold N.V. (Royal Ahold)." In *International Directory of Company Histories,* edited by Tina Grant, Vol. 16, 312–314. Detroit: St. James Press, 1997. *Gale Virtual Reference Library.* Web. 18 Apr. 2010.

National Farmers Union. "Royal Ahold/Ahold USA: Vertical Integration, Horizontal Integration and Globalization." National Farmers Union, 2001. Accessed January 12, 2011. http://www.foodcircles.missouri.edu/charts2.pdf.

"Royal Ahold Acquires Parkway Food Service." *Nation's Food Restaurant News,* February 26, 2001. Accessed January 12, 2011. http://findarticles.com/p/articles/mi_m3190/is_9_35/ai_71326546/.

Kuwait Petroleum Corporation

Safat
P.O. Box 26565
Kuwait City, 13126
Kuwait
Telephone: (965) 1 85 85 85
Fax: (965) 2499 4991
Web site: http://www.kpc.kw

State-Owned Company
Founded: 1980 as Kuwait Petroleum Company
Employees: 18,500 (est., 2010)
NAICS: 324110 Petroleum Refineries; 211111 Crude Petroleum and Natural Gas Extraction

■ ■ ■

Kuwait Petroleum Corporation (KPC) operates as a state-owned integrated oil and gas concern. Its operations include onshore and offshore upstream exploration and production, refining, marketing, retailing, petrochemical production, and marine transportation. These operations are carried out by self-descriptive subsidiaries such as the Kuwait Oil Tanker Company and the Kuwait Aviation Fuelling Company. Through over 4,000 service stations, subsidiary Kuwait Petroleum International uses the brand Q8 to sell petroleum products (fuel, lubricants) across Europe and the Middle East.

KPC has estimated reserves of around 100 billion barrel of oil, along with approximately 1.8 trillion meters of natural gas. The company maintains regional offices across the globe in Houston, London, Mumbai, Singapore, and Tokyo.

EARLY HISTORY

Although KPC was established only in January 1980, it took over a number of companies that had been active in Kuwait for much longer. The most important of these was the Kuwait Oil Company (KOC), which was incorporated in London on February 2, 1934, with an initial issued capital of £50,000 owned in equal shares by the Anglo-Persian Oil Company and Gulf Oil Corporation of the United States. (The Anglo-Persian Oil Company then became Anglo-Iranian Oil Company, then the British Petroleum Company, then BP.) On December 23 of the same year, the ruler of Kuwait granted an exclusive concession to KOC to explore for, produce, and market Kuwait's oil. The concession covered the whole country and was to last for 75 years.

The formation of Kuwait Oil had been in part the result of a prolonged diplomatic dispute between Britain, then the dominant power in the Middle East, and the United States, which supported U.S. oil companies' claims to participate in petroleum development in the region. KOC formed part of a network of consortia of major U.K. and U.S. oil companies that controlled the Middle Eastern oil industry and that had made its first appearance in the Iraq Petroleum Company formed in 1928.

KOC began drilling for oil in 1936. Oil had been discovered in Iraq in 1927 and in Bahrain in 1932, and it was widely believed that Kuwait held equally good

COMPANY PERSPECTIVES

Kuwait Petroleum Corporation (KPC) is a corporation of economic character. KPC's mission is to manage and operate these integrated activities worldwide in the most efficient and professional manner, in addition to growing shareholder value whilst ensuring the optimum exploitation of Kuwait hydrocarbon resources. KPC has an important role in contributing to the support and development of the Kuwaiti economy, developing national manpower, maintaining superior commercial and technical expertise, and pro-actively managing the environmental, health, and safety aspects related to KPC's businesses.

prospects. In May 1936, the first drilling began at Bahra, in north Kuwait, but eventually reached 7,950 feet without producing oil. Meanwhile, drilling had also started in October 1937, at Burgan, in south Kuwait. On the night of February 23, 1938, the drillers struck high-pressure oil in large quantities. This was the start of the Kuwait oil industry. Eight more wells were drilled at Burgan before July 1942, when all operations had to be suspended and all completed wells plugged with cement because of the wartime emergency. After World War II ended in 1945, operations resumed, and in June 1946 the first Kuwaiti oil exports began.

A NEW INDUSTRY FOR KUWAIT:
1946–58

Between 1946 and 1950 Kuwaiti oil production grew from 5.93 million barrels to 125.72 million barrels, making Kuwait the third-largest Middle Eastern oil producer after Iran and Saudi Arabia. However, the real breakthrough came with the cessation of oil exports from Iran between 1951 and 1954 because of the dispute between the Iranian government and the Anglo-Iranian Oil Company. KOC rapidly increased Kuwaiti output to replace the Iranian crude. By 1955 it had 185 producing wells in operation in Kuwait, and annual production had reached nearly 400 million barrels, the highest output in the Middle East. Throughout almost all of the next 15 years, Kuwaiti oil production retained this leading position, until it was gradually overtaken by Saudi Arabia and Iran toward the end of the 1960s.

Oil transformed Kuwait. In the 1930s the country was largely desert, with most of its population of 70,000 concentrated around the mud-walled trading and fishing port of Kuwait town. An average annual rainfall of four inches and a lack of irrigation permitted little agriculture. Almost all food and all drinking water were imported, and the economy was based on pearl fishing, shipbuilding, and entrepôt trade. Oil revenues transformed the situation, especially after 1952 when it was agreed that the net profits of the industry would be shared evenly between Kuwait and the oil companies. By 1961 Kuwait, with a total population of 320,000, of whom only 50 percent were nationals, had one of the highest per capita incomes in the world. Nationals were given free medical treatment and free education, and the infrastructure of an advanced welfare state was created.

This wealth did nothing to reduce a growing irritation in Kuwait (and elsewhere) with Western control over its oil resources. The consortium system limited the bargaining power of host governments, for they faced only one producer. Iran's dispute in 1951 with the Anglo-Iranian Oil Company was just the first sign of general resentment at the system which spread throughout the Middle East in the 1950s and 1960s. In 1958 the Kuwaiti government granted a concession to the Arabian Oil Company, a Japanese venture in which the Kuwaiti government had a 10 percent shareholding. In 1960 Kuwait joined the Organization of Petroleum Exporting Countries (OPEC) as a founder member. OPEC's objective was to unify and coordinate the petroleum policies of its members and protect their interests against the Western oil companies. In the same year, the government organized the Kuwait National Petroleum Company (KNPC) as a joint enterprise owned 60 percent and 40 percent by the government and private sectors, respectively. For the next two decades, this element of private ownership distinguished KNPC from most other national oil companies in the Middle East. In 1962 KOC was made to relinquish 60 percent of the areas included in its concession to KNPC.

INTERNATIONAL TENSION:
1960–76

During the 1960s the Kuwaiti government sought to increase the share of oil income staying in Kuwait, especially by promoting downstream development. The government attempted to persuade KOC to begin refining operations but the company resisted. Economically, there was an overwhelming case for locating refineries near centers of consumption rather than of production, and the vast majority of new refining capacity installed in the decades after World War II was in Western Europe and the United States. However, KOC, like the other Western oil companies in this period, underestimated the extent to which nationalist feelings

KEY DATES

1934: The Kuwait Oil Company (KOC) incorporates.

1938: KOC strikes oil in south Kuwait.

1946: Kuwait begins exporting oil.

1960: Kuwait joins OPEC as a founding member; Kuwait National Petroleum Company (KNPC) is organized.

1975: The Kuwaiti government takes full control of KOC.

1980: Kuwait Petroleum Company (KPC) is established to act as a holding company.

1988: The firm launches its own brand (Q8) in Europe.

1990: Iraq invades Kuwait; KPC sets up an alternative head office in the London premises of Kuwait Petroleum International.

1997: The Equate polyolefin plants opens.

2000: KPC is awarded $15.9 billion by the United Nations for damages related to the 1990 Iraqi invasion.

2004: CEO Nader Sultan retires and is replaced by Hani Hussain.

2010: Farouk al-Zanki is appointed CEO.

were growing, even in conservative and pro-Western states such as Kuwait and Saudi Arabia. Kuwait also had a special interest in building refining capacity. It would not only provide for technology transfer into Kuwait and create jobs, but by using advanced refinery technology it could counterbalance Kuwait's relatively weak export position, the result of its rather poor-quality crude oil. Eventually, KNPC decided to enter refining itself, and it started operating a refinery at Shuaiba (near the oil pipeline terminal) in 1968.

The Western oil consortia in the Middle East collapsed in the early 1970s during a dramatic restructuring of the industry. The most obvious manifestation of the restructuring was the huge rise in world oil prices in 1973. During the opening years of the 1970s, there was a rush of agreements designed to give producer-governments a stake in oil companies. In 1974 one such participation agreement transferred 60 percent of KOC's ownership to the state of Kuwait, the remaining 40 percent being divided equally between BP and Gulf Oil. In 1975 the Kuwaiti government took over this remaining 40 percent. In 1976 the Kuwait Oil Tanker Co. (KOTC), established in 1957 by private Kuwaiti

interests, was converted to 49 percent state ownership, and it was fully nationalized in 1979. Also in 1976, a minority private sector shareholding in Petrochemical Industries Co. (PIC), established in 1963, was similarly bought out.

KUWAIT PETROLEUM COMPANY: 1980–90

In January 1980 Kuwait Petroleum Company (KPC) was established as a holding company responsible for the overall management of this group of companies, together with the government's share of the capital of the Arabian Oil Company of Japan. Operations were rationalized, with KOC restricting its activities to exploration and production and KNPC to refining and distribution. In 1981 KPC established two new companies, the Kuwait Foreign Petroleum Exploration Company (KUFPEC), a subsidiary empowered to undertake crude oil and natural gas exploration, development, and production operations outside Kuwait, and the Kuwait International Petroleum Investment Co., owned 70 percent by KPC and 30 percent by private Kuwaiti investors and empowered to engage in refining and petrochemical operations outside Kuwait.

KPC developed an ambitious strategy to integrate its oil industry from the well-head to the petrol pump in consumer countries. Considerable attention was given to expanding and upgrading Kuwait's refinery capacity, in order to enhance Kuwait's ability to respond rapidly to changes in the pattern of export demand. By 1983 the share of product exports in total oil exports was more than 40 percent by volume and more than 50 percent by value. By 1989 KPC had three modern refineries (the Mina Abdullah, Mina al-Ahmadi, and Shuaiba plants) and plans were being made to integrate their operations to attain the greatest possible economic efficiency. When the expanded Mina Abdullah refinery came on stream in February 1989, Kuwait had a refined-products capacity of over 700,000 barrels per day.

KPC's most dramatic move, however, was to expand overseas. In 1981 it acquired Santa Fe International, a California-based exploration-services company, for $2.5 billion. Santa Fe owned or operated, among other things, rig joint ventures in various regions, including the North Sea and Australia. Another important step came in February 1983, when KPC purchased Gulf Oil's refining and marketing networks in the Benelux countries, adding those in Sweden and Denmark a month later. Over the next two years, KPC would acquire over 2,300 service stations across Europe. By 1989 through its London-based subsidiary Kuwait Petroleum International, KPC owned more than 4,500 petrol stations in seven countries, plus refineries in Rotterdam and in Gulfhaven, Denmark. In 1988 KPC launched its own brand, Q8, in Europe.

Although the construction of a retail network in Europe was at the heart of KPC's strategy in the 1980s, the company also was active in exploration activities in foreign countries through its KUFPEC and Santa Fe subsidiaries. In 1984 KUFPEC acquired two petroleum concessions, in Bahrain and Tunisia. Offshore discoveries in Egypt and Indonesia were developed in 1985 and 1986, and in 1986 an agreement was signed to participate in the development of the Yacheng gas field in China.

KPC was a remarkably successful national oil company. During the 1980s it achieved a far greater degree of integration than any other OPEC producer, with the possible exception of Petroleos de Venezuela. At the time, KPC was the first (and only) state-owned oil company from the Third World to sell its oil under its own brand name and through its own service stations. However, there were problems. Some analysts considered that KPC had paid excessive amounts for some of its acquisitions, especially the purchase of Santa Fe in 1981. KPC's consolidated net profits were impressive, rising from $488.6 million in 1986–87 to $606.9 million in 1987–88, but it was likely that this disguised poor performance from certain downstream operations. KPC also faced resistance to its growth from established international oil companies, which partly explained its failure to penetrate the U.S. market in the 1980s. More fundamentally, there was some conflict between the strategies of expanding refinery capacity within Kuwait and that of seeking to become an integrated oil major, which might dictate more refining operations nearer markets.

WAR AND EXPANSION: 1990–99

KPC's state ownership created political problems. KPC's attempts to buy downstream assets in Japan, for example, were blocked in part because it was owned by a foreign government. The Kuwait Investment Office's purchase of over 20 percent of British Petroleum's shares in 1988 as a consequence of the British government's privatization program was attacked on these grounds, and the Kuwaitis were forced to reduce their stake to 10 percent. At the time, there was speculation that this purchase was aimed at further advancing KPC's downstream integration strategy, because relations between the Kuwait Investment Office (KIO) and KPC were known to be close. KPC's greatest liability, however, was the geographical location of its home country. KPC relied entirely on sea transport through the Persian Gulf to export its oil, and during the Iran-Iraq War in the 1980s, the resulting vulnerability of KPC was evident. A number of KOTC tankers were hit by Iranian raids, prompting the Kuwaitis to reregister some of their fleet in the United States and United Kingdom. However, this was a minor irritant and inconvenience compared to the Iraqi invasion and occupation of Kuwait in August 1990, which took place after a period of tension over Kuwait's reluctance to see an increase in oil prices.

The Iraqi invasion devastated Kuwait, but it did not devastate KPC which, because of its international diversification strategy, survived. Senior staff of KPC escaped with the bulk of crucial management information intact, and within days had set up an alternative head office in the London premises of Kuwait Petroleum International. Saudi Arabia guaranteed KPI's European downstream commitment. In exile, KPC was granted immunity from the asset freeze which was imposed on Kuwait's overseas interests by the European Economic Community, the United States, and Japan, allowing it to continue normal commercial operations. Eight of KPC's ten directors were outside the country at the time of the Iraq invasion, enabling the company to continue functioning with a legal quorum. Shortly after the invasion, KPC's UK Lubricants business was relaunched as Kuwaiti Petroleum Lubricants. In October 1990 the diversification strategy was furthered when KIO acquired over 10 percent of the shares of the Singapore Petroleum Company, an oil-refining group. The continued vigor of KPC in the midst of the greatest crisis ever faced by Kuwait was a tribute to the strength of the business organization that had been created in a single decade.

The United States and its allies ousted Iraq from Kuwait during the Persian Gulf War. Allied forces led by the United States began their attack on Iraq in January 1991, and the war ended one month later. In the aftermath of the invasion, KPC was left to rebuild and recover from oil fires and damage. The oil concern recovered quickly, however, and was exporting oil products by June 1991. By early 1993 its refining capacity was nearing pre-invasion levels.

KPC spent the remaining years of the 1990s focused on its international expansion. Its upstream operations were bolstered by ventures in the South China Sea, Australia, Congo, Egypt, Indonesia, Tunisia, and Yemen. KPI expanded into Spain in 1992 and acquired BP's Luxembourg-based assets in 1994. The company also made key investments in Italy, Belgium, Sweden, and Thailand. In 1995 KPC reentered the Italian refining market with the purchase of 300 service stations from Eni, Italy's state-owned chemicals firm. In 1998 157 service stations in Belgium were acquired from British Petroleum Co. Encouraged by growth in the contract drilling market, KPC sold 31 percent of its Santa Fe International subsidiary in 1997, raising $997.5 million in one of the largest public offerings of the year.

A NEW CENTURY AND NEW CHALLENGES: 2000–04

Through its petrochemical development business, KPC was also involved in the development of the Equate facility, which was designed to reduce Kuwaiti dependence on oil production and refining. The Equate project was significant in several ways. It was the first major project to be completed in Kuwait since 1990, and it also marked the first joint venture between a local and international company in Kuwait. Owned by KPC's Petrochemical Industries Co. and Union Carbide Corp., Equate manufactured polyethylene, ethylene glycol, and polypropylene.

As KPC entered the new century, it was awarded $15.9 billion by the United Nations Compensation Commission for losses and damages related to the 1990 Iraqi invasion. The company's Santa Fe unit merged with Global Marine Inc. in a $3 billion deal to create Global Santa Fe Corp., the world's second-largest offshore drilling contractor. KPC also made a significant move in 2001 when it announced plans to allow foreign oil companies to develop its oil fields in Northern Kuwait.

While KPC did indeed stand on stronger ground than it had just a decade earlier, world events began to threaten its position. The terrorist attacks against the United States on September 11, 2001, made crude oil prices fluctuate from $30 per barrel to just over $15 per barrel. The global economy also entered a downturn, with overall growth falling from 3.9 percent in 2000 to 1.5 percent between April 2001 and March 2002. Global demand for oil remained stagnant during this time period. According to KPC, this was the first time in 20 years that oil demand did not increase on an annual basis.

In August 2004 longtime CEO and deputy chairman Nader Sultan announced his retirement. Sultan had been with KPC since its inception in 1980, and as CEO since 1993. KNPC managing director Hani Hussain was appointed to replace Sultan. Hussain's experience and reputation as a man free from political and financial ties made him an attractive candidate. His appointment resulted in a reshuffling of management down the line, including the appointment of Farouk al-Zanki as the new director of KOC, replacing Ahmed al-Arbeed, who became the managing director of Project Kuwait, KPC's

long-awaited initiative to invite international oil companies to participate in drilling northern fields.

DIVESTITURE AND REORGANIZATION: 2005 AND BEYOND

Kuwait's status as a government-owned company made for a difficult turn of the century for KPC. Project Kuwait was never fully approved, and several key projects failed due to government disapproval. The company began to divest some resources to refocus efforts.

In late 2004 KPC divested its retail interests in Great Britain, selling subsidiary Kuwait Petroleum Great Britain (KPGB) to the UK's Refined Holdings. By the end of 2006, KPC sold 30 percent of its foreign arm, Kuwait Foreign Petroleum Exploration. This move allowed the company to focus on exploration and production of natural oil and gas, which were still state-controlled ventures.

In 2007 Hani Hussain resigned his position as CEO, four months prior to his contract ending, after disagreement with oil minister Sheikh Ali Jarrah al-Sabah. Disillusioned with the industry, Hussain turned down several opportunities for government positions. Saad al-Shuwaib was appointed as acting CEO effective May 1. Al-Shuwaib also managed the Petrochemical Industries Company (PIC), managing many of the privatization projects in the petrochemicals business at KPC.

In 2008 PIC joined up with DOW Chemical Company to form K-Dow to produce polymers for Kuwait. However, the Supreme Petroleum Council in Kuwait did not support the deal, and the joint venture collapsed.

Another failed deal in March 2009 was the building of a new refinery in Al-Zour. KNPC had awarded deals to four South Korean firms and one Japanese company in May 2008. Again, members of Kuwait's parliament said that the contracts did not meet with standard bidding procedures.

In November 2010 Farouk al-Zanki was appointed CEO. Al-Zanki had broad experience at KPC, managing both flagship subsidiaries KOC and KNPC. Al-Zanki had earned a reputation for boosting production despite the failed Project Kuwait initiative. His success contrasted to al-Shuwaib's failure to negotiate satisfactory resolutions to government criticisms. By the end of 2009, there were no international energy companies actively involved in Kuwait's energy industry, a situation that would hinder future production and development.

Since Sultan's departure, no CEO has been able to make progress on KPC's need to open business to international oil companies.

In the early 2010s, Al-Zanki took on that challenge with a focused strategy. His key strategic initiatives included continuing the push for greater involvement with international oil companies and stressing projects that produced clean fuels. However, Kuwait's government has adamantly resisted the globalization of its business, and this has hindered production. Experts considered it likely that Kuwait's reserves would last less than 100 years without international expertise to assist in drilling reserves inaccessible with current resources.

Geoffrey Jones
Updated, Christina M. Stansell; Sara K. Huter

PRINCIPAL SUBSIDIARIES

Kuwait Gulf Oil Company; Kuwait Oil Company; Kuwait National Petroleum Company; Kuwait Oil Tanker Company; Kuwait Foreign Petroleum Exploration Company; Kuwait Petroleum International Ltd.; Kuwait Aviation Fueling Co.; Oil Development Company; Oil Services Company; Petrochemicals Industry Co.

PRINCIPAL COMPETITORS

Abu Dhabi National Oil Company; National Iranian Oil Company; Saudi Arabian Oil Company.

FURTHER READING

"All Change at KPC, KOC and KNPC." *MEED Middle East Economic Digest* 48, no. 34 (2004): 12.

Chisholm, A. H. T. *The First Kuwait Oil Concession Agreement.* London: Frank Cass, 1975.

Dutta, Ashok. "Project Kuwait Puts Its Case." *MEED Middle East Economic Digest* 45, no. 20 (2001): 4.

Ford, Neil. "Project Kuwait on the Brink: a Turnaround in Kuwaiti Policy Could See Major Oil Projects Developed by Foreign Companies for the First Time Since Nationalisation, Over 30 Years Ago." *The Middle East,* December 2005, 42+.

Kaye, Daniel, and Alice Bourret. "Profile Upgrade: with Oil Activities Held Tightly in State Hands, Kuwait Faces Huge Challenges in Modernizing Its Flagship Industry. Limited Internationalization Is Taking Shape." *Oil and Gas Investor* 25, no. 6 (2005): K-2(5).

"Kuwait Introduces Oil Plan." *Oil Daily,* January 4, 2001.

Luciani, Giacomo. *The Oil Companies and the Arab World.* London: Croom Helm, 1984.

"Reshuffle Complete in Oil Sector." *MEED Middle East Economic Digest* 48, no. 36 (2004): 9.

Sleight, Chris. "Commission Fines Bitumen Cartel 267 Million [Euro]: the European Commission Has Handed Out Fines Totaling 267 Million [Euro] to 14 Companies That It Says Operated a Cartel in the Netherlands' Bitumen Market for at Least Eight Years." *Construction Europe* 17, no. 8 (2006): 6.

Thomas, David, and Jimmy Burns, "The Gulf War; Kuwaitis Prepare for the Ultimate Oil Disaster." *Financial Times,* February 13, 1991, 3.

LB≡BW

Landesbank
Baden-Württenberg

Am Hauptbahnhof 2
Stuttgart, 70173
Germany
Telephone: (49) 711 127-0
Fax: (49) 711 127-43544
Web site: http://www.lbbw.de

State-Owned Company
Founded: 1999
Employees: 13,630 (2009)
Assets: EUR 412 billion ($512 billion) (2009)
NAICS: 521110 Monetary Authorities - Central Bank;
522110 Commercial Banking; 522230 Financial
Transactions Processing, Reserve, and Clearinghouse
Activities

■ ■ ■

Landesbank Baden-Württemberg (LBBW) is the central
bank for the savings banks in the German states of
Baden-Württemberg, Rhineland Palatinate, and Saxony.
As such, it handles wholesale banking transactions that
are too large for any of the smaller savings banks. It is
one of Germany's largest banks, with main offices in
Stuttgart, Karlsruhe, Mannheim, and Mainz as well as
international offices in New York, London, Singapore,
Seoul, and Mexico City.

LBBW also provides retail banking services through
over 200 branches in Germany. The Savings Bank Association of Baden-Württemburg owns around 40
percent of LBBW, while the state of Baden-
Württemburg, city of Stuttgart, and Landesbeteiligun-

gen BW (an investment vehicle linked to the state of
Baden-Württemburg) each own about 20 percent.

PUBLIC BANKING IN GERMANY

Although the Landesbank Baden-Württemberg was
formed in 1999, it can trace its roots back to the Württemberg Sparkasse (Savings Bank) which was founded in
1818 by the royal family of Württemberg for the benefit
of the poor among the population.

Landesbanks are German financial institutions usually owned in whole or in part by state or local
governments. They are legally deemed independent
institutions and are protected by law. In essence, they
are publicly owned banks.

Most Landesbanks were formed in the late 19th
century by municipalities or districts to encourage saving by the local population and to assist in the development of the regional economy. They also provided
services for the smaller local savings banks or Sparkasses,
often acting as centralized clearinghouses.

As they evolved, they developed a tripartite role. In
addition to being the central banks for local sparkasses,
they became banks for state governments and competitors for the private sector banks. Landesbanks came to
be seen as symbols of prestige and power for state and
municipal governments and the local politicians who sat
on the bank boards.

Following World War II, Germany entered into a
period of reorganization and reconstruction of both its
society and its government. Constitutionally, the government of the Federal Republic of Germany became

COMPANY PERSPECTIVES

The aim of LBBW is to consolidate its position as a partner of small and medium enterprises in the regional core markets of its retail banks by deploying its market knowledge and enhancing its customer proximity and thereby also to secure the future provision of lending to the economy.

responsible for broad national economic policies, which were implemented by the regions. Economic power was diffused to the states, and the states retained considerable autonomy.

The federal banking system developed a three-pillar approach consisting of private banks, public banks, and cooperatives. The public banks, which were largely the state-controlled Landesbanks, became as much political institutions as they were financial institutions. They were prone to interference from state and local politicians, and the protection they enjoyed under the law made them resistant to change. Attempts to reform the banking system with respect to Landesbanks often met with strong political reaction.

Protection under the law was not the only advantage the Landesbankes enjoyed. With their state and municipal owners acting as guarantors, Landesbankes were able to raise funds on the capital markets at a much lower cost than private sector banks. With double and triple A ratings (guaranteed by the taxpayer), Landesbanks not only raised money at lower rates, they were able to loan it out at preferred rates, undercutting other financial institutions.

While the three-pillar approach may have served Germany well during its period of reconstruction, by the 1990s it appeared to have run its course. Deregulation and privatization were already sweeping over Europe and would soon help to reshape the German financial services industry.

GERMAN BANKS AND THE EUROPEAN UNION: 1991–99

By the last decade of the 20th century, German reconstruction seemed complete, and the country, unified by the dissolution of East Germany, was once again the economic powerhouse of Europe. As government-owned and operated institutions became passé, the privatization of state enterprises and expansion of free markets through deregulation began to change the face

of the European banking industry. In Great Britain, France, and Italy, deregulation had resulted in consolidation and the creation of large and profitable conglomerates. The German system, however, remained rooted in the past, and Germany's private sector banks were falling behind.

With their access to cheap funds and taxpayer guarantee, the Landesbanks and their partners the Sparkassen accounted for 39 percent of all domestic corporate and retail deposits and a full 35 percent of all German bank lending. The German private banks were aware that if they could not compete within Germany, they would stand little chance beyond their borders in the European Union. In 1994 the German private banks took their case before the European Commission. They argued that state guarantees offered to Landesbanks gave the publicly owned banks an unfair advantage and placed private institutions at a competitive disadvantage. The private banks also claimed that state guarantees distorted the cost of capital in the free market system.

In 1999 the European Banking Federation also launched a complaint against the public banking system in Germany and the protection it received under the law and system of state support.

The issue would become the basis of a protracted dispute between the European Union and Germany. It would also become an important issue for the federal government, which was determined to influence bank reform and the states. Landesbanks were still influenced by local politics, and public sector banks in Germany provided in excess of 38,000 jobs. In 2001 an agreement was finally reached between Germany and the European Union to end the state guarantees, but the agreement would not take effect until 2005, leaving all parties ample time to adjust.

LBBW AS "UNIVERSAL BANK": 1999–2002

Unable to resist the forces of the global free market, the German banking system responded like other banking systems did by mergers and amalgamations. In 1999 the Landesbank Baden-Württemberg (LBBW) was formed by a merger of three other financial institutions. These were the Südwestdeutsche Landesbank Girozentrale, Landesgirokasse-öffentliche Bank und Landessparkasse, and the commercial banking business of Landeskreditbank.

From its beginning the LBBW was well placed as a financial competitor. In addition to the commercial banking business of the Landeskreditbank, it inherited a large wholesale banking business from Südwestdeutsche and the second-largest savings bank in Landesgirokasse.

KEY DATES

1818: Württemberg Sparkasse is established by the royal family of Württemberg to aid the poor.
1994: Private German banks push European Commission to help end competitive advantage enjoyed by Landesbanks.
1999: Establishment of Landesbank Baden-Württemberg.
2005: Landesbanks lose state guarantees; LBBW expands into Rhineland-Palatinate.
2008: LBBW losses exceed EUR 2 billion.
2009: LBBW begins restructuring plan and returns to profitability.

The bank set its sights on becoming a customer-orientated institution with a strategy based on the five main divisions of corporate clients, retail clients, savings banks, financial markets, and real estate financing.

A board of managing directors headed by Chairman Hans Dietmar Sauer, a German banking veteran, handled the day-to-day operations of the bank at the senior level. The owners of the bank included the State of Baden-Württemberg, the City of Stuttgart, and the Savings Bank Association of Baden-Württemberg, and were represented by the Guarantors Meeting, headed by a politician named Erwin Teufel, prime minister of Baden-Württemberg. Perhaps as a testament to its political pedigree, the bank had not one but three head offices located in Stuttgart, Mannheim, and Karlsruhe.

The LBBW established itself as a "universal bank," which meant it offered the full range of financial services. The common banking services such as taking deposits, lending, foreign exchange, and real estate financing would be augmented by additional services such as underwriting, leasing, securities trading, and portfolio management. Unlike other jurisdictions such as North America, where the distinction between commercial and investment banking was clear, in Germany universal banks combined both functions in one institution.

The bank became a significant player in the state of Baden-Württemberg, one of the most prosperous states in Germany. In addition to large corporate clients, LBBW aggressively sought out clients in the market called the *mittelstand*. These are the mass of small and medium-size companies that are the backbone of the German economy. (There are approximately 3.1 million mittelstand companies, and they account for 35 percent

of all investment in the German economy and over 55 percent of all investment in the corporate sector.) LBBW also continued to provide clearinghouse and other services to the savings banks.

NEW STRATEGIES FOR THE NEW CENTURY: 2003–07

The strategy of LBBW appeared to be working, and by 2003 the bank reported a net profit of EUR 366 million. The time had come for the bank to plan for the future. The 2001 agreement reached between the European Union and Germany to eliminate the state guarantees for the Landesbanks would come into effect in 2005, and LBBW knew it needed to identify new strategies to participate in the marketplace as a state-controlled business. Previously, the focus had been on providing credit, but the open market would force the bank to see things in a different light. Consolidation and reorganization would be required to improve earnings and capitalize on strengths.

The company created several independent subsidiaries to expand its market. If formed the Baden-Württembergische Bank (BW Bank) as a major force in private sector banking. It had a leasing company operating as Südleasing GmbH and a real estate arm operating as LEG GmbH. By the end of 2004 net income had climbed to EUR 502 million.

The LBBW group would experience significant changes in 2005. In addition to the end of state guarantees, the bank's chairman of the board of managing directors, Hans Sauer, retired. His replacement was Dr. Siegfried Jaschinski, another banking veteran who had served as LBBW's head of financial markets. Also retiring was Erwin Teufel, who as prime minister of Baden-Württemberg had represented the owners. He was replaced, both as prime minister and at the bank, by Günter H. Oettinger.

The bank expanded beyond the borders of its home state when it took over the assets of the Landesbank Rheinland-Pfalz in the neighboring state of Rhineland Palatinate. Rhineland Palatinate, with a population of just over 4 million, is a major wine-growing region as well as home to BASF, a major chemical company. Similar to Baden-Württemberg, the region was heavily dependent on small and medium-sized companies as its economic engine.

By 2006 LBBW had become the largest Landesbank in Germany with total assets under management of EUR 415 billion and net income of EUR 828 million. However, the German banking market was crowded, so in the spring of 2007, Jaschinski outlined a new strategy for growth, which included expanding operations abroad. To increase its global presence, Jaschinski planned to use LBBW Securities LLC, a New York-based subsidiary, which held an investment banking license and had $100 million in equity. The strategy would entangle LBBW in the subprime mortgage crisis in the United States and prove disastrous.

DOWNWARD SPIRAL AND GRADUAL RECOVERY: 2007 AND BEYOND

In August 2007 the LBBW group took over the troubled Sachsen Landesbank, based in Leipzig in the state of Saxony. The Sachsen LB, which had been established in 1992 and had assets of EUR 68 billion, was on the verge of financial collapse when the LBBW stepped in with an emergency rescue package of EUR 250 million.

Saxony, which is located in southeast Germany, could provide LBBW with a base from which they could tap into corporate and high-net-worth clients in eastern Germany. It could also provide access to markets in central and Eastern Europe, especially in Poland and the Czech Republic. Jaschinski felt these economic areas offered good prospects for growth.

His theory was soon put to the test when in April 2008, LBBW purchased the assets of BAWAG Bank CZ from its Austrian-based owners. The bank was small with total assets of EUR 1 billion, 300 employees, and only 20 branches, but it did give LBBW direct access to customers in the Czech Republic. The bank was renamed LBBW Bank CZ.

However, the year 2008 saw financial markets worldwide thrown into tumult. Losses spiraled throughout the year, and by November losses at LBBW for the first nine months of 2008 amounted to EUR 884 million. The crisis was quickly becoming a disaster, and some type of rescue plan was required.

Prime Minister Oettinger, who was still the chairman of the owners' group, felt the need to take some action. If the LBBW were to fail, the small and medium-size mittelstand companies, which were vital to Baden-Württemberg's economy, would be in peril. The owners furnished an immediate injection of EUR 5 billion of new equity and sought the approval of the EU later.

Despite the new capital, losses at the Landesbank Baden-Württemberg for 2008 would exceed EUR 2.0 billion.

In May 2009 Prime Minster Oettinger announced that Jaschinski's contract, which was due to expire at end of the year, would not be renewed, and that he would be replaced as chairman of the board of managing directors by Hans-Jörg Vetter.

The EU gave approval for the new equity injection, contingent on the Landesbank Baden-Württemberg providing a workable restructuring plan. In October 2009 the bank produced the plan, which called for the bank to refocus on its core business in Germany, particularly in the area of corporate customers and small and medium-size enterprises. It would offer project financing only in connection to a customer's business, and it was to withdraw from aircraft and ship financing. Real estate financing would center on projects in Germany and be severely curtailed in other parts of the world, particularly the United Kingdom and the United States. Cost cuts would include the elimination of 2,500 jobs and reductions of EUR 700 million per year until the balance sheet was reduced by 40 percent.

While the bank continued to lose money in 2009, a total of EUR 1.48 billion, the situation did begin to improve. LBBW returned to the black in the third quarter of 2010 with a profit of EUR 143 million. For the early 2010s, LBBW planned to focus primarily on its core areas, so a rapid expansion of either services or geographic reach was unlikely.

Ian MacDonald

PRINCIPAL SUBSIDIARIES

Baden-Württembergische Equity; BWK GmbH; Baden-Württembergische L-Finance; BW Capital Markets Inc. (USA); Cellent AG; Cellent Finance Solutions AG; Deutsche Mittelstandsinformatik GmbH; Landesbank Baden-Württemberg Capital Markets plc (England); LBBW Asset Management Investmentgesellschaft mbH; LBBW Bank CZ, a.s. (Czech Republic); LBBW Dublin Management GmbH; LBBW Equity Partners GmbH & Co. KG; LBBW Immobilien GmbH; LBBW Leasing GmbH; LBBW Pensionsmanagement GmbH; LBBW (Schweiz) AG (Switzerland); LBBW Structured Investment LLC (USA); LBBW Venture Capital GmbH; LHI Leasing GmbH; MKB Mittelrheinische Bank GmbH; SüdFactoring GmbH; SüdLeasing GmbH; Süd Beteiligungen GmbH; Vorarlberger Landes- und Hypothekenbank AG.

PRINCIPAL DIVISIONS

PRINCIPAL COMPETITORS

Commerzbank AG; Deutsche Bank Aktiengesellschaft; UBS AG; UniCredit Bank AG.

FURTHER READING

Eglin, Darrel R. "Federal Republic of Germany." *Countries of the World,* January 1, 1991.

Marshal, Tom. "A Splattering of Public Bank Mergers." *Euromoney,* March 1, 2003.

Moore, Philip. "German Bank Issuance Set to Prosper." *Euroweek,* November 1, 2002.

"Slow Progress: Why an End to State Guarantees May Change Less Than It Should." *Economist,* June 30, 2005. Accessed March 13, 2011. http://www.economist.com/node/4137866,

"Unity in Adversity: Only a Crisis Turns Bad Banks into Bedfellows." *Economist,* September 6, 2007. Accessed March 13, 2011. http://www.economist.com/node/9769382.

Wiesmann, Gerrit, and James Wilson. "Germany's Weak Link." *Financial Times,* September 28, 2010.

Libya Insurance Company

Aman Building
Sana'a Street
P.O. Box 2438
Tripoli, 50676
Libya
Telephone: (218) 214 444 177
Fax: (218) 214 444 176
Web site: http://www.libtamin.com

Public Company
Founded: 1964
Employees: 1,000 (est., 2010)
Stock Exchanges: Libya
Ticker Symbol: Libya Insurance
NAICS: 524113 Insurance Carriers

■ ■ ■

Founded in 1964, Libya Insurance Company (LIC) is the oldest insurance company in Libya. The insurance company is headquartered in Tripoli and operates seven branches in the major Libyan cities of Benghazi, Gharian, Misurata, Al-Zawia, Sebha, Alkhums, and Derna. The company also distributes its services through small office establishments spread throughout all parts of Libya. LIC is easily the largest insurance company in Libya, controlling more than 36 percent of the country's insurance market. The company's stake in the insurance market is set to increase as liberalization takes root in Libya following the improved political and economic environment in the country.

LIC provides a wide range of insurance products. Its major products are split into numerous options that suit the varying needs of customers. The liabilities insurance product covers employer civil, medical, product, and professional liabilities. The motor insurance product covers compulsory insurance, private vehicle comprehensive, commercial vehicle comprehensive, third part liability, fire, theft, Arab unified card (an orange card that gives the owner the right to drive through various Arab states), and green card. (Similar to the orange card, a green card gives its owner the right to drive in any countries that accept its validity.) The company' product mix for life assurance includes whole life, term life, group life, and individual life assurance.

Aviation insurance is one of the key pillars of LIC's insurance products. This includes the options of aircraft hull, liabilities of air carrier, pilot, and crew, personal accident, and loss of licenses. Fire insurance is packaged with options such as burglary, lightning, and additional risks such as energy and petroleum risks. The marine hull insurance product provides a full range of insurance options for marine transportation. The company boasts marine insurance varieties such as institutional fishing vessels, hull and machinery, port risks clauses, stevedore's liabilities, and personal accident for mariners. Marine insurance and fire insurance policies are the most active segments of the company's product, accounting for more than 23 percent of its overall business.

Transporters of bulk goods by sea, air, or land also have the option of LIC's cargo insurance that covers all risks associated with domestic and international transportation of goods. The company's miscellaneous insurance segment deals with the safety of cash in transit and cash in a safe as well as personal accident, fidelity guarantee, and bankers policy. Contractors' all risks and engineering insurance subproducts are also offered as part of miscellaneous insurance product range.

Libya Insurance Company is one of the few companies to be listed on the Libya Stock Market (LSM), a fledgling market that opened in 2007. In late 2010 the company's share price averaged LYD 9.40, a figure that translated to a market capitalization value of LYD 472 million ($378 million) as of November 2010.

COMPANY FOUNDING AND NATIONALIZATION: 1964–79

LIC was founded in 1964 as a privately owned insurance business entity. LIC was the first insurance company to be established and registered in Libya as per the provisions of the country's Supervision and Control of Insurance Act. The company's start-up capital consisted of a paid-up capital valued at 100,000 Libyan pounds. (Pounds were the currency denomination used in Libya between 1951 and 1971.)

The insurance company experienced relatively moderate growth as the private sector thrived in Libya in the postindependence period of the 1960s. However, the company's growth prospects suffered a major setback in 1969 following an unexpected political occurrence in Libya. The government was toppled on September 1, 1969, by the *Al-Fateh* revolution movement led by Colonel Muammar Gaddafi. (This last name may also be spelled Qaddafi and Ghadafi.) The revolutionary coup completely changed the course of politics and the economy in Libya as the new government introduced new policies and laws. The Gaddafi-led government declared the nationalization of all private companies in the country immediately after assuming power.

The formalization of the nationalization process of Libyan private companies began in the 1970s. The full nationalization of LIC was formalized in 1971 as the government subsequently expanded the company's paid-up capital to LYD 1 million. The government banned all other insurance companies in 1972 with the exception of the Al-Mukhtar Insurance Company. Multinational giants such as the Royal Group, American Life, and Eagle Star were some of the private insurance companies that operated in the country before the

blanket ban. As such, the LIC and Al-Mukhtar Insurance Company became the only players in Libya's insurance industry throughout the 1970s.

LOW MARKET PENETRATION AND POLITICAL DIFFICULTIES: 1981–99

In 1981 the Al-Mukhtar Insurance Company was dissolved through a merger with the LIC. The government of Libya transferred all the assets and liabilities of the Al-Mukhtar Insurance Company to LIC. The government further strengthened the capital base of LIC by expanding the company's paid-up capital by another LYD 1 million. The company was renamed Libya National Insurance Company and effectively became a monopoly state-controlled insurance corporation in Libya. The company, however, continued to operate within a restricted market because of low market penetration rates. The low rating of the insurance industry in the country was largely attributed to the religious inclination of its people.

Like many other Islamic countries, the attitudes of Libyan Muslims towards insurance products were guided by the Sharia laws. Insurance policies were generally considered to be a contravention of the fundamental principles of the Sharia laws. As such, the country's insurance industry was accorded a mild reception by its population throughout the 1980s. In their book *The Libyan Economy: Economic Diversification and International Repositioning,* Wanis Otman and Erling Karlberg observed that the "conventional form of the life insurance product was forbidden in 1903 by prominent Islamic scholars in the Arab world."

The future of the insurance industry in the Islamic world was accorded a reprieve in 1985 when a Sharia-compliant insurance system referred to as *Takaful* was introduced. Otman and Karlberg attributed the development to the approval of the *Takaful* system by the "Grand Counsel (*Majma-al-Fiqh*) of Islamic Scholars of Makkah in Saudi Arabia." Expectations were rife that the approval of this alternative, Sharia-compliant insurance system by the highly respected Islamic authority heralded the acceptance of insurance throughout the Islamic world in the long term.

The growing prospects in the insurance industry prompted the Libyan government to channel greater financial support to its underperforming insurance sector. In 1989 the government enhanced the LIC's capacity to underwrite a wide range of insurance risks by increasing the paid-up capital of the company to LYD 30 million. Libya however, experienced unprecedented political and economic challenges in

```
┌─────────────────────────────────────────────┐
│                                               │
│              KEY DATES                        │
│                  ■                            │
│  ───────────────────────────────────────     │
│  1964:  Libya Insurance Company (LIC) established. │
│  1981:  Al-Mukhtar Insurance Company merges with │
│         LIC.                                  │
│  2000:  Medical Insurance Board merges with LIC. │
│  2007:  Libya Insurance Company privatized.   │
│  2010:  Libya Insurance Company establishes *Al* │
│         *Takaful* branch.                     │
│                                               │
└─────────────────────────────────────────────┘
```

1989 after two citizens from the country were implicated in the Lockerbie bombing. (In December 1988 an explosion onboard Pan Am Flight 103 as it flew over Lockerbie, Scotland, killed all 259 passengers and crew as well as 11 people on the ground.) The incident economically isolated Libya from the rest of the world after the United Nations (UN) and the United States imposed stringent economic sanctions on the country.

EMERGENCE OF MARKET-DRIVEN ECONOMY: 1999–2006

The successful experimentation of the *Takaful* insurance system in Malaysia in the 1990s was good news for the isolated insurance industry in Libya. The diminished international business opportunities in the country following economic sanctions truncated LIC's market considerably, but it did not mean that a vibrant domestic insurance market could not exist.

Imbued with such optimism, the first privatization in Libya's insurance industry since 1969 was initiated in 1999 when the United Insurance Company was formed through a public-private joint venture. The government further streamlined the regulatory structure of the insurance industry in 2000 by merging the Medical Insurance Board with LIC. The merger was followed by the increase of the company's paid-up capital by 66.7 percent to LYD 50 million.

In 2004 the United States and the UN lifted economic sanctions that had been in place since 1989 following the Lockerbie bombing. The European Union and other regional blocs followed suit. The country's economy experienced renewed prospects as the country gradually opened up to the world for private sector investment opportunities.

The Libyan government demonstrated its commitment to economic liberalization in 2006 by establishing the Libyan Investment Authority (LIA) in a move that consolidated its key economic portfolios. As such, the government eliminated its direct regulation and control over the economy by competitively securing its interests in the market-driven economy through corporate entities. LIA became the umbrella body that was charged with the responsibilities of managing government institutional funds. LIA therefore formed a critical component for the anticipated privatization of LIC in the third quarter of 2007.

PRIVATIZATION AND EXPANSION: 2007–08

The Libyan government continued to pursue expanded economic opportunities for the country by developing closer economic ties with countries and regional economic bodies throughout the globe. The country's leadership particularly warmed up to Italy and the European Union because of past trading links. Former British prime minister Tony Blair visited Libya in 2007 in what was largely perceived to be increasing economic engagement between Libya and the West. The success of the intensified international reengagement strategy impacted heavily on the long-term prospects of LIC that relied on the speedy recovery of the country's economic sector.

The liberalization wave that swept across Libya's key economic sectors led to the privatization of LIC in 2007. The shares of the company were floated in the Libyan stock market through an initial public offering (IPO) that was conducted in 2007. A total of 4 million shares of the company were floated at the rate of LYD 7 per share during the IPO that recorded a 10 percent oversubscription. LIC recorded impressive performance in the year as its premium sales soared to LYD 82 million despite an overall loss ratio of 65 percent.

However, trading of the shares at the LSM was temporarily suspended until January 2008 because of operational adjustments that were being implemented at this newly created exchange. Even so, the company's share price soared by 80 percent to LYD 12.60 within the first six months of trading. The IPO resulted in the increase of the company's total paid-up capital to LYD 70 million. The government retained the majority shareholding in the company through its Economic and Social Development Fund, an investment arm that fell under the Libyan Investment Authority.

The regulation and oversight responsibilities of Libya's liberalized insurance industry was transferred to the Insurance Supervision and Control Authority in January 2008 when the state corporation was officially launched. The investment portfolio of LIC was expanded significantly in December 2008 with the signing of multiple contracts of investment. The sale of land, hotel, and administrative buildings were some of the major investment contract signings.

AL TAKAFUL AND UNREST: 2010 AND BEYOND

LIC announced the establishment of its Al Takaful branch in May 2010, designed to enhance the delivery of the company's Sharia-compliant insurance policies. The branch became operational on July 1, 2010. Published information at the Shariah Tamin Web site indicates that "the decision for the establishment of the independent branch was made by the key government economic agencies in consultation with the President of the Board of Libya Insurance Company." The Al Takaful branch was founded in accordance with LIC's principles of distinctive, high-quality and fast service provision in compliance with the principles of the *Takaful* system of insurance.

In early 2011 Libya plunged into civil unrest, following similar upheavals in Tunisia and Egypt that saw long-standing autocrats removed from power. With Libyans fighting one another across the country, in March of that year it was still uncertain how the conflict would end, but the final outcome is sure to influence the future of LIC and all Libyan companies.

Paul Ingati

PRINCIPAL COMPETITORS

African Insurance Company; Libo Insurance Company; Sahara Insurance Company; United Insurance Company.

PRINCIPAL DIVISIONS

Administrative Affairs Department; Department of Aviation Insurance; Department of Car Insurance; Depart-

ment of Fire Insurance; Department of General Insurance; Department of Legal Affairs; Department of Marine Insurance.

FURTHER READING

Allen, Franklin, Isaac Otchere, and Lemma W. Senbet. "African Financial Systems: A Review." Wharton School, University of Pennsylvania, March 6, 2010. Accessed November 4, 2010. http://fic.wharton.upenn.edu/fic/papers/10/10–11.pdf.

"Company Overview: Libya Insurance Company." *Bloomberg BusinessWeek.* Accessed November 5, 2010. http://investing.businessweek.com/research/stocks/private/snapshot.asp?privcapId=105774645.

Financial Standards Foundation. "Country Brief: Libya." estandardsforum.org, July 30, 2010. Accessed February 6, 2011. http://www.estandardsforum.org/system/briefs/272/original/brief-Libya.pdf?1282315016.

"Libya Insurance Co." FirstGlobalSelect.com, 2010. Accessed November 4, 2010. http://www.firstglobalselect.com/scripts/cgiip.wsc/globalone/htm/quote_and_news.r?pisharetype–id=21110.

"Libya Insurance Company." Libyan Stock Market. Accessed November 4, 2010. http://www.lsm.ly/English/Inclusion/Pages/LibyaInsuranceCompany.aspx.

"Libya Insurance Company: Establishment of Al Takaful Branch." shariahtamin.ly, May 19, 2010. Accessed November 5, 2010. http://www.shariahtamin.ly/en/?reset-settings.

"Libya Insurance Company Signed Three Investment Contracts." libyaninvestment.com, December 2, 2008. Accessed November 5, 2010. http://www.libyaninvestment.com/archive/libya_news.php?page=page&pageNo=67&Info=8591.

Martinez, Luis. *The Libyan Paradox.* New York: Columbia University Press, 2007.

"North African Insurance Report 2009." *Business Monitor International,* March 26, 2009. Accessed November 5, 2010. http://www.marketresearch.com/map/prod/2200615.html.

Otman, Waniss A., and Erling Karlberg. *The Libyan Economy: Economic Diversification and International Repositioning.* New York: Springer, 2007.

Oxford Business Group. *The Report: Libya 2008.* Oxford Business Group, 2008.

LogMeIn, Inc.

500 Unicorn Park Drive
Woburn, Massachusetts 01801
U.S.A.
Telephone: (781) 638-9050
Toll Free: (800) 993-1790
Fax: (781) 998-7792
Web site: http://www.logmein.com

Public Company
Founded: 2003
Employees: 338 (2009)
Sales: $74.41 million (2009)
Stock Exchanges: NASDAQ
Ticker Symbol: LOGM
NAICS: 541512 Computer Systems Design Services;
    511210 Software Publishers

■ ■ ■

LogMeIn, Inc., is a software-as-a-service (SaaS) vendor that offers a platform of network-based remote-connectivity solutions that allow one computing device to take control of another. With such technology, individuals have the capability to access an office or home PC from any location using a laptop or other portable device. Small and medium-sized businesses (SMBs) and IT professionals use LogMeIn to manage and back up multiple laptops, desktop computers, on-site servers, point-of-sale (POS) machines, and kiosks. In addition, IT and customer service providers use LogMeIn products to take control of a user's machine in order to fix computer problems remotely. LogMeIn has

the capability to support Macintosh computers, Windows PCs, smartphones, and iPads.

The majority of LogMeIn's profits come from IT service providers, SMBs, consumers, and mobile workers all over the world. However, large companies such as Best Buy, Sony, Toshiba, AT&T, and Lenovo have increasingly turned to LogMeIn services. While two of the company's services are free, their premium ones are available on a subscription basis.

LogMeIn houses research and development divisions in Budapest and Szegad, Hungary, as well as offices in Amsterdam, the Netherlands; Sydney, Australia; and London, England. With services available in 12 different languages used in over 200 countries, LogMeIn had over 20 million registered customers in 2010.

COMPANY BACKGROUND: 2003–06

LogMeIn was founded as 3am Labs, Inc., in Budapest, Hungary, in 2003 by software engineers Michael Simon and Marton Anka. Simon, who in 1995 founded Uproar, Inc., a highly successful software company that created Web-based versions of online games, including *Family Feud* and trivia games, had traveled to Budapest in 1992 seeking entrepreneurial opportunities in software development. The Hungarian-born Anka was a consultant for Uproar while independently working on a RemotelyAnywhere application, remote control and administration software. After debuting in 1999 to high accolades, the product went on to become the foundation of LogMeIn's remote-connectivity software. In February 2003 Simon and Anka partnered to form the start-up 3am Labs, Inc., which was incorporated under the laws of Bermuda but remained based in Hungary. According to the founders, overhead expenses in Budapest were much lower than they would be if the company were to operate in California's Silicon Valley, often referred to as a tech mecca.

From the outset, 3am released free versions of its basic PC software but charged for upgraded versions. The company's early growth was financed through investments made by Simon, who had profited from the sale of Uproar, and another Uproar colleague. Soon after it was launched, 3am drew praise from professionals in technology support who could assist customers by dialing remotely into their computers rather than making on-site office visits. Unlike other similar software platforms, 3am's products were both less expensive and less complicated to use because clients were not required to know complex computer configurations.

In August 2004 3am incorporated in Delaware and expanded to the United States, establishing headquarters in Woburn, Massachusetts, 11 miles north of Boston. Simon and Anka believed that its proximity to the larger city would allow 3am to take advantage of Boston's pool of software engineering talent while keeping the business within range of its Budapest development center. Ninety people, chiefly in sales and marketing, were hired for the Woburn office. Two years later the name 3am Labs, Inc., was changed to LogMeIn, Inc.

Under the LogMeIn name, the company continued to develop a variety of remote-access products while securing its reputation as a Web-based services provider. Suites offered included LogMeIn Rescue, a tool that helped technicians work more efficiently and effectively by allowing them to connect remotely to multiple PCs at once, and LogMeIn Pro, which gave mobile consumers high-security remote access to home or business computers with such productivity features as large file sharing and transfer and remote printing. Additionally,

LogMeIn IT Reach was gaining widespread attention for its management and support tools that helped IT personnel diagnose, track, and repair remote PC problems. From 2006 to 2007, LogMeIn added almost 12 million users to its customer base, reflecting a 500 percent growth rate.

PRODUCT DEVELOPMENT: JANUARY–JUNE 2007

LogMeIn kicked off 2007 with accolades from Network World's Clear Choice Test Award for LogMeIn IT Reach, followed by recognition from *PC Magazine* as a provider of the industry's Best Free Software, LogMeIn Hamachi, originally released in 2005. At the time, Hamachi users were adding around 800,000 new computers each month, allowing computers connected through Hamachi to communicate over the Internet as if they were operating on the same local area network (LAN). In April 2007 LogMeIn Hamachi was named a winner of the 2007 Global Product Excellence in VPN Customer Trust Award.

LogMeIn Ignition hit the technology scene in March 2007, paving the way for customers to use any portable USB storage device (such as a digital camera, memory stick, or cellular phone) plugged into a remote computer to gain full-screen access to the desktop of a host PC. This application soon became popular, as mobile devices continued to inundate the market. Two months later, LogMeIn released Ignition for IT, giving IT specialists one-click remote access to enhanced interactivity and support service features.

In June 2007 the company previewed LogMeIn Free for Mac, the first Web-based remote access product that allowed users to control their Apple Macintosh from any device connected to the Internet. That same month, LogMeIn announced the creation of LogMeIn Rescue+Mobile, an on-demand remote control and IT diagnostic tool for supporting smartphones running the Microsoft Windows Mobile operating system. One of the first Web-based support application for smartphones, LogMeIn Rescue+Mobile enabled IT departments and customer support representatives to securely and quickly access and control smartphones in order to diagnose and fix problems. When the service was officially launched in September, it worked solely with the Palm Treo mobile device. However, subsequent versions of LogMeIn+Mobile that would serve Symbian and Blackberry operating systems were already in the works.

PRODUCT RECOGNITION: JUNE–DECEMBER 2007

LogMeIn released updated versions of LogMeIn Free, LogMeIn Pro, and LogMeIn IT Reach in September

```
┌─────────────────────────────────────────────┐
│              KEY DATES                        │
│                    ■                          │
│  ───────────────────────────────────────     │
│  2003:  Company begins in Hungary.            │
│  2006:  3am Labs, Inc., changes its name to Log- │
│         MeIn, Inc.                            │
│  2007:  Company unveils LogMeIn Free for Mac, the │
│         first Web-based remote access product for │
│         Apple Macs.                           │
│  2008:  Company debuts LogMeIn Pro for Small  │
│         Business and LogMeIn POS and Kiosk for │
│         business owners.                      │
│  2009:  LogMeIn becomes publicly traded on    │
│         NASDAQ.                               │
│  2010:  Company opens office in London, England. │
└─────────────────────────────────────────────┘
```

2007. In addition to a new user interface with simplified menus and controls, improved features of the products included remote sound, meaning that sounds and music on the remote computer could be heard on the local computer being used. Another well-received productivity-enhancing feature allowed for drag and drop file transfers between PCs.

LogMeIn made headlines in December 2007 when it entered into a marketing and service agreement with Intel Corporation. Under this joint venture, LogMeIn adapted its service delivery platform to work with specific technologies of Intel hardware and software products. Intel, in turn, paid a quarterly license and service fee to LogMeIn, in addition to marketing and selling LogMeIn products to consumers. By the end of 2009, this partnership would bring in $6 million in revenue for LogMeIn. Due to a lack of demand, however, Intel would end this marketing agreement in September 2010, paying LogMeIn a termination fee of $2.5 million, plus license fees for the rest of the year.

EXPANSION: 2008

During 2008 LogMeIn initiated changes in its business strategies. In January LogMeIn announced that it had filed a registration statement with the Securities and Exchange Commission (SEC) in connection with the proposed initial public offering (IPO) of its common stock. In July LogMeIn opened a European headquarters in Amsterdam, the Netherlands, and hired two vice presidents at the Woburn office to lead the company's European development efforts. As part of the Amsterdam expansion, LogMeIn launched a Dutch-language Web site.

The year 2008 also saw further improvements and updated releases of LogMeIn's signature products. Responding to increases in Mac usage, for instance, LogMeIn added remote Apple Mac support to LogMeIn Rescue and debuted LogMeIn Pro for Small Business. The LogMeIn POS and Kiosk program became available in July. This was a program to serve companies that carried out business through point-of-sale (POS) systems and Windows-based interactive kiosks. With this new remote support tool, IT personnel could connect to and manage POS and kiosk devices remotely through any computer connected to the Internet, significantly reducing the time and cost of making on-site service calls.

In September LogMeIn Rescue+Mobile was reengineered to be an on-demand service supporting Mac, Windows, Windows Mobile, Symbian, and Blackberry devices. This led to the installation of LogMeIn products on more than 50 million computers, servers, and other apparatus by October. LogMeIn extended its reach into the Apple market by offering LogMeIn Ignition for the iPhone and iPod touch, a user-friendly application that facilitated remote access to home or office computers from mobile Apple devices. As a result of its sustained growth, LogMeIn placed 88th on Deloitte's 2008 Technology Fast 500, a ranking of the fastest-growing technology, media, telecommunications, and life sciences companies in North America.

BUSINESS VENTURES: 2009

Besides steadily adding features and functionality to updated releases of its products, LogMeIn ventured into other areas in 2009. In January 2009 LogMeIn introduced LogMeIn for Ford Work Solutions, remote access software that enabled drivers of Ford's F-150, SuperDuty, E-Series, and Transit Connect models to stay connected to their office computers from their vehicles. The software, which worked through an in-dash computer with Internet connectivity, was factory installed and featured tool and inventory tracking and fleet management telematics. It also allowed for mobile workers to print invoices and other documents on an optional wireless printer in their Ford vehicle.

A strong global presence remained a priority for LogMeIn. To accommodate greater demand in Australia and New Zealand, LogMeIn opened an office in Sydney, its first in the Asia Pacific region, in February 2009. The move was designed not only to support the company's existing customers but also to market its products more effectively to potential consumers. Several months later, LogMeIn revealed that it had signed a distribution contract with NEC BIGLOBE, a Japanese Internet service and broadband media provider. Under this agreement, NEC BIGLOBE would operate as an official distributor of LogMeIn products in Japan.

Another significant action by LogMeIn that year was becoming a publicly traded company on Wednesday, July 1. Offering 6.67 million shares of common stock at $16.00 per share, the company pulled in $107 million with its IPO. By midday on Wednesday, shares had risen to $20.77, a gain of almost 30 percent. In November LogMeIn announced a secondary offering of 3.13 shares of its common stock at $18.50 per share.

THE APPLE MARKET AND BEYOND: 2010

Many of LogMeIn's services during 2010 were designed to enhance the productivity of Apple devices. With the release of the LogMeIn Rescue update in February, for instance, came an iPhone e-mail configuration application that helped iPhone users set up corporate e-mail accounts in less time by contacting live-chat technicians who could remotely push out settings to the mobile devices. Later that month, LogMeIn unveiled new applications for Apple iPhones, as well as Android smartphones, at the GSMA Mobile World Congress in Barcelona, Spain. Among these innovations was a mobile viewer that allowed users, through their iPhones, to view other people's desktops. LogMeIn Pro2 for Mac became available in March, offering users more and faster features than the LogMeIn Free for Mac that had debuted in 2007. With the ability to control a Mac remotely from any location with an Internet connection, LogMeIn Pro2 users could communicate from Mac to Mac, iPhone to Mac, or Windows to Mac.

As the public response to LogMeIn's Apple-related solutions grew, LogMeIn continued to focus on that market sector. A new release of LogMeIn Ignition in April 2010 could be used with an iPad as well as with an iPhone or iPod. As with previous LogMeIn Ignition packages, the updated version allowed users access to both home and office computers from virtually anywhere using Wi-Fi and 3G technology. In July 2010 LogMeIn debuted a new version of LogMeIn Rescue for the increasingly popular iPad. This service gave IT help-desks the capability to provide support for iPad users through live chats. Another update of LogMeIn Ignition was released in August, this one with direct mode navigation that combined touch and click navigation to allow users interaction with remote computers as if they were original applications.

Other notable moves for LogMeIn during 2010 included the June opening of an office in London with the intent of expanding the company's international presence and better meeting the remote access needs of the United Kingdom. In addition, LogMeIn formed a partnership with Zendesk, a leading SaaS help desk trouble ticket and customer support tool. By integrating Zendesk software and LogMeIn Rescue to create LogMeIn Rescue for Zendesk, the two companies allowed users to streamline, and thereby expedite, the trouble ticket process, which involves tracking the detection, reporting, and resolution of a problem. The service was offered free to consumers who already had subscriptions to both LogMeIn Rescue and Zendesk. Another free service LogMeIn debuted was join.me, a screen-sharing product that allowed users to conduct online meetings for up to 250 people, with no account requirements.

After honoring LogMeIn with a prestigious Macworld Awards 2010 award for "Best iPad Application" for LogMeIn Ignition in June, Apple revealed in December 2010 that LogMeIn Ignition had finished fourth on the list of the top 10 highest-grossing iPad applications for the year.

As people continued to seek greater and greater interconnectivity for their electronic devices, LogMeIn was well positioned to continue its success during the 2010s.

Alicia Elley

PRINCIPAL SUBSIDIARIES

3am Labs Kft. (Hungary); Border Development Kft. (Hungary); LogMeIn Australia Pty. Ltd.; LogMeIn Europe B.V. (The Netherlands); LogMeIn UK, Ltd.; RemotelyAnywhere, Inc.

PRINCIPAL COMPETITORS

Apple Inc.; Bomgar Corporation; Cisco Systems, Inc.; Citrix Systems, Inc.; Microsoft Corporation; NTRglobal; NetViewer AG; TeamViewer GmbH.

FURTHER READING

Clancy, Heather. "3am Labs." *CRN,* August 19, 2005. Accessed February 18, 2011. http://www.crn.com/news/channel-programs/169400309/3am-labs.htm.

Gralla, Preston. "Editorial Review of LogMeIn Free." *PCWorld,* August 12, 2010. Accessed February 18, 2011. http://www.pcworld.com/downloads/file/fid,24507-order,4/description.html.

"LogMeIn Says Intel to End Services Deal." *Reuters,* September 10, 2010. Accessed February 18, 2011. http://www.reuters.com/article/2010/09/10/logmein-idUSSGE68909E20100910.

McLaughlin, Kevin. "SaaS Vendor LogMeIn Shares Jump 30 Percent in IPO." *CRN,* July 1, 2009. Accessed February 18,

2011. http://www.crn.com/news/applications-os/218102335/saas-vendor-logmein-shares-jump-30-percent-in-ipo.htm.

Soule, Alexander. "Budapest Startup, 90 Jobs Coming to Woburn." *Boston Business Journal,* September 20, 2004. Accessed February 18, 2011. http://www.bizjournals.com/boston/stories/2004/09/20/story4.html.

Spence, Nick. "Zendesk, LogMeIn Team to Bring Remote Support, Ticketing." *PC World,* September 17, 2010. Accessed February 18, 2011. http://www.pcworld.com/businesscenter/article/205641/zendesk_logmein_team_to_bring_remote_support_ticketing.html.

Vance, Ashlee. "In Hungary, Mogul Finds Fertile Area for Software." *New York Times,* October 11, 2010. Accessed February 18, 2011. http://www.nytimes.com/2010/10/12/technology/12simon.html?_r=1&scp=1&sq=Hungary,%20Mogul%20Finds%20Fertile%20Area%20for%20Software&st=cse.

Lonely Planet Publications

90 Maribyrnong Street
Footscray, Victoria 3011
Australia
Telephone: (61) 3-8379-8000
Fax: (61) 3-8379-8111
Web site: http://www.lonelyplanet.com

Wholly Owned Subsidiary of BBC Worldwide
Incorporated: 1973
Employees: 500 (2011)
Sales: $65.6 million (2010)
NAICS: 511130 Book Publishers; 512110 Motion Picture and Video Production; 516110 Internet Publishing and Broadcasting

■ ■ ■

Lonely Planet Publications is a travel publisher, producing guidebooks and television shows about destinations all across the world. The company has over 300 authors, and most of its books and publications are aimed at the more adventurous traveler, someone more interested in hiking a desolate mountain range than taking an air-conditioned bus tour of Paris.

In addition to its core travel guides, Lonely Planet offers phrasebooks, food guides, Web content, and a magazine. The company maintains offices in Australia, United Kingdom (London), and the United States (Oakland, California). Since 2011 Lonely Planet is wholly owned by BBC Worldwide, a company which bought a 75 percent stake in the company in 2007.

MEETING IN THE PARK

The partnership of Tony and Maureen Wheeler, the founders of Lonely Planet, began on a park bench in London in 1970. Tony Wheeler, in his mid-20s at the time, had earned a master's degree in automotive engineering at the London Business School. According to Tony Wheeler's recollection, he was sitting on the park bench reading a car magazine while Maureen, whom he did not then know, was sitting next to him, reading a novel by Tolstoy. The pair introduced themselves, struck up a conversation, and moved in with each other several days later. Tony Wheeler, born in Bournemouth, England, and Maureen Wheeler, a native of Ireland, were married a year later. The young couple flirted with a conventional lifestyle following their wedding, but wanderlust proved to have a stronger attraction than working in London. Tony Wheeler deferred accepting a well-paying job at Ford Motor Co., and Maureen Wheeler left her job working for a London wine importer. "The plan was to get the travel bug out of our systems, then settle down for good," Tony Wheeler recalled in an October 1994 interview with *Smithsonian* magazine.

In 1972 the Wheelers embarked on what was supposed to be the last big adventure of their lives. They emptied their bank accounts and used the $1,400 they obtained to purchase a few maps and a used Austin minivan. With much dependent on the reliability of the $130 Austin, the Wheelers boarded a boat, crossed the English Channel, and began driving eastward. As the young couple began their trek, they observed a daily budget of $6, crossing Western Europe, the Balkans, Turkey, and into Iran. Once they arrived in Afghanistan, the next country in a dizzying itinerary, the Wheelers sold the Austin and resorted to any transportation mode made available to them. The couple traveled by bus, train, boat, and rickshaw, hitchhiking whenever the need arose. Impulse served as their guidebook, taking the Wheelers on a meandering course snaking through Pakistan, Kashmir, India, Nepal, Thailand, Malaysia, and Indonesia.

The itinerant Wheelers came to rest in Sydney, Australia, nine months after they left London. The journey left the couple virtually penniless, whittling their savings down to 27 cents. "Our original intent had been to find jobs in Sydney and work there for three or four months until we'd earned enough for plane tickets, then fly back to London and get on with our lives," Tony Wheeler explained in his October 1994 interview with *Smithsonian*. He found a marketing job at a pharmaceutical company, but the attempt to return to London soon was shelved. When other travelers heard of the Wheelers' trip, they pressed the couple for details and advice. The interest convinced the Wheelers to write an account of their trip in guidebook form, a project neither of them had entertained before or during the trip. They sat at the kitchen table in their small Sydney apartment and began writing their first travel guide. The effort was truly homespun, a hand-collated, trimmed, and stapled guidebook that was 96 pages long.

With the book completed, the Wheelers needed a name for their kitchen-table company. The inspiration came from "Space Captain," a song by Joe Cocker and Leon Russell that contained the words "lovely planet." When he sang along to the song, Tony Wheeler had a habit of replacing "lovely" with "lonely," preferring his version of the lyrics even after his wife informed him of the mistake. Thus, Lonely Planet Publications became the name of the Wheelers' enterprise.

A 96-PAGE TRAVEL BOOK TAKES OFF

The 96-page travel book, which eventually became a collector's item, was titled *Across Asia on the Cheap*, published in 1973. "It was a crude, totally handmade book," Tony Wheeler remembered in his October 1994 interview with *Smithsonian*, "but when we took it 'round to book shops in Melbourne and Sydney it was

surprisingly easy to sell." The book sold for $1.80. The first printing sold out in 10 days, necessitating another, larger print run. The second print run sold out as well, requiring another run. Within its first year on bookstore shelves, *Across Asia on the Cheap* sold 8,500 copies, prompting the Wheelers to plan a second adventure for the substance of the next Lonely Planet publication.

With the profits from their first travel guide, the Wheelers were able to finance their second trip throughout Asia. They purchased a 250cc Yamaha and rode the motorcycle through Indonesia, Burma, Malaysia, Laos, and Thailand. After spending a year gathering thorough information, the Wheelers spent the next three months in a $2-a-night Singapore hotel room, where they wrote their second guidebook, *South-East Asia on a Shoestring*, published in 1975. Reverently referred to as the "Yellow Bible" by its readers due to the color of its cover, *South-East Asia on a Shoestring* trumped the success of its predecessor, selling twice as many copies as *Across Asia on the Cheap*.

With *South-East Asia on a Shoestring*, Lonely Planet established several of its defining characteristics. The information within the guidebook was meticulously researched, conveyed to the reader in frank, sometimes witty prose. A Lonely Planet travel guide contained conventional and unconventional information, offering advice on hotels and restaurants as well as how to change money on the black market. Equally as important as how well the Wheelers did their work was where they did it, particularly during Lonely Planet's formative years of development. They chose destinations that largely had escaped the attention of their competitors, focusing on countries, cities, and regions guidebook publishers such as Frommer's ignored. In an article he wrote for the July/August 1999 issue of *UNESCO Courier*, Tony Wheeler explained the importance of eschewing the world's more popular destinations. "We started with a very simple philosophy: we were the small time operator who couldn't compete head on with the big publishers in London or New York. So we would produce guidebooks to the places nobody had ever thought of writing about. In retrospect, it was an amazingly clever idea. By the time the 'big guys' had woken up to the tourist boom that was taking off from airports all over the world, we had carved out a name for ourselves as publishers for the new destinations suddenly topping the statistics lists. This hard-won reputation gave us the stature to move on to the more established and familiar destinations."

The success of *South-East Asia on a Shoestring* firmly established Lonely Plant as a guidebook publisher, albeit a decidedly small publisher. Using Melbourne as the base of their operations, the Wheelers spent the latter

KEY DATES

1973: Lonely Planet publishes its first book, *Across Asia on the Cheap.*

1980: The success of a guidebook on India gives Lonely Planet financial security.

1984: Company establishes a sales office in the United States.

1994: Lonely Planet launches its Web site.

2001: Terrorist attacks against the United States on September 11 lead to global decrease in tourism.

2002: Company decreases staff as revenue drops.

2007: BBC Worldwide purchases 75 percent stake in Lonely Planet for £89 million ($120 million).

2011: BBC Worldwide purchases remaining 25 percent stake in company.

half of the 1970s traveling in and writing about a series of countries, publishing travel guides for Nepal, Africa, New Zealand, and New Guinea. The books sold well, but the profits barely paid for the travel and publishing expenses incurred. Maureen Wheeler, in an October 1994 interview with *Smithsonian,* described their financial status in the years immediately following the publication of *South-East Asia on a Shoestring:* "We couldn't afford a decent car, the house we lived in didn't even have an indoor toilet, and the books remained pretty amateurish because we didn't have the money to do things as well as we should have. I didn't think Lonely Planet was ever really going to support the two of us." By the end of the 1970s, the Wheelers had published a dozen books, but the financial future of Lonely Planet remained uncertain. Certainty arrived at the beginning of the 1980s, when the publishing company's fervent yet limited readership shed the characteristics of a cult-like following.

A GUIDEBOOK FOR INDIA

Lonely Planet needed popularity on a higher level to ensure its survival and the Wheelers' financial well-being. The turning point in the publishing company's development occurred after the Wheelers decided in 1979 to write a guidebook for India, a project that quickly overwhelmed them and the two writers they hired to help produce the book. In scope and scale, the travel guide to India eclipsed all other Lonely Planet titles preceding it. Once completed, the book was 700 pages long, nearly four times the length of the publisher's other books. The extra length demanded an increased price tag, but when the $10 copies of the India guidebook arrived in bookstores in 1980, the higher price did not deter buyers in the least. The book was an immediate success, selling 100,000 copies in its first print run and earning a prestigious British literary award hailing it as the best travel book of the year. Eventually, the book sold 500,000 copies, giving Lonely Planet financial stability for the future.

In the wake of the seminal success of the India guidebook, the Wheelers were able to expand the size of their operation both in terms of personnel and physical presence. They could afford to hire editors, cartographers, and writers, all of whom worked on a contract basis, to assist in the production of a steady stream of Lonely Planet publications. As the library of Lonely Planet books increased, giving coverage to nearly every corner of the world, a small network of Lonely Planet sales offices emerged. In 1984 an office was opened in San Francisco, followed by the establishment of an office in London six years later.

AT THE FRONT OF THE TRAVEL GUIDE BUSINESS

Roughly 20 years after the first Lonely Planet books appeared in stores in Australia, Lonely Planet stood as one the most recognized names in travel guide publishing. By 1994 the company's staff had written and published 155 guide books, titles that were advertised as "travel survival kits." Offices in Australia, the United States, the United Kingdom, and France employed a full-time staff of 75 editors and cartographers, generating revenues exceeding $22 million a year.

As Lonely Planet pressed ahead during its third decade of existence, the company averaged annual sales growth of 24 percent. Part of the reason the company was able to maintain its momentum was its willingness to exploit new revenue-generating streams. In 1994, for instance, the company launched the Lonely Planet Web site, through which it fostered the development of a sizeable online community. To mark its 25th anniversary in 1998, the company published its first hardcover coffee-table book, *Chasing Rickshaws.* Another factor contributing to the unflagging strength of the company was the Wheelers' insistence that the tone and style of Lonely Planet books change to meet the changing tastes and needs of their readership. Travelers who were the Wheelers' contemporaries during the 1970s had different lifestyles and traveling desires by the 1990s. The Wheelers of the 1990s brought their children along on their adventures, took shorter trips, and stayed in more expensive accommodations than they had 25 years earlier. Lonely Planet guidebooks reflected the changes, ensuring that the publishing company did not lose touch with the demographic that had fueled its rise.

By its 25th anniversary, Lonely Planet had more than 350 titles in print, a total that was expanding by 20 to 25 new titles each year. "The thing that sets us apart from other travel guide companies is that right from the beginning, Tony Wheeler planted the seeds for worldwide distribution," explained the company's U.S. general manager in an October 12, 1998, interview with *Publishers Weekly.* "And that puts us in the unique position that we can publish a guidebook about almost any place in the world, and it will still make a reasonable return." Worldwide, Lonely Planet was generating annual sales in excess of $40 million, drawing 44 percent of the total from Europe, its largest market. North and South America ranked as the company's second-largest market, accounting for 36 percent of sales. Next on the list was Australia, accounting for 20 percent of sales, with Asia and Africa accounting for the rest.

The company began the 21st century by diversifying into restaurant and cultural guidebooks. However, the terrorist attacks against the United States on September 11, 2001, caused global tourism rates to plummet. When March 2002 arrived and Lonely Planet still had not recovered from the financial fallout that the attacks caused to global businesses, the travel guide firm decided to cut 75 jobs in Britain and the United States, particularly at its London and Oakland, California, locations. Prior to making the cuts, Lonely Planet offered its employees the chance to volunteer to take an extended leave in the hope that the savings would make up for some of the losses caused by the drop in international travel.

One hundred employees took up to five months off, and they were paid 15 percent of their regular salary. However, the impact of the September 11, 2001, attacks was larger than 100 employees opting to take time off at a reduced salary could absorb. Lonely Planet's Muslim travel guide sales dropped by 20 percent. Travel guide sales to various Middle East countries saw a 90 percent drop between late 2001 and early 2002. When the *Independent* asked Lonely Planet about the cuts, a company spokesperson, Jennifer Cox, commented, "After 11 September we needed to ask questions about the business. We had enough resources in the company to keep going but we had to make provision if such a thing happens again."

CONTINUOUS CHANGE

As a result of its review of its business, Lonely Planet moved its production departments to its Melbourne,

Australia, headquarters. As it continued to seek ways to adjust to changes, both in the publishing market and the global political and economic environment, in 2003 the company standardized its guidebook layouts after it inked a deal with Adobe Systems Incorporated to use its InDesign software to print its titles. In part because InDesign supported a variety of fonts, including Unicode fonts, the software helped Lonely Planet to reduce the time it took to steer a guidebook from layout to production. It also streamlined the multilanguage process.

In 2004 a few Lonely Planet staff members did something similar to what helped get the company started in the first place, as they packed up their belongings and traveled over 5,500 miles across the United States in the Lonely Planet RV. The group stopped at over 100 independent bookstores in 26 states. One reason for the tour was so that Lonely Planet could strengthen its existing ties with independent U.S. booksellers. Hitting the road again proved beneficial. By the end of the year, Lonely Planet posted more than $74 million in revenues.

By 2006 the company was one of the largest independent travel guidebook publishers in the world, with nearly 600 titles. Lonely Planet had weathered the global downturn in tourism.

NO LONGER INDEPENDENT

Thirty years after Tony and Maureen Wheeler wrote their first guidebook that helped to launch Lonely Planet, the couple announced in October 2007 that they were selling Lonely Planet to BBC Worldwide. The *Guardian* reported that BBC acquired Lonely Planet for £89 million ($120 million). The deal allowed the Wheelers to maintain 25 percent ownership in Lonely Planet. A year later, during the global economic downturn, Lonely Planet posted a loss. People around the world were focused on keeping their jobs and paying necessary household expenses. Traveling was not at the front of their thoughts.

The following year there were rumors that BBC was planning to sell Lonely Planet. However, BBC had spent between £5 million and £10 million on Lonely Planet's digital platform that launched in 2009, and it was not eager to toss that money aside. The digital platform allowed Internet users to download Lonely Planet guidebook chapters. By 2010 the Lonely Planet digital platform would grow by 37.2 percent, comprising 22.1 percent of Lonely Planet's total revenues.

In 2010 Lonely Planet posted £51.4 million in annual revenues, up from the previous year's £43 million. A majority of the growth came from sales in the United

Kingdom, United States, and Australia. Globally, print book sales were down 25 percent, but digital sales offset this decline.

In 2011 BBC Worldwide purchased the remaining 25 percent of Lonely Planet. In the early 2010s Lonely Planet's growth appeared to be fueled primarily by non-print channels, an unsurprising development given the explosion in usage of digital media devices. Although tourism could be deeply affected by global events, Lonely Planet had carved itself a well-defined position in the travel market as an adventure-oriented travel publisher, and it seemed likely that this position would be maintained.

Jeffrey Covell
Updated, Rhonda Campbell

PRINCIPAL DIVISIONS

Lonely Planet Digital; Lonely Planet Images; Lonely Planet Magazine; Lonely Planet Television.

PRINCIPAL COMPETITORS

Avalon Travel Publishing; Fodor's Travel; Let's Go Publications, Inc.

FURTHER READING

Beard, Matthew. "Lonely Planet Cuts 75 Staff in Downturn." *Independent,* March 22, 2002. Accessed March 7, 2011. http://www.independent.co.uk/arts-entertainment/books/news/lonely-planet-cuts-75-staff-in-downturn-654993.html.

Conlan, Tara. "BBC Worldwide Rules Out Lonely Planet Sale." *Guardian,* October 27, 2009. Accessed March 7, 2011. http://www.guardian.co.uk/media/2009/oct/27/bbc-worldwide-lonely-planet.

De Ramos, Abe. "Lonely Planet's Carolyn Sutton." *CFO,* March 22, 2006. Accessed March 7, 2011. http://www.cfo.com/article.cfm/5622298.

Farmanfarmaian, Roxane. "Lonely Planet Celebrates 25th Anniversary." *Publishers Weekly,* October 12, 1998, 17.

"Hitting the Road with a Lonely Planet Man." *Time International,* June 1, 1998, 6B.

Izon, Lucy. "New, Improved Guide to Russia." *Los Angeles Times,* May 5, 1996, 16.

Krakauer, John. "All They Really Wanted Was to Travel a Little." *Smithsonian,* October 1994, 132.

"Lonely Planet Signs First Multi-Platform Deal with Local Visitor & Convention Bureau." *Eye For Travel,* October 8, 2010. Accessed March 7, 2011. http://www.eyefortravel.com/news/marketing/lonely-planet-signs-first-multi-platform-deal-local-visitor-convention-bureau.

Object Consulting. "Object Backs Lonely Planet's Windows Phone 7 Travel Picks." Melbourne, Victoria: Object Consulting, October 11, 2010. Accessed March 7, 2011. http://touchingthesurface.com.au/latest-news/lonely-planet-phone-7.

Roether, Barbara. "Lonely Planet Adds Spanish Line." *Publishers Weekly,* March 5, 2001, 20.

Sweney, Mark. "BBC Worldwide's Magazines and Lonely Planet Hit by Downturn." *Guardian,* July 14, 2009. Accessed March 7, 2011. http://www.guardian.co.uk/media/2009/jul/14/bbc-worldwide-magazines-lonely-planet.

Wheeler, Tony. "Philosophy of a Guidebook Guru." *UNESCO Courier,* July-August 1999, 54.

"Words of Wisdom; Back to 'Lonely' Roots." *Advertiser,* June 23, 2001, M34.

Mace Security
International, Inc.

240 Gibraltar Road
Suite 220
Horsham, Pennsylvania 19044
U.S.A.
Telephone: (267) 317-4009
Fax: (215) 672-8900
Web site: http://corp.mace.com

Public Company
Founded: 1987
Employees: 310 (2010)
Sales: $28.2 million (2009)
NAICS: 561621 Security Systems Services

■ ■ ■

Mace Security International, Inc. (Mace), first attracted attention during the early 1990s for its manufacture of the less-than-lethal defense spray Mace. Although most of the general public probably still identifies the company with its brand domination in the pepper spray industry, MSI has two operating segments. The company's Security Segment offers a product line which includes various security products including security cameras, intrusion fencing, access control, and security digital recorders, in addition to its well-known Mace spray and other personal defense items. This segment also operates a security monitoring center which services more than 30,000 accounts. Nearly 66 percent of the company's revenues for 2009 came from the Security Segment.

The Digital Media Marketing Segment sold the company's products, as well as third-party products, on Internet promotional sites for several years. However, this segment was sold at the end of 2010. For a number of years, the company also operated a Car Wash Segment, which had as many as 62 car and truck washes at one point. However, most of these had been sold by 2011, with the exception of a few remaining operations in Texas yet to find buyers.

BUILDING A BRAND: 1987–93

Mace Security International was formed in 1987. Its first product was Mace, which became so well known that it was used as the generic name for all pepper sprays. The company was founded by Jon E. Goodrich, who located its headquarters in Bennington, Vermont. Goodrich launched an entrepreneurial career after graduating from St. Lawrence University in 1967 and studying real estate law at Northwestern University. Among the firms he launched were Home Security Inc. and Smith & Wesson Chemical Company.

When the International Chiefs of Police met in St. Louis in 1993, officials identified rising fears about crime as one of the factors in the increase in the personal safety business. "Everyone is jumping on the band wagon," said Mace training director Tom Archmbault, according to the *St. Louis Dispatch*. "Violent crime is escalating everywhere. People want to feel safe. And it's impossible for the police to be everywhere."

This increased emphasis on safety created a good environment for Mace Security International's initial

COMPANY PERSPECTIVES

In the current environment, Mace is aware of the importance of security in North America. Mace plans to continue developing and marketing cutting-edge security products and services aimed at allowing our customers to improve their safety and security needs.

public offering (IPO) in 1993. The first nine months of that year resulted in sales of $7 million. The fourth quarter of 1993, however, was disappointing for the company and resulted in a loss. CEO Jon Goodrich attributed the loss to "internal expansion costs" and the added expenses of sales and marketing people, attending trade shows, and anticipating growth.

EXPANSION IN THE INDUSTRY: 1994–95

In 1994 Mace acquired the assets of the Federal Laboratories division of TransTechnology Corporation. Federal Laboratories was the nation's oldest producer of tear gas as well as grenades and projectiles for purchase by law enforcement and correctional facilities. Mace hoped to bring Federal Laboratories back to profitability. Mace continued its expansion efforts in 1994 when it acquired Kindergard Corporation. Kindergard, a developer, manufacturer, and marketer of child safety products, provided another avenue for Mace's security and safety business. Kindergard's 18-item product line included cabinet latches, outlet plugs, and doorknob guards.

While Mace continued to focus on safety and security, the staple product, Mace pepper spray, occupied a lower percentage of the total sales of the company. In 1993 90 percent of sales were attributed to the spray, but by the third quarter of 1994, only 52 percent of sales came from pepper sprays. Acquisitions and growth in other areas assisted Mace with diversification within the safety industry. The diversification led the way to record net sales in the third quarter of 1994 of more than $3.9 million, an increase of more than 100 percent over the same period in 1993.

In March 1995 Mace began distributing its products in Canada through distribution company Feelin' Secure Ltd. The first product to be distributed was Muzzle, a pepper spray dog repellent.

PERSONNEL CHANGES AND ACQUISITIONS: 1995–96

In October 1995 the board of directors of Mace delegated the responsibilities of CEO, which had been the position of founder Jon Goodrich, to a three-member committee consisting of Goodrich, Robert Gould (a principal stockholder), and Robert D. Norman, the vice chairman. While Goodrich remained in charge of daily operations, all other matters required the consent of the committee. This situation did not last long, however, as in 1996, Goodrich officially resigned his positions as president and co-CEO. Robert D. Norman was named as his replacement. Goodrich remained as chairman and retained his stock in the company.

In the first quarter of 1996, the company announced three acquisitions to double Mace's annual revenues. The three companies, Howard Uniform Company, Balco Uniform Cap Corp., and Gould & Goodrich Leather, Inc., provided the law enforcement industry with uniforms and accessories.

Just nine months after resigning as CEO, Goodrich as well as Gould announced that they were jointly negotiating the sale of their stock (56.2 percent collectively) to a competitor. Mace ultimately avoided the threat of this takeover, but as part of the maneuvering Goodrich emerged again as chief executive officer of the company.

DIVERSIFICATION: 1997–99

In 1997 Mace purchased MSP, Inc., to further diversify itself in the personal safety industry. MSP, Inc., based in Aurora, Colorado, marketed consumer safety products under the names of Global Security, Safetynet, and Safeguard. Despite continued acquisitions, the company announced a loss in the first quarter of 1998 and reported that continuing operations for the quarter declined 1.9 percent. The company reported a net loss of $240,341 compared with a net loss of $8,573 for the previous year in the same period. The information about losses excluded reports from the company's Law Enforcement division, which was scheduled to be sold in the second quarter to Armor Holdings. The proceeds from the eventual transaction amounted to approximately $5.2 million.

The end of the first quarter of 1999 brought big changes to Mace Security International. The board reported that it had been reviewing the company's options to maximize profits. Opportunity came in the form of Louis D. Paolino, Jr., and his car wash company, American Wash Services Inc. The two companies merged, and Paolino was named chairman and chief executive officer of the company. With the

KEY DATES

1987: Mace Security International is founded; its first product, Mace, becomes the world's best-known defense spray.

1993: Company joins NASDAQ with initial public offering.

1997: Company continues to bolster personal safety division through acquisitions.

1999: Mace begins diversification into car wash industry with the purchase of American Wash Services; Louis D. Paolino, Jr., founder of American Wash Services, is named president, CEO, and chairman of Mace; Mace acquires four additional car wash companies.

2001: Low stock price leads to threat of delistment.

2005: Mace begins selling off its car and truck wash businesses.

2007: Company creates a digital media marketing division.

2009: Mace agrees to fine levied by the EPA regarding storage of hazardous chemicals.

2010: Company delisted from NASDAQ.

2011: Mace seeks to gain funding through rights offering.

merger, Mace became the first publicly traded national car wash chain. The company's headquarters moved from Bennington, Vermont, to Mt. Laurel, New Jersey. Former CEO Jon Goodrich retained the presidency of the Mace consumer division, and that portion of operations remained in Vermont.

SUCCESS IN A NEW INDUSTRY: 1999–2000

The stock market responded favorably to the company's change in direction. Trading as low as $1.12 per share before the announcement, the stock shot up to nearly $6 per share after the merger was announced. The share price continued to rise through the year, and revenues exceeded $38 million, compared with $9.2 million in 1998.

In 1999 alone, the company acquired four additional car wash companies as part of its strategy to dominate the industry. More acquisitions were made the following year, during which revenue reached $48 million. The year 2000 also marked further separation of Mace from its security roots. The company entered

into an agreement with Goodrich and his company, Mark Sport, whereby Goodrich would pay $20,000 per month to Mace. In exchange, Mark Sport would assume operations for all of the security products division, both risks and profits.

As Mace forged ahead in the car wash industry, it selected Super Bright Car Wash as the new brand name for the chain nationally. The transition to the new brand was slow, however, as acquired car wash businesses retained their existing names for some time.

NEW MARKETS: 2000–07

Aggressive acquisitions and losses in 2000 led to the stock price for Mace dropping to less than a dollar in the first quarter of 2001. Because of the drop, the company was in danger of being delisted by NASDAQ. The company avoided being delisted by meeting the NASDAQ requirement of maintaining a bid price of more than one dollar for 10 consecutive days.

The company started fiscal 2001 favorably, reporting increased revenue. Mace's car wash facilities were in Arizona, Delaware, Florida, New Jersey, Pennsylvania, and Texas, with truck washes located in Arizona, Indiana, Ohio, and Texas. Although by 2003 its number of car washes, as well as its revenues, had essentially remained constant, it continued to explore potential acquisitions, merger, and strategic alliances. In addition, it had returned, as of May 2002, to the direct sale of chemical defense sprays, following the expiration of the marketing agreement with Jon Goodrich, still a member of the board of directors.

The company expanded its foothold in the security market in August 2002 when it added electronic surveillance equipment to its product line. Mace acquired the assets of security products company Micro-Tech Mfg. Inc., which specialized in security cameras and other surveillance equipment.

The inventory and customer accounts of Securetek, Inc., were acquired by Mace in November 2005, further strengthening the company's position in the security field. Securetek specialized in electronic surveillance products, selling these items to dealers and installers of security alarm systems. Following the acquisition, the business was integrated into Mace's security operations.

The car wash business never really succeeded for Mace. Sales in that area peaked in 2001 and remained mostly flat thereafter. That year was also the last for some time in which Mace would post a profit. Net losses began in 2002 and continued throughout the decade.

As might be expected from a company in the red, Mace spent much of the first decade of the new century continuously making moves in order to return to profitability. After building up its Car Wash segment, in 2005 the company began exiting that industry by selling off its assets. Two years later Mace International acquired Promopath, which became the company's on-line marketing division in July 2007. Promopath assisted advertising clients in finding customers by publishing promotions online. In return, the clients, which included NetFlix and Discover credit cards, paid Promopath for each customer or prospect acquired. Also in July 2007, Mace purchased all outstanding common stock of Linkstar Interactive, Inc., for about $10.5 million. Linkstar became the company's e-commerce division. In late 2007 Mace launched Purity, a line of mineral cosmetics sold through the company's Linkstar e-commerce division.

CHALLENGES AND CHANGES: 2007–08

Despite the company's expansion into new arenas, revenues continued to fall. Financial concerns were not the only challenges facing Mace at this time. The U.S. Enviromental Protection Agency (EPA) conducted a site investigation of Mace's rented building space at the Bennington, Vermont, location in January 2008 to determine if hazardous materials were being properly stored. The company was required to remediate certain hazardous materials and waste. Such action was taken within the allotted time period, and the final report was accepted by the EPA in September 2009. The company and the owner of the property were also fined more than $240,000 for the EPA's oversight costs. Mace expected to pay approximately $190,000, with the property owner paying the remaining portion. This fine was in addition to the approximately $786,000 the company had already spent related to the remediation.

The Digital Media Marketing Segment underwent changes in 2008. To this point, the segment consisted of the e-commerce and online marketing business divisions. In June of that year, the online marketing services were discontinued to outside customers, and the segment basically only operated the Linkstar e-commerce division. Promopath, the online marketing division, then focused on increasing the distribution of Linkstar's products.

Other changes were in store during that year as well. Paolino was terminated as CEO of the company in May 2008, and Dennis Raefield was appointed as the CEO and president of Mace in October of that year. At the end of 2008 and into the beginning of 2009, the company reorganized in order to save money. The total number of employees was reduced, and the electronic surveillance equipment operations were consolidated, which included the sale of one of the warehouses used by this division.

FOCUSING ON SECURITY: 2009–10

In the midst of these changes, the company continued to grow its security business. In April 2009 Mace purchased all outstanding common stock of Central Station Security Systems, Inc. (CSSS), for about $3.7 million. CSSS, a wholesale monitoring company, became part of Mace's Security Segment and allowed the company to expand its security products line.

During the first quarter of 2010, Mace International resumed its online marketing division through Promopath, which accounted for a small portion of the Digital Media Marketing Segment's business. Products sold through this division included a variety of items from teeth whitening and skin care products to dietary supplements and pet vitamins.

On March 22, 2010, Mace once again received notification from NASDAQ that the company's bid price had closed for less than $1.00 per share for 30 consecutive days, which was out of compliance of the Listing Rule. Mace was given 180 days to regain compliance by having a closing price of at least $1.00 per share for 10 consecutive business days, otherwise the stock would be delisted. The company had received similar notification in October 2009 and was able to regain compliance by January 2010. However, the company faced a different outcome following this second noncompliance notification. As a result of not meeting the minimum price for shares, Mace was delisted in 2010.

Another major change occurred for the company during the fourth quarter of 2010 when it sold Linkstar Corp. for $1.1 million. By divesting this operation, Mace was able to continue toward its goal of focusing on security.

LEGAL MATTERS AND FALLING REVENUES: 2011

The Bennington, Vermont, factory, which was previously investigated by the EPA, was also under investigation by the United States Attorney for the District of Vermont regarding allegations of not disposing hazardous materials and waste according to the Resource Conservation and Recovery Act. These alleged violations of environmental law occurred between 1998 and 2008. In January 2011 a plea agreement was signed to settle the suit, and the company's subsidiary Mace Personal Defense pled guilty to one felony charge of storing hazardous waste without a permit, and paid a $100,000 fine.

Also in January 2011, the company made a final payment to former CEO Louis D. Paolino, Jr., under a settlement agreement entered into several months earlier. Paolino was awarded more than $4.1 million in damages as well as nearly $740,000 in legal fees related to claims he filed regarding his termination with Mace. He was found innocent of willful misconduct, and an arbitration panel determined that he was entitled to severance according to his employment agreement with the company. In order to make the payments, Mace began selling noncore assets such as the remaining car washes, a warehouse in Texas, and the Digital Media Marketing business. These funds would also be used to grow the Security Segment.

As revenues continued to decrease, Mace announced plans early in 2011 for a rights offering. This would help the company finance its growth in the security field. Under the plan, each Mace shareholder would be able to purchase three shares of common stock for every share currently owned. The offering was expected to take place during the first half of 2011.

In 2011 Mace appeared to be a company in trouble. Profitability remained elusive, revenue was weak, and the company had been delisted. However, Mace did possess a well-known brand name in the security industry, so any return to profitability would be through its core security holdings.

Updated, Diane Milne

PRINCIPAL SUBSIDIARIES

Care Investment, Inc.; CRCD, Inc.; ESG Marketing, LLC; Mace CSSS, Inc.; Mace Personal Defense, Inc.; Mace Security International, Inc.; Mace Security Products, Inc.; Mace Trademark Corp.

PRINCIPAL DIVISIONS

Business and Home Security Systems; Industrial Vision Source; Mace CS; Mace Pro Security Products; Personal Defense.

PRINCIPAL COMPETITORS

Armor Holdings, Inc.; Panasonic Corporation; Security Equipment Company, Inc.; Sony Corporation.

FURTHER READING

Librach, Phyllis Brasch. "New Products Breed Civilian Crime Fighters; Personal Protection Business Thrives as Fear of Crime Grows." *St. Louis Post-Dispatch,* October 18, 1993, 1A.

"Mace Enters Plea Agreement with U.S. Attorney for Its Vermont Subsidiary EPA Issue." *Manufacturing Close-Up,* January 13, 2001.

"Mace Security International Acquires Micro-Mfg." *American Clean Car,* 31, no. 5 (October 2002): 42.

"Mace Security International Inc. Moves Trading of Stock to OTCQB Marketplace." *Investment Weekly News,* October 16, 2010, 24.

"Mace Security Makes Final Payment to Former CEO; Secures Short-Term Financing; Plans Rights Offering." *Manufacturing Close-Up,* January 11, 2011.

Marquard & Bahls AG

Admiralitaetstrasse 55
Hamburg, 20459
Germany
Telephone: (49) 40-37 004-0
Fax: (49) 40-37-004 242
Web site: http://www.mbholding.de

Private Company
Founded: 1947
Employees: 3,692 (2009)
Sales: EUR 9.31 billion ($13 billion) (2009)
*NAICS:*221119 Other Electric Power Generation; 424710 Petroleum Bulk Stations and Terminals; 454311 Fuel Dealers; 488190 Other Support Activities for Air Transportation

■ ■ ■

Marquard & Bahls AG (M&B) has been successfully operating in the international oil and energy business for more than 60 years. The company's original and oldest subsidiary is Mabanaft, which is the oil trading arm of Marquard & Bahls. While Mabanaft's historic base is in northwest Europe, it trades in all import regions of the world. Mabanaft also operates a network of more than 500 service stations, which operate under the trade names of OIL! in central Europe, B.W.O.C. in the United Kingdom, and Tirex Petrol in Moldova.

Two other prominent M&B subsidiaries are its oil-tanking and skytanking units. Oiltanking GmbH operates approximately 70 terminals in 21 countries worldwide, with a storage capacity of over 17 million cubic meters. Europe is the primary market, but the company also has storage in the Americas, the Middle East, and Asia. M&B subsidiary Skytanking Holding gmbH provides a similar fuel storage service for 21 airports in Europe, the United States, and India. The volume of fuel handled is about 8.5 billion liters.

Finally, M&B subsidiary GEE Energy offers quality management services, while subsidiary Mabagas is focused on renewable energy, primarily biogas.

HANSEATIC VALUES

It is often said that business people in the Hamburg area of Germany possess "Hanseatic values," which are defined as honesty, reliability, responsibility, caution, and a willingness to form partnerships. It appeared that Theodor Weisser had all of these qualities when he founded Marquard & Bahls in the city of Hamburg in 1947.

It was a difficult time to start any type of a business in Germany. The country had been under occupation by the victorious Allied powers since the end of World War II in 1945, and these powers had been trying to diminish German industrial capacity. In the British Sector, which included Hamburg, industrial development was simply not allowed, especially by German nationals.

Undeterred by such restrictions and determined to get into the oil supply business, Theodor Weisser found a way to skirt the regulations simply by purchasing an existing business. The fact that the existing business was unrelated to the oil industry was only a temporary obstacle. The original Marquard & Bahls was a grain handling company that had been established in 1913.

COMPANY PERSPECTIVES

Independent, sound, and individual.

Having acquired a business without violating regulations, Weisser simply changed the focus of that business from grain handling to oil handling.

Entering the oil trading business in postwar Germany would prove to be a profitable venture. With most of the country's infrastructure destroyed, scarcity and shortages abounded, and Weisser saw a market opportunity in supplying domestic heating oils and lubricating oils. Marquard & Bahls established its subsidiary Mabanaft in 1947 and began trading.

The introduction of the Marshall Plan for the reconstruction of Europe in 1948 shifted the focus of the Allied powers that occupied western Germany. The stranglehold on German industrial development would begin to diminish, at least in the zones occupied by British, French, and U.S. forces.

TRADING WITH THE SOVIETS

The postwar years would be an opportune time to engage in the oil business. In 1950 global oil consumption would be 10.4 million barrels per day, but by 1960 that figure would more than double to 21.3 million barrels. It would double again by 1980 and reach a daily consumption of 62.9 million barrels.

In the mid-1950s, Marquard & Bahls passed the first milestone in its development when it began to import heating oil from the Soviet Union. In the decade that had passed since the end of the war, the former arch foe had become a trading partner.

For the Soviet Union, with an abundant supply of energy at home, trading oil with Germany would allow it to acquire foreign credits. It would use these credits to purchase materials and technology strategic to its own economic development.

DIVERSIFICATION AND EXPANSION

In 1972 Marquard & Bahls, which had operated a small petroleum tank terminal business through its subsidiary Mabanaft, reorganized its tank terminal business and created a new entity named Oiltanking GmbH.

The Oiltanking subsidiary was tasked with developing a network of storage terminals, often in partnership with local private or state enterprises. With a decentralized management structure, Oiltanking allowed its on-site management team considerable autonomy to respond to local opportunities. The company would not be involved in the ownership of the products it stored, but instead it would act as a "custodian of valuable liquids," as it described itself. Each facility would act as a profit center.

Oiltanking inherited the small terminal structure already established by Mabanaft, which had facilities in Hamburg, Karlsruhe, Frankfurt, Copenhagen, and Ghent. The company soon expanded beyond storage for oil to include chemical, gases, and biofuel storage, as well as pipeline operations in Europe, Asia, and the Americas.

In 1974 the company began operations in the United States by creating Oiltanking Houston LP. M&B continued to expand operations by opening facilities in the Texas cities of Beaumont, Pasadena, Texas City, and Port Neches.

In 1975 Oitanking began construction of a terminal in Amsterdam, and in 1982, the first oil from the Dutch continental shelf was piped to the facility. By 1983 additional wells in the area were piping 60,000 barrels per day.

In 1989 Oiltanking began construction of a facility in Singapore. In 1992 Oiltanking Malta opened, and in 1996 the company expanded to India. Operations would eventually extend to Argentina, Peru, Venezuela, Bulgaria, Finland, Estonia, China, Indonesia, and the Middle East.

AVIATION FUELING AND RENEWABLE ENERGY: 1999–2002

Marquard & Bahls would spot another opportunity for growth and expansion in the aviation fueling business. In 1999 it formed a wholly owned subsidiary named Skytanking and purchased a 50 percent interest in a fueling company at Munich airport.

As with the oil business, Marquard & Bahls' move into the aviation fueling business came at an opportune time. Massive restructuring was taking place in the airline business, and multiple airline operators were shredding noncore assets. Many airlines had storage facilities and fueling infrastructure, and many of those facilities were in need of repair and upgrading.

Marquard & Bahls, through Skytanking, purchased facilities and made investments in infrastructure with an eye toward long-term gain. The company was also willing to manage facilities on behalf of airlines unwilling to sell.

Skytanking specialized in the design, operating, and financing of aviation fuel storage and hydrant systems as well as into-plane fueling. It also provided independent aviation fuel handling to airlines, airports, and oil companies.

The renewable energy market was another area in which Marquard & Bahls saw potential. In 2002 it formed a subsidiary named GEE Energy to enter the wood pellet industry in Germany. GEE purchased sawdust and shavings from local wood mills and then processed and compressed them into briquettes. These briquettes could then be used as fuel for fireplaces and in wood-burning stoves.

INTERNATIONAL EXPANSION: 2003–07

In 2003 Marquard & Bahls would expand on its original business of home heating by obtaining controlling interest of Viterra Contracting, one of Germany's leading suppliers of energy to residential estates and special purpose buildings. That same year Skytanking won its first U.S. contract at Miami International Airport. It would go on to win contracts with Southwest Airlines at Dallas (Love Field), Raleigh Durham Airport, and Frontier Airlines at Denver. It would also win the contract to manage the fuel storage and hydrant operations at the Indianapolis International Airport.

As Marquard & Bahls continued to grow and expand internationally, it reorganized itself at home. In 2005 the company moved all of its international trading activities from its head office in Hamburg to its offices in Rotterdam, in the Netherlands. It also expanded to Turkey by entering into a joint venture with Enerji Petrol Denizcilik Ticaret Ve Sanayi A.S., a major supplier of bunker fuel oil.

Marquard & Bahls would make its first major foray into the Peoples' Republic of China in 2006 when Oiltanking established its first terminal at the Daya Bay Petrochemical Industrial Park. The next year it would acquire a major interest in the Xiba storage terminal at Nanjing China. In a joint venture with the Port Author-ity of Nanjing, Oiltanking operated this terminal as a chemical storage facility. Nanjing, which is the center of the East China chemical market, is strategically located on the Yangtze River. It is a major transfer point from ocean-going vessels to barge traffic.

In 2007 Skytanking signed a 30-year contract with Stuttgart International Airport to build and operate a new fuel storage facility. The contract was termed a "BOOT" contract, which stands for Build, Own, Operate, Transfer. It allowed the Stuttgart Airport to outsource the design, construction, and operation of the facility to Skytanking. In return for a 30-year concession, Skytanking would build, own, and operate the facility and at the end of 30 years transfer the facility back to the airport.

AGGRESSIVE GROWTH STRATEGY: 2009 AND BEYOND

To expand its presence in renewable energy, in 2009 the company formed another subsidiary, Mabagas, to concentrate on the biogas market. Marquard and Bahls saw biogas as one of the most rapidly growing sectors of the renewable energy market, and it hoped that Mabagas would be able to market on a national and international scale.

Marquard & Bahls has been a privately held international company since it was founded by Theodor Weisser in 1947. It has, however, occasionally raised money in the open market. In a 2009 private placement, the company acquired millions to allow it to pursue an aggressive growth strategy.

Until 2003 the chief executive officer had always been a Weisser family member. However, in that year Helmuth Weisser, son of the founder, turned control over to Wim Lokhorst, a company veteran who assumed the position of chairman of the board and CEO. In January 2011 Lokhorst retired and another company veteran, Christian Flach, was appointed chairman of the board and CEO.

Flach guided Marquard & Bahls in the early 2010s with a goal of expanding the company's forays into renewable energy and other energy-related revenue streams. While it was uncertain how well these new ventures would fare, it seemed likely that M&B's older subsidiaries would keep the company on a solid financial foundation. As long as petroleum remained the dominant global fuel, it would always need to be traded or stored.

Ian MacDonald

PRINCIPAL SUBSIDIARIES

GMA — Gesellschaft für Mineralölanalytik und Qualitätsmanagement GmbH & Co. KG; Mabagas GmbH & Co. KG; Mabanaft GmbH & Co. KG; OIL! Tankstellen GmbH & Co. KG; natGAS Aktiengesellschaft; Oiltanking GmbH; Skytanking Holding GmbH.

PRINCIPAL COMPETITORS

A.P. Møller-Maersk A/S; BP plc; Royal Vopak N.V.

FURTHER READING

Carlin, Wendy. "West German Growth and Institutions 1945–1990." London: Center for Economic Policy Research, January 1994.

Sucher, Joern. "Helmuth Weisserm, the Anti-Patriarch." *Manager Magazine,* September 22, 2004.

"Threat of Soviet Oil." *Saudi Aramco World,* March 1962.

"Wim Lokhorst – Oil Is His Job." *Hamburger Abendblatt,* June 24, 2004.

Massey Energy Company

4 North Fourth Street
Richmond, Virginia 23219
U.S.A.
Telephone: (804) 788-1800
Fax: (804) 788-1870
Web site: http://www.masseyenergyco.com

Public Company
Incorporated: 1920
Employees: 7,359 (2010)
Sales: $3.04 billion (2010)
Stock Exchanges: New York
Ticker Symbol: MEE
NAICS: 212111 Bituminous Coal ad Lignite Surface Mining; 212112 Bituminous Coal Underground Mining

■ ■ ■

Massey Energy Company is one of the largest coal mining and services company in the United States. In 2011 the company had 84 mining complexes in Central Appalachia (Virginia, West Virginia, and Kentucky), including 66 underground mines and 18 surface mines that produce 40 million tons of coal each year. Massey is the largest coal producer in the region. Massey transformed itself from a small coal brokerage firm into a large coal mining conglomerate through a succession of determined Massey family members and later under the guidance of men with coal mining in their blood.

Massey has had a difficult, if not hostile, relationship with both labor unions and nature that has put a shadow over its history. Massey's management, though admirable in their achievements, has made some catastrophic, even criminal, choices with regard to both the environment and labor, with dire consequences. Over the course of its history Massey has been responsible for financial malfeasance, environmental devastation, and loss of human life, including the collapse of the Upper Big Branch mine in 2010 that cost the lives of 29 miners, the worst U.S. mining accident in over 40 years.

In 2011 Massey agreed to be bought by competitor Alpha Natural Resources for over $7 billion.

FROM BROKERAGE TO DIGGING HOLES

A. T. Massey founded the A.T. Massey Coal Company (ATM) in 1920 as a coal brokering business and became its first president. A. T.'s sons, Evan and William, took over the company in 1945 with Evan serving as president. The company did not venture into mining until E. Morgan Massey, Evan's son, exerted his influence on the company. There are conflicting accounts of E. Morgan's transformation of ATM from a coal brokerage to a coal mining company. According to company documents, ATM acquired its first mining operation in 1945, but E. Morgan was still a student at the University of Virginia at that time. According to the *Cincinnati Enquirer*, ATM acquired its first mine in West Virginia in 1949. A 1985 *BusinessWeek* profile of Massey reported that after E. Morgan graduated from college he joined the family business and "asserted his independence by pushing to move the brokerage company into the profitable but troublesome mining business," and that his first move was a $10,000 investment in a coal mining venture. He had to make this move without his father's consent or even knowledge. When the company finally agreed to let him go forward with his plans, he could only use profits from his own ventures to expand his plans. Despite the tight restrictions, he succeeded and led ATM into the industry that would become its central business.

Even though E. Morgan was a manager of the West Virginia operation he shoveled coal alongside his workers. When the United Mine Workers (UMW) arrived and organized his employees E. Morgan signed up along with them. Six months later, the union representative told E. Morgan that as a manager he could not join the union. This experience as well as others would seed a deep antipathy between Massey's management and unions that would last for decades.

In 1962 E. Morgan's uncle, William E. Massey, became president of ATM. Under William's leadership the company continue to expand its mining interests. ATM acquired Peerless Eagle Coal Company in 1965 and established the Martin County Coal Corporation in 1969. The company expanded the operations of its subsidiary Omar Mining Company to cover from Logan County, West Virginia, to Boone County, West Virginia. In 1972 E. Morgan, at 46 years of age, became president of the company. Two years later, he, along with his uncle and his brother, sold ATM to St. Joe Minerals Corporation for 14 percent of St. Joe Minerals stock, valued at approximately $56 million.

E. Morgan remained president of what had become the ATM subsidiary of St. Joe Minerals. As the oil crisis took hold of the nation in the 1970s, coal as a source of energy grew in importance. The value of ATM grew accordingly. Companies like ATM were optimistic about the future and began expanding their capacity and increasing their holdings in the coal industry. In 1974 ATM bought Rawl Sales & Processing Company. In 1976 it acquired the Tennessee Consolidated Coal Company, and in 1978 the company launched two new companies, Massey Coal Services and Elk Run Coal Company.

In 1980 St. Joe Minerals sold half its interest in ATM to Royal Dutch Shell Group, an oil company. The resulting entity was Massey Coal Partnership. A year later Los Angeles-based Fluor Corporation bought St. Joe Minerals, including its interest in Massey Coal. At the time, the price of commodities such as coal, gold, and lead were soaring. Fluor, a major construction and engineering firm, bought St. Joe Minerals as a strategy to hedge against the downward turns in its own industry. It turned out to be a poor bet because commodity prices soon plunged, and in the mid-1980s Fluor sold St. Joe Minerals' gold and lead assets. In 1987 Flour bought out Royal Dutch Shell's interest in the partnership. As a result, Massey Coal was reorganized under the name A.T. Massey Coal Company (ATM) and as a wholly owned subsidiary of Fluor. In 1989 ATM acquired Vantage Mining from Pittston, and in 1991 the company acquired Big Creek and established the subsidiary Long Fork Coal Company.

During the mid-1980s the coal industry suffered from excess supply, the result of overexpansion in the late 1970s and early 1980s. Coal prices fell or remained flat, and coal companies resorted to cutting costs in order to counterbalance inflation and maintain profits. ATM cut costs by using small contractors to mine its less desirable deposits while retaining the richer coal seams under its own management. With contractors ATM could squeeze out what it could from them while reducing its overhead costs. Smaller contractors could fly under the radar of both regulators and unions and thus remain much more profitable.

VIOLENCE AND VICTORY, BLANKENSHIP RISES

ATM also maintained profitability by reducing labor costs. In the mid-1980s, Massey became involved in one of the most bitter labor disputes in decades when the company faced off with the UMW. Then manager Don Blankenship urged the company to take on the union in 1984. The UMW wanted to negotiate one contract that would cover all of ATM's 120 mines and subsidiaries. The company wanted each mine to negotiate its own contract. Blankenship argued that each mine served as a separate profit center and operated under different conditions. For UMW, the confrontation with ATM was an opportunity to demonstrate its power. Moreover, unions in general were looking to prove that they were still relevant in the United States. However, the trends at the time did not run in UMW's favor. Membership was down from 160,000 in 1978 to 110,000 members in 1985. The coal industry was moving west, where companies could engage in lower-cost surface mining,

KEY DATES

1920: A. T. Massey founds A.T. Massey Coal Company (ATM).

1945: ATM acquires first mining operation. Evan Massey becomes president of ATM.

1962: William E. Massey becomes president of ATM.

1972: E. Morgan Massey becomes president of ATM.

1974: St. Joe Minerals acquires ATM.

1980: Royal Dutch Shell Group and St. Joe Minerals form the Massey Coal Partnership.

1981: The Fluor Corporation acquires St. Joe Minerals (with Massey Coal Partnership).

1987: ATM becomes a wholly owned Fluor subsidiary.

1990: ATM names Don Blankenship as president.

2000: The Fluor Corporation splits into two publicly traded companies, one of which is Massey Energy Company.

2008: Massey Energy pays fine of $20 million to EPA for water pollution violations.

2010: Upper Big Branch mine explodes, killing 29 mine workers; Don Blankenship retires; Baxter F. Phillips, Jr., becomes president.

2011: Massey Energy agrees to sell itself to Alpha Natural Resources for $7.1 billion.

and the UMW had less of a presence. UMW mines at that time contributed to less than 40 percent of all coal products, so the union lacked the clout to command a massive strike across all ATM's mines. Instead, the union initiated strikes at selected mines and demanded a uniform contract.

The first strike was at the Rawls Sales & Processing Company, which was run by Blankenship. The mine was located in the Tug Fork Valley section of West Virginia, near the Kentucky border and where the legendary "Matewan Massacre" took place some 65 years earlier. An attempt to unionize area miners led to violence that cost the lives of nine people. In 1985 the labor fight pitted 1,500 UMW members against ATM, and once again violence broke out. An article in *Time* magazine described the conflict: "Violence has become almost monotonous. In the latest incident, a midnight explosion last week rocked the three-story brick district headquarters of the UMW in Pikeville, Kentucky, incidentally shattering a huge portrait of the late union

leader John L. Lewis that hung on the wall. ... Gunfire has been commonplace. Snipers killed a nonunion coal-truck driver, Hayes West, 35, in a convoy crossing Co-eburn Mountain in late May. Gunfire wounded miner Judy Mulins, 40, in the hand in July while she was picketing in Canada, Kentucky." On a single day 11 bullets were fired into Blankenship's office. One smashed through his Zenith television.

The strike lasted for 15 months until the UMW called it off, agreeing to negotiate separate contracts with ATM's 17 major subsidiaries. Blankenship kept that old Zenith television near his desk until the day he left the company many years later, most likely to remind him of the company's survival through such tumultuous times.

During the late 1980s many rival coal companies were abandoning the central Appalachian area, but ATM was buying up reserves. In particular, ATM bolstered its supply of metallurgical coal, which was a high-quality product suitable for making steel. An influx of low-priced foreign steel had crippled U.S. steel companies, so many coal companies dropped out of the metallurgical coal business, leaving an opportunity for ATM to grab these reserves at discounted prices. This strategy was so successful that ATM was soon producing over a third of Fluor's operating profit despite generating only 10 percent of its revenues.

After running two more of ATM's operating operations since the strike at Rawls Sales, Blankenship became president of ATM in July 1990. The son of a grocer, he was raised in the coalfields of West Virginia and worked in the coal mines during college breaks. Blankenship became the first leader of the company who was not a member of the Massey family. E. Morgan Massey assumed the newly created position of chairman and chief executive officer. E. Morgan retired in 1992, and Blankenship was given the position of chairman and CEO. Under Blankenship's leadership the company continued to buy up reserves through the rest of the 1990s. Blankenship was especially interested in the new federal clean air requirements, which he believed would bode well for low-sulfur coal producers such as ATM. The bet paid off. Demand rose for low-sulfur coal and with it ATM'sprofits, making the company one of Fluor's crown jewels by 1997, while Fluor's engineering and construction businesses were suffering a downturn.

ACCIDENTS, POLLUTION, AND LEGAL BATTLES

In 2000 Fluor split its company into two publicly traded companies, one composed of the engineering and construction assets and the other ATM. The deal was structured as a reverse spin-off. The construction business became a new public company, and the old Fluor Corporation retained the coal operations and changed its name to Massey Energy Company. Massey had $2 billion in assets and $500 million in debt. Blankenship remained CEO and chairman of the company.

Massey Energy started its new independence on rocky ground as it suffered several public relations disasters starting in October 2000. A wastewater reservoir collapsed above an abandoned mine and sent 230 million gallons of black sludge coursing through a tributary of the Big Sandy River. Fish and plants were killed over 36 miles downstream of the reservoir, and the water supply of several towns was shut down for weeks. ATM ultimately paid $40 million in cleanup costs. Management maintained that the spill was an "act of God," but the Kentucky's Mine Safety and Health Administration and its Office of Surface Mining concluded that the barrier between the mine and river was too thin. Several months later, a pump in another ATM mine developed a leak, and before it could be shut down the leak sent 30,000 gallons of sludge into a nearby stream. ATM failed to report the incident to authorities. The authorities learned of it when citizens called to complain that Robinson Creek had turned black.

Other incidents of the company committing illegal discharges of toxins followed. Over its first two years as Massey Energy Company, the company was cited 501 times by West Virginia officials for violating regulations. Regulators, citing a pattern of violations, slapped Massey with "show cause" orders and threatened to revoke their permits in some cases. A revoked permit is, in effect, a death sentence to a mining company because it makes it difficult for other permits to be issued or the old one to be renewed. The company argued that such an action would hurt the state as well as the company.

At the same time, demand for electricity rose and the spot price for central Appalachian coal jumped from $24 per ton to $48 per ton. Mining companies scrambled to source more coal. They also hired more workers and pushed up wages to attract them. Blankenship, however, refused to raise workers' pay, and as a result the company's miners quit in droves. By the end of 2001 half of his 5,000 employees were new hires. This coincided with Blankenship setting forward a goal to increase coal production for the coming year from 44 million tons to 56 million tons. The company would have to squeeze more output out of less experienced employees. However, productivity fell and so did operating margins.

Massey Energy endured more bad news in 2002 and 2003. In a jury trial, the company was found guilty

of defrauding the Harman Mining Company, which had to close operations due to the losses incurred. Massey Energy was hit with a $50 million verdict, which it appealed. The appeal took four years to reach the West Virginia Supreme Court's docket. In the interim, Blankenship spent $3 million on a campaign to unseat one of the members of the state Supreme Court, Justice Larry Starcher, who evidently had said negative things about Massey Energy to the press. Also, the judgment rose to $75 million as legal costs and interest mounted. Blankenship's campaign to unseat Justice Starcher failed, but Massey Energy still won its appeal, and the Harman Mining verdict was overturned with a vote of three to two. Then, in January 2008, the plaintiff filed papers with the state Supreme Court questioning the impartiality of Justice Elliott Maynard, who vacationed with Blankenship in 2006. The papers included 34 photographs of Maynard and Blankenship vacationing in Monte Carlo at the time the case was before the court. Maynard had been asked before to recuse himself because of a $3 million campaign contribution from Blankenship, but he refused.

Based on this new evidence the court was forced to reconsider the case. Maynard reluctantly agreed to recuse himself from the reconsideration. Justice Brent Benjamin had also received a large campaign contribution from Blankenship but refused to recuse himself. Four months after the initial reversal the state supreme court remained steadfast to its original decision. Justice Benjamin was the deciding vote, and the case was decided three to two in Massey Energy's favor.

At the same time that Massey Energy was fighting the Harman Mining verdict the company was hit with a much larger verdict by a circuit court jury over a contract dispute with the Wheeling-Pittsburgh Steel Company. Wheeling-Pitt claimed that instead of delivering 104,000 tons of coal as agreed Massey Energy diverted the coal to customers who were willing to pay a higher price. The verdict demanded that Massey Energy pay Wheeling-Pittsburg $239 million. Massey Energy appealed this case, and it was to come before the state supreme court. Again, Justice Maynard's relationship with Blankenship became the focus of the plaintiff, and he was forced to recuse himself. The Harman Mining and Wheeling-Pitt cases launched a statewide discussion of corruption in the state supreme court and initiated a proposal for a new recusal board to investigate issues of bias among justices. In the end, the state supreme court refused to review the Wheeling-Pitt verdict, as did the U.S. Supreme Court when Blankenship demanded that it review it. In December 2008 Massey Energy was forced to pay Wheeling-Pitt a total of $267 million, including the original award plus charges and interest.

Massey Energy faced other legal difficulties during the first decade of the 21st century. A group of disgruntled shareholders sued Massey Energy, Blankenship, and 10 other current or former officers. They claimed the defendants sold shares shortly before the price of the stock dropped from $22 to $12 per share. Early in 2003 Massey lost $10 million in an arbitrated case with Duke Energy over a coal supply contract. A few days later the company announced that the Securities and Exchange Commission was reviewing its corporate financial filings. In April 2003 the company agreed to make changes to its 2001 and 2002 filings, but according to Blankenship the impact on shareholders was minor. Instead of a loss of $30 million in fiscal 2002, it now recorded a loss of $32.6 million. Nevertheless, the news did little to improve the public image of Massey Energy.

The year 2005 brought a spike in demand for coal, specifically metallurgical coal. Much of the increase was due to the surge of economic growth in China, India, and other parts of Asia. Coal companies were sent scrambling for new workers but found that skilled workers were in short supply. Massey Energy was no exception and aggressively pursued new workers. The industry also faced increased production costs mainly due to soaring energy prices and rising material costs. While Massey Energy's revenues increased almost 25 percent in 2005, the company showed a net income loss of $101.6 million. The company returned to profitability in 2006, but over the next four years the company's revenues and profitability fluctuated. While revenues rose 25 percent from 2007 to 2008, net income fell 49 percent. Revenues fell 10 percent from 2008 to 2009, and net income rose 118.4 percent. Much of the company's instability had more to do with the ramifications of managerial malfeasance rather than any factors in the marketplace since the coal industry was booming in the latter half of the decade.

In May 2007 the U.S. Environmental Protection Agency (EPA) filed a lawsuit against Massey Energy, claiming that the company owed an estimated $2.4 billion in fines for violations of the Clean Water Act. The suit claimed that the company poured pollutants into the West Virginia and Kentucky waterways 4,633 times within the previous six years. In April 2008 the company settled with the EPA and paid a fine of $20 million, setting the record for the largest fine ever in a water-pollution case. The company also agreed to invest millions of dollars in pollution control improvements at its facilities in West Virginia and Kentucky.

TRAGEDY BRINGS AN END TO MASSEY ENERGY

On April 5, 2010, there was an explosion that collapsed the Upper Big Branch mine, which was owned and managed by Performance Coal Company, a subsidiary of Massey. The whole country watched and prayed as rescuers attempted to dig out survivors, but there were none. The explosion resulted in the deaths of 29 miners. It was the worst U.S. mining disaster since 1970, when 38 coal miners were killed at Finley Coal Company's No. 15 and 16 mines in Hyden, Kentucky. Later, Massey Energy's poor safety record for the Upper Big Branch mine emerged. The mine had been cited for 204 violations that were deemed serious. The government had also failed in its duty to institute a more stringent oversight of the mine after it showed a pattern of violations. Blankenship made statements to the press during the rescue attempt, but the once bold leader seemed chastened by the circumstances.

An investigation into the Upper Big Branch tragedy ensued, and investigators suspected that the explosion was caused by the buildup of methane gas and coal dust. In late 2010 federal regulators issued a preliminary report saying the cause of the explosion was poor mining practices and improper equipment maintenance. It said that the buildup of coal dust in the mine was ignited by a small flare-up of methane gas. Massey Energy denied this charge and claimed that the explosion was the result of a seep of natural gas from the mine floor. Neither the federal regulators nor Massey Energy could determine the source of the spark that caused the flare-up.

In December 2010 the embattled Blankenship resigned as CEO and chairman. After 30 years with the company he had become a liability, especially with regard to relations between the company and federal regulators. Baxter F. Phillips, Jr., took over the CEO position, and retired admiral Bobby Inman took over as a nonexecutive chairman. While still in the midst of a public relations nightmare, several lawsuits filed by families of the dead miners, a federal investigation, and a changeover of management, Massey Energy started pursuing takeover suitors and set up an auction. Alpha Natural Resources' bid won over that of Arch Coal. In January 2011 Massey agreed to sell itself to Alpha Natural Resources for $7.1 billion in cash and stock. The deal would create a large coal mining interest with more than 110 mines and about five billion tons of combined reserves throughout the Appalachian region, the Midwest, and Wyoming. The deal would not close until the middle of 2011. In the meantime, the company still faced a battle with regulators over the Upper Big Branch disaster and other legal complications due its past behavior.

Ed Dinger
Updated, Aaron Hauser

PRINCIPAL SUBSIDIARIES

A.T. Massey Coal Company, Inc.; Massey Coal Sales Company, Inc.; Massey Coal Services, Inc.; Omar Mining Company; Rawl Sales & Processing, Co.; Road Fork Development Company, Inc.; Sidney Coal Company, Inc.; Spartan Mining Company.

PRINCIPAL COMPETITORS

Alliance Resource Partners, L.P.; Arch Coal, Inc.; CONSOL Energy Inc.; International Coal Group, Inc.; NACCO Industries, Inc.; Peabody Energy Corporation.

FURTHER READING

Boyer, Mike. "Massey Coal Has Had Tumultuous Past." *Cincinnati Enquirer,* October 22, 2000.

Condon, Bernard. "Not King Coal." *Forbes,* May 26, 2003, 80–82.

De La Merced, Michael J. "Massey Energy Says It Will Be Sold." *New York Times,* January 30, 2011, 20. Accessed March 7, 2011. http://query.nytimes.com/gst/fullpage.html?res=9E03E0D91331F933A05752C0A9679D8B63&scp=1&sq=Massey%20Energy%20Says%20It%20Will%20Be%20Sold&st=cse.

Krauss, Clifford. "Massey's Energy Chief is Quitting, Renewing Talk of a Takeover." *New York Times,* December 4, 2010, 7.

Lubove, Seth. "Massey Coal Strike Is Testing UMW Strategy." *Wall Street Journal,* June 3, 1985, 1.

Miles, Gregory, and Cynthia Green. "The Coalfield Heavyweight Who's Going the Distance." *Business Week,* October 21, 1985, 123.

Trippett, Frank. "Violence in the Coalfields." *Time,* August 26, 1985, 17.

Urbina, Ian. "U.S. Fines Mine Owner $20 Million for Pollution." *New York Times,* January 18, 2008, 14. Accessed March 7, 2011. http://www.nytimes.com/2008/01/18/us/18mine.html?_r=1&scp=1&sq=U.S.%20Fines%20Mine%20Owner%20%2420%20Million%20For%20Pollution&st=cse.

Urbina, Ian, and John Leland. "A Mine Boss Inspires Fear, But Pride, Too." *New York Times,* April 8, 2010, 1. Accessed March 7, 2011. http://www.nytimes.com/2010/04/08/us/08blankenship.html?scp=1&sq=A+Mine+Boss+Inspires+Fear%2C+But+Pride%2C+Too.&st=nyt.

McIlhenny Company

Highway 329
Avery Island, Louisiana 70130
U.S.A.
Telephone: (337) 365-8173
Web site: http://www.tabasco.com

Private Company
Founded: 1868
Employees: 200 (est., 2011)
NAICS: 31194 Seasoning and Dressing Manufacturing

■ ■ ■

McIlhenny Company is a family-owned and operated manufacturer of Tabasco brand pepper sauce. Tabasco, perhaps the most famous of 150 pepper sauces available on the market, actually created the pepper sauce industry. The company remains a leader in domestic pepper sauce commanding an estimated 20 to 25 percent of the U.S. market in 2010 and is a longstanding provider of pepper sauce across the globe. The plant produces up to 600,000 bottles of Tabasco sauce a day. McIlhenny has added five other flavors to its line of Tabasco sauces, but its sales pale in comparison to the company's original red sauce. International sales make up 40 percent of the company's overall sales.

AVERY ISLAND AND A TREASURE TROVE OF SALT

The history of the McIlhenny Company begins with Avery Island, located 140 miles west of New Orleans and 150 feet above sea level. The Tabasco sauce depends on the island's salt and peppers. The 2,300-acre island is located in the bayou country of Louisiana and is the uppermost portion of a salt mountain. It is the largest of five such salt domes and features rich soil, Cyprus-lined waterways, exotic flora, and ancient oaks. The earliest artifacts found on the island, stone weapons for hunting, date back 12,000 years. Evidence of mastodons and mammoths, saber-toothed cats, and tiny three-toed horses has also been found there. Other evidence, including basket fragments, stone implements, and Indian pottery indicate that a salt brining industry began on the island in 1300 A.D.

French explorers discovered the island sometime during the 18th century, and white settlers arrived by the century's end, around the same time that Indians disappeared from the island. The salt brine springs, however, remained active, and were a source of salt for Andrew Jackson's forces as they fought the Battle of New Orleans in the War of 1812.

In 1818 Sara Craig Marsh's father purchased land on the island, then known as Ile Petite Anse. Sara Craig Marsh later married Daniel Dudley Avery, and their descendants came to control the entire island. During the mid-1800s, Edmund McIlhenny, an East Coast bank agent, visited New Orleans, which had become one of the nation's fastest-growing cities. Edmund was a fifth-generation U.S. citizen of Scottish and Irish descent. He was also an accomplished marksman, yachtsman, and prize-winning horse breeder who loved good food. A story goes that he ate at the famous Antoine's restaurant and commented, "I enjoyed this so much. I feel like starting all over again," and he did. He then ate another entire full-course dinner.

In 1859, at the age of 43, Edmund married Mary Eliza Avery, daughter of Sarah Craig Marsh and Daniel Dudley Avery. Daniel Avery, a lawyer and judge in Baton Rouge, Louisiana, also operated a sugar plantation on Ile Petite Anse. In 1862 they discovered a large rock salt deposit on the island, and the Averys moved from New Orleans to the island to oversee the quarrying of the salt deposit. The Averys supplied salt to the Confederate states, which were suffering under a blockade. The family grew wealthy cultivating the island's rock salt and marketing the salt as a meat preservative.

EDMUND MCILHENNY AND HIS GARDENING EXPERIMENTS

Edmund enjoyed gardening as a hobby at the family's plantation on the island. Legend has it that in 1848 a friend gave him some extra-spicy pepper seeds from Mexico's Tabasco region. The friend brought them back with him after fighting in the Mexican-American war. Another version says that a confederate soldier gave him the peppers, and he extracted the seeds from them to grow more. While promoting the construction of a Tabasco museum in New Orleans in 2004, the future curator of the museum (since abandoned as a project) stated that this was a myth and was unverifiable, and that nobody knew the true source of Edmund's original pepper seeds. The peppers Edmund grew in his garden were later identified as *capsicum frutescens*. Although about 20 wild species were known in the New World, mostly in South America, only about five species had been cultivated domestically. Despite claims that Edmund introduced Tabasco peppers and sauce to North America there is evidence that another man, plantation owner Maunsel White, produced a sauce made from Tabasco peppers as early as 1849, much earlier than Edmund, and used them in recipes for his lavish dinner parties. White bottled the sauce and began marketing it in 1853 as "Maunsel White's Concentrated Essence of Tabasco Pepper," which later became known by the shorter name of "Maunsel White's." Maunsel died in 1863, but his family continued to market and sell "Maunsel White's" sauce until the 1870s. There is no evidence that White and Edmund contacted each other or shared pepper sauce recipes, but it seems evident that Edmund was at least inspired by White's pepper sauce and his success.

Edmund planted his seeds and began experimenting with recipes for a pepper sauce to season local southern Louisiana dishes, including those influenced by Spanish, French, American Indian, and African traditions. In 1863 his efforts were interrupted by the Civil War. Union troops invaded the island and captured the salt quarries. The McIlhennys and Averys fled to Texas. When they were finally able to return they found a very different climate in Louisiana. The Averys and McIlhennys relocated to Ile Petite Anse permanently and began to rebuild their home there. The island, the salt quarry, and the sugar cane fields were in ruins. The pepper plants, however, had thrived. Edmund discovered that the humidity on the island helped the plants grow heartily. Motivated by the blandness of Reconstructionist food, he resumed his pepper sauce experiments until he perfected a recipe that everyone enjoyed, the same recipe used in today's McIlhenny Tabasco sauce.

Edmund's recipe was elegantly simple. He mashed the peppers on the same day he harvested them. Then he mixed a half coffee cup of Ile Petite Anse salt for each gallon of crushed peppers and aged the mixture for 30 days in wooden barrels. After aging he added French wine vinegar and aged the mixture for another 30 days while frequently stirring by hand to blend the flavors. Finally, he strained the naturally bright red sauce into perfume bottles topped with shakers and sealed with green wax. Family and friends suggested selling the sauce for additional income, so Edmund started marketing his new creation. Edmund considered naming his pepper sauce "PetiteAnse Sauce," but his family disliked this choice, so he named it Tabasco.

TABASCO SAUCE GETS OFF TO A SLOW START

In 1869 Edmund ordered cologne bottles from a nearby glass factory and bottled his Tabasco sauce in them. Initially, he sold them to Union soldiers still billeted in the South. Later, he established a relationship with a

KEY DATES

1869: Edmund McIlhenny formulates his recipe and begins selling his Tabasco sauce to Union soldiers.

1870: Edmund McIlhenny wins a U.S. Letters Patent for his Tabasco sauce.

1874: Company sells Tabasco in Europe for the first time.

1890: Founder Edmund McIlhenny dies. John Avery McIlhenny takes over business.

1907: McIlhenny Company incorporates; company establishes trademark on the word "Tabasco"; Edmund Avery "MisterNed" McIlhenny becomes president.

1942: McIlhenny Company discovers oil on Avery Island.

1949: Walter Stauffer McIlhenny becomes president.

1985: Edward McIlhenny Simmons becomes president.

1991: McIlhenny Company acquires Trappey's Fine Foods.

1998: Paul McIlhenny becomes president.

2010: Elizabeth II, queen of the United Kingdom, names Tabasco as "HerMajesty's Hot Sauce" and bestows upon the McIlhenny Company her Royal Warrant.

large national distributor and sold them around the country. In 1870 Edmund received a U.S. Letters Patent for his Tabasco brand pepper sauce. While there was some initial success it took almost a decade for Tabasco to gain popularity. Two elements contributed substantially to the success of Tabasco sauce, the consistency of the formulation and Edmund's business acumen. Often hot sauces varied in taste, even between small drops of the sauce, but Edmund's formulation of Tabasco remained the same with each drop. This made it popular with both consumers and professional chefs, who depended on consistency in their recipe ingredients.

Edmund eventually committed all his time to manufacturing and selling Tabasco sauce, and he proved to be a savvy distributor and seller of his product, quickly establishing a whole new market. It was not long before Edmund's efforts penetrated the European market. He exported Tabasco sauce to London for the first time around 1874 and began sending large quantities there a few years later.

In 1890 Edmund died. His son, John Avery McIlhenny, assumed control of the company. John set forward a new direction for Tabasco sauce. He visited commercial customers throughout the United States to familiarize himself with them and to court new customers. He instituted new marketing efforts including bill posters, large wooden signs in fields near cities, drummers canvassing house-to-house in selected cities, exhibits at food expositions, circulars and folders, and free trial-size samples. He even commissioned an opera company to perform the "Burlesque Opera of Tabasco," and in 1893 Harvard's Hasty Pudding Club asked permission to perform the opera as one of its reviews. John bought the rights to the review and staged it in New York. Samples of Tabasco were given away during the show's matinee performances. Other marketing efforts included promotions such as a grocery contest with a $3,000 prize and offers for famous painting reproductions in exchange for a Tabasco coupon and a 10 cents handling charge. Under John's leadership the family's Tabasco business grew tenfold.

THE MCILHENNY COMPANY ESTABLISHES A TRADEMARK

In 1898 John joined the First Volunteer Calvary of the U.S. Army, serving as a Rough Rider with Theodore Roosevelt, and fought at the Battle of Juan Hill. John traveled extensively after the Spanish-American War ended. After returning, he left home again in 1906 to work for then President Roosevelt at the U.S. Civil Service Commission. He would later become the U.S. minister plenipotentiary to Haiti. It was in 1906 that the family secured its trademark for the word Tabasco, which was controversial then and remains so because it is one of the few times the government has allowed a trademark for a generic ingredient that is also the name of a geographic region. Some believe John's friendship with President Roosevelt helped secure the patent, but the company's right to the word has stood the test of time, surviving several challenges in court. Also, sometime in the late 1800s, the family renamed Ile Petite Anse as Avery Island.

In 1907 the family incorporated the McIlhenny Company (McIlhenny) and named Edmund Avery "MisterNed" McIlhenny ("E.A."), John's younger brother, as president of the newly formed company. Another brother, Rufus Avery McIlhenny, became the production supervisor. His responsibilities included engineering and purchasing as well.

E.A. grew McIlhenny's reach domestically and internationally. He also ardently and successfully defended the company's brand against several cases of trademark infringement by taking the offenders to court. Several regional companies attempted to sell imitations of the Tabasco brand. In addition to developing the McIlhenny Company, E.A. made an effort to preserve the natural environment of Avery Island. Before becoming president of the company he was a self-trained biologist and traveled the world on scientific expeditions. When he returned to Avery Island to join the company he discovered that the snowy egret, a native bird to Louisiana, was close to extinction from plume hunters pillaging the species for feathers to be used in ladies' hats. E.A. captured eight snowy egrets and established a colony for them where they could multiply and live safely from any threats. Since then, thousands of egrets and other migratory birds have found a home in the "BirdCity" rookery on Avery Island.

E.A. also became a nutria breeder. Nutria are brown furry rodents with webbed feet and long, hairless tails from South America. He released many of them into the wild when a hurricane threatened the island. The nutria population in Louisiana has grown exponentially over the years since that time, and they have been blamed for eating the Louisiana coastal wetlands and causing harmful erosion. As a result, McIlhenny has borne the brunt of the opprobrium concerning this environmental problem. However, historians have proved that there were other nutria farmers active long before E.A. started and that they were equally, if not more, responsible for the nutria problem. E.A. also made an effort to protect the plant life on the island. When the family discovered oil on the island in 1942, E.A. insisted that work crews bury pipelines or paint them green to blend in with the surrounding park, which they named "JungleGardens."

POPULARITY ABROAD AND WITH THE MILITARY

Tabasco sauce had become highly popular in England. When the product's availability in Great Britain became threatened by the "Buy British" campaign of the isolationist British government in 1932, a crisis of national proportions erupted. Unhappy without their pepper sauce (a staple in the House of Commons dining room) members of Parliament protested and, with support of the press, they changed the "Buy British" motto to "Buy Tabasco." Also, the Queen Mother asked her staff to search London for Tabasco sauce. Her deputy controller wrote in his memoir that "The Queen (Mother), when she was told that there was no more Tabasco sauce, took the news philosophically."

John McIlhenny's son, Walter Stauffer McIlhenny, succeeded E.A. as president of McIlhenny. Walter McIlhenny joined the company around 1940, but World War II interrupted his business training. Nicknamed "Tabasco Mac" by his fellow Marine Corps reservists, Walter McIlhenny served his country with distinction. Stationed at Guadalcanal, he received the Navy Cross and a Silver Star before earning the rank of Brigadier General. He returned to the McIlhenny Company in 1946 and became president in 1949. He built a brick Tabasco sauce manufacturing plant and brought new management techniques to the company, but the marketing efforts of the company did not venture far afield of those established by his father. They still relied heavily on print ads in trade and consumer periodicals to market Tabasco sauce. Walter also defended the company against several offers to purchase the company and the pressure to tinker with the Tabasco recipe. Under Walter's leadership the production process for Tabasco remained virtually unchanged from that of his predecessors. The plantation had grown to 75 acres of peppers, and the peppers were still hand-picked by workers. Walter McIlhenny took personal responsibility for weighing the daily harvest and inspecting pepper mash. He also selected the pepper seeds for the next crop. The seeds were treated, dried, and stored on the island and in a bank vault until the next year's planting.

Until the 1960s all plants used for Tabasco sauce were grown on Avery Island. In the 1960s McIlhenny became increasingly concerned about maintaining a constant supply of peppers. The company faced a shortage of harvesters, high labor costs, crop diseases and harsh weather conditions (i.e., hurricanes). The company turned to Central and South American countries. All pepper plants were planted in greenhouses on the island, but increasingly the company grew the pepper plants to maturity in countries like Mexico, Colombia, Honduras, and Venezuela. Eventually 90 percent of the company's peppers were harvested abroad.

The military was never far from Walter McIlhenny's heart. During the Vietnam War, he created a C-ration cookbook for use by members of the U.S. Armed Forces. He knew that the U.S. Armed Forces used Tabasco sauce liberally on their C-rations. He titled the book the "Charley Ration Cookbook or, No Food Is Too Good for the Man up Front." Copies were sent to soldiers with bottles of Tabasco sauce. He even designed a Tabasco bottle holster that attached to a cartridge belt. This tradition continued, and during the Gulf War in 1991 every third MRE (Meals Ready to Eat) contained a small package of Tabasco sauce and a recipe booklet. Eventually every MRE included Tabasco sauce. In the 21st century, U.S. soldiers carried Tabasco sauce as part of their MRE in the Iraq and Afghanistan wars.

FACING CHALLENGES AND DIVERSIFYING

Walter McIlhenny remained president of the company until the day he died in 1985. He was succeeded by his nephew Edward McIlhenny Simmons. Together they instituted a new policy to safeguard against crop loss, storing 20 pounds of the pepper seeds in a bank vault in New Iberia, Louisiana, and 50 pounds at the company's headquarters on the island instead of keeping the entire batch on the island. Larger changes came under Simmons. The company ventured beyond John McIlhenny's marketing formula to include print and television advertising, and for the first time, the company expanded its product line. For years, the company had been facing strong competition from salsa, Buffalo wings, and other spicy foods, so McIlhenny added a chili powder, a seasoned salt, and popcorn seasonings to its product line. The company also offered a Bloody Mary mix, a seven-spice chili recipe, and a picante sauce.

In addition, McIlhenny made its first corporate acquisition in 1991. McIlhenny purchased Trappey's Fine Foods from its Connecticut-based parent company JEM Brands, Inc. Trappey's Fine Foods manufactured its Red Devil pepper sauce and other seasoning-related products in nearby New Iberia. McIlhenny marketed these acquired products under the name McIlhenny Farms. This new company gave McIlhenny the freedom to offer a wider variety of products including pepper jelly, ketchup, and molasses.

During the 1990s the company sold millions of bottles of Tabasco throughout the world with labels in over 15 languages. McIlhenny also introduced five new varieties under the Tabasco brand including a Chipotle Pepper Sauce, a Green Jalapeño Sauce, Habanero Sauce, Garlic Pepper Sauce, and SWEET & Spicy Pepper Sauce. By 1996 more than 50 million bottles of Tabasco sauce were sold in at least 105 countries. Canada alone used 250,000 bottles in one year. Japan became the largest consumer of Tabasco abroad, importing it to use for sushi, spaghetti, and pizza. The Avery Island factory operated four production lines, producing a maximum of 450,000 two-ounce bottles of Tabasco a day. In addition, the company launched its first Web site and marketed it under the name "Pepperfest."

A MORE COMPLICATED COMPANY CELEBRATES 140 YEARS

In 1998 Edward Simmons was elevated to chairman of the board and Paul McIlhenny became president of the company. Paul McIlhenny inherited a much more complex company than many of his ancestors, including having to answer to over 200 shareholders, all of them McIlhenny family heirs, and a crowded marketplace with over 150 competing pepper sauces. Also, the company was still involved in salt mining, oil and gas production, and running the island's nature preserve that attracted thousands of eco-tourists every year.

In 2001, in an effort to broaden the product's name recognition, the company inked its first cobranding deal with Hormel Foods Corporation. Hormel put the Tabasco logo on Hormel products, cobranding items like chili, pepperoni, Little Sizzlers sausage, and Spam, all under the "Hot&Spicy" name. In 2004 the company announced plans to build a Tabasco museum in New Orleans in order to promote the brand as a historical landmark and to set the record straight on some aspects of the company's colorful history, but Hurricane Katrina hit New Orleans in August 2005 and Hurricane Rita hit the Gulf coast a month later. Both hurricanes caused significant damage to the museum construction and flooding on Avery Island. Thanks to the high elevation of the salt dome the flooding caused very little damage, and production was able to resume after only two weeks downtime. Also, employees' homes on the island were spared any serious damage.

During the crisis, McIlhenny gave refuge to employees escaping from Hurricane Katrina and Hurricane Rita. Many of them roomed with McIlhenny employees residing on Avery Island until they could work out their next move. The following year, the company cancelled the Tabasco museum in favor of a levee project to protect the island from future hurricane threats.

The McIlhenny Company celebrated its 140th anniversary in 2008. As of 2009 McIlhenny sold Tabasco sauce and its other products in over 165 countries with bottle labels in 22 different languages. Japan has become its largest importer, with Canada, Mexico, Germany, and the United Kingdom filling out the top five. In the early 2010s the company was engaged in an expansion into Brazil, China, and Eastern Europe. In April 2010 Elizabeth II, queen of the United Kingdom, named Tabasco as "HerMajesty's Hot Sauce," bestowing upon the McIlhenny Company her Royal Warrant. The Royal Warrant enabled the company to advertise that it supplied the royal family.

McIlhenny keeps its financials private, but journalists estimated the company was taking in about $250 million in annual revenue. McIlhenny remained under family control despite offers of around $1 billion from corporate suitors. While McIlhenny and its workhorse Tabasco sauce enjoyed classic status across the world, the prospect for significant growth was uncertain. The company faced increasing competition from regional and national brands. As president, Paul McIlhenny faced pressure from younger shareholders who demanded that the company break away from its traditional mindset and move aggressively into the future.

Charity Anne Dorgan
Updated, Aaron Hauser

PRINCIPAL DIVISIONS

McIlhenny Farms.

PRINCIPAL COMPETITORS

B&G Foods, Inc.; Bruce Foods Corporation; H. J. Heinz Company.

FURTHER READING

Burdeau, Cain. "Tabasco Museum Aimed at Setting the Record Straight."*Associated Press,* March 17, 2004.

Burton, David. "Tabasco Chief Visits Local Market."*Retail World,* September 28, 2009, 14.

King, Ronette. "'TabascoUniversity' Means Business; Black Collegians Get Taste of Retail World."*Times-Picayune,* July 26, 2009, 1.

Mandell, Pat. "Louisiana Hot."*Americana,* February 1991, 26–32.

Montgomery, Mike. "StillSizzlin'Mcilhenny Basks in the Glow of 125 Years of Tobasco."*Times-Picayune,* July 4, 1993, F1.

Naj, Amal. *Peppers: A Story of Hot Pursuits.* New York: Alfred A. Knopf, 1992.

Pepitone, Sara. "142 Years Old and Still Hot." *CNN Money. com,* March 1, 2010. Accessed March 8, 2011. http:// money.cnn.com/2010/03/01/smallbusiness/tabasco/index. htm.

Rice, William. "Tabasco Sauce Stands Up to a Hurricane. "*Detroit Free Press,* November 18, 1992.

Robichaux, Mark. "Ingredients of a Family Fortune; The Hot Story of Tabasco Sauce."*Wall Street Journal,* October 10, 2007.

———. "Tabasco Sauce Maker Remains Hot after 125 years. "*Wall Street Journal,* May 11, 1990, B2.

"Tabasco Honored as Her Majesty's Hot Sauce."*PR Newswire,* April 13, 2009.

Thomas, Greg. "Tabasco Maker Kills Museum; New Factory Levee Is Deemed a Priority."*Times-Picayune,* December 14, 2006, 12.

Tuohy, William. "Avery Island: Where Egrets Roam and Tabasco Is King."*International Herald Tribune,* January 23, 1998, 9.

Medidata Solutions, Inc.

79 Fifth Avenue
Eighth Floor
New York City, New York 10003
U.S.A.
Telephone: (212) 918-1800
Toll Free: (877) 511-4200
Fax: (212) 918-1818
Web site: http://www.mdsol.com

Public Company
Founded: 1999
Employees: 700+ (est., 2011)
Total Revenues: $166.4 million (2010)
Stock Exchanges: NASDAQ
Ticker Symbol: MDSO
NAICS: 511210 Software Publishers

■ ■ ■

Medidata Solutions, Inc., is a global provider of software as a service (SaaS) solutions that are used to collect and manage data throughout the entire clinical trial process. Medidata's customer base consists of biotechnical, pharmaceutical, and medical device companies, as well as academic institutions, contract research organizations, and other entities that conduct clinical trials for medical products. These customers, located in more than 80 countries, purchase multiyear subscriptions to Medidata's Web-based systems. Medidata's technology allows users to design protocols; capture, manage, and report data from clinical trials; and analyze the results of that data.

The company's products include Medidata Designer for protocol development, and iMedidata for user and learning management. Medidata Grants Manager and Medidata CRO Contractor are used for trial planning and management, while Medidata Balance allows for randomization and clinical supply management. Data capture, management, and reporting is carried out through Medidata Rave, the company's original product. Monitoring of data is handled through Medidata Rave Monitor and Medidata Rave Targeted SDV, and Medidata Rave Safety Gateway offers tools for serious adverse events.

Most of Medidata's offices are in the Unites States, but the company also has offices in Japan and the United Kingdom.

CLINICAL TRIAL DATA COLLECTION

Sponsored primarily by the pharmaceutical industry, which is made up of branded pharmaceutical companies, biotechnical organizations, and generic drug manufacturers, clinical trials are used to test the efficacy and safety of new drugs and therapies on human volunteers. Clinical trial studies represent a multimillion-dollar business. Besides pharmaceutical companies, there are government agencies, research foundations, medical device manufacturers, academic institutions, and individual clinicians that fund clinical trials. Since the 1940s, U.S. clinical trials have been subject to stringent regulations by federal government agencies, such as the Food and Drug Administration, as well as foreign governments and regulatory authorities if

```
┌─────────────────────────────────────────┐
│                                          │
│     COMPANY PERSPECTIVES                 │
│                   ▪                      │
│   ─────────────────────────────────      │
│                                          │
│   Medidata's mission is to provide       │
│   innovative clinical development        │
│   solutions that safely and              │
│   efficiently improve quality of life.   │
│                                          │
└─────────────────────────────────────────┘
```

pharmaceutical products manufactured in the United States are marketed abroad. Increased clinical trial regulation has necessitated more precise documentation measures.

An integral part of clinical trial studies is the collection of data. Although electronic data capture (EDC) and clinical data management (CDM) tools had been available since the 1980s, the clinical trial industry was slow to convert from paper data collection methods. By replacing the paper-based process of collecting information with a computerized system, EDC experts reasoned, clinical trial sponsors could increase efficiency, reduce transcription errors, improve data quality, and better ensure patient safety.

Recognizing the market potential of a comprehensive electronic data capture and clinical data management system, business executive Tarek Sherif, software developer Glen de Vries, and physician Ed Ikeguchi founded Medidata Solutions as a New York corporation in 1999. A primary goal of the company, which began with eight employees, was to develop a user-friendly product that clinicians could adapt to all kinds of clinical trials in all stages. The software needed to be based on clinicians' individual study needs and professional skills, not on their computer knowledge.

INITIAL GROWTH: 2000–05

Created by de Vries, Medidata's original product was Medidata Rave, and it would remain the company's leading seller, as many subsequent software solutions were integrated with its operating framework. Medidata Rave, the clinical trial industry's first single-system EDC/CDM platform, allowed for the capture, management, and reporting of clinical trial data in all types and phases of clinical studies. One of the product's most valuable benefits was that it allowed clinicians to identify and correct erroneous data early in the clinical trial process.

Medidata's early growth was explosive. From 2000 to 2003, the company achieved a sustained revenue increase of 2,510 percent, earning it the number 10 spot on the 2003 Deloitte Technology Fast 500, a ranking of the 500 fastest-growing technology companies in North America. After receiving $1 million in investment funding from Milestone Venture Partners, Medidata made moves to enlarge its sales and technical support staff. After announcing a marketing alliance with Praxis Life Sciences, Medidata joined Praxis Life Sciences in 2003 to present a series of educational seminars addressing the benefits of EDC technology. Also that year, de Vries confirmed that Medidata's Rave platform and Medidata Vision software were compatible with Apple's recently-released Safari 1.0 Web browser, demonstrating to the biopharmaceutical field that Medidata was committed to meeting the needs of all end users.

In 2004 Medidata released Rave 5.0, as well as established its European headquarters in the United Kingdom. The company also received $20 million in financing led by Insight Venture partners.

Medidata continued to set EDC industry standards throughout 2005. In April the company announced AS-P*ire* to Win, a partner program that enabled contract research organizations (CROs) and other specialty service providers to streamline Medidata Rave technology with their own data management expertise. In July the company announced its 18th quarter of consecutive growth, which reflected a 149 percent increase in year-over-year revenue. (However, while the revenue growth was continuous, the company remained unprofitable until 2009.)

PRODUCT EXPANSION: 2006

In 2006 Medidata took steps to address the expanding global clinical trial market. Since more pharmaceutical companies around the world were taking advantage of decreasing clinical study costs, Medidata saw an opportunity to streamline data collection and management in foreign markets. The Japanese pharmaceutical industry was the second largest in the world behind the United States and held almost 70 percent of the Asia-Pacific market. To strengthen its presence in Japan, Medidata added two new executives to head its Tokyo office. That same year, Medidata also focused on meeting the EDC needs of China's pharmaceutical industry, which had maintained significant annual growth for 20 years.

Considering the impact of foreign markets, Medidata introduced an update of Medidata Rave in March 2006. Rave 5.5 was the first EDC production that gave sponsors the capability of running all of their clinical trial operations on one global platform. While other industry products required different versions of software to be installed for different languages, Rave 5.5 offered the Local Language Translation Workbench, a suite of

1999: Medidata is cofounded by Tarek Sherif, Glen de Vries, and Ed Ikeguchi.

2003: Medidata is number 10 on the 2003 Deloitte Technology Fast 500.

2004: Company opens European headquarters in the United Kingdom.

2005: Medidata introduces its ASP*ire* to Win program, allowing contract research organizations (CROs) to integrate Medidata Rave technology with their own data management technologies.

2009: Company issues IPO at $14.00 per share.

2011: Jim Attardi, vice president of information technology, is named one of *Computerworld*'s 2011 Premier 100 IT Leaders.

Web-based tools that allowed clinicians to access a centrally managed electronic storehouse of clinical data that would be automatically translated into the appropriate language. Additionally, Rave 5.5 included Double Data Entry, through which paper and EDC hybrid studies could be executed from a common platform. Another feature of the enhanced Rave was Central Lab Data, a function that could automatically compare such information as sex and age against user-defined lab range values. If data was flagged as out of range, users were immediately notified.

In June 2006 Medidata partnered with Cytel Inc., a provider of clinical trial consulting services and statistical software, to randomize patients in all types of trials directly through an EDC system. At the time, most clinical trials used separate management tools for data capture and for patient randomization. By integrating Cytel's FlexRandomizer into Medidata Rave, the two companies created a product that uniformly checked eligibility criteria across all investigator sites and maintained all randomization dates within one secure system.

INDUSTRY LEADER: 2006–08

By the end of 2006, Medidata had been recognized by several esteemed organizations. Besides being ranked number 59 on the *Inc.* 500 list of America's fastest-growing entrepreneurial companies, Medidata sat at number 70 on Deloitte's Technology Fast 500 of North American businesses. The company was also honored by Frost & Sullivan as 2006 Healthcare IT Entrepreneurial

Company of the Year. Based on such accomplishments as turning a 181 percent increase in year-over-year revenue and expanding in the Asian and European markets, Medidata was named a finalist in the Best Overall Company category in the 2006 American Business Awards.

At the beginning of 2007, Medidata launched another update of Rave, Medidata Rave 5.6, based on feedback from customers who used existing versions of the platform. The new program offered several enhancements intended to help all members of a clinical study team throughout the entire trial process. Tools to improve productivity included Data Clarification Forms, Local Lab Enhancements, Report Localization, Architect Loader, Amendment Manager Enhancements, and a Global Library.

A continuous flow of new products helped keep Medidata a leader in its field. In May 2008 Medidata Designer was selected from a group of over 30 companies to receive *Bio-IT World* magazine's Best of Show award in the Clinical Trials and Research category. At the end of the year, Medidata boasted contracts with a number of large pharmaceutical companies all over the world, including AstraZeneca, Bristol-Myers Squibb, and Pharmaxis Ltd.

MARKET REACH: 2009

In January 2009 Medidata filed a registration statement with the Securities and Exchange Commission for an initial public offering of its common stock, in a bid to raise $86 million. In November the company filed a registration statement for a secondary offering of common stock, priced at $15 per share.

At the close of 2009, Medidata had signed multi-year, multistudy agreements with a total of 173 companies, a number that reflected a growing presence in the academic and research center market. In the fourth quarter, Medidata took on eight new subsidiaries, most of them located in China, Europe, and Japan. The company also gained its first ASP*ire* to Win partner in Korea. Net revenues for the year were $140.4 million, up 33 percent from 2008.

CONTINUED GROWTH: 2010 AND BEYOND

During 2010 Medidata launched several new products, including Rave 5.64. Among its features were improved Web-based application programming interfaces (APIs) for customers integrating Rave into their own corporate IT platforms. In the third quarter of 2010, Medidata released upgrades to iMedidata, its clinical trial portal platform, and Medidata Balance, a product for patient randomization and clinical supply management.

Although most of Medidata's revenues in 2010 were generated from sales to U.S. customers, the company saw a significant portion of its revenues come from foreign markets. At the end of the third quarter, approximately 24 percent of total revenues were generated from European customers, while 13 percent came from partners in Asia.

Medidata's net revenues for 2010 were $166.4 million, an increase of 19 percent from 2009. The company added 63 new customers during the year and at year end had a total of 219 customers, which represented a compound growth rate of 34 percent over the past three years.

At the onset of 2011, Medidata added a contracting module to its Grants Manager Web-based budgeting application, allowing customers to negotiate, report, and manage clinical trial budget tasks directly online. At the same time, Medidata was adding to its customer base, signing agreements with Chugai Pharmaceutical Co., Ltd., one of Japan's leading pharmaceutical companies, as well as U.S. drug development service company Phar-Point Research, Inc. In February Jim Attardi, vice president of information technology at Medidata, was named one of *Computerworld*'s 2011 Premier 100 IT Leaders for his work in supervising all of Medidata's IT operations around the world.

As a profitable company with a history of high growth, in the 2010s Medidata hoped to continue to extend its global reach and capitalize on the ever-expanding clinical trial industry, especially in Asian countries.

Alicia Elley

PRINCIPAL SUBSIDIARIES

Medidata FT, Inc.

PRINCIPAL DIVISIONS

Professional Services; Support.

PRINCIPAL COMPETITORS

BioClinica, Inc.; Datatrak International, Inc.; EMC Corporation; Merge Healthcare Incorporated; Omni-Comm Systems, Inc.; Perceptive Informatics, Inc.; Phase Forward Incorporated.

FURTHER READING

Bellucci, Neal M. "China Welcomes EDC." *R&D Directions,* January 2006.

Benson, Barbara. "Glen de Vries, 37." *Crain's New York Business,* March 29, 2010.

Johnson, Holland. "Mediata Tests IPO Waters with $75.9 Million Offering." *Medical Device Daily,* June 26, 2009, 2.

"Leading Japanese Pharma Chugai Standardizes on Medidata Rave Clinical Technology." *Business Wire,* January 31, 2011. Accessed March 16, 2011. http://www.businesswire.com/news/home/20110131005386/en/Leading-Japanese-Pharma-Chugai-Standardizes-Medidata-Rave.

"Medidata Solutions Reports Record Fourth Quarter and Full Year 2009 Results." *Business Wire,* March 4, 2010. Accessed March 16, 2011. http://www.businesswire.com/news/home/20100304006579/en/Medidata-Solutions-Reports-Record-Fourth-Quarter-Full.

"Medidata Solutions Reports Record Fourth Quarter and Full Year 2010 Results." *EuroInvestor,* March 15, 2011. Accessed March 18, 2011. http://www.euroinvestor.co.uk/news/story.aspx?id=11656161&bw=20110315005717.

"Medidata Solutions Sets Up Technology Partner Program." *Medical Device Daily,* July 1, 2009, 3.

"Medidata Solutions Worldwide." *Applied Clinical Trials,* December 2010, 110.

"Q3 2010 Medidata Solutions, Inc. Earnings Conference Call—Final." *Fair Disclosure Wire (Quarterly Earnings Reports),* November 9, 2010.

MedQuist Inc.

1000 Bishops Gate Boulevard
Suite 300
Mount Laurel, New Jersey 08054-4632
U.S.A.
Telephone: (856) 206-4000
Toll Free: (800) 233-3030
Fax: (856) 206-4020
Web site: http://www.medquist.com

Public Company
Founded: 1970 as Transcriptions Ltd.
Employees: 5,382 (2010)
Net Revenues: $307.2 million (2009)
Stock Exchanges: NASDAQ
Ticker Symbol: MEDQ
NAICS: 518210 Data Processing, Hosting, and Related
Services

■ ■ ■

MedQuist Inc. is the largest medical transcription company in the United States. The company provides medical transcription software technology and services to assist more than 1,500 health systems, hospitals, and medical offices to manage all stages of clinical documentation. Health care providers dictate a patient's medical history, operative reports following surgeries, and discharge summaries via telephone to a dictation recording service in one of MedQuist's offices. These reports, which are the key parts of an electronic medical record, are then transcribed by the company and downloaded into the patient's computerized medical chart within 24 hours.

Software offered by MedQuist covers a range of tasks, including voice input and voice capture, mobile or premise-based dictation products, speech recognition, transcription, and electronic signature, as well as systems and services for medical coding. The company's products and services eliminate paper records and allow doctors to sign reports electronically. This reduces the costs of record storage and allows physicians and hospitals to instantly access patient records. The company contends that more than 30 percent of acute care hospitals in the United States which are not government-owned use at least one of MedQuist's products or services.

MedQuist employs more domestic medical transcriptionists than any other company worldwide and transcribes in excess of 1.5 billion lines of text each year. Nearly all of the company's transcriptionists work from their own homes. Over 80 percent of the company's net revenues typically comes from its medical transcription technology. Maintenance services, speech recognition programs, coding services, and digital dictation management systems provide the remaining portion of the company's annual revenue.

CBay Systems Holdings Limited, a holding company which owns a variety of medical services firms worldwide, is the majority shareholder in Medquist, controlling 69.5 percent of all MedQuist stock in 2010.

CHANGING THE INDUSTRY: 1970–87

MedQuist Inc. was founded in 1970 as Transcriptions Ltd. As former CEO David A. Cohen explained in *Journal of Healthcare Management,* "We started out as a company in 1970 in East Brunswick, New Jersey, on a card table doing transcription for a couple of doctors." At the time, most medical transcription involved using cassette recorders with digital recording equipment, typewriters, and carbon paper, as compared to today's digital systems and wireless devices. Transcriptions Ltd. was one of the first companies to develop a computer-based package for medical transcription. Twenty years later, the company developed an in-depth report distribution system to meet the changing workflow needs and demands of the health care industry.

The company was incorporated in New Jersey in 1984, and reorganized three years later as a group of outpatient health care businesses which were associated with a nonprofit provider of health care. In 1987 the company implemented its first computer-based transcription system.

TRANSCRIPTIONS LTD. BECOMES MEDQUIST: 1994

Several years after introducing the new system, in May 1994 Transcriptions Ltd. was purchased by MedQuist, a nationwide provider of medical business and information services. As a result of the transaction, Transcriptions became a division of its new company owner. MedQuist's revenues were expected to double as a result of adding Transcriptions Ltd., which had revenues of $26.75 million during the previous year.

At the time of the acquisition, *PR Newswire* quoted MedQuist's chairman and CEO Richard J. Censtis when he explained the benefit of the purchase.

"Transcriptions brings to our company the added value of a technological leader in its industry with 900 skilled transcriptionists serving approximately 450 hospitals. This new service is highly complementary with our medical records services and receivables management services."

GROWTH AND CHANGES: 1994–99

Over the next few years, sales and the acquisitions of smaller transcription companies caused MedQuist to grow quickly. During the fall of 1995, MedQuist expanded its transcription services when its subsidiary Transcriptions, Ltd., acquired a privately owned transcription company, Transcriptions Limited of Michigan. This newly acquired medical transcription company had an annual revenue of about $1.8 million at that time.

A few months later, in December of that year, MedQuist spun off its non-transcription-based businesses as part of the company's restructuring. The proceeds from this were used to eliminate some of MedQuist's debt. This also allowed the company to focus entirely on the medical transcription aspect of the business and helped prepare the company for a second public offering the following year to raise additional money.

JOINING OTHER COMPANIES: 1999–2000

During 1999 MedQuist's revenues exceeded $330 million. By 2000, MedQuist had shown growth of about 25 percent each year since its founding. This growth could be attributed in part to new business, and in part to the company's acquisition of approximately 30 small transcription companies in its first 30 years. By that time, MedQuist was providing services to 700 hospitals, and was approximately seven times larger than its closest competitor, according to a May 2000 article in *Healthcare Strategic Management.* The article also stated that MedQuist "serves more than 1,300 clients in 700 hospitals, and does about $400 million worth of medical-transcription business each year." At the time, the company estimated that approximately 75 percent of hospitals outsourced their transcription of medical records, and that this number would reach 90 percent in the future. Part of the reason so much hospital transcription was outsourced to companies such as MedQuist was that this provided a savings of approximately 15 to 20 percent, as compared to hospitals using their own internal medical transcriptionists.

In April 2000 MedQuist formed an alliance with A-Life Medical, a natural language processing (NLP)

KEY DATES

1970: Company founded as Transcriptions Ltd.
1994: Transcriptions Ltd. is purchased by
MedQuist.
2000: Royal Philips Electronics purchases majority
interest in MedQuist.
2008: Royal Philips Electronics sells its interest in
MedQuist to CBay Systems Holdings, Ltd.
2010: MedQuist and CBay purchase Spheris.

technology company, and also purchased approximately 20 percent of the company. A *Reuters* report noted that A-Life's NLP engine was also added to MedQuist's "existing transcription technology and workflow process to allow free-form dictation to be automatically coded and readied for billing submission to third party payers." This acquisition gave MedQuist the opportunity to step into the medical coding market.

In June 2000 Royal Philips Electronics, a large manufacturer of consumer electronics in Europe, purchased approximately a 60 percent interest in MedQuist for $1.2 billion and later purchased an additional 10 percent. Philips acquired the company as part of a plan to expand its offerings of services related to health care. Philips Medical Systems division was already an established leader in diagnostic imaging systems and services, offering X-ray, MRI, ultrasound, and imaging information systems to its customers. The acquisition of MedQuist allowed Philips to add medical transcription to its imaging services. Radiology departments, where most of the company's imaging products were used, were also one of the largest users of medical dictation services. In addition to the offerings of its medical systems division, Philips was also a worldwide market leader in speech recognition technologies prior to the acquisition. Adding MedQuist's capabilities in the area of transcription allowed Philips to work toward advancing transcription technology.

EXPANSION OF PRODUCTS AND SERVICES: 2001–06

During 2001 and 2002 MedQuist acquired several other companies in order to gain the technology and expertise needed to provide a complete line of document workflow management products and solutions. One of the companies purchased by MedQuist was Lanier Healthcare, a company specializing in health care document workflow, such as dictation, speech recognition, and

electronic signatures, as well as transcription. This acquisition provided MedQuist with an additional sales force to sell its products.

MedQuist also acquired Speech Machines, an application service company known for its use of a Web-based transcription system. Digital Voice Inc., a provider of digital dictation, was also purchased by MedQuist during this period. Along with the offerings MedQuist had prior to these acquisitions, the new companies provided technologies that worked together to allow MedQuist to develop an extensive package of products to meet the needs of the health care industry.

FACING LEGAL MATTERS: 2003–08

Despite the success of the company's products, the years 2003 through 2008 were a turbulent period for MedQuist. As a result of allegedly overbilling customers, the company faced a number of lawsuits and federal investigations. Hefty costs associated with the review of its historical billing practices, review of allegations and billing history, legal fees, and settlement costs caused the company to post significant net losses during this period, ranging between $15.2 million in 2007 to $111.6 million in 2005, even though revenues exceeded $300 million each year. Although the majority of suits were settled by 2008, some litigation continued for several years beyond this period, and included both class action suits and civil suits filed by customers, shareholders, and the Securities and Exchange Commission (SEC) not only against the company, but also against Philips and MedQuist's former executives. One of these suits was brought about as a result of allegations that the company overbilled federal agencies, and MedQuist was subsequently subjected to an investigation by the U.S. Department of Justice. The suit was resolved in 2008 when the company paid $6.6 million.

The pending lawsuits and associated fees were not the only issues MedQuist faced during this period. In June 2004 the company's stock was delisted from the NASDAQ as a result of the company not filing its Form 10-K Annual Report for 2003, or the Form 10-Q for the first quarter of 2004, with the SEC, despite receiving an extension from the SEC for the 10-K. These forms were delayed due to a pending review of MedQuist's possibly improper billing practices and an audit of the company's financial statements. The stock was relisted in 2008.

CHANGES AND FINANCES: 2008–09

In the early months of 2008, MedQuist terminated about 10 percent of its nontranscriptionist staff, which amounted to 200 employees. These positions were eliminated as part of a workforce restructuring plan to balance expenditures with the company's operational needs at the time. MedQuist also closed 60 of its local service centers, transforming its transcriptionists from on-site to home-based employees, and hiring overseas transcriptionists. The investigations into the company and the costs of resolving the allegations made such changes necessary.

Philips sold its holdings in MedQuist in August 2008 to CBay Systems Holdings Ltd. The new majority holder of MedQuist was a holding company whose portfolio of investments included businesses in the fields of medical transcription, as well as health care technology and financial services. As of 2010, CBay Systems owned approximately 69.5 percent of the outstanding MedQuist common stock.

Net revenues for 2009 were $307.2 million and net income was nearly $23.3 million. The revenue declined by approximately 6 percent from the previous year, due in part to lower prices in the area of transcription service. The company noted that many of its customers were trying to reduce costs in this area by using offshore labor for transcription and relying more heavily on speech recognition. Another factor contributing to lower annual revenues was the company's decrease in product maintenance revenues as customers did not renew maintenance contracts for some of the company's systems.

OUTLOOK FOR THE FUTURE: 2010 AND BEYOND

MedQuist and CBay Inc. received approval from the United States Bankruptcy Court of the District of Delaware to purchase nearly all assets of Spheris, a leading provider of clinical documentation technology and services worldwide. Based in Franklin, Tennessee, Spheris was the "second-largest medical transcription company in the US including mobile voice capture devices and speech recognition Web-based workflow platforms having its operations in North America and India," according to the *Information Company*.. Although the company had 1,900 employees in India specializing in the area of medical language, Spheris had not included its Indian operations in the bankruptcy. MedQuist acquired the U.S. assets of the company, and CBay acquired stock of its subsidiary, Spheris India Private Limited.

As U.S. president Barack Obama and his administration voiced commitment to helping to fund the adoption of electronic health records (EHR) for all U.S. citizens by 2014, MedQuist expected that increased opportunities would arise for the company.

Diane Milne

PRINCIPAL SUBSIDIARIES

MedQuist Canada Company (Nova Scotia); MedQuist CM Corporation; MedQuist IP Corporation; MedQuist of Delaware, Inc.; MedQuist Transcriptions, Ltd.; Speech Machines Limited (UK).

PRINCIPAL COMPETITORS

Cerner Corporation; Epic Systems Corporation; Nuance Communications, Inc.; Transcend Services, Inc.; WebMedex, Inc.

FURTHER READING

"CBaySystems Acquires Spheris for $116.3 Million." *Information Company,* April 19, 2010.

Egger, Ed. "MedQuist Prospers as Hospitals Step Up Outsourcing of Medical Record Transcription." *Healthcare Strategic Management,* May 2000, 14.

Johnson, James A. "Interview with David A. Cohen, Chairman and Chief Executive Officer of MedQuist Inc." *Journal of Healthcare Management* 45, no. 6 (2000): 353.

"Medical Coding Software Smooths Transition to ICD-10." *Product News Network,* 2010.

"MedQuist and CBay Receive Court Approval to Acquire Spheris." *Investment Weekly News,* May 1, 2010, 396.

"MedQuist Enters Medical Transcription Field; Transaction Doubles Annual Revenues." *PR Newswire,* May 31, 1994: 531PH004.

"MedQuist, Inc. Forms Strategic Alliance with A-Life Medical, Inc." *Reuters,* April 6, 2000.

"MedQuist Reports Fourth Quarter and Year End 2008 Results." *PR Newswire,* March 11, 2009, 396.

"MedQuist to Make a 20 Percent Equity Investment in A-Life Medical, Inc. and Form Broad-Based Strategic Alliance." *Business Wire,* April 6, 2000, 1238.

"Philips Moves Further into Health Services." *Mergers & Acquisitions Journal* 35, no. 7 (2000).

Metropark USA, Inc.

5750 Grace Place
Los Angeles, California 90022
U.S.A.
Telephone: (323) 622-3600
Fax: (323) 389-1599
Web site: http://www.metroparkusa.com

Private Company
Incorporated: 2003 as Santa Barbara Street Asylum, Inc.
Employees: 2,000 (2011)
Annual Sales: Approximately $100 million
NAICS: 448110 Men's Clothing Stores; 448120 Women's Clothing Stores; 448150 Clothing Accessories Stores

■ ■ ■

Metropark USA, Inc., is a mall-based specialty chain that fuses eclectic fashion, music, and art in a retail experience. Metropark, which targets adults age 20 to 35, offers contemporary apparel and accessories for both women and men through 70 stores in metropolitan areas across the United States. Modeled after stylish hotels, bars, and street boutiques, the company's stores offer customers a high-energy shopping experience that is enhanced by fashion shows, art installations, and live DJ performances on weekends.

DEMOGRAPHIC

Incorporated in Delaware in November 2003 under the name Santa Barbara Street Asylum, Inc., Metropark USA, Inc., opened its first stores in 2004 under the Metropark name. Cofounded by Orval Madden, Jay Johnson, and Lawrence Tannenbaum, the company was headquartered in City of Industry, California, with Madden serving as CEO and chairman, Johnson as CFO, and Tannenbaum as president. The concept behind Metropark was attributed to Madden, who had founded Hot Topic, a successful mall-based chain specializing in Goth clothing and accessories targeted to teenagers, in 1988. After leaving that company in 2000, Madden turned his focus to developing a store that would appeal to people born between 1977 and 1994, a group commonly referred to as Generation Y (or Gen Y). Madden realized that the teenagers who had once shopped at Hot Topic were in their twenties, and he saw great potential in catering to that older crowd.

Specifically, the demographic Metropark sought was 20- to 35-year-old hipsters, both male and female, whose lifestyle was influenced not only by fashion but also by music and art. They were young professionals who did not yet have either children or mortgages. Because popular reality shows, MTV programming, E! Entertainment Television, and the Internet gave everyone access to the same information, Metropark executives banked on the fact that young adults all over the country, not just those in New York or Los Angeles, knew what was fashionable and trendy in the urban scene. Studies showed Gen Y individuals to be brand-driven consumers with sophisticated tastes who spent five times the amount the previous generation did at the same age. At the time Metropark was conceived, some 73 million Gen Y shoppers accounted for $200 billion in spending, and Madden estimated that the figure

COMPANY PERSPECTIVES

Transcending the traditional retail experience, Metropark offers an exciting alternative for those who demand more fashion sophistication.

would increase as more of this demographic finished college over the next 10 years.

AMBIANCE

Although Madden, Johnson, and Tannenbaum chose to house Metropark stores in malls, the ambiance of the stores was unlike that of typical mall retail locations. In large part, the Metropark model was inspired by New York's chic SoHo neighborhood. As Tannenbaum explained to *Display & Design Ideas'* contributor Roy Sree, "For us, the term 'metro' signifies that we wanted to bring the street store boutique ambiance to the mall in a way that hasn't been done. We selected the name 'park' to signify that the store is intended as a fun gathering place for people." With this concept in mind, the Metropark design was drawn from trendy nightclubs, restaurants, lounges, and hotels, as well as stylish street boutiques, in metropolitan areas around the country.

An integral component of the Metropark business model was a high-energy social atmosphere. According to Ken Nisch, chairman at JGA, the design firm that worked on the Metropark project, the nightclub appeal of Metropark was apparent to shoppers well before they walked into the store. The view into the store was obscured by green-case shutters, but potential customers could see a platform window that showcased mannequins backed by a translucent acrylic Krinklglas panel. Nisch told Sree in *Display & Design Ideas*, "Krinklglas...has an iridescent quality and evokes an image of a steamed-up window in a bar." On the other side of the shutters was a high-tech DJ booth that played music selected to draw in shoppers. The principal idea was that Metropark customers could have the same kind of experience in a retail setting that they did when they went out to a bar at night.

Once inside, customers could relax in a lounge area toward the back of the store, close to the fitting rooms. There, they could enjoy energy drinks and flip through such publications as *Law of Inertia* and *Juxtapoz Art and Culture Magazine*. Metropark walls were covered with original artworks that were for sale, and customers could also browse a selection of jazz CDs. In addition,

customers could watch music videos and proprietary video content on multiple flat-panel plasma screens located throughout the store in fitting rooms, behind the customer service counter, and inside accessories cases. On weekends, live disc jockeys were hired to spin records, and Metropark frequently staged art and fashion shows, as well as VIP events featuring fashion, food, and entertainment in a nightclub environment.

MERCHANDISE

Metropark offered upscale apparel and accessory lines that were typically impossible to find at chain retailers. The company selected vendors whose goods were traditionally seen only in small, edgy street boutiques in such places as West Hollywood and New York City. A number of vendors were artists who had branched out into the fashion industry or designers who had partnered with artists in order to develop lines of clothing. As a result, it was not uncommon to see designs on garments that reflected some kind of artistic interpretation. Metropark carried only a limited run of any item, which helped make those customers interested in exclusiveness feel confident that they stood little chance of seeing anyone else wearing the same outfit. Furthermore, the strategy of offering new merchandise in limited quantities was designed to create a sense of urgency in buyers' minds.

Metropark carried the premium clothing brands Acrylic, Affliction, Ed Hardy, English Laundry, Howe, Monarchy, Obey, Rock & Republic, Salvage, and True Religion, among others, for men and women. On average, prices were higher at Metropark than at other mall-based chain stores, with jeans retailing for upwards of $200. Other merchandise offered included cosmetics, leather belts and bags, watches, costume jewelry, seasonal gifts, books and magazines, niche artwork, and CDs. Most items were edgy. A black-and-white design on a scarf, for example, was revealed to be a pattern of machine guns upon closer inspection. Metropark stores also featured novelty housewares, such as candleholders, vases, and figurines of famous personalities. The company had its own line of pet supplies as well, called MetroBark. Acknowledging the fact that owning pets, especially miniature dogs, was trendy because of such celebrities as Paris Hilton, MetroBark offered pink pet carriers, leopard-print dog beds, and T-shirts that read, "Bite Me."

EARLY OPERATIONS

The first four Metropark stores were opened in the fall of 2004 in the Los Angeles and San Francisco metropolitan areas, with the prototype at Glendale Gal-

KEY DATES

2003: Metropark USA, Inc., is incorporated as Santa Barbara Street Asylum, Inc., in City of Industry, California.

2004: Metropark opens its first four stores in California.

2005: A Metropark store is opened at Mall of America in Bloomington, Minnesota.

2006: The social network Meez creates virtual clothing for avatars based on actual Metropark apparel.

2007: Renee Bell is named company CEO.

2008: Metropark files for IPO.

2010: Cynthia T. Harriss replaces Renee Bell as company CEO; company withdraws IPO.

2011: Metropark launches online scavenger hunt.

leria in Glendale. The other stores were located at The Oaks in Thousand Oaks, Valley Fair in Santa Clara, and Oakridge in San Jose. By the end of the year, Metropark had entered into lease agreements for additional stores at Galleria at Tyler in Riverside and Irvine Spectrum Center in Irvine, where the store would include a 3,200-square-foot lounge area.

In May 2005 the company extended its reach out of state when it opened a store in Bloomington, Minnesota, at Mall of America, the nation's largest retail and entertainment complex. At the grand opening, Metropark featured a Dogtown skateboarding exhibit, as well as a display of artist Shepard Fairey's OBEY Giant sticker campaign, which was the inspiration behind the OBEY Clothing line carried by Metropark. As 2005 drew to a close, Metropark planned to expand its base of stores by 15 during 2006, not only in California, but also in Texas, Georgia, and Oregon.

Even as it launched new stores in such locales as Perimeter Mall and Lenox Square in Atlanta, Georgia, and Willowbrook Mall in Houston, Texas, Metropark explored new marketing techniques in 2006. The retailer gained widespread attention when it partnered with Meez, a social network service headquartered in San Francisco. Meez, which combines avatars, Web games, and virtual worlds, created virtual versions of Metropark's apparel at no cost to the clothing company. Beginning in May 2006, Meez users could outfit their avatars in representations of Metropark shirts, jackets, and dresses that could actually be found in Metropark stores. In return, Metropark featured Meez on its Web

site and on videos shown in stores. The promotion resulted in an estimated 400 visitors each day to Metropark's Web site, and Metropark's virtual clothing was seen on various Internet sites, including Facebook and YouTube.

From 2005 to 2007, Metropark's net sales went from $11.5 million to $71.6 million. One factor in this growth was improved visibility, as the company explored new ways to expand its public profile. In 2007, for instance, Metropark teamed with the Bawls Guarana energy drink company and Havianas Sandals in an "Ultimate Fashion Experience" contest. Part of the grand prize was a shopping spree at a Los Angeles Metropark store. Future promotions would pair Metropark with Gibson Guitar, Logic Wireless, and imeem, a social media service, to sponsor a contest in conjunction with Live Nation's "Let It Rock" tour starring multigenre musician Kevin Rudolf. As before, a shopping spree at a Metropark store was one of the prizes.

MANAGEMENT CHANGES

In 2007 Metropark underwent changes in its top management. Remaining on the board of directors, Madden stepped down as CEO. He was replaced by Robert Allison on an interim basis in April. Six months later, Metropark announced that general merchandising manager Renee Bell would move into the position of CEO. Bell, who had 20 years of retail experience, including serving as general manager of the women's apparel chain bebe and vice president of merchandising for Rampage clothing stores, would continue Metropark's business strategy of offering exclusive, high-end labels. According to Bell, the company planned to open 25 stores in 2008 in existing and new markets, followed by 25 to 30 stories per year in the future, with the ultimate goal of operating at least 300 stores in locations that varied from malls to upscale outdoor shopping centers to street locations in retail-oriented neighborhoods.

In June 2008 Metropark, which by then operated 43 stores in 17 states, filed a registration statement with the U.S. Securities and Exchange Commission to raise up to $100 million in an initial public offering. However, the company withdrew its IPO registration statement in June 2010, citing unstable market conditions. That same month, Metropark named Cynthia T. Harriss CEO, replacing Bell, who moved into the position of company president and chief merchandising officer. At the time Harriss was appointed to the post, Metropark operated 69 stores across the country with around $100 million in annual sales. Harriss brought 37 years of retail experience to Metropark. In addition to serving as president of Gap Inc. and Disney Resorts, Harriss had been senior vice president of Disney Store and was instrumental in expanding the chain from 140 to 460 stores throughout North America. While Bell would be responsible for inventory planning, merchandising, marketing, and e-commerce, Harriss was to lead Metropark's growth initiatives.

Under this new leadership structure, Metropark continued to improve its operations, both on-site and online. In November 2010 Metropark opened its 70th store, located in McLean, Virginia, at Tysons Corner Center, the largest shopping mall in Washington, D.C. To celebrate the grand opening, Metropark offered customers champagne and gave away $10 American Express Give Style Gift Cards to the store's first 200 shoppers. In February 2011 Metropark announced an online scavenger hunt that required visitors to its Web site to find style codes and status updates for merchandise. Users who successfully completed the activity had the chance to win Metropark gift cards worth up to $500.

In the early 2010s Metropark expected to open 10 new stores over the course of the year. In its short life the company has carved a distinct niche for itself that should help it continue to draw in trendy Gen Y shoppers.

Alicia Elley

PRINCIPAL COMPETITORS

Aéropostale, Inc.; bebe stores, inc.; H&M Hennes & Mauritz AB; Urban Outfitters, Inc.

FURTHER READING

Chandler, Michele. "Boutiques Hope to Capture Hip Mall Crowd in San Jose, Calif. Area." *San Jose Mercury News,* November 5, 2004.

Corcoran, Cate T. "Metropark Dresses Up Meez." *Women's Wear Daily,* October 10, 2007.

Cruz, Sherri. "Hot Topic Encore Metropark Headed to Irvine Spectrum." *Orange County Business Journal,* June 6, 2006, 17.

"Metropark to Bring High-Energy Shopping Experience to Mall of America: New Specialty Store Concept Heads to the Heartland Following Successful California Launch." *PR Newswire,* February 15, 2005.

Moin, David. "Metropark Appoints Cynthia Harriss CEO." *Women's Wear Daily,* June 2, 2010.

Pallay, Jessica. "Metropark Aims at Generation Y, Plans 200 Stores." *Daily News Record,* December 13, 2004.

Sree, Roy. "In the Club: Metropark Targets 20- to 30-Somethings with a Nightlife Feel." *Display & Design Ideas,* March 2005, 52.

York, Emily Bryson. "Goth to Guys: Hot Topic Founder Markets to Men at Malls." *Los Angeles Business Journal,* October 23, 2006.

Young, Vicki M. "Metropark Takes Step Toward IPO." *Women's Wear Daily,* June 18, 2008.

Miner Enterprises, Inc.

—■—

1200 East State Street
Box 471
Geneva, Illinois 60134
U.S.A.
Telephone: (630) 232-3000
Fax: (630) 232-3055
Web site: http:// www.minerent.com

Private Company
Founded: 1894 as the W.H. Miner Company
Employees: 280 (est., 2010)
Sales: $160 million (est., 2010)
NAICS: 336510 Railroad Rolling Stock Manufacturing

■ ■ ■

Based in Geneva, Illinois, Miner Enterprises, Inc. (Miner), supplies equipment and components for the railcar and related industries. Miner's operations consist of four business units, W.H. Miner, Powerbrace, Autoquip, and Miner Elastomer Products.

W.H. Miner supplies components for the freight car industry, including draft gears, side bearings, gates and unloading systems, hatch covers, brake beams, and Tecs-Pak springs. Miner also provides testing services and replacement parts for customers.

Powerbrace Corporation manufactures heavy-duty door securement for trailers and containers. Powerbrace sells both Miner and Powerbrace brands, all certified by the American Association of Railroads (AAR). Autoquip is a leader in lifting and materials handling equipment. Autoquip's products primarily consist of dock products,

in-plant products, freight lift products, and custom products. Since the late 1990s, the company has focused on custom products.

Miner Elastomer Products Corporation (MEPC) supplies thermoplastic elastomer energy management systems, or shock absorption systems. MEPC's Thermoplastic Elastomer Compression Spring Package (TecsPak) system was patented in 1985. While an excellent application for the railcar industry, TecsPak products serve many markets. Customers include the automotive, transportation, mining, appliance, and sports equipment industries.

COMPANY FOUNDED: 1894

Miner Enterprises, originally the W.H. Miner Company, was established in 1894 by William H. Miner when he patented a new concept for draft gears. (A draft gear is part of the mechanism that connects railroad cars to one another.) At the time, Miner worked for Hutchins Refrigerator Car Co., a company that transported fruit from California to New York. Miner was tasked with solving the problem of draft gear failures, which caused the product to spoil before it reached its destination. Miner designed a spring draft rig and received U.S. Patent 461,443 on October 20, 1891. Miner's flexible design also provided shock absorption, or "cushioning." The invention was useful to an industry that was developing faster engines, which caused more devastation when the cars would collide.

The railroad industry was a dangerous place to work in the late 19th century, with rail workers often identified by their missing fingers. The process of coupling two railcars required that a man stand between the cars to rig the coupler device, a dangerous and tricky task. An Iowa farmer and former Civil War chaplain led the reform to improve safety in the industry. In 1873 Eli H. Janney invented the knuckle coupler, which is still used today. Miner's invention included this automatic coupling, a design that slid two hooks together to interlock instead of the pin and trailer system. This improvement reduced accidents by 60 percent.

William Miner was born in Juneau, Wisconsin, in 1864. Miner's mother died when he was four and his father when he was ten. Miner's father had sought his fortune by moving west from Chazy, New York, but never quite found success. After his father's death, young William moved back to Chazy to live with his uncle John and aunt Hulda to work the Miner family farm founded by Miner's grandfather in 1820. When he turned 18, he followed his father's footsteps to seek his fortune in the West. He trained as a mechanic's apprentice at the Pray Manufacturing Company and attended night school for mechanical engineering. In 1891, the same year he received his first patent, he met Alice Trainer. They married and had one child that died.

THE GOLDEN AGE OF THE RAILROAD: 1890–1920

The late 19th century was the era when the railroad industry attracted the brightest engineers, as railroad transportation provided for the explosion of commerce, transporting bulk amounts of product that was previously impossible. As the space exploration and software industries do today, engineers could make their fortunes with inventions for the rail industry. The industry also provided a new form of passenger transportation prior to the automobile. In this business environment, Miner received over 100 patents over the next 30 years.

By the 1890s there were over 163,000 miles of railroad track. Miner's patents provided much of the standardization and efficiency advances necessary for the

industry to flourish. During the last part of the 19th century up through the 1920s, the industry enjoyed growing profitability. In 1916 the miles traveled by rail peaked at over 254,000. Railroads transported both passengers and cargo and were the primary means of transportation for both.

During the 1930s the Great Depression softened demand for cargo. The emergence of the affordable automobile also affected the rail industry, as those that could afford to travel now had a choice.

World War II spiked demand again as transportation of troops and equipment made the railways critical to the war effort. However, after the war ended, rail transportation declined and never again reached the 1916 peak. In the early 21st century, miles traveled by rail averaged approximately 160,000 annually.

INTERNATIONAL GROWTH AND NEW OWNERSHIP

As the U.S. rail industry slowed beginning in the early 20th century, Miner developed internal plans for global expansion. In the mid-1920s, Miner first sold draft gears overseas. In 1947 the company opened an Office of International Operations and hired foreign sales representatives. Later, in 1986, the company focused efforts on the needs of its foreign customers and developed programs to target potential growth markets. Throughout the late 1980s and mid-1990s, Miner opened sales offices in Europe, Canada, and South America. Miner engineers were tasked with modifying products to meet the standards of foreign customers while also satisfying international regulatory requirements. The company's marketing department prepared sales and technical documents in six different languages.

While a company that continued to thrive well over 100 years after its inception might be thought of as legacy enough for the founder, Miner's true legacy began after he returned to his childhood home of Chazy in 1903. There he founded schools, hospitals, and a museum dedicated to his wife. The family farm of Chazy had always struggled due to the arid temperature and rocky soil, but Miner brought hydration technology to the area. His contribution to the city made Chazy a place where young people might come to find their fortune, not leave it. William Miner died in 1933 from complications due to a tonsillectomy.

After Miner's death, the company was owned by a foundation in his name. In 1968, following a ruling by the Internal Revenue Service that foundations could not own businesses, the company, under CEO William E. Withall, merged with Enterprise Railway Equipment.

KEY DATES

1891: William H. Miner receives a patent for a new concept for the draft gear, filling a need for standardization.

1894: W. H. Miner receives first order for his invention, establishing the W.H. Miner Company.

1968: Merger between W.H. Miner Company and Enterprise Railway Equipment establishes Miner Enterprises, Inc.

1970: The Withall family takes ownership of Miner Enterprises.

2000: Miner Enterprises acquires Buffalo Brake Beam.

In 1960 Powerbrace subsidiary opened its doors to manufacture and develop door securement products. Powerbrace's flagship product, the lockrod, had been patented in 1913 and was an industry standard for semi-trailer door security. In addition to products for railcars, Powerbrace's products served the truck and farm industries.

INNOVATION AND GLOBAL EXPANSION

While Miner pursued international growth, the company continued to innovate, building lighter, stronger draft gears and products to complement them. A key component of the company's TF-880 draft gear was its patented Thermoplastic Elastomer Compression Spring Package, or TecsPak. TecsPak, a shock absorption system, was patented in 1985. The invention led to the founding of subsidiary Miner Elastomer Products Corporation (MEPC), which offered supplies to diversified industries globally.

In 1992 Miner won its first award for export excellence, the President's E-certificate, indicating worldwide acceptance of its products. International sales tripled over the next few years, reaching 20 percent of overall sales by the company's 100th birthday in 1994.

CAUTIOUS ACQUISITIONS: 2000–10 AND BEYOND

As the rest of the industry consolidated, Miner chose its acquisitions selectively. In 2000 Miner bought the assets of Buffalo Brake Beam Company, a manufacturer of rail car components, in Lackawanna, New York. In 2009 Miner's subsidiary Autoquip purchased American Lifts from the Columbus McKinnon Corporation for $2.4 million. American Lifts designs and manufactures scissor lift technology, complementing Autoquip's specialty in in-plant and dock material handling products.

Miner has continued its legacy of innovation, developing and patenting solutions for the rail and cargo industry. Its Aggregate loading and unloading systems are preferred for ballast, coal, and other dry bulk products. In 2008 Miner introduced the new Series 2008 Brake Beam. The enhancement ensured a tenfold increase in the life of struts and also prevented brake shoe loss. In October 2009 Miner introduced DuraShield, a hatch cover with a lightweight, durable design and high-performance seal, allowing uniform clamping and maximizing car capacity.

During the global economic recession of 2008 and 2009, Miner reduced its operations in Mexico and also cut back on its labor force, although it tried to do this as much as possible through attrition. While it weathered the slowdown, the company continued to focus on finding additional markets for its innovations. As of 2009, Miner exported to 56 countries worldwide, with 25 percent of the company's business generated outside of North America. Its largest global customer was Russia, followed by Europe, Australia, South Africa, and Brazil.

In the 2010s, the company expected its largest growth in international sales to take place in India and Russia. The key to success in those countries, Miner's president Kris Jurasek, told Kathy Keeney for the *Pocket List of Railroad Officials,* would be "patience and persistence. ... It takes a long time. We were involved in Russia on some level for 10 years before we had a sale."

Miner's executive management believed that part of the reason Miner was able to cope with the economic recession was because of its excellent customer service. The company prided itself on standing behind its products and using research and development efforts to lower customers' costs. As Jurasek explained to Keeney, "Today, you need to deliver more than the product that shows up at the company's dock. ... If you don't, somebody else can duplicate the processes and take the business away from you."

While Miner has experienced reduced sales in the early 21st century, management remained optimistic that the company would retain its prominent position in an industry that, while it may decline, will never disappear as long as products need inexpensive transport.

Sara K. Huter

PRINCIPAL SUBSIDIARIES

Autoquip Lifting Solutions Corporation; Miner Elastomer Products Corporation; Powerbrace Corporation.

PRINCIPAL COMPETITORS

A. Stucki Company; General Bearing Corporation; Trinity Industries, Inc.; Westinghouse Air Brake Technologies Corporation.

FURTHER READING

"Railroads in the 20th Century: The 'Golden Age' of Railroading Comes to a Close." American-Rails.com. Accessed December 20, 2010. http://www.american-rails.com/railroads-in-the-20th-century.html.

Burke, Joseph C. *William H. Miner: The Man and the Myth.* Minneapolis: Langdon Street Press, 2009.

Chazy Central Rural School. "William Henry Miner: The Man Behind the School." Chazy, NY: Chazy Central Rural School. Accessed December 22, 2010. http://www.chazy.org/history/whminer.html.

Keeney, Kathy. "Railcar Components Maker Rides Out Cyclical Business with Steady Course." *Pocket List of Railroad Officials,* 2nd quarter, 2009. Accessed February 17, 2011. http://www.minerent.com/news/index.asp.

"Powerbrace Turns 50." *Fleet Owner.* 2010.

Pozil, Scott. "'E' and 'E-Star' Awards Are Given to Two Maryland Firms." *Business America* 119, no. 2 (1998).

Tuzik, Robert E. "Miner Joins the Century Club." *Railway Age,* June 1994.

MIPS Technologies, Inc.

955 East Arques Avenue
Sunnyvale, California 94085
U.S.A.
Telephone: (408) 530-5000
Fax: (408) 530-5150
Web site: http://www.mips.com

Public Company
Founded: 1984 as MIPS Computer Systems, Inc.
Employees: 141 (2010)
Net income: $70.96 million (2010)
Stock Exchanges: NASDAQ
Ticker Symbol: MIPS
NAICS: 334413 Semiconductor and Related Device Manufacturing; 334419 Other Electronic Component Manufacturing

■ ■ ■

MIPS Technologies, Inc., is a leading microprocessor design company. Processors based on MIPS architectures and cores are used in millions of digital home entertainment, communications, networking, and mobile and portable media devices created by such names as Linksys, Sony, Pioneer, Motorola, Cisco, Microchip Technology, and Hewlett-Packard. The company has locations in China, Taiwan, Japan, Germany, and Israel, as well as the United States.

MIPS's designs are found in numerous digital consumer products such as set-top television boxes and offer features such as high-definition, video-on-demand, and Internet video access. Other consumer products us-

ing MIPS technology include automotive driver assistance and navigation products such as GPS and automotive accident prevention technology, video games, digital television, broadband products, Wi-Fi, Blu-ray disk players, digital still and video cameras, and mobile handsets. The company's business products are used for office automation products such as laser and multifunction printers, and networking equipment such as routers and switches.

The company has more than 370 license agreements with approximately 125 companies in networking, digital home products, and mobile devices. These companies use MIPS-based architecture in their products, and include Broadcom Corporation, Cavium Networks, ICT, NEC Electronics, and Toshiba Corporation. In the period between 2000 and 2010, more than 2.2 billion MIPS-Based Systems on Chips (SoCs) were sold by these licensees. These companies then pay royalties to MIPS for licensing their products. Royalties typically account for approximately two-thirds of the company's annual revenue, with the remaining one-third coming from licenses and contracts.

In addition to the United States, MIPS operates subsidiaries in China, Germany, Israel, Japan, South Korea, Switzerland, and Taiwan.

THE EARLY YEARS: 1984–89

Prior to becoming president of Stanford University, John Hennessey worked at the school as an assistant professor of electrical engineering. During this time, he led an engineering team to initiate the MIPS RISC architecture project in 1981. The advantage of the Reduced Instruc-

COMPANY PERSPECTIVES

MIPS Technologies is a leading provider of industry-standard processor architectures and cores for digital consumer and business applications. We design and license the industry's highest performance 32- and 64-bit architectures and cores, which also offer some of the smallest silicon footprints and lowest power consumption of any embedded microprocessors. Our customers include more than 100 of the world's leading OEM, fabless and ASIC semiconductor companies, and our technology is driving many high-growth embedded markets including digital set-top boxes, digital televisions, DVD recordable devices, broadband access devices, digital cameras, laser printers and network routers.

tion Set Computer (RISC) was its use of a simpler computer structure which not only increased the computer's performance but also decreased costs. According to *Newsmakers,* the *Stanford Online Report* stated that this advancement "revolutionized the computer industry."

Three years later, in 1984, Hennessey took a sabbatical from the university to see if the RISC concept had any business potential. He founded MIPS Computer Systems, Inc., a privately held maker of computer chips. MIPS, which is an acronym for "millions of instructions per second," supplied chip sets, the building blocks of computer systems, to manufacturers of minicomputers and work stations. According to Computer Design, "Compared to traditional semiconductor companies, MIPS Computer Systems is a systems company that adopted a different philosophy in developing its RISC architecture." One way MIPS accomplished this was by moving the complexity of the system from the processor to the compilers, causing the microprocessor to be simple, while giving it exceptional speed and efficiency. Also, the company moved many hardware functions to the computer's software. This allowed the hardware to be available to manage computational tasks.

During its first two years of operation, the company reported net losses of $6.4 million. Despite $7.8 million in revenue in 1986, the company still showed a loss of $9 million for the year. Product sales in 1988 increased significantly, however. This, combined with income from licensing the RISC chip technology, gave the

company over $39 million in revenue, lowering MIPS's annual loss to $3.7 million for the year.

Five years after its inception, MIPS Computer Systems became profitable for the first time and went public in 1989. The company announced plans to issue 4.75 million shares of common stock, with plans to use the proceeds as working capital to fund inventories and acquire equipment.

NEW PRODUCTS AND AWARDS: 1990–95

Over the next few years, MIPS created the industry's first 64-bit microprocessor, the R4000. This new technology was named "Microprocessor of the Year" by Microprocessor Report in 1991. Despite this new development, the company continued to face financial hardships. Hennessey and his partners responded to the situation by selling MIPS Computer Systems to Silicon Graphics, Inc. (which later became Silicon Graphics International), in 1992 for $333 million. SGI renamed the company MIPS Technologies and continued development of the MIPS microprocessor through its internal MIPS Group.

SGI also incorporated its wholly owned subsidiary MIPS Technologies, Inc., during this same year. The costs associated with the acquisition of MIPS caused SGI to post an annual loss of $118.4 million for 1992. However, taking over ownership of MIPS ensured the supply of the company's RISC microprocessors, which were considered crucial technology at that time. Following the acquisition, eight high-tech companies around the word announced plans to purchase 1.5 million shares of SGI, indicating support of SGI's new purchase.

Under the umbrella of SGI, MIPS continued to develop new products. A MIPS product was again recognized by Microprocessor Report as being the "Microprocessor of the Year" in 1995. This time, the honor was awarded to R4700.

SUCCESS AND DEVELOPMENT: 1995–99

Twelve years after its development, the MIPS architecture was not only the highest-volume RISC architecture in the world but also the fastest growing. In 1996 19.2 million of the processors were shipped by MIPS licensees. The following year, the number of processors shipped increased to 48 million. This was the first RISC architecture to exceed the volume of Motorola's 32-bit 68000 CISC. Also, in 1997 an estimated 30 million video game units were sold. Such products represented the first high-volume use for 32- and 64-bit

KEY DATES

1984: MIPS Computer Systems, Inc., is founded by Dr. John Hennessey of Stanford University.
1989: Company goes public for the first time.
1992: Hennessey sells MIPS to Silicon Graphics (SGI) for $333 million.
1998: SGI spins off MIPS, which is renamed MIPS Technologies, Inc.
2009: MIPS joins the Open Handset Alliance and assists in development of Android, a platform for smartphones.

microprocessors for consumer application, and approximately 90 percent of those sold incorporated technology developed by MIPS, including the Nintendo 64 and the Sony PlayStation.

In 1998 SGI divested some of its noncore business assets, which included the spin-off of MIPS Technologies, Inc. On June 30 of that year, MIPS became a publicly traded company when it made its initial public offering as MIPS Technologies. The IPO was one of the most successful in the area of technology for the year, and within six months, the shares had more than doubled in value.

During its first few years as the newly named MIPS Technologies, Inc., the company introduced a number of new developments which were quickly licensed by highly recognizable leaders in the technology industry. MIPS introduced its MIPS64 and MIPS32 architecture standards in 1999, which incorporated all of the previously developed MIPS instruction-set architectures, while providing a foundation for processor development in the future. Enhancements to these formats were introduced two years later as "Release 2" of the architecture. The company also introduced the highest performance, synthesizable 32-bit cores available for licensing in the industry. Known as the MIPS32 4KE family, LSI Logic was one of the first licensees of one of the new cores.

Along with Gemplus, a leader in smart cards, MIPS Technologies also released its high-performance Smart-MIPS architecture and smart card core. One of the first licensees of the products was Philips Semiconductors. The company also introduced the first synthesizable 64-bit core which included an integrated floating-point unit during this same year. This product was licensed by a number of companies, including LSI Logic, Texas Instruments, Atmel Corp., and Broadcom.

GROWTH IN A NEW CENTURY: 2000–06

The beginning of the new century brought more recognition for MIPS products. Microprocessor Reports awarded Sony Computer Entertainment and Toshiba America the "Best Embedded Processor" award in 2000 for their MIPS-based design used in the Sony PlayStation 2. The same publication also named Broadcom's MIPS64-based BCM1250 the "Best High-Performance Embedded Processor" in 2002.

The early years of the 21st century also brought about growth within the company through acquisitions, expansion, and market growth. MIPS Technologies acquired Algorithmics, a leading GNU tool chain vendor. (GNU is a form of operating system, and a tool chain is a group of programming tools that can be used to create software.) This acquisition allowed MIPS to improve its tools, software, and design services support. Another acquisition during this time was design services and development tools company First Silicon Solutions (FS2). MIPS believed that purchasing FS2 would improve the company's performance analysis abilities as well as its debugging capabilities. It was also expected that this acquisition would help to decrease the time to market the company's products.

The company also opened a new, larger office in Japan, a new office in Taiwan, and a research and development center in Shanghai. This expanded the company's Asian presence and helped established MIPS's operations in China. SinoSys Technologies, a company based in Shanghai, was appointed as the first Chinese MIPS Authorized Training Center.

MIPS Technologies and Microsoft worked together with leading vendors of silicon to get MIPS-based designs in more digital consumer devices. By 2004 MIPS was the most widely used architecture in the integrated digital television and digital video reecorder markets. Shortly thereafter, the company achieved a 97 percent market share in the area of cable modems. In 2006 Mobileye licensed one of MIPS Technologies' cores to be used for next-generation driver assistance products.

One result of the expansion and growth in the first few years of the 21st century could be seen in the company's profits. MIPS showed reported a net income of more than $11 million during the fiscal year ending June 30, 2006.

GROWTH BUT ALSO LOSSES: 2006–09

MIPS's growth continued over the next few years with the acquisition of Chipidea, a company that was the world leader in analog and mixed-signal intellectual property (IP) cores at that time. By purchasing this new company, MIPS was able to expand its product base and become a global leader in semiconductor design. After acquiring Chipidea, which was the company's largest acquisition to that time, MIPS organized itself into two business groups. The first was the Processor Business Group, and the second was the Analog Business Group (ABG). Chipidea operated as the ABG.

More than 350 million units were shipped by MIPS licensees during fiscal 2007, and the company showed a net income of $8.48 million during this year. However, a net loss of $131.8 million was reported during the 2008 fiscal year. MIPS explained the loss by noting that it had used all of its "available cash and short term investments to complete the acquisition of Chipidea and in connection with the acquisition incurred debt under a revolving credit agreement."

The market for analog processors was strong at the time MIPS acquired Chipidea, and the move appeared to offer the potential for long-term growth. "Unfortunately," according to John Bourgoin, then CEO of MIPS Technologies, in a 2009 article in Fair Disclosure Wire, "after two good quarters, the analog market went into a sharp downturn and marcoeconomic conditions have continued to slow affecting our entire business." As a result, MIPS sold its ABG division to Synopsis, Inc., for $22 million and began operating as a single business group. The company believed the divestiture would not only improve the value of its shares and increase profitability but also allow MIPS to focus on its processor business. The company reported a net loss of $9.44 million for the 2009 fiscal year. However, the loss was considerably lower than that of the previous year.

INNOVATION FOR THE FUTURE OF TECHNOLOGY

Also during 2009, MIPS joined the Open Handset Alliance. This group of more than 45 companies (in the field of technology and mobile devices) worked together with the goal of developing a better mobile experience at a lower price for customers. The group developed the first "complete, open, and free mobile platform," known as Android. After joining the group, MIPS planned to contribute to the creation of innovative Internet-connected technologies. By the following year, Android was a leading platform for smartphones in the United States, enjoying a healthy market share.

MIPS shipped a record 510 million products during the 2010 fiscal year and entered the following fiscal year with $65 million in the bank, with all debts paid off as of April of that year. Not only was MIPS first in the digital home arena but was also widely replacing PowerPC in the area of enterprise networking. Total revenue was 70.96 million, and net profits for the 2010 fiscal year were $12.8 million, the company's first net profit since 2007.

In 2011 the first MIPS-based cell phones became available. MIPS expected that in the future, even more consumer electronic devices would provide Internet connections and would be networked together. The company believed that its products would continue to provide the performance, price, and power that these devices would require.

Diane Milne

PRINCIPAL SUBSIDIARIES

MIPS Technologies B.V. Germany Branch; MIPS Technologies B.V. Israel Branch; MIPS Technologies B.V. Japan Branch; MIPS Technologies B.V. (Netherlands); MIPS Technologies B.V., Korea Branch; MIPS Technologies B.V. Taiwan Branch; MIPS Technologies International Ltd. (Cayman Islands); MIPS Technologies International AG (Switzerland); MIPS Technologies (Shanghai) Co., Ltd. (China).

PRINCIPAL COMPETITORS

Advanced Micro Devices, Inc.; Applied Micro Circuits Corporation; ARM Holdings plc; Freescale Semiconductor, Inc.; Intel Corporation; International Business Machines Corporation; Tensilica, Inc.

FURTHER READING

"10-K: MIPS Technologies Inc."*EDGAR Online-Glimpse,* September 15. 2008.

Cuff, Daniel F., and Lawrence M. Fisher. "Business People; Data General Executive Joins MIPS Computer."*New York Times,* April 14 1987.

Khan, Ashis. "MIPS RISK: An Overview of the Architecture. "*Computer Design* 28, no. 22 (1989): S12+.

Kovsky, Steven. "Mips, in the Black, Going Public; Inks Service Deal with Tandem."*Digital Review* 6, no. 47 (1989): 50.

"MIPS Technologies Announces Divestiture of Its Analog Business Group–Final."*Fair Disclosure Wire,* May 8, 2009.

Sanches, Brenna. "Hennessy, John L. (1952 –)MIPS RISK: An Overview of the Architecture."*Newsmakers,* edited by Laura Avery. Detroit: Gale Group, 2002.

"SGI." In *International Directory of Company Histories,* edited by Tina Grant. Vol. 29. Detroit: St. James Press, 2000.

Mirion Technologies, Inc.

—————————■—————————

3000 Executive Parkway
Suite 222
San Ramon, California 94583
U.S.A.
Telephone: (925) 543-0800
Web site: http://www.mirion.com

Private Company
Incorporated: 2006
Employees: 700+ (2011)
Revenues: $228.1 million (2010)
NAICS: 334513 Instruments and Related Products
Manufacturing for Measuring, Displaying, and
Controlling Industrial Process Variables; 334515
Instrument Manufacturing for Measuring and Test-
ing Electricity and Electrical Signals; 334519 Other
Measuring and Controlling Device Manufacturing

■ ■ ■

Mirion Technologies, Inc., headquartered in the San
Francisco Bay Area, is a portfolio company of American
Capital Strategies that specializes in radiation detection,
measurement, and analysis solutions, along with associated monitoring products and services. With 13 production facilities in Canada, China, Finland, France,
Germany, the United Kingdom, and the United States,
Mirion is a global provider to the nuclear, defense, and
medical end markets. Among the company's offerings
are dosimeters, contamination and clearance monitors,
detection and identification instruments, radiation

monitoring systems, and electrical penetration assemblies for nuclear power plants.

Mirion operates through the five industry segments
of Health Physics, Radiation Monitoring Systems, Sensing Systems, Dosimetry Services, and Imaging Systems.
In addition to dosimeters and contamination and clearance monitors, the Health Physics division provides
equipment that detects radioactive isotopes. The largest
of Mirion's divisions, it was the company's top revenue
producer at $73 million, or 32 percent of Mirion's total
revenue in 2010. The Health Physics division works
with nuclear power and utility companies, medical and
specialized industries, government agencies, NATO
military and civil defense organizations, and engineering
companies. The Health Physics division offers a line of
radiation detection devices for homeland security and
military personnel, as well as a BioChem detection solution that allows for real-time identification of biological
pathogens.

The Radiation Monitoring Systems division of
Mirion has specialized in the nuclear radiation field for
over 50 years. Employing 260 people across Europe,
North America, and Asia, the RMS Division develops,
produces, qualifies, and markets a range of electronic
instruments for nuclear radiation monitoring. Its
products, available as standard or customized, have the
capability of detecting and controlling gamma radiation,
alpha and beta contamination of gases and particulates,
gamma contamination for iodine and liquids, neutron
dose rates for radiation protection, and neutron flux
density for reactor power monitoring. RMS customers
include research laboratories, universities, government

```
COMPANY PERSPECTIVES

Protecting people, property, and the environment.
```

agencies, and engineering businesses, as well as power and utility companies.

Mirion's Sensing Systems division manufactures radiation detection and measurement solutions, electrical penetration assemblies, and control equipment components used in nuclear power plants and nuclear research reactors all over the world. Formerly known as the Imaging and Sensing Technology Corporation, this sector has been in operation for almost 25 years. Under the Mirion name, it serves the U.S. Navy, power and utility companies, and engineering groups.

Also once part of the Imaging and Sensing Technology Corporation is Mirion's Imaging Systems division. This segment provides specialized closed- circuit camera systems for inspection and surveillance in hazardous nuclear radiation environments. Besides power and utility companies, the markets for this equipment include waste management plants, petrochemical facilities, and cement kilns.

Mirion Technologies Dosimetry Services division, formerly known as Global Dosimetry Solutions, is a supplier of radiation monitoring and analytical products and services that help determine employees' levels of radiation exposure in the nuclear and medical end markets. Radiation measurement is offered mainly through film, thermoluminescent, and track etch technologies. The main customers of this segment are power and utility companies, hospitals, government agencies, veterinarians, dentists, and other medical professionals.

PREDECESSOR COMPANIES: 1955–2006

In the first decade of the 21st century, many private equity groups explored new ways to leverage their portfolio holdings in order to increase their size and scale. American Capital Strategies, Ltd., was one such organization, merging three of its portfolio companies to form Mirion Technologies in January 2006. Two of those, Global Dosimetry Solutions Inc. and Imaging and Sensing Technology Corporation, were U.S. companies, while the third, SynOdys Group SA, was based in France. The result was a new company with a prominent global presence in the industries of health physics, nuclear power instrumentation, and civil and military defense.

Although Mirion Technologies was a new entity, the three companies from which it was formed had been in the radiation detection industry for over 50 years. Incorporated in 1988, Imaging and Sensing Technology Corporation (IST) had built a reputation as a leading manufacturer of radiation detectors and related control systems. By the early 1990s the company had built a solid reputation, establishing a sales office in the United Kingdom, buying Reuter-Stokes in Canada, and initiating a technology transfer program with Skoda in the Czech Republic. In 1994 *USA Today* named IST a Quality Vendor for the Defense Logistics Agency, the U.S. Department of Defense's largest combat support agency. At the same time IST was developing technologies that were used in a wide range of products, from space satellites to film productions, it was acquiring companies both at home and abroad at the close of the decade. In 2002 IST moved to a new corporate headquarters in Horseheads, New York, which would also stand as the headquarters of Mirion's Imaging Systems division. IST continued to expand its company base by purchasing Microprocessor Designs in the United Kingdom and Auxitrol SA in France in 2002 and 2004, respectively. Following the American Capital Strategies merger in 2006, IST became the foundation of Mirion's Sensing Systems division and Imaging Systems division.

Before merging into Mirion Technologies in 2006, Global Dosimetry Solutions Inc. had long been an industry leader in radiation monitoring services. The company, founded in 1969 as ICN Worldwide Dosimetry Services, was involved in pilot studies that led to the development of the Nuclear Regulatory Commission's National Voluntary Laboratory Accreditation Program. ICN Worldwide Dosimetry was accredited through the U.S. Department of Energy's Laboratory Accreditation Program (DOELAP) in 1996 and the Health and Safety Executive of the United Kingdom in 2001. In September 2003 American Capital acquired ICN Worldwide Dosimetry Services for $49 million, and the company's name was changed to Global Dosimetry Solutions, Inc. Based in Irvine, California, Global Dosimetry also operated other offices worldwide, serving such customers as Exelon, University of California at Los Angeles, Dominion Power, and Pfizer.

The company known as SynOdys at the time it was merged with IST and Global Dosimetry Solutions in 2006 traced its origins to a group spun off from the Technical University of Munich in 1955. It had been founded as a research and development group for nuclear radiation measurement equipment under the

KEY DATES

2006: American Capital Strategies, Ltd., merges three of its portfolio companies to form Mirion Technologies.

2007: Mirion is contracted by NUKEM Limited, one of the United Kingdom's largest nuclear decommissioning and disposal service providers.

2008: Mirion signs an agreement to supply radiation detection equipment for the 2008 Summer Olympics held in Beijing.

2009: The company showcases its products at the Eighth International Exhibition on the Nuclear Power Industry in China.

2010: Mirion withdraws its IPO due to market conditions.

industrial leadership of AEG. In 1968 AEG acquired Hartmann & Braun (H&B), a German company well known for industrial measurement and automation, merging it with the Munich group to form H&B Nuclear Measurement. Over the course of the next 20 years, products with the H&B brand were delivered to all nuclear power plants in Germany. Throughout the 1990s H&B Nuclear Measurement underwent a series of ownership changes. In 2001 it was purchased by MGP Instruments, a Smyrna, Georgia, company that had developed a new generation of radiation monitoring systems in 1993. In 2002 the SynOdys Group was formed, joining the brand marks Rados Technology, MGPI-H&B, and MGP Instruments. When Mirion Technologies was formed in 2006, SynOdys became the RMS division of Mirion Technologies and sold under the SynOdys, MGP Instruments, and Rados brands.

EARLY CONTRACTS: 2006–08

Several early contracts negotiated under the Mirion Technologies umbrella were with international companies. In April 2006 the Sensing Systems division was awarded a contract by AREVA NP to provide electrical penetration assemblies for the first European pressurized water reactor, to be built in Finland. In October that same year, the Sensing Systems division signed an agreement with Korea Hydro & Nuclear Power to provide electrical penetration assemblies for two new power plants to be built in the Republic of Korea. One month later, Mirion announced that Electricité de France (EDF), one of the largest nuclear power

plant operators in the world, would upgrade its body monitors with Mirion products. While EDF had previously purchased radiation monitoring systems through Mirion's MGPI brand, the November deal expanded the relationship between the two companies with an order for contamination and clearance portal products and services.

The nuclear power industry increasingly recognized Mirion as a leader for a wide range of nuclear system technologies. In 2007 the company was contracted by NUKEM Limited, one of the United Kingdom's largest nuclear decommissioning and disposal service providers, to deliver a radiation-tolerant closed-circuit television system to be used for monitoring the safe storage of intermediate level nuclear waste. In the United States, Exelon Nuclear, the nation's largest nuclear utility, renewed its agreement with Mirion's Dosimetry Services division in January 2008. At that time, Mirion was one of the leading dosimetry service providers in the nuclear sector, providing products and services to 58 of the 104 nuclear reactors in the country.

During the first two quarters of 2008, Mirion unveiled several enhanced products and services. One updated product was the newly designed Thermo Luminiscent Dosimeter Badge, which offered better environmental protection and ergonomic improvements over previous badges. Another enhanced device was the IST-Rees Allrad Mk2 inspection camera platform, a tool with advanced capabilities to meet in-vessel visual inspection (IVVI) requirements in high-radiation environments. In June 2008, the IST-Rees branded camera systems were used in the testing of NASA's Phoenix Mars Lander. In addition to releasing version 2.0 software for its popular IST Quadtek Spyrometer 3 system, Mirion launched a new corporate Web site arranged around the company's five operating divisions. Also that year, the company sold radiation detection security equipment to China Customs for the 2008 Summer Olympics held in Beijing.

BUSINESS OPERATIONS: 2009 AND BEYOND

Mirion's international reach remained strong in 2009. Dosimetry contracts were signed not only with EDF but also with the Swedish Rescue Service Agency, the Gösgen Nuclear Power Plant in Switzerland, and the Polish army. Mirion also entered into agreements to supply radiation detection and monitoring systems to the Swiss army, as well as to nuclear power plants in Russia, China, Lithuania, and Korea. China, which was aggressively expanding its nuclear power capacity, had 11 reactors under construction, in addition to the 11 that were already in operation throughout the region. Mirion, which had products installed in all of those reactors, predicted future support from the Chinese nuclear industry and showcased its products at China's Eighth International Exhibition on the Nuclear Power Industry in March 2009.

Mirion filed an IPO registration statement with the U.S. Securities and Exchange Commission on August 13, 2009, to raise around $100 million in a public offering, $8 million of which would be paid to American Capital Financial Services. Mirion also planned to use funds gained from the sale of its common stock to make strategic acquisitions of other companies. The price for Mirion's 11 million share offering was set between $15 and $17 per share. In May 2010, however, Mirion issued a statement indicating that it was postponing its IPO due to market conditions. As of February 2011, the company remained a private entity.

In addition to carrying out domestic operations, Mirion continued to be an international presence, conducting business in Italy, Slovakia, Spain, and Germany throughout 2010. In June 2010 Mirion's RMS Division launched MI-RMS, an online forum for radiation monitoring systems professionals across the globe. Besides allowing users to communicate about RMS products and services, the forum provided information about nuclear power plants and related Web links, as well as current events, such as trade shows and product notifications. By the end of 2010 Mirion products and services had been sold, directly and indirectly, to all nuclear power producers in the United States, 397 of the global installed base of 436 nuclear power reactors, and 17 of the 28 NATO militaries.

Having filed to go public, it seemed quite likely that Mirion would have its IPO sometime in the early 2010s when market conditions were favorable. After that, the company may use proceeds to pay down debt and begin acquiring smaller companies that fit into its five business segments.

Alicia Elley

PRINCIPAL DIVISIONS

Dosimetry Services; Health Physics; Imaging Systems; Radiation Monitoring Systems; Sensing Systems.

PRINCIPAL COMPETITORS

AREVA; General Atomics; Landauer, Inc.; Thermo Fisher Scientific Inc.

FURTHER READING

Dickinson, Casey J. "ITS's Parent Merges It with Two Other Nuclear-tech Companies." *Business Journal,* February 10, 2006, p. 1B–13B.

"Inspection Camera Platform." *Nuclear Plant Journal,* May/June 2008, 18.

"Mirion Technologies Imaging Systems Division Releases IST Quadtek Spyrometer 3 System Software 2.0." *Product News Network,* March 5, 2008.

"Mirion Technologies Launches On-Line Radiation Monitoring System User Forum." *Business Wire,* June 16, 2010.

"Mirion Technologies Postpones Initial Public Offering." *Datamonitor Financial Deals Tracker,* May 27, 2010.

"Standard & Poor's LCD Daily Loan Market Wrap-Up." lcdcomps.com, December 13, 2010.

"'Unmatched Expertise:' IST Offers a Variety of Products for Nuclear, High-Temperature Industrial and General Industrial Applications." *Manufacturing Today,* Fall 2008, 98.

Mountain Equipment
Co-operative

———■———

149 West Fourth Avenue
Vancouver, British Columbia V5Y 4A6
Canada
Telephone: (604) 707-3300
Toll Free: (888) 847-0700
Fax: (604) 731-6483
Web site: http://www.mec.ca

Co-operative
Founded: 1971
Employees: 1,500 (2009)
Sales: CAD 262.06 million ($266.70 million) (2009)
NAICS: 451110 Sporting Goods Stores

■ ■ ■

Mountain Equipment Co-operative (MEC) is the largest
retail co-operative in Canada. MEC offers a wide range
of sporting and outdoor products, such as hiking gear,
mountain bikes, and related outdoor apparel, from 14
stores across Canada. As a co-operative that emphasizes
a healthy, outdoors-oriented lifestyle, MEC is similar to
Recreation Equipment Incorporated (REI) in the United
States. Both organizations provide their members with
dividends after all costs are accounted for.

Since enjoyment of the outdoors is a central theme
of MEC, the organization promotes a variety of
environmental sustainability issues, eschewing disposable
products when possible and doing its best to be "green"
and minimize its ecological footprint.

THE NEED FOR OUTDOOR EQUIPMENT

Mountain Equipment Co-op was founded in the summer of 1971 by a group of six outdoor enthusiasts at the
University of British Columbia in Vancouver. Members
of the Varsity Outdoor Club, their main interests were
in mountaineering, rock climbing, and hiking in the
nearby mountains. The group was dissatisfied with the
quality, selection, and price of outdoor equipment available from local commercial outlets, so they did
something about it.

Despite being a modern cosmopolitan city, Vancouver, because of its geographic location and mild climate,
lends itself to an active outdoor lifestyle. It is often possible to combine snow skiing, a round of golf, and a
visit to the beach all in one day. Vancouver also serves as
the gateway to the beautiful but rugged interior of British Columbia. Made up largely of the Canadian Rockies, the interior attracts outdoor enthusiasts and ecotour-
ists from around the world.

With a population of just over four million in a
landmass of 947,800 square kilometers (365,000 square
miles), much of the province is sparsely populated and
well suited to nature enthusiasts, but those who venture
into the interior on adventure holidays need the right
equipment to make the most of their recreation time
and to keep themselves safe and injury free. It was this
necessity that drove the original founders of MEC to
form their co-op, and the same necessity of good gear is
required today. According to the British Columbia
Search and Rescue Association, more than 1,300 people
are reported lost, missing, or injured every year.

FORMING A CO-OP

A co-op can be defined as an organization which is owned by its members, who use its services or are employed there. In the case of Mountain Equipment Co-op, the choice of forming a co-operative as opposed to some other form of commercial venture may have been a sign of the times, or it could have rested on a lack of start-up capital and the favorable tax status that co-ops enjoy.

Co-operatives are popular in Canada and make significant contributions to the economy. The earliest co-ops were formed in the 1840s when the country was still known as British North America. According to the government of Canada, there are 8,400 co-ops in Canada. Combined, the co-operatives employ some 152,000 people and hold more than CAD 209 billion in assets. According to a study conducted in 2008 by the Province of Quebec's Ministry of Industry and Commerce, co-op enterprises survive nearly twice as long as investor-owned enterprises.

With an original mandate to "sell good gear at fair prices for self-propelled activities," MEC went into business. To buy or rent equipment an individual was required to become a member of the co-op. Life time memberships were, and still are, CAD 5. A membership not only entitled members to shop at the co-op, it also entitled them to vote on issues affecting the organization and to a share of the profits in the form of a patronage dividend.

A year after its formation, and largely dependent on volunteers as staff, MEC was able to move into its first tiny store.

GROWING PAINS

Competing in the marketplace created some problems for the co-op. The original focus on supply gear for mountaineering, rock climbing, and hiking was too narrow to build a business on. The product line needed to be expanded, so it soon came to include running and fitness apparel, snow and water sports gear, tents, and other outdoor apparel and accessories.

Another problem was in the pricing of its goods. With a mandate to provide top gear at reasonable prices, MEC would retail its merchandise based on earning enough to cover salaries and overhead. As the primary goal of the co-op was to serve its members as opposed to making a profit, MEC was often selling goods for less than its competitors were. This led to problems with suppliers, who on occasion stopped supplying merchandise to the co-op. MEC dealt aggressively with suppliers to keep its costs low and once successfully sued a sunglass supplier who had cut the co-op off. It also began to manufacture its own line of equipment.

By the early 1990s Mountain Equipment had become the largest retailer of outdoor recreation equipment in Canada. Sales were growing at 25 percent per year and reached CAD 37 million in 1991.

There were several reasons why Mountain Equipment Co-op was doing so well. In addition to keeping costs low, the co-op focused on its products and lines. It strived to hire employees who shared an enthusiasm for the outdoors and for adventure sports, and who were passionate about social and environmental concerns. It emphasized product knowledge and paid employees to attend training seminars, placing more weight on expertise than seniority.

Another factor was the relationship between the consumer and the store. Customers had to be members of the co-operative, and in many instances that created a bond of trust between the consumer and the store. MEC determined that the three most important features that its customer/members were looking for were quality, value, and service. Co-op sales staff were trained to discover the needs of the membership and find products to fit those needs.

Mountain Equipment Co-op also set itself up as an information source, often offering seminars and slide shows on the products it sold and on adventure sports. Its business practices seemed to be working, and by the end of 1991 membership in MEC had grown to 360,000.

SUCCESS AND GROWTH:
1990–2000

Through the 1990s, Mountain Equipment Co-op enjoyed phenomenal success and cautious growth. In 1996 sales topped CAN 100 million for the first time. By 1997 it had opened new stores in Calgary, Toronto, and Ottawa and had developed one of the largest mail-order businesses in the country with more than 925,000 members on the mailing list.

KEY DATES

1971: Mountain Equipment Co-op founded.
1972: Company opens first store.
1996: Sales exceed CAD 100 million for first time.
2002: Paul Robinson appointed CEO.
2009: Membership in the Co-op reaches three million.

One of the quirks of operating a co-operative in Canada was of great assistance in planning growth. By law, members of a co-op were entitled to share in the profits of the organization in the form of a patronage dividend. The dividend was based upon a percentage of the amount the member had purchased, in the sense that the more the purchases, the higher the dividend. In order to accomplish this, co-operatives had to keep accurate records of what members purchased and where they purchased it. In addition, the mailing list and number of catalogs sent out to members rendered an accurate measure of how many members were in each geographic locality. This allowed MEC to carefully and accurately plan when and where to open new stores.

In 2000 Mountain Equipment Co-op made a significant move when it hired Paul Robinson as its chief executive officer. Robinson was raised in British Columbia and had studied geography at university prior to becoming a government park ranger. Twice decorated for bravery by the governor general of Canada, Robinson also led BC Housing, a crown corporation that developed social housing. He had joined MEC as a member in 1974. The Robinson years would be marked by growth and expansion and a renewed commitment to the environment, sustainability, and social projects.

ETHICAL STANDARDS AND ENVIRONMENTAL CAUSES: 2001–07

In 2001 the MEC Web site was revamped, allowing members to buy online. Its product mix was approximately 50 percent apparel and 50 percent equipment. Nearly half of the products it distributed were designed and manufactured by the co-operative itself, and MEC applied strict ethical standards to the way it conducted its business. While design was handled internally, manufacturing was contracted out to various suppliers. MEC established a supplier's code of conduct to ensure goods were made in an ethical manner. It would occasionally audit suppliers' facilities looking for compliance with employment standards, worker pay, safety, and environmental practices. Suppliers who did not measure up were dropped.

Since 1987 MEC had contributed a portion of sales to social and environmental causes. This resonated well with its membership, but protecting and preserving the environment also made good business sense. MEC funded community grants and promoted Canadian parks and protected areas. By 2008 MEC had contributed more CAD 12 million.

In 2003 MEC opened the first green retail outlet in Quebec when it opened a store in Montreal. The 45,000-square-foot store featured solar and geothermal energy for heating and cooling, natural sunlight to replace electric lights, and a rooftop garden to filter smoggy air and to provide insulation.

In 2007 Robinson left MEC for a position with the David Suzuki Foundation, an environmental group. Under his watch, MEC had grown from five to 11 stores and 2007 sales were CAD 239 million. The co-op donated CAD 2.4 million to environmental causes.

In the winter of 2007 the Mountain Equipment Board selected David Labistour as the new CEO. It was the first time in the co-operative's history that the CEO was an internal appointment. Labistour, a South African immigrant to Canada, had been Mountain Equipment's head of design since 2003. Previously, he had been employed by adidas.

LONG-TERM GOALS: 2007 AND BEYOND

In 2007 MEC published its first Accountability Report, a comprehensive analysis of the social, environmental, and economic impact of the business. It followed this up with a second report in 2009 in which it established three new long-term goals for the organization. The first, termed Active Canadians, was to increase participation in wilderness-oriented recreation throughout the country. The second goal, Conservation, saw the co-op support the stewardship of a comprehensive network of parks, wilderness areas, and outdoor recreation opportunities in Canada. The final long-term goal, Marketplace Change, hoped to foster change toward environmental, social, and economic sustainability in the marketplace.

Under Labistour, MEC introduced its own line of bicycles in 2009. Designed in-house and manufactured to the co-op's standards for quality value and performance, the bikes came in four categories: mountain, road, special, and urban.

In May 2010 MEC unveiled a revamped Web site. Having surpassed the three million mark for memberships in 2009, the co-op Web site was busier than ever. Online visits had jumped 25 percent over 2008, and the site was now recording more than 12 million visits per year.

In November 2010 MEC opened its 14th store, in Barrie, Ontario. It seemed likely that the organization would continue to grow steadily throughout the 2010s, and while competition from REI and other retailers would always be a potential damper on growth, the loyalty and dedication of MEC's co-op members would help insulate the company from its competitors.

Ian MacDonald

PRINCIPAL DIVISIONS

Activity; Clothing; Gear; Special Assortments.

PRINCIPAL COMPETITORS

Coast Mountain Sports; Recreation Equipment, Inc.; Patagonia, Inc.; SportChek.

FURTHER READING

Cayo, Don. "Gear-without-Guilt, Co-op Now a Goliath." *Vancouver Sun,* April 28, 2007.

MacQueen, Ken. "The Anti-Retailer." *MacLeans,* April 29, 2002.

"A Monument to the Environment." *Montreal Gazette,* November 22, 2003.

"Mountain Equipment Boss Leaps to Suzuki Foundation." *Vancouver Sun,* September 7, 2007.

Threndyle, S. "Mountain Magic, Market Savvy." *Canadian Business,* February 1992.

Mumias Sugar Company Limited

Kakamega-Bungoma Highway
P.O. Box Private Bag
Mumias, Western Province 50102
Kenya
Telephone: (56) 641620/1
Fax: (56) 641234
Web site: http://www.mumias-sugar.com

Public Company
Founded: 1971
Employees: 1,523 (2010)
Sales: KES 15.6 billion ($192 million) (2010)
Stock Exchanges: Nairobi
NAICS: 111930 Sugarcane Farming; 221119 Other Electric Power Generation; 311312 Cane Sugar Refining

■ ■ ■

Mumias Sugar Company Limited (MSC) is located in the Butere-Mumias district of Kenya's Western Province. The company engages in the principal activities of production and distribution of sugar and sugar byproducts in Kenya. The company also supplies sugar to international destinations under opportunities presented by regional and international commerce bodies such as Common Market for Eastern and Southern Africa (COMESA) and the African-Caribbean Protocol (ACP).

In 2010 MSC processed over 2.3 billion tons of sugar cane, yielding approximately 235,000 tons of sugar. This scale of production allowed MSC to command roughly three-fifths of the market for sugar in Kenya. However, MSC is in the process of diversifying its operations, and as such, and company operates a power plant designed to burn waste material derived from the sugar production process. In 2010, this allowed MSC to generate 34 MW of electricity.

MUMIAS SUGAR COMPANY ESTABLISHED: 1971

In 1967 the government of Kenya granted Bookers Agricultural and Technical Services the responsibility to conduct a feasibility study for growing sugarcane in Mumias. This decision paved the way for the establishment of one of the most successful companies in the country. In addition to conducting the study, Bookers Agricultural and Technical Services also initiated pilot projects that demonstrated the viability of sugarcane production in Mumias. The feasibility study report recommended the establishment of a sugar production factory in Mumias. The report further recommended the establishment and recognition of an outgrower farmers' scheme as the main supplier of cane to a specified factory. (In this type of contract farming arrangement, cane growers work together with sugar processors to ensure quality, quantity, and delivery schedules throughout the entire farming and production process.)

Mumias Sugar Company was finally established on June 29, 1971, following the government's adoption and implementation of the feasibility study findings. The government took up 70.76 percent of the total shares to become the majority shareholder of the company. The company's management services were contracted to Bookers Agricultural and Technical Services under the leadership of Booker Tate.

Production operations in Mumias Sugar Company commenced July 1973. The factory supported an hourly production capacity of 80 tons of cane, a rate that produced a total of 194,217 tons in the first year of production. Sugar production capacity was later expanded to an hourly processing rate of 125 tons of cane in July 1976. In 1979 the company's management initiated strategies for doubling the production capacity of the factory to meet the ever-growing demand for sugar in the local and international markets. The target was to expand the factory's hourly processing capacity to 300 tons of cane. The expansion task was substantive because it involved the construction of a new factory and required a number of years to achieve. Given that the company's management had already awarded the contracts for supplies required for the project in August 1976, the government granted consent for the commissioning of the project in 1979.

Mumias Sugar Company maintained a low profile for the most of the early 1980s because of insufficient sugarcane yields. Nonetheless, the company engaged in several conspicuous strategic activities. The completion of the production expansion project in 1985 was one of the major accomplishments by the company in the decade. The factory's expansion was a tremendous success because the annual milling capacity of the company was increased to 210,000 tons of cane. The new milling capacity, however, was exceeded in 1987 when annual processing capacity reached 220,000 tons of cane. The unexpected performance set in motion plans to expand the company's production capacity once again to match the prevailing market demand conditions.

Mumias Sugar Company also dedicated much of the 1980s to the initiation of many social development programs that promoted education and sports among communities in Mumias. The company concentrated on the development of Mumias Sugar Football Club, Mumias Sugar Central Primary School, Mumias Complex Primary School, and Mumias Booker's Academy.

FACTORY RATIONALIZATION PROJECTS: 1993–2000

In 1993 Mumias Sugar Company initiated a five-year project for rationalizing production processes in the factory. The project involved a phase-by-phase enhancement of the different core and support components of production. The company constructed a new boiler with an hourly production capacity of 110 tons in addition to installing a turbo alternator with an output of 7.0 megawatts. Customized clarifier components and evaporators for juice as well as diffusing equipment suited for sugarcane milling machinery were also introduced and enhanced. The successful completion of the project in rationalization 1997 expanded the company's daily production capacity to 7,000 tons. Moreover, the sugar extraction efficiency was also enhanced to 86 percent, up from 82 percent. The achievement of the twin objectives of production expansion and efficiency marked a major milestone in the company's strategic objectives.

The rationalization of the company's systems and work processes was extended to the human resources team in 1999. This development came after appraisals revealed the redundancy of a significant portion of the company's staff when compared to existing operational requirements. Some of the redundancy was caused by the automation of certain labor-intensive operations. To deal with this situation, the company initiated an innovative scheme that encouraged workers in overstaffed departments to take early retirement. The early retirement scheme enabled the management of the company to achieve a 26 percent reduction in the number of employees to 3,400 by the fourth quarter of 2000.

Mumias Sugar Company experienced a major strategic shift in its marketing and product diversification at the beginning of the 21st century. The company employed more aggressive approaches toward marketing, diversification, and product distribution processes, with the aim of cementing and expanding its market leadership position nationally and regionally. In addition to establishing an intensive distribution network with a nationwide reach, the company introduced the 2-kilogram branded packaging of its sugar product in 2000. The conclusion of a power supply deal in 2000 for the sale of 10,000 MWh of electricity annually to Kenya Power and Lighting Company (KPLC) marked a major diversification achievement for Mumias Sugar Company.

GROWTH AND EXPANSION: 2001–06

Mumias Sugar Company conducted a successful initial public offering (IPO) in November 2001. The Kenyan

KEY DATES

1971: After various government feasibility studies, the Mumias Sugar Company is established.

1993: Upgrades to sugar factory help increase sugar yields.

2001: Mumias Sugar Company Limited lists on the Nairobi Stock Exchange.

2006: Company floats a secondary share offer.

2009: MSC commissions a power cogeneration plant.

government offloaded 300 million of its shares in the company, and the IPO raised a total of KES 1.12 billion. The IPO reduced the government's shareholding in the company to 38.4 percent. The company was subsequently listed and commenced trading on the Nairobi Stock Exchange.

The company registered mixed fortunes in 2002 when the sugar industry was hit by erratic declines in sugar prices. However, the company's revenue shortfall was partially offset by increased sales of its 2-kilogram branded sugar. The expiry of the management contract with Bookers Agricultural and Technical Services in 2003 paved the way for the appointment of a new management team. Dr. Evans Kidero was appointed as the managing director through a competitive recruitment process.

The year 2004 marked a major turning point in the operational and growth activities of Mumias Sugar Company Limited following the achievement of unprecedented after-tax profits. The growth of the company's sugar production volume by 11 percent in 2004 resulted from the processing of 264,000 metric tons of cane. Market penetration strategies were also intensified through the enhancement of national distribution and supply networks. The capacity of the 2-kilogram branded packaging was doubled in addition to the introduction of half- kilogram and quarter-kilogram Mumias Sugar branded packets.

The revitalized operational capacity of the company resulted in the production of more than 269,000 metric tons of sugar in 2005. This was the highest production the company had registered since it was founded. The company marked another milestone when the long-awaited strategic plans for the exploitation of power cogeneration and establishment of a plant for ethanol production gained the approval of the Board of Directors. The management further reviewed and refurbished the production capacity of the factory to an hourly rate of 410 tons. The enormous successes of 2005 were crowned by the signing of a power sale contract with KPLC for the supply of electricity at the rate of 2.2 MWh to the national grid.

In 2006 Mumias Sugar Company launched a KES 700 million expansion project targeted at increasing the annual sugar production capacity to 300,000 tons by 2012. The company also awarded a $40 million contract for the upgrade of the electricity cogeneration unit to Avant Garde Engineers and Consultants (P) Limited, an India-based company. The upgrading project involved new installations of turbine alternators and 45 bar boilers. The revitalization was designed to expand the power production capacity to 35 MW. The company would then achieve the potential to export as much as 25 MW to the national grid. The upgrade of the cogeneration plant effectively advanced the company's objective of exploiting 50 percent of its potential for generating electricity.

The signing of a 10-year carbon trading agreement with the Japanese Carbon Finance Company Limited was the other landmark achievement of Mumias Sugar Company in 2006. In a deal that would be implemented between 2009 and 2019, the company would be rewarded with carbon credits as a token for substituting thermal electricity production with a green (baggase) energy production alternative. The company confirmed its commitment to complete the power cogeneration plant by January 2009. Plans to venture into a KES 3.6 billion ethanol production plant were also initiated in 2006. March 2009 was agreed upon as the appropriate commencement date of the ethanol project.

Mumias Sugar Company conducted a secondary sale in December 2006 to float an additional 18 percent of the government's shareholding in the company. The offer price for the secondary sale was KES 49.50 at a time when the company's share price was KES 55 per share. The secondary sale raised a total of KES 4.3 billion, and the government's stake in the company was reduced to 20.4 percent.

SOCIAL RESPONSIBILITY AND OTHER PROJECTS: 2008–10

The business environment in Kenya was briefly scuttled by the post-election crisis in the first half of 2008. (The disputed presidential election in late December 2007 led to violence in several areas in which up to 1,500 people were killed and as many as 250,000 displaced from their homes.) Many companies struggled to regain lost business opportunities, and Mumias Sugar Company was no exception. Nonetheless, the business performance prospects of the company received a major boost in September 2008 following a government policy intervention on regional international trade in sugar products. The minister of agriculture issued a directive stopping the importation of sugar products from the COMESA region. This development led to a steep reduction in the importation of inexpensice sugar into the country. The company realized increased sales volumes because decreased importation stabilized sugar prices in Kenya.

The company also benefited from the shortfall of global sugar supply that rocked the markets in 2008 and led to an increase in sugar prices. The company's 2008 calendar climaxed with the opening of the Nabongo Cultural Center and Matawa Bridge in December in ceremonies presided over by Kenya's prime minister, Raila Odinga. The commissioning of the two projects marked a major milestone in the company's corporate social responsibility commitments. The Shibale Water project was the other major community development initiative spearheaded by the company in 2008.

The year 2009 was associated with prosperity for Mumias Sugar Company. The volume of sugar sales sold by the company stabilized at 231,014 tons despite the adverse effect of the 2008 postelection skirmishes in Kenya. The year was also marked by the successful completion of key strategic projects and initiation of several other new projects. The ethanol production project was commenced in March 2009. This was followed by the commissioning of the cogeneration plant in May 2009, when the company started exporting power from the cogeneration project to KPLC's national grid. The cogeneration plant realized a total of KES 13 million in gross revenues between May 2009 and the close of the financial year in June 2009.

Mumias Sugar Company experienced a 2 percent growth in sugar production to 235,792 metric tons in 2010. The production growth saw the company's sales increase by 32 percent to KES 15.6 billion in the financial year ended 30 June 2010, up from KES 11.28 billion in the previous financial year.

The company however, registered a 2.5 percent drop in profits after tax in the financial year ending June 30, 2010. The slight reduction in annual profits was attributed to the substantial impact of the tax credit benefits awarded to the company in August 2009, following 150 percent investment deductions on the power cogeneration plant. Notably, the gross revenue from the power cogeneration plant shot to KES 359 million in the financial year ending June 2010.

FUTURE PLANS

As it looked toward the future, Mumias Sugar Company planned to enter a private joint venture with the Tana Athi River Development Authority (TARDA). With the pilot project already underway, the eventual signing of the private joint venture would pave the way for the cultivation of 20,000 hectares of sugarcane in the Tana River Delta. The joint venture gained approval from the National Environmental Authority (NEMA) in June 2008 despite objections from environment organizations. Mumias Sugar Company had plans to commission the ethanol production plant under construction by December 2011. A prefeasibility study conducted by the company to ascertain the economic and infrastructural viability of ethanol indicated the possibilities of achieving an annual output of 22 million liters of ethanol from molasses.

Plans to optimize the factory's production capacity by increasing sugar production from 265,000 tons to 300,000 tons annually by 2012 were also underway. The company's prospects for future growth in revenues and profits before tax were set at KES 22 billion and KES 5 billion, respectively, by 2012. The management of the company also planned to enhance its product diversification program by completing the development of a water bottling plant by June 2011. Moreover, the company's plans to acquire a number of sugar milling companies were well on course after the government of Kenya divested its interests in four major sugar mills in October 2010. The government divestiture set the pace for privatization of the sugar millers and provided an opportunity for Mumias Sugar Company to pursue expansion through strategic acquisitions.

Paul Ingati

PRINCIPAL COMPETITORS

Chemelil Sugar Company; Muhoroni Sugar Company; Nzoia Sugar Company; South Nyanza Sugar Company; Western Kenya Sugar Company.

FURTHER READING

Bonyo, Joseph. "Sugar Company to Start Production of Ethanol Next Year, Says Chief." *All Africa,* September 27, 2010. Accessed October 14, 2010. http://allafrica.com/stories/20 1009271790.html.

"Kenya: Projected Sugar Cane Plantations May Wipe Out Invaluable Tana River Delta." World Rainforest Movement, Bulletin 145, August 2009. Accessed October 15, 2010. http://www.wrm.org.uy/bulletin/145/Kenya.html.

Okoth, Jackson. "Mumias Sugar Share: Was the Market Misled?" *Financial Post,* Issue 120, April 2007. Accessed

October 17, 2010. http://www.financialpost.co.ke/Pdfs/FP 0ISSUE%20126.pdf.

Ombok, Eric. "Mumias Sugar Rises Most in 2 Weeks on Loan Agreement." *Bloomberg Business Week,* September 17, 2009. Accessed October 16, 2010. http://www.businessweek.com/ news/2010-09-27/mumias-sugar-rises-most-in-2-weeks-on-loan-agreement.html.

———. "Mumias Sugar's Annual Profit Falls on Earlier Tax Credit, Company Says." *Bloomberg Business Week,* August 26, 2010. Accessed October 17, 2010. http://www.bloom berg.com/news/2010-08-26/mumias-sugar-s-annual-profit-falls-on-earlier-tax-credit-company-says.html.

"Mumias Sugar Company Limited." Rich.co.ke. Accessed October 20, 2010. http://www.rich.co.ke/rcdata/company. php?i=Mzg%3D.

National Cattlemen's Beef Association

———— ■ ————

9110 East Nichols Avenue
Suite 300
Centennial, Colorado 80112
U.S.A.
Telephone: (303) 694-0305
Toll Free: (866) 233-3872
Fax: (303) 694-2851
Web site: http://www.beefusa.org

Nonprofit Organization
Founded: 1898 as National Live Stock Association
Budget: $42.2 million (2011)
NAICS: 813910 Business Associations

■ ■ ■

The National Cattlemen's Beef Association (NCBA) is a national trade association and marketing organization that serves approximately one million U.S. cattle famers. What began as a grassroots organization in 1898 continues to protect the economic, political, and social interests of the U.S. cattle industry. With over 28,000 individual members and 64 state affiliate, breed, and industry organization members, the NCBA is the largest national marketing and trade association dedicated solely to U.S. cattle producers. The organization receives funding from the federal Beef Checkoff program, as well as member dues, which it uses to back research in the areas of beef safety and human nutrition. Additionally, the NCBA sponsors the Cattle Industry Annual Convention and NCBA Trade Show, an event that draws more than 6,000 attendees each year.

EARLY CATTLE ASSOCIATIONS

While the history of the NCBA dates back to the U.S. cattle industry of the 1800s, the first cattlemen's association was established long before then. The Western Hemisphere's first cattlemen's association, known as the *Mesta,* was organized in the early 16th century in Mexico City. Formed to help control theft, the Mesta, which required cattle owners to have a distinctive brand that was registered in an official log in Mexico City, would serve as a model for other organizations hundreds of years later.

As it was not unusual for cattle to run away from ranches in Mexico, the animals eventually made their way to what would become the United States, many migrating to Texas and California. During the 1500s and 1600s, European settlers established the cattle industry in Virginia, Florida, and New England when they brought the livestock with them to the new world. However, a formal association for cattle growers was not formed in the United States until the founding of the Colorado Stock Growers in 1867. Several other similar organizations followed, although none were successful as a national organization.

A national cattle producers organization was finally born in 1898 when John W. Springer and Charles F. Martin, both members of the Livestock Committee of the Denver Chamber of Commerce and Trade Board, coordinated a National Stock Growers Convention in Denver, Colorado. At the convention, which hosted over 2,000 attendees, what would become the National Cattlemen's Beef Association was formed as the National Live Stock Association (NLSA), an organization that, founders hoped, would be free from the sway of political promoters. The NLSA served every sector of the livestock industry, not just cattle but hogs, sheep, chickens, goats, and horses. After one year, NLSA represented approximately 5,000 producers with nine million head of livestock at a combined investment of $300 million. It sponsored the 1899 National Stock Growers Convention, which focused on such important industry issues as humane rail transportation, the modernization of meat packing houses, national and state quarantines, livestock inspections, and highbred stock.

The NLSA continued to prosper over the next few years until economic hardships and land disputes caused dissent among members, leading to the formation of several splinter groups. Cattle production took a devastating downturn in the early 20th century, when prices dropped from an average of $24 to $15 per animal, while rail rates increased, only adding to the growing tensions within the industry. In 1901 the American Cattle Growers Association was created to represent only cattlemen, particularly against sheep herders. In 1905 a group attempted to deny NLSA membership to railroads. When this movement was defeated, another splinter group was formed, the American Stock Growers Association. Throughout those troubling times, NLSA directors sought to restore harmony among the different groups, eventually succeeding in 1906 when the NLSA and the American Stock Growers Association merged into the American National Live Stock Association (ANLSA).

GOVERNMENT REGULATION: 1906–34

That same year, *The Jungle* by Upton Sinclair was published. An immediate best-seller, the novel exposed the unsanitary conditions and corruption found in meat packing plants. U.S. president Theodore Roosevelt was so horrified by descriptions of dead rats being ground into sausage and diseased cows being slaughtered and sold that he called for sweeping reform of the meat packing industry. As a result, Congress passed the Pure

Food and Drugs Act of 1906 and the Meat Inspection Act of 1906, both of which reshaped the beef industry, as they established the nation's first regulations for the quality and safety of meat. ANLSA successfully lobbied for meat inspectors to be paid by the federal government, not by meat packing plants.

From 1906 to 1914, ANLSA focused on a number of the same issues that would face the organization in the upcoming decades, including export and trade concerns, control of public land, and declines in beef consumption. As in previous years, livestock transportation was a major bone of contention, with members fighting railroad companies over high rates, slow service, and limited car availability. Other areas of concern were the spread of animal disease, increased livestock commission charges, livestock lost to predators, and wildly fluctuating market prices. Many cattlemen thought that the extreme rise and fall of prices was caused by anti-competitive activities among the "Beef Trust," or "Big Five" meat packers, companies that were seeing record profits.

A 1919 investigation by the Federal Trade Commission revealed that the packers were indeed running a monopoly, prompting ANLSA and other associations to petition for federal regulation of the packing industry. Their efforts were rewarded with the creation of the Packers and Stockyards Act of 1921. This law granted the secretary of agriculture the authority to oversee the operations of meat packers and live poultry dealers and to regulate livestock marketing activities at public stockyards. One year later, the National Live Stock and Meat Board was formed by representatives from all sectors of the beef industry for the purpose of promoting all red meats (beef, lamb, and pork). In 1926 federal meat grading was introduced.

The U.S. beef industry did not escape the devastating effects of the Great Depression of the 1930s. Beef exports were down because World War I had financially devastated many European countries. Cattle prices plunged, while unemployment rates grew. A drought hit the Great Plains, drying up wells and watering holes all over the country. Although cattlemen hauled water long distances, cattle died by the thousands. Certainly the situation was bleak when President Franklin D. Roosevelt took office, and one of the first actions he took was initiating the New Deal, which consisted of such programs as the Agricultural Adjustment Act. This legislation, the first government attempt to manage agriculture, paid farmers to reduce their planted acreage and to store commodities. Another product of the New Deal was the Taylor Grazing Act of 1934, a law that regulated grazing on public lands.

KEY DATES

1898: The National Cattlemen's Beef Association is founded as the National Live Stock Association (NLSA).

1906: The NLSA and the American Stock Growers Association merge to form the American National Live Stock Association (ANLSA).

1906: Congress passes the Pure Food and Drugs Act of 1906 and the Meat Inspection Act of 1906, reshaping the beef industry.

1921: The Packers and Stockyards Act of 1921 is created for the federal regulation of the packing industry.

1951: ANLSA's name is changed to the American National Cattlemen's Association (ANCA).

1973: President Richard Nixon places a price freeze on beef, causing "the wreck."

1996: Beef sales plummet after a segment about "mad cow" disease airs on the *Oprah Winfrey Show*.

2010: An audit reveals that NCBA officials have misappropriated funds.

POSTWAR LEGISLATION: 1945–86

World War II brought new challenges for the beef industry. As incomes doubled nationwide, cattlemen struggled to meet the supply and demand of consumers, especially since 30 percent of all beef production was reserved for the military. Despite frustrations with price controls, rationing, and black market trading, ANLSA members pledged to provide the United States with an adequate beef supply for both consumers and the armed forces.

ANLSA changed its name to the American National Cattlemen's Association (ANCA) in 1951. When the Korean War began that year, cattlemen once again tackled issues of supply and demand, price controls, and the black market. As drought hit the Great Plains in 1953, many ranchers were glad to receive government aid. ANCA president Jay Taylor, however, realized that these subsidies were temporary and encouraged cattlemen to improve their situations through beef promotion. He set the precedent for the NCBA educational programs, seminars, and conferences that would be the cornerstone of the organization's support for people involved in the beef industry.

Protests against rising beef prices and boycotts of beef by consumer activists during the 1960s and early 1970s drove President Richard Nixon to impose a price freeze on beef in March 1973. This move led to what was known as "the wreck." Anticipating high prices when the freeze would be lifted in September, cattle feeders delayed the marketing of cattle, which resulted in a surplus of animals when the freeze ended and a significant price drop. As losses ran $100 to $200 per head, a large number of cattlemen went bankrupt, and numerous feed yards closed. It was estimated that the entire beef industry had sustained losses of $5 billion. ANCA, joining with the National Livestock Feeders Association into the National Cattlemen's Association (NCA) in 1977, and other cattlemen's organizations rallied by lobbying for a national beef checkoff program.

After two failed attempts, the Beef Promotion and Research Act, or the Beef Checkoff Program, was enacted by Congress with the passage of the 1985 Farm Bill. Under the act, which went into effect in October 1986, beef producers were required to pay $1 per head every time an animal was sold throughout its lifetime. Most in the industry considered it a self-help program. Out of every dollar collected, 50 cents was appropriated to the NCA for national programs, and 50 cents went to the beef council in each state, allowing cattlemen as a group to decide how the money would be invested. Intended to encourage producers to sell more beef, money from the checkoff program was used for advertising, research and development of new products, and public relations.

NATIONAL CONTROVERSY: 1990–2000

Throughout the 1990s, the NCA, which joined with the Beef Industry Council of the Meat Board to form the National Cattlemen's Beef Association in 1996, found itself at the center of controversy concerning the safety of U.S. beef. In 1989 the European Union had instituted a ban on U.S. beef in protest against the feeding of growth hormones to 90 percent of cattle in the United States. Although the NCBA cited studies showing that hormones were safe, many European countries continued to boycott U.S. beef over the course of the decade, resulting in estimated losses of $140 million each year for the U.S. cattle industry. The World Trade Organization eventually ruled that the sanction violated fair trade agreements and gave the European Union until May 13, 1999, to lift the ban.

Due to a growing belief that beef was unhealthy because of its fat and cholesterol content, the industry was experiencing a decline in consumption by U.S. consumers as well, prompting the NCBA to launch a multimillion-dollar advertising campaign. One highly successful commercial launched in 1992 featured the slogan "Beef: It's What's for Dinner," and recipes for quick and nutritious meals appeared in magazines. The organization also lobbied in the mid-1990s to have libel and defamation laws passed in 13 states. These food libel laws gave agribusiness the right to sue individuals, including journalists and citizen groups, who made false and disparaging statements about perishable food products.

The beef industry invoked those libel laws in April 1996 after talk show host Oprah Winfrey interviewed former rancher Howard Lyman. The topic of the show was the outbreak of bovine spongiform encephalopathy, or "mad cow" disease, that had recently affected Great Britain's cattle population. In March 1996 British health officials reported that consumption of beef infected with mad cow disease had been linked to a similar fatal human brain disease. Although there had been no cases of mad cow disease in the United States at the time, Lyman criticized the U.S. cattle industry's practice of feeding rendered cattle and sheep by-products to livestock, a practice that had spread the disease in Great Britain. Winfrey responded, "It has just stopped me cold from eating another burger!"

As a result of the show and fears about mad cow disease in general, beef consumption plummeted, costing the industry an estimated $10 million to $12 million. NCBA's Pal Engler and a group of Texas cattlemen sued both Winfrey and Lyman, seeking damages of $11 million. In a trial that lasted six weeks in early 1998, an Amarillo, Texas, jury ruled Winfrey and Lyman not liable for the statements they had made on the *Oprah Winfrey Show.* The plaintiffs appealed the case. However, a federal appeals court in 2000 decided that although Winfrey had "melodramatized" mad cow disease she had not given false information about it or defamed U.S. cattlemen. While Winfrey celebrated the verdicts as victories for the freedom of speech, the NCBA took advantage of the media attention to reassure the public that beef produced in the United States was not infected with mad cow disease.

HEALTH SCARES AND GLOBAL EXPORTS

In the first decade of the 21st century, the NCBA continued to face backlash from health scares associated with cattle. Recognizing that *E. coli,* a bacteria that causes severe intestinal disturbance in humans, was a consumer concern significantly impacting the sale of beef, NCBA in 2003 led the beef industry's initiative to develop and distribute science-based practices to help reduce the risk of outbreaks. Whereas per capita beef consumption had once seen an all-time high of 94 pounds, that number had dropped to 65 pounds by 2007 due in part to the public's fear of *E. coli.* In 2006 an outbreak of *E. coli* in spinach was traced to cattle feces in fields where the produce was grown. On December 24, 2009, the U.S. Food Safety and Inspection Services issued a recall of 248,000 pounds of beef products after an investigation of an *E. coli* outbreak showed that most of the sick people had consumed beef, many in restaurants. In an effort to combat the spread of *E. coli,* the NCBA continued to dedicate a large portion of its budget to food safety research.

NCBA's financial records came under scrutiny in July 2010 when an audit revealed insufficient documentation and noncompliance. According to the report, expenditures had been improperly billed to the Beef Checkoff fund from January 2008 to February 2010. After further review, NCBA arranged an agreement with the federal government to repay $216,944 to the Beef Checkoff program in January 2011.

At the onset of 2011, the NCBA addressed increased production demands from global markets. According to industry experts, 75 percent of all U.S. beef exports were going to Canada, Japan, Mexico, South Korea, and Vietnam. Korea alone had imported 24,000 tons of beef from the United States, up from 9,000 tons the previous year. Although total domestic supplies and cattle heads would be lower in 2011, NCBA's outlook for the cattle industry was optimistic based on the production and export numbers projected by economists.

Alicia Elley

PRINCIPAL DIVISIONS

Federation Division; Policy Division.

PRINCIPAL COMPETITORS

Ranchers-Cattlemen Action Legal Fund (R-CALF); U.S. Cattlemen's Association.

FURTHER READING

American Meat Institute. "U.S. Meat and Poultry Production & Consumption: An Overview." meatami.com, April 2009. Accessed February 23, 2011. http://www.meatami.com/ht/d/sp/i/286/pid/286.

Ball, C. E. "Historical Overview of Beef Production and Beef Organizations in the United States." *Journal of Animal Science* 79 (2000): 1–8. Accessed February 23, 2011. http://jas.fass.org/cgi/reprint/79/E-Suppl_1/1-e.

Dunn, Barry, T. G. Jenkins, and C. B. Williams. "Enhancing Management Decisions—History of the Decision Evaluator for the Cattle Industry." Range Beef Cow Symposium. University of Nebraska – Lincoln, December 14–16, 1999. Accessed March 1, 2011. http://digitalcommons.unl.edu/rangebeefcowsymp/131/.

National Cattlemen's Beef Association. "NCBA Eyes Expanding Trade Opportunities in 2011." *Drovers CattleNetwork,* February 4, 2011. Accessed February 23, 2011. http://www.cattlenetwork.com/cattle-news/latest/NCBA-eyes-expanding-trade-opportunities-in-2011.html.

Neuman, William. "Audit Finds Problems in Cattlemen's Spending." *New York Times,* August 2, 2010.

"Oprah Show Verdict Over Ranchers Is Upheld." *New York Times,* February 10, 2000.

"Understanding Your Beef Checkoff Program." mybeefcheckoff.com, 2009. Accessed March 1, 2011. www.beefboard.org/producer/CBBFinalUnderstandingBrochure.pdf.

Norddeutsche Landesbank Girozentrale

Friedrichswall 10
Hanover, 30159
Germany
Telephone: (49) 511 361-0
Fax: (49) 511 361-2506
Web site: http://www.nordlb.de

Private Company
*Founded:*1970
Employees: 6,463 (2009)
Sales: EUR 2.3 billion ($2.8 billion)(2009)
NAICS: 522110 Commercial Banking

■ ■ ■

Norddeutsche Landesbank Girozentrale (NORD/LB) is one of the largest banks in northern Germany. The bank serves as the Landesbank for the German states of Lower Saxony and Saxony Anhalt and acts as the central bank for 62 savings banks in Lower Saxony, Saxony Anhalt, and Mecklenburg-Western Pomerania. It also operates banks in Northeastern Europe.

NORD/LB specializes in the areas of investment, agriculture and real estate, corporate finance, ship and aircraft leasing, export and trade finance, and private banking. It is one of the top banks for national and international bond issues and maintains foreign offices in London, New York, Shanghai, and Singapore.

NORD/LB is owned by the State of Lower Saxony (41.75%), the State of Saxony Anhalt (8.25%), the Savings Banks Association of Lower Saxony (37.25%), the Savings Banks Holding Association of Saxony Anhalt (7.

53%), and the Special Purpose Holding Association of the Savings Banks of Mecklenburg-Western Pomerania (5.22%).

THE CROWDED BANKING SYSTEM

NORD/LB is one of the publicly owned financial institutions, unique to Germany, known as a Landesbank. The bank was formed in 1970 by the merger of four local banks, Niedersächsische Landesbank, Braunschweigische Staatsbank, Hannoversche Landeskreditanstalt, and Niedersächsische Wohnungskreditanstalt-Stadtschaft. All these banks had a long history before this merger. For instance, Braunschweigische Staatsbank was formed in 1765 and Hannoversche Landeskreditanstalt was created in 1840, making the two Niedersächsische financial institutions, formed in the 1920s, relative newcomers to the scene.

The German banking systems is based on a three-pillar approach which includes public banks, cooperatives, and commercial banks. The public banking sector is largely composed of Sparkassen, or savings banks, and Landesbanks, state-owned regional banks. Cooperatives are owned by their members and may not necessarily be profit orientated. Commercial banks operate on the principles of the free market system.

Landesbanks, which got their start in the 19th century, are generally owned at the state or municipal level. Historically, they functioned mainly as the state bank of the provinces in which they were located and as central banks to local sparkassens. They were able to borrow and lend money at preferred rates, backed by

```
┌─────────────────────────────────────┐
│                                     │
│    COMPANY PERSPECTIVES             │
│                 ■                   │
│    Do business locally, think globally. │
│                                     │
└─────────────────────────────────────┘
```

the usually excellent credit rating of state governments. However, since 2005, credit guarantees provided by state governments have been removed, and since then Landesbanks have competed with private sector banks in the open market.

The marketplace for financial services in Germany presents some unusual challenges. Most analysts agree that in spite of Germany's strong and robust economy, the German banking system is one of Europe's weakest. In general, the system is largely fragmented, earns poor returns, and has low profitability.

One of the major problems facing the industry is that there are just too many banks. It is estimated that there are some 2,700 lending institutions in Germany, and these institutions have more than 42,000 branches in the country. More than half (1,500) of these banks are deemed to be small or very small institutions with less than EUR 1 billion in business volume. Germany has twice as many banks relative to its population as Britain, Canada, or Japan.

With so many banks, it is perhaps not surprising that long-term growth of employment in the banking sector has been phenomenal. In 1960 an estimated 250,000 people were employed in the banking sector, but by 2005 that number had ballooned to 672,000.

The sheer number of banks, and by association bank employees, makes the banking system expensive. It is estimated that, on average, Germans spend 33 percent more on banking charges than other Europeans.

A second anomaly is the relationship between the corporate sector and banking sector in the Germany economy. Unlike other free-market areas, corporate financing in Germany is largely provided by bank loans as opposed to the sale of shares. More than 40 percent of corporate financing is made up of bank loans, whereas equity raised in the stock market accounts for 25 percent. In the United States, equity typically provides 50 percent of corporate finance.

Banks can also exert a considerable amount of power over corporations by voting on behalf of the owners of shares who have invested their shares in bank-managed portfolios.

These processes have led to a close relationship between banking and industry, and a good deal of intermingling of boards.

GROWTH AFTER MERGING

Smaller institutions such as NORD/LB needed to be aggressive and creative in order to survive and compete in this marketplace. In 1983 NORD/LB joined forces with Bremer Landesbank Girozentrale, based in Bremen, Germany. Bremer had been developing a decent business in ship financing. NORD/LB would grow the business to a portfolio volume of EUR 10 billion, mostly in the areas of container shipping, tanker shipping, and dry bulk. Limited passenger shipping financing was also available. For instance, in 2006 the bank provided U.S.-based Norwegian Cruise Lines (NCL) with a $610 million revolving credit facility.

The group also branched into aircraft financing in 1999 with a financial package for Dubai-based Emirates Airlines, which allowed it to purchase an Airbus A330-200 airliner. NORD/LB maintained a close relationship with Emirates Airlines, helping to finance further aircraft acquisitions in 2002 and 2003.

Continuing in this area, NORD/LB grew its aircraft financing business further by providing financing for both Atlas Air of the United States and Cargolux of Luxemburg for the purchase of Boeing 747 cargo aircraft. It also provided funding for an engine repair facility in Ireland.

In 2007 the bank arranged financing for the purchase of 13 new medium-range passenger jets for Air Berlin, Germany's second-largest airline, and in 2008 NORD/LB helped arrange financing for Singapore Airlines to purchase three Airbus A380 super jumbo passenger aircraft.

MEETING THE FREE MARKET

Free-market forces arrived on the German banking sector courtesy of the waves of deregulation and privatization that were sweeping over Europe in the 1990s. Despite its convoluted banking system, aggressive new players were entering the market. By the late 1990s U.S.-owned Citibank had 300 branches in Germany and was serving 2.8 million customers.

In addition to its forays into ship and aircraft financing, NORD/LB expanded its geographic reach as well by opening branches in Vilnius, Lithuania, and Stockholm, Sweden, in 1999. One year later the bank acquired a large interest in Prima Banka of Latvia. In 2002 the Government of Lithuania put the last of its state-owned banks up for sale. NORD/LB took majority share in Zemes Ukio Bankas (LZUB), an agricultural bank. It would operate these various enterprises under the brand name of NORD/LB.

In 2004 NORD/LB began to restructure and reorganize itself to meet the challenges which would

KEY DATES

1970: Norddeutsche Landesbank Girozentrale (NORD/LB) created from merger of four banks.

1998: Bremer Landesbank joins the NORD/LB group.

2000: NORD/LB acquires interest in Pirma Banks, Latvia.

2002: NORD/LB buys Zemes Ukio Bankas from Government of Lithuania.

2006: Opens BANK DnB NORD in partnership with DnB NOR of Norway.

2008: Company takes over German mortgage bank Deutsche Hypo.

arise in 2005 when the state-backed guarantees for Landesbanks were set to expire. The loss of taxpayer-based, state government guarantees would mean that Landesbanks would have to raise money based on their own creditworthiness as determined by rating agencies.

In response, the bank developed a new business model, which it termed the five "C's." The focus would be on capital market access, concentration on customers and products, core competencies, core regions, and applying a standard corporate approach. The central goal was to focus on returns, and three business divisions were created consisting of core business, growth business, and opportunistic business. It also dedicated itself to reinforcing its relationships with the regional savings banks in its core areas.

The process appeared to pay off as net profit, which had stood at EUR 13.9 million in 2003, rose sharply to EUR 50.8 million at the end of 2004.

In 2005 NORD/LB, Sparkasse Hannover, and Japan's Shinsei Bank founded a joint venture named SGK Servicegesellschaft Kreditmanagement GmbH. The venture was founded to sell and restructure nonperforming loans, and many viewed this as an attempt by NORD/LB to clean up its balance sheet in the face of independent ratings.

The bank would make one other important decision in 2005 when it sold off its interest in NILEG Immobilien Holdings Gmbh, a real estate company, to Fortress Investments. With this transaction NORD/LB had completely divested itself of its real estate holdings.

Continuing its expansion in Northern Europe, the bank entered into a joint venture with Norway's largest

financial group DnB NOR. In 2006 Bank DnB NORD began operations to serve the northeastern European markets of Denmark, Finland, Estonia, Lithuania, Latvia, and Poland. The area has a population of 56 million inhabitants and a gross domestic product of EUR 600 billion.

SURVIVING THE GLOBAL FINANCIAL CRISIS

The global financial crisis of 2008 and 2009, which began in the United States, had a profound effect on the German banking sector. According to the Organization for Economic Cooperation and Development (OECD), so-called toxic securities held by German banks amounted to EUR 230 billion, and write-downs by German banks amounted to approximately 7 percent of the global total.

Landesbanks accounted for nearly one-third of German banking losses, yet their share of business volume was only 20 percent. It appeared that state-owned banks demonstrated weak financial and managerial supervision, as foreign investments by Landesbanks had nearly doubled between 2005 and 2008. As a consequence of this perceived laxity, the European Union would demand significant changes to business models, governance, and ownership.

NORD/LB managed to escape the global financial crisis relatively unscathed. Consolidated profit for 2008 did drop by 50 percent from 2007 levels but was still EUR 151 million. Although the bank had taken a big hit, it did not sink into the mire, unlike many other financial institutions.

GREEN ENERGY

Despite a conservative risk strategy, during this period the bank was exploring new markets for its products. Under the direction of Dr. Gunter Dunkel, a member of the management board who specialized in structure finance, the bank helped to finance the expansion of a solar cell plant in China. It was one of NORD/LB first ventures into financing a renewable energy project. Dunkel, who would become chairman of the board of management and CEO in 2009, saw renewable energy projects as a major growth area for the bank.

Through 2008 and 2009, the bank financed wind farm projects with Renewable Energy Systems Group in the United Kingdom and ABO Wind AG of Wiesbaden, Germany. It also helped to finance the world's second-largest solar park in the state of Brandenburg, Germany, and the first renewable energy project in the Republic of Cyprus.

In addition to its new focus on green energy, in 2008 the bank reentered the real estate market when it took over Deutsche Hypothekenbank, or Deutsche Hypo for short. Deutsche Hypo was a mortgage bank which specialized in large-scale commercial financing and the construction of residential investment properties.

In 2009 earnings surpassed EUR 2 billion for the first time and the organization successfully passed the European Union's bank stress test. As a result, NORD/LB entered the 2010s on a better footing than many other banks, and the company's foray into renewable energy project financing may prove very beneficial in a decade with rising energy demands and a volatile global petroleum market.

Ian MacDonald

PRINCIPAL SUBSIDIARIES

Braunschweigische Landessparkasse; Bremer Landes-bankBremer LandesbankBremer LandesbankBremer Landesbank (92.5%); Deka Group; Deutsche Hypo; Norddeutsche Facility Management GmbH; NORD/LB Asset Management Holding GmbH; NORD/LB Norddeutsche Landesbank Luxembourg S.A. (Luxembourg); Öffentliche Versicherung Braunschweig (75%).

PRINCIPAL DIVISIONS

Financial Markets; International Business; Structured Finance; Retail Business; Association Business.

PRINCIPAL COMPETITORS

Commerzbank AG; Deutsche Bank Aktiengesellschaft; UniCredit Bank AG.

FURTHER READING

Eglin, Darrel R. "Federal Republic of Germany." *Countries of the World,* January 1, 1991.

Hüfner, F. "The German Banking System: Lessons from the Financial Crisis." *OECD Economics Department, Working Papers,* no. 788, OECD Publishing, 2010. Accessed March 13, 2011. doi: 10.1787/5kmbm80pjkd6-en.

Marshal, Tom. "A Splattering of Public Bank Mergers." *Euromoney,* March 1, 2003.

Moore, Philip. "German Bank Issuance Set to Prosper." *Euroweek,* November 1, 2002.

"Slow Progress: Why an End to State Guarantees May Change Less Than It Should." *Economist,* June 30, 2005. Accessed March 13, 2011. http://www.economist.com/node/413786 6?story_id=4137866.

Tiwari, Rajnish, and Stephen Buse. "The German Banking System, Competition, Consolidation & Contentment." Social Science Research Network, August 1, 2006. Accessed March 13, 2011. http://papers.ssrn.com/sol3/papers.cfm?a bstract_id=1583824.

"Unity in Adversity; Only a Crisis Turns Bad Banks into Bedfellows." *Economist,* September 6, 2007. Accessed March 13, 2011. http://www.economist.com/node/9769382.

Wiesmann, Gerrit, and James Wilson. "Germany's Weak Link," *Financial Times,* September 28, 2010.

Nutraceutical
International Corporation

1400 Kearns Boulevard
Second Floor
Park City, Utah 84060
U.S.A.
Telephone: (435) 655-6106
Toll Free: (800) 669-8877
Fax: (800) 767-8514
Web site: http://www.nutraceutical.com

Public Company
Founded: 1993
Employees: 685 (2010)
Sales: $180.05 million (2010)
Stock Exchanges: NASDAQ
Ticker Symbol: NUTR
NAIC: 325411 Medicinal and Botanical Manufacturing;
    445299 All Other Specialty Food Stores

■ ■ ■

Nutraceutical International Corporation develops, manufacturers, and markets a wide variety of vitamin, mineral, herbal, and nutritional supplements that are sold in the United States and many other nations. Over its history, the company has acquired approximately 30 other companies to fulfill its original goal of consolidating a fragmented industry. Unlike some supplement firms that sell their products in supermarkets and other mass and discount retail outlets, Nutraceutical sells its brand-name products to 7,000 natural and health food stores in the United States, as well as abroad via the Au Naturel unit. It offers some 5,000 products (vitamins,

supplements, and other natural products) sold under a variety of brand names, including Solaray, KAL, Nature's Life, LifeTime, Natural Balance, bioAllers, Herbs for Kids, NaturalCare, Health from the Sun, Life-flo, Organix-South, Pioneer, and Monarch Nutraceuticals.

The company also makes bulk nutritional products that are used in its own products, as well as being sold to other supplement companies under the trade names Monarch Nutritional Laboratories and Great Basin Botanicals. It owns a number of natural food markets, which operate under the names The Real Food Company, Thom's Natural Foods, and Cornucopia Community Market, as well as health food stores that operate under the names Fresh Vitamins and Granola's.

THE EARLY YEARS

Nutraceutical's beginnings date to 1993, when Bain Capital, Inc., a Boston-based private equity company, paired with senior management to organize Nutraceutical and consolidate what its leaders thought was a very divided nutritional supplements industry. Bain Capital's leader was Mitt Romney, who later became governor of Massachusetts (2003–07) as well as a 2008 Republican presidential candidate.

Nutraceutical's first acquisition in 1993 was Solaray, Inc., of Ogden, Utah. The company had begun making capsules of herbal products in 1973 under the company name Solar Products, Inc. The following year, the company was incorporated as a Utah entity known as Solaray.

By 1984 Solaray had added vitamins and minerals to its product lines. Later, in 1990, Solaray received funds from the Utah Department of Agriculture to work with Weber State College's Department of Chemistry to develop new products made from whey, a byproduct of cheese making that normally was discarded.

When Nutraceutical was founded in the early 1990s, it joined a natural products industry in Utah that had a long and colorful history. For example, in a 1979 article, writer Elaine Jarvik noted that six Utah herbal companies were not only "the first companies in the world to put herbs in capsules, but they now account for 85 percent of the nation's herb business." Other Utah herbal firms in the 1990s included Murdock Madaus Scwabe, Nature's Herbs (part of Twin Labs), Nature's Sunshine, Enrich International, USANA, NuSkin, Weider Nutrition, E'Ola, Morinda, and Neways. Unlike Nutraceutical, many Utah herbal products firms used multilevel marketing to distribute their products.

In 1998 the *Los Angeles Times* ran a four-part series on alternative health. The third article focused on how Utah became what writer David R. Olmos called the "Silicon Valley of herbs." He pointed out that the state's herbal and supplement industry was "bigger even than the skiing trade." In addition to entrepreneurship, Olmos credited Utah's Mormon culture. Although the Latter-day Saints (LDS) church had long accepted modern scientific medicine, many of its members used herbs and other forms of alternative healing. Thus, herbalism, capitalism, and religious factors all took part in creating the history of Utah's herbal products industry.

The early years of the herbal and supplement industry were tough, but times had improved by the time Nutraceutical was founded. "It wasn't always easy to be in this business," said Grace Rich, marketing director for Nature's Herbs in the August 16, 1998, *Salt Lake Tribune.* She continued, "There were plenty of people out there who thought we were all quacks trying to take their money." Ken Murdock, chairman of Utah's Nature's Way, said the growing emphasis on preventive care and individuals taking responsibility for their own

health had helped to end what he called "the Dark Ages of health care when doctors had all the answers." A new federal law helped the vitamin and herbal industry, however. Sponsored by Utah's Republican senator Orrin Hatch, the 1994 Dietary Supplement Health and Education Act prevented what the industry considered to be overregulation by the U.S. Food and Drug Administration (FDA). Following the passage of the new law, the nutritional supplement industry rapidly expanded.

ACQUISITIONS AND OTHER DEVELOPMENTS: 1994–98

In October 1994 Nutraceutical acquired Premier One Products, Inc., a Nebraska corporation. Premier One had been founded in July 1984 in Omaha, Nebraska, as one of the first companies to sell items made completely from bee products. Nutraceutical's third acquisition came in January 1995, when the company acquired the California-based Makers of KAL, Inc. Nutraceutical also acquired Healthway Corporation, a company that had been founded in 1958, as part of its KAL acquisition. KAL's beginnings dated to 1932, when the company was formed in Southern California as a pioneering firm providing supplements. Soon after its start, it switched from selling powdered products to tablets.

In 1995 Nutraceutical started VegLife as a separate brand, following its previous origin in 1992 as a line of products marketed under the Solaray brand. VegLife consisted of strictly vegetarian products, including encapsulated items and the beverages Peaceful Planet (a soy protein drink) and Peaceful Kava.

To sell its products overseas, Nutraceutical in fiscal year 1995 organized a wholly owned subsidiary called Au Naturel, Inc. Operating as a separate business, Au Naturel reformulated some Nutraceutical products and labels to meet the regulatory demands of the foreign nations where it operated.

A couple years later, in April 1997, Nutraceutical introduced a new line of supplements called Solar Green. The product line included tablets containing different kinds of algae and cereal grasses, and also a drink mix used to prepare a beverage supplement.

By early 1998 Nutraceutical products were being sold through Au Naturel in about 30 countries. However, foreign sales accounted for just 6.3 percent and 6.5 percent of Nutraceutical's total net sales in 1996 and 1997, respectively. Nutraceutical saw this area as a great opportunity for future growth. In 2010 global revenue for Nutraceuticals remained small (11%), with Norway being the company's largest international market.

KEY DATES

1993: Nutraceutical International is founded.
1993: The company purchases Solaray, Inc.
1995: The company acquires the Makers of KAL, Inc.
1997: The Solar Green brand is introduced in April.
1998: Stock is first sold on the NASDAQ.
2000: The company buys Thompson Nutritional Products.
2002: Nutraceutical acquires three natural food markets based in San Francisco.
2003: Company purchases Nature's Life brand of nutritional supplements and of Arizona Health Foods stores.
2009: Company rejects takeover bid by California investor Ryan Drexler.

A 1997 survey sponsored by *Health Supplement Retailer* found that Solaray ranked as the top-selling brand of nutritional supplements, and the second-best-selling line of herbal products. The survey also found that Solaray's St. John's wort was the best-selling herbal product, and Nutraceutical had the best customer service. By 1998 Nutraceutical employed 450 individuals, including 70 at its Park City, Utah headquarters.

COMPANY ADDITIONS AND INNOVATIONS: 1998–2000

In the summer of 1998 Nutraceutical acquired Action Labs Inc. for about $13.7 million cash. Started in 1988, Action Labs marketed and distributed some 65 brand name nutritional supplements sold mainly in health food stores, so it fit well with Nutraceutical's general distribution strategy. The acquisition of the Long Island, New York, company gave Nutraceutical "additional market penetration in the eastern United States," said Nutraceutical chairman and CEO Bill Gay in the August 3, 1998, edition of the *Enterprise*, a Salt Lake City business newspaper. Within a year, Nutraceutical was making its own Action Labs products instead of buying them from other manufacturers.

In September 1998 Nutraceutical introduced a new brand of products called Natural Sport. Designed for athletes and avid exercisers, the Natural Sport line included two beverages called Pre-Burn and Post-Up, a soy protein beverage supplement called ProSoy, creatine monohydrate, and Phyto Sport multivitamins.

The following year, Nutraceutical purchased Woodland Publishing, Inc., a publisher of books and other literature for the natural products industry. Based in Lindon, Utah County, Utah, near many large herbal products manufacturers, Woodland had been started in 1975 to publish the writing of some of Utah's well-known herbalists, such as John Christopher. In 1985 Woodland published *Today's Herbal Health,* of which over 750,000 copies had been sold by 1999. In 1995 Woodland began publishing its popular specialized booklets for sale mostly in health food stores. By 2000 Woodland had published over 160 titles.

On May 26, 2000, Nutraceutical announced that it had purchased a division of Rexall Sundown, Inc., called Thompson Nutritional Products. For over 60 years, Thompson had been making nutritional supplements. At the start of the 21st century, Nutraceutical had acquired numerous companies, folding most of them into the company and retaining their recognized names as brands.

BUSINESS IN A NEW MILLENNIUM

Meanwhile, the herbal and supplements business was evolving. For many years, consumers had been able to buy herbal products in health food stores but not in grocery stores or other outlets. In the late 1990s, however, large supermarket chains and mass retailers like Wal-Mart realized the consumer demand and opened new sections for supplements. "Paced by positive press," wrote Renee M. Kruger in the January 1999 edition of *Supermarket Business,* "once strange-sounding herbal supplements such as St. John's Wort, echinacea and gingko biloba have now moved into the mainstream as viable health enhancers, especially to aging baby boomers who are trying to maintain a higher quality of life."

Despite increasing competition, Nutraceutical reported a profit of $7 million for fiscal year 2001, up from $5.6 million in fiscal year 2000. One year later, Nutraceutical acquired three natural food markets based in San Francisco and owned by The Real Food Company. Nutraceutical, which paid approximately $2.7 million in cash for the markets in 2002, wanted a retail presence in an area considered by some to be a birthplace of the health food industry. In addition, they believed that the chain of successful natural food markets would provide direct consumer feedback both on the company's products and also on emerging trends and interests in the industry.

Named one of the "200 Best Small Companies" in the October 28, 2002, issue of *Forbes* magazine, Nutraceutical continued to have a strong performance despite an industry-wide slowdown. According to Kieffer, part of the company's positive financial performance was its continued focus on selling its product to health food stores rather than discounters such as Costco and Wal-Mart. "We're committed and loyal to health food stores," Kieffer told *Salt Lake Tribune* contributor Lesley Mitchell, pointing out that health food store customers focus more on selection and quality than just price.

CONTINUED ACQUISITIONS SPUR GROWTH

In 2003 Nutraceutical acquired the Nature's Life brand of nutritional supplements via a purchase of 100 percent of the stock of MK Health Food Distributors Inc., paying approximately $10.8 million in cash. The company also expanded its retail presence in the United States through the acquisition of Arizona Health Foods, which operated 11 health food stores that focused primarily on branded nutritional supplements. Nutraceutical paid approximately $3.5 million in cash for the stores. Nutraceutical's sales for fiscal year 2003 rose 12.3 percent to $124.5 million, marking the company's first double-digit revenue gain in six years. "The strong ones persevered and are turning the corner," analyst David Block of The Seidler Cos. told *Investor's Business Daily* contributor Marilyn Alva, referring to the slump in the supplements industry. He added: "Nutraceutical is one of them."

Nutraceutical continued to grow in 2004, first acquiring the Natural Balance brand of nutritional supplements by paying approximately $9 million in cash for nearly all of the operating assets of Natural Balance, Inc. Next, the company acquired Montana Big Sky brand of nutritional supplements via the purchase of selected assets of Montana Naturals for about $600,000 in cash. In its June 7, 2004, issue, *BusinessWeek* magazine named Nutraceutical as one of its 100 Hot Growth Companies with a ranking of 61. The company continued to make acquisitions, including six acquisitions in 2007, such as the NaturalCare brand of homeopathic products. In July 2009 Baywood International Inc. announced that it was selling the assets of Nutritional Specialities Inc. to Nutra Inc., a subsidiary of Nutraceutical, for $8.25 million in cash.

COMPANY SPURNS TAKEOVER BID

In August 2009 Nutraceutical spurned the offer of California investor Ryan Drexler, a former chief executive of Country Life Vitamins, to buy all the outstanding shares of Nutraceutical's stocks. Drexler already owned 341,000 shares of Nutraceutical, amounting to 3.1 percent of the company's outstanding stock. According to Drexler, Nutraceutical was not operating up to its full potential. On its part, Nutraceutical claimed that selling the shares to Drexler was not in the best interest of its stockholders.

Despite Drexler's criticisms of the company, Nutraceutical reported net sales for the end of the fiscal year 2010 at $180.1 million, compared to $162.3 million for the end of fiscal year 2009. Bill Gay, Nutraceutical's chairman and CEO, noted that the company's overall net sales and income were strong for fiscal year 2010. However, According to Gay, a weak economy continuing into 2011 left many uncertainties on the horizon for the company, especially in terms of future business opportunities. Nevertheless, he noted that the company looked to maintain its areas of financial strength and focus on improving the company in the long term via new acquisitions, integration improvements, raw improvement savings, and inventory reductions. The company was also looking to make improvements in manufacturing and distribution to become more cost efficient.

David M. Walden
Updated, David Petechuk

PRINCIPAL SUBSIDIARIES

Au Naturel, Inc.; Beehive Organics, Inc.; FunFresh Foods, Inc.; Monarch Nutraceuticals, Inc.; Nutra, Inc.; NutraSource Trading (Shanghai) Limited (China); Vita-Dollar, Inc.

PRINCIPAL COMPETITORS

Country Life LLC; The Hain Celestial Group, Inc.; NBTY, Inc.; Schiff Nutritional International, Inc.

FURTHER READING

Alva, Marilyn. "Nutraceutical International Corp. Park City, Utah; Vitamin Supplier Brews Up a Winning Plan." *Investor's Business Daily,* February 26, 2004, A08.

Carricaburu, Lisa. "The Changing Nature of Supplements." *Salt Lake Tribune,* December 20, 1998, 1, 4.

Campbell, Joel. "Nature's Own." *Deseret News,* June 28, 1998, M1.

Greenwald, John. "Herbal Healing." *Time,* November 23, 1998, 56–58.

Hinds, Gary. "Nutritional Supplement Maker Reports $7 Million Profit." *Standard-Examiner,* (Ogden, UT), December 15, 2001.

Jarvik, Elaine. "Underground Health." *Utah Holiday,* November 1979, 24–36.

Kruger, Renee M., "High Times for Herbals." *Supermarket Business,* January 1999, 65–68.

Mitchell, Lesley. "Nutraceutical International Corp. Grows Despite Supplement Industry Slump." *Salt Lake Tribune,* December 13, 2002.

"Nutraceutical Reports Fiscal 2010 Year End Results." *PR Newswire,* November 23, 2010.

Olmos, David R., "Herbal Medicine Sets Firm Roots in Utah." *Los Angeles Times,* September 1, 1998, 1.

"Park City Firm Buys Laboratory Assets for $13.7 Million Cash." *Enterprise,* (Salt Lake City), August 3, 1998, 15.

OpenTable, Inc.

———————■———————

799 Market Street
Fourth Floor
San Francisco, California 94103
U.S.A.
Telephone: (415) 344-4200
Toll Free: (800) 673-6822
Fax: (415) 267-0944
Web site: http://www.opentable.com

Public Company
Founded: 1998
Employees: 319 (2009)
Revenues: $68.60 million (2009)
Stock Exchanges: NASDAQ
Ticker Symbol: OPEN
NAICS: 561599 All Other Travel Arrangement and
Reservation Services

■ ■ ■

OpenTable, Inc., is an online restaurant reservation
service that serves the needs of both restaurants and
guests. The service allows diners to book reservations 24
hours a day at over 15,000 different restaurants using
the Internet or a smartphone application. When making
reservations, individuals can search for restaurants by
neighborhood, cuisine, and price, as well as read
restaurant reviews from other OpenTable customers and
reviews from travel guides such as Fodor's and Zagat.

For restaurants, OpenTable offers guest management software and hardware solutions that help dining
establishments maximize revenues. Through the

company's electronic reservations booking (ERB) system,
restaurants have the ability to keep more seats filled,
foster customer relations, and create effective e-mail
marketing techniques customized for its clientele.
OpenTable is a real-time operating system, with reservation requests traveling instantly over the Internet from a
guest's computer or mobile device to a restaurant's host-
stand computer, which immediately determines if tables
are available in the restaurant to accommodate the
request. If so, the reservation is booked automatically,
and a confirmation e-mail is sent to the diner.

OpenTable charges restaurants an installation fee for
its ERB system, a monthly subscription fee, and a fee
for each diner that makes a reservation through its
system. Diners use the service for free.

In addition to working with hundreds of distribu-
tion partners, including Google and TripAdviser,
OpenTable also carries out operations in Canada,
Mexico, Japan, Germany, and the United Kingdom.
However, North America remains the company primary
markets, accounting for over 90 percent of all revenue.

COMPANY ESTABLISHED: 1998–99

Listening to his wife grow increasingly frustrated as she
tried to book dinner reservations over the phone for
visiting relatives, Chuck Templeton, a product marketer
for a semiconductor equipment manufacturer, was
struck by the idea of creating an online reservation
network that would benefit customers as well as
restaurants. Thus inspired, he incorporated OpenTable
under Delaware state law in October 1998. Backed by
$2 million secured in May 1999 from several venture

COMPANY PERSPECTIVES

As our network of reservation-taking restaurants and diners grows, the value we deliver grows as well. Because the foundation of our network is building a critical mass of computerized reservation books, we enhance our offering to diners by adding new restaurant customers. In turn, as more diners use OpenTable to make their dining decisions and book their reservations, we deliver more value to our restaurant customers by helping them fill more of their seats. In this process, we grow the value of our business.

capitalists, the San Francisco-based company was officially launched in August 1999 as OpenTable.com.

The OpenTable site, which originally had around 20 restaurants in its reservations system, allowed diners to search for restaurants based on type of cuisine, neighborhood location, or available tables and times. After selecting a restaurant, diners could specify table preferences and notify restaurant staff of any dietary restrictions. Once they made reservations (which could be booked for up to 12 people and up to a year in advance), customers received instant confirmation and were given the option of having notification e-mails automatically sent to members of their party. In addition, they could get maps with driving directions to the restaurant. Most importantly, people could use the service around the clock at no cost, although a credit card number was required to book reservations. If a cancellation was not made at least three hours ahead of time, the diner's credit card was charged $20.

In a society in which flights and hotels were being booked online in record numbers, OpenTable quickly caught the attention of diners, restaurants, and investors alike. The site added restaurants daily so that by the end of 1999, it had signed up 130 clients in San Francisco, New York, Chicago, and Seattle. With $10 million in funding from new investors, OpenTable planned to add restaurants in Boston, Los Angeles, Washington, D.C., and Vail, Colorado, over the course of 2000.

ESTABLISHING A HOLD IN THE RESTAURANT INDUSTRY: 1999–2000

From the time of its inception, OpenTable was dependent on the host-stand operations of the restaurant industry. The company's focus was always on full-service restaurants, or those that accepted reservations, as opposed to quick-service ones that did not. Unlike the travel industry, which saw a significant rise in the number of people making reservations online rather than over the telephone during the late 1990s and the first decade of the 21st century, the restaurant industry was slow to computerize its traditional pen-and-paper host-stand procedures. Taking reservations at a restaurant was typically uncomplicated, consisting of little more than recording diners' names and phone numbers in a reservation book, with no advance payment required. As a result of this, many restaurant owners were reluctant to consider special reservation-taking services.

OpenTable, however, emphasized to restaurants the disadvantages of not having an online reservation system. A number of full-service dining establishments, for example, lost business because of the inefficiency of phone reservations. If a customer called to make reservations and got a busy signal, was placed on hold, or missed a return call, then that person was likely to try another restaurant, especially if it had a more convenient booking system. Also, no-shows commonly occurred because people thought calling to cancel a reservation was inconvenient, resulting in revenue losses for restaurants, which profit from filling as many seats as possible. Another problem with relying on written reservations was the potential for human error and miscommunication, as names and times could be recorded incorrectly, entries could be duplicated, or reservations could be lost.

With these factors in mind, OpenTable developed its electronic reservation book (ERB) to improve restaurants' profit margins through streamlined host-stand operations. OpenTable's ERB solution consisted of proprietary software, security tools, and computer hardware installed at the restaurant, complete with a touchscreen computer at the host stand. After verifying Internet connectivity on site, OpenTable customized the system according to the restaurant's needs and provided training on how to use it. Ongoing services included nightly data backups and 24-hour technical support.

Despite the services OpenTable offered, the company still faced several challenges early on. Five-star restaurants in New York and Los Angeles, in particular, were resistant to making the transition, as these establishments regarded a long waiting list for reservations to be a sign of status. Furthermore, maître d's at upscale restaurants often prided themselves on the practice of turning away everyday diners. According to Templeton, another major barrier to OpenTable's system

```
┌─────────────────────────────────────────┐
│                                          │
│              KEY DATES                   │
│                   ■                      │
│                                          │
│  1999:  OpenTable.com is officially      │
│         launched.                        │
│  2001:  Company acquires ProHost and     │
│         RSViP software brands.           │
│  2004:  OpenTable establishes office in  │
│         Miami, Florida.                  │
│  2007:  Jeff Jordan is hired as CEO.     │
│  2008:  Free applications for smartphones│
│         debut.                           │
│  2009:  OpenTable acquires guest         │
│         management solutions provider    │
│         GuestBridge, Inc.                │
│  2010:  Company acquires Toptable.com, a │
│         leading United Kingdom           │
│         reservation site.                │
│                                          │
└─────────────────────────────────────────┘
```

was that diners were accustomed to calling restaurants in order to make reservations.

GROWTH THROUGH EARLY PARTNERSHIPS: 2000–02

Nevertheless, interest in OpenTable's online reservation system gradually increased, and in the first quarter of 2000, well-known entities in the business world began to form partnerships with the start-up. The American Express Company, for instance, invested an undisclosed amount in OpenTable, believing that the ERB concept would help American Express develop new financial products and services for the restaurant industry. OpenTable announced an agreement with NYToday.com, an online entertainment guide owned by the *New York Times,* to operate a cobranded Web site for making reservations in New York restaurants. This was soon followed by a similar arrangement with the *Los Angeles Times.* America Online announced that it had made a deal with OpenTable that allowed diners to book reservations through AOL's Digital City network, which included AOL.com, CompuServe, and Netscape's Netcenter. In August, OpenTable joined with Worldspan, a reservation system that served around 21,000 travel agencies, to create a service that allowed customers to book dining reservations along with their travel reservations.

Such partnerships proved profitable, and OpenTable received $42 million from investors in October 2000, opening the door to more revenue-enhancing enterprises in 2001. Partly in response to industry analysts who indicated that OpenTable needed to broaden its product line in order to become profitable, the company acquired ProHost Table Management and RSViP

Reservations Administration software brands from Restaurant Solutions Group of Dallas in February 2001. Ownership of the software, created in 1992 and 1996, respectively, meant that OpenTable eliminated two competitors in the ERB sector, building its public profile. Even as such online reservations services as Eseated.com and Foodline.com, shut down, OpenTable continued to expand, with the number of registered users increasing 140 percent from August 2001 to August 2002.

PUBLIC RESPONSE: 2003–07

A major media focus in the middle of the first decade of the 21st century was OpenTable's computerized database that allowed restaurants to record personal information about diners. For instance, an entry might alert the restaurant to a customer's allergy to shellfish, the kind of drink someone favors, a person's vegan preferences, or a couple's anniversary. While many restaurant managers viewed the service as an invaluable resource for ensuring top-quality customer relations, some people, both within and without the industry, believed the database to be an invasion of privacy. An April 2003 *L.A. Times* article reported that some entries contained derogatory staff comments about a diner. One read, "Very cheesy guy … always comes in with a different girl. Doesn't tip well." This level (and manner) of detail, argued critics, was unnecessary and offensive. However, a number of guests appreciated the personal VIP service that the OpenTable system helped restaurants provide.

As people became more accustomed to the benefits of technology beyond the workplace, OpenTable saw steady growth in both the number of diners and restaurants using the service. Diners took advantage of the convenience online booking offered. In fact, OpenTable reported that around one quarter of all diners booked reservations between 10:00 P.M. and 9:00 A.M., when restaurants were closed. When restaurants began to take full advantage of e-mail marketing techniques, OpenTable partnered with VerticalResponse Inc. to give member restaurants the tools they needed to send graphically enhanced e-mails to their customers.

OpenTable furthered its U.S. reach when it opened an additional office in Miami, Florida, in 2004, hiring an account executive to target Sarasota, Bradenton, Tampa, and Orlando. By January 2005 OpenTable had extended into markets in Canada, Mexico, Puerto Rico, and Singapore. A little more than one year later, the company was seating over one million diners per month, with that number increasing to over two million customers per month by mid-2007.

A CHANGE IN FOCUS: 2007 AND BEYOND

In May 2007 OpenTable hired Jeff Jordan, the former president of PayPal who had also run eBay in North America, as the company's CEO. One of Jordan's primary goals was moving OpenTable beyond its narrow focus of adding restaurants to its network. One year after Jordan assumed his position with the company, OpenTable released a mobile version of its site, giving diners the capability to book reservations quickly over their smartphones. In November 2008 the company debuted the highly successful OpenTable for iPhone, a free real-time application for iPhone and iPod touch users. An app for the Blackberry was made available in August 2009, followed by one for smartphones using Android in September. Just one month later, OpenTable announced that it had seated over one million diners through mobile applications, a number that had reached over five million by November 2010.

Another area in which OpenTable branched out was the customer-written restaurant review. In May 2008 OpenTable introduced its Diners' Choice Lists, a program designed to help people select the establishment that best suited their particular dining needs and occasions. Only people who had dined at a restaurant using reservations from OpenTable were permitted to leave reviews on the company's Web site. Based on feedback from thousands of people, the Diners' Choice Lists were updated regularly to ensure that restaurants new to the OpenTable system were included in the rankings. Examples of Diners' Choice lists included the top 50 eating establishments with the best scenic views, restaurants that were good for groups, the top 50 Italian restaurants in the United States, and the most romantic places to dine. The program became such a popular feature of the OpenTable service that seven million diners had submitted reviews to the site by August 2010.

In May 2009 the same month it went public at $20 per share, OpenTable unveiled version 8.0 of its Electronic Reservation Book, an update that included 50 new features for restaurant partners. According to Jordan, OpenTable's software, especially its actual Web site, had received only cosmetic improvements since the founding of the company. Based on feedback from customers in the restaurant industry, the modernized ERB was designed to help dining establishments seat more diners and manage their reservation-related business more efficiently through real-time data. In addition to allowing restaurant professionals to create custom fields for recording more detailed guest information, OpenTable 8.0 gave them a dashboard view of table turn times, server performance, and wait times. The update also supported Payment Card Industry (PCI) security standards that had been recently released at the time.

At the close of 2009, OpenTable moved once again to expand its operations by acquiring providers of guest management services in the United States and abroad. In the last quarter of 2009, OpenTable bought Guest-Bridge, Inc., a leading developer of reservation and guest management software. In 2010 OpenTable completed an acquisition of Tabletop.com, a London-based restaurant reservation site that seated close to three million diners annually in the United Kingdom. With consistent user traffic, OpenTable continued to post record numbers of diners and restaurants using its services at the end of the decade, and its prospects of continuing to expand its services to more restaurants looked positive heading into the 2010s.

Alicia Elley

PRINCIPAL SUBSIDIARIES

OpenTable Canada, Inc.; OpenTable EURL (France); OpenTable Europe Ltd. (UK); OpenTable GmbH (Germany); OpenTable Kabushiki Kaisha (Japan); OpenTable Mexico S de la RL; OpenTable Spain S.L.

PRINCIPAL COMPETITORS

Restaurant.com, Inc.; SavvyDiner.com, Inc.; Yelp, Inc.

FURTHER READING

Hafner, Katie, "Restaurant Reservations Go Online." *New York Times,* June 18, 2007. Accessed February 18, 2011. http://www.nytimes.com/2007/06/18/business/18opentable.html?scp=1&sq=Restaurant+Reservations+Go+Online&st=nyt.

Needleman, Rafe. "OpenTable Files for IPO, Finally." *cnet News,* January 30, 2009. Accessed February 18, 2011. http://news.cnet.com/8301-17939_109-10153937-2.html.

"OpenTable.com, *Los Angeles Times* Announce Partnership." *Nation's Restaurant News,* October 23, 2000. Accessed February 18, 2011. http://findarticles.com/p/articles/mi_m3190/is_43_34/ai_66709550/.

Schonfeld, Erick. "OpenTable Files for IPO and Reveals Its Finances." *Tech Crunch,* January 30, 2009. Accessed February 18, 2011. http://techcrunch.com/2009/01/30/opentable-files-for-ipo-and-reveals-its-finances/.

Shaw, David. "They Have a File on You," *Los Angeles Times,* April 23, 2003.

Stross, Randall. "The Online Reservations That Restaurants Love to Hate." *New York Times,* December 11, 2010. Accessed February 18, 2011. http://www.nytimes.com/2010/12/12/business/12digi.html.

"Worldspan and OpenTable.com Announce Alliance." *Business Wire,* August 30, 2000. Accessed February 22, 2011. http://findarticles.com/p/articles/mi_m0EIN/is_2000_August_30/ai_64996433/.

The Pantry, Incorporated

---

305 Gregson Drive P.O. Box 8019
Cary, North Carolina 27511
U.S.A.
Telephone: (919) 774-6700
Toll Free: (877) 798-4792
Fax: (919) 774-3329
Web site: http://www.thepantry.com

Public Company
Founded: 1967
Employees: 6,378 (full time, 2010)
Revenues: $7.27 billion (2010)
Stock Exchanges: NASDAQ
Ticker Symbol: PTRY
NAICS: 447110 Gasoline Stations with Convenience
  Stores

■ ■ ■

The Pantry, Incorporated, runs convenience stores across the southeastern United States. In 2010 the company had 1,670 stores, of which most were named Kangaroo Express. The Pantry's operation coves 13 states, with over half of all stores in Florida, North Carolina, and South Carolina. While merchandise sales accounted for only one-quarter of revenue (gasoline sales account for the rest), merchandise accounted for almost 70 percent of gross profit in 2010. Tobacco products (39.1%), packaged beverages (15.3%), and beer and wine (15%) are the leading merchandise products.

SOUTHERN BEGINNINGS

The Pantry was founded in 1967 in North Carolina by businessmen Sam Wornom and Truby Proctor, Jr. The company expanded slowly at first and was described as being "steady and stable," and a "a quiet organization niched in the Carolinas, Kentucky, Tennessee, and Indiana." Wornom and Proctor acquired new stores by borrowing against existing stores and paying off debt with new sales. The Pantry was profitable during the 1960s and 1970s and faced few obstacles. Its situation changed in the 1980s, however. Like many other companies, The Pantry was affected by the savings-and-loan bailouts and leveraged buyouts. Its sales dropped. Without cash for renovations, its stores deteriorated. The Pantry had no direction and little hope for the future.

Founder Wornom sold his stake in The Pantry to Montrose Capital in 1987. Montrose was renowned for its famous shareholders, including Dave Thomas, the founder of Wendy's, and Wayne Rogers, the former Trapper John on the TV series *M*A*S*H*. The company was founded by former Duke University professor Clay Hamner. Montrose gained control of The Pantry in 1990 when it purchased half of cofounder Proctor's shares, although Proctor remained CEO.

The Pantry was still struggling in the 1990s. In an effort to get back on track, the company restructured. It closed unprofitable stores and remodeled others. These efforts were futile, however. The Pantry posted losses in 1991 and 1992. It posted a small income in 1993 but another loss in 1994. To make matters worse, The

Pantry had too much debt to acquire new stores, which would have helped increase its sales.

Tension between cofounder Proctor and Montrose's Hamner led Proctor to sell his remaining shares in The Pantry in 1995 to Freeman Spogli & Co., a Los Angeles-based investment firm specializing in management-led buyouts. Chase Manhattan Capital acquired the rest of the company from Montrose. Freeman Spogli & Co. had tremendous financial resources and the buyout presented great opportunities for The Pantry. Gene Horne, the company's president and CEO, concluded that with Freeman Spogli & Co. The Pantry had "the infrastructure to go to 1,000 to 2,000 stores." Horne was right but was not destined to be a part of it.

The following year, Peter J. Sodini took Horne's place as president and CEO. Prior to his appointment, Sodini was the CEO of Purity Supreme, Inc., a grocery store chain in New England. Industry analysts credited Sodini with attacking The Pantry's problems head-on and turning the company around.

At the time of his appointment, Sodini described The Pantry as being "in flux." Using resources from Freeman, Spogli & Co. he gave the company direction. Unlike some competitors, Sodini decided against turning its convenience stores into elaborate food stores and decided instead to concentrate on the sale of gas and tobacco. "We like to focus on what we think we do well, which is to run a basic convenience store selling gasoline and the usual amenities you find in the store," he explained.

MORE CHANGES AT THE TOP

Sodini was displeased with The Pantry's management, so he replaced many executives with allies from his former employer, the Purity Supreme Grocery Store chain. "Although they didn't have gasoline experience, what they brought in terms of being able to further enhance the merchandise side of their business was significant," Sodini said in *Convenience Store News*.

When it came to gasoline, Sodini himself had no experience. Ironically, this worked to his advantage. Ac-

cording to *Investor's Business Daily*, Sodini quickly realized that most convenience stores selling a lot of gas were not making as much money as they could be, since merchandise brings in higher profits than gasoline. Sodini thought this was also true of The Pantry's stores. "Not much thought was going into the adjoining stores and merchandise," he said. Using his supermarket expertise, he struck deals with suppliers and stocked the company's stores with 25 percent more merchandise than other convenience stores.

Sodini realized, however, that while merchandise helped boost sales, the sale of gasoline was still critical to the company's success. What made him different from competitors was the way he viewed gasoline. Said one analyst in *Investor's Business Daily*, "Most of the top convenience store operators are owned by oil companies, whose focus is to sell more gas. But to Sodini, pumping gas is like selling milk. It's a commodity that has to be competitively priced." The Pantry lowered the price of gas and cigarettes, which helped it compete better with other convenience stores.

Like many other convenience stores in the Southeast, The Pantry was plagued with a high employee turnover and a shortage of employees. To entice employees to sign on and stay, The Pantry paid higher-than-average wages. It also offered many opportunities for advancement and remodeled its stores. "People would rather work in a nice store versus a dump," Sodini commented in *Petrogram*.

Some of the renovations Sodini initiated included increased lighting in its stores, a new logo, and fresh paint. The Pantry painted many of its stores in local college colors. Its efforts proved worthwhile. The company's sales went up, and it further implemented its strategy of cutting prices to increase sales.

TAKING ON A CHAMPION

In late 1997 The Pantry got word that the 479-store Lil' Champ convenience store chain was for sale. (The Lil' Champ chain was named after founder Julian Jackson, a bantamweight boxing champion in the 1930s.) Analysts believed the Tosco Corporation, the leading independent oil refiner and oil maker in the United States, would buy the chain. Tosco had purchased Circle K, the second-largest convenience store operator in the country, two years earlier. The Pantry emerged victorious, however, and acquired the chain for $132.7 million and outstanding debt. Lil' Champ Food Stores, Inc., had 430 stores in northern Florida and 49 in southeastern Georgia.

Although The Pantry was delighted with its new acquisition, Sodini was quick to point out that the situ-

KEY DATES

1967: Businessmen Sam Wornom and Truby Proctor, Jr., found The Pantry Incorporated.
1987: Wornom sells his stake in the company to Montrose Capital.
1990: Montrose purchases half of Proctor's share in The Pantry Incorporated.
1996: Peter J. Sodini is hired as CEO and president of The Pantry Incorporated.
1997: The Pantry purchases the Lil' Champ convenience store for $132.7 million.
1999: The company launches its initial public offering.
2002: The Pantry spends $16.8 million to upgrade its convenience stores and gasoline equipment.
2005: Purchase of D&D Oil bolsters company presence in Alabama.
2009: Terrance Marks is named president and chief executive officer.
2010: Company expands into Kansas and Missouri.

were located in high-traffic tourist markets such as Myrtle Beach. Sodini believed the Food Chief acquisitions would significantly enhance the company's already strong presence in South Carolina.

During the same year, The Pantry acquired 49 convenience stores operating under the trade name Kangaroo, from Kangaroo, Inc. The purchase helped establish the company's presence in Georgia.

In 1999 The Pantry rose from being ranked the 33rd-largest chain in *Convenience Store News* Top 50 Companies to the 10th. Under the direction of Sodini and his new management team, the company had grown from about 400 stores to more than 1,200. Revenues had risen from $427 million to $985 million.

To pay off debt from its many acquisitions, The Pantry went public in June 1999. The company sold 6.25 million shares of common stock to raise $75.6 million in net proceeds. With its debt under control, the company was positioned for further expansion. Some of its many acquisitions included 12 On-the-Way Foods stores from the McKnight Oil Company. The Pantry also purchased 14 MiniMart stores from Oates Oil Company, located in South Carolina. The MiniMart purchase made The Pantry the largest convenience store operator in South Carolina.

Also in 1999 The Pantry purchased 19 stores from Tip Top Convenience Stores, Inc., operating under the name Big K. Big K stores were located mostly in Mississippi and Alabama. The Pantry also acquired the five-store Market Express convenient store chain in Sumter, South Carolina, and an Amoco station in Hilton Head, South Carolina.

ation was not perfect. "Many of the Lil' Champ stores were outdated. Many featured only single-hose product dispensers instead of the more popular multi-product dispensers. About 125 facilities didn't meet federal underground storage tank standards," Sodini said in *Convenience Store News.* "You could say that it was the ugliest mass of stores, but it was still a critical mass," he explained. The Pantry decided to immediately remodel most of the Lil' Champ stores and update them to meet federal standards.

The Lil' Champ acquisition was the beginning of a buying spree for The Pantry. In 1998 The Pantry acquired almost 155 stores through the acquisition of smaller chains. Included in these purchases was the acquisition of Quick Stop, a 75-store chain in the Carolinas, and 41 Zip Mart stores in North Carolina and eastern Virginia.

GROWTH THROUGH ACQUISITIONS

The following year The Pantry acquired 126 Handy Way stores in central Florida from Miller Enterprises. Many of the Handy Way stores had fast-food outlets such as Hardee's and Subway. The Pantry also purchased 28 stores operating under the Food Chief name from Dilmar Oil Company in South Carolina. The stores

GASOLINE REVENUES INCREASE IN VOLATILE MARKETS

As of September 2000, merchandise sales (e.g., soft drinks, tobacco and dairy products, video games) accounted for 37.3 percent of The Pantry's total revenues, an increase over the previous year's 33.1 percent. Acquisitions made during the previous year, like the MiniMart and On-The-Way-Food stores, were the primary reason for the increase.

Gasoline revenues saw an even greater increase. Fluctuating oil prices saw The Pantry's gasoline revenues reach $1.49 billion, up from the previous year's $923.8 million. This $1.49 billion represented 61.6 percent of The Pantry's total revenues. Volatile domestic crude oil prices swung from $21 per barrel in October 1999 to $37 a barrel in September 2000. Nearly 80 percent of The Pantry's stores sold gasoline under branded name suppliers including Amoco, BP, Citgo, Exxon, Shell,

Texaco, and Chevron. The remaining 20.4 percent of gasoline was purchased from independent fuel distributors. The Pantry owned gasoline operations at 1,250 of its stores, while gasoline sold at another 17 locations was operated under third-party arrangements.

Despite its growing gasoline revenues, due to a slowdown in the U.S. economy, The Pantry slowed down the numbers of locations it acquired and started focusing on developing its existing stores to grow its revenues. It spent $21.7 million in 2001 and another $16.8 million in 2002 to upgrade its convenience stores and gasoline equipment. Approximately 60 stores were remodeled while another 66 were upgraded in 2002, the same year The Pantry opened only three new stores. Re-imaging to grow sales was the goal. The focus on branding saw The Pantry's total revenues go from $2.64 billion as of September 2001 to $2.49 billion in 2002.

In October 2003 The Pantry bought Golden Gallon from Ahold USA, Incorporated for $187 million. The purchase added an additional 138 stores to The Pantry's operations. Ninety of the stores were located in Tennessee, while the other 48 were located in northwest Georgia. Acquiring Golden Gallon had been a dream of Pete Sodini's for three years. At the close of 2004, The Pantry's gasoline revenues were at $2.32 billion, up from the previous year's $1.74 billion.

SENIOR MANAGEMENT CHANGES

The Pantry's next major acquisitions would come in 2005, when it picked up D&D Oil Company Incorporated, holder of about 53 stores, as well as an additional 23 convenience stores from Angus I. Hines Incorporated. The Angus I. Hines Inc. purchase cost $21.4 million, while the D&D Oil Company Inc. purchase cost The Pantry $23.7 million. It also helped The Pantry to expand its Alabama market.

The company would name Terrance Marks as its president and chief executive officer (CEO) in September 2009 after Peter Sodini announced his retirement in May 2009. Marks had previously served as the president of Coca-Cola Enterprises, Incorporated. One

year later The Pantry purchased 47 stores from Presto Convenience Stores. The stores, located in Kansas and Missouri, marked an expansion away from the company's traditional southeastern base. In the 2010s The Pantry sought to strengthen its Kangaroo Express brand, and it seemed likely that the Presto purchase signaled its intention to expand geographically across the United States.

Tracey Vasil Biscontini
Updated, Rhonda Campbell

PRINCIPAL SUBSIDIARIES

Angler's Mini-Mart, Inc.; Coastal Petroleum Company, Inc.; D&D Oil Co., Inc.; Shop-a-Snak Food Mart, Inc.

PRINCIPAL COMPETITORS

7-Eleven, Inc.; Circle K Company; QuikTrip Corporation; RaceTrac Petroleum, Inc.

FURTHER READING

Gervickas, Bicki. "Stocking Up the Pantry." *Petrogram,* May/June 1999.

Grugal, Robin M.. "Supermarket Guru Revamps Minimart Chain." *Investor's Business Daily,* August 18, 1999.

Lofstock, John. "The Pantry to Acquire Golden Gallon." *Convenience Store News,* August 26, 2003. Accessed February 20, 2011. http://www.allbusiness.com/retail-trade/food-stores /4479976-1.html.

Morrison, Mitch. "The Pantry Stocks Up On C-Stores." *Convenience Store News,* February 8, 1999.

"The Pantry Acquires 47 Presto C-Stores." *Convenience Store News,* January 10, 2011. Accessed February 20, 2011. http://www.csnews.com/article-the_pantry_acquires_47_ presto_c_stores-1389.html.

"The Pantry, Inc." *Convenience Store News,* August 3, 1988, 74.

"Pantry President and CEO Peter J. Sodini to Retire in 2009." StreetInsider.com, April 23, 2009. Accessed February 20, 2011. http://www.streetinsider.com/Management+Changes/ Pantry+(PTRY)+President+and+CEO+Peter+J.+Sodini+to+ Retire+in+2009/4583382.html.

Playboy Enterprises, Inc.

680 North Lake Shore Drive
Chicago, Illinois 60611
U.S.A.
Telephone: (312) 751-8000
Fax: (312) 751-2818
Web site: http://www.playboyenterprises.com

Private Company
Founded: 1953
Employees: 547 (2009)
Sales: $215.2 million (2010)
NAIC: 511120 Periodical Publishers; 512110 Motion Picture and Video Production; 515120 Television Broadcasting.

■ ■ ■

Playboy Enterprises, Inc., is a global media company initially known for its signature magazine *Playboy,* which features lifestyle articles, political commentary, works of fiction, and beautiful women in various stages of undress. The prevalence of attractive nude women is central to the appeal of most of Playboy's ventures, for the company's media holdings include television networks (Playboy TV, Spice Digital), Web sites (Playboy.com, Cyber Club), and radio shows. The company also licenses its distinctive bunny logo to a variety of apparel and other products.

The company is closely identified with pajama-clad founder Hugh Hefner, who enjoys a well-photographed existence at the famous Playboy Mansion in Beverly Hills, California. However, circulation levels for the flag-ship magazine have plummeted, and revenue decreased by over one-third between 2007 and 2010. In 2011 Icon Acquisitions, an investment firm controlled by Hefner, acquired Playboy Enterprises for $207 million and took the company private.

THE MEN'S MAGAZINE, ONE STEP FURTHER

Hugh Hefner was born in 1927 in Chicago, Illinois. Hefner's family was traditional German-Swedish Protestant and his parent forbade him and his younger brother to drink, smoke, swear, and attend movies on Sunday. Their father worked as an accountant for an aluminum company and was rarely home. Their austere and imposing mother influenced their upbringing the most. The subject of sex was taboo, considered horrid and something never to be discussed. Hefner developed into an introverted young man and escaped into his own fantasy world through writing, drawing cartoons, and collecting butterflies.

Hefner graduated from high school in 1944. He served as a clerk in military installations throughout the United States for the remainder of World War II and was discharged from service in the summer of 1946. He followed his high school sweetheart, Millie Williams, to the University of Illinois at Urbana-Champaign and attended classes, working toward a psychology major. Hefner gained renown as a contributor of cartoons to the campus humor magazine. After graduating in 1949, Hugh and Millie married and moved back to Chicago. He worked in the personnel department of a printed carton manufacturing company to support them.

Hefner hated this job and soon quit to take graduate courses in psychology at Northwestern University. However, he dropped out of the graduate program to take a copywriting position in the advertising department of *Esquire* magazine. When his boss refused to give him a five-dollar raise, he quit. It was 1952, and Hefner was finding it difficult to find steady employment. Meanwhile, his marriage was barely surviving.

While working at *Esquire* magazine, Hefner developed an idea for a new product. *Esquire* magazine had been successful in creating an image of what it meant to be an urbane young man. This was a sophisticated, worldly person interested in fancy sports cars, good food, expensive clothing, exotic wines, hi-fi equipment, and women. Hefner took this formula and decided to take it one step further by including photographs of nude females in the magazine. He approached Art Paul, a freelance art director, and asked him to help design the magazine in exchange for private shares in the company. Hefner pawned his possessions and worked odd jobs to finance the magazine. In the evenings, he and Paul assembled the first issue of the magazine on his kitchen table in a small Chicago apartment. Hefner wanted to name the publication *Stag Party,* but there was a copyright conflict with another publication, so he settled on *Playboy* magazine. Paul designed the Playboy logo, a rabbit wearing a tuxedo bow tie, that would appear on the cover of every issue of the magazine.

Hefner purchased the famous nude calendar picture of Marilyn Monroe for $200 and inserted some risqué cartoons and jokes of his own. He rounded up a few literary pieces that had been previously published in other magazines, and in November 1953 the first issue went to press. Hefner published the issue using $600 of his own money and $8,000 raised through the sale of private stock to friends and supporters. His mother contributed $1,000 of the initial investment, although she never read an issue during her life. (He also hired his father as an accountant, and he never read an issue either.) The first issue carried no date because Hefner was not sure whether he would have the money to publish a second issue.

The bold and brash new magazine sold 55,000 copies at 50 cents a copy. By the publication of the fourth issue, Hefner had made enough money to rent an office in downtown Chicago and begin hiring staff. He retained control of all aspects of the magazine's production. The nude woman featured in each magazine became known as the "Playmate," and later as the "Playmate of the Month." What was unknown to many people was the initial difficulty Hefner had convincing women to pose nude for the centerfold, and at one point he ran out of options. As the story goes, an attractive female subscription manager came to ask him for an addressograph machine, and Hefner responded that she would have it if she would pose as the playmate of the month. She agreed to the deal, and soon after, word got around that the photo sessions were conducted with respect, good humor, and consummate professionalism. Before long Hefner was deluged with photos from women working at the Playboy offices in Chicago and from models across the United States. Eventually, the nude section or "pictorial" included a series of pictures of the playmate in progressive stages of undress and in various poses.

The nude pictures published during the first 15 years or so would be considered tame by contemporary standards. The pictures did not show even a slight glimpse of the woman's pubic hair until 1968, and it was not until January 1972 that the pictorial included full frontal nudity.

In 1959 Hugh Hefner and Millie Hefner divorced. The marriage had produced two children, Christie and David. The line between Hugh Hefner's private life and his professional life had pretty much dissolved, such that he took on the persona of the successful, freewheeling, and sophisticated bachelor as defined in the pages of his magazine. It became hard to distinguish the company from the man and vice versa. Hugh Hefner became the face of *Playboy* magazine, and any attention the magazine attracted was almost always directed mostly at him.

THE NIGHT LIFE, PLAYBOY STYLE

By 1960 *Playboy* magazine had become one of the most successful publications in the United States. Circulation had surpassed one million, and advertising revenues had skyrocketed to $2.3 million. Buoyed by his success, Hefner opened Playboy Clubs in major cities across the country. These were private clubs where tired businessmen could eat good food, drink, and be entertained while being waited on by the Playboy "bunnies." The bunnies wore only a one-piece corset with a cottontail fixed to the bottom and rabbit ears on their head. At the same time, Playboy diversified into more standard clubs, casinos, and resorts. In Chicago, Hefner purchased the old Knickerbocker Hotel and transformed it into the

KEY DATES

1953: Hugh Hefner publishes the first issue of *Playboy* magazine.

1960: The first Playboy Club opens in Chicago, Illinois.

1972: Magazine reaches highest circulation in its history at 7.2 million subscribers; Playboy publishes *Oui* magazine.

1976: Derick Daniels becomes president; Hugh Hefner remains publisher.

1981: Company sells *Oui* magazine to French publisher.

1986: Christie Hefner becomes president; the Meese Commission designates *Playboy* magazine as pornographic; the last Playboy Club closes in Lansing, Michigan.

1989: Playboy at Night, its first pay-per-view cable service, launches.

1997: Playboy Cyber Club launches.

2008: Christie Hefner resigns as CEO; Jerome Kern takes over as president on interim basis.

2010: Hugh Hefner offers to take company private.

2011: Board recommends to shareholders that they accept Hefner's offer to take company private.

posh and elegant Playboy Towers. In 1955 Hefner invested over $55 million to develop resort hotels. Other investments included Playboy apartment complexes, an agreement with Columbia Pictures to develop first-run movies, the production of television shows and records, and the production of sheet music. From 1965 to 1970, sales at Playboy Enterprises jumped dramatically from $48 million to just over $127 million.

Hefner carefully created his own Playboy myth. He purchased a huge Victorian estate in the heart of the most fashionable Gold Coast area on Chicago's north side, and he proceeded to decorate it with a combination of Renaissance and contemporary furnishings. Hefner lived in a room off the great hall, complete with a $5 million circular bed. Bunnies and former playmates of the month occupied other rooms on the upper two floors of the mansion. The swimming pool in the backyard was decorated with the trappings of a Roman temple. Neighbors complained about the seemingly endless parties. The "Friday Night Party" became a regular event at the mansion with Hefner as the master of ceremonies as his guests enjoyed swimming, drinking, eating, dancing, and, of course, lots of voyeurism. He

invited Playboy bunnies, playmates, casts of stage plays, movie stars, and other celebrities to his parties, and he strutted among his guests with a pipe in his mouth, looking quite similar to a reincarnation of the Great Gatsby.

"I JUST READ IT FOR THE ARTICLES"

In the late 1950s and through the 1960s, *Playboy* magazine also became known for content beyond the nude photographs, including articles and fiction written by the best journalists and authors of the times. Hefner himself wrote a Playboy Philosophy series addressing the major social issues of the times, opening up the magazine to debates on its pages. As early as 1954, *Playboy* magazine published Ray Bradbury's famous *Fahrenheit 451* in serial form. The magazine published works by other major authors like Norman Mailer, Jack Kerouac, Ernest Hemingway, Ian Fleming, and John Steinbeck. The magazine also became well known for a regular interview that was usually exhaustive and fairly confrontational with a celebrity, politician, or controversial public figure. The journalists interviewed a wide variety of people, including Miles Davis, Jean-Paul Sartre, Malcolm X, Princess Grace, Jimmy Hoffa, The Beatles, Fidel Castro, Cassius Clay (later Muhammad Ali), and Woody Allen.

The early 1970s were the best years for Playboy, benefitting from the "sexual revolution" and in many ways contributing to it. The company became a lightning rod for feminist activists, most notably Gloria Steinem who, after working as a bunny in a Playboy club, wrote an article attacking the company. Despite such attacks (or perhaps due to them), the magazine's circulation grew to its highest level ever at 7.2 million readers in 1972. The company also went public in 1971, trading under the symbol "PLA." At the same time, the magazine faced competition from a new upstart, *Penthouse* magazine, first published in Great Britain but then in the United States in 1969. *Penthouse* offered more explicit photographs of its "Penthouse Pets." Playboy created a new publication, *Oui* magazine, with equally explicit photographs, to compete with *Penthouse*.

Hefner grew dissatisfied with the lack of celebrity access and general conservative attitudes in Chicago, so he moved his residence to Beverly Hills, California. By this time, Hefner had lost interest in managing the company. He hired Derick Daniels to take charge of managing Playboy's operations and its growing business interests. Daniels had been instrumental in growing Knight-Ridder Newspapers into a newspaper behemoth. When he arrived at Playboy he found a company in disarray. Pretax profits had shrunk to $2 million in 1975 and barely topped $5 million in 1976. The new entertainment division, which included movies, television, records and sheet music, was operating at a significant loss.

A PAINFUL TRANSITION TO MODERNITY

Hefner gave Daniels full rein to reorganize the company and make improvements to operations. Daniels made a clean sweep of management at all levels, eliminating 100 positions within the company ranging from vice presidents to assistant publicists. He withdrew Playboy's interests in movies and television shows and discontinued its record and sheet music business. Playboy retained its licensing arrangements and reassessed the kind of advertisements run in the magazine. In an effort to stop the red ink, Daniels redirected the entertainment division toward developing the company's gambling operations. Although Playboy's nightclub and resort division was losing money, its London-based casinos were generating the majority of the company's cash flow. Daniels upgraded the London casinos, opened a new casino in Cable Beach, the Bahamas, and made plans for a hotel-casino in Atlantic City, New Jersey.

Despite Daniel's steady leadership and effective management, Playboy continued to languish in the early 1980s. The company lost over $69 million total over 1980 and 1981. In 1982 Playboy's financial loss was 50 percent of sales. The number of Playboy clubs had decreased precipitously from 22 to 3. In 1981 the cities of London and Atlantic City accused Playboy of various regulatory breaches and challenged its casino licenses. The company was forced to divest from its most profitable business activity and sell all of its casinos to other companies. Also, the company's more sexually explicit magazine, *Oui* magazine, had failed to compete with *Penthouse* and the younger *Hustler*. Instead, *Oui* magazine was losing money and stealing readers away from the company's own *Playboy* magazine. In 1981 Playboy sold *Oui* magazine to a French publisher. Hefner fired Daniels and replaced him with someone he knew more intimately and trusted more thoroughly, his own daughter.

THE CORPORATE DAUGHTER

Christie Hefner was a Phi Beta Kappa and summa cum laude graduate of Brandeis University. She graduated in 1974 and joined the company a year later. In 1982 she was made president of the company, a very quick rise even for someone with her qualifications. Her father remained editor-in-chief and majority stockholder in the

company. Christie projected a highly professional image and remained far away from the libertine excesses of her father. She quickly installed a new management team with more corporate experience to help her revitalize the company's fortunes. She inherited a sprawling mess of a company with investments in hotels, casinos, restaurants, movie and record production, book clubs, night clubs and, of course, magazines. A painful decision she made quickly was to sell off the company's casino holdings, and by 1984 Playboy was out of the gambling business. In addition, she consolidated several divisions and sold or closed various unprofitable ventures, including its night clubs.

One of her most daunting challenges was figuring out how the company's publications would adjust to the dramatic changes in the public's attitudes toward sex that had occurred over the last 30 years. During the 1950s, breaking the taboos of guiltless sex and nudity had catapulted Playboy to success, but in the 1980s, everything seemed tolerated, if not completely accepted. The company not only needed to achieve financial viability, but it needed to redefine *Playboy* magazine's credo of "Entertainment for Men." *Playboy* magazine needed a new direction, so it updated its editorial image by championing free speech and first amendment rights. The magazine contracted authors to write about social issues, supporting gay rights, AIDS research, and the plight of battered women. The magazine used its international publications as a forum for political dissidents, bringing attention to abuses of power and government corruption. The first issue of the company's Taiwan edition of *Playboy* magazine featured an interview with one of the leaders of the Tiananmen Square student uprising in China. The magazine continued to feature nude pictorials of busty women, but the new leaders of the company worked hard to transform the image of the company and attract a more diverse audience.

Regardless of any internal changes, events and the economic and political environment conspired against Playboy in the 1980s. The magazine continued to face tough competition from *Penthouse* and *Hustler*. In 1985 Hugh Hefner suffered a mild stroke, which left the business without its mascot and almost entirely in his fairly inexperienced daughter's control. In 1986 the Reagan administration's Meese Commission designated *Playboy* magazine as pornographic. Major vendors such as 7-Eleven and newsstands around the country refused to sell the magazine. Traditionally, 75 percent of all sales of *Playboy* magazine had come from full-price newsstand sales. When this source of revenue all but vanished, Playboy implemented a successful subscription campaign. By the end of the decade circulation had leveled off at approximately 3.4 million readers, with over

75 percent coming from subscription sales, but the change in direction took time and profits remained stagnant.

NEW VENTURES, OLD MAGAZINE

One of the bright spots in the company's fortunes was the reinvention of the entertainment division. The company had formed a Playboy Channel in the early 1980s to take advantage of the burgeoning cable television market. Television subscribers decreased from a high of 750,000 in 1985 to 430,000 in 1989, so Playboy replaced the ailing cable channel with a pay-per-view service called "Playboy At Night." The new service offered soft-core pornographic movies and Playmate videos. Playboy At Night quickly gained access to over four million homes and suddenly became the third-largest pay-per-view service in the United States. At the same time, Playboy put more money into producing videos. By the end of the decade Playboy was the third-largest nontheatrical distributor of videos, just behind Walt Disney and Jane Fonda (workout videos). The company's "ForCouple'sOnly" collection, which included the highly regarded massage videos, was the company's best-selling series.

In 1989 Hugh Hefner married Playmate of the Year Kimberley Conrad. Playboy entered the 1990s with strength, especially in overseas markets. Overseas circulation jumped from 500,000 during the mid-1980s to over 1.5 million. The company licensed 14 foreign editions and started developing television programming for Western Europe, where the cultures were more tolerant of nudity. Another licensee opened 20 sportswear boutiques that sold jogging suits, jeans, dress shirts, and attaché cases, all featuring the Playboy logo. The company initiated a Playboy Channel in Japan in partnership with the Tohokushinsha Film Corporation. Playboy also revived its gaming interests, taking a 12 percent stake in a casino to be built on the Greek Island of Rhodes.

By 1995 the battle between *Playboy* magazine and *Penthouse* magazine and other competitors had moved to the Internet. *Playboy* magazine was the first national magazine to have a Web site, and early on, Playboy.com registered 500,000 visitors in one 24-hour period. It quickly became one of the most popular Web sites. By 1997 the site registered as many as 7 million visits a day and was making a profit from online advertising. Later, the company launched the Playboy Cyber Club, a subscription and pay-per-view Web site. Subscribers paid a monthly or annual fee for access to playmate photos, artwork, cartoons, articles, and interviews going back to the beginning of the magazine. The site also offered chat rooms with playmates and a cyber tour of Hugh Hefner's Playboy mansion. Christie Hefner's vision for a new Playboy seemed to be taking hold, with an increased international presence, a new and ambitious Internet foothold, and a push into alternative television solutions like pay-per-view and satellite television broadcast. At the same time, circulation of *Playboy* magazine was at 3.2 million with 15 international editions and periodic issues such as *Playboy's Book of Lingerie*.

PERSONAL TRANSITIONS, BOLD VISIONS

In 1998 Hugh Hefner and his wife Kimberley separated. The marriage had produced two children, and Kimberley and her sons moved into a house next door that was connected to the mansion. On the verge of the new millennium, the corporate-minded Christie Hefner set a goal for the company directed mainly at Wall Street. She wanted the company to grow from its current capitalization of $350 million to above $1 billion in five years. Her vision was to build Playboy into a global multimedia giant, and she often said Playboy would be an adult version of the Walt Disney Company.

As Playboy crossed into the new millennium, the magazine and Playboy.com faced new competition from a new category of men's lifestyle magazines. Magazines like *Maxim, Details, Stuff,* and *FHM* (For Him Magazine) were more in line with the modern trends in magazine publishing. They published shorter, less content-intensive articles that could be read quickly. They featured women, mostly celebrities, photographed as close to nude as possible without actually being nude. The lack of nudity meant that retailers could place these magazines next to more mainstream publications. They did not have to restrict them by keeping them behind the counter or on the shelf behind a barrier that obscured the cover, as was the case with *Playboy* magazine and similar magazines. They also attracted advertisers who traditionally refused to advertise in the magazines with nude pictures.

In response, Playboy attempted to shift away from the antiquated image that Hugh Hefner had created for the magazine to an image that appealed to a new, younger market. As part of this effort, the company diverted attention from the old Playboy mansion and purchased an apartment in New York City on Fifth Avenue and 57th street. The company nicknamed it the "party lounge," or "Playboy East." While the parties at the apartment still featured playmates and Playboy bunnies the atmosphere was more urban and conservative as opposed to the wild glitz of the Playboy mansion. As the company shifted its image it also made inroads into the international market by expanding into Romania and Hungary.

The latter half of the first decade of the 21st century brought several challenges as Playboy faced rising printing, paper, and distributions costs, and the company came under the threat of free Internet porn. While the company's licensing ventures continued to be successful, its media properties, including the magazines and Internet venues, were dragging down the bottom line. In 2006 Playboy reentered the gambling industry through a joint venture with the Palms Casino Resort and N9NE Group, a restaurant and entertainment company. The concept was a nightclub similar to the old Playboy Clubs of the 1970s with gambling and a cover charge for entry. The club quickly became one of Playboy's most profitable ventures.

THE DAUGHTER'S SUDDEN EXIT

In 2008 Christie Hefner suddenly resigned her position as chairman and chief executive of Playboy. Her announcement surprised everyone, including her own staff. During her tenure, Christie had taken great strides to bring Playboy into the modern era, but the company still seemed to be lagging behind its competitors at leveraging its brand. Many thought her efforts were hampered by her father's devotion to the magazine, which operated at a loss through most fiscal quarters. Christie Hefner was replaced by Jerome Kern on an interim basis.

Playboy posted a loss of $160.4 million in 2008, and while it had a profit of $910,000 in 2007, the years 2005 and 2006 had also ended in losses. As a result of this unprofitability, the company announced that it was willing to entertain a buyer for the company. Playboy refused calls by investors to sell parts of the company off to buyers. Investors wanted Playboy to focus on its profitable licensing business and leave the magazine and Web site to be managed by a company that could concentrate on making it more profitable. Playboy continued to post losses through 2009 as the company entertained suitors.

In July 2009 Playboy hired Scott Flanders as CEO of the company. Flanders had been president and CEO of Freedom Communications, a $1 billion media company. Before that, he was chairman and CEO of the Columbia House Company, a direct marketer of music and video products. The company promoted executive vice president Alex Vaickus to the position of president. The new executive team directed the company through further reorganization and cost cutting in an effort to return it to profitability.

STRANGE OFFER BRINGS UNCERTAINTY

After a 12-year separation, Hugh Hefner and Kimberley Hefner finally divorced in early 2010. In July, Hefner, who was still the majority shareholder in Playboy, announced his intention to buy up the remaining shares of the company at $5.50 per share and take the company private. Investors were mystified by the move because they believed the value of the company to be overinflated, not underinflated as Hefner's offer implied. Later that year, at the age of 84, Hugh Hefner announced plans to marry 24-year-old Crystal Harris, who was *Playboy* magazine's playmate of the month for December 2009.

In early 2011 Hugh Hefner purchased Playboy Enterprises and took it private. The deal still looked questionable to Wall Street onlookers, mainly because they saw a difficult road ahead for Playboy. The company faced difficulties on two fronts. On one side, free pornography and more explicit X-rated pornography available on the Internet threatened the company's Internet and cable television pay-per-view model. On the other side, younger publications like *Maxim, Stuff,* and *FHM* continued to siphon away readers and Web site visitors. The magazine's circulation had dropped to 1.5 million at the end of 2010.

Originally, Playboy was a unique voice in a desert of sexuality. The magazine defined itself as a cultural force and dealt with the social and political issues of the times. As the company aged it responded to market pressures by moving into more explicitly pornographic media. As a result, Playboy became just another purveyor of male advice and pornography in a very crowded field. While it was uncertain if Playboy would be able to return to steady profitability in the 2010s, it did control one of the most recognized entertainment brands in the world.

Thomas Derdak
Updated, Aaron Hauser

PRINCIPAL SUBSIDIARIES

Playboy.com, Inc.; Playboy Clubs International, Inc.; Playboy Entertainment Group, Inc.; Playboy Forum Shops, Inc.; Playboy Gaming International, Inc.; Spice Entertainment, Inc.; The Hugh Hefner Foundation.

PRINCIPAL DIVISIONS

Entertainment; Licensing; Print/Digital.

PRINCIPAL COMPETITORS

Alpha Media Group, Inc.; FriendFinder Networks, Inc.; LFP, Inc.; New Frontier Media, Inc.; Vivid Entertainment, LLC.

FURTHER READING

Clifford, Stephanie. "Christie Hefner Stepping Down as Chief at Playboy." *New York Times,* December 9, 2008, 2.

Farhi, Paul. "Christie Hefner, Playboy Empire." *Austin American-Statesman,* August 24, 1997, J1.

Farzad, Roben. "It's Not Her Father's Playboy." *New York Times,* September 24, 2005, 3.

Jones, Tim. "Playboy Widening Its Use of the Web." *The Record,* June 23, 1997, H09.

Kaufman, Joanne. "Playboy Has a Losing Quarter, and It's Chief Talks of Media Transformation." *New York Times,* May 12, 2008, 4.

Machan, Dyan. "The Hef and Christie Saga." *Forbes,* August 28, 1995, 89.

McGrath, Charles. "How Hef Got His Groove Back." *New York Times,* February 6, 2011, 24.

Miller, Russell. *Bunny: The Real Story of Playboy.* New York: Holt, Rinehart and Winston, 1985.

Parks, Louis B. "Playboy Turns 50." *Houston Chronicle,* December 14, 2003, 1.

Peters, Jeremy W. "Hefner Bids to Buy All of Playboy." *New York Times,* July 13, 2010, 1.

Steinberg, Brian. "No Longer 'YourFather's' Playboy Works a Mellow Swagger." *Wall Street Journal,* December 13, 1999.

Weinraub, Bernard. "Reviving an Aging Playboy Is a Father-Daughter Project." *New York Times* February 4, 2002, 1.

Weyr, Thomas. *Reaching for Paradise: The Playboy Vision of America.* New York: New York Times Books, 1978.

Wiles, Russ. "Playboy Enterprises CEO Wants to Increase Company's Worth on Wall Street." *Arizona Republic,* June 9, 1998.

Playtech Limited

Upper Church Street
St. George's Court
Second Floor
Douglas, Isle of Man IM1 1EE
United Kingdom
Telephone: (44) 1624-645-999
Fax: (44) 1624 645-955
Web site: http://www.playtech.com

Public Company
Founded: 1999
Employees: 800 (2010)
Sales:£114.8 million ($184 million) (2009)
Stock Exchanges: London
Ticker Symbol: PTEC
NAICS: 713290 Other Gambling Industries

■ ■ ■

Playtech Limited is one of the largest online and land-based gaming software developers and vendors in the world. Headquartered in the United Kingdom's Isle of Man, Playtech enjoys an international presence and operates subsidiaries in Estonia, Bulgaria, Israel, and the Philippines. Playtech principally operates as a business to business (B2B) supplier and licensor of land-based and unified online gaming software platforms.

Playtech's gaming product portfolio includes iPoker, one of the foremost online poker networks worldwide. Other products, ranging from bingo to mahjong, come in a variety of platforms such as online, mobile, or fixed.

THE BIRTH OF PLAYTECH LIMITED INCORPORATED

Playtech Limited was founded as Playtech B.V. in 1999 by Teddy Sagi, an Israeli entrepreneur in the software engineering industry at the time. Sagi enlisted the help of his entrepreneur associates and registered the business as a B2B provider of gaming software platforms. The founders of the company spent the first two years on market research and planning, recruitment of information technology and software engineering experts, and the configuration of the blueprint gaming software for the company. The newly formed company completed its first gaming software package in 2000. In April 2001 Sagi and his shareholding associates proceeded to transform the company into an international entity with limited liabilities by incorporating Playtech (Cyprus) Limited in Cyprus. Playtech B.V. landed its first software vending deals with an online gaming operator in 2001.

The company established its presence in Israel in April 2002 by incorporating Techplay Marketing Limited as a wholly owned subsidiary for advertising and marketing the company's operations in Cyprus. The company made its first acquisition the same month when Playtech Cyprus secured the buyout of Technogama N.V. The company also purchased the entire share capital of OU Estonia in August 2002 and renamed it OU Playtech Estonia. OU Estonia designed, developed, and manufactured a wide range of sophisticated gaming software applications at the time of its acquisition.

COMPANY PERSPECTIVES

Our philosophy is based on a deep and stable partnership foundation and our success is based first and foremost on a commitment to achieving excellence through cooperative discourse with our clients. We believe that our practice of fostering open channels of communication with licensees is the best means of generating profitability, as it enables us to fine tune our management tools and product lines to suit our customers' specific requirements.

Playtech was officially incorporated as a limited liability offshore company in September 2002, with offices in the Isle of Man. For most of 2003, the management of Playtech Limited concentrated on the growth and development of its core business segments. The company introduced live gaming, live dealer tables, and real-time video streaming broadcast gaming software applications during the year. The company made its first acquisition for that year in October, when the Playtech Cyprus subsidiary purchased the share capital of Networkland Limited, a company based in the British Virgin Islands.

NICHE STRATEGIES AND AN IPO: 2004–2007

Playtech launched its iPoker network in 2004 as its software vending business prospects flourished following the integration of casinos and variety gaming applications by the leading betting and sportsbook companies. The company's gaming software authenticity was accorded recognition when the company was officially issued with BMM International's Certificate of Evaluation in March 2004. The company also expanded its offering for land-based gaming platforms by launching the Videobet subsidiary in the year.

Playtech Limited initiated a niche-targeted market strategy in April 2005 by releasing customizable gaming software applications for sportsbook operators. The release featured 13 fixed-odds games that included virtual horse racing.

Playtech's shares began trading at the London Stock Exchange on March 28, 2006, after a successful initial public offering (IPO) of 46 percent of the company's shares that raised £590 million. The IPO included 25 percent of the shareholding of the company's founder, Teddy Sagi. The company's founder retained 40 percent shareholding of the company.

Playtech introduced a new strategy angle in the gaming industry by establishing the Playtech Academy in Estonia in the first quarter of 2006. Playtech Academy was founded as a training institution for computer science courses tailored toward the gaming industry. The institution was based in Tartu and enrolled 40 students in its first session. The first batch of Playtech Academy students graduated in September 2006. The company also recruited 20 employees specializing in information technology to serve in its Bulgarian development center. This was established to facilitate the training of its employees in the country.

The company introduced Videobet, a mobile offering for casino games, and Asian-market-specific games in 2006. The Videobet software product was designed to suit both land-based and online-based gaming terminals. The mobile offering featured an integrated platform for both online casino and stand-alone applications for online bingo and poker. The company also launched Mahjong, its first gaming application tailored for the Asian gaming market.

Playtech enhanced business opportunities for its poker gaming platform by acquiring Tribeca Poker Network in December 2006. Acquired at a cost of $75 million, Tribeca Poker Network was a leading online poker gaming provider at the time of its acquisition. The admission of Playtech into the Remote Gambling Association (RGA) in 2006 marked a major milestone in the responsibile gaming initiatives of the company.

The enactment of the Unlawful Internet Gambling Enforcement Act 2006 (UIGEA) in the United States in September 2006 was a game changer in the gambling entertainment industry. UIGEA prohibited the acceptance by financial institutions of any payments from entities involved in betting or wagering businesses, in effect outlawing gambling on the Internet. The new anti-online gambling laws consequentially sealed off Playtech's B2B market opportunities in the United States. Playtech officially stopped licensing its U.S.-based gaming software operators in November 2007. The company, however, adopted an immediate strategy shift and directed its focus toward expansion in the European and Asian markets.

LICENSING AGREEMENTS AND REVENUE GROWTH: 2007–09

The success of the strategic shift was evidenced in 2007 when the company posted revenues in excess of those it posted prior to the enactment of UIGEA in 2006. The company compensated for the loss of its U.S. market share by entering a record 15 new licensing agreements

KEY DATES

1999: Israeli entrepreneur Teddy Sagi begins work on a software gaming platform.
2002: Playtech Limited incorporates.
2006: Playtech lists on the London Stock Exchange.
2008: Agreement with Paramount Digital Entertainment allows Playtech to feature popular brands of Paramount Pictures in its gaming offerings.
2010: Playtech acquires Virtual Fusion Limited, an online bingo gaming provider.

with European and Asian companies for its gaming software platforms. Playtech also witnessed the successful completion of the migration of Tribeca, the major international poker network, to its online gaming platforms after its acquisition. The development contributed to the transformation of iPoker into one of the largest poker network in the world in 2007, streaming to as many as 30,000 live real money players during peak sessions.

In 2008 Playtech's product portfolio continued to grow at the same pace as its growing number of licensees. Playtech further strengthened its market position by signing a guaranteed licensing agreement with Paramount Digital Entertainment that allowed the licensees of Playtech to feature popular brands of Paramount Pictures in its gaming offerings.

The emergence of new regulations in Playtech's target markets in Europe remained one of the big challenges confronted by the company expansion strategy. Nonetheless, the company was able to register commendable milestones by establishing a clientele in newly regulated markets of Spain and Italy in 2009. The signing of a licensing agreement with the Casino Gran Madrid (CGM) for the supply of land-based poker and casino gaming products was one such milestone achieved by the company in 2009. CGM is a prestigious gaming giant that boasts unrivaled grandeur in Europe.

Italy was the other newly regulated market where Playtech achieved an impact by establishing a network for its poker product segment. The company entered multiple licensing agreements that brought on board major Italian land-based gaming operators such as SNAI S.p.A., Eurobet Italia S.p.A., and Sisal S.p.A. In 2009 the company also secured gaming software licensing deals with Estonia's Olympic Online Casino Company and Serbia's state-run lottery in 2009.

In October 2009 William Hill Online migrated from its previous online gaming software providers to Playtech's online software, thereby marking the commencement of joint venture operations between the two companies. Playtech also secured software licensing agreements with Betfair, a betting giant in the United Kingdom, and Marvel Entertainment Inc. The multiple licensing agreements of 2009 facilitated the introduction of live television shows, sports betting, and a range of top-ranking branded games to Playtech's varied product portfolio. Playtech purchased Gaming Technology Solutions (GTS) at a total cost of $32.4 million in December 2009 to record one of the largest acquisitions in its history. GTS operated the EDGE open-architecture gaming platform under which 20 providers of gaming content extended more than 500 games at the time of its acquisition.

Playtech defied all odds to register growth in the financial year 2009 when many companies in the leisure and entertainment industry reported steep declines in performance. The adverse effects of the global economic crisis affected the performance of many companies in the industry and across the board. The company posted a 3 percent revenue growth in 2009 to reach £114.8 million compared to £111.5 million in 2008. The impressive performance of the company in the financial year 2009 was attributed to continued expansion of the company's B2B product portfolio and customer base. The cost measures adopted by the company during the year also contributed immensely to the successful performance. The company was granted associate membership to the World Lottery Association in recognition of its commitment to the principles of responsible gaming.

EXPANSION: 2010 AND BEYOND

Playtech continued to pursue its expansion strategies in 2010 through partnerships, mergers, and acquisitions. In January 2010 Playtech announced the establishment of a major gaming software licensing agreement with SEGA Games Limited. Playtech also finalized a strategic partnership deal with Scientific Games, a software development company based in the United States. The partnership deal is also defined by exclusivity clauses for the development of gaming terminal software for Scientific Games by Playtech's subsidiary, Videobet.

Playtech expanded its interest in the bingo gaming segment in February 2010 through the acquisition of Virtual Fusion Limited's business and assets at a cost of $36 million. Virtual Fusion was a top-ranking company in the development and licensing of online bingo gaming products. The buyout of Virtue Fusion effectively transformed Playtech into the world's largest network for bingo gaming products. The company landed a major deal for its bingo products soon after through the signing of an agreement with Boylesports Ltd., one of the largest bookmakers in Ireland, for the provision of online bingo solutions.

Continuous growth and expansion through partnerships, acquisitions, and licensing agreements remained at the core of the long-term plans of Playtech. The company also planned to develop gaming software programs tailored for the fast-emerging business-to-government (B2G) opportunities. The company launched the B2G plans in response to the emergence of newly regulated gambling markets in European countries such as Italy and Serbia.

Paul Ingati

PRINCIPAL SUBSIDIARIES

OU Playtech (Estonia); Playtech Software Ltd. (British Virgin Islands); Techplay Marketing Ltd. (Israel); VS Gaming Limited; VS Technology Lmited.

PRINCIPAL COMPETITORS

888 Holdings Limited; Betonsports plc; Ladbrokes plc; Party Gaming plc; The Rank Group plc.

FURTHER READING

Digital Look. "Playtech Ltd. (PTEC)." London: Digital Look Ltd. Accessed February 8, 2011. http://www.digitallook.com/cgi-bin/dlmedia/security.cgi?username=&ac=&csi=176573.

Edwards, H. L. "iPoker Network's Playtech Ltd Up 29 Percent." PokerRoomReview.com, May 13 2010. Accessed November 17, 2010. http://pokerroomreview.com/poker-news/6656-ipoker-network-playtech-up-29-percent.

Google. "Playtech Limited" Google Finance UK. Accessed October 14, 2010. http://www.google.co.uk/finance?q=LON:PTEC.

"Online Casino Software Providers." GamblingPlanet.org. Accessed November 19, 2010. http://www.gamblingplanet.org/casino_software.php.

"Playtech Acquires Gambling Company GTS." CasinoPeople.com, December 13, 2009. Accessed November 15, 2010. http://www.casinopeople.com/news/playtech-acquires-gambling-company-gts.html.

"Playtech Announces Licensing Agreement with SEGA Games Limited Operators of www.SEGACasino.com and wwwSEGAPoker.com." *PR Newswire,* January 14, 2010. Accessed November 17, 2010. http://www.prnewswire.com/news-releases/playtech-announces-licensing-agreement-with-sega-games-limited-operators-of-wwwsegacasinocom-and-wwwsegapokercom-81472297.html.

"Playtech Launches French iPOK." MoneyAM.com, July 20, 2010. Accessed November 17, 2010. http://moneyam.uk-wire.com/cgi-bin/articles/201007200700105879P.html.

"Playtech Ltd." *Bloomberg BusinessWeek.* Accessed November 17, 2010. http://investing.businessweek.com/research/stocks/snapshot/snapshot.asp?ticker=PTEC:LN.

"Playtech Up; Buys Online Bingo Firm." *Reuters,* February 15, 2010. Accessed November15, 2010. http://www.reuters.com/article/idUKLDE61E0VW20100215?type=companyNews.

"SEGA Casino Launched." *Gambling Gazette,* January 25, 2010. Accessed February 8, 2011. http://www.gambling-gazette.com/blog/gambling-news/sega-casino-launched.

Shuttleworth, Jenni. "Playtech Wins 2010 International Company of the Year Award." *Intergame Online,* October 15, 2010. Accessed February 8, 2011. http://www.intergameonline.com/intergamingi/news/4469/playtech-wins-2010-international-company-of-the-year-award/.

Watson, Katy. "Playtech, Gaming Software Designer, Plans London IPO." *Bloomberg,* February 17, 2006. Accessed November 15, 2010. http://www.bloomberg.com/apps/news?pid=newsarchive&sid=aBFn6CvPCZNA&refer=canada.

World Lottery Association. "Scientific Games Announces Strategic Partnership with Playtech." World Lottery Association, January 21, 2010. Accessed November 15, 2010. http://www.world-lotteries.org/cms/index.php?option=com_content&task=view&id=3551&Itemid=30.

The Princeton Review, Inc.

———■———

111 Speen Street
Framingham, Massachusetts 01701
U.S.A.
Telephone: (508) 663-5050
Toll Free: (877) 312-7022
Web site: http://www.princetonreview.com

Public Company
Founded: 1981
Employees: 996 (2009)
Sales: $143.5 million (2009)
Stock Exchanges: NASDAQ
Ticker Symbol: REVU
NAIC: 611691 Exam Preparation and Tutoring

■ ■ ■

The Princeton Review, Inc. (Princeton), was originally established to coach high school students taking the Scholastic Aptitude Test (SAT) and has grown to provide preparation materials for a wide variety of undergraduate and graduate admission tests and professional licensing tests. The company diversified into the for-profit online high school, vocational, and college industries when it acquired the Penn Foster Career School at the end of 2009. Princeton has also diversified into services for high school students, including college and career counseling and preparation for tests related to the federal No Child Left Behind Act of 2001 (NCLB).

BEFORE TEST PREP, THE TEST

In 1901 the nonprofit College Entrance Examination Board (College Board) started conducting essay-based admissions tests for a small number of colleges. It was not until 1926 that the SAT, with its multiple-choice format, was added to the College Boards. In 1947 the College Board joined forces with the American Council on Education and the Carnegie Foundation for the Advancement of Teaching to create the Educational Testing Service (ETS). The ETS administered the SAT to 75,000 students in 1948 and grew rapidly, doubling its sales every five years from 1948 to the early 1970s. It broadened its scope to include a variety of tests and other educational activities. Eventually, it grew more powerful than its founder, the College Board, which became little more than a rubber stamp for ETS's decisions. The organization essentially answered to no one and commanded enormous power over the fate of countless high school students. Students could not even verify that their tests had been accurately scored.

In 1979 the New York State legislature passed the Educational Testing Act, also called the "truth in testing" law, despite intense lobbying against it by ETS. The law allowed students to review their tests and required that ETS be more transparent about its testing and grading methods. Most importantly, ETS was required to make old SAT tests available. For years, tutors or coaches had been teaching wealthy students on how to prepare for the test. With the new rule, they had the opportunity to study more closely the structure of the SAT.

In 1938 Stanley Kaplan, a former high school teacher, founded the test-preparation industry. He started his company in the basement of his Brooklyn, New York home. His method was to help students raise their SAT scores through a concerted study of basic vocabulary, reading comprehension, and math. Kaplan embraced the SAT as an effective method of testing the aptitude of students, and in turn, the ETS viewed his company as an ally. When John Katzman founded the Princeton Review in the 1980s he challenged both the ETS and Kaplan and received a much more unfriendly response from both.

KATZMAN BREAKS DOWN THE TEST

John Katzman was the product of a self-described entrepreneurial family. His grandfather invented the electric vaporizer and his father ran the manufacturing operation for the device. While raising their three children, Katzman's mother worked as a part-time interior decorator. Katzman was interested in math as a youth. He scored 1,500 out of a possible 1,600 on the SAT and attended Princeton University, majoring in electrical engineering. To earn extra money while in school he worked for an SAT coaching school called Pre-test Review. The school was operated by Bob Scheller, a Wharton Business School graduate. Scheller used a computer to analyze old SAT tests and figure out how to outwit the test writers.

Katzman graduated in 1981 with a degree in architecture and went to work in the computer department of a Wall Street firm. He quit after only six weeks. He asked his parents for a loan of $3,000 and for the use of their Manhattan apartment to start his own SAT coaching school. Katzman named it The Princeton Review, taking the name from his alma mater.

Katzman started the company with just 19 students in the fall of 1981. He increased to 43 students by the spring of 1982 mostly through word of mouth. The business soon grew too big for the apartment, and his mother asked him to move it. Katzman resorted to renting rooms at Hunter College on the Upper East Side of Manhattan. His success at improving his students' scores led to more students. He claimed to be producing the best results of any SAT course in the city, and Adam Robinson, another former protégé of Bob Scheller, telephoned him to challenge the claim. The conversation led not to a rivalry but to a partnership. They joined together to expand Princeton. They began a practice of hiring teachers from a pool of ex-students who had become true believers in the Princeton method. Many of them worked part-time. The company's management and teachers exhibited brazen disdain for the SAT. They took great pleasure at exposing the SAT as merely testing a student's ability to take the test.

Katzman and Robinson taught their students how the SAT was constructed. They taught how the ETS designed questions so that the highest-scoring students would know the answers while the lowest-scoring students would not be able to arrive at the right answer because they were applying the wrong method. Also, ETS offered choices that were meant to trap the average test taker. Robinson invented a character he called Joe Bloggs, who represented the average target for the pitfalls of the test. Princeton taught its students how to think like Joe Bloggs to eliminate deceptive choices on each question. Instructors also helped students to spot experimental sections. ETS included experimental sections in each test to help it develop future tests, but these sections did not count toward the student's score. At the time, the experimental sections were fairly obvious. The experimental math section would be six pages instead of the actual four it was supposed to be. Princeton taught its students to answer these sections at random and move on to the sections that actually counted toward their score. Later, ETS developed countermeasures to prevent this tactic. Princeton also taught its students the 100 most likely vocabulary words that appeared on the SAT, what Robinson called the "Hit Parade." For the math sections, Princeton instructors taught how to solve geometry questions using the edge of the test booklet as a ruler and protractor. In essence, Princeton made the SAT a puzzle to solve rather than a wealth of material to master.

Katzman and Robinson were not alone in their contempt for ETS and the SAT. Writer David Owen took on ETS in a 1983 article for *Harper's* magazine. Owen joined Princeton in arguing that the SAT measured nothing of value, but he went further and claimed that the test was culturally biased. Owen was the first to claim that the people best suited to score well on the SAT were those students who shared the same prep school background and mindset as the people who created the test. Later, Owen authored a book on the subject, *None of the Above: The Truth Behind the*

KEY DATES

1901: The College Entrance Examination Board creates the first standardized admissions test.

1926: The Scholastic Aptitude Test (SAT) uses multiple choice test format for the first time.

1947: The College Entrance Examination Board, the American Council on Education, and the Carnegie Foundation for the Advancement of Teaching form the Educational Testing Service (ETS).

1979: New York passes "truth in testing" law.

1981: John R. Katzman founds the Princeton Review.

1984: *Cracking the SAT* makes the *New York Times* best-seller list.

1993: Princeton Review launches its first Web site.

1995: Random House acquires a stake in the company.

1996: Company establishes Princeton Review Publishing division.

2001: Company makes an initial public offering and lists as REVU on the NASDAQ exchange; The U.S. Congress passes the No Child Left Behind Act.

2004: Princeton introduces "Prep for the SAT" mobile phone service.

2009: Company acquires Penn Foster Educational Group for $170 million.

SATs in which he praised the Princeton Review. In March 1985 *Rolling Stone* published an excerpt from the book, including the praise for the Princeton Review. Katzman said that Owen "made me look more political than I was. But the response by ETS was so strong that I sort of became that political."

PRINCETON WINS BY LOSING

ETS openly expressed its low opinion of Katzman and Robinson. In 1982 Princeton became embroiled in controversy when the ETS accused Robinson of taking an SAT booklet from a test site. In response, Princeton agreed to refrain from using authentic SAT materials, but in 1985 ETS asked the courts to issue a restraining order to prevent both Princeton and Pre-test Review from using copyrighted materials. ETS filed a lawsuit claiming damages due to copyright infringement. They accused Katzman of using questions from tests stolen by students. At other occasions, Katzman took the test himself, often using false identities, and either copied or memorized questions for future use by Princeton to train students. Katzman admitted he took as many tests as he could but said he never broke the law. ETS also claimed that because of Princeton's tactics it had to retire over 300 "secure" questions that it had used repeatedly on its tests. In the end, ETS won the battle but lost the war. In 1987 the court approved a settlement agreement requiring that Princeton pay $52,000 in damages to ETS. Princeton was allowed to continue operating but the agreement barred Katzman from sitting for any of ETS's standardized tests for two years. Also, ETS was granted the right to inspect and copy Princeton's test preparation materials for the next four years. ETS had wanted to put Princeton out of business and failed, so Princeton claimed victory even though it lost in court. Scheller'sPre-test Review was not so fortunate. The company closed operations in 1987.

Despite its victory ETS lost credibility due in large part to Princeton's efforts, and the testing organization was forced to redesign the SAT. It also renamed it the Scholastic Assessment Test, but critics saw its changes as superficial. The essential nature of the test that had attracted criticism remained intact. At the same time, however, Princeton also became the target of criticism. The same people who criticized ETS for designing a meaningless test said that Princeton taught affluent students how to beat the SAT and therefore perpetuated the cycle of the rich attending the better schools while the less fortunate lost out. The criticism may have been unfair since Katzman made Princeton's services available to low-income and minority students, and he had set up a foundation to serve as an advocate and legal advisor to parents and students on testing issues.

GROWTH DESPITE CONFLICTS

Drawing the ire of ETS was in some ways good for Princeton's business. In 1985 Princeton taught 5,000 students at 10 states. The next year, the company operated at 30 sites and earned $8 million in revenues. By 1987 the company had 35 sites and revenues of $12 million. Katzman grew the business using franchising. In the early years, the company charged between $15,000 and $150,000 for a franchise, depending on the size of the market. Princeton also charged 8 percent in annual royalties. Princeton sold its test materials to each franchise. The company expanded so rapidly that in 1988 *Inc.* magazine listed it as the 106th fastest-growing company in the United States. It soon outpaced Kaplan in enrollment in the SAT business. Harcourt Brace Jovanovich offered $1 million for the company but Katzman turned it down.

The squabbles between Princeton and ETS, Kaplan, and its critics obscured another conflict, that between Katzman and Robinson. The *Wall Street Journal* reported that there were times when the two refused to speak to each other for weeks at a time. Despite such difficulties they managed to collaborate with Owen on a book about Princeton's methods titled *Cracking the SAT.* The book became a best-seller, and Robinson proposed that Princeton publish a line of books, tapes, and computer software. In 1989 Katzman and Robinson agreed to formalize their partnership. Katzman offered Robinson a salary of $100,000 per year plus a 3 percent equity stake. Robinson expected at least a 10 percent stake and was insulted by the offer. They eventually agreed on a 4 percent stake. Soon after their agreement, Robinson cashed in his share of the business for $200,000 and severed his relationship with Princeton. Katzman and Robinson remained coauthors on the Princeton books. Katzman decided to expand the publishing part of the business in 1991, and he arranged a royalty agreement to use Robinson's techniques in future books. In 1994 Random House approached Princeton to acquire a 20 percent stake in the company. Before finalizing the deal Katzman sought complete control over the company's backlist of titles. Owen and the literary agent sold their rights, but Robinson refused a $2 million offer, saying he wanted to see an accounting of Princeton's publishing unit. Despite this hitch, Katzman finalized the Random House deal. Katzman and Robinson ended up in court to resolve their disagreement but the case was not resolved for several years.

In the late 1980s Princeton started expanding beyond SAT preparation. The company added preparation classes for the ACT (the SAT equivalent in some Midwestern states), the LSAT, GMAT, MCAT, and GRE. In 1993 Princeton developed Inside the SAT, a software study aid that became a best-seller. The company also established an early presence on the World Wide Web. The company launched Princeton Review Publishing in 1996 and dramatically increased its number of book titles covering a wider range of subjects. Kaplan, which was still the leading test preparation company, quickly found itself playing catch-up.

Princeton owed a great deal of its success to Kaplan. In the beginning, Princeton simply played off the Kaplan model. The company used Kaplan's rate as a floor to establish a premium price. Princeton also offered smaller class sizes using Kaplan's as a benchmark. Princeton positioned itself as the rebel taking on the SAT and portrayed Kaplan as the establishment's toady. Kaplan changed its style and spent considerable advertising dollars attacking Princeton. The two companies became bitter rivals. In 1994 Princeton appropriated the Internet address Kaplan.com before Kaplan could register it. The supposed joke landed both companies in court, where Kaplan was eventually awarded the rights to the domain name. The two companies also wrangled over advertising claims and often threatened court action. Both regularly sent spies to attend each other's classes.

GROWING AN UNPROFITABLE BUSINESS

Their competition helped neither company enjoy good financial health during the 1990s. Both were private companies but the press reported the woes of both. Princeton in particular was reported to be suffering losses in the mid-1990s. The company returned to profitability in 1998 but took a downward trend again after that as it built up its Internet business. Princeton lost $2 million in 1999 and $8.2 million in 2000, despite earning $43 million in revenues.

Princeton and Kaplan faced stiff competition from new online businesses that also offered electronic college application services and online guidance counselor services. In 1999 Princeton rolled out Homeroom.com to help K-12 students improve their scores on state mandated exams. The company's other Web site, Review.com, targeted college-bound students and college students applying to graduate school.

In August 2000 Princeton announced that it would make a public offering of stock to raise money to pay off debt and fund the growth of its Internet business. It hoped to sell 5.4 million shares of stock at $11 to $13 per share. Some analysts questioned the initial public offering (IPO), maintaining that there was no compelling reason to own the stock. Nevertheless, the company arranged a $25 million line of credit in order to buy back its franchises and prepare for the offering. Princeton owned 450 sites and 16 franchises in the United States and 13 sites in 10 other countries. However, the IPO on the NASDAQ exchange in June 2001 was a disappointment. Shares sold at $11, raising only $59.4 million. The stock showed little strength on the exchange and quickly dropped in price. At the end of the day it had dropped to $9.50 per share. Toward the end of 2001 Princeton acquired Embark.com, a company that offered online admissions products and services to students. This represented the company's biggest move into offering online admissions products and services beyond test preparation. The distraction of the IPO and a year of acquisitions did not hinder the company from increasing revenues by 58 percent to $69.1 million, but it did take its toll on the bottom line. The company showed a net income loss of $16.7 million.

By 2003 the U.S. government had passed the No Child Left Behind Act (NCLB), which became a boon for supplemental service providers, including Princeton. Princeton's Homeroom.com let teachers give mini-tests to see whether their students were on track to pass the state exam. The site gave back instant results and identified the students's areas of weakness, offering them exercises to improve in those areas. Unlike the SAT and the other tests Princeton took on in its classes, there were other companies than ETS designing the tests required under NCLB. Harcourt Educational Measurement, a unit of publisher Harcourt Inc. also got in the game of designing and selling the tests to various states.

In late 2004 Princeton introduced its innovative "Prep for the SAT" mobile phone service. Parents had the option to receive a progress report via e-mail or text message. Princeton also engaged in another growing trend, corporate contracts. The college admissions process grew increasingly competitive in the 21st century. Corporations saw many of their employees become distracted by the stresses of the search for the right schools, the essays, admissions deadlines, and financial aid. Large corporations such as Goldman Sachs, I.B.M. and American International Group (AIG) set up counseling sessions and workshops as an employment benefit for their employees. Law firms, businesses, and banks contracted Princeton Review to provide these consulting services, and it became one of the company's fastest-growing segments of its business. Princeton's services (as well as Kaplan's) emphasized a more one-on-one personal consulting rather than group workshops.

CONTINUING WOES

The vast number of investments Princeton directed into new business projects took its toll on the company's bottom line. While the company generated revenues of $113.8 million in 2004 it showed a dismal net income loss of $30.4 million. Princeton boasted that it helped prepare 120,000 students in its courses and millions more with its books, but its investments in K-12 educational services and its online ventures, especially Embark.com, were not paying off as quickly as the company wanted. The company also made some missteps with a redesign of its LSAT prep course that cost it enrollment.

Another significant challenge was the transition to the new SAT. The College Board announced in 2003 a complete redesign of the SAT exam. There had been talk in 2001 of the death of the SAT as some large states began questioning whether the test adequately reflected what students actually learned in the classroom. In 2002 a University of California faculty committee recom-

mended that the SAT be replaced by a "core test" supplemented by subject matter tests that covered up to 22 subjects such as world history and physics. The College Board and its rival ACT moved quickly to halt a trend that could spread to other large institutions. They met with University of California officials to work out a redesign of both the SAT and ACT. The new test included a tougher math test, longer reading passages in the verbal portion, and a writing exam that carried as much weight as the other sections. The addition of the writing section shifted more weight (two-thirds) to verbal skills. However, the new design did not quell Katzman's criticism of the test. He said of the writing test that "rather than improving the teaching of writing, it will dumb it down." He stated that the "whole SAT is a middle-school test, and this new version is not going to make college-bound students better writers or better thinkers."

Nonetheless, the new SAT helped Princeton. In 2005 its revenues rose 19 percent to $93.8 million, but the company remained unprofitable and continued to be so for the next few years. It posted losses of $4.1 million in 2005, $10.4 in 2006, and $29.9 million in 2007. Princeton had proved that it had the marketing muscle to sell its products and services but it had not proven that it could make its business profitable. The losses continued to the end of the decade. Despite such losses the company poured further investment into its K-12 educational and other ventures.

In 2009 the *Wall Street Journal* published an article regarding a study showing that test prep courses did help students boost scores but not by very much. The article questioned whether the high price of the courses was worth it and whether the companies' claims of effectiveness were truthful. In addition, Princeton and Kaplan increasingly faced competition online from companies like Grockit.com that were less expensive and more nimble, quickly integrating newer technologies into their courses. For example, Grockit.com allowed students to instant message each other and openly discuss strategies as they worked on questions.

A LATE RESPONSE BRINGS HOPE

At the end of 2009, Princeton acquired the Penn Foster Educational Group for $170 million in cash and debt. Penn Foster ran three distance-learning schools for more than 223,000 students. The college offered inexpensive, self-paced classes in areas such as automotive technology, legal studies, and health care. The acquisition was a move to diversify its business and increase its potential for profitability. It was also a very late response to its major competitor. By 2009 Kaplan had been in the for-profit education business for nine years, first as Kaplan College (Kaplancollege.com), and later as Kaplan University. It achieved university status in 2004. Since then, Kaplan University acquired several small colleges around the country and grew its online business to become a major profit center for Kaplan Inc. and for its parent company, The Washington Post Company. Test prep revenue amounted to 80 percent of Princeton's revenues, and 4 percent of those revenues was attributable to its online services. The purchase of online-based Penn Foster would change the company's direction and increase its online presence.

The for-profit college business had been highly lucrative for decades, but there was a concern that Princeton was late to the game. By the time it purchased Penn Foster the federal government had instituted new regulations governing the for-profit education industry. Regulators were concerned about the institutions abusing the federal student loan system and making false claims to prospective students concerning their job prospects upon graduating. Regulators were not satisfied with the 2010 round of rules and more rules were proposed for coming years.

The significant revenue increase and high profit margins that might be gained through the Penn Foster acquisition offered Princeton a chance to bring its bottom line into the black on a consistent basis. Soon after acquiring Penn Foster, Princeton announced plans to create a new college for AFL-CIO union members and their families, a move that would grow its new division significantly. In the past, Princeton has not proven itself adept at integrating new ventures into its business model. In 2011 the company faced a test as to whether it would be able sustain its original brand as one of the premier test prep companies in the country, as well as achieve long-term profitability, while moving into a wholly new educational market.

Ed Dinger
Updated, Aaron Hauser

PRINCIPAL SUBSIDIARIES

ICS Canada Operations Ltd. (Canada); Penn Foster Education Group, Inc.; Test Services, Inc.

PRINCIPAL DIVISIONS

Penn Foster; Supplemental Educational Services (SES); Test Preparation Services.

PRINCIPAL COMPETITORS

Apollo Group, Inc.; Courier Corporation; ITT Educational Services, Inc.; Kaplan, Inc.; McGraw-Hill Education.

FURTHER READING

Bongiorno, Lori. "The Test Tutors Try to Settle a Score. "*BusinessWeek,* November 21, 1994, 62.

De Lisser, Eleena. "Test Case: Dysfunctional Duo Built SAT Prep Firm."*Wall Street Journal,* October 18, 1999, A1.

Hammer, Joshua. "Cram Scram."*New Republic,* April 24, 1989, 15–18.

Hechinger, John. "SAT Coaching Found to Boost Scores— Barely."*Wall Street Journal,* May 20, 2009, D1. Accessed March 18, 2011. http://online.wsj.com/article/SB12427 8685697537839.html.

Korn, Melissa. "Princeton Builds Online Test Business." *Wall Street Journal,* February 17, 2010.

Lewin, Tamar. "College Board to Revise SAT After Criticism by University."*New York Times,* March 23, 2002, 10.

Lombardi, Kate Stone. "Guiding a Child Into College Is Now Part of the Job."*New York Times,* August 18, 2004, 7.

McGrath, Charles. "Writing to the Test."*New York Times,* November 7, 2004, 24.

Mossberg, Walter S. "The Mossberg Solution: Can You Quiz Me Now? Turning a Cellphone into an SAT-Prep Tool."*Wall Street Journal,* August 25, 2004, D1.

Murphy, Anne. "Enemies, A Love Story." *Inc.,* April 1995, 77.

Owen, David. "Adam and John Say Put Your Pencil Down. "*Rolling Stone,* March 28, 1985, 74–80.

———. *None of the Above: The Truth Behind the SATs.* Lanham, MD: Rowman & Littlefield, 1999.

Professional Basketball
Club, LLC

■

2 Leadership Square
211 North Robinson Avenue, Suite 300
Oklahoma City, Oklahoma 73102
U.S.A.
Telephone: (405) 208-4800
Fax: (405) 429-7900
Web site: http://www.nba.com/thunder

Private Company
Founded: 1967 (as Seattle SuperSonics)
Employees: 135 (est., 2010)
Sales: $80 million (est., 2010)
NAICS: 711211 Sports Teams and Clubs

■ ■ ■

Professional Basketball Club, LLC, is the name of the company that operates the Oklahoma City Thunder (Thunder), a professional basketball team with the United States National Basketball Association (NBA). The Thunder is part of the Northwest Division of the Western Conference of the NBA. The team was formerly the Seattle SuperSonics (Sonics), which moved to Oklahoma City, Oklahoma, in July 2008. Since receiving its franchise charter from the NBA in 1967 the Thunder (as the Sonics) has been inconsistent at best, achieving only one national title, but the owners and team have been at the center of some of the most important legal actions throughout the history of the NBA.

TWO AMATEURS, TWO HOLLYWOOD PROS

In 1967 businessman Dick Vertlieb was a typical armchair general manager watching sports on television. At work, he would talk to anyone who would listen about what he thought were mistakes made by the team's management. Then he read about two Southern Californian investors, Eugene Klein and Sam Schulman, who purchased the National Football League (NFL) San Diego Chargers for $10 million, which at the time was a record price for an NFL franchise. Vertlieb and Don Richman, a University of Southern California fraternity brother, made a cold call to Klein and Schulman and convinced them to invest in an NBA expansion franchise for Seattle. Vertlieb also convinced them to put him and Richman in charge of the franchise. The NBA awarded the franchise to Schulman and his group of investors, who paid a $1.75 million expansion fee. They named the franchise the Seattle SuperSonics after the supersonic transport (SST) contract that had just been awarded by the government to Boeing, a Seattle corporation (the SST contract was later cancelled).

Schulman and Klein made their fortune as Hollywood moneymen, but they worked mostly behind the scenes. Their names almost never appeared on any movie credits. The only notable movie that ever carried Schulman's name was William Friedkin's 1985 film *To Live and Die in L.A.* He was listed as executive producer. After securing the Sonics franchise Vertlieb and Richman flipped a coin to determine who would be business manager and who would be general manager. Richman served as general manager for the first year, but Vertlieb ultimately took over both positions in the

---

COMPANY PERSPECTIVES

■

Rise together

---

second year. They hired Al Bianchi as the team's first coach. Bianchi was an assistant coach with the Chicago Bulls and a former player for the Philadelphia 76ers and Chicago Bulls. The team would play in the Seattle Center Coliseum (the Coliseum), later renamed KeyArena, a venue that would be the team's home on and off through most of its tenure in Seattle. During the first few seasons, the team averaged 6,524 fans per game at the Coliseum.

Management of the team got off to a rocky start. Vertlieb and Schulman were never able to work well together and butted heads many times over management decisions. The final straw came when Vertlieb hired Tom Meschery as assistant coach of the team without consulting Schulman. Schulman fired Vertlieb during a rather hostile phone call in the middle of the night. Bianchi got the team off to a dismal start for the 1968–69 season, and Houbregs fired him midseason and replaced him with Lenny Wilkens. Wilkens was at the time playing for the Sonics so he acquired the dual role of coach and player.

LEGAL WRANGLING

During those early years there were two professional basketball leagues in the United States, the NBA and the American Basketball Association (ABA). The NBA was founded in 1946 and the ABA in 1967. In 1970 the leagues agreed to merge. Sonics owner Schulman was a member of the ABA-NBA merger committee and was an ardent supporter of the merger, so much so that he announced publicly that if the NBA did not accept the merger agreement they had worked out with the ABA he would move the Sonics from the NBA to the ABA. The merger was delayed by legal action concerning free agency, but eventually the two leagues did merge.

In 1970 Schulman faced another legal action when the Sonics signed Spencer Hayward to a six-year, $1.5 million contract, which was in direct defiance of an NBA rule that a team could not sign a player who had not been out of high school at least four years. After various trials and appeals (all the way to the Supreme Court), the NBA and Hayward reached an out-of-court settlement, which allowed him to stay with the Sonics. Despite the court's ruling Schulman was forced by the

league to pay a $200,000 fine for breaking league rules. The Hayward settlement had significant repercussions for the league and eventually led to an increase of players leaving college early or coming straight out of high school to play in the NBA.

The season after Hayward joined the Sonics was the organization's first winning season (47–35), but due to late-season losses they fell short of making the playoffs. Before the next season, Schulman told Wilkens he had to choose between playing and coaching. Wilkens agreed to give up the coaching position and focus on playing. The team hired Tom Nissalke, who had been coaching the ABA Dallas Chaparrals, to replace him as coach. Nissalke had a long-term plan, and keeping a 35-year-old point guard was not part of the team's future. Without discussing it with Wilkens he negotiated a deal to trade him to the Cleveland Cavaliers. This was a terribly unpopular trade with the fans who had a great love for Wilkens. Unfortunately for Nissalke, his plan for the team did not result in many wins. Before the season was over Schulman fired Nissalke and replaced him with Bucky Buckwalter on an interim basis. The next year, an article in *Sports Illustrated* said that the players intentionally dumped a game against the Philadelphia 76ers in order to get Nissalke fired. Evidently, the players did not take well to Nissalke's tough style of coaching. The league investigated these charges but they were never proven.

Following the 1973 season, Schulman faced angry shareholders. They complained about his frequent and questionable personnel changes and mounting financial losses. To quell their anger Schulman hired NBA legend Bill Russell to serve as both general manager and head coach. He signed Russell to a five-year contract at $125,000 a year. Russell was a retired player who won eleven national championships, received five most valuable player awards, and was selected twelve times as an all-star while playing for the Boston Celtics. In 1975, under Russell's leadership, the Sonics made the playoffs for the first time. The team defeated the Detroit Pistons in the first round but fell to the Golden State Warriors. The win for Golden State was turnabout justice for Warriors' general manager, Dick Vertlieb, who had been fired by Schulman. The Warriors went on to win the NBA championship.

By the late 1970s, the NBA was beginning to experience the negative effects of free agency, a trend that was plaguing other professional sports leagues as well. The number of players seeking better deals with other teams increased significantly, which resulted in an escalation of salaries. Many teams were reporting losses even though attendance at games was high. Schulman was one of the major reasons for the escalation of

KEY DATES

1967: Sam Schulman and investment team found the Seattle SuperSonics.

1973: Sonics hire NBA legend Bill Russell as coach.

1979: Sonics win NBA national championship.

1983: Schulman sells Sonics to Barry Ackerley for $21 million.

1991: Renovation of the Seattle Center Coliseum begins; Sonics move to Tacoma Dome in Tacoma, Washington.

1995: Sonics move back to the newly renovated Coliseum.

2001: Ackerley sells the Sonics to Starbucks executive Howard Schultz and a private investment group for $200 million.

2006: Schultz sells the Sonics to Clay Bennett and a group of investors for $350 million.

2008: Sonics move to Oklahoma City, Oklahoma, and the team is renamed the Oklahoma City Thunder.

salaries, spending haphazardly in the 1970s for players such as Spencer Haywood, Jim McDaniels, and John Brisker. Later in the decade, he claimed to have seen the error of his ways and decried others for inflating salaries, but by that point it was too late. Owners were offering large salaries to attract the best talent available regardless of what effect this might have on the profitability of the league overall.

NEW REALITIES AND TRYING TO KEEP ABOVE WATER

In early 1983 the NBA owners proposed a salary cap in an effort to slow down the escalation of player salaries and bring back some franchises from the brink of financial failure. At that time, the average salary had grown to $246,000 a season, making it, with baseball, one of the two highest-paying major league sports. Also, the average basketball franchise lost $700,000 in the previous season. The players union agreed in principle with the cap but wanted revenue sharing as part of the deal to offset their lost bargaining power. A strike deadline was set as part of negotiations, and the players' union wielded that deadline strongly during negotiations. At one point Schulman spoke to the press and dared the players to strike. No other owner came out so brazenly against the players. A deal was finally reached three days before the strike deadline. A salary

cap was set with yearly increases, and the players retained free agency and gained a 53 percent share of gross revenues. Because the deal modified the 1976 Oscar Robertson court decision, both parties would have to ask court approval before it went into effect, which they later received. Schulman was the only owner who voted against the deal. He stated that he had not had a chance to review the agreement and had asked for a few weeks to review it with his lawyers.

A NEW OWNER AND THE FIGHT FOR A NEW ARENA

In October 1983 Schulman sold the Sonics to Barry Ackerley for $21 million. Ackerley was founder and president of the Ackerley Group, which owned a large outdoor advertising business (billboards) and several radio and television stations. Ackerley assumed $8 million in liabilities, which reduced the purchase price to $13 million. Schulman claimed that diversification of his own interests forced him to sell the team, and he stated publicly that he regretted selling the team almost as soon as he had done it. Three years later, when the team was going through difficult seasons and attracting very low attendance, Schulman said that giving up the team was a mistake and that he wished he could undo it. Regardless, Schulman would go on to achieve great success as chairman of New Century Productions in Hollywood.

Under Ackerley the team floundered for several years, although they did manage to make a run to the 1989 Western Conference Finals. They were seeded seventh in the playoff series and were not expected to make it so far in the playoffs. To help refurbish the team's image and fortune, Ackerley began looking for a new arena for the Sonics. The Coliseum was almost thirty years old and no longer met NBA standards. Ackerley threatened to take the team to another city if the city council did not allow him to build a new arena. The mayor and Ackerley joined together to propose an $80 to $100 million privately owned arena and parking garage. Under the plan the city would contribute $47 million. The plan was not well received by the city council, but Ackerley and the council negotiated back and forth and finally came to an agreement that allowed plans for the new arena to move forward. Then a group of employees of the Coliseum and a group called "Save the Seattle Center" sued to stop the new arena. Their legal basis was a $1 million tax rebate that was part of the deal. They argued that the rebate represented a donation of city money to a corporation and was therefore unconstitutional. The city countered that they would save taxpayer money by building the new arena and that upgrading the current Coliseum to current

NBA standards would cost at least $82 million. Also, they argued that Ackerley would most likely move the team if they did not build a new arena. The court case caused construction to be delayed, and in June 1991 Ackerley backed out of the new arena deal. He said that with the legal fees and other considerations the arena was not a financially viable project. Ackerley lost $5.6 million in development costs due to the failure of the new arena.

In the wake of the failure of the project, the Sonics organization began assessing what it would take to renovate the Coliseum and bring it up to NBA standards. Ackerley decided not to move the team, a decision that may have been prompted by financial difficulties. During the summer of 1991 the Ackerley Group missed four debt payments and faced a $246.1 million bill due in September 1991. The difficulties had less to do with sports and more to do with a nationwide advertising slump and credit crunch. Some feared that Ackerley would sell the team, but Ackerley said they would work out a debt restructure that would allow him to keep the team. After several renovation plans were paraded in front of the City Council and Ackerley, they finally came to an agreement on a $74 million project to renovate the existing Coliseum facilities. The plan would mean that the team needed a temporary home while the Coliseum underwent construction. The team chose to play on an interim basis at the Tacoma Dome in Tacoma, Washington.

In 1992 George Karl took over the head coaching job. This change marked the team's return to winning ways. Under Karl, the team achieved a 55–27 record in the 1992–93 season and went to the playoffs. They made it to the Western Conference final but lost to the Phoenix Suns in seven games. The following year they had the NBA's best record at 63–19.

The team moved back to the Coliseum, now renamed KeyArena, for the 1995–96 season. The renovation ended up costing the city of Seattle $74.5 million and the Sonics $21 million. KeyCorps purchased the rights to rename the arena for $15.1 million. The new arena featured 3,000 additional seats and 58 luxury suites. In 1996 the team reached the NBA finals but lost to the Michael Jordan-led Chicago Bulls in six games. At the end of the 1997–98 season, management decided not to renew Karl's contract even though he had led the team to the playoffs every year he coached the team. When Ackerley fired Karl he famously asked him "Where are my rings?" meaning that while the team had been successful Karl had not delivered a championship, so he was out. Ackerley went on to clean house by letting go of the rest of the coaching staff. The Sonics replaced Karl with former Sonics

player Paul Westphal. This marked the beginning of another period of mediocrity for the team. Westphal's tenure was plagued with discord between him and the players, culminating in a shouting match between Westphal and star point guard Gary Payton during a game against the Dallas Mavericks. A few days later, 15 games into the 2000–01 season, the Sonics fired Westphal and replaced him with interim coach Nate McMillan. McMillan eventually became the permanent coach but not before Ackerley decided to sell the team.

THE STARBUCKS EXECUTIVE AND ANOTHER ARENA FIGHT

In late 2000 Ackerley started looking for a buyer for the SuperSonics as well as his other sports interest, the Women's National Basketball Association (WNBA) team the Seattle Storm. While the Sonics were underperforming the Storm was proving to be a terrible financial drain. Ackerley found a buyer in Howard Schultz, the chairman and chief global strategist for Starbucks. On January 11, 2001, Ackerley announced the sale of the Sonics for $200 million to a private investment group led by Schultz that included the Sonics president and general manager Wally Walker. The deal included the Storm. Schultz owned 42 percent of the resulting package.

Under the new management, the team made McMillan the permanent coach, and Schultz hired Rick Sund as general manager. Sund had previously been successful general manager for the Detroit Pistons. For the next four seasons the Sonics had limited success. During the 2004–05 season, the team managed to surprise the experts by winning the division title and reaching the playoffs. The team came close to ousting the defending champion San Antonio Spurs but lost in six games.

During Schultz's tenure the team performed poorly, and Schultz gained a reputation for being rather naïve and showing a lack of understanding of the sports business. Schultz's decision-making seemed influenced too much by whether the team was winning or losing rather than the overall business. He also was ever-present courtside and risked technical fouls by screaming at the officials and coming onto the court to celebrate a critical basket with the team.

In February 2006 Schultz and his investment group demanded that the state legislature approve a $200 million earmark to update KeyArena or they would consider selling or moving the team to another city. Schultz claimed that the team had lost $56 million over the last five years and blamed it on the poor conditions of KeyArena and the unfair revenue-sharing deal they had with the city of Seattle. Under the deal the city received 60 percent of money from the luxury suites. Both the city and the state balked at Shultz's demands. They wanted the Sonics to take on more of the cost of the renovation. The city and state had already invested $672 million for new stadiums for the Seahawks and Mariners, and the public was averse to another big-ticket project, especially one seen as having no economic benefit to the city. Also, the Sonics still had three years left on their lease with KeyArena, which left them in a poor negotiating position. Lastly, while the Sonics were in the dumps the Seattle Seahawks were on the ascent and appearing in their first Super Bowl. As a result, the Sonics looked like a poor public investment.

As a result of these factors, the governor and state legislature refused to consider an earmark until the city and the team agreed to a deal on the renovation costs and future revenues. The legislature set a deadline, but Schultz and the city could not come to an agreement. The deadline passed, and the legislature adjourned until the following year. In April 2006 Schultz and his investment group met to discuss the future of the team. Selling the team was almost a foregone conclusion and moving it was also considered. Four cities emerged as potential new homes for the Sonics: Norfolk, Virginia; San Jose, California; Kansas City, Missouri; and Oklahoma City, Oklahoma.

SALE TO AN OKLAHOMA BUSINESSMAN

In July 2006 a deal was reached to sell the team to Professional Basketball Club LLC (PBC), a group of investors led by Oklahoma City businessman Clay Bennett. Bennett had been instrumental in bringing the New Orleans Hornets to Oklahoma City as an interim home following Hurricane Katrina that devastated the Gulf Coast in late August 2005. However, the Hornets were to return to New Orleans before the 2007–08 season. The PBC bought the Sonics and its sister team the Storm for $350 million.

Bennett said he hoped to bring basketball to Oklahoma City, but he intended to keep the team's lease obligation with KeyArena. He also gave the city of Seattle 12 months to come up with a deal to keep the team, either to finance a renovation of KeyArena or build a new arena. The city was ready to move forward until a group called Citizens for More Important Things gathered enough signatures on a petition to put Initiative 91 on the November ballot. Initiative 91 prohibited the city of Seattle from funding any new sports ventures unless it was in the form of a loan. On November 7, 2006, the initiative passed and effectively tied the hands of the city council. Bennett vowed to continue working with the county or state governments to reach a deal.

Meanwhile, the team started off the 2006–07 season poorly (13–17), and at the end of the season the fate of the team was still uncertain. In April 2007 a bill came before the state legislature to contribute $300 million of public funds to a new $500 million arena, but the bill never came to vote, and again the legislature adjourned without considering it. On October 31, 2007, the 12-month grace period ended, and Bennett informed the NBA he intended to move the team to Oklahoma City, but their KeyArena lease did not end until 2010. Bennett asked Seattle to let the team out of their lease early. The city of Seattle refused. Then Bennett asked the courts to set up arbitration between the parties. The judge rejected this request, and Seattle sued the PBC to enforce its lease. At stake were the revenues the city derived from the luxury suites. In July 2008, just hours before the judge was to make a decision, both parties announced a settlement that released the team from the lease and allowed it to move earlier. The team agreed to pay the city $45 million immediately and another $30 million if Seattle was not given a replacement team in five years. Also, the Oklahoma team could not use the Sonics name and colors. Lastly, the Oklahoma team would retain the franchise history of the Sonics but could be shared by any future Seattle team. Bennett announced that the team would move immediately and play the 2008–09 season in Oklahoma City.

Later that year, the former owners, Schultz and his investors, filed a lawsuit against PBC claiming that PBC never intended to keep the team in Seattle and negotiated the purchase in bad faith. As restitution they wanted the purchase rescinded and the team returned to them. Of course, they would keep the team in Seattle. The NBA intervened in federal court and argued that Schultz's lawsuit would interfere with the stable operation of the franchise and the transfer would violate NBA regulations. The NBA also argued that Schultz had signed a release as part of the sale agreeing not to sue PBC. Therefore, the lawsuit was invalid. At the same time, the city of Oklahoma City threatened to sue for damages if Schultz's lawsuit succeeded and the team did not move. After weeks of court wrangling, Schultz dropped the lawsuit, claiming the case could not be won. Echoing the words of the Sam Schulman, Schultz apologized to the city of Seattle for selling the team.

NEW NAME, NEW CITY

In Oklahoma City on March 3, 2008, the voters approved a $120 million renovation of the Ford Center, including the construction of a new practice facility. Two weeks later, Bennett and the city agreed to a 15-year lease. The new team was named the Oklahoma

Thunder. The Thunder got their first season off to a bad start. After a 10-game losing streak, Bennett fired coach P. J. Carlesimo and assistant coach Paul Westhead. Assistant Scott Brooks took over, but the team went 3–29 before it started winning more than losing. They finished their first season at 23–59. However, the team's financial fortunes changed for the better. In December 2008 *Forbes* valued the franchise at $300 million, a 12 percent increase from the previous year. Also, the team was selling out games at the Ford Center. The next season, the Thunder improved to a 50–32 record and secured a spot in the playoffs but lost in the first round to the defending champion Los Angeles Lakers.

At the end of the 2009–10 season the Thunder reported an operating profit of $12.7 million, the first profit in many years. Reincarnated as the Thunder, the team had left behind a shocked and hurt fan base in Seattle but had discovered a new lease on life with a new owner, a new city, and new fans excited to support their team.

Aaron Hauser

PRINCIPAL COMPETITORS

Denver Nuggets Limited Partnership; Minnesota Timberwolves Basketball LP; Trail Blazers; Jazz Basketball Investors, Inc.

FURTHER READING

Bruscas, Angelo. "Ownership: Worth the Risk?" *Seattle Post-Intelligencer,* June 20, 2002, p. C7.

Cour, Jim. "Sonics Revamp Organization, Make Wilkins General Manager." *Associated Press,* April 24, 1985.

Demasio, Nunyo. "Starbucks Executive Might Buy Seattle Supersonics Basketball Team." *Seattle Times,* January 8, 2001, Back Page.

Goldaper, Sam. "N.B.A. Strike Averted With Accord On 4-Year Pact." *New York Times,*, April 1, 1983, NYTF.

Gross, Jane. "Sonics, Slot Machine Firm Seek Merger." *New York Times,* January 8, 1982, NYTF.

Hughes, Frank. "Starbucks' Schultz Will Buy Sonics." *News Tribune,* January 8, 2001, p. A1.

Hu, Janny. "Things Aren't Super for Sonics in Seattle." *San Francisco Chronicle,* February 5, 2006, p. C8.

Johnson, Roy S. "N.B.A. Thinks About Changes." *New York Times,* January 31, 1982.

O'Neil, Danny. "Sam Schulman: 1910–2003." *Seattle Post-Intelligencer,* June 14, 2003, p. D1.

"Owner Dares Union to Strike." *New York Times,* February 18, 1983.

Raley, Dan. "End Game." *Seattle Post-Intelligencer,* August 12, 2004, p. D1.

———. "Spencer Haywood." *Seattle Post-Intelligencer,* November 22, 2006, p. C1.

"Seattle Won't Enter Bidding War to Keep SuperSonics." *Associated Press,* May 26, 1987.

"Sonics Consider Moving." *Record,* February 5, 1989, p. s07.

"The Sonics Through the Years." *Seattle Post-Intelligencer,* July 19, 2006, p. D4.

"Sports People: Owner's About-Face." *New York Times,* November 17, 1982.

"Starbucks Chief Leads Group Buying SuperSonics Team." *Business Line,*, January 13, 2001.

"Supersonics Rule Out Gambling-Firm Merger." *New York Times,* June 10, 1982.

Vescey, George. "In Sports, Money Is the Main Issue." *New York Times,* March 16, 1981.

Watts, Slick, and Frank Hughes. *Slick Watts's Tales from the Seattle Supersonics.* Champaign, IL: Sports Publishing, 2005.

PSA Peugeot Citroën S.A.

75, avenue de la Grande–Armée
Paris, 75116
France
Telephone: (33) 1 40 66 55 11
Fax: (33) 1 40 66 54 14
Web site: http://www.psa-peugeot-citroen.com

Public Company
Incorporated: 1896 as Peugeot S.A.
Employees: 186,220 (2009)
Sales: EUR 48.4 billion ($62.6 billion) (2009)
Stock Exchanges: Euronext Paris; OTC
Ticker Symbol: UG; PEUGY
NAICS: 336111 Automobile Manufacturing; 423110
    Automobile and Other Merchant Vehicle Wholesal-
    ers; 423120 Motor Vehicle Supplies and New Parts
    Merchant Wholesalers

■ ■ ■

PSA Peugeot Citroën S.A. (PSA) is Europe's second-
largest automotive manufacturer, trailing only
Volkswagen. and in 2009 it was the world's sixth-largest
company in terms of vehicle production. PSA produces
passenger cars and light commercial and utility vehicles
under the famous Peugeot and Citroën brand names, as
well as motorbikes and scooters, and vehicles for
military use.

In 2009 PSA employed almost 186,220 people,
through operations in more than 160 countries. While
much of the company's manufacturing is done outside
of France, Europe, and especially France, remains the

company's chief focus, with roughly two-thirds of all
vehicle sales occurring in this region. The company is
also focused on eco-friendly vehicles, as it leads Europe
in the production of low-carbon- emitting vehicles.

In addition to vehicle manufacturing, PSA owns
Gefco, a transportation and logistics company, as well as
a majority stake in Faurecia, an auto parts supply firm.
The company's Banque PSA Finance subsidiary operates
with both dealers and customers.

FOUNDING THE FRENCH AUTOMOBILE INDUSTRY IN THE 1890S

The Peugeot and Citroën names held a prominent position in the emerging French automotive industry of the
19th century. The Peugeot family was already among
the country's prominent manufacturers, operating a
textile mill in France's Alsace region. In the early part of
the 19th century, the family turned to steel production,
after Jean-Pierre and Jean-Frederic Peugeot invented the
cold-roll method of manufacturing spring steel. The
bicycle craze of the 1880s brought the family into
wheeled vehicle production, as Armand Peugeot,
grandson of Jean-Pierre and a cyclist himself, joined the
family business. It was Armand Peugeot who would turn
the Peugeot name into one of the most respected
automotive manufacturers in the world.

Peugeot's success in the manufacture of machine
tools resulted in his gaining recognition and influence,
and many of his colleagues feared the risks entailed in
devoting his complete resources to the manufacture of
an automobile. However, this did not deter Peugeot.

The company has four main ambitions: to be a step ahead in pioneering vehicles and service, to be a global player, to be an industry benchmark for operational efficiency, and to develop responsibly.

Production of the first Peugeot passenger vehicle, a three- wheeled, steam-powered motoring car, was launched at the end of the 1880s. However, Peugeot quickly recognized the potential of the newly emerging internal combustion engine. In 1891 Peugeot traveled to Germany in search of the perfect twin-cylinder engine, resolved that he would not come back empty-handed. Two months later he returned with the 525-cc version, which was being manufactured by Daimler for its own hand-built cars. This purchase, Peugeot told his colleagues, was the beginning of something "grand."

Peugeot's motor car would quickly make its mark, winning some of the world's first automobile races and establishing the Peugeot name among the top of the profession. Peugeot soon introduced a new type of automobile, the station wagon, before the turn of the century. Armand Peugeot was also credited with producing the world's first compact car, dubbed "Le Bébé" (the Baby), in 1905. Within 15 years Peugeot had established manufacturing facilities throughout France. The first Peugeot factories were established in Valentigney and Audincourt, and then in Lille and Sochaux. For a few years after the Sochaux plant was opened, production primarily involved the manufacture of trucks. The first of these to bear resemblance to modern trucks was the type 109 which, with a maximum load of three tons, could still reach 20 km/hr. Industrial vehicle production increased dramatically during World War I, but as the war ended it began to recede.

In the period leading up to the war Peugeot cars won many races, including the 1913 Indianapolis 500. However, Peugeot mainly specialized in the production of utilitarian models like the Bébé. The Quadralette, engineered along the same lines as the Bébé and introduced at the Brussels Motor Show in 1920, subsequently led to the development of the model 5 CV, which hit a record production figure of 83,000 chassis.

By then, a new name had appeared on the French automotive scene. André Citroën's father, a Dutch diamond merchant, had moved to Paris in the 19th century. André Citroën graduated from the École Polytechnique, France's most prestigious university, in 1900

and turned to manufacturing. In 1913 Citroën established the company's precursor, the Citroën Gear Company. In order to work smoothly, the teeth on the gears had the form of chevrons, the shape that became the emblem of the Citroën name. André Citroën soon began importing modern industrial working methods to France during World War I, and Citroën's introduction of mass production methods enabled the country to supply its war machine. Citroën himself turned production to munitions. These same production methods, inspired by Citroën hero Henry Ford would later allow Citroën to produce economical cars in large quantities and transform the automobile from an elite possession to a common consumer good in Europe. In 1916 M. Citroën began preparations to convert his Paris munitions factory on the Quai de Javel into a car factory. By the end of 1919, the factory was producing 30 cars a day.

The factory produced the Type A, appearing in June 1919, the first European car to be mass produced and the first low-cost car to be sold fully equipped (with, among other things, electric starter and lighting, hood, spare wheel, and tire). It was also the first car designed with the intention of reaching the popular market.

In 1920 Citroën's fame took off at rapid speed after the company won the fuel economy grand prix at Le Mans. As a result, the company greatly increased its rate of production. From a total of 2,810 cars built in 1919, the company had a production total of 12,244 in 1920.

The following year, Peugeot would make its own contribution to the automotive engine market, introducing the first diesel-powered passenger automobile. Peugeot continued to handcraft its automobiles, as Citroën moved its postwar production in two directions.

In 1921 production began on three types of "half-trucks," bearing the Citroën name and incorporating the B2 engine. The new truck type would accomplish the first vehicle crossing of the Sahara. This mission, led by Haardt and Audouin Dubreuil, left Algiers in December 1922 and arrived successfully in Timbuktu in February 1923. In the ensuing decades, Citroën gained world renown by participating in motor expeditions, rallies, and mass treks across desert landscapes in both Asia and Africa.

On the consumer side, Citroën was also innovating. In 1922 the company began offering credit sales, with repayments spread over 12 or 18 months. These arrangements helped to jumpstart the popularization of the automobile throughout France. Also in 1922, the company presented the 5CV Type C, a model that contributed to the "democratization" of the automobile because it was economical and easy to drive. It was so

KEY DATES

1913: Citroën establishes the company's precursor, the Citroën Gear Company.
1916: M. Citroën begins preparations to convert his Paris munitions factory on the Quai de Javel into a car factory.
1922: The company begins offering credit sales, with repayments spread over 12 or 18 months.
1924: Automobiles Citroën officially commences.
1928: Citroën's factories employ 30,000 workers and maintain a total production capacity of 1,000 vehicles per day.
1954: The company designs constant height hydropneumatic rear suspension. The system combines the actions of a gas and a liquid to achieve greatly improved road handling.
1998: PSA puts the finishing touches on the merging of the Citroën and Peugeot organizations, retaining the separate brand identities while merging production to a single operation.
2000: PSA Peugeot Citroën incorporates new diesel particulate filter system designed to lower emission rates greatly.
2008: Company suffers as global economic downturn depresses global car purchases.

easy, in fact, that it was dubbed the first "ladies' car." The model was mostly painted yellow; hence its popular nickname was "petite citron," or little lemon.

Citroën first became known in foreign markets in 1921, when it exported a total of approximately 3,000 cars. This move sent the company on a long trek of expansion through numerous international territories throughout the century. André Citroën established the basis of a network of subsidiaries in Brussels, Amsterdam, Cologne, Milan, Geneva, and Copenhagen in 1924, and the company exported a total of 17,000 vehicles during that year.

The year 1924 marked the official beginning of Automobiles Citroën. André Citroën founded the Société Anonyme Automobiles Citroën with a capital of FFR 100 million. In the same year, the company presented the B10, the first automobile to have an all-steel body instead of the conventional mixed wood and steel construction. Made of cold-pressed panels welded together, the new body offered much better resistance to

impact. Production increased in 1924 to 300 vehicles per day, for a total output that year of 55,387 automobiles.

By 1928 Citroën's factories employed 30,000 workers and maintained a total production capacity of 1,000 vehicles per day; the company had 14 distributors in France and North Africa, 10 subsidiary companies, and four factories in foreign countries. Overseas sales represented 45 percent of all French motor industry exports.

Peugeot would turn to the new automotive technologies in the late 1920s yet remained committed to its tradition of handcraftsmanship. The first "modern" Peugeot automobile, the 201, was introduced at the 1929 Paris Motor Show. This completely new car earned Peugeot its reputation as a manufacturer of reliable vehicles. What distinguished Peugeot from other car companies of its time was the number of technological developments that the company incorporated into its product designs year after year. A steady stream of innovations formed the core of the company's history during its first century.

After the crash of the New York Stock Exchange in 1929, Citroën, along with the rest of the world, entered an era of economic crisis. The company's yearly production fell in 1932 to 41,348 vehicles. However, Citroën, like Peugeot, continued to introduce new automobile models and innovations. Milestones in the 1930s included Citroën's first bus, a 22-passenger vehicle with all-steel bodywork and a six-cylinder engine, built at the Levallois factory in 1931. In 1932 the company announced the C4G and C6G, containing the first engines carried on soft mountings to eliminate vibration.

Even as the Depression continued to dampen the high spirits of the French motor industry, André Citroën clung to his belief that the greater the number of products, the less expensive production would become. In 1933 he set goals of production of 1,000 vehicles per day and the introduction of a new front-driven model developed by Citroën designer André Lefebvre. The company announced the 7A in April 1934, the first of a line of Traction Avant models that were produced until 1957.

M. Citroën's plans came to a standstill, however, when the company's financial difficulties led to an inability to pay its debts. In 1934 the French government asked the Michelin company, Citroën's principal creditor, to take financial control and refloat the company. Under the direction of Michelin, 8,000 layoffs took place. The company's production plummeted from 51,546 in 1934 to 29,101 in 1935. By that time, André Citroën was already ill, and he died in 1935 of stomach cancer. Yet Citroën's legacy would remain that of a pioneer of the European motor industry and the man most responsible for creating the automobile as a mass-consumer item in Europe.

REBUILDING IN THE POSTWAR ERA

The loss of the company's independence, and the death of its founder, did not end Citroën's record of innovation. In 1936 Citroën conceived one of its all-time classics, the legendary 2CV (or "deux chevaux"). The idea was for a low-priced car with a very small engine, described by the design department as "four wheels under an umbrella." In 1939 the outbreak of war prevented the company from announcing the 2CV, and the company destroyed all but one of its 250 prototypes to maintain secrecy. In 1940 the Quai de Javel factory was bombed, and Citroën's Belgian factory was partly destroyed. The company's production gradually fell to zero in 1943, partly due to management's refusal to comply with the demands of the Vichy government.

Peugeot, too, was crippled by World War II. Production slowed and almost ground to a halt as a result of the damage inflicted by Allied bombing. It picked up again immediately after the war with the 202 model, which had originally been introduced in 1938. This was replaced towards the end of 1947 by the 203 model, of which over 685,000 were built. With a unitary body and a 1300-cc 45 hp engine, this vehicle remained in production for almost 12 years without any major modifications.

On the Citroën side, production rebuilt slowly from 1,600 in 1945 to 12,600 in 1946. In 1948 the 2CV appeared at the Paris Motor Show. From October 1949 to the end of 1984, the company built over three million examples of the immensely popular and inexpensive vehicle. A cult developed around the 2CV, for it became something of a national symbol for the proletariat. Manifestations of popular enthusiasm for the 2CV included odes, sculptures, and water races (contestants removed the car's tires and floated the chassis on oil drums). As the company entered the 1950s, the demand for the 2CV stretched the delivery delay to six years.

In 1953 Citroën began decentralizing its production organization with the opening of the Rennes-la Barre Thomas factory in Brittany. It was not until the end of the 1970s, however, that the company achieved a balance between the Paris region and the provinces.

In 1954 Citroën's design and development department pioneered a technical breakthrough known as constant height hydropneumatic rear suspension. The system combined the actions of a gas and a liquid to achieve greatly improved road handling. In 1955 the

company announced the DS19, with no front grille and a completely smooth nose. This model was revolutionary not only because of its aerodynamic shape, but also because of its technical features, including the newly developed hydropneumatic suspension. All major systems (gear change, clutch, steering, and brakes) were power operated. The model was an instant success, and Citroën received 12,000 orders by the end of the first day.

In 1958 the factory of the Société Citroën Hispania at Vigo (Spain) began to produce 2CV vans for the Spanish market and for export. This gave the company representation in a market where imports were strictly limited by quotas. Also in 1958, the company announced the four-wheel drive 2CV Sahara, especially useful for oil exploration and mining teams in desert areas. The vehicle was capable of climbing a sandy, 40 percent slope fully laden.

As Citroën entered the 1960s, the company expanded by establishing subsidiaries and signing joint ventures in foreign locations. In 1960 it reached an agreement with the Yugoslav Tomos concern for the assembly of the 2CV in Yugoslavia. In 1962 Citroën established sales companies in Montreal and Vienna. In 1963 the company set up a subsidiary in Chile for assembly and sales, and it also reached an agreement with the Sedica company for the assembly of the 2CV and 3CV in Madagascar. In 1964 the Mangualde factory in Portugal came into operation to manufacture the 2CV. This move again allowed Citroën access to a market with severe restrictions on the import of fully assembled cars.

New Citroën models in the 1960s included the Ami 6, a model categorized as top-of-the-range, and the Dyane, a model categorized between the 2CV and Ami 6. In 1965 Citroën acquired the Panhard factory at Reims (France), a facility specializing in the manufacture of mechanical components for commercial vehicles. In 1967, after signing an industrial collaboration agreement for the production of common designs, Citroën took a majority shareholding in the company Berliet, the European Economic Community's largest producer of commercial vehicles.

Citroën underwent major reorganization the following year. Citroën SA, a holding company, was created to oversee the activities of Citroën, Berliet, and Panhard. Citroën SA gathered within its structure more than 20 subsidiary companies, including the Société Anonyme Automobiles Citroën (handling production) and the Société Commerciale Citroën (handling sales).

Citroën signed a technical and commercial agreement in 1968 with the Italian sports car company Maserati. It also signed an agreement with Fiat to set up a holding company, Pardevi, which would hold the majority of Citroën shares, and in which Fiat would have a 49 percent shareholding and Michelin, 51 percent.

JOINING FORCES IN THE 1970S

The Arab oil embargo of the 1970s and the resulting worldwide recession prompted Michelin to sell its Citroën holding to Peugeot. Peugeot was then eyeing international expansion to enable it to compete on a global scale. Two years later, the newly named PSA Peugeot Citroën SA purchased Chrysler's struggling European operations, including the Simca brand name. That name would soon be transformed to Talbot. The acquisition proved a disappointment, however, and the Talbot name disappeared in the 1980s.

Peugeot and Citroën, meantime, continued to be operated independently, with their own factories and distribution networks. The merging of the two companies took place over the following decades, especially under the leadership of Jacques Calvet, who took over as head of PSA in 1984. By 1998 Peugeot and Citroën, while retaining their brand identities, had nevertheless been streamlined into a more efficient organization, exemplified by the Citroën Xsara, a sedan featuring Citroën styling and Peugeot parts.

A new recession in the early 1980s propelled PSA into net losses. The company was also crippled by a weeks-long strike in its Parisian facilities. However, the successful launch of a number of new models, including the popular Citroën BX and the luxury XM models, and the extension of the Peugeot 05 range, enabled a restructured PSA to emerge with profits of more than FFR 8 billion by the end of the decade. During the 1980s, also, PSA entered a number of new markets, including the fast-developing Pacific region, particularly the Chinese market.

The European and world economies would contract again in the early 1990s. By then, the European auto market, facing the looming entry of Japanese carmakers, began taking on a new shape, as companies formed strategic partnerships, not only for sales and distribution but for production as well, with many models sharing the same platforms among different makes. These moves helped PSA maintain its leading position in France, despite intense competition from French government-owned rival Renault, and kept PSA among the top automotive manufacturers in Europe.

PSA's balance sheet was further enhanced by the successful launches of new generation models, including the extended Peugeot 06 line and the highly successful Citroën Xantia and Xsara midrange sedans. In 1998

PSA put the finishing touches on the merging of the Citroën and Peugeot organizations, retaining the separate brand identities while merging production to a single operation. Closing out the year, PSA recorded sales of FFR 221.44 billion.

ECO-FRIENDLY AUTOMOTIVE ENGINES: 2000–07

In 2000 PSA Peugeot Citroën achieved a major technological leap by enhancing its fuel-efficient HDi engine with a new technology called diesel particulate filter system (DPFS). The DPFS was an innovative automotive engine production technology that reduced the emission of toxic gases to the environment by destroying even the smallest particles of diesel. The DPFS was applied for the first time in the Peugeot 607 model in what was largely perceived to be one of the most successful exploits of the company at the turn of the new millennium.

In another development, PSA Peugeot Citroën entered a technological cooperation agreement with BMW with the objective of enhancing the design of the company's car engines with regards to performance and efficiency. The cooperation between the two carmakers led to the development of the 1.61 automotive engines that reduced fuel consumption and carbon dioxide emissions. In the beginning of 2006, the company continued to tout the success of its technological exploits with the presentation of two demonstration vehicles for "hybrid diesel-electric" drivetrain, the Peugeot 307 and C4 Hybrid HDi.

SALES DECLINE FOLLOWING PLUNGE IN AUTOMOTIVE MARKETS: 2008

The presentation of Hybrid 4 at the 2008 Paris Motor Show was one of the biggest achievements of PSA Peugeot Citroën during the year. The unique model was equipped with all utilities associated with hybrid car models, including energy recovery during deceleration, energy boost during acceleration, and reduced fuel consumption.

However, PSA Peugeot Citroën experienced a harsh macroeconomic environment in 2008 as a result of the global economic crisis. The drop of the group's sales by 4.9 percent, from 3,326,000 units in 2007 to 3,260,000 units in 2008, resulted from a 5.7 percent overall decline in the global automotive industry. The company's sales in its Western European markets were particularly hard hit by the global economic crisis, dropping by 8.8 percent when compared to 2007. Nonetheless, the group maintained its hold of 5 percent share of the global market as well as a 13.8 percent share of the Western European market.

PSA Peugeot Citroën also experienced positive growth in Eastern Europe, and Russia in particular, where its automobile registrations rose by 67 percent. Generally, the impressive performance of the company in 2008 in a difficult macroeconomic environment was attributed to a variety of factors. These included a receptive market for the Peugeot 308 model, the launch of the 308 station wagon, and the entry of the Citroën C5, Citroën Sedan, Peugeot Bipper, and Peugeot Partner, among others.

The continued focus of the company on the production of eco-friendly and low-cost vehicles had a positive impact on its overall performance in 2008. The worldwide sales of the company's automobile units that had engine capacities of less than 130g of carbon dioxide emission per kilometer increased in 2008 by 7.4 percent, to reach 921,000 vehicles.

PSA Peugeot Citroën posted mixed results in 2009. The company experienced a 21.8 percent decline in revenues in the first half of the year but was able to return to profit in the second half with a 2.6 percent growth in revenues. Growth in all areas continued in 2010. Successful launches included the new Citroën DS line in March and the Citroën DS3 and the new Peugeot RCZ in May. The company's sales of new vehicles rose 13 percent to 3,602,200, and its market share in Europe increased from 13.8 percent in 2009 to 14.2 percent. Global automotive markets grew in 2010 by 10 percent, and the proportion of the company's sales outside of Europe grew to 39 percent. This expansion reflected the company's success in its designated growth regions of Latin America (26.5% increase in sales), China (38%), and Russia (37%). The company expected those markets to continue to grow during the 2010s and set a target for 50 percent sales outside Europe in 2015.

Continuing its strategy of optimizing conventional engine technology, PSA Peugeot Citroën developed plans to introduce a new family of 1-liter, 3-cylinder petrol engines with power generation capacities of between 50KW and 70KW. The company also planned to introduce in 2011 the new family of petrol engines in smaller town models such as the Peugeot 107 before gradually spreading the technology to the more compact models.

Also part of the company's strategy for the future was the development of hybrid technologies and the promotion of electric vehicles. The Peugeot i0n and Citroën C-ZERO electric vehicles were introduced in late 2010, as was a micro-hybrid system on the Citroën C4, C4 Picasso, and C5. Plans called for the same system to be introduced on the Peugeot 508 and 308 in 2011. The world's first diesel hybrid, the Peugeot 3008 HYbrid4, was scheduled for launch in 2011.

As a leading maker of eco-friendly, fuel-efficient vehicles, it seemed likely that PSA would fare well if the trend toward all things "greener" continued.

Dorothy Walton
Updated, M. L. Cohen; Paul Ingati

PRINCIPAL SUBSIDIARIES

Banque PSA Finance; Faurecia (57%); Gefco.

PRINCIPAL DIVISIONS

Peugeot; Citroën.

PRINCIPAL COMPETITORS

Bayerische Motoren Werke AG; Ford Motor Company; General Motors Ltd; Hyundai Motor Company; Toyota Company Ltd; Volkswagen AG.

FURTHER READING

PSA Peugeot Citroën. "Clean, Economical Engines to Cut Greenhouse Gas Emissions.", Accessed January 13, 2011. http://www.psa-peugeot-citroen.com/en/psa_group/technology_b3.php.

———. "PSA Group History." Accessed January 13, 2011. http://www.psa-peugeot-citroen.com/en/psa_group/history_b4.php.

———. "PSA Peugeot Citroën Sales Hold Up against the Sharp Drop in Automotive Markets." Accessed January 13, 2011. http://www.psa-peugeot-citroen.com/en/psa_group/market_b5.php.

———. "Record Sales Performance in 2010: Worldwide Sales Up 13% to 3.6 Million Units." Press Release, January 13, 2011. Accessed January 14, 2011. http://www.psa-peugeot-citroen.com/en/psa_espace/press_releases_details_d1.php?id=1199.

"World Motor Vehicle Production." OICA Correspondents Survey. Accessed January 13, 2011. http://oica.net/wp-content/uploads/ranking-2009.pdf.

PT Bank UOB Buana Tbk

Jalan Asemka, No. 32–36
Jakarta Barat, 11110
Indonesia
Telephone: (21) 6922901
Fax: (21) 6922005
Web site: http://www.bankbuana.com

Subsidiary of United Overseas Bank Ltd.
Founded: 1956 as PT Bank Buana Tbk
Employees: 5,000 (est., 2010)
Assets: IDR 38 trillion ($4 billion) (2010)
NAICS: 522110 Commercial Banking

■ ■ ■

One of Indonesia's top 20 banks, PT Bank UOB Buana Tbk (Bank Buana) focuses on the trade finance segment, especially targeting small and mid-sized businesses. The retail distribution market is also a primary target of the group. Bank Buana offers a full range of retail and commercial banking services, including a range of savings products and e-banking services. The company's loans include working capital loans, export-import loans, bank guarantees, and investment loans. Bank Buana serves its market through nearly 35 branches throughout Indonesia.

ORIGINS AND DEVELOPMENT: 1950S TO 1975

UOB Bank Buana Indonesia was founded in 1956 as privately owned PT Bank Buana Indonesia Tbk. The bank remained small, and by the early 1960s found it difficult to keep afloat. In 1965 the bank was bought up by a group of five Indonesian industrial companies, each of which took an approximately equal share in Bank Buana. Among the bank's new owners were a producer of glass and a textile manufacture. Owning a bank for these modestly sized businesses was not merely a matter of prestige but was also a way of cutting back on their own banking charges. However, the equal shareholder status of the five owners made it difficult to reach agreement over the bank's management policies and long-term strategy. This situation led the bank to adopt a highly conservative approach to growth and to focus its customer portfolio on the trade finance market rather than on the consumer market.

Nonetheless, Bank Buana grew strongly in the 1970s. Mergers and acquisitions marked the group's expansion during this period, beginning with the 1972 merger with PT Bank Pembinaan Nasional, in Bandung. In 1974 Bank Buana expanded its operations again by absorbing PT Bank Kesejahteraan Masyaraka, in Semarang, and then again in 1975 by merging with PT Bank Aman Makmur, based in Jakarta.

GROWTH FOLLOWED BY STAGNATION: 1976–93

A turning point for Bank Buana came in 1976, when it was awarded a foreign exchange license. Only about 20 percent of Indonesia's many banks were to achieve this status. As such, Bank Buana was able to develop into one of the country's leading foreign currency and trade finance specialists. The bank stepped up its growth

COMPANY PERSPECTIVES

We strive to focus our service to customers who are retailers, distributors, and industry with small-medium scale enterprises. This sector has proven to be the most dynamic economic sector, one that is able to survive and grow even when economic times are difficult.

through the 1980s, opening more than 100 branch offices throughout the country. By 1990 Bank Buana had become Indonesia's 12th- largest bank.

By the late 1980s, however, Bank Buana's five-way ownership structure, and the inability to reach consensus, had left the bank vulnerable in the buoyant Indonesian banking market. Starting in about 1989, the bank went into a period of relative stagnation, and by 1994 it had slipped back to 35th place among the country's top 50 banks. As both its loan portfolio and assets base slipped, the bank continued to lose ground in the booming Indonesian banking sector.

Fueled by increasingly liberal government banking policies, the Indonesian economy, and its banking sector, grew quickly in the late 1980s and early 1990s. Bank Buana, however, appeared to sit on the sidelines while its competitors increasingly gained ground. By the early 1990s Bank Buana seemed at a standstill in what some observers described as an "overbanked" Indonesian financial market.

Instead of growing its own business, Bank Buana concentrated on forming joint ventures, partnering with foreign banks seeking entry into the fast-growing Indonesian market. As such, the group formed a joint venture with Japan's Mitsubishi Bank, named PT Mitsubishi Buana Bank, in 1989. The following year, Bank Buana partnered with DBS Bank and TatLee Bank of Singapore to create DBS Buana TatLee Bank. DBS later took over Mitsubishi's stake in the former bank, which changed its name to DBS Buana Bank, then sold out its stake in the Buana-TatLee partnership, which became Keppel TatLee Buana Bank.

RESTRUCTURED FOR GROWTH: 1994–2002

The year 1994 marked a significant change for Bank Buana. In that year, the company changed its shareholder structure, placing more than 89 percent of its shares into a newly created holding company, PT Sari Dasa Karsa. At the same time, the bank installed a new

management team, which began a more aggressive growth policy. The bank's new management targeted expansion of the bank's loan policy, which grew by some 40 percent into the middle of the decade.

In the second half of the 1990s, Bank Buana's new growth drive had returned it to Indonesia's top 20 banks. However, concerns that the bank was expanding too fast led management to scale back its growth. Although analysts consistently referred to the group's management strategy as conservative, Bank Buana itself favored "prudent" as a more descriptive term for its strategy. Nonetheless, Bank Buana began preparing for an initial public offering, initially slated for 1997.

The crash of Indonesia's financial community amid the economic crisis that swept through Asian markets in the late 1990s put a temporary halt to the group's plans for a stock listing. As the Indonesian banking sector reeled from the sudden collapse of the country's economy, and as many of Bank Buana's competitors slipped into bankruptcy, Bank Buana's more conservative approach enabled it to emerge relatively unscathed from the crisis. When the Bank of Indonesia reviewed Bank Buana, it became one of only a few to receive certification as a Class A financial institution.

Bank Buana once again began preparations for its public listing at the end of the 1990s. As part of that process, the bank sold off its share of the DBS Buana joint venture. Bank Buana went public in July 2000, listing on the Jakarta and Surubaya stock exchanges in a successful offering that was several times oversubscribed. The bank continued expanding its shareholder base, adding two new major shareholders in the first few years of the 21st century, including PT Makindo Tbk, which boosted its stake in the bank to 6.92 percent.

Bank Buana split its stock for the first time, in a two-for-one split, near the end of 2002. Soon after, Bank Buana was admitted to the New York Stock Exchange as well, where its shares began trading as American Depositary Receipts (ADRs). In April 2003 the International Finance Corporation, a subsidiary of the World Bank, acquired nearly 7 percent of the bank, underscoring Bank Buana's status as one of the country's most stable smaller banks. That purchase reduced PT Sari Dasa Karsa's stake in the bank to just over 55 percent.

GOING PRIVATE: 2004–05

Bank Buana's plans to expand took an unexpected turn in 2004 with an acquisition that ultimately took the bank back to a private ownership status. In early 2004 Bank Buana issued $60 million in bonds to prepare for further acquisitions. However, profit declined 12 percent in 2003, despite a growth expectation of 10 percent,

KEY DATES

1956: PT Bank Buana Indonesia is established in Jakarta.

1965: Bank Buana is acquired by a partnership formed by five industrial companies.

1972: The bank merges with PT Bank Pembinaan Nasional, in Bandung.

1975: The bank merges with PT Bank Aman Makmur, based in Jakarta.

1976: Bank Buana is granted a foreign currency license.

1994: A new holding company is created, PT Sari Dasa Karsa, which acquires nearly 90 percent of Bank Buana's shares and installs new management.

1999: The bank receives class A certification from Bank of Indonesia and sells out its share of DBS Buana Bank.

2000: Bank Buana goes public with a listing on the Jakarta Stock Exchange.

2003: International Finance Corporation, a subsidiary of the World Bank, acquires a 7 percent stake in Bank Buana.

2005: UOB Singapore acquires controlling stake in Bank Buana.

2007: Bank Buana changes its name to UOB Bank Buana.

2008: UOB Bank Buana privatizes.

2010: UOB merges subsidiary UOB Indonesia into UOB Buana.

and the acquisitions did not materialize. On April 6, 2004, United Overseas Bank Ltd. (UOB), Singapore's second-largest bank, announced its intention to acquire 23 percent of Bank Buana's shares.

In theory, the acquisition would benefit both parties by opening up new markets for each. For UOB, the acquisition would offer access to a market of 210 million people. Bank Buana would have an expanded product base to offer its customers. With this move, the company raised its loan-to-deposit ratio (LDR) from 56 to 70 percent in 2005, effectively increasing its risk position.

The move toward a less risk-averse position was also an indication of the intentions of OUB, which had hinted that it planned to take a majority stake in Bank Buana over time. In 2005 UOB acquired another 30

percent of Bank Buana's shares, making its holdings total 53 percent.

However, by becoming a major shareholder, UOB's stake violated Indonesia's Single Presence policy, under which a foreign investor cannot own a controlling stake in more than one bank in Indonesia. The additional shares were acquired from PT Sari Dasa Karsa, which was no longer the majority shareholder. UOB already owned a majority share of Bank UOB Indonesia. UOB opted to establish a holding company in Indonesia for the two banks. The two banks would merge in July 2010.

GROWTH AND LABOR PROBLEMS: 2007 AND BEYOND

In January 2007 Bank Buana changed its name to UOB Buana to accommodate its majority stakeholder. Bank Buana effectively privatized in late 2008 when UOB Singapore acquired another 38 percent of Buana shares, making its ownership 98.99 percent of Bank Buana.

Bank Buana's profitability increased steadily after its initial merger with UOB due to rising interest rates and expanded loan activity. This success did not go unnoticed by the bank's workers, who requested pay raises and bonuses. In April 2009 workers went on strike after receiving no indication of a favorable response from management. The strike lasted two days. Of the bank's 5,800 workers, 4,000 joined the strike, affecting 23 of the 35 branches nationwide. Negotiations were only partially successful. Management refused the requested 26 percent pay raise, citing the international economic crisis that hindered the banking industry and Bank Buana's cash flow. However, 2009 and 2010 proved again to be growth years for the company. While workers did not receive all that they demanded, management did make some concessions. Relationships between workers and management remained strained, yet after repeated threats, the workers did not strike again over the issue in 2010.

In 2010 11 banks in Indonesia, including Bank Buana, received $1 billion from the Export-Import Bank of the United States (Ex-Im Bank) to sponsor U.S. exports to Indonesia. The financial backing provided important support for Bank Buana's move toward becoming a truly international bank.

M. L. Cohen;
Updated, Sara K. Huter

PRINCIPAL COMPETITORS

PT Bank Central Asia Tbk; PT Bank Danamon Indonesia Tbk; PT Bank Negara Indonesia Tbk; PT Bank Rakyat Indonesia Tbk.

FURTHER READING

"Bank Buana Indonesia to List on NYSE." *Asia Pulse* December 27, 2002.

"Bank Buana to Go Public." *Jakarta Post,* June 16, 2000.

"Bank UOB Buana Assets Reach Rp 38t After Merger." *Jakarta Post,* June 13, 2010.

"Indonesia's Bank Buana Hopes to Complete Delisting This Year." *AsiaPulse News,* June 23, 2008.

"Indonesia's Bank Buana Posts 5.58% Decline in Net Profit." *Asia Pulse,* October 31, 2002.

"UOB to Buy Bank Buana Shares." *America's Intelligence Wire,* April 7, 2004.

"UOB Workers to Wait Until April 15 Before Another Strike." *Jakarta Post,* April 2009.

Queensland Treasury Corporation

61 Mary Street
Level 14
GPO Box 1096
Brisbane, Queensland 4001
Australia
Telephone: (61 7) 3842-4600
Fax: (61 7) 3221-4122
Web site: http://www.qtc.com.au

State-Owned Company
Founded: 1988
Employees: 200 (est., 2010)
Assets: AUD 74.39 billion ($74.2 billion, 2010)
Stock Exchanges: Australian Securities Exchange (ASX)
Ticker Symbol: XQL
NAICS: 921130 Public Finance Activities

■ ■ ■

As the Australian state of Queensland's corporate treasury services provider, Queensland Treasury Corporation (QTC) is also the Queensland government's central financing authority. As a conduit between the government and the private sector, the company's responsibilities include providing financial risk management services and advice to the state and the state's public sector organizations. The company also sources the state's long-term debt funding requirements. Another major responsibility includes investing the state's short- to medium-term cash surpluses with the aim of maximizing returns to Queensland's public sector

bodies within a conservative risk management framework.

In terms of debt funding, QTC borrows funds in the domestic and international markets with the goal of minimizing the state's and QTC's liquidity and rollover risk. The company then lends these funds to customers or uses them to manage customers' debt or to refinance maturing debt. Debt expertise developed through relationships with domestic and international markets is used to provide customers with short- to medium-term investment solutions. The company's financial risk management services work closely with public sector customers to help manage risk in financial transactions while achieving the best financial solution for the organizations and the state.

QTC does not formulate policy but works within the policy framework developed by the government and Queensland Treasury. Although the company does not take direct equity in products, it may, at the government's direction, invest equity in special purpose vehicles established to achieve a specific outcome for the state.

COMPANY FOUNDED AND RESTRUCTURED: 1988–91

The Queensland Treasury Corporation (QTC) was created to provide a range of independent financial services to the government and its public sector entities. It was founded in 1988 as a "corporation sole" constituted by the under treasurer in accordance with the Queensland Treasury Corporation Act 1988 (QTC Act). Essentially, a "corporation sole" is a corporation, or company, that

COMPANY PERSPECTIVES

As partners in financial sustainability, the mission of Queensland Treasury Corporation is to provide corporate treasury services to our customers and the State by striving to understand our customers' current and future needs, and by delivering solutions to meet those needs.

consists solely of a nominated office holder as opposed to the more usual type of corporation that has at least two members, with those members being appointed personally. Unlike most companies in Australia, QTC was not established under the Corporations Act but rather by the QTC Act. The QTC Act specifically stated that QTC is excluded from and not subject to the Corporations Act.

The establishment of QTC continued the financial operations of its predecessor, the Queensland Government Development Authority, which was the investment branch of the Queensland Treasury Department. Although QTC initially operated as a division of the Queensland Treasury, a restructuring took place on July 1, 1991, that made QTC a separate, autonomous, and accountable central financing authority. The restructuring also resulted in the establishment of the QTC board, which increased representation from independent board members. Ultimately, the board was responsible to the Australian Parliament through the under treasurer. Participation in QTC activities was voluntary for local authorities, statutory bodies, and government-owned enterprises. However, participation was mandatory for government departments.

As the autonomous and accountable central financing authority, QTC became responsible for the state's wholesale and medium- to long-term investments. In August 1991 Sir Leo Hielscher AC was appointed QTC's chairman, and the QTC Capital Markets Board was established. Hielscher had served as deputy under treasurer of Queensland for 10 years before he became the under treasurer from 1974 to 1988. He was appointed as chairman of the Queensland Treasury Corporation Advisory Board in 1988 before becoming inaugural chairman of the Queensland Treasury Corporation Board.

CONSOLIDATING DEBT

In the beginning QTC's primary goal was to consolidate Queensland's debt as it took on the role as the state's only debt issuer. This allowed QTC to reduce the number of state entities approaching the debt markets and help eliminate competition between different local government-related authorities. The consolidation resulted in an economy of scale that benefited overall operations. Furthermore, QTC committed itself to open and transparent communication with the markets.

QTC was credited with achieving many firsts, including establishing a global transferable note (TRN) program specifically targeting offshore investors. It also issued global bonds at yields below those typically achieved in the domestic market. At the same time, QTC supplemented its Global TRN program by establishing multicurrency medium-term note programs in both the United States and Europe. In 1992 QTC became the lowest-priced Australian semigovernment issuer, a position that QTC has maintained throughout the years.

QTC also established a Cash Fund to help customers manage their short-term cash balances. Traditionally the fund has done well, delivering competitive returns for customers' short- to medium-term investments. In 1994 QTC broadened its capabilities and established an independent corporate advisory service.

ADVISING THE STATE

In its role as a financial adviser to the state of Queensland, QTC has served as an adviser in some capacity on most of the state's key infrastructure projects. In 1995 QTC played an integral role in the leasing of wind turbines by Stanwell Corporation Limited, a Queensland-owned electrical power producer. At the time, the lease had a transaction amount of AUD 1.365 billion. The project's success ultimately led to QTC leading the way in a series of other lease arrangements for major assets, including power lines and rolling stock.

QTC also played a major role in negotiating the 1996 merger of Suncorp, the Queensland Industry and Development Corporation, and Metway Bank to form Suncorp-Metway Limited. The effort to join public and private corporations and bring them into public ownership resulted in one of Australia's largest banks and its largest general insurance group.

FOCUS ON CUSTOMERS AND TRAINING: 1996–2002

By 1996 QTC had achieved significant economics of scale and scope for its customers. As a result, QTC began to reconsider its strategic approach and ultimately decided to commit to a customer loyalty operating model. To better develop and deliver customized

```
┌─────────────────────────────────────────┐
│             KEY DATES                     │
│               ▪                           │
│  1988:  Queensland Treasury Corporation   │
│         (QTC) founded as a division of    │
│         the Queensland Treasury.          │
│  1991:  QTC is restructured as a          │
│         separate, autonomous, and         │
│         accountable central financ-       │
│         ing authority.                    │
│  1992:  Company becomes the lowest-priced │
│         Australian semigovernment issuer. │
│  2005:  QTC and the Local Government      │
│         Association (LGA) of Queensland   │
│         establish LG Infrastructure       │
│         Services Pty Ltd.                 │
│  2007:  QTC conducts a major review of    │
│         the financial sustainability of   │
│         109 of Queensland's local         │
│         governments.                      │
└─────────────────────────────────────────┘
```

financial and risk management solutions, QTC set out to acquire a comprehensive understanding of its customers and their businesses, as well as the financial challenges they faced then and in the future.

In 1997 QTC established its Central Treasury Management course. The course was designed to help customers' understand the concepts, financial instruments, and practices integral to managing debt and interest rate risk. Five years later, in 2002, QTC hosted its first corporate financial management course. This course helped customers understand key issues in financial management, such as determining capital structure, evaluating projects and assessing their risks, and establishing a framework for interest rate risk management. Both courses included simulated models designed to reinforce the courses' teachings.

QTC also set out to provide more targeted support for customers working on major projects. As a result, it established a secondment program in 2002. The program consisted of sending QTC employees to work for various customers for a certain period of time to help with key strategic and operational roles within customers' businesses. Since that time, QTC has placed employees in more than 100 such positions.

HELPING GOVERNMENT FINANCE INFRASTRUCTURE: 2005–07

In 2005 QTC joined with the Local Government Association (LGA) of Queensland to launch a new organization called LG Infrastructure Services Pty Ltd.

The goal was to provide targeted support to the procurement of local government infrastructure development. Established as a corporations law company owned by QTC and the LGA, LG Infrastructure Services provided its services to local governments using a fee-for-service system. The service was created in response to the fact that large infrastructure projects were rare for many local councils, especially smaller ones, and in recognition that these councils did not have expertise for the most effective operation of such projects. For example, LG Infrastructure helped determine waste management solutions for a group of 14 councils.

In 2007 QTC collaborated with various government stakeholders to help develop the innovative Supported Debt Model (SDM). A variant of the traditional privately financed Public Private Partnership (PPP) model, the SDM differs from a traditional PPP in that it is partly financed from the public sector. The SDM provided the Queensland government with a responsible option for using PPPs to achieve various infrastructure objectives, especially in a challenging market environment. SDM also helped fund projects at a lower cost to taxpayers.

The SDM model was used to fund the South East Queensland Schools project. The project involved the construction and maintenance for 30 years of seven new schools in Australia's rapidly growing Sunshine Coast, Western Corridor, the Gold Coast, and Redlands areas. Although the construction phase of the project was entirely debt-funded by the private sector, 70 percent of that debt eventually was to be taken out by QTC at various milestones during the project.

FOCUS ON FINANCIAL SUSTAINABILITY

One of QTC's most significant projects took place in 2007 when QTC completed a major review of the financial sustainability of 109 of Queensland's local governments. The review was an assessment of the Queensland government's capacity to meet its commitments in both the short and long term. One of the review's goals was to provide various local governments with insights into the financial health of its business from the current time and forward for a 10-year period. The review helped to identify whether or not changes needed to be made to government business based both on current forecasts and potential risks and issues in the future.

As a part of the review, QTC assessed 94 Queensland Councils and found that 49 percent were either "weak," "very weak," or "financially distressed." Andrew

Fraser, Queensland's minister for Local Government, Planning and Sport, was quoted in an article in Brisbane's *Courier-Mail* as saying: "Without reform we face a situation where many local governments will collapse under the weight of mounting pressure. There are challenges ahead but doing nothing is not an option." Ultimately, the information obtained from QTC's review helped the Queensland's Reform Commission determine the boundaries for going forward with an amalgamation that reduced Queensland's existing local governments from 156 to 72.

In 2010 Sir Leo Hielscher retired as chairman of the Queensland Treasury Corporation Board. The company's CEO Stephen Rochester was elevated to the chairmanship. In addition, Philip Noble was named QTC's chief executive. New challenges, however, quickly arose for the new chief executive and chairman. Massive flooding in Queensland in early 2011 was estimated to cost the local economy AUD 13 billion. A cyclone that arrived on the heels of the flooding also complicated recovery efforts. Overall cost to the state government was estimated to be at least AUD $2.5 billion. Some analysts predicted that QTC was going to have to issue more bonds to help pay for construction and other costs associated with the damage.

Despite the negative impact of these disasters on the economy of Queensland, the company planned to remain focused on future needs as well. Such plans included establishing a new customer transaction system that would provide customers with significant autonomy, especially in routine financial transactions.

David Petechuk

PRINCIPAL COMPETITORS

ASX Ltd.; Commonwealth Bank of Australia; Esanda Finance Corporation Ltd.

FURTHER READING

Bell, Paul. "Reforming Local Government Funding to Meet Community Needs." Speech to the Building and Financing Local Governemnt Infrastructure Conference, Sydney Australia, March 12, 2008. Australian Local Government Association. Accessed February 19, 2011. http://www.alga.asn.au/newsroom/speeches/2008/20080312_PaulBell.php.

Maynard, Neale. "Poor Councils Named." *Courier-Mail,* May 18, 2007. Accessed February 22, 2011. http://www.couriermail.com.au/news/queensland/poor-councils-named/story-e6freoof-1111113563680.

Paxton, Paul, and Minter Ellison. "Australia Innovative Funding Models—Breaking the Mould." Practical Law Company, May 4, 2010. Accessed February 19, 2011. http://www.practicallaw.com/3-502-2137#null.

QuinStreet Incorporated

950 Tower Lane
Sixth Floor
Foster City, California 94404
U.S.A.
Telephone: (650) 578-7700
Fax: (650) 578-7604
Web site: http://www.quinstreet.com

Public Company
Founded: 1999
Employees: 637 (2010)
Revenue: $334.8 million (2010)
Stock Exchanges: NASDAQ
Ticker Symbol: QNST
NAICS: 541890 Other Services Related to Advertising

■ ■ ■

Founded by a team of entrepreneurs including Bronwyn Syiek and Doug Valenti, QuinStreet Incorporated serves more than 200 global clients. QuinStreet makes its money from revenue generated through pay-per-click (PPC) sales. It also uses opt-in e-mail, newsletters, and third-party publishers to generate revenue. It owns and manages a suite of online proprietary networks. QuinStreet's clients span a range of industries including financial services, health care, education, career services, and business-to-business (B2B) firms.

Primary client verticals at the company are within the education and financial services industries. (A vertical marketing strategy is one that targets a specific industry.) Websites that QuinStreet operates include ArmyStudyGuide.com, ElderCarelink.com, Insure.com (an online insurance quote service and brokerage business), Insurance.com, and ReliableRemodeler.com (a Web site that specializes in online home renovation and contractor referrals).

COMPANY FOUNDING AND EARLY YEARS: 1995–2001

Prior to starting QuinStreet, Doug Valenti was a general partner at Rosewood Capital. He also worked at Proctor & Gamble Company as a manager and at McKinsey & Company as a consultant. It was at McKinsey & Company that he crossed paths with Brownyn Syiek, who (prior to McKinsey) had worked as director of business development at De La Rue, a European security products and services provider.

Under Valenti and Syiek's guidance, QuinStreet got its start during the peak of the dot-com bubble (1995–2000). To help finance its early business ventures, QuinStreet raised approximately $60 million of venture capital equity investment between 1999 and 2000. Financers included Granite Global Ventures, Split Rock Partners, Sutter Hill Ventures, Charter Growth Capital, and Rosewood Capital (one of Doug Valenti's former employers). QuinStreet would need the money when the dot-com bubble started to burst.

During the dot-com bubble, venture capitalists pumped billions into start-up firms that showed the promise of quick returns. Technology and online firms were the rage. However, by the close of 2002, when it was all over, some businesses were forced to close their

COMPANY PERSPECTIVES

We have become the leader in vertical marketing and media online because we have consistently delivered the right leads at the right volumes of qualified customer prospects to thousands of industry-leading consumer and business brands since 1999.

doors. Others issued rounds of heavy layoffs or instituted hiring freezes.

Amidst this climate, and to compete effectively on the changing virtual turf, QuinStreet took steps to strengthen its technological infrastructure. It started using BEA Systems Incorporated's WebLogic Server as the means to drive its direct marketing business model. The e-commerce platform allowed QuinStreet to launch its first revenue-generating Web sites in June 2000.

Before the close of 2000, QuinStreet had launched six commercial Web sites. The Web sites sold Kiss My Face beauty products, Rainbow Light Nutritional Systems, Select Comfort air beds, Balducci's specialty foods, Ariat boots, and Hooked on Phonics home reading programs. Senior vice president and chief technology officer, Aida Scott, had this to say about QuinStreet's initial six commercial sites in an October 31, 2000, press release: "Right now, our six merchant sites serve about 40,000 member sellers, and we are planning for the number of merchant sites we run to grow to more than 25 by next June, with upwards of 200,000 members."

In October 2001 QuinStreet launched GiftGiving. com. Collectible and licensed gift items were sold to QuinStreet's 100,000 Web site members through this portal. In 2001 revenues for QuinStreet were $1.5 million.

A START-UP REALIZING PROFITS

In April 2001 QuinStreet entered into an agreement with Topica, a privately held e-mail content provider, hosting, and marketing service company. The agreement allowed QuinStreet to provide promotional data to Topica's more than 70,000 list publishers. Topica list publishers would earn commissions based on sales they generated through QuinStreet's merchant partners.

On the heels of their deal with Topica, QuinStreet reported its first profits in 2002, $12.7million. QuinStreet clients included DeVry University, University of Phoenix, Hooked on Phonics, Countrywide Home

Loans, Ariat, and CSFBDirect. A big part of QuinStreet's success centered around its marketing efforts.

To continue to attract targeted Internet users to its own and its clients' Web sites, QuinStreet brought Aurelie Guerrieri on as senior marketing manager in 2003. Prior to joining QuinStreet, Gurerrieri worked as a business analyst at McKinsey and Company in their Paris office. Guerrieri was charged with growing QuinStreet's home and business verticals. She would also oversee the digital media customer acquisition (e.g., online customer ad click-through leads) functions at the firm. Her efforts paid off. By April 2004 QuinStreet had delivered four million prequalified sales leads for its clients.

Guerrieri's efforts were not enough to keep cyber squatters (people who register domain names with the intent of selling them for a profit to the trademark name owners) from encroaching on its own and its clients' Web sites. QuinStreet took the cyber squatters to court in 2005. The case was based on rights afforded trademark name owners under the Anti-Cyber Squatting Consumer Protection Act (ACPA) of November 1999. Under the act, QuinStreet would have to prove that the defendants had "bad faith" intent to profit from the use of its trademark business names. QuinStreet won its lawsuit in July 2006. Owners of Web sites with the same domain name as QuinStreet Web sites were ordered by the courts to shut down their Web sites that illegally mirrored the design and content of actual QuinStreet Web sites.

Growth in its revenues and its number of commercial Web sites caused QuinStreet to strengthen its financial oversight capabilities. The firm brought Kenneth Hahn on board as its chief financial officer (CFO) in 2006. Hahn had previously worked as senior vice president and CFO of Borland Software, a tech firm based in Cupertino, California. According to QuinStreet CEO Doug Valenti, Hahn was brought on board to help manage QuinStreet's growing capital. Another change to QuinStreet's senior management ranks would come in February 2007 when the company announced that Bronwyn Syiek (one of the company's founders) would take over as president. She would also continue to serve as chief operating officer (COO). With its senior management team firmly in place, the following year would be a year of acquisitions.

A FLURRY OF ACQUISITIONS AND ONLINE LEARNING

QuinStreet picked up Oregon-based ReliableRemodeler for $25.5 million in February 2008. Two months later, in April 2008, the online marketing firm picked up Arkansas-based CardRatings.com for $15.4 million and

```
┌─────────────────────────────────────────────┐
│                                             │
│              KEY DATES                      │
│                   ■                         │
│  ─────────────────────────────────────────  │
│                                             │
│  1999:  Doug Valenti is named chief executive officer │
│         at QuinStreet.                      │
│  2001:  QuinStreet launches GiftGiving.com. │
│  2002:  QuinStreet reports its first profits, $13 │
│         million.                            │
│  2008:  QuinStreet purchases Cyberspace Com- │
│         munication Corporation for $46.4 million. │
│  2010:  QuinStreet offers its initial public offering of │
│         10 million shares at $15 per share. │
│                                             │
└─────────────────────────────────────────────┘
```

Cyberspace Communication Corporation for $46.4 million ($28.4 million in cash and $18 million in potential earn-out payments). A month later QuinStreet announced plans to acquire New Jersey-based VendorSeek for $14.5 million. The deal closed in June 2008. VendorSeek, a B2B lead generation firm founded in 2002 by Ken Wisnefski, specialized in accounting, credit card, and payroll software and services. In addition to the above purchases, QuinStreet acquired 20 online publishing businesses in 2008.

The shift toward consumers getting information online rather than via television and print media formats played a sizable role in QuinStreet's profitability. As Forrester Research's 2009 "Consumer Behavior Online" report noted, in the United States alone consumers spent 33 percent of their time viewing or accessing media-related content online rather than through other means. QuinStreet positioned itself to realize profits from the shift.

DeVry University, a school that offers undergraduate and graduate online degree programs, became one of QuinStreet's largest clients. In 2009 DeVry made up 19 percent of the marketer's net revenues. This represented a 4 percent decrease over the previous year's 23 percent. QuinStreet would continue to focus on broadening is client base in efforts to ensure that no single client comprised more than 10 percent of its net revenues.

QuinStreet generated $260.52 million in net revenues in 2009. It also celebrated its 10th anniversary in May 2009. Even while Valenti addressed his colleagues during their 10th anniversary celebration, the company was in talks to acquire additional businesses. In October 2009 QuinStreet purchased the brand name, related media assets, and Web site of Insure.com for $16 million. In November 2009 Alan Meckler, a leader in the tech trade business, sold Internet.com (a leading

news source for technology professionals and a division of WebMediaBrands) to QuinStreet for $15.9 million in cash and $1.7 million in a non-interest-bearing promissory note. The deal was announced in August 2009. QuinStreet's next major acquisition would come less than one year later.

GOING PUBLIC

Winter of 2009 brought another milestone change to QuinStreet. One of its largest clients (DeVry University) inked a deal with an advertising agency and reduced the amount of business it did with QuinStreet. The change could not go unnoticed. Over half (58 percent) of QuinStreet's revenue came from the education sector. Financial services was another industry that the company generated the bulk of its annual revenues from. In 2009 financial services comprised 31 percent of QuinStreet's revenues. This represented a 17 percent decrease over the previous year's 48 percent of revenues generated from the financial sector. The recession of 2008 and 2009 and its continuing impact on the economy had negatively affected several of QuinStreet's clients, particularly those who operated in the mortgage and credit card sectors.

Working with clients across several industries (e.g. financial, educational) helped QuinStreet post $260.52 million in net revenues in 2009, an increase over its $192.03 million 2008 net revenues. In December 2009, two months after it purchased the brand name Insure.com, QuinStreet announced its plans to go public. Although initial shares were at $15, lower than the anticipated $17 to $19 per share offerings, the company's initial public offering (IPO) brought in $140 million.

Results of its IPO out, QuinStreet found itself dealing with another challenge. Following DeVry's decision to reduce its lead generation business with QuinStreet, the U.S. Department of Education issued a June 2010 proposal to repeal existing safe harbors regarding recruiter incentive compensation. The move, if approved, would impact the ability of QuinStreet's academic-based clients to spend millions on direct advertising.

In an effort to continue to grow its non-academic-based business, in July 2010 QuinStreet paid $35.6 million to purchase Insurance.com, an online auto insurance agency. Insurance.com was based in Solon, Ohio, and had approximately 140 employees. The company allowed users to compare prices and services for auto, life, home, and health insurance rates across several firms.

LEGAL ACTIONS AND LOOKING TO THE FUTURE

At the end of the summer of 2010 the firm became part of a legal action. In September QuinStreet was named as a defendant (along with Adchemy Incorporated and NextTag) in a lawsuit brought forth by LendingTree LLC (which later became part of Tree.com, Inc.). In the lawsuit, LendingTree accused QuinStreet and the other two defendants of patent infringement. The infringement lawsuit stated that QuinStreet copied LendingTree's method of matching borrowers and lenders.

In the early 2010s, then, QuinStreet faced some uncertainties regarding its education and finance markets. If the Department of Education ruling and the lawsuit were to come out against QuinStreet, the company would face some financial hardship. However, as a well-established Internet marketing company, QuinStreet was well positioned to reap the continued benefits associated with Internet commerce.

Rhonda Campbell

PRINCIPAL SUBSIDIARIES

3041486 Nova Scotia Company (Canada); QuinStreet Media, Inc.; WorldWide Learn, Inc. (Canada); WorldWide Learn Partnership (Canada).

PRINCIPAL COMPETITORS

Bankrate, Inc.; IAC/InterActiveCorp; Monster Worldwide, Inc.; NexTag, Inc.; Tree.com, Inc.

FURTHER READING

Hoge, Patrick. "Online Marketer to Hit $300M in Revenue," *San Francisco Business Times,* August 23, 2009. Accessed February 16, 2011. http://www.bizjournals.com/sanfrancisco/stories/2009/08/24/story7.html.

Morningstar. "QuinStreet, Inc. QNST." Chicago: Morningstar, Inc., 2011. Accessed February 16, 2011. http://www.nasdaq.com/MorningStarProfileReports/QNST_USA.pdf.

Morris James LLC. "QuinStreet vs. Parallel vs. Microsoft Corporation," Wilmington, DE: Morris James LLC. Accessed February 16, 2011. http://depatentlaw.morrisjames.com/uploads/file/06%20495%20334.pdf.

"QuinStreet Adds GiftGiving.com to Its Online Network." AllBusiness.com, October 9, 2001. Accessed February 16, 2011. http://www.allbusiness.com/retail-trade/4292037-1.html.

"QuinStreet and Topica Launch Joint Marketing Program; Topica to Offer QuinStreet's Specialty." *Business Wire,* April 3, 2001. Accessed February 16, 2011. http://www.allbusiness.com/marketing-advertising/marketing-advertising/6092912-1.html.

Stobbart, George. "Acquisition: Quinstreet Acquired Insurance.com for $35m." news-insurances.com, September 10, 2010. Accessed February 16, 2011. http://www.news-insurances.com/acquisition-quinstreet-acquired-insurance-com-for-35m/0167320206.

U.S. Government Accountability Office. "Higher Education: Stronger Federal Oversight Needed to Enforce Ban on Incentive Payments to School Recruiters." October 2010. Accessed February 16, 2011. http://www.gao.gov/new.items/d1110.pdf.

"Verdict: $35.6 Million Insurance.com Acquisition Wasn't Just The Domain Name." *Domain Name Wire,* August 10, 2010. Accessed February 16, 2011. http://domainnamewire.com/tag/quinstreet.

Zimmett, Nora. "Ex-Sen. Bill Bradley Sits on Board of Major Spamming Firm." *Fox News,* April 24, 2009. Accessed February 16, 2011. http://www.foxnews.com/story/0,2933,517622,00.html.

RESERVE BANK OF AUSTRALIA

Reserve Bank of Australia

———————————— ■ ————————————

65 Martin Place
Sydney, New South Wales 2000
Australia
Telephone: (61) 2 9551 8111
Fax: (61) 2 9551 8000
Web site: http://www.rba.gov.au

State-Owned Company
Founded: 1959
Employees: 1,010 (2010)
Sales: AUD 2.094 billion ($2.09 billion) (2010)
NAICS: 522320 Financial Transactions Processing, Reserve, and Clearing House Activities

■ ■ ■

The Reserve Bank of Australia (RBA) is Australia's central bank. Its role is to conduct monetary policy, work to maintain a strong financial system, and issue Australia's currency. Wholly owned by the Australian government, the bank is also a policymaking body that provides banking and registry services to various Australian government agencies, as well as to overseas central banks and official institutions. In addition, the bank manages Australia's gold and foreign exchange reserves. RBA's overall operation is overseen by two boards, the Reserve Bank Board and the Payments System Board, both chaired by the RBA's governor, or chairman.

RBA's activities, powers, and responsibilities are underpinned by various pieces of government legislation, including the Reserve Bank Act of 1959, the Bank-

ing Act 1959, the Financial Corporations Act of 1974, and the Commonwealth Authorities Companies Act 1977. RBA has the power to regulate bank lending and interest rates and to influence banks' asset holdings. Its transactional banking services include deposit and check processing services, processing and distribution of bulk electronic direct credit and direct debit transactions, various paper-based electronic collection services, and check reconciliation, repository, and verification services. RBA also manages the government's annual borrowing program and, as an agent for the commonwealth, sells government treasury bonds and notes.

The bank's overall responsibility is to ensure that its monetary and banking policies contribute to the stability of the Australian economy and the Australian peoples' welfare, including protecting the deposits of the Australian banks. As an independent central bank, RBA is accountable to the Australian Parliament. Headquartered in Sydney, Australia, the company also has representative offices in London and New York City.

ORIGINS AND EARLY YEARS: 1911–59

The origins of the Reserve Bank of Australia (RBA) can be traced back to 1911 when the Commonwealth Bank of Australia (CBA) was established by an act of Parliament. The CBA commenced operations in 1912 and was empowered to conduct both savings and general banking business, with the security of a federal government guarantee. No other Australian institution at that time was involved in both of these traditionally separate areas of banking. In addition, no other bank had a federal government guarantee.

COMPANY PERSPECTIVES

The Reserve Bank of Australia's duty is to ensure that the bank's monetary and banking policy is directed to the greatest advantage of the Australian people. The powers of the bank are to be exercised in such a manner that will best contribute to the stability of the currency of Australia, the maintenance of full employment in Australia, and the economic prosperity and welfare of the people of Australia. Both the Reserve Bank and the Government agree on the importance of low inflation and low inflation expectations to assist businesses in making sound investment decisions, underpin the creation of jobs, protect the savings of Australians, and preserve the value of currency. Furthermore, monetary policy needs to be conducted in an open and forward-looking manner.

CBA opened for business on July 15, 1912. Its solitary bank facility was located in Melbourne, but the bank also had 489 agencies located in post offices throughout the Australian state of Victoria. Over the following year, capital city branches and postal agencies were established across Australia. In 1916 the bank moved its headquarters to Sydney. Via mergers with state banks in Tasmania in 1912 and Queensland in 1920, the bank's infrastructure and customer base began to expand. In addition, during World War I CBA assisted various federal authorities to organize war loans, primary production pools, and a merchant shipping fleet. It also provided regular banking services to military personnel both in Australia and abroad.

In 1920 the Australian government transferred responsibility for note issue from the Commonwealth treasury to CBA, beginning two decades during which CBA's responsibilities expanded to encompass those of a central bank. These responsibilities evolved primarily because of pressure placed on the economy by the Great Depression and World War II. In the midst of the Great Depression in 1931, the bank became significantly larger as it was combined with the State Bank of Western Australia and the State Bank of New South Wales.

In the 1940s, during World War II, the bank served as an agent of the federal government. Its powers were temporarily expanded to include exchange control and various other wide-ranging controls over the banking system, such as the authority to determine interest rates.

In addition, similar to its duties during World War I, the CBA served as the banker for numerous Australian and allied service personnel scattered across the country and overseas.

Following the end of World War II in 1945, the Commonwealth Bank Act and the Banking Act were passed to formalize CBA's powers concerning the administration of monetary and banking policy and of exchange control. As the bank conducted government business, it also operated as a private bank, opening hundreds of new branches and agencies as Australia's population grew and spread throughout the country. The bank also made special efforts to help migrants via the establishment of the Migrant Information Service.

RESERVE BANK CREATED: 1959–60

Despite CBA's successes in serving the government and as a private enterprise, controversy over the organization's dual functions as a central bank and as a trading and savings bank grew throughout the 1950s. As the decade came to a close, most observers and government officials came to see the CBA's position as untenable to both regulate and compete with private banks. As a result, legislation was based via the Commonwealth Bank Act of 1959 and the Reserve Bank Act of 1959 to formally divide the two operations.

The Reserve Bank Act of 1959 preserved the original corporate body under the new name of the Reserve Bank of Australia (RBA). RBA's role was to carry on the central banking functions previously conducted by the Commonwealth Bank. On January 14, 1960, RBA opened for business with 1,800 staff from the CBA, including RBA's governor, Dr. H. C. "Nugget" Coombs, who had served as the governor of the CBA since 1949. In addition to Coombs, the RBA maintained the same board and charter, which is inscribed on the RBA's head office building in Sydney. This charter charged the bank with the obligation to conduct policies that would help the stability of Australia's currency, the maintenance of full employment in Australia, and the economic prosperity and welfare of the people of Australia.

At the dedication of the RBA's headquarters in Martin Place in Sydney, Coombs observed that the building's architectural style reflected the spirit of modernism. As noted on the Reserve Bank of Australia's Web site, Coombs commented on the connection between the architectural style and RBA's goals: "Here, contemporary design and conceptions express our conviction that a central bank should develop with growing knowledge and a changing institutional

KEY DATES

1911: Australian Parliament establishes the Commonwealth Bank of Australia (CBA).
1959: Reserve Bank Act of 1959 establishes the Reserve Bank of Australia.
1960: Reserve Bank's new headquarters in Sydney's Martin Place is dedicated.
2008: Reserve Bank establishes robust stimulus package to counter global economic crisis.
2010: Reserve Bank celebrates its 50th anniversary.

structure and adapt its policies and techniques to the changing needs of the community within which it works."

NEW FUNCTIONS AND POWERS

Over the next two decades, the RBA experienced little change in its functions and goals. However, there was a gradual change from a system of direct controls on banks to market-oriented methods of implementing monetary policy. In 1979 the Australian government had appointed a major financial system inquiry called the Campbell Committee. With the abolition of Exchange Control, which followed the float of the Australian dollar in 1983, the Australian financial landscape was transformed to virtually a fully deregulated system. At about the same time, the RBA began to build up a specialized banking supervision function.

Another major inquiry into the Australian banking system, the Wallis Committee, took place in 1996. As a result of this inquiry, beginning on July 1, 1998, banking supervision function was transferred from RBA to a new authority called the Australian Prudential Regulation Authority, which became responsible for the supervision of all institutions that took deposits. Furthermore, the Reserve Bank Act was changed to create the Payment Systems Board to promote the safety and efficiency of Australia's payment system. The Payment Systems (Regulation) Act of 1998 and the Payment Systems and Netting Act 1998 gave RBA relevant powers in this area.

One of RBA's mandates over the years has been to enhance the community's understanding of its responsibilities and policies through a broad communications program. The bank also joined the Australian Stock Exchange Ltd., Macquarie Bank Ltd., and Reuters Australia Pty. Ltd, in developing STARLab.

This partnership between academia and business was launched in 1999 and focused on forming a financial risk-management training venture at the University of New South Wales in Sydney.

RECOGNITION FOR FINANCIAL POLICY MANAGEMENT

In 2002 RBA's governor Jim McFarlane was named Central Bank Governor of the Year by *Asiamoney* magazine. It was the second time in three years that McFarlane had received the award for helping Australia to attain a better economic position than many other countries after a global economic downturn. Noting that Australian's position in the global economy was relatively good and that its terms of trade had increased since 1999 in spite of a global recession, a contributor to *Asiamoney* wrote that some observers thought that Australia's ability to weather the storm might have been a fluke. However, the *Asiamoney* contributor argued that such a view " would be a disservice to the intelligent decisions of the Reserve Bank."

Part of Australia's good financial position in 2002 was due to Macfarlane and RBA instituting an aggressive interest rate policy that began before the global slowdown. The RBA under Macfarlane also made quick cuts to interest rates in the second half of 2001, which according to the *Asiamoney* contributor, "earned the admiration of the market for being decisive and sensible in a tight spot." RBA and Mcfarlane were also praised for being "transparent and open" about economic issues.

FACING A CRISIS: 2008

Australia and RBA faced a financial global downturn that reached crisis proportions in 2008 as the world economy was confronted with the worst recession in 75 years. Under Glenn Stevens, who had taken over as governor of RBA after beginning his career as a research assistant there more than 25 years earlier, the RBA oversaw a robust stimulus package and moved quickly to slash interest rates by 4.25 percent beginning in September 2008. According to a contributor to the *Banker*, this moved played "a key role in defending the Asia-Pacific economy from a global downturn."

The RBA also acted quickly during the economic crisis to provide liquidity and to introduce guarantees on deposits and wholesale funding, moves that helped Australia's financial system continue to provide credit.

With the international financial system stabilizing in late 2009 and through 2010, RBA gradually withdrew some of the exceptional measures it had taken in 2008 to assist the Australian economy. For example, it largely unwound the provision of additional liquidity by the end of 2009 and generally removed or discontinued most exceptional monetary policy stimulus packages. Nevertheless, RBA continued some policies including a guarantee on deposits of up to AUD 1 million until October 2011.

However, the RBA did not come through the financial crisis completely unscathed. Factors such as Australia's large open foreign currency position contributed to RBA's record net losses for fiscal year 2009–10 of approximately AUD 3.8 billion, which according to Stevens in the company's 2010 annual report, "was the largest loss, in absolute terms, the Bank has ever experienced."

RBA headed into the 2010s with a much healthier balance sheet, having dealt with the 2009 to 2010 write-downs. As for setting future monetary policies, RBA planned to remain focused on medium-term prospects for economic activity and inflation issues.

David Petechuk

PRINCIPAL DIVISIONS

Banking and Payments Group; Corporate Services Group; Currency Group; Economic Group; Financial Markets Group; Financial System Group.

PRINCIPAL COMPETITORS

Australia and New Zealand Banking; Commonwealth Bank of Australia; National Australia Bank.

FURTHER READING

"Central Bank Governor of the Year–Other Winners." *Banker,* January 1, 2010.

"Jin and Macfarlane Lead the Region." *Asiamoney,* May 2002, 24.

Reserve Bank of Australia. "Reflections of Martin Place." Accessed February 4, 2011. http://www.rba.gov.au/about-rba/history/anniversary/reflections-gallery.html.

"Risk Management Education Growing in Australia: Interest from Professional Community Sparks Efforts." *Business Insurance,* October 25, 1999, G2.

Stevens, Glenn. "Governor's Foreword." *Reserve Bank of Australia Annual Report 2010.*

Ricola Limited

P. O. Box 130 Laufen CH-4242
Switzerland
Telephone: (41) 061-765-4121
Fax: (41) 061-765-4122
Web site: http://www.ricola.com

Private Company
Incorporated: 1930
Employees: 420 (est., 2010)
Sales: CHF 300 million ($330 million, est., 2010)
NAICS: 311340 Nonchocolate Confectionary Manu-
facturing

■ ■ ■

Ricola Limited has been soothing the throats of over
three generations of consumers. The family-owned
company is based in Laufen, near Basel, Switzerland,
where it produces its famous herb-based throat lozenges
and related products. Ricola's flagship product remains
its Ricola Swiss Herb Candy, a hard candy based on a
blend of 13 herbs found in the Swiss mountains and
created by company founder Emil Richterich. Exports
to over 50 countries comprise the majority of company
revenue.

Raw materials come from some 100 farmers in
Switzerland, who provide Ricola with organic herbs
grown according to company specifications. Ricola
remains wholly owned by the founding Richterich
family.

WHAT BUYING A BAKERY BRINGS ABOUT

Ricola's success began with Emil Richterich, who
acquired the Bleile bakery in the small town of Laufen,
near the city of Basel, Switzerland, in 1924. Richterich
carried on the bakery's candy making, cooking toffee
candies in a kettle over a wood fire. He later expanded
the business to include some 100 different confectionery
types, including "fünfermocken," a traditional caramel
candy that had long been popular in the region. Richterich himself handled sales and delivery, riding his
bicycle throughout the local area to deliver candies to
customers.

Richterich also began developing confectioneries
based on herbs found in the mountainous region around
Laufen, where herbal preparations and remedies had
remained widely used. In the late 1920s, Richterich
developed a cough drop, Hustenwohl, based on herbs.

The bakery's products gained increasing recognition
in the region, and, with demand rising, Richterich
turned to the full-time manufacture of candies and
confectionery. In 1930 he created a new company, Con-
fiseriefabrik Richterich & Co. Laufen, and added more
modern production equipment, such as a coal-fired
stove, cooling tables, presses, and molds.

Richterich continued working on new recipes and
finally hit on the formula that was to turn the former
bakery into a globally operating company. In 1940 he
debuted his "Swiss Herb Candy." This was a blend of
13 herbs including peppermint, sage, thyme, as well as
ribwort, horehound, burnet, mallow, yarrow, and others.
The candy's unusual flavor, and its ability to soothe

COMPANY PERSPECTIVES

Ricola believes that success is not an end in itself. It is a company that takes its responsibilities to its employees, to society, and to the environment seriously. As a company with close ties to nature, Ricola assigns top priority to first-class raw materials. Ricola only uses herbs grown under controlled conditions which do no harm to the environment. Such herbs are not only more aromatic; they are also endowed with the inner vital force of nature.

minor throat irritations (later proven clinically), quickly became a company flagship product.

The new drop, with its own distinctive shape, became a popular product in the region before spreading throughout much of Switzerland. In order to keep up with demand, Richterich built his first factory in 1950. Joining the company then was Richterich's son, Hans Peter, who recognized the potential for a new product line. Customers had taken to dissolving the Ricola drops in hot water, creating a herbal tea. In the 1950s Richterich extended its product range with its own herbal tea blend based on the original Herb Candy formula.

During the 1960s the Richterich family company remained focused on the Swiss market. When Hans Peter Richterich took over the company's leadership during that decade, he turned to conquering the international market. As part of that effort, the company changed its name, combining the first two initials of Richterich & Co. Laufen to form Ricola. The company also converted its status to that of a joint-stock company, although shares remained controlled by the Richterich family.

Whereas Emil Richterich had focused on inventing candies for the local market, Hans Peter Richterich's interests lay in developing the company's business and sales operations. He turned the company toward the international market by launching sales initiatives in nearby Germany, Italy, and France, and preparing to establish the company as a global brand.

At the end of the 1960s, the company, which had continued to manufacture a wider assortment of candy and confectionery products, decided to focus its production around its herb-based flagship product. The company phased out its noncore products, then built a new factory just outside of Laufen. The expanded production enabled the company to enter new markets.

Success in the German, Italian, and French markets came swiftly during the late 1960s, and by the early 1970s the company's 70 employees were producing more than 90 tons per year.

The longstanding European interest in herbal products and remedies gave Ricola fertile ground to grow its sales throughout the 1970s. The popularity of herbal preparations in Asia also led the company to expand into that market during the decade. In the early 1970s Ricola began selling its throat lozenges in Japan through a partnership with family-owned trading house Nisshoku. Hong Kong also became an important market for Ricola's products. At the same time, interest in herbal formulas had also been growing in the United States, and Ricola entered that market on a modest scale, with sales remaining limited to the health and natural foods retail channels.

PRODUCT EXPANSION

Ricola's emphasis on its niche specialty led it to begin developing new herb-based products. In 1976 the company released its first new major product line, the sugar-free Pearls. The new candy, which contained the same herbal formula as its predecessor, featured a gum arabic base, making it a chewy alternative to the Swiss Herbal Formula.

Ricola also began developing a wider assortment of flavors for its products. The original formula was soon joined by a range of flavors, including orange, menthol-eucalyptus, and, in support of the group's effort to increase its penetration of the U.S. market, cherry-mint.

Entry into the United States got underway in earnest during the mid-1980s. In 1986 the company decided to switch from its previous distributor, a specialty products group, to a more mainstream brokerage network with a commission-based sales force. Ricola also established a U.S. subsidiary in New Jersey in 1986. The company at that time expanded beyond the health foods retail channel to claim a position on the shelves and cashier counters of mainstream drugstore chains. By the beginning of the 1990s, Ricola had succeeded in placing its products in nearly all of the major drugstore groups in the United States. As in Europe, the company also began a drive to get its products into the still-broader supermarket channel.

Supporting the group's expansion efforts was a new line of herbal candy, a sugar-free lozenge, prepared using hard-boiled isomalt. That product was launched in 1988. In addition to the United States, the company also began targeting the wider market in the Asia Pacific, where consumption of herbal-based remedies had long been integral to the lifestyle of the region. In

KEY DATES

1924: Emil Richterich takes over a small bakery making candies and confectionery in Laufen, Switzerland.

1930: Increasing sales lead Richterich to found a dedicated candy business, Confizerie Richterich & Co. Laufen.

1940: Richterich develops a recipe for a new Swiss Herbal Candy, a throat and cough drop that features a blend of 13 herbs.

1985: The company establishes a U.S. subsidiary.

1997: The company launches a cough syrup.

2002: Ricola launches a new line of elderberry flower-based lozenges.

2004: Adrian Kohler is named chief executive officer.

2006: Company establishes a Milan-based subsidiary, Divita S.r.I.

2007: Sales top CHF 300 million ($308 million) for first time.

2009: Ricola names Lil' Drug Store Products its exclusive distributor of cough and throat drops to U.S. convenience stores.

1992 the company established a new sales subsidiary in Singapore to service its growing sales in this market. That initiative was taken by the group's new CEO, Felix Richterich, who took over from his father in 1991. By then, Ricola had succeeded in introducing its products in some 40 national markets. Felix Richterich then took the group's strategy a step further and began working on developing the company's name into a recognized specialty brand.

In support of its new strategy, the company built a new marketing office in its Laufen home base and also constructed a packaging plant in Brunstatt, in the French Alsace region, not far from the Swiss border. The company then began work on expanding its product range.

Ricola rolled out a new series of products during the second half of the 1990s, including a throat syrup based on its herbal formula. The company also debuted its own Ricola-branded line of breath mints. In 1998 the company added to its line of throat and cough products with the release of a new range of echinacea-based lozenges. In another extension of its reputation for quality herbal products, Ricola debuted its own line of Herbal Health Supplements in 1999.

Ricola's brand expansion continued into the 21st century with the introduction of sage-based drops in 2001 and, in 2002, a new line of lozenges based on elderberry flowers. As part of that launch, the company participated in the planting of some 5,000 new elderberry bushes near its home base in Laufen. Ricola had by then become one of the world's most recognized herbal specialists.

To continue to be a leader in the herbal cough suppressant industry, in 2003 Ricola launched a new product, Nature's Protection. The vitamin C supplement drops rolled out to the United States first.

ENTERING NEW MARKETS

The following year the family-owned, Swiss-operated firm appointed Adrian Kohler as its chief executive officer (CEO). Felix Richterich, grandson of the founder, continued to serve as the company's chairman of the board. Kohler focused on day-to-day business objectives, part of which involved growing the company's offshore accounts. After all, 90 percent of Ricola's business came from international sales.

In 2005 Ricola celebrated its 75th year in business. That year also, Ricola expanded its operations in the duty-free market. The company had been selling duty- or tax-free products for 15 years in selected airports throughout Europe and other duty-free areas like Andorra. Ricola created gift boxes, bags, and tins to sell its products in duty-free markets. It made its distribution agreement to get the products in select European stores and airports with the Valora Group, a Swiss-based trading company.

The company opened a new facility in Switzerland in 2006. The new production plant would make and ship approximately 250 million units of the company's 30 different herbal products by the close of 2007.

HITTING A MILESTONE

Ricola hit a milestone in 2007 when its sales topped the CHF 300 million ($308 million) mark for the first time. Its next success would come in the sports arena. The company's products were distributed during the Union of European Football Association's (UEFA) 2008 football tournament. With soccer (European football) being more popular than American football, it was like advertising to every sports fan who attended the U.S. Super Bowl.

At the same time it was expanding its presence in Europe, Ricola continued to focus on international regions, Japan being one of its primary targets. In the June 2009 *Japan Times* article, "Giving the World a

Sweet Taste of Switzerland," Kohler said, "Due to the aging population in Japan, health is an important concern and Ricola has made a positive contribution to Japan with its herbal candy." He continued, "We have been successful in Japan through our partner Nisshoku for many years and 2009 will see us working with Frente, a private Japanese company, to gain direct access to the Japanese retail market."

The United States was another region where Ricola focused its attention. In October 2009 Ricola and Lil' Drug Store Products, a U.S. distribution firm, entered into an agreement that made Lil' Drug Store Ricola's exclusive distributor of cough and throat drops to U.S. convenience stores.

If aging populations in Japan, the United States, and elsewhere continued to turn to herbal remedies, it seemed likely that Ricola and its products would fare well in the 2010s.

M. L. Cohen
Updated, Rhonda Campbell

PRINCIPAL SUBSIDIARIES

Ricola Asia Pacific PTE. Ltd. (Singapore); Ricola Inc. (USA).

PRINCIPAL COMPETITORS

Alliance Boots GmbH; GNC Acquisition Holdings, Inc.; Herbalife Ltd.; Mother Nature, Inc.; Nature's Sunshine Products, Inc.

FURTHER READING

"A Balanced Approach." *Supermarket Business,* December 15, 1999, 55.

"Giving the World a Sweet Taste of Switzerland." *Japan Times,* June 30, 2009. Accessed March 8, 2011. http://classified. japantimes.com/ads/pdfs/20090630-wer-switzerland.pdf.

"Global Herbal Supplements and Remedies Market to Reach US$93.15 Billion by 2015, According to a New Report by Global Industry Analysts, Inc." *Earth Times,* January 12, 2011. Accessed March 8, 2011. http://www.earthtimes.org/articles/press/global-industry-analysts-inc,1612011.html.

Gold, Daniel. "Ricola Cough Drops Hack Away at a Crowded Market." *Adweek's Marketing Week,* February 19, 1990, 24.

"New High-Quality Production Boosts Flexibility for Ricola." *Packazine,* 2010. Accessed March 8, 2011. http://www.boschpackaging.com/boschpackagingworld/eng/media/packazine_01_10_Food_ENG.pdf.

Payne. "Payne Helps Ricola Support Switzerland in 'Euro 08.'" Payne Press Release, December 4, 2008. Accessed March 8, 2011. http://www.payne-worldwide.com/home/news/2008-press-releases/ricola-support-switzerland.htm.

"Ricola Adds New Formula," *Chain Drug Review,* May 22, 2000, 19.

"Ricola Introduces Throat Syrup." *Chain Drug Review,* June 23, 1997, 86.

"A Swiss Alpine Meadow in Your Mouth." *Japan Times,* August 2, 2002.

Zammit, Deanna. "MRGL to Introduce Ricola Refreshers." *Adweek,* August 6, 2003. Accessed March 8, 2011. http://www.allbusiness.com/marketing-advertising/4128465-1.html.

Royal Bank of Scotland Group PLC

---

36 Saint Andrew Square
Edinburgh,
United Kingdom EH2 2YB
Telephone: (44) 131-556-8555
Fax: (44) 131-557-6140
Web site: http://www.rbs.com

Public Company
Founded: 1727
Employees: 183,700 (2009)
Revenue: £29.4 billion ($47.5 billion, 2009)
Stock Exchanges: New York; London
Ticker Symbol: RBS
NAICS: 522120 Commercial Banking

■ ■ ■

Royal Bank of Scotland Group PLC (RBS) is one of Europe's largest banking groups. Through subsidiaries Royal Bank of Scotland and National Westminster Bank, it provides retail banking to 15 million Britons through 2,000 branches. Subsidiary Ulster bank provides retail banking in the Republic of Ireland and Northern Ireland, while Citizens Bank does the same in the United States. RBS also offers wealth management services and financial and insurance products through subsidiaries such as Coutts and Adam & Company. After a series of bailouts in 2008 and 2009, RBS is roughly 80 percent owned by the British government.

17TH CENTURY BEGINNINGS

After one failed attempt, the Royal Bank of Scotland was established on May 31, 1727. The first attempt to establish the bank came in the late 17th century when Scotland tried to improve its economic position with the so-called Darien scheme. The Darien scheme was a plan to establish a Scots trading colony, designed along the lines of England's London East India Company, in Panama. With a population of only around 1.1 million at the end of the 17th century, Scotland could not hope to raise the requisite capital alone, so the scheme's architects relied on England for the bulk of their subscriptions. English investors, however, withdrew their money at the last minute when the English government realized that a successful Scottish venture could jeopardize the position of the London East India Company. Forced to finance the venture alone, the Scots raised £238,000 for the enterprise. Unfortunately, the entire sum was lost when the venture collapsed in 1699 due to difficulties with the heat, the Spanish, and outbreaks of fever.

The failure was devastating to Scotland, which had lost a quarter of its liquid assets in the disaster. Feelings ran so high against England for its lack of support that when the two countries were joined by the 1707 Act of Union, the English government deemed it wise to agree to pay compensation. The government provided for an 'Equivalent' of £398,085 (and 10 shillings) to cover the Darien losses and other debts, and allowed for an 'Arising Equivalent,' which would be a percentage of tax revenue. Because only £150,000 of the promised money was actually available in cash, many Scottish creditors were given debentures bearing interest at 5 percent.

Little of this interest actually materialized, however, until 1719, when an act was passed establishing an annual fund of £10,000 to be raised by Scotland's customs and excise.

Organizations such as the Society of the Subscribed Equivalent Debt arose in both Scotland and England to aid in collecting the interest due, to buy more debenture stock, and to issue loans to members based on the value of their holdings. In 1724 these organizations were joined and regularized by Parliament to create the Equivalent Company. By 1727 this company, which was essentially acting as a bank to its members, chose to take the next logical step and officially become a bank. It was impossible to do so in England, where the Bank of England's monopoly was firmly fixed, but the field was open in Scotland, where the monopoly of the Bank of Scotland, established by an act of the Scottish Parliament in 1695, had expired in 1716. The Equivalent Company was granted a charter for banking on May 31, 1727, and was incorporated as the Royal Bank of Scotland.

The new bank opened in Edinburgh on December 8, 1727, with an authorized capital of £111,347 and a governor, a court of directors, and a staff of eight. It was a modest beginning but the new bank received a welcome boost in the form of £20,000 from the government, which chose that occasion to finally honor a commitment undertaken as part of the 1707 Act of Union, which provided for that sum to be lent out at interest for the development of Scottish fisheries and general manufacturing.

The Royal Bank learned to compete well against the Bank of Scotland and other banks as they were subsequently established. Circulation wars were an especially popular way of discomfiting the competition. At the time, official government-backed banknotes did not exist. Each bank issued its own, and a favorite ploy was to amass as many of a rival's banknotes as possible and present them for payment all at once, causing frequent embarrassment and occasional temporary closures. Before long, however, an efficient counter tactic was mounted when competitors demanded redemption of banknotes be paid entirely with sixpences. Eventually the practice died out.

RESPONDING TO COMPETITION

Although the tricks may have been discontinued, the rivalry among competing banks remained. By the later 18th century the struggle for dominance shifted to Glasgow, Scotland's second-largest city, which was rapidly gaining prominence as a center for industry and commerce. Smaller banks had already sprung up there to satisfy new demand, and the big two, the Royal Bank and the Bank of Scotland, both Edinburgh-based, soon reacted to the threat of more competition. The Royal's first Glasgow branch opened in 1783, and the bank became deeply involved in the city's booming industries of cotton, steam ships, sugar, and tobacco. Before long the Royal dominated the financial market in Glasgow. By the 1810s the bank's Glasgow trade eclipsed its business in Edinburgh.

By the early 19th century a new threat faced the Royal and its arch-rival the Bank of Scotland. As large banking institutions whose clients tended to be big companies and very wealthy individuals, the two were perceived (accurately) as being removed from the interests of the general public. The average small customer's banking needs were served by small private banks which in turn banked with the Royal or the Bank of Scotland. The system, which struck many as unsatisfactory, changed with the arrival in 1810 of the new Commercial Bank of Scotland, which billed itself as "the Bank of the Citizens." The new bank did well, having built up a branch network in Scotland of 30 banks by 1831, when it was granted a Royal Charter of Incorporation. The Commercial's success was watched with interest, and other, similar banks soon appeared, most notably the National Bank of Scotland, incorporated in 1825.

Increased competition notwithstanding, the Royal continued to thrive as the 19th century progressed. As its success in Glasgow had proved, the bank was keenly aware of the opportunities afforded by the expansion of industry. In 1826 it financed Scotland's first steam-powered railway, the first of several successful transport ventures. As the bank prospered it also expanded. By 1836 five new outlets had been established in Dundee, Paisley, Perth, Rothesay, and Dalkeith. The Royal Bank began a policy of aggressive acquisition, taking over many new branches after the 1857 failure of the Western Bank of Scotland and in 1864 acquiring the Dundee Banking Company, which had been founded in 1763. The Royal Bank also expanded its operations into England in 1874.

The Royal increased its presence in England in the early 20th century. In 1924 the bank acquired Drummonds Bank, a small but highly regarded London bank (whose clients had included George III and Beau Brum-

KEY DATES

1727: The Equivalent Company becomes Royal Bank of Scotland.
1783: Royal Bank opens branch in Glasgow.
1826: Company finances Scotland's first steam-powered railway.
1864: Royal Bank acquires Dundee Banking.
1924: Royal Bank acquires Drummonds Bank.
1930: Royal Bank acquires William Deacon's Bank, third of the Three Banks Group.
1968: Royal Bank and National Commercial merge to form the Royal Bank of Scotland.
1972: Easing of restrictions by the Bank of England gives Royal Bank greater access to British market.
1988: Citizens Financial Group, based in New England, is acquired by RBS.
1993: RBS acquires Adam & Company, an Edinburgh-based private bank.
2000: Royal Bank acquires NatWest.
2007: Company acquires ABN AMRO, a holding company with sizable banking assets.
2008: RBS reports £28.83 billion in losses.
2009: British government continues to provide financial support for RBS.

mel) originally founded in 1717 by an expatriate Scotsman. Six years later the Royal acquired the Bank of England's West End Branch and also Williams Deacon's Bank, whose branch network in Manchester and the northwest provided the Royal with its first English presence outside the capital. The trend toward acquisition continued in 1939 with the addition of another private London bank, Glyn, Mills & Co. This bank and Williams Deacon's continued to operate under their own names as subsidiaries, and together with their parent the Royal Bank were known as the Three Banks Group.

TECHNOLOGY AND CONSOLIDATION: POST-WORLD WAR II

As the bank grew it took advantage of technology. At this time the Royal Bank introduced telephones, typewriters, adding machines, and teleprinters. After World War II the bank founded a residential banking college to train staff for an increasingly sophisticated financial world.

By 1959 banking trends clearly favored consolidation. Scottish banks needed to match the financial might of their English counterparts if they were to be able to accommodate the needs of growing Scottish industry and commerce. Accordingly, the National and Commercial banks merged to form the National Commercial Bank of Scotland, and in 1966 further strengthened their position by acquiring the English and Welsh branches of the National Bank. Three years later, however, the National Commercial Bank merged with the Royal Bank. A new holding company was formed called National and Commercial Banking Group Ltd., which included the Scottish side, the Royal Bank of Scotland, and the English concerns, Glyn, Mills & Co., Williams Deacon's, and the National Bank. In 1970 the latter came together as Williams & Glyn's Bank Ltd.

WATERSHED ECONOMIC CHANGES: 1971–95

Greatly strengthened by the amalgamation, the group was ideally placed to take full advantage of the two watershed economic events of the 1970s. In 1971 the regulatory Bank of England eased restrictions on Scottish banks operating in England, allowing the Royal Bank to compete freely for the first time. The range of financial services that banks could provide was also substantially broadened. Perhaps even more significant, the rise of the North Sea oil industry in the 1970s proved an unprecedented boom to the Scottish economy, especially to banks, such as the Royal, which were quick to recognize the tremendous potential of the new industry. Taking advantage of its newfound strength, the bank expanded its foreign interests, establishing branches in New York and Hong Kong and opening representative offices in Chicago, Houston, Los Angeles, and San Francisco. At decade's end, the group's holding company was renamed the Royal Bank of Scotland Group plc., or RBS.

The group adopted a more aggressive program of expansion and diversification. In 1985 the bank created the Royal Bank of Scotland Group Insurance Company Limited, a telephone-based general insurance business. The subsidiary, soon renamed Direct Line, proved a runaway success, becoming the largest motor insurer in the United Kingdom. It soon offered household and life insurance. In 1988 RBS acquired the Rhode Island-based Citizens Financial Group, the fifth-largest bank in New England, and promptly set upon a course of aggressive expansion. By late 1995, following the acquisition of a number of banks in the region, Citizens had established major presences in Connecticut and Massachusetts in addition to its home state of Rhode Island. It became the third-largest commercial bank in New England with the April 1996 purchase of First New

Hampshire Bank, which had been a subsidiary of Bank of Ireland. Following this transaction, Bank of Ireland held a 23.5 percent stake in Citizens.

MANAGING ITS SUBSIDIARIES

The tremendous success of Direct Line and Citizens led to speculation in the early 1990s that the RBS would sell one or both of these subsidiaries, but the rumored divestments did not occur. In fact the subsidiaries played a fundamental role not only in keeping profits high but also in protecting the group from fluctuations. In theory, if one sector of the RBS's business were to suffer a reverse, the others could carry the group for a time. Meanwhile, under the new leadership of George Mathewson, who became chief executive in 1992, RBS in 1993 acquired Adam & Company, an Edinburgh-based private bank that had been founded 10 years earlier.

With astonishing rapidity RBS diversified into new financial services, products, and initiatives. In 1994 the bank pioneered its 'finance shops,' which offered an extensive realm of mortgage and savings products to customers. The bank also placed a new emphasis on credit card services, making this an independent operation. Also, RBS established a specialist group to finance public sector projects in 1994. The bank also captured an increasing share of the U.K. mortgage lending market, traditionally the province of the building societies (the rough equivalent of U.S. savings and loan associations).

In the United States, RBS regained full ownership of Citizens in September 1998 when it purchased Bank of Ireland's minority holding. The following year Citizens acquired the commercial banking business of State Street Corporation, then in January 2000 Citizens acquired Boston-based UST Corp.

Somewhat audaciously, RBS pursued an acquisition of the much larger Barclays Bank in 1999, during a period when that bank was without a chief executive, but this initiative was rebuffed. Later in 1999, however, the RBS commenced a prolonged takeover battle with longtime rival Bank of Scotland, the prize being London-based National Westminster Bank. RBS ended up on the winning side and acquired NatWest in March 2000.

Moving quickly in the wake of its long sought-after acquisition of a major English bank, RBS started the integration of NatWest and began the process of slashing 18,000 NatWest jobs over a three-year period, including 9,000 in 2000 alone. Although NatWest no longer existed as an independent firm, the NatWest name lived on in the retail banking arena, giving Royal Bank two main U.K. retail banking brands. NatWest's corporate banking units, however, were integrated into those of RBS.

BEFORE THE BAILOUT

The next years would see RBS continue to focus its attention on acquisitions. In April 2001 RBS purchased International Aviation Management (IAM), an independent aviation advisory and transaction agreement firm. That same year in July, RBS made plans to acquire The Regional Franchise, a U.S. financial institution, and Euro Sales Finance, a leading provider of invoice discounting and factoring services. The next pickup for Royal Bank came in June 2002, when the bank purchased Medford Bancorp, Incorporated, a savings bank headquartered in Massachusetts.

As RBS entered into new acquisition agreements, it worked to complete the integration of NatWest, a company it picked up at the start of the new century. NatWest IT was fully integrated into RBS as of October 2002. Approximately another 18,000 employees were given walking papers as a result of redundancies in job roles at the two organizations.

The years 2003 through 2004 were heavy acquisition years for RBS. Additional companies it picked up during this period included the credit card business of People's Bank of Connecticut, Bank Von Ernst, and the Churchill Insurance Group.

MOVING INTO THE HEADWINDS

Local acquisitions saw RBS add one million new savings accounts in the United Kingdom to its balance sheet in 2007. Aggressive in its intent to grow by acquisition, RBS set its sights on ABN AMRO, a Dutch holding company with massive commercial and investment banking operations, in November 2007. ABN AMRO had more than six million retail clients and nearly half a million business clients. RBS paid over £70 billion for ABN AMRO, making it one of the largest financial industry takeovers in history.

However, 2008 was not a good year to be a heavily overstretched bank. As the global financial sector melted down, RBS found itself holding billions in bad assets. The company lost £28.83 billion (over $40 billion) in 2008, and its very survival was in question. To stop the bleeding, the British government underwrote RBS's capital-raising efforts by infusing £37 billion ($50 billion) of capital into the bank group, a move that gave the government a 58 percent stake.

The salary, including bonuses, that RBS CEO Fred Goodwin received while the recession rocked the United

Kingdom and the rest of the world left more than a few people aghast. Government bailouts and companies attempting to recover from errors made by high-priced executives by cutting jobs did not sit well with RBS customers. In 2009 alone, RBS cut nearly 19,000 jobs. At the heart of the recession, Goodwin was reported to have received a £2.9 million ($1.6 million) bonus on top of a £1.3 million ($1.7 million) a year regular salary. He tendered his resignation in October 2008, and Stephen Hester was named chief executive officer. Prior to joining RBS, Hester had served as chief executive officer at The British Land Company PLC.

Hester's job was unenviable, to say the least. As Royal Bank continued to struggle to regain its footing, Hester forewent his £1.6 million ($2.75 million) bonus in 2009, his first full year of service at RBS. In that year also, the British government infused another $300 billion into RBS, bringing its ownership in RBS to roughly 80 percent.

In the early 2010s, CEO Hester expressed cautious optimism about the company's future. RBS was focusing much of its efforts on selling noncore assets and moving itself into profitability and out of government control.

Robin Dublanc
Updated, David E. Salamie; Rhonda Campbell

PRINCIPAL SUBSIDIARIES

Citizens Financial Group, Inc. (USA); Coutts & Company; National Westminster Bank Plc; RBS Securities Inc.; The Royal Bank of Scotland plc; Ulster Bank Limited.

PRINCIPAL DIVISIONS

Citizens Bank; Global Banking Markets; Global Transaction Services; RBS Insurance; Ulster Bank; United Kingdom Corporate and Commercial; United Kingdom Retail; Wealth Management.

PRINCIPAL COMPETITORS

Bank of Ireland; Barclays plc; HSBC Holdings plc; Lloyds Banking Group plc.

FURTHER READING

Ashby, J. F. *The Story of the Banks.* London: Hutchinson, 1934.

Bray, Nicholas. "NatWest Chooses a Cautious Offensive." *Wall Street Journal,* February 28, 1992, A5A.

Financial Services Authority. "FSA Fines Royal Bank of Scotland pls 750,000 for Money Laundering Control Failings." FSA, December 17, 2002. Accessed February 23, 2011. http://www.fsa.gov.uk/Pages/Library/Communication/PR/2002/123.shtml.

Gapper, John. "Losing Lots of Layers." *Financial Times,* June 8, 1993, 16.

Graham, George. "The Awful History of Unhappy Banking Acquisitions in the United States." *Financial Times,* December 20, 1995, 20.

Inman, Phillip. "Government May Start Sale of RBS Stake in 2011, Says Chief Executive." *Guardian,* July 4, 2010. Accessed February 23, 2011. http://www.guardian.co.uk/business/2010/jul/04/rbs-government-sale-stake.

"The Law Firm of Laurie and Weiss Investigates The Royal Bank of Scotland Group plc." *MSN Money,* February 1, 2011. Accessed February 23, 2011. http://money.msn.com/business-news/article.aspx?feed=BW&date=20110201&id=12857507.

"Law Office of Howard G. Smith Announces Class Action Lawsuit Against the Royal Bank of Scotland Group, plc." *Business Wire,* January 26, 2011. Accessed February 23, 2011. http://www.businesswire.com/news/home/20110126007090/en/Law-Offices-Howard-G.-Smith-Announces-Class.

Munro, Neil. *The History of the Royal Bank of Scotland, 1727–1927.* Edinburgh: R. & R. Clark, 1928.

Tobin, Lucy. "Big Bonuses May Be Fairer Than We Think." *Guardian,* October 19, 2010. Accessed February 23, 2011. http://www.guardian.co.uk/education/2010/oct/19/kingston-university-bonus-research.

Royal KPN N.V.

Maanplein 55
The Hague,
Netherlands 2516 CK
Telephone: (31) 70 343 43 43
Fax: (31) 70 332 44 85
Web site: http://www.kpn.com

Public Company
Incorporated: 1989
Employees: 25,086 (2009)
Sales: EUR 13.51 billion ($16.8 billion, 2009)
Stock Exchanges: Amsterdam
Ticker Symbol: KPN
NAICS: 517110 Wired Telecommunications Carriers;
    517212 Cellular and Other Wireless Telecomm-
    unications

■ ■ ■

Royal KPN N.V., also known as Koninklijke KPN or simply KPN, is the top telecommunications provider in the Netherlands, offering both landline and wireless services. At the beginning of 2010 the company had over 33 million wireless customers, as well as 4.7 million fixed line and 2.5 million Internet customers. The Netherlands is easily the company's primary market, accounting for about 70 percent of all revenue, although KPN's Mobile International division does have operations in Germany (E-Plus Gruppe), Belgium (KPN Group), Spain, France, and elsewhere.

In addition to its telecommunications work, KPN provides information technology services to companies through its business division and its Getronics subsidiary. Services provided included application management, enterprise communications solutions, and data networking services.

IMPACT OF DUTCH POSTAL SERVICE

The history of KPN may be traced through the history of Dutch communications, a system which until the 1990s was controlled by the government. Although postal services had long been in place in the collection of city-states that later became the Netherlands, it was not until the end of the 18th century that the Dutch postal services were reformed into a single, national system, modeling its organization after the system developed by the French. This system, officially established in 1799, provided the foundation of what would soon become known as the PTT Post.

The Dutch postal service inherited a variety of postal tariffs and collection and delivery methods. In 1807, however, the Post was placed under the administration of the Ministry of Finance. This body passed the country's first Postal Act, a series of regulations providing for a more standardized collection, carrying, and delivery system, while also establishing a single rate system (based on distance and weight) for the entire country. However, the Post was still not conceived of as a public service. Instead, it was expected to operate more along the lines of a tax collection service, providing funds for the national treasury.

COMPANY PERSPECTIVES

It is our mission to enable all our customers, whether they're using our consumer products or our business solutions, to enrich their work and leisure time with our range of communication services.

A shift in the vision of the Netherlands' postal services came in the mid-19th century. The passage of the Postal Act of 1850 established the postal service as a service in the public interest. While remaining under the finance ministry, the Post shed its role as tax collector to become a public service. The Postal Act of 1850 further codified the postal service's domestic monopoly and created a simplified postal rate structure. Two years later the postal service began the implementation of a nationally organized network of postal service facilities. By the 1870s the Post's network of post offices covered most of the country.

In the meantime, the Netherlands had begun to install its first telegraph transmission networks. In 1852 the country formally organized its telegraph utility, the Rijkstelegraaf, under the Ministry of the Interior, which assumed responsibility for installing a roadside network of telegraph poles and cables. Use of the telegraph as a communication means remained relatively limited, however.

The postal system and the telegraph service, which was soon to add the newly invented telephone, operated as separate government agencies until the 1880s. Given the limited growth of the telegraph in the Netherlands, it was decided that the two services should be joined into one agency, under a single ministry in 1886. Combining the two services offered the pragmatic benefit of allowing both to operate from the postal services' national network of post offices. With the addition of telephone services, this agency would become known as the PTT (for Post, Telegraph, and Telephone) and would remain a state-run monopoly for more than 100 years.

The combination of postal services with the country's telegraph and telephone systems was never wholeheartedly performed. Even though the two services were available through the same post offices, operations remained more or less separate, with each branch retaining its own personnel and culture. For the most part, the two services operated in parallel, each with its own personnel, budget and finances, and infrastructure.

DIFFICULT ECONOMIC CLIMATE

The Depression era forced the PTT to modernize. The introduction of more efficient sorting systems enabled the PTT to cut back on the number of its delivery rounds. Instead of the three deliveries per day, PTT postmen performed only two. The growth of the telephone network, and the rising number of telephone users, was also slowly changing the communication habits of the Dutch commercial and private user, who would soon reach for the telephone rather than the pen.

The difficult economic climate presented an opportunity for the PTT, in that government allowed the agency to operate more and more as a commercial enterprise. Unlike other government agencies, which were provided for in the national budget, the PTT was given a more corporate status, enabling the company to make the necessary capital investments and take write-offs on its balance sheet rather than depend on government approval for each investment. The PTT was also given its own press and publicity departments, enabling the agency to compete for consumer attention. While most of Europe's postal services and telephone companies remained under government control, the PTT's relative independence allowed it to present a more modern appearance to consumers, who were treated also with original postal stamp designs.

The Nazi takeover of the Netherlands during World War II interrupted the PTT's independent activities, as the Germans seized control of the country's communications systems. With the Liberation, the PTT was faced with rebuilding its telephone infrastructure. By the end of the 1940s, the agency was reporting heavy losses, especially from its postal services. In this way, the PTT was no different from most of its government-run counterparts in other countries. Telephone services, nevertheless, would provide a means to maintain a positive balance sheet for PTT, as the telephone quickly imposed itself as a mainstay in the postwar home. The PTT's telephone monopoly allowed the government-run service to maintain relatively high rates. As in most of its European counterparts, the telephone service charged by the minute for all calls, including local ones.

ERA OF INNOVATION

Through the 1960s and 1970s, the PTT continued to improve the quality of its phone lines and telephone transmissions. The telephone industry was by then preparing to enter a new era of innovation. The use of telex equipment and facsimile machines, joined in later decades by electronic messaging systems, and Internet-based voice and video communication technology, as well as portable telephone systems freed of dependence

KEY DATES

1886: Dutch postal service and telegraph service combined into a single ministry.
1989: Dutch postal and telephone monopoly, PTT Post, privatizes and reorganizes.
1994: PTT Nederland lists on the Amsterdam exchange.
1998: PTT Nederland splits into two entities, one of which is Royal KPN.
2001: Ad Scheepbouwer appointed company CEO; KPN debt reaches EUR 23 billion.
2005: KPN reduces its debt to EUR 8 billion.
2010: KPN appoints Eelco Blok as its chief executive officer.

on a physical telephone wiring system, threatened a drastic transformation of traditional communication systems.

While the telephone industry was facing a time of great change, the postal world was also changing. The arrival of dedicated express mail and other courier services, led by such companies as Federal Express and United Parcel Service in the United States, presented new challenges to traditional postal services.

END OF GOVERNMENT MONOPOLIES

By the 1980s, the era of government-run, monopoly services had reached the beginning of the end. Restructuring was quickly becoming a necessity, not only to enable the PTT to compete in a rapidly transforming marketplace but also to give the consumer more options (and potentially lower rates). During the 1980s, the PTT focused on expansion activities, buying up interests in domestic cable and television networks and moving toward international expansion of its telecommunications services. In 1989 the PTT was finally privatized.

That year the PTT was reorganized as a private business, PTT Nederland N.V., under the direction of CEO Wim Dik. Under the new structure, the postal service, renamed PTT Post, joined the larger telecommunications industry sister company, PTT Telecom, as an independently operating subsidiary. Despite no longer being a government agency, the new PTT remained nonetheless wholly owned by the Dutch government. The change, however, allowed the company

to pursue its own growth strategy into the 1990s, unhampered by the slower governmental decision-making process. Privatization also enabled the company to seek new international partners, some of which had balked at the prospect of pursuing projects with a government agency.

Partnering would prove essential if PTT Telecom, with its relatively small Netherlands market, was to be able to compete on an international scale. The coming of telephone deregulation in the European market, scheduled for the late 1990s, also presented PTT Telecom with new opportunities. In 1992 PTT Telecom joined with Sweden's telecommunications monopoly Telia to form the Unisource alliance. This partnership quickly gained more weight with the addition of Swiss Telecom in 1993. By the following year, Unisource had reached an international cooperation agreement with AT&T to form the joint venture Uniworld. Launched in 1996, Uniworld targeted commercial customers with integrated data-voice telephone packages. Uniworld also gave PTT Telecom a position in the Far East, as a member of WorldPartners with AT&T, Japan's KDD, and Singapore Telecom.

In 1994 PTT Nederland went to the stock market, as the Dutch government sold off some 30 percent of its shares on the Amsterdam exchange. Interest in the new shares was high, with most investor attention going to PTT Telecom. Two years later, PTT Nederland offered another 25 percent of its shares, effectively ending the Dutch government's control of the country's post and telecommunications services. At that time, PTT Nederland took listings on the New York, London, and Frankfurt stock exchanges as well.

The public offering not only enhanced PTT Telecom's profile in the telecommunications industry, it also gave the company maneuvering room in the rapidly changing telecommunications landscape. This would prove especially necessary, as PTT Telecom faced the end of its domestic telephone monopoly, as well as competition for the Netherlands' mobile telephone customers. With the increase in capital, PTT Telecom began an international expansion drive. In 1994 the company bought a 30 percent interest in Bakrie Electronics Company (BEC) of Indonesia, partnering with that country's telephone monopoly to build and operate new telephone networks.

The Eastern European market would also be targeted by PTT Telecom as part of its international expansion. In partnership with Swiss Telecom and AT&T, PTT Telecom bought up a 27 percent share in SPT, the Czech telecommunications provider. Moreover, PTT Telecom's partnership in the Pannon GSM digital mobile telephone network brought the company to

Hungary. PTT Telecom also began building a fixed line and mobile telephone infrastructure in Ukraine, in partnership with other providers.

THE SPLIT, AND NEW SERVICES: 1998–2005

In 1998 PTT Nederland announced that it was splitting into two entirely independent, publicly listed companies, Royal KPN, which contained the company's telecommunications activities, and TNT Post Group (TPG), which took over the company's postal, logistics, and express mail services wing, including both companies' shares of the GDEW partnership. Both KPN and TPG retained listings on the Amsterdam, New York, London, and Frankfurt stock exchanges.

The retirement announcement of KPN chief Wim Dik in 1999 fueled industry opinion that KPN itself would become a takeover candidate early in the new century. Even as rumors of a takeover ensued, KPN enlarged its footprint in the world of mobile communications in 2000 when it started providing wireless Internet services on its mobile telephone networks, a fairly advanced concept at the time. In addition to rolling out these services, KPN continued to seek out companies to acquire or increase its stake in. In July 2000 it met with Japan's mobile operator, NTT DoCoMo to discuss buying a stake in Hutchinson Whampoa's British division. While NTT DoCoMo did not agree to this deal, it did spend $3.56 billion to buy a 15 percent stake in KPN's mobile telephone business.

All the years KPN had spent acquiring other telecommunications companies came at a cost. By mid-2001 the company was nearly $31.23 billion in debt. Talks of a takeover increased. To get out from beneath the mounting debt and quiet takeover rumors, KPN named Ad Scheepbouwer as its chief executive officer in November 2001. Scheepbouwer set about the task of increasing KPN's cash flow and margins. He also entered merger discussions with Belgian telco Belgacom, a leading Belgium telecommunications operator. The deal fell through when the Belgian government refused to fund the deal.

From 2002 through 2003, KPN focused on strengthening its bottom line. By third quarter 2003, the company had added nearly half a million new customers. Additionally, it rolled out wireless LAN connections to customers located in the Netherlands and Germany. To continue to grow its customer base, in 2004 KPN started hosting mobile telephone systems for other companies on its servers.

By 2005 KPN's debt was down to $10.86 billion, a considerable drop from four years earlier. After the firm celebrated its 125th anniversary in 2006, it turned its sights on offering its customers fiber-optic cabling services. The services allowed customers to access the Internet at faster speeds.

ACQUISITION AND ECONOMIC CHALLENGES: 2007 AND BEYOND

As it began to regain financial strength, KPN returned to growth by acquisition when it bought Getronics, a global information and communications technologies (ICT) services firm, for $1 billion in 2007. About the pickup, Schweepbouwer told *Forbes* in its July 30, 2007, article, "KPN Gets Getronics for $1 Billion," that "Telecommunications and IT services are increasingly becoming two sides of the same coin." He continued, "More and more companies are converging their telecoms and IT requirements, sourcing all services from a single end-to-end vendor."

IBM, Dell, and Hewlett-Packard had also showed interest in the ailing Getronics. Although the purchase brought 22,000 additional employees to KPN, the company had its hands full making Getronics profitable. During the first half of 2007, Getronics posted a net loss of $147.5 million, down from the previous year's profit of $30.1 million.

The following years would not be easy for the company, as it struggled through the global economic recession. Revenue fell by 8.7 percent from 2008 to 2009. In October 2010 KPN appointed Eelco Blok as its chief executive officer, replacing Scheepbouwer. Blok had served on KPN's board since 2004.

In the early 2010s, Blok and KPN faced a declining market for landlines and a competitive market for wireless communications. However, KPN's wireless services revenue had been increasing, and subsidiary Getronics had increased revenues from 2008 to 2009, giving the company reason to believe that KPN could continue to find success in some, if not all, of its business segments.

Marc Du Ry
Updated, M. L. Cohen; Rhonda Campbell

PRINCIPAL SUBSIDIARIES

E-Plus Mobilfunk Geschäftsführungs GmbH (Germany); Getronics N.V.; iBasis Inc. (USA); KPN Mobile N.V.

PRINCIPAL DIVISIONS

Consumer; Business; Getronics; Wholesale & Operations; E-Plus Gruppe; KPN Group Belgium.

PRINCIPAL COMPETITORS

Belgacom SA; Deutsche Telekom AG; France Telecom; Tele2 Netherlands Holding N.V.

FURTHER READING

"Citibank Announces Global Offering Including Royal KPN N.V. ADSs and ADNs; Premier Dutch Telecommunications Provider Expands Its NYSE-Listed ADR Program." *Business Wire,* November 24, 2000. Accessed February 25, 2011. http://www.thefreelibrary.com/Citibank+Announces+Global+Offering+Including+Royal+KPN+N.V.+ADSs+and...-a0673 64423.

Dickey, Allan. "Public Services at Private Prices." *Eurobusiness,* March 1994, 57.

"Dutch KPN Divests PharmaParners to TSS." *Internet Business News,* January 11, 2011. Accessed February 25, 2011. http://www.allbusiness.com/health-care/health-care-overview/15438254-1.html.

Hastings, Phillip. "Rush to Repackage." *Financial Times,* June 17, 1999.

"Hitting the Mail on the Head." *Economist,* April 30, 1994, 69.

Resener, Madeleine. "How the Dutch Did It." *Institutional Investor,* April 1995, 66.

"Royal KPN NV Q2 2010 Earnings Call Transcript." *Seeking Alpha,* July 28, 2010. Accessed February 25, 2011. http://seekingalpha.com/article/216972-royal-kpn-nv-q2-2010-earnings-call-transcript.

"TNT Sale May Signal Industry Trend." *Logistics Management,* January 1997, 26.

Van Gaal, Maud, and Chiara Remondini. "Royal KPN Appoints Eelco Blok as Chief Executive to Replace Scheepbouwer." *Bloomberg,* October 18, 2010. Accessed February 25, 2011. http://www.bloomberg.com/news/2010-10-18/royal-kpn-appoints-eelco-blok-as-chief-executive-to-replace-scheepbouwer.html.

Woodford, Julian. "KPN." *Utility Week,* January 23, 1998, 24.

Sammons Enterprises, Inc.

5949 Sherry Lane
Suite 1900
Dallas, Texas 75225
U.S.A.
Telephone: (214) 210-5000
Fax: (214) 210-5099
Web site: http://www.sammonsenterprises.com

Private Company
Founded: 1938 as the Reserve Life Insurance Company
Employees: 3,800 (est., 2009)
Sales: $2.9 billion (est., 2009)
NAICS: 5511 Management of Companies and Enterprises

■ ■ ■

One of the largest privately owned companies in Texas, Sammons Enterprises, Inc., is a diversified holding company that concentrates its business on three sectors: financial services, equipment distribution, and hospitality and real estate.

Sammons Financial Group is a group of insurance companies based primarily in the northern and midwestern United States. The group shares resources and services, but the companies are separately managed and separately regulated by the state in which they do business. Member companies include Midland National in Sioux Falls (South Dakota), North American in Chicago, Sammons Annuity Group in Des Moines (Iowa), and Sammons Securities Company in Ann Arbor, Michigan. In total, Sammons Financial has ap-

proximately $25 billion in assets with $245 billion in total life insurance policies.

Sammons' businesses in the equipment distribution sector consist of the Briggs Equipment companies, including Briggs International, Briggs Equipment UK, Briggs Equipment U.S., and Briggs Equipment Mexico. Briggs is an international equipment distribution company that rents, sells, and services Yale and Caterpillar brands in North America and Europe.

Sammons' hospitality and real estate companies are SRI Ventures and the Grove Park Inn Resort and Spa. SRI Ventures, with assets of $40 billion, operates an equity fund that seeks joint ventures in office, retail, hospitality, residential, and industrial development projects. Grove Park Inn Resort and Spa is a historic getaway originally built in 1913 and acquired by Sammons in 1955. After a major renovation, the inn offers 512 rooms, a full-service spa, and a world-class golf course designed by the famed golf course architect Donald Ross. Grove is listed on the National Register of Historic Places and is a member of Historic Hotels of America.

YOUNG ENTREPRENEUR: 1898–1917

Charles Addison Sammons, Jr., was born on June 5, 1898, and was orphaned by the time he was 13, when his parents died within a year of each other. Charles, the middle son, was sent to Plano, Texas, to live with his aunt while his two sisters were sent to separate relatives. Sammons' father, Charles Sammons, Sr., had become wealthy as a lumberyard owner in the new Oklahoma

COMPANY PERSPECTIVES

Seventy years of success has taught us to protect and preserve the values that guide our relationships with our colleagues and business partners. Our values are evident in our behavior and our decisions: how we treat each other, our involvement in the community, and how we decide to invest our time and capital.

territory. He had also been an avid traveler, taking his family on vacation regularly. Charles Jr. inherited his father's business acumen and love for travel, both of which would influence Charles Jr. and Sammons Enterprises in the future. In later years, Charles Jr. wrote, "My hobbies are reading, travel, some swimming and bicycling. However, perhaps attempts to solve business problems [and] help make companies grow and prosper is my most interesting activity."

Although separated from his sisters, Charles Jr. remained close with them and felt responsible for their well-being. During high school, he began a laundry service, earning enough to put both siblings through college, although Sammons did not attend college himself.

In 1917 Sammons moved to Dallas to start his own business. He obtained credit from local banks and helped facilitated the transport of grain and livestock from shippers and producers to market. When the banks discovered that Sammons was not of legal age to borrow money, Sammons petitioned the courts to have his minor status removed so that he was legally accountable for his debts. Integrity was a value Sammons held throughout his career.

INSURANCE: 1928–58

In 1928 Sammons met local businessmen Abe Marker and Harold Goodman, who proposed a partnership. Marker and Goodman were involved in the health insurance business, with limited success. Sammons offered an excellent credit rating and knowledge of office operations, which Marker and Goodman lacked. The three named the company Postal Indemnity Company, a mutual assessment insurance company that wrote accident and life insurance coverage.

In 1938, after the death of Marker, Sammons bought out Marker's widow and separated from Goodman, who took the Indianapolis branch for his own. Sammons used the remaining branches and expanded to

form Reserve Life Insurance Company (RLI), the company that would eventually become the first company of Sammons Enterprises.

Sammons continued expansion through World War II and after. The health insurance industry went through drastic changes during this time. The Baylor Plan, the precursor to Blue Cross and Blue Shield, offered hospital care at a low monthly premium to school teachers. In 1946 RLI offered a similar product and emphasized the relatively new concepts of preventive health care and the family health plan.

Sammons' strategy for expansion was to buy existing licensed insurers as subsidiaries in the state that they operated. This allowed RLI to expand its product line to these subsidiaries without having to go through the licensing process in each state.

In 1958 Sammons acquired Midland National, a life insurance company based in South Dakota. Midland National, known for weathering the influenza pandemic of 1916 to 1918 (nicknamed "Spanish flu") and the Dust Bowl, offered innovative products such as the Hog Contract. Under the Hog Contract plan, Midland offered a female pig to all farmers that renewed their life insurance policies. The company achieved double-digit growth under Sammons every year. (It reached $119 billion in assets by 2009.) Midland eventually became the flagship insurer of Sammons Financial Group after the sale of RLI's health insurance business in 1989.

The health care industry became personal to Sammons when both of his sisters were afflicted with breast cancer at an early age. This prompted Sammons to partner with the Baylor University Medical Center, contributing to research projects and encouraging other business leaders to do the same. In 1973 Sammons' $1 million gift funded a new virology lab and nuclear medicine department, leading to the establishment of the Charles A. Sammons Cancer Center.

A FULLY DIVERSIFIED COMPANY: 1952–62

In 1952 Sammons purchased Briggs-Weaver, marking its entrance into the equipment distribution industry. Under Sammons, Briggs grew at an average of 20 percent per year. (In 1996 Briggs became a separate working operation under Sammons. Briggs expanded to Mexico in 1996 and the United Kingdom in 2004.)

In 1955 Sammons purchased Grove Park Inn Resort and Spa, marking its entrance into the hospitality industry. Built in 1913 and located in Asheville, North Carolina, the hotel's history included presidents and business leaders. F. Scott Fitzgerald stayed at the Groves

KEY DATES

1938: Charles Sammons opens the Reserve Life Insurance Company.

1952: Sammons diversifies to the equipment distribution sector with the purchase of Briggs-Weaver.

1955: Sammons diversifies to the hospitality sector with the purchase of the Grove Park Inn.

1962: Sammons Enterprises is established.

1978: Sammons launches the company's Employee Stock Ownership Plan (ESOP).

1988: Charles Sammons dies.

2008: Company continues philanthropy efforts with a $20 million donation to the Baylor Health Care System Foundation.

to be near his wife Zelda, who was hospitalized in Asheville's Highland Hospital. During World War II the hotel housed Axis diplomats waiting for repatriation as well as war-weary U.S. soldiers. In 1982 Sammons' wife, Elaine, pioneered a multimillion-dollar renovation that added a 40,000-square-foot underground spa and 27-hole golf course.

Sammons continued his expansion of real estate and hospitality sites. In the early 1950s, he purchased the Jack Tar Hotel in Galveston, and in 1959 he purchased the Grand Bahama Hotel and Country Club off Florida's coast. In 1986 Sammons Realty was formed to acquire and develop real estate ventures. Sammons Realty became a part of SRI Ventures, an equity fund that specialized in real estate joint ventures with partners that had local expertise.

In 1962 Sammons Enterprises was established to hold the diverse collection of companies that Sammons had accumulated. Sammons Enterprises had grown to almost 70 companies in communications, ceramics, printing, insurance, and real estate.

DIVERSIFICATION INTO CABLE: 1961–86

The regular cash flow of health care premiums appealed to Sammons, and he sought diversification opportunities with a similar cash flow pattern. In 1961 he partnered with Bill Daniels, a cable broker based in Colorado. Sammons bought cable, radio, and antenna systems. In 1972 he formed Sammons Communications, Inc., which generated revenues of $14 million. In 1974 Sam-

mons Communications became the seventh-largest cable television system operator.

The cable industry grew rapidly in the 1970s and 1980s. More channels were offered, and the new technologies offered multiple opportunities for expansion. Satellite technology allowed channels such as HBO and WTBS to broadcast nationally. These "premium" channels were charged an increased monthly subscription rate. By the mid-1980s, Sammons had increased subscribership to 700,000 customers.

Another important development in the 1970s concerned employee stock ownership. In 1973 Ken Mutzel, CFO of Sammons Enterprises, approached Charles Sammons about an employee stock ownership plan (ESOP). ESOP plans were developed by investment banker Louis Kelso, who coauthored the *Capitalist Manifesto*. Kelso argued that employee ownership would strengthen the capitalist ideals within companies. By allowing employees to own a portion of the value they created with their employers, both parties would achieve success. However, because ESOP plans were not yet tested, Sammons did not fully commit to the idea until 1978. Eventually, Sammons not only saw the value of ESOPs, but he changed his will so that the ESOP plan would become the primary beneficiary of his estate.

SUCCESSION AND SALE: 1988–96

On January 1, 1988, Sammons appointed Bob Korba, the company's general counsel, to succeed him as CEO. Sammons died on November 12, 1988. Korba's promise to Sammons upon his death was first to take care of his family and second to take care of Sammons Enterprises, thus honoring Sammons' devotion to both. Elaine Sammons, Sammons' wife and business advisor of 25 years, became chairman of the board until her death in 2009.

In 1996, eight years after Sammons died, Korba sold the cable business for $1.8 billion due to the tighter profit margins and increased capital required to keep up with competition. Customers were demanding lower rates and more services due to competition from other providers that offered combined telephone, Internet, and cable services. The large capital investment that Sammons would have had to make to offer these services, combined with tighter margins, motivated the sale.

SAMMONS ENTERPRISES: 2006 AND BEYOND

Sammons continued its expansion in its core sectors in the early years of the 21st century. In 2006 Sammons acquired Finning U.K.'s materials handling division, naming the company Briggs Equipment U.K. The acquisition increased Brigg's lift truck fleet by 25,000.

In 2008 Sammons entered into a $1.8 billion deal with Kroll Development Co. and E2M Partners to build 90 office buildings in Chicago, Washington, D.C., Houston, and San Francisco. The deal expanded Sammons' real estate sector, a move that took advantage of the soft real estate market. Also that year, the company completed the creation of a comprehensive career development program for senior and mid-level staff, with plans to extend it to line staff. In addition, the company continued its commitment to cancer research. In 2008 a donation of over $20 million to the Baylor Health Care System Foundation led to the funding of a new cancer complex, making it the largest outpatient cancer center in North Texas.

In January 2009, after 20 years at the helm of Sammons Enterprises, Bob Korba retired as CEO, remaining as chairman of the board upon Mrs. Sammons' death. In retirement, Korba founded Y Street Ventures and VERUS Real Estate Advisors. VERUS offered comprehensive brokerage, asset, and property management, and advisory services to owners of commercial real estate.

Replacing Korba was Michael Masterson, previous CEO and chairman of Sammons Financial Group. Masterson joined Sammons in 1995 as executive vice president and chief marketing officer of Midland National. In 1996 he was promoted to CEO and president of that company. In 2002 he became CEO of Sammons Financial Group.

In 2010 Sammons Enterprises was poised to take advantage of the soft real estate cycle, using its core competencies in the hospitality and real estate investment industries. The insurance and financial services industries were set to undergo drastic changes as a result of the Patient Protection and Affordable Care Act, which U.S. President Barack Obama signed into law in March 2010. However, Sammons Enterprises, a traditionally conservative company with little debt and ample capital, was well positioned to cope with the complexities of both industries.

Sara K. Huter

PRINCIPAL SUBSIDIARIES

Briggs Equipment; Briggs Equipment – Mexico City; Briggs Equipment UK Limited; The Grove Park Inn Resort & Spa; Midland National Life Insurance Company; North American Company for Life and Health Insurance Company; Sammons Annuity Group; Sammons Corporate Markets Group; Sammons Corporation; Sammons Realty Corporation; SRI Ventures.

PRINCIPAL COMPETITORS

Deere & Company; MetLife, Inc.; NES Rentals Holdings, Inc.; Prudential Financial, Inc.

FURTHER READING

"Briggs Equipment Parent Acquires Finning U.K.'s Forklift Business." *Rental Equipment Register,* September 18, 2006.

"Charles Sammons, 90, Executive. (Obituary)." *New York Times,* November 14, 1988.

"Elk River Real Estate Partners with Y Street Ventures to Form VERUS Real Estate Advisors and Appoints Bob Korba as Chairman." *Business Wire,* April 12, 2010.

Knowles, Robert G. "Reserve Life Exits Health Market." *National Underwriter Life & Health–Financial Services Edition,* 43, 1989.

"Koll Development Teams with 2 Investors on Major Expansion." *Dallas Morning News,* July 1, 2008.

"Sammons Support for Baylor Health Care System Foundation Tops $20 Million." *PR Newswire,* September 24, 2009.

Satcon Technology Corporation

27 Drydock Avenue
Boston, Massachusetts 02210
U.S.A.
Telephone: (617) 897- 2440
Toll Free: (888) 728-2664
Fax: (617) 897-2401
Web site: http://www.satcon.com

Public Company
Founded: 1985
Employees: 226 (2009)
Sales: $52.54 million (2009)
Stock Exchanges: NASDAQ
Ticker Symbol: SATC
NAICS: 334413 Semiconductor and Related Device
    Manufacturing

■ ■ ■

Satcon Technology Corporation (Satcon) produces components used in renewable energy projects. The company's power inverters are utilized at large-scale solar installations, and the company markets fuel cell power inverters as well. Satcon also provides design services for renewable energy projects.

Power inverters are the latest product for Satcon, which has attempted to make its mark in many different markets. However, the company has had very few profitable years, and at the end of 2009 its accumulated debt was $231.7 million.

COMPANY FOUNDING AND EARLY YEARS: 1985–1990

Despite its small size, the city of Cambridge, Massachusetts, is home to two of the leading academic institutions in the United States, Harvard University and the Massachusetts Institute of Technology (MIT). In 1985 a group of engineers with strong academic backgrounds and ties to MIT came together to form the Satcon Technology Corporation.

These engineer-entrepreneurs established Satcon with the goal of developing new and improved power and energy management technologies. They believed that as global electrification began to spread, the demand for energy would increase. They also believed that the use of computers would transform the way in which countries generated, distributed, and used electrical power.

The development of new technologies and products with a view to applying them to commercial use would be a reoccurring theme at Satcon. Although the company would change its focus and reinvent itself several times, the application of new ideas and processes would be a constant theme.

The original focus for Satcon Technology, at its founding in 1985, was on the space program. The development of new space vehicles and particularly the proposal to establish a permanent space station in orbit around the Earth was raising some interesting engineering challenges. The space station and its human crew would require new methods of generating, storing, and managing power. New technologies would need to be

COMPANY PERSPECTIVES

Rugged, reliable, and backed by world-class warranty and support programs, Satcon solutions are chosen by the world's leading businesses and utility companies to convert renewable energy into efficient and stable power.

developed in order to permit humans to live and work in space for extended periods of time.

The competition between the United States and the Soviet Union to explore and conquer space was intense. While single-mission space flights were expensive, the costs of building, maintaining, and supporting a permanent space station were prohibitive. In the 1970s, the United States had launched Skylab, an orbital space station, but abandoned the program by mid-decade. The Soviet Union, with its more rigid and structured economy, took the lead in developing an orbiting laboratory, first with the Salyut program and then with the launch of the Mir Space Station.

Delays and cost overruns in the creation of a U.S. space station forced Satcon to change its focus. The company began to search out new markets for energy management in order to survive. Satcon turned its attention to developing active motion control technology. This type of technology is used in electromechanical controlled motion technology. While the space station program floundered, the United States was developing new space- and land-based defense systems, and Satcon played a role in developing technology for the armed services.

With funding from the Ballistic Missile Defense Organization (BMDO), an agency of the U.S. Department of Defense, the company developed vibration control systems, frictionless magnetic bearings, and electrical drive systems. The idea was that all of these components would be needed during the construction of a missile defense system. In addition to money received from BMDO, Satcon also received funding from the United States Navy and the National Aeronautics and Space Administration (NASA).

The company also received research funding from the Small Business Innovation Research program (SBIR). Under this program, the federal government assisted small business in research and technical innovation. The program sought to adapt new technical innovation into commercial applications. SBIR funding was a key link in Satcon's growth strategy.

PUBLIC COMPANY: 1992

The last decade of the 20th century brought significant developments in the history of the company. In 1992 Satcon reformed itself and became a publicly traded company when it incorporated in the State of Delaware, and its stock began to trade on the NASDAQ exchange.

The company remained dedicated to developing new technology and adapting it to commercial use, particularly in the area of energy and power. It also sought to expand by acquiring other companies that could complement its business.

Two of the original founders assumed vital roles within the new company. David B. Eisenhaure became president and CEO of the new public entity. Eisenhaure, who held a degree in mechanical engineering, had led the organization since its inception. Dr. James L. Kirtley, who held a Ph.D. in electrical engineering, had been a consultant with Satcon since 1985. He now took a position as a director of the company. Both men were academics who had taught at MIT, Eisenhaure as a lecturer in the Department of Mechanical Engineering and Kirtley as a professor of electrical engineering.

Since its inception in 1985, Satcon had received virtually all of its funding from research and development contracts. It now started to transform itself from a technology-based research company to a technology-driven manufacturer.

In 1993 Satcon began working with the Chrysler Motor Corporation on a turbine electric vehicle. Chrysler set out to build a world-class race car using hybrid technology. The "Patriot," as the vehicle was known, used a flywheel energy storage system developed by Satcon. Although some testing of the technology was conducted, Chrysler ultimately dropped funding of the project.

Even with the loss of the Chrysler contract, Satcon remained interested in automotive technology and was the recipient of several contracts for the development of Hybrid Electric Vehicle (HEV) propulsion technology. Both the U.S. Department of Energy and the automotive industry were exploring alternatives to the gasoline-powered internal combustion engine.

However, the company was not dedicated to any single industry and would create products for a diverse range of markets. For instance, in one of its unique projects, Satcon developed a laser system to detect pathogens in meat products. Developed in cooperation with the North Plains Premium Beef Cooperative, the Remote Inspection Biological Sensor (RIBS) used lasers to detect the presence of harmful *e.coli* and *salmonella* bacteria in meat supplies. It was hoped that the laser would not only speed up the inspection process but

```
┌─────────────────────────────────────────────────┐
│                                                 │
│              KEY DATES                          │
│                   ■                             │
│                                                 │
│  1985:  Satcon Technology Corporation founded in│
│         Massachusetts.                          │
│  1992:  Satcon becomes a public company.        │
│  1993:  Company enters into Patriot project with│
│         Chrysler Motors.                        │
│  2005:  Company begins to develop solar power   │
│         business.                               │
│  2007:  David Eisenhaure, company founder, steps│
│         down as president and CEO.              │
│  2009:  Accumulated debt reaches $231.7 million.│
│                                                 │
└─────────────────────────────────────────────────┘
```

would also reduce the chances of human error. While this device was a technological innovation, like many of Satcon's creations, RIBS did not become a huge commercial success.

REORGANIZATION AND EXPANSION: 1997–2001

As part of its growth strategy, the company began to reorganize and expand. In 1997 it formed Beacon Power Company to manufacture and distribute its flywheel energy storage systems. These systems were designed for industries which required an uninterrupted power supply (such as utilities, telecommunications, and cable television businesses).

It also began to acquire companies which could complement its electrometrical business. It purchased K + D Magmotors, a manufacturer of custom electric motors. The motors produced by Magmotors were used in factory automation and medical equipment.

In April 1997 Satcon purchased Film Microelectronics Incorporated (FMI). Through FMI, Satcon would manufacture custom integrated circuits with target markets such as aerospace, the military, and communications.

In 2001 Satcon became a transnational corporation when it completed the acquisition of Inverpower Controls of Burlington, Ontario, Canada. Renamed Satcon Power Systems Canada, the company manufactured power electronic modules and high-speed digital controls for industrial power supply, power conversion, and power quality systems.

With its acquisitions completed, the company organized itself into three business units: Satcon Power Systems, Satcon Semiconductor Products, and Satcon Applied Technology.

NEW DIRECTION FOR A NEW CENTURY

As a company, Satcon had been on the leading edge of new technology and product development, but as with many new technology companies, profit remained elusive. Technology companies often fall victim to the fact that new technology, by its very definition, is not mainstream. New technology can be expensive and time-consuming to develop and there is often a lag time before it is accepted. The longer it takes for new technology to garner political, business, and consumer support, the greater the chance that it can stall the growth of the companies that develop it. Satcon experienced some, if not all, of these problems.

By 2005 Satcon Technology Corporation had incurred its 10th straight year of operating losses. Its accumulated operating losses since its inception stood at $137.9 million. Once again, it would begin to seek new commercial avenues to expand its technological base.

One such area that Satcon felt was a potential growth field was alternative energy, particularly solar energy. Solar energy involved the capture, conversion, storage, and transmission of power to generate electricity, processes familiar to the engineers at Satcon. The company began to establish itself in the solar energy industry through the development of commercial grade inverters.

In the next year, 2006, Satcon developed a strategy for competing in the alternative energy sector. It was be a four-step plan, which included leveraging its technical breadth, achieving commercial scale, partnering with other companies, and exapanding globally. Company revenues from this alternative energy technology would rise to $11.0 million.

Satcon was leaving behind the motion control industry and transforming itself into a clean technology force. Clean technology can be defined as a process that delivers value using limited or zero nonrenewable resources. It also creates less waste than conventional technology. Some widely known examples of clean technology would be solar power, wind power, bio-fuels, fuel cells, and hybrid vehicles. Clean technology, with its emphasis on energy and transportation, appeared a good fit for Satcon.

In 2007 the company restructured. David Eisenhaure, who had helped found the company and had led it since 1985, stepped down as president and CEO. He would continue to serve on the board of directors. His replacement would be Stephen Roades, a veteran of the energy business. Roades, who held a masters degree in physics, had done previous stints with companies such as Advanced Energy and Applied Materials.

The company began to cut costs and tried to reduce its expenditures. In order to focus on its core business of renewable energy it sold off its electronics and power systems business and its applied technology business.

The company began to concentrate on converting renewable energy into efficient and stable sources of power. Satcon developed solar photovoltaic converters and fuel cell converters under the PowerGate brand, and also developed Solstice, an energy distribution system.

In 2008 the company became a supplier of high-efficiency converters for a large rooftop solar array in North America, located at the Atlantic City Convention Center in New Jersey. Later that same year it provided a 12-megawatt system for the General Motors car plant at Figueruetas, Zaragoza, Spain.

In some ways, Satcon's restructuring plan had worked. Revenue rose from $14.1 million in 2006 to $33 million in 2007, and 2008 saw another increase to $54.29 million. Like many companies, adverse economic conditions caused a decrease in 2009 revenue, but the decline was only to $52.4 million. More troubling, however, was that even while revenue was increasing, profitability remained out of reach. Net losses for 2006 to 2009 were in excess of $13 million each year, with 2009 net losses almost $30 million ($29.87 million). In the 2010s, it remained to be seen whether Satcon's clean technology business could bring the company into profitability, or if its commercial grade inverters would be another technological innovation that failed to translate into a commercially viable product.

Ian MacDonald

PRINCIPAL SUBSIDIARIES

Satcon Applied Technology, Inc.; Satcon Electronics, Inc.; Satcon Power Systems, Canada, Ltd. (Canada).

PRINCIPAL COMPETITORS

Advanced Energy Industries, Inc.; Power-One, Inc.; Pv Powered, Inc.; Schneider Electric SA; Siemens Corporation; SMA Solar Technology AG; Sungrow Power Supply Co., Ltd.

FURTHER READING

Howe, Peter J. "New Laser System May Shine Light on Tainted Contaminated Meat Supplies." *Boston Globe,* September 1, 1997.

Pernick, Ron, and Clint Wilder. *The Clean Tech Revolution.* New York: HarperCollins, 2007.

Petersen, Gordon. "Spotlight on Industry – Satcon Technology Corporation." *Sea Power,* October 1, 2002.

"Satcon Gets $4.1 Million Contract for Shipboard Power." *Industrial Environment,* March 1, 2002.

"Satcon Tapped for Motor Research." *Energy Conservation News,* November 1, 1996.

The Seattle Times Company

1120 John Street
Seattle, Washington 98109
U.S.A.
Telephone: (206) 464-2111

Subsidiary of Blethen Corporation
Founded: 1896
Employees: 220 (est. 2010)
Sales: $25 million (est. 2010)
NAIC: 511110 Newspaper Publishers

■ ■ ■

The Seattle Times Company operates as a news and information company. Owner and operator of one of the last independent and locally owned metropolitan newspapers in the United States, the company publishes the *Seattle Times.* In addition, the company owns the *Yakima Herald-Republic,* the *Walla Walla Union-Bulletin,* and several regional weekly newspapers in Washington state. The Seattle Times Company also operates online news and advertising Web sites, such as NWclassifieds.com, an online classified and employment advertising site, and NWsource.com, a guide to entertainment, restaurants, outdoor activities, and shopping. In addition, the company provides newspaper and online advertising, direct marketing, market analysis, media planning, promotions, and design and copywriting, as well as commercial printing services. The *Seattle Times* was founded in 1896 by Alden Blethen and is headquartered in Seattle, Washington. The Blethen family continues to own 50.5 percent of the company,

which is a subsidiary of Blethen Corporation. Newspaper holding firm The McClatchy Company owns 49.5 percent of the company.

PREDECESSORS: 1881–96

When Colonel Alden J. Blethen stepped off the steamship *Walla Walla* in 1896, the city of Seattle gained its newest and most vocal newspaper publisher, a man who reportedly walked with a defiant strut and carried a heavy, gold-headed cane for protection against those riled by his decided and purposeful invectiveness. Blethen would impart his unhesitatingly frank and unabashedly bold personality to the *Seattle Times,* transforming the struggling evening newspaper into the largest daily in Washington State and creating a newspaper publishing dynasty that would employ generations of Blethens to follow. The ownership stability established by Colonel Blethen stood in sharp contrast to the newspaper's early years, a 15-year span before Blethen's arrival when ownership of the *Seattle Times'* direct predecessor, the *Seattle Chronicle,* changed hands frequently. Shortly after Blethen's arrival in Seattle, however, the shaky and fitful beginnings of the *Seattle Times* gave way to a century of ownership stability, as the paper flourished under the stewardship of its most colorful leader.

When Blethen acquired the *Seattle Times,* ownership of the newspaper had devolved into the hands of C. A. Hughes and T. A. Davies, who had no intention of continuing its publication, hoping only to sell the paper to the first interested party able to pay a price that would yield the two businessmen a profit. The newspaper Hughes and Davies had purchased represented a combination of several Seattle daily papers that descended from the *Seattle Chronicle,* the newspaper from which the *Seattle Times* inherited its Associated Press franchise. The *Seattle Chronicle,* an evening paper issued every day except Sunday, had been founded by Kirk C. Ward, who published the first copy on October 10, 1881. The following year, the *Seattle Chronicle* changed from an evening to a morning paper and began printing Associated Press dispatches, then in 1884 resumed evening publication, concurrent with its securing of the Associated Press franchise for the day report.

Two years later, the *Seattle Chronicle* was sold and consolidated with another daily newspaper, the *Daily Call,* forming the *Daily and Weekly Press.* When the former owners of the *Daily Call* were given positions at the newly formed newspaper, displacing a group of *Chronicle* employees, another Seattle daily newspaper was organized. This was the *Times,* published by the Times Publishing Company, founded by the *Chronicle* employees who had lost their jobs in the consolidation of the *Chronicle* and the *Daily Call.*

Change had been rampant during the five years following the founding of the *Chronicle,* the pace of which would not slacken much in the years leading up to Blethen's arrival in Seattle. Ownership of the *Daily and Weekly Press* changed twice in the three years following its formation, the second of which, in 1889, touched off a bitter feud between Seattle's two evening papers, the *Times* and the *Daily and Weekly Press.* The cloud of acrimony pervading the battle between the two evening newspapers was cleared away by the most ameliorative means possible in the business world when the *Daily and Weekly Press* acquired the *Times* in 1891 and began publishing the newspaper as the *Seattle Press-Times.*

Ownership of the *Seattle Press-Times* passed through several receiverships during the ensuing years, as the newspaper's financial woes mounted. In March 1895

Hughes and Davies purchased the floundering evening newspaper, becoming perhaps the most uninterested of all the newspaper's owners. As Colonel Blethen would write of the 17-month Hughes-Davies ownership, the pair operated the *Seattle-Press Times* "as a mere incident to [their] job—a printing business which had already been established," demonstrating a carelessness that would require, once again, a name change for the newspaper. Under the management of Hughes and Davies, an incorrect circulation figure was reported to the George P. Rowell Newspaper Directory, resulting in the newspaper being blacklisted from the directory. Consequently, "Press" was dropped from the newspaper's official name to obscure its identity, and the newspaper continued as the *Seattle Times,* less than a year before Blethen's arrival.

ESTABLISHING A GROWING BUSINESS: 1896–1906

Blethen disembarked from the steamship *Walla Walla* on July 26, 1896, having already lost two businesses by the age of 40. Born in Knox, Maine, Blethen had previously published a newspaper but lost the business to a fire, then founded a bank, which collapsed as well in the bank panic of 1893. His business failures, neither of which were attributable to his mismanagement, did not dilute Blethen's willingness to assume the mantle of responsibility once again, something he promptly did 15 days after arriving in Seattle when he purchased the *Seattle Times* from Hughes and Davies on August 10, 1896.

Decisive leadership was apparent from the outset, as Blethen strategically positioned the newspaper as a working man's alternative to the larger, more successful, and entrenched *Seattle Post-Intelligencer* (*P-I*), a morning newspaper founded in 1863. By consistently baiting the *P-I* into controversies and adopting an editorial position that distinguished his newspaper from the *P-I,* Blethen increased the circulation of the *Seattle Times.* Through his newspaper, Blethen was bitingly blunt about his views, particularly if they butted against the perspective espoused in the *P-I.* As a result, Blethen exposed himself to wave after wave of criticism, but enemies and friends alike were readers of the *Seattle Times,* enabling the outspoken publisher to establish a solid base of readership that would serve as the newspaper's foundation for the remainder of the century.

Growth came quickly to the *Seattle Times* under the leadership of Blethen, securing the newspaper's financial future, which for several years before Blethen assumed control had threatened to cause the newspaper's collapse. From a circulation of less than 8,000 copies in 1896, the *Seattle Times* had increased its circulation to

KEY DATES

1881: The *Seattle Chronicle*, a predecessor of the *Seattle Times*, begins publication.

1896: Alden Blethen purchases *Seattle Chronicle*.

1902: The *Seattle Times* becomes the largest published newspaper west of Chicago and north of Los Angeles.

1921: Alden's son C. B. Blethen assumes control of the *Seattle Times*.

1968: C.B.'s youngest son John is named publisher.

1983: A 50-year joint operating agreement is made between the *Seattle Times* and the *Seattle Post-Intelligencer*.

1989: Company acquires the *Yakima Herald-Republic*.

2000: The *Seattle Times* switches from evening to morning publication.

2007: Company ends court battle with the *Seattle Post-Intelligencer* and its parent company the Hearst Corp.

2009: Company sells its regional Maine newspapers.

25,000 by 1901, eclipsing the circulation of the rival *P-I*, then reached 40,000 by 1906, by which time the newspaper's annual revenues had jumped to roughly $580,000 from the $60,000 it generated at the beginning of Blethen's ownership. Revenue growth had enabled the construction of a new printing plant in 1898 and supported the newspaper's expansion from four pages in 1896 to more than 20 pages by 1906. Encouraged by his success, Blethen had launched a Sunday version of the *Seattle Times* in February 1902, which in four years' time recorded more robust growth than the daily version, exceeding 51,000 in circulation, making it the largest published newspaper west of Chicago and north of Los Angeles.

UNDER NEW LEADERSHIP: 1915–40

Blethen died in 1915, having completed the transformation of the *Seattle Times* from an upstart newspaper to a market leader that ranked as the largest daily newspaper in Washington. As it would for decades to come, leadership of the *Seattle Times* was handed down to the next generation, Blethen's sons, Joseph Blethen and Clarence Brettun (C.B.) Blethen, who assumed the titles of president and managing editor, respectively. Six years later, in 1921, when William Randolph Hearst acquired

the *P-I*, C. B. Blethen bought out his brother's share in the family company, grabbing a firm hold on the *Seattle Times* and wielding his authority with a style entirely distinct from his father. It was C.B.'s intent, insiders noted, to make the *Seattle Times* a mass-circulation newspaper, an objective he pursued by running the newspaper like a business, taking particular care, unlike his father, to avoid controversy in order to increase circulation. Wishing to produce a newspaper that no person would be ashamed to have around the house at night, C.B. sanitized the *Seattle Times*' editorial posture, eliminating crime news from the front page and prohibiting reporters from using words such as "gun" and "blood" in their published accounts of the daily news. Meanwhile, the newspaper's orientation was altered to embrace the more cautious middle-class members of Seattle's society.

Under C.B.'s leadership, heart-warming local news stories filled the *Seattle Times*' front page, creating a newspaper that could offend no one. Nonetheless, despite C.B.'s solicitous approach to running the company he came close to losing the family business in the early 1930s when the cost of constructing new corporate offices for the newspaper raised debt to a dangerous level. C.B. saved the company from potential failure by selling a 49.5 percent interest in the company to a hostile minority partner that later became known as Knight-Ridder Inc. It was a necessary but regrettable move on C.B.'s part, leading to periodic takeover attempts by Knight Ridder that continued until after C.B.'s death in 1941, with the last formal challenge mounted in 1949 and ending in a victory for the Blethen family.

Despite his uncharacteristic slip in the early 1930s, no one was more responsible for the *Seattle Times*' financial success than C. B. Blethen, whose business-first approach to running the newspaper fueled two decades of steady growth. His years in charge left a lasting impression for the generations of Blethen leaders to follow, setting a conservative journalistic tone at the newspaper that would predicate its growth, yet prompt critics to accuse the *Seattle Times* of being overly cautious and bland in its reporting. In the decades after C.B.'s death, his legacy lived on, leading one former reporter to characterize the *Seattle Times* in the late 1960s as "the good, gray place," a newspaper that lacked the stinging editorial stance prevalent in Alden Blethen's day, yet one that had grown enormously successful, ranking as the largest newspaper in Washington.

COMPETITORS UNITE: 1983

After C.B.'s death in 1941, Elmer Todd, his best friend and attorney, took control of running the newspaper, the first nonfamily member to steward the *Seattle Times*.

Todd was succeeded after an eight-year stint by two of C.B.'s sons, William K. Blethen, Sr., who was named publisher, and Frank A. Blethen, Sr., who became president. The two Blethen brothers were then succeeded by their younger brother John Blethen, who was named publisher in 1968, by which time the daily version of the newspaper had a circulation of slightly more than 250,000, or nearly 50,000 more than the *P-I*, while the Sunday edition had a circulation of 310,000, 52,000 more than the *P-I* could claim. Carrying roughly 60 percent of the advertising appearing in both papers, the *Seattle Times* had established a solid lead over its morning rival, a lead that would widen during the 1970s and early 1980s.

For years, the two newspapers had competed fiercely against each other, at times opposing each other as bitter foes, with each closely monitoring how the other was reporting the news. By the early 1980s, however, intense competition had created the need for the two newspapers to seek each other's help, particularly the *P-I*, which was beginning to succumb to the financial pressures resulting from the stronger market position enjoyed by the *Seattle Times*. In 1983 the two newspapers ended their sometimes contentious battle not by a figurative handshake but by a full embrace of each other.

On May 23, 1983, after narrowly surviving legal challenges to defeat it, a 50-year joint operating agreement between the *Seattle Times* and the *P-I* took effect, enabling the two newspapers to legally cooperate in order to ensure their mutual survival in the marketplace. Editorially, the two newspapers remained separate, but the *Seattle Times* Company took control of all *P-I*-related production, advertising, and circulation matters, removing the costly expense of waging a circulation war. Under the joint operating agreement, the *Seattle Times* ceased publication of its daily morning edition, begun in 1980, and was awarded the lion's share of the profits generated by both newspapers. In addition to taking a management fee equal to 6 percent of any profits earned by both newspapers in a year, the *Seattle Times* also took 66 percent of the remaining profits, leaving the balance for the *P-I*.

A PERIOD OF UNPRECEDENTED GROWTH: 1985–96

Buoyed by the financial boost provided by the joint operating agreement, the *Seattle Times* faced a brighter economic outlook as it moved toward the future and its greatest period of financial growth. Leading the company during this stretch of energetic growth was Frank Blethen, Jr., great-grandson of Colonel Alden Blethen. Frank Blethen, Jr., took the reins at the *Seattle Times* when his predecessor, W. J. Pennington, a nonfamily member who succeeded John Blethen in 1983, died unexpectedly in 1985. When Frank Blethen, Jr., was thrust into the leadership of the *Seattle Times* in 1985, he became the newspaper's sixth publisher and chief executive officer, gaining authority he would use to steer the newspaper toward what company officials described as unprecedented financial growth.

To realize this financial growth, Frank Blethen, Jr., launched several spin-off niche publications, acquired three regional weeklies, and in 1989 acquired the *Yakima Herald-Republic,* a daily newspaper with a circulation of more than 40,000. Three years after the purchase of the *Yakima Herald-Republic,* the *Seattle Times* company opened a $175 million, state-of-the-art satellite printing plant, then began operating its Infoline service, a telephone reader-information line supported financially through advertisers.

CHANGING TIMES: 1998–2000

In 1998 the *Seattle Times* announced that it would buy the Maine newspapers of Guy Gannett Communications. These papers including the *Portland Press Herald, Kennebec Journal, Morning Sentinel,* and other nonbroadcast media properties in Maine. "The excellent quality of the Maine newspapers and the Blethen family's strong ties to Maine were very motivating for us," Frank A. Blethen, publisher and chief executive officer was quoted as saying in a *Business Wire* report.

The following year, the *Seattle Times* and the *P-I* amended their joint business and publishing agreement. The changes were designed to strengthen the ties between the two newspapers and to allow the *Seattle Times* to change from an evening to a morning publication. The reasoning behind the new agreement was twofold. First, newspaper readers nationwide were demonstrating a preference for morning newspapers. Second, the city of Seattle had grown over the years, increasing highway congestion in the greater Seattle region and making it more difficult to meet afternoon delivery times. To avoid evening delivery delays, the company would have had to increase capital and operating costs. On March 6, 2000, the *Seattle Times* published its first morning edition.

AN ONGOING COURT BATTLE: 2003–07

Despite the relationship between the two newspapers, many observers saw the *Seattle Times'* switch to morning publication as likely to increase the heated rivalry with the *P-I*. "Expect the battle to get ugly quickly," wrote

MediaWeek contributor Vincent Coppola. The rivalry was compounded by tougher economic times beginning in 2001, which led to declining advertising revenues. True to many observers predictions, the competition between the two took a drastic turn when in April 2003 the *Seattle Times* announced its plans to end the joint operating agreement (JOA) with the *P-I.*

In response to the *Seattle Times* move to cut ties with the *P-I,* the paper's parent company, the Hearst Corp., announced that it was suing, declaring that the *Seattle Times* was seeking to put the *P-I* out of business. The *Seattle Times'* primary argument in ending the JOA was that it could not make a profit under the agreement. The court case went on for the next year with both sides at times winning decisions. In May 2005, the U.S. Justice Department concluded an investigation and announced that it had found no evidence of any wrongdoing on the part of the *Seattle Times* in terms of the paper endangering the *P-I's* long-term survival.

However, the court battle waged on until 2007 when, just before going into a binding arbitration, the two papers announced that they had agreed to a much-changed JOA that insured the *P-I's* continued existence. "Both newspapers were at risk due to the dramatic erosion of the newspaper revenue model in this decade," noted Frank Blethen, according to an article in *Editor & Publisher.* "Now we can each focus on publishing newspapers that are relevant to our community while we work at adjusting the old business model to the new realities."

LOOKING TOWARD THE FUTURE

With the court battle over, the *Seattle Times,* like other major newspapers throughout the country, was still facing difficult times due to declining readership and advertising revenues. The newspaper had already cut 86 positions and let go some of its circulation staff. It was also trying to outsource its trucking operation, which would lead to eliminating 74 more positions. In 2008 the company decided to sell its newspapers in Maine and focus solely on its Washington state papers. The sale was completed in June 2009.

Despite the difficult times for the newspaper industry, the *Seattle Times* remained intact, unlike the *P-I,* which stopped publishing in March 2009, although it maintained its Web site. The *Seattle Times* also remained a family-run business, as reflected by the appointment of Ryan Blethen as the editorial page editor while still continuing his role as the newspaper's associate publisher. The newspaper had also established a successful online presence with more than five million visitors per month. In 2011 the *Seattle Times* boasted a readership of 1.8 million adults, counting both the print and online versions of the paper. The company continued to seek out new and innovative ways to meet the needs of its readers and advertisers.

Jeffrey L. Covell
Updated, David Petechuk

PRINCIPAL DIVISIONS

News; New Media; Operations; Information Technology; Finance, Contracts, and Supply Management.

PRINCIPAL COMPETITORS

Gannett Co., Inc.; The Hearst Corporation; The New York Times Company.

FURTHER READING

Brewster, David. "Behind the Times." *Seattle Magazine,* November 1969, 33–38.

Coppola, Vincent. "War & Peace." *MediaWeek,* February 21, 2000, 32.

"The First Fifty Years." *Seattle Times,* August 11, 1946, 1–3.

"Labor Disputes Which Closed Times for 95 Days Are Detailed." *Seattle Times,* October 19, 1953, 1.

Park, Clayton. "Times Hangs onto Its Roots as Family-Owned Paper." *Puget Sound Business Journal,* November 17, 1995, 7A.

"The Seattle Times to Buy the Maine Newspapers of Guy Gannett Communications." *Business Wire,* September 1, 1998.

"Settlement: Seattle JOA Will Change, but Live On." *Editor & Publisher,* April 16, 2007.

Smile Brands Group, Inc.

8105 Irvine Center Drive
Suite 1500
Irvine, California 92618
U.S.A.
Telephone: (714) 668-1300
Web site: http://www.smilebrands.com

Private Company
Founded: 1998
Employees: 1,826 (2009)
Revenues: $456 million (2009)
NAICS: 561110 Office Administrative Services; 621210
Offices of Dentists

■ ■ ■

Helping dentists care for over 2.5 million patients across the nation, the Smile Brands Group, Inc., is the largest dental practice management company in the United States. The company provides business support services, nonclinical personnel, facilities, and equipment for dentists and hygienists. Services offered include staff recruiting, payroll, accounting, billing, marketing, patient financing, risk management, real estate development and management, operational support, quality assurance, call centers, and information technology. Each office under the Smile Brands umbrella is staffed with qualified dentists and hygienists who provide clients with comprehensive dental care and hygiene. Specialty services include orthodontic, endodontic, periodontal, and pediatric dentistry, along with oral surgery and a range of cosmetic dentistry.

Smile Brands Group, Inc., was incorporated in 2005 for the purpose of acquiring Smile Brands, Inc., which had operated since 1998 under the name Bright Now! Dental, and its subsidiaries. Smile Brands conducts business through affiliate dental groups that operate principally through one of three brands, Bright Now! Dental, Castle Dental, and Monarch Dental. Besides these, there are other affiliated brands in California and Virginia. Operating in California are Newport Dental and various "city branded" offices, such as San Jose Dental. Affiliated Virginia locations all conduct business under the Mazin Alayssami, D.M.D. & Associates brand. Smile Brands supports more than 300 affiliated dental offices in 17 states.

COMPANY BEGINNINGS: 1998

During the mid-1990s, the consolidation of dental offices under a single management company was a new trend in the health care industry. At the time, around 85 percent of all dentists were practicing alone or with one other dentist. Supporters of dental management companies argued that providers who became part of a large business group had access to more efficient resources, such as better collections and billing systems. By turning over their front-office administrative functions to dental practice management companies, proponents maintained, dentists could focus on treating their patients rather than on completing paperwork.

One person who saw the financial potential of dental practice management companies was Richard Matros, former CEO of Care Enterprises and Regency Health Services Inc. The history of Smile Brands dates

COMPANY PERSPECTIVES

The mission of Smile Brands is to deliver smiles for everyone! Whether you call it our vision, mission, or purpose, it is the reason for Smile Brands' existence, and what each employee and affiliated dental provider strives for every day. It means ensuring that all the groups who interact with Smile Brands—patients, doctors and employees—are enriched by their experience.

back to May 1998, when Matros partnered with Gryphon Investors, a San Francisco private equity firm that focused on middle market investment opportunities, to incorporate the Consumer Dental Services Organization in Northern California. Initially comprising 19 Bay Area offices that specialized in union and employer-group care, Consumer Dental Services Organization acquired 16 Southern California offices of Newport Dental three months later.

Under the executive leadership of Matros, Consumer Dental Services Organization acquired Megdal Dental Care Clinic, which had been in difficulty since 1997 due to the death of a young patient in one of its offices. In part to avoid the controversy involving the Megdal brand, Consumer Dental Services Organization officially changed its name to Bright Now! Dental in October 1998. The name change also allowed the company to launch a universal advertising campaign highlighting the advantages of larger offices to a public that was accustomed to dental care from small, independent offices, the perception being that a large operation would not be focused on customer service. Bright Now! selected advertising agency Towsend & O'Leary to develop a new corporate identity program and head its $2 million campaign. Soon, the dental practice management company was administered under the name of Smile Brands Inc.

By November 1998 the Smile Brands umbrella included 48 dental offices in California, Oregon, and Washington with annual revenues around $60 million. Matros focused on the goal of making Smile Brands a leader in the dental practice management sector. In addition to plans to open eight to ten new affiliate dental offices in the Bay Area and Pacific Northwest throughout 1999, to be followed by more West Coast operations, the company set its sights on expanding nationwide. While Smile Brands continued to open offices under the Bright Now! brand and boost its market

share through affiliations with a number of dental care service providers, the company did not see major expansion until it acquired two key players in the dental market, Castle Dental Centers and Monarch Dental Corp.

CASTLE DENTAL EXPANSION FOLLOWED BY DEBT: 1981–2001

Founded in Houston in 1981 by Jack Castle Jr. and his father, Castle Dental Centers had grown to be the largest dental group in Texas during the 1990s. Castle was an early entrepreneur in the dental practice management industry, bringing together both general dentists and specialists in the same office in order to reduce overhead expenses and capture more patient revenue. He was also one of the first in the business to apply such traditional retail strategies as payment plans, multiple locations, and extended office hours to the dental industry. As a result, Castle Dental was poised to go public when many Wall Street players turned their focus to dental practice consolidation. After debuting on the NASDAQ in September 1997, Castle Dental underwent rapid expansion.

Castle Dental targeted cities with a minimum population of 250,000, aiming to establish one center for every 100,000 people. In February 1998 the company revealed that it would purchase 80 percent ownership of Dental Consulting Services, a California-based dental practice management company that provided administrative services to five dental offices in the Los Angeles area. That deal was followed by the acquisition of five dental centers in Florida. Three of these offices were in the Sarasota area, one was in North Fort Lauderdale, and one was in Delray Beach. In November of that year, Castle Dental announced that its revenues for the third quarter had increased 72 percent, reaching a record $20.2 million, and it was recognized as one of the largest dental practice management companies in the United States.

In early 1999 the company acquired Dental Centers of America, a move that gained Castle Dental 16 Texas offices. Seven of these were in the Dallas-Fort Worth region, two in Austin, and seven in San Antonio, an area that had been one of Castle Dental's targets for expansion not only because of its population, but also because the city was the home of the University of Texas Dental School in San Antonio. Upon completion of this transaction, Castle Dental had a significant presence in the four largest metropolitan areas in Texas.

Despite such growth, Castle Dental reported second-quarter earnings that fell below company expectations. This setback was attributed to an underperforming office in Florida, as well as a conversion of management systems in California that slowed operations. Financial troubles, including a $1.4 million payout to settle a lawsuit brought against a dental practice acquired in 1996, persisted, and by April 2000 Castle Dental's accountants had expressed concerns about the company's future. In default on $63.8 million in debt, Castle Dental posted a $10.5 million loss in September 2000, an amount that reflected an $11.5 million write-off with $8.5 million of uncollectable patient debt. In response, Castle Dental took steps to eliminate jobs, close unprofitable offices, and write off lease agreements in offices where it had planned to add locations. In February 2001 Jack Castle Jr. stepped down as CEO.

Castle Dental's revenues continued to fall throughout 2001 and 2002, despite corporate restructuring efforts to implement operational changes and communications programs. In July 2002 the company announced that it had reached an agreement with lenders to restructure around $70 million in debt. In September that same year, Castle Dental entered into talks with Monarch Dental about a possible merger.

MONARCH DENTAL'S BACKGROUND: 1987–2002

Like Castle Dental, Monarch Dental was a Texas-based dental practice management company. Founded in Dallas in 1987, Monarch Dental Corp. incorporated in 1994 and went public two years later. In the late 1990s Monarch focused on entering new markets through acquisitions. During the second quarter of 1998, the company took over Managed Dental Care Centers Inc., a dental group practice comprising nine offices in New

Mexico and Austin, Texas. Additionally, Monarch Dental acquired two San Antonio private practices and one in Wisconsin, and it opened four new offices, two of which were located in Houston, one in San Antonio, and one in Houston. These transactions added a combined $8 million to Monarch Dental's annual revenues. Another series of acquisitions in 1998 included Valley Forge Dental Associates in Pennsylvania, Williams Dental Group in the Dallas-Fort Worth Metroplex, and Talbert Dental Group, a dental practice management company affiliated with MedPartners, Inc. By the close of 1999 Monarch Dental would own 190 offices in Arizona, Arkansas, Colorado, Georgia, Florida, Indiana, New Jersey, New Mexico, Ohio, Pennsylvania, Texas, Utah, Virginia, and Wisconsin.

Financial difficulties struck Monarch Dental in 1999. Rapid acquisitions and inexperienced management contributed to the company's monetary problems, along with $42 million in debt that had been assumed from the deal involving Valley Forge Dental Associates. Monarch Dentals' shares dropped nearly 50 percent over several months, and the company's earnings remained disappointing.

In April 1999 a class action suit was filed with the United States District Court for the Northern District of Texas against Monarch Dental on behalf of stockholders who had purchased the company's common stock between February 24, 1998, and December 22, 1998. According to the complaint filed by attorney Steven E. Cauley, Monarch Dental issued false and misleading information that artificially inflated the price of its stock to almost $20 per share. When the company announced fourth quarter losses in 1998, Monarch Dental stock fell to around $3 per share. Other class action lawsuits followed, with plaintiffs alleging that Monarch Dental had knowingly engaged in securities fraud. In February 2000 Monarch Dental agreed to pay $3.5 million in settlement of all claims in the litigation.

Monarch Dental received its sixth debt extension in October 2000, the same month that both the chairman and CEO of the company resigned. As a result of its situation, Monarch Dental faced delisting by the NASDAQ at the onset of 2001. After a year of net losses, the company sold off its Wisconsin operations, a total of 26 offices, for $9.7 million. After considering a merger with Castle Dental in September 2002, Monarch Dental struck a deal with Smile Brands.

GROWTH: 2003 AND BEYOND

In February 2003 Smile Brands purchased Monarch Dental and its affiliates for $12.07 million. One year later, Smile Brands bought Castle Dental for $34.4 million, making the publicly traded company a private subsidiary of Smile Brands As a result of this acquisition, 64 percent of Smile Brands was located in Texas. Executives within each organization were confident that the mergers would enable Smile Brands to become the nation's leading company in the dental practice management industry.

Following the acquisition of Castle Dental and Monarch Dental, Smile Brands turned its focus toward a *de novo* infrastructure, meaning that new dental offices were built rather than acquired. Convenience being a driving factor in the success of the organization, Smile Brands established locations in densely populated, middle-income areas. The locales themselves were required to be visible and easily accessible and to have good parking. In addition to being located in such high-traffic areas as shopping centers or complexes with a theater and grocery store, offices offered extended hours to better accommodate patients' schedules. Smile Brands carried on with its expansion all through the first decade of the 21st century.

In May 2005 Gryphon Investors sold its controlling stake in Smile Brands Inc. to Freeman Spogli & Co., a private equity firm based in Los Angeles, for an undisclosed amount. At the time of the deal, Smile Brands, incorporated under Smile Brands Group, Inc., that year, posted annual revenues of approximately $300 million. By the end of 2007, that number had reached $427.2 million. Smile Brands filed an initial public offering (IPO) registration statement with the U.S. Securities and Exchange Commission on April 29, 2009, to raise around $144 million in a public offering of more than seven million shares of common stock under the symbol "GRIN," with the initial offering price expected to be between $16.00 and $18.00. In April 2010 Smile Brands scaled back the size of its IPO to between $112 million and $125 million. However, Smile Brands canceled its IPO in May because the price per share of $14 was weaker than the company was willing to accept. In December 2010 Smile Brands sold majority interest to private equity investment firm Welsh, Carson, Anderson & Stowe. The deal left Freeman Spogli & Co., which had previously owned 77.3 percent of Smile Brands, a minority investor.

Having changed private equity firms as majority owners, Smile Brands was well poised to continue its consolidation of the dental management practices industry during the 2010s.

Alicia Elley

PRINCIPAL SUBSIDIARIES

ConsumerHealth, Inc.; Ivory Intermediate Co., Inc.; SB Holdings 1, Inc.; SB Holdings 2, Inc.; SB Holdings 3, Inc.; SB Holdings 4, Inc.; Smile Brands East, Inc.; Smile Brands, Inc.; Smile Brands of Abilene, L.P.; Smile Brands of Arkansas, Inc.; Smile Brands of Cleveland, Inc.; Smile Brands of Indiana, Inc.; Smile Brands of Midland/Odessa, L.P.; Smile Brands of Pennsylvania, Inc.; Smile Brands of Tennessee, Inc.; Smile Brands of Texas, L.P.; Smile Brands Southwest, Inc.; Smile Brands West, Inc.; Smile Now! Finance, Inc.

PRINCIPAL COMPETITORS

American Dental Partners, Inc.; Aspen Dental Management Inc.; InterDent Inc.; Pacific Dental Services; Western Dental Services Inc.

FURTHER READING

Darwin, Jennifer. "King of the Castle." *Houston Business Journal,* April 10, 1998.

Norman, Jan. "Majority Ownership of O.C. Firm Sold." *Orange County Register,* November 4, 2010. Accessed March 9, 2011. http://jan.ocregister.com/2010/11/04/majority-ownership-of-o-c-firm-sold/48696/.

Pema, Gabe. "Bright Now! Dental: Delivering Smiles for Everyone!" *Exec Digital,* January 30, 2009. Accessed March 9, 2011. http://www.execdigital.com/Bright-Now--Dental--Delivering-Smiles-for-Everyone-_15541.

Reed, Vita. "Bright Now's Dental Plan Yields $500M in Sales." *Orange County Business Journal,* March 12, 2007. Accessed March 9, 2011. http://www.ocbj.com/news/2007/mar/12/bright-nows-dental-plan-yields-500m-in-sales/.

———. "Profitable Dentist Group Set to Test Public Waters." *Orange County Business Journal,* January 4, 2010. Accessed March 9, 2011. http://www.ocbj.com/news/2010/jan/04/profitable-dental-group-set-test-public-waters/.

Schlegel, Darrin. "Houston-Based Dental Firm in Talks to Merge with Dallas Company." *Houston Chronicle,* September 20, 2002.

———. "Houston Dental Firm to Be Bought for $34.4 Million." *Houston Chronicle,* April 27, 2004.

Yu, Roger. "Monarch Dental Enjoys Clean Slate after Merger." *Dallas Morning News,* March 8, 2003.

Solyndra, Inc.

47488 Kato Road
Fremont, California 94538
U.S.A.
Telephone: (510) 440-2400
Toll Free: (877) 511-8436
Web site: http://www.solyndra.com

Private Company
Founded: 2005 as Gronet Technologies, Inc.
Employees: 1,050 (2011)
Revenues: Approximately $140 million (2010)
NAICS: 334413 Semiconductor and Related Device
Manufacturing

■ ■ ■

With offices in the United States, Germany, Italy, France, and Switzerland, Solyndra, Inc., is a global leader in rooftop solar technology. Combining proprietary cylindrical modules and thin-film technologies, Solyndra designs and manufactures photovoltaic panel systems that cost less to install and generate more electricity output than conventional solar panels. Solyndra's systems, which are wholly produced at the company's Fremont, California, factory, are mounted on commercial, industrial, and institutional rooftops. At the end of 2010, Solyndra had installed systems on over 1,000 rooftops in more than 20 countries.

PROPRIETARY DESIGN: 2005 TO 2007

Founded by Dr. Chris Gronet, who initially served as CEO, Solyndra was incorporated in May 2005 in

Delaware as Gronet Technologies, Inc. Renamed Solyndra, Inc., in January 2006, the company raised $79 million in venture capital funding in 2007, backed by Virgin Green Fund, Rockport Capital Partners, Madrone Capital Partners, and CMEA Ventures. Until early 2007 Solyndra's main focus was on the research and development of its photovoltaic systems and related manufacturing equipment and processes. Installation of equipment for high-volume production at the company's first manufacturing facility, known as Fab 1, commenced in 2007.

While several Silicon Valley companies made thin-film solar panels using CIGS, a semiconductor material composed of copper, indium, gallium, and selenium, Solyndra developed a technology unique to the industry. Instead of flat photovoltaic solar panels, the company's proprietary design consisted of cylindrical solar cells that collected solar energy from all directions. The cylindrical modules could absorb both direct and diffused sunlight, as well as sunlight that passed through the gaps between the solar cells and was reflected off white, or "cool," rooftops. Because this shape allowed the photovoltaic array to capture more light over the course of a day than traditional solar panels, more power was generated. Solyndra's cylindrical solar system was designed for flat, commercial rooftops, such as those found on warehouses, malls, and office buildings.

Conventional solar panels had to be bolted into rooftops or weighted down with heavy ballast. Mounted at an angle to gather as much sunlight as possible, these panels had to be rotated to follow the course of the sun throughout the day in order to obtain the best results. The flat-panel design was susceptible to wind damage from all directions, with some rooftops stressed to the breaking point from strong downward winds.

Solyndra's product avoided such problems. The company's photovoltaic array consisted of 40 tubes laid out a few inches apart and connected to a self-ballasting steel frame. Mounted horizontally, the panels could be installed close together, covering more roof area and producing more energy than traditional solar panels. In addition to facilitating a 360-degree collection of sunlight, the slat-like openings between each cylinder allowed for more advantageous operations in a variety of weather conditions. Since wind could blow through and around the tubes, most issues with air resistance were eliminated. Additionally, Solyndra's photovoltaic array experienced less energy loss due to snow, as the cylindrical modules, which would not be completely covered in snow as were flat panels, could capture reflected light from a snowfall. Solyndra's design also attracted less dirt, and moisture that landed on the modules helped clean the cylinders. According to the company, energy lost to soiling was around half of that for traditional flat panels.

SALES BEGIN: 2008

In the first and second quarters of 2008, Solyndra's photovoltaic systems were certified by the Canadian Standards Association, the International Electrotechnical Commission, and the VDE (Germany's Association for Electrical, Electronic and Information Technologies). In July 2008 Solyndra began low-volume commercial production and shipment of solar panels. This operation expanded into a full-scale, highly-automated production line at Fab 1, achieving a production rate of 7.8 megawatts (MW) by the end of the year. When Solyndra formally announced in October 2008 that it was entering the solar power market with its proprietary photovoltaic array, information about the new technology quickly spread within the solar power sector, and the company opened an office in Germany.

With the industry receptive to its design, Solyndra signed agreements with several companies, both within the United States and abroad, in 2008. In addition to a $325 million contract with Solar Power Inc. to deliver solar panels through 2012, Solyndra signed a $681 million deal with Phoenix Solar AG, Germany. In October Solyndra announced a $250 million contract with solar integrator GeckoLogic in Wetzlar, Germany. In December, Solyndra formed a strategic partnership with Carlisle Construction Materials that would allow Carlisle Construction Materials to offer Solyndra's proprietary cylindrical photovoltaic modules as part of a reflective membrane/PV roof system.

LOAN GUARANTEE: 2009

In March 2009 Solyndra became the first company to receive a loan guarantee offer from the U.S. Department of Energy under Title XVII of the Energy Policy Act of 2005, legislation that provided financial backing for innovative technologies that reduced emissions of greenhouse gases. With $535 million in federal funding, the company set out to expand its solar manufacturing capacity in Fremont, California, by building a manufacturing plant that would produce 300 MW of solar panels per year. That location would also house Solyndra's headquarters, as well as a customer demonstration center. Construction on the 300,000-square-foot facility, known as Fab 2, began in September.

The Fab 2 project was recognized by the Obama administration as part of the American Recovery and Reinvestment Act, which was enacted in February 2009 for the purpose of creating new jobs and saving existing ones, at the same time spurring economic activity. Along with creating approximately 3,000 on-site construction jobs, Fab 2 was expected to result in new jobs across the United States. In Arkansas, Pennsylvania, Washington, Wisconsin, and 18 other states, workers were hired to produce the building materials that were used in the construction of the Fremont facility. In Arizona, Colorado, Michigan, Tennessee, and eight other states, employees built the manufacturing equipment that was installed in the factory. Hundreds of other jobs would be created to carry out the installation of the finished solar panels once the facility began production.

After the loan guarantee announcement, Solyndra significantly increased its customer base. It signed a long-term sales contract worth $189 million with Sun-Connex B.V., a solar integrator based in Amsterdam, followed by another contract worth up to $238 million with Umwelt-Sonne-Energie GmbH in Holzgerlingen, Germany. Although Solyndra did conduct some business with U.S. companies (its products were used by Solar Power, Inc., to equip a Hazlet, New Jersey, Costco store with an air conditioning system run by solar power), the

KEY DATES

2005: Solyndra is incorporated by Dr. Christian Gronet.
2006: The company establishes headquarters in Fremont, California.
2007: Solyndra begins the installation of manufacturing equipment at its first high-volume production factory, known as Fab 1.
2008: The company officially announces its entry in the solar power market.
2009: Solyndra receives a $535 million loan guarantee from the U.S. Department of Energy.
2009: The company files an IPO registration statement.
2010: Solyndra surpasses 1,000 installations around the world.
2011: Construction is completed on Fab 2.

majority of its dealings were with foreign customers. In 2009 over 85 percent of all Solyndra's sales were to customers located in Europe, where local government incentives for solar products were prevalent.

Solyndra had received a Prism Award for Photonics Innovations and was named the winner in the Emerging Tech Green/Clean Technology category by the *San Jose Business Journal* in 2008. The year 2009 brought additional honors for the company. It received a 2009 Excellence in Renewable Energy Award from *Renewable Energy World Magazine.* In addition, Solyndra was named to the Global Cleantech 100, a list recognizing leading innovators in cleantech technology.

FINANCIAL DIFFICULTY: 2010

In 2010 it became evident that Solyndra was facing financial difficulties. Even after raising $1 billion in venture capital and receiving money from the Department of Energy, the company had yet to show a profit. It had lost $558 million since its inception. At the close of 2009, Solyndra had filed an initial public offering (IPO) registration statement with the U.S. Securities and Exchange Commission, seeking to raise $300 million from the sale of its common stock. Critics soon accused the company of squandering the federal funding it had been given. Some industry analysts blamed Chinese producers for driving down the price of solar panels. Others, however, had reservations about whether Solyndra would ever expand beyond a niche market.

Although Solyndra's cylindrical photovoltaic system was less expensive to install than conventional flat panels, the cylinders were more expensive to produce, making the overall price of Solyndra's product less competitive in comparison to those of other players in the solar power market. Manufacturing costs in China, for example, ranged from $1.10 to $1.20 per watt, while Arizona-based First Solar, a leader in thin-film panel technology, weighed in at 75 cents per watt. Solyndra's manufacturing costs at the time were approximately $3.00 per watt.

After a March audit conducted by Pricewaterhouse-Coopers raised questions about Solyndra's financial viability, the company cancelled plans for an IPO in June, citing adverse market conditions. In lieu of offering common stock, the company announced that it had raised $175 million from the sale of promissory notes to existing investors. In July Gronet was replaced as CEO by Brian Harrison, whose first major moves were to shut down Fab 1, consolidate manufacturing at Fab 2, cancel the company's plans to add 1,000 jobs, and scale back total production by half to 300 MW per year. Amid all of these changes, Solyndra's executive board remained confident that the company could increase sales, adjust expenditures, and reduce manufacturing costs.

Despite its financial problems, Solyndra continued to have a presence in the solar power market in 2010. The company earned ISO 9001: 2008 certification, an internationally recognized standard for quality management systems. In keeping with ISO 9001: 2008 specifications, Solyndra was required to demonstrate its ability to provide a product that consistently met both customer demands and regulatory mandates. Furthermore, the company had to commit to the continual improvement of its products.

As of July 2010 the company had produced 16 million modules and shipped 65 MW all over the globe. Besides completing its largest project in Europe, a 3 MW operation in Belgium, Solyndra undertook its largest U.S. installation, a 1 MW project for Frito Lay. By the end of the year, Solyndra had exceeded 1,000 installations around the world. One of these projects, a 2030-panel 370Wp rooftop solar system on an architectural landmark in the Piedmont region of Italy, was nominated as one of the best Italian rooftop PV installations for 2010. Solyndra was also named to the 2010 *Wall Street Journal* "Top 10 Venture-backed Clean-Tech Companies" and included in MIT's *Technology Review* magazine's list of the "50 Most Innovative Companies in the World," proving that the solar energy industry remained interested in Solyndra's proprietary technology.

FUTURE PLANS: 2011 AND BEYOND

From the time it was founded, Solyndra operated in quiet mode and otherwise attempted to keep a low public profile. Under Harrison's leadership, however, the company increased its visibility in 2011 by presenting at trade shows and granting interviews to journalists. Sales and marketing staffs were expanded, and Harrison himself made a point of being more accessible to both customers and company employees.

In February Solyndra announced that it was experimenting with a new application for its cylindrical modules in Italy. By installing the company's solar panels on agricultural shade structures and greenhouses, growers were able to generate electricity while supporting existing agricultural operations. Solyndra's panels could be integrated onto the roof of a greenhouse or shade structure, capturing solar energy while providing shade and supporting plant growth.

The company reached a milestone when construction on Fab 2 was completed in February 2011. The building included a 1.23 MW rooftop cylindrical solar system that provided a portion of the building's power. Full installation of production equipment was expected to be finished by the end of that year, with production capacity reaching 300 MW in 2012. Solyndra executives predicted that the new facility would enable the company to manufacture products at a cost of approximately $2.00 per watt by the first quarter of 2013. It seemed likely that Solyndra's ability to meet these cost per watt goals would factor greatly in its long-term viability.

Alicia Elley

PRINCIPAL SUBSIDIARIES

Solyndra Fab 2 LLC; Solyndra Operator LLC.

PRINCIPAL COMPETITORS

First Solar, Inc.; Global Solar Energy, Inc.; HelioVolt Corp.; Nanosolar, Inc.; OptiSolar Inc.; SCHOTT AG.

FURTHER READING

"Cylindrical-Shaped Photovoltaics Harness Sunlight from Every Direction." *Building Design & Construction,* December 2008. Accessed March 20, 2011. http://www.bdcnetwork. com/product/cylindrical-shaped-photovoltaics-harness-sun light-every-direction.

Hull, Dana. "Fremont's High-Flying Solyndra Hits a Rough Patch." *MercuryNews.com,* January 30, 2011. Accessed March 20, 2011. http://www.mercurynews.com/business/ci_17221170?nclick_check=1.

Rae-Dupree, Janet. "Solyndra's Technology Is Ahead of the Curve," *San Jose Business Journal,* December 7, 2008.

"Solyndra Breaks Ground on New 500 MW Solar Plant." *Space Daily,* September 13, 2009.

"Solyndra Cylindrical Modules Offer Greenhouse Energy Generation Solution." *Wireless News,* February 25, 2011.

"Solyndra Enhances Architectural Landmark in Italy." *Space Daily,* December 7, 2010.

"Solyndra to Close Factor, Slash Production Goal," *SustainableBusiness.com,* November 4, 2010. Accessed March 20, 2011. http://www.sustainablebusiness.com/index.cfm/go/news.display/id/21355.

"Tubular Sunshine." *Economist,* October 11, 2008, 110.

Yang, Tony C. "Solar Company Solyndra Plans Expansion in Fremont." *San Jose Business Journal,* October 5, 2008.

Sonangol E.P.

—■—

Rua Rinha Ginga, Number 22
Caixa Postal 1316
Luanda,
Angola
Telephone: (244) 226 643967
Fax: (244) 332 578
Web site: http://www.sonangol.co.ao

State-Owned Company
Founded: 1976
Sales: $22.4 billion (2009)
NAICS: 211111 Crude Petroleum and Natural Gas Extraction; 213112 Support Activities for Oil and Gas Operations

■ ■ ■

The largest public company in Angola, Sonangol E.P. undertakes exploration, production, refinery, marketing, and distribution of all state-controlled hydrocarbon resources in Angola. The company principally operates as an upstream company by serving as the concessionaire of hydrocarbon exploration in Angola, but it also participates in downstream activities that include production, marketing, and distribution of oil and its derivatives. The company has further diversified its service and production portfolio through the establishment of multiple subsidiaries that deal in air transport, maritime transport, professional training, telecommunications, and retailing industries.

Headquartered in the country's capitol, Sonangol E.P.'s operations and strategies are principally driven by the core objective of achieving sustainable social development of Angola. The company, however, remains a major business force despite its socially oriented founding objectives. Sonangol achieved an estimated daily oil production of 3 million barrels (3 million bpd) in 2010, a capacity that makes Angola the second-largest oil producer in sub-Saharan Africa (after Nigeria). The company concessions both offshore and land-based oil mining fields according to confirmed oil deposits blocks. Block 0, an oil block leased to Chevron Texaco until 2030, remains the most profitable oil block in Angola. Blocks 15 and 17 remain the most productive oil blocks, accounting for more than 50 percent of oil production in Angola.

Sonangol E.P. boasts an international presence in the United States (Houston), Europe (London), Asia (Singapore), and Africa (Brazzaville, Congo).

COMPANY FOUNDING AND EARLY YEARS: 1976–79

The founding of some major corporate institutions in Angola was associated with the country's deep economic ties with Portugal both before and after independence from the European country. Many Portuguese companies established subsidiaries in Angola as they expanded their sources of raw materials and markets for their finished products. SACOR was one such Portugal-based company that established its commercial presence in Angola in 1953 when it founded the *ANGOL Sociedede de Lubrificantes e Combustíveis Sarl* (ANGOL) in the Angolan capital of Luanda. ANGOL operated as SACOR's privately owned subsidiary for marketing and distributing energy fuels, lubricating products, and liquefied gas throughout Angola.

In the years leading to Angola's independence, a strategically poised working group consisting of the indigenous business community and other experts was formed to support and fast-track the transformation of the country's oil industry in preparation for independence. The economic landscape in Angola was finally transformed in 1975 after the country attained political independence from Portugal. The country's first African-led government began to implement economic nationalization policies immediately after independence. ANGOL was nationalized by the Angolan government in 1976 and split into two independent, state-owned entities, the *Direcção Nacional de Petroleós* and Sonangol U.E.E.

The mandate of Sonangol U.E.E. was narrowed down to the exploration of hydrocarbon resources while *Direcção Nacional de Petroleós* remained with the oil marketing and distribution task. The working group that was formed during the preindependence period to support the oil industry was transformed into a management committee before its subsequent transformation into the board of directors of the newly formed state corporation. The company was structurally transformed in accordance with the company's articles of incorporation and other regulations that govern the operation of state corporations in Angola.

Civil war had erupted in Angola immediately after independence in 1975. As such, the combination of state-sponsored nationalization programs and a bloody civil war made the country unattractive to many foreign and private investors, leading to an exodus of major multinational corporations. Between 1976 and 1978 Sonangol U.E.E. embarked on an expansion spree by purchasing the business assets of oil exploration companies that left the country, including Texaco, Shell, and Fina. The company further entered into an agreement with Mobil for the acquisition of Mobil's business assets and interests in Angola. In the meantime, the company contracted Marc Rich & Company to provide oil trading agency services for steering its crude oil and associated derivatives business.

The Council of Ministers in Angola ratified a hydrocarbon law in 1978 that effectively expanded the mandate of Sonangol U.E.E. into Angola's sole hydrocarbon exploration and production concessionaire. Sonangol U.E.E., however, experienced challenges over its future human resources capabilities as the oil industry experienced a shortage of specialized employees. In the mid-1970s, the company crafted and began implementing a training program targeted at sponsoring students for specialized training in different disciplines relevant to oil industry operations. This first batch of students was dispatched to Italy under the cosponsorship of Sonangol U.E.E. and ENI-Italian Oil Group. A second and larger group of trainees was dispatched to Algeria. The first group of trainees began returning home in 1979 after completing their studies in Italy, and more and more trainees were sent abroad.

EXPANSION OVERSEAS: 1983–98

Sonangol U.E.E. opened its first trading office in London in 1983 as its oil trading agency contract with Marc Rich & Company came to a close. Incorporated in London as Sonangol Limited, the trading office was Sonangol U.E.E.'s first international subsidiary. Sonangol Limited assumed all the functions that were previously undertaken by Marc Rich & Company that included trading of oil and its derivatives in the international markets.

Sonangol U.E.E. sanctioned its first deep sea oil concession to Chevron Texaco in 1991. The concession for deep sea oil exploration and production was located in block 16 and was leased to Chevron Texaco. Sonangol U.E.E. continued to operate as the principal exclusive lease concessionaire in Angola until 1992, when it made entry into oil exploration and production activities through the establishment of the Pesquisa & Produção (P&P) subsidiary. As a lease concessionaire, the company's activities had previously been limited to regulating and granting exploration and production rights to foreign companies. The establishment of P&P was therefore a significant step toward optimizing the company's revenue generation through active participation in oil exploration and production both in the mainland and offshore.

Sonangol E.P. began enhancing its corporate social responsibility (CSR) programs in the early 1990s as the company forged closer ties with the community as one of its key stakeholders. The company collaborated with the Angolan Writers Union in instituting the Sonangol

```
┌─────────────────────────────────────────────┐
│                                               │
│              KEY DATES                        │
│                    ━                          │
│  ─────────────────────────────────────────    │
│                                               │
│  1976:  Sonangol U.E.E. is established.        │
│  1983:  Company opens first international trading │
│         subsidiary.                           │
│  1999:  Sonangol E.P. is incorporated.         │
│  2003:  Sonangol launches first oil production │
│         operations.                           │
│  2008:  Sonangol E.P. restructures shareholding in │
│         subsidiaries.                         │
│  2009:  Company publishes audited annual financial │
│         statements for the first time.        │
│                                               │
└─────────────────────────────────────────────┘
```

Literature Award in 1992. The first winner of the prestigious literary award was honored with monetary prizes in addition to career development and media-supported exposure of literary works. The distinctive annual award was targeted at encouraging continuous literary development in Angola.

The company continued to expand its international markets through the mid-1990s and incorporated its second international office, Sonangol USA Company (SONUSA) in Houston, Texas, in 1997. The company also acquired a shareholding stake in Empresa Nacional de Combustíveis SARL (ENACOL) in Cape Verde in 1997. ENACOL specifically marketed oil derivatives in Cape Verde and internationally.

Sonangol also extended its expansion strategies in the African continent in 1998, a mission that was enhanced with the opening of the Sonangol Congo subsidiary in Brazzaville. The Sonangol Congo subsidiary was established to specialize in downstream activities in Congo, including marketing, storing, and transporting oil as well as importing processed oil products.

INCORPORATION AND FURTHER EXPANSION: 1999–2002

The Law of Public Companies that was introduced by the Angolan government in 1999 necessitated the legal and structural review of Sonangol U.E.E. in accordance with the provisions of the new laws. The changes involved the incorporation of Sonangol E.P. on August 20, 1999, through the transformation of Sonangol U.E.E. from the status of a state department into the status of an E.P. (public company). Angola's Council of Ministers appointed Manuel Vicente to be chairman and CEO of the newly transformed company.

Sonangol E.P. 's management was also transformed when the Administration Council was established to manage its operations in three-year term limits. Angola's new discoveries of oil deposits had risen to 1.3 billion barrels by the end of 1999, a development that placed the country as the third-leading country worldwide in new discoveries of oil. Sonasing Kuito, a subsidiary for export, crude oil preparation, and storage, was established in 1999 through a joint venture deal with Single Buoy Moorings Ltd.

The company embarked on the enhancement of its CSR approaches in 2000, as demonstrated by the establishment of Cooperativa Cajueiro, Sociedad Cooperativa de responsabilidade Limitada, an organization that was mandated to manage a welfare program affordable to the company's employees. The establishment of the employee welfare and housing unit was preceded by the formation of a social project committee that supervised the housing complexes for its employees.

The dawn of the 21st century marked a new phase in the expansion of Sonangol's upstream and downstream activities as well as expansion into service provision industries both in Angola and internationally. The first deep sea oil field in Angola began production operations in Kuito in January 2001. The deep sea oil field located at block 16 came into operation under a joint venture between Sonangol and Chevron Texaco. The company established AAA, an insurance services subsidiary, in January 2001. The head office of AAA was based in Luanda from where it was mandated to manage the group's risks in the oil industry, provide brokerage services for insurance products, and manage pension funds.

In 2002 Angola achieved peace for the first time since independence when the chief architect and leader of the UNITA-fronted civil war, Jonas Savimbi, was killed in his hideout in a remote part of the country. The other members of Savimbi's revolutionary movement accepted a political amnesty that was offered by the Angolan government and surrendered. Peace initiatives were conducted and the former rebels were gradually absorbed into the different state organs and institutions. The achievement of peace in Angola marked a very important event in the history of the country because mineral exploration activities were extended to the former strongholds of the rebels that had substantial oil and diamond deposits.

INCREASED OPERATIONS AND TRANSPARENCY: 2003–08

In 2003 the company began offshore oil production in shallow waters in block 3 with a daily capacity of 12,000 barrels. The company subsequently launched deep sea oil exploration in block 34. These developments illustrated the metamorphosis of Sonangol E.P. from a purely concessionary entity to both an upstream and downstream oil production entity in Angola's oil industry.

The government of Angola began to implement transparency and accountability procedures in all state-owned corporations in the country through the guidance of the International Monetary Fund (IMF). Sonangol's accounts were audited for the first tome in 2003 when the government hired Ernst & Young to undertake annual audits of the company's accounts. The development was hailed as a first step in the right direction, although the government did not publish the audited accounts. Sonangol achieved an oil production capacity of 965,000 bpd in 2003, statistics that indicated accelerated production rates following the achievement of peace throughout the country.

Sonangol made an entry into Asia in January 2004 when the company's Sonasia subsidiary was opened in Singapore. Sonasia was principally mandated to undertake oil exploration, marketing, and distribution activities in Singapore. The government, through the Ministry of Finance, began publishing oil production statistics for each oil block on the government Web site in 2004. In May 2004 the government announced that Chevron had paid a total of $290 million to Sonangol for the signing and social bonuses for extending Chevron's Block 0 concession until 2030. This was confirmation of the government's commitment to embracing transparency and accountability. It was the first time the Angolan government had made such disclosures.

The company enhanced its presence in Asia by establishing the China Sonangol International Holding (CSIH) in Hong Kong in June 2004. The activities of CSHI were focused on investment in mineral and oil as well as well as crude oil trading throughout Hong Kong and mainland China. The company also established the Sonangol SGPS subsidiary in 2004 to complement P&P's activities through the provision of specialized drilling services. Sonangol further expanded its operations in Europe in 2005 by establishing Stena Sonangol through a partnership with Stana, a Swedish tanker operator. The partnership effectively increased the company's distribution capacity in European markets.

In 2006 Sonangol made public the winning bids for oil blocks concession licensing as part of Sonangol's continued commitment to transparency. Sonangol reviewed some of its CSR programs in 2006 and introduced amendments that included giving the Sonangol Literary Award once every five years rather than annually. The geographical scope of the award was expanded to include writers from all Portuguese-speaking countries in the African continent.

In 2008 Angola earned 97.7 percent of its exports from petroleum after raising revenues in excess of $62 billion from the petroleum industry. The impressive statistics demonstrated the continued significance of Sonangol E.P. to Angola's economy.

The IMF placed pressure on Sonangol to begin publishing its audited financial results because of concerns over improprieties in the management of the company's financial resources. The first Oil Diagnostic Study's revelation of a $2.1 billion underpayment of Sonangol's funds to the Central Bank of Angola increased concerns over accountability of the company. The increased pressure for accountability prompted Sonangol to commit to an IMF-sponsored arrangement to begin publishing its audited financial results in 2008. The IMF agreed to disburse tranches of its Stand-By Arrangement loan to Angola only on condition that the government publish the 2008 audited financial reports for Sonangol.

FINANCIAL STATEMENTS AND EXPANSION: 2009 AND BEYOND

The delayed publication of Sonangol's 2008 financial results was a major achievement in the government's commitment to economic transparency through financial disclosures in public corporations. The 2008 annual financial results reported a 55 percent growth in the company's revenue from $17.3 billion in 2007 to 26.8 billion in 2008. Sonangol E.P.'s unpublished financial report for the 2009 financial year indicated that the company experienced a 16 percent drop in its revenues to 22.4 billion in 2009. The company's reduced production output was attributed to the adverse effects of the global economic recession.

In January 2010 Sonangol announced its plans to invest $1 billion in Brazilian oil exploration projects. The expansion program involved the acquisition of shareholding in Starfish, a Brazilian company specializing in oil production and exploration. The company announced another successful deal with the Ministry of Oil in Iraq on January 26, 2010. The deal secured Sonangol the licensing rights for oil production in two oil fields in northern Iraq. The deal was a major achievement in the company's expansion strategies, given the high volume of oil deposits in Iraq.

Sonangol E.P. continued to pursue expansion strategies through acquisitions, partnerships, and joint ventures in order to continue achieving sustained growth. Continued diversification into other industries remained at the core of the company's future plans.

Paul Ingati

PRINCIPAL SUBSIDIARIES

China Sonangol International Holdings (China); ENA-COL (Cape Verde); MSTelcom; SonAir; Sonangol Congo; Sonangol Shipping; Sonasia.

PRINCIPAL COMPETITORS

Angola Telecom; Cabinda Gulf Oil Ltd; Secil Marítima.

FURTHER READING

Campos, Indira, and Alex Vines. "Angola and China: A Pragmatic Partnership." Working Paper Presented at the CSIS Conference, "Prospects for Improving U.S.-China-Africa Cooperation," December 5, 2007. Washington, DC: Center for Strategic and International Studies, March 2008. Accessed November 26, 2010. http://csis.org/files/media/csis/pubs/080306_angolachina.pdf.

Human Rights Watch. "Transparency and Accountability in Angola: Reforms since 2004." April 13, 2010. Accessed November 26, 2010. http://www.hrw.org/en/node/89454/section/3.

Leigh, Lamin, Yuan Xiao, and Nir Klein. "IMF Lends Angola $1.4 Billion to Support Reserves, Reforms." *IMF Survey Magazine,* November 23, 2009. Accessed November 27, 2010. http://www.imf.org/external/pubs/ft/survey/so/2009/car112309b.htm.

Morias, Rafael Marques de. "Manuel Vicente's Raid on Sonangol." Maka–Anti-Corruption Watchdog, May 5, 2010. Accessed November 26, 2010. http://allafrica.com/stories/201005050596.html.

"Our House: Angola's Pavilion at Expo in Shanghai Is Proving to Be a Big Draw." *Universo,* September 2010. Accessed November 27, 2010. http://www.sonangol.co.ao/wps/wcm/connect/f7a7220044065e08b75bf7f058c402b9/SU27-web.pdf?MOD=AJPERES.

Perry, Alex. "Africa's Oil Dreams." *Time,* May 31, 2007. Accessed November 27, 2010. http://www.time.com/time/magazine/article/0,9171,1626751-2,00.html.

"Sonangol Becomes Superleague Formula Title Sponsor for 2009 and 2010 Seasons." Sport Convergence, July 13, 2010. Accessed February 9, 2011. http://www.sportconvergence.fr/en/news/sonangol_becomes_superleague_formula_title_sponsor_for_2009_and_2010_seasons/1359.html.

"Sonangol Clinches Deals for Iraqi Oil Fields." *Rigzone,* January 26, 2010. Accessed November 26. 2010. http://www.rigzone.com/news/article.asp?a_id=86419.

"Sonangol Plans $1bn Brazil Spend." upstreamonline.com, January 20, 2010. Accessed November 26, 2010. http://www.upstreamonline.com/live/article204049.ece.

Southern Company

———————— ◼ ————————

30 Ivan Allen Jr. Boulevard, N.W.
Atlanta, Georgia 30308
U.S.A.
Telephone: (404) 506-5000
Fax: (404) 506-0455
Web site: http://www. southerncompany.com

Public Company
Incorporated: 1947
Employees: 26,112 (2009)
Sales: $15.74 billion (2009)
Stock Exchanges: New York
Ticker Symbol: SO
NAICS: 221111 Hydroelectric Power Generation; 221112 Fossil Fuel Electric Power Generation; 221113 Nuclear Electric Power Generation; 221119 Other Electric Power Generation; 221121 Electric Bulk Power Transmission and Control; 221122 Electric Power Distribution

■ ■ ■

Southern Company is a utility holding company whose principal subsidiaries provide power in Alabama, Georgia, Florida, and Mississippi. Roughly 4.4 million U.S. customers receive electricity from subsidiaries Alabama Power, Georgia Power, Gulf Power, and Mississippi Power. In addition to its core electrical generation and distribution operations, Southern Company also sells electricity in the wholesale market via its Southern Power subsidiary, while subsidiary SouthernLINC Wireless provides digital wireless communications to about 215,000 customers. Southern also operates three nuclear plants and is a fiber-optic cable wholesaler.

SOUTHERN POWER ENTREPRENEURS

Southern Company traces its roots to a group of entrepreneurs in Alabama and Georgia. Alabama's early power industry was led by James Mitchell and Thomas Martin. Mitchell worked for the Thomson-Houston Company, a predecessor of General Electric, and later built power plants and railroads in Brazil. After leaving Brazil he met with the United Kingdom's financial community and then came to the southern United States, where he scouted sights for hydroelectric installations. Eventually he decided to build a dam on the Cherokee Bluffs site along Alabama's Tallapoosa River.

Seeking to acquire the necessary land, in November 1911 Mitchell met Thomas Martin of Tyson, Wilson & Martin, a law firm handling the title work for hydroelectric developers along the Tallapoosa. Mitchell's technical expertise and access to U.K. capital meshed with Martin's legal training and local knowledge, and the two decided to join forces.

After the Cherokee Bluffs site became embroiled in a lawsuit brought by the owner of a waterwheel plant nearby, Mitchell and Martin turned to a site on the Coosa River at Gadsden, Alabama. The Gadsden site was owned by William P. Lay, who in 1906 had organized the Alabama Power Company to dam the river. Lay had been unable to secure capital and readily agreed to join with Mitchell and Martin on the project.

COMPANY PERSPECTIVES

In addition to providing affordable and reliable electricity, Southern Company works to reduce its environmental impact, invest in our personnel, and be stewards of the community.

Others also were planning hydroelectric projects along the Coosa and Tallapoosa Rivers. To prevent ruinous competition, Mitchell and 14 investor groups joined in the Alabama Traction, Light and Power Company, Ltd., a holding company organized in Canada to attract U.K. investment. Through Alabama Traction, Light and Power Mitchell raised British capital for Lay's dam. Built by engineer Eugene Adams Yates, Lay Dam was completed in 1914.

At this time Alabama Traction, Light and Power also was acquiring small hydroelectric power companies already in existence. During 1912 and 1913 it bought a 10,000-kilowatt steam electric plant in Gadsden, Alabama, and a 2,000-kilowatt hydroelectric plant at Jackson Shoals, Alabama. By 1913 the company was supplying electricity to Talladega and Gadsden.

Alabama Power Company, the operating subsidiary of Alabama Traction, Light and Power, expanded rapidly, but World War I depleted British capital and left Alabama Power overextended. Unable to meet his obligations Mitchell went to the United Kingdom and convinced bondholders to defer interest payments and authorize the sale of new bonds and preferred stock.

James Mitchell died in 1920 and was replaced as president by his lawyer partner Tom Martin. Martin helped Alabama Power grow by buying up small electric systems, sponsoring industrial development, and pushing rural electrification. He remained a force in the southern power industry through the 1950s.

ENTERING THE HYDROELECTRIC FIELD

Georgia's first hydroelectric project was built by S. Morgan Smith. In the 1870s Smith had invented a water turbine that won wide acceptance in Pennsylvania grist mills. Later he adapted his turbine to hydroelectric purposes and built a facility for clients at Appleton, Wisconsin. Around 1900 he began looking for a major city where he could build his own facility. Eventually he organized the Atlanta Water & Electric Power Company and dammed up the Chattahoochee River 17 miles north of Atlanta.

Smith died in 1903, so his sons Elmer and Fahs finished the dam, ran the S. Morgan Smith Company, and took over the Atlanta Water & Electric Power Company. They expanded the operation, built new plants, and sold turbines to other power projects, often taking an equity share in the new ventures as payment for their product.

Another person working on hydroelectric power in Georgia was A. J. Warner. Warner and investors formed the North Georgia Electric Company and built a dam, transmission lines, and an office building in the Atlanta area.

Soon after completing the dam the company fell on economic hard times. To strengthen cash flow, Warner worked out a deal with Elmer Smith in which Smith would buy Warner's electricity and sell it in Atlanta through the newly organized Atlanta Power Company. Despite the new business Warner's situation continued to worsen, and in 1910 Fahs Smith bought North Georgia Electric at a foreclosure sale.

Harry Atkinson, a young banker, also was active in the electric power industry in Georgia. In 1883 the Georgia Electric Light Company of Atlanta had received a franchise to supply the city. Georgia Electric Light of Atlanta got off to a poor start and became heavily indebted to the Thomson-Houston Company. In 1891 Atkinson and a group of Boston financiers gained control of the company and reorganized as the Georgia Electric Light Company.

Despite Atkinson's failures in sidelines such as shipping and railroads, Georgia Electric Light grew. With attorney Jack Spalding, Atkinson conducted a series of acquisitions, mergers, and consolidations. In 1912 he gathered a variety of Georgia utilities, including the Smith brothers' North Georgia Electric, into the Georgia Railway and Power Company. Most of the leading lights of the Georgia power industry sat on Georgia Railway and Power's board, and the company was the natural predecessor of Atkinson's Georgia Power Company, which in 1927 consolidated most of the state's remaining electric power companies.

Steps toward the union of Alabama and Georgia Power began in 1924 when Tom Martin and Eugene Yates created Southeastern Power & Light Company, a holding company whose purpose was to amalgamate and integrate utilities throughout the state. Southeastern's first acquisition was Alabama Power, then owned by Alabama Traction, Light and Power of Canada. In 1925 Martin began negotiations with Georgia Railway and Power. A union seemed advantageous for both companies. The Georgia company needed new capital and supplementary power for dry seasons when rivers ran low. Southeastern was seeking

KEY DATES

1912: Harry Atkinson forms Georgia Railway and Power Company.

1914: Construction of Lay Dam at Gadsden, Alabama, is completed.

1926: Southeastern Power and Light acquires Georgia Railway and Power Company.

1947: Securities and Exchange Commission approves the creation of Southern Company.

1982: Southern Energy is formed.

1998: Southern Energy joins Vastar to form Southern Company Energy Marketing.

1999: Environmental Protection Agency files civil action suit against Southern Company.

2000: Southern Company participates in the Alabama Direct Fuel Cell Demonstration Project.

2001: Southern Company spins off its international operations.

2004: Southern Company becomes involved in a lawsuit regarding carbon dioxide emissions.

2010: Southern Company and Ted Turner announce plans to build a solar photovoltaic power plant.

new markets. In 1926 Southeastern acquired all the common stock of Georgia Railway and Power, which subsequently became Georgia Power Company.

Southeastern also acquired smaller utilities. In 1926 it bought properties in Augusta, Columbus, Macon, and Rome, Georgia, and amalgamated them into Georgia Power. The same year it acquired disparate electric properties in South Carolina, northwest Florida, and eastern Mississippi. The South Carolina properties became the South Carolina Power Company, the Florida operations became the Gulf Power Company, and the Mississippi properties became the Mississippi Power Company.

Martin's general manager, Yates, led the move toward technical interconnection. Southeastern also set up a wholesale power division to help convert factories from steam to electric power. Among early industrial converts were textile mills and coal mines.

GROWTH AND EXPANSION

The late 1920s saw electrical consolidation on a national scale. In 1929 a New York holding company called

Commonwealth & Southern acquired all of Southeastern Power and Light's utilities. Commonwealth & Southern's chairman was a merger and acquisitions man named B. C. Cobb. In addition to the Southeastern properties, Commonwealth & Southern had a variety of midwestern utilities and one other southern one, the Tennessee Electric Power Company, whose service area was contiguous to Southeastern's.

With the acquisition, Southeastern's president, Tom Martin, became president of Commonwealth & Southern. Cobb and Martin did not get along, nor at least initially did the northern and southern subsidiaries of Commonwealth & Southern. Within two years, Martin returned to the presidency of Alabama Power.

In 1932 Cobb retired and was replaced by Wendell Willkie. Willkie had been the company's general counsel and would later run for president of the United States. The Great Depression had caused a drop in industrial production and thus a drop in industrial consumption of electricity. Willkie needed to increase consumption and cut costs. To increase consumption, he pushed the sale of electric appliances. To reduce costs, he made draconian cuts in wages and personnel. Despite his efforts, the company lost money in the mid-1930s.

Willkie also had to face the Tennessee Valley Authority (TVA) and the Public Utility Holding Company Act of 1935, both of which threatened Commonwealth & Southern. In 1933 Congress created the TVA, chartered to develop surplus power from navigation and flood control dams. The TVA competed directly with the southern subsidiaries of Commonwealth & Southern. These subsidiaries and other utilities sued to question the TVA's constitutionality but lost. Commonwealth & Southern sold Tennessee Electric Power to the TVA for $78 million in 1939, and in 1940 it sold sections of Alabama Power, Georgia Power, and Mississippi Power to the authority.

The Public Utility Holding Company Act of 1935 was written in response to the abuses of utility financiers such as Samuel Insull and Howard Hopson. The act permitted only contiguous and integrated systems and thus called for divestiture of some of Commonwealth & Southern's subsidiaries. Court challenges, negotiations, and World War II delayed dissolution until 1947, when the Securities and Exchange Commission (SEC) approved the creation of Southern Company, comprising Alabama Power, Georgia Power, Mississippi Power, and Gulf Power. The company had to sell South Carolina Power to South Carolina Electric & Gas Company.

Southern Company's first president was Eugene A. Yates, former general manager of Southeastern Power & Light. Tom Martin, still a power in the organization, backed him.

Southern Company lacked certain facilities. Among Yates's first acts was the creation of Southern Company Services, which ran power pooling operations, provided engineering for major projects, furnished pension and insurance services, and contributed staff services such as accounting and internal auditing. First owned jointly by the four operating subsidiaries, Southern Company Services became a directly owned subsidiary in 1963. Other housekeeping chores Yates was faced with included the sale of gas and transportation businesses, as required by the SEC.

The postwar years saw an increase in demand for power and a consequent increase in the need for capital. Southern made its first sale of common stock (1.5 million shares) in December 1949.

In 1950 Southern Company acquired Birmingham Electric Company (BECO), which had long been pursued by Tom Martin. BECO's owner, the Electric Bond & Share Company of New York, put it up for sale in 1950 after the SEC ordered Electric Bond & Share to divest its holdings.

Also in 1950 Yates became chairman of Southern Company, and Eugene McManus, president of Georgia Power, was promoted to president of the holding company. McManus gained nationwide attention for taking a new, friendlier approach in government-utility relations. He offered to supply municipalities and rural electric cooperatives at cost, and he ended opposition to government hydroelectric projects.

In the mid-1950s Southern Company became involved in a conflict-of-interest controversy. The Eisenhower administration had challenged the industry to provide 600,000 kilowatts for the Atomic Energy Commission's (AEC) southern installation. Southern Company and Middle South Utilities proposed a plant that would sell electricity to the TVA, which in turn would sell it to the AEC. The Southern Company-Middle South venture won the contract but was dropped after it was discovered that a First Boston Corporation investment banker, working temporarily with the Bureau of the Budget, also had advised the utilities. In the end, the city of Memphis, Tennessee, built a municipal power plant to take up the load.

CAPITAL CONSTRUCTION

The late 1950s marked the beginning of a dramatic period of capital construction. In 1956 the company organized Southern Electric Generating Company (SEGCO), as a cooperative venture between Georgia Power and Alabama Power. With no coal deposits of its own, Georgia Power wanted a power plant in Alabama where it could be close to the source of energy and not

pay rail costs. Alabama Power was attracted by economies of scale. Built on the Coosa River near Wilsonville, Alabama, and completed in 1962, the plant consisted of four 250,000-kilowatt units as well as two fully mechanized coal mines.

At the same time that SEGCO was gearing up, Tom Martin of Alabama Power was pushing for a series of dams on Alabama's Coosa and Warrior Rivers. The extensive project, which eventually provided 852,525 kilowatts of energy, took 10 years and $245 million to build.

In January 1957 McManus left the presidency and was elected vice chairman. Harllee Branch, president of Georgia Power, became president of Southern Company. When Yates died in October 1957, McManus became chairman of the board. Branch's tenure was a long and satisfying one. As president and, later, chairman he served until June 1971. In Branch's first year, Georgia Power paid $11 million to acquire Georgia Power and Light, which served 38,000 customers in southern Georgia.

The 1960s were a time of construction, expansion, and profits. Sales, income, and dividends all increased yearly. Between 1960 and 1969 sales rose from $317 million to $666 million, net income went from $46 million to $94 million, and dividends rose from 70 cents to $1.15 per share.

By the late 1960s Southern Company was showing the fruits of its huge building campaign. In 1969 it had 21 steam-electric plants and 30 hydroelectric power projects. Of the system's capacity, 81 percent came from steam-electric plants and 19 percent from hydroelectric dams. Overall, 31 percent of capacity had been constructed in the previous five years. The late 1960s also marked the beginning of a nuclear construction program.

In 1969 Harllee Branch, who had been president and chairman, retired as president in favor of Alvin W. Vogtle, Jr. The following year Vogtle became chief executive officer in anticipation of Branch's retirement as chairman.

The energy crisis of the early 1970s left Southern Company virtually unscathed. At that point 84 percent of its electricity was generated by coal-fueled steam-electric plants, and only 7.5 percent of the system's energy came from oil or natural gas.

Two concerns the company did have at this point were cleanliness of coal in an increasingly environmentally conscious nation and the availability of capital at a time when the company was spending more than $1 billion annually on construction. In the late 1970s a series of rate disputes between Southern's subsidiary Alabama Power and the Alabama Public Service Commission depressed earnings and caused the subsidiary to leave some jobs vacant and the parent to freeze its dividend payment.

The early 1980s saw a return to growth. In January 1982 Southern Company formed Southern Electric International Inc. to market Southern Company's technical expertise to utilities and industrial concerns. Large building programs also were continued. In 1984 Southern Company announced that it would spend $7.1 billion over three years to complete seven generating plants including two nuclear units at a site near Augusta, Georgia.

As the decade came to a close, Southern, like many utilities, found that its nuclear building program was over budget. In 1985 Southern had pledged not to pass through to ratepayers any more than $3.56 billion, which was then its share of the $8.35 billion estimated total cost of the Vogtle plant, which also had several smaller utilities as investors. Southern said any amount above that cap would be charged to its shareholders. When the estimated price of the project increased by $522 million in 1986, Southern posted a charge of $229 million against 1987 earnings. Problems with construction costs and regulators led to a series of disappointing earnings years and stagnant dividends.

In March 1988 Southern Company acquired Savannah Electric & Power Company of Savannah, Georgia, for approximately 11 million common shares, exchanging 1.05 Southern shares for each Savannah Electric common share, a stock transaction valued at $239.3 million. Later that year the U.S. Attorney General's office in Atlanta began investigating Southern's tax accounting practices regarding spare parts, and it also began investigating whether executives at Gulf Power had made illegal political contributions. In 1989 Gulf Power pleaded guilty to conspiring to make political contributions in violation of the Public Utility Holding Company Act and impeding the Internal Revenue Service in its collection of income taxes. In accordance with the plea agreement, Gulf Power paid a fine of $500,000.

The year 1990 brought another disappointment as Georgia regulators refused to allow Southern to charge customers for a portion of its investment in the Vogtle nuclear plant. On a positive note, Southern agreed to sell a unit of Georgia Power's Scherer Plant to two Florida utilities for $810 million and formed Southern Nuclear Operating Company to provide services for nuclear power plants. Also in 1990, the Attorney General's office dropped its investigation of Southern's spare parts accounting practices.

The Energy Policy Act of 1992 inaugurated the era of deregulation in the utilities industry. By encouraging competition in the nation's regional power markets, the new laws compelled major utilities to expand and diversify to survive. Southern Company responded aggressively to deregulation, both at home and abroad. In 1998 it merged with Houston-based Vastar to form Southern Company Energy Marketing, with the purpose of exploring possible acquisitions in Texas and the Southwest. That same year, Southern purchased generating facilities in New England, New York, and California. While Southern Company's regulated utilities in the Southeast continued to perform well throughout the 1990s, expansion into the unregulated market transformed the company into the nation's largest supplier of electricity by decade's end, when it could claim nearly 50,000 megawatts of power generation.

Southern Company also led the charge into the rapidly growing world energy market. It obtained its first overseas holding with the purchase of a 50 percent stake in Bahamian utility Freeport Power in 1992. This initial expansion was followed in 1994 with acquisitions in Trinidad and Tobago and in 1995 with the purchase of South Western Electricity in Great Britain. In 1996 Southern Company negotiated an agreement with Hong Kong billionaire Gordon Y. S. Wu to take over 80 percent of Consolidated Electric Power Asia (CEPA), gaining complete control of the company the following year. Under Southern's ownership, CEPA's earnings rose from $68 million in 1998 to $175 million in 1999. Sual, a 1,218 megawatt coal-burning generating facility in the Philippines, was up and running by the end of the decade. Southern Company was also the first U.S. utility to break into the German market with its 1997 purchase of a 25 percent share of Bewag. In 1999 Southern established a marketing operation in Amsterdam, with the goal of exploring potential growth areas in central Europe. Southern Company's European earnings reached $170 million by 1999.

ENVIRONMENTAL PROTECTION AGENCY CONCERNS

The 1990s also saw increased friction between the Environmental Protection Agency (EPA) and the major utilities. The Clean Air Act Amendments of 1990 imposed stricter standards on the reduction of harmful emissions from generating plants, establishing annual emissions reduction goals and requiring utilities plants to cease making repairs on outdated coal-burning facilities that lacked adequate pollution control equipment. In 1999 the EPA filed a civil action suit against seven major utilities, including Southern Company, for alleged noncompliance with these regulations. The companies also were cited for emitting illegal levels of smog-causing nitrogen oxides and sulfur dioxide.

In spite of these allegations, Southern Company had taken measures in the 1990s to establish itself as an industry leader in the reduction of harmful emissions. Over the course of the decade, Southern reduced its nitrogen oxide emissions by more than 20 percent, and its sulfur dioxide emissions by 30 percent, all the while increasing production of electricity by 20 percent. The company devoted more than $4 billion over the course of the decade to environmental protection measures, including the country's largest electric vehicle leasing program for its employees. Southern Company also volunteered for the U.S. Department of Energy's Climate Challenge Program to Reduce Carbon Dioxide. In 2000 Southern Company participated in the Alabama Direct Fuel Cell Demonstration Project, an effort to develop cleaner power generation through electrochemical technology.

A partial settlement of the lawsuit was announced in 2006, under which Southern Company's subsidiary Alabama Power Company would reduce emissions of sulfur dioxide and nitrogen oxides, with costs that would reach $200 million.

DOMESTIC AND INTERNATIONAL SUBSIDIARIES

While its domestic business grew, Southern Company spun off its international subsidiary, Southern Energy, into a separate company in January 2001. After the transition, Southern Energy became Mirant Corporation. Approximately 80 percent (272 million shares) of Mirant was distributed to Southern Company shareholders in April 2001 when the spin-off was finalized. To continue to grow its business Southern Company focused its energies in the key areas of its retail business in the southeastern United States, wholesale generation, and energy-related products and services.

January 2001 was also when the Securities and Exchange Commission (SEC) granted Southern Company approval to form Southern Power. The new Southern Power subsidiary owned, managed and financed generating assets in the southeastern United States. Its target market was the area's wholesale customers.

The following year, in July 2002, the Georgia Public Service Commission gave Southern Company certification to start serving retail customers in the gas market. Southern Company marketed its gas products and services to customers of its recently acquired New-Power Company Incorporated, a national residential and small business energy provider. The purchase came on the heels of NewPower Company's June 2002 Chapter 11 reorganization filing.

Southern Company paid approximately $28 million for the NewPower Company customer contracts, and an additional $32 million for NewPower's natural gas inventory and risk management systems. Southern Company formed the subsidiary Southern Power Gas to meet the needs and demands of its newly acquired gas customers. The subsidiary would remain in the Georgia retail natural gas market until January 2006, at which time it was sold to Cobb EMC's affiliate, Gas South.

AN EYE ON GLOBAL WARMING

Despite its business growth by way of acquisitions and new customer accounts, Southern Company faced challenges. In July 2004 three environmental groups, the City of New York, and attorneys general from eight states (California, Connecticut, Iowa, New Jersey, New York, Rhode Island, Vermont and Wisconsin) sued Southern Company, the Tennessee Valley Authority, the American Electric Power Company, Xcel Energy Incorporated, and Cinergy Corporation. In the lawsuit, the plaintiffs required the defendants to reduce heat-trapping carbon dioxide emissions, a greenhouse gas that was thought to cause global warming, at their plants. Together the eight utility companies owned or operated 174 fossil fuel-burning power plants in 20 states. Annually, the plants emitted nearly 650 million tons of carbon dioxide.

Southern Company was named in the lawsuit as emitting 171 million tons of carbon dioxide, making it the second-highest polluter of the utility companies named in the lawsuit. Monetary damages were not sought in the lawsuit. In September 2005 the United States District Court for the Southern District of New York granted the utility company's motion to dismiss the case. One month later, the plaintiffs filed an appeal with the United States Court of Appeals for the Second Circuit. The judge ruled in favor of the plaintiffs, and Southern Company and the other utility firms were again charged with reducing the amount of carbon dioxide created at their power plants. In November 2009 the utility companies sought a rehearing on the appeal.

Lawsuit notwithstanding, Southern Company focused on expansion and growth. In early 2010 it joined forces with Ted Turner, media mogul and founder of Renewable Energy. In March of that year Southern Company and Turner announced plans to purchase the rights to build one of the largest solar photovoltaic power plants in the United States. The 30-

megawatt plant was expected to be constructed by the end of the year. The plant was designed to provide power to approximately 9,000 homes. First Solar Incorporated was selected as the contractor for the project.

As a company with over 100 years of experience, Southern Company was capable of generating and providing electricity to its customers for many years to come, and a continued transition towards cleaner forms of generating plants seemed likely during the 2010s.

Jordan Wankoff
Updated, Stephen Meyer; Rhonda Campbell

PRINCIPAL SUBSIDIARIES

Alabama Power Company; Georgia Power Company; Gulf Power Company; Mississippi Power Company; SouthernLINC Wireless Company; Southern Nuclear Company; Southern Power Company; Southern Renewable Energy Company.

PRINCIPAL COMPETITORS

American Electric Power Company, Inc.; Duke Energy Corporation; Entergy Corporation; Tennessee Valley Authority (TVA).

FURTHER READING

Barringer, Felicity. "Flooded Village Files Suit, Citing Corporate Link to Climate Change." *New York Times*, February 27, 2008. Accessed February 18, 2011. http://www.nytimes.com/2008/02/27/us/27alaska.html.

Burnett, Richard. "Power Player: An Atlanta-Based Utility Giant Prepares for Deregulation and a Move into Florida." *Orlando Sentinel*, March 2, 1997, H1.

Carter, Janelle. "Clean Air Law Sparks Suits: DOJ Targets Utilities with Coal-Burning Plants." *Associated Press*, November 3, 1999.

Crist, James F., *They Electrified the South*. Atlanta: Southern Company, 1981.

"Eight States & NYC Sue Top Five U.S. Global Warming Polluters." nyc.gov, July 21, 2004. Accessed February 18, 2011. http://www.nyc.gov/html/law/downloads/pdf/pr072104.pdf.

Quinn, Matthew C. "Southern Wins Race to Asia: Acquisition Will Turn It into World's Largest Independent Power Company." *Atlanta Journal and the Atlanta Constitution*, October 10, 1996, F01.

"Southern Company Gas Plans to Sell Georgia Assets to Electricity Provider." *Atlanta Journal-Constitution*, July 10, 2005. Accessed February 18, 2011. http://www.redorbit.com/news/science/169705/southern_company_gas_plans_to_sell_georgia_assets_to_electricity.

"Southern Company & Ted Turner Acquire First Solar Project." *Renewable Energy World*, March 15, 2010. Accessed February 19, 2011. http://www.renewableenergyworld.com/rea/news/article/2010/03/southern-company-ted-turner-acquire-first-solar-project.

U.S. Environmental Protection Agency. "Alabama Power Company to Spend More Than $200 Million Under Clean Air Act Settlement." Washington, DC: EPA, April 25, 2006. Accessed February 19, 2011. http://yosemite.epa.gov/opa/admpress.nsf/a8f952395381d3968525701c005e65b5/9800b064764883568525715b005ac17b!OpenDocument.

Spyker Cars N.V.

—■—

Edisonweg 2
Zeewolde, NL-3899 AZ
Netherlands
Telephone: (31) 036 535 87 87
Fax: (31) 036 535 87 80
Web site: http://www.spykerworld.com

Public Company
Founded: 1999
Employees: 3,600 (2010)
Sales: EUR 6.6 million ($8.40 million) (2009)
Stock Exchanges: Amsterdam
Ticker Symbol: SPYKR
NAICS: 336111 Automobile Manufacturing; 423110
   Automobile and Other Motor Vehicle Merchant
   Wholesalers

■ ■ ■

Based in the Netherlands, Spyker Cars N.V. (Spyker) is a manufacturer of high-end sports cars. Bearing the name and logo of a defunct Dutch car company that ceased to exist in 1929, today's Spyker hearkens back to its namesake's role in building innovative, top of the line automobiles. Spyker made international headlines in 2010 when it acquired the venerable Swedish car company Saab Automobile from General Motors. Spyker is also branching out into motor sports and Formula One racing. A young company, Spyker is aggressively expanding from a specialty car manufacturer to a mid-level player in the international automotive industry. With the acquisition of Saab, Spyker is in a

transitional phase, moving away from boutique manufacturing and into the international market.

SPYKER, MARK ONE: 1898–1929

Dutch brothers Jacobus and Hendrik-Jan Spijker started their carriage company in 1880 and quickly established themselves as premier carriage makers. By 1898 their prestige was such that the company was contracted by the Dutch royal government to build the Golden Carriage for Queen Wilhelmina's investiture. The carriage was still in use by the royal family in the 21st century.

The same year they built the Golden Carriage, the Spijker brothers decided to begin transitioning into the emerging automotive industry. By 1900 their first cars, mounting two-cylinder engines that generated three to five horsepower, were being offered for sale. Three years later, the company changed its spelling from Spijker to Spyker in an effort to broaden its appeal beyond the Netherlands.

Spyker continued its tradition of excellence into its automobiles, building the world's first six-cylinder engine and seeing its cars compete in races, including second place in the grueling 1907 Peking to Paris motor rally. Its autos were hailed for their craftsmanship and quality, earning the nickname "the Rolls Royce of the Continent." Unfortunately, the company was also beset by repeated financial crises. The same year as the Peking to Paris race, Hendrik-Jan Spijker died in a ferry accident, and the company went bankrupt. It was bought by a group of investors and Jacobus retired. By 1915 Spyker was again insolvent and was once again bought out.

Although the Netherlands was officially neutral during World War 1 (1914–18), several Dutch companies manufactured and sold arms to belligerent countries. Spyker was one such company, branching out into the aeronautical industry, and it was at this time that an airplane propeller was added to the Spyker logo. Throughout the war, Spyker built over 100 fighter planes and 200 aircraft engines. Despite its wartime expansion, Spyker was once again facing bankruptcy by 1922. Bought out again, this time by a British company, Spyker limped along for the remainder of the decade, but by 1929 the company's time was finally up and it was shuttered for good.

SPYKER RESURGENT

Spyker would likely have remained a footnote in automotive history were it not for two Dutch entrepreneurs reviving the brand name a century after the Spijker brothers began building their first cars. In 1999 Victor Muller and Maarten de Bruijn brought back the Spyker name with a plan to produce high-end, high-performance sports cars. The company also revived the old logo, an airplane propeller superimposed over a wire-spoke wheel, and the Latin motto *Nulla tenaci invia est via,* meaning "For the tenacious, no road is impassable."

The new company goals were to build cars "for those discerning connoisseurs who do not just buy a car but have one built for them, to their exacting specifications." Design of the new line of cars was to be heavily influenced by the original Spyker's commitment to excellence as well as its involvement in aircraft and aerodynamic design. As an antidote to the standard assembly line approach to car manufacture, each car built by Spyker would have a unique chassis number and individual modifications specified by its buyer. Later, Web-based gimmicks were added, such as an individual Web page for each car that featured a dedicated Webcam feed streaming live footage of the individual car's assembly process, 24 hours a day, seven days a week.

This commitment to high quality, predictably, came at a high price. Spyker's "supercars" retailed for $200,000 and up. In 2009, an average year for sales, the company sold a mere 36 cars. Despite the high price on each car, Spyker struggled to turn a profit, especially since deciding to begin trading publically in 2004.

Spyker's commitment to balancing performance and engineering won it immediate attention and acclaim. In 2000 its flagship C8 Spyder sports car won an award for engineering excellence from the Institute of Vehicle Engineers. In 2005 the C8 was voted "Best New Exotic Car 2006" by duPont Car Registry's Exotic Car Buyers Guide. In 2006 Spyker picked up recognition in the highly competitive Asian car market, winning second place in the Chinese Hurun Report's "Favorite Sport Cars" list as well as being named "Luxury Sports Car of the Year" by QQ.com, a leading Chinese Web site.

In addition to producing high-end supercars, Spyker also branched out into the luxury car market, producing luxury commercial vehicles and sport utility vehicles, including the D8 Peking-to-Paris, named for the 1907 rally that made the original Spyker cars a household name across Europe. Furthermore, in 2006 Spyker expanded into the world of motorsport, buying out Formula One racing team Midland F1 Racing for $106 million. The company's factory racing team, Spyker Squadron, went on to enter cars, many of them almost factory standards, in races and endurance competitions such as the 24 Hours at Le Mans.

ACQUIRING SAAB

The global financial crisis that began in 2008 brought an unexpected opportunity for Spyker to expand. Saab, the legendary Swedish car manufacturer, had been under the General Motors umbrella since 1990. With GM's near collapse and subsequent government bailout, the motor giant was looking to unload its less profitable ventures, and this included Saab. Initially, a deal was brokered with Swedish company Koenigsegg Group AB, but that deal fell through in November 2009. GM, anxious to be rid of Saab one way or the other, announced a self-imposed deadline of the end of the year for other offers to be considered. Spyker was among several companies to submit bids.

So began a rapid-fire series of back-and-forth, last-minute negotiations between GM and Spyker. As 2009 wound down, it looked like Saab would go out of business as GM ordered the factories closed and began the process of winding the company down. Its chief objection to Spyker's offer was the involvement of Russian banker Vladimir Antonov. GM's official position was that it was concerned that Russian involvement in the deal would allow intellectual property to make its way to Russian manufacturers. In addition, there were also allegations that Antonov was part of a family involved with Russian organized crime, allegations hotly debated

KEY DATES

1898: Two Dutch coach builders, the Spijker brothers, begin manufacturing motorcars.

1929: Four years after building its last car, Spyker goes out of business.

1999: The Spyker brand name is revived by Dutch entrepreneurs Victor Muller and Maarten de Bruijn as a specialty car manufacturer.

2004: Spyker begins trading publicly on the Euronext exchange.

2009: Spyker moves production to Britain.

2010: After considerable legal wrangling, Spyker acquires Swedish car company Saab from General Motors.

by Antonov and Muller. Ultimately, two independent investigations cleared Antonov of any connections to organized crime, but by that point the Saab sale had already gone through with GM's stipulations that Antonov be bought out of his involvement with the deal.

Antonov's 29.9 percent share in Spyker was bought out by a holding company controlled by Muller. In addition, Spyker paid $74 million in cash along with $326 million in shares. GM also kept about $100 million in Saab's operating capital. The final ingredient in the deal was Spyker's securing of a $563 million loan secured by the Swedish government. By January 26, 2010, Saab had been saved from dissolution and plans were under way to make the company profitable again.

THE ROAD AHEAD

With the Saab deal finalized, Vladimir Antonov soon made his return, a move heralding a radical reimagining of Spyker's business plan. In February 2011 it was announced that Antonov would buy out Spyker's sports car division for $21 million. Further payments over a six-year period would follow based on the division's performance and profits.

Prior to the Antonov buyout, Spyker had already been undergoing significant reorganization in the wake of its Saab deal. As mentioned earlier, the company had been losing money since going public in 2004. As the deal with General Motors was playing out in late 2009, the company was simultaneously looking to cut costs by moving its manufacturing operations from its traditional homebase in Zeewolde across the Channel to Coventry, England. The move was announced in late November of

that year, with Victor Muller stating that "[M]oving closer to our suppliers and engineering partners will result in substantial savings and tangible efficiency improvements."

With auto sales in 2009 nearing 14 million units in China, the Asian auto market was quickly becoming the new frontier for Western manufacturers, and in 2010 Spyker made a move to tap into China's luxury market. A deal was made shortly after closing the Saab purchase to secure distributorship and after-sales service in China. Spyker intended to market its full line of supercars, luxury sport utility vehicles, and luxury commercial vehicles through one of China's major importers, China Automobile Trading Co.

In the wake of the Antonov buyout, Spyker increasingly focused on its Saab brand. In May 2011 Spyker announced its intention to change its name to integrate the Saab brand. The company hoped to have Saab profitable by 2012, which would involve raising production above 2010 levels, when the production target had to be reduced from 45,000 to 35,000 vehicles. By 2012, Saab needed to be moving 100,000 to 120,000 units to achieve the desired profitability.

The company hoped that moving away from the supercar boutique market would help in this regard. Spyker chairman Hans Hugenholtz issued a statement after the deal with Antonov was announced, summing up the company's desire that the deal "will allow Spyker Cars N.V. to focus on the Saab Automobile business exclusively, will eliminate the requirement for us to make further capital investment in the Spyker business and will reduce our debt." As a further sign of its realignment, CEO Muller, who was set to step down in 2011, announced that the company was contemplating a move to the Stockholm stock exchange.

The venerable Saab's brush with oblivion under General Motors mobilized its international base of fans and customers, who cheered its last-minute reprieve at the hands of Spyker. In the wake of Spyker's divestment of its original *raison d'etre,* Saab's fortunes became Spyker's fortunes. The company hoped that Saab's loyal customer base would make sure the new Spyker enjoyed fairer fortunes than its earlier, 20th-century namesake.

David Larkins

PRINCIPAL DIVISIONS

Spyker Cars; Spyker Squadron; Saab.

PRINCIPAL COMPETITORS

Ferrari S.p.A.; Group Lotus plc; Maserati S.p.A.

FURTHER READING

"At Last, GM Finds a Buyer; Saving Saab." *Economist,* January 30, 2010, 72EU.

"Dutch Car Maker Plans Move to UK." *BBC News,* November 21, 2009. Accessed March 12, 2011. http://news.bbc.co.uk/2/hi/uk_news/england/coventry_warwickshire/8372121.stm.

"Saab Sale–Full Details." *Autocar.co.uk,* January 26, 2010. Accessed March 14, 2011. http://www.autocar.co.uk/News/NewsArticle/AllCars/246896/.

Kinnander, Ola. "Spyker to Sell Sports-Car Unit to Vladimir Antonov in Focus on Saab Brand." *Bloomberg,* February 24, 2011. Accessed March 14, 2011. http://www.bloomberg.com/news/2011-02-24/spyker-agrees-to-sell-sports-car-unit-to-vladimir-antonov-to-reduce-debt.html.

Spyker Cars. "Annual Report 2009." Accessed March 13, 2011. http://www.spykercars.nl/download/investor/JVSpyker2009Compleet.pdf.

"Spyker Taps into China's Luxury Car Market." *Xinhua Economic News,* April 25, 2010.

Strayer Education, Inc.

1100 Wilson Boulevard
Suite 2500
Arlington, Virginia 22209
U.S.A.
Telephone: (703) 247-2500
Fax: (703) 527-0112
Web site: http://www.strayereducation.com

Public Company
Founded: 1892
Employees: 2,099 (2010)
Sales: $636.7 million (2010)
Stock Exchanges: NASDAQ
Ticker Symbol: STRA
NAIC: 611310 Colleges, Universities, and Professional
    Schools; 611410 Business and Secretarial Schools

■ ■ ■

Strayer Education, Inc., is the education services holding company for Strayer University. Strayer University was founded in Baltimore, Maryland, in 1892 as Strayer Business College. Strayer University is a proprietary institution of higher learning offering undergraduate and graduate degree programs in accounting, business administration, and computer information systems. Strayer offers its courses online and at 89 physical campuses in 21 states and Washington, D.C. Its student body consists mostly of working adults. For the fall 2010 term, Strayer had more than 60,000 students enrolled in its programs.

A SHORTHAND LAUNCH TO SUCCESS

Dr. S. Irving Strayer founded Strayer's Business College in 1892 in Baltimore, Maryland. Strayer had spent years developing a method of shorthand that improved upon the widely popular Pitman system. First copyrighted in 1890, "Strayer's Universal Shorthand" became one of the main courses of study at his new college. The college's original focus was secretarial skills, so the other primary course of study was bookkeeping.

Shortly after the college opened, a typewriter distributor named Thomas W. Donoho bought half ownership in the institution by making a significant investment and donating all the typewriters the college needed for its students. Donoho became president and general administrative officer of the college in 1902. He immediately took steps to improve and expand the college. He took an extensive survey and used it to improve the curriculum, textbooks, and quality of the teaching faculty. He opened two new branches of the college in 1904, one in Washington, D.C., and one in Philadelphia, Pennsylvania. Donoho bought the Washington, D.C., and Baltimore campuses from Irving Strayer in 1910. Thomas W. Donoho was the first of three generations of Donohos to serve as president of the college.

From the beginning, Strayer emphasized its commitment to making its educational opportunities available to industrious individuals at whatever hours those individuals had available to study. The college established a night school to accommodate students who held jobs during the day. Strayer presented itself as a

---

COMPANY PERSPECTIVES

The mission of Strayer University is to make higher education achievable for working adults.

---

rigorous institution and distanced itself from other business colleges that offered lower cost, quicker, but also less thorough, training. Strayer was committed to finding its graduates employment, which led to close affiliations with businesses. Businesses came to rely on Strayer as a good source of new employees.

In 1929 Strayer founded the Strayer College of Accountancy. The Board of Education of the District of Columbia licensed the new college to grant degrees. The school was governed by its own board of trustees but operated in conjunction with the business college. The two schools merged in 1959 under the newly incorporated Strayer Junior College. After the merger, the college started broadening its range of courses. The school added programs in court reporting and health facilities management, two areas of employment experiencing shortages.

NEW TECHNOLOGIES BRING NEW CURRICULUM

Strayer launched an effort to modernize its curriculum in September 1964. The college added data processing as a degree prerequisite for the accounting program. The school devoted significant funds to rent and install IBM equipment in new laboratory environments where students could receive instruction and practice using data processing machines.

By 1969 approximately 1,500 students were enrolled in Strayer. The college employed 32 full-time faculty members and 52 part-time instructors. Strayer received licensure to award bachelor of science degrees and became a four-year institution. The college changed its name to Strayer College. By 1974 Strayer was fully accredited and gained legitimacy as a four-year institution. In 1977 enrollment reached 1,775, a 14 percent increase over the previous year.

In 1980 Dr. Charles E. Palmer was elected chairman of Strayer's board of directors. Palmer had headed nine proprietary business colleges and associate degree-granting junior colleges of business in North Carolina, South Carolina, Virginia, and Washington, D.C. He had served as leader of a number of educational and civic organizations. He also coauthored 11 McGraw-Hill textbooks for accounting and business subjects. Palmer brought Strayer significant credibility during his 10-year tenure.

In 1981 the Commission of Higher Education of the Middle States Association endorsed Strayer, making it the first proprietary school in the country to receive regional accreditation. That same year, the State Council of Higher Education of Virginia approved Strayer's request to open a campus in Arlington, Virginia. This marked the beginning of a period of geographic expansion for Strayer.

RON K. BAILEY GRABS AN OPPORTUNITY

In 1989 Ron K. Bailey bought Strayer College for $5 million and took over as president of the institution. Bailey received his bachelor of science degree from Strayer and returned to the college in 1974 as a part-time instructor of business courses. Bailey rose to a leadership position and was serving as executive vice president when he was presented with the opportunity to purchase the college.

There were several reasons why for-profit education was such an attractive business to Bailey. The for-profit schools offered flexible hours, an accelerated degree path, and a near 100 percent acceptance rate. In exchange, schools charged higher tuition than most public state schools. Strayer's tuition and fees were, on average, more than three times higher than those at state universities. Also, the schools operated with significantly lower overhead and labor costs because they emphasized a more focused, on-the-job training rather than a broad liberal arts education. Campus facilities were less extensive, and the faculty consisted of predominantly part-time instructors.

When he took over as president, Bailey understood that managing Strayer required vigilant cost containment while maintaining the school's reputation for top-quality educational services. He accelerated Strayer's program of regional expansion and committed himself to a further broadening of Strayer's curriculum and degree programs. He also set about improving the caliber of the faculty and opening up more campus locations. By 1991 Strayer had added six new campus locations in Maryland and Virginia.

The exponential growth of Strayer coincided closely with the high-tech boom of the 1990s. Computer skills became a crucial requirement for more and more jobs, and demand for computer education skyrocketed. Similarly, the bull market for technology-related stocks brought stocks of for-profit education companies along for the ride. Stock analysts liked for-profit education

KEY DATES

1892: Dr. S. Irving Strayer founds Strayer Business college in Baltimore, Maryland.

1910: Thomas W. Donoho purchases the company from Strayer.

1928: Strayer establishes the Strayer College of Accountancy.

1959: The business college and the school of accountancy merge and incorporate under name Strayer Junior College.

1969: Strayer Business College gains licensure to award bachelor of science degrees, becomes Strayer College.

1974: Strayer College receives accreditation by the Association of Independent Colleges and Schools.

1989: Ron K. Bailey buys Strayer College from Charles Palmer.

1996: Strayer establishes Strayer Education, Inc., as holding company and goes public, trading under symbol "STRA."

1998: District of Columbia awards university status to Strayer College.

2000: New Mountain Capital, LLC, and DB Capital Partners purchase a controlling interest in Strayer Education, Inc.; Robert S. Silberman becomes president and CEO.

2002: Strayer Education gains regulatory approval to open campuses in North Carolina.

2010: Enrollment at Strayer College is approximately 60,000 on 87 campuses.

companies because they believed them to be recession-proof. When the economy slumped, people who were laid off tended to go back to school to improve their skills and employability.

NEW LOAN PROGRAM

To expand enrollment Strayer introduced the Strayer Education Loan Program in 1995. The program served as an alternative source of funding to government-sponsored loans. The school formed a subsidiary named Education Loan Processing, Inc. (ELP). The service offered highly competitive loan terms and interest rates because it managed to service the loans at a lower cost than the government. ELP tailored its services to the needs of working adults, and it offered a dual benefit for

Strayer. It accommodated its particular brand of student and it was good for business.

In 1996 the school established Strayer Education, Inc., as the parent company of Strayer College in preparation for going public. The company listed on the NASDAQ under the ticker symbol "STRA." Its initial public offering raised $30 million in capital. Nine months later, Strayer returned to the market for a secondary offering of 1.15 million shares.

In July 1997 Dr. Donald Stoddard became president of Strayer College. Ron K. Bailey continued as president and CEO of Strayer Education. At the time, the college had over 8,000 students enrolled at nine campuses in Washington, D.C., Virginia, and Maryland. With new leadership and substantial capital at its disposal, Strayer had the tools to move aggressively in three strategic directions. First, the company expanded its regional presence, opening a new campus every year for the next five years. Second, Strayer increased the number of educational programs, including its Internet-based school, Strayer Online. Third, the company continued to expand the courses tailored for its corporate and government clients. As part of the third direction, Strayer formed a new subsidiary called Professional Education, Inc. (ProEd). Strayer had begun offering on-site computer training courses for corporations like AT&T and federal agencies like the Internal Revenue Service. These corporate and government affiliations were particularly lucrative, because Strayer charged for teaching the courses without having to provide the equipment or facilities. Strayer designed ProEd to deliver specialized professional development curriculum, especially computer training, to employees of corporations and government entities.

A NEW OWNER ACCELERATES GROWTH

In January 1998 Strayer Education was granted university status. This was rare for a proprietary institution and conferred new respectability on Strayer. The new status could not have come at a better time since Strayer was about to embark on a major expansion. By 2000 the District of Columbia Education Licensure Commission had approved the university's right to offer a master of science degree in communications technology as well as master of arts degrees in computer networking and acquisition and contract management.

In 2000 Strayer Education signed an agreement with a group of investors headed by New Mountain Capital, LLC, which was a New York investment that specialized in education companies. New Mountain Capital and co-investor DB Capital Partners purchased a controlling stake in Strayer Education for $150 million. Ron K. Bailey retired and sold his 52 percent stake in the company. Robert S. Silberman, a New Mountain Capital executive, succeeded Bailey as president and CEO. New Mountain's founder and CEO, Steven B. Klinsky, became the nonexecutive chairman of Strayer-Education's board of directors.

Silberman accelerated the company's rate of growth. Bailey's rate of one new campus each year became three per year. Strayer Education made its way across the Mid-Atlantic region then turned its sights on a national presence. In the electronic realm, the company aggressively pursued foreign students to attend its online courses.

EXPANDING INTO NEW STATES: 2002–08

In March 2002 Strayer Education was granted regulatory approval to open campuses in North Carolina, its first move beyond its established geographic footprint. Within the year, the company quickly opened three campuses, two in Charlotte and one in Raleigh-Durham. At the same time, Strayer Education established alliances with more than 80 corporate and government entities to provide training to their employees.

In 2003 Strayer opened campuses in Nashville and Memphis, Tennessee. Also, online enrollment jumped to 6,372 students, a 69 percent increase from the previous year. Some industry analysts believed that the online school had begun to take students away from the classroom business. Even though overall enrollment had increased 17 percent, classroom enrollment at Strayer had fallen slightly.

Strayer continued to expand through the rest of the decade. In 2005 it opened new campuses in South Carolina, Georgia, and Florida. By the end of 2007 the company had spread its reach to Delaware, Alabama, New Jersey, and Kentucky. Strayer surpassed Silberman's original goal of three new campuses a year and started opening around eight new campuses a year. The university boasted over 36,000 students enrolled, an increase of 4,500 over the previous year. Strayer claimed that its increase of students was equal to the total enrollment of some U.S. colleges.

In 2008 Strayer added eight more campuses, mostly expanding its presence among the states in which it already operated. Enrollment swelled to over 45,000 students in 25 metropolitan areas.

THRIVING UNDER FIRE

As Strayer grew in size it faced increasing competition from larger, national entities like the Apollo Group (University of Phoenix), ITT Educational Services, and DeVry Educational Development Corporation. Also, while Strayer enjoyed growing revenues and healthy profit margins, the college could not help but suffer from the negative public relations that engulfed its industry. Around 2009 the U.S. Department of Education and industry experts raised questions concerning the student loan practices of for-profit colleges. They also expressed concern about the quality of education offered by these colleges. Evidence emerged that these schools were behaving more like high-pressure sales organizations. They aggressively pursued students, intent on grabbing up student loan dollars without much concern for whether the students could repay the loans once they graduated. For-profit colleges were depending heavily on the Education Department's grants and loans program such that some of them were using federal money to fund 100 percent of the student's tuition.

In addition, a multitude of testimonials came to light about students having difficulties professionally. Many said the colleges misled them about the health of the employment markets. Others said the poor quality of their education made it difficult for them to obtain jobs. Some lost their jobs because they could not function as well as others with equal experience who came from more traditional nonprofit institutions. Poor marketability or lack of employability made it difficult for students to repay their loans. Also, since these were federally guaranteed student loans, the taxpayer was left holding bad loans. The Education Department's statistics showed that the industry's dropout rate of 37 percent was about the same as public colleges and well above the 29 percent for nonprofit private institutions. Also, just 34 percent of for-profit students attained their bachelor's degrees after six years, compared to 45 percent at public colleges and 52 percent at nonprofit private colleges.

In 2010 the U.S. Department of Education proposed new regulations governing proprietary colleges. Up until then, proprietary colleges had pretty much avoided stringent oversight since the Department of Education traditionally focused on nonprofit institutions. That same year, proprietary colleges showed double digit declines in enrollment. For the fall term, new student enrollments decreased 2 percent.

Many of the for-profit institutions threatened that they would have to increase tuition to achieve profitability, but much of this looked like scare tactics to stop the government from imposing regulations on their industry. Most, if not all, of the institutions reported very healthy revenues and profits despite the downturn. Strayer reported annual revenue in 2010 of $636.7 million, an increase of 24 percent over 2009. Strayer reported a net 2010 income of $131.3 million, an increase of 25 percent over 2009.

Most of the new federal regulations were scheduled to go into effect on July 1, 2011. These regulations were intended to protect students from being misled by recruitment practices and from running up huge debts. Some parts of the regulations were delayed when the industry successfully generated thousands of comments. Most of the comments to regulators were regarding the "gainful employment" proposal. This proposal required that a program seeking financial aid prove that its training is linked to occupations actually demanded on the employment market. Many thought this would limit students' choices for programs if they were deemed by regulators to be unproductive. Regulators agreed to meet with a group of for-profit institutions in early 2011 to discuss the rule.

GROWTH PROSPECTS: 2010 AND BEYOND

Despite a potential slowdown in enrollment, Strayer was in a good position for steady growth through the 2010s. While new regulations may slow Strayer's growth somewhat, it was doubtful that they would have much impact on its long-term growth. The company was expanding at about eight new campuses a year, either moving into new geographic areas or increasing its footprint in existing cities. During 2009 and 2010, Strayer expanded into Mississippi, Arkansas, Texas, and Utah. At the end of 2010, Strayer was operating 87 campuses, 34 less than three years old, 53 older than three years.

Also, Strayer's online school was still growing, especially from outside the United States. Another factor that helped Strayer was the effect of the recession of 2008 and 2009 on employment levels. Unemployment at the beginning of 2011 was an estimated 9 percent,

and an estimated 25 million people were unemployed. The unemployment rate was not expected to decrease significantly until 2012, so it seemed likely that Strayer would reap the benefit of a transitioning economy as people sought retraining to take advantage of the next wave of job creation.

Erin Brown
Updated, Aaron Hauser

PRINCIPAL SUBSIDIARIES

Education Loan Processing, Inc.; Strayer University.

PRINCIPAL COMPETITORS

Apollo Group, Inc.; Bridgepoint Education, Inc.; Corinthian Colleges, Inc.; DeVry Inc.; ITT Educational Services, Inc.

FURTHER READING

Alpert, Bill. "Leveraging Up to Learn."*Barron's,* November 9, 2009, 26.

Appel, Rebecca. "For-Profit Colleges Oppose Tighter Regulation in U.S."*New York Times,* October 24, 2010. Accessed March 18, 2011. http://www.nytimes.com/2010/10/25/us/25iht-educSide25.html.

Hamilton, Martha McNeil. "Like Its Students, Strayer Is Advancing."*Washington Post,* September 15, 2003, E01.

Knight, Jerry. "Learning from Strayer's Ron Bailey." *Washington Post,* July 9, 2001, E01.

Korn, Melissa. "Strayer Blames Bad Press for Low Enrollment. "*Wall Street Journal,* January 10, 2011. Accessed March 18, 2011. http://online.wsj.com/article/SB10001424052748703779704576073942667054086.html.

McTague, Jim. "Strayer Education's Lofty Growth Plans Mirror the Expanding Market for Professional Training."*Barron's Online,* August 5, 2002.

Morey, Ann. "The Growth of For-Profit Higher Education. "*Journal of Teacher Education,* September, 2001, 300.

Soley, Lawrence. "Higher Education … or Higher Profit; For-Profit Universities Sell Free Enterprise Education."*Institute for Public Affairs,* September 28, 1998, 14.

SUNGARD®

SunGard Data Systems
Incorporated

—■—

680 East Swedesford Road
Wayne, Pennsylvania 19087
U.S.A.
Telephone: (484) 582-2000
Toll Free: (800) 825-2518
Web site: http://www.sungard.com

Private Company
Incorporated: 1982
Employees: 20,700 (est., 2009)
Sales: $5.51 billion (2009)
NAICS: 518210 Data Processing, Hosting, and Related
Services; 541519 Other Computer Related Services

■ ■ ■

SunGard Data Systems Incorporated is an information technology services company serving governmental, financial, and educational institutions. Its largest operating market is its financial services sector, where SunGard has almost 14,000 of its more than 25,000 customers. The company's software and products can handle almost any type of financial transaction, including monitoring cash flow, managing assets and their derivatives, and trading and processing securities. SunGard also provides disaster recovery services, information availability consulting services, and software for enterprise resource planning. SunGard is controlled by a consortium of investment firms.

OUTGROWING SUN COMPANY

SunGard began as a subsidiary of the oil giant Sun Co. In the mid-1970s, Sun Information Services (SIS) had served as the data processing arm of Sun Co. and also provided data processing services to companies in the greater Philadelphia area. As Sun's business became increasingly dependent on the use of computers, SIS president John Ryan noted that the company could lose up to $3 million by the third day if its computer system failed. His division developed a disaster contingency plan for Sun, in which daily transactions were recorded on backup tapes and stored at an off-site area. Should Sun's mainframe computer fail, these could then be loaded into an alternate mainframe, and business could continue running as usual.

In 1978 SIS received a request for a proposal from a group of Philadelphia businesses searching for a similar disaster recovery system. Based on its own program, SIS then presented itself as a "commercial hot site vendor," offering subscriptions to data storage and emergency off-site data processing on an IBM 370/158 mainframe computer. According to the program, should a disaster prevent a subscriber from accessing its computer system, SIS would load the subscriber's backup data into its system and allow access to its computers so that business could begin running as usual the next day. SIS won the contract and immediately began soliciting subscriptions from other businesses. Within the first year, 80 companies had subscribed to the service. By 1980 SIS had 110 subscribers, each paying between $3,500 and $12,000 per month for services.

In the late 1970s, having diversified into several non-oil related businesses, Sun Co. maintained four computer-related subsidiaries (SunGard Services Co., Applied Financial Systems Inc., Catallactics Corp., and NMF Inc.) in addition to SIS. When oil prices hit $30 a barrel in the early 1980s, Sun decided to spin off a number of its subsidiaries and asked SIS president Ryan to search for potential buyers. Convinced that SIS and these four companies could form a profitable business, Ryan and a group of venture capitalists arranged to purchase an 80 percent share of the five subsidiaries for $19.5 million in cash and notes in 1983.

That proved to be a fortuitous year for the spin-off company. In 1983 the Comptroller of the Currency began requiring national banks to have a testable backup plan should their computer systems fail. SunGard and a rival firm, Comdisco Disaster Recovery Services Inc., were the only two companies in the United States offering emergency backup services. Thanks to the new banking regulations, SunGard's disaster recovery customer base more than doubled to 280 subscribers. Each company paid upwards of $50,000 in subscriptions fees, plus an additional user fee of $25,000 or more for use of SunGard's computer systems. By 1985 disaster recovery services brought in 49 percent of the company's $58.5 million total revenues; financial processing software and services accounted for 47 percent.

GOING PUBLIC

In March 1986 the company went public on the NASDAQ exchange under the name SunGard Data Systems Inc. Its disaster recovery services became a wholly owned subsidiary under the name SunGard Recovery Services Inc. The initial public offering raised $23.7 million dollars. SunGard paid its debts to Sun Co. and other venture capital firms that financed the spin-off, reinvesting the remaining $10.2 million. Profits that year totaled $5.5 million, on revenues of $69 million.

During this time, SunGard sought to improve its offerings in the data processing arena, acquiring a total of 27 companies between 1986 and 1994, primarily in the investment support services arena. SunGard made four acquisitions in 1987, the largest of which was Devon Systems International, a provider of software for currency and interest rate options trading, purchased for $20 million in cash, notes, and common stock. That

year, profits rose 50 percent to $8.2 million on revenues of $91.1 million. Fifty percent of revenues came from software sales and operation, and 50 percent were attributable to disaster recovery services.

By 1988 SunGard Recovery had "hot sites" in Chicago, San Diego, Philadelphia, St. Paul, and London. That year, the company also began offering downtime services, which allowed customers to cope with lost time caused by more regular computer failures in communications and processor systems. The following year, SunGard entered a joint venture with STM Systems Corp., a Toronto-based firm, to provide disaster recovery services in Canada under the name STM-SunGard Recovery Services.

In 1989 another competitor entered the disaster recovery arena. International Business Machines Corporation (IBM), whose mainframe computers SunGard used to backup client data at its hot sites, began offering backup services for many of its own systems, including System?36, System?38 and AS?400 computers. SunGard issued a press release welcoming IBM's entry into the industry and told *American Banker* that competition with IBM would "make us a better company." At that time, SunGard Recovery and Comdisco had penetrated less than 50 percent of the disaster recovery market. Both believed there was room for a third competitor.

IBM initially captured some big accounts from SunGard's customers who worked with large IBM systems. However, SunGard took measures to prevent further sales erosion, and, by 1991, had curtailed the loss of customers to its new competitor. Despite increased competition, disaster recovery sales grew by over 30 percent in 1990, fueled by the earthquakes that shook California as well as several other natural disasters across the United States. In 1990 company-wide sales hit $262 million, up 59 percent from 1988.

In 1989 SunGard merged with Daytron Corp., a large supplier of bank data processing software, and also purchased Warrington Financial Systems, Inc., a British supplier of bank treasury software, for $65.3 million in cash. Following this acquisition, the company formed a new division, SunGard Financial Systems, which included subsidiaries Warrington, Devon Systems International Inc., Wismer Associates Inc., Money Management Systems Inc., and SunGard Investment Systems Inc. In 1990 SunGard expanded into the securities trading management arena, purchasing Phase3 Systems, Inc., a supplier of "integrated, real-time securities transaction processing systems for equity and fixed-income instruments" for undisclosed terms. Phase3 served about 35 corporate customers across the United States.

KEY DATES

1986: SunGard makes an initial public offering.
1987: SunGard acquires Devon Systems International.
1989: SunGard merges with Daytron Corporation.
1991: SunGard sells its Daytron Mortgage Systems Division to Stockholder Systems Incorporated.
1995: SunGard rolls out its OMNIPLUS accounting system.
2002: Cristobal Conde is named chief executive officer.
2005: Silver Lake Partners and six private equity firms acquire SunGard.
2007: SunGard acquires VeriCenter.
2010: Company acquires Ireland-based Hosting 365.

SunGard's growth in investment support services soon began to outpace its disaster recovery division. In 1991 investment support services brought in approximately 58 percent of the $262 million in sales. Following its long string of mergers and acquisitions, SunGard sought to pare down some of its services, selling its Daytron Mortgage Systems Division to Stockholder Systems Inc. in 1991 for an undisclosed price. It then acquired Shaw Data Services, a top supplier of portfolio management services to banks and other institutional investors, for approximately $35 million. This was all in keeping with what Richard C. Tarbox, vice president of corporate development, said was SunGard's growth strategy: "To provide investment support on a service basis ... [and have] something to offer all managers of money."

By its 10th anniversary in 1993, SunGard had firmly established itself as a leading provider of investment management software and disaster recovery services. That year, SunGard shares began trading on the London Stock Exchange, and earnings rose 49 percent from 1992 to $38 million on revenues of $381 million.

ADDRESSING A GROWING ELECTRONIC MARKET

Increasing its electronic product line was one of the ways SunGard addressed the ever-expanding market for its services. PowerImage, a document imaging and workflow software system, was purchased by SunGard in 1994. The system made it possible for SunGard custom-

ers to create and send copies of documents electronically. It was marketed primarily to SunGard's accounting system customers.

Known for its business continuity products and services, SunGard also expanded its Philadelphia and Chicago MegaCenters, including adding a mainframe command center in the locations. This allowed SunGard's business continuity customers to recover their critical documents more efficiently when they worked out of the MegaCenters during natural and human-made disasters.

An early 1995 pickup would position SunGard to expand its product line for its remote and on-site business continuity customers. In March 1995 SunGard reached an agreement with CHI/COR Information Management Incorporated and acquired its disaster recovery planning software business. This came on the heels of SunGard purchasing Computervision Corporation's disaster recovery business in October 1994.

To support its banking and financial investment customers' defined contribution and defined benefit retirement plans, SunGard developed the OMNIPLUS accounting system. The product rolled out in 1995. Despite the fact that it was widely known for its business continuity sites, products, and services, it was clear that SunGard was creeping further into the electronic financial investment business.

Further evidence of this came in May 1996 after SunGard closed on its deal to acquire NCS Systems, a subsidiary of National Computer Systems. SunGard paid $95 million for NCS, a company that had 350 employees in Atlanta, Georgia, and Cambridge, Massachusetts, at the time of the close. NCS' turnkey trust accounting and corporate trust systems allowed SunGard to offer its banking and financial investment clients additional accounting tools.

From 1994 through 1998, the company focused on consolidating its investment support products (e.g., PowerImage, FrontArena). Acquisitions were the primary reason for the consolidation efforts. Product unification and enhancement were a big part of this effort as SunGard worked to provide its customers access to multiple technological systems through common interfaces and shared databases. It also developed personal computer and workstation front-end products (e.g. iWorks Prophet, Adaptiv, Infinity) so that it could convert systems to client-server technology. Additionally, the company focused on expanding its presence in the international market.

In March 1999 SunGard announced its plans to acquire Oshap Technologies Ltd, an Israeli software company, for approximately $210 million in a share-exchange deal. The Oshap Technologies purchase strengthened SunGard's portfolio management software product line. Banking and financial investment customers, particularly global asset managers, could use the software to track trade orders and ensure they were in compliance with exchange laws.

The acquisitions and products consolidations paid off. Year end 1999 through 2001, SunGard posted international sales of $297 million, $347.5 million, and $381.2 million, respectively.

THE TECHNOLOGY GIANT IS ACQUIRED

SunGard's trend of growing through acquisitions would deliver the technology firm a surprise hand in 2005. According to a *Business Week* article by Justin Hibbard, Glenn Hutchins, cofounder of Silver Lake, a venture capital consortium, got word in February 2004 that the SEC was drafting a regulation that would guarantee that investors got the best prices able to be executed electronically. Hutchins anticipated that the number of mergers involving electronic trading businesses would increase. He had already been pursuing SunGard for the last several months, and the news regarding the SEC proposal only whet his appetite further. Not only would the deal make Hutchins and his Silver Lake partners lots of money, it was expected to strengthen SunGard's position in the IT world.

In April 2005 SunGard announced plans to offer Silver Lake a leveraged buyout (LBO). A group of Silver Lake Partners raised $11.4 billion to close the deal, making it the largest LBO since the 1989 RJR Nabisco deal. Other private equity firms associated with the deal were Bain Capital Partners, The Blackstone Group, Goldman Sachs & Co., Kohlberg Kravis Roberts & Co., Providence Equity Partners, and the Texas Pacific Group.

SunGard reported total revenues of $1.30 billion in 2005, up from the previous year's $1.16 billion. Expectations of major changes in the SunGard senior management ranks following the Silver Lake LBO did not materialize. Cristóbal Conde remained SunGard's president and chief executive officer (CEO). He had served as CEO since 2002, and had served on Sun-Gard's board since 1999. A senior management change would not come until 2010 when Robert Woods was named SunGard's chief financial officer (CFO). Prior to joining SunGard in January 2010, Woods served as CFO at IKON Office Solutions from 2004 to 2009.

Continuing to grow in large part through acquisitions, SunGard acquired the Ireland-based Hosting 365 in March 2010. Hosting 365 is a hosted infrastructure provider offering on-demand computing services. At the time of purchase, it also operated two secure data centers, locations which were expected to strengthen SunGard's international business continuity efforts.

Further acquisitions like the Hosting 365 one were expected throughout the 2010s, as SunGard continued to bolster its formidable presence as an IT provider to the global financial services sector.

Maura Troester
Updated, Rhonda Campbell

PRINCIPAL DIVISIONS

Availability Services; Financial Systems; Higher Education; Public Sector.

PRINCIPAL SUBSIDIARIES

365 Hosting Limited (Ireland); Advanced Portfolio Technologies, Inc.; Decalog N.V. (The Netherlands); Decision Software, Inc.; FNX, L.L.C.; GL Settle, Inc.; Guardian iT (England and Wales); Integrity Treasury Solutions, Inc.; Morris Software, Inc.; Ubitrade OSI (Tunisia).

PRINCIPAL COMPETITORS

Fidelity National Information Services, Inc.; First Data Corporation; Fiserv, Inc.; Total System Services, Inc.;

FURTHER READING

Hibbard, Justin. "Wall Street's New Alchemist." *BusinessWeek*, August 8, 2005. Accessed February 19, 2011. http://www.silverlake.com/pdfs/2005-08-08.pdf.

"Hosting 365 Acquired by IT Services Giant SunGard." *Silicon Republic*, December 3, 2010. Accessed February 19, 2011. http://www.siliconrepublic.com/business/item/15547-hosting-365-acquired-by-it.

Koselka, Rita. "Blue-Chip Backup." *Forbes*, January 26, 1987, 80.

Millman, Joel. "The Great Escape," *Forbes*, November 11, 1990, 234.

"SunGard Data Systems, Inc. Announces Definitive Agreement to Acquire Oshap Technologies Ltd." *Business Wire*, March 10, 1999. Accessed February 19, 2011. http://www.allbusiness.com/technology/software-services-applications-information/6651233-1.html.

"SunGard – The Biggest Leveraged Buyout in 16 Years." AnalystViews.com, April 19, 2005. Accessed February 2011. http://wp.bitpipe.com/resource/org_1090505793_180/20050419-SunGuard.pdf.

Tyson, David O. "IBM to Compete with Major Vendors in Disaster Recovery Market." *American Banker*, April 5, 1989, 9.

Zipser, Andy. "SunGard Shines Again: After a Dull Year, It's Set for Fresh Growth." *Barron's News and Investment Weekly*, October 21, 1991, 15.

Synergetics USA, Inc.

———————————— ■ ————————————

3845 Corporate Centre Drive
O'Fallon, Missouri 63368
U.S.A.
Telephone: (636) 939-5100
Toll Free: (800) 600-0565
Fax: (636) 939-6885
Web site: http://www.synergeticsusa.com

Public Company
Founded: 1991 as Synergetics, Inc.
Employees: 342 (2010)
Sales: $52.1 million (2010)
Stock Exchanges: NASDAQ
Ticker Symbol: SURG
NAICS: 334510 Electromedical and Electrotherapeutic Apparatus Manufacturing

■ ■ ■

Synergetics USA, Inc., designs and manufactures precision instruments for the ophthalmologic and neurosurgical applications. Its products are designed for minimally invasive procedures. Synergetics also manufactures and markets accessories and supplies for use with surgical instruments.

Products for the ophthalmology unit include illumination, magnification, and viewing products for retinal surgery, surgical lasers and probes, scrapers, injection kits, and other supplemental products for ophthalmologists and retinal surgeons. Synergetic's products in the retinal and ophthalmology fields are

necessary for the precise maneuvers in retinal surgical operations.

Products for the neurosurgery unit consist of two primary products. The Lumen Light Source provides superior illumination using microfiber technology. The Malis Advantage is a bipolar generator that uses Dual-Wave technology or waveforms for cutting and coagulation with minimal damage to surrounding tissue.

The company receives the majority (68% in 2010) of revenue from the United States, but it does have offices in France, Germany, and Italy. Roughly three-fifths of all revenue derives from its ophthalmic products.

FOUNDING AND GROWTH: 1991–99

Synergetics, Inc., was founded by business partners Gregg Scheller and Kurt Gampp. Synergetics was Scheller's second successful venture. In 1986 he founded Advanced Surgical Products, a company later purchased by investors and renamed Infinitech. In 1991 Scheller and Gampp founded Synergetics in Scheller's garage.

The idea for the company began with Scheller's job at Storz Instruments. He discovered that retinal surgical devices had no quick turnaround for repair, usually averaging six months. Synergetics entered the market by offering a one-week turnaround for the repair of retinal surgical devices.

Whereas Scheller specialized in engineering, Gampp specialized in manufacturing. With Gampp's manufacturing expertise and the assistance of Matthew Thomas of Barnes Hospital, the company patented and offered its own line of retinal surgical devices in 1992. Thomas was in the process of developing a new procedure to remove vascular netting that grows behind the retina of some patients with histoplasmosis (a disease caused by fungus spores). Thomas needed special instruments and approached his Dutch supplier to develop and manufacture them. The supplier's slow response time to deliver a prototype eventually led him to Synergetics. Scheller and Gampp developed a prototype within a week, and after another week, Thomas had a workable instrument for surgery.

In 1993 the company, at that time with 10 employees, moved out of Scheller's garage to its first office location in Chesterfield, Missouri. A flood in the area required that the company relocate temporarily to Ellisville, Missouri. While in Ellisville, the company outgrew its Chesterfield location and bought manufacturing space in St. Charles County with the help of the St. Charles County Economic Development center. As growth continued, the company moved to O'Fallon, Missouri in 1996, allowing the company to consolidate its manufacturing and administrative functions.

The company grew at a rate of 465 percent between 1994 and 1998 as both its products and retinal instrument repair services gained acceptance in the marketplace and received ISO 9000 certification. Synergetics, until then, was the only U.S. manufacturer of retinal surgical instruments. The immediate availability and ease of customer service allowed Synergetics to serve an unmet need in the ophthalmology field in the United States.

In 1998 Synergetics entered the neurosurgical market when the company began a long-term partnership with Japanese medical device manufacturer Mutoh Co. Ltd. Mutoh developed technology for an ultrasonic surgical aspirator for neurosurgery applications. Synergetics brought the technology to the United States and further developed the product to make the tips

disposable. Synergetics named the product OMNI. The device was quickly adopted in neurosurgery because it allowed surgeons to remove bone tissue from the cranium more easily without damaging surrounding tissue. The device also had the ability to cut dense tissue such as bone or fibrous lesions but was also gentle enough for soft tissue procedures.

After 1998 the company continued to grow at an average of 30 percent per year. The company committed 8 percent of its revenues to research and development. By 1999 the company was selling its products in 54 countries.

MERGER AND MORE GROWTH: 2005–06

In 2005, after a brief foray into plastic surgery and ear, nose, and throat instruments, the company focused on its core markets of the retinal surgical instruments and neurosurgery instruments. The company's revenues of $16.9 million attracted investors, and in May, the company announced a merger agreement with Valley Forge Scientific Corp. (Valley Forge), a company with approximately $4.8 million in revenues. Valley Forge was a publicly held company at the time of the merger.

With the merger, Synergetics effectively became a publicly held company. The new company was named Synergetics USA with Scheller as its new president and CEO and Gampp as executive vice president and COO. Jerry Malis, former CEO of Valley Forge, became executive vice president and chief scientific officer.

Valley Forge Scientific was formed in 1981 by brothers Leonard I. Malis and Jerry Malis. The technology was originally developed by the elder brother, Leonard I. Malis, MD, professor and chairman emeritus of the Mount Sinai School of Medicine Department of Neurosurgery. Valley Forge was a leader in the development and manufacture of bipolar electrosurgical systems. Its DualWave (TM) technology allowed surgeons to safely cut and coagulate during brain and spinal cord surgeries.

In July 2005 Synergetics hired Pamela Boone as CFO. Boone was previously vice president and acting CFO of Missouri-based Maverick Tube Corporation, a producer of tubular steel products used for industrial purposes. Boone brought experience with a publicly held company and had been serving as acting CFO for Maverick.

In October 2005 Synergetics announced a new product, the Malis Advantage, a fourth-generation, multifunctional, electrosurgical generator, which had been developed to replace other monopolar electrical systems

KEY DATES

1991: Synergetics, Inc., founded as a retinal instrument repair company.
1998: Synergetics enters the neurosurgery instrument market.
2005: Synergetics merges with Valley Forge Scientific Corp. and goes public. The company is renamed Synergetics USA.
2008: Synergetics settles longtime patent infringement lawsuit with IRIDEX.
2009: David Hable replaces founder Greg Scheller as CEO.

and lasers. At the same time, Synergetics inked an agreement with Codman & Shurtleff, a subsidiary of Johnson and Johnson, to distribute MALIS and other disposables and accessories.

In 2005 Synergetics was actively increasing its marketing partnerships. In August the company extended an agreement with Stryker, which had originally been an agreement with Valley Forge. The agreement was also a distribution agreement for Stryker to distribute a radio frequency generator for the treatment of pain. One month later, the company inked an agreement with Volk Optical for Synergetics USA to distribute Volk's products, including lenses and the company's Optiflex Surgical Assistant, a product designed to enhance visibility into the retina for surgeons.

INFRINGEMENT AND LAWSUITS: 2004–08

As U.S. competitors entered the market for retinal surgery, patents and intellectual property became a bitterly contested asset. In 2005 Innovatech Surgical, Inc., filed suit against Synergetics for unfair competition, trade libel, injurious falsehood, and tortious interference with business relationships. This suit was actually a countersuit, in response to Synergetic's previous suit filed against Innovatech.

Synergetics had filed suit in 2004 against two former employees, Charles Richard Hurst, Jr., and Michael McGowan, the principals of Innovatech. The suit focused on who was the original owner of drawings used to develop retinal surgical instruments. In addition, both Synergetics and Innovatech claimed that the other had made false and harmful statements about the other company's products to customers.

In September 2005 the courts awarded Synergetics $2.3 million in damages. As a result of this ruling, Innovatech dismissed its suit but appealed the ruling. Innovatech held that a contractor, IRIDEX, had actually used the intellectual property material without the knowledge of the principals of Innovatech.

IRIDEX subsequently filed suit against Synergetics for patent infringement. The product in question was called EndoProbe, a laser probe technology. Other products under the same patent were also included in the lawsuit. Synergetics responded by filing a motion that stated that IRIDEX had known about Synergetics' products since 1998 and had responded to IRIDEX's charges at the time. At that time, Synergetics also sought the courts to declare a summary judgment that Synergetics did not infringe the patent.

Synergetics also claimed that statements by IRIDEX employees weakened the patent infringement claim. Gregg Scheller claimed that IRIDEX employees had stated that Synergetics' products were unsafe and damaging. Scheller held that these claims by IRIDEX's employees significantly weakened the infringement case, because the IRIDEX employees effectively differentiated its own product. While the court found in favor of Synergetics, it also ruled in 2008 that Synergetics had participated in unethical practices related to the case and awarded Hurst and McGowan sanctions.

ACQUISITIONS AND PERSONNEL CHANGES: 2008 AND BEYOND

In early 2008 Synergetics made a small acquisition of an injection molding shop for precision surgical instrument design. The acquisition totaled $80,000. Plans for the acquisition were to convert many of the metal instruments to plastic moldings and to convert other products to disposable products. Overall, the company would cut costs, increase usage, and offer presterilized products to its customers.

In August 2008 Scheller abruptly resigned from the company. While a board member indicated that Scheller would continue to collaborate with Synergetics, there was no announcement regarding Scheller's plans for the future, indicating that the resignation may have been requested by the board, perhaps related to the settlement and lawsuits that had plagued the company since 1999. In February 2009 the company announced the appointment of David Hable as the new CEO, previously of Johnson and Johnson's Codman & Shurtleff.

In November 2009 Stryker announced the acquisition of Mutoh Co. Ltd., Synergetics' longtime strategic partner in the distribution and sale of the OMNI Ultrasonic Aspirator product line. This required Synergetics to expand its partnership with Stryker and to sell certain assets to it associated with marketing and sales of the consoles, hand pieces, and other products used in conjunction with OMNI. This presented an opportunity to Synergetics to expand its relationship with Stryker, which it did in 2010. The agreement also covered new development projects that the companies would pursue together.

Compared to 2009, 2010 revenue was flat, but profits actually increased as Synergetics shifted much of its direct selling of neurosurgical products to marketing partners. Although the Patient Protection and Affordable Care Act of 2010 changed certain aspects of medical care in the United States, Synergetics remained well placed to continue as a niche producer of ophthalmic and surgical instruments.

Sara K. Huter

PRINCIPAL SUBSIDIARIES

Medimold, L.L.C.; Synergetics Delaware, Inc.; Synergetics France, SARL (France); Synergetics Germany GmbH (Germany); Synergetics IP, Inc.; Synergetics Italia, Srl (Italy);

PRINCIPAL COMPETITORS

Alcon, Inc.; B. Braun Melsungen AG; Bausch & Lomb Incorporated; Covidien plc; Dutch Ophthalmic Research Corp.; IRIDEX Corporation.

FURTHER READING

"Always Improving: Synergetics USA Inc. Has Grown By Improving Products, Maintaining Quality and Responding to Market Demands." *Manufacturing Today,* January-February 2008, 106.

Armstrong, Michael W. "A Pact Fused By Long Friendship. "*Philadelphia Business Journal* 9, no. 34 (1991): 3.

"Garage Was First Home of Medical-Tool Maker; Founders' Take Advantage of Opportunities to Fill Doctors' Needs." *St Louis Post-Dispatch,* November 25, 2005.

Gillespie, Luke. "Building Synergy: Synergetics Has Evolved from a Small Basement Operation into a World Leader in the Ophthalmic and Neurosurgical Medical Devices." *US Business Review* 10, no. 1 (Winter 2010): 47.

"Gregg Scheller, 43." *St. Louis Business Journal* 20, no. 8 (1999): 52.

"Gregg Scheller to Leave Synergetics USA." *Health & Beauty Close-Up,* August 9, 2008.

"Innovatech Lawsuit Dismissed Against Synergetics on Heels of Synergetics' Win Against Innovatech's Principals." *PR Newswire,* September 23, 2005.

TAAG Angola Airlines (Linhas Aéreas de Angola, E.P.)

Rua da Missao 123
P.O. Box 79
Luanda,
Angola
Telephone: (224) 923 190 000
Web site: http://www.taag.com

State-Owned Corporation
Founded: 1938
NAICS: 481111 Scheduled Passenger Air Transportation

■ ■ ■

TAAG Angola Airlines (Transportes Aéreas de Angola, E.P.) is the largest airline in Angola. The state-owned airline provides passenger and cargo flights to more than 33 destinations around the world. TAAG Angola Airlines boasts a fleet of 11 modern Boeing aircraft, which sets it apart from other African airlines that consist mainly of secondhand planes. The Quatro de Fevereiro Airport in Luanda serves as TAAG's main operational hub.

The airline's operations are organized into three main segments identified as domestic flights, regional flights, and international flights. The domestic flights and regional flights segments specialize in passenger and cargo flights to destinations within Angola and Africa respectively. The international flights, the largest operational segment, consist of a global route network providing flight services to various destinations in North America, South America, Europe, Asia, and Australia.

TDA FOUNDED: 1938

Air transport was introduced in Angola in 1937 when Joaquim Almedia Baltazar, a Portuguese aviation expert, was invited by the Aéro Club de Angola to train the club's aviation students. Initially the aviation club lacked an aircraft, so it instructed Baltazar to acquire one. Baltazar purchased a de Havilland Tiger Moth and transferred it to Luanda, Angola, with the assistance of F. A. Bossa. The aviation club proceeded to acquire additional light aircraft that included a Cessna C37 Airmaster and a Piper J3 Cub. The aviation advancements in the Aéro Club de Angola drew the attention of the colonial government that was increasingly appreciating the need to establish air transport in the country.

The then Portugese president, Óscar Carmona, and the country's minister of colonies, António Machado, ordered Baltazar to spearhead the formation of an aviation company in the colony of Angola. Baltazar, in conjunction with government officials, formed the Divisão dos Transportes Aéreos de Angola (DTA) in 1938. DTA served as the overall administration unit for air, maritime, and railway transport. Baltazar was appointed to serve as general manager of the newly formed DTA.

The colonial government spent the next two years constructing an airport in Luanda and fixing the appropriate infrastructure in preparation for the introduction of light aircraft. The Portuguese government had issued the authorization for the release of funds for the acquisition of a light aircraft fleet consisting of de Havillands and Junkers. However, the delivery of the Junkers was derailed by the anticipated outbreak of World War II in Europe in 1939. In the meantime, the young avia-

COMPANY PERSPECTIVES

TAAG works to be the company leading the modernization of air transport and associated services in Angola, through an operation that is reliable, financially sustainable, and that promotes the image of Angola in the world.

tion company utilized aircrafts borrowed from the Aéro Club de Angola until the de Havillands were delivered.

INITIAL FLIGHTS AND NEW AIRCRAFT

DTA launched its operations in July 17, 1940, when three de Havilland biplanes made their maiden domestic flights from Luanda to Namibe. The company premiered its aviation services through two main routes that had been created by the Aéro Club de Angola. The first route that connected Luanda to Namibe mainly cut through the coastal areas. The second route was largely an inland route that connected Luanda and Benguela through Lobito. The second route was later extended to Macadames.

Baltazar quit the general manager position in 1940 after he was requested to return to Portugal to attend to urgent domestic issues as a result of war in Europe. DTA was also rebranded to DTA Linhas Aéreas de Angola (DTA Angola Airlines) in 1940. The second inland route was extended to Cabinda in 1941.

TDA Angola Airlines recorded few flights from 1940 through to 1943 because of a severe aircraft parts shortage that was precipitated by World War II. Baltazar returned to the company in 1944 and resumed the general manager position that he previously occupied. The company expanded its fleet in 1944 when it purchased two Stinson Reliants light aircraft from Belgian Congo. In early 1946 TDA purchased several Douglas DC-3s aircraft from the U.S. military and four additional Beech 18s later in the year. Some of the additional fleet was used to launch flights to Kinshasa, Zaire, in 1946.

DTA Linhas Aéreas de Angola began extending regular weekly flights to all its major destinations in Angola. The company acquired additional aircrafts in 1948 by purchasing a Douglas DC-3. DTA was operating seven DC 3s and four Beech D-18s in 1959. The Beech aircrafts were used for charters, training, and government communications. The DC-3s were operat-

ing all the scheduled routes and were beginning to show their age. It was becoming clear that new aircraft were needed. In response, the airline ordered two new Fokker F-27-200 Friendship aircraft in June 1961 in an event that became the airlines' first purchase of new aircraft. The two Fokker F-27-200 Friendship aircraft were delivered in 1962 and were used to replace the aged DC-3s in December the same year. DTA ordered the third Fokker F-27-200 Friendship aircraft in 1965 and received it in 1966.

TDAs first recorded air crash occurred on May 21, 1972, when one of its Fokker F-27-200 Friendship aircraft crashed into the Atlantic sea approximately two miles from Lobito. The worst plane crash ever to occur in Angola at the time, it killed 20 of the 23 people who were aboard.

INDEPENDENCE AND INTERNATIONALISM

The airline served as a domestic carrier until 1973 when it was renamed Transportes Aéreos de Angola (TAAG Angola Airlines) and subsequently upgraded to international carrier. TAAG Angola Airlines launched its maiden operations as an international carrier with flights to São Tomé and Príncipe and Namibia (Windhoek) in 1973.

The transformation of Angola from a Portuguese colony to an independent state on November 11, 1975, brought with it many changes in the country's corporate sector, including TAAG Angola Airlines. The airline was converted into Angola's national carrier wholly owned by the government of Angola. The carrier's management board was restructured and the first Angolan citizens were nominated to the board. The carrier made its first intercontinental flight to Lisbon Portugal in 1975 as the country experienced the realities of independence. The opening of the European route increased the pressure on the airline's service capacity, a development that prompted the acquisition of its first Boeing jet, a Boeing 737, in 1976.

The 1980s marked the period when TAAG Airlines Angola recorded unprecedented growth in its operational capacity and route network. Increase in oil and diamond production in Angola in this decade opened up demand for cargo and passenger transport services in Angola and to international destinations. The acquisition of a new Boeing 707 in 1980 heralded a period of accelerated expansion in the carrier's domestic and international markets. According to the airline, TAAG recorded "more than 30,000 hours and 18 million kilometers (approximately 11 million miles) in 1980," a clear manifestation of the company's positive growth trends.

KEY DATES

1938: Government officials form the Divisão dos Transportes Aéreos de Angola.

1975: TAAG Angola Airlines proclaimed the Angolan national carrier.

1980: Company acquires first Boeing 707.

1997: Company acquires First Boeing 747.

2008: The European Union bans TAAG Angola Airlines.

2010: The European Union lifts ban on TAAG Angola Airlines.

Angola, however, continued to be plagued by a bitter civil war that erupted in 1975 immediately after the country's independence. The UNITA rebels that were fighting the government employed guerrilla tactics by committing acts of sabotage to destabilize the government. The rebels also destroyed key infrastructure components including roads and railroads in their strongholds. Rail transport, one of the key means of passenger and bulk cargo transportation in Angola, was completely stalled in the mid-1980s because of lack of security. A majority of the roads in the country's interior became impassable as well, due to destroyed bridges and frequent attacks against travelers by revolutionary rebels.

The airline experienced the first fatal aircraft accident involving its Boeing fleet on November 8, 1983, when a scheduled domestic flight crashed during takeoff from Lubango Airport, killing all 130 people aboard. The Luanda-bound aircraft had successfully taken off the runways and ascended to an altitude of 200 feet but began a sudden descent that saw it crash on its left wing before bursting into flames less than a mile from the runway. The exact cause of the accident remained controversial. The Angola authorities blamed technical failures, but the UNITA guerilla movement claimed to have shot down the aircraft. The aircraft was mainly ferrying Angolan soldiers who were traveling for their leave.

The stalling of railroad transport combined with the unreliable state of roads left air transport as the only reliable (although not entirely safe) means of transport in inland Angola. TAAG Airlines adjusted accordingly to the increase in demand for its passenger and cargo transports services. The carrier's customer numbers continued to swell as it recorded its one millionth passenger in 1986, a year during which its employee numbers also increased to 5,000. The magnitude of the airlines' expanded operational capacity in 1986 was a clear indication of the growing dependence of Angola's economic activities on the airline's services.

DIFFICULT SKIES: 1987–97

In 1987 TAAG Angola Airlines created a new subsidiary, the Angola Air Charter, in response to the ever-growing demand for its services. The Angola Air Charter helped to ease operational pressure by launching chartered and scheduled flights to mainly regional and international destinations that included Johannesburg, Ostend, and Lisbon. TAAG Angola Airlines, however, experienced a major setback in July 1988 following the crash of a Boeing belonging to its subsidiary. The aircraft was completely destroyed, killing all six passengers on board, in a crash that occurred near Lagos, Nigeria. TAAG Angola Airlines was subjected to unfavorable news again in July 1990 when another aircraft belonging to its Angola Air Charter subsidiary, a Lockheed, crashed as it landed in Menongue, Angola.

The airline was restructured in 1991 when a new subsidiary, Sociedad de Aviação Ligeira (SAL) was formed to focus on the key flight segments of multipurpose flights and aero-taxi services. The establishment of the SAL subsidiary facilitated the concentration of TAAG Angola Airlines' operational activities on core domestic and international routes by delegating its noncore air charter services to the newly created subsidiary.

Angola Air Charter was converted into a partnership entity in 1992 when ENDIANA, Angola's leading state-owned diamond mining company, acquired 49 percent of the shareholding in the subsidiary. TAAG Angola Airlines held on to 51 percent, and in 1993 a new livery for Angola Air Charter was created to draw a clear distinction in the identities of the two airlines. TAAG Angola Airlines opened the Luanda-Harare and the Luanda-Johannesburg Routes in 1993 and 1994, respectively. However, the company's safety standards were again called into question in April 1994 when a Lockheed operated by Angola Air Charter crashed as it landed in Malange, Angola.

TAAG Angola Airlines resumed operations in the Luanda-Lusaka route in 1995, several years since the route was suspended because of insufficient passenger and cargo traffic. In July 1997 TAAG Angola Airlines boosted its operational capacity through the purchase of a Boeing 747. According to the airline's Web site, the acquisition of the largest Boeing aircraft at the time was a momentous achievement for the airline, which also captured the mood in the country by christening the jet "Cidade do Kuito" as a dedication to the martyrs of

Kuito. (From 1993 to 1994, between 20,000 and 30,000 people died in the city of Kuito as a result of an 18-month siege by UNITA rebels.)

TROUBLE IN EUROPE

The unrivaled expansion strides that had been achieved by TAAG Angola Airlines in the early years of the 21st century were dealt a major blow when a Boeing 737-2M2 of the carrier crashed in northern Angola in June 2007. The aircraft, destined for M'banza-Kongo, crashed at that airport after undershooting the runway, killing one crew member and four passengers out of the 78 people who were on board. The accident also killed one person on the ground and injured many others as the plane crashed through stationary vehicles and two buildings.

Nonetheless, in November 2007 the airline proceeded with expansion of its regional route network in Northern Africa when it entered a bilateral agreement with Ethiopian Airlines for the extension of connecting flights between the two carriers. The agreement facilitated TAAG Angola Airlines' objective of increased access to high-traffic air transport opportunities in North African, Middle East, and Asian markets. The carrier made its first trip to Addis Ababa, Ethiopia on November 24, 2007.

In July 2008 TAAG Angola Airlines faced one of the biggest challenges in its history when it was blacklisted as an unsafe airline by the European Union (EU) and banned from flying in EU's airspace. The EU further issued travel advisories warning European citizens against flying with the Angolan carrier. The ban effectively reduced TAAG's operations by a significant margin because the EU market accounted for more than a third of the carrier's passenger enplanements and cargo transport. The EU ban on TAAG Angola Airlines was extended in November 2008 when a report for an audit conducted in October 2008 identified the persistence of safety loopholes in the airline's operations.

BETTER SAFETY AND NEW MARKETS: 2009 AND BEYOND

TAAG Angola Airlines continued to upgrade its fleet in a bid to achieve internationally recommended safety standards. In April 2009 the carrier announced it had ordered two new state-of-the-art Boeing 777s at an approximate cost of $544 million. The deal also included rights for the purchase of two additional 777s for Boeing. The strategy shift in TAAG Angola Airlines also involved searching for alternative markets in southeastern Asia, eastern Europe, and the Middle East

with particular focus in China and Dubai. The strategy paid off as the airline was able to compensate for the loss of the EU market.

The situation began to change in May 2009 when the carrier successfully passed an Operational Safety Audit (IOSA) by the International Air Transport Association (IATA). This accreditation renewed the carrier's hopes of being cleared by the EU. On March 30, 2010, the EU released the updated list of its blacklisted carriers, and TAAG Angola Airlines was granted a conditional ending of the ban. The EU made it clear that TAAG Angola Airlines would remain under tight safety surveillance and risked another ban if it did not achieve sustained safety for its flight operations.

The carrier demonstrated its commitment to continuous service improvement by signing a 10-year agreement worth $50 million with OnPoint Solution Services for the maintenance, repair, and overhaul of 10 of its GE90 engines. The agreement was hailed as strategy toward achieving sustainable high-quality standards in the airline's operational equipment and material repairs and maintenance activities.

As it looked to the future, TAAG Angola Airlines remained committed to continuous service improvement through expansion of its domestic, regional, and international route networks. The company planned to acquire more Boeing 777-300ERs aircraft so as to serve the increasing traffic in the European routes. TAAG Airlines was also destined for privatization as soon as the government of Angola approved privatization laws in the country.

Paul Ingati

PRINCIPAL SUBSIDIARIES

Angola Air Charter.

PRINCIPAL COMPETITORS

Aero Tropical; Angola Aeronautica; Diexim Espresso; SonAir Airlines Services, S.A.; Transafrik International.

FURTHER READING

"Accident Digest Boeing 737-200 TAAG Angola." *Flight Story, Aviation Blog.* Accessed November 26, 2010. http://blog. flightstory.net/196/accident-digest-boeing-737-200-taag-angola.

"Ethiopian, TAAG Angola Enter into Agreement." *Africa News,* December 3, 2007. Accessed November 27, 2010. http://www.africanews.com/site/list_messages/13606.

"EU Bans All Indonesian Airlines." *BBC News,* June 28, 2007. Accessed November 27, 2010. http://news.bbc.co.uk/2/hi/europe/6248490.stm.

European Commission. "Commission Updates the List of Airlines Banned from the European Airspace." Brussels, Europe.eu, March 30, 2010. Accessed November 26, 2010. http://europa.eu/rapid/pressReleasesAction.do?reference=IP/10/388&format=HTML&aged=0&language=EN&guiLanguage=en.

Guttery, Ben R. *Encyclopedia of African Airlines.* Jefferson, N.C.: McFarland, 1998.

Harrison, Pete. "EU Bans Sudan, Philippine Airlines; Clears TAAG." *Reuters,* March 3, 2010. Accessed November 27, 2010. http://af.reuters.com/article/investingNews/idAFJOE62T0KJ20100330.

Stead, Mike, and Sean Rorison. *Angola.* Chalfont St. Peter, Buckinghamshire, UK: Bradt Travel Guides, 2010.

"TAAG Air Angola." airlinesinfocare.com. Accessed November 25, 2010. http://www.airlinesinfocare.com/international-airline-flights/taag-air-angola.html.

"TAAG Angola Airlines – Accident Description." Aviation Safety Network, 2010. Accessed November 25, 2010. http://aviation-safety.net/database/record.php?id=20070628-0.

TAAG Angola Airlines. "Boeing, TAAG Linhas Aéreas de Angola Announces Order for Two 777-300ERs." TAAG Angola Airlines, Press Release, April 29, 2009. Accessed November 26, 2010. http://www.taag.com/en/press-release.aspx.

"TAAG Passes IATA's Test." *ANGOP: Agência Angola Press,* May 29, 2009. Accessed November 27, 2010. http://www.portalangop.co.ao/motix/en_us/noticias/transporte/TAAG-passes-IATA-test,0b2303c4-c4b5-411a-a51c-bfb7c5139548.html.

Taiheiyo Cement
Corporation

■

Daiba Garden City Building, 2-3-5
Daiba, Minato-Ku
Tokyo, 135-8578
Japan
Telephone: (3) 6226-9018
Fax: (3) 6226-9154
Web site: http://www.taiheiyo-cement.co.jp

Public Company
Founded: 1881 as Onoda Cement
Employees: 16,909 (2010)
Sales: ¥728.6 billion ($9 billion) (2010)
Stock Exchanges: Tokyo
Ticker Symbol: 5233
NAICS: 327310 Cement Manufacturing

■ ■ ■

Taiheiyo Cement Corporation operates as Japan's largest cement manufacturer. The company has over 570 subsidiaries in its arsenal, all of which are involved in the construction, construction materials, and real estate sectors. Taiheiyo's core business segments include cement and minerals and aggregates, along with its zero-emissions division, an environmentally friendly unit that focuses on turning waste materials into resources. Chichibu Onoda Cement Corp. and Nihon Cement Co. Ltd. merged in 1998 to form Taiheiyo, the fifth-largest cement concern in the world.

ORIGINS IN THE LATE 19TH CENTURY

The history of the Onoda Cement Company, a major predecessor in the Taiheiyo group, begins during Japan's Meiji era (1867 to 1912). During this time, the Japanese social structure changed from feudal to Western forms through government-sponsored industrial expansion. One of the first steps taken by the Meiji government to modernize was the construction of port and harbor facilities. The first cement in Japan, imported from France in 1870, was used in the construction of piers in the port of Yokosuka. As the demand for infrastructure increased, so did the demand for cement and other imported goods. In an effort to reduce the outflow of gold and silver due to increased imports, the Meiji government began a domestic industrial development program.

Except in military industries and strategic communications systems, private concerns carried out this industrial development program. In certain industries, however, the Meiji government sponsored and constructed pilot plants. One of these industries was cement. The construction bureau of the Ministry of Finance built Japan's first cement plant at Fukagawa, Tokyo, in 1873. Portland cement was manufactured there two years later, in 1875.

One of the crucial features of the Meiji era, the disbanding of the samurai warrior class in 1869, helped provide the financial basis for Onoda Cement Company. After their dismissal from government service, the samurai received pensions from the government that amounted to a percentage of their original salary and

COMPANY PERSPECTIVES

Our mission is to contribute to social infrastructure development by providing solutions that are environmentally efficient, enhance our competitive position, and bring value to our stakeholders.

varied in value. After about seven years, the pensions became too expensive and were replaced with interest-bearing, nonconvertible bonds. The samurais' incomes fell to a fraction of their original levels, and only a few of them had enough commercial experience to go to work to replace their lost incomes. At the same time, inflation due to weakened paper currency and increased government expenditures reduced the real value of their fixed holdings. Inflation later became a principal reason for the government's decision to sell its various pilot plants.

In May 1881 at Onoda-Mura, Yamaguchi Prefecture, Junpachi Kasai founded Onoda Cement, the first privately owned cement company in Japan. A year later, Onoda Cement purchased the government's pilot plant at Onoda. Kasai, himself an ex-samurai warrior, led a group of samurai who pooled their pensions to capitalize the company. Kasai became one of Japan's leading industrialists and part of a group of business leaders who helped reinforce Japan's national integrity. Through their industrial successes, these businesspeople resisted the expansion of Western interests into Japan during a period of global colonization. During the presidency of Kasai's son, Shinzo Kasai, between 1900 and 1930, Onoda became the largest cement firm in Japan.

Transportation was crucial to profitability in the cement industry because cement was traditionally a high-bulk, low-value good. Manufacturers maximized revenues by placing plants near either the final market or a water transportation facility, since water transport was the least expensive mode of bulk carriage. Prior to World War II, Onoda solely produced cement. It did not have its own sales and distribution network. Mitsui Bussan, a large *zaibatsu*, or conglomerate, was Onoda's sales and distribution agent in both foreign and domestic markets. The relationship did not compromise Onoda's independence. Onoda was not a subsidiary of Mitsui Bussan but rather a client of its trading services. From its founding Onoda had been proud of maintaining its corporate independence.

The firm expanded extensively before World War II, especially into China and the Japanese colony of Korea, the closest areas for increasing market size. By the beginning of the war, over 60 percent of the firm's assets, roughly 19 plants, were in Korea and China.

OVERCOMING PROBLEMS

In 1924 the cement federation Rengokai, a cartel organization, was formed to control output. The cartel set uniform curtailment rates that required cement manufacturers to limit production to 60 percent of capacity. Uniform production curtailment rates favored established firms over newer firms. Established firms retained older equipment, normally scrapped in a competitive environment, simply for the purpose of counting it as production capacity. Older firms could curtail production to 60 percent of capacity by using 100 percent of their new equipment and none of their older equipment. Newer firms with a higher percentage of newer equipment found that the 60 percent cap cut into the machinery they could use in a competitive market, putting them at a disadvantage.

The cement federation agreements covered Japan proper, the colonies, Manchukuo, and the South Seas Mandatory territories. Tensions within the cartel, intensified by the Great Depression, prompted the formation of sales associations to fix exclusive sales territories with sales quotas and standard prices. In 1932 Onoda's Dairen factory seceded from the cartel over a dispute about Manchurian quotas. In December 1933 the cartel responded to this challenge by setting up a mechanism by which to divide markets, the Cement Exporters Association.

In 1934 Onoda and the Oita Company withdrew from the cartel on the grounds that the industry's leader, the Asano Group, gained an unfair advantage from the uniform curtailment rates because it had predominantly older equipment. When the cartel lost its control, it appealed to the government for intervention. In December 1934 the minister of commerce and industry enforced Article 2 of Japan's Major Industries Control Law, for the first time ever, on the cement industry. The government's intervention forced the "outsiders" to comply with the cartel's curtailment rates but actually did very little to control competition since the law applied only to production in Japan proper.

To get around this constraint, Onoda built plants in Korea, Kwantung, and Manchukuo and supplied the home market from these sources. This move was easy to accomplish because Onoda and the other "outsiders" operated mainly in western Honshu, Kyushu, and Korea. The national and municipal governments became

KEY DATES

1881: Junpachi Kasai establishes Onoda Cement.

1924: Rengokai, a cement federation, is formed to control output.

1945: Onoda loses 60 percent of its assets as a result of World War II.

1974: P.T. Semen Nusantara is set up in Indonesia to operate a cement plant.

1988: The company enters the U.S. market.

1998: Chichibu Onoda joins forces with Nihon Cement Co. Ltd. to form Taiheiyo Cement Corp.

2000: Taiheiyo acquires a 28 percent stake in South Korea-based Ssangyong Cement Co. Ltd. and a majority interest in Grand Cement Co. of the Philippines.

2004: Management announces sweeping reforms to its organization and structure.

2009: Head office is relocated to Minato Ward.

2011: Earthquake and tsunami devastate Honshu.

some of Onoda's biggest customers, since the company now could undercut cartel prices. The cartel responded to these Onoda successes by having the Asano, Mitsubishi, and Yasuda zaibatsu set up their own colonial companies. It also secured the 1936 revision of the Major Industries Control Law, which extended the government's control into the colonies as well. The government's solution to the conflict was to have agents of the Rengokai and Onoda meet every three months to set prices and production limits. This arrangement lasted until the eve of World War II, at which time Onoda operated 27 plants with an annual production of 3.5 million tons.

POSTWAR GROWTH

As a result of World War II, Onoda lost 60 percent of its assets, or a total of 19 plants, including its foreign holdings in China and all of its holdings in what had been its colony, Korea. The plants left to Onoda after World War II included Ofunato, Fujiwara, Tahara, Hikone, Atetsu, Onoda, Yahata, Tsunemi, and Oita. Together with the loss of plants, Onoda lost its distribution arrangement with Mitsui Bussan when that zaibatsu was broken up by the occupation government of the Allied powers. The new arrangement called for Onoda to operate its own domestic sales and distribution network while employing Mitsui as its foreign sales and distribution agent.

After the war, Onoda president Toyoroku Ando rebuilt the business to reemerge as the industry's leader in Japan. Ando was a 1921 graduate of Tokyo University and a lifelong employee of Onoda. He spent his first 25 years with the company in Korea, where he rose to manage the Pyongyang factory in 1944. Ando became president in 1945 and improved the efficiency of Onoda's production, distribution, and transportation systems. Under his direction, the company began extensive diversification plans.

Onoda began to expand outside Japan in the 1960s with a joint venture with two partners, Mitsui Bussan and Hong Leong Corporation. This joint venture, Singapore Cement, was a bulk importer of Onoda's "Dragon Brand" cement. In 1974 Onoda set up P.T. Semen Nusantara in Indonesia to operate a cement plant at Cilacap, in central Java. Later, Onoda expanded into several markets, including Hong Kong, Australia, Hawaii, Malaysia, and regions of the Pacific Rim. In the late 1980s Onoda began to expand into both the Chinese and continental U.S. markets.

Onoda's entry into the United States began with a joint venture with Lone Star Industries of Greenwich, Connecticut, in 1988. The $60 million operation, Lone Star Northwest, conducted business in Washington, Oregon, and Alaska. The venture imported cement and manufactured concrete and aggregates (crushed stones used in making cement and in highway construction).

Onoda's second entry into the U.S. market that year was the purchase of the CalMat Company's cement division, California Portland Cement Company, for $310 million. CalMat was a Los Angeles-area firm dealing in sand, gravel, asphalt, concrete, and land development. The purchase included 13 ready-mix concrete plants, three cement plants, and a cement-importing terminal, and it made Onoda the largest cement producer in California. In 1989 Onoda invested in China in a joint venture with Mitsui Bussan and two Chinese firms, Huaneng Raw Material Corporation and Dalian Cement Factory.

The company's principal innovations at that time included the reinforced suspension preheater (RSP), an advanced cement-manufacturing process developed in 1964 that substantially reduced the amount of energy used in the manufacture of cement. The RSP system was used in more than 20 countries and was recognized as an industry standard. The O-sepa separator was an air separation system sold worldwide. The system, developed in the late 1970s, saved electric energy and improved particle-size distribution. A third product, Bristar, was an efficient, nonexplosive demolition agent used in urban areas to minimize the traditional side effects of explosives, such as flying debris, noise, vibration, gas, and dust. Another innovation was Chemicolime, developed in the late 1960s. This quicklime technology, which stabilized wet soils, was used by the U.S. military in Vietnam to strengthen jungle and marshland roads. Its contemporary uses involved construction projects near coastal regions.

ECONOMIC CHALLENGES, EXPANSION, AND REFORM; 1991–2003

By the early 1990s, Japan's cement industry was plagued with problems. Onoda faced intense competition while struggling against a downturn in government works projects and overcapacity. In addition, the country's economy was faltering. Many of Japan's leading companies were forced into merger activity, an uncommon occurrence in the Japanese business world. Sure enough, Onoda, positioned as one of Japan's largest cement manufacturers, and Chichibu Cement Co. Ltd., Japan's sixth-largest cement concern, joined forces in October 1994. The merger created Chichibu Onoda Cement Corp., Japan's largest cement manufacturer with a 24 percent share of the market.

Changes continued into the late 1990s as the company once again found itself in the midst of a major deal. Chichibu Onoda solidified its leading position in the industry by teaming up with Nihon Cement Co. Ltd. in 1998. Taiheiyo Cement Corp. was born out of the union and controlled over 40 percent of the domestic cement market. Even with its enviable position, Taiheiyo faced tough times due to continued weak demand. As part of a restructuring effort, the firm initiated a round of job cuts, reduced production capacity, and took other cost-cutting measures with a plan of saving ¥37 billion per year through 2001.

As Taiheiyo entered the 21st century, the company looked to international expansion as a means of shoring up profits. The firm acquired a 28 percent stake in South Korea-based Ssangyong Cement Co. Ltd. and a majority interest in Grand Cement Co. of the Philippines in 2000, making it the fifth-largest cement concern in the world based on output capacity. Despite these positive steps, Taiheiyo and its domestic counterparts continued to deal with falling demand, among other obstacles. In April 2000 the *Nikkei Weekly* reported that "Japan's cement industry seems immune to economic recovery. The problem can be traced to the sector's distribution structure, which negates the benefits of manufacturer cost-cutting by fostering intense competition among suppliers of ready-mix concrete. Complex conflicts of interest have made it extremely

difficult for cement manufacturers to address the issue."

Nevertheless, Taiheiyo began to reform its distribution and logistics practices during this time period. It raised cement prices, stopped paying sales commissions, and began utilizing a uniform pricing structure in hopes of bolstering its financial position. In 2002 the company launched a new three-year program aimed at reducing debt. It sold off various real estate and securities assets and slashed capital spending.

During 2003 the operating environment in the cement industry remained challenging, especially for Taiheiyo. Demand in the government sector, which had accounted for nearly 60 percent of domestic cement demand in the past, continued to dwindle, forcing the company to look down different avenues for growth. One such area was recycling waste, which the company participated in through its zero-emission promotion business.

SWEEPING ORGANIZATIONAL REFORMS: 2003–07

While Taiheiyo posted a net profit in 2003, difficulties continued as the company faced reduced demand, management restructuring, and decreased market values. However, the company continued to acquire subsidiaries, particularly in the United States.

In early 2004 Taiheiyo announced sweeping organizational reforms. The first reform was to establish a mid-term management plan to commit to strengthening the company's financial position. Taiheiyo would focus on liquidating unprofitable assets and investments, and on growth areas. In addition, a new executive committee was established to determine and guide company strategy. The executive committee would be made up of one board director, the company's president, and executive officers from the corporate, professional, and research and development divisions. In addition, the executive officers' terms were limited to two years. The plan further specified that decision making would become decentralized, and it established divisions to operate as in-house companies.

Taiheiyo specified its medium-term plan to become the leading cement company in the Pacific Rim by 2007 fiscal year end (March 31, 2008). In doing so, the company would increase its operating cash flow through profitability, focus on growth businesses, and strengthen its group management functions. Areas of focus would be operating profit, cash flow, and debt reduction. By 2008 the company's cash flow and debt projections were on target, but net income figures missed their target by ¥20 billion due to extraordinary losses from the sale of its assets, estimated losses from decreased market value on overseas investments, and increased allowances for doubtful accounts due to economic deterioration of credit quality of its customers.

Problems compounded when Taiheiyo's products were tainted with chromium-6 at high levels, which is hazardous to the soil and in violation of the Basic Environment Law. The company took a loss on these products as it remedied the problem through dealer recalls and daily testing.

ACQUISITIONS AND A RECESSION: 2008 AND BEYOND

Amid the challenges, Taiheiyo continued to acquire assets, particularly in the United States. In January 2008 Taiheiyo acquired the business assets of IMIX Group, a ready-mix concrete and aggregate company in Phoenix, Arizona. Phoenix was a growing market for the construction industry. The acquisition added seven ready-mix plans that produced 450,000 metric tons annually, and two aggregate quarries that produced 600,000 tons annually.

The early months of 2008 also brought two acquisitions for Taiheiyo's subsidiary California Portland Cement Company (CPC). In March 2008 Taiheiyo acquired the common stock of Union Asphalt, a California construction business that also sold ready-mix and aggregate. As a consequence of California's prohibitive policies for developing new aggregate resources, Union Asphalt was attractive because its resources were already developed, allowing CPC access to the coastal region along California. In April, CPC announced the acquisition of SSMC Holdings which owned Silver State Materials LLC, based in Las Vegas, to take advantage of construction opportunities offered due to the area's growing population. This acquisition added eight ready-mix plants and an aggregate business to Taiheiyo's asset base. However, the collapse of global financial markets eventually led to drastically reduced rates of new construction, making these acquisitions ill-timed.

In May 2009 Taiheiyo relocated its head office to Minato Ward to simplify operational efficiency of the group management. The move consolidated business units and simplified R&D and administrative departments. This move also discontinued the previously planned decentralization that created in-house companies. Instead, the businesses of construction materials, ceramics, and electronics were housed in the same location where oversight could be consolidated.

In early 2010 Taiheiyo announced that it would discontinue cement production domestically due to the drastic decline in demand. The move would substantially reduce fixed costs. The company anticipated that the discontinuation of this line of business would result in a reduction of ¥15 billion in FY 2010. Later that year, the company sold the assets associated with the move.

The company remained profitable through FY 2008, but the global economic recession significantly affected the company's profitability in 2009 and 2010, when it lost ¥35 billion and ¥37 billion, respectively. While the company's management plans were on track to take advantage of growth opportunities, and operating cash flows allowed the company to make attractive acquisitions, it was possible that the company's declining sales and rising debt level would hinder its ability to continue to do so as interest payments may strap its liquidity. Devastation to Japan caused by a massive earthquake and resulting tsunami in March 2011 also increased the uncertainty regarding Taiheiyo's long-term business prospects.

John C. Bishop
Updated, Christina M. Stansell; Sara K. Huter

PRINCIPAL SUBSIDIARIES

CalPortland Company (USA); Dalian Onoda Cement Co., Ltd. (China); Jiangnan-Onoda Cement Co., Ltd. (China); Kalahari Dry (Thailand) Co., Ltd. (Thailand); Nghi Son Cement Corporation (Vietnam); PNG-Taiheiyo Cement Limited (Papua New guinea); Qinhuangdao Asano Cement Co., Ltd. (China); Shanghai Sanhang Onoda Cement Co., Ltd. (China); Shenzhen Haixing Onoda Cement Co., Ltd. (China); Ssangyong Cement Industrial Co., Ltd. (South Korea); Taiheiyo Cement Philippines, Inc. (Philippines); Taiheiyo International (Thailand) Co., Ltd. (Thailand); Yuko Mining Co., Ltd.

PRINCIPAL COMPETITORS

Holcim Ltd.; Lafarge S.A.; Mitsubishi Materials Corporation; Sumitomo Osaka Cement Co., Ltd.

FURTHER READING

"The Cement Industry of Japan." *Far Eastern Economic Review,* August 8, 1957.

Masson, R. H. P. *A History of Japan.* New York: Free Press, 1972.

"Raw Materials Costs Driving Cement Prices Higher in Japan." *AsiaPulse News,* February 16, 2011.

Sapsord, Jathon. "Mergers' Growing Acceptance in Japan Is Fortified by Fair Trade Panel's Move." *Wall Street Journal,* January 12, 1994, A7.

"Taiheiyo Cement Mounts Drive into Asian Markets." *Nikkei Weekly,* October 16, 2000.

"Two Cement Firms in Japan Announce Plans for a Merger." *Wall Street Journal,* November 13, 1993, A7.

Tanzania Breweries Limited

———————— ■ ————————

Plot 79, Block AA
Uhuru Street, Mchikichini, Ilala District
P.O. Box 9013
Dar es Salaam, 35091
Tanzania
Telephone: (22) 218 2779
Fax: (22) 218 1457
Web site: http://www.sabmiller.com

Wholly Owned Subsidiary of SABMiller plc
Founded: 1930
Employees: 1,300 (est., 2010)
Sales: TZS 464 billion ($310 billion) (2009)
Stock Exchanges: Dar es Salaam
Ticker Symbol: TBL-TZ
NAICS: 312120 Breweries

■ ■ ■

Tanzania Breweries Limited (TBL) is the largest manufacturer of malted beer and alcoholic beverages in the Republic of Tanzania. TBL is one of the subsidiaries of SABMiller plc, a leading international brewing company based in South Africa. Tanzania Breweries is headquartered in Dar es Salaam and runs a chain of three other breweries in Mwanza, Arusha, and Mbeya, in addition to a malting plant in Moshi. TBL also owns a 65 percent stake and participates in the management of Tanzania Distilleries Limited, a leading distiller of spirits in Tanzania.

TBL boasts an overall market share of 83 percent and its brands dominate Tanzania's beer and alcoholic fruit beverage market. Safari Lager, Konyagi, and Kilimanjaro Premium Lager are the company's leading brands. TBL also engages in licensed production and distribution of SABMiller plc's and Kenya's East Africa Breweries Limited (EABL) brands. Castle Lager, Redd's Premium, and Castle Milk Stout are the main SABMiller plc's brands produced and distributed by TBL in Tanzania. Tusker Lager, Guinness, and Pilsner Lager are the main EABL brands that the company is licensed to manufacture and distribute in Tanzania.

TBL distills Konyagi Ice on behalf of Tanzania Distillers Limited under a license agreement defined by the subsidiary relationship between the two companies.

FOUNDING AND LATER NATIONALIZATION

TBL has a long and inspiring history that goes back to the 1930s. The company was founded as Tanganyika Breweries in Dar es Salaam in 1930. Mainly owned by foreign investors, the company rolled out its production activities in 1933. Tanganyika Breweries was acquired by Kenya Breweries in 1935 through a successful buyout of the majority ownership stake in the company. Kenya Breweries was under the stewardship of its founders, H. A. Darling and Charles Hurst, at the time of the Tanganyika Breweries acquisition. In 1936 Tanganyika Breweries was officially merged with Kenya Breweries to form East African Breweries Limited (EABL). The acquisition of a financial stake in Uganda Breweries in 1959 effectively spread the influence of EABL to the entire East African region.

COMPANY PERSPECTIVES

We believe that for SABMiller and Tanzania Breweries to achieve competitive advantage, and ultimately better profitability, sustainable development needs to be part of what we do every day. It needs to be integrated into our decision-making and the way we run our business. To this end, in addition to goals such as discouraging irresponsible drinking, the company also works toward reducing its carbon footprint, implementing zero-waste operations, and making more beer but using less water.

EABL asserted its dominance in the Tanzanian market with the acquisition of a controlling interest in Kilimanjaro Breweries in 1963. The unification of Tanganyika mainland and Zanzibar islands to form the Republic of Tanzania in 1964 presented major transformations in the country's political, economic, and social landscapes. The political and economic realities that defined the country's transformation at the time meant that the impending conversion of the nation's leading brewery into a state corporation was inevitable.

The emergence of socialist and Marxist political ideologies in Tanzania immediately after independence led to the nationalization of many privately owned companies in the country. The nationalization process of Tanzania Breweries commenced in 1964. The Tanzanian subsidiary of the East Africa Breweries was restructured and renamed Tanzania Breweries. By 1967 the Tanzanian Government had secured 45 percent shareholding in the company. Tanzania Breweries was fully converted into a state corporation in 1979.

PRIVATIZATION AND EXPANSION: 1993–95

Tanzania's gradual shift from socialism to capitalism in the mid-1980s opened the doors for the liberalization of the country's political economy. The exit of President Julius Nyerere's government in 1985 and election of a new government under President Ali Hassan Mwinyi marked the end of socialism in Tanzania. Privatization of companies in Tanzania's mainstream economic sector became the norm as the country experienced a transition to capitalism. The Tanzania Parastatal Sector Reform Commission was established with the mandate of spearheading the transformation of more than 200 state-owned companies into privately owned entities.

Tanzania Breweries was one of the first big parastatal businesses to be privatized by the newly established commission. The privatization began in 1993 after it became evident that the profitability and production capacity of the company had been compromised by its nationalization. Safari Lager was the corporation's only brand and its market share had drastically dropped to 30 percent. The government of Tanzania offered a 50 percent joint venture stake of Tanzania Breweries to SABMiller, which accepted. The enhanced capital and liquidity capacity of the company deriving from this agreement was immediately channelled towards the modernization and restructuring of the dilapidated production plants and equipment. The company also invested $87 million toward the construction of a new Greenfields brewery to enhance its production volume.

The improving fortunes of the company were taken a notch higher in 1995 with the successful completion of the Mwanza Brewery Plant. The construction of the Mwanza Brewery was aided by an $18 million loan from the International Finance Corporation (IFC), part of the World Bank Group. Around the same time as this plant was completed, TBL started importing and distributing Castle Milk Stout and Castle Lager from South Africa's SABMiller parent company. By the end of 1995, Tanzania Breweries had managed to raise its overall market share to 45 percent. As such, the company's management was evidently pursuing capacity expansion and product portfolio strategies with the objective of achieving the market leadership position in Tanzania.

NEW PRODUCTS AND AN IPO: 1996–99

In 1996 the Tanzanian government further diluted its ownership stake in the company through a rights issue of 13 percent of its 50 percent shareholding. SABMiller won part of the share auction with assistance from IFC and effectively acquired the majority ownership status of the company. IFC was allocated 9 percent of the 13 percent common shares in Tanzania Breweries that were offered by the government. TBL committed much of the raised capital to the expansion of production capacity and development of new products. The company commenced local production of Castle Lager in 1996 and launched the popular Kilimanjaro brand as well.

Tanzania Breweries also began experiencing the benefits of the government's five-year tax holiday scheme initiated in 1996. The tax holiday scheme was one of the government's numerous incentives that were designed to stimulate private sector development and foreign investments. Moreover, the Mwanza Brewery Plant outperformed expectations and the company

KEY DATES

1930: Company begins as Tanganyika Breweries.
1964: Republic of Tanzania is created, leading to nationalization movement for many companies.
1979: Tanzania Breweries becomes wholly owned state company.
1993: With capitalism on the ascent politically, privatization of Tanzania Breweries commences.
1998: Tanzania Breweries goes public.
2002: TBL acquires the production and distribution license in Tanzania of East Africa Breweries Limited (EABL).
2010: EABL negotiates for reentry into the Tanzania beer market.

repaid the IFC loan and other related loans in a shorter period than earlier projected. The company proceeded to enhance its brand portfolio with the launch of the Ndovu beer brand and importation of the Redd's beer cans in 1997.

The incorporation of Tanzania Breweries into a fully fledged public limited company occurred in 1998. The government floated 20 percent of its shares in the company to the public through an initial public offer (IPO). The IPO, however, presented some disappointment as lack of enthusiasm among local investors in the country resulted in a 75 percent share subscription. The IPO reduced the government's shareholding in the company to 15 percent. Whereas SABMiller increased its majority shareholding to 66 percent, IFC opted to maintain its 9 percent shareholding. Local investors in Tanzania were allocated the remaining 10 percent of the company's shares.

The unrivalled advancement of TBL into the leading company in the brewing industry was further evidenced by the addition of Bia Bingwa into its brand portfolio in 1998. The volume of beer production had risen from 400,000 hectoliters annually in 1993 to 1.6 million hectoliters in 1998. The company's sales revenue reached $36 million in the 1998 financial year, which was a 400 percent increase on the 1993 financial year.

Market demand for the company's beers and alcoholic fruit beverages outstripped its production capacity in 1998. The company was prompted to expand its annual production capacity to 2.2 million hectoliters. The expansion project was supported by $75

million equity funding from SABMiller and other funds that were generated internally. The launch of Draught and Balimi beer brands in 1999 cemented the dominance of the company's brands in Tanzania's beer market.

GROWTH OF REVENUES AND PRODUCTION CAPACITY: 2001–08

TBL recorded relative success in the first decade of the 21st century as demonstrated by the constant growth of the company's revenues and production capacity throughout the decade. TBL engaged in a spree of strategic acquisitions, mergers, divestitures, and partnerships for most of this decade. Apart from acquiring a barley malting plant in Moshi in 2001, the company entered a license agreement with Kenya's EABL for the brewing and distribution of the latter's brands. In May 2002 TBL cemented its market share domination in Tanzania by offering EABL a 20 percent shareholding stake. In return, EABL forfeited its subsidiary in Kibo and exited the Tanzanian market. The agreement accorded the company the license to produce and distribute the brands formerly produced by EABL at the Kibo subsidiary.

In a similar agreement in Kenya, TBL forfeited its operations in Kenya by taking up a 20 percent shareholding in EABL. The company agreed to close its Castle Breweries in Thika and accorded EABL the license to produce and distribute its brands previously produced by the Thika Castle Brewery. However, although the two companies registered major strategic achievements in their respective markets, EABL's eventual closure of the Castle Brewery in Thika caused massive job losses in the region.

TBL contracted High-Tech Systems to conduct a three-month refurbishment project targeting electrical control installations and equipment. The refurbishment exercise focused on the installation of temperature control systems for the tanks in addition to the replacement of the old programmable logic controller with updated versions. The company added a new chapter in its supplies and distribution prowess with the opening of the Ubungo Distribution Warehouse in November 2008. The new warehouse enhanced efficiency in the distribution processes and logistical operations of TBL.

COURT CASE AND PLANS FOR NEW MARKETS: 2009 AND BEYOND

TBL marked the beginning of 2009 with a change in its top leadership. Robin Goetzshe was appointed to the board on January 6, 2009, and subsequently elevated to serve as the managing director of the company. TBL's continued growth was shown in 2009 revenue of TZS 464,199 million, up from TZS 383,181 million the previous year.

The 2002 agreement between SABMiller plc and EABL that saw the latter cease operations in Tanzania suffered a major setback in 2009. EABL entered an agreement with Serengeti Breweries Limited (SBL) in July 2009 for the purchase of a significant shareholding stake in the company. EABL's change of strategy was influenced by the fact that SBL was the second-largest brewing company in Tanzania with a gross asset value of $56.7 million. SBL enjoyed 17 percent of the market share in Tanzania's beer market and operated breweries in Dar es Salaam, Moshi, and Mwanza.

Consequently, EABL offered to terminate its relationship with SABMiller through the sale of its 20 percent stake in TBL. The revelations about the planned return of EABL into the Tanzanian market sparked a legal controversy that prompted SABMiller to file a court petition against EABL. In a similar development, SABMiller initiated plans for resuming beer production and distribution in Kenya upon realization that a successful bid by EABL would render the 2002 agreement irrelevant.

The two companies reportedly reached an agreement in February 2010 after SABMiller plc agreed to lift the court injunction filed against EABL. The legal stalemate between the two companies was further diluted by the Tanzania Fair Competition Commission (FCC) in October 2010 through a ruling that required EABL to sell its stake in TBL to the public as the precondition for the approval of the planned acquisition in SBL. EABL agreed to the preconditions set by the FCC and commenced consultations with the Tanzania Capital Markets and Securities Authority on the procedures of the share sale.

TBL intensified its water efficiency programs in 2010 through the launch of an in-house efficient water usage campaign. The company's initiative was born out of the need to respond to the acute water shortages in Dar es Salaam. As such, the efficient use of water in brewing operations would ideally allow the company to meet one of its core corporate social responsibility initiatives by providing the surrounding communities with access to clean drinking water.

As it looked toward the future, the realization of a fully unique brand portfolio ranked high in the core

plans of TBL. The company was also planning to review and consolidate its supply chain structures and distribution strategies to enhance uptake at the point of purchase through favourable retail pricing. The exploitation of new markets through the exploration of innovation-motivated opportunities defined the company's long-term prospects.

Paul Ingati

PRINCIPAL SUBSIDIARIES

Kibo Breweries Limited; Mountainside Farms Limited; Tanzania Distilleries Limited (65%).

PRINCIPAL COMPETITORS

East Africa Breweries Limited; Serengeti Breweries Limited.

FURTHER READING

Bruyn, Chanel de. "Local Company Supplies Electrical Equipment to Brewery, Beverage Projects." *Engineering News,* November 16, 2007. Accessed October 18, 2010. http://www.engineeringnews.co.za/article/local-company-supplies-electrical-equipment-to-brewery-beverage-projects-2007-11-16.

"Diageo's East African Subsidiary, East African Breweries Limited, Issues Statement in Respect of Tanzania Operations to Kenyan Stock Exchange." London Stock Exchange, July 27, 2009. Accessed October 19, 2010. http://www.londonstockexchange.com/exchange/news/market-news/market-news-detail.html?announcementId=10122953.

"EABL to Sell Stake in Tanzania Breweries: Paper." *Reuters,* October 10, 2010. Accessed February 6, 2011. http://af.reuters.com/article/investingNews/idAFJOE6990682010 1010.

Kimani, Mwaura. "How Tanzania Brewer Drew EABL into a Court Battle." *Business Daily (Nairobi),* October 21, 2009. Accessed October 25, 2010. http://allafrica.com/stories/20 0910201185.html.

"Tanzania Breweries Limited." CreditRiskMonitor.com. Accessed October, 17 2010. http://www.crmz.com/Report/ReportPreview.asp?BusinessId=9495917.

"Tanzania Breweries Limited Company Comparison." FirstGlobalSelect.com. Accessed October 17, 2010. http://www.firstglobalselect.com/scripts/cgiip.wsc/globalone/htm/securitycompare.r?pisharetype-id=13645.

"Tanzania: Diageo's EABL to Take Serengeti Breweries Stake." just-drinks.com, March 1, 2010. Accessed October 17, 2010. http://www.just-drinks.com/news/diageos-eabl-to-take-serengeti-breweries-stake_id99987.aspx.

Telephone and Data Systems, Inc.

—■—

30 North LaSalle Street
Suite 4000
Chicago, Illinois 60602
U.S.A.
Telephone: (312) 630-1900
Fax: (312) 630-1908
Web site: http://www.teldta.com

Public Company
Founded: 1969
Employees: 12,400 (2010)
Sales: $5.02 billion (2009)
Stock Exchanges: New York
Ticker Symbol: TDS
NAICS: 517110 Wired Telecommunications Carriers

■ ■ ■

Telephone and Data Systems, Inc., or TDS, is a telecommunications service company operating primarily in the southeastern, central, and midwestern United States. Roughly four-fifths of TDS's revenue comes from its U.S. Cellular wireless phone service subsidiary (82% owned), which has 6.1 million customers in 26 states. Wholly owned subsidiary TDS Telecommunications Corporation (TDS Telecom) offers various landline services such as local and long distance voice service, broadband services, and network access to rural and suburban markets. TDS Telecom also operates as a competitive local exchange carrier in five states under the TDS Metrocom name. All told, TDS Telecom services over 1.1 million customers and accounts for almost one-fifth of total revenue for its parent company.

Son of the founder, president/CEO Leroy T. Carlson, Jr., along with his siblings on the board of directors (Letitia, Prudence, and Walter Carlson), are members of a trust which controls the majority of voting power in TDS.

GROWTH VIA ACQUISITIONS

Earlier in his career, Leroy T. Carlson had been a product development director for Acme Steel. In 1950 he acquired the Suttle Equipment Company, a small supplier of business forms, equipment, and other supplies for independent telephone companies. Through his sales efforts, Carlson was well acquainted with many of these small, primarily rural companies and the difficulties they faced. In 1956 a business associate suggested that Carlson consider buying a small telephone company in Calvert City, Kentucky, that had 218 customers. When he learned that Southern Bell was about to take over the company, Carlson quickly examined the situation and, over the course of a weekend, bought the company. He subsequently purchased a hodgepodge of other small telephone companies, a directory publisher, and some manufacturing operations, assembling them into a minor conglomerate called Telephones, Inc. The publicly listed common shares of the holding company were sold to Continental Telephone Company in 1964, but Carlson continued to dabble in the market by buying and selling several other small telephone companies.

By 1967 Carlson decided to play a bolder role in the industry. Driven by the rewards of investment in

```
┌─────────────────────────────────────────┐
│                                           │
│   COMPANY PERSPECTIVES                    │
│                    ■                      │
│  ─────────────────────────────────────   │
│   At TDS, our mission is to provide out-  │
│   standing communications services to     │
│   our customers and meet the needs of     │
│   our shareholders, our people, and our   │
│   communities.                            │
│                                           │
└─────────────────────────────────────────┘
```

new technologies and economies of scale, he began searching for telephone properties located adjacent to one another. The task was made harder by the fact that large independent companies like General, United Telephone, and Continental had already snapped up many of the best prospects. Carlson and his associates concentrated their search on Wisconsin, where they identified several rural companies that together would provide the critical mass for an efficient operation.

Negotiations were often difficult for Carlson, who was forced to make his pitch to busy owners who were farmers, store keepers, and struggling rural entrepreneurs, but the extraordinary effort paid off. Beginning with the Central State Telephone Company in September 1967, Carlson acquired nine more companies over the next 14 months. He set up an operations group in Madison and a corporate staff in his hometown of Chicago. With help from his father-in-law, a corporate attorney, the new company was incorporated on January 1, 1969, as Telephone and Data Systems, Inc. Carlson's son, Leroy T. Carlson, Jr., was a member of the original board.

Certain that the future growth of his company would turn on its reputation, Carlson invested heavily in improvements for his 25,000 customers. TDS eliminated multiparty service, installed new electronic switching systems, and introduced direct distance dialing. It preserved the local flavor of each company and built on their established goodwill by maintaining local managements, who were well known in each community and provided valuable public relations counsel. In 1969 TDS bought out six more companies, five of which were in Wisconsin. Suddenly, TDS was the third-largest telephone company in the state and was beginning to encounter mounting, potentially disastrous opposition from General, Continental, and other established holding companies. For these reasons, TDS abruptly shifted its acquisition activity to the Northeast, and during 1970 snapped up five companies in New Hampshire, Vermont, and Maine. In each case, state regulatory commissions noted the company's good reputation for service improvement.

REGULATORY PROCEEDINGS

TDS benefitted from centralized purchasing and standardized systems and engineering, but it quickly outgrew the capabilities of its small organization and was obliged to establish specialized subsidiaries to provide management and engineering services. The company also outgrew its financial resources and in 1971 issued more than $4 million in long-term debentures. However, with the rise of the consumerist movement, TDS found itself increasingly unable to push rate increases past state regulators. These increases made network improvements harder to fund and made it difficult to float debentures and other investment papers. Carlson personally spearheaded his company's case in rate proceedings and often produced favorable results, earning a reputation as a formidable negotiator. He also won a favorable arrangement with the Bell System that would provide more equitable distribution of interconnection fees.

Between 1971 and 1973, TDS added 19 more companies in the Northeast and Midwest as well as in Oregon, Idaho, North Carolina, Alabama, and Mississippi. The geographical diversity of TDS was further enhanced in 1974 and 1975 when eight more companies were added in Virginia, Pennsylvania, and Tennessee, bringing TDS its 100,000th customer. By that time, even with 503 employees, it became impossible to properly administer the growing TDS system. In July 1974 the company reorganized into groups comprising the Wisconsin, Northeast, Southeast, and Mid-Central regions, and an "Assigned" group for companies outside those regions. In 1976 TDS created a computer services subsidiary to implement centralized, automated bill processing. The company also acquired Carlson's old Suttle equipment company and transferred its operations from Lawrenceville, Illinois, to Waunakee, north of Madison, Wisconsin.

LeRoy Carlson was active in regulatory policy proceedings and emerged as a strong opponent of the Justice Department's attempts to break up the Bell System. He argued that the task of providing affordable telephone service to everyone in the United States could be completed only through subsidies from American Telephone and Telegraph Company's (AT&T) long-distance revenues. The position of AT&T and other monopoly providers, however, gradually eroded. Even TDS began to experience competition in its key systems and PBX sales from companies that were not obligated to do business in unprofitable areas. Nevertheless, TDS finished 1978 as the twelfth-largest telephone company in the United States, serving 173,500 customers. It operated 52 telephone companies and recorded $33.7

KEY DATES

1969: LeRoy T. Carlson founds Telephone & Data Systems, Incorporated.

1976: Telephone & Data Systems, Incorporated acquires Suttle Press.

1981: Company trades on the New York Stock Exchange for the first time.

1981: LeRoy T. Carlson, Jr., named president of Telephone & Data Systems, Incorporated.

1997: Telephone & Data Systems, Incorporated enters an agreement with EchoStar that allows customers to purchase DISH Network satellite TV service through TDS Telecom.

1998: Company divests itself of its paging business.

2003: TDS upgrades more than 75 percent of its wireless networks to a faster technology, Code Division Multiple Access.

2009: Total revenue dips slightly from previous year.

2010: Telephone & Data Systems, Incorporated acquires TEAM Technologies, LLC.

million in revenue, 10 times the figure it recorded in 1969.

In 1978 also, TDS switched the focus of its expansion from acquiring individual companies to taking over franchises from other independents. TDS acquired several companies from United and Continental, including Tennessee Telephone, a company with 15 exchanges serving 39,000 customers. These acquisitions helped TDS to amass more than 250,000 customers in 22 states by 1983. They also necessitated the creation of a new Tennessee operating division. As great as the company's strides had been, it remained a regulated company earning a prescribed rate of return. To achieve greater rates of growth, TDS needed to expand into a range of unregulated services. Such a move required additional financing. Having been listed on the American Stock Exchange in 1981, TDS distributed four million new common shares, raising $25 million dollars.

TDS became involved with paging services in Wisconsin in 1972. After battling to win the right to serve more populous adjacent communities where it did not provide telephone service, TDS built up a highly profitable paging service territory that included Madison, Green Bay, Milwaukee, and all the areas in between. Spurred on by the Bell companies' reluctance to develop paging systems, TDS later won the right to offer paging services in Chicago, Miami, San Antonio,

and Tucson, and established a special subsidiary called American Paging to operate these franchises.

PRODUCT EXPANSION

Another area TDS developed was cable television. The company acquired its first cable franchise in April 1975, when it took over the Calhoun City Telephone Company in Mississippi. Additional systems were added later as TDS acquired other telephone companies that also operated cable franchises. By 1978 it had become apparent that cable television companies could develop the capability to displace telephone companies by offering switched voice connections, as well as television service, over their coaxial networks. TDS quickly applied for licenses and cross-ownership waivers to set up cable television systems within its other existing telephone service territories.

In many cases, TDS's staff lacked the experience to properly administer these new ventures. A separate cable television operation was thus established. Carlson, who turned 65 in 1981, relinquished his post as president to his son Leroy Carlson, Jr., or Ted, who bolstered the company's engineering group by hiring experienced cable television and radio systems managers. He also expanded the managerial hierarchy to accommodate the company's growing range of interests. Cable operations were centralized in 1984 under the newly created TDS Cable Communications Company. By the next year, the company operated 16 cable systems serving more than 30,000 homes. Meanwhile, a new, much more promising technology was emerging.

ENTERING THE CELLULAR MARKET

Cellular telephones were first tested by Illinois Bell in 1979. However, while the Bell companies were slow to develop cellular service, hundreds of other companies, including TDS, saw tremendous new opportunities for the technology. The company quickly planned to establish a series of cellular communications networks, beginning with an application to serve Indianapolis. The Federal Communications Commission (FCC), which granted cellular licenses, was overwhelmed by the tremendous number of applications it received and a myriad of challenges to its rulings. To speed the process, the FCC asked the hundreds of applicants to work out their own partnership agreements before applying for a license. TDS eventually abandoned its bid for Indianapolis in favor of a 5 percent stake in the Los Angeles market. TDS spent a quarter million dollars on its first filing, developing detailed business and engineering plans, but later applications brought the average cost to below $10,000.

Unable to handle its growing cellular activities, TDS established a new subsidiary called United States Cellular Corporation on December 23, 1983. The small company was frequently steamrollered by larger companies. The arrogance of these companies raised the ire of LeRoy Carlson, Jr., who fought tenaciously for United States Cellular, and often prevailed. Through an industry-wide agreement, the company was awarded licenses for cellular networks in Knoxville, Tennessee, and Tulsa, Oklahoma. TDS made the development of its cellular unit a major priority in March 1985, when it decided to sell its cable television holdings and devote its full attention to United States Cellular Corporation. The cellular market promised considerably higher growth and rates of return than cable, and it also posed a greater threat to wireline services than cable. TDS generated $41 million from the sale of its cable systems, the last of which was disposed of in November 1986.

By 1987 United States Cellular Corporation was highly influential in the cellular industry. The company applied for more than 70 additional licenses and won franchises in Peoria, Illinois; Des Moines, Iowa; and Poughkeepsie, New York. The same year, TDS diluted its control of United States Cellular Corporation by issuing additional shares in the unit to Coditel, a Belgian cable television company. It planned to sell an additional block of shares to the public. However, the sale had to be postponed until May 1988, after the Black Monday stock market collapse of October 1987. More than three million shares were distributed, reducing TDS's interest in United States Cellular Corporation to just over 80 percent. In 1988 United States Cellular Corporation was active in 31 regions, including Wichita, Kansas; Atlantic City, New Jersey; and Columbia, Missouri. Meanwhile, TDS greatly expanded its American Paging business and was serving 127,600 customers in 31 major metropolitan areas, including San Francisco, St. Louis, and Pittsburgh.

GROWTH AND EXPANSION: 1989–99

Between 1989 and 1992, TDS Telecom brought the number of telephone companies it operated up to 88. Over the previous 20 years, however, TDS and companies such as Rochester Telephone and Century Telephone had purchased so many independent companies that the number of remaining prospects had dwindled considerably. TDS Telecom was forced to look for new companies in areas well outside its established operating territories. Still, the geographical remoteness of some companies did not preclude them from taking advantage of the centralized purchasing, engineering, and billing services that had made TDS's existing companies able to operate so much more efficiently.

Again, to fund the company's expansion, TDS issued more shares, diluting the existing shareholder base by 24 percent over just 18 months. Since financial demands were even greater in the cellular market, the number of United States Cellular Corporation shares grew by 61 percent over the same period. Meanwhile, TDS held its ownership in United States Cellular Corporation at 82.3 percent, which meant that it took on four-fifths of all the new shares in United States Cellular Corporation that were issued. Due to the high start-up costs associated with cellular systems, the investments had a profound effect on TDS's earnings growth. Once these investments were made, however, the way was clear for a steady return from United States Cellular. This growth was first realized in 1992, when United States Cellular Corporation registered a 58 percent increase in the number of subscribers, to 182,500. The number of subscribers rose above 260,000 in 1993.

The same year, the company's American Paging group registered 36 percent growth, serving 321,000 customers. The division's strength was due mainly to excellent marketing and customer retention efforts, as well as the introduction of enhanced-function paging systems. In 1993 American Paging served more than 433,000 units. Within TDS's core wireline business, TDS Telecom, the customer base grew by nearly 6 percent to 321,700 access lines in 1992. TDS Telecom acquired five additional telephone companies during 1992, bringing the total number of TDS telephone companies to 90. In 1993 the customer base rose to 350,600 and the number of telephone companies to 92. This made TDS the ninth-largest non-Bell local telephone company in the country, with a presence in 28 states. The consolidated customer units of TDS topped one million in 1993.

TDS maintained a reputation for superior customer service and the technological upgrade of rural and small-town systems. This stemmed from the company's commitment to the rural economies it served, and its dedication to ensuring that the telecommunications infrastructure contributed to the growth of these markets.

Although the company was doing well in the mid-1990s, TDS' paging operations saw only modest growth over the coming years. This was due, in large part, to the fact that pagers were not being used in the United States as heavily as they had been a few years earlier. From 1996 through 1997, TDS would decrease radio paging operating revenues from $104,187 to $94,413, a 9 percent drop. Offsetting its lagging paging business was the TDS cell phone business. Cell phone operations would realize a 59 percent jump in customer accounts and a 29 percent growth in roaming service business. Additionally, cell phone revenues would grow from $663 million in 1996 to $853 million in 1997. TDS eventually divested itself of its paging business in 1998.

Due to its expanding cellular business which operated under the subsidiary, U.S. Cellular, TDS enjoyed healthy profits in 1997. Revenues grew by 12 percent to $444 million. This growth came on the heels of the passing of the Telecommunications Act of 1996. The act opened the door for local telephone companies to compete for voice and data communications customer business against established telecommunications providers. However, nearly three quarters of U.S. Cellular's customers lived in metropolitan areas where competition for customer accounts, due to the Telecommunications Act of 1996, was heating up.

TDS realized that it had to shore up its core business. To do this it focused on strengthening its marketing and sales efforts. Over the next year, marketing and sales operating expenses increased by 24 percent, to $27.8 million. However, the average cost to acquire a new customer decreased from $335 to $309 over the same period. TDS also entered into an agreement with EchoStar, a satellite television provider, to allow its customers to purchase DISH Network Satellite television services through TDS. The efforts paid off. TDS reported total assets of $5.52 billion in 1998, up from the previous year's $4.97 billion.

NEW TECHNOLOGY AND ACQUISITIONS: 21ST CENTURY

The 2001 pickup of Chorus Communications Group, Ltd., a Wisconsin-based telecommunications firm, helped TDS to strengthen its ability to provide Internet services to its growing customer base. The merger brought TDS approximately 27,000 new Internet customers.

In 2003 TDS upgraded more than 75 percent of its wireless networks to a faster technology, Code Division Multiple Access. It also added 500 cell sites to the network to increase speeds at which customers could access the Internet. These upgrades helped to add 447,000 net new customers to TDS in 2003. Other improvements and additional services increased TDS' customer accounts to 5.4 million in 2005. This represented an 11 percent increase over the previous year.

During the coming years, the global economic downturn would force TDS to continue to find ways to grow its revenues. The challenge would see TDS return to growth through acquisitions. In 2009 TDS acquired New Hampshire's Union Telephone Company. The purchase gave TDS an additional 8,500 access lines

covering about 150 square miles in eastern New Hampshire. Even with the pickup, 2009 revenue decreased slightly from the previous year.

A year later, as the U.S. economy started to rebound, TDS would hone its disaster recovery, data security, and information technology services when it acquired TEAM Technologies LLC in December 2010. TDS bought the privately owned data center services provider for approximately $47 million.

In the early 2010s, TDS primary business remained its U.S. Cellular operations. Although the wireless communications market was saturated, the company hoped that it could continue to promote growth by maintaining its high levels of customer service and satisfaction.

John Simley
Updated, Rhonda Campbell

PRINCIPAL SUBSIDIARIES

TDS Telecommunications Corporation; United States Cellular Corporation (82%); Suttle-Straus, Inc. (80%).

PRINCIPAL DIVISIONS

Wireless Operations; Incumbent Local Exchange Carriers; Competitive Local Exchange Carriers.

PRINCIPAL COMPETITORS

AT&T Mobility LLC; Sprint Nextel Corporation; T-Mobile USA, Inc.; Verizon Communications Inc.

FURTHER READING

August, K. C. *TDS: The First Twenty Years.* Madison, WI: Telephone and Data Systems, Inc., 1989.

"Chorus Acquisition Completed." *Business Journal,* September 5, 2001. Accessed February 28, 2011. http://www.bizjournals.com/milwaukee/stories/2001/09/03/daily14.html.

"Company News; Airtouch to Purchase Cellular Stakes for $245 Million." *New York Times,* December 2, 1997. Accessed February 28, 2011. http://www.nytimes.com/1997/12/02/business/company-news-airtouch-to-purchase-cellular-stakes-for-245-million.html?ref=telephoneanddatasystemsinc.

"Company Watch." *Financial World,* September 15, 1992, 12–13.

Federal Communications Commission. "Telecommunications Act of 1996." Last modified November 15, 2008. Accessed February 28, 2011. http://www.fcc.gov/telecom.html.

"TDS." *Telephone News,* April 14, 1985, 8; September 9, 1989, 1.

"Telephone and Data Systems, Inc. Acquires Team Companies." *New York Times,* December 16, 2010. Accessed February 28, 2011. http://markets.on.nytimes.com/research/stocks/news/

press_release.asp?docTag=201012151633PR_NEWS_USPR X____CG18367&feedID=600&press_symbol=266391.

"US Cellular President and CEO John E. Rooney to Retire in 2010." *Street,* February 24, 2010. Accessed February 28, 2011. http://www.thestreet.com/story/10688783/us-cellular-president-and-ceo-john-e-rooney-to-retire-in-2010.html.

TeliaSonera AB

Stureplan 8
Stockholm, SE-106 63
Sweden
Telephone: (46) 8-504-550-00
Fax: (46) 8-504-550-01
Web site: http://www.teliasonera.com

Public Company
Founded: 2003
Employees: 29,734 (2009)
Sales: SEK 106.6 billion ($16.5 billion, 2010)
Stock Exchanges: OMX Stockholm
Ticker Symbol: TLSN
NAICS: 517212 Cellular and Other Wireless Telecommunications; 518111 Internet Service Providers

■ ■ ■

TeliaSonera AB is a leading telecommunications provider to the Scandinavian and Baltic regions. The company has approximately 135 million mobile subscribers worldwide. In addition to its strong presence in Norway, Sweden, Finland, Denmark, Lithuania, Estonia, and Latvia, TeliaSonera also has mobile operations in Spain (Yoigo), Kazakhstan, Azerbaijan, Tajikistan, Nepal, and elsewhere.

TeliaSonera also provides landline phone services in its primary regions of Scandinavia and the Baltic states, although this market is decreasing as more people migrate to wireless communications only. However, the company does provide broadband access (Internet, cable television, and voice over IP) to this region as well.

TeliaSonera was created in 2003 by the merger of Sweden's Telia AB and Finland's Sonera.

STARTING WITH ELECTRIC TELEGRAPHS

Both Telia and Sonera had their roots in the 19th century. Sweden introduced its first electric telegraph line between Uppsala and Stockholm in 1853 (the company had in fact pioneered an optical telegraph network in 1794). From the start, the country's telegraph market was placed under the control of the government, which formed Kongliga Elektriska Telegraf Verket. The state body continued extending its telegraph network and, as early as 1854, had connected Sweden into a line that reached to the European mainland through central Europe. Elektriska Telegraf Verket shortened its name, to Telegrafverket, in 1860.

Finland's political situation was different. At the time the country existed as an autonomous Grand Duchy under the Russian Empire, and this resulted in a more limited extension of the telegraph in that country. In 1855 the Russian government connected Helsinki to St. Petersburg. Traffic was initially restricted, however, to Russian governmental and military uses, and the Finnish Telegraph Office remained under imperial control until Finland's declaration of independence in 1917.

By then, however, the telegraph had given way to a new device. Telegrafverket laid Sweden's first telephone line in 1877, just one year after Alexander Graham Bell was awarded his patent. The country's first private exchange was built in Stockholm in 1880. Sweden's poor road and transport system made the company

COMPANY PERSPECTIVES

TeliaSonera is an international group with a global strategy, but wherever we operate we act as a local company. We provide network access and telecommunication services that help people and companies communicate in an easy, efficient and environmentally friendly way.

fertile ground for the new communication system. By the end of the century, Telegrafverket's own phone network had more than 60,000 customers, and by World War I the country boasted more than 170,000 subscribers.

The Swedish government was somewhat unusual in its tolerance of private telephone networks, as most other governments had moved to take control of the sector by the beginning of the 20th century. A major contributor to developing the early Swedish phone system was H. T. Cedergrens, who founded Stockholms Allmanna Telefonaktiebolag (SAT) in 1883 in order to counter the entry of the United States' Bell, which had already achieved dominance in a number of countries. SAT itself was to gain market dominance, setting up the country's largest telephone exchange.

In 1918, with Sweden's economy under pressure, SAT was merged into telephone equipment manufacturer Ericsson. The telephone exchange was then sold to Telegrafverket, giving the state body the monopoly on the country's telephone system. Telegrafverket, which became Televerket, or Swedish Telecom, in 1953, had never been formally established as the country's telecom monopoly, however.

EVOLVING TELEPHONE SYSTEMS

The evolution of Finland's telephone system continued to reflect the country's political situation. The Finnish government was eager to prevent imperial Russia from gaining control of the country's telephone system. While the Finnish government created its own telephone body, which became Telecom Finland, overseeing the installation of the country's first phone lines in 1877, private companies were encouraged to wire the country as well. By the early 1880s a number of private phone lines had been set up, linking harbors or railroad stations or warehouses. In 1882 the first private local telephone company was established. The Finnish government favored the creation of a large number of local telephone companies rather than creating a single, statewide organism, reasoning that it would be more difficult for the czarist government to take over such a fragmented market.

Regulation of the Finnish telecommunications market began in 1886, with the passage of the Imperial Telephone Decree, which created legislation requiring telephone companies to apply for licensing. However, these were granted only to local, Finnish-owned companies, effectively locking Russia out of the market. By 1938 there were more than 800 local telephone companies operating in Finland, very nearly one company for each village. These small companies were later brought more or less under local government control, essentially becoming owned by their subscribers.

Meanwhile, the Finnish government, following the country's independence in 1917, established the Telegraph Office as the state-owned telecommunications arm. In 1927 the Telegraph Office was merged with the country's Post Office, forming the Finnish Post and Telegraph Office, or PTT. That body was charged with hooking up the country's sparsely populated northern and eastern regions, where setting up private telephone operations would have been too costly. The PTT, which became the country's regulatory body, also began acquiring a number of local companies, yet in the early 1930s the PTT's share of the Finnish market amounted only to 1.2 percent. In 1935, however, the PTT bought out the country's largest long-distance provider and gained a monopoly on Finland's long-distance and international telecommunications markets.

Over the next decades, the high cost of investment in new technology led to a concentration in the Finnish telecommunications sector. By the mid-1950s, the number of telephone companies had dropped to 550. By the beginning of the 1960s, the number had shrunk to just 200, then to 73 in 1970. By the 1990s there were only 49 predominantly regional telephone companies in Finland.

Telegrafverket remained at the forefront of the telecommunications industry, particularly through the presence of the Ericsson company, which established itself as one of the world's leading telecommunications equipment suppliers. The state-owned body had begun automating the country's telephone system as early as the 1930s. In the late 1940s Telegrafverket debuted one of the world's first mobile telephone systems using a closed radio circuit. By then, the country's telephone market was undergoing a boom in connections, and by the 1950s Sweden boasted one of the world's highest per-capita telephone connection rates.

Televerket, as it was called after 1953, began offering data transmission services in 1965, then, forming

KEY DATES

∎

1853: The first electrical telegraph line is opened between Uppsala and Stockholm; the Swedish government creates Kongliga Elektriska Telegraf Verket to oversee the telegraph network.

1880: The first private telephone exchange in Stockholm is opened.

1917: The newly independent Finnish government establishes the Telegraph Office to oversee the telecommunications sector.

1953: Telegrafverket becomes Televerket.

1984: Televerket is separated from the Swedish government and becomes a for-profit state-owned enterprise.

1990: Televerket forms a Unisource partnership with KPN of the Netherlands.

1993: Televerket changes its name to Telia.

2000: Telia lists on the Stockholm stock exchange.

2002: Telia and Sonera announce their agreement to merge operations.

2003: TeliaSonera begins operations as a combined company.

2004: TeliaSonera acquires Orange Denmark.

2008: Company subscriber base reaches 135 million.

2010: Company enters agreement with Ericcson to deploy four Long Term Evolution (LTE) mobile broadband networks.

the Ellemtel partnership with Ericsson in 1970, began developing the world's first digital switching network. The company also began offering satellite-based services that year. The company later began diversifying its operations, launching a cable television service and an early cellular telephone network. In 1978 Televerket, which had been publishing telephone directories for Sweden since 1889, began commercial telephone directory services, launching the Gula Sidorna (Yellow Pages) that year, then publishing business-to-business directories starting in 1982. The directories operation was later developed into a separate division, InfoMedia (later Eniro), which began providing directory publishing services on an international basis.

DEALING WITH DEREGULATION

By the mid-1980s, most of the Scandinavian countries began preparing to deregulate their telecommunications industries. Sweden proved a pioneer in this development, ending government funding of Televerket in 1984. Televerket was then expected to operate as a for-profit business, although it remained owned by the Swedish government. Through the remainder of the decade, the government began taking steps to liberalize the Swedish telecommunications market. As Televerket saw its monopoly positions compromised on the domestic front (the country fully liberalized the telecommunications sector in 1991), it began seeking international partners to protect it against the expected incursion of the world's largest telecommunications groups. In 1990 Televerket created Unisource in partnership with the Netherlands' KPN partnership. Later joined by Swiss Telecom, Belgacom, and others, the Unicom partnership, which intended to provide telecommunications services to large corporations, produced only limited results.

Nonetheless, the 1990s marked the start of Televerket's internationalization. In 1993 Televerket, underscoring its international ambitions as well as the shift in the telecommunications market away from a focus on telephone communications, changed its name to Telia AB. By the mid-1990s Telia faced competition from some 30 different companies yet remained the dominant player in the Swedish market, especially by capturing a leading share of the booming mobile telephone market. In 1995 Telia launched its own Internet access service, quickly gaining a leading share in the country.

By then, too, Finland had deregulated its telecommunications sector, a process begun in 1981 with the renaming of the Post and Telegraph Office as Posts and Telecommunications of Finland, a step toward converting the state-controlled body into a limited liability company. In 1987 the Finnish government passed a new National Telecommunications Act, replacing the original Imperial Telephone Decree of 1886. Among other things, this created new registration rules for telecommunications companies and removed the Post and Telecommunications' regulatory powers, which were transferred to the Ministry of Transport and Communications.

In 1990 Post and Telecommunications took the next step toward private enterprise when government funding was cut off and the company was expected to operate on a for-profit basis. In 1994 the two functions, postal services and telecommunications, were separated, and a new limited liability company was formed, Telecom Finland. In that year, Telecom Finland lost its monopoly on the country's long-distance market. By then, the Finnish telephone market had been reduced to just 49 companies, which joined together to create Telegroup of Finland in 1991 (renamed Finnet Group in 1995).

Telecom Finland remained controlled by the Finnish government until 1998, when the company was formally privatized. Renamed Sonera, the company went public, listing on the Helsinki stock exchanges and NASDAQ. By then, Sonera was regarded as one of the most technologically advanced telecommunications companies in the world. While the group held an approximately 30 percent share of the Finnish fixed line market, it had been particularly active in the mobile telephone arena, capturing some 65 percent of a market that had already reached 60 percent of the country's population by the late 1990s, the highest penetration in the world at the time. Sonera was also the first to offer mobile Short Message Service (SMS) and to link the mobile system into the Internet through Wireless Access Protocol (WAP) services. Sonera also became the country's leading Internet service provider.

Sonera's ambitions turned decidedly international as the Finnish market matured at the end of the 1990s. The company began buying stakes in mobile telephone operations in other countries, particularly in Latvia, Lithuania, Estonia, Russia, and Hungary. The company also bought up 41 percent of Turkey's Turkcell for $116 million, an investment that was valued at some $7.5 billion by 2000. From Turkey, Sonera turned to the former Soviet republics of Azerbaijan, Georgia, and Kazakhstan, building mobile networks in those countries. Back at home, the company, aided by fellow Finn Nokia, was building one of the world's most advanced mobile Internet networks, including its wireless Internet portal Zed. The company's developments in this area helped boost its share price, and by 2000 the company's market value had soared to some $25 billion. In that year, the Finnish government moved to cut its stake in the company, reducing its position to 54.5 percent.

BIDDING FOR LICENSING RIGHTS

In 2000 Sonera also had launched an ambitious attempt to enter the bidding war for Europe's next-generation UTMS high-speed mobile telephone licenses. The company spent billions of Euros, winning a 48 percent share in a German UTMS license. The purchase sank the company heavily in debt at a time when the global telecommunications industry was experiencing a massive downturn. By the end of 2000 Sonera's share price had plunged by some two-thirds. By then, the company had already acknowledged its interest in being acquired by a larger telecommunications group, with Vodaphone stepping up as a potential suitor. The collapse of the telecommunications market put an end to that effort, however.

Telia, too, had been emphasizing its international growth, particularly in the Scandinavian region, where it acquired a stake in the Norwegian and Danish mobile telephone markets. Telia also entered the mobile telephone markets in the Baltic states, where its investments found the company working alongside Sonera. After leaving Unisource in 1998, Telia began looking about for a new international partner. In 1999 the company announced that it had agreed to a merger with Telenor, of Norway. The "merger of equals" soon collapsed, however, notably because of disagreements about where to locate the new group's headquarters.

Instead Telia turned to smaller Sonera, and in 2002, the two companies announced their agreement to merge into a new entity, TeliaSonera. To avoid the mistakes of the Telenor merger attempt, the two sides agreed to maintain their existing Finnish and Swedish operations more or less intact, creating a corporate headquarters in Stockholm only for company-wide decisions. Telia and Sonera also agreed to bring in a "neutral" CEO with no connection to either firm, choosing Anders Igel, former head of stationery company Esselte, for the role.

This time the merger proved a success, and in January 2003 the new company was born, marking the first of an expected wave of cross-border European telecommunications mergers. With nearly EUR 9 billion in pro forma 2002 sales, TeliaSonera remained somewhat of a minnow in the fast-moving telecommunications sector. Nonetheless, the company held key positions in its core Scandinavian market as well as a major role in the mobile telephone markets in the Baltic regions.

TeliaSonera's next acquisition would come the following year when it picked up Orange Denmark, a mobile telecommunications firm owned by the French telecommunications operator, France Telecomm. The purchase allowed TeliaSonera to increase its footprint in Denmark, and it expanded TeliaSonera's cell phone customer base, as Orange Denmark was primarily a cell phone provider. The company would expand its global footprint further when it opened Third Generation (3G) networks in Finland and Sweden. Application services associated with the networks gave TeliaSonera customers wireless options like mobile Internet access, the ability to hold video conference calls, and to enjoy television programs on their wireless equipment.

IN COURT WITH CUKUROVA

Legal wrangling in 2005 would find TeliaSonera dueling with the Cukurova Group, owner of one of Turkey's leading mobile operators, Turkcell. As the Cukurova Group worked to maintain its tight grip on Turkcell, TeliaSonera accused it of backpeddling on a two-year-old agreement. In the agreement, the Cukurova Group was said to have stated that it would sell the bulk of its stake in Turkcell. The deal was made after two of Cukurova's banks collapsed in 2000. The Turkish government, under the leadership of the Justice and Development Party, loaned Cukurova $264 million so that the company could stay afloat. When Cukurova still had difficulties paying its debts three years later, it cut the deal with TeliaSonera. Details of the deal required that Cukurova sell its controlling stake in Turkcell to Telia-Sonera for $3.1 billion.

Rather than keep its agreement with TeliaSonera, Cukurova backed out when it received what it thought was a better offer, from Alfa Telecom, a Russian telecommunications firm. Alfa Telecom loaned Curko-rova $1.7 billion for a 49 percent stake in Turkcell. Two years later, Curkorova started dragging its feet when it came time to pay back the loan. TeliaSonera's lawsuit put it in a group with other companies that Curkorova had defaulted on a promise with.

Turkcell was attractive to TeliaSonera and Alfa Tele-com because it was a front-runner in the Turkish mobile communications market. By the close of 2005 Turkcell had nearly 32.3 million subscribers. Nearly half of the Turkish population (46%) used its services. Further-more, Turkcell's profits rose from $47 million in 2002 to $833 million in 2006.

In 2009 Alfa and Telia Sonera reached a tentative agreement over ownership of Turkcell, with Telia Sonera ending up with about a two-fifths stake in the company. Some legal issues remained, however, and in 2011 Telia-Sonera was still seeking to gain majority control of the company. The long-standing litigation continued to cloud the ownership issue in the early 2010s, but Turk-cell was the market leader in Turkey with 36 million customers, making it an attractive commodity.

UNDER NEW LEADERSHIP

In September 2007 the telecommunications giant named Lars Nyberg as its president and chief executive officer. Prior to joining TeliaSonera, Nyberg served at NCR Corporation as its chairman and chief executive officer. The year that Nyberg came aboard, TeliaSonera set its sights on opening a 4G network. TeliaSonera hoped to reach growing markets of young people in the three countries that had a keen interest in mobile devices.

In 2009 the company debuted its first 4G network in Stockholm. The network opened with a maximum speed of 40 megabytes per second (Mbps). The network allowed TeliaSonera to provide some of the world's fast-est and most reliable Internet access using fixed

broadband and mobile services. Increasing numbers of TeliaSonera customers could watch television and listen to the radio directly from their computers using the network. TeliaSonera would go on to launch 4G networks in several cities including Oslo, Copenhagen, and Helsinki.

Although the 4G networks were impressive, Telia-Sonera entered the 2010s with somewhat flat revenues. Sales increased slightly from 2008 and 2009 but then dipped again in 2010, mostly due to a decline in broadband services revenue. Also in 2010 the company increased its ownership in Nepal's Ncell and Uzbeki-stan's Ucell. Along with its continued efforts to gain outright control of Turkcell, these efforts illustrated Te-liaSonera's stated goal of increasing its ownership stake in existing assets. Along with a slight decrease in employee levels, TeliaSonera hoped that greater control of its subsidiaries would result in a healthier financial performance.

C. J. Gussoff
Updated, M. L. Cohen; Rhonda Campbell

PRINCIPAL SUBSIDIARIES

Halebop AB; NextGenTel (Norway); Omnitel (Lithua-nia); TeleFinland (Finland); UCell (94%, Uzbekistan); Yoigo (76.6%, Spain).

PRINCIPAL DIVISIONS

Mobility Services; Broadband Services; Eurasia.

PRINCIPAL COMPETITORS

DNA Ltd.; Elisa Corporation: Tele2 AB; Telenor ASA.

FURTHER READING

Brown-Humes, Christopher. "Telia and Sonera Look for New Partners After Euros 18bn Merger." *Financial Times,* March 27, 2002, 21.

"Crossing the Border." *Global Telecoms Business,* May-June 2002, 20.

Junkkari, Marko. "History of Sonera and Telia Goes Back to Telegraph Days." *Helsingin Sanomat,* March 27, 2002.

Koza, Patricia. "Sonera-Telia Back on Track." *Daily Deal,* November 8, 2002.

Morais, Richard C. "The Sonera Also Rises." *Forbes,* December 27, 1999, 10.

Roberts, Dan. "Sonera Surreptitiously Seeks Best Deal." *Financial Times,* August 4, 2000, 27.

"Sweden's TeliaSonera to Cut 800 Jobs." *Bloomberg Business-week,* February 3, 2011. Accessed February 24, 2011. http://www.businessweek.com/ap/financialnews/D9L59AKO1.htm.

"TeliaSonera AB Closes Acquisition of Orange Denmark." *Tele-comworldwire,* October 11, 2004. Accessed February 28, 2011. http://findarticles.com/p/articles/mi_m0ECZ/is_2004_Oct_11/ai_n6283394.

"Telia/Sonera Promises, but Will It Deliver?" *Corporate Finance,* May 2002, 7.

"Turkcell: Controlling Interest." Global Technology Forum, July 10, 2007. Accessed February 28, 2011. http://globaltechforum.eiu.com/index.asp?layout=rich_story&channelid=3&categoryid=1&title=Turkcell%3A+Controlling+interest&doc_id=11041.

Uimonen, Terho. "Telia Has an Eye on an Overseas Expansion as IPO Draws Closer." *InfoWorld,* March 20, 2000, 54.

Wireless Federation. "Ericsson & TeliaSonera AB Together for a Commercial LTE Network (Sweden)." London: Wireless Federation, January 16, 2009. Accessed February 28, 2011. http://wirelessfederation.com/news/14107-ericsson-teliasonera-ab-together-for-a-commercial-lte-network-sweden.

Tesla Motors, Inc.

—————— ■ ——————

3500 Deer Creek
Palo Alto, California 94304
U.S.A.
Telephone: (650) 681-5000
Fax: (650) 681-5101
Web site: http://www.teslamotors.com

Public Company
Founded: 2003
Employees: 800 (est., 2010)
Revenues: $111.9 million (2009)
Stock Exchanges: NASDAQ
Ticker Symbol: TSLA
NAICS: 336111 Automobile Manufacturing; 33632
    Motor Vehicle Electrical and Electronic Equipment
    Manufacturing

■ ■ ■

Tesla Motors, Inc., designs and manufactures electric vehicles and electric powertrains. Tesla boasts the world's first high-performance, sporty electric vehicle, the Roadster, which car enthusiasts praise as fun to drive as well as environmentally responsible. In addition to its popular Roadster models, Tesla has production plans for a four-door sports sedan to be delivered to the public in 2012. By working with other automakers, Tesla believes that its technology will eventually lead to more affordable electric cars being driven all over the world. In addition to corporate offices in Palo Alto, California, and Windsor, United Kingdom, in 2010 the company had

29 retail locations in North America, Europe, and the Asia-Pacific region.

COMPANY BACKGROUND

The history of electric cars dates back to the early 19th century, when Scottish inventor Robert Anderson developed an electric carriage powered by nonrechargeable battery cells. While electric vehicles were popular in the early 20th century, interest in such transportation declined after the introduction of the mass-produced gasoline-powered Model T Ford and people sought faster vehicles that could travel longer distances. Interest revived in the 1990s, and from 1997 to 2000 such automakers as Honda, Ford, General Motors, and Toyota manufactured all-electric vehicles, most of which were available only by lease. In the early 21st century, however, all major automobile manufacturers had discontinued their all-electric vehicle programs although some continued to work with hybrid technologies. To some people, however, the resulting cars were unattractive in both style and high-level performance. Martin Eberhard was one of those people.

Tesla Motors was the brainchild of Eberhard, an engineer and entrepreneur who in 2003 had begun to investigate the feasibility of a zero-emissions luxury sports car. After examining different power sources for such a vehicle, including diesel, hydrogen fuel cells, natural gas, and hybrid technologies, he determined that electricity was the most efficient option. Eberhard persuaded Al Cocconi of AC Propulsion, an electric vehicle company that had developed the tzero, a prototype that ran off lead-acid batteries, to power the tzero with lighter lithium ion laptop batteries. The result was an electric vehicle that could travel over 300 miles on one charge and accelerate from 0 to 60 mph in less than four seconds. Although Eberhard had pushed for Cocconi to start producing the tzero commercially, Cocconi had not been interested. Instead, the AC Propulsion leader agreed to allow Tesla Motors to use the tzero to attract investors by demonstrating its performance power.

Thus encouraged, Eberhard convinced Marc Tarpenning, a former partner software engineer, to join his venture to create a high-performance electric car. On July 1, 2003, Eberhard and Tarpenning incorporated Tesla Motors in the state of Delaware. The company was named for Nikola Tesla, who invented, among a number of other things, the alternating current induction motor in the late 19th century and explored ways to apply the technology to electric vehicles. Without Tesla's genius, Eberhard believed, Tesla Motors could not exist. By the end of the year, Ian Wright had joined Tesla as vice president of vehicle development, and the company actively sought financial backing.

In February 2004 Eberhard and Wright met with Elon Musk, cofounder of PayPal. Like the other men, Musk had been interested in putting electric vehicles on the road for several years, and he was ready to front the money to do so. With an initial investment of $7.5 million, Musk led Tesla's first round of financing by venture capitalists. In return, he became chairman of the board of Tesla, established a business plan for the company, and soon appointed engineer JB Straubel chief technical officer of the company.

THE ROADSTER INTRODUCED: 2006

The prototype for the zero-emissions Tesla Roadster debuted in Santa Monica, California, in July 2006. Built in Hethel, England, on a Lotus chassis modified for Tesla's electric vehicle, the Roadster captured the attention of car aficionados across the globe for its sleek styling, its ability to go from 0 to 60 mph in about four

seconds, and a speed topping out around 130 mph. The electric vehicle also came at a price of $109,000. Despite the price, the limited edition Signature One Hundred series of the Tesla Roadster had sold out by mid-August, only three weeks after its appearance, even though the vehicle was not slated to be distributed for at least one year. By October the second planned production run of 100 vehicles was sold out as well.

The Roadster used 6,831 lithium-ion batteries, which Tesla claimed had over four times the storage capacity of other kinds of batteries. While the battery pack was manufactured in California, the electric motor used in the car was made in a factory in Taiwan. With a range of approximately 250 miles, the Roadster out-ranged electric vehicles from major automakers by 100 miles. Roadster owners could have a recharging station installed in their home garages that allowed for a complete recharge in 3.5 hours, making charging the Roadster much like charging a cell phone. For drivers on the go, the car could be recharged at any electrical outlet through the use of a mobile kit. Initial estimates showed that the Roadster cost around one to two cents per mile to operate.

Almost immediately, Tesla Motors was recognized all over the world. In October 2006, for instance, Tesla Motors received a Product/Industrial Design Award from Global Green, an organization created in 1993 by Mikhail Gorbachev, former president of the Soviet Union, to increase awareness of environmental issues. Tesla was also named a recipient of a 2006 *Popular Mechanics* Breakthrough Award, becoming the first automobile ever to receive the honor. Additionally, *Time* magazine named the Roadster one of 2006's best inventions. According to a November 2006 Tesla Motors press release, even California governor Arnold Schwarzenegger remarked during a speech about clean alternative fuel vechicles, "I test drove this vehicle, and it is hot."

TROUBLED TIMES: 2007–08

Even as Tesla Motors was enjoying its public presence, the company was experiencing discord behind the scenes. As Tesla transitioned from a focus on development to operations, Eberhard found himself under the scrutiny of Musk and other board members, who had begun to question his understanding of the company's financial matters, particularly in regard to meeting its August 27, 2007, production date. After months of dissent, Musk replaced Eberhard with interim CEO Michael Marks, an investor in Tesla with a background in corporate finance.

One of Marks' first tasks was to announce a revised production schedule for the Roadster. He reported in

KEY DATES

2004: Tesla Motors receives financial backing and begins developing prototype.
2006: The Tesla Roadster debuts in Santa Monica, California.
2006: *Time* magazine names the Roadster one of the year's best inventions.
2007: Martin Eberhard replaced as CEO.
2008: Tesla opens sales and service centers in Santa Monica and Menlo, California.
2010: Tesla Motors goes public.

September that 50 cars would be manufactured in the first quarter of 2008, while 600 additional vehicles would be produced during the rest of the year. In December 2007 Ze'ev Drori, a retired technology entrepreneur, assumed the position of Tesla CEO, and Eberhard was fired from the company the following month. Ten percent of Tesla's employees were laid off at the same time. (In 2009 Eberhard would initiate legal proceedings against Tesla Motors. Eventually he withdrew his petition, which led to speculation that a settlement had been made outside of court.) Commercial production of the Roadster did not begin until March 17, 2008, well behind the originally scheduled date.

EXPANSION: 2008–09

Despite delays in production, the Tesla Roadster continued to be in high demand in 2008. Over 1,000 vehicles had been ordered by the time production was initiated in March. In April Tesla started to accept reservations from European customers for delivery in the spring of 2009. The production run of 250 would be a special edition with European specs, priced at EUR 99,000. In May Tesla opened a showroom in Santa Monica, followed by one in Menlo, California, two months later. Even though the dealerships had no floor models to sell, eager customers visited the stores to preview the luxury sports electric vehicle and to place their orders for future models.

In September 2008 Tesla announced that it would build a $250 million manufacturing facility for its next vehicle, the Model S, in San Carlos, California, rather than in Albuquerque, New Mexico, as had been previously planned. This statement came one week after the California Alternative Energy and Advanced Transportation Financing Authority approved a new program offering tax exemptions to zero-emission vehicle manufacturers. In addition to receiving these exemptions for purchasing equipment for its new San Carlos plant, Tesla was eligible for over $1 million in Employment Training Panel Workforce Development Funds. Like the Roadster, the Model S, a four-door car with a base price of $60,000, was engineered to be a luxury sports sedan and included a 17-inch touchscreen with 3G connectivity. In addition, the vehicle offered consumers a choice of three battery packs with 160, 230, or 300 miles per charge. All were rechargeable in 45 minutes from any electrical outlet.

With delivery for the Model S scheduled for 2012, Tesla began taking orders for the Roadster Sport in January 2009. The Roadster Sport, a higher-performance vehicle than its predecessor, had an upgraded powertrain that allowed the vehicle to accelerate from 0 to 60 mph in 3.7 seconds as opposed to the original Roadster's 3.9 seconds. At a base invoice price of $128,500 in the United States, the Roadster Sport also featured an improved suspension that drivers could customize, including comfort and sport settings. As with the Roadster, the Roadster Sport had car enthusiasts praising its innovation in both design and performance.

In 2009 Tesla Motors launched dealerships in the United States and abroad. Over the course of the year, the company opened sales and service centers in Seattle, Chicago, New York City, Miami, London, and Monaco, and set its sights on Washington, D.C., Toronto, and Atlanta. After considering Denver as a possible location, Tesla opened a gallery in Boulder, Colorado, in October. There, potential customers could test drive a Roadster during a special weekend promotion. As deliveries to Europe increased, Tesla opened its first store in continental Europe in Munich, Germany. At the 2009 Frankfurt Motor Show, the company officially unveiled the production version of the Roadster Sport, as well as debuted the Model S to the European market.

Tesla expanded its operations beyond development and production in October 2009 when it introduced a mobile service program for Tesla owners in the United States and Canada. Known as Tesla Mobile Service Rangers, specialized technicians would service customers' vehicles at their homes or offices, or even in parking garages. Services included annual inspections, and customers paid $1 per roundtrip mile from the nearest Tesla service center.

MAKING HEADLINES: 2010 AND BEYOND

Tesla continued to make headlines in 2010 as a leader in the electric vehicle industry, garnering accolades from the global automotive and technology industries alike. On April 30, 2010, Tesla made history when a Tesla Roadster traveling around the world in the Odyssey of Pioneers tour received official authorization to park in Moscow's Red Square. The Roadster was the first vehicle without components made in Russia ever to be granted such clearance. Sponsored by Tesla Motors and TAG Heuer, a Swiss watch maker, the specially equipped TAG Heuer Tesla Roadster traveled approximately 12,000 miles to over 165 towns and cities on three continents. Included on the tour was a stop in Budapest, Hungary, the place where Nikola Tesla engineered his alternating-current induction motor in 1882. Along the way, the Roadster demonstrated its recharging adaptability as it was charged from standard outlets in such locations as churches, private homes, hotels, and a barn in rural Switzerland.

In May Tesla attracted attention when it purchased a former Toyota factory in Fremont, California. The two companies announced that they had made a deal to collaborate on the development of electric vehicles and parts, with a strategy to market a Toyota with a Tesla powertrain within two years. Only a few days later, Tesla opened a sales and service center in Zurich and made its first Roadster deliveries to Canada.

Tesla Motors was listed on NASDAQ and went public on June 29, 2010. In an effort to move closer to its goal of raising $213 million to finance manufacturing facilities and purchase equipment, Tesla increased the size of its initial public offering (IPO) from 11.1 million to 13.3 million shares, offered at a cost of $14 to $16 per share. From the time of Tesla's filing with the Securities and Exchange Commission, investors were highly interested. As reported by Sharon Silke Carty in *USA Today*, Scott Sweet, senior managing partner at IPO Boutique, declared that the IPO "has become a cult following. It's huge." Many financial experts, however, criticized investor interest in a company that had sold only 1,000 cars since its conception and had yet to turn a profit. (Tesla had lost approximately $246 million over the previous years.) The fact that the Tesla Roadster cost $109,000, analysts argued, meant that the electric car manufacturer would most probably lose even more money until it could launch a less expensive vehicle.

Nevertheless, Tesla remained the world's foremost high-performance electric vehicle at the onset of 2011. By early January the company had delivered more than 1,500 Roadsters in over 30 countries. In addition to seeing the completion of its initial Model S production

run, Tesla was also expected to commence delivery for the Roadster 2.5, an updated version of its original Roadster model, in 2011.

Alicia Elley

PRINCIPAL SUBSIDIARIES

Tesla Motors Australia, Pty Ltd. (Australia); Tesla Motors Canada Inc. (Canada); Tesla Motors Denmark ApS (Denmark); Tesla Motors GmbH (Germany); Tesla Motors HK Limited (China); Tesla Motors Japan K.K. (Japan); Tesla Motors Leasing, Inc.; Tesla Motors Ltd; Tesla Motors New York, LLC; Tesla Motors SARL (Monaco); Tesla Motors Switzerland GmbH (Switzerland); Tesla Motors Taiwan Limited (Taiwan).

PRINCIPAL COMPETITORS

Fisker Automotive, Inc.; Ford Motor Company; General Motors Company; Honda Motor Company; Toyota Motor Corporation.

FURTHER READING

Baker, David R. "Auto Plant Deal Better for Tesla Than for Toyota." *San Francisco Chronicle,* October 1, 2007, A1.

Carty, Sharon Silke. "Demand for Tesla Motors IPO 'Getting Ridiculous.'" *USA Today,* June 29, 2010.

Clark, Amy S. "Silicon Valley Takes on Detroit." *CBS News,* July 22, 2006. Accessed February 20, 2011. http://www.cbsnews.com/stories/2006/07/22/eveningnews/main1826843.shtml.

Copeland, Michael V. "Tesla's Wild Ride." *Fortune Magazine,* July 9, 2008. Accessed February 20, 2011. http://money.cnn.com/2008/07/10/technology/copeland_tesla.fortune/index.htm.

Corcoran, Elizabeth. "Can Silicon Valley Reinvent the Car?" *Forbes.com,* March 19, 2007. Accessed February 20, 2011. http://www.forbes.com/2007/03/18/tesla-electric-car-tech-cz_ec_0319valleyletter.html.

Fuhs, Allen E. *Hybrid Vehicles and the Future of Personal Transportation.* Boca Raton, FL: CRC Press, 2009.

Grabianowski, Ed. "How the Tesla Roadster Works." auto.howstuffworks.com, October 24, 2006. Accessed February 20, 2011. http://auto.howstuffworks.com/tesla-roadster.htm.

Taylor, Michael, "Hot Sports Car with No Gas Tank." *SFGate,* August 9, 2006. Accessed February 20, 2011. http://articles.sfgate.com/2006-08-09/news/17307225_1_tesla-motors-tesla-roadster-electric-cars.

"Tesla Motors." *Red Herring,* April 29, 2007, 81.

UGI Corporation

460 North Gulph Road
King of Prussia, Pennsylvania 19406
U.S.A.
Telephone: (610) 337-1000
Fax: (610) 992-3254
Web site: http://www.ugicorp.com

Public Company
Incorporated: 1882
Employees: 9,800 (2010)
Sales: $5.59 billion (2010)
Stock Exchanges: New York
Ticker Symbol: UGI
NAICS: 221210 Natural Gas Distribution

∎ ∎ ∎

UGI Corporation is a holding company with subsidiaries in various energy markets. AmeriGas Partners L.P. (44% owned) is the nation's largest retail propane distributor, serving approximately 1.3 million customers in the United States. Overseas, wholly owned subsidiaries Antargaz and Flaga distribute liquified petroleum gases (LPGs) in France and eastern Europe, respectively. UGI Utilities operates as a natural gas utility for over 500,000 customers in Pennsylvania, and it also operates as an electrical utility for 60,000 customers in two Pennsylvania counties (Luzerne and Wyoming). Finally, UGI Energy Services is an energy marketer that operates under the name GASMARK.

IT ALL STARTED IN PHILADELPHIA

UGI is the oldest public-utility holding company in the United States, having been incorporated in 1882 as the United Gas Improvement Co. The company was founded by Philadelphia businessmen to introduce a new process for the manufacture of "water gas," made by combining air and steam with coal (in place of the older method of making illuminating gas from the distillation of coal). The new Lowe process exposed water-gas vapors to a thin stream of petroleum naphtha, enriching the gas with hydrocarbons from the oil and producing almost twice the candle power of coal gas at less cost. United Gas Improvement manufactured, sold, and installed equipment needed for the Lowe process. The company also leased the production and distribution facilities of existing gas works, operated the plants, and sold the gas.

Within its first year of operation, United Gas Improvement began acquiring interests in local gas works in various parts of the country, in what was perhaps the first attempt to bring several independent and geographically separated public utilities under one management. United Gas Improvement (or UGI, as it became known) also acquired extensive interests in electric utilities and electric street railways, particularly in New York, Connecticut, northern New Jersey, and eastern Pennsylvania.

The establishment of UGI initially required some rather complex business transactions. The stocks of the gas companies acquired were placed in the hands of a trustee, since Pennsylvania law did not allow one corporation to hold the securities of another. To simplify this cumbersome process, UGI's founders acquired the charter of the Union Co. Formerly known as the Union Contract Co., this company had been granted a charter in 1870 by a special act of the Pennsylvania legislature and was thereby allowed to purchase and own the securities of other corporations. The name of the Union Co. was changed to The United Gas Improvement Co. in 1888, and the following year the new company acquired the assets of the old United Gas Improvement Co. By 1902 the company held interests in 45 firms providing gas, electric, and railway service across the country.

In 1897 UGI secured a 30-year lease from Philadelphia to run the city gas works. UGI would continue to lease and manage Philadelphia's gas works until the early 1970s, when it was replaced by a city-owned nonprofit corporation. By that time, the works was the largest municipally owned gas operation in the United States.

In 1925 UGI merged with the American Gas Co., and, two years later, it acquired the Philadelphia Electric Co. The company diversified into heavy construction during this time, forming, through United Engineers & Constructors, Inc., the largest general engineering and construction firm in the United States. UGI also held a minority interest in Samuel Insull's Midland Utilities, which operated in more than 5,000 communities in over 32 states. By the end of 1934, UGI directly or indirectly had interests in 55 subsidiary companies, stretching from New Hampshire to Arizona. Most of these companies were fully owned by UGI.

SURVIVING THE GREAT DEPRESSION

Thanks to conservative management, the utility holding company suffered relatively little from the Great Depression. Dividends paid by its utility subsidiaries fell only 10.6 percent between 1931 and 1938. However, according to some critics at the time, UGI was doing too well. Writing in *The Nation,* Isidor Feinstein alleged that "The same group sits on both sides of the table in fixing management fees, construction costs, and financing charges," and that without federal regulation the

consumer was paying "a premium on inefficient operation, costly management, and a bloated capital structure." UGI's various subsidiaries, Feinstein noted, were providing the parent company with average annual returns ranging from 11 percent to as high as 84 percent.

In 1935 the U.S. Congress passed the Public Utility Holding Company Act, which required utility holding companies to register with the Securities and Exchange Commission (SEC). The act also gave the Federal Power Commission and the Federal Trade Commission authority to regulate interstate transmission of electric power and gas, respectively, and restricted electric and gas holding companies to single and concentrated systems confined to a single area. Contending that the act was unconstitutional, UGI management sought injunctions to restrain the government from enforcing it.

Although UGI eventually lost its court battle, the company continued to grow, and by the end of 1940 was at the peak of its power. Operating in 11 states, UGI held investments in four subholding companies, 38 gas and electric utilities, and 48 nonutility companies, including water, transit, ice, and cold-storage firms. It had 120,000 stockholders and assets of $846 million.

In 1941 the SEC directed UGI to divest itself of properties in Arizona, Connecticut, Illinois, Indiana, Michigan, New Hampshire, New Jersey, Ohio, and Tennessee. As a result, UGI was restricted to one compact property largely intrastate in character. In 1943 UGI's subsidiaries were selling electricity or gas to more than five million customers in seven states, but, by the end of 1953, these operations were limited to eastern Pennsylvania. Ironically, when the company's government-mandated divestiture plan was filed in 1942, investors decided that less was more. UGI's common stock jumped from $4 to $6 per share and reached $9.88 in 1943, before UGI distributed to shareholders stock representing some two-thirds of its assets.

REORGANIZING AND SWITCHING TO NATURAL GAS

In 1952 the SEC approved a plan to reorganize UGI by dissolving the holding company structure, merging its remaining subsidiaries into UGI, which became a Pennsylvania public-utility operating company, dissolving its nonutility subsidiaries, and disposing of its stock in nonsubsidiary companies. On the last day of 1952, seven Pennsylvania public-utility subsidiaries, including management of the city-owned Philadelphia Gas Works Co., were merged into the new UGI. The company's assets of $75 million were less than one-tenth of its prewar total. The name of the parent company was officially changed to UGI Corporation on July 1, 1968.

KEY DATES

1882: Business incorporates as the United Gas Improvement Company.
1897: United Gas Improvement Company secures a 30-year deal from Philadelphia to run the city gas works.
1925: Company merges with the American Gas Company.
1968: Name of company changes to UGI Corporation.
1977: Company establishes new subsidiary, AmeriGas.
1994: UGI Corporation acquires interest in and management of Petrolane, Incorporated.
1996: Pennsylvania governor Tom Ridge signs the Pennsylvania Electric Generation Customer Choice & Competition Act, opening up electrical market.
1999: UGI acquires Unisource Worldwide Incorporated.
2006: UGI purchases natural gas utility PG Energy.
2010: Company invests $300 million in infrastructure projects in the Marcellus Shale region.

The UGI system converted from manufactured gas to natural gas during the 1950s. Most of UGI's customers were residential, with industrial sales accounting for only 15 percent of gas consumption in 1955. To promote greater industrial use of natural gas, the company instituted a special summer industrial rate to drum up business during the slack season. At the same time, UGI was striving to convince homeowners to convert to gas heat as well as to win business from buyers of new homes. Only 11 percent of all homeowners in the company's area of operation had gas heat in 1956, excluding the territory of the Philadelphia gas works, where most households were cooking and heating with manufactured gas. UGI's efforts were so successful that between 1955 and 1971 its gas sales increased fivefold.

EXPANDING SUBSIDIARIES

A majority-owned UGI subsidiary called Ugite Gas, Inc., entered the unregulated liquefied petroleum gas (LPG) business in 1959 by acquiring three companies serving communities in eastern Pennsylvania and Maryland. Operations soon were extended to western

Pennsylvania and eastern Ohio as well. By 1973 Ugite had expanded its "bottled gas" service to 35 locations in eight states, including Kentucky and Tennessee. Between 1974 and 1976, the subsidiary acquired more LPG properties in Florida, Alabama, and Georgia, adding annual volume of nine million gallons to its propane sales.

The principal LPGs, propane and butane, were separated from natural gas at processing plants and from crude oil at refineries. Stored and transported in a liquid state, propane vaporized to a clean-burning gas with properties similar to natural gas. The retail segment of the propane business was attractive to UGI because it was a distribution business similar to that of a local natural gas company and one with the same types of customers, who used the fuel primarily for heating. Moreover, unlike a natural-gas utility, the retail sale of propane was unregulated and free to spread geographically. Perhaps most importantly, however, it required only small capital investment. In 1977 additional propane distribution and storage facilities in New York, Pennsylvania, and North Carolina brought sales up to approximately 78 million gallons of propane.

During this time, Ugite was the company's LPG Division and a holding company for UGI's expansion in compressed gases. Newly acquired SEC Corp. of El Paso, Texas, a producer and distributor of carbon dioxide and other gases in 16 states, became the Carbon Dioxide Division. In 1977 a new subsidiary, AmeriGas, was established, succeeding Ugite as the parent of the LPG and Carbon Dioxide Divisions. A year later AmeriGas acquired Northern Gases and Manitowoc Gases, the only producers of industrial gases in Wisconsin. This acquisition formed the new Industrial Gases Division, a producer and distributor of oxygen, nitrogen, argon, and acetylene. AmeriGas also produced and sold welding equipment and supplies.

RESPONSE TO ENERGY CRISIS

UGI responded to the energy crisis of the 1970s by forming a division to explore for natural gas. It acquired oil and gas rights on 75,000 acres in western and central Pennsylvania and began exploratory drilling in 1974. Three years later, UGI formed a joint venture with Amoco Production Co. to search for oil and gas on more than a million acres of southwestern Pennsylvania. In 1979 all of the company's oil and gas activities were transferred to a new wholly owned subsidiary, UGI Development Co., the consolidation of which was completed in 1981. Gas production began in 1977, and four drilling rigs were operating in 1980.

By 1980 UGI was shifting its focus from its core gas and electric distribution to substantial interests in a half-dozen energy-related activities. Company president Thomas Lefevre related that UGI intended to shift its income ratio from three-fourths regulated utility business to half utility and half nonutility business within three to four years. Propane and industrial gases appeared to be a lucrative field for expansion, with operating income from AmeriGas having risen 48 percent during the period between mid-1979 and mid-1980, compared to 8 percent from natural gas and electric utilities.

By the end of 1981 UGI was the leading supplier of carbon dioxide to the nation's oilfields, where it was used to stimulate well production. AmeriGas was producing carbon dioxide from eight production plants and two natural wells. The company also expected other industrial gases to enjoy rapid growth in the upcoming years. It completed an air-separation plant in 1981 to produce nitrogen for oilwell stimulation and had begun construction on a second plant.

The early 1980s were a period of rapid expansion for UGI, as it acquired several companies that serviced oilfields. However, by the mid-1980s the oil and gas drilling activity stimulated by the hikes in energy prices during the 1970s had collapsed, forcing UGI to make cuts. In 1983 UGI sold half of its LPG Division and formed AP Propane, Inc., a joint venture with the Prudential Insurance Company. In mid-1986 only five UGI oil and gas drilling and supplying companies in three markets were still operating, as compared to 12 in seven markets at the end of 1985. Moreover, UGI's oil and gas work force was cut from 1,130 to less than 500. The company took a $45.7 million writedown of oil and gas assets and other investments in 1985 and reported a rare annual loss.

NEW MARKETS AND ACQUISITIONS: 1986–99

Between 1986 and 1987 UGI Development Co. discontinued all its oil and gas activities, including selling a significant portion of its oilfield service operations to UTI Energy Corp. In 1987, as part of UGI's strategy of focused growth in propane, AmeriGas, through the AP Propane joint venture, acquired Cal Gas Corporation and instantly became the nation's fourth-largest propane marketer. At the time, Cal Gas was three times the size of the AmeriGas propane operations. Over the next few years, AmeriGas withdrew from the industrial gases industry in a series of seven transactions, selling practically all the operating assets of its industrial gases and carbon dioxide divisions to the BOC Group, Inc., for about $146 million. James A. Sutton, chair and chief executive officer, told shareholders at UGI's 1990 annual meeting that its divestiture of oil and gas and

industrial gases businesses since 1986 had "transformed the company from one operating in four distinct industries through over 20 separate businesses into a company focused in two industries with three businesses."

In 1990 AmeriGas took total control of the joint venture established with Prudential in 1983, buying Prudential's 49 percent stake in AP Propane Inc. for $63 million. This company was then merged into AmeriGas Propane. The following year, UGI was reincorporated in Pennsylvania, emerging as a restructured holding company by the same name. The former UGI Corporation was renamed UGI Utilities, Inc. This subsidiary operated the regulated Pennsylvania electric and gas utilities, while AmeriGas, Inc., conducted propane distribution through AmeriGas Propane, Inc., its wholly owned subsidiary.

In 1993 UGI acquired a significant interest in and management of debt-laden Petrolane, Inc., one of the nation's largest marketers of propane, through a prepackaged plan of reorganization under Chapter 11 of the U.S. Bankruptcy Code. The company hoped to turn Petrolane around financially and to combine it with its AmeriGas Propane operations. By early 1994 Amerigas and UGI had acquired 35 percent of Petrolane. UGI also announced plans to acquire the remaining 65 percent in 1995 and to form a master limited partnership in which AmeriGas would hold a majority interest.

In April 1995 UGI completed the acquisition of the remaining 65 percent of Petrolane and combined the operations of Petrolane and AmeriGas Propane into one entity. This was AmeriGas Partners, L.P., owner and operator of the nation's largest retail propane marketing organization. AmeriGas then owned 59 percent of the partnership.

UGI started 1996 by entering talks to acquire Norstar Energy, a privately owned natural gas utilities company. The deal was expected to increase UGI's customer base by nearly 3,000 people. This was also the year that Pennsylvania governor Tom Ridge signed the Pennsylvania Electric Generation Customer Choice & Competition Act. The law opened the way for Pennsylvanians to shop around for an electric provider of their choice. Competition was phased in from November 1997 through January 2001. Utility companies had until 1997 to set their rates which would remain effective through 2001. The law also required utility companies to unbundle their rates that they reflected on customer bills. Customer invoices were separated into generation, transmission, distribution, and transition.

In 1997 UGI looked at purchasing Unisource Worldwide Incorporated. The cost of the pickup was expected to be $1.5 billion. Just as UGI was the largest U.S. seller of propane, Unisource was the largest distributor of paper and janitorial supplies in the United States. However, UGI shares dropped at news of the proposal, and it was not long before UGI backed away from the deal. Before the close of the year, Unisource was picked up by Georgia-Pacific Corporation for $842 million in cash.

Following the collapse of the Unisource deal, UGI shifted its focus from entering the paper business and worked on strengthening its core business, propane. It bought interest in Antargaz, one of France's largest propane distributors. The move helped UGI to strengthen its position in Europe's propane business. Even before the deal, UGI was already selling more than 34 million retail gallons of propane each year in Austria, the Czech Republic, and Slovakia via its Flaga subsidiary.

GROWTH AND ECONOMIC CHALLENGES: 21ST CENTURY

The next several years would bring warmer temperatures to the regions UGI provided the bulk of its services to. This, in turn, caused UGI to turn to acquisitions to help grow domestic revenues. In August 2001 UGI purchased Columbia Energy Group, a subsidiary of Columbia Propane Corporation. The deal added 186 locations to UGI. The pickup of Horizon Propane LLC in 2003 brought 90 locations in twelve states to UGI. Southern Union Company's natural gas utility business, PG Energy, was another purchase UGI made to grow its business. The deal closed in 2006 for nearly $580 million. It also added about 158,000 customers in the northeastern and central Pennsylvania region to UGI. A result of the acquisitions was $5.47 billion in revenues for UGI in 2007, an increase over the previous year's $5.22 billion in revenues.

In 2008 the economic downturn that gripped the United States and the world caused UGI's electricity business to lag. Revenues generated from its electric business fell from $13.7 million in 2007 to $13.1 million in 2008. The company responded to the slowdown by shifting its focus toward getting consumers to convert their homes from electricity and oil to natural gas.

UGI's next steps would expand its international markets. Through its subsidiaries Antargaz and Flaga, it boosted its European LPG business. In September 2010 UGI cut a deal with BP and purchased its Denmark's LPG business Kosan Gas. It also acquired Shell Gas Hungary Zrt, another LPG business.

Growth in Europe appeared to be one avenue UGI was taking to bolster its revenue. However, while the company showed a profit in 2010, total revenue declined for the second straight year. The company planned to invest $300 million to develop infrastructure around the Marcellus Shale, an Appalachian Basin region with promising oil and gas deposits. Increased output from this region, combined with continued growth in Europe, were two prime areas expected to contribute to UGI's growth in the 2010s.

Robert Halasz
Updated, Rhonda Campbell

PRINCIPAL SUBSIDIARIES

AmeriGas Partners, L.P. (44%); Antargaz S.A. (France); Flaga GmbH (Austria); UGI Energy Services, Inc. (GASMARK); UGI HVAC Services, Inc.

PRINCIPAL DIVISIONS

AmeriGas Propane; International Propane—Antargaz; International Propane—Other; Gas Utility; Electric Utility; Midstream& Marketing.

PRINCIPAL COMPETITORS

Allegheny Energy, Inc.; Energy Transfer Partners, L.P.; Ferrellgas Partners, L.P.; FirstEnergy Corp.; Suburban Propane Partners, L.P.

FURTHER READING

Bemis, Samuel. "Some Recent Municipal Gas History." *Forum*, March 1998, 72–75.

Campanella, Frank W. "UGI Sweetens Mix." *Barron's*, June 30, 1990, 36–37, 41.

Commins, Kevin. "UGI Strategy for the 1980s: Diversification of Operations." *Journal of Commerce*, July 25, 1980, 3.

"Company News; Georgia-Pacific Agrees to Acquire Unisource." *New York Times*, May 26, 1999, http://www.nytimes.com/1999/05/26/business/company-news-georgia-pacific-agrees-to-acquire-unisource.html?src=pm.

"Company News; UGI Stock Plunges After Offer for Unisource." *New York Times*, March 2, 1999. Accessed February 28, 2011. http://www.nytimes.com/1999/03/02/business/company-news-ugi-stock-plunges-after-offer-for-unisource.html?ref=ugicorporation.

"Death Sentence." *Business Week*, February 1, 1941, 14–15.

Feinstein, Isidor. "Corporate Tammany Halls." *Nation*, December 18, 1935, 710.

Pratt, Tom. "Smith Barney Unveils LP for UGI's Petrolane Deal." *Investment Dealers' Digest*, November 14, 1994, 10–11.

"Resignation to Revolt," *Time*, December 2, 1935, 62–63.

UGI Corp. *UGI Corporation: The First 100 Years.* Valley Forge, PA: UGI Corp., 1982.

"UGI to Acquire Unisource for $1.5 Billion." *Journal Record* (Oklohoma City), March 2, 1999. Accessed February 28, 2011. http://findarticles.com/p/articles/mi_qn4182/is_19990302/ai_n10125393.

Universal Health Services, Inc.

———■———

367 South Gulph Road
P.O. Box 61558
King of Prussia, Pennsylvania 19406
U.S.A.
Telephone: (610) 768-3300
Fax: (610) 768-3336
Web site: http://www.uhsinc.com

■ ■ ■

Public Company
Incorporated: 1978
Employees: 28,100 (2009)
Sales: $5.2 billion (2009)
Stock Exchanges: New York
Ticker Symbol: UHS
*NAICS:*622110 General Medical and Surgical Hospitals

■ ■ ■

Universal Health Services, Inc. (UHS), owns and operates for-profit medical facilities such as behavioral health centers, acute care hospitals, surgical centers, and radiation oncology centers. In 2010 the company had roughly 200 behavioral centers and 25 acute care hospitals in 32 states in the United States, the District of Columbia, and Puerto Rico. Combined, facilities in Nevada (24%), Texas (20%), and California (10%) account for over half of all revenue.

Although UHS has a presence in some large U.S. cities (Las Vegas, Washington, D.C.), many of the company's acute care hospitals and behavioral centers are located in smaller cities like Enid, Oklahoma, or Sparks, Nevada. In 2009 the company received roughly one-fourth of its revenue from its behavioral centers, with the remaining three-fourths coming from its hospitals, surgical centers, and radiation oncology centers. However, this ratio is likely to change following UHS's 2010 acquisition of 94 treatment centers from Psychiatric Solutions.

Founder Alan Miller, who retains the post of board chairman and CEO, controls over 80 percent of UHS voting stock.

FROM UNEMPLOYMENT TO BUSINESS OWNERSHIP

Universal Health Services was founded in September 1978 by Alan B. Miller, a businessman with experience in the health care industry. Although Miller had started his career as an executive at advertising agency Young & Rubicam after a stint in the U.S. Army, he left that field in 1969 when a former classmate at the Wharton School of Business invited him to join American Medicorp, a hospital management company. Within four years, Miller had become chief executive officer of the company, at the age of 35. Under his leadership, American Medicorp became the second-largest hospital management firm in the business, with 56 hospitals, 15,000 employees, and yearly revenues of $550 million. Unwittingly, however, Miller had transformed his employer into a tempting target, and he lost his job when it was purchased in a hostile takeover by Humana, Inc., the largest U.S. hospital chain, in 1978.

Enraged, Miller filed suit against Humana in the wake of the deal and then picked himself up and started over. The newly unemployed chief executive and six of

COMPANY PERSPECTIVES

UHS Seeks to provide superior quality healthcare services that patients recommend to families and friends, physicians prefer for their patients, purchasers select for their clients, employees are proud of, and investors seek for long-term results.

his former colleagues at Medicorp set out to found another hospital chain. The seven executives chipped in three quarters of a million dollars of their own funds and borrowed $3.2 million from a consortium of venture capital banks to start Universal Health Services, Inc. They based their new venture in King of Prussia, Pennsylvania, a suburb of Philadelphia.

In 1979 the fledgling company made its first acquisition when it purchased Doctors' Hospital. Miller bought the hospital because he thought it showed great potential for improvement, and after just one full year of Universal management, Doctors' Hospital had increased its profits tenfold, to almost $1.2 million.

To finance additional acquisitions, Universal borrowed more money and issued shares in the company. Since he had seen one successful company yanked out from underneath him when its outstanding shares were bought up by a hostile suitor, Miller structured Universal's stock offering so that the class of stock publicly traded, one of four classes overall, represented nearly four-fifths of the company's equity but less than 5 percent of its voting power. Voting power remained in the hands of Universal's executives. This allowed Miller to rest assured that control of the company he was working to build would not be taken away from him, but still gave Universal the means to acquire additional acute care hospitals in Texas and Nevada. In June 1979 the company bought Memorial Hospital in Panama City, California, from Texas International, an equipment manufacturer.

From the start, Universal focused its activities on markets where dramatic growth in population was predicted, reasoning that an ever-increasing number of residents would help to keep hospital beds filled. These markets included the Sun Belt states of California, Nevada, Texas, and Florida, where Universal made its first acquisitions, and which experienced population growth of more than two and a half times the national average during Universal's first full decade in operation.

Universal continued its steady pace of acquisitions through the end of 1981, when it looked north to purchase five nonprofit hospitals from the Stewards Foundation, a Christian organization, at a cost of $40 million. The acquisition was the first time that nonprofit hospitals had been taken over by a publicly owned management company. The move brought Universal two properties in Chicago and three facilities in the state of Washington. All together, the hospitals contained 600 beds. After Universal implemented a series of changes designed to shorten the length of time the average patient stayed in the hospital, increase the percentage of private-paying patients, and raise the productivity of the hospitals' employees, pretax revenues for the facilities tripled.

BUILDING ITS OWN HOSPITALS

In 1983 Universal opened the first hospital that the company had constructed rather than purchased. Sparks Family Hospital, outside Reno, Nevada, was the first new hospital to be opened in the fast-growing area in over 40 years. Eventually, Universal would construct many of its facilities. 'We didn't just acquire companies,' Chairman Miller later told *Forbes,* 'We built maybe a third of our acutes, a half of our psychiatrics. We aren't in it for the fast play.'

In operating the facilities that it had purchased, Universal implemented a business philosophy that allowed it to reduce costs and increase profits from the hospitals it owned. The company typically improved the facility's technical capabilities, set up more effective purchasing systems, standardized fees for services, and reviewed plans for renovation and expansion. In addition, Universal sought to smooth relations between doctors and the hospital, and with the community as a whole, and it instituted aggressive marketing to seek out the patients it most desired.

Despite the steady growth that these policies brought, Universal found its profitability limited on several fronts. There was an oversupply of acute care hospital beds in many areas, which pushed earnings down and also controlled prices through competition. In addition, a significant portion of acute care hospital revenue was derived from patients whose treatment was paid for by Medicare. With its strict caps on fees and reimbursements, Medicare made it difficult for hospital owners to reap large sums.

In response to these conditions, in May 1983 Universal branched out from its original mission of running acute-care hospitals to the field of psychiatric services. The company began by purchasing Qualicare, which operated 15 psychiatric hospitals, for $120

KEY DATES

1978: Alan B. Miller and a team of executives found Universal Health Services.

1982: Universal Health Services purchases five hospitals from Stewards Foundation.

1983: Company purchases Qualicare for more than $100 million.

1992: UHS moves trading to New York Stock Exchange.

1996: Company acquires Northwest Texas Healthcare System.

2005: Hurricane Katrina damages many UHS hospitals in Louisiana.

2007: Company acquires Dover Behavioral Health System.

2009: Marc Miller, son of founder Alan, takes over as company president.

2010: UHS adds 94 behavioral treatment centers by purchasing Psychiatric Solutions, Inc.

million. Since psychiatric facilities did not suffer from excess capacity and were not largely dependent on Medicare payments, their operators could earn larger profits, allowing the business to grow at a faster rate.

Two months after its Qualicare purchase, Universal acquired an additional property in its Sun Belt base when it bought Stevens Park Osteopathic Hospital in Dallas for $7 million. The facility had 117 beds, and the company announced that it would operate the existing hospital only as long as it took to construct an $18 million replacement. With this purchase, the number of hospitals owned by Universal grew to 24.

The company's string of acquisitions continued in 1984, as Universal purchased the Forest View Psychiatric Hospital in Grand Rapids, Michigan, for $8.5 million, and leased Doctor's Hospital, in Shreveport, Louisiana. After divesting itself of the River West Medical Center, a general hospital in Plaquemine, Louisiana, Universal had 30 facilities on its roster, and in March 1984 it reported annual earnings of $9.8 million.

By the spring of 1985 Universal's steady growth had made it the sixth-largest hospital management firm in the United States, but the company's aggressive pace of acquisitions had come at the cost of a sizable debt. In August, Universal announced that it would issue an additional two million shares of stock in an effort to reduce its debt.

CONTINUING GROWTH AND EXPANSION

In November 1985 Universal further rearranged its stock structure in an effort to strengthen its already formidable defenses against an unwanted corporate takeover. One month later, the company made two additional acquisitions, purchasing another Florida health care facility in the town of Plantation and McAllen Medical Center in McAllen, Texas.

By January 1986 Universal's yearly profits had reached $21.7 million. With this domestic base to build on, the company turned its focus to operations overseas, investing $40 million in three hospitals in the United Kingdom. The company built one hospital each in London and the town of Shirley, and a third outside London. Universal's U.K. facilities were designed to appeal to the growing number of wealthy Britons, who, the company hoped, would opt out of the country's system of socialized medicine and instead pay handsomely for top-notch private medical care. Expecting that Britain's Conservative government, under Prime Minister Margaret Thatcher, would implement measures to encourage private health insurance and allow service in private hospitals, Universal looked forward to large profits from its overseas venture.

Unfortunately, Britain's economy went into a decline, limiting the number of Britons wealthy enough to afford Universal's health services, and the company's United Kingdom hospitals remained unprofitable. In addition, by the end of 1986, Universal's debts had reached $317 million, and its seven-year streak of rising profits had come to an end. Net income fell to $1.7 million, a drop of $20 million from the year before.

In response to this growing fiscal crisis, in 1987 Universal's Chairman Miller adopted a novel financial solution. In order to reduce the company's debt, he placed 10 of Universal's hospital properties in a real estate investment trust, the Universal's Health Realty Income Trust. Shares in this trust were then given to Universal's creditors and traded on the New York Stock Exchange, where almost 10 percent of the shares were purchased by the Bass family of Texas. After its reorganization, Universal had one-third less equity and $75 million less debts. However, the company had also saddled itself with $13 million a year in rental payments on the properties it had previously owned. As a result of this move, Universal's profits rose during 1987 to $11.8 million but still did not attain their previous levels.

In the late 1980s Universal entered a period of retrenchment and solidification of its holdings, following its rapid, debt-generating growth in the earlier part of the decade. The company moved to sell off hospitals whose profits did not meet expected levels, generate cash from its operations, and reduce its debts overall. As part of this process, in 1988 Universal sold its Centralia Hospital, in Centralia, Washington, to a religious order for $9.5 million. Streamlining its operations, in June 1988 Universal sold its share in a health maintenance organization in Nevada it had entered into as a joint venture.

AN EXPANDING FIELD AND RISING PROFITS: 1988–91

In place of these facilities, Universal picked up property in the more lucrative psychiatric treatment field in 1988, when it bought La Amistad, a 43-bed psychiatric hospital in Florida, for $3.7 million. Revenues from the company's psychiatric treatment centers had been rising since 1987 and would soon come to represent a third of Universal's profits, despite the fact that they made up less than a sixth of its gross revenues.

In the spring of 1990 Universal continued its policy of purchasing psychiatric treatment centers, as it agreed to acquire the assets of the Ridgeview Institute, in Rhode Island, the company's 15th such facility, and entered into negotiations for a 16th. 'We still don't have an oversupply of psychiatric hospital beds,' Miller told *Forbes* magazine, explaining his acquisitions philosophy. 'There are opportunities to build if you do it very selectively.'

Also in 1990 Universal inaugurated a quality management department in an effort to make its existing properties more profitable. These efforts started to pay off as the company's gross revenues topped $1 billion for the first time at the end of that year, and profits almost doubled from the year before, to $11.6 million.

In February 1991 Universal's bottom line got a further boost when the company received a generous offer for its hospitals in Britain. Although Chairman Miller had continued to predict their imminent profitability, the facilities had never turned a profit, and had, in fact, constituted a significant drain on the company's earnings as they racked up losses of $5 million a year. Universal had been unsuccessfully trying to sell the hospitals for some time, and its earnings outlook was bolstered by the $51.1 million offer for the properties from Compass Group, plc, one of Great Britain's largest hospital management firms.

Two months later, Universal moved to heighten its public profile when it voted to list its stock on the New York Stock Exchange, a more prominent marketplace than the American Stock Exchange, which it had previously used. The company also made a tentative foray into the managed-care industry, with a pilot program at one of its Florida hospitals, and the purchase of a 166-bed psychiatric hospital in Torrance, a suburb of Los Angeles, that was home to a leading treatment center for sexual addiction. These moves helped Universal to rack up profits of $20.3 million in 1991, its fourth consecutive year of improved profits.

CORE MARKETS: 1991–99

In the early 1990s, Universal's net revenues grew in each of the company's principal businesses of psychiatric hospitals, acute care hospitals and ambulatory treatment centers. To continue to grow its outpatient revenues, Universal focused on acquiring and constructing ambulatory treatment centers. Forty percent of Universal's revenues were generated from fixed payment services received through Medicare and Medicaid.

Universal took a step to expand its treatment centers in 1994 when it acquired Manatee Hospital, a 512-bed acute care facility located in Manatee, Florida. It also picked up Aiken Regional Medical Centers, a 225-bed medical facility located in Aiken, South Carolina. It spent $71 million to build several new medical facilities including the 129-bed Edinburg Hospital in Edinburg, Texas. Before the year closed, the company entered into an agreement to purchase the Westlake Medical Center in Westlake, California, as well as the 104-bed Dallas Family Hospital.

Growth via acquisitions would continue through 1999 for Universal Health Services. In 1997 it acquired the 501-bed acute care hospital George Washington University Hospital. A year later, it acquired three hospitals in Puerto Rico for a combined price of $186 million. In 1999 it entered into an agreement with The Cooper Companies and purchased Hampton Behavioral Health Center, Hartgrove Hospital, and the Midwest Center for Youth and Families. The acquisitions would see annual revenues for Universal increase to $2 billion at the end of 1999.

HURRICANE KATRINA AND FURTHER GROWTH: THE 21ST CENTURY

Annual revenues for Universal would reach $3.9 billion in 2004. However, the impact of Hurricane Katrina would chew away at some of the revenues. The hurricane hit the Gulf coast from central Florida to Texas in late August 2005 and was especially devastating in Louisiana, a state where Universal operated two medical facilities in New Orleans and an additional two facilities in Chalmette. The company's four Louisiana-based hospitals suffered substantial water and wind damage.

In 2009 founder Alan Miller relinquished the post of company president to his son Marc Miller, who had been a company director since 2006. The elder Miller retained the title of CEO and board chairman.

In 2010 Universal purchased Psychiatric Solutions, Incorporated, for nearly $3.1 billion. This gave Universal ownership of an additional 94 treatment centers located in 32 states, Puerto Rico, and the U.S. Virgin Islands. By boosting its behavioral treatment center business, UHS entered the 2010s with two main business lines that it believed would help keep the company's earnings robust.

Elizabeth Rourke
Updated, Rhonda Campbell

PRINCIPAL SUBSIDIARIES

ASC Property Management, Inc.; Auburn Regional Medical Group; District Hospital Partners, L.P.; Fort Duncan Medical Center, L.P.; Frontline Hospital, LLC; Keystone Education and Youth Services, LLC; Lakewood Ranch Therapy, LLC; Laredo Holdings, Inc.; McAllen Holdings, Inc.; UHS Holding Company, Inc.; Wellington Regional Medical Center Incorporated.

PRINCIPAL COMPETITORS

Community Health Systems, Inc.; HCA Holdings, Inc.; Health Management Associates, Inc.; Tenet Healthcare Corporation.

FURTHER READING

"Baptist Hospitals and Health Systems, Inc. and Universal Health Services, Inc. (UHS) Announce the Signing of a Letter of Intent for UHS To Acquire Mantee Memorial Hospital." *PR Newswire,* November 9, 1994. Accessed February 28, 2011. http://www.thefreelibrary.com/BAP TIST+HOSPITALS+AND+HEALTH+SYSTEMS,+INC. +AND+UNIVERSAL+HEALTH...-a015908265.

Hazelton, Lynnette. "Simple Formula Leads to Universal Success." *Focus,* September 25, 1985.

Cook, James. "Once Burned ...," *Forbes,* April 16, 1990.

George, John. "UHS's Success Builds upon Learned Lessons." *Philadelphia Business Journal,* May 27, 1991.

"Universal Health Buys Windmoor Owner Psychiatric Solutions." *Tampa Bay Business Journal,* May 17, 2010. Accessed February 28, 2011. http://www.bizjournals.com/ tampabay/stories/2010/05/17/daily2.html.

"Universal Health Services, Inc. Reports Damage Sustained From Hurricane Katrina." *PR Newswire,* September 1, 2005. Accessed February 28, 2011. http://www.prnewswire.com/ news-releases/universal-health-services-inc-reports-damage- sustained-from-hurricane-katrina-54688032.html.

U.S. Department of Health & Human Services. "Disproportionate Share Hospital (DSH).", Accessed February 28, 2011. http://www.hhs.gov/recovery/cms/dsh.html.

U.S. Department of Health & Human Services and U.S. Department of Justice. "US Files Complaint Against Virginia Medicaid Providers (Civil Division)." March 2, 2010. STOPMedicareFraud.gov. Accessed February 28, 2011. http://www.stopmedicarefraud.gov/innews/virginia. html.

USEC Inc.

Two Democracy Center
6903 Rockledge Drive
Bethesda, Maryland 20817
U.S.A.
Telephone: (301) 564-3200
Fax: (301) 564-3201
Web site: http://www.usec.com

Public Company
Founded: 1992 as United States Enrichment Corporation
Employees: 2,949 (2010)
Sales: $2.04 billion (2010)
Stock Exchanges: New York
Ticker Symbol: USU
NAICS: 3251188 All Other Basic Inorganic Chemical Manufacturing

■ ■ ■

USEC Inc. is a global energy company and a major supplier of low-enriched uranium (LEU) for nuclear power plants. The LEU is necessary to make nuclear fuel needed for reactors to produce electricity. LEU is produced using natural uranium, mined from sites in Canada, Australia, and other countries. The company produces LEU at the Paducah Gaseous Diffusion Plant (GDP) located on a 750-acre site in Paducah, Kentucky. This plant, as well as the company's Portsmouth GDP in Piketon, Ohio, is leased from the U.S. Department of Energy (DOE).

LEU is also acquired by buying dismantled Russian nuclear missiles. This is done in accordance with the Megatons to Megawatt agreement with that country. Fissile material from Russia accounts for roughly one-half of the company's supply mix annually. The 20-year Megatons to Megawatts agreement was signed in January 1994, and states that USEC will purchase about 5.5 million SWU each year through 2013. (The Russian government indicated that the country would not extend the contract beyond that time.) By the end of 2010, the equivalent of about 16,500 Soviet-era nuclear warheads had been eliminated.

USEC provides LEU to approximately 150 nuclear reactors around the world and is the only uranium enrichment plant in the United States. Most of USEC's customers are utilities that operate nuclear power plants. In 2010 large utilities customers included Entergy Corporation and Exelon Corporation. The U.S. government is also a prominent customer. USEC also performs contract work for the DOE and other DOE contractors at the Paducah and Portsmouth GDPs. USEC provides systems for the transportation and storage of spent nuclear fuel, and provides nuclear fuel cycle and energy consulting services through its subsidiary NAC.

COMPANY FOUNDING AND EARLY YEARS: 1992–96

On October 24, 1992, the Energy Policy Act of 1992 was signed, which created the United States Enrichment Corporation (USEC), a corporation completely owned by the government. USEC began operating on July 1 of the following year. This was the first step in transferring the Department of Energy's uranium enrichment opera-

COMPANY PERSPECTIVES

USEC's mission is to supply enriched uranium and nuclear industry related services in a safe and environmentally responsible manner. Our vision is to be the world's most reliable and competitive supplier of enriched uranium and related services and to expand our role in the global resurgence of nuclear power.

tion from the government to the private sector. One requirement of the act was that the corporation would later be sold to private investors. USEC took over operations of two existing plants, which served in excess of 60 electric utility companies in 11 countries at the time. Profits from the corporation, which were $30 million for 1993, $55 million in 1994, and $120 million in 1995 and 1996, went to the U.S. Treasury.

The USEC Privatization Act was signed in 1996, and privatization of USEC was approved by President Bill Clinton the following year. However, the sale of the company into the private sector did not happen immediately. According to *Government Executive,* the privatization was "held up for a variety of reasons, ranging from finding an acceptable calculation of USEC's value to concerns about whether a privatized USEC would follow through on potentially unprofitable deals to purchase Russian uranium to keep it off the black market."

OPERATING AS A PUBLIC COMPANY: 1998–2002

After considering bids from private companies interested in purchasing USEC, the company's board of directors decided to privatize the company through an initial public offering (IPO), although many lawmakers did not support this plan and believed it would be a risk to national security. Despite these concerns, USEC transitioned from government corporation to publicly traded company in July 1998. The IPO was the first privatization for the U.S. government in more than 10 years, and it was rather large, as the sale reached $1.425 billion. Along with the IPO, the name was changed to USEC Inc. All of the U.S. government's interest in the business were transferred to USEC, except for certain liabilities from the government's earlier operations.

Revenues for 1999 exceeded $1.5 billion. However, oversupply among competitors created a need for the

company to reduce labor costs early in 2000. The company announced that 850 of its 4,000 employees would be laid off. The privatization agreement limited employee layoffs to 500 during the first two years following the IPO, but this number of people were laid off voluntarily, allowing the company to further limit its workforce.

Within two years of becoming a public company, stock prices for USEC plummeted by 70 percent. Lower prices for uranium and uranium enrichment worldwide, a decrease in demand for both, and an increase in costs for materials caused the company to lower production, which resulted in increased unit costs. Executives also stated that the agreement with Russia was partly to blame, because the cost of purchasing the materials exceeded the price for which USEC could sell them. The impact of the program contributed to the company's loss of $62.4 million during the fourth quarter of 2000. Profits for the year fell by more than $110 million as compared to 1999.

In addition, the company faced class action lawsuits by investors claiming that fraudulent statements were made at the time of the IPO. Critics also accused USEC executives of considering personal gain when selecting an IPO rather than a private sale of the company, which would have given the new owners the opportunity to bring in their own management team.

As a result of financial hardship, uranium enrichment operations were discontinued at the Portsmouth GDP in June 2001. The plant was maintained in a state of "cold standby," under a contract with the DOE. In this state, the plant could more easily return to full operation or be reengineered for new technology being tested by the DOE.

Things began to look up a bit for USEC in 2002 when the International Trade Commission (ITC) approved import duties on uranium from international firms. USEC had previously claimed that competitors from Europe were selling their enriched uranium at prices that were lower than the cost of production. The import duties were a result of the ITC's investigations into these claims. Another boost came later that year when USEC negotiated a new pricing contract for the uranium being purchased from Russia. The previous contract included a fixed price that was below market value at the time of the agreement, but which caused a significant loss of profit for USEC when the market price dropped considerably. The new contract based prices on an average international market price over the period of the previous three years, minus a discount. The new pricing agreement, which would be in effect until the end of the uranium contract in 2013, gave USEC room for profit when selling the materials.

PREPARING FOR THE AMERICAN CENTRIFUGE PLANT: 2006–08

In 2006 USEC and the DOE entered a lease agreement for the long-term use of the Portsmouth GDP for the American Centrifuge Plant (ACP), which was expected to be the most advanced uranium enrichment technology in the world. There are two methods of enriching uranium for use in nuclear power plants. The first is gaseous diffusion, which has historically been used by USEC. The second is gas centrifuge. The company planned to deploy the new gas centrifuge technology to replace the previous method. USEC began developing this new technology in 2002, although the DOE had been working on it several decades earlier.

The company was considering whether to locate the facility in Piketon, Ohio, or Paducah, Kentucky. The Piketon location was eventually chosen based on the fact that the former Portsmouth GDP facility was already in that location, seismic faults near Paducah would cause higher risk and costs, and the state of Ohio offered $100 million in grants, a loan, and tax incentives for selecting the Piketon site. The ACP would replace the gaseous diffusion plant, decrease power costs, and improve production.

FINANCING AND THE ACP: 2008–09

By the spring of 2008, the initial designs for the gas centrifuge machines to be used in the ACP were finalized. Between 40 and 50 of the machines were expected to be used in the new plant, which the company planned to have in operation by spring of 2009. During the summer of 2008, the company applied for a loan guarantee from the DOE to help finance the project, which had an estimated cost of $3.5 billion. This budget included money the company had already spent on the project but did not include any financing costs or financial assurance. These would be covered by the loan guarantee.

In further preparation for the American Centrifuge Project, the company created four subsidiaries during September 2008. Once the project was launched, the subsidiaries would not only own the plant and equipment but also operate, maintain, and manufacture machines related to the project, as well as continue research and development on the centrifuge. This business structure was put in place to help the company obtain DOE loan financing and other investors. It would also help to facilitate future expansion of the plant.

The company was counting on the money from the loan to complete the project, but in July 2009 the DOE asked USEC to withdraw its application in order to resolve specific technology issues. The company was told that the application could be reconsidered in a year to a year-and-a-half. USEC refused to withdraw the application, and planned to attempt to secure financing from another source. However, construction of the ACP was put on hold as a result of the uncertainty surrounding funding, causing the loss of about 120 at USEC. Although work on the project was halted, the company continued to incur costs associated with contractual obligations.

By the end of 2010, USEC had invested almost $2 billion in the project. However, in order to complete construction of the plant, not only was more money needed, it was also expected that the final cost of the project would exceed the initial budget due to the demobilization, higher costs, and the cost of remobilizing the project once financing was secured.

Despite the challenges associated with the ACP, USEC did find success in other aspects of the company during 2009. That year USEC and one of its subsidiaries settled a legal dispute associated with an antidumping order. USEC sought recoveries related to the order, known as the Byrd Amendment, and was awarded $70.7 million following a unanimous Supreme Court ruling in the company's favor.

THE FUTURE OF USEC: 2010S

In May 2010 USEC received an investment of $100 million each from the Babcock & Wilcox Company

(B&W, a U.S. energy contractor) and Toshiba Corporation, a leader in the electric and nuclear power industry. These funds were to be used for general purposes as well as continued progress on ACP. The money would be invested in three phrases, and the companies would receive USEC stock in exchange. Also, according to the *Information Company*, " USEC could provide enriched uranium for bundling with Toshiba's nuclear power plant proposals. USEC and B&W also plan to complete the joint venture announced last year to manufacture USEC's commercial AC100 centrifuge machines for the American Centrifuge Plant." The joint venture was known as American Centrifuge Manufacturing (ACM).

The company received $75 million in September 2010 as the first phase of the investment by Toshiba and B&W. The ACP project took a huge step forward in the fall of 2010. The DOE loan guarantee for USEC was approved in October 2010, putting the company on track to continue construction on the ACP. An anticipated 8,000 jobs would be created by the project. The loan would be granted following the submission of final documentation and the meeting of the loan's closing conditions.

In February 2011 USEC and the DOE modified the agreement made in 2002 regarding the timeline for deploying the ACP. Under the new agreement, USEC had until November 2011 to secure financing for the plant and must begin operations by May 2014 at a certain capacity. The agreement took into account the fact that approximately two years would be needed to begin operations at the plant after the necessary financing was received, and approximately three years to complete the plant once initial commercial operations had begun.

USEC's fate during the 2010s was closely tied to its ACP venture. There was reason to believe that if the plant were to operate as the company hoped, it would aid the company's bottom line considerably.

Diane Milne

PRINCIPAL SUBSIDIARIES

NAC International Inc.; United States Enrichment Corporation.

PRINCIPAL COMPETITORS

AREVA; OAO Tekhsnabexport; Urenco, Inc.

FURTHER READING

Kochaniec, Joanne Wojcik. " Taking Stock of Purchase Plan; Employer Facing Challenges After Shares Plummet." *Business Insurance* 34 (2000): 1.

"Lawmakers Criticize Privatization of Uranium Processor." *American Metal Market* 108, no. 73 (2000): 20

Moses, Eric. " Uranium, Inc." *Government Executive,* April 1, 1997.

Schmitt, Bill. "Government Exits Uranium Scene; New Firm to Represent US Key Supplier Role." *American Metal Market* 101, no. 130 (1993): 4.

Scoblic, J. Peter. " United States, Russia Approve New 'HEU Deal' Contract. (News and Negotiations)." *Arms Control Today,* July-August 2002, 20+.

"Toshiba, Babcock & Wilcox to Invest $200 Million in Uranium Producer USEC." *Information Company,* May 26, 2010.

Weinstock, Matthew. "Meltdown." *Government Executive,* February 1, 2001.

VicSuper Pty Ltd

Level 6
90 Collins Street
Melbourne, Victoria 3000
Australia
Telephone: (61) 3 9667-9679
Fax: (61) 3 9667-9610
Web site: http://www.vicsuper.com.au

Private Company
Founded: 1994
Employees: 178 (2010)
Sales: AUD $491.34 million ($490 million) (2010)
NAICS: 525120 Health and Welfare Funds

■ ■ ■

VicSuper Pty Ltd is a private company specializing in pension and retirement funds, called superannuation funds in Australia. Based in the Australian state of Victoria, it is one of Australia's largest public offer superfunds with 255,000 members and almost 15,000 active employers participating as of 2010. Any eligible individual in Australia can become a member, and any Australian employer can choose to pay superannuation contributions into VicSuper Fund on behalf of their employees. The company's headquarters are in Melbourne, but it also has major offices in the cities of Bendigo, Blackburn, Geelong, Melbourne, and Traralgon.

VicSuper offers superannuation plans designed to range from the start of participants' working lives through to their retirement years. The company also provides superannuation advice and comprehensive education programs at no cost to its members. VicSuper operates and invests based on economic, governmental, social, and environmental considerations with an emphasis on long-term investment profitability.

To conrol risk and achieve members' return objectives, VicSuper invests according to a strategic asset allocation that sets the percentage of each option to be invested in one or more of four asset classes. These are equities (or company shares), cash, fixed interest, and property. VicSuper offers members the opportunity to invest in one or more of VicSuper's seven investment options based on risk tolerance and return expectations. The Cash Option features safe but low return investing, the Capital Secure Option features moderate risk and low to moderate returns, and the Capital Stable Option includes a 40 percent allocation to growth assets. Other options are the Balanced Option, which has a 60 percent allocation to growth assets and expected moderate to high returns, and the Growth Option, which features an 80 percent allocation to growth assets and higher returns expected over the long term. The last two options are the Equity Growth Option, which features a 100 percent allocation to growth assets and expected very high returns, and the Equity Growth Sustainability Option, which focuses on companies with optimal sustainability practices. While these companies are considered high- to very high-risk investments, there is also the possibility of very high returns.

SUPERANNUATION IN AUSTRALIA

Although superannuation, or retirement plans, as a form of savings dates back more than a century in Australia,

COMPANY PERSPECTIVES

VicSuper's purpose is to help people prepare for and meet their income needs in later life by making sense of their superannuation. Our central operating principle is to create value for VicSuper shareholders by building a sustainable superfund through the integration of economic, social, and environmental considerations into all of VicSuper's decision support system. Our core values focus on our member services and emphasize making sense, respect and encouragement, trust and integrity, learning, and quality. Our ultimate goal is to be the preferred superannuation fund for Australians living in the state of Victoria.

for many years these plans affected only a minority of people working in Australia. For the most part, these employees were white-collar staff in large corporations, finance sector employees, government employees, and members of the armed forces. It was not until the 1970s that superannuation started to become more widely available to a broader spectrum of Australian workers.

Institutionalized employee superannuation began in Australia in September 1985 when the Australian Council of Trade Unions, as part of its national Wage Case claim with the Conciliation and Arbitration Commission, sought a 3 percent employer superannuation contribution to be paid into an industry fund. The Australian government supported the claim, and the commission announced in 1986 that it would approve industrial agreements that would approve contributors for approved superannuation funds. At this time, the funds approved were primarily multiemployer industry funds that had joint sponsorship from trade unions and employer associations.

Although superannuation coverage for Australians rapidly grew, nearly one-third of private sector employees remained uncovered by 1991. In addition, not all the employees entitled to superannuation received it, partly because the only avenue to enforce compliance was a laborious case mounted with the Australian Conciliation and Arbitration Commission. On July 1, 1992, the Australian government announced that a new system known as the superannuation guarantee would require employers to make tax-deductible superannuation contributions on behalf of their employees. Employers who failed to provide the required amount of superannuation support would be liable to a charge equivalent to the individual employee

shortfall in contributions, as well as an interest component and an administrative charge.

COMPANY FOUNDING AND EARLY YEARS: 1994–2000

The Victorian Superannuation Fund, or VicSuper Fund, was founded in 1994. The fund was initially a Victorian public sector fund overseen by the Victorian Superannuation Board (VSB), a special government organization established specifically to administer the superannuation benefits of many public servants in Victoria. On July 1, 1999, the VSB was replaced as Trustee and administrator of the fund by VicSuper Pty Ltd. At the same time, the State Superannuation Fund (SSF) and the state's Emergency Services Superannuation Scheme merged for administration purposes and was named the ESSSuper.

In July 2000 the VicSuper Fund became a public offer fund, meaning that participants no longer had to be employed by a VicSuper Fund participating employer. As a result, any eligible person in Australia could join VicSuper's public offer benefit plans, which included VicSuper Beneficiary Account, VicSuper Commutable Pension, and VicSuper Non-Commutable Pension. Although VicSuper represented a nonprofit company, it nevertheless adopted a corporate governance framework to administer and manage the fund.

FOCUSING ON SUSTAINABILITY

VicSuper, under the leadership of its chief executive Bob Welsh, incorporated sustainability as its central operating principle in 2000. According to Welsh, the move toward these types of investments stemmed from the wishes of many of its customers. As a result, VicSuper hired the Swiss business firm Sustainable Asset Management to begin screening investments for suitability as investment vehicles for AUD 60 million worth of superannuation funds. VicSuper also established the Equity Growth Sustainability fund. This fund was offered to any investor who desired to place funds into sustainable investments only. "We and many of our fund members are also concerned about the future viability of the planet and its people so this initiative gives us the opportunity to meet our financial responsibilities to members while doing something positive for the planet," Welsh was quoted as saying in the *Australasian UNEP Finance Initiatives Newsletter.*

By the end of 2001 VicSuper began a review of its investment strategy with an eye toward outsourcing some mandates in active international and domestic small caps, international and domestic private equity, and enhanced passive domestic equities. The following

```
┌─────────────────────────────────────────────┐
│                                             │
│            KEY DATES                        │
│                                             │
│              ■                              │
│                                             │
│  1994:  The Victorian Superannuation Fund, or Vic- │
│         Super Fund, is founded.             │
│  1999:  VicSuper Pty Ltd becomes trustee and │
│         administrator of VicSuper Fund.     │
│  2000:  VicSuper Fund becomes a public offer fund. │
│  2005:  VicSuper enters a 10-year agreement to work │
│         with EPA Victoria to protect the environment │
│         and work toward a sustainable Victoria. │
│  2010:  VicSuper's chief executive, Bob Welsh, retires. │
│                                             │
└─────────────────────────────────────────────┘
```

year, the company decided to invest about AUD 40 million in international and domestic private equity and to hire money managers to oversee the investments. By July 2002 the company announced that it was increasing its strategic allocation to international equity by 10 percent at the expense of domestic equity. The move was made to provide access to some sectors Australia's marketplace had a traditionally limited exposure to, such as IT.

In July 2003 VicSuper received two awards from the Banksia Environmental Foundation. It was named the winner in the categories of "Business Environmental Responsibility and Leadership" and "Leadership in Socially Responsible Investment." At about the same time VicSuper announced its plan to expand its educational efforts targeting its fund members. At the time, in addition to its advisers based in Melbourne, the company had 17 traveling advisers to serve fund members who did not live in Melbourne.

ESTABLISHING A SUSTAINABILITY COVENANT: 2005–07

VicSuper also made sustainability covenants with EPA (Environmental Protection Authority) Victoria. The first such covenant was designed to further the resource use efficiency of VicSuper's operations. The second, signed on August 17, 2005, was a 10-year agreement to work with EPA Victoria to protect the environment and contribute to a more sustainable Victoria.

VicSuper increased its commitment to sustainability investments by becoming one of the first pension funds in the world to publish what would become the company's annual comprehensive sustainability reports, the first of which was published in 2004. As part of its sustainability covenant, the company's report provided information on the company's activities, initiatives, and outcomes of the previous year and commitments for the

year ahead. In recognition of VicSuper's commitment to integrating sustainability principles into all the asset classes of VicSuper's pension fund, Welsh, the company's chief executive, received the SAM/SPG Sustainability Pioneer Award in 2005. (SAM is a global investment boutique focused exclusively on sustainability investing, and SPG is an investment company managed by SAM.)

As a part of its effort to find good investments for its superannuation fund while incorporating sustainability principles, VicSuper began investing in Victorian farms in 2007. The state had been suffering through severe drought conditions for several years, and the properties purchased by VicSuper were properties near Kerang, a town in northern Victoria that was heavily affected by the drought. The AUD 40 million agricultural investment was bolstered by a study to find the most suitable crops to grow in the area with a focus on environmental impact. The purchase was made via a new venture called the Australian Farms Fund, which provided superfunds the opportunity to invest in the industry and the environment.

VicSuper was recognized in 2009 as the first Australian superfund to direct its members' retirements savings into an investment portfolio designed to achieve the same return on investments as the wider international share marked but with half the carbon footprint. The company's low-carbon investment portfolio, managed by Vanguard Investments, was begun with AUD 150 million investment and included 700 companies that collectively emit significantly less carbon emissions than other similar industries. "At VicSuper, we firmly believe that low carbon investments offer less risk and the likelihood of higher long-term investment returns," Welsh noted in an article in *Briefing,* a newsletter of the UNEP Finance Initiative.

WORKING THROUGH THE GLOBAL FINANCIAL CRISIS: 2008 AND BEYOND

Like most investment portfolios, the VicSuper Fund suffered significant losses in investment returns in 2008 and 2009 due to the worldwide economic downturn. Most of the various aggressive investment groups suffered double digit or close to double digit percentage losses over the period. However, the fund rebounded in fiscal year 2009–10 with annual investment returns for the year being positive for all asset classes. For example, higher risk asset classes posted double digit or near double digit percentage gains.

As of June 30, 2010, VcSuper's net assets had increased by more than AUD 1 billion to AUD 7.201

billion, equaling a growth rate of 23 percent per annum since VicSuper Fund became a regulated fund open to any employer in 1999. This growth in assets was due primarily to higher gross investment returns and dividend payments following the recovery of global markets. Another factor was the continuing high levels of member contributions to the Superfund. A major growth area within the company was the VicSuper Pensions, which for the first time exceeded AUD 1 billion in members assets. Other positive aspects of fiscal year 2009–10 included a net membership increase of 6,000 for the year.

VicSuper experienced a momentous change at the end of 2010 with the retirement of Welsh, who had led the fund since its inception in 1999 and was recognized as the fund's pioneer in building a sustainable superfund. VicSuper chair Barbra Norris noted in an *InvestorDaily* article that Welsh's departure would not alter the company's focus. The company "is synonymous with sustainability and it will remain central to our operations and investments," Norris said. VicSuper deputy chief executive Michael Geragthy was named acting chief executive as the company searched for a new chief executive.

In 2010 VicSuper had over AUD 7 billion in assets under management. Continued financial stability and growth remained at the core of the company's investing strategy. The company's future plans included extending sustainability investing deeper into VicSuper's core listed equities, property, and infrastructure assets and fixed-interest portfolio. The company also planned to continue to address risks and opportunities due to climate change and other sustainability challenges.

David Petechuk

PRINCIPAL SUBSIDIARIES

VicSuper Ecosystem Services Pty Ltd.

PRINCIPAL COMPETITORS

AustralianSuper Pty Ltd; FSS Trustee Corporation; Health Super Pty Ltd; Westscheme Pty Ltd.

FURTHER READING

"Good Clean Funds." *Personal Investor,* December 2001, 48.

Hunter, Jenny. "VicSuper Leads Australian Superannuation Funds in Sustainability Investing." *Australasian UNEP Finance Initiatives Newsletter,* January 2002.

Klijn, Wouter. "VicSuper Chief to Depart at End of Year." *InvestorDaily,* December 17, 2010. Accessed March 9, 2011. http://investordaily.com.au/archive/10778.xml.

"VicSuper Takes the Lead on Low Carbon Superannuation." *Briefing: UNEP Finance Initiative News from Australasia,* July 2009. Accessed March 9, 2011. www.unepfi.org/fileadmin/documents/epavic_newsletter_issue16.pdf.

Washington Nationals
Baseball Club, LLC

■

1500 South Capitol Street, SE
Washington, District of Columbia 20003
U.S.A.
Telephone: (202) 675-6287
Fax: (202) 640-7999
Web site: http://washington.nationals.mlb.com

Private Company
Founded: 1969 as the Montréal Expos
Employees: 100 (est., 2010)
Sales: $180 million (est., 2010)
NAICS: 711211 Sports Teams and Clubs

■ ■ ■

Washington Nationals Baseball Club, LLC, owns and operates the Nationals, or "the Nats," a professional baseball team located in Washington, D.C. Part of Major League Baseball (MLB), the Nationals are in the East Division of the National League. The Washington Nationals was formerly the Montréal Expos (Expos), which moved to the Washington, D.C., area in 2004. The team's home field is Nationals Park, located in Southeast Washington, D.C., near the Anacostia River. The Nationals is owned by Theodore Lerner, a successful commercial real estate developer who purchased the team in 2006.

TROUBLED BEGINNINGS:
SNYDER'S LONG FIGHT

Even before the Montréal Expos got started, they were in trouble. Well before 1969, there had been an effort to

bring professional baseball to Montréal, Canada. At the beginning of the decade the city lost its International Baseball team, the Montréal Royals, and for many years local politician Gerry Snyder had been trying to bring a professional baseball team back to the city. In 1967 Snyder, then a city councilor, presented a proposal to the MLB at the owners' meeting in Mexico City. He proposed that they award an expansion team to the city of Montréal. In May 1998 MLB approved the Montréal expansion team. Montréal beat out Buffalo, New York, and Dallas-Fort Worth, Texas, for the bid. It was a controversial choice, mainly because U.S. baseball fans did not like the idea of an MLB team belonging to a foreign city. Even the U.S. Congress condemned the decision. Regardless, MLB moved forward with its plans.

As MLB decided to move forward, the Canadians took a step or two backward. The investment group assembled by Snyder and Montréal mayor Jean Drapeau started to fall apart. J. Louis Levesque, an industrialist and the majority investor in the team, suddenly dropped out of the deal. As a result, the remaining investors let the $10 million franchise fee become past due. Also, full investment or not, the group could not come up with a commitment for a ballpark, and opening day was only nine months away. Mayor Drapeau scrambled to find new investors and eventually managed to convince Charles Bronfman, owner of beverage company Seagram, to come in as their anchor investor. Bronfman had been looking for a project to forge his own identity. Even though he ran the family business and was the largest distiller in the world, he did so under the shadow of his legendary father, Samuel Bronfman. Drapeau's proposal was a perfect opportunity for Bronfman, and he funded his commitment out of his own money.

However, the deal was still on shaky ground because they had not secured a ballpark. The MLB commissioner became concerned that this last obstacle might be insurmountable, since the city had very few venues that met MLB standards. The commissioner sent his aide John McHale to Montréal to see if he could help keep the deal alive. McHale, Drapeau, and others toured the city. Two local reporters showed them Jarry Park, which was serving as a junior baseball stadium at the time. In what seemed a last resort decision and a severe compromise, all parties agreed that the 3,000-seat ballpark in the northwest corner of the city would be the interim solution until the owners built a professional stadium. The Expos renovated the ballpark and enlarged it to seat around 28,500, which was still very small for an MLB team. At the time, they expected to play in Jarry Park for at most three years, at which point they would move into a larger ballpark that met MLB standards.

UNCOMFORTABLE BALLPARK, UNCOMFORTABLE BEGINNINGS

In 1969 the MLB officially expanded by four teams, two in the American League and two in the National League. The two American League teams were the Kansas City Royals and the Seattle Pilots (later the Milwaukee Brewers). The two National League teams were the San Diego Padres and the Montréal Expos. The Montréal team was the first MLB team outside the United States. Charles Bronfman named the team the Montréal Expos (or Les Expos de Montréal) after the Expo 67 World's Fair that had just been held in Montréal.

On April 8, 1969, the Montréal Expos played their first game against the New York Mets and won 11–10. They played their first home game at Jarry Park on April 14 in front of a sell-out crowd and won 8–7 over the St. Louis Cardinals. The team's star player was outfielder Rusty (Le Grand Orange) Staub. However, once the team began playing in Jarry Park, the venue proved to have other problems than being small. The field was outdoors and exposed to the elements, and because of the orientation of the field the sun shined directly in the first baseman's eyes. Also, Montréal's summers were very

short, so the team was forced to postpone many games at the beginning and end of the season to protect the fans from the elements. Regardless of where they played, the Expos were not making baseball very attractive to their fans. In their first season they lost 110 games and won only 52, and the next few seasons were not much better.

By 1971 it became apparent to everyone that the team's new ballpark, Olympic Stadium, would not be ready for the 1972 season. MLB threatened to move the team to another city, but the Expos managed to get the owners to agree not to move the team for another year. These delays continued for the next five years, the main culprit being a labor strike, until the stadium opened in 1977. However, even as the team played its first game in the new stadium in April 1977 the stadium still lacked a roof. The planned roof sat in a warehouse in France for almost 10 years. It was not until 1987 that the team played an indoor game at Olympic Stadium.

ROCKY BEGINNINGS

The club spent much of its early history losing. The year 1978 brought another losing season and frustration throughout the organization. Late in the season, General manager Charlie Fox was involved in a clubhouse altercation with pitcher Steve Rogers, during which Fox punched Rogers. However, fortunes changed one year later. In 1979 the team achieved a winning season for the first time in its history with 95 wins and 65 losses. In 1981 despite a delay in the season due to a players' strike, the team started strongly. Because of the strike, the season was significantly shortened, forcing the league to cancel 713 games. The Expos seemed to benefit from the shortened season and avoid a late-season collapse. The team finished the season in first place in their division and went to their first playoff series. They won the first round against the Phillies 3–2 but lost in the second round to the Los Angeles Dodgers, 2–3. In the last game, Dodger Rick Monday hit a home run in the ninth inning to win the game. This game became referred to by Montréal fans as "Blue Monday." The next season the team had a winning record but failed to make the playoffs.

By 1984 the team had gone through seven managers in 10 years and was plagued with poor play on the field and internal discontent. Also, the Expos were mired with bitter fans and an unfriendly hometown press. Much of the frustration had to do with the fact that the team's management had achieved many of its goals without much to show for it. They had made it through the rough early expansion years and moved into their new home. They had built up and developed an arsenal of star players, including Andre Dawson, Gary

```
┌─────────────────────────────────────────────────┐
│                                                 │
│                 KEY DATES                       │
│                    ■                            │
│                                                 │
│   1969:  Charles Bronfman and investment group start │
│          the expansion team the Montréal Expos in │
│          Montréal, Canada.                      │
│   1977:  Montréal Expos move into Olympic Stadium. │
│   1991:  Bronfman sells the Expos to Claude Brochue │
│          and a consortium of investors for CAD 100 │
│          million.                               │
│   1999:  Consortium sells the Expos to Jeffrey Loria, │
│          Steven Bronfman, and other investors for │
│          CAD 125 million.                       │
│   2001:  Loria and investors sell the Expos to MLB. │
│   2005:  The Expos move to Washington, D.C., and │
│          are renamed the Washington Nationals   │
│   2006:  MLB sells the Nationals to Lerner Enterprises │
│          Group for $450 million.               │
│   2008:  The Nationals play their first game in │
│          National Park, their new $611 million │
│          stadium.                               │
│                                                 │
└─────────────────────────────────────────────────┘
```

Carter, and Tim Raines. They had put the team in a good position to contend for a championship, but thus far that dream had gone unfulfilled. Even owner Bronfman was quoted as saying that there needed to be management changes. The team hired Murray Cook to replace McHale.

One of the difficult economic factors affecting the Expos from the very beginning was foreign exchange. The team traveled around the United States, supported farm teams based in the United States, and paid their players in U.S. dollars, but much of their revenue depended on the Canadian dollar. Sixty-seven percent of the Expos' revenues came from home games and merchandise sales, which was in Canadian dollars. As a result, currency shifts had a profound effect on the team's profitability from year to year. In 1984 the Canadian dollar dropped below $0.80 to the U.S. dollar and the costs of operations skyrocketed for the Expos as well as the Toronto Blue Jays. Also, attendance in 1984 was at its lowest since the team moved into Olympic Stadium. The Blue Jays raised their ticket prices, but the Expos set forward a new pricing structure that actually lowered the prices for a majority of its 59,149 seats. Management hoped that the lower prices would bring in more fans and increase revenues through increased attendance, but the strategy did not seem to work. Attendance plummeted to less than 1.6 million for the year, and the team failed to make the playoffs. The

Canadian dollar continued its slide against the U.S. dollar, and the Expos were rumored to have experienced a CAD 3 million loss in 1985. The team had not had a profit since 1981 ($1.86 million). However, Bronfman was not concerned about the losses. He was quoted as saying that he and his fellow owners were not in the business of making hefty profits. He said, "Seagrams I need, baseball I love." Nonetheless, the loss in 1985 was hard to ignore, and Bronfman replaced McHale as president with Claude Brochu, who had been vice president of marketing for Joseph E. Seagram & Sons, a Bronfman-controlled distilling company.

THE SEASON THAT BROKE BRONFMAN'S HEART

The fortunes of the team did not improve over the next five years as the team never finished higher than third place. Before the 1990 season Bronfman announced that the team was for sale. The 1989 season was the breaking point. The team had made major trades with the intention of being a viable contender for the national title that year, and the strategy worked for most of the season. The Expos led the National League East from the end of June to the start of August, but then the team went into a slump and fell back to finish fourth with a .500 record. Then many of the star players left the team as free agents. Bronfman searched for a buyer who would keep the team in Montréal. A Miami group made an offer of CAD 135 million, but Bronfman rejected it and said he was willing to take a lower offer if it would keep the team in Montréal. In an ironic turn of fate, Bronfman found plenty of interest among the Montréal business community, but he was having trouble finding a majority investor, the same problem that Mayor Drapeau brought to him back in 1969. Hurting Bronfman's chances was a report by a Montréal brokerage firm estimating that the Expos had lost CAD 42.2 million since the team's inception and the owners had sunk CAD 25.2 million into the franchise. The report indicated that the only reason the team remained in operation was due to the passion Bronfman and his partners brought to baseball.

When Bronfman had exhausted his efforts, the team's president Claude Brochu took the lead in searching for an investment group to keep the team in Montréal. Bronfman agreed to extend the deadline for bids to allow Brochu time to put together a deal. While Brochu searched for investors, a Washington, D.C. group expressed interest in purchasing the team, but Bronfman told them he was not interested in selling to anyone outside Quebec. A group of Canadian, U.S., and Japanese investors offered CAD 100 million to move the team to Toronto, thinking Toronto could support two MLB teams, but again, Bronfman rebuffed the offer. Finally, after several months of searching, Brochu managed to put together a consortium of Canadian investors to purchase the team for CAD 100 million. The consortium consisted of a diverse group of 13 investors, including Brochu and the City of Montréal, which contributed CAD 15 million to the deal. As a goodbye to the fans, Bronfman said he and his partners would purchase 200,000 tickets a year for the next 10 years and donate them to disadvantaged children and persons involved in amateur sports.

NEW OWNERSHIP BRINGS THE ALOU ERA

In the early 1990s the Expos began to find success under manager Felipe Alou, the first Dominican-born manager in MLB history. However, the one season that gave them the best chance to win a championship ended in frustration and disappointment that had nothing to do with the actual performance of the team. On August 12, 1994, the players went on strike as union contract negotiations broke down. The negotiations concerned a proposed salary cap to protect teams from the escalating salaries and a revenue-sharing agreement to help smaller market teams say alive during difficult times. At the time of the strike, the Expos had the best record in the league at 70–40, and the team would surely have gone to the playoffs. The strike and negotiations dragged on, and on September 12, 1994, Commissioner Bud Selig cancelled the rest of the season, including the playoffs. The strike continued until the following March, which shortened the 1995 season by 18 games. Montréal fans could not help but feel cheated out of their best chance at a championship.

HOW TO GUT A TEAM IN FOUR EASY STROKES

Before the 1995 season, Brochu instructed general manager Kevin Malone to let go four of the team's stars. Larry Walker left as a free agent, but John Wetteland, Ken Hill, and Marquis Grissom were traded. Brochu believed they had enough talent to fill the void left by the departing players and still win a championship. These trades gave the Expos the lowest payroll in the MLB, and soon after the trades, Malone resigned, saying, "I'm in the building business, not in the dismantling business." Brochu replaced Malone with Jim Beattie, the director of player development for the Seattle Mariners. Beattie became the Expos' fourth general manager in five years, but the team never recovered from the loss of player talent and star power. Seeing that management was not committed to win-

ning, other top players left the team for teams where they had a better chance of earning a championship.

The team floundered under mounting financial losses and a drop in attendance. Attendance at Olympic Stadium never topped 20,000 for the team's remaining 10 years in Montréal, and Brochu faced networks unwilling to televise the Expos' games. The networks were not convinced there were enough English-speaking Canadians who cared whether the team won or lost.

By 1997 several teams had built new ballparks, each costing hundreds of millions of dollars. The new thinking was that stadium revenues rather than television money would drive the economics of baseball. Brochu thought a new ballpark would solve the Expos' financial problems, and he ordered architectural, engineering, and financing studies to assess the economic impact of a new stadium. He tried to sell this idea to the Montréal community during difficult economic times and when the team's finances were deep in the red. In June 1997 Brochu stated that the team lost over CAD 13 million. He also revealed that the team lost CAD 16 million in 1994 and CAD 7 million in 1995. The numbers were somewhat suspect since the team had one of the lowest payrolls in the league at $18,255,500 and received almost $10 million in revenue-sharing funds from the league. Also, the team received almost $45 million in expansion fees from the newly added Arizona and Tampa Bay franchises. However, the team's financial woes became increasingly obvious as they continued to trade away young and talented players to avoid paying higher salaries. Despite the obstacles before him, Brochu started plans to sell 62 luxury boxes (suites) and 18,000 seat licenses for the new stadium. His goal was to raise CAD 70 million. He set a deadline with the threat that if the team did not get a new stadium he would move the team to another city, most likely in the United States.

By 1998 Brochu had cut the total payroll in half to $9.1 million, which was less than the annual salary of some individual star players in the league. Attendance had dropped to about 10,000 a game. Many of the star players the team had cut from its roster had gone on to win championships with other teams, and the current Expos were playing terrible baseball, with the lowest number of runs scored and a team batting average of .240. The team did report a profit in 1998 but this was mainly because Brochu had pared down the payroll to a bare minimum. Also, the team pocketed the league's revenue-sharing income contributed from richer teams instead of using that money as the league intended, to bring in new and better players.

OWNERSHIP COUP BRINGS
TURMOIL

In October 1998, at a team owners' meeting, Brochu was ousted as president of the club and asked to divest his interest in the consortium. Brochu agreed to sell his 7.1 percent ownership and take himself out of the team's future. The owners immediately put the team up for sale to local interests. The consortium set a deadline of 150 days to come up with local buyer and a financing plan for the new stadium. Also, the consortium proposed a smaller, less expensive stadium and one with less public investment than Brochu formulated. If they failed to meet the deadline they would have to sell the team to out-of-town buyers.

Finding a local buyer and getting rid of Brochu turned out to be more difficult than the consortium anticipated. No local buyers stepped forward, and Brochu refused several offers for his share in the team, including an offer of CAD 10 million. As the 150-day deadline approached, the team had failed to find a local buyer and establish a plan to finance the new stadium. Also, Brochu was still holding on to his shares. It seemed that he was hoping the ownership would be forced to sell the team to deeper pockets outside Quebec and bring a more lucrative payoff.

After months of negotiations and deadline extensions, the owners announced they had found new investors who would infuse CAD 125 million into the team, including $75 million from Jeffrey Loria, an art dealer from New York City. Loria had put in a failed bid to purchase the Baltimore Orioles several years earlier. Another major investor joining the bid was Steven Bronfman, son of the original owner Charles Bronfman. Jacques Menard, a member of the consortium, upped Brochu's buyout figure to around $15 million, and Brochu accepted. Then a deal was worked out with Quebec to contribute the interest on a $100 million loan, all in a bid to keep the team in Montréal. By September 1999 the team had a new owner.

The new owners committed to keeping the Expos in Montréal, and Loria made a good faith effort to make it happen. He used the team's newfound deep pockets to sign three star players for high salaries and attempted to rebuild the team into a winner. Loria came in as another white knight who would save baseball in Montréal, but instead he ended up making the same old problems even worse. Loria bullied the Montréal investors as he vied for power over the team. He waited too long to ask for bids from the television and radio broadcasters, who had already set their schedules and budgets for the year. As a result, Loria failed to secure television and radio contracts for the 2000 season, which did not endear him to the fans or the press. He

interceded in management decisions that were the purview of the general manager, even making trades that were ill advised and unpopular. He also fired a critical member of the coaching team without consulting Alou.

Then there was the proposal for a new stadium. As soon as Loria and his investment partners took control they proposed a new stadium, but the financing once again became an issue. Having estranged his investment partners, they balked at any further fundraising efforts, and Quebec balked at any further public investment, especially since the government was having trouble even keeping public hospitals open. Eventually, the stadium plans were cancelled. Attendance dropped again to fewer than 10,000 and the team fired the very popular manager Alou early in the 2001 season. Soon enough, Loria and his partners were talking about selling or moving the team to another city.

BARELY SURVIVING IN
MONTRÉAL

On November 6, 2001, the MLB owners voted to contract the league by two teams. The teams likely to be eliminated, the Expos and the Minnesota Twins, voted against the plan. Then an owner shuffle occurred. John W. Henry, owner of the Florida Marlins, purchased a controlling interest in the Boston Red Sox, and Loria purchased the Marlins from Henry with financial help from MLB. Loria sold the Expos to MLB under a subsidiary named Expos Baseball, LLP. Loria took his entire front office staff with him to Miami, leaving the Expos with empty offices. The writing was on the wall that the Expos would be shut down. Then the operators of the Metrodome, where the Twins played, won an injunction requiring that the Twins play there for another year. Since the league could not eliminate the Twins, eliminating the Expos would create an odd number of teams in the league. This meant on any given day a team would be sitting idle, making it impossible for the league to maintain its 162-game season. As a result, the league postponed the contraction for another year. There was not enough time to find the Expos a new home in time for the 2002 season, so they were forced to keep the team in Montréal. MLB made Tony Tavares team president, Omar Minaya vice president, and Frank Robinson manager. Later that year, the league negotiated an agreement with the players' union that required the contraction to be postponed even longer, to 2006.

The Expos played the next three seasons in Montréal on life support. In 2003 the team played 22 of its home games in San Juan, Puerto Rico, and became more popular there than they were at home. The team began winning and was seen as a potential wild card entry in the playoffs, but late in the season MLB decided it could not afford to bring up players from the minor league to energize the final stretch for the playoffs. The team languished through the end of the season and failed to make the playoffs. In 2004 the team went a dismal 67–95, and at the end of the season MLB announced the team was moving to Washington, D.C. The Expos played their final game in Montréal on October 3, 2004, against the New York Mets, the same team they played in their first game in 1969. They lost 8–1. Meanwhile, the MLB owners approved the move 28–1. The Baltimore Orioles owner was the lone dissenter, believing a second team in the Baltimore-D.C. area would take from his team's revenues. The former owners of the Expos sued MLB and Loria in an attempt to keep the team in Montréal, but the lawsuit was struck down by the by arbitrators on November 15, 2004. Meanwhile, MLB hired Jim Bowden as general manager of the team. He would lead them through five tumultuous years.

A NEW LIFE SOUTH OF THE BORDER

Washington, D.C.,'s history with baseball was filled by two teams, both named the Senators. The first played in D.C. from 1905 to 1960 and moved to Minnesota to become the Twins. The second team, from 1961 to 1972, moved to Arlington, Texas, to become the Texas Rangers. MLB considered naming the new team the Senators but the Texas Rangers were unwilling to give up their rights to the name. The MLB also considered naming the team the Grays, which was the name of the Negro league team that played most of its games in the D.C. area in the 1940s. In the end, the team chose the Nationals, which was the unofficial nickname of the 1905–60 Senators team.

Even before the Nationals could start playing baseball in 2005 there was a business deal in place that would hinder the team's financial beginnings. Orioles owner Peter Angelos and MLB negotiated a compensation deal to offset any losses due to the introduction of the Nationals into the Baltimore-D.C. market. The agreement established a new cable television network to broadcast both the Orioles' and the Nationals' games. The Orioles were given controlling interest, but the network had no deals in place with the local cable providers. Over the next two years the network made an effort to secure contracts with the cable providers with little success. As a result, almost the entire first two seasons of the Nationals were not televised. It was generally thought that the MLB went into the negotiations with a conflict of interest and made a bad deal that only hurt the future owners, once MLB managed to sell the team.

The move to D.C. was contingent on a deal to build a new stadium, and after much wrangling over public investment and a stadium lease MLB negotiated a deal with the city that set a public funding cap of $611 million. The team played its first three seasons in Robert F. Kennedy Memorial Stadium (RFK Stadium), where the DC United of Major League Soccer play and where the NFL Washington Redskins once played football. Robinson moved with the team from Montréal to D.C. and continued as manager. Fueled by fan excitement, the team achieved a .500 record in its first season, but they could not maintain their success. In 2006 the team went 71–91, and attendance at RFK Stadium dropped to an average of 24, 217, from 33,651 in 2005.

At the end of the 2006 season, MLB sold the Nationals to Lerner Enterprises Group, led by the 80-year-old shopping mall magnate Theodore "Ted" Lerner. Lerner Enterprises bought the team for $450 million. Also, in September 2006, cable provider Comcast finally agreed to broadcast the Nationals' games. The team also fired Frank Robinson and replaced him with Manny Acta, a third-base coach for the New York Mets.

On March 30, 2008, the Nationals played their first game in their new stadium, Nationals Park. The stadium featured 41,888 seats, 78 luxury boxes, four restaurants, and three stores. The stadium cost the city of Washington, D.C. $611 million and was the first stadium in the nation to receive the environmental LEED Certification (silver level). President George W. Bush threw out the first pitch. Despite the new stadium and the enthusiasm it produced in the fans, the team continued its dismal performance on the field. During its first year in the new ballpark the team lost an embarrassing 102 games, and the next year it lost 103 games. The team was yet to top its inaugural season .500 record.

In early 2009 a federal investigation focused on the Nationals and several managers who may have skimmed money off player signing bonuses for Dominican players. Other teams had come under the same scrutiny in the recent past, since the Dominican Republic, a country with a very poor population, offered a rich pool of baseball talent. Under the pressure of the investigation but denying culpability, Jim Bowden resigned as general manager, and several staff people involved with recruitment in the Dominican Republic were fired. The team also fired Acta as manager midseason and replaced him with Jim Riggleman. Mike Rizzo became general manager. Going into 2010, the Nationals started to take baby steps toward improving their prospects for becoming a winning team, but it was uncertain whether

Lerner had a firm grasp on how to make the Nationals into a national champion.

Aaron Hauser

PRINCIPAL COMPETITORS

Atlanta National League Baseball Club, Inc.; Florida Marlins, L.P.; The Phillies: Sterling Mets L.P.

FURTHER READING

Beacon, Bill. "Where Did It All Go Wrong for the Montréal Expos." *Canadian Press,* September 27, 2004.

Blair, Jeff. "Expos Staying Put in '99, Brochu Confirms." *Globe and Mail,* June 12, 1998, p. S7.

Brunt, Stephen. "Brochu Off Base on Expos." *Globe and Mail,* March 25, 1997, p. C14.

Crary, David. "Expos' Last Stand in Montréal." *The Record,* May 17, 1998, p. s10.

Davidson, James. "Montréal Dome Wins Praise; Expos Lose Game." *Globe and Mail,* April 21, 1987, p. D1.

"Expos' G.M. Decides to Go." *New York Times,* October 3, 1995.

"Expos Shake-up McHale Takes Over as General Manager." *Globe and Mail,* October 19, 1978, p. 49.

Hadekel, Peter. "Expos a Tough Sell: Club President Wants Downtown Stadium." *Hamilton Spectator,,* April, 5, 1997, p. C3.

Hunter, Jennifer. "Bronfman 'Seagrams I Need, Baseball I Love,' Billionaire Says." *Globe and Mail,* August 25, 1984, p. S1.

Kovacevic, Dejan. "The Big Uh-Oh." *Pittsburgh Post-Gazette,* April 11, 1999, p. D-3.

Marsh, James. "Canadians in Baseball: The Lost Tribe." *Calgary Herald,* May 18, 2002, p. OS5.

———. "Expos Owner Trashes Once-Proud Franchise." *Rocky Mountain News,* August 15, 2000, p. 2C.

Scott, Terry. "Expo Sale Completed." *Globe and Mail,* June 15, 1991, p. N12.

"Simply Déjà Vu for Montréal's Baseball Fans; Franchise Could Use a White Knight." *Toronto Star,* December 17, 2004, p. B06.

"Things They Don't Know." *Financial Post,* October 22, 1992, p. 44.

York, Marty. "At Large: Expos Expect Record Financial Loss." *Globe and Mail,* June 25, 1997, p. D14.

———. "Jays Outscore Expos All the Way to the Bank." *Globe and Mail,* July 23, 1985, p. P1.

WaterFurnace Renewable Energy, Inc.

———■———

9000 Conservation Way
Fort Wayne, Indiana 46809
U.S.A.
Telephone: (260) 478-5667
Toll Free: (800) 436-7283
Fax: (260) 747-2828
Web site: http://www.waterfurnace.com

Public Company
Founded: 1983 as WaterFurnace International, Inc.
Employees: 285 (est.)
Sales: $129 million (2009)
Stock Exchanges: Toronto
Ticker Symbol: WFI
NAICS: 221330 Steam and Air-Conditioning Supply

■ ■ ■

WaterFurnace Renewable Energy, Inc., designs, develops, and sells geothermal and water-source HVAC systems for residential, commercial, and institutional customers. These products are marketed with the brand names WaterFurnace and GeoStar. The company serves customers throughout North America. The company operates two subsidiaries, WaterFurnace International (WFI) and LoopMaster International, Inc.

WFI manufactures geothermal heat pumps for the residential market. Geothermal heating and cooling systems are high-efficiency, energy-saving systems for the home. Geothermal systems are solar-powered systems that tap into the earth's solar energy for power. Unlike traditional solar systems that exchange power with the air, geothermal systems use the consistent temperature underground to exchange power, making the system much more efficient.

LoopMaster is a geothermal loop contractor that serves residential customers in the Midwest and commercial customers throughout the United States. Loop-Master specializes in vertical loops and pond loops. Vertical loops are used for institutional and commercial applications. Pipes are bored deep into the ground, 15 feet apart, and connected to conduct heat and cooling capacities of one ton or more per pipe. Pond loops use the water's heating and cooling properties to provide climate control for industrial buildings. Pipes are fitted to the bottom of the body of water, where temperatures stay consistent year-round in most climates. Pond loops are generally less expensive to install, as excavation is not needed. Horizontal loops are similar to vertical loops except that the pipes are laid horizontally, generally five to eight feet deep. Horizontal loops require more surface area but are effective for smaller buildings with massive land space.

FOUNDING AND GROWTH 1983–99

In the late 1970s, two geothermal engineers worked separately to alter existing HVAC systems to create geothermal systems. Dan Ellis of Fort Wayne, Indiana, and Dave Hatherton of Toronto, Canada, were introduced to each other by a common supplier, who suggested that they team up. The third founder, James Shields, had already enjoyed success as a stockbroker for Merrill Lynch and had retired in 1972. The two engineers ap-

COMPANY PERSPECTIVES

Since 1983, we've pioneered the development of "closed loop" geothermal systems with three generations of ground-breaking products. Each has shattered previously existing efficiency benchmarks. To this day, WaterFurnace products are recognized as the most efficient HVAC systems available.

proached him for the initial capital of $70,000 to get started. Shields provided both the capital and his garage. In 1983 WaterFurnace International, Inc., began manufacturing geothermal products for the residential market in Fort Wayne, Indiana.

Shield's success can be traced years prior to his founding of WaterFurnace. After serving in World War II, Shields took a job with brokerage firm Merrill Lynch. He bought private stock in Merrill Lynch and earned a significant profit when the company went public. Although he did not need to come out of retirement, Shields would stay with WaterFurnace as the chairman of the board until his second retirement in 2004, when he was honored by the International Ground Source Heat Pump Association for his contributions to the geothermal heat pump industry. His son Timothy Shields would take over the role.

Dave Hatherton's interest in geothermal energy began in high school when he worked for his father, a water well driller. His father advised him to warm his ice-cold hands in the well water. Hatherton realized that the earth contained and stored solar energy that could be tapped. Nearly half the sun's energy is absorbed by the earth's surface. Only a few meters below, the earth maintains the temperature of 10 degrees Celsius year-round. Hatherton went on to found NextEnergy in Elmira, Ontario, in 1998. (In 2007 he was awarded the Lifetime Leadership Award by the Canadian GeoExchange Coalition.)

Dan Ellis served as WaterFurnace's president and CEO until 1995 when he moved to work for ClimateMaster. In 2000 he was named president of ClimateMaster.

For the first seven years of its existence, WaterFurnace grew, but it did so at a fairly modest rate. However, in 1990 there were several significant events for the company, beginning with its introduction of the most efficient water source heat pump on the market. The compressor was the first with a variable-speed motor, a technology developed by General Electric. This product

was the jumping point for WaterFurnace's explosive sales over the next five years, as revenue increased from $5 million to $25 million. The technology would become a standard for HVAC systems.

Also in 1990, WaterFurnace moved out of Shield's garage to an 115,000-square-foot facility in Fort Wayne. The facility also served as a model for its products, as the company's pond loop and 41 geothermal units heated and cooled the facility. Finally in 1990, WaterFurnace publicly offered shares on the Toronto Stock Exchange.

The 1990s were years of varying profitability for the company. In 1996 the company extended its product line to the commercial sector, a move seen as a logical extension of its product line. This move may have been a factor in the company's success, as WaterFurnace posted consistent profits between 1999 through 2008. The company was also aided by the construction boom during this time period, as sales of WaterFurnace products were linked to rates of new construction.

WATER AND INTERNATIONAL GROWTH: 2001–04

The year 2001 might be called the "water" year in the company's history. WaterFurnace formed a going venture with Hardin GeoTechnologies to market a process that used municipal water to lower heating, cooling, and refrigeration costs for homes and commercial buildings. The system rerouted water through the structure back to the water utility plant. In the process, the water was naturally cooled or heated. What was important about this product was that for the first time, WaterFurnace offered a product that could compete based on price. Traditional geothermal products were quite a bit more expensive than traditional HVAC systems. The new product was named "Water+" and was positioned as an independent company.

In December 2003 WaterFurnace began a joint venture with Aqua Comfort Technologies (ACT) to build swimming pool heaters that provided efficient, high-capacity heating with computerized control system with built-in logic. (Four years later, the company expanded its line to supply a high-efficiency pool heater that used the heat of the air.)

Also in 2003 the company WaterFurnace announced the formation of a new international division, WFI Global. This group was formed to serve markets outside North America and to take advantage of the Kyoto Protocol, an international agreement to reduce greenhouse gas emissions by embracing renewable energy technologies. WFI focused its efforts on Europe,

KEY DATES

1983: Company founded by James R. Shields, Daniel Ellis, and Dave Hatherton as Water-Furnace International, Inc.

1993: Stock publicly offered on the Toronto Stock Exchange.

1998: Bruce Ritchey joins WaterFurnace International as CEO.

2008: Company changes its name to WaterFurnace Renewable Energy, Inc.

2009: Bruce Ritchey retires; Tom Huntington joins WaterFurnace Renewable Energy as new CEO.

2011: Company acquires Hyper Engineering Pty in New South Wales, Australia.

China, and South Korea. The new company quickly formed a strategic alliance with Fedders Corporation to build water source heat pumps in China. The Fedders Xinle Co. Ltd. in Ningbo, China, would manufacture heat pumps using WaterFurnace's technology under the WaterFurnace brand.

In February 2004 WFI Global and Geothermal Heating (GHI) entered into a strategic alliance to distribute WaterFurnace branded water source and geothermal heat pumps in Europe. GHI was a company with a strong presence in Europe. Manufacturing would take place at the WFI Fort Wayne plant, and GHI would distribute and sell products throughout Europe.

Another China joint venture was announced in June 2004 with the Ningbo Shenglong Group. The Ningbo Shenglong Group was established in 1996 as an automobile component producer but then expanded through joint ventures with U.S. partners to build viscous fan drives, water pumps, and other machinery products for both the automobile and construction industries. WFI and Ningbo Shengleng teamed up to build geothermal heating and air conditioning products for distribution throughout China.

CAPITALIZING ON GOING GREEN: 2007 AND BEYOND

WaterFurnace was one beneficiary of the Economic Stability Act of 2008. The act contained provisions to promote renewable energy, and in particular, provided a $2,000 tax credit for homeowners and a 10 percent tax credit for businesses to install geothermal heat pumps. A similar law was passed in Canada for a $3,500 tax rebate for customers that replaced a traditional pump with a geothermal heat pump. This resulted in rapid sales growth for WaterFurnace's products. WaterFurnace offered a package specifically geared to renewable energy sources for new construction for homeowners and businesses. The company later took advantage of the stimulus package incentives for consumers that also included provisions for reducing carbon emissions.

On June 18, 2008, WaterFurnace Industrial changed its name to WaterFurnace Renewable Energy, Inc., to cement its reputation as a manufacturer of sustainable heating and cooling products.

In September 2009 the *Air Conditioning Heating & Refrigeration News* magazine gave WaterFurnace an honorable mention in its Dealer Design Award program, for its WaterFurnace Savings Calculator and its Synergy3D services hydronic system. That same month, ContractingBusiness.com awarded WaterFurnace's Envision NXW Series of reversible chillers a top rank in the HVAC Comfortech 2009 Product Showcase Awards.

In addition to the numerous awards, WaterFurnace received recognition by television shows and celebrities. In September 2008 the company's products were installed in an episode of *Extreme Makeover: Home Edition*. In 2010 the PBS series *Hometime* featured WaterFurnace's products. Jeff Gordon, famed NASCAR driver, publicized his "going green" commitment by installing WaterFurnace's Envision geothermal vertical system for his home in Charlotte, North Carolina.

Accolades aside, not all was rosy for the company. By the end of 2009 WaterFurnace's sales finally succumbed to the global recession, having decreased from $137 million in 2008 to $129 million in 2009. In response, the company focused its efforts on replacement systems to make up for the reduction in new construction projects. Sales for 2010 also lagged from the 2008 high, although they were improved from 2009. While the company's sales lagged, its profitability remained consistently positive.

In January 2011 WaterFurnace acquired the assets and technologies of Hyper Engineering Pty in South Wales, Australia, for $2.8 million. Hyper Engineering builds devices that extend the life of electric motors by reducing the inrush current when motors are started up. WaterFurnace planned to use this technology in its own products to increase their efficiency.

WaterFurnace's continuing success was likely a result of two major factors. The "going green" movement received support from both the consumer market and the government's sponsorship of sustainable products. The company also serendipitously made its international push shortly before the U.S. housing market crashed in 2008. The international joint ventures in China were particularly successful as the Chinese market continued to grow tremendously due to the massive population and opportunities in a previously closed market. Given these favorable conditions, it seemed likely that WaterFurnace's success would continue in the 2010s.

Sara K. Huter

PRINCIPAL SUBSIDIARIES

LoopMaster International, Inc.; WaterFurnace International, Inc.

PRINCIPAL COMPETITORS

AAF-McQuay Inc.; Carrier Corporation; Trane Inc.

FURTHER READING

"Heat Beneath Our Feet." *Vancouver Sun,* October 25, 2004.

Held, Shari. "Jim Shields Down to Earth." *Indiana Business Magazine* August 2007.

Mazurkiewicz, Greg. "Using Municipal Water to Help Lower Energy Bills." *Air Conditioning, Heating & Refrigeration News* 213, no. 17 (2001).

McCammon, Val. "2009 Junior Achievement BEL Honorees: James R. Shields." *Business People,* May 2009.

Murphy, Mike. "Don't Dis the Geo (Thermal). Please Don't Let Me Be Misunderstood." *Contracting Business,* April 2003.

"New Idea Makes Geothermal Cheaper." *Contractor* 48, no. 4 (2001).

"People." *Air Conditioning, Heating & Refrigeration News* 209, no. 9 (2000).

"Ritchey Named WFI President/CEO." *Contracting Business,* May 1999, 24.

Slack, Eric. "Grounded Power: The US Leader in Geothermal Heating and Cooling Systems Is Bringing Its Renewable Source of Energy to Your Backyard. Bruce Ritchey Explains." *American Executive* 6, no. 7 (2008).

"WaterFurnace Names President/CEO." *Air Conditioning, Heating & Refrigeration News* 237, no. 5 (2009).

"WaterFurnace: Renewable Energy Could Contribute to Economic Recovery." *National Driller* 30, no. 4 (2009).

Wood-Mode Incorporated

One Second Street
Kreamer, Pennsylvania 17833
U.S.A.
Telephone: (570) 374-2711
Toll Free: (877) 635-7500
Fax: (570) 374-2700
Web site: http://www.wood-mode.com

Private Company
Founded: 1942
Employees: 1,200
Sales: $258 million (est., 2009)
NAICS: 337110 Wood Kitchen Cabinet and Counter Top Manufacturing; 337215 Showcase, Partition, Shelving, and Locker Manufacturing.

■ ■ ■

Wood-Mode Incorporated is a leading cabinetry manufacturer. The company offers semicustom and custom cabinetry for the kitchen and also for other rooms of the home in several woods and styles and a great variety of finishes, including cherry, maple, oak, and pine. The company produces two lines of customized cabinetry built to customer specifications under the Wood-Mode as well as the Brookhaven names. In addition to its factory and office headquarters in Kreamer, Pennsylvania, the company has showrooms in the United States, Canada, Mexico, and Bermuda.

COMPANY FOUNDING AND EARLY YEARS: 1942–56

The company that would eventually be called Wood-Mode was founded by four men who had been salesmen for Whitehead Monel Kitchens Co., a division of International Nickel Co. that was selling the white metal kitchen cabinets popular throughout the 1930s. Ted Gronlund and Dick Nellis, Sr., of New York City, and Charles Wall, Sr., and Caswell Holloway of Philadelphia, realized that, with the imminent involvement of the United States in World War II, the production of steel would be shifted to the war effort, leaving them with nothing to sell. The four founded Wood-Metal Industries, Inc., in 1942 in a small lumber-planing mill in Kreamer, Pennsylvania.

Wood-Metal's initial client was Uncle Sam, seeking production of military needs such as cook's tables, coops for the army's carrier pigeons, shell cases, ladders, and Signal Corps equipment cases. The government set exacting specifications for these products, especially for the finishes applied to the Signal Corps cases. These cases, earmarked for use in the South Pacific, had to be sealed against fungal growths and waterproofed by varnish that sometimes required as many as 11 coats. The company's experience in meticulous wood finishing during this period would prove invaluable in the development of its cabinetry finishes.

As World War II neared its end, military contracts began to dwindle, and Wood-Metal turned its attention to making kitchen cabinets. The company met its difficulty in buying top-grade lumber by purchasing timber rights on a tract of land in the Beaver Springs,

Pennsylvania, area for $2,000 in 1943 and building a sawmill to provide the raw material. Wood-Metal never made a metal cabinet in Kreamer, but it acquired a manufacturing plant in Beech Bottom, West Virginia, to make such cabinets once steel became available after the war. This operation was moved in the 1950s to McClure, Pennsylvania, where it began making and marketing a line of institutional and residential cabinets.

By 1945 Wood-Metal was producing enameled finishes for a contemporary cabinet-door style and had begun to offer special purpose items that included a telescoping towel rack, cutlery trays with linoleum bottoms, and a broom/linen-closet combination. During the late 1940s the company was also designing and manufacturing cabinets and casework for schools, hospitals, and other institutional customers. By the mid-1950s, the institutional line was offered in three woods, with a choice of six natural and 12 enameled finishes.

All four founders had other business interests in New York and Philadelphia, so C. K. Battram, Sr., was brought in as general manager in 1944. Holloway withdrew from participation in the firm in 1948, but Nellis, the company's president since its inception, moved to Kreamer to assume day-to-day leadership, while Gronlund and Wall also began to devote greater time to the fledgling company. When the firm celebrated its 50th anniversary in 1992, members of the Battram, Gronlund, and Wall families were still active in management. Corporate headquarters remained, however, on Park Avenue in New York, until 1953.

The Wood-Metal product line in 1950 included 14 enameled finishes and one natural wood finish. The company also introduced "customized" natural finished doors and drawers on enameled cabinets and manufactured the first built-in unit to accommodate a Thermador range/grill-and-oven combination. The first Wood-Metal knotty-pine cabinets were introduced in 1951 to accommodate the Early American home decor so popular at the time. These cabinets featured authentic V-joint construction and were in the forefront of design.

Wood-Metal originally shipped cabinets to its customers by commercial carrier. This proved less than ideal because at times the products were not properly handled, leading to damage and delays in installation. In 1952 the company began to use its own fleet of trucks to deliver to markets in the eastern United States, thereby greatly improving service to dealers and customers. The following year Wood-Metal decided to launch a modest advertising and promotional program to support its sales representatives and dealers. Its first advertisement in a national consumer magazine appeared in January 1954. The number of sales representatives reached 21 by the end of 1955. Advertisements were placed in magazines such as *House and Garden* and *Good Housekeeping* (the latter in conjunction with the famous seal of approval).

CABINETRY INTO EVERY ROOM: 1956–89

The name of the company's residential line of cabinets was changed to Wood-Mode Kitchens in 1956 because wood, rather than metal, kitchen cabinets were growing in popularity, reaching 70 percent of the total installed that year. (The corporate name was not changed to Wood-Mode, however, until 1990.) In a full-page ad appearing in *Kitchen Business* that year, the company explained its decision as intended "to better describe the finest line of all-wood kitchens." For a 1958 issue of *House and Garden,* Wood-Mode designed and built a kitchen that could be taken along when the homeowner moved. The company's products also appeared on several television game shows, including *The Price Is Right,* in which the grand prize was a custom-built kitchen.

Nellis resigned as president in 1959 and was succeeded by Wall. In 1961 the company initiated a "picturebook" that afforded a view of actual installations of Wood-Mode cabinets in oak, maple, and pine, in four different styles and 22 natural and 12 enamel finishes, with a variety of hardware and a choice of more than 50 special purpose cabinets and accessories. Wood-Mode was letting it be known that its custom-built cabinetry could be made to order for any room in the house. In 1970 the company logo was changed from "Wood-Mode Kitchens" to "Wood-Mode Cabinetry."

Gronlund succeeded Wall as president in 1963. He died in 1967, and Battram, his successor, passed away in 1969. Charles Wall, Jr., succeeded Battram as president. In 1970 Wood-Mode added 180,000 square feet of manufacturing and warehousing space, and in 1972 it opened a factory showroom across the highway from the plant. This facility contained a full working kitchen and an auditorium that would be used for the longest continuing training school in the industry. By 1992

KEY DATES

1942: Founded as Wood-Metal Industries, Inc.

1954: Company's first advertisement in a national consumer magazine appears.

1956: Company's line of residential cabinets changed to Wood-Mode from Wood-Metal.

1974: Robert Gronlund, son of one of the company's founders, is named president of the company.

1980: Sales increase to $30 million.

1988: Company installs cogeneration plant to produce electricity from scrap wood and sawdust.

1990: Company name is changed to Wood-Mode, Inc.

2001: Robert Gronlund becomes sole owner of the company.

2010: R. Brooks Gronlund, grandson of the company's cofounder and Robert Gronlund's son, is named president and COO.

more than 6,500 students had attended classes there. In the early 1970s *Kitchen Business* named Wood-Mode one of the two largest manufacturers of custom cabinetry in the nation. Robert Gronlund, Ted's son, succeeded Wall as president of the company in 1974. The company honored nine representatives in 1975 whose territorial sales volume reached or exceeded $1 million a year.

During this period Wood-Mode introduced two new special purpose units. These were an improved version of its chef's pantry, and a hutch that was the company's first small step into "furniture" manufacturing. The latter helped to popularize the idea of built-in cabinetry in every room of the house, a concept the firm called "RoomScaping." Wood-Mode was offering its clientele custom and built-in cabinetry as an alternative to the limits of freestanding furniture, in a choice of six different styles available in three woods and more than 35 finishes, including wood-grain PVC plastic laminate. The company also introduced vinyl interiors and five new door styles and, in the late 1970s, Hallmark cherry cabinets and the Alpha and Citation door styles.

By the end of 1981 Wood-Mode had expanded its distribution into the Southwest and Pacific Northwest. At that time it held about 20 percent of the total factory-built custom-cabinetry market. Sales grew from

$30 million in 1980 to $75 million by 1988. Wood-Mode introduced a line of six door styles of frameless cabinets in 1984, and this line in turn inspired the creation of new door styles.

Often at the forefront of environmentally conscious manufacturing, Wood-Mode in 1988 added a 600,000-pound thermal incinerating system to eliminate potentially harmful emissions from the finishing process. It also installed a cogeneration system using scrap wood and sawdust to produce electricity for both its own needs and the local power system. In 1989 the company added a second floor to its warehouse in order to create 160,000 additional square feet of manufacturing space. This brought its total amount of production and warehouse space to 1 million square feet.

INCREASED GROWTH AND NEW PRODUCTS: 1991–99

Brookhaven, a made-to-order, semicustom cabinetry series introduced for the mid-range market in 1988, garnered $26 million in sales within three years. This helped to resuscitate Wood-Mode's growth rate, which had been slowed at the close of the 1980s by a leveling off of new housing and the consequent demand for high-end home furnishings. Company sales reached $96 million in 1994, of which semicustom, rather than custom, cabinetry accounted for 56 percent of the total.

Wood-Mode was offering cabinetry in cherry, oak, maple, and pine woods, and laminate in traditional, country, and contemporary styles in 1997. Design Group 42 offered traditional framed-construction cabinetry, including 30 door styles. Design Group 84 offered an extensive collection of frameless cabinetry in the same woods, including 24 door styles. In addition, 12 specialty cabinet-door styles were available, included leaded glass and mullion styles. Drawers and shelves were also offered. A wide variety of hand-rubbed stained, opaque, glazed, and cottage finishes were available in a palette of more than 50 colors.

Wood-Mode's customized solutions to manage storage space were numerous and included a rollout serving cart, several chef's pantries, a pull-out table, a wine rack, and an appliance garage. Cabinetry for rooms other than the kitchen included living room/den bookshelves and bookcases, family-room entertainment centers, TV and bar cabinets, and shelving for art, collectibles, and trophies. There were also dining room hutches, home office storage drawers; bedroom dressers, armoires, bathroom cabinets, "his and her" vanities, and even storage units for laundry and utility rooms.

COMPANY CONTINUES TO THRIVE: 2002–07

By 2002 Wood-Mode had increased sales by 200 percent over the previous 10 years to approximately $180 million. It was producing an estimated 1,600 cabinet units per day. The vertically integrated company maintained complete quality control over its products, from lumber processing to final delivery. Another unique aspect of the company was that 90 percent of its products were sold via independent dealers, with 10 percent sold through homebuilders and other contractors. Approximately 75 percent of its business was through remodeling accounts.

In a *Wood & Wood Products* article, Wood-Mode's chairman Robert Gronlund told Karen Koenig that the company's unique place in the market stemmed from its decision back in 1993 not to follow its competitor and market the company's various products in the growing number of home center chain stores throughout the nation, such as Home Depot and Lowe's. "We've always taken the position that we don't want to be at a stock cabinet price point," Gronlund noted. "It's very competitive, oftentimes with low (profit) margins." According to Gronlund, Wood-Mode preferred to focus on customized factory-built cabinetry, leading the company to have approximately 800 dealers throughout the United States in 2002 selling Wood-Mode cabinetry.

Over the years, Wood-Mode had also invested hundreds of thousands of dollars for upgrades throughout its plant and by 2005 had recently upgraded its lumber processing and rough mill areas. In addition, when Gronlund became the sole owner of the company in 2001 after purchasing his brothers' shares, he initiated a total quality management (TQM) program to improve various aspects of its business, including customer service and supplier relationships. In 2005 Wood-Mode was producing 2,000 cabinetry units per day and had more than 2,100 employees. Overall, Wood-Mode had become a more than $225 million company, compared to 1972 when its annual sales were $6 million to $7 million. In 2005 Gronlund received *Wood & Wood Products'* third annual Jerry Metz Achievement Award.

In addition to its success as a business, Wood-Mode was long recognized as having a friendly environmental stewardship in terms of the company's materials and manufacturing process. For example, its Regenerative Thermal Oxidizer (RTO) system helped destroy emissions during the cabinetry finishing process. Furthermore, beginning in the 1980s, the company had used all of the sawdust and wood scrap produced during the manufacturing process as fuel to heat the company's 1.4-million-square-foot factory and office complex, as well as to provide steam to operate its dry kilns. In 2009 the company earned certification in the Environmental Stewardship Program (ESP) sponsored by the Kitchen Cabinet Manufacturer's Association (KCMA).

SLUMP IN HOUSING MARKET: 2007 AND BEYOND

Like most businesses associated with the building and construction industries, Wood-Mode faced some difficult times because of the economic downturn and housing market slump that began in late 2007. In November 2007 the company let approximately 50 workers go, followed by another layoff of 120 workers in 2008. Although the economy began to rebound in 2009, the company laid off another 95 workers in October of that year. The total layoffs over three years, which included more layoffs in early 2010, had reduced the company's number of employees to approximately 1,200, largely because the custom cabinet industry still lagged behind other areas in the rebounding construction industry.

In November 2010 the company announced that R. Brooks Gronlund, grandson of the company's cofounder and Bob Gronlund's son, had been named president and COO of the company. He had joined the company in 2001 as vice president of operations after having served as director of finance for Hewlett Packard and Agilent Technologies.

As of January 2011 the company had not hired any new employees. However, despite the slowdown in the cabinet industry market, Wood-Mode remained one of the largest custom cabinet-makers in the United States.

Robert Halasz
Updated, David Petechuk

PRINCIPAL COMPETITORS

Armstrong World Industries, Inc.; Masco Corporation; MasterBrand Cabinets, Inc.

FURTHER READING

Christianson, Rich. "2005 Metz Award Winner: Stays Ahead of the Curve." *Wood & Wood Products,* October 2005, 11.

"A Family Custom: The Wood-Mode Story." *Wood & Wood Products.* Annual 1995, 290.

A Half Century of Fine Cabinetmaking. Kreamer, PA: Wood-Mode Cabinetry, 1992.

Koenig, Karen. "Gronlund's Commitment to Quality and Service — Success in Action: Bob Bronlund's Hands-On

Management Style and Commitment to Customer and Community Service Help Make Wood-Mode One of the Top Cabinet Companies in North America — and Earn Him the Third Annual Jerry Metz Achievement Award." *Wood & Wood Products,* October 2005, 40.

———. "Wood-Mode Deals a Winning Strategy: Inherent to Wood-Mode Inc.'s Marketing Strategy Is Its Decision to Remain Loyal to Dealers by Not Selling Its Products Through Nationwide Home Centers." *Wood & Wood Products,* March 2002, 53.

Wyllie Group Pty Ltd

225 St. Georges Terrace
St. Georges Square
Nineteenth Floor
Perth, Western Australia 6000
Australia
Telephone: (61) 8 9322-6699
Fax: (61) 8 9322-2075
Web site: http://www.wylliegroup.com

Private Company
Founded: 1991
NAICS: 523920 Portfolio Management

■ ■ ■

The Wyllie Group Pty Ltd is a family-owned boutique investment company with a wide range of investments across all asset classes. The group's range of activities include property investment, commercial and residential property development, farming, financial services, share trading, and holding of strategic investments in public and private companies.

The company's diverse investments across Australia range from office buildings and shopping centers in Western Australia and New South Wales to residential towers on the Queensland Gold Coast and land development in Darwin. Wyllie Group investments focus on four major groups, which are property, equities, private equity, and lifestyle. In its real estate investments, the company has used a flexible approach that features spreading the risk while maximizing opportunities. The company owns outright or a substantial share in numerous important building projects, including the Perth Convention Exhibition Center, Sorrento Quay, and St. Georges Square.

The group's resource and industrial equities have also contributed substantially to company profits. The establishment of a funds management division led to its first private equity fund offering investing in a variety of latter-stage private equity situations, but primarily investments in private industrial companies with a nexus to Western Australia. Over the years, through the lifestyle interests of the company's founder, Bill Wyllie, various investments have been made in areas such as farming, aviation, horse racing, and art work.

BILL WYLLIE: HUMBLE BEGINNINGS

The Wyllie Group was founded by Western Australian businessman Bill Wyllie, who was known as a "corporate doctor" in Hong Kong. Based in Southeast Asia for nearly 38 years, Wyllie was born in Perth, Western Australia, and faced difficult times as a youth, including spending a brief time in an orphanage after his parents divorced. He quit school at the age of 13 and went to work in the timber mills with hopes of becoming a motor mechanic. Working toward that goal, he completed correspondence courses in automotive and aeronautical engineering.

In 1952 Wyllie joined Wearne Brothers and was based in Singapore, where he honed his business skills in the automotive, truck, and heavy equipment distribution company. Over the years he worked in various branches in Singapore, Malaya, Sarawak, and British

COMPANY PERSPECTIVES

The Wyllie Group Pty Ltd has shown faith in Australia's future and, as a result, has been able to profit from the growth now seen across the country. The company uses a flexible approach designed to spread risk and maximize its opportunities. The investment team has a diverse range of skills and experience. They are forward thinking and have a common desire to succeed based on the qualities of hard work, high standards, and good values.

North Borneo. Wylie also developed an interest in racing and became an accomplished race car driver. He competed in a car he built himself.

At the 1958 Macau Grand Prix, he developed a friendship with Bob Harper, whose company was a race sponsor. In 1963 Harper asked Wyllie to look over the operations of his struggling automotive business in Hong Kong, Wallace Harper and Company Ltd, the Ford and Lotus distributor there. In particular, Harper's company was suffering from continuing operating losses due to bad investments into other unrelated businesses. In addition, the Ford Motor Company had established a new dealer for Hong Kong and Kowloon, thus taking away a substantial portion of Wallace Harper's business.

Wyllie agreed to help Harper and spent two weeks in Hong Kong interviewing the managers of Wallace Harper's businesses and going over the company's financial records and accounts. Wyllie's review resulted in his recommendation to reduce staffing and eliminate all subsidiaries that were losing money. He also reported that improvements were needed in management and its performance. Wyllie became managing director of Wallace Harper with an option for one-third ownership of the company over five years.

WYLLIE CONTINUES TO "DOCTOR" COMPANIES

Despite bank failures and political turmoil in the region over the next several years, Wallace Harper began to prosper and report steadily increasing profits, changing its name to Harper International Ltd in 1967. Over the next 20-plus years, Wyllie went on to play a major role in fixing financially ailing companies, reaping substantial financial reward for himself in the process. For example, in late 1974 China Engineers (Holdings) Limited, which had bought out Harpers International in 1972,

asked Wylie to become chairman and CEO of Sime Darby of Singapore, which was experiencing financial difficulties. In addition to a generous salary, Wylie was to receive an option for more than 10 million shares at par. Under Wyllie's guidance, the company made a dramatic recovery.

Wyllie's most famous rescue of a company began in 1975 when he was named chief executive of Hutchinson International Limited, one of Hong Kong's largest companies at the time. Hutchinson, however, was in dire financial straits and close to bankruptcy. Wyllie went to work, closing down or selling more than 100 of Hutchinson subsidiaries. He also acquired several key businesses, including the Hong Kong and Whampoa Dock Co. (HWD). Under the advice of a merchant bank, Wyllie eventually formed a new holding company to merge Hutchinson International and HWD to form Hutchison Whampoa Limited (HWL) in 1977. Wyllie and his team gained worldwide business renown for completing what was, at the time, the largest and most complex company merger ever achieved in Hong Kong.

Wyllie became chairman and chief executive of HWL, which had wide-ranging interests in areas such as commodity trading, property development, supermarkets, textiles, construction, and more. The company thrived and was in line to report its first HKD 1 billion in profit in 1981 when Wyllie resigned. Wyllie stated that he had achieved his objectives for the company and was going to concentrate on his private company, Asia Securities Limited (ASL). That company's interests included financial services and investment dealings, high-technology electronics, and a significant amount of property holdings in Hong Kong, the United States, and Australia.

WYLLIE GROUP FOUNDED: 1991

Despite running his own company, Wyllie was not through turning other companies' fortunes around, including the British company BSR Limited in 1981 and a restructuring of the Regal Hotel Group and Paliburg Investments. In 1991 Wyllie decided that he was going sell Asia Securities and retire from active business in Hong Kong. He wanted to spend more time with his family but was by no means ready to completely retire. Instead, with some of the HKD 800 million he had garnered for Asia Securities, Wyllie established Wyllie Group Pty Ltd in 1991. The following year he returned to live in Australia permanently.

Over the next 14 years, Wyllie guided the company in a series of successful real estate investments to create a sprawling empire that stretched across Australia. Among its notable investments is the Perth Convention Exhibi-

```
┌─────────────────────────────────────────────────┐
│                                                 │
│              KEY DATES                          │
│              ───────■───────                    │
│                                                 │
│  1991:  Company founded by Bill Wyllie.         │
│  2004:  Perth Convention Exhibition Center opens.│
│  2005:  Melissa Karlson named managing director.│
│  2006:  Company founder Wyllie dies.            │
│  2007:  Company establishes private equity subsidiary│
│         Viburnum Funds Pty Ltd.                 │
│                                                 │
└─────────────────────────────────────────────────┘
```

tion Center, built by the Multiplex Construction company for the Wyllie Group and then leased to Spotless Group for 25 years. The center opened in 2004. Other investments include the Sorrento Quay Boardwalk retail and tourism center, the St Georges Square office tower, as well as a AUD 65 million stake in Multiplex Construction. Wyllie also owned 10 percent of the Burswood Casino before selling its interest to Publishing and Broadcasting Limited in 2004.

CHANGES IN MANAGEMENT AND DIRECTION: 2005

In 2005 Wyllie, who was battling cancer, turned over the company's reins to his daughter Melissa Karlson, who became managing director of the company in August of that year. At the time, the company's estimated worth was AUD 450 million. Karlson had insisted on working her way up in the company, taking an assistant accountant position in 2000 while studying for her commerce degree. By 2003 Karlson had worked her way up to director of Property Management. "No one could ever say a job was created for me," Karlson noted in an interview with Jame Thomson for *Business Review Weekly.* "I've done every job at Wyllie Group. If all my staff didn't show up, I'd happily answer the phones."

While the company focused primarily on property under its founder's direction, Karlson began to focus more attention on the share market. Karlson's appointment also triggered several of the Wyllie Group's executives to retire, leaving Karlson to build a new team. "If I had to blow my own trumpet, that's the best thing I've done since I've been there," she told *Business Review Weekly* contributor Thomson. "To be able to recruit the people I have, in a market where no one else can find staff just makes me really happy."

Karlson also initiated a thorough review of the company's assets, noting that she had become somewhat bored with some of the long-term investments. However, with a new management team and the strengths they brought to the company, Karlson began

to reappraise her thoughts about many of the company's assets. Although Karlson did not expect to make sweeping changes, she made a major strategic move by selling 50 percent of the company's stake in the St. George's Square office building for AUD 55 million. She also sold off her father's antique fighter plane collection and stable of thoroughbred race horses.

Karlson went on to guide the company in acquiring stakes in several groups. For example, in 2006 the company group acquire slightly more than 5 percent of Nomad Building Solutions, which supplied modular buildings to various building sectors. The company also acquired stakes in Automotive Holdings Group and Lignor Ltd. However, the company's new managing director did not forget about the holdings the company already had as she pushed forward further development of the Sorrento Quay Boardwalk in the northern outskirts of Perth. Karlson's plans for the boardwalk, which had become the third most visited tourist site in Perth, included an expansion with a new tavern and jetty, as well as the purchase of a parcel of adjacent land to further expand the project.

ESTABLISHES PRIVATE EQUITY ARM

In July 2007 the Wyllie Group invested AUD 30 million into the first fund-raising for its newly established alternative asset fund manager. Called Viburnum Funds Pty Ltd, the fund's investment focus was on a variety of latter stage private equity situations. The focus was to be on small and medium-sized private industrial companies connected to Western Australia and with a value of less than AUD 100 million. Wyllie Group also moved back into the energy sector in 2008 despite a troubled involvement with Tap Oil. After an unsuccessful attempt to initiate a board change at Tap Oil, the Wyllie Group divested its 6.2 percent holding in the company in November 2007. Nevertheless, Western Australia's booming natural resources sector still held promise for good returns. As a result, Wyllie Group paid AUD 15 million for a 15 percent stake in the Perth-based, oil and gas company Amadeus Energy Ltd.

The company's efforts in the private equity market were bolstered by the market's evolution in Western Australia. Companies that once would have listed had begun to steer away from the stock market, leading to good opportunities in the private equity market as a source of capital. Wyllie Group made another major move through its Viburnum Funds arm to acquire control of the Western Australia franchise Dome Coffees from the Asia-based Navis Capital Partners.

Wyllie Group managing director Melissa Karlson took a sabbatical overseas in 2010. Although rumors swirled that the sabbatical was due primarily to her mother's increased involvement in the company, these claims were denied. Nevertheless, Karlson remained overseas as of February 2011 but still remained on the company's board. After suffering AUD 36.1 million in losses in 2009 due to the economic downturn, the company posted a small profit in 2010. The company planned to continue to examine potential investments in Perth's natural resources enterprises but also maintain a strong set of investments in the real estate market.

David Petechuk

PRINCIPAL SUBSIDIARIES

Viburnum Funds Pty Ltd.

PRINCIPAL COMPETITORS

Australian Surety Corporation Pty Limited; Leveraged Equities Limited; Plenty Credit Co-Operative Limited.

FURTHER READING

Burrell, Andrew, and Marsha Jacobs. "Wyllie Loses Battle with Cancer." *Australian Financial Review,* March 14, 2006.

Orlando, Adam. "Private Equity Shows Strength." *Business News,* August 14, 2008, 10.

Thomson, James. "Wealth Becomes Them." *Business Review Weekly,* December 7, 2006.

"Wyllie Boss Maps Out Blueprint." *West Australian,* January 26, 2007.

"Wyllie Launches New 'Niche within a Niche' Company." *Financial Standard,* July 7, 2007, 8.

Zynga Inc.

4104 Twenty-Fourth Street, Number 363
San Francisco, California 94114
U.S.A.
Toll Free: (800) 762-2530
Web site: http://www.zynga.com

Private Company
Founded: 2007
Employees: 1,300 (est., 2010)
Revenue: $500 million (est., 2010)
NAICS: 713990 All Other Amusement and Recreation Industries; 541519 Other Computer Related Services

■ ■ ■

Zynga Inc. is the largest social game developer in the world. The company has more than 215 million active users playing its games each month, as well as more than 65 million daily active users, on various worldwide platforms such as Facebook, MySpace, Yahoo, MSN Games, the iPad, and iPhone. FarmVille is the company's most popular game and in 2011 is played by approximately 75 million people each month. The company offers puzzle games, card games, role-playing games, and virtual word games. Some of these titles include FrontierVille, Mafia Wars, Zynga Poker, Café World, Treasure Isle, YoVille, FishVille, and PetVille. Ninety percent of the company's revenue comes from the purchase of virtual goods within the games. While there is no charge to play the games, approximately 1 to 3 percent of players purchase virtual items within the games, such as seeds, a hot rod tractor, or a farmhouse within FarmVille.

While video games are generally thought to appeal mostly to 18- to 34-year-old male players, three of Zynga's most popular games have found appeal outside of that range. The majority of players on FarmVille, Café World, and Fishville are females outside of the 18- to 34-year-old age range.

The company is committed to helping the world through virtual social goods. More than $6 million has been raised by Zynga players for international nonprofit organizations through Zynga.org since it was founded in October 2009. These funds have helped earthquake victims in Haiti, wildlife in the Gulf Coast following the BP oil spill, victims of poverty worldwide, and other recipients.

COMPANY FOUNDING AND FINANCING: 2007–08

Zynga was founded in January 2007 by Mark Pincus, a Harvard MBA and Silicon Valley investor. He believed that gaming experiences were a missing piece in daily use of the Internet. His vision for the company, which he named after his late American bulldog, was to allow people to build social connections through playing games. In other words, Zynga combined online gaming with social networking through Facebook. According to *CNN Tech,* Pincus said "We built the games so they could be played in a tab on your browser while you're on a conference call." His plan was to create simple games that players could easily set aside.

COMPANY PERSPECTIVES

At Zynga, our mission is to connect people through games. We make social games that are free and accessible for everyone to play. Every day millions of people interact with their friends and express their unique personalities through our games, which range from harvesting plants to baking apple pies to playing poker.

Prior to founding the company, Pincus launched Tribe.net, which was one of the first social networking sites, in 2003. He also founded Support.com, a tech-support company, and launched FreeLoader, a Web-based company for gathering information, before selling it a few months later. Pincus was also an early investor in Facebook.

About a year after its founding, Zynga received $10 million in its first round of funding during February 2008. Then in July it received $29 million in additional funding, led by Kleiner Perkins Caulfiend & Byers, a venture capitalist firm which had previously invested in companies such as Google and Amazon.com. John Doerr, one of the firm's investors, later said that the investment in Zynga was one of the best the company ever made. In November 2010, according to *GamesBeat*, Doerr said, "Zynga is the most-profitable, fastest-growing, and has the happiest customers of any company that Kleiner Perkins has invested in."

OFF TO A RUNNING START: 2008–09

A few months after its founding, Zynga released Texas Hold'Em Poker on Facebook. Many of the company's first games were card games or other traditional games. However, within a short time, the company created new games and virtual communities that would quickly gain popularity among users.

In early 2008 Zynga launched its virtual goods transactions with Poker and also acquired YoVille, a game in which players choose their homes, clothes, and friends in a virtual world. Then in June, Mafia Wars went live on Facebook. This role-playing game was the first to offer a single player activities that could be enhanced by working with other players. This combination quickly become popular with social gaming formats. Within one year, Mafia Wars was voted Best Game of the Year in the Webby People's Voice Awards,

and the game's Facebook page had more than two million fans.

By March 2009, one year after its introduction, Poker was the number one game on Facebook. It was also the first game to have 10 million active users each month. The following month, the company announced that Zynga was the top application developer on Facebook and had more than 40 million monthly active users on this format.

VIRTUAL WORLDS AND THE REAL WORLD: 2009

In June 2009 FarmVille was released on Facebook. This game, which allows players to grow crops and raise animals on their own virtual farms, quickly became popular with users. Players invite online friends to become neighbors on their farms, send gifts to each other, and help with the farming activities. Within two months, it had 10 million daily active players. By December 2010 there were 30 million farms in FarmVille, which is 15 times more than the number of actual farms in the United States.

Café World, which gives players the opportunity to design their own cafés (including choosing recipes and cooking for friends), was released on Facebook in October 2009. During that same month, Zynga.org was launched to raise money for nonprofit organizations around the world. Players are able to purchase items through Zynga games, with half of the money being used to make positive contributions internationally. At first, resources were used to benefit families in Haiti, with $487,500 being donated during the first month. Shortly after Zynga.org began, Haiti was hit by a devastating earthquake. Zynga players raised $1.5 million for the Haiti Relief Fund in only five days.

In November 2009 Zynga announced that it had in excess of 100 million unique users each month, making the company the largest destination for online gaming. By this time, the company had more than 200 million active monthly users across all of its games, and one million players purchasing virtual items each month.

EXPANSION: 2009–10

In December 2009 Zynga sold company securities to Digital Sky Technologies (DST) and other investors for $180 million in order to raise capital to fund company growth. DST, a Russian company, would be a passive investor, with no positions on Zynga's board of directors. Soon after receiving this injection of capital, in February 2010 Zynga acquired Serious Business, a U.S.-based company known for creating social games on

KEY DATES

2007: Zynga founded by Mark Pincus; Texas Hold'Em Poker is released on Facebook within the first few months.

2008: Mafia Wars goes live on Facebook; voted Best Game of the Year in the Webby People's Voice Awards.

2009: In June FarmVille is released on Facebook; within two months it becomes the first game on Facebook to reach 10 million daily active players. By December there are 30 million farms in FarmVille.

2009: In October Zynga.org is launched to raise money for international nonprofit organizations.

2010: Zynga expands internationally by opening offices in India, China, and Japan.

Facebook. The company's employees joined Zynga's San Francisco offices.

Another expansion for the company during that same month offered opportunities outside of the United States. Zynga opened its first international offices in Bangalore, India. At the time, the popularity of online gaming was expanding quickly in India, with 41 percent of active Internet users playing games online in 2008. This was an increase of 89 percent from 2007. With such growth, and approximately 81 million Internet users in the country, it was expected that India would be the third-largest online market by the year 2013, behind China and the United States. According to a press release by the company, Pincus stated, "Social gaming combines the best of web technical talent with game storytelling." He went on to state, "India offers some of the world's most sophisticated and rich technical talent bases and we are thrilled to have a local presence."

Shortly after its expansion into India, Zynga acquired XPD Media, a social gaming company based in Beijing. This acquisition marked Zynga's first move into the Asian market. XPD Media was launched in 2008 and focused on developing social games for Asian and international networks.

Zynga acquired the Austin, Texas-based social gaming company Challenge Games in June 2010, renaming it Zynga Austin. This location focused on product development and retained Challenge Games' cofounder and CEO as vice president, as well as Challenge's 35 employees. Challenge was also founded in 2007 and developed online games including Warstorm and Ponzi.

Zynga's worldwide expansion continued in July 2010 when the company announced a venture with SOFTBANK, a leading technology company in Japan, to develop social games to be distributed across that country through Tokyo-based Zynga Japan. At the same time, SOFTBANK completed a $150 million investment in Zynga. The joint venture capitalized on SOFTBANK's mobile and Web technology capabilities and Zynga's social games expertise to reach a wider international audience with mobile Internet and social Web experiences.

Zynga's acquisition of other gaming companies continued with its purchase of Bonfire Studios, which became Zynga Dallas in October 2010. Bonfire was founded in 2008 and had created video games for the PC and Xbox 360. These titles included Age of Empires and Halo Wars. Bonfire's founders were given management positions within Zynga Dallas, which planned to continue developing new games across a variety of platforms.

NEW GAMES IN 2010

The year 2010 was not only marked by a number of acquisitions but also by the introduction of several new Zynga games. Treasure Isle was introduced in April, giving players the chance to travel to different islands to dig for treasure, harvest plants, and decorate their own islands. FrontierVille was introduced in June and enjoyed the largest game launch for Zynga to that time, attracting approximately 116,000 players within the first day. This game gave players the chance to become pioneers in a virtual wilderness, build a homestead, and test their survival skills.

CityVille was launched in November 2010 and offered players the opportunity to build and manage the city of their dreams. Within 24 hours of the game's launch, there were 290,000 players, making this the largest launch of any game to date for the company. FrontierVille had quickly grown and had 6.5 million daily players by this time. Within about three weeks of the launch of CityVille, 2.7 million residences had been built, five million sections of road had been laid, and nearly one-fourth of the players had set up a franchise on another player's game board.

In December 2010 Zynga acquired Newtoy, Inc., a mobile game development company responsible for games such as Words with Friends and Chess with Friends. This acquisition increased Zynga's worldwide presence. Newtoy was founded in 2008 and quickly developed some of the most popualor social games available on a mobile platform. In fact, at the time of the acquisition, the company's Games with Friends franchise had more than a million users that played the game for at least one hour each day and was the most popular gaming series on the iPhone, iPod Touch, and iPad.

LOOKING FORWARD

Zynga and American Express entered a relationship that was the first of its kind in December 2010. American Express announced that customers would be able to use their Membership Rewards points to purchase virtual items on Zynga, such as manors and windmills in Farm-Ville, fountains and stoves in Café World, or roadsters and robots in YoVille. Points could also be used to buy physical and virtual game cards for Zynga. Other exclusive offers would also be available to customers of both companies. This marked the first time a financial services provider had offered its customers the opportunity to use reward points for virtual games.

While Zynga does not comment on its value, *Bloomberg Businessweek* reported that the value of the company was estimated at $5.51 billion in the fall of 2010, up from an estimated $2.61 million in March of that year. During the second half of 2010, Zynga raised in excess of $350 million in private capital, acquired six new companies, and increased its workforce by approximately one-third during the final quarter.

Following such expansion, it was anticipated that Zynga's revenues would be in excess of $1 billion for 2011. The company had not formally announced plans for an initial public offering as of the end of 2010, but according to the *San Francisco Chronicle* it was widely speculated that Zynga would file for an initial public offering (IPO) in the near future.

Diane Milne

PRINCIPAL COMPETITORS

Big Fish Games, Inc.; eGames, Inc.; Electronic Arts Inc.

FURTHER READING

"American Express and Zynga Announce Strategic Relationship to Make Virtual Goods and Game Cards Available for Purchase Using Membership Rewards Points." *Investment Weekly News,* December 18, 2010.

Arrington, Michael. "Google Secretly Invested $100+ Million in Zynga, Preparing to Launch Google Games." *Tech Crunch,* July 10, 2010. Accessed December 21, 2010. http://tech crunch.com/2010/07/10/google-secretly-invested-100-million-in-zynga-preparing-to-launch-google-games/.

Gross, Doug. "The Facebook Games That Millions Love (and Hate)." *CNN Tech,* February 23, 2010. Accessed December 23, 2010. http://www.cnn.com/2010/TECH/02/23/face book.games/index.html.

Levy, Ari. "Zynga Tops Electronic Arts as Social Games Spread." *Bloomberg Businessweek,* October 26, 2010. Accessed December 29, 2010. http://www.businessweek.com/news/2010-10-26/zynga-tops-electronic-arts-as-social-games-spread.html.

Nusca, Andrew. "Zynga Acquires Challenge Games; Expands Social Gaming Footprint." *The Toy Box,* (blog) *Zdnet,* June 3, 2010. Accessed December 28, 2010. http://www.zdnet.com/blog/gadgetreviews/zynga-acquires-challenge-games-expands-social-gaming-footprint/15272.

Takahasi, Dean. "Google Investor Jon Doerr: Zynga Is Our Best Company Ever." *GamesBeat,* November 16, 2010. Accessed December 29, 2010. http://venturebeat.com/2010/11/16/google-investor-john-doerr-zynga-is-our-best-company-ever.

Temple, James. "Zynga Signing Biggest S.F. Office Lease in Years." *San Francisco Chronicle,* September 25, 2010. Accessed December 29, 2010. http://www.sfgate.com/cgi-bin/article.cgi?f=/c/a/2010/09/24/BUOR1FHJ4Q.DTL&tsp=1.

Zynga. "Zynga Acquires Chinese Social Gaming Company XPD Media." Zynga Press Release, May 20, 2010. Accessed December 28, 2010. http://www.zynga.com/about/article.php?a=20100520.

"Zynga Touts Top Ranking as App Developer on Facebook." *Entertainment Close-up,* April 2009. General One File. Accessed December 21, 2010.

Cumulative Index to Companies

AECOM Technology Corporation, 79 10–13

Aecon Group Inc., 121 17–21

Aeffe S.p.A., 119 21–25

AEG A.G., I 409–11

Aegean Marine Petroleum Network Inc., 89 18–21

Aegek S.A., 64 6–8

Aegis Group plc, 6 15–16

AEGON N.V., III 177–79; 50 8–12 (upd.) *see also* Transamerica–An AEGON Company

AEI Music Network Inc., 35 19–21

AEON Co., Ltd., V 96–99; 68 6–10 (upd.)

AEP *see* American Electric Power Co.

AEP Industries, Inc., 36 17–19

Aer Lingus Group plc, 34 7–10; 89 22–27 (upd.)

Aero Mayflower Transit Company *see* Mayflower Group Inc.

Aeroflot - Russian Airlines JSC, 6 57–59; 29 7–10 (upd.); 89 28–34 (upd.)

AeroGrow International, Inc., 95 20–23

Aerojet-General Corp., 63 6–9

Aerolíneas Argentinas S.A., 33 17–19; 69 9–12 (upd.)

Aeronca Inc., 46 6–8

Aéroports de Paris, 33 20–22

Aéropostale, Inc., 89 35–38

Aeroquip Corporation, 16 7–9 *see also* Eaton Corp.

Aerosonic Corporation, 69 13–15

The Aérospatiale Group, 7 9–12; 21 8–11 (upd.) *see also* European Aeronautic Defence and Space Company EADS N.V.

AeroVironment, Inc., 97 13–16

The AES Corporation, 10 25–27; 13 12–15 (upd.); 53 14–18 (upd.)

Aetna, Inc., III 180–82; 21 12–16 (upd.); 63 10–16 (upd.)

Aetna Insulated Wire *see* The Marmon Group, Inc.

AFC Enterprises, Inc., 32 12–16 (upd.); 83 9–15 (upd.)

Affiliated Computer Services, Inc., 61 12–16

Affiliated Foods Inc., 53 19–21

Affiliated Managers Group, Inc., 79 14–17

Affiliated Publications, Inc., 7 13–16

Affinion Group, Inc., 121 22–24

Affinity Group Holding Inc., 56 3–6

Affymetrix Inc., 106 18–24

Aflac Incorporated, 10 28–30 (upd.); 38 15–19 (upd.); 109 6–11 (upd.)

African Rainbow Minerals Ltd., 97 17–20

Africare, 59 7–10

After Hours Formalwear Inc., 60 3–5

Aftermarket Technology Corp., 83 16–19

AG Barr plc, 64 9–12

Ag-Chem Equipment Company, Inc., 17 9–11 *see also* AGCO Corp.

Ag Services of America, Inc., 59 11–13

Aga Foodservice Group PLC, 73 18–20

AGCO Corp., 13 16–18; 67 6–10 (upd.)

Agence France-Presse, 34 11–14

Agere Systems Inc., 61 17–19

Agfa Gevaert Group N.V., 59 14–16

Aggregate Industries plc, 36 20–22

Aggreko Plc, 45 10–13

Agilent Technologies Inc., 38 20–23; 93 28–32 (upd.)

Agilysys Inc., 76 7–11 (upd.)

AGL Resources Inc., 116 12–15

Agland, Inc., 110 6–9

Agnico-Eagle Mines Limited, 71 11–14

Agora S.A. Group, 77 5–8

AGRANA *see* Südzucker AG.

Agri Beef Company, 81 5–9

Agria Corporation, 101 9–13

Agricultural Bank of China, 116 16–19

Agrigenetics, Inc. *see* Mycogen Corp.

Agrium Inc., 73 21–23

Agrofert Holding A.S., 117 5–9

AgustaWestland N.V., 75 18–20

Agway, Inc., 7 17–18; 21 17–19 (upd.) *see also* Cargill Inc.

AHL Services, Inc., 27 20–23

Ahlers, 123 1–5

Ahlstrom Corporation, 53 22–25

Ahmanson *see* H.F. Ahmanson & Co.

AHMSA *see* Altos Hornos de México, S.A. de C.V.

Ahold *see* Koninklijke Ahold NV.

AHP *see* American Home Products Corp.

AIA Engineering Ltd., 119 26–30

AICPA *see* The American Institute of Certified Public Accountants.

AIG *see* American International Group, Inc.

AIMCO *see* Apartment Investment and Management Co.

Ainsworth Lumber Co. Ltd., 99 18–22

Air & Water Technologies Corporation, 6 441–42 *see also* Aqua Alliance Inc.

Air Berlin GmbH & Co. Luftverkehrs KG, 71 15–17

Air Canada, 6 60–62; 23 9–12 (upd.); 59 17–22 (upd.)

Air China Limited, 46 9–11; 108 15–19 (upd.)

Air Express International Corporation, 13 19–20

Air France–KLM, 108 20–29 (upd.)

Air-India Limited, 6 63–64; 27 24–26 (upd.)

Air Jamaica Limited, 54 3–6

Air Liquide *see* L'Air Liquide SA.

Air Mauritius Ltd., 63 17–19

Air Methods Corporation, 53 26–29

Air Midwest, Inc. *see* Mesa Air Group, Inc.

Air New Zealand Limited, 14 10–12; 38 24–27 (upd.); 119 31–36 (upd.)

Air Pacific Ltd., 70 7–9

Air Partner PLC, 93 33–36

Air Products and Chemicals, Inc., I 297–99; 10 31–33 (upd.); 74 6–9 (upd.)

Air Sahara Limited, 65 14–16

Air T, Inc., 86 6–9

Air Wisconsin Airlines Corporation, 55 10–12

Air Zimbabwe (Private) Limited, 91 5–8

AirAsia Berhad, 93 37–40

Airborne Freight Corporation, 6 345–47; 34 15–18 (upd.) *see also* DHL Worldwide Network S.A./N.V.

Airborne Systems Group, 89 39–42

AirBoss of America Corporation, 108 30–34

Airbus Industrie *see* G.I.E. Airbus Industrie.

Airgas, Inc., 54 7–10

Airguard Industries, Inc. *see* CLARCOR Inc.

Airlink Pty Ltd *see* Qantas Airways Ltd.

Airsprung Group PLC, 121 25–27

Airstream *see* Thor Industries, Inc.

AirTouch Communications, 11 10–12 *see also* Vodafone Group PLC.

Airtours Plc, 27 27–29, 90, 92

AirTran Holdings, Inc., 22 21–23

Aisin Seiki Co., Ltd., III 415–16; 48 3–5 (upd.); 120 10–14 (upd.)

Aitchison & Colegrave *see* Bradford & Bingley PLC.

Aiwa Co., Ltd., 30 18–20

AIXTRON AG, 118 11–14

Ajegroup S.A., 92 1–4

Ajinomoto Co., Inc., II 463–64; 28 9–11 (upd.); 108 35–39 (upd.)

AK Steel Holding Corporation, 19 8–9; 41 3–6 (upd.); 122 9–13 (upd.)

Akal Security Incorporated, 119 37–40

Akamai Technologies, Inc., 71 18–21

Akbank TAS, 79 18–21

Akeena Solar, Inc., 103 6–10

Akerys S.A., 90 17–20

AKG Acoustics GmbH, 62 3–6

Akin, Gump, Strauss, Hauer & Feld, L.L.P., 33 23–25

Akorn, Inc., 32 22–24

Akro-Mills Inc. *see* Myers Industries, Inc.

Aktiebolaget SKF, III 622–25; 38 28–33 (upd.); 89 401–09 (upd.)

Akzo Nobel N.V., 13 21–23; 41 7–10 (upd.); 112 1–6 (upd.)

Al Habtoor Group L.L.C., 87 9–12

Al-Tawfeek Co. For Investment Funds Ltd. *see* Dallah Albaraka Group.

Alabama Farmers Cooperative, Inc., 63 20–22

Alabama National BanCorporation, 75 21–23

Aladdin Knowledge Systems Ltd., 101 14–17

Alain Afflelou SA, 53 30–32

Alain Manoukian *see* Groupe Alain Manoukian.

Alamo Group Inc., 32 25–28

Alamo Rent A Car, 6 348–50; 24 9–12 (upd.); 84 5–11 (upd.)

ALARIS Medical Systems, Inc., 65 17–20

Alascom, Inc. *see* AT&T Corp.

Alaska Air Group, Inc., 6 65–67; 29 11–14 (upd.)

C.F. Martin & Co., Inc., 42 55–58

The C.F. Sauer Company, 90 86–89

C.H. Boehringer Sohn, 39 70–73

C.H. Guenther & Son, Inc., 84 39–42

C.H. Heist Corporation, 24 111–13

C.H. Robinson Worldwide Inc., 11 43–44; 40 78–81 (upd.); 116 87–91 (upd.)

C. Hoare & Co., 77 76–79

C.I. Traders Limited, 61 44–46

C. Itoh & Co., I 431–33 *see also* ITOCHU Corp.

C.O. Bigelow Chemists, Inc., 114 117–20

C.R. Bard, Inc., 9 96–98; 65 81–85 (upd.)

C.R. Meyer and Sons Company, 74 58–60

CA Inc., 116 92–95

CAA *see* Creative Artists Agency LLC.

Cabela's Inc., 26 49–51; 68 74–77 (upd.)

Cable & Wireless HKT, 30 95–98 (upd.)

Cable and Wireless plc, V 283–86; 25 98–102 (upd.)

Cabletron Systems, Inc., 10 193–94

Cablevision Electronic Instruments, Inc., 32 105–07

Cablevision Systems Corporation, 7 63–65; 30 99–103 (upd.); 109 87–94 (upd.)

Cabot Corporation, 8 77–79; 29 79–82 (upd.); 91 74–80 (upd.)

Cabot Creamery Cooperative, Inc., 102 65–68

Caché, Inc., 30 104–06; 124 54–57 (upd.)

CACI International Inc., 21 85–87; 72 49–53 (upd.)

Cactus Feeders, Inc., 91 81–84

Cactus S.A., 90 94–97

Cadbury plc, 105 60–66 (upd.)

Cadbury Schweppes PLC, II 476–78; 49 75–79 (upd.)

Cadence Design Systems, Inc., 11 45–48; 48 75–79 (upd.)

Cadence Financial Corporation, 106 88–92

Cadmus Communications Corporation, 23 100–03 *see also* Cenveo Inc.

CAE USA Inc., 48 80–82

Caere Corporation, 20 101–03

Caesars World, Inc., 6 199–202

Café Britt Coffee Corporation Holdings NV, 119 93–96

Café de Coral Ltd., 122 65–69

Caffè Nero Group PLC, 63 87–89

Caffyns PLC, 105 67–71

Cagle's, Inc., 20 104–07

Cahill May Roberts Group Ltd., 112 77–80

Cahners Business Information, 43 92–95

Cains Beer Company PLC, 99 76–80

Caisse des Dépôts et Consignations, 90 98–101

CAL *see* China Airlines.

Cal-Maine Foods, Inc., 69 76–78

CalAmp Corp., 87 84–87

Calavo Growers, Inc., 47 63–66

CalComp Inc., 13 126–29

Calcot Ltd., 33 84–87

Caldor Inc., 12 54–56

Calgon Carbon Corporation, 73 76–79

California Cedar Products Company, 58 51–53

California Dairies Inc., 111 66–68

California Pizza Kitchen Inc., 15 74–76; 74 61–63 (upd.)

California Sports, Inc., 56 49–52

California Steel Industries, Inc., 67 85–87

California Water Service Group, 79 85–88

Caliper Life Sciences, Inc., 70 37–40

Callanan Industries, Inc., 60 77–79

Callard and Bowser-Suchard Inc., 84 43–46

Callaway Golf Company, 15 77–79; 45 74–77 (upd.); 112 81–86 (upd.)

Callon Petroleum Company, 47 67–69

Calloway's Nursery, Inc., 51 59–61

CalMat Co., 19 69–72 *see also* Vulcan Materials Co.

Calpine Corporation, 36 102–04; 113 66–70 (upd.)

Caltex Petroleum Corporation, 19 73–75 *see also* Chevron Corp.

Calumet Specialty Products Partners, L.P., 106 93–96

Calvin Klein, Inc., 22 121–24; 55 84–88 (upd.)

CAMAC International Corporation, 106 97–99

Camaïeu S.A., 72 54–56

Camargo Corrêa S.A., 93 114–18

CamBar *see* Cameron & Barkley Co.

Cambrex Corporation, 16 67–69; 44 59–62 (upd.)

Cambridge SoundWorks, Inc., 48 83–86

Cambridge Technology Partners, Inc., 36 105–08

Camden Property Trust, 77 80–83

Cameco Corporation, 77 84–87

Camelot Group plc, 110 68–71

Camelot Music, Inc., 26 52–54

Cameron & Barkley Company, 28 59–61 *see also* Hagemeyer North America.

Cameron Hughes Wine, 103 88–91

Cameron International Corporation, 110 72–76

Camp Dresser & McKee Inc., 104 47–50

Campagna-Turano Bakery, Inc., 99 81–84

Campbell Brothers Limited, 115 97–100

Campbell-Ewald Advertising, 86 56–60

Campbell Hausfeld, 115 101–04

Campbell-Mithun-Esty, Inc., 16 70–72 *see also* Interpublic Group of Companies, Inc.

Campbell Scientific, Inc., 51 62–65

Campbell Soup Company, II 479–81; 7 66–69 (upd.); 26 55–59 (upd.); 71 75–81 (upd.)

Campeau Corporation, V 25–28

The Campina Group, 78 61–64

Campmor, Inc., 104 51–54

Campo Electronics, Appliances & Computers, Inc., 16 73–75

Campofrío Alimentación S.A, 59 101–03

Canada Bread Company, Limited, 99 85–88

Canada Council for the Arts, 112 87–90

Canada Packers Inc., II 482–85

Canada Trust *see* CT Financial Services Inc.

Canadair, Inc., 16 76–78 *see also* Bombardier Inc.

Canadian Broadcasting Corporation, 37 55–58; 109 95–100 (upd.)

Canadian Imperial Bank of Commerce, II 244–46; 61 47–51 (upd.)

Canadian National Railway Company, 6 359–62; 71 82–88 (upd.)

Canadian Pacific Railway Limited, V 429–31; 45 78–83 (upd.); 95 71–80 (upd.)

Canadian Solar Inc., 105 72–76

Canadian Tire Corporation, Limited, 71 89–93 (upd.)

Canadian Utilities Limited, 13 130–32; 56 53–56 (upd.)

Canal Plus, 10 195–97; 34 83–86 (upd.)

Canam Group Inc., 114 121–24

Canandaigua Brands, Inc., 13 133–35; 34 87–91 (upd.) *see also* Constellation Brands, Inc.

Canary Wharf Group Plc, 30 107–09

Cancer Treatment Centers of America, Inc., 85 45–48

Candela Corporation, 48 87–89

Candie's, Inc., 31 81–84

Candle Corporation, 64 62–65

Candlewood Hotel Company, Inc., 41 81–83

Canfor Corporation, 42 59–61

Canlan Ice Sports Corp., 105 77–81

Cannon Design, 63 90–92

Cannon Express, Inc., 53 80–82

Cannondale Corporation, 21 88–90

Cano Petroleum Inc., 97 92–95

Canon Inc., III 120–21; 18 92–95 (upd.); ; 79 89–95 (upd.)

Canstar Sports Inc., 16 79–81 *see also* NIKE, Inc.

Cantel Medical Corporation, 80 55–58

Canterbury Park Holding Corporation, 42 62–65

Cantine Cooperative Riunite *see* Banfi Products Corp.

Cantine Giorgio Lungarotti S.R.L., 67 88–90

Cantor Fitzgerald, L.P., 92 38–42

CanWest Global Communications Corporation, 35 67–703

Cap Gemini Ernst & Young, 37 59–61

Garan, Inc., 16 231–33; 64 140–43 (upd.)

The Garden Company Ltd., 82 125–28

Garden Fresh Restaurant Corporation, 31 213–15

Garden Ridge Corporation, 27 163–65

Gardenburger, Inc., 33 169–71; 76 160–63 (upd.)

Gardner Denver, Inc., 49 158–60

Garmin Ltd., 60 135–37

Garst Seed Company, Inc., 86 156–59

Gart Sports Company, 24 173–75 see also Sports Authority, Inc.

Gartner, Inc., 21 235–37; 94 209–13 (upd.)

Garuda Indonesia, 6 90–91; 58 138–41 (upd.)

Gas Natural SDG S.A., 69 190–93

GASS see Grupo Ángeles Servicios de Salud, S.A. de C.V.

Gasunie see N.V. Nederlandse Gasunie.

Gate Gourmet International AG, 70 97–100

GateHouse Media, Inc., 91 196–99

The Gates Corporation, 9 241–43

Gateway Corporation Ltd., II 628–30 see also Somerfield plc.

Gateway Group One, 118 158–61

Gateway, Inc., 10 307–09; 27 166–69 (upd.); 63 153–58 (upd.)

The Gatorade Company, 82 129–32

Gatti's Pizza, Inc. see Mr. Gatti's, LP.

GATX, 6 394–96; 25 168–71 (upd.)

Gaumont S.A., 25 172–75; 91 200–05 (upd.)

Gaylord Bros., Inc., 100 178–81

Gaylord Container Corporation, 8 203–05

Gaylord Entertainment Company, 11 152–54; 36 226–29 (upd.)

Gaz de France, V 626–28; 40 191–95 (upd.) see also GDF SUEZ.

Gazprom see OAO Gazprom.

GBC see General Binding Corp.

GC Companies, Inc., 25 176–78 see also AMC Entertainment Inc.

GDF SUEZ, 109 256–63 (upd.)

GE see General Electric Co.

GE Aircraft Engines, 9 244–46

GE Capital Aviation Services, 36 230–33

GEA AG, 27 170–74

GEAC Computer Corporation Ltd., 43 181–85

Geberit AG, 49 161–64

Gecina SA, 42 151–53

Gedeon Richter plc, 122 175–79

Gedney see M.A. Gedney Co.

Geek Squad Inc., 102 138–41

Geerlings & Wade, Inc., 45 166–68

Geest Plc, 38 200–02 see also Bakkavör Group hf.

Gefco SA, 54 126–28

Geffen Records Inc., 26 150–52

GEHE AG, 27 175–78

Gehl Company, 19 172–74

GEICO Corporation, 10 310–12; 40 196–99 (upd.)

Geiger Bros., 60 138–41

Gelita AG, 74 114–18

GEMA (Gesellschaft für musikalische Aufführungs- und mechanische Vervielfältigungsrechte), 70 101–05

Gemini Sound Products Corporation, 58 142–44

Gemplus International S.A., 64 144–47

Gen-Probe Incorporated, 79 185–88

Gencor Ltd., IV 90–93; 22 233–37 (upd.) see also Gold Fields Ltd.

GenCorp Inc., 9 247–49

Genentech, Inc., I 637–38; 8 209–11 (upd.); 32 211–15 (upd.); 75 154–58 (upd.)

General Accident plc, III 256–57 see also Aviva PLC.

General Atomics, 57 151–54; 112 194–98 (upd.)

General Bearing Corporation, 45 169–71

General Binding Corporation, 10 313–14; 73 159–62 (upd.)

General Cable Corporation, 40 200–03; 111 154–59 (upd.)

The General Chemical Group Inc., 37 157–60

General Cigar Holdings, Inc., 66 139–42 (upd.)

General Cinema Corporation, I 245–46 see also GC Companies, Inc.

General DataComm Industries, Inc., 14 200–02

General Dynamics Corporation, I 57–60; 10 315–18 (upd.); 40 204–10 (upd.); 88 105–13 (upd.)

General Electric Company, II 27–31; 12 193–97 (upd.); 34 183–90 (upd.); 63 159–68 (upd.)

General Electric Company, PLC, II 24–26 see also Marconi plc.

General Employment Enterprises, Inc., 87 172–175

General Growth Properties, Inc., 57 155–57

General Host Corporation, 12 198–200

General Housewares Corporation, 16 234–36

General Instrument Corporation, 10 319–21 see also Motorola, Inc.

General Maritime Corporation, 59 197–99

General Mills, Inc., II 501–03; 10 322–24 (upd.); 36 234–39 (upd.); 85 141–49 (upd.)

General Motors Corporation, I 171–73; 10 325–27 (upd.); 36 240–44 (upd.); 64 148–53 (upd.)

General Nutrition Companies, Inc., 11 155–57; 29 210–14 (upd.) see also GNC Corp.

General Parts, Inc., 122 180–83

General Public Utilities Corporation, V 629–31 see also GPU, Inc.

General Re Corporation, III 258–59; 24 176–78 (upd.)

General Sekiyu K.K., IV 431–33 see also TonenGeneral Sekiyu K.K.

General Signal Corporation, 9 250–52 see also SPX Corp.

General Tire, Inc., 8 212–14

Generale Bank, II 294–95 see also Fortis, Inc.

Générale des Eaux Group, V 632–34 see also Vivendi.

Generali see Assicurazioni Generali.

Genesco Inc., 17 202–06; 84 143–149 (upd.)

Genesee & Wyoming Inc., 27 179–81

Genesis Health Ventures, Inc., 18 195–97 see also NeighborCare, Inc.

Genesis HealthCare Corporation, 119 185–89

Genesis Microchip Inc., 82 133–37

Genesys Telecommunications Laboratories Inc., 103 184–87

Genetics Institute, Inc., 8 215–18

Geneva Steel, 7 193–95

Genmar Holdings, Inc., 45 172–75

Genovese Drug Stores, Inc., 18 198–200

Genoyer see Groupe Genoyer.

GenRad, Inc., 24 179–83

Gentex Corporation, 26 153–57

Genting Bhd., 65 152–55

Gentiva Health Services, Inc., 79 189–92

Genuardi's Family Markets, Inc., 35 190–92

Genuine Parts Co., 9 253–55; 45 176–79 (upd.); 113 150–55 (upd.)

Genworth Financial Inc., 116 250–53

Genzyme Corporation, 13 239–42; 38 203–07 (upd.); 77 164–70 (upd.)

geobra Brandstätter GmbH & Co. KG, 48 183–86

Geodis S.A., 67 187–90

The Geon Company, 11 158–61

GeoResources, Inc., 101 196–99

Georg Fischer AG Schaffhausen, 61 106–09

Georg Jensen A/S, 110 173–77

George A. Hormel and Company, II 504–06 see also Hormel Foods Corp.

The George F. Cram Company, Inc., 55 158–60

George P. Johnson Company, 60 142–44

George S. May International Company, 55 161–63

George W. Park Seed Company, Inc., 98 145–48

George Weston Ltd., II 631–32; 36 245–48 (upd.); 88 114–19 (upd.)

George Wimpey plc, 12 201–03; 51 135–38 (upd.) see also Taylor Wimpey PLC.

Georgia Gulf Corporation, 9 256–58; 61 110–13 (upd.)

Georgia-Pacific LLC, IV 281–83; 9 259–62 (upd.); 47 145–51 (upd.); 101 200–09 (upd.)

Geotek Communications Inc., 21 238–40

Geox S.p.A., 118 162–65

Gerald Stevens, Inc., 37 161–63

K

KeySpan Energy Co., 27 264–66
Keystone Foods LLC, 117 207–10
Keystone International, Inc., 11 225–27
see also Tyco International Ltd.
KFC Corporation, 7 265–68; 21 313–17 (upd.); 89 290–96 (upd.)
Kforce Inc., 71 188–90
KfW Bankengruppe, 116 317–23 (upd.)
KGHM Polska Miedz S.A., 98 223–26
KHD Konzern, III 541–44
KI, 57 206–09
Kia Motors Corporation, 12 293–95; 29 264–67 (upd.); 56 173
Kiabi Europe, 66 199–201
Kidde plc, I 475–76; 44 255–59 (upd.)
Kiehl's Since 1851, Inc., 52 209–12
Kiewit Corporation, 116 324–30 (upd.)
Kikkoman Corporation, 14 287–89; 47 203–06 (upd.)
Kimball International, Inc., 12 296–98; 48 243–47 (upd.)
Kimberly-Clark Corporation, III 40–41; 16 302–05 (upd.); 43 256–60 (upd.); 105 264–71 (upd.)
Kimberly-Clark de México, S.A. de C.V., 54 185–87
Kimco Realty Corporation, 11 228–30
Kimpton Hotel & Restaurant Group, Inc., 105 272–75
Kinder Morgan, Inc., 45 227–30; 111 252–57 (upd.)
KinderCare Learning Centers, Inc., 13 298–300
Kinetic Concepts, Inc., 20 321–23
King & Spalding LLP, 23 315–18; 115 267–71 (upd.)
The King Arthur Flour Company, 31 292–95
King Kullen Grocery Co., Inc., 15 259–61
King Nut Company, 74 165–67
King Pharmaceuticals, Inc., 54 188–90
King Ranch, Inc., 14 290–92; 60 186–89 (upd.)
King World Productions, Inc., 9 306–08; 30 269–72 (upd.)
Kingfisher plc, V 106–09; 24 266–71 (upd.); 83 235–242 (upd.)
King's Hawaiian Bakery West, Inc., 101 282–85
Kingston Technology Company, Inc., 20 324–26; 112 237–41 (upd.)
Kinki Nippon Railway Company Ltd., V 463–65
Kinko's Inc., 16 306–08; 43 261–64 (upd.) *see also* FedEx Office and Print Services, Inc.
Kinney Shoe Corp., 14 293–95
Kinray Inc., 85 209–12
Kinross Gold Corporation, 36 314–16; 109 344–48 (upd.)
Kintera, Inc., 75 225–27
Kirby Corporation, 18 277–79; 66 202–04 (upd.)
Kirin Brewery Company, Limited, I 265–66; 21 318–21 (upd.); 63 227–31 (upd.)
Kirkland & Ellis LLP, 65 194–96

Kirlin's Inc., 98 227–30
Kirshenbaum Bond + Partners, Inc., 57 210–12
Kiss My Face Corporation, 108 290–94
Kit Manufacturing Co., 18 280–82
Kitchell Corporation, 14 296–98
KitchenAid, 8 298–99
Kitty Hawk, Inc., 22 309–11
Kiva, 95 225–29
Kiwi International Airlines Inc., 20 327–29
KKR *see* Kohlberg Kravis Roberts & Co.
KLA-Tencor Corporation, 11 231–33; 45 231–34 (upd.)
Klabin S.A., 73 204–06
Klasky Csupo, Inc., 78 193–97
Klaus Steilmann GmbH & Co. KG, 53 192–95
Klein Tools, Inc., 95 230–34
Kleiner, Perkins, Caufield & Byers, 53 196–98
Kleinwort Benson Group PLC, II 421–23; 22 55 *see also* Dresdner Kleinwort Wasserstein.
Klement's Sausage Company, 61 147–49
KLM Royal Dutch Airlines, 104 239–45 (upd.) *see also* Air France–KLM.
Klöckner-Werke AG, IV 126–28; 58 201–05 (upd.)
Kluwer Publishers *see* Wolters Kluwer NV.
Kmart Corporation, V 110–12; 18 283–87 (upd.); 47 207–12 (upd.) *see also* Sears Holding Corp.
KMG Chemicals, Inc., 101 286–89
KN *see* Kühne & Nagel Group.
Knape & Vogt Manufacturing Company, 17 277–79
Knauf Gips KG, 100 245–50
K'Nex Industries, Inc., 52 206–08
Knight-Ridder, Inc., IV 628–30; 15 262–66 (upd.); 67 219–23 (upd.)
Knight Trading Group, Inc., 70 147–49
Knight Transportation, Inc., 64 218–21
Knights of Columbus, 120 197–200
Knitting Factory Entertainment, 108 295–98
Knoll, Inc., 14 299–301; 80 184–88 (upd.)
Knorr-Bremse AG, 84 226–231
Knorr Co. *see* C.H. Knorr Co.
The Knot, Inc., 74 168–71
Knott's Berry Farm, 18 288–90
Knouse Foods Cooperative Inc., 102 200–03
Knowledge Learning Corporation, 51 197–99; 115 272–77 (upd.)
Knowledge Universe, Inc., 54 191–94
KnowledgeWare Inc., 9 309–11; 31 296–98 (upd.)
KOA *see* Kampgrounds of America, Inc.
Koala Corporation, 44 260–62
Kobe Steel, Ltd., IV 129–31; 19 238–41 (upd.); 109 349–54 (upd.)
Kobold Watch Company, LLC, 121 268–72
Kobrand Corporation, 82 191–94

Koç Holding A.S., I 478–80; 54 195–98 (upd.)
Koch Enterprises, Inc., 29 215–17
Koch Industries, Inc., IV 448–49; 20 330–32 (upd.); 77 224–30 (upd.)
Kodak *see* Eastman Kodak Co.
Kodansha Ltd., IV 631–33; 38 273–76 (upd.)
Koenig & Bauer AG, 64 222–26
Koenigsegg Automotive AB, 115 278–80
Kohlberg Kravis Roberts & Co. L.P., 24 272–74; 56 190–94 (upd.)115 281–87 (upd.)
Kohler Company, 7 269–71; 32 308–12 (upd.); 108 299–305 (upd.)
Kohl's Corporation, 9 312–13; 30 273–75 (upd.); 77 231–35 (upd.)
Kohn Pedersen Fox Associates P.C., 57 213–16
Kolbenschmidt Pierburg AG, 97 249–53
The Koll Company, 8 300–02
Kollmorgen Corporation, 18 291–94
Kolmar Laboratories Group, 96 240–43
Komag, Inc., 11 234–35
Komatsu Ltd., III 545–46; 16 309–11 (upd.); 52 213–17 (upd.); 113 189–95 (upd.)
Konami Corporation, 96 244–47
KONE Corporation, 27 267–70; 76 225–28 (upd.)
Konica Corporation, III 547–50; 30 276–81 (upd.)
König Brauerei GmbH & Co. KG, 35 256–58 (upd.)
Koninklijke Ahold N.V., II 641–42; 16 312–14 (upd.); 124 178–82 (upd.)
Koninklijke Grolsch BV *see* Royal Grolsch NV.
Koninklijke Houthandel G Wijma & Zonen BV, 96 248–51
Koninklijke KPN N.V. *see* Royal KPN N.V.
Koninklijke Luchtvaart Maatschappij N.V., I 107–09; 28 224–27 (upd.) *see also* Air France–KLM.
Koninklijke Nederlandsche Hoogovens en Staalfabrieken NV, IV 132–34
N.V. Koninklijke Nederlandse Vliegtuigenfabriek Fokker, I 54–56; 28 327–30 (upd.)
Koninklijke Nedlloyd N.V., 6 403–05; 26 241–44 (upd.)
Koninklijke Numico N.V. *see* Royal Numico N.V.
Koninklijke Philips Electronics N.V., 50 297–302 (upd.); 119 282–90 (upd.)
Koninklijke PTT Nederland NV, V 299–301 *see also* Royal KPN NV.
Koninklijke Reesink N.V., 104 246–50
Koninklijke Vendex KBB N.V. (Royal Vendex KBB N.V.), 62 206–09 (upd.)
Koninklijke Wessanen nv, II 527–29; 54 199–204 (upd.); 114 254–60 (upd.)
Koo Koo Roo, Inc., 25 263–65
Kookmin Bank, 58 206–08
Kooperativa Förbundet, 99 245–248

PCL Construction Group Inc., 50 347–49

PCM Uitgevers NV, 53 270–73

PCS *see* Potash Corp. of Saskatchewan Inc.

PDI, Inc., 52 272–75

PDL BioPharma, Inc., 90 322–25

PDM Group *see* Prosper De Mulder Limited

PDO *see* Petroleum Development Oman.

PDQ Food Stores Inc., 79 310–13

PDS Gaming Corporation, 44 334–37

PDVSA *see* Petróleos de Venezuela S.A.

Peabody Energy Corporation, 10 447–49; 45 330–33 (upd.); 118 343–48 (upd.)

Peabody Holding Company, Inc., IV 169–72

Peace Arch Entertainment Group Inc., 51 286–88

The Peak Technologies Group, Inc., 14 377–80

Peapod, Inc., 30 346–48

Pearl Musical Instrument Company, 78 297–300

Pearle Vision, Inc., 13 390–92; 115 383–88 (upd.)

Pearson plc, IV 657–59; 46 337–41 (upd.); 103 320–26 (upd.)

Peavey Electronics Corporation, 16 408–10; 94 352–56 (upd.)

Pechanga Resort & Casino, 122 334–38

Pechiney S.A., IV 173–75; 45 334–37 (upd.)

PECO Energy Company, 11 387–90 *see also* Exelon Corp.

Pediatric Services of America, Inc., 31 356–58

Pediatrix Medical Group, Inc., 61 282–85

Peebles Inc., 16 411–13; 43 296–99 (upd.)

Peek & Cloppenburg KG, 46 342–45

Peet's Coffee & Tea, Inc., 38 338–40; 100 333–37 (upd.)

Peg Perego SpA, 88 300–03

Pegasus Solutions, Inc., 75 315–18

Pegasystems Inc., 122 339–42

Pei Cobb Freed & Partners Architects LLP, 57 280–82

Pelican Products, Inc., 86 331–34

Pelikan Holding AG, 92 296–300

Pella Corporation, 12 384–86; 39 322–25 (upd.); 89 349–53 (upd.)

Pemco Aviation Group Inc., 54 283–86

PEMEX *see* Petróleos Mexicanos.

Penaflor S.A., 66 252–54

Penauille Polyservices SA, 49 318–21

Pendleton Grain Growers Inc., 64 305–08

Pendleton Woolen Mills, Inc., 42 275–78

Pendragon, PLC, 109 441–45

Penford Corporation, 55 296–99

Pengrowth Energy Trust, 95 323–26

The Penguin Group, 100 338–42

The Peninsular and Oriental Steam Navigation Company, V 490–93; 38 341–46 (upd.)

Peninsular and Oriental Steam Navigation Company (Bovis Division), I 588–89 *see also* DP World.

Penn Engineering & Manufacturing Corp., 28 349–51

Penn National Gaming, Inc., 33 327–29; 109 446–50 (upd.)

Penn Traffic Company, 13 393–95

Penn Virginia Corporation, 85 324–27

Penney's *see* J.C. Penney Company, Inc.

Pennington Seed Inc., 98 301–04

Pennon Group Plc, 45 338–41

Pennsylvania Blue Shield, III 325–27 *see also* Highmark Inc.

Pennsylvania Power & Light Company, V 693–94

Pennwalt Corporation, I 382–84

PennWell Corporation, 55 300–03

Pennzoil-Quaker State Company, IV 488–90; 20 418–22 (upd.); 50 350–55 (upd.)

Penske Corporation, V 494–95; 19 292–94 (upd.); 84 305–309 (upd.)

Pentair, Inc., 7 419–21; 26 361–64 (upd.); 81 281–87 (upd.)

Pentax Corporation, 78 301–05

Pentech International, Inc., 29 372–74

The Pentland Group plc, 20 423–25; 100 343–47 (upd.)

Penton Media, Inc., 27 360–62

Penzeys Spices, Inc., 79 314–16

People Express Airlines Inc., I 117–18

Peoples Energy Corporation, 6 543–44

People's United Financial Inc. , 106 349–52

PeopleSoft Inc., 14 381–83; 33 330–33 (upd.) *see also* Oracle Corp.

The Pep Boys—Manny, Moe & Jack, 11 391–93; 36 361–64 (upd.); 81 288–94 (upd.)

PEPCO *see* Potomac Electric Power Co.

Pepco Holdings, Inc., 116 382–85

Pepper *see* J. W. Pepper and Son Inc.

The Pepper Construction Group, LLC, 111 385–88

Pepper Hamilton LLP, 43 300–03

Pepperidge Farm, Incorporated, 81 295–300

The Pepsi Bottling Group, Inc., 40 350–53

PepsiAmericas, Inc., 67 297–300 (upd.)

PepsiCo, Inc., I 276–79; 10 450–54 (upd.); 38 347–54 (upd.); 93 333–44 (upd.)

Pequiven *see* Petroquímica de Venezuela S.A.

Perdigao SA, 52 276–79

Perdue Incorporated, 7 422–24; 23 375–78 (upd.)119 362–67 (upd.)

Perfection Bakeries, Inc., 123 313–16

Perfetti Van Melle S.p.A., 72 270–73

Perficient, Inc., 119 368–71

Performance, Inc., 120 317–20

Performance Food Group, 31 359–62; 96 329–34 (upd.)

Perini Corporation, 8 418–21; 82 274–79 (upd.)

PerkinElmer, Inc., 7 425–27; 78 306–10 (upd.)

Perkins & Marie Callender's Inc., 107 345–51 (upd.)

Perkins Coie LLP, 56 268–70

Perkins Family Restaurants, L.P., 22 417–19

Perkins Foods Holdings Ltd., 87 371–374

Perma-Fix Environmental Services, Inc., 99 338–341

Pernod Ricard S.A., I 280–81; 21 399–401 (upd.); 72 274–77 (upd.)

Perot Systems Corporation, 29 375–78

Perrigo Company, 12 387–89; 59 330–34 (upd.); 118 349–55 (upd.)

Perry Ellis International Inc., 41 291–94; 106 353–58 (upd.)

Perry's Ice Cream Company Inc., 90 326–29

The Perseus Books Group, 91 375–78

Personna American Safety Razor Company, 119 372–76 (upd.)

Perstorp AB, I 385–87; 51 289–92 (upd.)

Pertamina, IV 491–93; 56 271–74 (upd.)

Perusahaan Otomobil Nasional Bhd., 62 266–68

Pescanova S.A., 81 301–04

Pet Incorporated, 7 428–31

Petco Animal Supplies, Inc., 29 379–81; 74 231–34 (upd.)

Peter Kiewit Sons' Inc., 8 422–24 *see also* Kiewit Corporation.

Peter Pan Bus Lines Inc., 106 359–63

Peter Piper, Inc., 70 217–19

Peterbilt Motors Company, 89 354–57

Petersen Publishing Company, 21 402–04

Peterson American Corporation, 55 304–06

Pete's Brewing Company, 22 420–22

Petit Bateau, 95 327–31

Petland Inc., 110 363–66

PetMed Express, Inc., 81 305–08

Petrie Stores Corporation, 8 425–27

Petro-Canada, IV 494–96; 99 342–349 (upd.)

Petrobrás *see* Petróleo Brasileiro S.A.

Petrobras Energia Participaciones S.A., 72 278–81

Petroecuador *see* Petróleos del Ecuador.

Petrof spol. S.R.O., 107 352–56

Petrofac Ltd., 95 332–35

PetroFina S.A., IV 497–500; 26 365–69 (upd.)

Petrogal *see* Petróleos de Portugal.

Petrohawk Energy Corporation, 79 317–20

Petróleo Brasileiro S.A., IV 501–03

Petróleos de Portugal S.A., IV 504–06

Petróleos de Venezuela S.A., IV 507–09; 74 235–39 (upd.)

Standard Commercial Corporation, 13 490–92; 62 333–37 (upd.)

Standard Federal Bank, 9 481–83

Standard Life Assurance Company, III 358–61

Standard Microsystems Corporation, 11 462–64

Standard Motor Products, Inc., 40 414–17

Standard Pacific Corporation, 52 319–22

The Standard Register Company, 15 472–74; 93 419–25 (upd.)

Standex International Corporation, 17 456–59; 44 403–06 (upd.)

Stanhome Inc., 15 475–78

Stanley Furniture Company, Inc., 34 412–14

Stanley Leisure plc, 66 310–12

The Stanley Works, III 626–29; 20 476–80 (upd.); 79 383–91 (upd.)

Staple Cotton Cooperative Association (Staplcotn), 86 373–77

Staples, Inc., 10 496–98; 55 351–56 (upd.); 119 423–30 (upd.)

Star Banc Corporation, 11 465–67 *see also* Firstar Corp.

Star of the West Milling Co., 95 386–89

Starbucks Corporation, 13 493–94; 34 415–19 (upd.); 77 404–10 (upd.)

Starcraft Corporation, 30 434–36; 66 313–16 (upd.)

Starent Networks Corp., 106 446–50

StarHub Ltd., 77 411–14

Starkey Laboratories, Inc., 52 323–25

StarKist Company, 113 368–72

Starrett *see* L.S. Starrett Co.

Starrett Corporation, 21 471–74

StarTek, Inc., 79 392–95

Starter Corp., 12 457–458

Starwood Hotels & Resorts Worldwide, Inc., 54 345–48; 119 431–35 (upd.)

Starz LLC, 91 445–50

The Stash Tea Company, 50 449–52

State Auto Financial Corporation, 77 415–19

State Bank of India, 63 354–57

State Farm Mutual Automobile Insurance Company, III 362–64; 51 341–45 (upd.)

State Financial Services Corporation, 51 346–48

State Grid Corporation of China, 108 470–74

State Street Corporation, 8 491–93; 57 340–44 (upd.)

Staten Island Bancorp, Inc., 39 380–82

Stater Bros. Holdings Inc., 64 364–67

Station Casinos, Inc., 25 452–54; 90 390–95 (upd.)

Statnett SF, 110 439–42

Statoil ASA, 61 344–48 (upd.)

The Staubach Company, 62 338–41

STC PLC, III 162–64 *see also* Nortel Networks Corp.

Ste. Michelle Wine Estates Ltd., 96 408–11

The Steak n Shake Company, 41 387–90; 96 412–17 (upd.)

Steamships Trading Company Ltd., 82 353–56

Stearns, Inc., 43 389–91

Steel Authority of India Ltd., IV 205–07; 66 317–21 (upd.)

Steel Dynamics, Inc., 52 326–28

Steel Technologies Inc., 63 358–60

Steelcase Inc., 7 493–95; 27 432–35 (upd.); 110 443–50 (upd.)

Stefanel SpA, 63 361–63

Steiff *see* Margarete Steiff GmbH.

Steilmann Group *see* Klaus Steilmann GmbH & Co. KG.

Stein Mart Inc., 19 423–25; 72 337–39 (upd.)

Steinberg Incorporated, II 662–65

Steiner Corporation (Alsco), 53 308–11

Steinway Musical Instruments, Inc., 19 426–29; 111 446–51 (upd.)

Stelco Inc., IV 208–10; 51 349–52 (upd.)

Stelmar Shipping Ltd., 52 329–31

Stemilt Growers Inc., 94 407–10

Stepan Company, 30 437–39; 105 438–42 (upd.)

The Stephan Company, 60 285–88

Stephens Inc., 92 344–48

Stephens Media, LLC, 91 451–54

Steria SA, 49 382–85

Stericycle, Inc., 33 380–82; 74 316–18 (upd.)

Sterilite Corporation, 97 382–85

STERIS Corporation, 29 449–52

Sterling Chemicals, Inc., 16 460–63; 78 356–61 (upd.)

Sterling Drug Inc., I 698–700

Sterling Electronics Corp., 18 496–98

Sterling European Airlines A/S, 70 300–02

Sterling Financial Corporation, 106 451–55

Sterling Software, Inc., 11 468–70 *see also* Computer Associates International, Inc.

STET *see* Società Finanziaria Telefonica per Azioni.

Steuben Glass *see* Corning Inc.

Steve & Barry's LLC, 88 377–80

Stevedoring Services of America Inc., 28 435–37

Steven Madden, Ltd., 37 371–73; 123 384–88 (upd.)

Stew Leonard's, 56 349–51

Stewart & Stevenson Services Inc., 11 471–73

Stewart Enterprises, Inc., 20 481–83

Stewart Information Services Corporation, 78 362–65

Stewart's Beverages, 39 383–86

Stewart's Shops Corporation, 80 360–63

Stickley *see* L. and J.G. Stickley, Inc.

Stiebel Eltron Group, 107 411–16

Stiefel Laboratories, Inc., 90 396–99

Stihl *see* Andreas Stihl AG & Co. KG.

Stiles Machinery Inc., 123 389–92

Stillwater Mining Company, 47 380–82

Stimson Lumber Company Inc., 78 366–69

Stinnes AG, 8 494–97; 23 451–54 (upd.); 59 387–92 (upd.)

Stirling Group plc, 62 342–44

STMicroelectronics NV, 52 332–35

Stock Yards Packing Co., Inc., 37 374–76

Stoddard International plc, 72 340–43

Stoll-Moss Theatres Ltd., 34 420–22

Stollwerck AG, 53 312–15

Stolt-Nielsen S.A., 42 356–59; 54 349–50

Stolt Sea Farm Holdings PLC, 54 349–51

Stone & Webster, Inc., 13 495–98; 64 368–72 (upd.)

Stone Container Corporation, IV 332–34 *see also* Smurfit Kappa Group plc

Stone Manufacturing Company, 14 469–71; 43 392–96 (upd.)

Stonyfield Farm, Inc., 55 357–60

The Stop & Shop Supermarket Company, II 666–67; 24 460–62 (upd.); 68 350–53 (upd.)

Stora Enso Oyj, IV 335–37; 36 447–55 (upd.); 85 396–408 (upd.)

Storage Technology Corporation, 6 275–77

Storage USA, Inc., 21 475–77

Storehouse PLC, 16 464–66 *see also* Mothercare plc.

Stouffer Corp., 8 498–501 *see also* Nestlé S.A.

Strabag SE, 113 373–79

Strand Book Store Inc., 114 390–93

StrataCom, Inc., 16 467–69

Stratagene Corporation, 70 303–06

Stratasys, Inc., 67 361–63

Strattec Security Corporation, 73 324–27

Stratus Computer, Inc., 10 499–501

Straumann Holding AG, 79 396–99

Strauss Discount Auto, 56 352–54

Strauss-Elite Group, 68 354–57

Strayer Education, Inc., 53 316–19; 124 380–84 (upd.)

StreamServe, Inc., 113 380–83

Stride Rite Corporation, 8 502–04; 37 377–80 (upd.); 86 378–84 (upd.)

Strine Printing Company Inc., 88 381–84

Strix Ltd., 51 353–55

The Strober Organization, Inc., 82 357–60 *see also* Pro-Build Holdings Inc.

The Stroh Brewery Company, I 290–92; 18 499–502 (upd.)

Strombecker Corporation, 60 289–91

Strongwell Corporation, 110 451–54

Stroock & Stroock & Lavan LLP, 40 418–21

Strouds, Inc., 33 383–86

The Structure Tone Organization, 99 427–430

U

United Paper Mills Ltd., IV 347–50 *see also* UPM-Kymmene Corp.
United Parcel Service, Inc., V 533–35; 17 503–06 (upd.); 63 414–19; 94 425–30 (upd.)
United Plantations Bhd., 117 427–30
United Press International, Inc., 25 506–09; 73 354–57 (upd.)
United Rentals, Inc., 34 466–69
United Retail Group Inc., 33 426–28
United Road Services, Inc., 69 360–62
United Service Organizations, 60 308–11
United Services Automobile Association, 109 559–65 (upd.)
United States Cellular Corporation, 9 527–29 *see also* U.S. Cellular Corp.
United States Filter Corporation, 20 501–04 *see also* Siemens AG.
United States Health Care Systems, Inc. *see* U.S. Healthcare, Inc.
United States Pipe and Foundry Company, 62 377–80
United States Playing Card Company, 62 381–84
United States Postal Service, 14 517–20; 34 470–75 (upd.); 108 516–24 (upd.)
United States Shoe Corporation, V 207–08
United States Soccer Federation, 108 525–28
United States Steel Corporation, 50 500–04 (upd.); 114 494–500 (upd.)
United States Sugar Corporation, 115 465–68
United States Surgical Corporation, 10 533–35; 34 476–80 (upd.)
United States Tennis Association, 111 503–06
United Stationers Inc., 14 521–23; 117 431–36 (upd.)
United Surgical Partners International Inc., 120 451–54
United Talent Agency, Inc., 80 392–96
United Technologies Automotive Inc., 15 513–15
United Technologies Corporation, I 84–86; 10 536–38 (upd.); 34 481–85 (upd.); 105 455–61 (upd.)
United Telecommunications, Inc., V 344–47 *see also* Sprint Corp.
United Utilities PLC, 52 372–75 (upd.)
United Video Satellite Group, 18 535–37 *see also* TV Guide, Inc.
United Water Resources, Inc., 40 447–50; 45 277
United Way Worldwide, 36 485–88; 112 451–56 (upd.)
UnitedHealth Group Incorporated, 103 476–84 (upd.)
Unitika Ltd., V 387–89; 53 341–44 (upd.)
Unitil Corporation, 37 403–06
Unitog Co., 19 457–60 *see also* Cintas Corp.
Unitrin Inc., 16 503–05; 78 427–31 (upd.)
Unitymedia GmbH, 115 469–72

Univar Corporation, 9 530–32
Universal American Corp., 111 507–10
Universal Compression, Inc., 59 402–04
Universal Corporation, V 417–18; 48 403–06 (upd.)
Universal Electronics Inc., 39 405–08; 120 455–60 (upd.)
Universal Foods Corporation, 7 546–48 *see also* Sensient Technologies Corp.
Universal Forest Products, Inc., 10 539–40; 59 405–09 (upd.); 122 455–60 (upd.)
Universal Health Services, Inc., 6 191–93; 124 429–33 (upd.)
Universal International, Inc., 25 510–11
Universal Manufacturing Company, 88 423–26
Universal Security Instruments, Inc., 96 434–37
Universal Stainless & Alloy Products, Inc., 75 386–88
Universal Studios, Inc., 33 429–33; 100 423–29 (upd.)
Universal Technical Institute, Inc., 81 396–99
Universal Truckload Services, Inc., 111 511–14
The University of Chicago Press, 79 451–55
University of Phoenix *see* Apollo Group, Inc.
Univision Communications Inc., 24 515–18; 83 434–439 (upd.)
UNM *see* United News & Media plc.
Uno Restaurant Holdings Corporation, 18 538–40; 70 334–37 (upd.)
Unocal Corporation, IV 569–71; 24 519–23 (upd.); 71 378–84 (upd.)
UNUM Corp., 13 538–40
UnumProvident Corporation, 52 376–83 (upd.)
Uny Co., Ltd., V 209–10; 49 425–28 (upd.)
UOB *see* United Overseas Bank Ltd.
UPC *see* United Pan-Europe Communications NV.
UPI *see* United Press International.
Upjohn Company, I 707–09; 8 547–49 (upd.) *see also* Pharmacia & Upjohn Inc.; Pfizer Inc.
UPM-Kymmene Corporation, 19 461–65; 50 505–11 (upd.)
The Upper Deck Company, LLC, 105 462–66
UPS *see* United Parcel Service, Inc.
Uralita S.A., 96 438–41
Uranium One Inc., 111 515–18
Urban Engineers, Inc., 102 435–38
Urban Outfitters, Inc., 14 524–26; 74 367–70 (upd.)
Urbi Desarrollos Urbanos, S.A. de C.V., 81 400–03
Urbium PLC, 75 389–91
URS Corporation, 45 420–23; 80 397–400 (upd.)
URSI *see* United Road Services, Inc.
US *see also* U.S.
US 1 Industries, Inc., 89 475–78

US Airways Group, Inc., I 131–32; 6 131–32 (upd.); 28 506–09 (upd.); 52 384–88 (upd.); 110 472–78 (upd.)
USA Interactive, Inc., 47 418–22 (upd.)
USA Mobility Inc., 97 437–40 (upd.)
USA Track & Field, Inc., 122 461–64
USA Truck, Inc., 42 410–13
USAA, 10 541–43; 62 385–88 (upd.) *see also* United Services Automobile Association.
USANA, Inc., 29 491–93
USCC *see* United States Cellular Corp.
USEC Inc., 124 434–37
USF&G Corporation, III 395–98 *see also* The St. Paul Companies.
USG Corporation, III 762–64; 26 507–10 (upd.); 81 404–10 (upd.)
Ushio Inc., 91 496–99
Usinas Siderúrgicas de Minas Gerais S.A., 77 454–57
Usinger's Famous Sausage *see* Fred Usinger Inc.
Usinor SA, IV 226–28; 42 414–17 (upd.)
USO *see* United Service Organizations.
USPS *see* United States Postal Service.
USSC *see* United States Surgical Corp.
UST Inc., 9 533–35; 50 512–17 (upd.)
USTA *see* United States Tennis Association
USX Corporation, IV 572–74; 7 549–52 (upd.) *see also* United States Steel Corp.
Utah Medical Products, Inc., 36 496–99
Utah Power and Light Company, 27 483–86 *see also* PacifiCorp.
UTG Inc., 100 430–33
Utilicorp United Inc., 6 592–94 *see also* Aquilla, Inc.
UTStarcom, Inc., 77 458–61
UTV *see* Ulster Television PLC.
Utz Quality Foods, Inc., 72 358–60
UUNET, 38 468–72
Uwajimaya, Inc., 60 312–14
Uzbekistan Airways National Air Company, 99 470–473

V

V&S Vin & Sprit AB, 91 504–11 (upd.)
VA TECH ELIN EBG GmbH, 49 429–31
Vail Resorts, Inc., 11 543–46; 43 435–39 (upd.); 120 461–67 (upd.)
Vaillant GmbH, 44 436–39
Vaisala Oyj, 104 459–63
Valassis Communications, Inc., 8 550–51; 37 407–10 (upd.); 76 364–67 (upd.)
Vale S.A., 117 437–42 (upd.)
Valeo, 23 492–94; 66 350–53 (upd.)
Valero Energy Corporation, 7 553–55; 71 385–90 (upd.)
Valhi, Inc., 19 466–68; 94 431–35 (upd.)
Valio Oy, 117 443–47
Vall Companys S.A., 120 468–71
Vallen Corporation, 45 424–26
Valley Media Inc., 35 430–33
Valley National Gases, Inc., 85 434–37
Valley Proteins, Inc., 91 500–03

Wincor Nixdorf Holding GmbH, 69 370–73 (upd.)
Wind River Systems, Inc., 37 419–22
Windmere Corporation, 16 537–39 *see also* Applica Inc.
Windstream Corporation, 83 462–465
Windswept Environmental Group, Inc., 62 389–92
The Wine Group, Inc., 39 419–21; 114 515–18 (upd.)
Winegard Company, 56 384–87
Winmark Corporation, 74 392–95
Winn-Dixie Stores, Inc., II 683–84; 21 528–30 (upd.); 59 423–27 (upd.); 113 465–71
Winnebago Industries, Inc., 7 589–91; 27 509–12 (upd.); 96 462–67 (upd.)
Winpak Ltd., 121 434–38
WinsLoew Furniture, Inc., 21 531–33 *see also* Brown Jordan International Inc.
Winston & Strawn, 35 470–73
Winterthur Group, III 402–04; 68 402–05 (upd.)
Wintrust Financial Corporation, 106 497–501
Wipro Limited, 43 465–68; 106 502–07 (upd.)
The Wiremold Company, 81 428–34
Wirtgen Beteiligungsgesellschaft mbh, 120 480–84
Wirtz Corporation, 72 374–76
Wisconsin Alumni Research Foundation, 65 365–68
Wisconsin Bell, Inc., 14 551–53 *see also* AT&T Corp.
Wisconsin Central Transportation Corporation, 24 533–36
Wisconsin Dairies, 7 592–93
Wisconsin Energy Corporation, 6 601–03; 54 417–21 (upd.)
Wisconsin Public Service Corporation, 9 553–54 *see also* WPS Resources Corp.
Wise Foods, Inc., 79 468–71
Witco Corporation, I 404–06; 16 540–43 (upd.) *see also* Chemtura Corp.
Witness Systems, Inc., 87 461–465
Wizards of the Coast LLC, 24 537–40; 112 497–501 (upd.)
WLR Foods, Inc., 21 534–36
Wm. B. Reily & Company Inc., 58 372–74
Wm. Morrison Supermarkets plc, 38 496–98; 110 487–90 (upd.)
Wm. Wrigley Jr.company, 7 594–97; 58 375–79 (upd.)
WMC, Limited, 43 469–72
WMF *see* Württembergische Metallwarenfabrik AG (WMF).
WMS Industries, Inc., 15 537–39; 53 363–66 (upd.); 119 528–33 (upd.)
WMX Technologies Inc., 17 551–54
Wolfgang Puck Worldwide, Inc., 26 534–36; 70 364–67 (upd.)
Wolohan Lumber Co., 19 503–05 *see also* Lanoga Corp.
Wolseley plc, 64 409–12

Wolters Kluwer NV, 14 554–56; 33 458–61 (upd.)
The Wolverhampton & Dudley Breweries, PLC, 57 411–14
Wolverine Tube Inc., 23 515–17
Wolverine World Wide, Inc., 16 544–47; 59 428–33 (upd.); 118 494–501 (upd.)
Womble Carlyle Sandridge & Rice, PLLC, 52 421–24
WonderWorks, Inc., 103 521–24
Wood Hall Trust plc, I 592–93
Wood-Mode Incorporated, 23 518–20; 124 453–57 (upd.)
Woodbridge Holdings Corporation, 99 482–485
Woodcraft Industries Inc., 61 398–400
Woodstream Corporation, 115 493–96
Woodward Governor Company, 13 565–68; 49 453–57 (upd.); 105 498–505 (upd.)
Woolrich Inc., 62 393–96
The Woolwich plc, 30 492–95
Woolworth Corporation, V 224–27; 20 528–32 (upd.) *see also* Kingfisher plc; Venator Group Inc.
Woolworths Group plc, 83 466–473
Woot, Inc., 118 502–05
WordPerfect Corporation, 10 556–59 *see also* Corel Corp.
Workflow Management, Inc., 65 369–72
Working Assets Funding Service, 43 473–76
Working Title Films Ltd., 105 506–09
Workman Publishing Company, Inc., 70 368–71
World Acceptance Corporation, 57 415–18
World Bank Group, 33 462–65
World Book, Inc., 12 554–56
World Color Press Inc., 12 557–59 *see also* Quebecor Inc.
World Duty Free Americas, Inc., 29 509–12 (upd.)
World Fuel Services Corporation, 47 449–51; 112 502–05 (upd.)
World Kitchen, LLC, 104 474–77
World Publications, LLC, 65 373–75
World Vision International, Inc., 93 494–97
World Wide Technology, Inc., 94 469–72
World Wrestling Entertainment, Inc., 32 514–17; 107 470–75 (upd.)
WorldCorp, Inc., 10 560–62
World's Finest Chocolate Inc., 39 422–24
Worldwide Pants Inc., 97 481–84
Worldwide Restaurant Concepts, Inc., 47 452–55
WorleyParsons Ltd., 115 497–500
Worms et Cie, 27 513–15 *see also* Sequana Capital.
Worthington Foods, Inc., 14 557–59 *see also* Kellogg Co.
Worthington Industries, Inc., 7 598–600; 21 537–40 (upd.); 114 519–25 (upd.)

WPL Holdings, 6 604–06
WPP Group plc, 6 53–54; 48 440–42 (upd.); 112 506–11 (upd.)
WPS Resources Corporation, 53 367–70 (upd.)
Wray & Nephew Group Ltd., 98 468–71
WRG *see* Wells Rich Greene BDDP.
Wright Express Corporation, 80 419–22
Wright Medical Group, Inc., 61 401–05
Writers Guild of America, West, Inc., 92 416–20
WS Atkins Plc, 45 445–47
WSI Corporation, 102 453–56
WTD Industries, Inc., 20 533–36
Wunderman, 86 429–32
Württembergische Metallwarenfabrik AG (WMF), 60 364–69
Wüstenrot & Württembergische AG, 121 439–43; 123 442–47
WuXi AppTec Company Ltd., 103 525–28
WVT Communications *see* Warwick Valley Telephone Co.
WWRD Holdings Limited, 106 508–15 (upd.)
Wyant Corporation, 30 496–98
Wyeth, Inc., 50 535–39 (upd.); 118 506–11 (upd.)
Wyle Electronics, 14 560–62 *see also* Arrow Electronics, Inc.
Wyllie Group Pty Ltd, 124 458–61
Wyman-Gordon Company, 14 563–65
Wyndham Worldwide Corporation, 99 486–493 (upd.)
Wynn's International, Inc., 33 466–70
Wyse Technology, Inc., 15 540–42

X

X-Rite, Inc., 48 443–46
Xantrex Technology Inc., 97 485–88
Xcel Energy Inc., 73 384–89 (upd.)
Xeikon NV, 26 540–42
Xerium Technologies, Inc., 94 473–76
Xerox Corporation, III 171–73; 6 288–90 (upd.); 26 543–47 (upd.); 69 374–80 (upd.)
Xilinx, Inc., 16 548–50; 82 435–39 (upd.)
XM Satellite Radio Holdings, Inc., 69 381–84
XO Holdings, Inc., 119 534–40
XOMA Ltd., 117 453–56
Xstrata PLC, 73 390–93
XTO Energy Inc., 52 425–27

Y

Yageo Corporation, 16 551–53; 98 472–75 (upd.)
Yahoo! Inc., 27 516–19; 70 372–75 (upd.)
Yak Pak, 108 542–45
Yamada Denki Co., Ltd., 85 470–73
Yamaha Corporation, III 656–59; 16 554–58 (upd.); 40 461–66 (upd.); 99 494–501 (upd.)
Yamaichi Securities Company, Limited, II 458–59

Index to Industries

Accounting

American Institute of Certified Public Accountants (AICPA), 44
Andersen, 29 (upd.); 68 (upd.)
Automatic Data Processing, Inc., III; 9 (upd.); 47 (upd.)
BDO Seidman LLP, 96
BKD LLP, 96
CPP International, LLC, 103
CROSSMARK, 79
Deloitte Touche Tohmatsu International, 9; 29 (upd.)
Ernst & Young Global Limited, 9; 29 (upd.); 108 (upd.)
FTI Consulting, Inc., 77
Grant Thornton International, 57
Huron Consulting Group Inc., 87
JKH Holding Co. LLC, 105
KPMG International, 33 (upd.); 108 (upd.)
L.S. Starrett Co., 13
LarsonAllen, LLP, 118
McLane Company, Inc., 13
NCO Group, Inc., 42
Paychex Inc., 15; 46 (upd.); 120 (upd.)
PKF International, 78
Plante & Moran, LLP, 71
PRG-Schultz International, Inc., 73
PricewaterhouseCoopers International Limited, 9; 29 (upd.); 111 (upd.)
Resources Connection, Inc., 81
Robert Wood Johnson Foundation, 35
RSM McGladrey Business Services Inc., 98
Saffery Champness, 80
Sanders\Wingo, 99
Schenck Business Solutions, 88
StarTek, Inc., 79

Travelzoo Inc., 79
Univision Communications Inc., 24; 83 (upd.)

Advertising & Business Services

1-800-FLOWERS.COM, Inc., 26; 102 (upd.)
4imprint Group PLC, 105
24/7 Real Media, Inc., 49
ABM Industries Incorporated, 25 (upd.)
Abt Associates Inc., 95
Accenture Ltd., 108 (upd.)
AchieveGlobal Inc., 90
Ackerley Communications, Inc., 9
ACNielsen Corporation, 13; 38 (upd.)
Acosta Sales and Marketing Company, Inc., 77
Acsys, Inc., 44
Adecco S.A., 36 (upd.); 116 (upd.)
Adelman Travel Group, 105
Adia S.A., 6
Administaff, Inc., 52
The Advertising Council, Inc., 76
The Advisory Board Company, 80
Advo, Inc., 6; 53 (upd.)
Aegis Group plc, 6
Affiliated Computer Services, Inc., 61
Affinion Group, Inc., 121
AHL Services, Inc., 27
Alibaba.com, Ltd., 119
Allegis Group, Inc., 95
Alloy, Inc., 55
Amdocs Ltd., 47
American Building Maintenance Industries, Inc., 6
Amey Plc, 47
Analysts International Corporation, 36

aQuantive, Inc., 81
The Arbitron Company, 38
Ariba, Inc., 57
Armor Holdings, Inc., 27
Asatsu-DK Inc., 82
Ashtead Group plc, 34
Avalon Correctional Services, Inc., 75
Bain & Company, 55
Barrett Business Services, Inc., 16
Barton Protective Services Inc., 53
Bates Worldwide, Inc., 14; 33 (upd.)
Bearings, Inc., 13
Berlitz International, Inc., 13; 39 (upd.)
Bernard Hodes Group Inc., 86
Bernstein-Rein, 92
Big Flower Press Holdings, Inc., 21
Billing Concepts, Inc., 26; 72 (upd.)
Billing Services Group Ltd., 102
The BISYS Group, Inc., 73
bofrost Dienstleistungs GmbH and Company KG, 123
Booz Allen Hamilton Inc., 10; 101 (upd.)
Boron, LePore & Associates, Inc., 45
The Boston Consulting Group, 58
Bozell Worldwide Inc., 25
BrandPartners Group, Inc., 58
Bright Horizons Family Solutions, Inc., 31
Broadcast Music Inc., 23; 90 (upd.)
Bronner Display & Sign Advertising, Inc., 82
Buck Consultants, Inc., 55
Bureau Veritas SA, 55
Burke, Inc., 88
Burns International Services Corporation, 13; 41 (upd.)
Cambridge Technology Partners, Inc., 36
Campbell-Ewald Advertising, 86
Campbell-Mithun-Esty, Inc., 16
Cannon Design, 63

Aerospace

Agribusiness & Farming

Airlines

Beverages

Todhunter International, Inc., 27
Triarc Companies, Inc., 34 (upd.)
Trinchero Family Estates, 107 (upd.)
Tropicana Products, Inc., 73 (upd.)
Tsingtao Brewery Group, 49
Tully's Coffee Corporation, 51
Underberg AG, 92
Unilever, II; 7 (upd.); 32 (upd.); 89 (upd.)
Unión de Cervecerias Peruanas Backus y Johnston S.A.A., 92
V&S Vin & Sprit AB, 91 (upd.)
Van Houtte Inc., 39
Vermont Pure Holdings, Ltd., 51
Veuve Clicquot Ponsardin SCS, 98
Vin & Sprit AB, 31
Viña Concha y Toro S.A., 45
Viña San Pedro Tarapacá S.A., 119
Vincor International Inc., 50
Vinmonopolet A/S, 100
Vranken Pommery Monopole S.A., 114
Warsteiner Group, 113
Whitbread PLC, I; 20 (upd.); 52 (upd.); 97 (upd.)
Widmer Brothers Brewing Company, 76
Willamette Valley Vineyards, Inc., 85
William Grant & Sons Ltd., 60
Wine Group, Inc., The, 39; 114 (upd.)
Wolverhampton & Dudley Breweries, PLC, The, 57
Wray & Nephew Group Ltd., 98
Young & Co.'s Brewery, P.L.C., 38
Young's Market Company, LLC, 32; 118 (upd.)

Bio-Technology

Actelion Ltd., 83
Affymetrix Inc., 106
Agria Corporation, 101
Amersham PLC, 50
Amgen, Inc., 10; 30 (upd.)
ArQule, Inc., 68
Becton, Dickinson and Company, I; 11 (upd.); 36 (upd.); 101 (upd.)
Biogen Idec Inc., 14; 36 (upd.); 71 (upd.)
bioMérieux S.A., 75
Bio-Rad Laboratories, Inc., 93
Bio-Reference Laboratories, Inc., 122
BTG Plc, 87
Caliper Life Sciences, Inc., 70
Cambrex Corporation, 44 (upd.)
Cardiac Science Corporation, 121
Celera Genomics, 74
Centocor Inc., 14
Charles River Laboratories International, Inc., 42
Chiron Corporation, 10; 36 (upd.)
Covance Inc., 30; 98 (upd.)
CryoLife, Inc., 46
Cytyc Corporation, 69
Delta and Pine Land Company, 33
Dionex Corporation, 46
Dyax Corp., 89
Ebro Foods S.A., 118
Embrex, Inc., 72
Enzo Biochem, Inc., 41
eResearch Technology, Inc., 115
Eurofins Scientific S.A., 70

Genentech, Inc., 32 (upd.)
Gen-Probe Incorporated, 79
Genzyme Corporation, 38 (upd.)
Gilead Sciences, Inc., 54
Hindustan Lever Limited, 79
Howard Hughes Medical Institute, 39
Huntingdon Life Sciences Group plc, 42
IDEXX Laboratories, Inc., 23; 107 (upd.)
ImClone Systems Inc., 58
Immunex Corporation, 14; 50 (upd.)
IMPATH Inc., 45
Incyte Genomics, Inc., 52
Inverness Medical Innovations, Inc., 63
Invitrogen Corporation, 52
Judge Group, Inc., The, 51
Kendle International Inc., 87
Landec Corporation, 95
Life Technologies, Inc., 17
LifeCell Corporation, 77
Lonza Group Ltd., 73
Luminex Corporation, 122
Martek Biosciences Corporation, 65
Medarex, Inc., 85
Medtronic, Inc., 8; 30 (upd.); 67 (upd.)
Meridian Bioscience, Inc., 115
Millipore Corporation, 25; 84 (upd.)
Minntech Corporation, 22
Mycogen Corporation, 21
Nektar Therapeutics, 91
New Brunswick Scientific Co., Inc., 45
Novozymes A/S, 118
Omrix Biopharmaceuticals, Inc., 95
Pacific Ethanol, Inc., 81
Pharmion Corporation, 91
QIAGEN N.V., 39; 121 (upd.)
Quintiles Transnational Corporation, 21
RTI Biologics, Inc., 96
Seminis, Inc., 29
Senomyx, Inc., 83
Serologicals Corporation, 63
Sigma-Aldrich Corporation, I; 36 (upd.); 93 (upd.)
Starkey Laboratories, Inc., 52
STERIS Corporation, 29
Stratagene Corporation, 70
Talecris Biotherapeutics Holdings Corp., 114
Tanox, Inc., 77
TECHNE Corporation, 52
Trinity Biotech plc, 121
TriPath Imaging, Inc., 77
Viterra Inc., 105
Waters Corporation, 43
Whatman plc, 46
Wilmar International Ltd., 108
Wisconsin Alumni Research Foundation, 65
Wyeth, Inc., 50 (upd.); 118 (upd.)

Chemicals

A. Schulman, Inc., 8; 49 (upd.)
Aceto Corp., 38
Air Products and Chemicals, Inc., I; 10 (upd.); 74 (upd.)
Airgas, Inc., 54
Akzo Nobel N.V., 13; 41 (upd.); 112 (upd.)
Albaugh, Inc., 105

Albemarle Corporation, 59
AlliedSignal Inc., 9; 22 (upd.)
ALTANA AG, 87
American Cyanamid, I; 8 (upd.)
American Vanguard Corporation, 47
Arab Potash Company, 85
Arch Chemicals Inc., 78
ARCO Chemical Company, 10
Arkema S.A., 100
Asahi Denka Kogyo KK, 64
Atanor S.A., 62
Atochem S.A., I
Avantium Technologies BV, 79
Avecia Group PLC, 63
Azelis Group, 100
Baker Hughes Incorporated, III; 22 (upd.); 57 (upd.); 118 (upd.)
Balchem Corporation, 42
BASF SE, I; 18 (upd.); 50 (upd.); 108 (upd.)
Bayer AG, I; 13 (upd.); 41 (upd.); 118 (upd.)
Betz Laboratories, Inc., I; 10 (upd.)
BFGoodrich Company, The, 19 (upd.)
BOC Group plc, I; 25 (upd.); 78 (upd.)
BorsodChem Zrt., 113
Braskem S.A., 108
Brenntag Holding GmbH & Co. KG, 8; 23 (upd.); 101 (upd.)
Burmah Castrol PLC, 30 (upd.)
Cabot Corporation, 8; 29 (upd.); 91 (upd.)
Calgon Carbon Corporation, 73
Caliper Life Sciences, Inc., 70
Calumet Specialty Products Partners, L.P., 106
Cambrex Corporation, 16
Campbell Brothers Limited, 115
Catalytica Energy Systems, Inc., 44
Celanese Corporation, I; 109 (upd.)
Celanese Mexicana, S.A. de C.V., 54
CF Industries Holdings, Inc., 99
Chemcentral Corporation, 8
Chemi-Trol Chemical Co., 16
Chemtura Corporation, 91 (upd.)
China Petroleum & Chemical Corporation (Sinopec Corp.), 109
Church & Dwight Co., Inc., 29
Ciba-Geigy Ltd., I; 8 (upd.)
Clariant Ltd., 123
Clorox Company, The, III; 22 (upd.); 81 (upd.)
Croda International Plc, 45
Crompton Corporation, 9; 36 (upd.)
CVR Energy Corporation, 116
Cytec Industries Inc., 27
Degussa-Hüls AG, 32 (upd.)
DeKalb Genetics Corporation, 17
Dexter Corporation, The, I; 12 (upd.)
Dionex Corporation, 46
Dow Chemical Company, The, I; 8 (upd.); 50 (upd.); 114 (upd.)
DSM N.V., I; 56 (upd.)
Dynaction S.A., 67
E.I. du Pont de Nemours & Company, I; 8 (upd.); 26 (upd.); 73 (upd.)
Eastman Chemical Company, 14; 38 (upd.); 116 (upd.)

Conglomerates

Construction

Education & Training

Electrical & Electronics

Foxconn Technology Co., Ltd., 121
Freescale Semiconductor, Inc., 83
Frequency Electronics, Inc., 61
FuelCell Energy, Inc., 75
Fuji Electric Co., Ltd., II; 48 (upd.)
Fuji Photo Film Co., Ltd., 79 (upd.)
Fujitsu Limited, III; 16 (upd.); 42 (upd.);
    103 (upd.)
Funai Electric Company Ltd., 62
Galtronics Ltd., 100
Gateway, Inc., 63 (upd.)
Gemini Sound Products Corporation, 58
General Atomics, 57; 112 (upd.)
General Dynamics Corporation, I; 10
    (upd.); 40 (upd.); 88 (upd.
General Electric Company, II; 12 (upd.)
General Electric Company, PLC, II
General Instrument Corporation, 10
General Signal Corporation, 9
Genesis Microchip Inc., 82
GenRad, Inc., 24
GM Hughes Electronics Corporation, II
Goldstar Co., Ltd., 12
Gould Electronics, Inc., 14
GPS Industries, Inc., 81
Graybar Electric Company, Inc., 54; 123
    (upd.)
Grote Industries, Inc., 121
Grundig AG, 27
Guillemot Corporation, 41
Hadco Corporation, 24
Hamilton Beach/Proctor-Silex Inc., 17
Harman International Industries,
    Incorporated, 15; 101 (upd.)
Harmonic Inc., 109 (upd.)
Harris Corporation, II; 20 (upd.); 78
    (upd.)
Hayes Corporation, 24
Hemisphere GPS Inc., 99
Herley Industries, Inc., 33
Hewlett-Packard Company, 28 (upd.); 50
    (upd.); 111 (upd.)'
High Tech Computer Corporation, 81
Hitachi, Ltd., I; 12 (upd.); 40 (upd.); 108
    (upd.)
Hittite Microwave Corporation, 106
Holophane Corporation, 19
Hon Hai Precision Industry Company,
    Ltd., 59; 117 (upd.)
HON INDUSTRIES Inc., 13
Honeywell International Inc., II; 12
    (upd.); 50 (upd.); 109 (upd.)
Hubbell Inc., 9; 31 (upd.); 76 (upd.)
Hughes Supply, Inc., 14
Hutchinson Technology Incorporated, 18;
    63 (upd.)
Hynix Semiconductor Company Ltd., 111
Hypercom Corporation, 27
IDEO Inc., 65
IEC Electronics Corp., 42
Illumina, Inc., 93
Imax Corporation, 28
Immersion Corporation, 124
In Focus Systems, Inc., 22
Indigo NV, 26
InFocus Corporation, 92
Ingram Micro Inc., 52
Innovative Solutions & Support, Inc., 85

Inphi Corporation, 124
Integrated Defense Technologies, Inc., 54
Intel Corporation, II; 10 (upd.); 75 (upd.)
Intermec Technologies Corporation, 72
International Business Machines
    Corporation, III; 6 (upd.); 30 (upd.);
    63 (upd.)
International Electric Supply Corp., 113
International Rectifier Corporation, 31; 71
    (upd.)
Intersil Corporation, 93
Ionatron, Inc., 85
Itel Corporation, 9
Jabil Circuit, Inc., 36; 88 (upd.)
Jaco Electronics, Inc., 30
JDS Uniphase Corporation, 34
Johnson Controls, Inc., III; 26 (upd.); 59
    (upd.); 110 (upd.)
Juniper Networks, Inc., 122 (upd.)
Juno Lighting, Inc., 30
Katy Industries, Inc., I; 51 (upd.)
Keithley Instruments Inc., 16
KEMET Corporation, 14; 124 (upd.)
Kent Electronics Corporation, 17
Kenwood Corporation, 31
Kesa Electricals plc, 91
Kimball International, Inc., 12; 48 (upd.)
Kingston Technology Company, Inc., 20;
    112 (upd.)
KitchenAid, 8
KLA-Tencor Corporation, 45 (upd.)
KnowledgeWare Inc., 9
Kollmorgen Corporation, 18
Konami Corporation, 96
Konica Corporation, III; 30 (upd.)
Koninklijke Philips Electronics N.V., 50
    (upd.); 119 (upd.)
Koor Industries Ltd., II
Kopin Corporation, 80
Koss Corporation, 38
Kudelski Group SA, 44
Kulicke and Soffa Industries, Inc., 33; 76
    (upd.)
Kyocera Corporation, II; 21 (upd.); 79
    (upd.)
L-3 Communications Holdings, Inc., 111
    (upd.)
LaBarge Inc., 41
Lamson & Sessions Co., The, 13; 61
    (upd.)
Lattice Semiconductor Corp., 16
LDK Solar Co., Ltd., 101
LeCroy Corporation, 41
Legrand SA, 21
Lenovo Group Ltd., 80
Leoni AG, 98
Lexmark International, Inc., 18; 79 (upd.)
Linear Technology Corporation, 16; 99
    (upd.)
Littelfuse, Inc., 26
Loewe AG, 90
Loral Corporation, 9
LOUD Technologies, Inc., 95 (upd.)
Lowrance Electronics, Inc., 18
LSI Logic Corporation, 13; 64
Lucent Technologies Inc., 34
Lucky-Goldstar, II
Lunar Corporation, 29

Lynch Corporation, 43
Mackie Designs Inc., 33
MagneTek, Inc., 15; 41 (upd.)
Magneti Marelli Holding SpA, 90
Marconi plc, 33 (upd.)
Marquette Electronics, Inc., 13
Marshall Amplification plc, 62
Marvell Technology Group Ltd., 112
Matsushita Electric Industrial Co., Ltd.,
    II; 64 (upd.)
Maxim Integrated Products, Inc., 16
McDATA Corporation, 75
Measurement Specialties, Inc., 71
Medis Technologies Ltd., 77
MEMC Electronic Materials, Inc., 81
Merix Corporation, 36; 75 (upd.)
Methode Electronics, Inc., 13
Micrel, Incorporated, 77
Midway Games, Inc., 25; 102 (upd.)
MIPS Technologies, Inc., 124
Mirion Technologies, Inc., 124
Mitel Corporation, 18
MITRE Corporation, 26
Mitsubishi Electric Corporation, II; 44
    (upd.); 117 (upd.)
Molex Incorporated, 11; 54 (upd.)
Monster Cable Products, Inc., 69
Motorola, Inc., II; 11 (upd.); 34 (upd.);
    93 (upd.)
N.F. Smith & Associates LP, 70
Nam Tai Electronics, Inc., 61
National Instruments Corporation, 22
National Presto Industries, Inc., 16; 43
    (upd.)
National Semiconductor Corporation, II;
    26 (upd.); 69 (upd.)
NEC Corporation, II; 21 (upd.); 57
    (upd.)
Network Equipment Technologies Inc., 92
Nexans SA, 54
Nintendo Company, Ltd., III; 7 (upd.);
    28 (upd.); 67 (upd.)
Nokia Corporation, II; 17 (upd.); 38
    (upd.); 77 (upd.)
Nortel Networks Corporation, 36 (upd.)
Northrop Grumman Corporation, 45
    (upd.); 111 (upd.)
Oak Technology, Inc., 22
Océ N.V., 24; 91 (upd.)
Oki Electric Industry Company, Limited,
    II
Omnicell, Inc., 89
OMRON Corporation, II; 28 (upd.); 115
    (upd.)
Onvest Oy, 117
Oplink Communications, Inc., 106
OPTEK Technology Inc., 98
Orbit International Corp., 105
Orbotech Ltd., 75
Otari Inc., 89
Otter Tail Power Company, 18
Pacific Aerospace & Electronics, Inc., 120
Palm, Inc., 36; 75 (upd.)
Palomar Medical Technologies, Inc., 22
Parlex Corporation, 61
Peak Technologies Group, Inc., The, 14
Peavey Electronics Corporation, 16
Philips Electronics N.V., II; 13 (upd.)

Engineering & Management Services

Entertainment & Leisure

Financial Services: Banks

International Assets Holding Corporation, 111

Inter-Regional Financial Group, Inc., 15

Investcorp SA, 57

Island ECN, Inc., The, 48

Istituto per la Ricostruzione Industriale S.p.A., 11

J. & W. Seligman & Co. Inc., 61

JAFCO Co. Ltd., 79

Janus Capital Group Inc., 57

JB Oxford Holdings, Inc., 32

Jefferies Group, Inc., 25

John Hancock Financial Services, Inc., 42 (upd.)

John Nuveen Company, The, 21

Jones Lang LaSalle Incorporated, 49

Jordan Company LP, The, 70

JTH Tax Inc., 103

Kansas City Southern Industries, Inc., 26 (upd.)

Kleiner, Perkins, Caufield & Byers, 53

Kleinwort Benson Group PLC, II

Knight Trading Group, Inc., 70

Kohlberg Kravis Roberts & Co. L.P., 24; 56 (upd.); 115 (upd.)

KPMG Worldwide, 10

La Poste, V; 47 (upd.); 109 (upd.)

LaBranche & Co. Inc., 37

Lazard LLC, 38; 121 (upd.)

Legal & General Group Plc, III; 24 (upd.); 101 (upd.)

Legg Mason, Inc., 33; 110 (upd.)

Lehman Brothers Holdings Inc. (updates Shearson Lehman), 99 (upd.)

LendingTree, LLC, 93

LifeLock, Inc., 91

Lilly Endowment Inc., 70

Liquidnet, Inc., 79

London Scottish Bank plc, 70

London Stock Exchange Limited, 34

M.H. Meyerson & Co., Inc., 46

M.R. Beal and Co., 102

MacAndrews & Forbes Holdings Inc., 28; 86 (upd.)

Madison Dearborn Partners, LLC, 97

Man Group PLC, 106

MasterCard Worldwide, 9; 96 (upd.)

MBNA Corporation, 33 (upd.)

Merrill Lynch & Co., Inc., II; 13 (upd.); 40 (upd.)

Metris Companies Inc., 56

Morgan Grenfell Group PLC, II

Morgan Stanley Dean Witter & Company, II; 16 (upd.); 33 (upd.)

Mountain States Mortgage Centers, Inc., 29

NASD, 54 (upd.)

NASDAQ Stock Market, Inc., The, 92

National Association of Securities Dealers, Inc., 10

National Auto Credit, Inc., 16

National Discount Brokers Group, Inc., 28

National Financial Partners Corp., 65

Navy Federal Credit Union, 33

Neuberger Berman Inc., 57

New Enterprise Associates, 116

New Street Capital Inc., 8

New York Stock Exchange, Inc., 9; 39 (upd.)

Newedge Group S.A., 122

Nikko Securities Company Limited, The, II; 9 (upd.)

Nippon Shinpan Co., Ltd., II; 61 (upd.)

Nomura Securities Company, Limited, II; 9 (upd.)

Norwich & Peterborough Building Society, 55

NovaStar Financial, Inc., 91

Oaktree Capital Management, LLC, 71

Old Mutual PLC, 61

Ontario Teachers' Pension Plan, 61

Onyx Acceptance Corporation, 59

ORIX Corporation, II; 44 (upd.); 104 (upd.)

PaineWebber Group Inc., II; 22 (upd.)

PayPal Inc., 58

Piedmont Investment Advisors, LLC, 106

Piper Jaffray Companies, 22; 107 (upd.)

Pitney Bowes Inc., III; 19 (upd.); 47 (upd.)

PLS Financial Services, 119

Providian Financial Corporation, 52 (upd.)

Prudential Financial Inc., III; 30 (upd.); 82 (upd.)

Quick & Reilly Group, Inc., The, 20

Quicken Loans, Inc., 93

Rathbone Brothers plc, 70

Raymond James Financial Inc., 69

Resource America, Inc., 42

Robert W. Baird & Co. Incorporated, 67

Royal Gold, Inc., 117

Ryan Beck & Co., Inc., 66

Safeguard Scientifics, Inc., 10

St. James's Place Capital, plc, 71

Salomon Inc., II; 13 (upd.)

Sanders Morris Harris Group Inc., 70

Sanlam Ltd., 68

SBC Warburg, 14

Schroders plc, 42; 112 (upd.)

Scottrade, Inc., 85

SEI Investments Company, 96

Shearson Lehman Brothers Holdings Inc., II; 9 (upd.)

Siebert Financial Corp., 32

Skipton Building Society, 80

SLM Corp., 25 (upd.); 116 (upd.)

Smith Barney Inc., 15

Soros Fund Management LLC, 28

Spear, Leeds & Kellogg, 66

State Street Boston Corporation, 8

Stephens Inc., 92

Student Loan Marketing Association, II

Sun Life Financial Inc., 85

T. Rowe Price Group, Inc., 11; 34 (upd.); 122 (upd.)

Teachers Insurance and Annuity Association-College Retirement Equities Fund, 45 (upd.)

Texas Pacific Group Inc., 36

Thrivent Financial for Lutherans, 111 (upd.)

Total System Services, Inc., 18

TradeStation Group, Inc., 83

Trilon Financial Corporation, II

United Jewish Communities, 33

United Services Automobile Association, 109 (upd.)

USAA, 10; 62 (upd.)

Vanguard Group, Inc., The, 14; 34 (upd.)

Verband der Vereine Creditreform e. V., 117

VeriFone Holdings, Inc., 18; 76 (upd.)

VicSuper Pty Ltd, 124

Viel & Cie, 76

Visa Inc., 9; 26 (upd.); 104 (upd.)

Wachovia Corporation, 12; 46 (upd.)

Waddell & Reed, Inc., 22

Washington Federal, Inc., 17

Waterhouse Investor Services, Inc., 18

Watson Wyatt Worldwide, 42

Western Alliance Bancorporation, 119

Western Union Company, 112 (upd.)

Western Union Financial Services, Inc., 54

WFS Financial Inc., 70

Working Assets Funding Service, 43

World Acceptance Corporation, 57

Wyllie Group Pty Ltd, 124

Yamaichi Securities Company, Limited, II

Ziegler Companies, Inc., The, 24; 63 (upd.)

Zurich Financial Services, 42 (upd.); 93 (upd.)

Food Products

A. Duda & Sons, Inc., 88

A. Moksel AG, 59

Aachener Printen- und Schokoladenfabrik Henry Lambertz GmbH & Co. KG, 110

Aarhus United A/S, 68

Adecoagro LLC, 101

Agri Beef Company, 81

Agway, Inc., 7

Ajinomoto Co., Inc., II; 28 (upd.); 108 (upd.)

Alabama Farmers Cooperative, Inc., 63

Albert Fisher Group plc, The, 41

Alberto-Culver Company, 8; 36 (upd.); 91 (upd.)

Albert's Organics, Inc., 110

Alfesca hf, 82

Alfred Ritter GmbH & Co. KG, 58

Allen Brothers, Inc., 101

Allen Canning Company, 76

Alpine Confections, Inc., 71

Alpine Lace Brands, Inc., 18

American Crystal Sugar Company, 11; 32 (upd.)

American Foods Group, 43

American Italian Pasta Company, 27; 76 (upd.)

American Licorice Company, 86

American Maize-Products Co., 14

American Pop Corn Company, 59

American Rice, Inc., 33

Amfac/JMB Hawaii L.L.C., 24 (upd.)

Amy's Kitchen Inc., 76

Annie's Homegrown, Inc., 59

Archer-Daniels-Midland Company, 32 (upd.)

Archway Cookies, Inc., 29

Arcor S.A.I.C., 66

Food Services, Retailers, & Restaurants

Health, Personal & Medical Care Products

Health Care Services

Hotels

Information Technology

Insurance

HCC Insurance Holdings Inc., 116
HDI (Haftpflichtverband der Deutschen Industrie Versicherung auf Gegenseitigkeit V.a.G.), 53
HealthExtras, Inc., 75
HealthMarkets, Inc., 88 (upd.)
Hilb, Rogal & Hobbs Company, 77
Home Insurance Company, The, III
Horace Mann Educators Corporation, 22; 90 (upd.)
Household International, Inc., 21 (upd.)
Hub International Limited, 89
HUK-Coburg, 58
Humana Inc., III; 24 (upd.); 101 (upd.)
Humphrey Products Company, 110
Inventec Corp., 113
Irish Life & Permanent Plc, 59
Jackson National Life Insurance Company, 8
Japan Post Holdings Company Ltd., 108
Jefferson-Pilot Corporation, 11; 29 (upd.)
John Hancock Financial Services, Inc., III; 42 (upd.)
Johnson & Higgins, 14
Kemper Corporation, III; 15 (upd.)
LandAmerica Financial Group, Inc., 85
Legal & General Group Plc, III; 24 (upd.); 101 (upd.)
Liberty Corporation, The, 22
Liberty Mutual Holding Company, 59
Libya Insurance Company, 124
LifeWise Health Plan of Oregon, Inc., 90
Lincoln National Corporation, III; 25 (upd.); 113 (upd.)
Lloyd's, 74 (upd.)
Lloyd's of London, III; 22 (upd.)
Loewen Group Inc., The, 40 (upd.)
Lutheran Brotherhood, 31
Manulife Financial Corporation, 85
Mapfre S.A., 109
Markel Corporation, 116
Marsh & McLennan Companies, Inc., III; 45 (upd.); 123 (upd.)
Massachusetts Mutual Life Insurance Company, III; 53 (upd.)
MBIA Inc., 73
Meiji Mutual Life Insurance Company, The, III
Mercury General Corporation, 25
Metropolitan Life Insurance Company, III; 52 (upd.)
MGIC Investment Corp., 52
Midland Company, The, 65
Millea Holdings Inc., 64 (upd.)
Mitsui Marine and Fire Insurance Company, Limited, III
Mitsui Mutual Life Insurance Company, III; 39 (upd.)
Modern Woodmen of America, 66
Munich Re (Münchener Rückversicherungs-Gesellschaft Aktiengesellschaft in München), III; 46 (upd.)
Mutual Benefit Life Insurance Company, The, III
Mutual Life Insurance Company of New York, The, III
Mutual of Omaha Companies, The, 98

Mutuelle Assurance des Commerçants et Industriels de France, 107
N.V. AMEV, III
National Medical Health Card Systems, Inc., 79
Nationale-Nederlanden N.V., III
Nationwide Mutual Insurance Company, 108
Navigators Group, Inc., The, 92
New England Mutual Life Insurance Company, III
New Jersey Manufacturers Insurance Company, 96
New York Life Insurance Company, III; 45 (upd.); 118 (upd.)
Nippon Life Insurance Company, III; 60 (upd.)
The Northwestern Mutual Life Insurance Company, III; 45 (upd.); 118 (upd.)
NYMAGIC, Inc., 41
Ohio Casualty Corp., 11
Ohio National Financial Services, Inc., 118
Old Republic International Corporation, 11; 58 (upd.)
Oregon Dental Service Health Plan, Inc., 51
Pacific Mutual Holding Company, 98
Palmer & Cay, Inc., 69
Pan-American Life Insurance Company, 48
PartnerRe Ltd., 83
Paul Revere Corporation, The, 12
Pennsylvania Blue Shield, III
The Phoenix Companies, Inc., 115
PMI Group, Inc., The, 49
Preserver Group, Inc., 44
Principal Financial Group Inc., 116
Principal Mutual Life Insurance Company, III
Progressive Corporation, The, 11; 29 (upd.); 109 (upd.)
Provident Life and Accident Insurance Company of America, III
Prudential Financial Inc., III; 30 (upd.); 82 (upd.)
Prudential plc, III; 48 (upd.)
Radian Group Inc., 42
Regence Group, The, 74
Reliance Group Holdings, Inc., III
Riunione Adriatica di Sicurtà SpA, III
Royal & Sun Alliance Insurance Group plc, 55 (upd.)
Royal Insurance Holdings PLC, III
SAFECO Corporaton, III
Sagicor Life Inc., 98
St. Paul Travelers Companies, Inc., The, III; 22 (upd.); 79 (upd.)
SCOR S.A., 20
Skandia Insurance Company, Ltd., 50
Sompo Japan Insurance, Inc., 98 (upd.)
StanCorp Financial Group, Inc., 56
Standard Life Assurance Company, The, III
State Auto Financial Corporation, 77
State Farm Mutual Automobile Insurance Company, III; 51 (upd.)
State Financial Services Corporation, 51

Stewart Information Services Corporation, 78
Sumitomo Life Insurance Company, III; 60 (upd.)
Sumitomo Marine and Fire Insurance Company, Limited, The, III
Sun Alliance Group PLC, III
Sun Life Financial Inc., 85
SunAmerica Inc., 11
Suncorp-Metway Ltd., 91
Suramericana de Inversiones S.A., 88
Svenska Handelsbanken AB, 50 (upd.)
Swett & Crawford Group Inc., The, 84
Swiss Reinsurance Company (Schweizerische Rückversicherungs-Gesellschaft), III; 46 (upd.)
T&D Holdings Inc., 114
Teachers Insurance and Annuity Association-College Retirement Equities Fund (TIAA-CREF), III; 45 (upd.); 119 (upd.)
Texas Industries, Inc., 8
Thrivent Financial for Lutherans, 111 (upd.)
TIG Holdings, Inc., 26
Tokio Marine and Fire Insurance Co., Ltd., The, III
Torchmark Corporation, 9; 33 (upd.); 115 (upd.)
Transatlantic Holdings, Inc., 11
Travelers Corporation, The, III
UICI, 33
Union des Assurances de Pans, III
United National Group, Ltd., 63
United Services Automobile Association, 109 (upd.)
Unitrin Inc., 16; 78 (upd.)
Universal American Corp., 111
UNUM Corp., 13
UnumProvident Corporation, 52 (upd.)
USAA, 10; 62 (upd.)
USF&G Corporation, III
UTG Inc., 100
Victoria Group, 44 (upd.)
VICTORIA Holding AG, III
Vision Service Plan Inc., 77
W.R. Berkley Corporation, 15; 74 (upd.)
Washington National Corporation, 12
Wawanesa Mutual Insurance Company, The, 68
WellCare Health Plans, Inc., 101
WellChoice, Inc., 67 (upd.)
WellPoint, Inc., 25; 103 (upd.)
Westfield Group, 69
White Mountains Insurance Group, Ltd., 48
Willis Group Holdings Ltd., 25; 100 (upd.)
Winterthur Group, III; 68 (upd.)
Wüstenrot & Württembergische AG, 121; 123
Yasuda Fire and Marine Insurance Company, Limited, The, III
Yasuda Mutual Life Insurance Company, The, III; 39 (upd.)
Zurich Financial Services, 42 (upd.); 93 (upd.)

Zürich Versicherungs-Gesellschaft, III

Legal Services

Manufacturing

Jenoptik AG, 33
Jervis B. Webb Company, 24
Johns Manville Corporation, 64 (upd.)
Johnson Outdoors Inc., 28; 84 (upd.)
Johnstown America Industries, Inc., 23
Jotun A/S, 80
JSP Corporation, 74
Jungheinrich AG, 96
Kaman Corporation, 12; 42 (upd.)
Kansai Paint Company Ltd., 80
Karsten Manufacturing Corporation, 51
Kaydon Corporation, 18; 117 (upd.)
KB Toys, Inc., 35 (upd.); 86 (upd.)
Kelly-Moore Paint Company, Inc., 56;
112 (upd.)
Kennametal Inc., 68 (upd.)
Keramik Holding AG Laufen, 51
Kewaunee Scientific Corporation, 25
Key Technology Inc., 106
Key Tronic Corporation, 14
Keystone International, Inc., 11
KHD Konzern, III
KI, 57
Kit Manufacturing Co., 18
Klein Tools, Inc., 95
Knape & Vogt Manufacturing Company,
17
Koala Corporation, 44
Koch Enterprises, Inc., 29
Kohler Company, 7; 32 (upd.); 108
(upd.)
Komatsu Ltd., 113 (upd.)
KONE Corporation, 27; 76 (upd.)
Korg, Inc., 111
KraftMaid Cabinetry, Inc., 72
Kreisler Manufacturing Corporation, 97
KSB AG, 62
Kwang Yang Motor Company Ltd., 80
L.A. Darling Company, 92
L.B. Foster Company, 33
L.S. Starrett Company, 64 (upd.)
Lacks Enterprises Inc., 61
LADD Furniture, Inc., 12
Ladish Company Inc., 30; 107 (upd.)
Lakeland Industries, Inc., 45
Lalique S.A., 123
Landauer, Inc., 51; 117 (upd.)
Lane Co., Inc., The, 12
La-Z-Boy Incorporated, 14; 50 (upd.)
Le Creuset S.A.S., 113
Leatherman Tool Group, Inc., 51
Leggett & Platt, Inc., 11; 48 (upd.); 111
(upd.)
Leica Camera AG, 35
Leica Microsystems Holdings GmbH, 35
Lennox International Inc., 8; 28 (upd.)
Lenox, Inc., 12
Liebherr-International AG, 64
Linamar Corporation, 18; 114 (upd.)
Lincoln Electric Co., 13
Lindsay Manufacturing Co., 20
Line 6, Inc., 117
Lionel L.L.C., 16; 99 (upd.)
Lipman Electronic Engineering Ltd., 81
Little Tikes Company, 13; 62 (upd.)
Loctite Corporation, 8
Lodge Manufacturing Company, 103
LoJack Corporation, 48; 120 (upd.)

Longaberger Company, The, 12; 44 (upd.)
LSB Industries, Inc., 77
Lucas Industries PLC, III
Lucite International, Limited, 121
Lydall, Inc., 64
M.A. Bruder & Sons, Inc., 56
Mabuchi Motor Co. Ltd., 68
Mace Security International, Inc., 57
Mace Security International, Inc., 124
(upd.)
Madeco S.A., 71
Madison-Kipp Corporation, 58
Mag Instrument, Inc., 67
Makita Corporation, 22; 59 (upd.)
Manhattan Group, LLC, 80
Manitou BF S.A., 27
The Manitowoc Company, Inc., 18; 59
(upd.); 118 (upd.)
Margarete Steiff GmbH, 23
Mark IV Industries, Inc., 7; 28 (upd.)
Martin Industries, Inc., 44
Masco Corporation, III; 20 (upd.); 39
(upd.); 111 (upd.)
Masonite International Corporation, 63
Master Lock Company, 45
Master Spas Inc., 105
MasterBrand Cabinets, Inc., 71
Mattel, Inc., 7; 25 (upd.); 61 (upd.)
Matthews International Corporation, 29;
77 (upd.)
Maverick Tube Corporation, 59
Maytag Corporation, III; 22 (upd.); 82
(upd.)
MBI Inc., 120
McKechnie plc, 34
McWane Corporation, 55
Meade Instruments Corporation, 41
Meadowcraft, Inc., 29; 100 (upd.)
Mecalux S.A., 74
Meguiar's, Inc., 99
Meidensha Corporation, 92
Melissa & Doug, LLC, 123
Memry Corporation, 72
Mentor Corporation, 26; 123 (upd.)
Mercury Marine Group, 68
Merillat Industries, LLC, 13; 69 (upd.)
Mestek Inc., 10
MetoKote Corporation, 120
Mettler-Toledo International Inc., 30; 108
(upd.)
Meyer International Holdings, Ltd., 87
MGA Entertainment, Inc., 95
Microdot Inc., 8
Miele & Cie. KG, 56
Mikasa, Inc., 28
Milacron, Inc., 53 (upd.)
Mine Safety Appliances Company, 31
Minebea Co., Ltd., 90
Miner Enterprises, Inc., 124
Minolta Co., Ltd., III; 18 (upd.); 43
(upd.)
Minuteman International Inc., 46
Misonix, Inc., 80
Mitsubishi Heavy Industries, Ltd., III; 7
(upd.); 40 (upd.); 120 (upd.)
Mity Enterprises, Inc., 38
Mocon, Inc., 76

Modine Manufacturing Company, 8; 56
(upd.)
Moelven Industrier ASA, 110
Moen Inc., 12; 106 (upd.)
Mohawk Industries, Inc., 19; 63 (upd.)
Monnaie de Paris, 62
Montblanc International GmbH, 82
Montres Rolex S.A., 13; 34 (upd.)
Morgan Crucible Company plc, The, 82
Moulinex S.A., 22
Movado Group, Inc., 28; 107 (upd.)
Mr. Coffee, Inc., 15
Mr. Gasket Inc., 15
MTD Products Inc., 107
Mueller Water Products, Inc., 113
Multi-Color Corporation, 53
Musco Lighting, 83
MXL Industries, Inc., 120
National Picture & Frame Company, 24
National Standard Co., 13
NCI Building Systems, Inc., 88
Neenah Foundry Company, 68
Newcor, Inc., 40
Newell Rubbermaid Inc., 9; 52 (upd.);
120 (upd.)
Newport Corporation, 71
NGK Insulators Ltd., 67
NHK Spring Co., Ltd., III
Nidec Corporation, 59
Nikon Corporation, III; 48 (upd.)
Nippon Electric Glass Co. Ltd., 95
Nippon Paint Company Ltd., 115
Nippon Seiko K.K., III
Nobia AB, 103
The NORDAM Group, Inc., 121
Nordex AG, 101
NordicTrack, 22
Nordson Corporation, 11; 48 (upd.)
Norton Company, 8
Novellus Systems, Inc., 18
NSS Enterprises Inc., 78
NTK Holdings Inc., 107 (upd.)
NTN Corporation, III; 47 (upd.)
Nu-kote Holding, Inc., 18
Nypro, Inc., 101
Oak Industries Inc., 21
Oakwood Homes Corporation, 15
Ocean Bio-Chem, Inc., 103
ODL, Inc., 55
Ohio Art Company, The, 14; 59 (upd.)
Oil-Dri Corporation of America, 20; 89
(upd.)
Oilgear Company, The, 74
Okuma Holdings Inc., 74
Oldcastle, Inc., 113
Oldenburg Group Inc., 113
Olympus Corporation, 106
Oneida Ltd., 7; 31 (upd.); 88 (upd.)
Optische Werke G. Rodenstock, 44
Orange Glo International, 53
Oreck Corporation, 110
Osmonics, Inc., 18
Osram GmbH, 86
O'Sullivan Industries Holdings, Inc., 34
Otis Elevator Company, Inc., 13; 39
(upd.)
Outboard Marine Corporation, III; 20
(upd.)

Mining & Metals

Acindar Industria Argentina de Aceros
S.A., 87
African Rainbow Minerals Ltd., 97
Aggregate Industries plc, 36
Agnico-Eagle Mines Limited, 71
AIA Engineering Ltd., 119
AK Steel Holding Corporation, 122
(upd.)
Aktiebolaget SKF, III; 38 (upd.); 89
(upd.)
Alcan Aluminium Limited, IV; 31 (upd.)
Alcoa Inc., 56 (upd.)
Aleris International, Inc., 110
Alleghany Corporation, 10
Allegheny Ludlum Corporation, 8
Allegheny Technologies Incorporated, 112
(upd.)
Alliance Resource Partners, L.P., 81
Alrosa Company Ltd., 62
Altos Hornos de México, S.A. de C.V., 42
Aluar Aluminio Argentino S.A.I.C., 74
Aluminum Company of America, IV; 20
(upd.)
AMAX Inc., IV
AMCOL International Corporation, 59
(upd.)
Ampco-Pittsburgh Corporation, 79
Amsted Industries Incorporated, 7
Angang Steel Company Ltd., 117
Anglo American Corporation of South
Africa Limited, IV; 16 (upd.)
Anglo American PLC, 50 (upd.); 118
(upd.)
Aquarius Platinum Ltd., 63
ARBED S.A., IV; 22 (upd.)
Arcelor Gent, 80
ArcelorMittal, 108
Arch Coal Inc., 98
Arch Mineral Corporation, 7
Armco Inc., IV
ASARCO Incorporated, IV
Ashanti Goldfields Company Limited, 43
Atchison Casting Corporation, 39
Aubert & Duval S.A.S., 107
Barrick Gold Corporation, 34; 112 (upd.)
Battle Mountain Gold Company, 23
Benguet Corporation, 58
Bethlehem Steel Corporation, IV; 7
(upd.); 27 (upd.)
BHP Billiton, 67 (upd.)
Birmingham Steel Corporation, 13; 40
(upd.)
Boart Longyear Company, 26
Bodycote International PLC, 63
BÖHLER-UDDEHOLM AG, 73
Boliden AB, 80
Boral Limited, III; 43 (upd.); 103 (upd.)
British Coal Corporation, IV
British Steel plc, IV; 19 (upd.)
Broken Hill Proprietary Company Ltd.,
IV, 22 (upd.)
Brush Engineered Materials Inc., 67
Brush Wellman Inc., 14
Bucyrus International, Inc., 17; 103
(upd.)
Buderus AG, 37
California Steel Industries, Inc., 67
Cameco Corporation, 77

Campbell Brothers Limited, 115
Caparo Group Ltd., 90
Carpenter Technology Corporation, 13;
95 (upd.)
CEMEX, S.A.B. de C.V., 122 (upd.)
Centamin Egypt Limited, 119
Chaparral Steel Co., 13
Charter Manufacturing Company, Inc.,
103
China Shenhua Energy Company
Limited, 83
Christensen Boyles Corporation, 26
CITIC Pacific Ltd., 116 (upd.)
Cleveland-Cliffs Inc., 13; 62 (upd.)
Cloud Peak Energy Inc., 116
Coal India Limited, IV; 44 (upd.); 115
(upd.)
Cockerill Sambre Group, IV; 26 (upd.)
Coeur d'Alene Mines Corporation, 20
Cold Spring Granite Company Inc., 16;
67 (upd.)
Cominco Ltd., 37
Commercial Metals Company, 15; 42
(upd.)
Companhia Siderúrgica Nacional, 76
Compañia de Minas Buenaventura S.A.A.,
93
CONSOL Energy Inc., 59
Corporacion Nacional del Cobre de Chile,
40
Corus Group plc, 49 (upd.)
CRA Limited, IV
Cyprus Amax Minerals Company, 21
Cyprus Minerals Company, 7
Daido Steel Co., Ltd., IV
De Beers Consolidated Mines Limited/De
Beers Centenary AG, IV; 7 (upd.); 28
(upd.)
Debswana Diamond Company Proprietary
Limited, 124
Degussa Group, IV
Diavik Diamond Mines Inc., 85
Dofasco Inc., IV; 24 (upd.)
Duro Felguera S.A., 120
Dynatec Corporation, 87
Earle M. Jorgensen Company, 82
Echo Bay Mines Ltd., IV; 38 (upd.)
Eldorado Gold Corporation, 122
Empire Industries Ltd., 114
Engelhard Corporation, IV
Eramet, 73
Evergreen Energy, Inc., 97
Evraz Group S.A., 97
Falconbridge Limited, 49
Fansteel Inc., 19
Fluor Corporation, 34 (upd.)
Freeport-McMoRan Copper & Gold, Inc.,
IV; 7 (upd.); 57 (upd.)
Fried. Krupp GmbH, IV
Gencor Ltd., IV, 22 (upd.)
Geneva Steel, 7
Georg Jensen A/S, 110
Gerdau S.A., 59
Glamis Gold, Ltd., 54
Gold Fields Ltd., IV; 62 (upd.)
Goldcorp Inc., 87
Golden Star Resources Ltd., 117
Grupo Mexico, S.A. de C.V., 40

Gruppo Riva Fire SpA, 88
Handy & Harman, 23
Hanson Building Materials America Inc.,
60
Hanson PLC, III; 7 (upd.); 30 (upd.)
Hanwa Company Ltd., 123
Harmony Gold Mining Company
Limited, 63
Harsco Corporation, 8; 105 (upd.)
Haynes International, Inc., 88
Hebei Iron & Steel Group, 111
Hecla Mining Company, 20
Hemlo Gold Mines Inc., 9
Heraeus Holding GmbH, IV; 54 (upd.)
Highland Gold Mining Limited, 95
Highveld Steel and Vanadium
Corporation Limited, 59
Hitachi Metals, Ltd., IV
Hoesch AG, IV
Homestake Mining Company, 12; 38
(upd.)
Horsehead Industries, Inc., 51
Hudson Bay Mining and Smelting
Company, Limited, The, 12
Hylsamex, S.A. de C.V., 39
IAMGOLD Corp., 117
Imatra Steel Oy Ab, 55
IMCO Recycling, Incorporated, 32
Imerys S.A., 40 (upd.)
Imetal S.A., IV
Inco Limited, IV; 45 (upd.)
Indel Inc., 78
Industrias Peñoles, S.A. de C.V., 22; 107
(upd.)
Inland Steel Industries, Inc., IV; 19 (upd.)
INTERMET Corporation, 32; 77 (upd.)
Iscor Limited, 57
Ispat Inland Inc., 30; 40 (upd.)
JFE Shoji Holdings Inc., 88
Jiangsu Shagang Group Company Ltd.,
117
Johnson Matthey PLC, IV; 16 (upd.); 49
(upd.)
Joy Global Inc., 104 (upd.)
JSC MMC Norilsk Nickel, 48
K+S Aktiengesellschaft, 112
K.A. Rasmussen AS, 99
Kaiser Aluminum Corporation, IV; 84
(upd.)
Kawasaki Heavy Industries, Ltd., III; 63
(upd.)
Kawasaki Steel Corporation, IV
Kennecott Corporation, 7; 27 (upd.)
Kentucky Electric Steel, Inc., 31
Kerr-McGee Corporation, 22 (upd.)
KGHM Polska Miedz S.A., 98
Kiewit Corporation, 116 (upd.)
Kinross Gold Corporation, 36; 109 (upd.)
Klockner-Werke AG, IV
Kobe Steel, Ltd., IV; 19 (upd.); 109
(upd.)
Koninklijke Nederlandsche Hoogovens en
Staalfabrieken NV, IV
Laclede Steel Company, 15
Layne Christensen Company, 19
Lonmin plc, 66 (upd.)
Lonrho Plc, 21
LTV Corporation, The, I; 24 (upd.)

Nonprofit & Philanthropic Organizations

Easter Seals, Inc., 58
EMILY's List, 109
Feed The Children, Inc., 68
Feeding America, 120 (upd.)
Food For The Poor, Inc., 77
Ford Foundation, The, 34
Gifts In Kind International, 101
Girl Scouts of the USA, 35
Goodwill Industries International, Inc.,
    16; 66 (upd.)
Greenpeace International, 74
Harlem Children's Zone, Inc., 121
Heifer Project International, 112
Heritage Foundation, The, 114
Humane Society of the United States,
    The, 54
International Brotherhood of Teamsters,
    37; 115 (upd.)
International Youth Hostel Federation,
    118
J. Paul Getty Trust, The, 105
John D. and Catherine T. MacArthur
    Foundation, The, 34
John Simon Guggenheim Memorial
    Foundation, 118
Knights of Columbus, 120
Lance Armstrong Foundation, Inc., 111
Make-A-Wish Foundation of America, 97
March of Dimes, 31
Médecins sans Frontières, 85
Mothers Against Drunk Driving
    (MADD), 51
National Association for the Advancement
    of Colored People, 109
National Cattlemen's Beef Association,
    124
National Council of La Raza, 106
National Organization for Women, Inc.,
    55
National Rifle Association of America,
    The, 112 (upd.)
National Trust, The, 110
National Wildlife Federation, 103
Operation Smile, Inc., 75
Outward Bound USA, 111
Oxfam GB, 87
Pew Charitable Trusts, The, 35
RAND Corporation, 112
Recording for the Blind & Dyslexic, 51
Rockefeller Foundation, The, 34
Rotary International, 31
Salvation Army USA, The, 32
Smile Train, Inc., 122
Special Olympics, Inc., 93
Sundance Institute, 122
Susan G. Komen Breast Cancer
    Foundation, 78
Ten Thousand Villages U.S., 108
Theatre Development Fund, Inc., 109
United Nations International Children's
    Emergency Fund (UNICEF), 58
United Negro College Fund, Inc., 79
United Service Organizations, 60
United States Tennis Association, 111
United Way of America, 36
United Way Worldwide, 112 (upd.)
USA Track & Field, Inc., 122
Volunteers of America, Inc., 66

World Vision International, Inc., 93
YMCA of the USA, 31
YWCA of the U.S.A., 45

Paper & Forestry

AbitibiBowater Inc., IV; 25 (upd.); 99
    (upd.)
Ainsworth Lumber Co. Ltd., 99
Albany International Corporation, 51
    (upd.)
Amcor Ltd, IV; 19 (upd.); 78 (upd.)
American Business Products, Inc., 20
American Pad & Paper Company, 20
API Group plc, 118
Aracruz Celulose S.A., 57
Arjo Wiggins Appleton p.l.c., 34
Asplundh Tree Expert Co.,20; 59 (upd.)
Avery Dennison Corporation, IV; 17
    (upd.); 49 (upd.); 110 (upd.)
Badger Paper Mills, Inc., 15
Beckett Papers, 23
Beloit Corporation, 14
Bemis Company, Inc., 8; 91 (upd.)
Billerud AB, 100
Blue Heron Paper Company, 90
Bohemia, Inc., 13
Boise Cascade Holdings, L.L.C.,, IV; 8
    (upd.); 32 (upd.); 95 (upd.)
Bowater PLC, IV
Bunzl plc, IV
Canfor Corporation, 42
Caraustar Industries, Inc., 19; 44 (upd.)
Carter Lumber Company, 45
Cascades Inc., 71
Catalyst Paper Corporation, 105
Central National-Gottesman Inc., 95
Champion International Corporation, IV;
    20 (upd.)
Chesapeake Corporation, 8; 30 (upd.); 93
    (upd.)
Clondalkin Group PLC, 120
Collins Companies Inc., The, 102
Consolidated Papers, Inc., 8; 36 (upd.)
CPP International, LLC, 103
Crane & Co., Inc., 26; 103 (upd.)
Crown Vantage Inc., 29
CSS Industries, Inc., 35
Daio Paper Corporation, IV; 84 (upd.)
Daishowa Paper Manufacturing Co., Ltd.,
    IV; 57 (upd.)
Dalhoff Larsen & Horneman A/S, 96
Deltic Timber Corporation, 46
Dillard Paper Company, 11
Doman Industries Limited, 59
Domtar Corporation, IV; 89 (upd.)
DS Smith Plc, 61
Empresas CMPC S.A., 70
Enso-Gutzeit Oy, IV
Esselte, 64
Esselte Leitz GmbH & Co. KG, 48
Esselte Pendaflex Corporation, 11
Exacompta Clairefontaine S.A., 102
Federal Paper Board Company, Inc., 8
Fellowes Inc., 28; 107 (upd.)
FiberMark, Inc., 37
Fletcher Challenge Ltd., IV
Fort Howard Corporation, 8
Fort James Corporation, 22 (upd.)

Georgia-Pacific LLC, IV; 9 (upd.); 47
    (upd.); 101 (upd.)
Gould Paper Corporation, 82
Graphic Packaging Holding Company, 96
    (upd.)
Groupe Rougier SA, 21
Grupo Portucel Soporcel, 60
Guilbert S.A., 42
Hampton Affiliates, Inc., 77
Herlitz AG, 107
Holmen AB, 52 (upd.); 111 (upd.)
Honshu Paper Co., Ltd., IV
International Paper Company, IV; 15
    (upd.); 47 (upd.); 97 (upd.)
James River Corporation of Virginia, IV
Japan Pulp and Paper Company Limited,
    IV
Jefferson Smurfit Group plc, IV; 49 (upd.)
Jujo Paper Co., Ltd., IV
Kadant Inc., 96 (upd.)
KapStone Paper and Packaging
    Corporation, 122
Kimberly-Clark Corporation, III; 16
    (upd.); 43 (upd.); 105 (upd.)
Kimberly-Clark de México, S.A. de C.V.,
    54
Klabin S.A., 73
Koninklijke Houthandel G Wijma &
    Zonen BV, 96
Kruger Inc., 17; 103 (upd.)
Kymmene Corporation, IV
Longview Fibre Company, 8; 37 (upd.)
Louisiana-Pacific Corporation, IV; 31
    (upd.)
Mackay Envelope Corporation, 45
MacMillan Bloedel Limited, IV
Mail-Well, Inc., 28
Marvin Lumber & Cedar Company, 22
Matussière et Forest SA, 58
Mead Corporation, The, IV; 19 (upd.)
MeadWestvaco Corporation, 76 (upd.)
Menasha Corporation, 8; 59 (upd.); 118
    (upd.)
Mercer International Inc., 64
Metsa-Serla Oy, IV
Metso Corporation, 30 (upd.); 85 (upd.)
Miquel y Costas Miquel S.A., 68
Mo och Domsjö AB, IV
Mohawk Fine Papers, Inc., 108
Monadnock Paper Mills, Inc., 21
Mosinee Paper Corporation, 15
M-real Oyj, 56 (upd.)
Myllykoski Oyj, 117
Nashua Corporation, 8
National Envelope Corporation, 32
NCH Corporation, 8
Newark Group, Inc., The, 102
NewPage Corporation, 119
Norske Skogindustrier ASA, 63
Nuqul Group of Companies, 102
Oji Paper Co., Ltd., IV
P.H. Glatfelter Company, 8; 30 (upd.); 83
    (upd.)
Packaging Corporation of America, 12
Papeteries de Lancey, 23
Plum Creek Timber Company, Inc., 43;
    106 (upd.)
Pope & Talbot, Inc., 12; 61 (upd.)

British-Borneo Oil & Gas PLC, 34
Broken Hill Proprietary Company Ltd.,
 22 (upd.)
Bronco Drilling Company, Inc., 89
Burlington Resources Inc., 10
Burmah Castrol PLC, IV; 30 (upd.)
Callon Petroleum Company, 47
Caltex Petroleum Corporation, 19
Calumet Specialty Products Partners, L.P.,
 106
CAMAC International Corporation, 106
Cano Petroleum Inc., 97
Carrizo Oil & Gas, Inc., 97
Chevron Corporation, IV; 19 (upd.); 47
 (upd.); 103 (upd.)
Chiles Offshore Corporation, 9
The China National Offshore Oil Corp.,
 118
China National Petroleum Corporation,
 46; 108 (upd.)
China Petroleum & Chemical
 Corporation (Sinopec Corp.), 109
Chinese Petroleum Corporation, IV; 31
 (upd.)
Cimarex Energy Co., 81
CITGO Petroleum Corporation, IV; 31
 (upd.)
Clayton Williams Energy, Inc., 87
Coastal Corporation, The, IV; 31 (upd.)
Compañia Española de Petróleos S.A.
 (CEPSA), IV; 56 (upd.); 123 (upd.)
Complete Production Services, Inc., 118
Compton Petroleum Corporation, 103
Comstock Resources, Inc., 47
Conoco Inc., IV; 16 (upd.)
ConocoPhillips, 63 (upd.)
CONSOL Energy Inc., 59
Continental Resources, Inc., 89
Cooper Cameron Corporation, 20 (upd.);
 58 (upd.)
Cosmo Oil Co., Ltd., IV; 53 (upd.)
CPC Corporation, Taiwan, 116
Crimson Exploration Inc., 116
Crown Central Petroleum Corporation, 7
Daniel Measurement and Control, Inc.,
 16; 74 (upd.)
Dead River Company, 117
DeepTech International Inc., 21
Delek Group Ltd., 123
Den Norse Stats Oljeselskap AS, IV
Denbury Resources, Inc., 67
Deutsche BP Aktiengesellschaft, 7
Devon Energy Corporation, 61
Diamond Shamrock, Inc., IV
Distrigaz S.A., 82
DOF ASA, 110
Double Eagle Petroleum Co., 114
Dril-Quip, Inc., 81
Duvernay Oil Corp., 83
Dyneff S.A., 98
Dynegy Inc., 49 (upd.)
E.On AG, 50 (upd.)
Edge Petroleum Corporation, 67
Egyptian General Petroleum Corporation,
 IV; 51 (upd.)
El Paso Corporation, 66 (upd.)
Elf Aquitaine SA, 21 (upd.)
Empresa Colombiana de Petróleos, IV

Enbridge Inc., 43
EnCana Corporation, 109
Encore Acquisition Company, 73
Energen Corporation, 21; 97 (upd.)
ENI S.p.A., 69 (upd.)
Enron Corporation, 19
ENSCO International Incorporated, 57
Ente Nazionale Idrocarburi, IV
Enterprise GP Holdings L.P., 109
Enterprise Oil PLC, 11; 50 (upd.)
Entreprise Nationale Sonatrach, IV
EOG Resources, 106
Equitable Resources, Inc., 54 (upd.)
Ergon, Inc., 95
Etablissements Maurel & Prom S.A., 115
Exxon Mobil Corporation, IV; 7 (upd.);
 32 (upd.); 67 (upd.)
F.L. Roberts & Company, Inc., 113
Ferrellgas Partners, L.P., 35; 107 (upd.)
FINA, Inc., 7
FJ Management, 121 (upd.)
Flotek Industries Inc., 93
Fluxys SA, 101
Flying J Inc., 19
Forest Oil Corporation, 19; 91 (upd.)
Frontier Oil Corporation, 116
Galp Energia SGPS S.A., 98
GDF SUEZ, 109 (upd.)
General Sekiyu K.K., IV
GeoResources, Inc., 101
Giant Industries, Inc., 19; 61 (upd.)
Global Industries, Ltd., 37
Global Marine Inc., 9
Global Partners L.P., 116
GlobalSantaFe Corporation, 48 (upd.)
Grant Prideco, 57
Grey Wolf, Inc., 43
Gulf Island Fabrication, Inc., 44
Gulfport Energy Corporation, 119
Halliburton Company, III; 25 (upd.); 55
 (upd.)
Hanover Compressor Company, 59
Hawkeye Holdings LLC, 89
Helix Energy Solutions Group, Inc., 81
Hellenic Petroleum SA, 64
Helmerich & Payne, Inc., 18; 115 (upd.)
Hindustan Petroleum Corporation Ltd.,
 116
Holly Corporation, 12; 111 (upd.)
Hunt Consolidated, Inc., 7; 27 (upd.)
Hunting plc, 78
Hurricane Hydrocarbons Ltd., 54
Husky Energy Inc., 47; 118 (upd.)
Idemitsu Kosan Company Ltd., IV; 49
 (upd.); 123 (upd.)
Imperial Oil Limited, IV; 25 (upd.)
Indian Oil Corporation Ltd., IV; 48
 (upd.); 95 (upd.); 113 (upd.)
INPEX Holdings Inc., 97
Input/Output, Inc., 73
Iogen Corporation, 81
Ipiranga S.A., 67
Irving Oil Limited, 118
Kanematsu Corporation, IV; 24 (upd.);
 102 (upd.)
KBR Inc., 106 (upd.)
Kerr-McGee Corporation, IV; 22 (upd.);
 68 (upd.)

Kinder Morgan, Inc., 45; 111 (upd.)
King Ranch, Inc., 14
Knot, Inc., The, 74
Koch Industries, Inc., IV; 20 (upd.), 77
 (upd.)
Koppers Industries, Inc., 26 (upd.)
Korea Gas Corporation, 114
Kuwait Petroleum Corporation, IV; 55
 (upd.); 124 (upd.)
Libyan National Oil Corporation, IV
Louisiana Land and Exploration
 Company, The, 7
Lufkin Industries Inc., 78
Lyondell Petrochemical Company, IV
Mansfield Oil Company, 117
MAPCO Inc., IV
Marathon Oil Corporation, 109
Mariner Energy, Inc., 101
Marquard & Bahls AG, 124
Maxus Energy Corporation, 7
McDermott International, Inc., III; 37
 (upd.)
MDU Resources Group, Inc., 114 (upd.)
Merit Energy Company, 114
Meteor Industries Inc., 33
Mexichem, S.A.B. de C.V., 99
Mitchell Energy and Development
 Corporation, 7
Mitsubishi Oil Co., Ltd., IV
Mobil Corporation, IV; 7 (upd.); 21
 (upd.)
MOL Rt, 70
Motiva Enterprises LLC, 111
Murphy Oil Corporation, 7; 32 (upd.);
 95 (upd.)
N.V. Nederlandse Gasunie, V; 111 (upd.)
Nabors Industries Ltd., 9; 91 (upd.)
National Fuel Gas Company, 6; 95 (upd.)
National Iranian Oil Company, IV; 61
 (upd.)
National Oil Corporation, 66 (upd.)
National Oilwell, Inc., 54
Neste Oil Corporation, IV; 85 (upd.)
Newfield Exploration Company, 65
Nexen Inc., 79
NGC Corporation, 18
Nigerian National Petroleum Corporation,
 IV; 72 (upd.)
Nippon Oil Corporation, IV; 63 (upd.);
 120 (upd.)
Noble Affiliates, Inc., 11
NuStar Energy L.P., 111
OAO Gazprom, 42; 107 (upd.)
OAO LUKOIL, 40
OAO LUKOIL, 109 (upd.)
OAO NK YUKOS, 47
OAO Siberian Oil Company (Sibneft), 49
OAO Surgutneftegaz, 48
OAO Tatneft, 45
Occidental Petroleum Corporation, IV; 25
 (upd.); 71 (upd.)
Odebrecht S.A., 73
Oil and Natural Gas Corporation Ltd.,
 IV; 90 (upd.)
Oil States International, Inc., 77
Oil Transporting Joint Stock Company
 Transneft, 93
OMV AG, IV; 98 (upd.)

Publishing & Printing

U.S. News & World Report Inc., 30; 89 (upd.)
United Business Media Limited, 52 (upd.); 114 (upd.)
United News & Media plc, IV; 28 (upd.)
United Press International, Inc., 25; 73 (upd.)
University of Chicago Press, The, 79
Valassis Communications, Inc., 8
Value Line, Inc., 16; 73 (upd.)
Vance Publishing Corporation, 64
Verlagsgruppe Georg von Holtzbrinck GmbH, 35
Verlagsgruppe Weltbild GmbH, 98
Village Voice Media, Inc., 38
VistaPrint Limited, 87
VNU N.V., 27
Volt Information Sciences Inc., 26
W.W. Norton & Company, Inc., 28
Wallace Computer Services, Inc., 36
Walsworth Publishing Co., 78
Washington Post Company, The, IV; 20 (upd.); 109 (upd.)
Waverly, Inc., 16
WAZ Media Group, 82
Wegener NV, 53
Wenner Media, Inc., 32
West Group, 7; 34 (upd.)
Western Publishing Group, Inc., 13
WH Smith PLC, V; 42 (upd.)
William Reed Publishing Ltd., 78
Wilmington Group plc, 122
Wizards of the Coast LLC, 112 (upd.)
Wolters Kluwer NV, 14; 33 (upd.)
Workman Publishing Company, Inc., 70
World Book, Inc., 12
World Color Press Inc., 12
World Publications, LLC, 65
Xeikon NV, 26
Yell Group PLC, 79
Zebra Technologies Corporation, 14; (53 (upd.)
Ziff Davis Media Inc., 12; 36 (upd.); 73 (upd.)
Zondervan Corporation, 24; 71 (upd.)

Real Estate
Acadia Realty Trust, 106
Akerys S.A., 90
Alexander's, Inc., 45
Alexandria Real Estate Equities, Inc., 101
Alico, Inc., 63
AMB Property Corporation, 57
American Campus Communities, Inc., 85
Amfac/JMB Hawaii L.L.C., 24 (upd.)
Apartment Investment and Management Company, 49
Archstone-Smith Trust, 49
Associated Estates Realty Corporation, 25
AvalonBay Communities, Inc., 58
Baird & Warner Holding Company, 87
Berkshire Realty Holdings, L.P., 49
Bluegreen Corporation, 80
Boston Properties, Inc., 22
Bouygues S.A., I; 24 (upd.); 97 (upd.)
Bramalea Ltd., 9
British Land Plc, 54
Brookfield Properties Corporation, 89

Burroughs & Chapin Company, Inc., 86
Camden Property Trust, 77
Canary Wharf Group Plc, 30
CapStar Hotel Company, 21
CarrAmerica Realty Corporation, 56
Castle & Cooke, Inc., 20 (upd.)
Catellus Development Corporation, 24
CB Commercial Real Estate Services Group, Inc., 21
CB Richard Ellis Group, Inc., 70 (upd.)
Central Florida Investments, Inc., 93
Chateau Communities, Inc., 37
Chelsfield PLC, 67
Cheung Kong (Holdings) Limited, IV; 20 (upd.)
Christie Group plc, 122
CITIC Pacific Ltd., 116 (upd.)
City Developments Limited, 89
Clayton Homes Incorporated, 13; 54 (upd.)
Cohen & Steers, Inc., 119
Coldwell Banker Real Estate LLC, 109
Colliers International Property Consultants Inc., 92
Colonial Properties Trust, 65
Corcoran Group, Inc., The, 58
Corky McMillin Companies, The, 98
CoStar Group, Inc., 73
Cousins Properties Incorporated, 65
CSX Corporation 79 (upd.)
Cushman & Wakefield, Inc., 86
Cyrela Brazil Realty S.A. Empreendimentos e Participações, 110
Del Webb Corporation, 14
Desarrolladora Homex, S.A. de C.V., 87
Developers Diversified Realty Corporation, 69
Douglas Emmett, Inc., 105
Draper and Kramer Inc., 96
Ducks Unlimited, Inc., 87
Duke Realty Corporation, 57
Durst Organization Inc., The, 108
EastGroup Properties, Inc., 67
Edward J. DeBartolo Corporation, The, 8
Enterprise Inns plc, 59
Equity Office Properties Trust, 54
Equity Residential, 49
Erickson Retirement Communities, 57
Fairfield Communities, Inc., 36
First Industrial Realty Trust, Inc., 65
FirstService Corporation, 121
Forest City Enterprises, Inc., 16; 52 (upd.); 112 (upd.)
Gale International Llc, 93
Gecina SA, 42
General Growth Properties, Inc., 57
GMH Communities Trust, 87
Great White Shark Enterprises, Inc., 89
Griffin Land & Nurseries, Inc., 43
Grubb & Ellis Company, 21; 98 (upd.)
Guangzhou R&F Properties Co., Ltd., 95
Habitat Company LLC, The, 106
Haminerson Property Investment and Development Corporation plc, The, IV
Hammerson plc, 40
Hang Lung Group Ltd., 104
Harbert Corporation, 14
Helmsley Enterprises, Inc., 39 (upd.)

Henderson Land Development Company Ltd., 70
Holiday Retirement Corp., 87
Home Properties of New York, Inc., 42
HomeAway, Inc., 116
HomeVestors of America, Inc., 77
Hongkong Land Holdings Limited, IV; 47 (upd.)
Hopson Development Holdings Ltd., 87
Hovnanian Enterprises, Inc., 29; 89 (upd.)
Hyatt Corporation, 16 (upd.)
Icahn Enterprises L.P., 110
ILX Resorts Incorporated, 65
IRSA Inversiones y Representaciones S.A., 63
J.F. Shea Co., Inc., 55
Jardine Cycle & Carriage Ltd., 73
JMB Realty Corporation, IV
Jones Lang LaSalle Incorporated, 49
JPI, 49
Kaufman and Broad Home Corporation, 8
Kennedy-Wilson, Inc., 60
Kerry Properties Limited, 22
Kimco Realty Corporation, 11
Koll Company, The, 8
Land Securities PLC, IV; 49 (upd.)
Lefrak Organization Inc., 26
Lend Lease Corporation Limited, IV; 17 (upd.); 52 (upd.)
Liberty Property Trust, 57
Lincoln Property Company, 8; 54 (upd.)
Loewen Group Inc., The, 40 (upd.)
Long & Foster Companies, Inc., The, 85
Macerich Company, The, 57
Mack-Cali Realty Corporation, 42
Macklowe Properties, Inc., 95
Manufactured Home Communities, Inc., 22
Maui Land & Pineapple Company, Inc., 29; 100 (upd.)
Maxco Inc., 17
Meditrust, 11
Melvin Simon and Associates, Inc., 8
MEPC plc, IV
Meritage Corporation, 26
Mid-America Apartment Communities, Inc., 85
Middleton Doll Company, The, 53
Mills Corporation, The, 77
Mitsubishi Estate Company, Limited, IV; 61 (upd.)
Mitsui Real Estate Development Co., Ltd., IV
Morguard Corporation, 85
Nature Conservancy, The, 28
New Plan Realty Trust, 11
New World Development Company Ltd., IV
Newhall Land and Farming Company, 14
Nexity S.A., 66
NRT Incorporated, 61
Olympia & York Developments Ltd., IV; 9 (upd.)
Panattoni Development Company, Inc., 99
Park Corp., 22
Parque Arauco S.A., 72

Retail & Wholesale

Textiles & Apparel

Tobacco

UST Inc., 9; 50 (upd.)
Vector Group Ltd., 35 (upd.)

Transport Services

A.P. Møller-Mærsk A/S, 57; 119 (upd.)
ABC Rail Products Corporation, 18
Abertis Infraestructuras, S.A., 65
Adams Express Company, The, 86
Aegean Marine Petroleum Network Inc., 89
Aéroports de Paris, 33
Ahlers, 123
Air Express International Corporation, 13
Air Partner PLC, 93
Air T, Inc., 86
Airborne Freight Corporation, 6; 34 (upd.)
Alamo Rent A Car, Inc., 6; 24 (upd.); 84 (upd.)
Alaska Railroad Corporation, 60
Alexander & Baldwin, Inc., 10, 40 (upd.)
Allied Worldwide, Inc., 49
AMCOL International Corporation, 59 (upd.)
AMERCO, 6; 67 (upd.)
American Classic Voyages Company, 27
American Commercial Lines Inc., 99
American President Companies Ltd., 6
Anderson Trucking Service, Inc., 75
Anschutz Corp., 12
APL Limited, 61 (upd.)
Aqua Alliance Inc., 32 (upd.)
Arlington Tankers Ltd., 101
Arriva PLC, 69
Atlas Van Lines Inc., 14; 106 (upd.)
Attica Enterprises S.A., 64
Austal Limited, 75
Avis Group Holdings, Inc., 75 (upd.)
Avis Rent A Car, Inc., 6; 22 (upd.)
Avondale Industries, 7; 41 (upd.)
BAA plc, 10
BAE Systems Ship Repair, 73
Bekins Company, 15
Belships ASA, 113
Bénéteau SA, 55
Berliner Verkehrsbetriebe (BVG), 58
Bollinger Shipyards, Inc., 61
Boyd Bros. Transportation Inc., 39
Brambles Industries Limited, 42
Brink's Company, The, 58 (upd.)
British Railways Board, V
Broken Hill Proprietary Company Ltd., 22 (upd.)
Buckeye Partners, L.P., 70
Budget Group, Inc., 25
Budget Rent a Car Corporation, 9
Burlington Northern Santa Fe Corporation, V; 27 (upd.); 111 (upd.)
C.H. Robinson Worldwide, Inc., 40 (upd.); 116 (upd.)
Canadian National Railway Company, 71 (upd.)
Canadian National Railway System, 6
Canadian Pacific Railway Limited, V; 45 (upd.); 95 (upd.)
Cannon Express, Inc., 53
Carey International, Inc., 26

Carlson Companies, Inc., 6; 22 (upd.); 87 (upd.)
Carolina Freight Corporation, 6
Carver Boat Corporation LLC, 88
Cascade General, Inc., 65
Celadon Group Inc., 30
Central Japan Railway Company, 43
Chantiers Jeanneau S.A., 96
Chargeurs International, 6; 21 (upd.)
CHC Helicopter Corporation, 67
CHEP Pty. Ltd., 80
Chicago and North Western Holdings Corporation, 6
Chicago Transit Authority, 108
Christian Salvesen Plc, 45
Coach USA, Inc., 24; 55 (upd.)
Coles Express Inc., 15
Compagnie Générale Maritime et Financière, 6
Compagnie Maritime Belge S.A., 95
Compañia Sud Americana de Vapores S.A., 100
Conrad Industries, Inc., 58
Consolidated Delivery & Logistics, Inc., 24
Consolidated Freightways Corporation, V; 21 (upd.); 48 (upd.)
Consolidated Rail Corporation, V
Con-way Inc., 101
Correos y Telegrafos S.A., 80
Covenant Transportation Group, Inc., 119
CR England, Inc., 63
Crete Carrier Corporation, 95
Crowley Holdings, Inc., 6; 28 (upd.); 120 (upd.)
CSX Corporation, V; 22 (upd.); 79 (upd.)
Ctrip.com International Ltd., 97
Dachser GmbH & Co. KG, 88
Danaos Corporation, 91
Danzas Group, V; 40 (upd.)
Dart Group PLC, 77
Detyens Shipyards, Inc., 120
Deutsche Bahn AG, V; 46 (upd.); 122 (upd.)
Deutsche Post AG, 108 (upd.)
DHL Worldwide Network S.A./N.V., 6; 24 (upd.); 69 (upd.)
Diana Shipping Inc., 95
Dot Foods, Inc., 69
DP World, 81
DryShips Inc., 95
East Japan Railway Company, V; 66 (upd.)
Echo Global Logistics Inc., 116
EGL, Inc., 59
Eitzen Group, 107
Electric Boat Corporation, 86
Emery Air Freight Corporation, 6
Emery Worldwide Airlines, Inc., 25 (upd.)
Enterprise Rent-A-Car Company, 6
Estes Express Lines, Inc., 86
Eurotunnel Group, 37 (upd.)
EVA Airways Corporation, 51
Evergreen International Aviation, Inc., 53
Evergreen Marine Corporation (Taiwan) Ltd., 13; 50 (upd.)
Executive Jet, Inc., 36
Exel plc, 51 (upd.)

Expeditors International of Washington Inc., 17; 78 (upd.)
Federal Express Corporation, V
FedEx Corporation, 18 (upd.); 42 (upd.); 109 (upd.)
Ferretti Group SpA, 90
Ferrovie Dello Stato Societa Di Trasporti e Servizi S.p.A., 105
FirstGroup plc, 89
Forward Air Corporation, 75
Fountain Powerboats Industries, Inc., 28
Four Winns Boats LLC, 96
FreightCar America, Inc., 101
Fritz Companies, Inc., 12
Frontline Ltd., 45
Frozen Food Express Industries, Inc., 20; 98 (upd.)
Garuda Indonesia, 58 (upd.)
GATX Corporation, 6; 25 (upd.)
GE Capital Aviation Services, 36
Gefco SA, 54
General Maritime Corporation, 59
Genesee & Wyoming Inc., 27
Genmar Holdings, Inc., 45
Geodis S.A., 67
Go-Ahead Group Plc, The, 28
Greenbrier Companies, The, 19
Greyhound Lines, Inc., 32 (upd.)
Groupe Bourbon, 60
Grupo Aeroportuario del Centro Norte, S.A.B. de C.V., 97
Grupo Aeroportuario del Pacífico, S.A. de C.V., 85
Grupo TMM, S.A. de C.V., 50
Grupo Transportación Ferroviaria Mexicana, S.A. de C.V., 47
Gulf Agency Company Ltd., 78
GulfMark Offshore, Inc., 49
Hanjin Shipping Co., Ltd., 50
Hankyu Corporation, V; 23 (upd.)
Hapag-Lloyd AG, 6; 97 (upd.)
Harland and Wolff Holdings plc, 19
Harmon Industries, Inc., 25
Harper Group Inc., 17
Heartland Express, Inc., 18; 120 (upd.)
Hertz Corporation, The, 9; 33 (upd.); 101 (upd.)
Holberg Industries, Inc., 36
Horizon Lines, Inc., 98
Hornbeck Offshore Services, Inc., 101
Hornblower Cruises and Events, 122
Hospitality Worldwide Services, Inc., 26
Hub Group, Inc., 38
Hvide Marine Incorporated, 22
IAP Worldwide Services, Inc., 119
Illinois Central Corporation, 11
Ingalls Shipbuilding, Inc., 12
Ingram Industries Inc., 122 (upd.)
International Shipholding Corporation, Inc., 27
ITOCHU Corporation, 116 (upd.)
J Lauritzen A/S, 90
J.B. Hunt Transport Services, Inc., 12; 119 (upd.)
Jack B. Kelley, Inc., 102
James Fisher and Sons Public Limited Company, 118
John Menzies plc, 39

Utilities

Waste Services

Geographic Index

Germany

Loctite Corporation, 8; 30 (upd.)
Lodge Manufacturing Company, 103
LodgeNet Interactive Corporation, 28; 106 (upd.)
Loehmann's Holdings Inc., 24; 107 (upd.)
Loews Corporation, I; 12 (upd.); 36 (upd.); 93 (upd.)
Logan's Roadhouse, Inc., 29
Logicon Inc., 20
LogMeIn, Inc., 124
LoJack Corporation, 48; 120 (upd.)
London Fog Industries, Inc., 29
Lone Star Steakhouse & Saloon, Inc., 51
Long & Foster Companies, Inc., The, 85
Long Island Bancorp, Inc., 16
Long Island Power Authority, V; 102 (upd.)
Long Island Rail Road Company, The, 68
Long John Silver's, 13; 57 (upd.)
Longaberger Company, The, 12; 44 (upd.)
Longs Drug Stores Corporation, V; 25 (upd.); 83 (upd.)
Longview Fibre Company, 8; 37 (upd.)
Loos & Dilworth, Inc., 100
Loral Space & Communications Ltd., 8; 9; 54 (upd.)
Lorillard, Inc., 112
Los Angeles Turf Club Inc., 102
Lost Arrow, Inc., 22; 121 (upd.)
LOT$OFF Corporation, 24
Lotus Development Corporation, 6; 25 (upd.)
LOUD Technologies, Inc., 95 (upd.)
Louis Berger Group, Inc., The, 104
Louisiana Land and Exploration Company, The, 7
Louisiana-Pacific Corporation, IV; 31 (upd.)
Love's Travel Stops & Country Stores, Inc., 71
Lowe's Companies, Inc., V; 21 (upd.); 81 (upd.)
Lowrance Electronics, Inc., 18
LPA Holding Corporation, 81
LSB Industries, Inc., 77
LSI Logic Corporation, 13; 64
L-3 Communications Holdings, Inc., 48; 111 (upd.)
LTV Corporation, The, I; 24 (upd.)
Lubrizol Corporation, The, I; 30 (upd.); 83 (upd.)
Luby's, Inc., 17; 42 (upd.); 99 (upd.)
Lucasfilm Ltd., 12; 50 (upd.); 115 (upd.)
Lucent Technologies Inc., 34
Lucille Farms, Inc., 45
Lucky Stores, Inc., 27
Lufkin Industries Inc., 78
Luigino's, Inc., 64
Lukens Inc., 14
Lumber Liquidators, Inc., 111
Luminex Corporation, 122
Lunar Corporation, 29
Lunardi's Super Market, Inc., 99
Lund Food Holdings, Inc., 22
Lund International Holdings, Inc., 40
Lutheran Brotherhood, 31
Lydall, Inc., 64
Lykes Brothers Inc., 110

Lyman-Richey Corporation, 96
Lynch Corporation, 43
Lynden Incorporated, 91
Lyondell Chemical Company, IV; 45 (upd.)
M&F Worldwide Corp., 38
M.A. Bruder & Sons, Inc., 56
M.A. Gedney Co., 51
M.A. Hanna Company, 8
M. A. Mortenson Company, 115
M.D.C. Holdings, Inc., 118
M.H. Meyerson & Co., Inc., 46
M.R. Beal and Co., 102
M. Rubin and Sons Inc., 110
M. Shanken Communications, Inc., 50
Mac Frugal's Bargains - Closeouts Inc., 17
Mac-Gray Corporation, 44
MacAndrews & Forbes Holdings Inc., 28; 86 (upd.)
MacDermid Incorporated, 32
Mace Security International, Inc., 57; 124 (upd.)
Macerich Company, The, 57
MacGregor Golf Company, 68
Mack Trucks, Inc., I; 22 (upd.); 61 (upd.)
Mackay Envelope Corporation, 45
Mack-Cali Realty Corporation, 42
Mackie Designs Inc., 33
Macklowe Properties, Inc., 95
Macmillan, Inc., 7
MacNeal-Schwendler Corporation, The, 25
MacNeil/Lehrer Productions, 87
Macromedia, Inc., 50
Macrovision Solutions Corporation, 101
Macy's, Inc., 94 (upd.)
Madden's on Gull Lake, 52
Madelaine Chocolate Novelties, Inc., 104
Madison Dearborn Partners, LLC, 97
Madison Gas and Electric Company, 39
Madison Square Garden, LP, 109
Madison-Kipp Corporation, 58
Mag Instrument, Inc., 67
MaggieMoo's International, 89
Magic Seasoning Blends Inc., 109
Magma Copper Company, 7
Magma Design Automation Inc., 78
Magma Power Company, 11
MagneTek, Inc., 15; 41 (upd.)
MAI Systems Corporation, 11
Maidenform, Inc., 20; 59 (upd.)
Maid-Rite Corporation, 62
Mail Boxes Etc., 18; 41 (upd.)
Mail-Well, Inc., 28
Maine & Maritimes Corporation, 56
Maine Central Railroad Company, 16
Maines Paper & Food Service Inc., 71
Majesco Entertainment Company, 85
Major Automotive Companies, Inc., The, 45
Make-A-Wish Foundation of America, 97
Malcolm Pirnie, Inc., 42
Malden Mills Industries, Inc., 16
Mallinckrodt Group Inc., 19
Malt-O-Meal Company, 22; 63 (upd.)
Mammoth Mountain Ski Area, 101
Management Action Programs, Inc., 123

Management and Training Corporation, 28
Manatron, Inc., 86
Mandalay Resort Group, 32 (upd.)
Manhattan Associates, Inc., 67
Manhattan Beer Distributors LLC, 114
Manhattan Group, LLC, 80
Manheim, 88
The Manitowoc Company, Inc., 18; 59 (upd.); 118 (upd.)
Mannatech Inc., 33
Manning Selvage & Lee (MS&L), 76
MannKind Corporation, 87
Manor Care, Inc., 6; 25 (upd.)
Manpower Inc., 9; 30 (upd.); 73 (upd.)
Mansfield Oil Company, 117
ManTech International Corporation, 97
Manufactured Home Communities, Inc., 22
Manufacturers Hanover Corporation, II
Manville Corporation, III; 7 (upd.)
MAPCO Inc., IV
MAPICS, Inc., 55
Maple Grove Farms of Vermont, 88
Maples Industries, Inc., 83
Marathon Oil Corporation, 109
Marble Slab Creamery, Inc., 87
Marc Ecko Enterprises, Inc., 105
Marc Glassman, Inc., 117
March of Dimes, 31
Marchex, Inc., 72
marchFIRST, Inc., 34
Marco Business Products, Inc., 75
Marco's Franchising LLC, 86
Marcus Corporation, The, 21
Marie Callender's Restaurant & Bakery, Inc., 28
Marine Products Corporation, 75
MarineMax, Inc., 30
Mariner Energy, Inc., 101
Marion Laboratories, Inc., I
Marisa Christina, Inc., 15
Marisol S.A., 107
Maritz Holdings Inc., 38; 110 (upd.)
Mark IV Industries, Inc., 7; 28 (upd.)
Mark T. Wendell Tea Company, 94
Mark Travel Corporation, The, 80
Markel Corporation, 116
Marks Brothers Jewelers, Inc., 24
Marlin Business Services Corp., 89
Marmon Group, Inc., The, IV; 16 (upd.); 70 (upd.)
Marquette Electronics, Inc., 13
Marriott International, Inc., III; 21 (upd.); 83 (upd.)
Mars Petcare US Inc., 96
Mars, Incorporated, 7; 40 (upd.); 114 (upd.)
Marsh & McLennan Companies, Inc., III; 45 (upd.); 123 (upd.)
Marsh Supermarkets, Inc., 17; 76 (upd.)
Marshall & Ilsley Corporation, 56
Marshall Field's, 63
Marshalls Incorporated, 13
Marshfield Clinic Inc., 82
Martek Biosciences Corporation, 65
Marten Transport, Ltd., 84

Praxis Bookstore Group LLC, 90
Pre-Paid Legal Services, Inc., 20; 120 (upd.)
Precision Castparts Corp., 15; 111 (upd.)
Precision Foods, Inc., 120
Preferred Hotel Group, 103
Premark International, Inc., III
Premcor Inc., 37
Premier Industrial Corporation, 9
Premier Parks, Inc., 27
Premiere Radio Networks, Inc., 102
Premium Standard Farms, Inc., 30
PremiumWear, Inc., 30
Preserver Group, Inc., 44
President Casinos, Inc., 22
Pressman Toy Corporation, 56
Presstek, Inc., 33
Preston Corporation, 6
PRG-Schultz International, Inc., 73
Price Communications Corporation, 42
Price Company, The, V
Price Pfister, Inc., 70
PriceCostco, Inc., 14
Priceline.com Incorporated, 57
PriceSmart, Inc., 71
PricewaterhouseCoopers International Limited, 9; 29 (upd.); 111 (upd.)
Pride International Inc., 78
Primark Corp., 13
Prime Hospitality Corporation, 52
Primedex Health Systems, Inc., 25
Primedia Inc., 22
Primerica Corporation, I
Prince Sports Group, Inc., 15
Princess Cruise Lines, 22
Princeton Review, Inc., The, 42; 124 (upd.)
Principal Financial Group Inc., 116
Principal Mutual Life Insurance Company, III
Printpack, Inc., 68
Printrak, A Motorola Company, 44
Printronix, Inc., 18
Prison Rehabilitative Industries and Diversified Enterprises, Inc. (PRIDE), 53
Pro-Build Holdings Inc., 95 (upd.)
Procter & Gamble Company, The, III; 8 (upd.); 26 (upd.); 67 (upd.)
Prodigy Communications Corporation, 34
Professional Basketball Club, LLC, 124
Professional Bull Riders Inc., 55
Professional Golfers' Association of America, The, 41
Proffitt's, Inc., 19
Pro-Football, Inc., 121
Programmer's Paradise, Inc., 81
Progress Energy, Inc., 74
Progress Software Corporation, 15; 120 (upd.)
The Progressive Corporation, 11; 29 (upd.); 109 (upd.)
Progressive Inc., The, 110
ProLogis, 57
Prometheus Global Media, LLC, 122
Promus Companies, Inc., 9
Proskauer Rose LLP, 47
Protection One, Inc., 32

Provell Inc., 58 (upd.)
Providence Health System, 90
Providence Journal Company, The, 28
Providence Service Corporation, The, 64
Provident Bankshares Corporation, 85
Provident Life and Accident Insurance Company of America, III
Providian Financial Corporation, 52 (upd.)
Prudential Financial Inc., III; 30 (upd.); 82 (upd.)
PSI Resources, 6
PSS World Medical, Inc., 115 (upd.)
Psychemedics Corporation, 89
Psychiatric Solutions, Inc., 68
Pubco Corporation, 17
Public Service Company of Colorado, 6
Public Service Company of New Hampshire, 21; 55 (upd.)
Public Service Company of New Mexico, 6
Public Service Enterprise Group Inc., V; 44 (upd.)
Public Storage, Inc., 52
Publishers Clearing House, 23; 64 (upd.)
Publishers Group, Inc., 35
Publix Super Markets, Inc., 7; 31 (upd.); 105 (upd.)
Pueblo Xtra International, Inc., 47
Puget Sound Energy Inc., 6; 50 (upd.)
Pulaski Furniture Corporation, 33; 80 (upd.)
Pulitzer Inc., 15; 58 (upd.)
Pulte Corporation, 8
Pulte Homes, Inc., 42 (upd.); 113 (upd.)
Pumpkin Masters, Inc., 48
Pure World, Inc., 72
Purina Mills, Inc., 32
Puritan-Bennett Corporation, 13
Purolator Products Company, 21; 74 (upd.)
Putt-Putt Golf Courses of America, Inc., 23
PVC Container Corporation, 67
PW Eagle, Inc., 48
Pyramid Breweries Inc., 33; 102 (upd.)
Pyramid Companies, 54
Q.E.P. Co., Inc., 65
Qdoba Restaurant Corporation, 93
QRS Music Technologies, Inc., 95
QSC Audio Products, Inc., 56
QSS Group, Inc., 100
Quad/Graphics, Inc., 19
Quaker Chemical Corp., 91
Quaker Fabric Corp., 19
Quaker Foods North America, 73 (upd.)
Quaker Oats Company, The, II; 12 (upd.); 34 (upd.)
Quaker State Corporation, 7; 21 (upd.)
QUALCOMM Incorporated, 20; 47 (upd.); 114 (upd.)
Quality Chekd Dairies, Inc., 48
Quality Dining, Inc., 18
Quality Food Centers, Inc., 17
Quality King Distributors, Inc., 114
Quality Systems, Inc., 81
Quanex Corporation, 13; 62 (upd.)
Quanta Services, Inc. 79

Quantum Chemical Corporation, 8
Quantum Corporation, 10; 62 (upd.)
Quark, Inc., 36
Quest Diagnostics Inc., 26; 106 (upd.)
Questar Corporation, 6; 26 (upd.)
Quick & Reilly Group, Inc., The, 20
Quicken Loans, Inc., 93
Quidel Corporation, 80
Quigley Corporation, The, 62
Quiksilver, Inc., 18; 79 (upd.)
QuikTrip Corporation, 36
Quill Corporation, 28; 115 (upd.)
Quinn Emanuel Urquhart Oliver & Hedges, LLP, 99
QuinStreet Incorporated, 124
Quintiles Transnational Corporation, 21; 68 (upd.)
Quixote Corporation, 15
Quiznos Corporation, 42; 117 (upd.)
Quovadx Inc., 70
QVC Inc., 9; 58 (upd.)
Qwest Communications International, Inc., 37; 116 (upd.)
R&B, Inc., 51
R&R Partners Inc., 108
R.H. Kuhn Company, Inc., 117
R.T. Vanderbilt Company, Inc., 117
R.B. Pamplin Corp., 45
R.C. Bigelow, Inc., 49
R.C. Willey Home Furnishings, 72
R.G. Barry Corporation, 17; 44 (upd.)
R.H. Macy & Co., Inc., V; 8 (upd.); 30 (upd.)
R.J. Reynolds Tobacco Holdings, Inc., 30 (upd.)
R.L. Polk & Co., 10; 123 (upd.)
R. M. Palmer Co., 89
R.P. Scherer, I
R.R. Bowker LLC, 100
R.R. Donnelley & Sons Co., IV; 9 (upd.); 38 (upd.); 113 (upd.)
Racal-Datacom Inc., 11
RaceTrac Petroleum, Inc., 111
Racing Champions Corporation, 37
Rack Room Shoes, Inc., 84
Radian Group Inc., 42
Radiant Systems Inc., 104
Radiation Therapy Services, Inc., 85
@radical.media, 103
Radio Flyer Inc., 34; 118 (upd.)
Radio One, Inc., 67
RadioShack Corporation, 36 (upd.); 101 (upd.)
Radius Inc., 16
RAE Systems Inc., 83
Rag Shops, Inc., 30
RailAmerica, Inc., 116
RailTex, Inc., 20
Rain Bird Corporation, 84
Rainbow Media Holdings LLC, 109
Rainforest Café, Inc., 25; 88 (upd.)
Rainier Brewing Company, 23
Raley's, 14; 58 (upd.); 123 (upd.)
Rally's, 25; 68 (upd.)
Ralphs Grocery Company, 35
Ralston Purina Company, II; 13 (upd.)
Ramsay Youth Services, Inc., 41
Ramtron International Corporation, 89

TruFoods LLC, 114
Truman Arnold Companies, Inc., 114
Trump Organization, The, 23; 64 (upd.)
TruServ Corporation, 24
Trustmark Corporation, 106
TRW Automotive Holdings Corp., 75 (upd.)
TRW Inc., I; 11 (upd.); 14 (upd.)
T-3 Energy Services, Inc., 119
TTX Company, 6; 66 (upd.)
Tubby's, Inc., 53
Tucson Electric Power Company, 6
Tuesday Morning Corporation, 18; 70 (upd.)
Tully Construction Co. Inc., 114
Tully's Coffee Corporation, 51
Tultex Corporation, 13
Tumaro's Gourmet Tortillas, 85
Tumbleweed, Inc., 33; 80 (upd.)
Tumi, Inc., 112
Tupperware Corporation, 28; 78 (upd.)
TurboChef Technologies, Inc., 83
Turner Broadcasting System, Inc., II; 6 (upd.); 66 (upd.)
Turner Construction Company, 66
Turner Corporation, The, 8; 23 (upd.)
Turtle Wax, Inc., 15; 93 (upd.)
Tuscarora Inc., 29
Tutogen Medical, Inc., 68
Tuttle Publishing, 86
TV Guide, Inc., 43 (upd.)
TVI Corporation, 99
TVI, Inc., 15
TW Services, Inc., II
Tweeter Home Entertainment Group, Inc., 30
Twentieth Century Fox Film Corporation, II; 25 (upd.)
Twin Disc, Inc., 21
Twinlab Corporation, 34
Twitter, Inc., 118
II-VI Incorporated, 69
Ty Inc., 33; 86 (upd.)
Tyco Toys, Inc., 12
Tyler Corporation, 23
Tyler Perry Company, Inc., The, 111
Tyndale House Publishers, Inc., 57
Tyson Foods, Inc., II; 14 (upd.); 50 (upd.); 114 (upd.)
U.S. Aggregates, Inc., 42
U.S. Army Corps of Engineers, 91
U.S. Bancorp, 14; 36 (upd.); 103 (upd.)
U.S. Borax, Inc., 42
U.S. Can Corporation, 30
U.S. Cellular Corporation, 31 (upd.); 88 (upd.)
U.S. Delivery Systems, Inc., 22
U.S. Foodservice, Inc., 26; 120 (upd.)
U.S. Healthcare, Inc., 6
U.S. Home Corporation, 8; 78 (upd.)
U.S. Music Corporation, 108
U.S. News & World Report Inc., 30; 89 (upd.)
U.S. Office Products Company, 25
U.S. Physical Therapy, Inc., 65
U.S. Premium Beef LLC, 91
U.S. Robotics Corporation, 9; 66 (upd.)

U.S. Satellite Broadcasting Company, Inc., 20
U.S. Silica Company, 104
U.S. Timberlands Company, L.P., 42
U.S. Trust Corp., 17
U.S. Vision, Inc., 66
U S West, Inc., V; 25 (upd.)
UAL Corporation, 34 (upd.); 107 (upd.)
UAW (International Union, United Automobile, Aerospace and Agricultural Implement Workers of America), 72
UGI Corporation, 12; 124 (upd.)
Ugly Duckling Corporation, 22
UICI, 33
Ukrop's Super Markets, Inc., 39; 101 (upd.)
Ulta Salon, Cosmetics & Fragrance, Inc., 93
Ultimate Electronics, Inc., 18; 69 (upd.)
Ultimate Software Group Inc., 123
Ultra Pac, Inc., 24
Ultra Petroleum Corporation, 71
Ultrak Inc., 24
Ultralife Batteries, Inc., 58
Ultramar Diamond Shamrock Corporation, 31 (upd.)
Umpqua Holdings Corporation, 87
Uncas Manufacturing Company, 117
Uncle Ben's Inc., 22
Uncle Ray's LLC, 90
Under Armour Performance Apparel, 61
Underwriters Laboratories, Inc., 30
Unica Corporation, 77
Unicom Corporation, 29 (upd.)
Unifi, Inc., 12; 62 (upd.)
Unified Grocers, Inc., 93
UniFirst Corporation, 21
Uni-Marts, Inc., 17
Union Bank of California, 16
Union Camp Corporation, IV
Union Carbide Corporation, I; 9 (upd.); 74 (upd.)
Union Electric Company, V
Union Pacific Corporation, V; 28 (upd.); 79 (upd.)
Union Planters Corporation, 54
Union Texas Petroleum Holdings, Inc., 9
UnionBanCal Corporation, 50 (upd.)
Unique Casual Restaurants, Inc., 27
Unison HealthCare Corporation, 25
Unisys Corporation, III; 6 (upd.); 36 (upd.); 112 (upd.)
Unit Corporation, 63
United Airlines, I; 6 (upd.)
United Auto Group, Inc., 26; 68 (upd.)
United Brands Company, II
United Community Banks, Inc., 98
United Dairy Farmers, Inc., 74
United Defense Industries, Inc., 30; 66 (upd.)
United Dominion Industries Limited, 8; 16 (upd.)
United Dominion Realty Trust, Inc., 52
United Farm Workers of America, 88
United Foods, Inc., 21
United HealthCare Corporation, 9
United Illuminating Company, The, 21
United Industrial Corporation, 37

United Industries Corporation, 68
United Jewish Communities, 33
United Merchants & Manufacturers, Inc., 13
United National Group, Ltd., 63
United Nations International Children's Emergency Fund (UNICEF), 58
United Natural Foods, Inc., 32; 76 (upd.)
United Negro College Fund, Inc. 79
United Online, Inc., 71 (upd.)
United Parcel Service of America Inc., V; 17 (upd.)
United Parcel Service, Inc., 63; 94 (upd.)
United Press International, Inc., 25; 73 (upd.)
United Rentals, Inc., 34
United Retail Group Inc., 33
United Road Services, Inc., 69
United Service Organizations, 60
United Services Automobile Association, 109 (upd.)
United States Cellular Corporation, 9
United States Filter Corporation, 20
United States Pipe and Foundry Company, 62
United States Playing Card Company, 62
United States Postal Service, 14; 34 (upd.); 108 (upd.)
United States Shoe Corporation, The, V
United States Soccer Federation, 108
United States Steel Corporation, 50 (upd.); 114 (upd.)
United States Sugar Corporation, 115
United States Surgical Corporation, 10; 34 (upd.)
United States Tennis Association, 111
United Stationers Inc., 14; 117 (upd.)
United Surgical Partners International Inc., 120
United Talent Agency, Inc., 80
United Technologies Automotive Inc., 15
United Technologies Corporation, I; 10 (upd.); 34 (upd.); 105 (upd.)
United Telecommunications, Inc., V
United Video Satellite Group, 18
United Water Resources, Inc., 40
United Way of America, 36
United Way Worldwide, 112 (upd.)
UnitedHealth Group Incorporated, 103 (upd.)
Unitil Corporation, 37
Unitog Co., 19
Unitrin Inc., 16; 78 (upd.)
Univar Corporation, 9
Universal American Corp., 111
Universal Compression, Inc., 59
Universal Corporation, V; 48 (upd.)
Universal Electronics Inc., 39; 120 (upd.)
Universal Foods Corporation, 7
Universal Forest Products, Inc., 10; 59 (upd.); 122 (upd.)
Universal Health Services, Inc., 6; 124 (upd.)
Universal International, Inc., 25
Universal Manufacturing Company, 88
Universal Security Instruments, Inc., 96
Universal Stainless & Alloy Products, Inc., 75